The Ultimate Guide to

★ THE BEST ★

1,000 Modern Movies
on DVD and Video

ReelViews 2

with a foreword by **Roger Ebert**

JAMES BERARDINELLI

creator of www.reelviews.net

Justin, Charles & Co.
Boston

FIRST U.S. EDITION 2005

Every effort has been made to fulfill requirements with regard to reproducing copyright material. The author and publisher will be glad to rectify any omissions at the earliest opportunity.

ISBN 1-932112-40-5

Library of Congress Cataloging-in-Publication Data is available.

Published in the United States by Justin, Charles & Co., Publishers, Boston
www.justincharlesbooks.com

Distributed by National Book Network, Lanham, Maryland
www.nbnbooks.com

10 9 8 7 6 5 4 3 2 1

PRINTED IN THE UNITED STATES OF AMERICA

For Sheryl

Many thanks to my parents & grandparents, for undying support;
to Martha Haigh and Roland LaVoie, for inspiring me to put pen to paper; and to Roger
Ebert and Harlan Jacobson for teaching me a few things about expressing opinions about
film.

Contents

FOREWORD

BY ROGER EBERT

Film critics are asked all the time: "Do you read the reviews of other critics?" The anticipated answer, I think, is "No, of course not! I exist in a pure and inviolate space occupied only by my own reviews." In this view, to read another critic would be cheating. My own answer is that I read other critics constantly. One of them, Stanley Kauffmann, I have been reading since 1960. I never took a film class—they were not offered when I was an undergraduate—but as a graduate student of English literature, I was expected to read the literature on an author or novel or poem before venturing to write my own essay. No serious scholar in any discipline would write about a subject without being familiar with the writing of those who had gone before.

That said, the experience of a film critic on deadline is a little different. James Berardinelli and I, and most of the other critics whose reviews appear on or before a movie's opening day, cannot read other critics most of the time, for the obvious reason that we are writing before any other reviews are available. If a film has already opened in England, say, or played for six months in San Francisco, there may be reviews online, but then there is another inhibiting factor: We don't want to come across an insight or a nice bit of phrasing that *we* might have thought of—and then feel that we can't use it, because we know that someone else already has.

Therefore, I prefer not to discuss movies with anyone before writing my review, and I rarely talk about them with other critics after a screenings. Case history. Some years ago there was a Chicago press screening of a film of truly awesome incompetence. As it happened, one of its reels was missing. In the dark, I smiled to myself, thinking, "If the missing reel contained the lost footage from *Greed,* it wouldn't help." The lights came up, a publicist appeared, and said "We have tracked down the missing reel and can show it to you after the second screening tomorrow." Gene Siskel said: "Even if it's the lost footage from *The Magnificent Ambersons,* it wouldn't help." Damn! Now how could I use my line?

So most of us write in a vacuum, sometimes by necessity, sometimes by choice. Once our reviews are written, however, of course I read others — especially if the movie is likely to divide critics, or is tricky or controversial in some interesting way. Most movies open on Fridays, and one of my Friday rituals is to visit a Web site like rottentomatoes.com, where the Tomatometer measures North American critical reaction and provides links to dozens of reviews. Other good sources are the Movie Review Query Engine (mrqe.com) and of course the invaluable Internet Movie Database (imdb.com).

For several years, one of my regular stops has been the ReelViews.net site of James Berardinelli, who was online even before the dawn of the Web. In an article about the best Web-based movie sites, for the first (June 1996) issue of *Yahoo! Internet Life* magazine, I wrote:

> . . . some of the Web-based critics are excellent, and there is one, James Berardinelli who stands above the crowd. Berardinelli describes himself as an electrical engineer from Morristown, N.J., who has written some 1,000 movie reviews over the last four years. That's more than many full-time critics manage. Berardinelli is literate, opinionated, well-informed and a good writer. He's also familiar with film history; unlike many Web critics, he knows the classics. A newspaper looking for a film critic would be well-advised to head for his URL and hire him immediately (assuming he could be wrenched away from electrical engineering).

Berardinelli and I struck up an e-mail friendship, and a year or so later I met him in person at the Philadelphia Film Festival. I found a man who was serious, focused, with a wry humor, fascinated by movies, and so thin that I never knew whether to talk movies with him, or take him out and try to get him to eat something.

I learned a little of his story. How his profession as a computer expert was matched with a passion for the cinema. How a sad loss in his life left him with a lot of free time, and he began posting reviews on the Web as a way of filling empty hours. How he had to drive to screenings in Philadelphia and New York. How nevertheless he found time to see a great many movies and to review them at full length, with insight and genuine feeling.

James and I have met several times since then, at the Toronto Film Festival and my own Overlooked Film Festival at the University of Illinois at Urbana-Champaign. I still believe a newspaper is missing a bet by not hiring him full-time, but I also understand that James is not looking for that: He likes the mix between his day job and his movies.

The Web is a remarkable democracy. Anyone can post a movie review there, and sometimes it seems like everyone does. Reviews appear on personal Web sites, on host sites, on newspaper and magazine sites, in webzines, at about.com and epinions.com, as "user comments" on the Internet Movie Database, as customer reviews on Amazon.com, and in places like the newsgroup rec.arts.movies.current-reviews. There are many sites dedicated to single directors or stars or genres. If you are a critic dealing with a genre you need to know more about, like Japanese anime, you can choose from dozens of sites via Google.

This vast and open democracy is like a testing-ground for the free marketplace of ideas. In theory, the best critics will rise to the top, and the lesser critics will find their sites visited only by their friends — maybe. Berardinelli's ReelViews now carries the top-page line, "The largest non-commercial movie site on the 'Net." Over a period of several years, many thousands of people looking for movie reviews have traveled the Web, and they have discovered Berardinelli, recognized the quality of his work, and kept coming back. As one who found him very early on, I agree with their discernment. I wanted to write this foreword because I admire the writing, and also because I admire the writer. Berardinelli is a valuable resource, and it is good to have his reviews — sane, accurate, passionate, generous in both praise and blame—between covers.

INTRODUCTION
BY JAMES BERARDINELLI

The process of watching a movie isn't what it used to be. Not that long ago, seeing a film meant hiring a babysitter, driving to a theater, standing in line to buy a ticket, enduring the rudeness of fellow patrons, and being at the mercy of uncaring projectionists. Now, with the advent of home theater, the movie-going experience can be replicated to a degree in the comfort of one's house. All it takes is a trip to the video store or a few minutes browsing online. DVDs have elevated the audio and video quality far beyond what could be achieved with VHS tapes and laserdiscs. With a high-end speaker system and a big screen TV, home viewing can be nearly as immersive as theater going. And you don't have to deal with the kid behind you kicking the back of your seat or your shoes getting stuck to the floor.

One of the most daunting aspects of programming a home theater's screenings is choosing the movies. Walk into a video store, and you're faced with hundreds of titles, only a few of which (those that are relentlessly hyped in TV ads) sound familiar. It's worse online, where the selection is broader. The average video store around the corner may stock 1,000 titles; the most popular Internet rental sites stock ten times that. Granted, it's a lot cheaper to rent a movie than it is to see one in a theater, but the cost is not zero, and wasted time is still wasted time. Better to be prepared than to take a shot in the dark. Hopefully, that's where this book comes in.

The purpose of the book is twofold: to provide a list of recommended movies for viewing, and, hopefully, to offer a few hours of reading enjoyment. My view has always been that reviews, like any form of written criticism, should be seen as pieces of literature, to be read and enjoyed in their own right, regardless of whether you are familiar with the movie, or whether you agree with the review. Reviews are not solely designed as consumer guides for video renters/buyers, but as sources of information, inspiration, and entertainment. So, in compiling this book, I decided to reduce the number of titles in order to be able to present lengthier reviews. Call it quality over quantity.

You don't have to agree with a critic for him or her to be valuable. There's no such thing as an objective review. Reviews are informed opinions. They are useful to any reader who understands where the critic is coming from. After browsing through a number of the reviews in this book, you'll figure out a lot about me, and, using that information, you should be able to determine with reasonable accuracy from the text of any given review, whether the movie will interest you. You can't do that with one of those "every title under the moon" tomes, which assign zero to five stars and offer a 50-word synopsis.

The reviews are presented by category, much as the movies are to be found in most video stores. The placement of some titles presented difficulties. For example, more than a few movies straddle both the "Action/Adventure" category and the "Thriller" category. And should a romantic comedy be considered a "Romance" or a "Comedy?" In all cases, I have done my best to place each title where I believe it most appropriately to belong, but there may be cases where reasonable people will disagree.

There are roughly 1,000 reviews presented here. All have one thing in common: I recommend them. The assigned ratings – "Recommended," "Highly Recommended," or "Must See" — are indications of my enthusiasm. But there are no mediocre or bad movies to be found in this book. To one degree or another, I enjoyed every film that is reviewed in these pages.

The majority of the reviews are of movies released between 1990 and 2002. Since most video stores stock more new movies than older ones, this represents a good cross section of the most widely available titles. Blockbusters and obscure titles get equal treatment. There's also a small selection of older "classics" — pre-1990 movies that can be found in almost any video store and without which I would have felt this book to be incomplete. What kind of book would this be if there were no reviews of *Casablanca* and *Citizen Kane*? Admittedly, the choice of older reviews is somewhat arbitrary, but hopefully there are enough of those titles to satisfy anyone who is interested in earlier material.

Since all of these reviews are available online (at http://www.reelviews.net), it's a fair question to ask why it's worth investing in this book. I can think of a couple of reasons. The first is that the reviews here have been edited and condensed with a view toward enhanced readability. A great deal of extraneous information has been cut away, leaving behind a final article that is leaner and in many ways more literate than the Web site version. The second reason is one of convenience. Books are far more portable than computers. It's a lot easier to bring a book to a video store, or to curl up on a couch with a book, than it is a computer. As much as I value the Internet, I would be lost without my small library of printed material. Online material will never entirely replace books, just as home video will never completely supplant theatrical viewing.

It is my hope that everyone reading this book enjoys it for what it is — a collection of film-related essays written over a span of more than 10 years by someone whose love of movies has deepened during that period. No matter how closely your tastes match mine, you won't agree with everything I have written, but hopefully you will be entertained by every word.

I'll see you in line and online.

Reel Views 2

Action/Adventure

The 13th Warrior [1999]

Starring: Antonio Banderas, Diane Venora, Omar Sharif Director: John McTiernan Screenplay: William Wisher & Warner Lewis Running Time: 1:42 Rated: R (Violence, bloody carnage, headless bodies) Theatrical Aspect Ratio: 2.35:1

Admittedly, anyone expecting Shakespeare will be disappointed. Depth is not one of *The 13th Warrior*'s strengths. In fact, probably as the result of hasty editing, two subplots (one about internal politics and one featuring a romance) have been pruned to the point where their inclusions raise more questions than they answer. On the other hand, the main storyline is lean and tightly plotted, with the best sword-and-spear battle sequences since *Braveheart*. The movie is a lavish spectacle and does an excellent job of creating atmosphere and establishing an involving scenario.

Antonio Banderas plays Ahmed Ibn Fadlan, a 10th century Arab ambassador from Baghdad whose mission is to interact with and learn the ways of the Vikings. Although initially horrified by the Northmen's barbaric customs and lack of hygiene, Ahmed unexpectedly becomes one of their number when the Vikings' leader, Buliwyf (Vladimir Kulich), includes him in a small band of adventurers. Their goal: report to aging King Hrothgar (Sven Wollter) and offer their assistance in protecting his people from a scourge that is causing supernatural terror and decimating the population — half-men, half-beasts that attack during the night, decapitating their victims. Soon, Ahmed is on the front lines, fighting alongside Bulifwyf and his right-hand man, Herger (Dennis Storhøi), to defeat the creatures known as the "Eaters of the Dead."

What's interesting about *The 13th Warrior* is that it purports to be a deconstruction of the legend of Beowulf. According to the classic heroic poem (composed around 1000 A.D.), Beowulf is a great Scandinavian warrior who answers King Hrothgar's pleas for help to kill the man-eating monster Grendel. Later, after slaying the creature, Beowulf enters Grendel's lair to destroy his mother. *The 13th Warrior* argues that "Grendel" is not actually one creature, but a host of costumed men who assault under cover of darkness, pretending to be fearsome, demonic apparitions. Buifwyf/Beowulf earns his reputation by driving them back then leading a small party of warriors on a search-and-destroy mission for the female leader of the attacking tribe.

Admittedly, most of those venturing into a theater to see *The 13th Warrior* won't know anything about Beowulf or Grendel. But it's not necessary to make the connection. The movie can be enjoyed for what it is — an action/adventure picture filled with violent, bloody battles and larger-than-life heroic deeds. Think *Conan the Barbarian* crossed with *Braveheart*. There's more than a little of both to be found here — great deeds by great men in a forgotten era.
RECOMMENDED

Alive [1993]

Starring: Ethan Hawke, Vincent Spano, Josh Hamilton Director: Frank Marshall Screenplay: John Patrick Shanley Running Time: 2:06 Rated: R (Language, disturbing images, cannibalism) Theatrical Aspect Ratio: 1.85:1

In 1972, a chartered plane carrying 37 people — friends, family, and members of a Uruguayan rugby team — crash-landed in the Andes en route to Chile. For 72 days, the survivors struggled to prolong their existence, resorting to cannibalism to stay alive. *Alive,* based on Piers Paul Read's bestseller, is their story.

Alive will not be shown on any airplanes. The plane crash sequence, perfectly prefaced and executed, is hair-raising — perhaps the most terrifying crash ever shown in a movie. The tension of the moment is heightened, rather than diminished, by the knowledge of what is to come. The unpleasant subject of cannibalism is confronted in *Alive.* Because it was such an important factor to the survival of the 16, it could not be glossed over, but it is dealt with sensitively rather than sensationalistically. There are no gruesome close-ups of half-eaten bodies. The characters react with genuine horror at what they have to do. The most graphic scene occurs past the mid-point of the film, in a wide shot of the crash/camp site, where several stripped skeletons can be seen half-covered by snow.

One of the disadvantages of having so many characters is that few of them attain independence from the mass as far as the audience is concerned. As a result, most of the deaths are meaningless. There are only three characters who have enough screen time, dialogue, and interaction to achieve depth: Nando Parrado (Ethan Hawke), Antonio Balbi (Vincent Spano), and Roberto Cannessa (Josh Hamilton). It is primarily around these three that the story centers.

Alive is an adventure that grapples with issues more profound than most movies of the genre. The moral implications of eating the body of a dead friend or relative are not overlooked, nor is the spiritual cost of such a decision. The will to live demands sacrifices, none of which come cheaply. Religion and the existence of God are themes that *Alive* constantly returns to. Well-produced, acted, and scripted, this is a film that has to be seen to be experienced, even by those who know the entire tale. **RECOMMENDED**

Apollo 13 [1995]

Starring: Tom Hanks, Kevin Bacon, Bill Paxton   Director: Ron Howard
Screenplay: William Boyles, Jr. & Al Reinert   Running Time: 2:20
Rated: **PG** (Bodily functions)   Theatrical Aspect Ratio: **2.35:1**

The Apollo program was first announced in 1961. The climax came on July 20, 1969, when Neil Armstrong stepped out of Apollo 11's lunar module and issued his famous quote. Nine months later, with astronauts Jim Lovell (Tom Hanks), Fred Haise (Bill Paxton), and Jack Swigert (Kevin Bacon) aboard, Apollo 13 left the launch pad. Since moonshots were now regarded as commonplace, none of the three networks chose to air Lovell's first broadcast to Earth. However, when an explosion left the crew with a dwindling oxygen supply and failing power, television took notice, as did the entire world. This is the story told by Ron Howard in *Apollo 13.*

Perhaps the most impressive feat of this film is sustaining white-knuckle tension even though the chain of events is well known. The conclusion of the mission is a matter of recent historical record, yet recalling how it ends does nothing to lessen the excitement or dampen the emotional impact of several key moments. Such deft filmmaking is a prime reason why *Apollo 13* is an unqualified success.

It's not the only reason, however. During the 140-minute running time, we are essentially given three stories: the astronauts' struggle to stay alive, the controlled chaos at NASA as experts are forced to come up with unexpected solutions, and the trauma faced by the families of the men whose lives are in danger. With inserts of news footage from the time (much of which features Walter Cronkite), *Apollo 13* attains a level of verisimilitude few current features can match.

The effective, understated special effects never upstage any of the fine performances. All three actors playing the astronauts — Hanks, Paxton, and Bacon — have gotten under their characters' skins. Ed Harris exudes a palpable intensity in a supporting performance as Mission Controller Gene Kranz, the coordinator of the teamwork that goes into saving the space craft. Gary Sinise, reunited here with *Forrest Gump* co-star Tom Hanks, plays Ken Mattingly, the member of Lovell's team who, after being refused medical clearance to fly, plays a crucial role in the rescue.

The villain here is the vastness of space — an antagonist that refuses direct confrontation. There isn't a traditional bad guy to be found, but *Apollo 13* needs no such useless embellishment. Reality has a taste the likes of which fiction can rarely match. Those who recall that week in April 1970 will enjoy seeing the full story unfold; those who are too young to remember will get a feeling not only of what the individuals endured, but how the country as a whole reacted. **MUST SEE**

Bandit Queen [India, 1995]

Starring: Seema Biswas, Nirmal Pandey, Manoj Bajpai
Director: Shekhar Kapur   Screenplay: Mala Sen   Running Time: **1:59**
Rated: **R** (Rape, violence, sexual situations)   In Hindi with subtitles

Two phrases encapsulate the backdrop against which *Bandit Queen* unfolds. The first is a quote shown on-screen at the film's start: "Animals, drums, illiterates, low castes and women are worthy of being beaten." The second is a statement by Phoolan Devi's father: "A daughter is always a burden . . ." It is into this male-centered culture that Devi is born in the late 1950s. Her entire life from the age of 11, when she is married to a much older man, is devoted to fighting for the rights of women and striking blows against a viciously prejudiced social structure.

After running away from her husband, Devi is captured and abused by bandits. Eventually, she joins a gang, and it isn't long before her reputation as a Robin Hood-like figure becomes known across India. She exacts revenge on those who betrayed her, becoming the chief instigator of 1980's Behmai Massacre, where 24 men are killed. The authorities prove unable to capture Devi, and she remains on the loose until 1983, when a deal with the Indian government brings about her surrender.

The picture of human indignity and suffering painted by *Bandit Queen* is on par with that of *Schindler's List*. As the Nazis treated the Jews like animals, so too do the upper caste Indians regard those born into poverty and squalor. Compared to some of the indignities experienced by Devi, death would have been quick and merciful. Multiple rapes and public humiliation are only a few of the torments she must endure, and each atrocity further hardens her heart. When it comes, Devi's revenge is indeed a dish best served cold.

Tightly-paced, powerfully-written, and well-acted, *Bandit Queen* is a first-rate adventure movie. Like *Schindler's List,* there is no political diatribe here. Actions and events are allowed to define the social climate. The film manages to grip the audience in a way that no preachy commentary ever will. Devi, as strikingly portrayed by actress Seema Biswas, becomes real, and it doesn't take long for us to feel her seething rage at the mountain of injustices rising above her. It is uncomfortable to sympathize with someone who becomes so ruthless and uncompromising, but that is the gut-wrenching path along which director Kapur drags us. *Bandit Queen* is not for the squeamish, or for those who prefer not to be challenged or unsettled by a motion picture. Because, whatever your feelings about the movie or its protagonist, *Bandit Queen* will not leave you apathetic. **HIGHLY RECOMMENDED**

Batman Forever [1995]

Starring: Val Kilmer, Tommy Lee Jones, Jim Carrey, Nicole Kidman, Chris O'Donnell Director: Joel Schumacher Screenplay: Lee Batchler, Janet Scott Batchler and Akiva Goldsman Running Time: 2:01
Rated: PG-13 (Violence, cartoonish garishness) Theatrical Aspect Ratio: 1.85:1

It's lighter, brighter, funnier, faster-paced, and a whole lot more colorful than before. There's a new actor underneath the cape, a new girlfriend on his arm, and a new partner by his side. The director is different and the composer has changed. The villains — Jim Carrey decked out in a neon question-mark jacket and Tommy Lee Jones with a face out of *The Elephant Man* — are making their debuts. Yet somehow, perhaps because of the costume, it still feels like the same *Batman* we've gotten to know in two previous films. The same, yet different — and much better.

This time around, the Caped Crusader (Val Kilmer) is faced with a new pair of dastardly bad guys: the Riddler (Carrey) and Harvey Two-Face (Jones). The Riddler, aka Edward Nigma, is a scientist working in Bruce Wayne's electronics factory. When he invents a device to beam television waves directly into the brain, then tries it on himself, he becomes unhinged ("wacko" is the "technical" term used). Now, he's out to control all of Gotham City and humiliate his former boss in the process. To that end, he joins up with Two-Face, who has a more modest goal: kill Batman, whom he blames for his disfigurement. Meanwhile, Bruce Wayne is falling for his third woman in three films. This time, it's a lady doctor with a name that sounds like two merged banks (Chase Meridian, played by Nicole Kidman). She's a psychiatrist who specializes in split personalities (something that afflicts just about everyone in this movie). And, in the person of Dick Grayson (Chris O'Donnell), who takes on the appellation Robin, Batman gets a sidekick to help use all his bat-gadgets and pilot his batmobiles, bat boats, bat planes, and bat subs.

Director Joel Schumacher's vision of Gotham is similar to, yet different from, Tim Burton's. The same bizarre, larger-than-life architecture is evident, but *Batman Forever*'s city is bigger and brighter. This is a jaunty, multi-hued place that reflects a lightening in the movie's tone. There's a lot going on in *Batman Forever* — probably much more than in either *Batman* or *Batman Returns* — yet Schumacher keeps things on an even keel, moving swiftly without creating such a strong undertow that the viewer loses his or her footing. The film is a blast and, ultimately, a very quick 2 hours. In a relatively short time, we get a solid action/adventure story, an odd romantic triangle, and the most detailed exploration of Batman's character to date. All-in-all, this is a very full motion picture. **RECOMMENDED**

Behind Enemy Lines [2001]

Starring: Owen Wilson, Gene Hackman, Joaquim de Almeida
Director: John Moore Screenplay: David Veloz & Zak Penn Running
Time: 1:43 Rated: PG-13 (Violence, profanity) Theatrical Aspect
Ratio: 2.35:1

Behind Enemy Lines takes place at some unspecified, not-too-distant time in Bosnia, and does not attempt to dissect or explain the complicated social and political situation there. Instead, we are presented with a straightforward scenario. An American reconnaissance plane veers off course during a flyover and is shot down because its crew sees something they aren't intended to see. Once downed, Lt. Chris Burnett (Wilson) must flee for his life from a bunch of Bad Guys (identified only as being Serbs) who are out to get him. Meanwhile, back on his home aircraft carrier of the USS Carl Vinson, Admiral Reigart (Gene Hackman) is trying to organize a rescue effort. But he is being stymied by NATO Admiral Piquet (Joaquim de Almeida), who is concerned that a U.S. incursion into Bosnia at this critical time could cause a peace accord to disintegrate.

The film develops parallel storylines. The first involves Burnett's danger-laden trip to the town of Hac, where he is supposed to be lifted to safety. Along the way, he must avoid the well-armed troops of the local Serbian military leader, Lokar (Olek Krupa), and an assassin (Vladimir Maskov) whom Lokar has assigned to kill him. Meanwhile, on the ship, Reigart risks his career by trying to find a way to get Burnett out of harm's way without directly disobeying an order. Piquet becomes a villain of sorts simply because he comes across as a bureaucrat standing in the way of a righteous mission, but his form of villainy pales in comparison to that of the ruthless butchers seeking to eliminate Burnett.

Owen Wilson is a shrewd choice to play the film's protagonist. Like Bruce Willis in *Die Hard*, Wilson brings an everyman quality to the role. We can easily identify with Burnett — he's not an Arnold Schwarzenegger, Sylvester Stallone, or Jean-Claude Van Damme. Gene Hackman, the consummate veteran, lends a hard-nosed dignity to the part of Admiral Reigart.

Even though this is only his debut, director John

Moore has a clear sense of what works in this sort of motion picture. The premise is familiar and the storyline formulaic, yet the execution is effective enough that it keeps us involved for the running length. *Behind Enemy Lines* is a crowd-pleaser, and Moore rarely gives us enough down time to reflect on its weaknesses. In addition, the movie doesn't wear out its welcome. At just under 105 minutes, it's the right length. **RECOMMENDED**

The Bourne Identity [2002]

Starring: Matt Damon, Franka Potente, Clive Owen, Chris Cooper
Director: Doug Liman Screenplay: Tony Gilroy & William Blake Herron,
based on the novel by Robert Ludlum Running Time: 1:58 Rated: R
(Violence, profanity) Theatrical Aspect Ratio: 2.35:1

In all likelihood, Robert Ludlum fans will not be pleased by this adaptation of one of the spy master's best-received novels. That's because *The Bourne Identity* uses the premise, a few character names, and some isolated incidents from the novel, then runs off in its own direction. This version is nicely paced and fits the bill for those in search of 2 hours of spy-based action and martial arts. The movie has credibility issues, but none are insurmountable in the name of entertainment.

The Bourne Identity doesn't have much of a story to speak of — the plot is a jumping-off point and a means to keep things rolling from one action sequence to the next. Jason Bourne (Matt Damon) is a CIA assassin who loses his memory after a failed mission that results in him being shot twice and left floating in the ocean. However, while Jason doesn't know exactly who (or what) he is, he recognizes that someone is after him, and his training kicks in. That "someone" is his boss, Ted Conklin (Chris Cooper), who sees Bourne as a loose end that has to be eliminated. Jason meets Marie Kreutz (Franka Potente), a German wanderer who leaps at the chance to earn $20,000 by driving Jason to his Paris apartment. Once there, however, they encounter hit men and dead bodies, and Jason decides that the only way to save himself is to find out who he is and why someone wants him dead.

Action-oriented tension drives *The Bourne Identity*. While the movie pays lip service to solving the "mystery" of Jason's identity, this is pretty much a red herring. We figure things out early in the proceedings, so there are no surprises around the corner. The real question posed by the screenplay is how Jason will survive the hit men sent after him, especially the deadly Professor (Clive Owen), who seems to be his equal. In addition to a number of high-octane fight scenes and some cat-and-mouse games, the movie contains a lengthy car chase through the streets of Paris.

The Bourne Identity does not rely on special effects or science fiction-like plot elements to get by. It's a straightforward story of good guys against bad guys, with most of the moral ambiguities leached out. No matter who comes out on top, this is the kind of movie where the audience — at least an audience looking for 120 minutes of adrenaline-propelled escapism — wins. RECOMMENDED

Braveheart [1995]

Starring: Mel Gibson, Patrick McGoohan, Sophie Marceau
Director: Mel Gibson Screenplay: Randall Wallace Running Time: 2:50
Rated: R (Graphic violence, brief nudity) Theatrical Aspect Ratio: 2.35:1

Borrowing from masters like Sam Peckinpah and David Lean, actor/director Mel Gibson has crafted an exceptional cinematic tapestry in only his sophomore effort. Most of the time, 3-hour movies have a few flat spots, but *Braveheart* is constantly on the move — riveting from start to finish.

The title character is William Wallace (Gibson), a hero of Scottish history whose legend has surely outstripped fact (in its own unique way, the film acknowledges this). Wallace fought for Scotland's freedom in the late 13th century, wielding his broadsword and influence to defeat the forces of King Edward I (Patrick McGoohan), the British monarch who had declared himself king of Scotland upon the former ruler's demise.

Braveheart builds slowly to its first gritty climax. Much of the early film concentrates on Wallace's love for Murron (Catherine McCormack). Their courtship is unhurried, yet this is all preparation. The real meat of the story, which includes political machinations, betrayal, and dramatic battles, is yet to come. Patrick Henry once said, "Give me liberty, or give me death!" That might well be Wallace's motto. The nobles of Scotland fight for land and riches, but Wallace stands for the individual, and earns respect with words and deeds.

Bulked up and wearing a long-haired wig, Gibson brings his usual wealth of charisma to the title role. Patrick McGoohan, best known from TV's *Secret Agent Man* and *The Prisoner,* is almost unrecognizable beneath a snowy beard. His Edward the Longshanks exudes an aura of cold menace. He's a worthy foe for Wallace because his intelligence matches his ruthlessness. Sophie Marceau, the French actress who plays Princess Isabelle, and Catherine McCormack are both immensely appealing.

Braveheart is a brutal, bloody motion picture, but the violence is not gratuitous. The maimings, decapitations, and other assorted gruesome details make Wallace's world seem real and immediate. In addition, few theatrical moments make a more eloquent statement against war than when Gibson shows women and children weeping over the dead on a body-littered battlefield. War is a two-headed beast, and both faces — the glorious and the tragic — are depicted. *Braveheart* offers an exhilarating, and occasionally touching, experience that has viewers leaving the theater caught up in an afterglow of wonder. These days, heroes like William Wallace are as rare as motion picture displays of this high, uncompromising quality. MUST SEE

Broken Arrow [1996]

Starring: John Travolta, Christian Slater, Samantha Mathis
Director: John Woo Screenplay: Graham Yost Running Time: 1:48
Rated: R (Violence, profanity) Theatrical Aspect Ratio: 2.35:1

According to the movie, a "broken arrow" is the military term for a lost nuclear weapon. Here, there are two, but they aren't really lost. Rather, they have been stolen by Air Force Major Vic Deakins (John Travolta at his most nasty). Vic thinks the military has done him a grave injustice by repeatedly passing him over for promotion, and he's out to get revenge. His demands are simple: $250 million or one major American city will be atomized.

The only things standing between Vic and a luxurious retirement are his ex-partner, Captain Riley Hale (Christian Slater), and a Utah park ranger, Terry Carmichael (Samantha Mathis). They hook up when Terry finds Riley after Vic ejects him from a stealth bomber. The rest of the film is a cat-and-mouse game, with Riley and Terry chasing Vic, or the other way around, depending on who has the missiles. There are all the requisite close calls and narrow escapes, but nothing quite as nerve-wracking as watching a bus thunder towards a gap in a freeway-under-construction.

The writer of *Broken Arrow,* Graham Yost, also wrote *Speed,* which accounts for many of the similarities. Director John Woo seems very much at home in this high-tech arena. His characteristic trademarks, such as someone leaping through the air with guns blazing in both hands, are all in evidence. As always, Woo choreographs action like a ballet, creating some of the most artistic violence to be found anywhere.

After being typecast as a good guy, John Travolta finally gets a chance to try his hand at a despicable-to-the-core villain. And, boy, is he *cool*. Christian Slater's Riley doesn't have Vic's twisted charisma, but Slater musters enough screen presence to get us on his side. And, while it's nice to see him teamed up again with Samantha Mathis (the two previously joined forces in *Pump Up the Volume*), the two never really click.

The preposterous thrills in *Broken Arrow* take the characters from a fight aboard a stealth bomber to a car chase across the flats of Utah to the bowels of a disused copper mine to a speeding train. The pace is relentless; Woo never allows the excitement to flag. In the end, *Broken Arrow* is an exhilarating, if empty, experience. It's the kind of thing where you turn off your brain and dig your fingernails into the armrest.
RECOMMENDED

Brotherhood of the Wolf [France, 2001]
Starring: **Samuel Le Bihan, Vincent Cassel, Emilie Dequenne, Monica Bellucci** Director: **Christophe Gans** Screenplay: Stéphane Cabel & Christophe Gans Running Time: 2:26 Rated: R (Violence, gore, nudity, sex) Theatrical Aspect Ratio: **2.35:1** In French with subtitles

Brotherhood of the Wolf is a period-piece action/adventure movie with elements of the following genres thrown in for good measure: martial arts, horror, and mystery/intrigue. The events represented herein are based on an actual historical event, although, to paraphrase a popular saying, director Christophe Gans never lets the facts get in the way of a good story. Most of what transpires here is pure fantasy and has little to do with the real "Beast of Gevaudan," which roamed the remote countryside in 1764 France, killing several dozen women and children.

When the story opens, and Grégoire de Fronsac (Samuel Le Bihan) and his faithful Iroquois companion, Mani (Mark Dacascos), have arrived in Gevaudan to hunt down and kill the fearsome beast that has been terrorizing the district. Rumors about it abound, but the common belief is that it's a wolf-like demon. Fronsac, a man of science, disputes this. He believes that there is something more prosaic at work than the devil. Soon after arriving in Gevaudan, Fronsac meets the twisted Jean-François de Morangias (Vincent Cassel), a bitterly sardonic young man who has lost one arm, and his pretty sister, Marianne (Emilie Dequenne), who falls for Fronsac.

With the exception of a couple isolated fights,

there's not much action during *Brotherhood of the Wolf*'s first hour — most of what transpires is exposition or used to establish characters and relationships. Indeed, we only catch half-glimpses of the Beast throughout the movie's first half. Once the action starts, however, it rarely lets up. We are treated to one martial arts showdown after another, leaving one to wonder whether an ancestor of Jackie Chan's roamed 18th century France dispensing fighting lessons.

Brotherhood of the Wolf isn't exactly a "guilty pleasure" — there is more artistry involved in the production than is immediately obvious — but its strongest appeal will be to those who don't mind movies that stray beyond the accepted boundaries of what we call "reality." The movie has something in it to appeal to just about everyone — religious politics, incestuous longing, a little gratuitous sex and nudity, savage fight scenes, a dollop of romance, and an impressive looking monster that is both more and less than it seems to be. In short, *Brotherhood of the Wolf* is daring in its approach and successful in its result — assuming the result is to provide pure entertainment to the viewer.
RECOMMENDED

Captain Corelli's Mandolin [United Kingdom/United States, 2001]
Starring: **Nicolas Cage, Penelope Cruz, John Hurt, Christian Bale** Director: **John Madden** Screenplay: Shawn Slovo Running Time: 2:07 Rated: R (Nudity, violence, sexual situations) Theatrical Aspect Ratio: **2.35:1**

Captain Corelli's Mandolin, based on the "unfilmable" novel by Louis de Bernieres, represents the kind of old-fashioned romantic melodrama that hardly ever seems to reach multiplexes these days. Although there's nothing ground-breaking or otherwise extraordinary about the film, it is expertly directed, beautifully photographed, and (for the most part) nicely acted.

The movie opens on the eve of World War II in Greece. On the island of Cephalonia, life continues as usual. One of those "usual" events is the courtship of Pelagia (Penelope Cruz), the daughter of the resident doctor, Dr. Iannis (John Hurt), and Mandras (Christian Bale), a fisherman. The two announce their engagement on the day before Mandras goes off to war. He promises to write, but Pelagia hears nothing from him, her letters going unanswered. Meanwhile, Cephalonia comes under Italian occupation. The officer billeted in Dr. Iannis's house is the mandolin-playing, opera-loving Captain Antonio Corelli (Nicolas Cage). After initially resisting the attraction, he and Pelagia fall in love — just in time for Mandras to return. But the Italian officers face a moral crisis when Mussolini surrenders to the Allies and the Germans move in to take over the Italian occupation: do they give in and let the Germans take over, or do they fight against their former allies alongside the Greek rebels?

The most interesting aspect of *Captain Corelli's Mandolin* is the way the film explores the shifting relationship between the occupiers (Italians and Germans) and the occupied (Greeks). At first, there is a great deal of animosity, but, with the passage of time, as the two sides come to know one another, a wary camaraderie develops, especially between the Italians and the Greeks.

As Captain Corelli, Nicolas Cage is somewhat miscast. This isn't one of those incidents when the actor's presence in the role torpedoes the entire film, but there are instances when Cage doesn't seem comfortable living in Corelli's skin. He goes over-the-top and makes the title character more fatuous than he is meant to be. Penelope Cruz and Christian Bale are solid, but unspectacular.

For director John Madden (*Shakespeare in Love*), *Captain Corelli's Mandolin* represents an opportunity to indulge his preference for character-driven dramas. The movie also has a message to impart about the inhumanity of men to other men in war. But the glue that holds the movie together, and the element that will draw most viewers into the theater, is the romance between Pelagia and Corelli. Theirs isn't a love affair for the ages, but it's strong enough that *Captain Corelli's Mandolin* is likely to appeal to the *English Patient* audience. RECOMMENDED

Cast Away [2000]

Starring: Tom Hanks, Helen Hunt Director: Robert Zemeckis
Screenplay: William Broyles, Jr. Running Time: 2:24 Rated: PG-13
(Harrowing material, mild profanity) Theatrical Aspect Ratio: 1.85:1

The year is 1995. Chuck Noland is an overworked Federal Express exec who zips from country to country troubleshooting problems and streamlining operations. Chuck is enjoying Christmas dinner with his girlfriend, Kelly (Helen Hunt), and his family, when a call comes in: he's needed in Malaysia. A short time later, he's airborne, flying through stormy skies over the South Pacific. Suddenly, there's an explosion, and Chuck finds himself underwater in the belly of a crashed plane. An inflatable life raft carries him to the surface and bears him to a deserted tropical island, where he learns that survival without the trappings of civilization is far more difficult than it's made out to be in books and in the movies. There may not be any humans on the island, but something is making noise in the jungle at night. And how is he to obtain food and fresh water? Without proper tools, simple tasks like opening a coconut or making a fire become herculean efforts.

Cast Away is divided into three clearly-defined acts: the setup, the main story, and the aftermath. Although the movie's centerpiece is the 75-minute portion detailing Chuck's experiences while marooned, it's the third act, which offers no easy solutions for difficult situations, that elevates the film from the level of a stirring, innovative adventure to a fully satisfying drama.

The scenes on the island are presented with uncommon intelligence. We follow Chuck on his step-by-step journey of survival, where even the smallest things become significant accomplishments. Zemeckis' approach to this segment of the film is flawless. He never cuts away from Chuck — there are no "back in Memphis" scenes that would have broken the mood, nor is there any incidental music. Also, the script doesn't cook up any hard-to-swallow, melodramatic situations or artificial conflicts.

For the level of his work in *Cast Away*, Hanks earned another Oscar nomination. The movie's success rests with him, since he is on screen by himself for more than half of the running time. It's one thing for an actor to triumph by playing off others; it's another thing altogether for him to excel with no one else around and virtually no dialogue to speak. In addition, the physical changes that Hanks had to go through to play the part are dramatic — he was forced to gain and lose weight quickly and in extraordinary amounts.

For as long as he works in Hollywood, Robert Zemeckis will be associated with *Forrest Gump*. As good a film as that was, it does not represent his finest work. In many ways, both *Contact* and *Cast Away* are stronger and more compelling features. *Cast Away* has all the hallmarks of a great motion picture: well-developed characters, solid drama, non-traditional adventure, and an intelligent script. It is one of the best of the year. MUST SEE

Charlie's Angels [2000]

Starring: Cameron Diaz, Drew Barrymore, Lucy Liu, Bill Murray
Director: McG Screenplay: Ryan Rawe, Ed Solomon & John August
Running Time: 1:38 Rated: PG-13 (Profanity, violence, sexual innuendo) Theatrical Aspect Ratio: 2.35:1

Charlie's Angels approaches its subject matter in much the same way that *The Brady Bunch Movie* did. With tongue planted firmly in cheek for the entire 98-minute running length, the film simultaneously pays homage to and makes fun of the first television show to have gotten dads and daughters to bond in front of the set. *Charlie's Angels* is designed camp — a movie that openly acknowledges its dubious appeal and revels in it.

There is a plot — not that the specifics matter much. The current group of Angels — blond Natalie (Cameron Diaz), busty Dylan (Drew Barrymore), and leather-loving Alex (Lucy Liu) — are summoned to the Townsend Detective Agency building by Bosley (Billy Murray in the role originated by the late David Doyle). There, speaking from a remote location, the disembodied Charlie (voice of John Forsythe — the only returning participant from the TV series) informs his employees about their new assignment. Their client, Vivian Wood (Kelly Lynch), has suffered a catastrophic loss — her best friend and boss, the genius behind Knox Electronics, has been kidnapped, presumably by his chief rival, the dastardly Roger Corwin (Tim Curry). The Angels are to save Knox (Sam Rockwell) and recover the stolen technology Corwin has hidden deep in an ultra-secret vault.

It's hard to say whether *Charlie's Angels* contains more action scenes or flashes of flesh. Regardless, both are present in abundance. The film's director, making his feature debut, "McG" (short for Joseph McGinty Mitchell), pumps up the visual and audio volume, making *Charlie's Angels* a kinetic experience, even during the few "slow" sequences.

Fortunately, the actors are all in synch with the material. None of them tries to play things too seriously or too broadly. Barrymore, in addition to being one of the driving forces behind getting the movie made, is arguably the most luminous of the stars. Diaz borrows liberally from her *There's Something About Mary* character, although she appears (for lack of a better term) a little washed out. Lucy Liu is at her best when playing the part of a dominatrix disciplining a room full of sun-deprived engineers.

Feminists have always debated the merits of *Charlie's Angels* whether it deals in female exploitation or empowerment. This movie certainly isn't going to resolve the issue, since there's plenty of both going on. Ultimately, however, *Charlie's Angels* is far too light to promote any sort of serious or introspective discus-

sion — and rightfully so. The movie is exactly what it needs to be to succeed: trashy, dumb, and flashy — in short, a guilty pleasure. RECOMMENDED

Courage Under Fire [1996]

Starring: Denzel Washington, Meg Ryan, Lou Diamond Phillips, Matt Damon   Director: Edward Zwick   Screenplay: Patrick Sheane Duncan   Running Time: 1:57   Rated: R (Profanity, violence, mature themes)   Theatrical Aspect Ratio: 1.85:1

Courage Under Fire shows us another face of war's horrors, although this particular perspective is less bleak than that of a *Platoon* or an *Apocalypse Now*. Those movies were brutally effective because they reveled in bleakness, cynicism, and carnage; *Courage Under Fire* gains its power by affirming that the cost of war isn't the inevitable eradication of every trace of human dignity and heroism.

Lieutenant Colonel Nat Serling (Denzel Washington) was a tank commander during the Gulf War. On the night of February 25, 1991, his troops engaged the Iraqis, and, during the confusion, Serling mistook one of his own tanks for the enemy. He gave the order to fire, and ended up killing his best friend. Since then, Serling has been burdened by guilt.

Six months after the war's conclusion, Serling is working on the staff of General Hershberg (Michael Moriarty), investigating potential medal recipients. In that capacity, he is asked to rubber-stamp the approval of a posthumous Congressional Medal of Honor for Captain Karen Walden, a helicopter pilot who is credited for saving 5 lives at the cost of her own. As Serling begins his investigation, however, he discovers discrepancies in the stories of those involved. He digs deeper, and uncovers contrasting perspectives of the same events. Ilario (Matt Damon), one of the men in Walden's medi-vac unit, claims that "the heavier the pressure, the calmer she got." Monfriez (Lou Diamond Phillips), another of Walden's men, has a different story, stating emphatically, "She was afraid. . . . She was a coward. That's the bottom line. . . ."

Akira Kurosawa's *Rashomon* depicted a murder from several different viewpoints. *Courage Under Fire* uses a similar technique for events in the desert. Which Karen Walden is the real one: Ilario's, Monfriez's, or someone else's? Or is the truth unknowable? For Serling, whose honor demands that he get to the bottom of things, understanding what happened when Walden crash-landed becomes an obsession. His quest is like putting together a puzzle with pieces missing, and we work alongside him to unravel the mystery.

The campaigns of *Courage Under Fire* that leave the deepest impression aren't those involving ground troops and air cover. Rather, they're the deeper, more personal struggles of Nat Serling as he sifts through the war-ravaged elements of the human spirit for that "one little piece of shining something for people to believe in." *Courage Under Fire* is as profound and intelligent as it is moving. MUST SEE

Crouching Tiger, Hidden Dragon [China/Taiwan/United States, 2000]

Starring: Chow Yun-Fat, Michelle Yeoh, Zhang Ziyi Director: Ang Lee Screenplay: Wang Hui-Ling, James Schamus & Tsai Kuo Jung Running Time: 2:00 Rated: PG-13 (Violence, sex) Theatrical Aspect Ratio: 2.35:1 In Mandarin with subtitles

One of many things that can be said about director Ang Lee is that he's not afraid to take a chance. For his latest, most ambitious outing, Lee has turned his focus to a mythical China of several hundred years ago. The critically celebrated *Crouching Tiger, Hidden Dragon* is an epic martial arts film that combines incredible action sequences with elements of romantic melodrama and superhero derring-do. As visually stunning as it is inventive, *Crouching Tiger, Hidden Dragon* has gained an international following.

Taking place during the era of the Qing dynasty, *Crouching Tiger, Hidden Dragon* gives us a trio of larger-than-life characters: the great martial arts master, Li Mu Bai (Chow Yun-Fat), whose near-invincibility makes him the Superman of his day; the love of his life (for whom he has never openly acknowledged his feelings), female warrior Yu Shu Lien (Michelle Yeoh); and the powerful-but-innocent Jen (Zhang Ziyi), who is wandering down a path towards evil. The story hinges on Li Mu Bai and Yu Shu Lien's attempts to retrieve the legendary sword Green Destiny, which has been stolen from its rightful owner, and the manner in which that quest places Li Mu Bai into conflict with his old adversary Jade Fox (Cheng Pei-pei), the woman who killed his master.

Crouching Tiger, Hidden Dragon unfolds much like a comic book, with the characters and their circumstances being painted using wide brush stokes. Subtlety is not part of Lee's palette; he is going for something grand and melodramatic. His protagonists are bigger than life and their quest is the kind of epic endeavor that pits good against evil, with an innocent caught in between. The hallmark of *Crouching Tiger,*

Hidden Dragon is its standout action sequences. All of them are eye-popping and spectacularly choreographed with special effects being used to enhance the natural athleticism of the participants.

Thematically, *Crouching Tiger, Hidden Dragon* has a rich underlying foundation. It ruminates on the true nature of freedom and how everyone, regardless of their circumstances, is a prisoner of one sort or another. Of equal importance is the way it balances the timeless equation of love, honor, and sacrifice. When viewed from any perspective, be it the lofty perch of a jaded critic or the less demanding vantage point of the average movie-goer, *Crouching Tiger, Hidden Dragon* stands out as one of the year's most complete, and exhilarating, motion picture experiences. HIGHLY RECOMMENDED

The Crow [1994]

Starring: Brandon Lee, Ernie Hudson, Michael Wincott Director: Alex Proyas Screenplay: David J. Schaw & John Shirley Running Time: 1:40 Rated: R (Graphic violence, profanity, sex, nudity) Theatrical Aspect Ratio: 1.85:1

The Crow is a gothic nightmare. With a view of Detroit that is every bit as bleak and dazzling as the urban panoramas presented in *Batman* and *Blade Runner,* this film makes it clear from the outset that wherever its flaws may lie, they will not be in the realm of visual presentation. Indeed, not only is *The Crow* a feast for the eyes, but it collides violently with another sense, utilizing a high decibel soundtrack to keep the energy level up.

There can be few in the audience upon whom the tragic irony of this picture will be lost. Lead actor Brandon Lee met his death in the final days of filming, killed as the result of a gun accident while acting the part of a man who returns from the dead to avenge his murder and that of his girlfriend (the film is dedicated to Lee and his fiancee, Eliza Hutton). It is a case of "art imitating death," and that specter will always hang over *The Crow*. Fortunately, however, the vision of director Alex Proyas lifts this film above its sad history.

Lee plays murdered rock star Eric Draven, who returns from the grave one year following his Devil's Night slaughter. His task is simple and bloody — avenge his death and that of his beloved Shelly by taking out each of the 4 killers. This he proceeds to do, with each murder becoming progressively more grizzly. Along the way, he teams up with a friendly cop (Ernie Hudson) who sympathizes with his goals.

The decision to tell the story, at least in part, from the perspective of young Sarah (Rochelle Davis) is an effective choice. By utilizing her point-of-view, *The Crow* attains an emotional level that it would not otherwise have reached. This is one of the few occasions when a voiceover works to advance, rather than hinder, the story.

Admittedly, the appeal of *The Crow* is entirely visceral. There's nothing intellectual about frying eyeballs and impaled bodies. No matter how stylish the direction and how captivating the action scenes, it's hard to see this film as much more than a highly-accomplished entry into the "revenge picture" genre. Nevertheless, as a project that the director and producer finished in memory of their young star, this film is a fitting epitaph. RECOMMENDED

Dangerous Lives of Altar Boys [2002]

Starring: Kieran Culkin, Jena Malone, Emile Hirsch, Vincent D'Onofrio, Jodie Foster Director: Peter Care Screenplay: Jeff Stockwell, Michael Petroni Running Time: 1:40 Rated: R (Profanity, violence, sexual situations, drug use) Theatrical Aspect Ratio: 1.85:1

Dangerous Lives of Altar Boys isn't your usual coming-of-age movie. Although elements of the film are reminiscent of *Stand By Me* (the group of male friends) and *Ghost World* (the dark, cynical undercurrent), *Dangerous Lives of Altar Boys* stands on its own legs. The serious issues are counterbalanced by a whimsical sense of humor. Among the most striking aspects of the movie are its occasional forays into animation.

Tim Sullivan (Kieran Culkin) and Francis Doyle (Emile Hirsch) are best friends and classmates at a Catholic high school. They spend their days and nights devising pranks and working on a comic book project that they call "The Atomic Trinity." Both Tim and Francis have graphic alter egos, and their nemesis is a caricature of the school's disciplinarian, Sister Assumpta (Jodie Foster). One day, Tim comes up with an idea for the ultimate prank — to drug a cougar at a local zoo, steal the dozing animal from its pen, and sneak it into Sister Assumpta's room. His plan is ambitious but seemingly without hope of success. Meanwhile, his constant co-conspirator, Francis, has fallen for pretty Margie Flynn (Jena Malone), who is receptive to his advances.

Dangerous Lives of Altar Boys is told from the perspective of a couple of high-school outcasts. Thus, their parents play virtually no part in the movie, the adult figures at school come across as one-dimensional bad guys, and they live life with a sense of invulnerability. In a way, their superhero alter egos are more than drawings — they're an extension of how Tim and Francis feel about themselves.

There's a lot to like about *Dangerous Lives of Altar Boys,* even if, in the final analysis, there are some things that don't work. The animated sequences — lively, colorful, and energetic — are amongst the movie's high points, and director Care does a good job evoking the tribulations of adolescence. The romance is handled with the sensitivity demanded by the subject matter it encompasses, and the friendship between Francis and Tim is credible. *Dangerous Lives of Altar Boys* isn't the best coming-of-age story to hit the big screen, but it skirts new territory, and does so with a flair that earns it a recommendation. RECOMMENDED

Deep Blue Sea [1999]

Starring: Samuel L. Jackson, Saffron Burrows, Thomas Jane, Stellan Skarsgård, LL Cool J Director: Renny Harlin Screenplay: Duncan Kennedy, Wayne Powers & Donna Powers Running Time: 1:45 Rated: R (Violence, profanity) Theatrical Aspect Ratio: 2.35:1

At first glance, *Deep Blue Sea* might look like just another dumb, pointless monster movie crawling from the depths. However, while I won't argue that this creature feature is going to enrich the mind, the script is characterized by a certain flair and Renny Harlin's direction keeps things moving at a breakneck pace.

I like the way *Deep Blue Sea* is constructed. It takes a short time to introduce the characters and set up the situation, then gets right into the action. And, once the mayhem starts, the level of tension doesn't let up until the closing credits. The script borrows liberally from *Jaws, Jurassic Park, Alien(s),* and *The Abyss,* but it doesn't try to hide its sources of inspiration. *Deep Blue Sea* knows it's not original, and it uses the audience's recognition of this as an asset rather than a detraction. The filmmakers play with our expectations by allowing events to happen in ways that they often don't in movies of this sort.

Nearly all of the action takes place on the Aquatica, an advanced deep sea research laboratory that looks like a "floating Alcatraz." It's there that a small group of marine biologists and other scientists are experimenting on three genetically altered Mako sharks that are bigger, smarter, faster, and deadlier than is typical for members of their species. The humans, led by Doctors Susan McAlester (Saffron Burrows) and Jim Whitlock (Stellan Skarsgård), believe that a protein found in the sharks' brains can cure Alzheimer's Disease. On the day that the project's funder, Russell

Franklin (Samuel L. Jackson), is on the Aquatica, all hell breaks loose. The sharks turn violent, a tropical storm hits, and a helicopter crashes into the station. A group of 6 — McAlester, Franklin, shark handler Carter Blake (Thomas Jane), engineer Tom Scoggins (Michael Rapaport), preacher/cook Dudley (LL Cool J), and scientist Janet Winters (Jacqueline McKenzie) — are trapped below the surface, struggling against rising water levels while avoiding 3 pairs of dangerous jaws.

While *Deep Blue Sea* is mostly played straight, it's clear that Renny Harlin isn't beyond having a little fun with the material. But humor and drama are not the reason why audiences see a movie like *Deep Blue Sea,* and Harlin recognizes that. He gives viewers exactly what they want — a taut, exciting thriller that takes movie-goers and characters deep under water and leaves them gasping for breath. **RECOMMENDED**

Die Hard [1988]

Starring: **Bruce Willis, Alan Rickman, Bonnie Bedelia** Director: **John McTiernan** Screenplay: **Jeb Stuart & Steven E. de Souza** Running Time: 2:11 Rated: R (Extreme violence, profanity, brief nudity) Theatrical Aspect Ratio: **2.35:1**

Die Hard represents the class of modern action pictures and the standard by which they must be judged. Few films falling into the "mindless entertainment" genre have as much going for them as this movie. Not only is it a thrill-a-minute ride, but it has one of the best film villains in recent memory, a hero everyone can relate to, dialogue that crackles with wit, and a lot of very impressive pyrotechnics.

John McClane (Bruce Willis) had intended to spend a nice, quiet Christmas with his wife Holly (Bonnie Bedelia) and children, ironing out his marital problems caused by his working in New York City as a cop while her career keeps her in Los Angeles. Unfortunately for John, a group of terrorists, led by the suave Hans Gruber (Alan Rickman), has other ideas. After taking over the high rise Nakatomi Tower and holding the attendees of the Christmas party (including Holly) hostage, they begin the time-consuming and complex procedure of breaking into the building's vault. However, one thing — perhaps the *only* thing — that Hans didn't plan on was John McClane, the self-professed "fly in the ointment," who is on the loose inside, and whose goals are in direct contradiction with those of the terrorists.

With *Die Hard,* director John McTiernan (*Predator*) has given us a modern action classic — a movie that doesn't slow down until the end credits are rolling to

the tune of "Let It Snow." McTiernan is a master of pacing, and on those few occasions when the script lets him down, the camerawork of Jan De Bont comes to the rescue. This film is explosive in more ways than one — a lavish, noisy extravaganza that gets the adrenaline flowing.

Bruce Willis is perfect as the wisecracking John McClane, an "everyday" sort of guy who gets caught up in circumstances that force him to play the reluctant hero. Alan Rickman's Hans Gruber redefines the action genre villain. His charm lies in that volatile mixture of violence and cunning, all sheathed in a gentlemanly civility.

Whether Bruce Willis is climbing up an elevator shaft, throwing himself off an exploding building, or racing barefoot across a floor littered with glass shards, his John McClane holds our attention while we hold our breaths. *Die Hard* isn't motion picture poetry, but it shows the kind of raucous entertainment that the industry is capable of delivering. For what it is, this is the top model — flash, bang, and witty one-liners all included. **MUST SEE**

Die Hard 2 [1990]

Starring: **Bruce Willis, William Sadler, John Amos** Director: **Renny Harlin** Screenplay: **Steven E. de Souza & Doug Richardson** Running Time: 2:04 Rated: R (Extreme violence, profanity, brief nudity) Theatrical Aspect Ratio: **2.35:1**

It's rare that the sequel to a good movie lives up to expectations. Such is the case with *Die Hard 2,* the somewhat-muddled but still entertaining return of Bruce Willis' John McClane. Fortunately, the original *Die Hard* was good enough that there's room for the second installment to be enjoyable while still not matching the pace or possessing the flair of its predecessor.

It's Christmas Eve, and John McClane (Bruce Willis) is in trouble . . . again. This time, the scene is Dulles International Airport in Washington D.C., where a group of terrorists led by the renegade Colonel Stewart (William Sadler) has taken command of the runways and control tower. Unless their demands, which include the immediate release of the drug lord on his way to the United States for trial, are met, Stewart's band intends to start crashing planes. And Holly McClane (Bonnie Bedelia) is on one of those planes, endlessly circling above while a winter blizzard envelopes the already crippled airport. As before, it's up to John to save the day.

Die Hard 2 is not as tightly focused as the original, and this leaches away some of the excitement. The movie is still a thrill-a-minute ride, but much of the action is more pedestrian than stylish. Renny Harlin is a fair replacement for John McTiernan in the director's chair, but he lacks a measure of his predecessor's refinement.

Die Hard 2 is, in the final analysis, a worthwhile action film, but it doesn't deliver nearly as much as the first *Die Hard*. Nevertheless, those who enjoyed spending a couple hours with John McClane atop the Los Angeles skyline will find much to savor about this outing. It's not as crisply directed, and the plot holes are easier to find, but *Die Hard 2* is filled with the same sense of good-natured, wisecracking fun that infused the original. This is one sequel where déjà vu doesn't necessarily mean a rehash of what went before. HIGHLY RECOMMENDED

The Dirty Dozen [1967]

Starring: **Lee Marvin, Ernest Borgnine, Charles Bronson, Jim Brown**
Director: **Robert Aldrich** Screenplay: **Nunnally Johnson & Lukas Heller**
Running Time: **2:30** Rated: No MPAA Rating (Violence, mild profanity)
Theatrical Aspect Ratio: 2.35:1

More than 30 years after its initial release, *The Dirty Dozen* remains one of the most popular war films ever to grace the silver screen. A quintessential "guys' movie," *The Dirty Dozen* is best remembered for its tightly choreographed action sequences and testosterone-boosted storyline, but it was also one of the first movies to show the darker side of war — that the best soldiers are often society's outcasts, the sociopaths and misanthropes who kill and rape. War is not civilized, and there's no place for order or manners amidst the carnage of a battlefield.

The time period is 1944. D-Day is approaching. In addition to the overall invasion plan, the United States military has come up with an auxiliary mission designed to interrupt the German chain-of-command: raid a secluded mansion where high ranking German officers often come with their mistresses, and kill everyone there. To accomplish this suicide operation, the army has decided to use criminals who are either awaiting the execution of a death sentence or who have been condemned to spend at least 20 years in prison.

The officer in charge of the operation, General Worden (Ernest Borgnine) has chosen Major John Reisman (Marvin) to train the men and lead them on the mission. Reisman is selected for a specific reason: he is a known discipline problem, and, if he fails, the army will be rid of him. Disgruntled but obedient, Reisman meets his group of 12 angry men — a

sullen, antisocial lot, many of whom are convicted murderers and rapists. After convincing them that he is in charge, Reisman starts his version of boot camp in an atmosphere thick with tension. But, as the men learn to work together, a growing sense of camaraderie begins to develop, and, when Reisman stands up to a pompous colonel on behalf of his troop, they accept him as their leader.

Those who are sticklers for detail will find plenty to nit-pick about *The Dirty Dozen*. Its view of the military and of military procedures is slipshod, its handling of the wargames sequence is at times absurd, and its setup of the climax is contrived. Nevertheless, it's a testimonial to Aldrich's skill as a director that these problems don't interfere with the viewer's overall enjoyment of the film. *The Dirty Dozen* flows nicely, keeping things moving and drawing the audience along in its rapid current. The movie may not be a masterpiece but recent history has shown it to be an important motion picture, and the passage of 33 years has not dated it, nor has it diminished *The Dirty Dozen*'s enjoyability. RECOMMENDED

Dr. No [United Kingdom, 1962]

Starring: **Sean Connery, Joseph Wiseman, Jack Lord, John Kitzmiller, Ursula Andress** Director: **Terence Young** Screenplay: **Richard Maibaum, Johanna Harwood & Berkely Mather** Running Time: **1:51**
Rated: PG (Violence, sexual innuendo) Theatrical Aspect Ratio: 1.75:1

Barring a television adaptation of *Casino Royale* in the 1950s, 1962's *Dr. No* was the first opportunity fans of Ian Fleming's James Bond had to watch the intrepid superspy in action. However, producers Harry Saltzman and Albert Broccoli wanted their movie to appeal to a wider audience than just Fleming's readers. To that end, they altered the 007 of the novels to better fit the screen. Bond became more suave and witty, and less cold-blooded.

Story-wise, *Dr. No* isn't all that different from most of the other Bond plotlines, although it is a little more "bare bones." When a British agent assigned to Jamaica disappears, M (Bernard Lee) sends 007 (Sean Connery) to the Caribbean to look into the situation. Upon arrival, Bond is immediately the target of a would-be assassin, and, as his investigation leads him closer to the truth, attempts on his life become more frequent. After joining forces with CIA operative Felix Leiter (Jack Lord), Bond enlists the aid of boat owner Quarrel (John Kitzmiller) to take him to Crab Key Island, which is ruled by the mysterious Dr. No (Joseph Wiseman). Once there, in addition to meeting a scantily-dressed young woman named

Honey Ryder (Ursula Andress), 007 learns why no one ever returns from Crab Key.

With the exception of the big explosion during the film's finale, *Dr. No* is a low-key adventure. There are no gadgets, forcing Bond to rely on his ingenuity (in one scene, when he needs to breathe while submerged, he uses hollowed-out reeds as air tubes). The single car chase is reasonably straightforward. And, for the only time in the series, 007 is unmistakably brutalized, appearing bloody, beaten, and disheveled as a result. Regardless, he still defeats the villain and gets the girl. All-in-all, *Dr. No* is a successful, if not superlative, motion picture. While it may appear tame by the standards of the later productions, it's an entertaining look back in movie history at a project that developed into a worldwide phenomenon.

RECOMMENDED

El Mariachi [United States/Mexico, 1992]

Starring: **Carlos Gallardo, Consuelo Gómez, Peter Marquardt, Reinol Martinez** Director: **Robert Rodriguez** Screenplay: **Robert Rodriguez** Running Time: **1:24** Rated: **R (Mature themes, violence)** Theatrical Aspect Ratio: **1.66:1** In Spanish with subtitles

The title character of *El Mariachi* is the mariachi (Carlos Gallardo), an itinerant musician who goes from town to town in Mexico looking for a new place to play his music. Dressed in black and carrying his guitar in a case, he inquires for employment at various bars and restaurants. Unfortunately for the mariachi, Azul (Reinol Martinez) has just broken out of prison and is on his way to kill crime boss Roco (Peter Marquardt). No one except Roco has seen Azul, so the description of the escaped criminal is sparse: he dresses in black and carries a guitar case (which, instead of containing a musical instrument, has a selection of knives and guns). An obvious case of mistaken identity arises as Roco's thugs think the mariachi is Azul and try to gun him down. Fortunately, he finds a sympathetic ear in the person of Domino (Consuelo Gómez), but her introduction into his life only adds new and previously unforeseen complications.

El Mariachi is the $7,000 wonder. For less money than it costs to film a major television commercial, Robert Rodriguez took his crew to Mexico and filmed a gripping, tautly-paced action flick that outdoes most of Hollywood's similar output. This is clear evidence that film quality often has little to do with a production's budget.

El Mariachi is an old-fashioned thriller based on a case of mistaken identity. It's the kind of film that Humphrey Bogart would have been at home in. The only noticeable difference between this movie and something produced in the 1940s is the level of graphic violence. Rodriguez doesn't pull punches when it comes to showing people getting shot. There's enough blood and gore in this film to earn it the R rating.

On only a few occasions is it obvious that Rodriguez is a novice director working with almost no money. *El Mariachi* doesn't look like something out of Hollywood — the subtitles and the cleverness of the script make that much obvious — but neither does it look like the $7,000 project of a film student.

RECOMMENDED

Escape from L.A. [1996]

Starring: **Kurt Russell, Stacey Keach** Director: **John Carpenter** Screenplay: **John Carpenter, Debra Hill & Kurt Russell** Running Time: **1:40** Rated: **R (Violence, profanity)** Theatrical Aspect Ratio: **2.35:1**

The prologue to *Escape from L.A.* takes place shortly after the conclusion of *Escape from New York*. On August 23, 2000, the "big one" hits the west coast, severing Los Angeles from the mainland. The new President of the Moral United States (Cliff Robertson, giving an eerily Reagan-esque performance) declares that L.A. is no longer part of the country. It becomes the deportation zone to which all those convicted of moral crimes are sent. Los Angeles is viewed as an island of depravity and violence, populated by psychos, criminals, and other assorted weirdoes — not that different, some would argue, from what it's like today.

Fast forward to 2013, where we once again meet the infamous criminal, Snake Plisskin (Kurt Russell). For a second time, the government needs him for a rescue-and-retrieval mission. This time, the object of his quest isn't a person, but a thing. The President's daughter, Utopia (A. J. Langer), has stolen the remote control unit for a doomsday weapon and given it to a guerrilla leader (George Corraface) on Los Angeles Island. So Snake, who has been injected with a virus that leaves him ten hours to live, has to go in, complete his mission, and escape to get the antidote.

If this premise sounds an awful lot like that of *Escape from New York,* it's no coincidence. John Carpenter isn't just making a sequel to the 1981 cult classic, but, armed with a considerable budget, he's also doing a partial remake. *Escape from L.A.* follows an almost-identical trajectory to its predecessor, only this time all the action takes place against the backdrop of the Hollywood Hills rather than under the shadow of the World Trade Center.

All things considered, *Escape from L.A.* is a significant improvement over the first Snake Plisskin adventure. The action sequences are better paced and directed. The erratic, tongue-in-cheek comedy of *New York* is back, but, in this picture, it is supplemented by a barbed satire of family values and political correctness. Best of all, however, the basic premise is satisfactorily explored rather than just existing as a jumping-off point.

The only returning actor is Kurt Russell, who slips effortlessly into his character as if a decade-and-a-half hadn't passed. Little has changed — Snake still talks with a Clint Eastwood-like rasp, sports a heavy five o'clock shadow, and openly despises authority. Though Snake may have aged, the self-deprecating, angry core that makes him more than a mere caricature hasn't changed one bit. Will Snake be back again? Probably not, but if he does return, at least there's no shortage of possibilities for the title. Anyone for *Escape from Chicago*? RECOMMENDED

Executive Decision [1996]

Starring: **Kurt Russell, Halle Berry, John Leguizamo, Oliver Platt, Joe Morton, David Suchet** Director: **Stuart Baird** Screenplay: **Jim Thomas & John Thomas** Running Time: 2:12 Rated: R (Violence, profanity)
Theatrical Aspect Ratio: 2.35:1

Kurt Russell as James Bond? Well, not quite, but in *Executive Decision*, it's not far off. As David Grant, PhD, Russell looks dashing and debonair in his tux as he sneaks on board a hijacked airplane to put pay to the bad guys. Using a mixture of brains and brawn, he performs some tricks that would make Sean Connery proud. The result is just the kind of tightly-scripted, well-paced white-knuckler that's needed to alleviate the late winter doldrums.

When it opens, *Executive Decision* looks suspiciously like a Steven Segal film. The stone-faced action hero portrays Lt. Col. Austin Travis, commander of an anti-terrorist operations unit. Fortunately, however, this isn't a Segal movie — in fact, those expecting a heavy dose of the martial arts master will be disappointed, since he's only on screen for about a quarter of the picture.

David Suchet plays the dastardly bad guy here, an Islamic fanatic named Nagi Hassan who hijacks a 747 bound from Athens to Washington D.C. On board are 406 passengers and a cache of nerve gas that, if it reaches the United States, could wipe out the Northeast. It's up to the anti-terrorist squad, led by Travis

and Grant, to thwart the hijackers. To that end, they make use of the new, super-secret military plane that allows them to board the 747 undetected, while in flight. Then, the war of nerves begins . . .

Obviously, *Executive Decision* is a *Die Hard* wannabe, right down to the final shot. It's not a great clone, but it's still pretty good. *Executive Decision* isn't a start-to-finish string of shoot-outs and standoffs. In fact, barring a few fast-paced sequences, there's not that much action. Instead, this film relies on a growing sense of impending disaster to bring its audience to the edge of their seats.

It's refreshing to see a group of heroes who are as smart as their opponents, don't blunder around while attempting the rescue, and aren't bickering amongst themselves. Although Grant isn't a military man, he doesn't have to spend three-quarters of the film earning the others' respect; once they realize that he has a plan, they follow him without question.

Executive Decision certainly isn't quantum physics or advanced philosophy. It doesn't have a message, it's not overly-concerned with character development, and a fairly rigorous suspension of disbelief is mandatory. But, for uncomplicated excitement, the film offers a solid 130 minutes. RECOMMENDED

Face/Off [1997]

Starring: **John Travolta, Nicolas Cage** Director: **John Woo** Screenplay: **Mike Werb & Michael Colleary** Running Time: 2:20 Rated: R (Violence, profanity) Theatrical Aspect Ratio: 2.35:1

Face/Off is in overdrive for about two-thirds of its running length. The rest of the movie is devoted to such mundane tasks as plot exposition, character and relationship development, and ruminations on philosophical issues like identity. While there's very little of the latter, there is enough to give *Face/Off* an interesting subtext. How much of who we are is determined by our physical appearance? And, if we're given the face of another, how like that person are we likely to become?

Such weighty questions are posed because the two main characters swap faces and identities. Sean Archer (John Travolta) is a dedicated federal officer whose obsession with bringing down one particular master criminal, Castor Troy (Nicolas Cage), has blinded him to all other concerns. Six years ago, Troy's attempt to kill Archer went wrong, and Archer's young son was killed. Since then, a thirst for revenge has driven the FBI agent to pursue Troy with a single-minded relentlessness that has alienated both his wife (Joan Allen) and his teenage daughter (Dominique Swain). When the latest confrontation between the two leaves the criminal in a coma, Archer is forced to undergo a face transplant with Troy's features so that he can go undercover in a prison, interact with Troy's paranoid brother, Pollux (Alessandro Nivola), and learn the location of a bomb that is ticking away somewhere in downtown L.A. But, while Archer is masquerading as his arch-enemy, the real Troy regains consciousness and hijacks Archer's face.

The biggest hurdle to overcome while watching *Face/Off* is suspending disbelief. After all, the scenario that enables Troy and Archer to swap identities is preposterous. No matter how desperately Woo tries to make the procedure seem logically and medically feasible, it's all a little too much to swallow. Appreciating the movie as anything more than a series of flashes and bangs demands that the viewer accept, if not believe, that Troy and Archer can exchange features without showing any lingering signs of surgery or physical trauma.

There's almost too much action in *Face/Off*. After a while, no matter how much flair Woo invests in the project, the intensity starts to wear off and things become repetitive. *Face/Off* is primarily for hard-core action junkies and those who appreciate Woo's inimitable style. The movie is brash, loud, and far from the intellectual cutting-edge, but, on those occasions when *Face/Off* gets everything right, it's capable of moments of rare cinematic perfection. That alone makes it worth the price of admission. RECOMMENDED

For Your Eyes Only [United Kingdom, 1981]
Starring: Roger Moore, Carole Bouquet, Julian Glover, Topol
Director: John Glen Screenplay: Richard Maibaum & Michael G. Wilson Running Time: 2:07 Rated: PG (Sexual innuendo, violence) Theatrical Aspect Ratio: 2.2:1

With *For Your Eyes Only*, Roger Moore's fifth appearance as Bond and the twelfth entry in the long-running series, 007 enters the 1980s with a return to the "glory days" of the '60s. Realizing it would be tough to top the technical glitz of *Moonraker*, the film makers wisely chose not to try, opting instead for a retro-Bond adventure that takes the intrepid superspy back into familiar territory: KGB involvement in a plan that centers on classified British secrets.

But that's not the only aspect of *For Your Eyes Only* that looks more to Bond's past than his future. Blofeld, the constant nemesis during the Connery years, makes a brief return appearance, and the film opens with 007 visiting the grave of his dead wife,

Tracy. Bond's mission this time, "for [his] eyes only," is to locate and, if possible, recover Great Britain's ATAC equipment — a ship-based weapons system that allows the user to take control of the country's nuclear submarines, ordering them to attack any target. ATAC was on board a freighter that sank in the Ionian Sea, and Bond has at least one major rival, a sly villain named Kristatos (Julian Glover), who's after it as well. Joining 007 on his quest is Melina (French actress Carole Bouquet), the daughter of a scientist killed by Kristatos, who has vowed revenge against her father's murderers. Also along for the ride is the good-natured smuggler Columbo (Topol), who Kristatos set up as a fall guy.

Alas, Julian Glover's Kristatos won't be remembered as one of the great 007 bad guys. While the actor's ability is beyond question, it's usually not talent that makes for a memorable Bond villain, and Glover just isn't over-the-top or nasty enough. (One wonders if the film makers might have done better keeping Blofeld around for more than the pre-credits sequence.) Locque (Michael Gothard), Kristatos' henchman, is as dull as his master — he looks evil, but in the wake of Jaws, comes across as rather pathetic.

In the final analysis, *For Your Eyes Only* is a solid adventure, although it could have been better. There's enough action to hold those with even a short attention span, and Roger Moore's deft charm hasn't yet begun to wear thin. By the end of the '80s, Bond would be viewed as something of a relic, but at least the decade opened with an enjoyable outing. RECOMMENDED

From Russia with Love [United Kingdom, 1963]
Starring: Sean Connery, Daniela Bianchi, Pedro Armendariz, Lotte Lenya, Robert Shaw Director: Terence Young Screenplay: Richard Maibaum & Johanna Harwood Running Time: 1:50 Rated: PG (Violence, sexual innuendo) Theatrical Aspect Ratio: 1.75:1

The elements of *From Russia with Love* move the movie closer to the recognizable "Bond formula" than was the case for its predecessor, *Dr. No*. Here, the action scenes are more numerous and generate added tension, the title sequence has a familiar flavor, John Barry's distinctive score replaces the workmanlike music of Monty Norman, Q makes his first appearance, and Connery tones up 007's sophistication while downplaying his cold-bloodedness.

Unlike the megalomaniacs in later Bond films, the villains in *From Russia with Love* aren't after world domination (at least not immediately). In fact, they want something significantly less ambitious: a Russian decoding device. Two of SPECTRE's top operatives are on the mission: #3, former KGB agent Rosa Klebb (Lotte Lenya), and #5, Kronsteen (Vladek Sheybal), a chess master who has meticulously plotted every move and weighed all alternatives. The pair reports directly to the mysterious #1, Blofeld.

Kronsteen's manipulative plan involves using Bond and Russian cipher clerk Tatiana Romanova (Daniela Bianchi) as pawns. Once the British agent has obtained the decoding device from Tatiana, SPECTRE thug Red Grant (Robert Shaw) is to take it from him, leaving behind a corpse. The plot is suitably complicated (but not so convoluted that the viewer will get lost), and, even though 007 suspects a trap, the lure of a beautiful woman and a valuable espionage coup is too enticing to resist. So he travels to Istanbul, where Tatiana has arranged to meet him.

From Russia with Love is among the most tightly-plotted of all the Bond films, and, as a result, is one of the shortest. It moves briskly, blending intrigue, romance, and action into an immensely satisfying whole. *Russia* exudes style, as typified by a fight in a gypsy camp where Bond offhandedly dispatches rogues to the strains of John Barry's "007 theme." This movie has several such memorable moments, including an inventively choreographed fight sequence with Bond and Grant going at it in the confined space of two train compartments. Shortly after that, there's a death-defying chase between Bond and a helicopter.

Standing at the pinnacle of the series, *From Russia with Love* shows how good a Bond film can be when all the ingredients mesh. This movie isn't just a fun popcorn-munching action adventure flick; it's a good motion picture by any standards. **HIGHLY RECOMMENDED**

The Fugitive [1993]

Starring: Harrison Ford, Tommy Lee Jones, Sela Ward, Jeroen Krabbe, Andreas Katsulas Director: Andrew Davis Screenplay: Jeb Stuart & David Twohy Running Time: 2:13 Rated: PG-13 (Violence, language, mature themes) Theatrical Aspect Ratio: 1.85:1

Despite his innocence, Dr. Richard Kimble (Harrison Ford) has been tried, convicted, and sentenced to die for the murder of his wife. On the bus ride that takes him to the prison where he will spend the rest of his days, Kimble is accompanied by 3 other prisoners. When they stage an attempted escape, the driver of the bus loses control and it plunges down an embankment. Kimble is free. Ninety minutes later, Federal Deputy Marshal Sam Gerard (Tommy Lee Jones) arrives on the scene to coordinate the search for the fugitive. So, while Kimble flees Gerard and his men, he begins his search for his wife's real killer — a mysterious one-armed man (Andreas Katsulas).

The Fugitive is loosely based on the 1960s television series that featured the late David Jansen in the title role. Even though *The Fugitive* is a chase movie, the scenes before the hunt begins are among the best of the movie. Everything surrounding the murder and trial, all told in a tremendously well-edited 15-minute prologue, is engrossing. The movie's pace flags somewhat during the second hour as the pursuit cools down and Kimble's own search for the one armed man takes up screen time. Most of *The Fugitive*'s problems center around this investigation. There are too many leaps of intuition and handily-placed clues. The murder mystery is not well-constructed; simplifying this aspect of the story might have resulted in a more tightly-constructed plot, and less confusion about the motivation of some of the characters.

With all apologies to Harrison Ford, the real stand-out is Tommy Lee Jones. He invests his character with charisma and energy and, as Gerard's grudging respect for Kimble grows, so does our appreciation of what Jones is doing with his seemingly-straightforward role.

While no one could accuse *The Fugitive* of having a masterful insight into human nature, that's not why this film was produced. There's an odd moment or two when an element of someone's behavior strikes a responsive chord, but basically the characters are developed only enough to keep us interested as the chase proceeds. They, like the sometimes overplotted story, are subordinate to the hunt. Fans of the old TV series will find echoes of the show here, but most of this version is new. "Innovative" is not a legitimate description of *The Fugitive*, but "entertaining" is. **RECOMMENDED**

Gladiator [2000]

Starring: Russell Crowe, Joaquin Phoenix, Richard Harris, Djimon Hounsou, Connie Nielsen Director: Ridley Scott Screenplay: David H. Franzoni, John Logan, William Nicholson Running Time: 2:35 Rated: R (Violence) Theatrical Aspect Ratio: 2.35:1

Gladiator is the kind of movie upon which Hollywood once built its reputation but rarely produces anymore: the spectacle. Filled with larger-than-life characters, gorgeous scenery, impressive set design, and epic storytelling, *Gladiator* is designed not just to entertain, but to enthrall. It draws audiences in and immerses them in a reality that is not their own. This is filmmaking on a grand scale.

Gladiator is set in 180 A.D., and uses actual historical personages and events for background. The latest Caesar, Marcus Aurelius (Richard Harris), is a scholar who has taken to the battlefield to repel a barbarian threat from Germania. To that end, he has invaded, relying upon the leadership and valor of his best general, Maximus (Russell Crowe), to win the day. Maximus does not disappoint, and the Emperor privately decides to name him as his successor — a decision that does not sit well with Commodus (Joaquin Phoenix), Marcus' son. In a fit of rage and grief, he kills his father, then has Maximus taken away to be executed. The general, however, escapes death, slaying his would-be killers, then races home to protect his wife and son. But he is too late — by the time he arrives, they are both dead, and he is soon taken prisoner by slave-traders. Along with his new friend Juba (Djimon Hounsou), he is bought by Proximo (Oliver Reed), an owner and trainer of Gladiators. Recognizing Maximus' potential, Proximo grooms him for a trip to Rome's Coliseum.

Gladiator weds the heroic scope of movies like *Ben-Hur, Spartacus, Braveheart,* and *Rob Roy* with the serpentine political treachery of *I, Claudius.* The film never fails to be involving and entertaining, and there are plenty of moments designed to stir the adrenaline. Additionally, the screenplay manages to avoid the trap of predictability. The villains are at least as smart as the heroes, and far more ruthless.

For New Zealand-born, Australian-bred actor Russell Crowe, *Gladiator* represents an opportunity to expand his reputation. This is Crowe's first opportunity to carry a big-budget motion picture, and he won a Best Actor Oscar for it.

One minor stumbling block is an occasional tendency towards moments of pretension. From time-to-time, a character will make a florid, preachy speech. There's nothing wrong with injecting social commentary about the bestial nature of human beings into a movie like *Gladiator* — my argument is that it should be more subtle. But that's a minor quibble. Like many of the great Hollywood historical epics, *Gladiator* is the story of the triumph of a heroic figure over seemingly-insurmountable odds. As spectacles go, *Gladiator* has a great deal to recommend it. **HIGHLY RECOMMENDED**

Goldeneye [United Kingdom, 1995]

Starring: Pierce Brosnan, Sean Bean, Izabella Scorupco, Famke Janssen Director: Martin Campbell Screenplay: Jeffrey Caine & Bruce Feirstein Running Time: 2:10 Rated: PG-13 (Sexual innuendo, violence) Theatrical Aspect Ratio: 2.35:1

Like everything else, James Bond (Pierce Brosnan) has had to change for the nineties. The venerable 007 has taken on his sixth face, changed his mode of transport from an Aston-Martin to a BMW, and now answers to a female "M" (played dryly by Judi Dench). Bond's attitudes towards women have been modified — although not greatly. Also, there's more action in *Goldeneye* than in previous 007 entries — enough to keep a 90-minute film moving at a frantic pace. Unfortunately, this movie isn't 90 minutes long — it's 130, which means that fully ¼ of *Goldeneye* is momentum-killing padding.

As for the leading man, he's a decided improvement over his immediate predecessor. Brosnan has a flair for wit to go along with his natural charm; Dalton was stoic and sober. Of course, the newest Bond doesn't come close to Sean Connery's definitive portrayal, but he lacks the fatuousness that marred Roger Moore's tenure. Brosnan's approach has invigorated 007 enough to overcome a movie that seemingly never wants to end.

The story is standard fare, mixing and matching cliches of the genre. The Russian mafia obtains a space-based weapons system called *Goldeneye* that works by exploding a nuclear device in orbit, then crippling a ground location with the resulting electromagnetic pulse. It's up to Bond to save London from a vengeance-crazed megalomaniac. Along the way, he runs into such diverse characters as a beautiful computer programmer (Izabella Scorupco), a former partner (Sean Bean), a wisecracking CIA agent (Joe Don Baker), an ex-KGB officer with a score to settle (Robbie Coltrane), and a psychotic woman who likes squeezing men to death between her legs (Famke Janssen). Brosnan is supported by an interesting troupe of actors, but the spotlight is always on him.

Goldeneye keeps Bond's comic book-like stunts at an appropriately absurd level. And, with its mixture of humor, interesting locales, high-speed chases, explosions, and action, *Goldeneye* represents solid entertainment. This updated Bond can stand toe-to-toe with today's crop of heroes. **RECOMMENDED**

Goldfinger [United Kingdom, 1964]
Starring: **Sean Connery, Gert Frobe, Honor Blackman, Harold Sakata**
Director: **Guy Hamilton** Screenplay: **Richard Maibaum & Paul Dehr**
Running Time: **1:52** Rated: **PG (Violence, sexual innuendo)** Theatrical
Aspect Ratio: **1.7:1**

With 1964's *Goldfinger*, the third James Bond story to reach the screen, the "Bond formula" had reached maturity. One of the last Bond films to clock in at under two hours, *Goldfinger* is tightly-paced and economical in its usage of extraneous material. The character development of *From Russia with Love* is replaced by a greater attention to action. There are several memorable fight sequences (including a climactic struggle between 007 and Goldfinger's nasty henchman, Oddjob) and a lengthy car chase that has Bond's Aston Martin trailing smoke screens and oil slicks, firing built-in guns, and ejecting the passenger seat. The level of excitement in *Goldfinger* is up a notch from its predecessors.

When the British Secret Service decides that they want supposedly-legitimate bullion dealer Auric Goldfinger (Gert Frobe) under observation, agent 007 is chosen for the job. After Bond (Sean Connery) finds a naked, dead woman on his bed, covered head-to-toe with gold paint, the investigation takes on a new urgency. It seems that Goldfinger is planning something big — "Operation Grand Slam" — and anyone who interferes is targeted for elimination, including, of course, Bond. But, when Goldfinger captures the British agent in Switzerland, he decides to keep him as a hostage rather than kill him. So Bond accompanies the criminal and his entourage to Kentucky, where Goldfinger plans to engineer the greatest crime in history: knock over Fort Knox.

Sean Connery, back for the third time in the role that made him famous, plays the lead character with the same easy elegance and wit he displayed in *From Russia with Love*. The title character (played by Gert Frobe) isn't the most sinister or vicious villain to stand against 007, but he is intelligent, ingenious, and obsessed with gold. In addition to being one of the most unforgettable of the "Bond Girls," Honor Blackman's Pussy Galore is one of the toughest and most self-sufficient women to cross 007's path. In her own words, she's immune to his charm, and, while this doesn't prevent her from sharing an intimate moment or two with him, she never yields her independence.

In the midst of Bond's "golden era" of the '60s, it's hard to single out one film as the best, but history has shown *Goldfinger* to be among the series' most enduring entries. Although more gimmicky than *From Russia with Love*, this film is equally as entertaining. And, of course, it takes the Bond films in a slightly different direction, blazing a trail that they have been following ever since. **HIGHLY RECOMMENDED**

Hellboy [2004]
Starring: Ron Perlman, Selma Blair, Jeffrey Tambor, Karel Roden, Rupert Evans, John Hurt, Doug Jones, David Hyde Pierce (voice)
Director: Guillermo del Toro Screenplay: Guillermo del Toro, based on the comic books by Mike Mignola Running Time: 1:52 Rated: PG-13 (Violence) Theatrical Aspect Ratio: 1.85:1

Hellboy opens in October 1944 Scotland, where a team of Nazis is trying to recruit otherworldly aid to Hitler's failing cause. Their efforts are foiled, but not before a creature passes through an open portal — a baby demon who is nicknamed "Hellboy." Taken under the wing of American scientist Professor Bruttenholm (John Hurt), Hellboy (Ron Perlman) grows up as an agent for the shady FBI Bureau of Paranormal Research and Defense. (Their purpose: "There are things that go bump in the night — we are the ones who bump back.") There, along with fellow "freaks" Abe Sapien (Doug Jones), an aquatic type, and Liz Sherman (Selma Blair), a firestarter, he defends the United States from supernatural dangers. The latest threat is Rasputin (Karel Roden), the resurrected Russian spiritualist who has made a pact with a group of dark gods. In return for everlasting life and great powers, he will open their way to Earth. In order to do so, he must convert Hellboy to his cause, or, at the very least, blackmail him. And Red (as his friends call him) has two weaknesses: his affection for his adopted father and his unvoiced love for Liz.

Director/screenwriter Guillermo del Toro knows what he's doing; this is not just a paycheck job. The film's look is perfect for the subject matter — dark and gothic, with even the "real" settings presented using rich colors and deep blacks. The action scenes are suitably over-the-top, and all the more fun for it. After a slow beginning, the pace doesn't flag, and the film does a decent job of developing Hellboy's character. The humor is what sets *Hellboy* apart from many of the other, recent comic book adaptations and, unlike in other offerings, it's not silly and inappropriate.

Coherence and plotting are not among *Hellboy*'s strong suits. The movie does not stand up to any kind of thoughtful inspection, and the muddled finale is nonsensical. The computer-generated effects look like something out of a video game. No matter how slick the CGI appears, there's never any doubt that these scenes were put together in postproduction. Sometimes, directors have too many toys to play with. It's a shame, because the makeup work (by Rick Baker) on Perlman is top-notch.

My sense is that most comic book aficionados, regardless of whether or not they are familiar with Mike Mignola's Dark Horse series, will enjoy what *Hellboy* has to offer. It's a throwback to the 80s, with a strong hero (15 years ago, this role would have been perfect for Schwarzenegger), well-crafted action sequences, and an undemanding story line. **RECOMMENDED**

Hero [HONG KONG/CHINA 2002]

Starring: Jet Li, Tony Leung, Maggie Cheung, Zhang Ziyi, Donnie Yen, Chen Daoming Director: Zhang Yimou Screenplay: Li Feng, Wang Bin, Zhang Yimou Running Time: 1:36 Rated: PG-13 (Violence, sensuality) Theatrical Aspect Ratio: 2.35:1 In Mandarin with subtitles

Hero represents Chinese director Zhang Yimou's first foray into the martial arts/action genre. While there are aspects of the film that recall Ang Lee's *Crouching Tiger, Hidden Dragon* (the movie that brought "wire-fu" Asian cinema to mainstream Western audiences), such a comparison is in many ways too facile. In fact, *Hero* actually has more in common with the work of Japanese master director Akira Kurosawa than with *Crouching Tiger*. This is an amazingly stylish and vivid motion picture, where images move the story forward more forcefully than the traditional methods of exposition, dialogue, and character development. If there's a drawback, it's that the plot is trite. *Hero* is an exemplary example of visual poetry. The narrative is clearly of secondary concern.

Hero takes place in feudal China, before the warring kingdoms were united into a single country. Jet Li plays the Nameless warrior, who has been brought before the king of Qin (Chen Daoming) to receive a reward for heroic deeds. The Nameless warrior has killed three assassins who sought the king's life: Long Sky (Donnie Yen), Broken Sword (Tony Leung), and Flying Snow (Maggie Cheung). At the king's behest, the Nameless warrior tells how he killed the assassins, but the king challenges his tales and offers a different interpretation.

From the *Rashomon*-influenced method of relating events from multiple perspectives to the dream-like state of the martial arts battles, the spirit of Kurosawa presides over Zhang's approach to the material. And this is the first movie by the director since *Raise the Red Lantern* to impart such a great importance to color. There are four distinct schemes: red, blue, white, and green. In each, all garments and many of the set pieces match the appropriate hue. At times, filters are used to enhance the colors. Wind is also a noticeable element — from the breezes that blow around the diaphanous draperies and curtains to the whirlwind used by Flying Snow to knock aside her opponents.

Hero's theme of self-sacrifice being necessary to serve the greater good isn't revolutionary, but it is presented with enough force that we don't dismiss it lightly. There's a universality to this that allows Western audiences to relate to it with as much immediacy as Asian audiences. But few who see *Hero* will be there for its thematic content. They will be there to enjoy the spectacle of wire-fu battles, of which there are many, and to appreciate the way in which Zhang Yimou and his cinematographer, Christopher Doyle, have chosen to populate their canvas. **RECOMMENDED**

The Horseman on the Roof [France, 1995]

Starring: Olivier Martinez, Juliette Binoche, Pierre Arditi, Carlo Cecchi Director: Jean-Paul Rappeneau Screenplay: Jean-Paul Rappeneau, Nina Companez & Jean-Claude Carriere Running Time: 1:57 Rated: R (Violence, nudity, cholera) Theatrical Aspect Ratio: 2.2:1 In French with subtitles

The year is 1832. Napoleon has fallen, leaving behind a vacuum of power. The Austrian empire is attempting a takeover of Italy, and many Italian patriots have fled to France to continue the fight from there. Meanwhile, a devastating cholera epidemic sweeps across France like wildfire, wiping out entire towns and generating a widespread fear of all strangers. Soldiers patrol the countryside, enforcing quarantines by lethal means. It's a grim era, and many superstitious folk think that God's judgment of the world has finally come.

This is the setting for Jean-Paul Rappeneau's *The Horseman on the Roof*, an old fashioned, historical, epic romance. These movies have certain common characteristics: a love affair involving two attractive protagonists; sweeping, beautifully-photographed backgrounds; and a tragic, tumultuous plot. Replete with heaving bosoms, thundering horses, energetic swordfights, and glorious widescreen cinematography, *The Horseman on the Roof* delivers what's expected.

The story opens with Angelo Pardi (Olivier Martinez), an Italian Carbonaro in exile, dodging a trio of Austrian assassins sent to Aix-en-Provence to murder him. With the killers hot on his trail, he flees to the city of Manosque. Before he can join up with a group of Italian refugees, he is accused of poisoning a water supply, and has to run from an angry mob. Angelo takes to the rooftops as riots break out in the streets below. When a thunderstorm strikes, he shelters in a house. The woman living there is Pauline (Juliette Binoche), a married French noblewoman, and, upon encountering Angelo, she reacts with unexpected calmness, inviting him to warm up and have some tea. Soon after, the two are paired in a flight across France to reunite Pauline with her husband and send Angelo back to Italy.

Although much of *The Horseman on the Roof* is more lighthearted than many sweeping melodramas, there are moments of stark, horrifying power. Most deal with the effects of cholera on France's unprepared populace. This is one of the most lavish, recent French exports, and the production values are topnotch. Rappeneau (*Cyrano de Bergerac*) directs with a sure hand, Martinez and Binoche do credible (if not spectacular) jobs, and cameos by Francois Cluzet and the ubiquitous Gerard Depardieu add a few brief moments of "star power." Despite all of this, however, *The Horseman on the Roof* is not a transcendent experience. But, while it doesn't have the power to get eyes misty and hearts aflutter, it's still entertaining nough to make the two hours pass quickly.

RECOMMENDED

House of Flying Daggers [CHINA/HONG KONG 2004]

Starring: Takeshi Kaneshiro, Andy Lau, Zhang Ziyi, Song Dandan Director: Zhang Yimou Screenplay: Li Feng, Wang Bin, Zhang Yimou Running Time: 1:59 Rated: PG-13 (Violence, sensuality) Theatrical Aspect Ratio: 2.35:1 In Mandarin with subtitles

One of the most colorful and stylish films of the end-of-the-year season is Zhang Yimou's *House of Flying Daggers*, his wire-fu follow-up to *Hero*. If you think *Hero* is a stunningly beautiful film, prepare to be blown away by *House of Flying Daggers*. The martial arts sequences are more exciting and elaborate than those in *Hero*, and, while this movie does not rely as heavily upon color schemes as its predecessor, it nevertheless contains some eye-poppingly beautiful sequences. Consider, for example, a battle that begins in the autumn, with all of the trees showing their glorious colors. It starts to snow, and soon everything is covered in white. When people talk about the magic of cinema, they're referring to moments like these.

The bare bones narrative opens in the ninth century. A rebel group fighting to bring down China's Tang Dynasty goes by the name of "House of Flying Daggers" and acts in a Robin Hood–like manner, stealing from the rich and giving to the poor. Two guard captains, Jin (Takeshi Kaneshiro) and Leo (Andy Lau), are sent on a mission to find the hidden rebel base. To do this, Jin courts the affections of Mei (Zhang Ziyi), a blind call girl who may actually be a key member of the Flying Daggers group. After breaking Mei out of prison, Jin goes on the run with her — and discovers that his growing feelings for her could interfere with his mission.

House of Flying Daggers features six amazing battle sequences, all of which are surrounded by an epic aura. The first fight occurs in the Entertainment House, where Mei duels with an expert swordsman. This is followed by the Echo Game. Later, there are conflicts in the forest, in the fields, and in the trees. Then there's the tragic, final struggle. Perhaps most notable is the conflict that is inexplicably *missing*. The movie leads viewers to believe that there will be a titanic clash between guards and rebels, but, despite the buildup being in place, the battle never happens. This curious omission causes *House of Flying Daggers* to end on an anticlimactic note.

The actors and stunt doubles do their jobs well. Most impressive is Zhang's current leading lady, Zhang Ziyi, who has grown considerably as an actress in recent years. She's more than just a pretty face, and she captures the arrogance and vulnerability of Mei perfectly. She can be sexy and seductive one moment and deadly the next. Her male counterpart, Takeshi Kaneshiro, is equally effective. *House of Flying Daggers* has a little something for everyone, and only the disappointing ending keeps it from being a truly memorable film on par with *Crouching Tiger, Hidden Dragon*. **RECOMMENDED**

Hulk [2003]

Starring: Eric Bana, Jennifer Connelly, Sam Elliott, Josh Lucas, Nick Nolte Director: Ang Lee Screenplay: John Turman and Michael France and James Schamus Running Time: 2:18 Rated: PG-13 (Violence, brief nudity) Theatrical Aspect Ratio: 1.85:1

Hulk represents the most involving superhero motion picture since *Superman* soared skyward in 1978. By taking its time to develop characters and situations, *Hulk* does what so many action/adventure movies fail to do — allow us to really *feel* for the protagonists. Director Ang Lee, fresh off his success from *Crouching Tiger, Hidden Dragon*, has re-imagined The Hulk as a tragic figure trapped by fate and the hubris of others into showing the inner beast whenever rage overwhelms him. In truth, the film has a greater synergy with classic monster movies like *Dr. Jekyll and Mr. Hyde*, *Frankenstein*, and (especially) *King Kong* than it does with the current crop of superhero motion pictures. *Spider-Man* or *X-Men,* this isn't.

Hulk begins with a short prologue in 1966, where a young Bruce Banner watches his unhinged father, a discredited military scientist, commit an unspeakable deed. Skip ahead about 35 years. Bruce (Eric Bana) is a scientist working at the Berkeley Nuclear Biotechnical Institute alongside his ex-girlfriend, Betty (Jennifer Connelly). Their current project has hit a few stumbling blocks, but that hasn't stopped sleazy corporate executive Talbot (Josh Lucas) from taking an interest. Also watching things with a careful eye is Betty's father, General Ross (Sam Elliot), who is wondering if the project has military applications. Then, one day, a lab accident exposes Bruce to a massive dose of radiation. Not only does he survive — he isn't even injured.

While lying in his hospital bed, he receives a visit from a grizzled old man who claims to be his father, David Banner (Nick Nolte). The distracted David speaks in riddles and half-truths, but Bruce understands the meaning when, in a later fit of rage, he is transformed into The Hulk — a 15-foot-high behemoth with green skin, massive strength, and a near-invulnerability to conventional weapons. Suddenly, everyone wants something. Bruce and Betty are looking for a cure. Ross and Talbot are wrangling over whether to kill Bruce or cultivate him. And David has something sinister in mind.

Although Lee injects plenty of philosophy and tragedy into the film (the tone is unusually somber for a popcorn movie, although not so dark that it kills the enjoyment), he never forgets that The Hulk is a comic book character. His direction is frequently wildly over-the-top, with kinetic camera movements and a wide variety of angles and distances. He also frequently uses multiple split screens that divide the viewing area into a multi-paneled canvas that looks very much like the page of a comic book. There are times when Lee's visual techniques seem excessive, but they stop short of being pretentious or irritating. Indeed, his vision of *Hulk* is exciting, and he has fashioned a motion picture that's a breath of fresh air. **HIGHLY RECOMMENDED**

In the Line of Fire [1993]
Starring: Clint Eastwood, John Malkovich, Rene Russo
Director: Wolfgang Petersen Screenplay: Jeff Maguire Running
Time: 2:03 Rated: R (Language, mature themes, violence) Theatrical
Aspect Ratio: 2.35:1

In 1963, Frank Horrigan was among the "best and brightest" of the Secret Service, the personal choice of President Kennedy. On November 22 in Dallas, an afternoon that Horrigan will never forget, he became one of the few living agents to lose a president. Now, decades later and only months before a presidential election, Mitch Leary (John Malkovich) is stalking the President. Believing there to be an intangible bond between himself and Horrigan (he says they were both betrayed by a government they had once loved), Leary makes contact with the Secret Service agent to discuss his intentions. Following his conversation with the potential killer, Horrigan acts quickly to get himself posted to protection duty. This time, he has no intention of failing and believes that, given the opportunity, he will take the bullet.

John Malkovich may be one of the screen's most overlooked actors. Or, at least he was until this performance. Hands down, Malkovich's assassin is the best thing about this solid thriller — a villain that rivals Hannibal Lecter for intelligence and cold, calculated viciousness.

Eastwood is Eastwood, albeit a more vulnerable version akin to what we saw in *Unforgiven.* He's still tough, and he isn't afraid to use his gun, but Frank Horrigan is haunted by his past. He's no longer sure whether it was simple indecision or an unwillingness to take a bullet that led to his not being there for Kennedy, and the possibility that the same situation might arise a second time troubles him day and night. Horrigan gives us the human side of Eastwood — the side we never see in a Dirty Harry film, the side that isn't afraid to shed a tear.

Plot-wise, *In the Line of Fire* is nothing extraordinary. It's basically a formula-type thriller with one or two twists thrown in to keep the viewer off-balance. However, strength of character, coupled with a consistently-high level of excitement, makes this film anything but ordinary. The most intriguing element of *In the Line of Fire* is the cat-and-mouse game between Horrigan and Leary. The relationship of these two is fascinating in a twisted way, as it explores psychological layers which many motion pictures find too difficult to convey realistically. For a couple of hours of entertainment, *In the Line of Fire* doesn't disappoint. **RECOMMENDED**

Iron Monkey [Hong Kong, 1993]
Starring: Donnie Yen, Yu Rong-gwong, Jean Wang Director: Yuen
Woo Ping Screenplay: Tsui Hark, Elsa Tang & Lau Tai Mok Running
Time: 1:25 Rated: PG-13 (Violence) Theatrical Aspect Ratio: 1.85:1
In Cantonese with subtitles

When it comes to action, *Iron Monkey* is every bit as astounding as either of Yeun Woo Ping's subsequent, more commercially successful features (he choreographed the fight scenes in both *Crouching Tiger, Hidden Dragon* and *The Matrix*). There are plenty of amazing fight scenes, each intent upon topping its predecessor. Many use wires, enabling the combatants to seemingly leap amazing distances and do all sorts of gravity-defying moves in mid-air. The climactic struggle, which features a duo of good guys against a mighty villain, has the participants balancing on poles over a raging inferno.

Iron Monkey is actually a prequel of sorts to the Tsui Hark/Jet Li 1991 collaboration, *Once Upon a Time in China*, about a 19th century Chinese folk hero named Wong Fei-hung. Here, Fei-hung is a 12-year old boy (played by a girl, Tsang Sze-man) who has come to the city of Chekiang with his father, kung fu master Wong Kei-ying (Donnie Yen). Shortly after their arrival, they are "recruited" by the corrupt governor (James Wong) to hunt down the notorious outlaw, Iron Monkey. Kei-ying is told that his son will be imprisoned until Iron Monkey is caught. But, as Kei-ying begins his task, he finds little help from the citizens of Chekiang. Iron Monkey is a popular figure, who, like Robin Hood, robs from the rich and gives to the poor. The only ones to show any sympathy to Kei-ying are the kindly Dr. Wang (Yu Rong-gwong) and his lovely assistant, Miss Orchid (Jean Wang). The irony is that, by night, Dr. Wang is Iron Monkey.

Iron Monkey doesn't possess the epic feel of a *Crouching Tiger*, nor are the characters as well developed or effectively drawn. The storyline, despite having supposed historical underpinnings (like most legends), seems as simple and straightforward as something out of a comic book (with very few deaths). It also has a clear sense of good and evil.

Of course, the primary reason to see *Iron Monkey* isn't for a history lesson. Instead, *Iron Monkey* is all about action, a goal that Yuen pursues relentlessly, pausing only occasionally for short bursts of exposition before getting the adrenaline pumping again. His fights are innovative and intense, whether they're a whirlwind one-on-one duel or one of many struggles featuring multiple combatants. And he truly saves the best for last. RECOMMENDED

Whack! Thworp! Crack! Sometimes, it's fun to sit back and enjoy the spectacle of bad guys getting their heads beaten in. No political correctness. No toning down the violence to obtain the teen-friendly PG-13 classification from the MPAA. These things make a movie like *Kiss of the Dragon* a pure, if somewhat guilty pleasure. Of course, it helps that the lead actor is Jet Li, a man who oozes equal parts coolness and charisma.

Kiss of the Dragon doesn't have much of a plot. It's about a Beijing cop, Liu Jian (Jet Li), who's on assignment in France where he is framed by a local, high-ranking law enforcement officer, Inspector Richard (Tcheky Karyo). Jian's best hope to prove his innocence is Jessica (Bridget Fonda), a North Dakota girl who is hooking on the streets of Paris, but she won't speak out against Richard until Jian agrees to save her daughter from the dirty policeman's clutches. So the whole film is essentially one long chase, with Richard trying to kill Jian before Jian can expose him as crooked.

As far as action icons go, Jet Li has more acting ability than most. Not only is he incredibly athletic and able to perform kicks, parries, and thrusts with blazing speed, but he has screen presence and is able to develop his character into a likable individual — at least to the degree allowed by the formula. Li has about a half-dozen standout action scenes, including one in which he goes up against an entire class of adult martial arts students, and one in which he faces off against two hulking Aryan brothers.

Kiss of the Dragon has been directed by newcomer Chris Nahoun, a protégé of French filmmaker Luc Besson (who co-wrote the script and co-produced the movie). Besson is one of a group of French directors who believe that for the French movie industry to be able to play on the international stage, it must make motion pictures that will succeed in the United States. As a result, even though events take place in Paris, everyone speaks English. *Kiss of the Dragon* stands out as a high-energy action movie that holds an audience's attention for its full running length, rather than losing viewers in a sea of plot contrivances and glitzy special effects. RECOMMENDED

Kiss of the Dragon [France, 2001]

Starring: Jet Li, Bridget Fonda, Tcheky Karyo Director: Chris Nahon
Screenplay: Luc Besson & Robert Mark Kamen, based on a story by
Jet Li Running Time: 1:38 Rated: R (Violence, sexual situations)
Theatrical Aspect Ratio: 2.35:1

The Last of the Dogmen [1995]

Starring: Tom Berenger, Barbara Hershey, Kurtwood Smith, Steve
Reevis Director: Tab Murphy Screenplay: Tab Murphy Running
Time: 2:00 Rated: PG (Violence, mild profanity) Theatrical Aspect
Ratio: 2.35:1

Take the mentality of an old-fashioned Hollywood Western, bleed in elements from Kevin Costner's *Dances with Wolves*, and start it out with a sequence culled from *The Fugitive*, and you get *The Last of the Dogmen* — a surprisingly entertaining, somewhat corny adventure film. And, while there's an obviously politically-correct slant to the story, that does nothing to dilute *The Last of the Dogmen*'s enjoyability.

Lewis Gates (Tom Berenger) is an old-time, macho cowboy who loves the rugged outdoors, carries a knife and a gun, and would rather not take a woman into "the roughest country God's ever put on a map." As the story opens, the local sheriff (Kurtwood Smith) has recruited Lewis, the best tracker in the area, to go into the Oxbow Quadrangle in search of three convicts. After some convincing, Lewis agrees, and it doesn't take him long to pick up his quarry's trail. But, by the time he catches up to them, all that's left are ripped clothes and a lot of blood. The bounty hunter returns to town empty-handed and full of questions.

For the answers, he goes to a leading Indian expert, Dr. Lillian Sloan (Barbara Hershey), telling her he believes there are lost warriors in the Oxbow. At first, she thinks he's deluded, but as he presents evidence accumulated from old newspaper clippings, her interest is piqued. Lewis wants one of her male associates to accompany him into the mountains — he needs someone who speaks Cheyenne. Much to his distress, however, she chooses to come herself, and together they go in search of the last of the Cheyenne dogmen — the possible descendants of survivors from 1864's Sand Creek Massacre.

Writer/director Tab Murphy pokes occasional fun at the macho cowboy image while simultaneously embracing it through Berenger's scruffy Lewis. But the main point of the movie is that when people finally find something they've spent their entire life searching for, they'll risk anything to protect it. The Cheyenne are Lewis' redemption, and his interaction with them saves a guilt-ravaged spirit. This simple theme lies at the core of an adventure that, while not original, is nevertheless satisfying. *The Last of the Dogmen* may recall *Dances with Wolves*, but it seems less a copy than a different story taking a similar path. **RECOMMENDED**

The Last of the Mohicans [1992]

Starring: Daniel Day-Lewis, Madeleine Stowe, Wes Studi, Russell Means, Jodhi May Director: Michael Mann Screenplay: Christopher Crowe, Michael Mann Running Time: 1:54 Rated: R (Violence, mature themes) Theatrical Aspect Ratio: 2.35:1

There is so little wrong with this film that I'll get the incidental negatives out of the way first. The introductory moments are somewhat confusing, and it takes about fifteen or twenty minutes to get the characters and situations straight. Madeleine Stowe's British accent is of the "now-you-hear-it, now-you-don't" variety, although her performance pretty much makes up for this inconsistency. Finally, the photography surrounding the waterfall is unconvincing. Other than that, *The Last of the Mohicans* is virtually flawless.

Cinematography and musical score combine in a breathtaking mosaic. Historical accuracy has been preserved (even if the movie takes liberties with James Fenimore Cooper's story). The battle scenes are easily the best choreographed since *Glory* — there's so much going on that one viewing isn't enough to pick up on everything.

From beginning to end, there isn't a weak performance. As the bare-chested central character, a native-raised white man named Hawkeye, Daniel Day-Lewis shines, bringing acting acumen to the role of romantic adventure hero. Madeleine Stowe, Richard Dreyfuss' girlfriend in *Stakeout*, is equally appealing as Hawkeye's upper-class British love interest. The major characters are fully fleshed-out, and there's more audience empathy for the minor characters here than the protagonists in many other films. As is common in a realistic depiction of a war, very little is absolutely good or evil.

Finally, there's the story, which, while not all that complex, is of epic nature — big, bold, and gloriously sweeping. It's about the love of Hawkeye, the adopted Mohican, and Cora, the daughter of a British commander stationed in America during the mid-1700s. War and tragedy swirl around them as they struggle to find their own kind of private solace. Bold and stirring with impeccable production values, *The Last of the Mohicans* is a memorable motion picture adventure. **MUST SEE**

The Last Samurai [2003]

Starring: Tom Cruise, Ken Watanabe, Tony Goldwyn, Timothy Spall, Koyuki, Hiroyuki Sanada, Billy Connolly, Shichinosuke Nakamura Director: Edward Zwick Screenplay: John Logan and Marshall Herskovitz & Edward Zwick Running Time: 2:24 Rated: R (Violence) Theatrical Aspect Ratio: 2.35:1

The Last Samurai opens in 1876 San Francisco, where Civil War hero Nathan Algren (Tom Cruise) is drowning his sorrows in booze. A warrior without a war to fight, Nathan spends his time shilling for a rifle company, making live appearances that pay him enough to afford his drink. That all changes when a delegation arrives from Japan, seeking to hire American army "heroes" to teach modern warfare to the emperor's forces. A band of rebels, led by the samurai Katsumoto (Ken Watanabe), is threatening to derail a cross-country railroad being built by the Japanese government, so troops are needed to intervene. When offered an obscene amount of money for his aid, Nathan cannot refuse, so he joins his good friend, Sergeant Zebulah Grant (Billy Connolly), and his former commander (with whom he has "issues"), Colonel Benjamin Bagly (Tony Goldwyn), on the trip to Japan. As he writes in his diary, referring to the days when he and Bagly slaughtered Indians: "I am hired to once again stop the rebellion of another tribal leader — apparently the only job for which I am qualified."

Once in Japan, Nathan wastes no time teaching the art of firing rifles to his sad group of conscripts, but when they are prematurely forced to face Katsumoto, they are unprepared. The engagement is a rout, and Nathan is captured. Through the long winter of 1876 and into the spring of 1877, he is held captive in Katsumoto's mountain settlement. During that time, he engages in many conversations with the samurai leader, who is attempting to master English. He learns about the samurai way of life, develops an attraction to Katsumoto's sister, Taka (Koyuki), and improves his fighting skills. When ninjas attack, he battles alongside the samurai to defend the village. Thereafter, he is seen as an equal and is no longer a captive. But a hard decision lies ahead: return to Tokyo and resume his commission, or side with Katsumoto and face almost certain death.

The Last Samurai is singularly effective in bridging the gap between today and the 1870s. We are transported back through time more than a century and halfway across the globe. Director Edward Zwick overcomes the language barrier by having Katsumoto be a student of English (that way, everything doesn't have to be subtitled). The battle sequences are frank and brutal, with none of the artistry and grace of many recent sword-fighting movies. *The Last Samurai* is about heroes of a different sort. The movie's title foreshadows a tragic denouement, but that in no way lessens *The Last Samurai*'s impact. The film is in many ways about the clash between the old ways (those of the samurai) and the new (those employed by the American-trained troops). There is, of course, something exceptionally dramatic about stories in which a grossly outnumbered group puts up a valiant, albeit ultimately doomed, defense. This element gives *The Last Samurai* much of its power and passion. It is in the grand storytelling tradition of the underdog achieving glory. **HIGHLY RECOMMENDED**

Licence to Kill [United Kingdom, 1989]

Starring: Timothy Dalton, Robert Davi, Carey Lowell, Talisa Soto, Anthony Zerbe Director: John Glen Screenplay: Richard Maibaum & Michael G. Wilson Running Time: 2:13 Rated: PG-13 (Sexual innuendo, violence) Theatrical Aspect Ratio: 2.2:1

Licence to Kill, Timothy Dalton's second and final outing as superspy James Bond is a most atypical adventure. Not since *Dr. No* has 007 been so cool and ruthless, and never has a plot been this close to realistic plausibility. The villain is not a megalomaniac, but a drug lord, and Bond's mission has nothing to do with Her Majesty's Secret Service. In fact, he's acting on a vendetta and the British government is trying to capture him and bring him back to London.

Paradoxically, while there are almost no gadgets in this film, the "gadget man" himself, Q (Desmond Llewelyn), has his biggest role to date. While taking a vacation, he seeks out Bond in South America and offers his help. Another returning character is Felix Leiter (David Hedison, the only man to play the part twice), who loses his leg to a shark. It's this brutal attack on Leiter and his wife (Priscilla Barnes) by drug kingpin Sanchez (Robert Davi) that leads to Bond's abrupt resignation from MI6 so he can carry out a personal plan of revenge.

The dark, almost-ominous tone of *Licence to Kill* is unprecedented. This is an edgy movie, almost completely lacking in humor or flippancy. Dalton's 007 is angry and focused, and this portrayal is, at times, very like that of Connery at the beginning of *Diamonds Are Forever* (where Bond was hunting down Blofeld to avenge his wife's death).

For the most part, action is toned down in favor of plot development. This overemphasis on story may be a mistake, because there are times when *Licence to Kill*'s narrative bogs down. There are still two impressive action sequences, however. One involves an underwater struggle that develops into a mid-air fight. The other is a spectacular downhill chase featuring four loaded tanker trucks roaring along winding mountain roads. *Licence to Kill* may be taut and gripping, but it's not traditional Bond, and that, as much as any other reason, may explain the public's rejection of this reasonably well-constructed picture.

RECOMMENDED

Light It Up [1999]

Starring: Usher Raymond, Rosario Dawson, Marcello Robinson, Vanessa L. Williams, Forest Whitaker Director: Craig Bolotin
Screenplay: Craig Bolotin Running Time: 1:37 Rated: R (Violence, profanity) Theatrical Aspect Ratio: 1.85:1

Light It Up has all the trappings of an exploitation thriller about a group of high school students who hole up in a library with a hostage. There's a police negotiator, an overanxious SWAT team, and a media circus. Despite all of that, however, it's a relatively actionless film that's more concerned with developing characters and conveying a message than with carnage and pyrotechnics. As the story unfolds, *Light It Up* surprises by veering off into unexpected territory and defying the bloodthirstiness of some audience members in favor of attacking issues.

The film takes place in Queens' Lincoln High School on a seemingly normal day. When popular teacher Mr. Knowles (Judd Nelson) is suspended, a group of students organizes a sit-in. The arrival of police officer Dante Jackson (Forest Whitaker), in his first day on the job at the school, escalates an already tense situation. He becomes involved in a scuffle with two kids, Ziggy (Robert Ri'chard) and Lester (Usher Raymond), and soon his gun is in Ziggy's hands, he has been shot in the leg, and the school is being evacuated. Six students remain behind to hold Jackson hostage. As a horde of cops gathers outside the building, the kids begin to realize the enormity of their situation, and the list of demands they present to the negotiator (Vanessa L. Williams) surprises nearly everyone.

Writer/director Craig Bolotin manages the difficult task of telling his story without exploiting current events — not an easy task considering how volatile the post-Columbine atmosphere is regarding kids and guns. Bolotin shines the spotlight on important social issues by developing a group of interesting characters and placing them in an untenable situation. He occasionally resorts to clichés (friction among the students, a cop who is anxious to drop the negotiations and storm the Bastille), but, for the most part, he keeps things fresh.

There are those who will see *Light It Up* as a left-wing sermon, but Bolotin de-politicizes the movie by highlighting the problem without offering specific solutions. In addition to being a cautionary tale, the movie also functions as a well-constructed, taut thriller. There's a great deal of tension in the situation, and Bolotin doesn't allow it to go to waste. Bolotin, his cast, and his crew have invested this motion picture with more than a flash of purpose and promise.

RECOMMENDED

Limbo [1999]

Starring: Mary Elizabeth Mastrantonio, David Strathairn, Vanessa Martinez, Kris Kristofferson Director: John Sayles Screenplay: John Sayles Running Time: 2:07 Rated: PG-13 (Profanity) Theatrical Aspect Ratio: 1.85:1

There is little doubt that the most discussed aspect of writer/director/editor John Sayles' *Limbo* will be the ending. Unconventional and unexpected, the conclusion will inspire outrage in some movie-goers. Others, however, will recognize that Sayles chooses a resolution that is in keeping with the tone and artistic intent of the rest of the picture. Anything else would have been a capitulation to convention and traditional storytelling. With the exception of the atypical ending, *Limbo* ranks as one of Sayles' most accessible pictures. But mainstream audiences will *hate* what happens at the 2-hour mark.

If it's not obvious at first why this film is called *Limbo*, it will be by the time the proceedings have finished. The movie is about 3 characters trapped in an emotional paralysis from which only death will free them. In their own way, each of them is deeply troubled. Joe Gastineau (David Strathairn) is an introverted, lonely man who is haunted by a past that includes a tragic fishing accident in which two of his friends died. Donna De Angelo (Mary Elizabeth Mastrantonio) is a second-rate lounge singer whose life has consisted of a series of failed relationships. Her daughter, Noelle (Vanessa Martinez), is a disturbed teenager who entertains thoughts of suicide and self-mutilation. These three meet and interact in the town of Port Henry, Alaska, where Donna lands a gig at the local bar.

For a while, *Limbo* seems like it might be a slow-burning romance and tale of redemption, but, as is often the case, Sayles takes his audience in unexpected directions (unexpected because they defy comfortable, traditional narrative routes). Joe ends up in the middle of the mother/daughter struggle because he is involved with them both, albeit in different ways. Then his brother, Bobby (Casey

Siemaszko), shows up in town looking for his help crewing a boat. Joe agrees, and invites Donna and Noelle to come along. Bobby is none-too-pleased by the inclusion of 2 passengers, and, after a while, it becomes apparent why: this isn't a routine trip; Bobby is being hunted by gangsters.

During the second half, when the 3 protagonists are stranded on a deserted island, Sayles enters seemingly familiar territory. It doesn't take long, however, for him to stake out his own patch of land. This is no lightweight romantic fantasy, nor is it an exploration of man's triumph over nature. As thrillers go, *Limbo* is a sedate film, but that's the point. It's not about vital characters striving to achieve great things; instead, it's about a trio of broken human beings who are trapped in stasis, heading for a dead-end. And, when you think about it, that's exactly what *Limbo*'s controversial conclusion depicts. **HIGHLY RECOMMENDED**

Mary Shelley's Frankenstein [United States/United Kingdom, 1994]

Starring: Kenneth Branagh, Robert De Niro, Helena Bonham Carter, Ian Holm, Tom Hulce Director: Kenneth Branagh Screenplay: Steph Lady & Frank Darabont Running Time: 2:04 Rated: R (Violence, gore) Theatrical Aspect Ratio: 1.85:1

With this cinematic depiction of Mary Shelley's classic monster movie, director (and uncredited co-writer) Kenneth Branagh has taken a less-traveled path. He has chosen to view *Frankenstein* as a tragedy of Greek (or, given his background, Shakespearean) proportions. What Branagh should recognize better than anyone, though, is that tragedy is at its most effective when allowed to cook slowly, basting in its own juices. This version of *Frankenstein* moves so frantically that far too many subtleties get lost along the way. The result is a rousing, occasionally-chaotic (especially during the choppily-edited first half-hour) piece of work that, while undeniably entertaining, lacks a depth that might otherwise have been attained.

As far as its faithfulness to the source material is concerned, *Mary Shelley's Frankenstein* frequently differs from the book on plot points, but the two are thematically in synch. The greatest strength of *Mary Shelley's Frankenstein* is that it illustrates both the good and evil qualities in each of its main characters. Of the two — Robert De Niro's creature and Kenneth Branagh's Frankenstein — the former is, perhaps surprisingly, the more sympathetic. In part because of the script and in part because of the acting (De Niro gives a far stronger performance than his director/

co-star), the creature seems almost the more "human" of the two. In its own words, it is capable of great love and great rage. Frankenstein, on the other hand, often comes across as petty, self-serving, and ambitious. Only towards the end, when he finally grasps the full consequences of his actions, does the scientist capture a measure of our understanding.

Comparison's with 1992's *Bram Stoker's Dracula* are inevitable, especially since both came from Francis Ford Coppola's American Zoetrope production company. Considering the merits of both movies, however, there is little doubt which is more effective. Kenneth Branagh's film is stronger thematically and visually, possesses more solid characterization, and boasts Robert De Niro and Helena Bonham Carter rather than Keanu Reeves and Winona Ryder. *Mary Shelley's Frankenstein* may not be the definitive version of the 1817 novel, and the director likely attempted more than is practical for a 2-hour film, but overambition is preferable to the alternative, especially if it results — as in this case — in something more substantial than Hollywood's typical, fitfully entertaining fluff. **RECOMMENDED**

The Mask of Zorro [1998]

Starring: Antonio Banderas, Anthony Hopkins, Catherine Zeta-Jones, Stuart Wilson Director: Martin Campbell Screenplay: John Eskow, Ted Eliot & Terry Rossio Running Time: 2:15 Rated: PG-13 (Violence, sexual innuendo) Theatrical Aspect Ratio: 2.35:1

The Mask of Zorro treats us to the sight of not one, but two, Zorros. When the film opens in 1821, the mask is worn by Don Diego De La Vega (Anthony Hopkins). He is the original Zorro, the mysterious avenger who defends Mexico against its foes, including his arch-enemy, Don Rafael Montero (Stuart Wilson), the cruel governor of the region. But, on the night of Zorro's final public appearance, Montero learns his identity and takes a squadron of guards to De La Vega's abode. There, in a tragic accident, De La Vega's beloved wife is killed. Montero then imprisons his enemy and takes De La Vega's infant daughter as his own.

Twenty years later, that daughter, Elena (Catherine Zeta Jones), has grown into a beautiful woman. With her by his side, Montero triumphantly returns from exile with plans to turn California into an independent republic. Montero's reappearance awakens a long-dormant passion in De La Vega, who has spent two decades in dungeons, and he escapes. Soon after, he encounters a thief on the run from the law, Alejandro Murrieta (Antonio Banderas), who, as a child, once did Zorro a favor. After a brief period of deliberation, De La Vega decides that fate has brought them together ("When the pupil is ready, the teacher will find him"), and he agrees to take the man on as his protégé and groom him as the new Zorro. For his part, Murrieta is willing to endure De La Vega's tough training regimen, because he wants revenge on his brother's killer, Captain Harrison Love (Matt Letscher), who happens to be Montero's right-hand man.

Most recent superhero movies have been dark, bleak, and heavily reliant upon special effects. *The Mask of Zorro* is none of these. In many ways, it's a throwback to simpler times, before every new movie of this sort had to mimic *Batman*. There's something in the tone and style that recalls *Raiders of the Lost Ark*, and, while *The Mask of Zorro* isn't on the same level, it's not an altogether ridiculous comparison. Even though *Zorro* doesn't feature the non-stop cliffhanger adventure of *Raiders*, there's still plenty of action, tumult, and derring-do. And, like *Raiders*, this film never takes itself too seriously.

Like all great heroes, Zorro is bigger than life, and we wouldn't have it any other way. If the film makers can produce another one like this, here's hoping that Zorro rides again. **RECOMMENDED**

Master and Commander: The Far Side of the World [2003]

Starring: Russell Crowe, Paul Bettany, Billy Boyd, James D'Arcy, Lee Ingleby, David Threlfall, Max Pirkis Director: Peter Weir Screenplay: Peter Weir & John Collee, based on the novels by Patrick O'Brian Running Time: 2:15 Rated: PG-13 (Violence) Theatrical Aspect Ratio: 2.35:1

Master and Commander: The Far Side of the World is based on the exploits of characters created by 20th-century author Patrick O'Brian, who wrote 20 novels centered around the adventures of Captain "Lucky" Jack Aubrey (Russell Crowe) and Dr. Stephen Maturin (Paul Bettany). Although *Master and Commander* uses the general plot thrust of O'Brian's *The Far Side of the World*, it changes and deletes key elements and borrows select details from many of the other books in the series.

When the movie opens, it is August 1805, and the Napoleonic War are in full swing. Nowhere is the fear of Napoleón becoming Emperor of the World more prevalent than in England, where the anti-French sentiment is the strongest. So, in April of that year, the HMS *Surprise*, commanded by Captain Aubrey, is stationed off the east coast of Brazil with the mission of stopping the French privateer *Acheron*. The first en-

gagement is a near-disaster for the *Surprise*; the French ship is bigger, faster, and has more guns. Only the presence of a fogbank saves Aubrey and his crew. Thereafter, a chase begins, with the *Surprise* pursuing the *Acheron* south through the Atlantic Ocean, around Cape Horn, and through the Pacific to the Galápagos Islands. The longer the chase goes on, the less clear it becomes who is the pursuer and who is the pursued in this high-stakes cat-and-mouse game.

Master and Commander opens and closes with rousing battle scenes. The interim 75-odd minutes include character building, crew interaction, and details concerning what life was like on a ship in Nelson's navy. There are a few tense moments, such as when the *Surprise* encounters a typhoon off the coast of Cape Horn, but much of the film's protracted middle segment concerns more mundane matters. Some of this stuff — such as Maturin teaching a willing "disciple" about his naturalist hobby — is fascinating. Other elements seem pointless. At least one subplot, involving an officer who is disliked by the enlisted men and wonders if he is cursed, could easily have been excised, resulting in a tighter story line. The biggest problem the film has is getting its audience from one battle scene to the other without putting them to sleep. A less deliberate pace during the middle third would have made the job easier.

The film looks marvelous from start to finish. In fact, this may be the best-looking film ever made about a seafaring vessel. The filmmakers carefully researched ships of the period and spent time and money doing the best possible job re-creating the era. Peter Weir is a veteran director whose films have always been characterized by their uncommon intelligence. For those with any interest in 18th and 19th-century seafaring or naval warfare, this is a must-see motion picture. **RECOMMENDED**

Maverick [1994]

Starring: Mel Gibson, Jodie Foster, James Garner Director: Richard Donner Screenplay: William Goldman Running Time: 2:09 Rated: PG (Mild profanity, implied sex) Theatrical Aspect Ratio: 2.35:1

Maverick may be as close as anything comes to perfect light entertainment (as opposed to a perfect movie). It has great action sequences, more than a splash of legitimately funny humor, solid performances from engaging actors, and a script that doesn't demand much mental exercise.

Lethal Weapon's Richard Donner and Mel Gibson have teamed up again in this comedy/adventure/

western that recalls, but does not imitate, the 1950s television series. Along for the ride is James Garner, who millions will remember as the original Bret Maverick, and Donner makes a wise decision in giving him more than a token speaking part. Garner's laid back persona is the perfect contrast to the high-voltage Gibson. Two-time Oscar winner Jodie Foster is effervescent in a role that requires little dramatic range but a flair for comedy. Foster's Annabelle Bransford is delightful, especially when paired with Gibson. There's a spark between them.

The story involves Maverick and Annabelle's attempts to get to a big Saint Louis riverboat poker game where the entry fee is $25,000. Each is short by a few grand, and they go from town-to-town trying to win, steal, or cheat others out of it. They meet in Crystal River, and soon find themselves on the same runaway coach out of town, in the company of itinerant lawman Zane Cooper (Garner).

Maverick features gun fights, fist fights, an attempted hanging, and a tête-à-tête with rattlesnakes — but none of these sequences are graphic or gory. The film is basically lighthearted, so there aren't too many deaths or maimings. Donner has a great deal of fun incorporating parodies of past movies into this one. The most inspired is a quick flash to his own *Lethal Weapon*. There's also an extended *Dances with Wolves* sequence, featuring *Wolves*' Graham Greene as a hip Indian who cheats the white man. *Maverick* also pays tribute to screenwriter William Goldman's *Butch Cassidy and the Sundance Kid*.

The strength of *Maverick* is the ease with which it switches from comedy to action, and back again. For the most part, the pacing is excellent, although at more than two hours, the film goes on for a little too long. No drama is needed, nor is it in evidence. The well-crafted *Maverick* does everything it sets out to do. To paraphrase the lead character, *Maverick* rarely bluffs and never, ever cheats its audience.

HIGHLY RECOMMENDED

Mission: Impossible II [2000]

Starring: Tom Cruise, Thandie Newton, Dougray Scott, Ving Rhames
Director: John Woo Screenplay: Robert Towne Running Time: 2:07
Rated: PG-13 (Violence, profanity) Theatrical Aspect Ratio: 2.35:1

Chef Emeril Legasse is known for "kicking up" his food concoctions by adding a liberal dash of hot spices. Working from Robert Towne's pedestrian screenplay for *Mission: Impossible II,* that's what director John Woo has done with this cinematic entrée. The movie illustrates the kind of impact a stylish filmmaker can have on a project. In other hands, *Mission: Impossible II* might have been a run-of-the-mill action movie, but, emblazoned with Woo's trademark flourishes, the motion picture has been transformed into a high-energy, adrenaline-and-testosterone boosted ride. This is most definitely "a John Woo film."

The story concerns the quest of an ex-secret agent, Sean Ambrose (Dougray Scott), to obtain samples of both the killer virus Chimera and its antidote from the scientist who created them for Biocyte Pharmaceuticals in Sydney, Australia. Once he has the virus, Ambrose plans to unleash it in the streets of Sydney and get rich as his stock options in Biocyte skyrocket, since the drug company will be the only one producing the antidote. Of course, the Impossible Missions Force (IMF) cannot allow this to happen, so their leader, M . . . err, make that Swanbeck (Anthony Hopkins), calls on his top agent, Ethan Hunt (Cruise), interrupting his mountain climbing vacation.

Swanbeck sends Hunt to recruit Ambrose's old girlfriend, Nyah Nordoff-Hall (Thandie Newton), to spy for the IMF. On this mission, Hunt brings along an old buddy, Luther (Ving Rhames), and a new Aussie cohort (John Polson). Complications occur when Hunt unexpectedly falls — and falls hard — for Nyah, and his feelings are returned. Suddenly, saving her life becomes as important as saving the world, and, since we're deep in 007 territory for most of the movie, there's little question that both likelihoods will arise.

Woo is in fine form, employing every weapon in his considerable arsenal: slow motion shots, billowing clothing (scarves, loose jackets, the dresses on flamenco dancers), pigeons taking flight, lots of martial arts/WWF moves, and a fluid but constantly-moving camera. The soundtrack, which features a relentless Hans Zimmer score liberally sprinkled with a souped-up version of the "Mission: Impossible" theme, hammers the viewer's ears. As always, Woo choreographs his action scenes like ballet. The final chase/fight sequence, which features motorcycles zig-zagging through traffic and ends with a lengthy hand-to-hand duel in which both participants display superhuman stamina, is edge-of-the-seat material. It may sound clichéd and familiar, but Woo elevates it to another level. *Mission: Impossible II* is an exciting assault on the senses that doesn't tax the brain. **RECOMMENDED**

Moonraker [United Kingdom, 1979]

Starring: Roger Moore, Lois Chiles, Michael Lonsdale, Richard Kiel
Director: **Lewis Gilbert** Screenplay: **Christopher Wood** Running
Time: **2:06** Rated: PG (Sexual innuendo, violence) Theatrical Aspect
Ratio: 2.2:1

Moonraker is a sort of James Bond meets *Star Wars*. While parts of *Moonraker* are rather silly (a trend during Roger Moore's tenure), solid special effects, well-executed action sequences, and a strict reliance upon the "Bond Formula" keep this film among Moore's better entries as the British superspy.

The film opens with the hijacking of a Moonraker space shuttle on loan from the United States to Great Britain. Anxious to get to the bottom of the situation, the British government sends agent 007 to investigate, beginning with Drax Industries in California, where the shuttle was produced. Bond arrives, starts poking around, and becomes the immediate target of several murder attempts. Along the way, he strikes up a relationship with Dr. Holly Goodhead (Lois Chiles), one of Drax's chief scientists, and encounters an old adversary — Jaws (again played by Richard Kiel).

While *Moonraker*'s centerpiece is the final half-hour, which takes place aboard an Earth-orbiting space station, this is actually the least entertaining portion of the film. It's essentially a special effects demonstration, with laser bolt shootouts and space shuttles firing at deadly satellites. Most of the tense action scenes occur before Bond blasts into outer space. If nothing else, this film proves that Bond is best on Earth.

Normally, characters in Bond films don't go through much development. Such is not the case with Jaws, however. One of 007's best adversaries returns for a second engagement (he was also in *The Spy Who Loved Me*). This time, however, the steel-toothed bad guy has mellowed as the direct result of falling in love. Although Jaws is still as indestructible as ever, we see a different side of him as *Moonraker* draws to a close. Just don't expect anything *too* dramatic — this is still a James Bond movie, after all.

As Roger Moore's fourth Bond outing, and the eleventh film in the series, *Moonraker* is a satisfying followup to *The Spy Who Loved Me*. Science fiction fans may be offended by some of the liberties taken here, but tolerance is necessary. The film is, after all, geared towards a specific audience. Accent the "fiction" in science fiction, and recognize that with Bond, realism is the last thing anyone expects — or wants.

RECOMMENDED

Once Upon a Time in Mexico [2003]

Starring: Antonio Banderas, Salma Hayek, Johnny Depp, Mickey Rourke, Eva Mendes, Danny Trejo, Enrique Iglesias, Cheech Marin, Rubén Blades, Willem Dafoe, Gerardo Vigil, Pedro Armendáriz
Director: **Robert Rodriguez** Screenplay: **Robert Rodriguez** Running
Time: **1:40** Rated: R (Violence, profanity) Theatrical Aspect Ratio: 2.35:1

Some times are easier than others to forgive a filmmaker his excesses. Such a case is *Once Upon a Time in Mexico*, a mess of a movie that nevertheless entertains because each individual piece stands high enough on its own merits that it's not necessary to look hard at the nonsensical linking material. *Once Upon a Time in Mexico* isn't so much a movie as it is a series of action/comedic sequences.

For those to whom it matters, there is the loose framework of a story. El Mariachi (Antonio Banderas), the hero of Rodriguez's first two films, *El Mariachi* and *Desperado*, is back, and this time he's out for revenge. He wants to assassinate General Marquez (Gerardo Vigil), the man who killed his beloved wife, Carolina (Salma Hayek), and their daughter. When a shady CIA agent (or so he claims to be) named Sands (Johnny Depp) comes to El Mariachi with a proposal that's too good to refuse, he agrees to eliminate Marquez. As it turns out, this is just one aspect of an attempt by drug lord Barillo (Willem Dafoe) to destabilize and topple the regime of the current president (Pedro Armendáriz). Or something like that.

Even though the shadow of a tragedy hangs over the movie (El Mariachi is motivated by revenge for his dead loved ones), Rodriguez's lively approach to moviemaking keeps things from becoming grim. In fact, parts of the film are downright hilarious. (Johnny Depp on his cell phone: "Can you hear me now?") The action sequences are brilliantly conceived and executed. They may not be much more than eye candy, but each one is a tasty morsel. The title is an homage to Sergio Leone, but the style, at least for the most part, pays tribute to the classic Hong Kong action films of the 70s and 80s, complete with the cheesy exuberance that characterized the best of, say, John Woo.

As has been true of his *Spy Kids* movies, Robert Rodriguez takes nearly every major behind-the-scenes role: director, coproducer, writer, editor, cinematographer, composer, production designer, special effects supervisor, and probably a few other things. Rodriguez is known as a guerrilla filmmaker. He makes pictures quickly, cheaply, and with a lot of energy. *Once Upon a Time in Mexico* is a bloody fairy tale with no moral and a lot of juice. **RECOMMENDED**

On Her Majesty's Secret Service
[United Kingdom, 1969]
Starring: George Lazenby, Diana Rigg, Telly Savalas Director: Peter Hunt Screenplay: Richard Maibaum Running Time: 2:15 Rated: PG (Violence, sexual innuendo) Theatrical Aspect Ratio: 2.2:1

With the exception of one production aspect, *On Her Majesty's Secret Service* is by far the best entry of the long-running James Bond series. The film contains some of the most exhilarating action sequences ever to reach the screen, a touching love story, and a nice subplot that has agent 007 crossing (and even threatening to resign from) Her Majesty's Secret Service. The problem is with Bond himself. Following Sean Connery's departure, the film makers had to come up with a replacement. The man they chose, a model named George Lazenby, is *boring,* and his ineffectualness lowers the picture's quality.

Lazenby can handle the action sequences, but that's about all he masters. Even considering the leading man's limitations, however, *On Her Majesty's Secret Service* is still a fine motion picture. It's the only Bond film where 007 genuinely falls in love. The object of his affection, Tracy (Diana Rigg), is the troubled daughter of a European crime boss, Draco (Gabriele Ferzetti). After Bond saves Tracy's life and pays off a 20,000-franc debt, Draco becomes interested in acquiring the British agent as a son-in-law. Bond declines his offer of one million pounds to marry Tracy, then proceeds to fall in love with her anyway.

The movie isn't all love-and-kisses, however. The main storyline involves the return of Blofeld (Telly Savalas in this incarnation). This time, he plans a campaign of biological warfare to be waged from a "research clinic" high in the Alps. Posing as a genealogist, Bond visits the place. Despite their face-to-face meeting in *You Only Live Twice,* Blofeld doesn't recognize his adversary (maybe the change to Lazenby confused him), but a minor mistake blows 007's cover.

The climactic half-hour of *On Her Majesty's Secret Service* is almost non-stop action. There's a stunning night ski sequence, a car chase down icy streets and through the heart of a stock car race, an avalanche, a helicopter raid on Blofeld's clinic, and fisticuffs on a speeding bobsled. Director Peter Hunt has a flair for these kinds of scenes, and he keeps viewers on the edge of their seats. Even featuring an inferior 007, *On Her Majesty's Secret Service* is a landmark change-of-pace, and an exhilarating and affecting piece of entertainment. **HIGHLY RECOMMENDED**

The Perfect Storm [2000]
Starring: George Clooney, Mark Wahlberg, Diane Lane, William Fichtner, Mary Elizabeth Mastrantonio Director: Wolfgang Petersen Screenplay: Bill Witliff, based on the novel by Sebastian Junger Running Time: 2:08 Rated: PG-13 (Profanity, intense weather-related scenes) Theatrical Aspect Ratio: 2.35:1

In 1997, almost 6 years after the Great Halloween Nor'easter, journalist Sebastian Junger published *The Perfect Storm,* an account of some of the most dramatic and memorable events associated with the late-October 1991 weather system. The primary focus of the film (as well as the book) is the 6-man crew of the swordfishing vessel *Andrea Gail* — Bobby Shatford (Mark Wahlberg), Dale Murphy (John C. Reilly), David Sullivan (William Fichtner), Bugsy Moran (John Hawkes), Alfred Pierre (Allen Payne), and the captain, Billy Tyne (George Clooney). After returning to shore with a poor haul that earns him less than $6,000 (and members of his crew under $3,000), Tyne decides to take the *Andrea Gail* out one more time this season. The trip to the Flemish Cap is relatively eventless, but, as the *Andrea Gail* heads east, bad weather is brewing behind them, blocking their return home. Later, after they have filled their cargo holds and are on their way back, they lose radio contact and are unaware of the strength of the storm ahead of them.

The movie is at its best when it stays with the crew of the *Andrea Gail,* which it does most of the time. The opening half-hour, before the ship sails, does a good job introducing the characters and letting us know what makes them tick. The only piece of character interaction that isn't effective is the bickering between Murph and Sully (which leads to more than one passage of badly written dialogue). The sequences with these 6 men braving the rough seas and bad weather represent some of *The Perfect Storm's* most suspenseful moments. For those who are unaware of the *Andrea Gail's* fate, there will be more than one nail-biting moment.

Making use of impressive visuals (many of which were enhanced, if not generated altogether, by digital technology), *The Perfect Storm* gives a sense of the awe-inspiring power of a raging sea. With mountainous swells that dwarf even large boats and no place to hide or take refuge, the ocean can easily become a very dangerous place. The movie is exciting, engaging, and, at times, majestic, but it does not change the historical facts to make for a more crowd-pleasing story. For the first time since *Das Boot,* Wofgang

Petersen has taken his cast, crew, and cameras back into the water; the result is definitely *not* all wet.
RECOMMENDED

Pirates of the Caribbean: The Curse of the Black Pearl [2003]

Starring: Johnny Depp, Geoffrey Rush, Orlando Bloom, Keira Knightley, Jack Davenport, Jonathan Pryce Director: Gore Verbinski Screenplay: Ted Elliott & Terry Rossio Running Time: 2:20 Rated: PG-13 (Walking dead, violence) Theatrical Aspect Ratio: 2.35:1

For those taking a global view of *Pirates of the Caribbean: The Curse of the Black Pearl*, it's very easy to be cynical. This is, after all, cross-promotion at its most blatant. What could be more marketable than one of Disney's most popular theme park attractions? The name recognition is already in place — all that's necessary to complete the puzzle is a story that will fit the ride. But there are two reasons why jaded ranting isn't the best way to proceed with this review. In the first place, no one really cares. And, more importantly, this is actually an entertaining experience.

Cap'n Jack Sparrow (Johnny Depp) is a pirate who's infamous for his ineptitude. After rescuing a damsel, Elizabeth Swann (Keira Knightley), he finds himself being thanked by her father (Jonathan Pryce) and her would-be betrothed (Jack Davenport) while simultaneously being arrested for piracy. He escapes, but after losing a duel with the heroic blacksmith Will Turner (Orlando Bloom), who pines for Elizabeth, he is sent back to jail. However, when the town comes under attack by the pirate ship *Black Pearl*, and its blackguard of a captain, Barbossa (Geoffrey Rush), kidnaps Elizabeth, Will springs Jack from prison so the pirate can help him retrieve his beloved. But Barbossa isn't interested in a ransom. He and his crew are cursed to walk the earth as the living dead until a blood sacrifice can restore their humanity.

Pirates of the Caribbean belongs to Johnny Depp. Keira Knightley (now a familiar face in the wake of *Bend It Like Beckham*) and Orlando Bloom (*The Lord of the Rings*' Legolas, sans ears and blond hair) make a cute couple, and Geoffrey Rush is typically over-the-top as the bad guy, but the star of every scene is Depp. With several gold teeth in his mouth and beads in his hair, Depp plays the part with an engaging goofiness that sets the movie's tone. In one scene, Sparrow becomes blind drunk, but his behavior isn't all that different from when he's sober — a clear indicator of where Depp elected to take the character. Sparrow is a rogue through-and-through and, al-

though he may have a heart of gold, it's definitely tarnished. Take away Depp and you're left with a derivative and dull motion picture.

As is mandated by the first rule of adventure movies — sustain the action — *Pirates of the Caribbean* is wall-to-wall battles, chases, and fights. The only pauses are those necessitated by the need to advance the plot through exposition. There's lots of swordplay, including a lengthy and memorable struggle between Sparrow and Will. It's probably the best example of cinematic sword fighting since *The Mask of Zorro*. **RECOMMENDED**

The Professional [France/United States, 1994]

Starring: Jean Reno, Natalie Portman, Gary Oldman Director: Luc Besson Screenplay: Luc Besson Running Time: 1:52 Rated: R (Violence, language, mature themes) Theatrical Aspect Ratio: 2.35:1

The career aspirations of Mathilda (Natalie Portman) aren't those of the average 12-year old girl. Instead of wanting to be a doctor, fashion model, teacher, lawyer, or nuclear physicist, Mathilda has decided to follow in the footsteps of her best friend, surrogate father, and protector, Leon (Jean Reno). The only problem is that Leon is a "cleaner" — a professional hit man. Mathilda comes from a *very* dysfunctional family. Her father is a drug dealer, his wife despises her, and her half-sister enjoys beating her up. Mathilda's chief pleasure is hanging out in her New York City tenement building's stairwell, smoking cigarettes.

One day, a crooked cop (played with typical over-the-top exuberance by Gary Oldman) decides to have Mathilda's whole family exterminated. When she arrives home to find them slaughtered, she goes to Leon, who lives down the hall, for help. Although he's at first reluctant to open his door to her, once he does, she worms her way into both his life and his heart. And she's not some wide-eyed innocent; her desire to learn about killing is fueled by the need to exact bloody revenge for her little brother's murder (she could care less about the other family members).

The real strength of *The Professional* is the central relationship between Mathilda and Leon. Although not well-founded in reality, these two characters mesh nicely. Despite an occasional low-key hint of sexual attraction, this is basically a father/daughter or mentor/apprentice relationship. There's nothing unique about a young girl melting the heart of a hardened loner except the manner in which Luc Besson approaches the theme.

Because of the non-American flavor brought to this film by Besson, *The Professional* is anything but typical fare. It is stylish, darkly humorous, and almost artsy in its approach to the genre. Nevertheless, it delivers what viewers want from any thriller: lots of action. With some surprisingly strong character interaction, there's a lot to like about this movie, at least for those willing to look beyond all the bloodshed.

At one point, Leon comments to an attentive Mathilda that "the closer you get to being a pro, the closer you can get to the client." Through the intimacy of the link forged by Besson with his audience, there's no doubt that he's as much the consummate professional as his implacable title character.
RECOMMENDED

Queen Margot [France/Italy/Germany, 1994]

Starring: Isabelle Adjani, Daniel Auteuil, Jean-Hugues Anglade, Vincent Perez Director: Patrice Chereau Screenplay: Daniele Thmopson & Patrice Chereau Running Time: 2:23 Rated: R (Violence, gore, sex, nudity) Theatrical Aspect Ratio: 1.85:1 In French with subtitles

The ageless Isabelle Adjani, one of France's most beautiful faces, has an undeniable screen presence. And, with his lean, well-toned body and finely-sculpted features, Vincent Perez is equally pleasing to the eye. However, put them together with the expectation that they'll play off one another, and the love affair that's supposed to sizzle instead fizzles. Not only is there no chemistry between these two, but the cold-as-ice Adjani never thaws, and Perez shows that in France, like elsewhere, physical attractiveness does not equate to acting talent.

Fortunately, there's a lot more going on in *Queen Margot* than the relationship between Perez' gallant La Mole and Adjani's title character. The film's primary focus is the bloody 16th-century struggle between French Catholics and Protestants, and the resulting political intrigue in the court of King Charles XI. *Queen Margot* opens in 1572 at the ostentatious wedding of Margot — the Catholic daughter of Catherine de Medici (Virna Lisi) and the brother of Charles (Jean-Hugues Anglade) — to Henri of Navarre (Daniel Auteuil) — the leader of the Huguenots. While this arrangement is intended to secure peace between the rival religious factions, it is a marriage of convenience only. Margot makes it clear that Henri is not welcome in her bed.

Six days after the marriage comes the Saint Bartholomew's Day massacre, an event that sees the wanton slaughter of thousands of Protestants, including the king's confidante. Henri, like many of his subjects, is forced to convert to Catholicism to save his life. Meanwhile, Margot has taken a new lover — a brave and dashing Huguenot by the name of La Mole. Yet the *I Claudius*-like scheming and political machinations have just begun.

Most of *Queen Margot* is a top-notch historical epic featuring impeccable costumes and grand scenery. Unlike the "typical" French film, this is not at all talky. In fact, amidst the swordfights, carnage, and battle scenes, there are occasions when dialogue is at a premium. *Queen Margot* is a sumptuous movie — except when the focus switches to the poorly realized romance between Margot and La Mole.

Queen Margot has enough pomp and pageantry — not to mention melodrama — to alienate viewers who don't enjoy that sort of film. However, for those who appreciate bigger-than-life historical sagas, Chereau's entry is often impressive and almost always entertaining. **RECOMMENDED**

The River Wild [1994]

Starring: Meryl Streep, David Strathairn, Joseph Mazzello, Kevin Bacon, John C. Reilly Director: Curtis Hanson Screenplay: Dennis O'Neill Running Time: 1:52 Rated: PG-13 (Violence, language) Theatrical Aspect Ratio: 2.35:1

As thrillers go, *The River Wild* is a cut below a "white-knuckler," but it still has its share of spills and chills. Crafted by Curtis Hanson, *The River Wild* represents for its audience just about what you might expect from a film with that title.

It's the 10th birthday for Roarke (Joseph Mazzello), and his mother Gail (Meryl Streep) has agreed to take him white water rafting to celebrate the occasion. She knows the territory well, having spent years working as a guide. Workaholic dad Tom (David Strathairn) at first refuses to accompany them but, after a guilty conscience prods him to join the family outing, he seems determined not to enjoy himself. Brooding, not boating, is his specialty.

Also on the river are Wade (Kevin Bacon) and Terry (John C. Reilly), a pair of inept rafters who have supposedly lost their guide. Gail, not wanting to strand them 5 days from civilization, agrees to let them join her party. Along the trip downstream, as both parents' distrust of the strangers grows, Roarke becomes fascinated by his new friends, especially when Wade shows him a loaded gun. From that point, the story moves in a sinister direction, with hostages being taken and lives threatened.

The River Wild has its share of tense moments. The

plot beneath the action is flimsy at best, but there's enough on-screen energy to overcome this deficiency. Adding noticeable value is the fine quality of the cast. These aren't just personalities thrown into suitable roles. Meryl Streep and David Strathairn are well-respected actors who have done some incredible work in the past. Kevin Bacon, who typically plays a "nice guy," is effective cast against type as a ruthless killer.

Top-of-the-line production values are of equal importance. Expansive cinematography and an apt score transfer a portion of the rafting experience to the audience. No one is likely to get seasick from *The River Wild*, but the roller-coaster pace of the picture easily matches the ups and downs of the rapids.

With *The Hand that Rocks the Cradle*, director Hanson showed that he could manipulate characters and situations within the comfortable confines of a formula plot. With *The River Wild*, he does considerably more. The thriller framework is still familiar, but the results exhibit a welcome freshness. With a pace and level of excitement designed to submerge implausibilities and minor gaffes, *The River Wild* braves the rapids while keeping the viewer afloat amidst its churning waters. **RECOMMENDED**

Rob Roy [1995]

Starring: Liam Neeson, Jessica Lange, John Hurt, Tim Roth Director: **Michael Caton-Jones** Screenplay: Alan Sharp Running Time: **2:15** Rated: **R** (Violence, mature themes, sex, nudity, rape) Theatrical Aspect Ratio: **2.35:1**

Ultimately, it's of minor import how much of *Rob Roy* is based upon historical fact and how much has been embellished by the pen of screenwriter Alan Sharp. As a hero of 18th century Scotland, Robert Roy MacGregor is known to have walked through the mists of the Highlands, living by the code that made his name a legend. This film takes the skeletal myth and builds a real person around those bones. As embodied by Liam Neeson, Rob Roy is a tremendous protagonist — a naive man whose belief in honor and whose love for a woman, family, and clan make him a figure to cheer for.

Rob Roy has a great villain as well. Tim Roth, one of today's finest character actors, plays Cunningham, a fop with effete mannerisms and a deadly blade. He's a sociopath who kills and rapes without compunction or remorse, and whose primary goal in life is to make the best out of a tormented existence in Scotland. Hunting down Rob Roy gives him something to do — something he enjoys.

It's the forcefulness of the characters and the talents of the actors who play them that give *Rob Roy* its soul. After all, almost everyone loves a movie with admirable heroes and detestable villains. But there is more to this film than that. The story is well-developed, exciting, and visceral, and works equally well as an epic drama or an historical adventure.

The picture is well-crafted, with expert editing, impressive camerawork, and an atmospheric musical score. Composer Carter Burwell has combined traditional Scottish folk songs with original material to form an audio tapestry that complements the lens work of Karl Walter Lindenlaub. With all the elements coming together so flawlessly, director Michael Caton-Jones can be justifiably proud of *Rob Roy*, sure to be one of 1995's most absorbing and exhilarating epic adventures. **HIGHLY RECOMMENDED**

The Rock [1996]

Starring: Sean Connery, Nicolas Cage, Ed Harris Director: **Michael Bay** Screenplay: David Weisberg, Donald S. Cook & Mark Rosner Running Time: **2:15** Rated: **R** (Violence, profanity, sex) Theatrical Aspect Ratio: **2.35:1**

As is often the case with action films, a simple premise is the most effective. Here, it's that a group of ex-Marines have stolen 15 VX gas rockets and are threatening to launch a lethal strike on the San Francisco Bay area if their demands aren't met. Led by war hero and living legend Brigadier General Frank Hummel (Ed Harris), the crack platoon has holed up on Alcatraz, where they're holding 81 civilians hostage. The U.S. government responds by sending a troop of Navy SEALS on a secret raid, using the labyrinth of tunnels beneath the island as their entranceway. Their guide is the only man ever to escape from the legendary prison: ex-SAS operative, John Mason (Sean Connery). Also in the party is FBI agent Stanley Goodspeed (Nicolas Cage), an admitted "chemical superfreak" who has the knowledge and experience to defuse Hummel's rockets.

The cast is first rate. But the real standout is, of course, Connery. Having lost none of his charisma with age, the veteran actor puts to use his mastery of mixing humor and action. Just like Bond, Mason does all his shooting and battling with tongue in cheek. Along the way, he develops a nice rapport with Goodspeed, with the two actors clicking in the best "buddy movie" fashion.

The Rock's running time could have been trimmed. There's no reason for it to last a bloated 135 minutes. Much of the early, character-building material could have been shortened without damaging the complexity of the principal trio, and certain aspects of the script might have benefiting from a little tightening up. Flaws aside, however, *The Rock* still represents a loud, fast-paced night's worth of entertainment. There are all the expected shoot-outs, explosions, and death-defying stunts. Director Michael Bay doesn't break new ground, but he displays his command of the genre by keeping the familiar from becoming boring. With Connery, Cage, Harris, and a host of harrowing action sequences, this is the kind of breath-stealing entertainment that audiences crave. Although not as expertly-crafted as *Die Hard* or *Speed, The Rock* is exhausting in its own right — and that's just one of several convincing reasons to see this film. RECOMMENDED

The Rocketeer [1991]

Starring: Bill Campbell, Jennifer Connelly, Alan Arkin, Timothy Dalton
Director: Joe Johnston Screenplay: Danny Bilson & Paul DeMeo
Running Time: 1:48 Rated: PG (Mild violence) Theatrical Aspect
Ratio: 2.35:1

The Rocketeer is a superhero movie, but it's a superhero movie of a different flavor. This isn't a *Batman* or a *Superman* clone. It isn't about a vigilante out to stomp out crime or a visitor from another world using his powers to advance truth, justice, and the American way. Instead, it's about an ordinary man who is briefly given the opportunity to do extraordinary things.

It's Hollywood, 1938. Although a war rages in Europe, the United States remains mostly isolated, and the West Coast mecca of motion pictures is deserving of the name of "Tinseltown." Cliff Secord (Bill Campbell) is a daredevil test pilot who enjoys his job but doesn't have much money. His girlfriend, Jenny (Jennifer Connelly), is an aspiring actress who loves Cliff, but thinks he takes her for granted. So it's no surprise that when the debonair Neville Sinclair (Timothy Dalton), the "third biggest box office draw," takes an interest in Jenny, she's smitten. Meanwhile, Cliff's career is in as much trouble as his love life. A plane he had hoped to fly in competition has crashed and burned, and he's left with too little money and too little time to set up something new. Then fate intervenes.

A gang of crooks has stolen a top-secret rocket backpack from Howard Hughes. Pursued by the FBI, they ditch it in Cliff's hanger, where he finds it. After a few experiments to see how it works, he straps it on and The Rocketeer (as the papers dub him) is born.

But, while Cliff's intentions are to use the pack only for honorable purposes and return it to the legitimate owner upon request, others want it for darker reasons. Soon, Cliff finds himself pursued by gangsters, Nazis, and a big, ugly man with a rubber mask.

The film has something of the feel of the Indiana Jones movies, albeit without the self-referential humor. There's a lot of action and more than a few "How's he going to get out of this?" moments. As is often the case with movies of this sort, character development is not a focal point. As a result, we get thinly-sketched types: the likable hero, his irascible mentor, the gorgeous girlfriend, and the charming villain. They're comic book type individuals, which shouldn't be all that surprising, considering *The Rocketeer*'s pedigree. *The Rocketeer* may not be perfect, but it's an excellent example of how to adapt a comic book to the screen. RECOMMENDED

The Rundown [2003]

Starring: The Rock, Seann William Scott, Rosario Dawson, Christopher
Walken, Ewen Bremner Director: Peter Berg Screenplay: R. J. Stewart
and James Vanderbilt Running Time: 1:42 Rated: PG-13 (Violence,
crude language) Theatrical Aspect Ratio: 2.35:1

The Rundown is a lot of fun because it's a throwback. The screen isn't polluted by excessive razzle-dazzle. The filmmakers have wisely kept their computer animators on a short leash. There are some obligatory pyrotechnics, but for the most part this is the kind of testosterone-charged action we saw often during the 1980s.

Beck (The Rock), a self-described "Retrieval Expert," finds himself in Brazil on his latest job. His mission: locate Travis (Seann William Scott), the son of his boss, and bring him to California. Unfortunately, Travis doesn't want to be caught. He is in pursuit of an artifact and he doesn't intend to leave the monkey-infested jungle before he finds it. Travis isn't the only one after the gold statue. Local bartender/fortune hunter Mariana (Rosario Dawson) wants it, as does the detested regional despot, Hatcher (Christopher Walken), who has turned the locals into a slave labor force. So Beck chases Travis while being pursued by Mariana, Hatcher, and Hatcher's goons.

Director Peter Berg, who has spent a fair amount of time in front of the camera during his career, crafts the film like a seasoned veteran. The action sequences are crisply framed and edited. The suspense is not stalled by too many cuts, and the movie never goes more than a few minutes without something happening, even if it is just The Rock being menaced by a horny baboon. Neither the actor nor the director takes things too seriously, which keeps the proceedings lighthearted. There is a fair amount of comedy sprinkled throughout, including a number of deliciously cheesy one-liners.

The Rundown offers everything a good movie of this sort should: plenty of suspenseful action, a few good laughs, and a share of obligatory "reluctant buddy" bonding. If you're in the mood for this sort of lighthearted entertainment, it's worth a rental. **RECOMMENDED**

Set It Off [1996]

Starring: Jada Pinkett, Queen Latifah, Vivica Fox, Kimberly Elise
Director: F. Gary Gray Screenplay: Takashi Bufford & Kate Lanier
Running Time: 2:00 Rated: R (Violence, profanity, sex, mature themes)
Theatrical Aspect Ratio: 2.35:1

Set It Off, which chronicles the attempts of 4 young black women to take control of their lives, may sound like it's treading a similar path to the one blazed by the tepid *Waiting to Exhale*, but nothing could be farther from the truth. In the first place, although *Set It Off* contains some dramatic elements, it is, first and foremost, an action/caper film. Secondly, all things considered, this is a much better picture.

Jada Pinkett is one of the crop of fine young actresses working today, and she deservedly gets more screen time than her co-stars. As Stony, she's the most sympathetic of the quartet, and the only one who comes close to having a well-rounded personality. The film opens with her prostituting herself to get the money for her younger brother's college tuition. Shortly thereafter, he is dead, the victim of an accidental police shooting. Stony is devastated, and her anger at the system makes her vulnerable to the seductive lure of easy money through a bank robbery.

Her accomplices in crime are her best friends. The four women, who have always been there to support one another, share not only a common history but the dream of one day escaping from the projects where they have lived their entire lives. The plan's mastermind is Frankie (Vivica Fox), an ex-bank employee who was fired when she reacted improperly during a hold-up. Tisean (Kimberly Elise) needs the money to keep her young son from becoming a ward of the State. And Cleo (Queen Latifah) wants in on the action so she can live the high life and buy nice clothes for her lesbian girlfriend. Together, after being kicked in the face once too often by society, these four don wigs, borrow some guns, walk into the South Los Angeles Bank, and take $12,000 in cash.

What sets this movie apart from the innumerable other entries into the action/caper genre is its social perspective. *Set It Off* doesn't preach, but you'd have to be blind not to recognize that there's a message here about the kind of desperation that can result from the familiar cycle of poverty, sexism, and racism. And, although the marketing for *Set It Off* is geared primarily towards African Americans, you don't have to be black to appreciate this effective, in-your-face style of film making. **RECOMMENDED**

Space Cowboys [2000]

Starring: Clint Eastwood, Tommy Lee Jones, James Garner, James
Cromwell, Donald Sutherland Director: Clint Eastwood
Screenplay: Ken Kaufman & Howard Klausner Running Time: 2:10
Rated: PG-13 (Profanity, brief nudity) Theatrical Aspect Ratio: 1.85:1

In 1958, the 4 men of Team Daedalus were the most experienced and daring that the Air Force had to offer. Eventually, the team broke apart, each of them heading in separate directions — until 40 years later, when the orbit of the Russian communications satellite *Icon* begins to decay. The satellite has only five weeks before it burns up in the atmosphere, and the Russians are worried that its loss will cripple their telecommunications infrastructure and perhaps start a civil war. *Icon*'s antiquated guidance system will not respond to commands sent from Earth and no one currently at NASA knows how to fix it. So, grudgingly, NASA approaches Frank Corvin (Eastwood), the leader of Team Daedalus and the creator of *Icon*'s "dinosaur" guidance system. Frank agrees to help, but there's a condition: he and the other three members of his team — pilot Hawk Hawkins (Tommy Lee Jones), navigator Tank Sullivan (James Garner), and structural engineer Jerry O'Neill (Donald Sutherland) — must be on the space shuttle when it launches.

Those going to *Space Cowboys* expecting aliens and space warfare will have wandered into the wrong theater. The premise is not designed to test a viewer's willing suspension of disbelief. *Space Cowboys* uses technology that is currently available. As *Apollo 13* taught viewers, it's possible to have a low-key space adventure with a great deal of tension — all that must happen is for something to go wrong. And that's exactly what fuels this movie's climactic segments.

A significant portion of *Space Cowboys*' appeal results from the four leads, all of whom possess high viewer recognition and comfort levels. We like these guys and enjoy being in their company for two hours. Eastwood is careful to balance the ensemble, not giving himself all the prime material. This allows him to do what he does best — stay calm under pressure and perform some low-key heroics. The sense of camaraderie within the group is more tangible than in many of the conventional buddy movies that invade multiplexes on a regular basis.

In the movies, putting senior citizens in space is nothing new, but this is the first time it has been done semi-realistically. The screenplay incorporates a lot of material, including secret cold war politics, cover-ups, political infighting, melodrama, media manipulation, male bonding, and, of course, science fiction action/adventure. Some of these elements work better than others, but, taken as a whole, they make for an entertaining ride. *Space Cowboys* is a blast for those who don't mind geriatric heroes. RECOMMENDED

Speed [1994]

Starring: Keanu Reeves, Dennis Hopper, Sandra Bullock Director: Jan De Bont Screenplay: Graham Yost Running Time: 1:55 Rated: R (Violence, profanity) Theatrical Aspect Ratio: **1.85:1**

It's an ingenious premise that first-time director Jan De Bont has turned into a tremendously well-executed motion picture. A mad bomber (Dennis Hopper) wants $3.7 million and to obtain a small measure of revenge on Jack Traven (Keanu Reeves), a cop who foiled one of his plots. So he rigs up a bomb on a bus that becomes armed when the vehicle goes over 50, and is primed to explode when it drops below that speed. And it's Jack's job to save all the people on board, including himself.

Good action movies are rare. Great action movies come along once every few years. *Speed* deserves a place in the latter category. This is a film that cries out for audience participation, whether it be the silent majority's digging of fingers into armrests or the vocal minority's cheers and catcalls.

With a single exception (that of the bus "flying" through the air), the stunts and special effects are flawlessly incorporated. And there are a lot of them. A *whole* lot. You could almost call this film *Planes, Trains, and Automobiles,* although for entirely different reasons than those behind the naming of the Steve Martin/John Candy flick. *Speed* is clearly divided into three acts, each no less draining than the others. The first and last (which involve an elevator and a train, respectively) bookend the longer and better sequence on the bus. The film may clock in at nearly 2 hours, but the time, like the various vehicles, races. There is, quite literally, never a dull moment.

Of course, there are plot contrivances. How could there not be? But these are subtle and convincingly woven into the fabric of the story. While watching *Speed,* you may notice one or two (for an example, consider how a bus traveling at 52 mph can slam into a car and have its speed not drop below the red line), but you won't care much. The low-level but persistent humor is used to blot the tension. Most of the one-liners aren't as good as those in *Die Hard,* but a few are worth a chuckle, and they serve their purpose. This is not, after all, supposed to be a comedy.

This movie is a winner, and the closest you can get to an amusement park ride in a theater. Perhaps the same warning that's used for roller coasters should be applied here. You know, the one about high blood pressure and heart problems. HIGHLY RECOMMENDED

Spider-Man [2002]

Starring: Tobey Maguire, Willem Dafoe, Kirsten Dunst Director: Sam Raimi Screenplay: David Koepp Running Time: 2:01 Rated: PG-13 (Violence, sensuality) Theatrical Aspect Ratio: **1.85:1**

Spider-Man is as critic-proof as movies come, so nothing that I say will make even a miniscule difference, but, for what it's worth, this represents the best kind of adventure movie — bold, colorful, and well-paced without numbing the mind or insulting the intelligence. On the scale of superhero movies, this one is about on par with *X-Men,* ahead of all of the *Batman* movies, but behind the grandly reverent *Superman.*

In comic book language, this is an "origin" story, meaning that it tells how Spider-Man came into being. The movie starts by introducing us to nerdy high school senior Peter Parker (Tobey Maguire), who is one of the least cool kids in school. He's shy and smart, and the girl of his dreams, Mary Jane Watson (Kirsten Dunst), doesn't know he exists. Peter's best friend is Harry Osborn (James Franco), the under-achieving son of the rich and arrogant scientist Norman Osborn (Willem Dafoe). Peter lives with his uncle, Ben (Cliff Robertson), and aunt, May (Rosemary Harris), who are like a father and mother to him.

Things change rapidly for Peter when, while visiting a lab at Columbia University, he is bitten by a genetically altered spider. Overnight, Peter gains arachnid powers — unnatural strength and endurance, amazing agility, and glands on his wrist that allow him to spin webs. Eventually, Peter is forced to make a choice between hiding his abilities or coming into the open and helping humanity. Meanwhile, Spidey's first arch-rival is also in the making, as Norman Osborn's scientific experimentation gives him equal parts superhuman strength and madness, and his access to the latest technology allows him to don a horrific metal suit and ride a one-man jet-propelled glider. After his first public appearance, at which he wreaks mayhem, the press dubs him The Green Goblin.

Although it is first and foremost an action/adventure film, *Spider-Man* is many other things, as well. There's a fairly high romance quotient — after all, many of Peter's motivations are centered around his near-obsession with Mary Jane. These two make a cute couple, but the better part of their love story is still to come (although their kiss, with Spider-Man hanging upside down as they lock lips, is memorable). *Spider-Man* also offers occasional doses of morality, the biggest one coming from Uncle Ben's words of warning to Peter: "With great power comes great responsibility." In the comic book, that phrase became Spider-Man's credo.

This is a pure popcorn movie — the kind of film one can unabashedly enjoy for what it is. There's plenty of visual flash and dizzying action, but not at the expense of the other qualities that make for a complete motion picture experience. As a character in a comic book, Spider-Man is 4 decades old. His leap into this new medium has rejuvenated the legend, and offers movie-goers an opportunity to sit back and enjoy the birth of a new cinematic superhero. RECOMMENDED

Spider-Man 2 [2004]

Starring: Tobey Maguire, Kirsten Dunst, James Franco, Alfred Molina, Rosemary Harris, J. K. Simmons, Donna Murphy Director: Sam Raimi
Screenplay: Alvin Sargent ·Running Time: 2:08 Rated: PG-13 (Violence)
Theatrical Aspect Ratio: 2.35:1

Spider-Man 2 has all the elements of a good, but not great, superhero motion picture. A worthy sequel to the 2002 blockbuster, *Spider-Man 2* will deposit fans somewhere on the satisfaction spectrum between quietly pleased and overjoyed. Although not as economical with its scenes as the first *Spider-Man,* this film nevertheless advances the leftover threads from its predecessor, tells its own self-contained tale, and dangles enough bait to hint at where *Spider-Man 3* will be heading.

Spider-Man 2 picks up a couple of years after the conclusion of the original *Spider-Man.* By this time, the costumed alter ego of geeky Peter Parker (Tobey Maguire) has become a New York City legend. Despite being decried by the *Daily Bugle* as a "menace,"

Spidey (as he is affectionately known) is as big a hero to some as he is a villain to others. In staying true to his calling as a crime fighter, Peter must stay away from the girl of his dreams. Mary Jane Watson (Kirsten Dunst) loves Peter, and Peter loves her, but he can never let her know, because he's afraid his enemies would use that information against them. So he pines in silence, and she becomes engaged to an astronaut. Meanwhile, a brilliant physicist named Dr. Otto Octavius (Alfred Molina), who is working for Peter's best friend, Harry Osborne (James Franco), has mastered a way to generate a controlled fusion reaction that can provide enough energy to fuel an entire city. Using mechanical arms grafted into his spinal column, he begins to manipulate the mini-sun he creates, but things go disastrously wrong. When the dust has settled, Dock Ock is no longer the man he was — he's insane and obsessed, and determined to rid Manhattan of Spider-Man. But, like Clark Kent in *Superman 2,* Peter has decided to abandon his powers so he can love a woman — and just at the time when the world most needs him.

Spider-Man 2 is essentially three movies rolled into one: a traditional superhero story, a coming-of-age tale, and a romance. Then there's the humor. One of *Spider-Man 2's* strengths is that it doesn't fear occasionally lightening up. So we get a lady singing the theme song from the animated *Spider-Man* TV series; Spidey taking an elevator and complaining that his costume is too tight in the crotch; Bruce Campbell playing a snooty usher; and Peter Parker displaying an aghast expression when learning that Aunt May (Rosemary Harris) gave away his comic book collection.

Spider-Man 2 is about 20 minutes too long. Although Sam Raimi's direction is generally solid (and, in some scenes, flawless), the film's middle act has instances when it seems repetitive and exposition-heavy. The strength of the climax and denouement almost renders such concerns moot, but they cannot be completely dismissed since they prevent this film from ascending to the pinnacle of superhero movies. Nevertheless, even though *Spider-Man 2* does not eclipse *Superman, Hulk,* or even *X-Men 2,* it proves that this series has plenty of juice left. RECOMMENDED

Spy Game [2001]

Starring: Robert Redford, Brad Pitt, Catherine McCormack
Director: Tony Scott Screenplay: Michael Frost Beckner & David Arata
Running Time: 2:05 Rated: R (Violence, profanity) Theatrical Aspect
Ratio: 2.35:1

Spy Game is an espionage thriller for viewers afflicted with Attention Deficit Syndrome. That's not to say it's a bad movie, but the frenzied approach doesn't allow much opportunity to absorb details. Despite the length, which exceeds 2 hours by a few minutes, *Spy Game* doesn't feel bloated or protracted. In fact, given the amount of ground covered by the storyline, this could easily have been a much longer endeavor.

Spy Game centers on the mentor/protégé relationship between Nathan Muir (Robert Redford), a jaded CIA agent on the verge of retirement, and Tom Bishop (Brad Pitt), a young idealist. On his latest mission, in Beijing, Bishop has been captured by the Chinese government. With only 24 hours until his execution, the CIA is attempting to distance themselves from Bishop so that this international incident will not endanger trade talks. Muir, on the other hand, is appalled by the idea of hanging Bishop out to dry, and covertly develops a plan to affect a rescue. Meanwhile, Muir must relate his entire history with Bishop — how they met, why the older man recruited the younger one, and which missions they worked on together — in front of a room full of CIA bigwigs.

By using flashbacks, *Spy Game* covers four time periods. The film's present-day is 1991, when a new world order is developing from the ashes of the cold war. Michael Frost Beckner and David Arata's script also takes us back to the Vietnam war, where Muir and Bishop first meet; to '70s Berlin, where Bishop is assigned to bring an informant through Checkpoint Charlie; and to 1985 Beirut, where the CIA recruits terrorists to eliminate other terrorists. The manner in which the flashbacks are grafted into the main story is a little clumsy, but it succeeds in filling in the gaps and illuminating why Muir is determined to save Bishop.

Spy Game does not offer the attention to detail evident in the best spy thrillers. There's also no real build-up in tension, although this is principally a result of Scott's style and the screenplay's approach (it's difficult to develop suspense when flashbacks continually interrupt the main narrative thread). Overall, *Spy Game* is an engrossing, if flawed, endeavor — the kind of movie that represents an evening's solid diversion. **RECOMMENDED**

The Spy Who Loved Me [United Kingdom, 1977]

Starring: Roger Moore, Barbara Bach, Curt Jurgens, Richard Kiel
Director: **Lewis Gilbert** Screenplay: Richard Maibaum & Christopher
Wood Running Time: 2:05 Rated: PG (Sexual innuendo, violence)
Theatrical Aspect Ratio: 2.35:1

Of Roger Moore's 7 James Bond pictures, *The Spy Who Loved Me* stands out as the best. Stripped of the extreme silliness of *The Man with the Golden Gun* and packed with style, action, and wit, *The Spy Who Loved Me* ranks alongside the Connery Bonds as a memorable cinematic representation of Ian Fleming's superspy (although the screenplay is not based on Fleming's novel of the same title).

As usual, Bond's chief nemesis is a megalomaniac. This time, his name is Stromberg (Curt Jurgens), and he's out to destroy the world to fulfill his dream of creating and populating an underwater city. The first part of his plan involves destroying the over-water civilization by a nuclear holocaust. To that end, he steals British and Soviet submarines with the intention of using their nuclear capacity against the superpowers. 007, along with his Russian counterpart, Major Anya Amasova, aka agent Triple-X (Barbara Bach), is dispatched to stop this. There are complications, however, because, although the USSR and England are cooperating on the mission, Anya has a personal grudge against Bond, and she makes it perfectly clear that she intends to kill him at the first favorable opportunity.

The Spy Who Loved Me marks the first appearance of Jaws (Richard Kiel), who would prove to be 007's most dangerous and persistent adversary. So massive and powerful is Jaws that there's little Bond can do against him physically. He's the perfect supervillain, and it's great fun to see how 007 survives confrontations with the steel-toothed giant. Barbara Bach proves to be a pleasant addition to the cast as the latest "Bond girl." Major Amasova is attractive, smart, sexy, and (of course) dangerous. Her repartee with Bond is scripted with the usual attention to double entendres and witty retorts.

The Spy Who Loved Me has no shortage of gadgets. These include noxious cigarettes, ski pole projectiles, and, most impressive of all, a Lotus Esprit that swims rather than sinks. But such toys are only part of 007's appeal. Bond films attract audiences because they're solid fun — light, uncomplicated entertainment that requires no more from a viewer than that he or she sits back and enjoys. Despite the recycled plot, *The Spy Who Loved Me* deserves its popularity as one of Bond's most engaging outings. Even those who swore off the films with Sean Connery's departure might consider checking this one out. **RECOMMENDED**

Supercop [Hong Kong, 1993]

Starring: Jackie Chan, Michelle Khan Director: Stanley Tong
Screenplay: Edward Tang, Fibe Ma & Lee Wai Yee Running Time: 1:36
Rated: R (Violence) Theatrical Aspect Ratio: 2.35:1 Dubbed into English

With its infectious mix of action and comedy, *Supercop* is vastly different from any big budget American picture. And the knowledge that Jackie Chan and his co-stars are doing their own stunts only sweetens the pot. Then there are the martial arts sequences (choreographed by director Stanley Tong), which are, quite simply, amazing, and remind the viewer that the fist is faster than the eye.

Supercop gives audiences an opportunity to appreciate the clown aspect of Chan's personality. Although he's best known as an action star, he's also a gifted comic. He has an expressive face — his features go through more contortions than his body. The dubbed English is actually an asset for this kind of film — the cheesy mis-synching of lips adds to the goofy fun.

Frankly, dialogue doesn't mean much in *Supercop*, nor does the plot. It's a framing device to get Chan into action. All we really need to know is which characters are the good guys and which ones are the bad guys, and, once that has been established, little else matters. For the record, *Supercop* pairs Chan's Hong Kong detective with a female Chinese security officer (Michelle Khan). Together, they go undercover to break a master criminal, Panther (Yuen Wah), out of prison, so he can lead them back to his drug lord brother (Ken Tsang). Their goal: infiltrate the organization and bring it down.

As is usual in a Chan film, the end credits (which show out-takes of failed stunts) are one of *Supercop*'s highlights. Ultimately, the closing montage points out one of the chief differences between Chan's stylized, fast-paced films and those of his American counterparts: this is action with a smile, not a grimace. **RECOMMENDED**

Swordfish [2001]

Starring: John Travolta, Hugh Jackman, Halle Berry, Don Cheadle
Director: Dominic Sena Screenplay: Skip Woods Running Time: 1:38
Rated: R (Violence, profanity, nudity, sex) Theatrical Aspect
Ratio: 2.35:1

Swordfish is escapist entertainment that requires a significant level of suspended disbelief. While this motion picture lacks the strong scripts and easy-to-identify-with central characters of its antecedents, its deficiencies in those areas don't detract significantly from its watchability. The screenplay, credited to Skip Woods, is silly and often preposterous, but it's not dumb. It pokes fun at itself on a fairly constant basis, although never straying so far over the line that it morphs into self-parody. Director Dominic Sena puts things into testosterone-and-adrenaline overdrive, delivering a healthy portion of chases leavened with high-tech gadgetry and a helping of raunchy under-the-table sex and high-profile nudity.

The story is presented in a convoluted manner, starting in the middle, flashing back for about an hour, then returning to the present. Gabriel Shear (John Travolta) is the film's charismatic villain, a man so wealthy and powerful that "he lives a life where nothing is beyond him." In this case, he's planning a $9.5 billion electronic bank robbery, the proceeds of which he can use to finance anti-terrorist terrorist activities. His surprisingly small crew includes the sexy Ginger (Halle Berry), who harbors a secret, and the stoic Marco (Vinnie Jones). Now, he wants to add ex-super hacker Stanley Jobson (Hugh Jackman) to his payroll. At first, Stanley isn't interested — he just got out of prison, and doesn't want to go back. Then Gabriel dangles an irresistible lure in front of him — the chance of regaining custody of his beloved daughter, Holly (Camryn Grimes), who is currently living with her porn-star mother. So Stanley agrees, and this places him once again into conflict with FBI agent Roberts (Don Cheadle), the man who previously busted him. Now, with his team assembled, Gabriel embarks upon the heist, using violent, amoral, pyrotechnic techniques and fooling his pursuers by pulling Houdini-like deceptions out of his bag of tricks.

By using computer hacking as a plot element, *Swordfish* attempts to be high-tech. There are some neat computer graphics and the dialogue occasionally sounds convincing (although those in the know will catch some laughable errors), but that's all window dressing for the caper action. The movie is loud, flashy, and violent, and certain viewers will probably offended by the casual manner in which some of the deaths occur. But, for those on the lookout for this sort of motion picture, that's irrelevant. **RECOMMENDED**

Tears of the Sun [2003]

Starring: Bruce Willis, Monica Bellucci, Cole Hauser, Johnny Messner, Tom Skerritt Director: Antoine Fuqua Screenplay: Alex Lasker & Patrick Cirillo Running Time: 1:58 Rated: R (Violence) Theatrical Aspect Ratio: 2.35:1

Tears of the Sun succeeds admirably at what it is trying to do: create a war movie for the new millennium that combines many of the old clichés with some of the darker, morally gut-wrenching realities that influenced the post-Vietnam genre. So there are times when one can imagine John Wayne inhabiting the uniform of title character A. K. Waters, while, on other occasions, the viewer is more likely to be reminded of the chaos of a *Platoon* or *Full Metal Jacket* than anything that starred the Duke. Director Antoine Fuqua has attempted the difficult task of fashioning a war movie that uses its backstory as more than an excuse for scenes of violent conflict.

Tears of the Sun opens with a brief voice-over explaining that Muslim rebels have staged a bloody coup in the country of Nigeria and, after assassinating the president and his family, they are in the process of encouraging the mass slaughter of Christians. The captain (Tom Skerritt) of the U.S.S. *Harry S. Truman,* stationed off the coast of Africa, has been ordered to send in his top team into hostile territory to evacuate Dr. Lena Hendricks (Monica Bellucci), a U.S. citizen who is in harm's way. Leading the mission is A. K. Waters (Bruce Willis), who is known for completing difficult assignments. Dr. Hendricks is easily located, but she refuses to leave unless every able-bodied individual at the mission where she is serving is allowed to accompany her. Waters initially balks, but when he observes the horrors perpetrated by the rebels, he relents and leads a group of several dozen refugees on a harrowing journey through the Nigerian jungle toward the safety of the Cameroon border.

Tears of the Sun has its share of effective moments. One of the most powerful occurs when passengers in a helicopter gaze down at the aftermath of a massacre. Another transpires when the soldiers enter a town that is currently being "cleansed" by the rebels. Most of the victims are beyond their help, but in a primal act of rage, they exact revenge. Finally, there's the last, hopeless battle, which features full portions of tragedy, glory, and heroism. It's rousing, but there's also an underlying sense of poignancy.

Much as he did with *Training Day,* Fuqua takes a genre picture and, by diverting the story onto an unconventional path, generates a sense of urgency. *Tears of the Sun* is not a great movie, but it is satisfy-ing, and represents an example of accomplished filmmaking. The film doesn't make the same kind of bold statement about war that is evident in productions like *Platoon* or *Apocalypse Now.* But, as might be presumed from the poetic title, there's more substance to be found here than one might initially expect from a Bruce Willis action flick. RECOMMENDED

Terminator 3: Rise of the Machines [2003]

Starring: Arnold Schwarzenegger, Nick Stahl, Claire Danes, Kristanna Loken, David Andrews Director: Jonathan Mostow Screenplay: John Brancato & Michael Ferris Running Time: 1:50 Rated: R (Violence, profanity, brief nudity) Theatrical Aspect Ratio: 2.35:1

Terminator 3 is not weighted down by plot, but it does have a recognizable story line featuring legitimate characters and a few nice (but minor) twists. Some degree of attention is helpful — *Terminator 3* is not an intellectual challenge, but neither is it vacuous. The film has plenty of action sequences, some of which are spectacular. Director Jonathan Mostow has wisely not relied too much on computer graphics for these. A fair amount of stunt work was required, and the computer components are incorporated seamlessly. Additionally, Mostow does not play the game of cutting every second or so, and the music never upstages the visuals. *Terminator 3* gets the most bang for its buck by letting the camera linger on the spectacle and allowing tension, not flashiness, to be its hallmark.

It's 10 years after *Terminator 2: Judgment Day,* and in the decade since we last entered this universe, Sarah Connor has died of leukemia and her son, John (Nick Stahl), has become a recluse. Even though he and his mother supposedly averted the nuclear war that would devastate the planet and allow the machines to take over, a part of him doubts that the future is secure. That uncertainty bears fruit when an unstoppable Termanatrix, the T-X (Kristanna Loken), enters the early 21st century on a mission to kill John and one of his lieutenants, Kate Brewster (Claire Danes). Following the T-X through the portal is the reliable, obsolete T-800 (Arnold Schwarzenegger), sent to protect John and Kate. Eventually, the human targets end up on the run from the T-X. Their goal is the same as it was in *Terminator 2:* avert a nuclear catastrophe. But this time, the odds are even more heavily stacked against them and time is not on their side.

Arnold Schwarzenegger effortlessly slides into the role that made him a superstar. Depending on where his political aspirations take him, this could either be a comeback or a farewell. Either way, this performance reminds us why, for all of his acting limitations, no one was a bigger action star during the 80s. Schwarzenegger has charisma and screen presence. Watching him here, it's hard to believe that he's in his 50s.

Will there be a *Terminator 4?* The ending allows for one, and parts of the story have yet to be told. But, from an action standpoint, is there any way that a fourth picture could be anything other than a rehash of its predecessors? It has taken a long time to get *Terminator 3* to the screen, and while the production doesn't rock the action motion picture industry to its foundation, it's a credible and entertaining movie and was worth the wait. RECOMMENDED

Thunderball [United Kingdom, 1965]

Starring: Sean Connery, Claudine Auger, Adolfo Celi, Luciana Paluzzi
Director: Terence Young Screenplay: Richard Maibaum & John Hopkins Running Time: 2:13 Rated: PG (Sexual innuendo, violence) Theatrical Aspect Ratio: 2.35:1

By the time *Thunderball,* the fourth in the "official" James Bond film canon, was released, the "Bond Formula" had already been perfected. It goes something like this: take the suave 007 (always impeccably dressed and ready with a witty one-liner) and add several beautiful, scantily-clad women, at least one exotic locale, a few neat gadgets, multiple polished action sequences, a megalomaniac villain, and a musical score by the inimitable John Barry. These elements, taken together, made Bond a huge success in the 1960s and have kept him riding a crest of financial profitability for more than three decades.

As *Thunderball* opens, SPECTRE is again on the move. This time, the mission — to blackmail the United States and Great Britain — is headed by Number Two, Emilio Largo (Adolfo Celi). The plot he has masterminded involves stealing two nuclear weapons, then threatening to blow up a major city if the two countries don't pay the ransom. After the threat has been issued, M (Bernard Lee) calls in the "00" agents and assigns them to tasks around the world with the goal of finding and stopping Largo. 007 draws Nassau, where he encounters old friend Felix Leiter (played this time by Rik Van Nutter), Largo's lovely mistress, Domino (Claudine Auger), and a host of deadly adversaries.

At 2¼ hours, *Thunderball* runs too long. Certain squences could have been trimmed, especially the climactic underwater battle, which seems to take forever. The villain of the piece is a little weak,

coming in the wake of such memorable adversaries as Dr. No and Goldfinger. While Adolfo Celi is suitably menacing, he plays Largo like a high-placed thug. There is some compensation for the deficiencies of the lead villain, however. It comes in the person of femme fatale Fiona (Luciana Paluzzi), whose sophisticated, black widow-like personality makes her more dangerous than any male SPECTRE agent.

The underwater sequences, which are choreographed and directed with great skill, are *Thunderball*'s standout feature. Connery is more often in a bathing suit than a tuxedo here. A fair amount of time is spent beneath the ocean's surface, and, down in Neptune's realm, the photography (by Lamar Boren) is clear and the action sequences are invigorating (when they don't seem to last forever, that is). *Thunderball* is classic 007 — not the best picture in the long-running series, to be sure, but a more-than-worthwhile diversion for the action-loving escapist in us all. RECOMMENDED

Titanic [1997]

Starring: Leonardo DiCaprio, Kate Winslet, Billy Zane Director: James Cameron Screenplay: James Cameron Running Time: 3:14 Rated: PG-13 (Mayhem, nudity, sex, profanity, mild violence) Theatrical Aspect Ratio: 2.35:1

Short of climbing aboard a time capsule and peeling back 8½ decades, James Cameron's magnificent *Titanic* is the closest any of us will get to walking the decks of the doomed ocean liner. Meticulous in detail, yet vast in scope and intent, *Titanic* is the kind of epic motion picture event that has become a rarity. You don't just watch *Titanic,* you experience it — from the launch to the sinking, then on a journey 2½ miles below the surface, into the cold, watery grave where Cameron has shot never-before seen documentary footage specifically for this movie.

Titanic is a romance, an adventure, and a thriller all rolled into one. It contains moments of exuberance, humor, pathos, and tragedy. In their own way, the characters are all larger-than-life, but they're human enough (with all of the attendant frailties) to capture our sympathy. Perhaps the most amazing thing about *Titanic* is that, even though Cameron carefully recreates the death of the ship in all of its terrible grandeur, the event never eclipses the protagonists. To the end, we never cease caring about Rose (Kate Winslet) and Jack (Leonardo DiCaprio).

Titanic sank during the early morning hours of

April 15, 1912 in the North Atlantic, killing 1500 of the 2200 on board. The movie does not begin in 1912, however — instead, it opens in modern times, with a salvage expedition intent on recovering some of the ship's long-buried treasure. The bulk of the film — well over 80% of its running time — is spent in flashbacks. We pick up the story on the day that *Titanic* leaves Southampton, with jubilant crowds cheering as it glides away from land. On board are the movie's three main characters: Rose, a young American debutante trapped in a loveless engagement because her mother is facing financial ruin; Cal Hockley (Billy Zane), her rich-but-cold-hearted fiancé; and Jack Dawson, a penniless artist who won his third-class ticket in a poker game. When Jack first sees Rose, it's from afar, but circumstances offer him the opportunity to become much closer to her. As the voyage continues, Jack and Rose grow more intimate, but, when circumstances in the Rose/Cal/Jack triangle are coming to a head, *Titanic* strikes an iceberg and the "unsinkable" ship begins to go down.

A dazzling mix of style and substance, of the sublime and the spectacular, *Titanic* represents Cameron's most accomplished work to date. It's important not to let the running time hold you back — these 3+ hours pass very quickly. Although this telling of the *Titanic* story is far from the first, it is the most memorable. **MUST SEE**

Titus [1999]

Starring: Anthony Hopkins, Jessica Lange, Alan Cumming
Director: Julie Taymor Screenplay: Julie Taymore, based on the play by William Shakespeare Running Time: 2:42 Rated: R (Extreme violence, frontal nudity, sex) Theatrical Aspect Ratio: 2.35:1

Based on Shakespeare's play, *Titus* is a gory story of betrayal and revenge. It opens with Titus Adronicus (Anthony Hopkins), an aging and respected Roman commander, returning to Rome in the wake of a successful campaign against the Goths. He is greeted by his brother, Marcus (Colm Feore), who attempts to install him as Emperor. Titus refuses, instead throwing his support behind another candidate, Saturnius (Alan Cumming), who is quickly confirmed. One of Saturnius' first declarations as Emperor is that he will take Titus' daughter, Lavinia (Laura Fraser), as his bride. When Saturnius' brother, Bassianus (James Frain), objects on the grounds that he and Lavinia are already engaged, the Emperor is enraged, but he agrees to choose another. His alternate is Tamora (Jessica Lange), the queen of the Goths who was recently captured by Titus. Dripping honey from her

forked tongue, she smoothes over quarrels and plays the peacemaker — all in preparation for a war of vengeance to be waged against Titus, who was responsible for the death of her eldest son. With the aid of her faithful Moor lover, Aaron (Harry J. Lennix), she causes the death of Bassianus, allows Lavinia to be raped and mutilated, and entraps two of Titus' sons. These actions drive the old commander into a state of towering rage and grief that sends him over the precipice of madness.

While the dialogue in *Titus* is taken verbatim from Shakespeare's text, the style is all Taymor's. In her feature debut, the acclaimed stage director categorically rejects a conventional interpretation of the play. Instead, she sets *Titus* in a nightmarish netherworld, where traditional Roman costumes and settings are married with trappings from other eras, particularly the 20th century.

Taymor's tone is not relentlessly bleak — there are bursts of kinetic action and certain scenes are suffused with wry, black humor. Also, she does not sensationalize the violence. Many of the bloodier acts are hidden from the camera's view. So, while we see the aftermath of the severing of hands and heads, we aren't afforded a direct shot of the actions occurring. Taymor finds the correct balance between indicating brutality and turning *Titus* into a bloodbath. One of the clearest indications that *Titus* succeeds is that, despite its nearly 3-hour running time, there are few dead spots. Taymor's visual flourishes prove to be an effective compliment for Shakespeare's text, rather than a distraction. **HIGHLY RECOMMENDED**

Tomb Raider [United States/United Kingdom, 2001]

Starring: Angelina Jolie, Daniel Craig, Iain Glen, Chris Barrie, Noah Taylor, Jon Voight Director: Simon West Screenplay: Patrick Massett & John Zinman Running Time: 1:38 Rated: PG-13 (Violence, profanity, brief nudity) Theatrical Aspect Ratio: 2.35:1

For what it is, *Tomb Raider* does a good job. It's like Indiana Jones meets James Bond with a female protagonist and most of the plot siphoned off. When you consider that Bond movies are not exactly known for their writing, this puts Lara Croft's first cinematic endeavor in perspective. Don't think too hard about the story — it simply won't stand up. Focus instead upon the action pieces, which are all expertly produced. (Although a slightly less hyperactive camera would have been appreciated — are all of those lightning-fast cuts really necessary?) *Tomb Raider* moves at a fast clip, and represents top notch eye candy.

It doesn't take a film critic to ascertain why *Tomb*

Raider works. Her name is Angelina Jolie, and she imbues her character with a third dimension that didn't exist on the written page, where Lara Croft is all height and width with no depth. She's action and sex appeal blended and personified. We even feel for Lara at times — a sure sign that the character has managed to attain a semblance of life. Lara Croft may hail from a video game, but her first movie is all comic book in style and approach.

The story sounds like recycled *Dr. Who*. A fabled artifact called the Triangle of Light has been broken into two pieces. Now, as the 9 planets are about to align for the first time in 5,000 years, a secret society of Illuminati are trying to find these two hidden pieces and bring them together. If they succeed, they will have control over time. In their employ is Manfred Powell (Iain Glen), who oozes the kind of charm that only a villain can. In their way is Lara Croft, who is acting on written instructions from her dead, beloved father, Lord Croft (Jon Voight, Jolie's real-life dad), to stop them. This results in a showdown for the ages, with all sorts of special effects and *Matrix*-inspired action. It's involving, although not quite exhausting. *Tomb Raider* is a great way to cure the blahs, provided, as always with this kind of film, you short-circuit the thinking parts of your brain.

RECOMMENDED

Tomorrow Never Dies [United Kingdom/United States, 1997]

Starring: Pierce Brosnan, Jonathan Pryce, Michelle Yeoh, Teri Hatcher Director: Roger Spottiswoode Screenplay: Bruce Feirstein Running Time: 2:00 Rated: PG-13 (Violence, mild profanity, sensuality) Theatrical Aspect Ratio: 2.35:1

Tomorrow Never Dies is a better film than *Goldeneye*. In fact, it's the best Bond film in many years. For the first time since the legendary Sean Connery left the part, this movie feels like a Connery Bond adventure. Pierce Brosnan, having left behind the jitters he occasionally exhibited during *Goldeneye*, now inhabits his character with a suave confidence that is very like Connery's. The villain of the piece, Elliot Carver (played with panache by Jonathan Pryce), is cut from the Blofeld/Goldfinger mold — sinister, cunning, and charismatic. Added to that are the usual Bond girls (Teri Hatcher and Michelle Yeoh), the gadgets, the chase scenes, the fights, the explosions, and a John Barry-esque score (by David Arnold) that makes repeated and effective use of the "James Bond Theme."

As is usually the case in a 007 flick, the bad guy is a megalomaniac. There's a twist, however — Carver doesn't want to rule the world, he wants to rule the world's media. Using the advanced technological capabilities of the Carver Media Group, he engineers a conflict in the South China Sea between two Chinese planes and the *HMS Devonshire*. War between China and Britain looms, with Carver having the inside story. And that's where Bond comes in.

Equipped with a brand new BMW that can almost drive itself, 007 goes undercover into Carver's empire, pretending to be a banker. At a posh party held by the tycoon, he meets Carver's wife, Paris (Teri Hatcher), an old flame. Also present is Wai Lin (Michelle Yeoh), a Chinese secret agent posing as a newswoman. It doesn't take long for Bond to rub someone the wrong way, and soon he's ducking behind a printing press to escape a hail of bullets, then racing through the streets of Hamburg in his souped-up car. With the clock ticking, Bond and Wai Lin have less than 48 hours to stop World War III.

The action sequences are suitably entertaining. It's impossible to count the number of bullets fired, and there are pyrotechnics aplenty, including exploding missiles, a fireworks show on the ground, and a fairly spectacular climactic conflagration. There are a couple of memorable chases, including one with a driverless car and another with a low-flying helicopter closing in on a motorcycle. For those who crave flashes, bangs, narrow escapes, and other action film staples, *Tomorrow Never Dies* delivers. **RECOMMENDED**

True Crime [1999]

Starring: Clint Eastwood, Isaiah Washington, Denis Leary, Lisa Gay Hamilton, James Woods Director: Clint Eastwood Screenplay: Larry Gross, Paul Brickman & Stephen Schiff Running Time: 2:07 Rated: R (profanity, violence, sexual situations) Theatrical Aspect Ratio: 1.85:1

True Crime has the potential to be a truly memorable film, and, for more than three-quarters of its running time, it is poised to live up to that potential. But then there are the final 20 minutes, which proffer the almost-painful experience of watching compelling drama devolve into mindless action. *True Crime*'s denouement is perplexing and exasperating, because, aside from generating some artificial tension, it contributes nothing to the story as a whole, and, consequently, serves only to cheapen it.

True Crime follows 24 hours in the lives of two men whose circumstances are vastly different, but whose destinies become intertwined. Frank Beachum (Isaiah Washington) is an innocent man on Death Row in San Quentin. A mere day away from his final meal,

Frank is calm and resigned to his fate. Last minute reprieves are unlikely. Frank's wife, Bonnie (Lisa Gay Hamilton) and his young daughter are less stoic. Meanwhile, in the aftermath of the death of a colleague at the Oakland Tribune, veteran reporter Steve Everett (Clint Eastwood) is given the assignment of covering Frank's execution. Something isn't right, and, after only a few hours' digging, he thinks he knows why: Frank has been wrongfully convicted. Of course, the difficulty lies in proving it, and, the more of himself Steve invests in the story, the more apparent it becomes that his personal redemption is fused with Frank's salvation.

True Crime is not afraid to tackle difficult issues. While it does not attack the subject of capital punishment as directly as *Dead Man Walking*, it presents the frightening scenario of an innocent man awaiting execution. Eastwood, who is functioning with three hats (director, producer, star), depicts Frank's final day with the assurance and meticulous detail of a seasoned professional. From the guard who sits at a typewriter recording his every activity to Frank's agonizing final meeting with his family and the long walk to the Lethal Injection Chamber, Eastwood doesn't miss a beat.

I'll never understand why otherwise-intelligent motion pictures occasionally resort to the contrived tactics employed at the end of *True Crime*. We don't need the high-speed car chase and the race against the clock. Even with its flaws, *True Crime* is a fine motion picture, but I can't avoid asking the simple, clichéd question of "What if?" RECOMMENDED

True Lies [1994]

Starring: Arnold Schwarzenegger, Jamie Lee Curtis, Tom Arnold, Tia Carrere Director: James Cameron Screenplay: James Cameron Running Time: 2:20 Rated: R (Language, violence) Theatrical Aspect Ratio: 2.35:1

In the past, James Cameron has proven himself to be a master of action and suspense. Titles like *The Terminator* and *Aliens* speak volumes about his talent. His least original film, *T2*, was still a rollicking good time, if a little limited when it came to a plot. Now, with *True Lies*, the director has not only reaffirmed his ability to keep viewers on the edge of their seats, but he has shown himself capable of making an audience laugh. One of the best things about *True Lies* is that it's genuinely funny.

The storyline isn't really all that inventive, although it contains a few original moments. Arnold plays Harry Tasker, a man who leads a double life. At home,

with his wife Helen (Jamie Lee Curtis) and daughter Dana (Eliza Dushku), he's a loving, if somewhat meek, husband and father. When he goes off to work, however, he doesn't travel to the sales office where Helen thinks he has a desk. Instead, he joins up with his partner Albert Gibson (Tom Arnold) to save the world. That includes romancing beautiful-but-deadly women like Juno Skinner (Tia Carrere) and squaring off against "wacko" terrorists like Salim Abu Aziz (Art Malik).

The point of *True Lies* is enjoyment. The plot is a little meatier than that of *Speed*, but until the last forty-five minutes, it doesn't thunder along at nearly the same breakneck pace. In fact, the main "terrorist-blackmailing-the-world" story stays in low gear until the film is 90 minutes along. Before then, a lot of time is spent examining the duplicitous relationship between Harry and Helen. When he suspects her of having an affair with a used car salesman (Bill Paxton), the results are hilarious.

There are the requisite spectacular explosions, coupled with an expectedly high body count. This is, after all, an Arnold Schwarzenegger motion picture, and certain things are expected. *True Lies* is an old-fashioned, high-tech, fun time at the movies. By not trying to "out-*Die Hard*" *Die Hard*, and relying instead on its own brand of mayhem and humor, this movie has injected some much-needed freshness into a genre that always threatens to turn stale. HIGHLY RECOMMENDED

Twister [1996]

Starring: Helen Hunt, Bill Paxton, Cary Elwes Director: Jan De Bont Screenplay: Michael Crichton & Ann-Marie Martin Running Time: 1:52 Rated: PG-13 (Violent weather) Theatrical Aspect Ratio: 2.35:1

Twister, which follows a team of tornado chasers as they track down storms, is exciting, if a little shallow. This particular disaster movie, which pits man against an implacable, unstoppable enemy, owes as much to *Godzilla* and *Jurassic Park* as to *The Towering Inferno* and *The Poseidon Adventure*. It's a perfect motion picture roller coaster — fun, fast, and furious . . . as long as you don't think too hard.

Twister opens with a short prologue in June 1969. It's one of the film's most effective sequences, as a family of three flees into a shelter to escape an oncoming storm. The father is killed, sucked into the vortex while his wife and 5-year-old daughter, Jo, watch. More than 25 years later, that little girl has grown up to be a tornado chaser. Played by

Helen Hunt, Jo is obsessed with increasing the pre-storm warning time. Accompanied by her old partner and soon-to-be-ex-husband, Bill Harding (Bill Paxton), her usual crew, and Bill's fiancee (Jami Gertz), Jo is about to try out "Dorothy," a specially-built instrument designed to spit out data from inside the vortex. So, in the midst of "the biggest series of storms in 12 years," Jo and Bill hit the road, vying with a rival scientist (Cary Elwes) to reach each new storm first.

Apparently, nature doesn't make a good enough villain, so the writers of *Twister* decided to add some nasty human rivals. Unfortunately, Cary Elwes' character is both unnecessary and irritating; the tornadoes are enough. Equally superfluous are the romantic complications in the relationship between Jo and Bill. It's a rather boring subplot, and, if these two had been together from the beginning, we would have been spared the presence of Jami Gertz' unappealing character.

Twister is peppered with bits of information about how to react if a tornado approaches, how dangerous the storms can be, etc. Despite these snippets of safety-conscious advice, the movie doesn't function as a public service announcement, nor should it. *Twister* doesn't have any pretensions. It is what it sets out to be: an effective piece of big money, early summer entertainment designed to blow viewers away. **RECOMMENDED**

U-571 [2000]

Starring: Matthew McConaughey, Bill Paxton, Harvey Keitel
Director: Jonathan Mostow Screenplay: Jonathan Mostow, Sam Montgomery, David Ayer Running Time: 1:55 Rated: PG-13 (Violence, mild profanity) Theatrical Aspect Ratio: 2.35:1

As submarine movies go, *U-571* gets the job done — that is to say, it tells an engaging (albeit predictable) story and features several scenes of nail-biting suspense. All of the usual plot staples are in evidence: tension between crew members, deep diving where the hull threatens to collapse, dodging depth charges, and sub-to-sub battles. Director Jonathan Mostow should be commended for taking a thin script and crafting a compelling film out of it. *U-571* doesn't hold together well upon reflection, but, while it's playing on screen, it works.

The storyline is simple enough. The crew of a U.S. submarine is sent on a top-secret mission to board a disabled German U-boat and steal a secret encoding device. The boarding crew is led by Lt. Andrew Tyler (Matthew McConaughey), whose relationship with his captain (Bill Paxton) is currently strained. Once Tyler's group has boarded the U-571, a German sneak attack destroys the U.S. sub, and the navy officers are forced to maneuver the crippled U-boat through enemy territory while being pursued by a German destroyer.

U-571 contains some great, sustained action sequences, the best of which is the climactic one, which features about ten minutes of nonstop tension as the submarine sinks to potentially fatal depths then ends up in a race against time. The battle scenes are well executed, with Mostow effectively conveying the confusion and chaos of what happens when a submarine is buffeted by depth charges that threaten to split it wide open. Bolts pop, water explodes through leaks, sparks fly, and fires start. The experience of watching these sequences is visceral.

On an intellectual level, the movie is less successful. The characters aren't just *under*developed — they are *un*developed. The only one with any backstory is Tyler, and all we know about him is that he was denied a promotion because his captain was unsure that he possessed the fortitude to send men to their deaths. We know nothing about the background or personality of any of the other men stuck on the U-571, except how they react to the crisis at hand. This complete lack of development makes it difficult to care about the characters. In terms of pure action/adventure, *U-571* is a strong contender, and its big name cast will give it a degree of visibility. Despite its weaknesses, this movie offers 2 hours of solid, kinetic entertainment. **RECOMMENDED**

Volcano [1997]

Starring: Tommy Lee Jones, Anne Heche, Don Cheadle, John Corbett
Director: Mick Jackson Screenplay: Jerome Armstrong & Billy Ray
Running Time: 1:53 Rated: PG-13 (Death and mayhem) Theatrical Aspect Ratio: 1.85:1

For *Volcano*, character development fits into the "obligatory" category. Here, we have Mike Roark (Tommy Lee Jones), the head of Los Angeles' Office of Emergency Management (OEM), who smells a disaster around every corner. When a mild earthquake (4.9 on the Richter Scale) shakes the city, he abandons a vacation with his 13-year-old daughter (Gaby Hoffman) to come into work, uncertain how his second-in-command, Emmett Reese (Don Cheadle), will handle the situation on his own. Soon, however, strange things start happening. Several men working underground are scalded to death. The water temperature of a lake goes up by 6 degrees in 12 hours.

And the La Brea tar pits begin to pop and bubble in earnest. Concerned that some geological cataclysm may be approaching, Roark requests the help of an expert. He gets Dr. Amy Barnes (Anne Heche), who believes that L.A. could be sitting atop a volcano that's about to become active.

In real life, I don't know anyone who believes that the residents of Los Angeles have anything to fear from volcanoes, but this film makes it very easy to suspend that particular disbelief. Not only is *Volcano* a hell of a ride, but the script has enough intelligence (relatively speaking, that is) that it's possible to become engrossed in the movie without constantly being jerked back to reality by stupid and obvious plot contrivances. Oh, there are missteps, such as an ill-conceived subplot about racial strife between a black youth and a white cop, but *Volcano* surprisingly manages to avoid many of the most common disaster movie pitfalls (probably because it keeps the number of major characters to a minimum).

All that most people want from a disaster movie is a jolt of adrenaline and a chance to "ooh" and "ahh," and *Volcano* fills both cravings. After all, there's a lot at stake — this isn't some sleepy Northwestern town, it's the second most populous city in the United States. The special effects are top-notch. When a lava river starts flowing down Wilshire Boulevard, we believe that it's actually happening. Although you see this film for the spectacle, the other stuff (characters, plot, etc.) doesn't get in the way, and that's the formula for success in this genre. *Volcano* triumphs with a resounding bang. **RECOMMENDED**

White Squall [1996]

Starring: **Jeff Bridges, Caroline Goodall, John Savage, Scott Wolf, Jeremy Sisto, Balthazar Getty** Director: **Ridley Scott** Screenplay: **Todd Robinson** Running Time: **2:08** Rated: **PG-13 (Profanity, mature themes, violence)** Theatrical Aspect Ratio: **2.35:1**

Based on the true-life memoirs of Chuck Gieg, *White Squall* introduces us to 13 high school students who have elected to spend the 1960-61 academic year on the American schoolship *Albatross* (a windjammer based out of Mystic, Connecticut). The Captain is Christopher Sheldon (Jeff Bridges), a man who preaches two lessons: the importance of unity among the crew and that "the ship beneath [them] is not a toy and sailing's not a game." His wife, Alice (Caroline Goodall), is the ship's doctor and the boys' science teacher. Other adults aboard are a Shakespeare-quoting English teacher (John Savage) and a Cuban cook (Julio Mechoso).

The young crew includes Chuck (Tom Cruise look-alike Scott Wolf), an all-American student who wants to break away from his parents' vision of what his future should be; Tod (Balthazar Getty), a tough-as-nails kid who hides a secret; Frank (Jeremy Sisto), who can't escape from under his rich father's thumbnail; and Gill (Ryan Phillipe), a young man with a desperate fear of heights. The trip on the *Albatross* is their rite of passage. By the end of *White Squall*, those who have survived are no longer boys, but men.

Given the title, it's no secret that the *Albatross* runs into real trouble. In nautical language, a "white squall" is a sudden, violent, wind-and-lightning storm that can take the sturdiest ship and snap it in two. However, this meteorological catastrophe doesn't make an appearance until the film's last 45 minutes. Until then, *White Squall* devotes itself to developing its young characters, their growing admiration for their skipper, and the relationships amongst them. While some of this drama relies on familiar formulas, a capable director like Scott can maintain the audience's attention through a long setup.

For nearly 2 hours, *White Squall* is a completely involving motion picture, keeping its comic, dramatic, and tragic elements in perfect balance. Unfortunately, the need to end with a *Dead Poets' Society*-like catharsis brings the conclusion down. Hopelessly corny and needlessly manipulative, the last scene is bad melodrama. Mercifully, it lasts only a few minutes, and the overriding image left with the viewer as the end credits roll is not of this silliness but of the *Albatross* riding the seas in the face of a hurricane-force wind. *White Squall* is a success because the good elements are so well orchestrated that they dwarf the few obvious flaws. This film offers just about everything, including a 20-minute white-knuckle sequence and a chance to shed a few tears. In short, it's first-rate entertainment. **RECOMMENDED**

The World Is Not Enough [United Kingdom/United States, 1999]

Starring: **Pierce Brosnan, Sophie Marceau, Denise Richards, Robert Carlyle** Director: **Michael Apted** Screenplay: **Bruce Feirstein, Neal Purvis & Robert Wade** Running Time: **2:08** Rated: **PG-13 (Violence, sexual innuendo, brief nudity)** Theatrical Aspect Ratio: **2.35:1**

When it comes to Bond films, there's really only one question: Does it entertain for the entire running length? For *The World Is Not Enough*, as for the previous two endeavors with Brosnan, the answer is "yes." There's nothing special, shocking, or precedent-setting about the film, but it functions on a level that 007 fans will appreciate — as eye and ear candy for those who prefer action to exposition and character development. There are plenty of bangs, flashes, and chase sequences (on foot, on skis, and in the water), plus the usual array of beautiful women with skimpy outfits and funny names, science fiction-inspired gadgets (cars that drive themselves, x-ray glasses, a jacket that inflates into a survival bubble), and exotic locales (Azerbaijan, Kazakhstan, Istanbul).

With its emphasis on personal revenge, *The World Is Not Enough* hearkens back to *Licence To Kill*. Only this time it's "M" (Judi Dench) who's making things personal. When a good friend of hers is killed while inside MI6 headquarters, "M" is determined to have the murderer hunted down and brought to justice. She assigns her best agent, Bond (Brosnan), to protect her dead friend's daughter, Elektra King (Sophie Marceau). Bond soon discovers that the man who killed Elektra's father, and is now trying to eliminate her, is a mysterious terrorist named Renard (Robert Carlyle), who is called "The Anarchist." Electra has previous ties to Renard. When she was younger, he kidnapped her, but she escaped before her father could pay the $5,000,000 ransom. But his purpose here seems more sinister than vengeance for a foiled plot. When Bond tracks him down, he finds Rendard about to steal a nuclear bomb from a group of scientists led by Dr. Christmas Jones (Denise Richards). And "M" arrives on the scene just in time to be captured.

The World Is Not Enough contains the usual array of eye-popping action sequences. In terms of genuine suspense, *The World Is Not Enough* is a cut below *Tomorrow Never Dies* — but only a tiny cut. For those who have enjoyed the other Bond movies or for anyone who appreciates fast-paced action films, *The World Is Not Enough* should prove to be a winner. Director Michael Apted may be best known for documentary efforts (the *Seven Up* series) and dramas (*Gorillas In the Mist, Nell*), but he proves to have a deft hand managing the taut pace and pyrotechnics of this kind of motion picture. When it comes to action and excitement, actors, directors, and screenwriters may change, but there's still only one James Bond. **RECOMMENDED**

X-Men [2000]

Starring: Patrick Stewart, Hugh Jackman, Ian McKellen, Halle Berry
Director: **Bryan Singer** Screenplay: **David Hayter** Running Time: **1:40**
Rated: PG-13 (Violence, mature themes, profanity) Theatrical Aspect Ratio: **2.35:1**

X-Men's action takes place in the near future, when the United States Senate is debating a bill that will require all mutants (human beings who possess special powers as a result of DNA mutations) to register with the government. The leader of this movement, Senator Kelly (Bruce Davison), is a McCarthy-like personality who has whipped public opinion into a frenzy. One of the most powerful of the mutants, Magneto (Ian McKellen), believes that Kelly's words are the first volley of a battle that will turn into a war, and he intends to launch a preemptive strike for mutantkind — something to head off the struggle before it begins. He is opposed by his old friend, the telepath Professor X (Patrick Stewart), and his band of "X-Men." The professor and those who study at his "School for Gifted Children" believe in the philosophy of peaceful co-existence. Meanwhile, a pair of newcomers have arrived at Professor X's school. They are Rogue (Anna Paquin), a frightened teenage girl who cannot touch another human being without draining that person's life energy, and Wolverine (Hugh Jackman), a fast healer with an adamantine skeleton and retractable claws that spring from the backs of his hands. These two, who have a big brother/little sister type of bond, are deciding whether to join Professor X when a move by Magneto takes matters out of the realm of free choice.

Compared to *Batman*, *X-Men* is an improvement. Style, not story, was that series' forte. The world created by Singer and his craftsmen is not as strange and gothic as Gotham City, but it is no less visually interesting. The climax, which involves the Statue of Liberty and Ellis Island, utilizes flawless, set-based duplications of reality (no significant footage was actually shot in or around New York). The giant spherical room within Professor X's school is impressive, as are chambers in Magneto's abode, and the glass-and-plastic apartment shown later in the film.

X-Men does not, however, top *Superman* as the most engaging superhero motion picture. The 1978 Richard Donner feature possessed an epic scope that *X-Men* doesn't approach. (Nor, in all fairness, does it aspire to.) This is a much simpler action/adventure effort, as the relatively short running length of 100 minutes betokens.

Most viewers will see *X-Men* as delivering what's expected of any summer movie. There are serveral in-jokes designed specifically for *X-Men* fans, none of which will confound someone who has never been exposed to this world before. *X-Men* brings to the screen the elements that any live comic book adaptation should offer, resulting in a lightly enjoyable cinematic experience. For escapism, *X* marks the spot.

RECOMMENDED

X2: X-Men United [2003]

Starring: Patrick Stewart, Hugh Jackman, Ian McKellen, Halle Berry, Famke Janssen, James Marsden, Rebecca Romijn-Stamos, Brian Cox, Alan Cumming, Bruce Davison, Anna Paquin, Kelly Hu, Shawn Ashmore, Aaron Stanford Director: Bryan Singer Screenplay: Michael Dougherty, Daniel P. Harris, Bryan Singer Running Time: 2:13 Rated: PG-13 (Violence, brief profanity, sexual situations) Theatrical Aspect Ratio: 2.35:1

The problem with *X2* is essentially the same one that plagued *X-Men*: too many characters, resulting in too little screen time for anyone. To be fair, *X2* does a better job than *X-Men*, primarily because it isn't saddled with the baggage of having to introduce everyone. The only new major mutant is the blue-skinned teleporter Nightcrawler (Alan Cumming); everyone else is a returning player. Nevertheless, most of the X-Men come across as no more three-dimensional than their comic book counterparts. There are a few exceptions, with tough guy Wolverine (Hugh Jackman) and telepath Jean Grey (Famke Janssen) leading the way. And one could make a case for teenager Rogue (Anna Paquin) and arch villain Magneto (Ian McKellen). But there's still a lot of underused talent. Patrick Stewart (as Professor X, who runs the show), for example, is completely wasted, as is Halle Berry (as weather-controlling Storm). James Marsden's Cyclops, with his laser beam eyes, has about the same amount of paltry screen time as

he had in *X-Men*. Shapeshifter Mystique (Rebecca Romjin-Stamos) gets more exposure, but her personality remains a black hole.

The story picks up where the first movie ended, preserving continuity. Wolverine is in the process of tracking down his roots, Magneto is trapped in his metal-deficient prison, and the mutant issue is being widely debated on a national, political level. Then, when the mysterious Nightcrawler sneaks into the White House and nearly assassinates the U.S. president, General William Stryker (Brian Cox), a man with a vendetta against mutants, is given special powers to raid Professor X's school and detain everyone there. Suddenly, the mutants are scattered and under siege; Professor X is captured and brainwashed to be used as a weapon of genocide against his people; Magneto is free and working with the X-Men; and Jean Grey has discovered the terrifying depths of her mental powers. As the war begins, the casualties mount on both sides.

The appeal of *X2* is probably less broad-based than that of a *Spider-Man* or *Superman*. Although it's possible to enjoy this movie without boasting any familiarity with the comic book (or, for that matter, having seen the first movie), director Bryan Singer has developed this project with the fans in mind. This is a Valentine to them, and they are likely to be the most enthusiastic respondents to the film. Yet, as big as Singer's canvas may be, he has yet to acquire the knack of how to metamorphose his ensemble from a group of comic book icons defined by their powers to multidimensional cinematic individuals. That's the quality that holds back *X2* — instead of being a great movie, it's merely a solidly entertaining one.

RECOMMENDED

Animated

Aladdin [1992]

Featuring the voices of: Robin Williams, Scott Weinger, Linda Larkin, Jonathan Freeman Directors: Ron Clements and John Musker Screenplay: Ron Clements & John Musker and Ted Elliot & Terry Rossio Running Time: 1:30 Rated: G Theatrical Aspect Ratio: 1.75:1

Like its immediate predecessors, *The Little Mermaid* and *Beauty and the Beast*, *Aladdin* features stunningly crisp visuals and wonderful song-and-dance numbers. Unlike those two films, however, the protagonist here is a boy. The other big change in *Aladdin* is the level of humor. *Beauty* and *Mermaid* had their comic moments, but they were essentially lightweight fantasy/dramas. Thanks to an incredibly lively vocal characterization by Robin Williams as the Genie, *Aladdin* is pretty much a straight comedy, with elements of romance, fantasy, and adventure thrown in almost as afterthoughts.

The story centers around the title character (voice of Scott Weinger), a homeless orphan living on the streets of the city of Agrabah. One day, while avoiding a contingent of the local law enforcement, Aladdin comes into contact with a young girl who is also hiding from the guards. She is actually the Princess Jasmine (Linda Larkin) in disguise, seeking shelter after having run away from home because of a disagreement with her father about his plans for her marriage. The gallant street urchin shows her his favorite place of concealment, then promptly falls in love with her. Soon, however, Aladdin has more to worry about than the guards or the sultan's daughter. The palace sorcerer, Jafar (voiced with relish by Jonathan Freeman), has divined that Aladdin represents the key to his plans. So, in the guise of an old man, Jafar tricks his unwitting victim into entering the mysterious Cave of Wonders, where undreamed-of treasures are hidden. There, Aladdin finds an ornate bottle, and, after accidentally rubbing it a few times, comes face-to-face with a blue genie (Williams), who is ready and willing to grant him 3 wishes. What follows is a basic formula tale as Aladdin, with the help of his sidekicks — a monkey named Abu and a flying carpet, seeks to win Jasmine's hand, defeat the evil Jafar and his vicious parrot, Iago (voiced with grating sarcasm by Gilbert Gottfried), and save Agrabah.

The mixture of Robin Williams' voice and the Disney animators' work makes the Genie a truly magical persona, stealing scene after scene from the rather bland title character. Even putting Williams' performance aside, there's still a lot to like about this film. The animation is almost as amazing as that in *Beauty and the Beast*. There are a number of wild action segments that are expertly executed. While the music isn't as important to *Aladdin* as it was to the previous two Disney animated films, there are still five new tunes, three of which are standouts. Perhaps best of all is that, as with *The Little Mermaid* and *Beauty and the Beast*, *Aladdin* can be enjoyed as much by adults as by children. This is a fun motion picture on all levels. **HIGHLY RECOMMENDED**

Anastasia [1997]

Featuring the voices of: Meg Ryan, John Cusack, Kelsey Grammer, Angela Lansbury, Christopher Lloyd, Hank Azaria Directors: Don Bluth, Gary Goldman Screenplay: Susan Ganthier & Bruce Graham, Bob Tzundiker & Noni White Running Time: 1:37 Rated: G Theatrical Aspect Ratio: 2.35:1

The first thing to note about this delightful animated adventure is that it should not be confused with an historical account of the Russian revolution. Aside from borrowing a few names, facts, and dates, this is pure, unadulterated fantasy. Someone expecting even a loose reliance upon history is going to be horrified, but then anyone who falls into that category probably doesn't belong at this movie in the first place.

The story opens in 1916 Russia, just before the revolution, and depicts the fall of Czar Nicholas II as the result of a curse placed upon him by the evil monk Rasputin (voice of Christopher Lloyd). Every member of the Romanov family is killed, except Nicholas' mother, Marie (Angela Lansbury), who escapes to Paris, and the Czar's youngest daughter, Anastasia (Kirsten Dunst), who is missing. Rasputin is also slain, but, because his curse was not fulfilled, he ends up languishing in limbo.

Fast-forward 10 years. Marie has offered a 10 million ruble reward for anyone who finds her granddaughter. Back in St. Petersburg, a pair of con artists, Dimitri (John Cusack) and Vladimir (Kelsey Grammer), are holding auditions for an "Anastasia" to take to Paris. When they discover Anya (Meg Ryan), little do they realize that the 18-year-old young woman is actually the real princess. Together, Dimitri and Vladimir teach Anya how to act like royalty, preparing her for an audience with Marie. Meanwhile, Rasputin finds a way out of his nether-domain and plots Anastasia's demise.

While the animation in *Anastasia* still doesn't quite match up to that of Disney's recent features, it's light years ahead of the likes of *The Land Before Time*, *Balto*, and even *An American Tail*. There are times when the characters' lips don't perfectly synch up with the vocals, and other occasions when the background detail is lacking, but, on the whole, *Anastasia*'s visual palette is quite rich.

Story-wise, *Anastasia* is every bit as strong as any new wave Disney film except *Beauty and the Beast*. There's a little adventure, a little romance, a little mysticism, and a little drama. The whole process of watching *Anastasia* is a thoroughly enjoyable one, and it proves that any studio willing to put forth the time, money, and effort can match Disney.

HIGHLY RECOMMENDED

Antz [1998]

Featuring the voices of: **Woody Allen, Sharon Stone, Gene Hackman, Sylvester Stallone** Directors: **Eric Darnell, Tim Johnson**
Screenplay: **Tod Alcott, Chris & Paul Weitz** Running Time: **1:17**
Rated: **PG (Mild profanity)** Theatrical Aspect Ratio: **1.85:1**

Antz is a very good movie, no matter how you look at it. Visually, it's more impressive than Disney's *Toy Story*, the pioneer in this burgeoning genre. On a script level, it was developed as much with a mature audience in mind as with the usual pre-pubescent crowd. A significant helping of *Antz*'s humor will go over the heads of the average under-12 viewer. Image-conscious adults should not feel embarrassed about sitting through this "kids' movie." The big-name vocal cast is expertly-selected. Where else can you find Woody Allen, Sylvester Stallone, Anne Bancroft, Christopher Walken, Sharon Stone, and Gene Hackman in the same film?

Antz follows the adventures of Z-4195 (Z for short), a neurotic worker ant whose voice is appropriately provided by Woody Allen. Z is in therapy because he's an individual in a colony where conformity is not only desirable, but mandatory. He's having trouble coming to grips with his insignificance and inadequacy. One night, while at a bar, he dances with Princess Bala (Sharon Stone), who's out incognito for a night of adventure. Z is immediately lovestruck and begins to plan a way to arrange another meeting with the princess. His scheme involves impersonating his friend, Weaver (Sylvester Stallone), a soldier ant. Things go wrong, however, when the evil General Mandible (Gene Hackman), arranges for the ant army to attack a nearby colony of termites, and Z finds himself in the midst of a battle. Surrounded by fierce fighters that look death in the face and laugh at it, this timid worker, whose preference is to "make belittling comments and snicker behind death's back," does the only thing he can: he hides.

Adults and children alike will be awestruck by *Antz*'s impressive production design. This animated effort has texture and depth. Story-wise, there's nothing here that is likely to confuse younger viewers. The basic plot is a cross between an adventure and a "Taming of the Shrew" romantic comedy. Or, as Z puts it, *Antz* is "your basic boy meets girl, boy likes girl, boy changes underlying social structure" tale. The dialogue is consistently smart, and has not been diluted to enable underage audience members to comprehend every line. Successful as an adventure, a surprisingly sophisticated comedy, a light romance, and a visual treat, there are few things that Eric Darnell and Tim Johnson's feature debut does not do. **HIGHLY RECOMMENDED**

Atlantis: The Lost Empire [2001]

Featuring the voices of: Michael J. Fox, James Garner, Cree Summer Directors: Gary Trousdale, Kirk Wise Screenplay: Tab Murphy Running Time: 1:33 Rated: PG (Cartoon violence) Theatrical Aspect Ratio: 2.35:1

Atlantis is from veteran Disney directors Gary Trousdale and Kirk Wise, whose previous credits include *Beauty and the Beast* and *The Hunchback of Notre Dame*. The vocal talents represent a large cross-section of Hollywood, including Michael J. Fox, James Garner, John Mahoney, Leonard Nimoy, and the late Jim Varney.

The story is simple enough. Nerdy Milo Thatch (voice of Michael J. Fox) is chosen to participate in an early 20th century expedition in search of the lost city of Atlantis. Milo, a linguist by trade (or, as some call him, an "expert in gibberish"), has earned that honor because his grandfather was the explorer who retrieved the journal that tells of the city's location. Milo is part of a party that includes a wisecracking cook, Cookie (Jim Varney); a bubbly teenage mechanic, Audrey (Jacqueline Obradors); an explosives authority, Vinny (Don Novello), a burly doctor, Sweet (Phil Morris); and The Mole (Corey Burton), an expert on digging. The group is led by the no-nonsense Commander Rourke (James Garner) and his equally humorless second-in-charge, Helga (Claudia Christian). After taking a submarine under water, battling a giant sea monster, and falling into the bowels of a dormant volcano, the group encounters the Atlantians, led by Princess Kida (Cree Summer) and her wary father, King Nedakh (Leonard Nimoy). Soon, Rourke's real objective in finding the city becomes apparent. He's not there for the "discovery, teamwork, and adventure" that drives Milo. His motive is purely mercenary — he sees dollar signs if he can bring back Atlantis' mysterious source of power. And the rest of the group is with him — at least to start with.

Atlantis contains less dialogue than some of the recent Disney animated features, replacing the songs and talking with some genuinely thrilling action sequences. There are submarine chase sequences, aerial dogfights, and a variety of daring escapes that feature all manner of pyrotechnics. Trousdale and Wise employ some bold camerawork, creating the animated equivalent of impressive tracking shots. There are also numerous panoramic sequences that involve a moving, rotating camera. The look of the characters is more angular than usual, giving the film a non-traditional appearance.

In terms of wit and character empathy, *Atlantis* is a notch below other recent Disney offerings, but, to a degree, the level of adventure spectacle compensates. On the whole, *Atlantis* offers 90 minutes of solid entertainment, once again proving that while Disney may be clueless when it comes to producing good live-action movies, they are exactly the opposite when it comes to their animated division. **RECOMMENDED**

Beauty and the Beast [1991]

Featuring the voices of: Paige O'Hara, Robby Benson, Jerry Orbach, David Ogden Stiers, Angela Lansbury Directors: Gary Trousdale, Kirk Wise Screenplay: Linda Woolverton Running Time: 1:30 Rated: G Theatrical Aspect Ratio: 1.66:1

"Irresistible" is an apt description of this film, because every frame is imbued with a magic that is rare for any motion picture, animated or otherwise. *Beauty and the Beast* is a triumph of artistry — a rare movie where all of the elements gel perfectly. It has set the standard for today's animated motion picture, establishing a level that no subsequent animated film has equalled.

Belle (voice of Paige O'Hara) is the most beautiful girl in a provincial town in France. Unfortunately for those who might want her as a wife, including the dim, narcissistic Gaston (Richard White), she's also one of the village's oddest denizens. She keeps to herself, helping her inventor father, Maurice (Rex Everhart), with his contraptions, and, in her spare time, devouring books. Then, one fateful day, her father disappears in the forest. Belle goes searching for him and stumbles upon a dark and scary castle. Venturing inside, she discovers a gallery of magical creatures — household objects that speak and move. Then there's the Beast (Robby Benson), the terrifying creature who rules over this domain and holds Maurice captive. Once a handsome prince, he has been cursed to remain a beast until he finds someone who truly loves him in spite of his appearance. Now, he is filled with equal parts hope and dread at Belle's arrival — hope that she might be "the one" to break the spell, and dread that she might be repulsed by his ugliness. Nevertheless, he agrees to release her father if she accedes to being his permanent guest. She makes the bargain, Maurice is set free, and she is trapped. In time, however, Belle discovers that life in the castle is not as dreadful as it initially seems.

As a romance, *Beauty and the Beast* is a delightful confection, creating a pair of memorable, three-dimensional characters and giving us reason to root for their union. Belle is strong-willed, independent, and smart. The real allure of the movie, however, is twofold: the amazingly-detailed animation and a half-dozen spectacular song-and-dance numbers. Visually, *Beauty and the Beast* is so carefully-constructed that repeated viewings reveal new details, like the wayward strands of hair that fall across Belle's forehead. The production numbers represent the best in Disney's considerable arsenal. They're the animated equivalent of Broadway show-stoppers, with all the energy and audacity of something choreographed by Busby Berkeley.

Combining all of these diverse elements, *Beauty and the Beast* attains a nearly-perfect mix of romance, music, invention, and animation. While many animated features claim to appeal equally to adults and children, *Beauty and the Beast* is one of the rare ones that actually achieves that lofty goal. It's a family feature that someone over the age of 18 can venture into without an accompanying child. **MUST SEE**

The Black Cauldron [1985]

Featuring the voices of: Grant Bardsley, Susan Sheridan, Nigel Hawthorne, John Byner, John Hurt Directors: Ted Berman and Richard Rich Screenplay: Ted Berman, Vance Gerry, Joe Hale, David Jones, Roy Monta, Richard Rich & Al Wilson Running Time: 1:20 Rated: PG (Potentially frightening moments) Theatrical Aspect Ratio: 2.35:1

The credits for *The Black Cauldron* claim that the film is based on Lloyd Alexander's "The Chronicles of Prydain." In actuality, it was inspired by *The Book of Three* and *The Black Cauldron*, 2 of the 5 books comprising the children's saga. While many of the characters and plot elements have survived the written page-to-screen transition, much of the depth and complexity is absent, turning *The Black Cauldron* into a fun-but-uninspired swords-and-sorcery story.

The film opens on a small farm in the mythical country of Prydain, where Taran the Assistant Pig Keeper (voice of Grant Bardsley) is caring for Hen Wen, a swine with clairvoyant capabilities. The farm is presided over by Dallben the Wizard (voice of Freddie Jones), who, upon viewing Hen Wen's latest prognostication sends Taran away from the farm to hide his pink charge. All does not go well, however, and Taran's journey turns into a rescue mission when Hen

Wen is captured by the agents of the evil Horned King (voice of John Hurt), who intends to use the animal to discover the whereabouts of the Black Cauldron, a talisman of malevolent power that will enable him to take over the world. Along the way, Taran is joined by a petulant-but-pretty princess, Eilonwy (voice of Susan Sheridan); a cute, cuddly creature named Gurgi (voice of John Byner); and Fflewddur Fflam (voice of Nigel Hawthorne), a bard with a penchant for telling tall tales.

The Black Cauldron is not populated with a gallery of interesting characters. Taran is nobility personified, and, as such, is pretty boring. Eilonwy, despite showing signs of the backbone that later Disney heroines would display, isn't much more compelling than Taran. Fflewddur is used more for comic relief than anything else. As far as the villain goes, the only thing we learn about the Horned King is that he's evil and wants to take over the world. He looks and acts scary, but that's about it.

For those weaned on the slick animation of Disney's new wave features, some of the drawing in *The Black Cauldron* may seem a little rough or unfinished. Frankly, though, even judging by today's high standards, the artwork is impressive, especially during the late sequences when the Black Cauldron spews its magical contents skyward and an army of corpses begins its march.

To date, Hollywood has yet to make a truly rousing animated fantasy feature, making it perhaps the only genre to have eluded those who weave movie magic. Maybe because it is animated, *The Black Cauldron* is one of the more successful attempts. While the movie probably plays better to those who have not read Alexander's "Chronicles of Prydain," it's far from the failure it was once branded as. Now that it's available on video, it should find favor with a generation that never had the opportunity to see it during its brief theatrical tenure. **RECOMMENDED**

Brother Boear [2003]

Featuring the voices of: Joaquin Phoenix, Jeremy Suarez, Jason Raize, Rick Moranis, Dave Thomas, D. B. Sweeney, Michael Clarke Duncan Directors: Aaron Blaise, Bob Walker Screenplay: Steve Bencich, Ron J. Friedman Running Time: 1:36 Rated: G Theatrical Aspect Ratio: 1.85:1

Brother Bear will not go down in the annals of traditional animation as a classic, but it is proof that Disney remains capable of producing enjoyable, family-oriented animated movies. This film looks and feels a little bit like a throwback to the kinds of pictures Disney was making when it was still at the top of the animation heap. There's drama and comedy, a message about tolerance and brotherhood, and a few songs to sell the sound track. The end result is a pleasant experience that is more appropriate for families than for adults unaccompanied by young offspring.

The movie takes us to the dawn of prehistoric human civilization and introduces us to three brothers: Sitka (voice of D. B. Sweeney), the eldest; Denahi (Jason Raize), the middle one; and impetuous Kenai (Joaquin Phoenix). After a large bear kills Sitka, Kenai avenges his brother's death by eliminating the animal. At that moment, an ancient spell transforms Kenai into the form of a bear, and Denahi mistakenly believes that Kenai killed Sitka. Thus begins a chase, with Denahi hunting Kenai, who soon befriends a motherless cub, Koda (Jeremy Suarez). Koda talks too much and can be annoying, but Kenai becomes protective of his younger companion. The bears are soon joined by a pair of moose, Rutt (Rick Moranis) and Tuke (Dave Thomas), but Kenai keeps moving because Denahi is only a step behind him.

The subject matter may be darker than usual for an animated film, but there's plenty of comic relief. The lion's share of it is provided by Rutt and Tuke, who are essentially SCTV's McKenzie brothers (right down to the exaggerated Canadian accents, eh) in animal form. The humor is reasonably broad-based: not so juvenile that adults will dismiss it, and not so sophisticated that children won't laugh. Phil Collins provides a few tunes. The target audience will probably enjoy these, but I think the film would have worked as well (if not better) without them. *Brother Bear* is not a musical; why bother to throw in a few random songs unless it's to sell more CDs, to get Collins an Oscar nomination, or both? RECOMMENDED

A Bug's Life [1998]

Featuring the voices of: Dave Foley, Kevin Spacey, Julia Louis-Dreyfus, Phyllis Diller Directors: John Lasseter, Andrew Stanton Screenplay: Andrew Stanton, Donald McEnery, Bob Shaw Running Time: 1:35 Rated: G Theatrical Aspect Ratio: 1.85:1

In *A Bug's Life*, the protagonist is Flik (voice of Dave Foley), an ant whose sole desire in life is "to make a difference." Flik is an inventor, and, when one of his experiments goes wrong, it brings the wrath of the grasshoppers, led by the dangerous Hopper (Kevin Spacey), down upon the denizens of the ant hill. To protect the community, Flik, with the blessing of the ant queen (Phyllis Diller) and Princess Atta (Julia

Louis-Dreyfus), ventures into the outside world and recruits "warrior insects" to defend the colony. The group of nine he collects is comprised of a praying mantis (Jonathan Harris, Mr. Smith from the TV version of "Lost in Space"), a butterfly (Madeline Kahn), a black widow spider (Bonnie Hunt), an unladylike ladybug (Denis Leary in a scene-stealing vocal performance), a walking stick (David Hyde Pierce), a caterpillar with a German accent (Joe Ranft), a rhino beetle (Brad Garrett), and a pair of unintelligible pillbugs (Michael McShane). There is a mistake in identity, however. Flik's "warrior bugs" are actually circus insects, and they accompany him under the false assumption that he is a talent scout. Things start to unravel once the ant and his elite corps discover the truth about each other.

The story presented in *A Bug's Life* works well on two levels. Children will appreciate the likable characters and fast-paced adventure; adults will marvel at the skillful animation and subtle humor. Visually, the film is both brilliantly detailed and wonderfully textured. *A Bug's Life* gives new dimensions to the diminutive world — a place where raindrops are dangerous projectiles, single berries provide full meals, and the most feared enemy is a bird.

Another thing *A Bug's Life* has is an ingenious series of end credits. Instead of just the latest lame Randy Newman song warbling over scrolling names, we are presented with a collection of mocked-up outtakes that parody the kinds of flubs and goofs which have come to decorate the credits of numerous comedies. It's brilliant in both conception and execution, and one could make a solid case that the last three minutes of *A Bug's Life* are its best.

Co-directors John Lasseter and Andrew Stanton understand that every story, even one with such an intense focus on visual elements, begins with a script and characters. *A Bug's Life*, like *Toy Story*, develops protagonists we can root for, and places them in the midst of a fast-moving, energetic adventure. HIGHLY RECOMMENDED

Chicken Run [United Kingdom, 2000]

Featuring the voices of: Mel Gibson, Julia Sawalha, Miranda Richardson Directors: Nick Park, Peter Lord Screenplay: Kerey Kirkpatrick & Jack Rosenthal Running Time: 1:25 Rated: G Theatrical Aspect Ratio: 1.66:1

If the overall storyline of *Chicken Run* strikes a vague chord of familiarity, that's because it borrows loosely from the classic World War II adventure, *The Great*

Escape. "Loosely," however, is the operative word. The movie is, appropriately enough, about a group of chickens, led by the hen Ginger (voice of Julia Sawalha), who are trapped on the farm of the stupid and greedy Mr. Tweedy (Tony Haygarth). Their lives are grinds: they produce eggs, which are collected by Tweedy and his wife (Miranda Richardson), then, when their egg-laying days are over, they become candidates for a chicken dinner. Unwilling to resign herself to such an existence, Ginger begins formulating escape plans. But, while getting one or two chickens off Tweedy's farm is feasible, freeing everyone seems to be an impossible task — until the unexpected arrival of Rocky the Flying Rooster (Mel Gibson), who crash-lands on the farm after escaping from a circus. In return for the hens hiding him, he agrees to teach them how to fly so they can sail over the fence penning them in. Unfortunately, Rocky isn't entirely trustworthy.

Although children will enjoy the film's likable animated protagonists and won't have any problem wrestling with the straightforward storyline, *Chicken Run*'s greatest appeal may be reserved for adults, who will appreciate the movie's singular wit. A fair amount of the dry, British humor is going to go over the heads of younger viewers. There are enough obvious jokes that kids won't be completely left out of the laughter loop, but my sense is that audience members over the age of 15 will find *Chicken Run* to be more amusing than those in the preteen and under-10 crowd.

Chicken Run is truly an unusual endeavor since, unlike every other animated motion picture reaching screens this year, its primary aim is not to astound viewers visually. In fact, with its old-fashioned approach to animation, it looks clunky in comparison to some of its competitors. Of course, that's part of *Chicken Run*'s charm.

At the dawn of the third millennium, animation has become the domain of the United States and Japan, so it's a rare pleasure to see another movie industry enter into the fray. With *Chicken Run*, Nick Park has taken all that was enjoyable about *Wallace & Gromit*, brought it into a barnyard, and extended it to feature length. Fans of the previous Aardman animated shorts (two of which have won Academy Awards) will undoubtedly shower Park with plaudits for what he has accomplished here. All that remains is for audiences at large to discover the simple-but-engaging entertainment of *Chicken Run*. **RECOMMENDED**

Dinosaur [2000]

Featuring the voices of: D.B. Sweeney, Julianna Margulies, Joan Plowright, Alfre Woodard Directors: Eric Leighton, Ralph Zondag Screenplay: John Harrison & Robert Nelson Jacobs Running Time: 1:24 Rated: PG (Dino violence) Theatrical Aspect Ratio: 1.85:1

While watching Disney's *Dinosaur*, with all of its incredibly rendered creatures and seamless blending of animated objects with real backgrounds, a question occurred to me: In movies like this, can the writing keep pace with the technology? As stunning as this movie is from a visual point-of-view, it boasts little else of great interest. Like so many big summer extravaganzas, this is a classic example of the triumph of style over substance.

Of course, since *Dinosaur* is a Disney animated effort and is geared primarily towards a younger audience, one has to make certain allowances. Kids will love the film. Although old and young alike will be awed by the spectacle of dinosaurs coming to life, the adventure, romance, and moralizing are all aimed squarely at the under-10 crowd. Children will enjoy *Dinosaur* as a fairly typical Disney-generated experience. Adults will appreciate it on another level, marveling at what cutting-edge special effects can accomplish while paying little or no attention to the rudimentary story and bland characterization.

There's not much to the plot. It's essentially a prehistoric road movie with a little *Tarzan* thrown in for good measure (once again, Disney recycles themes and ideas). Aladar (voiced by D.B. Sweeney) is a dinosaur who has been raised by a family of pre-monkey mammals. His mother (voice of Alfre Woodard), grandfather (Ossie Davis), and siblings are all cute, furry creatures that make the Ewoks look like grotesque monsters. Disney couldn't possibly have further ratcheted up the cuteness level. At any rate, after a good portion of the surrounding terrain is devastated by a meteor strike (not the Big One, apparently, since there's no lasting nuclear winter), Aladar and his mammal friends join a herd of dinosaurs who are on their way to The Nesting Ground (dino-speak for Eden). The journey is arduous, with danger coming from climate changes, roving predators, and infighting among the dinosaurs. In the end, it's up to Aladar to prove his mettle and be a hero.

Co-directors Eric Leighton and Ralph Zondag have crafted a film that will be an unqualified success with their primary target group. Children, more interested in fast-moving action than in a story with characters, will adore every moment of *Dinosaur*'s relatively

short, 84-minute running time. Adults may be more restrained in their praise, but, even though the traditional aspects of cinema are lacking, it's hard not to be impressed by the package as a whole. *Dinosaur* is worth *seeing*. And seeing, as they say, is believing.
RECOMMENDED

The Emperor's New Groove [2000]

Featuring the voices of: David Spade, John Goodman, Eartha Kitt, Patrick Warburton Director: Mark Dindal Screenplay: David Reynolds, Based on a story by Chris Williams & Mark Dindal Running Time: 1:15 Rated: G Theatrical Aspect Ratio: 1.85:1

The Emperor's New Groove represents Disney's first feature-length animated comedy. Although many of the Magic Kingdom's recent endeavors have included comedic characters (the genie in *Aladdin,* the dragon in *Mulan,* etc.), *The Emperor's New Groove* is the first motion picture to strive exclusively for comedy. Oh, there's a message buried in there (caring for others = good; selfishness = bad), but it isn't brought to the fore with sappy sentimentality. Instead, armed with what is arguably the most clever animated script in a long time, the movie makes its point through wit and gently barbed dialogue. The deeper one gets into *The Emperor's New Groove,* the less important the below average quality of the animation becomes.

Kuzco (voice of David Spade) is the emperor of all he can see — and has an ego to match his kingdom. With him, everything is "Me, Me, Me." Unbeknownst to Kuzco, his once-trusted advisor, the wizened witch Yzma (Eartha Kitt), is planning to depose him by poisoning a drink. Instead of causing the emperor's death as planned, however, Yzma's potion turns him into a llama. On all fours, he escapes from the clutches of Yzma's bumbling henchman, Kronk (Patrick Warburton), and joins forces with a kindly peasant, Pacha (John Goodman), who believes there is good in everyone — even the amazingly self-centered Kuzco. Together, these two work to restore Kuzco to his human body and his throne.

The screenplay offers plenty to laugh at for kids and adults. There's slapstick, self-mocking and self-referential humor, and amusing one-liners. The vocal casting is impeccable — perhaps the best Disney has done in 5 or 6 years. David Spade brings an edge to Kuzco, and he and John Goodman make an excellent team. Eartha Kitt finds the purr-fect tone for Yzma — bitchy, demanding, and over-the-top, but never frightening. The real scene-stealer, however, is Patrick Warburton, who sounds a great deal like Tim

Allen as Buzz Lightyear. Warburton's good-natured mindlessness makes Kronk the film's constant comic highlight.

The Emperor's New Groove has gone through a major overhaul since it initially went into pre-production. Originally called *Kingdom of the Sun,* the movie was to have been a romantic comedy musical in the "traditional" Disney style. Director Mark Dindal indicated that the film's shift in course forced his team to employ "out of the box" thinking. The result, while not a groundbreaking effort for Disney, takes the animated division in a fresh direction by rejecting a number of expected conventions. *The Emperor's New Groove* is good, solid fun. **RECOMMENDED**

Fantasia 2000 [2000]

Hosted by: Deems Taylor, Steve Martin, Quincy Jones, Bette Midler, Penn & Teller, James Levine, James Earl Jones, Angela Lansbury Running Time: 1:15 Rated: G Theatrical Aspect Ratio: 1.85:1

Comparing *Fantasia 2000* to the original *Fantasia* is in some ways unfair, especially considering the way movie-going tastes have changed over the past 6 decades. Yet, even though the hand-drawn animation has been helped along by the latest in computer imaging and the running length is considerably shorter, the two movies have the kind of kinship one would expect from motion pictures under the same umbrella.

Of the 7 new segments, there are a couple of throw-aways. The opening sequence featuring a swarm of abstract triangles flying and dancing to Beethoven's Fifth Symphony, is dull and uninspired. Equally wasteful is a sequence featuring yo-yo-ing flamingos set to Camille Saint-Saen's "The Carnival of the Animals." And, while the animation for "Rhapsody in Blue," which tells a New York story, is interesting (and said to be based on the work of caricaturist Al Herschfeld), it seems to belong in another movie.

Balancing out the weaker entries are some new classics. The best of the three is "The Steadfast Tin Soldier," which mixes music (Shostakovich's "Piano Concerto No. 2"), top-notch animation, and an emotionally-rewarding story. More visually ingenious is the sequence based on Stravinsky's "The Firebird." Chosen to close the movie, this shows how a dryad-like spirit renews the earth after it has been blasted by a volcanic eruption. Finally, there's *Fantasia 2000*'s lightest episode, a charming tale of Donald Duck on Noah's Ark set to the familiar strains of "Pomp and Circumstance." Children, who are not really *Fantasia*

2000's primary audience (this is much more of an "adult" movie), will enjoy this one the best — either that, or "The Sorcerer's Apprentice," which is as delightful now as it was 20, 30, 60, or however many years ago you first saw it.

Although the overall quality of *Fantasia 2000* is considerably more variable than that of *Fantasia*, certain aspects of the experience are the same — namely, the ability to sit in a theater and listen to great music while being presented with a choreographed visual accompaniment. *Fantasia 2000* does not soar the way its predecessor did, but neither does it plummet to the earth. Instead, it occupies a middle territory, often hovering and drifting, but occasionally flying. RECOMMENDED

Finding Nemo [2003]

Featuring the voices of: Albert Brooks, Ellen DeGeneres, Alexander Gould, Willem Dafoe, Brad Garrett, Allison Janney, Austin Pendleton, Stephen Root, Geoffrey Rush Director: Andrew Stanton Screenplay: Andrew Stanton Running Time: 1:41 Rated: G Theatrical Aspect Ratio: 1.85:1

Finding Nemo takes viewers on an offbeat road trip as an overprotective clown fish father, Marlin (Albert Brooks), teams up with a forgetful hippo tang, Dory (Ellen DeGeneres), to find Marlin's lost son, Nemo (Alexander Gould). While testing his boundaries and defying his father, Nemo wanders too close to a human scuba diving expedition and becomes an aquarium specimen. Now, he spends his days as a captive in a saltwater tank with several other inhabitants, including a royal gramma, a starfish, a puffer, and a butterfly fish, Gill (Willem Dafoe), whose lone goal is escape. Meanwhile, Marlin and Dory brave the dangers of the open seas — including a trio of would-be vegetarian sharks, a forest of jellyfish, and the belly of a whale — on their way to Australia, where Nemo is being held captive.

Pixar films always contain thematic content, and this one is no different. It touches on the issues of how a parent's natural protective instincts can drive away a child, and how children, no matter how desperately they crave independence, still need their families. None of this is presented in a heavy-handed manner. Instead, it's offered in such a way that even the younger members of the audience will understand what the film is saying without feeling like they're being subjected to a sermon. There's also a message about the importance of diversity and harmony, as a wide variety of animal species band together to help Marlin as he searches for his lost son.

Director Andrew Stanton opted to animate some of the fish realistically, while using artistic license with others. The clown fish and hippo tang, for example, look almost identical to their real-life counterparts. The sea horses and turtles, however, have some of their rough edges smoothed out, making them cuter and more child-friendly. Overall, *Finding Nemo* is a treasure trove of visual splendor. From the opening scenes on the coral reef with Marlin taking up residence in his new anemone to the cheesy insides of Nemo's aquarium cage, the film is colorful and amazingly detailed. Every time I view a Pixar film, I am stunned at how much there is to see. *Finding Nemo* proves that the computer animators can do as much underwater as above it. Pixar has done it again and, in the process, managed to salvage Disney's reputation — at least for a little longer. HIGHLY RECOMMENDED

Hercules [1997]

Featuring the voices of: Tate Donovan, Joshua Keaton, Roger Bart, Danny DeVito, James Woods, Susan Egan Directors: Ron Clements and John Musker Screenplay: John Musker, Ron Clements, Bob Shaw, Don McEnery, Irene Mecchi Running Time: 1:32 Rated: G Theatrical Aspect Ratio: 1.85:1

Students of mythology may be irritated by the changes made to the legend of Hercules. Many of these are understandable, given the studio's espousal of family values. After all, how much light-hearted fun can you have telling the tale of the bastard son of a god and mortal who grew up to kill his wife and children? So, instead, Disney has made Hercules the divine offspring of a couple that represents Olympian marital bliss: Zeus and Hera. Unfortunately, Hades, who is preparing a "hostile takeover bid" of the big mountain, has it on good authority that Hercules is the only one who can foul up his plans. So, using his inept assistants Panic and Pain, he has Hercules turned into a human. When Dad and Mom learn about this, they realize that their son, who is no longer immortal, cannot live on Olympus, and they allow him to be raised by Greek foster parents.

Hercules comes close to being a remake of the *The Little Mermaid* with a male hero. One could easily argue that all Disney animated films are similar, but *Hercules* is a little too blatant in its cannibalization of past themes and plot points. Besides that, this film has a distractingly episodic feel. Instead of coming together as a cohesive story, it's like a bunch of thinly-related events strung one-by-one to reach a ninety-minute running time.

The most disappointing aspect of *Hercules* is the amateurish quality of the artwork. The "excuse" for this is that the animators at Disney were trying a new, angular style. In fact, this approach makes the film look rushed and, at times, incomplete. It is never a visual marvel — even the computer-generated scenes fail to impress. The sequences intended to offer the biggest spectacle — Olympus and the Underworld — provoke little more than a yawn.

So, although *Hercules* is undoubtedly a lightly enjoyable motion picture, I couldn't shake the feeling that it could have been and done more. Those on the lookout for another Disney masterpiece won't uncover it here. However, anyone with the modest goal of finding a screen solution to the problem of a family outing need not worry: Disney's 35th animated motion picture fills the prescription. RECOMMENDED

The Hunchback of Notre Dame [1996]
Featuring the voices of: Tom Hulce, Tony Jay, Demi Moore, Kevin Kline
Directors: Gary Trousdale and Kirk Wise Screenplay: Tab Murphy
Running Time: 1:30 Rated: G Theatrical Aspect Ratio: 1.66:1

Out of respect for the stunning visuals and family entertainment value of Disney's 34th animated feature, I can do no less than recommend *The Hunchback of Notre Dame*. All things considered, *The Hunchback of Notre Dame* isn't bad, it's just a little disappointing. Despite the over-hyped and overexaggerated "darkness" of the production, kids will love it.

It's curious that the Disney movie to use the most adult source material has yielded the least potent results. Obviously, Victor Hugo's vision of *The Hunchback of Notre Dame* couldn't be made into a Disney cartoon — it violates almost every aspect of the studio's traditional, feel-good/happy ending formula. So, predictably, the screenwriters diluted it. In doing so, they siphoned off the elements that give the story its unique power. With the darkest and most unpleasant aspects of Hugo's tragedy eradicated, there's not much left. The poorly-focused remains are likely to appeal most strongly to the under-12 crowd. Unlike past efforts, there aren't many in-jokes and double-entendres to catch the attention of the adults in the audience.

The film loosely follows Hugo's narrative. After opening with a 6-minute prologue describing how Judge Claude Frollo (voice of Tony Jay) becomes the guardian of the deformed bell-ringer of Notre Dame, Quasimodo (voice of Tom Hulce), *Hunchback* launches into the meat of its story, which involves a curious love quadrangle. The center of attention is the gypsy Esmeralda (who looks and sounds like Demi Moore). Frollo, a powerful magistrate in 15th century Paris, whose self-proclaimed duty is to eradicate sin, wants all the gypsies dead, including Esmeralda. At the same time, however, he's having trouble fighting a lustful desire for her. The captain of his guards, Phoebus (voice of Kevin Kline), has fallen madly in love with the gypsy girl, as has Quasimodo, who becomes her friend and confidante. In Hugo's book, the interaction between these characters fuels a complex and multi-layered drama. Not so in this movie, where Quasimodo's 3 talking gargoyle companions exhibit more personality than the humans. For, although we come to feel for "Quasi," neither Esmeralda nor Phoebus makes a dent in our sympathy.

If you believe that the primary purpose for animated films is to enthrall children, *The Hunchback of Notre Dame* is an unquestionable success. If you're looking for entertainment for the whole family, this movie will fit the bill. But if you're anticipating something that's as diverting for adults as for younger viewers, *Hunchback* may disappoint. RECOMMENDED

Ice Age [2002]
Featuring the voices of: Ray Romano, John Leguizamo, Denis Leary
Director: Chris Wedge Screenplay: Peter Ackerman, Michael Berg, Michael Wilson Running Time: 1:22 Rated: PG (Mild violence)
Theatrical Aspect Ratio: 1.85:1

Discounting *Final Fantasy,* which was aimed at a much different audience, *Ice Age* is the 8th Hollywood-financed computer animated film. It follows in the wake of, and borrows liberally from, both of 2001's blockbusters, *Shrek* and *Monsters Inc.* In fact, if *Ice Age* hadn't been in development before those movies arrived in multiplexes, one might be tempted to argue that the screenplay for this film took elements from its two immediate predecessors, jumbled them together, then dumped them out in the middle of a frozen tundra. Kids, of course, will love *Ice Age*. Adults will be entertained, but no more.

The time period is the Dawn of Man. The dinosaurs have long since vanished from the Earth, and an ice age is fast approaching. The animals, at least most of them, are headed south for the long, hard winter. Among the exceptions are an industrious, frustrated squirrel, and 3 larger mammals: Manfred the Mammoth (voice of Ray Romano), Sid the Sloth (voice of John Leguizamo), and Diego the Sabertooth (voice of Denis Leary). These 3 have banded together on an unlikely quest: return a lost human baby to his tribe. However, while Manfred and Sid have the best intentions, Diego is pursuing his own agenda, which includes turning Manfred into dinner.

The contentious relationship turned to warm friendship between Manfred and Sid is virtually identical to that of Shrek and Donkey. The bonding that goes on between the animals and the baby recalls the way Boo worms her way into the big, bad monsters' affections. But, despite the many plot similarities, the humor and sophistication of *Ice Age* never quite reaches the level of the other computer animated endeavors — except on those occasions when the squirrel is on screen. Also, the quality of the animation is a notch lower. It's not *bad,* by any means, but it's a definite step backwards, often more resembling the look of a computer game than that of a big budget motion picture.

Ice Age's director is Chris Wedge, whose only previous experience behind the camera was making an animated short called "Bunny." His first foray into feature filmmaking is successful, although *Ice Age* is not a standout in the still-small subgenre of computer animated films. It's perfectly acceptable family entertainment — the kind of movie that parents can take their children to without worrying about inappropriate content (for either the youngsters or the adults). And, sometimes, that's about all you can ask for from a movie. **RECOMMENDED**

The Incredibles [2004]

Featuring the voices of: Craig T. Nelson, Holly Hunter, Samuel L. Jackson, Jason Lee, Wallace Shawn, Spencer Fox, Lou Romano, Sarah Vowell, Elizabeth Peña Director: Brad Bird Screenplay: Brad Bird Running Time: 1:55 Rated: PG (Cartoon violence) Theatrical Aspect Ratio: 2.35:1

One thing immediately noticeable about this picture is that it is markedly more mature in tone and approach than any previous digitally animated movie. That's not to say that kids, even young ones, won't enjoy *The Incredibles,* but it appears that writer/director Brad Bird composed his film with older children and their parents in mind. Also, because of the long running time (nearly two hours), boys and girls prone to restlessness may have trouble sitting through everything.

The Incredibles confronts the midlife crisis of a once-popular superhero. In his prime, Mr. Incredible (voice of Craig T. Nelson) was beloved by millions. Saving the world wasn't just his job; it was his passion. ("No matter how many times you save the world, it always gets in jeopardy again.") But things changed. People began filing lawsuits against the superheroes (starting with a suicide victim irate that his life was saved), driving them underground courtesy of the "Superhero Relocation Program," which offered a new life in return for a promise never to act as a superhero again. At first, Mr. Incredible and his beloved wife, Elastigirl (Holly Hunter), were happy to live as Bob and Helen Parr and raise their children, speedy Dash (Spencer Fox) and shy, shrinking Violet (Sarah Vowell). But, as his job at an insurance company becomes increasingly abrasive, Mr. Incredible yearns for the old days. Some nights, he and his old buddy, Frozone (Samuel L. Jackson), listen to the police scanner, then give the cops a little unexpected aid. But it's not enough. Then along comes a mysterious woman (Elizabeth Peña) with a job offer, and Mr. Incredible sees a chance to regain his self-confidence and convince himself that he can once again make a difference.

Although *The Incredibles* has plenty of action (including chases and battle scenes), its strength is that it makes the characters and their relationships more important than the fights and pyrotechnics. This is a close family — they just happen to possess some rather unusual abilities. The film's director is Brad Bird, who fashioned the uncommon *The Iron Giant,* a traditionally animated effort that has developed a large following among adults. For his latest outing, Bird keeps the same audience in mind. Where some animated movies attract adults using pop references and sly one-liners, Bird keeps older viewers interested by not dumbing down his screenplay. It's inevitable that some of *The Incredibles*' themes (such as that of a middle-age crisis) will go over the heads of kids, but it won't hurt the experience for them. They'll still thrill to the action scenes and laugh at the jokes. And they'll get the overall message about parents being the most important superheroes. But Bird's approach makes this a richer and more worthwhile experience for the over-18 crowd. *The Incredibles* is without question one of 2004's most accomplished and enjoyable family-oriented films. **HIGHLY RECOMMENDED**

The Iron Giant [1999]

Featuring the voices of: Eli Marienthal, Vin Diesel, Jennifer Aniston, Harry Connick Jr. Director: Brad Bird Screenplay: Brad Bird & Tim McCanlies, based on the book by Ted Hughes Running Time: 1:20 Rated: PG (Mild profanity, cartoon violence) Theatrical Aspect Ratio: 2.35:1

The reason for *The Iron Giant*'s success isn't hard to discern — it has to do with the writing. The script is crisp, smartly-paced, intelligent, and emotionally satisfying. It recalls the strengths of *E.T.* without the weaknesses. It introduces real, likable characters worth caring about and rooting for. It's the kind of story with the power to engross 6-year olds and 60-year olds alike because it doesn't condescend. *The Iron Giant* is filled with small moments that only older viewers will get, but which pass so quickly that kids won't realize they have missed anything.

The place is Rockwell, Maine. The year is 1957. Grade schooler Hogarth Hughes (voice of Eli Marienthal) is forever looking for a pet that his mother, Annie (voice of Jennifer Aniston), will allow him to keep. One night while his mother is working late at the diner where she waitresses, Hogarth hears a noise outside. By the time he goes to check, nothing is there, but he can see a swath of destruction: broken fences, trampled ground, and downed trees. So he follows the trail into the forest to a nearby power station. It's there that he first glimpses the Iron Giant (voice of Vin Diesel) — a 100-foot tall robot from space that eats metal. When it runs afoul of some live wires, Hogarth finds the station's "Off" switch to cut the power, saving the Iron Giant from electrocution.

After another chance encounter the next day, Hogarth and the Giant become friends, but danger is lurking in the wings. A dastardly government agent, Kent Mansley (voice of Christopher McDonald), who tracks down unexplained phenomenon, is convinced that Hogarth knows something about the strange goings-on around Rockwell, and he is determined to use any means necessary to learn the truth.

The Iron Giant teaches lessons about friendship, tolerance, and sacrifice, without turning preachy. Although Hogarth is initially frightened by his huge friend (who wouldn't be?), he soon comes to realize that he's actually quite childlike and gentle. Hogarth becomes both his friend and his teacher, giving him speech lessons and occasionally discussing philosophical issues, like whether a robot can have a soul. The film also has a fairly strong anti-gun message. In addition to its effective dramatic elements, *The Iron Giant* contains a share of successful comedy. Some of the humor is fairly sophisticated, but most has a broad enough base to be enjoyed by everyone in the audience, regardless of age, gender, or race. And there's even a little flatulence, although it's considerably more tame than in most of today's films.

The Iron Giant's real strength lies in the story and character development. It's in this arena that this movie proves to be vastly superior, making this a top-notch family feature. **HIGHLY RECOMMENDED**

James and the Giant Peach [1996]

Cast: Paul Terry, Joanna Lumley, Miriam Margoyles, Pete Postlethwaite; and the voices of Richard Dreyfuss, Susan Sarandon, Simon Callow Director: Henry Selick Screenplay: Karey Kirkpatrick, Jonathan Roberts, and Steve Bloom based on the book by Roald Dahl Running Time: 1:20 Rated: PG (Scary situations) Theatrical Aspect Ratio: 1.85:1

Based (rather faithfully) on Roald Dahl's children's story, *James and the Giant Peach* uses a combination of live-action sequences and stop-motion animation to tell the tale of a lonely boy, James (Paul Terry), who finds love during a bizarre, transatlantic voyage in the innards of a gargantuan peach. His companions on the journey are a grasshopper, a centipede, a spider, an earthworm, a glow worm, and a ladybug. In the hands of Henry Selick, this weird story has been transformed into a playful, visually arresting experience with more than a few allusions to *The Wizard of Oz*.

In this case, the destination isn't Oz, but New York City, which, as envisioned by Selick, is a magical, ethereal place. The story takes place during an era when the Empire State Building is the world's tallest building, and *James and the Giant Peach* becomes the second movie to place an overgrown object at its pinnacle. Between England (where the story begins, with James suffering under the repressive thumbs of two ogre-like aunts) and New York, the peach, which is propelled by a flock of harnessed birds, has an ocean splashdown and takes a detour to frozen northern reaches.

Of course, all but the youngest children (who could be frightened by certain scenes) will be delighted by the film, and the script is written to succeed on more than one level. There are some deliciously wicked lines that few youngsters will get. This crisp dialogue is delivered by the likes of Susan Sarandon (the spider), Simon Callow (the grasshopper), David Thewlis (the earthworm), and Richard Dreyfuss (the centipede), actors with effective vocal presences.

Dorothy, accompanied by a dog, a Scarecrow, a Tin Man, and a Cowardly Lion, followed the yellow brick road. James, along with a pack of oversized bugs, follows his dreams. Both reach their destinations, and, once there, discover that it's what they learned on the trip that really matters. In the final analysis, *James and the Giant Peach* is undemanding entertainment with a subtle message. **RECOMMENDED**

The Lion King [1994]

Featuring the voices of: Jeremy Irons, James Earl Jones, Matthew Broderick, Whoopi Goldberg, Moira Kelly Directors: Rob Minkoff and Roger Allers Screenplay: Irene Mecchi & Jonathan Roberts Running Time: 1:27 Rated: G Theatrical Aspect Ratio: 1.66:1

Hamlet meets *The Jungle Book* — that's what *The Lion King* is — adding, of course, a few special touches all its own. *The Lion King* is primarily about guilt and redemption. Simba, a young lion cub and heir to his father's throne, is led to believe that he was the cause of the king's death. The trauma caused by this is so great that Simba goes into exile, attempting to find peace-of-mind through anonymity in the company of a warthog and a meerkat. But it's never that easy to escape the past . . .

The *Hamlet* parallels are all there for the discerning adult to note. Mufasa, king of the lions, is killed by a treacherous brother who subsequently takes over the rule of the kingdom. Simba, the beloved son, is wracked by guilt and impotence until the ghost of his father gives him instruction on what actions he should take. Death, something not really touched on in the last 3 animated Disney tales, is very much at the forefront of *The Lion King*. In a scene that could disturb younger viewers, Mufasa's demise is shown. It is a chilling moment that is reminiscent of a certain incident in *Bambi*. The film also contains a fair share of violence, including a rather graphic battle between two lions. Parents should carefully consider before automatically taking a child of, say, under 7 years of age, to this movie.

Scar, Simba's treacherous uncle, is the latest in a long line of Disney antagonists. Gone is the buffoonery that has marked the recent trio of Ursula, Gaston, and Jafar. Scar is a sinister figure, given to acid remarks and cunning villainy. The cold-hearted manner in which he causes Mufasa's death lets us know that this is not a lion to be trifled with.

The animation, as expected from any Disney film, is superior. As usual, as much attention is given to small background details as to foreground principals. Lighting and color are used to highlight the shifting tone of the picture (the sunny warmth of Mufasa's kingdom to the dreary barrenness of Scar's), and the animators have never lost sight that their subjects are not human.

With each new animated release, Disney seems to be expanding its already-broad horizons a little more. *The Lion King* is the most mature (in more than one sense) of these films, and there clearly has been a conscious effort to please adults as much as children. Happily, for those of us who generally stay far away from "cartoons," they have succeeded. HIGHLY RECOMMENDED

The Little Mermaid [1989]

Featuring the voices of: Jodi Benson, Samuel E. Wright, Pat Carroll, Christopher Daniel Barnes Directors: Ron Clements and John Musker Screenplay: Ron Clements & John Musker Running Time: 1:22 Rated: G Theatrical Aspect Ratio: 1.66:1

Despite revitalizing Disney's fortunes and introducing the present wave of big-screen cartoons, *The Little Mermaid* was not a groundbreaking motion picture, although it was the first animated movie to so thoroughly incorporate songs into the narrative. With big production numbers like "Under the Sea" and "Kiss the Girl," and several other hummable melodies, the film makers did their best to create the cartoon equivalent of a musical. Like all musicals, much of the enjoyment comes as a result of simply enjoying the singing, rather than being carried away by the relatively uncomplicated story.

The Little Mermaid is loosely based on the Hans Christian Andersen fable, albeit with a radically changed ending. Ariel (voice of Jodi Benson) is the rebellious teenage mer-daughter of Triton, King of the Sea (Kenneth Mars). She is obsessed with the culture of those who live on land, and keeps a secret treasure trove of objects recovered from shipwrecks. One day, while swimming around with her fish pal, Flounder (Jason Marin), and her chaperone, the crab Sebastian (Samuel E. Wright), Ariel comes upon a sinking ship and saves a handsome young human, who turns out to be a prince named Eric (Christopher Daniel Barnes), from drowning. Ariel is smitten, but when her father finds out about her excursions to the surface, he is furious. Hurt and desperate, the young mermaid falls into the trap of the sea-witch Ursula (Pat Carroll), who offers her a deal: in return for being transformed into a human, Ariel must cause Eric to fall in love with her in less than 3 days, otherwise her soul will belong to Ursula. To seal the bargain, Ariel gives her voice to the witch. What the mermaid doesn't know, however, is that Ursula has stacked the deck so that Ariel can't possibly emerge victorious.

The animation in *The Little Mermaid* isn't quite as accomplished or eye-popping as that of its successors, but it's still impressive, and hurried or unfinished cels are almost impossible to spot. What the film does expertly is to weave together music, likable protagonists, thoroughly nasty villains, and a fun plot into a cohesive whole, with a result that is nothing short of magical. And, although *The Little Mermaid* isn't among Disney's most "mature" animated movies, it offers enough entertainment, innocent romance, and low-key humor to keep adults involved. Children, of course, will love it. For 90 minutes of pure escapism, it's difficult to beat *The Little Mermaid*. **HIGHLY RECOMMENDED**

Looney Tunes: Back in Action [2003]

Starring: Brendan Fraser, Jenna Elfman, Steve Martin, Timothy Dalton, Heather Locklear, Joan Cusack, voices of Joe Alaskey, Jeff Glenn Bennett, Billy West, Eric Goldberg   Director: Joe Dante   Screenplay: Larry Doyle   Running Time: 1:31   Rated: PG (Cartoon violence) Theatrical Aspect Ratio: 2.35:1

Looney Tunes: Back in Action is so jam-packed with self-referential humor, pop culture cameos, and nods to some of the greatest moments in animation that it's almost impossible not to like it. It's a breezy, fun-filled romp that owes as much of its success to nostalgia as it does to the cutting-edge computer animation that brings human actors and animated creatures together. Nearly the entire roster of Warner Brothers cartoon characters is on hand. Of course, the starring roles belong to Bugs and Daffy, but they are given able support by the likes of Wiley Coyote, Sylvester, Porky Pig, Tweety Bird, Marvin the Martian, Speedy Gonzalez, Yosemite Sam, and Elmer Fudd. Then there are the cameos, which include Shaggy and Scooby Doo, Roadrunner, Robbie the Robot, and a couple of Daleks from *Doctor Who*. Everyone gets his or her moments, most of which are reminiscent of what we remember from their golden age.

The movie has a plot, although it's best not to spend too much time thinking about it. It's clunky and uninteresting, and occasionally gets in the way of simply enjoying the clever bits. This is one of those times when it's better not to see the forest for the trees. Look instead at the leaves. At any rate, the chairman of Acme Corporation (played by Steve Martin doing an impersonation of Dr. Evil crossed with Arte Johnson) has a plan to take over the world by using a magical blue diamond that will turn human beings into monkeys. After getting superspy Damian Drake (played by ex-007 Timothy Dalton) out of the way, the chairman thinks everything is going his way, until Drake's son, DJ (Brendan Fraser), starts looking for his dad. He is aided in his quest by Kate (Jenna Elfman), a Warner Brothers executive, and a gaggle of Looney Tunes characters, including Bugs and Daffy. The chairman is not without his own animated henchmen, however.

The film has its share of inspired moments, the most obvious of which occur during a sequence in which Elmer Fudd chases Bugs and Daffy through the Louvre. The trio ends up running through paintings by Dalí (*The Persistence of Memory*), Seurat (*Sunday Afternoon on the Grande Jatte*), and Munch (*The Scream*) and being appropriately transformed as they enter each new landscape. For kids who aren't up on art, there's a scene that pays homage to *Star Wars*, complete with Bugs taking a crash course on the art of lightsaber dueling by reading *The Force for Dummies*.

Needless to say, the film's appeal is universal, much as the appeal of the Looney Tunes characters is universal. Seven-year old kids will be laughing at the same things that amuse their older siblings, parents, and grandparents. The movie works on a lot of different levels. The older you are, the more satire you'll see in *Looney Tunes: Back in Action,* but the picture offers plenty of laughs for viewers of all ages. **RECOMMENDED**

Monsters, Inc. [2001]

Featuring the voices of: Billy Crystal, John Goodman, James Coburn, Jennifer Tilly   Directors: Peter Docter, David Silverman Screenplay: Dan Gerson, Andrew Stanton   Running Time: 1:30 Rated: G   Theatrical Aspect Ratio: 1.85:1

There's a world out there, somewhere under the rainbow, where monsters live. The sprawling city where they go about their daily lives is called Monstropolis — a vast, bustling place populated by all sorts of misshapen creatures who would cause the average human child to crawl under the covers. Energy in Monstropolis comes from an unusual source — the screams of children. Employees working for megacorporation Monsters, Inc. go through gateways into the bedroom of human kids on Earth, frighten them into screaming, capture the energy from the screams, and convert it to electricity in Monstropolis. But, since children are becoming harder to scare, Monstropolis is facing a "scream shortage."

The most successful scream team at Monsters, Inc. is comprised of Sulley Sullivan (voice of John Goodman) and Mike Wazowski (Billy Crystal). Sulley, really a gentle giant, is the scary one; Mike is his wisecracking partner. Together, they're approaching the all-time scream record. Their lone challenger is Randall Boggs (Steve Buscemi), who will stop at nothing to move past them. One night, after hours, Randall decides to cheat by making some unauthorized trips to the other side. Sulley accidentally discovers his plot. When he opens a door Randall has set up, a catastrophe occurs — a little girl, Boo (Mary Gibbs), crosses the threshold into the monsters' world. Suddenly, the greatest imaginable horror in monster society has occurred — a child from Earth has entered Monstropolis. Chaos reigns as Sulley and Mike try to hide the girl, protect themselves, and expose Randall's secret scheme.

Everything that was true of the two *Toy Story* movies and *A Bug's Life* can be said about *Monsters, Inc.* — this is the kind of movie that works on multiple levels — as fast-moving, lively fun for children and as slyly written, visually impressive entertainment for adults. *Monsters, Inc.* is one of those rare family films that parents can enjoy (rather than endure) along with their kids. And childless individuals venturing into a theater showing this picture need not worry that they'll be viewed as deviants — *Monsters, Inc.* is capable of drawing audience members from across the age spectrum.

The great strength of the previous Pixar films, as well as *Shrek,* is that they offer a genuine emotional component that runs deeper than that of the run-of-the-mill animated feature. Such is the case here, where the attachment between burly Sulley and tiny Boo touches the heart. The little girl brings out Sulley's soft side and smoothes some of Mike's rough edges.

Monsters, Inc. reaffirms the fact that a good animated film can be every bit as stimulating and emotionally satisfying a motion picture as a high quality live action endeavor. **HIGHLY RECOMMENDED**

Mulan [1998]

Featuring the voices of: Ming-Na Wen, Eddie Murphy, B.D. Wong, Miguel Ferrer Directors: Tony Bancroft, Barry Cook Screenplay: Eugenia Bostwick-Singer, Rita Hsiao, Philip LaZebnik, Chris Sanders, Raymond Singer Running Time: 1:25 Rated: G Theatrical Aspect Ratio: 1.85:1

The setting for this adventure is feudal China. An army of Huns under the command of the ruthless Shan-Yu (voice of Miguel Ferrer), has invaded the country, spreading death and disaster far and wide. The Chinese Emperor (Pat Morita) commands that one able-bodied male from every family must serve in an emergency army. Meanwhile, in a remote village, an independent-minded young woman named Mulan (Ming-Na Wen) has been rejected by a local matchmaker on the grounds that she is too willful. "You will never bring your family honor," decrees the matchmaker, causing Mulan to begin a period of soul-searching. When the Emperor's decree arrives, Mulan cuts her hair, dresses like a man, and enters the army in her father's place. With the help of her inept mythical guardian, the tiny dragon Mushu (Eddie Murphy), she seeks to win the confidence of her captain, Li Shang (B.D. Wong), and the acceptance of her fellow peasant-turned-warriors, while keeping her sex concealed from everyone.

Mulan is the first Disney animated film to deal with war and death on a large scale. The subject is not glossed over — the movie features several poignant sequences showing the devastation in the aftermath of a battle, including hundreds of lifeless bodies lying in the snow. Oddly, because there's nothing exploitative or gruesome about these images, they're more likely to affect older viewers, who will better understand the implications, than younger ones, for whom death is often a nebulous concept. In no way can it be said that *Mulan* is glorifying war.

The main character is cut from a familiar cloth. Although she looks different from Ariel, Belle, Jasmine, and Pocahontas, Mulan is very much the same type of individual: a woman with a strong, independent streak who is unwilling to bend to the customs of her culture, which decree that the role of the female is to be ornamental. The film isn't very subtle in reinforcing the idea of equality between the sexes, but the script contains a few amusing lines in this vein that will fly high over the heads of younger viewers.

As all Disney movies must, *Mulan* features a pair of new sidekicks. One, the second best-known cartoon cricket in the history of motion pictures, doesn't have a voice. The other, Mushu, never shuts up. It's clear that, in his vocal characterization of the dragon, Eddie Murphy is trying to top (or at least equal) Robin Williams' genie from *Aladdin.* Amazingly, he comes close. With his high-energy, often hilarious delivery, Murphy flies away with his scenes. Mushu is the primary reason kids will love *Mulan,* and he's not so fundamentally juvenile that adults won't get a few chuckles out of him, as well. **HIGHLY RECOMMENDED**

The Nightmare Before Christmas [1993]

Featuring the voices of: Danny Elfman, Chris Sarandon, Catherine O'Hara, William Hickey, Ed Ivory Director: Henry Selick Screenplay: Caroline Thompson Running Time: 1:15 Rated: PG (Cartoon monsters) Theatrical Aspect Ratio: 1.66:1

The scene is Halloween Town where, not surprisingly, October 31 is the biggest night of the year. However, after arranging and carrying out his most devilish Halloween yet, Jack Skellington (voiced by Chris Sarandon when speaking, Danny Elfman when singing) is suffering the post-holiday blues. He craves something different in his life, something that can't be found in Halloween Town. Wandering out in a forest, he discovers gateways to different holidays, and finds his way to Christmas Town. There, he is captivated by the lights, the festivity, and the joy. He returns home to tell everyone that this year, Halloween Town is going to celebrate Christmas. To make things complete, he, Jack Skellington, will replace "Sandy Claws" on his yearly December 25 ride, delivering presents and spreading good cheer. Everyone is enthused by the idea except Sally (voiced by Catherine O'Hara), who has a premonition of doom if Jack goes through with his plans.

The Nightmare Before Christmas is a visual splendor. Done on the cheap, this could have been a gimmicky, unsatisfying experience, but, as the result of considerable time and effort, it is an unqualified success. All of the figures move smoothly and naturally, and the attention to detail is exquisite. We are given a group of cleverly-fashioned characters that look like refugees from Edward Gorey's sketchbook.

The film is designed for all but the youngest children, some of whom might be frightened by the bizarre inhabitants of Halloween Town. On its surface, the story is relatively straightforward, enabling younger viewers to enjoy the movie without becoming lost or bored. However, the film works on a second level, as well. The most deft humor is aimed at adults. Even those who aren't taken in by the charming tale or likable characters will be enthralled by the world Tim Burton and director Henry Selick have created. It is, quite frankly, an amazing achievement.

The Nightmare Before Christmas is *How the Grinch Stole Christmas* thrown into reverse (although clearly the Dr. Seuss tale had a part in formulating some of the images of Christmas Town). While the Grinch made Christmas better by trying to destroy it, Jack Skellington ruins the holiday by trying to improve it. But don't worry — everything turns out all right in the end. After all, this is a family film. **HIGHLY RECOMMENDED**

Pocahontas [1995]

Featuring the voices of: Irene Bedard, Mel Gibson, Russell Means, David Ogden Stiers Directors: Mike Gabriel and Eric Goldberg Screenplay: Carl Binder, Susannah Grant, Philip LaZebrik Running Time: 1:21 Rated: G Theatrical Aspect Ratio: 2.35:1

Anyone who expects historical accuracy from a Disney animated feature should be ashamed of themselves. Those approaching *Pocahontas* in anticipation of a true-to-history account of the early days of Jamestown are in for a rude awakening.

Despite obvious similarities — Menken's music, a heroine who doesn't want her father to choose her husband, and a small legion of animals — *Pocahontas* is actually something of a departure from the recent batch of releases. This film isn't quite as cute; deals with some reasonably serious, "adult" issues; and contains an element of poignancy. The cartoonish animal sidekicks, which include a raccoon, a hummingbird, and a pug, are amusing as ever, but this time around, they don't have voices.

Pocahontas presents a fictionalized chronicle of the arrival of English settlers in Virginia. Led by a greedy, bombastic governor (David Ogden Stiers) and Captain John Smith (Mel Gibson), the explorers have come to the New World in search of gold. They promptly begin cutting down trees, digging holes, and preparing to kill the Indians. Meanwhile, a young native woman, Pocahontas (speaking voice of Irene Bedard, who was also the physical model for the character; singing voice of Judy Kuhn), observes the newcomers with a mixture of curiosity and trepidation. Her father, Chief Powhatan (voice of Native American activist/actor Russell Means), is certain that the white mens' landing means war. And the only hope to avert a pitched battle arises as a result of the romance that develops between Smith and Pocahontas.

Several recognizable themes suffuse *Pocahontas*: the stupidity of wanton destruction, the need for tolerance between those of different races and cultures, and the forks in life's road offered by fate. While none is presented with any special subtlety (after all, children are supposed to get the message), there is surprisingly little preaching. It would have been easy to turn this into a "Native American good/White Man bad" film, but positive and negative traits are shown on both sides. **HIGHLY RECOMMENDED**

The Polar Express [2004]

Starring: Tom Hanks, Leslie Zemeckis, Eddie Deezen, Nona Gaye, Peter Scolari, Michael Jeter Director: Robert Zemeckis Screenplay: Robert Zemeckis & William Broyles, Jr., based on the book by Chris Van Allsburg Running Time: 1:30 Rated: G Theatrical Aspect Ratio: 2.35:1

The Polar Express is cinematic magic — a delightful tale guaranteed to enthrall viewers of all ages. Does that sound like advertising hype or the words of a publicist? Perhaps, but it's a reflection of how strongly this film pulled me under its spell. For children, this is a glorious adventure, full of excitement, splendor, and plenty of holiday good cheer. For adults, there are deeper meanings to be found, not to mention the bittersweet nostalgia of gazing back through the years to the point where innocence gave way to the curse of maturity.

As I was watching *The Polar Express*, I was reminded of *The Wizard of Oz*. The similarities are, at times, remarkable. The characters in this film are on a journey to a mythical place — not Oz, but the North Pole. And they're following train tracks, not the yellow brick road. But the four companions are all searching for something intangible. Our hero, an unnamed boy, is on a quest for faith. His companions are seeking confidence, courage, and humility. The entire story may be the figment of the main character's imagination. But at least there's no Wicked Witch or a surrogate. *The Polar Express* is a tale with plenty of heart and no traditional villain.

The story begins on Christmas Eve, with a boy who is unable to sleep. He's listening for sleigh bells. He wants to believe in Santa Claus, but his growing sense of logic tells him the annual ride is impossible: The presents would be too heavy, and the rate of travel would have to exceed the speed of light. But, instead of hearing the prancing and pawing of each little hoof, he is jarred to full wakefulness by the noise of a train coming to a halt outside of his house. "All aboard!" calls the conductor. "Where are you going?" asks the boy. "Why, the North Pole, of course! This is *The Polar Express*."

Thus begins the boy's odyssey. On board the train, he meets three of the other passengers: a know-it-all, a shy boy, and an outgoing girl who sometimes doubts herself. Later, the boy will meet a mysterious hobo and the engineers running the train. The conductor is always around, occasionally seeming more officious than helpful. And the journey sometimes turns into more of a roller coaster than a simple train ride.

There's no question that *The Polar Express* is destined to become a Christmas cinematic classic. Fortunately, DVDs do not wear out, or else some parents would find themselves having to buy multiple copies over the years. It has been a long time since there has been a family holiday movie that is this strong and endearing. *How the Grinch Stole Christmas* pales in comparison, and nothing recent comes close.

HIGHLY RECOMMENDED

The Prince of Egypt [1998]

Featuring the voices of: Val Kilmer, Ralph Fiennes, Sandra Bullock, Jeff Goldblum, Michelle Pfeiffer Directors: Brenda Chapman, Steve Hickner, Simon Wells Screenplay: Philip LaZebnik Running Time: 1:39 Rated: PG (Slavery) Theatrical Aspect Ratio: 1.85:1

The subject matter of *The Prince of Egypt* is fairly sophisticated for animated fare (witness the PG rating). In keeping with Exodus, the mistreatment of the Hebrew slaves is depicted (albeit not graphically), as is the mass slaughter of Egyptian firstborns that leads to the Pharaoh's freeing of the slaves. And, as if the story wasn't grim enough to begin with, the screenwriters invented a friendship between Ramses and Moses to elevate certain aspects of *The Prince of Egypt* to the level of a Shakespearean tragedy. At times, Moses is depicted as a brooding, Hamlet-like hero.

The Prince of Egypt neither skims over nor dwells upon the least happy elements of the story. Overall, it's a story of triumph and adventure — of oppression ended and freedom begun. The comedy elements that have become an integral part of animated features are downplayed. The Pharaoh's two chief priests are sly and fatuous, and some of their antics are amusing, but they offer little more than occasional, momentary comic relief. For the most part, *The Prince of Egypt* plays it straight.

The animation in *The Prince of Egypt* is truly top-notch. The artists effectively mix hand-drawn and computer-generated images to good effect, the colors are rich and vibrant, and the characters' lip movements are in synch with the soundtrack. The final product is polished, with a number of standout sequences (the chariot race, the plagues, and the parting of the Red Sea).

As far as vocal talents are concerned, the film makers have gathered an impressive cast, with even the minor characters being voiced by recognizable names. The plum roles of Moses and Ramses, the leader of the captive Hebrews and the King of Egypt, belong to Val Kilmer and Ralph Fiennes, respectively. Michelle Pfeiffer supplies the voice of Moses' wife, Zipporah; Sandra Bullock is his sister, the prophetess Miriam; Jeff Goldblum is his brother, Aaron; and Danny Glover is his father-in-law, Jethro. Other voices include Patrick Stewart and Helen Mirren as Ramses' parents, and the team of Martin Short and Steve Martin as the foolish Egyptian priests.

Jeffrey Katzenberg has gone out of his way to emphasize that *The Prince of Egypt* is not a religious movie, despite the nature of the source material. This is not intended to be a big budget Bible Story cartoon, but a rousing animated adventure. Consequently, this movie is worth a trip to the local multiplex by viewers of all ages, races, and religious persuasions. **HIGHLY RECOMMENDED**

Princess Mononoke [Japan/United States, 1999]

Featuring the voices of: Billy Crudup, Claire Danes, Gillian Anderson, Minnie Driver, Billy Bob Thornton Director: Hayao Miyazaki
Screenplay: Hayao Miyazaki, Neil Gaiman (English version) Running Time: 2:13 Rated: PG-13 (Violence) Theatrical Aspect Ratio: 1.85:1

The director of *Princess Mononoke* is something of a living legend: Hayao Miyazaki, whom Roger Ebert called "a [Japanese] national treasure." Fans of anime uniformly praise his work, stating with enthusiasm that it puts even Disney's best to shame. There's such attention to detail that it's easy to lose oneself in the animation. Perhaps the best way to put it is that Miyazaki's films have a texture that is absent from even some of the most technically adept animated motion pictures.

Princess Mononoke has been "Americanized" by Miramax. No content has changed and no scenes have been cut, but familiar English-speaking actors (Billy Crudup, Gillian Anderson, Billy Bob Thornton, Claire Danes, Minnie Driver) have been brought in to record a new soundtrack. That means no subtitles, and, because dubbing isn't a major problem with animation, there's no obvious mismatch between lip movements and words.

The film, which takes place in ancient Japan at the dawn of the Age of Iron, is loosely based on Japanese mythology and is fundamentally about the eternal conflict between man and nature (as such, there's actually a conservationist message). When the story begins, a Curse God is approaching a small village in Northeast Japan, destroying everything in its path. Ashitaka (Billy Crudup) rides out to stop it. However, while he succeeds in killing the creature, its touch afflicts him with a curse that will eventually kill him. The village wise woman tells Ashitaka that his only hope for survival is to travel West and find the Forest Spirit, who may deign to cure him. So, alone with his faithful mount, Ashitaka begins a long and perilous trek.

Eventually, Ashitaka comes to Irontown, a remote human settlement populated by society's outcasts and ruled by the Lady Eboshi (Minnie Driver). Irontown is under siege from samurai and is also waging a war with the Boar Gods and other Gods of the Mountains. During an attack by the Wolf God, Moro (Gillian Anderson), her two sons, and her human "daughter," San (aka "Princess Mononoke," voiced by Claire Danes), Ashitaka saves two men, and, as a result, is welcomed into Irontown by Eboshi. And, from that point, the story only grows more complex.

Is *Princess Mononoke* suitable for children? Probably not for the very young — the complexity of the story may confound them. (The violence isn't much of an issue, since it's not a great deal more intense than what kids see during some Saturday morning cartoons.) However, older boys and girls will be caught up in the film's adventure and impressed by its animation, although they will likely miss some of the plot's many subtleties. With a running length of nearly 2:15, this epic picture opens a vast world of romance, fantasy, and excitement that is unlike anything to emerge from a Western studio. **HIGHLY RECOMMENDED**

Shark Tale [2004]

Featuring the voices of: Will Smith, Robert De Niro, Renée Zellweger, Jack Black, Angelena Jolie, Martin Scorsese Directors: Bibo Bergeron, Vicky Jenson, Rob Letterman Screenplay: Rob Letterman, Damian Shannon, Mark Swift, Michael J. Wilson Running Time: 1:30 Rated: PG (Mild profanity) Theatrical Aspect Ratio: 1.85:1

The Mafia shark family consists of Don Lino (voice of Robert De Niro) and his sons, Frankie (Michael Imperioli) and Lenny (Jack Black). Frankie has inherited his father's love of violence, but Lenny is a sweetheart — and a vegetarian, to boot. Enter Oscar the wrasse (Will Smith), a worker at the Whale Wash, which is owned by the puffer fish Sykes (Martin Scorsese). After wandering into shark territory, Oscar has to flee from an enraged Frankie. An accident results in Frankie's death, but Oscar takes the credit and is redubbed by the fish community as "the Shark Slayer." As Oscar's popularity skyrockets, two female fish vie for his affections: the sexy Lola (Angelina Jolie), and the steady Angie (Renée Zellweger), who has swum by his side for years.

The best material in *Shark Tale* involves Don Lino and Sykes. The De Niro/Scorsese dialogue will be most amusing to adults since they'll get the sly references. They will also recognize the significance of the mole on Don Lino's face and Sykes's bushy eyebrows. Will Smith is perhaps a little too high energy as Oscar. Listening to him do his shtick is a little exhausting. I kept reflecting about how much better Eddie Murphy was in *Shrek* precisely because he was in a secondary part. Had Lenny been elevated to the main character with Oscar playing the wisecracking sidekick, things might have been more relaxed. (Even though Jack Black is known for being manic, Lenny is surprisingly mellow, despite his neuroses.)

When it comes to the new genre of digitally

animated films, *Shark Tale* falls around the middle (still an enviable place to be, considering the high quality of most of the entrees). It's not as good as *Shrek*, the *Toy Story* movies, or *Finding Nemo*, but it's better than *Ice Age* and *Shrek 2*. I would place it on about the same level as *Monsters Inc.* The key thing to note is that *Shark Tale* represents solid family entertainment and will find a special place in the hearts of those who adore the *Godfather* movies and the TV series *The Sopranos*. **RECOMMENDED**

Shrek [2001]

Featuring the voices of: Mike Myers, Eddie Murphy, Cameron Diaz, John Lithgow Directors: Andrew Adamson, Vicky Jenson Screenplay: Ted Eliot, Terry Rossio Running Time: 1:27 Rated: PG (Mild violence) Theatrical Aspect Ratio: 1.85:1

Dreamworks Pictures' wonderful, whimsical *Shrek* proves to be the latest family film to live up to its billing. With its blend of high adventure, light romance, and double-layered dialogue (which will take on a slightly different meaning for the under-and over-12 crowd), *Shrek* is capable of enthralling both children and their parents. In fact, this movie is so good that adults unaccompanied by offspring can venture into a theater without having to dress up in a disguise. *Shrek* is not a *guilty* pleasure for sophisticated movie-goers; it is, purely and simply, a *pleasure*.

Our protagonist is an ogre named Shrek (voice of Mike Myers, using a Scottish accent). Except for scaring off the odd knight who comes in search of his hide-out, Shrek leads a relatively peaceful life, until the day that he stumbles into Donkey (voice of Eddie Murphy). Donkey is fleeing soldiers who are rounding up all the fairy tale creatures with the intent of resettling them. Unfortunately for Shrek, the local landholder, Lord Farquaad (John Lithgow), has decided to deport them to Shrek's swamp. This causes the irritated ogre, accompanied by his new best friend, Donkey, to head for the city of Duloc, where Farquaad holds court. There, he makes a deal with the noble — in return for getting back his swamp, Shrek will perform a quest and rescue Princess Fiona (Cameron Diaz) from the tower where she is held prisoner. The catch: she's guarded by a fire-breathing dragon. Farquaad wants Fiona for his wife (he chose her over Cinderella and Snow White), and figures that the ogre might be his best chance to rescue her. But what he doesn't count on, and what Shrek doesn't expect, is that the beauty and the beast will develop feelings for each other.

The interplay between Shrek and Princess Fiona is sweet and tender, while the exchanges between the ogre and the ass are often barbed and subversively funny. Like *The Princess Bride*, *Shrek* breaks with convention, but not so far that viewers will be put off by it. And, while there is a happy ending (as there must be in any fairy tale, no matter how unconventional), it's not necessarily the conclusion that many people will be expecting (at least up until the 2/3 point, when the movie reveals its hand). First-time co-directors Andrew Adamson and Vicky Jenson have crafted a movie to be proud of, and one that will hopefully receive a lot of attention, even during the crowded summer season. *Shrek* is easily one of the genre's most magical experiences. **HIGHLY RECOMMENDED**

Shrek 2 [2004]

Featuring the voices of: Mike Myers, Eddie Murphy, Cameron Diaz, Julie Andrews, Antonio Banderas, John Cleese, Rupert Everett, Jennifer Saunders Director: Andrew Adamson Screenplay: William Steig, J. David Stern, Joe Stillman, David N. Weiss Running Time: 1:35 Rated: PG Theatrical Aspect Ratio: 1.85:1

A certain amount of credit must be given to the film-making team behind *Shrek 2* for overcoming a seemingly insurmountable obstacle and producing an entertaining motion picture. That obstacle is the ending of the original *Shrek*, which neatly wrapped up every conceivable aspect of the story, leaving little room for a sequel. Originally, *Shrek* had been designed as a one-off movie, but when it became a huge hit, DreamWorks decided that a second installment was warranted. However, with Shrek and Princess Fiona married and living happily ever after as ogres, some creative brainstorming had to be done to arrive at a sequel-worthy concept.

To be fair, *Shrek 2* doesn't have much of a story line. It's basically about the meeting between newlyweds Shrek (voice of Mike Myers) and Princess Fiona (Cameron Diaz) and the bride's parents, King Harold (John Cleese) and Queen Lillian (Juilie Andrews). To facilitate this encounter, Shrek, Fiona, and Donkey (Eddie Murphy) must travel to the kingdom of Far, Far Away. The grotesque appearance of the happy couple isn't to the liking of the ruling family or to study Prince Charming (Rupert Everett), who wants Fiona for his wife. With a little help from his mom, the Fairy Godmother (Jennifer Saunders), and a killer cat named Puss 'n Boots (Antonio Banderas), Charming seeks to win Fiona away from Shrek.

Although there isn't much in the way of a plot, *Shrek 2* is populated with clever and amusing sequences, parodies, and pop references. The dialogue includes plenty of double entendres and secondary meanings. The music is laced with contemporary tunes: Donkey croons (in his own inimitable fashion) the theme to *Rawhide,* and the whole cast joins in on "Livin' La Vida Loca." And what would a DreamWorks animated film be without a few knocks at Disney? It's these things, not the unimaginative story line, that give *Shrek 2* its energy and freshness.

The animation is on the same level as that of *Shrek,* which was, in its own time, groundbreaking. There haven't been many advances in computer animation since then, but *Shrek 2* hasn't done any backsliding. The film looks as bright and imaginative as its predecessor. The nonhumans are surprisingly lifelike, while the humans still retain the slightly awkward look of something designed on a computer. There are a lot of background jokes; I have a feeling that it will take multiple viewings to uncover some of the more subtle ones. As in the first film, it's clear that the *Shrek* animators had fun putting everything together.

With its appealing blend of animated comedy, romance, and adventure, *Shrek 2* follows the formula of its predecessor while maintaining enough originality not to come across as a direct copy. Fans of the first movie will be pleased. Although *Shrek 2* isn't as breezy as *Shrek,* it's a respectable effort and a solid example of family-friendly entertainment. **RECOMMENDED**

South Park: Bigger, Longer and Uncut [1999]

Featuring the voices of: Trey Parker and Matt Stone Director: Trey Parker Screenplay: Trey Parker & Matt Stone, Pam Brady Running Time: 1:22 Rated: R (Extreme profanity, cartoon nudity) Theatrical Aspect Ratio: 1.85:1

South Park is consistently rude, crude, and profane, with more than 200 obscenities being uttered in less than 90 minutes. The "R" rating is well deserved. But this production isn't all toilet humor, obscenities, and flatulence jokes. As is true of the TV series, there's a lot of subversive material to be found herein — satirical thrusts struck against a diverse array of opponents. Those include (but are not limited to) the MPAA and its ratings system, small town America, middle class "family values," traditional Judeo-Christian religious icons, Canada, wars, the Baldwin brothers, Bill Clinton, Bill Gates, and USO shows. In fact, it's hard to find a target that *South Park* doesn't savage in one way or another. And, while there aren't more than a handful of gut-busting, laugh-aloud moments, there is enough sly, slick humor to keep the average viewer chuckling throughout.

There is a plot, although the specifics of it don't much matter. Things get started when the 4 intrepid South Park heroes — Stan (Trey Parker), Cartman (Parker), Kyle (Matt Stone), and Kenny (Stone) — sneak into an R-rated movie to see a couple of Canadian stars singing profane songs and telling dirty jokes. The film makes such an impression on the youths that they can't stop swearing. Soon, everyone in school has seen the movie, and the classrooms have turned into hot beds of creative cursing. Canada gets the blame for this (after all, the movie was produced north of the border) and conservative organizations press President Clinton to declare war. Meanwhile, Kenny, who died after lighting fire to himself, is spending some time in Hell getting to know Satan and his gay companion, Saddam Hussein. When Kenny learns that the war between the U.S. and Canada could trigger the apocalypse, he decides to make a ghostly appearance to warn his former friends.

It will come as no surprise to fans of the show that *South Park* co-creators Trey Parker and Matt Stone are at the reins. Their trademark attacks on pop culture are much in evidence. *South Park* aficionados will doubtlessly be enthralled by the final product. Those who are new to the cartoon are advised to keep an open mind, and, since this is raw, ribald material, anyone who is easily offended should stay away. In the final analysis, *South Park* is an agreeable, albeit uneven, experience. **RECOMMENDED**

Spirit: Stallion of the Cimarron [2002]

Featuring the voices of: Matt Damon, James Cromwell, Daniel Studi Directors: Kelly Asbury, Lorna Cook Screenplay: John Fusco Running Time: 1:21 Rated: G Theatrical Aspect Ratio: 2.35:1

Spirit: Stallion of the Cimarron is a classic "kids' movie" — not a "family movie," as most recent animated movies have been described, but a "kids' movie." Frankly, aside from some gorgeous artwork, there's nothing in this movie to interest a viewer over the age of about 10. Dreamworks does try some interesting things with this movie. To begin with, it's a Western — a genre that has all but gone to Boot Hill. In the second place, the filmmakers have decided not to allow the animals to talk — a big plus as far as I'm concerned, albeit a risky proposition. I don't think it would have worked if the horses had engaged in deep conversations with each other.

"They say that the history of the West was told from the saddle of the horse. But it's never been told from the heart of one before." With those words from the narrator (Matt Damon), *Spirit* opens with the birth of the title character, a mustang colt who grows into a mighty stallion. As an adult, Sprit finds his world threatened by the arrival of the White Man to the frontier. After a wild chase, a group of these interlopers capture the horse by throwing nooses around his neck. For a while, Spirit is penned inside a fort under the watchful eye of an army colonel who is determined to break him. But luck intervenes and Sprit escapes from the cavalry — only to be caught by Indians. But his treatment at their hands is more kind, and he learns that all human beings are not interested in subjugation. Also, during his time with the Indians, he meets the mare of his dreams.

The storyline for *Spirit* is infused with the kind of reverse approach to Westerns that has been in favor since *Dances with Wolves*. The Indians are the good guys; the cowboys and soldiers are the villains. *Spirit*'s twin morals of tolerance and harmony with nature are simplistic and unsubtle (as one would expect from a children's feature). An area in which *Spirit* excels is its animation. Easily the equal of anything to come out of Disney's studios in the past decade, *Spirit*'s artwork is virtually without flaw. Since the horses do not talk, the task falls to the animators to have the animals communicate and convey emotion through actions. As a result, there's a distinctly "human quality" to the horses' facial expressions.

Those for whom *Spirit* was made will find this to be a thoroughly enjoyable production. As a "kids' movie," *Spirit* is a resounding success. **RECOMMENDED**

Spirited Away [Japan/United States, 2002]

Featuring the voices of: Daveigh Chase, Jason Marsden, Suzanne Pleshette, Michael Chiklis, Susan Egan Director: Hayao Miyazaki Screenplay: Hayao Miyazaki Running Time: 2:04 Rated: PG (Scary moments) Theatrical Aspect Ratio: 1.85:1

Spirited Away takes influences from *Alice in Wonderland* and *The Wizard of Oz* and uses them to fashion a highly original story about a 10-year-old girl, Chihiro (voiced by Daveigh Chase), who, along with her parents, ventures through a tunnel that leads to the world of spirits. After a witch, Yubaba (Suzanne Pleshette), turns Mom and Dad into pigs, Chihiro must find a niche in the spirit world, where humans are not well thought-of, and figure out a way to convince Yubaba to change her parents back into humans and send them all home. With help from Haku (Jason Marsden), Yubaba's boy apprentice, and Lin (Susan Egan), a "big sister" type, Chihiro gets a job at Yubaba's bathhouse for spirits, and there her quest to aid her family begins.

But, as complications arise, she finds additional tasks to perform and other allies willing to help her.

The nature of the story is tailor-made for animation. Many of the characters engage in shape-shifting (boys become dragons, adults become pigs, a giant baby becomes a bloated mouse) and the bathhouse is frequented by a variety of strange and unusual creatures. While a few of the inhabitants of the sprit world look human, most appear to be anything but that. Take the boiler operator Kamaji (David Ogden Stiers), for example. At first glance, he's just a cranky old man with a frizzy beard. Then we notice that he has 8 legs and walks like a spider. We also find out that he's not as intimidating as he looks. His initially surly disposition melts away and he becomes of one Chihiro's numerous friends.

Miyazaki is an environmentalist, and his films often contain strong pro-environment messages. (This was a cornerstone to *Princess Mononoke*.) The film's animation is stunning, with richly-detailed backgrounds and flawless foregrounds. Unlike many animators, Miyazaki still relies almost exclusively upon hand-drawn artwork and his meticulous care shows.

Miyazaki does not dumb down *Spirited Away*, even though his stated target audience is children. This is a true family film, in that adults will be as enchanted by the characters and situations as children will. The pace is a little slower than the average animated film — there is not as much frantic action — but not so languid that younger viewers will become restless. The dubbing into English is very good, so there is no subtitle barrier. Miyazaki has provided another triumph, and, in the midst of the quality fall-off of Disney's in-house animated projects, a reason for animation-lovers to rejoice. **HIGHLY RECOMMENDED**

Tarzan [1999]

Featuring the voices of: Tony Goldwyn, Minnie Driver, Glenn Close, Lance Henriksen, Rosie O'Donnell, Brian Blessed Directors: Chris Buck, Kevin Lima Screenplay: Tab Murphy Running Time: 1:30 Rated: G Theatrical Aspect Ratio: 1.85:1

One thing viewers should never reasonably expect from an animated movie is faithfulness to the source material. Adult themes and unhappy endings rarely make it into a Disney movie. So those expecting *Tarzan* to be a faithful recreation of the Edgar Rice Burroughs classic would do best to alter their expectations.

The movie opens on a high note, as Tarzan's mother and father, along with their baby boy, escape a burning shipwreck. They make it to shore, erect a treehouse, and start a life in Africa. Shortly thereafter, however, the two adults fall victim to a wild animal and the baby is adopted by a female gorilla. As he grows, Tarzan becomes an accepted member of the family, but he wonders why he looks different from everyone else. His questions — at least some of them — are answered with the arrival of Jane Porter, her father, and their guide, Clayton, to the jungle. Tarzan is surprised to find others like him, and, after he saves Jane from a band of angry baboons, he finds himself inexplicably drawn to her, and she to him.

From a purely visual standpoint, this may be the most impressive of all of Disney's traditionally animated features. The backdrops are lush, the characters are well realized, and the action sequences are dizzying, with frequent changes of perspectives and camera angles. No conventional animated film has been this ambitious before. Once again, Disney has made a series of wise decisions concerning vocal characterizations. Tarzan is voiced by Tony Goldwyn, who gives the hero a sort of ordinary voice. Minnie Driver's Jane is considerably more independent than the Rice Burroughs version, but she is allowed to keep her British accent. Nigel Hawthorne is Jane's father, Brian Blessed is the nefarious Clayton, Glenn Close is Tarzan's adopted mother, and Lance Henriksen is Kerchak, the fearsome leader of the gorillas.

One potential problem with *Tarzan* is the lack of a strong, central villain. Although Clayton eventually fulfills the bad guy role, he really doesn't assume the position until just before the anticlimactic final battle. Even then, he's not very frightening.

Through the years, Tarzan has proven to be an extraordinarily popular character with movie audiences. This new animated effort is sure to be a huge hit with children, and, while adults will find much to enjoy about the film, few will see this as the definitive screen version of the Edgar Rice Burroughs classic, and even fewer will herald this as one of Disney's greatest achievements. **RECOMMENDED**

Thumbelina [1994]

Featuring the voices of: Jodi Benson, Gary Imhoff, John Hurt, Carol Channing, Barbara Cooke, Gilbert Gottfried Directors: Don Bluth and Gary Goldman Screenplay: Don Bluth Running Time: 1:26 Rated: G Theatrical Aspect Ratio: **1.85:1**

As her name indicates, Thumbelina (voice of Jodi Benson) is about the size of a finger. She lives a generally happy day-to-day life with her human mother and several animal friends, but something is missing —

until she meets Cornelius (voice of Gary Imhoff), the Fairy Prince. One day, while out riding his bumblebee, Cornelius overhears Thumbelina singing. Circumstances bring the two together, and they are instantly smitten with each other. But, before Cornelius can propose marriage, Thumbelina is stolen away by a gruesome toad who also wants her for his wife.

The animation is crisp and visually striking, with careful attention paid to details. Thumbelina is perhaps not as completely-realized as Arielle, Belle, or Jasmine, but she's far better drawn than the women populating all the fringe big-screen cartoons. The same can be said of the other characters, most of whom are animals, and none of which embarrass their creators.

The storyline of *Thumbelina*, adapted from the popular Hans Christian Andersen fable, is relatively uncomplicated, and makes excellent material for an animated romance/adventure. There are several occasions when the plot seems rushed, especially towards the end. While children most likely won't notice this, adults will, although it shouldn't detract much from anyone's enjoyment of the film.

Entertainment comes in many forms, and *Thumbelina* is among the frothiest available. But the best thing is that not only is it fun — an eminently watchable — but it's a perfect "family film," capable of pleasing both children and their parents. With the exception of Disney fare, this has become an increasingly-rare commodity, and when an opportunity such as this occurs, it should be taken advantage of. **RECOMMENDED**

Titan A.E. [2000]

Featuring the voices of: Matt Damon, Drew Barrymore, Bill Pullman, Nathan Lane, Tone Loc Directors: Don Bluth, Gary Goldman Screenplay: Ben Edlund and John August and Joss Whedon Running Time: **1:34** Rated: PG (Violence, mild sensuality) Theatrical Aspect Ratio: **2.35:1**

Titan A.E. represents an ambitious attempt by co-directors Don Bluth and Gary Goldman to fuse traditional animated techniques with the latest in computer graphics, and to present it all through a plot that owes more to Japanese anime than to classic Disney.

The year is 3028, and Earth has been destroyed by the merciless attack of an alien race known as the Drej. There are survivors, although the ragtag bunch of humans is scattered to the far corners of the quadrant, and the Drej, bent on genocide, pursue them doggedly and seemingly without reason. For humanity, there is hope, however, in the form of a giant spaceship called *Titan*, which was successfully launched before the planet's destruction. But it is lost in deep space and only Cale, the young son of the *Titan*'s captain, possesses information about its location.

In 3042, Cale (voice of Matt Damon) is a young man living an aimless life on Salvage Station Tau 14. It is there that Captain Korso (Bill Pullman), an old friend of Cale's father, finds him. Korso has assembled a motley crew that includes a beautiful navigator, Akima (Drew Barrymore); an indolent first officer, Preed (Nathan Lane); a short-tempered weapons expert, Stith (Janeane Garafolo); and a brilliant-but-erratic scientist, Gune (John Leguizamo). Together, they have one goal: find the *Titan,* and they need Cale's help to do it. Although initially reluctant to join Korso's quest, Cale has a change of heart when he learns that the Drej are out to get him because they, like Korso, need the information he is in possession of.

Titan A.E. is action-oriented, with a number of high octane space chases and battles. The standout sequence occurs during the closing half-hour, when two ships are playing hide-and-seek in a field of giant, collapsing ice crystals. Not only are the visuals stunning, but there's a human element as well, because, by this point, we have come to care about the characters, so the sense of danger is genuine. Some of Bluth and Goldman's backgrounds are as impressive as the computer-generated foregrounds, featuring arrays of deep colors and brilliant detail. Despite technique mismatches, *Titan A.E.* is still a nice piece of visual candy.

Animation, especially of the non-Disney variety, is gradually moving in a more adult direction. *Titan A.E.* slides a little further down this slope, offering non-cute violence and blood. Such "innovations" may only be baby steps in the direction of *Heavy Metal* and countless Japanese features, but the payoff is evident: more challenging stories with interesting characters. **RECOMMENDED**

Toy Story [1995]

Featuring the voices of: Tom Hanks, Tim Allen Director: John Lasseter
Screenplay: Joss Whedon, Andrew Stanton, Joel Cohen & Alec
Sokolow Running Time: 1:21 Rated: G Theatrical Aspect Ratio: 1.85:1

Ever wonder how toys seem to get from one place to another with no human help? *Toy Story,* Disney's first feature-length foray into computer animation, postulates that they do it themselves. Toys have their own magical world which comes to life any time the lights are out or people aren't around. Any who doubt this should take a look at *Toy Story.* You'll never again feel quite the same way about Mr. Potato Head, Monkeys in a Barrel, or Slinkies.

Of course, the visual aspect is the centerpiece of *Toy Story.* The computer-generated effects are a marvel. Rich in unexpected detail (the grain of a wood floor, fingerprints and chipped paint on a door, reflections in polished surfaces, and so on . . .), this colorful and brilliantly-rendered aspect of the film would alone be worth the price of admission. It's something of a bonus that the characters, dialogue, and story provide entertainment value of their own.

Toy Story is a buddy movie/adventure tale with an understated lesson about the value of friendship. Parents might also be able to use some of what transpires to encourage their offspring to put away toys after playtime. While the screenplay isn't a marvel of originality, it is capable of holding the attention — light, undemanding fun that never gets too immature or syrupy. There's also quite a bit of intelligent wit that will go above the heads of younger viewers — that stuff's for Mom and Dad.

The two main characters are toys: cowboy Woody (voice of Tom Hanks), the old-time favorite, and space ranger Buzz Lightyear (voice of Tim Allen), the battery-operated newcomer. *Toy Story* opens with Buzz's arrival. Woody is upset that this high-tech neophyte has usurped his rightful place on the bedspread and in his 6-year-old owner's play time. The disgruntled cowboy comes up with a plan to eliminate Buzz, but it backfires, and soon the two rivals are out in the real world, forced to help each other in their struggle to escape the clutches of a toy-torturing juvenile delinquent.

How does *Toy Story* compare to Disney's more conventional animated features? They're really very different types of productions. This film is less artistic and more technologically impressive. Despite a few Randy Newman songs, it's not really a musical. Of course, the target audience is the same, and everything from Disney embraces "family values," but it's difficult — and unfair — to make an effective contrast of the two film making styles. **HIGHLY RECOMMENDED**

Toy Story 2 [1999]

Featuring the voices of: Tom Hanks, Tim Allen, Joan Cusack, Kelsey
Grammer Directors: John Lasseter, Lee Unkrich, Ash Brannon
Screenplay: Andrew Stanton, Rita Hsiao, Doug Chamberlin & Chris
Webb Running Time: 1:30 Rated: G Theatrical Aspect Ratio: 1.85:1

One would have to be a hopeless curmudgeon not to be entertained by *Toy Story 2*'s remarkable visual style, quick-moving storyline, endearing characters, and witty dialogue. The balance between what has been included for kids and what's there for adults is almost perfect. There are things that children will appreciate more than their parents, but other elements will go over the heads of shorter viewers. However, the majority of what *Toy Story 2* offers will delight everyone in the audience, regardless of their physical or mental age.

This film begins an unspecified time following the happily-ever-after conclusion to *Toy Story*. In the aftermath of their earlier adventures, Buzz (voice of Tim Allen) and Woody (voice of Tom Hanks) are now fast friends. One day, Andy's mother decides to have a yard sale, and she collects a few old toys from her son's room. Since one of these discards is a member of the moving toy gang, Woody goes to the rescue, leaving the safety of the house for the uncertainty of the front lawn in order to bring the toy back. Although his mission is successful, he is placed in a serious predicament when a toy collector named Al (voice of Wayne Knight) spies Woody while hunting through the wares available at the sale. The cowboy toy represents the final collectible needed to complete his collection of merchandise from the old TV series, "Woody's Roundup." If he can acquire Woody, Al can ship everything to a toy museum in Japan for a huge profit. So, after Andy's mother refuses to sell the wooden cowboy, Al steals him, and it's up to the other toys, led by Buzz, to go into the city to save their friend.

With all the elements working in perfect concert, *Toy Story 2* is a lot of fun. Viewers can expect a healthy dose of fast-moving action and broadly amusing comedy. And, although the primary thrust of the narrative is not drama, there is a moment of surprisingly affecting pathos where Jessie contemplates the pain of being outgrown by her child. It's a testimony to the skill of directors John Lasseter (who went solo on the original *Toy Story*), Lee Unkrich, and Ash Brannon that we develop such a strong bond with a group of computer generated toys. And, while *Toy Story 2* isn't quite the achievement that its predecessor represented, it is nevertheless a top example of family entertainment. **HIGHLY RECOMMENDED**

Treasure Planet [2002]

Featuring the voices of: Joseph Gordon-Levitt, Brian Murray, David Hyde Pierce, Emma Thompson Directors: Ron Clements, John Musker Screenplay: Kaan Kalyoun, Mark Kennedy, Sam Levine, Donnie Long, Frank Nissen Running Time: 1:35 Rated: PG (Mild violence, scary moments) Theatrical Aspect Ratio: 1.85:1

Treasure Planet is Disney's science fiction-style reimagining of Robert Louis Stevenson's *Treasure Island*. The film uses a fair amount of computer-generated imagery to enhance the hand-drawn visuals and, to a layman like myself, the result is stunning. *Treasure Planet* is rich and colorful, with vivid foregrounds and richly detailed backgrounds. There are a number of standout action scenes and one bravura sequence in which the camera zooms in on a spaceport, starting from far away, then gradually moving closer, until we're in the midst of the bustling streets.

Needless to say, the story is a variation on *Treasure Island*, using many of the same characters and situations. When teenager Jim Hawkins (voice of Joseph Gordon-Levitt) comes into possession of a map that purports to show the location of the legendary "Treasure Planet," where the dreaded pirate Flint hid his stash, his mother's friend, Dr. Doppler (David Hyde Pierce), decides to fund an expedition. Doppler hires a stern captain, Amelia (Emma Thompson), to guide the ship, and a crew that seems comprised primarily of cutthroats — especially the Master of the Galley, John Silver (Brian Murray). Amelia is distrustful of the men on the ship, calling them "a ludicrous parcel of galloping galoots." Her concerns are not without merit, since Silver is planning a mutiny as soon as the ship reaches Treasure Planet.

With the exception of Jim and his mother, none of the characters in *Treasure Planet* are human. Silver is a cyborg, Dr. Doppler has canine features, Amelia appears to be descended from cats that walk upright, and the crew is comprised of all manner of beasts. There's even an arachnid. In the sidekick category, Jim ends up accompanied by a small creature called Morph that can change its shape at will and the robot B.E.N., whose missing memory chips have resulted in a bad case of cybernetic dementia.

Treasure Planet is perfectly pleasing animated action/adventure movie that seems better designed and better motivated than many of the Magic Kingdom's recent forays into hand-drawn motion pictures. As family films go, this one offers an engaging and exciting 90 minutes. **RECOMMENDED**

Waking Life [2001]

Cast: Wiley Wiggins Director: Richard Linklater Screenplay: Richard Linklater Running Time: 1:37 Rated: R (Profanity, mature themes) Theatrical Aspect Ratio: 1.85:1

After a short three-year hiatus, filmmaker Richard Linklater has returned to the world of cinema with the offbeat and ambitious *Waking Life*, an animated excursion through the dreams and philosophical musings of the main character. *Waking Life* is clearly an experiment, and, as such, looks and feels much different from anything else recently seen on a movie screen. When he introduced the film at its Sundance 2001 premiere, Linklater posed one question to the audience, and it goes a long way towards setting the stage for *Waking Life*. "How many of you out there are on drugs?" he asked. When a number of hands went up, he added, "Good. This is for you. The rest of you, just bear with me."

Waking Life is animated, but not in tradition of Disney features. Linklater filmed the entire movie in live action, then digitally transferred the images to computers, where his animators went to work. The final result is disjointed and dreamy, with images that are sometimes finely detailed and sometimes almost crude. The backgrounds frequently waver, making it look like all of the action is taking place on board a gently rocking ship. This is all intentional, since every moment of *Waking Life* is meant to be transpiring inside a dream.

The nameless protagonist is played by Wiley Wiggins, who is perhaps reprising his role from an earlier Linklater offering, *Dazed and Confused*. Also making a return appearance are Ethan Hawke and Julie Delpy, picking right up where they left off in *Before Sunrise*. They are present in an interlude, having an intriguing discussion about dream activity and reincarnation. Indeed, *Waking Life* is comprised of a series of philosophical discussions ranging from how language evolved to the role of the media in modern life to free will & quantum mechanics to the meaning of identity. For those who enjoy this kind of rambling, talky motion picture, *Waking Life* offers a full platter. Guest appearances by the likes of director Steven Soderbergh and Speed Levitch (the motor-mouthed protagonist of *The Cruise*) only up the ante. *Waking Life* certainly isn't for everyone, but, in large part because of its fresh approach and its endlessly fascinating discourses, it ends up staying with you long after the jittery animated images have faded from the screen. **HIGHLY RECOMMENDED**

Classics

2001: A Space Odyssey [United Kingdom/United States, 1968]

Starring: Keir Dullea, Gary Lockwood, William Sylvester
Director: Stanley Kubrick Screenplay: Stanley Kubrick & Arthur C. Clarke Running Time: 2:19 Rated: PG (Mild violence, mild profanity) Theatrical Aspect Ratio: 2.35:1

In terms of its approach to the science fiction genre, *2001* stands alone. This is a space-based movie without zooming spaceships, laser shootouts, or explosions. The action, to the degree that there is action, is viewed from a detached perspective. Spacecraft move (relatively) slowly, they do not zip around at the speed of light. The result is a cold, majestic motion picture, a movie that seeks to remind us of the vastness of space and our relatively insignificant place in it. Kubrick's intention with *2001* was not to thrill us with battles and pyrotechnics, but to daunt us with the realization of how much there is that we do not understand. The movie's slowness (and it is slow) not only allows us to absorb the images, music, and atmosphere, but provides the opportunity to think about the implications of what Kubrick is saying. As enjoyable as *Star Wars* is, it does not encourage deep introspection. *2001* demands it.

Many viewers who understand *2001* through the first two hours leave the theater confused because the movie raises new questions during the last reel, when a conventional film would be providing solutions. However, for someone who enjoys the opportunity to ponder a filmmaker's intentions and delve deeply into a movie's subtext, the final act of *2001* is a godsend. As is true of every Kubrick film, the meticulous attention to detail is evident. Working in close concert with co-screenwriter Arthur C. Clarke and other scientific advisors, Kubrick made sure that every aspect of the film conformed to known scientific fact. His vision is eerily accurate, and, even though we have not attained Clarke's prophesied advancements, we are on the same track. Additionally, there isn't a moment in *2001* that seems dated.

2001 needs to be experienced to be appreciated. *2001* does not build bonds between the viewers and the characters or set up a straightforward, linear storyline. Instead, it challenges the audience and inspires wonder. Proponents argue that this is Kubrick's best film; regardless of whether or not that is true, there's no doubting that this movie represents the product of a great director at the height of his powers. Years after its release, *2001* has lost none of the qualities that make it an acknowledged masterwork.
MUST SEE

The Big Sleep [1946]

Starring: Humphrey Bogart, Lauren Bacall, John Ridgely, Martha Vickers, Charles Waldron Director: Howard Hawks Screenplay: William Faulkner & Leigh Brackett & Jules Furthman, based on the novel by Raymond Chandler Running Time: 1:54 Rated: No MPAA Rating (Violence, sexual innuendo) Theatrical Aspect Ratio: 1.33:1

The Big Sleep is credited with having one of the most confusing storylines of any motion picture ever made. The reason that so many people get lost is probably because plot really isn't *The Big Sleep*'s focus. We get so caught up watching Bogart and Bacall — every nuance of their interaction is fascinating — and enjoying the sharp, smart dialogue with all of its double entendres, that it's almost impossible to keep track of what's going on and who's responsible for which murder. The ending is satisfying not because the killer (or, more appropriately, "one of the killers") has been caught, but because Bogart and Bacall are together. *The Big Sleep* is about atmosphere, tone, and, above all, star power.

The Big Sleep opens with private detective Philip Marlowe (Bogart) entering the house of General Sternwood (Charles Waldron), after having been invited for a discussion. Before Marlowe meets the general, he is introduced to his youngest daughter, the flirtatious Carmen (Martha Vickers). Sternwood has a job for Marlowe — he wants the detective to investigate the details of why someone is demanding money from him to cover up one of Carmen's indiscretions, and, once the facts are uncovered, make the blackmailer "go away." On the way out of the house, Marlowe meets the general's other daughter, Vivian (Bacall), who is as alluring as Carmen, but more mature.

From there, the mystery begins, and it doesn't take long to heat up. Shortly, there are two corpses, but those deaths are only the beginning. There are double-crosses, chases, shoot outs, and the undeniable and growing heat between Marlowe and Vivian. In essence, however, *The Big Sleep* is two capers in one. The first, which involves Marlowe's investigation into the blackmail, is concluded by the half-way point. The second, in which the detective looks into a related (but not directly connected) death and disappearance, comprises the movie's second half. Common characters, circumstances, and coincidences bridge the two, but they can (at least to an extent) be decoupled.

The Big Sleep remains one of Hollywood's most intriguing and enduring examples of film noir. It's a movie that every film student should study and every movie lover should watch at least once. Things may not always make sense, but the film's numerous delights completely eclipse its few, small weaknesses. **HIGHLY RECOMMENDED**

Butch Cassidy & the Sundance Kid [1969]

Starring: Paul Newman, Robert Redford, Katharine Ross, Strother Martin Director: George Roy Hill Screenplay: William Goldman
Running Time: 1:50 Rated: PG (Violence, sexual situations) Theatrical Aspect Ratio: 2.35:1

Despite arriving during the era when this kind of movie was beginning a slow but inexorable fall from public favor, *Butch Cassidy and the Sundance Kid* re-

mains one of the best crafted and most beloved of all the Westerns. In addition to launching Robert Redford's career into orbit and polishing Paul Newman's reputation as a leading man, *Butch Cassidy* also solidified screenwriter William Goldman's position in Hollywood.

The primary differentiator between *Butch Cassidy* and the hundreds of other films littering the genre is its lighthearted tone. The movie is jovial without being silly; it retains the sense of adventure that characterizes the Western, but replaces the often somber mood with one that is airy and, at times, almost comedic. To go along with its upbeat tone, it has a little of everything — comedy, action, adventure, drama, romance, and whimsy. It's hard to ask for much more than what this movie delivers.

The film can be loosely divided into three sections: the introduction, the posse chase, and the Bolivia adventures. Each has its own distinct mood. The introduction, when we meet Butch & Sundance and see them in action robbing a train, allows us a leisurely opportunity to get to know the characters. The posse chase, with the two protagonists being pursued by a relentless and seemingly unstoppable group of faceless bounty hunters, is the film's most tense sequence — 30 minutes of close calls culminating in Butch & Sundance's decision to leave the country. The Bolivia segment contains both the most overtly comical and the most dramatic sequences. At one point, the two men rob a bank where their inability to speak Spanish causes communication problems. Later, after Butch & Sundance have gone straight, they are forced into a gunfight with bandits. It is here that Butch, who avoided killing as a bank robber, takes his first life. Then, of course, there's the final shoot-out in San Vincente (the two go out more heroically on screen than they did in real life).

The success of *Butch Cassidy and the Sundance Kid* made it a template for countless later films. Although *Butch Cassidy* wasn't the first movie to pair up a couple of wisecracking best friends in an action/adventure setting, this film became the model of how well that approach could work when done right. It's easy to see a little of Butch and Sundance in nearly every action duo to reach the screens during the last 30 years. And that, more than anything, is a testimony to the lasting influence of one of the most atypical of all the Westerns. **HIGHLY RECOMMENDED**

Casablanca [1942]

Starring: Humphrey Bogart, Ingrid Bergman, Paul Henreid, Claude Rains Director: Michael Curtiz Screenplay: Julius J. Epstein, Philip G. Epstein, and Howard Koch Running Time: 1:42 Rated: No MPAA Rating (Mature themes) Theatrical Aspect Ratio: 1.33:1

It's probably no stretch to say that *Casablanca,* arguably America's best-loved movie, has had more words written about it than any other motion picture. Ultimately, however, while it's fascinating to examine and dissect all that went into the making of *Casablanca,* the greatest pleasure anyone can derive from this movie comes through simply watching it. Aside from some basic knowledge of recent world history, little background is needed to appreciate the strength and power of the film. *Casablanca* accomplishes that which only a truly great film can: enveloping the viewer in the story, forging an unbreakable link with the characters, and only letting go with the end credits.

Just about everyone knows the story, which takes place about a year after the Germans invaded France. Ilsa (Ingrid Bergman) and her husband, Czech freedom fighter Victor Laszlo (Paul Henreid), wander into Rick's Cafe in Casablanca. The two are on the run from the Nazis, and have come to the American-owned nightspot to lie low. But the German-controlled local government, headed by Captain Louis Renault (Claude Rains), is on the move, and Laszlo has to act quickly to get the letters of transit he came for, then escape. Little does Ilsa know that the cafe is run by Rick Blaine (Humphrey Bogart), the one true love of her life. When the two see each other, sparks fly, and memories of an enchanted time in Paris come flooding back.

Bogart and Bergman. When anyone mentions *Casablanca,* these are the two names that come to mind. The actors are both so perfectly cast, and create such a palpable level of romantic tension, that it's impossible to envision anyone else in their parts. Bogart is at his best here as the tough cynic who hides a broken heart beneath a fractured layer of sarcasm. Ilsa's arrival in Casablanca rips open the fissures in Rick's shield, revealing a complex personality that demands Bogart's full range of acting. As Ilsa, Bergman lights up the screen. What man in the audience wouldn't give up everything to run away with her?

Although just about everyone involved with this legendary motion picture has departed this life, the film itself has withstood the test of more than a half-century to rise, like cream, to the top. One can only imagine that, in another 50 years, its position in the hierarchy of all-time greats will be even higher. **MUST SEE**

Chinatown [1974]

Starring: Jack Nicholson, Faye Dunaway, John Huston Director: Roman Polanski Screenplay: Robert Towne Running Time: 2:11 Rated: R (Violence, profanity, sexual situations, brief nudity) Theatrical Aspect Ratio: 2.35:1

Chinatown is unquestionably one of the best films to emerge from the 1970s, a period that has been called the "last great decade of American cinema" by more than one movie critic. The production, which went in front of the cameras without a final script, marks the high-water point in the careers of both lead actor Jack Nicholson and director Roman Polanski.

At first glance, Jake Gittes (Nicholson) seems like the kind of private investigator who would be at home in the pages of a Dashiel Hammett or Raymond Chandler novel. But that's an illusion. As we come to learn, Gittes isn't as thick-skinned as his numerous predecessors. He lives his life by a series of moral precepts that are not always governed by the principle of self-interest. Sure, Gittes can trade one-liners with the best of them, but his heart is bigger, and beats louder, than any of them.

Gittes' latest case starts innocently enough — those are the ones you have to watch out for — when a woman identifying herself as Mrs. Evelyn Mulwray (Diane Ladd) walks into his office and asks him to obtain evidence that her husband, Hollis (Darrell Zwerling), is having an affair. Jake does so, and soon finds that the photographs he has taken of Mr. Mulwray, the L.A. Water Commissioner, and a pretty blonde have been sold to a local paper. Into his office comes the *real* Mrs. Evelyn Mulwray (Faye Dunaway), and Jake knows he's been had. Someone has used him, and now he's determined to get to the bottom of it. Soon, however, his investigation leads to Mulwray's drowned body and Evelyn Mulwray's charming-but-sinister father, Noah Cross (John Huston), whose every word hints at past misdeeds too horrible to consider. Cross, who serves Jake a fish with the head still on for lunch, is clearly a man not to be trifled with. But Jake presses on.

Chinatown requires that the viewer pay attention, not because there are lots of twists, but because the plot is complex and doesn't stop every 10 minutes to bring slower audience members up to speed. Ever since film noir reached Hollywood, the detective has become a type, with film noir being his playground.

It takes a Herculean effort to transform this type into a character and to replace the formula with a story, and *Chinatown*'s success in both of these regards is one of the reasons it is universally viewed as a classic. The movie is a nearly flawless example of movie composition, with close examination revealing how carefully it was put together. For those who take a less studious and more visceral approach to movie viewing, it's also worth noting that *Chinatown* is a superior thriller — one that will keep viewers involved and "in the moment" until the final, mournful scene has come to a conclusion. **MUST SEE**

Citizen Kane [1941]

Starring: Orson Welles, Joseph Cotten, Dorothy Comingore, Agnes Moorehead Director: Orson Welles Screenplay: Herman J. Mankiewicz and Orson Welles Running Time: 1:59 Rated: No MPAA Rating (Mature themes) Theatrical Aspect Ratio: 1.33:1

Citizen Kane has been lauded as the greatest motion picture to come out of America during the black-and-white era (or any era, for that matter). It also represents the pinnacle of Orson Welles' film making career. For, although Welles lived for more than 40 years following the release of *Kane,* he never succeeded in recapturing the brilliance or fulfilling the promise of his first feature.

The movie opens with an unforgettable image of a distant, fog-shrouded castle on a hill. It's a classic gothic shot, and goes a long way towards establishing *Citizen Kane*'s mood. We quickly learn that this place, called Xanadu, is the dwelling of America's Kubla Khan, Charles Foster Kane (Welles), a one-time newspaper magnate who could have become President if not for an ill-advised extramarital affair. Xanadu, in the words of the faux newsreel that gives a brief history of Kane's life, is the "costliest monument of a man to himself." Any resemblance to The Ranch, William Randolph Hearst's real-life San Simeon abode, is *not* coincidental.

Within moments of the film's eerie, visually-stunning opening, Kane is dead, uttering the word "Rosebud" as he hunches over. When a reporter (William Alland) digs into Kane's past to learn the meaning of Rosebud, the mogul's history is unraveled through a series of extended flashbacks that represent the sometimes-overlapping, non-chronological accounts of five eyewitnesses. As the story unfolds, we see Kane, aided by his closest friend, Jedediah Leland (Joseph Cotton), build a nationwide newspaper empire out of one small paper with a circulation of less than 30,000. To do so, he displays equal parts ruth-lessness and generosity. By the time he marries Emily Norton (Ruth Warrick), the President's niece, Kane is one of the most powerful men in America.

Eventually, Kane moves into the political arena, but his bid for the governor's office crashes and burns when his rival, Boss Jim Gettys (Ray Collins), exposes Kane's affair with Susan Alexander (Dorothy Comingore). Following this failure, Kane divorces his first wife, marries Susan, then goes into seclusion in his unfinished palace of Xanadu. As the years pass, he becomes progressively more bitter and less approachable, until Susan, weary of Xanadu's isolation, leaves him. Alone and unloved, Kane awaits the inescapable hand of death.

As a film, *Citizen Kane* is a powerful dramatic tale about the uses and abuses of wealth and power. It's a classic American tragedy about a man of great passion, vision, and greed, who pushes himself until he brings ruins to himself and all around him. There's no denying the debt that the movie industry owes to Welles and his debut feature. Motion picture archives and collections across the world would be poorer without copies of this film, which will forever be recognized as a defining example of American cinema. **MUST SEE**

City Lights [1931]

Starring: Charlie Chaplin, Virginia Cherrill, Harry Myers Director: Charles Chaplin Screenplay: Charles Chaplin Running Time: 1:28 Rated: No MPAA Rating (Nothing offensive) Theatrical Aspect Ratio: 1.33:1

Charlie Chaplin's the Tramp is front and center in *City Lights*. One night when he's out and about town, he prevents a drunk Millionaire (Harry Myers) from drowning himself. The Millionaire, realizing his folly, is grateful, and brings the Tramp home with him, much to the chagrin of the Millionaire's snobbish butler (Allan Garcia). In the morning, when the Millionaire has sobered up, he doesn't remember the Tramp. By nightfall, however, with the drink again in his veins, he greets his friend with warmth and good spirits, while the butler looks on with a pained expression.

Meanwhile, the Tramp has fallen in love with a gentle, blind Flower Girl (Virginia Cherrill). Using his last cent, he buys a flower from her and wears it in the lapel of his natty suit. The next day, flush with money provided by the Millionaire, he purchases her entire stock, then drives her home in his new friend's car. She mistakenly thinks he's a wealthy man, and that impression is re-enforced when he provides her with the money to pay her rent and travel abroad to have an operation to cure her blindness.

City Lights' ending is well known and has justly been described as one of the most perfect conclusions in the history of cinema. The Tramp, recently released from prison, encounters the Flower Girl, who can now see. At first, she doesn't recognize her benefactor, and takes pity on him because he looks poor and down-and-out. But, when she touches his hand, she understands who he is. Title cards are used to convey their sparse dialogue. Yet words would have ruined the moment, which features heartbreaking performances through body language and facial expression from both Chaplin and Cherrill. It is an indelible exchange that is often presented as a clip to illustrate the strength of silent films, but is inexpressibly powerful when shown in the context of the entire movie.

As compelling as *City Lights'* dramatic element is, the film is still primarily a comedy, and features several instances of Chaplin at his best. Indeed, the movie is pieced together like a series of shorts with several common characters. It's an episodic endeavor, with a host of classic comic vignettes. There is a paradoxical aspect to *City Lights*. When recalling its charm and humor, I don't think of it as a "silent film." Instead, it springs to mind as an example of a spry narrative brought to life by wonderful performances and talented direction. Yet the means of *City Lights'* presentation — without talking — is a necessary part of its charm and power. Dialogue can become a crutch. Here, the characters must emote their feelings without voice, and it results in some astounding moments. **MUST SEE**

Dr. Strangelove [United Kingdom, 1964]

Starring: Peter Sellers, George C. Scott, Slim Pickens, Sterling Hayden Director: Stanley Kubrick Screenplay: Stanley Kubrick, Peter George, and Terry Southern Running Time: 1:33 Rated: No MPAA Rating (Mature themes, sexual innuendo) Theatrical Aspect Ratio: 1.33:1 & 1.66:1

Originally, director Stanley Kubrick envisioned Peter Sellers playing 4 unique roles. However, after filming 3 of them (President Merkin Muffley, RAF Group Captain Mandrake, and ex-Nazi scientist Dr. Strangelove), the actor broke his leg and was unable to complete the quartet. In his place, Slim Pickens was signed to portray Major "King" Kong. Other cast members include George C. Scott as General Buck Turgidson, Sterling Hayden as General Jack D. Ripper, and James Earl Jones (in his first film role) as Lieutenant Lothar Zogg.

The film opens with a deranged General Jack D. Ripper (Sterling Hayden) declaring a "Code Red," sealing off his airforce base, and ordering a nuclear attack on Russia. When his assistant, RAF Group Captain Mandrake (Peter Sellers), advises moderation, Ripper replies that he intends to launch a pre-emptive strike to stop a Communist infiltration which is "sapping and impurifying all of our precious bodily fluids."

In Washington D.C., an emergency meeting is called to determine how to react to the crisis. Present are President Merkin Muffley (Sellers), a man whose effete personality is adequately described by his name; General Buck Turgidson (George C. Scott), whose least favorite color is red; Dr. Strangelove, an ex-Nazi scientist who is now head of the United States' weapons development program; Soviet Ambassador de Sadesky (Peter Bull); and the rest of the higher-uppers at the Pentagon.

Meanwhile, aboard the bomber "Leper Colony," we are introduced to the crew that will play a vital role in the events about to transpire. Led by Major "King" Kong (Slim Pickens), an old-fashioned, gung-ho cowboy type (complete with hat and Texas accent), these men are as loyal and anti-Communist as they come.

As a story chronicling the potential countdown to humanity's end in a nuclear fireball, *Dr. Strangelove* is tightly-plotted and well-paced. As a black comedy, wielding a wit sharper than honed steel, the film is unparalleled. Kubrick's picture has so many targets that it's difficult to know where to begin. The genius of *Dr. Strangelove* is that it's possible to laugh — and laugh hard — while still recognizing the intelligence and insight behind the humor. The film is always saying something, and a viewer would have to be deaf and blind not to recognize the targets of the sarcasm. In fact, I'd worry about anyone who takes this movie *too* seriously. That, after all, isn't the kind of person *Dr. Strangelove* is aimed for; it's the kind this film takes aim at. **MUST SEE**

The Godfather [1972]

Starring: Marlon Brando, Al Pacino, James Caan, Robert Duvall Director: Francis Ford Coppola Screenplay: Francis Ford Coppola and Mario Puzo based on the novel by Mario Puzo Running Time: 2:51 Rated: R (Violence, mature themes, language, brief nudity) Theatrical Aspect Ratio: 1.85:1

Rarely can it be said that a film has defined a genre, but never is that more true than in the case of *The Godfather*. Since the release of the 1972 epic, all "gangster movies" have been judged by the standards of this one. If *The Godfather* was only about gun-toting Mafia types, it would never have garnered as many accolades. The characteristic that sets this film apart from so many of its predecessors and successors is its ability to weave the often-disparate layers of story into a cohesive whole. The picture is a series of mini-climaxes, all building to the devastating, definitive conclusion.

The film opens in the study of Don Vito Corleone (Marlon Brando), the Godfather, who is holding court. It is the wedding of his daughter Connie (Talia Shire), and no Sicilian can refuse a request on that day. The family has gathered for the event. Michael (Al Pacino), Don Vito's youngest son and a second world war hero, is back home in the company of a new girlfriend, Kay Adams (Diane Keaton). The two older boys, Sonny (James Caan) and Fredo (John Cazale), are there as well, along with their "adopted" brother, Tom Hagen (Robert Duvall), the don's right-hand man.

With the end of the war, the times are changing, and as much as Don Vito seems in control at the wedding, his power is beginning to erode. His refusal to do business with drug supplier Sollozzo (Al Lettieri) strikes the first sparks of a war that will last for years and cost many lives. Each of the 5 major mob families in New York will be gouged by the bloodshed, and a new order will emerge. Betrayals will take place, and the Corleone family will be shaken to its roots by treachery from both within and without.

We come to *The Godfather* like Kay Adams — outsiders uncertain in our expectations — but it doesn't take long for us to be captivated by this intricate, violent world. The film can be viewed on many levels, with equal satisfaction awaiting those who just want a good story, and those who demand much more. *The Godfather* is long, yes — but it is 170 minutes well-spent. **MUST SEE**

The Godfather Part II [1974]

Starring: Al Pacino, Robert DeNiro, Robert Duvall, Diane Keaton
Director: Francis Ford Coppola Screenplay: Francis Ford Coppola and Mario Puzo based on the novel by Mario Puzo Running Time: 3:20 Rated: R (Violence, mature themes, language) Theatrical Aspect Ratio: 1.85:1

The Godfather Part II is a more ambitious production than the original since it attempts not only to tell a pair of completely disconnected stories, but to do so in parallel. The less time consuming of the two presents the early life of Vito Corleone (played by Robert DeNiro) in Sicily and New York, and shows how he came into power. The other tale picks up approximately a decade after the conclusion of *The Godfather,* and shows the means by which Michael Corleone (Al Pacino), now secure in his position, attempts to expand the family empire into Las Vegas and Cuba.

Michael lives his life and runs his business by two of his father's creeds: "A man who doesn't spend time with his family can never be a real man" and "Keep your friends close, but your enemies closer." There are times, however, when those precepts fail as guiding principles, such as when a betrayal occurs from within the family. Broken trust arising from so intimate a source can be devastating.

For a man constantly battling to keep his family together, a mournful irony of *The Godfather Part II* is that Michael's efforts succeed only in fragmenting it. If the end of the first film was numbing, this one is shattering. The flashback preceding the final scene presents a stark differentiation of how things once were from what they have become.

The traditional elements of the Tragedy introduced in *The Godfather* reach their maturity in *Part II*. Much of the humanity remaining to Michael at the outset is leached from him with each deception and setback. Late scenes with a resentful Fredo (John Cazale) and a bitter Kay (Diane Keaton) emphasize the price for Michael of continuing his father's dominion. His flaw is his imperceptiveness and, as is the case for any hero in a story of this nature, its effects are crippling.

Combined, *The Godfather* and *The Godfather Part II* represent the apex of American movie-making and the ultimate gangster story. Few sequels have expanded upon the original with the faithfulness and detail of this one. Beneath the surface veneer of an ethnic period piece, *The Godfather* is not so much about crime lords as it is about prices paid in the currency of the soul for decisions made and avoided. It is that quality which establishes this saga as timeless. **MUST SEE**

Gone with the Wind [1939]

Starring: Clark Gable, Vivien Leigh, Leslie Howard, Olivia De Havilland
Director: Victor Fleming Screenplay: Sidney Howard based on the novel by Margaret Mitchell Running Time: 3:42 Rated: G Theatrical Aspect Ratio: 1.33:1

Gone with the Wind is, simply put, a tale of two halves. The movie is divided by an intermission into a pair of roughly-equal segments. The first, which is brilliant and consistently captivating, covers the time period of the Civil War, beginning shortly after the election of Abraham Lincoln, and ending during Sherman's march through Atlanta. The post-intermission half, which dishes out the suds, picks up at the end of the Civil War and concludes about 8 years later. This portion of *Gone with the Wind*, while still retaining a degree of appeal and narrative interest, spins its wheels frequently.

Gone with the Wind has one of the best-known storylines of any film, due in large part to the popularity of the source material, Margaret Mitchell's best-selling 1936 book. The main character is Scarlett O'Hara (Vivien Leigh), the spoiled, manipulative daughter of an Irish immigrant plantation owner (Thomas Mitchell). Scarlett is secretly in love with Ashley Wilkes (Leslie Howard), who is about to marry the gentle, demure Melanie Hamilton (Olivia De Havilland). When Scarlett confesses her love to Ashley, he admits his feelings for her, but notes that Melanie will make a much better wife. Immediately after this meeting, Scarlett has her first encounter with the irrepressible Rhett Butler (Clark Gable), the cynical, smart hero who eventually falls in love with her. They are two headstrong likes who simultaneously repel and attract one another.

The bulk of the film follows a romantic quadrangle as it unfolds against the backdrop of war and reconstruction in and around Atlanta and the O'Hara plantation, Tara. Scarlett is in love with Ashley, or thinks she is, but he won't leave his wife. Melanie loves both her husband and Scarlett, who improbably becomes her best friend. Rhett is smitten with Scarlett, and she is clearly interested in him, but the real question is how long it will take for her to recognize the depth of her feelings.

To date, no film has sold more box-office tickets than *Gone with the Wind*. Of course, when the movie was first released, it wasn't just another motion picture — it was a spectacle, an event. Even though the habits of movie-goers have changed over the years, it's easy to see why this film provoked such an outpouring of praise and adulation during its initial release, and why its stature has grown with the passage of decades. *Gone with the Wind* has flaws, but it's still undeniably a classic and a legend. **HIGHLY RECOMMENDED**

It's a *Wonderful Life* [1946]

Starring: James Stewart, Donna Reed, Lionel Barrymore, Thomas Mitchell Director: Frank Capra Screenplay: Frank Capra, Frances Goodrich, Albert Hackett, and Jo Swerling Running Time: 2:09

Rated: No MPAA Rating (Nothing offensive) Theatrical Aspect Ratio: 1.33:1

What is it about this film, an uplifting, sentimental fable about the importance of the individual, that strikes a responsive chord with so many viewers? Some might argue that it has something to do with the season, but I don't buy that reasoning. *It's a Wonderful Life* is just as good in July as in December — the time of the year has little to do with motion picture quality. Rather, I think *It's a Wonderful Life* has earned its legion of followers because it effectively touches upon one basic truth of life that we all would like to believe — that each of us, no matter how apparently insignificant, has the power to make a difference, and that the measure of our humanity has nothing to do with fame or money, but with how we live our life on a day-to-day basis. *It's a Wonderful Life* asks and answers a question that all of us think of at one time or another: "What would this world be like if I had never been born?"

As almost every avid movie-lover knows, *It's a Wonderful Life* tells the story of George Bailey (James Stewart), the unsung, beloved hero of Bedford Falls. As a child, George was selfless, risking his own life (and losing his hearing in one ear) to save his brother from drowning. As an adult, he gave up his dreams of traveling the world and going to college to stay home and manage the Bailey Building and Loan Society after his father passed away. Throughout his life, George lived by a creed that always placed human need above riches, and, as a result, his only wealth was in his friends and family.

The film's villain is a miserly old man named Potter (played with consummate nastiness by movie great Lionel Barrymore), who uses his considerable wealth to bleed the citizens of Bedford Falls dry. The Bailey Building and Loan Society is the only institution in town that he doesn't own, and he's willing to do anything to get his hands on it — lie, cheat, bribe, steal . . . There's no end to the schemes that Potter devises to destroy George. Yet the Baileys always seem to end up on top.

Combine the characters, the story, the message, and the acting, and it's easy to see why *It's a Wonderful Life* isn't just a holiday favorite, but a great movie by almost any standards. There are a few cynics who will disparage this film, but, in a "feel good" genre clogged with imitators and inferior features, *It's a Wonderful Life* stands high above the rest. Whether you view this film in the middle of the summer or at Christmas, Capra's greatest film represents one of the most transcendent and joyful experiences any movie-lover can hope for. **MUST SEE**

King Kong [1933]

Starring: Robert Armstrong, Bruce Cabot, Fay Wray Directors: Merian C. Cooper and Ernest B. Schoedsack Screenplay: James Creelman and Ruth Rose Running Time: 1:45 Rated: No MPAA Rating (Violence) Theatrical Aspect Ratio: **1.33:1**

When released in 1933, *King Kong* was greeted with unprecedented amazement. State-of-the-art visual effects, an entertaining story, and a touching ending combined to bequeath upon this film the coveted label of a "classic." In its era — and, indeed, for decades after — no monster movie (whether made in the United States, Japan, or elsewhere) approached the lofty perch of this one. The title character, the creation of stop-motion effects wizard Willis O'Brien (mentor to Ray Harryhausen), captivated audiences and started a world-wide love affair with a giant ape.

The plot is reasonably straightforward — not a bad thing for a monster movie. A film crew headed by Carl Denham (Robert Armstrong) arrives at the mysterious Skull Island to do some location shooting for a new picture. However, the dark-skinned natives take a liking to Denham's leading lady, Ann Darrow (Fay Wray, in the role that immortalized her scream), and kidnap her as an offering to their god, Kong. Just as the cavalry, led by Denham and a hunky sailor named Jack Driscoll (Bruce Cabot), rushes in to save Ann, Kong — a 25-foot high ape (actually, his size varies throughout the film) — makes his appearance, snatching his prize from the altar and heading off into the jungle. Denham, Driscoll, and a search party set off in pursuit. Various encounters with Kong and a series of prehistoric relics decimate the group. In the meantime, we get to see battles between the giant ape and several dinosaurs. Eventually, Driscoll sneaks Ann away from Kong and, when the beast arrives at the natives' village to retrieve her, Denham uses sleeping gas to capture him.

Weeks later, a live show opens in New York City's Radio City Music Hall, with a chained Kong as the main attraction. He is, as the marquee proclaims, "The Eighth Wonder of the World." Despite Denham's best precautions, Kong breaks free on opening night, grabs Ann, wreaks havoc in the city, then climbs to the top of the Empire State Building. There, high atop New York, in one of cinema's most unforgettable moments, Kong fights a duel to the death with a group of biplanes.

Despite its various deficiencies and occasionally antiquated style, *King Kong* remains not only a milestone of movie-making, but a magical experience. Ultimately, the mystique of the film lies not so much in what it offers today, but what it has contributed during the course of the last 6 decades. Watching *King Kong* reminds us of what movies once were and what they have the potential to be, and that's something that *Jurassic Park* will never be able to do.

HIGHLY RECOMMENDED

Lawrence of Arabia [United Kingdom, 1962]

Starring: Peter O'Toole, Alec Guinness, Anthony Quinn, Jack Hawkins, Omar Sharif Director: David Lean Screenplay: Robert Bolt, based on "The Seven Pillars of Wisdom" by T.E. Lawrence Running Time: 3:37 Rated: PG (Violence, mature themes) Theatrical Aspect Ratio: 2.20:1

Lawrence of Arabia recounts the larger-than-life exploits of T.E. Lawrence (Peter O'Toole), an officer in the British army serving in the Middle East during World War I, who, according to one observer, "was a poet, a scholar, and a mighty warrior. He was also the most shameless exhibitionist since Barnum & Bailey." The film opens in 1935, with a prologue that shows Lawrence's death as a result of a motorcycle accident, followed by his funeral. The time frame then shifts back more than 20 years to Cairo, where Lawrence is about to begin the greatest adventure of his career. His commanding officer orders him to enter the desert and make contact with the Bedouin Prince Feisel (Alec Guiness), who is a British ally in the fight against the Turks. What follows is not only an account of how Lawrence became a pivotal figure in the Arab revolt against the Turks, but of the nearly-Shakespearean rise and fall of his character.

The most compelling aspect of *Lawrence of Arabia* is the way in which it dissects the fluid, often-contradictory personality of the title character. Like many of the best classic "war" movies, this one uses the battles as a backdrop for a character study. The combat sequences in *Lawrence of Arabia* are perfunctory, with few of the details shown. This allows us to focus on the individual at the epicenter of the storm.

As important as the actors are, however, they are often rendered insignificant by the scenery, and by the manner in which the perfectionist Lean and his cinematographer, Freddie Young, chose to shoot it. *Lawrence of Arabia* is littered with majestic, unforgettable shots. There's the famous "mirage scene," where

Ali first approaches Lawrence on horseback, emerging from a shimmering haze on the horizon. There's a transition in which, after Lawrence blows out a match flame, the camera cuts to a blazing sunset. There are images of majestic dunes with camel riders making their way along them, silhouetted against the sky. And there are shots of rock formations that one normally does not associate with the desert. Add to these moments the grandeur of Maurice Jarre's score, and *Lawrence of Arabia* has the power to overwhelm.

For David Lean, widely regarded as one of the masters of epic filmmaking, *Lawrence of Arabia* represented the most ambitious undertaking of a fruitful career. Restored to its full length in 1989, the version available today shows the story as Lean intended it to be seen. **MUST SEE**

My Fair Lady [1964]

Starring: Audrey Hepburn, Rex Harrison, Stanley Holloway
Director: George Cukor Screenplay: Alan Jay Lerner, based on the play "Pygmalion" by George Bernard Shaw Running Time: 2:50 Rated: G
Theatrical Aspect Ratio: 2.35:1

It could easily be argued that *My Fair Lady* is one of the richest and most intelligent romantic comedies ever produced. The dialogue, adapted by Lerner from Shaw's material, is brilliant: a perfect amalgamation of well-honed wit and barbed satire. The verbal jousting between Eliza Doolittle (Audrey Hepburn) and Professor Henry Higgins (Rex Harrison) is a delight, as is that between the various other characters.

The basic storyline concerns Eliza, a poor Cockney from Covent Garden who is transformed into a lady under the tutelage of Higgins. Although at first reluctant, Higgins, intrigued by the challenge of re-making a woman, agrees. He is ruthless in pushing Eliza. In addition to cleaning her up, teaching her how to behave in society, and instructing her about what to wear, he completely re-shapes her language skills. By depriving her of sleep and forcing her to repeat phrases like "The rain in Spain falls mainly in the plain," he hopes to rid her of her ghastly accent. "Think what you're trying to accomplish," he tells her. "Think what you're dealing with. The majesty and grandeur of the English language, it's the greatest possession we have. The noblest thoughts that ever flowed through the hearts of men are contained in its extraordinary, imaginative, and musical mixtures of sounds. And that's what you've set yourself out to conquer Eliza. And conquer it you will."

Few genres of films are as magical as musicals, and few musicals are as intelligent and lively as *My Fair Lady*. It's a classic not because a group of stuffy film experts have labeled it as such, but because it has been, and always will be, a pure joy to experience. It's also one of a very few 3-hour films that justifies the seemingly long running time. Rarely have so many minutes in a theater been passed this enjoyably. **MUST SEE**

Patton [1970]

Starring: George C. Scott, Karl Malden Director: Franklin J. Schaffner
Screenplay: Edmund H. North and Francis Ford Coppola Running
Time: 2:50 Rated: PG (Violence, language) Theatrical Aspect
Ratio: 2.20:1

In early 1971, the Academy Awards saluted *Patton*. Capturing 8 Oscars — including best picture, best director, best actor, best screenplay, best editing, and best production design — the movie won every major battle of the evening. Such acclaim was richly deserved, for *Patton* remains to this day one of Hollywood's most compelling biographical war pictures.

With its larger-than-life, yet at the same time singularly human, portrayal of General George S. Patton, Jr., Franklin Schaffner's picture is an example of filmmaking at its finest. From production design and battle choreography to simple one-on-one dramatic acting, *Patton* has it all. There is no scene in all 170 minutes that doesn't work on some level.

The film opens in 1943 North Africa, with a brutal look at American casualties at the battle of Kasserine. Patton (George C. Scott) arrives from Morocco to take command of the U.S. army in Tunisia in preparation for fighting Rommel (Karl Michael Vogler) at el Gitar. From North Africa, Patton's forces move to Sicily, where they sweep north across the island, taking Palermo, then racing Montgomery (Michael Bates) to Messina. Along the way, Patton's verbal and physical abuse of a soldier suffering from "battle fatigue" — which the general brands as cowardice — becomes ammunition for his critics. He later offers a public apology, but this incident keeps him from the action for a while, and he must stand by as a decoy during the Normandy invasion. Later in the year, however, General Omar Bradley (Karl Malden) gives Patton command of the Allied Third Army, with which he pushes across Western Europe to stop the Germans at the Battle of the Bulge, the last major Nazi offensive of the war.

Those who have not seen *Patton,* or who have not watched the film carefully, might assume that this movie is about World War II and one of its most celebrated generals. In fact, they would be only partially correct. What *Patton* sets out to do is to demythicize its subject and show the forces that drove this man.

Brilliant tactician, merciless disciplinarian, tireless fighter, prima donna, and staunch patriot — Patton was all of these things and more. Life for him was the battlefield, and without war, his spirit was sapped. The German military recognized this when they noted that Berlin's fall would finish him. Patton was an anachronism — a man who belonged in another time. He was a warrior living in a time when victory in battle no longer meant the triumph it once had, a Roman conqueror who understood the meaning of the words that "all glory is fleeting." Above all, however, he was an icon whom millions cheered, millions hated, and few understood. **MUST SEE**

Psycho [1960]

Starring: Anthony Perkins, Vera Miles, John Gavin, Martin Balsam, Janet Leigh Director: Alfred Hitchcock Screenplay: Joseph Stefano based on the novel by Robert Bloch Running Time: 1:48 Rated: R (Violence) Theatrical Aspect Ratio: 1.85:1

With *Psycho*, Hitchcock dabbled in cinematic taboos, pushing the censorship envelope. For example, this was the first American motion picture to feature a toilet being flushed (most movies of the era didn't even acknowledge the existence of toilets). Also, Janet Leigh is shown in her underwear on more than one occasion, and, during the famous shower scene, it's possible to see hints of flesh (most of which belong to a body double). The script also features a man speaking the word "transvestite" — a line that survived in the film only after a Herculean struggle on Stefano's part.

The film starts out in traditional fashion for a Hitchcock thriller. A woman, Marion Crane (Janet Leigh), desperate to find a way to be with her lover, Sam Loomis (John Gavin), embezzles money from her boss, then goes on the lam. She's not an apt criminal, however, and she leaves a wide trail. A used car salesman assesses her nervous mood and uses it to bilk her out of some extra cash. A somewhat-ominous policeman shadows her, almost to the point of stalking. If anyone could ever be said to look and act guilty, it's Marion. Eventually, she ends up at the out-of-the-way Bates Motel, where the shy-but-kind manager, Norman Bates (Anthony Perkins), offers her a room, a meal, and a sympathetic ear. During her conversation with Norman, when he speaks

about the traps that life places everyone in, Marion resolves to return on the following morning and give back the money. Events of the night, which involve violence and the jealous rage of Norman's twisted mother, put an end to Marion's plans. Soon after, others arrive at the Bates Motel looking for her, including Loomis, a private investigator named Arbogast (Martin Balsam), and Marion's sister, Lila (Vera Miles). They all make horrifying discoveries.

Story-wise, *Psycho* is not extraordinary; its true ingeniousness lies in its construction. Hitchcock and Stafano have developed the movie in such a way that it consistently flouts expectations. There are 2 major surprises: the shower scene murder and the final revelation about Mother. A viewer who sees the film for the first time without knowing about either will experience the full impact of what Hitchcock intended.

Today, *Psycho* still holds up extraordinarily well. With the exception of *Halloween*, no latter-day horror/thriller has been capable of generating as many goosebumps. The painstaking care with which Hitchcock composed every scene is evident in the quality of the final product. *Psycho* may not represent the master director's pinnacle, but it is the motion picture for which he is best known, and its legacy is inarguably one of the most far reaching of any film to come out of a Hollywood studio. **HIGHLY RECOMMENDED**

Rear Window [1964]

Starring: James Stewart, Grace Kelley, Wendell Corey, Thelma Ritter, Raymond Burr Director: Alfred Hitchcock Screenplay: John Michael Hayes based on a short story by Cornell Woolrich Running Time: 1:53 Rated: PG (Mature themes, violence) Theatrical Aspect Ratio: 1.85:1

One of the most engrossing, and, in its own way, groundbreaking, studies of voyeurism is Alfred Hitchcock's *Rear Window*. The film is universally regarded as a classic, and a strong cadre of critics, scholars, and fans considers this to be the director's best feature. Not only does the movie generate an intensely suspenseful and fascinating situation, but it develops a compelling and memorable character: L.B. Jefferies (James Stewart), a top-flight photographer who, as the result of an accident that left him in a leg cast, is confined to his upper-story Manhattan apartment. He amuses himself by gazing out his window at the building opposite, and builds pictures of each of the inhabitants from the glimpses he catches of their lives. Some of them, like "Miss Torso," a lithe young ballerina who capers around in various stages of dress, and "Miss Lonelyhearts," a forlorn spinster, keep their curtains wide open. Others, like a newly-wed couple, pull down the blinds, leaving Jefferies to smile wryly as he guesses about their activities.

As Jefferies' days of confinement wear on, his fascination with his neighbors turns into an obsession. Their lives become more important than his. After all, they are vital and mobile; he is trapped and impotent. He has a charming and gorgeous young girl-friend, Lisa Fremont (Grace Kelly), but he is emotionally cool towards her, and their relationship is caught in the same stasis that paralyzes every other aspect of Jefferies' life. When he gropes for a reason why she wouldn't make a good wife, the only fault he can find is that she's "too perfect, too talented, too beautiful, and too sophisticated." Lisa may love him, but she is losing patience. Then, one day, Jefferies observes something that forces him to abandon his safe, co-cooned role as a voyeur and become a participant. He sees — or *thinks* he sees — one of his neighbors, Lars Thorwald (Raymond Burr), commit a murder. When the police don't believe Jefferies, he is forced to take action without their help. Abetted by Lisa, he works to uncover evidence to prove that a crime was committed. However, with his mobility restricted, Jefferies can only watch through his rear window as Lisa puts herself in harm's way, and, when danger strikes, he is helpless to go to her rescue.

Simply put, *Rear Window* is a great film, perhaps one of the finest ever committed to celluloid. All of the elements are perfect (or nearly so), including the acting, script, camerawork, music (by Franz Wax-man), and, of course, direction. The brilliance of the movie is that, in addition to keeping viewers on the edges of their seats, it involves us in the lives of all of the characters, from Jefferies and Lisa to Miss Torso. There isn't a moment of waste in 113 minutes of screen time. **MUST SEE**

Vertigo [1968]

Starring: James Stewart, Kim Novak, Barbara Bel Geddes Director: Alfred Hitchcock Screenplay: Samuel Taylor and Alec Coppel Running Time: 2:08 Rated: PG (Mature themes) Theatrical Aspect Ratio: 1.85:1

Vertigo opens with a short prologue that details the circumstances under which Detective John Ferguson (James Stewart) develops an acute case of acrophobia that leads to vertigo whenever he climbs a steep flight of stairs or gets more than a few feet above the ground. After leaving the police force because of this condition, John is approached by an old acquain-tance, ship yard magnate Gavin Elster (Tom Hel-more), to tail his wife, Madeleine (Kim Novak). Gavin is concerned about Madeleine's health — she has frequent black-outs and he believes that the spirit of a dead woman is attempting to possess her.

As John follows Madeleine, watching her day after day, he falls for her. Eventually, the two meet and discover that the attraction is mutual. But even love is not enough to overcome John's vertigo, and he is unable to save her from a fall from the top of a church bell tower. Madeleine's death causes John to suffer a breakdown, and, during his recovery, a chance encounter on the street brings him face-to-face with a woman, Judy Barton (Novak), who is the spitting image of his dead love.

Hitchcock does a masterful job blending all of *Vertigo*'s diverse elements together. It's a love story, a mystery, and a thriller all rolled into one. It deals with issues of obsession, psychological and physical paralysis, and the tenuous nature of romantic love. *Vertigo* should really be seen more than once to be fully appreciated. Many of the darker, deeper aspects only begin to bubble to the surface on subsequent viewings.

Stylistically, perhaps the two most noteworthy elements of *Vertigo* are its distinctive color scheme, which features reds and greens, and the memorable, haunting score turned in by composer Bernard Herrmann. There are numerous, lengthy passages that pass without dialogue (most of these occur while John is trailing Madeleine), and Herrmann's music sustains Hitchcock's carefully-crafted tone. **HIGHLY RECOMMENDED**

The Wizard of Oz [1939]

Starring: Judy Garland, Frank Morgan, Ray Bolger, Bert Lahr, Jack Haley, Billie Burke Director: Victor Fleming Screenplay: Noel Langley and Florence Ryerson and Edgar Allan Woolf Running Time: 1:41 Rated: G Theatrical Aspect Ratio: 1.37:1

Throughout the years, there have been dozens of live-action films, stage plays, animated features, and TV programs based on L. Frank Baum's classic Oz stories. To one degree or another, almost all have been influenced by Fleming's telling of the tale. When anyone thinks of *The Wizard of Oz*, they see Judy Garland, Ray Bolger, Bert Lahr, and Jack Haley, and hear "Somewhere over the Rainbow" and "Follow the Yellow Brick Road."

Probably the most interesting aspect of *The Wizard of Oz* comes from interpreting what really happens during the bulk of the film. The story opens by introducing us to Dorothy Gale (Judy Garland), a young girl in Kansas who finds her wanderlust stirred by dreams of going "somewhere over the rainbow." When a tornado strikes the farm where she lives with her aunt and uncle, she is knocked unconscious. Upon waking up, she finds herself in the magical land of Oz, where she journeys in the company of a Scarecrow (Ray Bolger), a Tin Man (Jack Haley), and a Cowardly Lion (Bert Lahr) to defeat the Wicked Witch of the West (Margaret Hamilton) and find the all-powerful Wizard (Frank Morgan), who has the power to send her home. But is this a real trip, or is it all a dream? A strong case can be developed for either possibility, although it's ultimately up to each viewer to make up his or her own mind. Whichever way you lean, it doesn't detract from the movie's boundless capacity to entertain.

The Wizard of Oz has been subjected to the kind of scrutiny reserved for only the greatest of motion pictures. Volumes have been written about it, analyzing everything from its look to the urban legends that have sprung up around it. Ultimately, however, it doesn't take a lengthy study to understand why multiple generations find the movie so compelling. Not only is it wonderfully entertaining, but the issues it addresses, and the way it presents them, are both universal and deeply personal. And therein lies *The Wizard of Oz*'s true magic. **MUST SEE**

Comedy

8 Women [France, 2002]

Starring: Danielle Darrieux, Catherine Deneuve, Isabelle Huppert, Emmanuelle Béart, Fanny Ardant, Virginie Ledoyen Director: François Ozon Screenplay: François Ozon and Marina de Van, based on the play by Robert Thomas Running Time: 1:43 Rated: R (Sexual themes) Theatrical Aspect Ratio: 1.85:1

The product of French director François Ozon, *8 Women* offers as much delicious enjoyment to the viewer as it obviously did to the cast and crew when they were assembling it. Part satire, part comedy, part musical, and part murder mystery, this motion picture criss-crosses genre lines at will, offering just about every kind of pleasure imaginable, guilty or otherwise.

The 8 women of the title are Gaby (Catherine Deneuve); her daughters, Catherine (Ludivine Sagnier) and Suzon (Virginie Ledoyen); her mother (Danielle Darrieux); her sister, Augustine (Isabelle Huppert); her sister-in-law, Pierrette (Fanny Ardant); and her two maids, Louise (Emmanuelle Béart) and Chanel (Firmine Richard). These characters are trapped together in a house during a snowstorm with one dead body (Marcel, Gaby's husband) and cut phone lines. Tensions run high, with each woman suspecting the others of being the killer. Secrets, some silly and some shocking, are revealed. Suzon begins acting like Hercule Poirot, and everyone else takes an occasional break to lapse into song and dance. A more enjoyable confection cannot be found.

What a cast! No director could dream of a more talented and beautiful group of actresses to grace his film. The names read like a who's who of French film across 3 generations: the youngsters (Ledoyen, Sagnier, and Béart), the middle-aged stars (Deneuve, Huppert, Ardant), and the venerable grande dame (Danielle Darrieux). All of them are in top form and completely in step with what Ozon is attempting. In addition to paying homage to, as well as spoofing, Agatha Christie (via a '60s play written by Robert Thomas), he is re-creating the look and feel of a '50s or '60s Technicolor movie, complete with brightly-hued costumes, old-fashioned set design, and a lushly melodramatic score. Plus, for good measure, he throws in 6 musical numbers, allowing nearly all of the characters an opportunity to play the canary.

In many ways, *8 Women* is the ultimate feel-good movie, Ozon's valentine to those who have stuck with him through all of his previous, serious work. *8 Women* has the life and energy of a manic comedy, the spirit of a musical, and the heart of a mystery. And, believe it or not, despite all of the madcap zaniness going on, viewers come to care about the characters and are interested in knowing the answer to the crucial question of "Whodunnit?" In true Agatha Christie fashion, there's as much of a twist to that as there is to just about everything else in this wonderfully entertaining motion picture. **HIGHLY RECOMMENDED**

13 Going on 30 [2004]

Starring: Jennifer Garner, Mark Ruffalo, Shana Dowdeswell, Jack Salvatore, Jr., Kathy Baker, Phil Reeves, Judy Greer Director: Gary Winick Screenplay: Cathy Yuspa & Josh Goldsmith and Niels Mueller Running Time: 1:30 Rated: PG-13 (Sexual situations, profanity) Theatrical Aspect Ratio: 1.85:1

There's something irresistible about a displaced-consciousness story, whether it's an adult occupying the body of a child, a child occupying the body of an adult, or a gender switch. *13 Going on 30* belongs to the same subgenre as *Big*, although many of the particulars are different. As films of this sort go, this one is solidly entertaining. It requires that the viewer exhibit a fair amount of willing suspension of disbelief, but buying into the essential premise is more than half the battle. Accept the magic that transports the mind of a 13-year-old girl into the future body of her 30-year old self, and little else that director Gary Winick throws out will be difficult to swallow.

The movie opens in 1987. On her 13th birthday, Jenna Rink (Shana Dowdeswell) wants nothing more than to be popular and date one of the cutest boys in school. When her best friend, Matt (Jack Salvatore, Jr.), remarks that she's better off trying to be original, she retorts, "I don't want to be original. I want to be cool!" (The refrain of so many high school students . . .) After her birthday party is a disaster, Jenna retreats to a closet to salve her tattered pride, and wishes she could be 30 years old. That's when a sprinkle of pixie dust descends upon her.

When she awakens the next morning, she's still Jenna Rink, but the year is 2004 and she's 30 years old (and now played by Jennifer Garner). She's has a powerhouse job as an editor for *Poise* magazine, lives with a star hockey player, and is friends with Lucy (Judy Greer), the girl whose companionship she craved at 13. Jenna goes through all the expected stages: confusion about what has happened to her life ("it's a dream"), exultation about how great everything is, then panic that she's adrift in a world she doesn't know or understand. So she tracks down the only one she believes she can trust: Matt (now played by Mark Ruffalo) — except he explains that their friendship ended years ago. He eventually relents and agrees to help Jenna, and she begins to feel things for him that she never experienced when they were teenagers.

The film's primary asset is Jennifer Garner, who is in the process of parlaying her success in the TV series *Alias* into a film career. Garner is wonderful as Jenna, and we have no trouble accepting her as a child trapped in an adult's body. Like Jamie Lee Curtis in the recent *Freaky Friday* remake, she gets all the mannerisms right, and nothing about the way she acts is over-the-top or too cute. Ultimately, the movie may not be as good, uplifting, or perceptive as *Big*, but it's one of the better teen girl–themed films of the

year, and can be enjoyed by viewers of either gender in any age group. **RECOMMENDED**

Adaptation [2002]

Starring: Nicolas Cage, Meryl Streep, Chris Cooper, Brian Cox, Tilda Swinton Director: Spike Jonze Screenplay: Charlie Kaufman and Donald Kaufman, based on *The Orchid Thief* by Susan Orlean Running Time: 1:50 Rated: R (Profanity, sexual situations, brief nudity, violence) Theatrical Aspect Ratio: 1.85:1

There is a concept in mathematics called "recursion." Charlie Kaufman and director Spike Jonze have apparently discovered the cinematic equivalent with *Adaptation,* an occasionally maddening and sometimes brilliant motion picture that varies between being insightfully sharp and insufferably self-indulgent. Regardless of whether you appreciate the movie or not, it's likely to stay with you.

Adaptation stars Nicolas Cage in a dual role as Kaufman and his fictitious brother, Donald. Meryl Streep is Susan Orlean, the writer of *The Orchid Thief;* Chris Cooper is Laroche; Brian Cox is Robert McKee, a real-life lecturer about the art of screenplay writing; and Tilda Swinton is Valerie, the one who commissions Kaufman to write the adaptation of the book. The film flips back and forth across time, alternating between the "present," in which Kaufman is trying to write the screenplay, and 3 years in the past, when the events recounted in *The Orchid Thief* are taking place. There are also various flashbacks and even an excursion to pre-historic times. Certain events take place on the set of Jonze and Kaufman's previous collaboration, *Being John Malkovich,* allowing actors like Malkovich and Catherine Keener to make cameos.

The title of *Adaptation* doesn't only refer to what Kaufman is doing to Orlean's book. It is also meant in the Darwinian sense — that humans adapt to circumstances. The movie is certainly as offbeat as *Being John Malkovich,* although it is neither as funny nor as accessible (if, indeed, *Malkovich* can be considered to be "accessible"). *Adaptation* has a serious point or two to divulge. In particular, it's about the importance of passion in every endeavor.

The movie comes across as chaotic, which I'm sure is intentional. With the multiple storylines, there's too much going on, and this damages *Adaptation*'s structure. Jonze does his best to bring a kind of order to the proceedings, but there are times when things get away from him. And there are instances when the movie comes across as being a little too clever. I can't imagine *Adaptation* having much mainstream appeal, but, for those who look for something genuinely off-the-wall in a motion picture, this will unquestionably strike a nerve. **HIGHLY RECOMMENDED**

The Adventures of Priscilla, Queen of the Desert
[Australia, 1993]
Starring: Terrence Stamp, Hugo Weaving, Guy Pearce
Director: Stephan Elliot Screenplay: Stephan Elliot Running Time: 1:32
Rated: R (Language, sexual themes, violence) Theatrical Aspect
Ratio: 1.85:1

The Adventures of Priscilla, Queen of the Desert is about the most fun you can have with 3 guys who like to dress up as women. The latest export from down under, *Priscilla* is the story of 3 drag queens — Bernadette/Ralph (Terrence Stamp), Mitzi/Tick (Hugo Weaving), and Felicia/Adam (Guy Pearce) — on their way across the Australian desert to play a gig. Along the way, their bus, Priscilla, breaks down, and they have to rely on help from strangers. And, while cross-dressing performers are accepted in the big city, their welcome in a less urban setting is not always warm and friendly.

The dance numbers are lavish and fun to watch, whether they're performed in the middle of the desert, atop a bar in some out-of-the-way town, or on a stage in Sydney. Mostly '70s disco hits (including once-popular tunes by Gloria Gaynor, the Village People, and ABBA), these songs are lip-synched and gyrated to with gusto by the transvestite trio as they don garish costumes and even worse makeup to wow their audiences.

There are moments of seriousness amidst all the zaniness as the twin specters of intolerance and homophobia (two sides of the same coin) cast a pall over the proceedings. Give director Stephan Elliot credit for not dwelling overmuch on these instances. He knows that their mere inclusion is sufficient to get the message across.

While each of the 3 leads is good, the standout performance belongs to normally-serious veteran actor Terrence Stamp, who has previously appeared in such diverse outings as *Billy Budd* and *Superman* (I and II). Here, he brings a quiet dignity to the role of Bernadette. That's not easy to do considering some of the outrageous costumes he's required to wear.

The Adventures of Priscilla, Queen of the Desert is a great deal more appealing than many might suppose it to be. It's a road movie that's anything but typical or traditional. So, whether or not you share the procliv-

ities of Bernadette, Mitzi, and Felicia, the trio's cinematic cabaret is nevertheless something to smile and laugh your way through. **RECOMMENDED**

American Pie [1999]
Starring: Jason Biggs, Thomas Ian Nicholas, Chris Klein, Eddie Kaye Thomas, Eugene Levy Director: Paul Weitz Screenplay: Adam Herz
Running Time: 1:37 Rated: R (Graphic sexual activities of various sorts, nudity, profanity) Theatrical Aspect Ratio: 1.85:1

The point of every gross, eccentric, and vulgar moment in *American Pie* is to make the audience laugh. First time director Paul Weitz and writer Adam Herz aren't going for anything remotely intellectual here — they're appealing to the least common denominator in us all. And it works. *American Pie* is consistently funny and sporadically hilarious. It should come as a surprise to no one that the most effective jokes involve some form of sex. There's also one instance of (literal) toilet humor that had the audience in stitches. *American Pie* descends into bad taste with its first scene and has the good sense never to rise above that level.

American Pie introduces us to a quartet of males with a serious problem: their high school senior year is coming to a close and they're all virgins. Jim (Jason Biggs), the film's ostensible hero, is an awkward guy who has trouble talking to females. Kevin (Thomas Ian Nicholas), the most average member of the group, is involved in a stable relationship with a beautiful girl, but he keeps stranding runners at third base. Oz (Chris Klein), a dumb jock, decides that the best way to meet members of the opposite sex is to join the glee club. And Finch (Eddie Kaye Thomas), the intellectual, is so tightly wound that he won't use the school restrooms. The egos of these 4 are badly bruised when evidence suggests that the biggest geek at East Great Falls High has had sex before them. So they make a pact to help each other lose their virginity before they graduate, and target one specific event: the Senior Prom.

Each of the guys is ultimately paired with a girl. For Jim, it's an oversexed exchange student named Nadia (Shannon Elizabeth), and, when that falls through, it's Michelle (Alyson Hannigan), a timid member of the school band. Oz falls for smart, pretty Heather (Mena Suvari), who generally has little time for jocks. Kevin's steady girlfriend is Vicky (Tara Reid), whose best friend, Jessica (Natasha Lyonne), encourages her to "do it." And Finch learns why *The Graduate* is such a popular movie.

The main difference between *American Pie* and most of the other teen-themed comedies flooding theaters these days is the take-no-prisoners edge. This film isn't going for "cute." It's not trying to earn a PG-13 for maximum exposure to the under-17 crowd. It takes risks; they don't always work, but, when they do, there's a payoff. There's nothing obtuse about the film's appeal. For those who think the moral level of Hollywood pictures is in a steep decline, *American Pie* provides evidence to support the theory. For just about everyone else, it's a guilty (or, in some cases, a not-so-guilty) pleasure. **RECOMMENDED**

American Psycho [2000]

Starring: Christian Bale, Willem Dafoe, Jared Leto, Reese Witherspoon, Samantha Mathis Director: Mary Harron Screenplay: Mary Harron & Guinevere Turner, based on the novel by Bret Easton Ellis Running Time: 1:42 Rated: R (Violence, sex, nudity, profanity) Theatrical Aspect Ratio: 1.85:1

First and foremost, *American Psycho* takes a scathing look at the "me first" mentality of the mid-to-late-'80s. In fact, one of the reasons the film works so well is because of a take no prisoners attitude. We are given a gallery of despicable, amoral characters to observe. Anyone who identifies with them needs to consider seeking immediate psychiatric help. The most disturbing of them is Patrick Bateman (Christian Bale), a successful, wealthy commodities broker who believes himself to be untouchable and perhaps indestructible. Not content to destroy lives in the conventional manner embraced by his colleagues, Patrick has taken things one step further and become a serial killer. In fact, he has murdered so many times that he is losing track of the body count.

A crucial aspect of the movie's effective satire is the performance of Christian Bale, whose dead-on, straight man approach to the role gives *American Psycho* its punch. Bale's cold, charismatic, misogynist turn as the 27-year-old psycho is riveting. The supporting cast contains a number of familiar names — Reese Witherspoon as Patrick's superficial fiancée, Evelyn; Chloë Sevigny as his faithful secretary, Jean; and Willem Dafoe as a police detective.

In a voiceover, Patrick informs us that "There is no real me. I simply am not there." He sees himself as a façade — a perfectly sculpted body encompassing a black hole where his soul and conscience should be. "I have all the characteristics of a human being but not one discernible emotion except greed and disgust." He's a huge fan of pop music. Some of the film's creepiest and funniest scenes occur when he plays Huey Lewis and the News, Phil Collins, and Genesis as foreplay to violence. During sex, he spends as much time preening in front of a mirror as he does playing with the girl (or girls) he's with. When introducing himself at nightclubs, he claims to be in "murders and executions" not "mergers and acquisitions." And the people he uses that line with think it's funny.

In the recent tradition of movies like *Fight Club*, *American Psycho* employs a surprise ending. There is enough ambiguity about the last act revelations that one can interpret them in more than one way, but the most likely choice forces the entire movie to be re-interpreted through a different filter. In retrospect, the film holds together no matter which approach you accept, and the seams never show. **HIGHLY RECOMMENDED**

America's Sweethearts [2001]

Starring: Julia Roberts, Billy Crystal, Catherine Zeta-Jones, John Cusack, Hank Azaria Director: Joe Roth Screenplay: Billy Crystal & Peter Tolan Running Time: 1:40 Rated: PG-13 (Sexual situations, profanity) Theatrical Aspect Ratio: 2.35:1

Bruce Willis & Demi Moore. Meg Ryan & Dennis Quaid. Tom Cruise & Nicole Kidman. These are only three of the highest profile Hollywood "supercouples" to have blown apart in recent years, their splits enflaming the interest of gossip-mongers everywhere. It was only a matter of time before a group of filmmakers decided to make a movie about "Divorce — Hollywood Style." The talented trio to tackle the subject are veteran producer-turned-director Joe Roth and screenwriters Billy Crystal & Peter Tolan — all 3 of whom have their satirical razors sharpened to a keen edge for this endeavor. *America's Sweethearts* is first and foremost a lampoon of today's Hollywood, and its targets are as diverse as the cast. No one emerges unscathed from this comedy — not high-powered, egotistical producers; not self-absorbed actors; not film critics; and (especially) not publicists.

Eddie Thomas (John Cusack) and Gwen Harrison (Catherine Zeta-Jones) were America's most beloved husband-and-wife acting duo, with such titles on their combined resume as *Autumn with Greg & Peg, Requiem for an Outfielder,* and *Sasha and the Optometrist*. Of the 9 films they made together, 6 grossed more than $100 million. Then, 18 months ago, their fairy-tale story came to an end when Gwen began an affair with Spanish heartthrob Hector (Hank Azaria) and Eddie suffered a nervous breakdown. Now, after her solo film career has gone into a downward spiral steeper than the stairs in *Vertigo* and he has spent countless months in a "rest clinic," Eddie and Gwen are about to meet again to promote their final motion picture together: a science fiction spectacular called *Time Over Time*. Two publicists, studio flack, Lee (Billy Crystal), and Gwen's sister, Kiki (Julia Roberts), have the unenviable task of attempting to convince all the journalists on the press junket that Eddie and Gwen might be headed for a reunion. But there are complications — Kiki's long-harbored crush on Eddie threatens to turn everything on its head.

America's Sweethearts is characterized by sharp dialogue, comedy that varies from tame to ribald (Billy Crystal's encounter with a friendly Doberman is priceless), and a romance that adds a little sugar to the otherwise salty circumstances. The movie is more about the shenanigans that go on during the course of a press junket than about any particular character or relationship. It's the way all of the stories spin out of control and entwine with each other that makes the movie so enjoyable. Sure, the ending is predictable, but 95% of the fun is getting there, and, whenever things start getting too soft, there's always a vicious one-liner just around the corner. **RECOMMENDED**

Analyze This [1999]

Starring: Robert De Niro, Billy Crystal, Lisa Kudrow Director: Harold Ramis Screenplay: Peter Tolan, Harold Ramis & Ken Lonergan Running Time: 1:45 Rated: R (Profanity, violence, sex) Theatrical Aspect Ratio: 1.85:1

The greatest asset evidenced by Harold Ramis' gangster comedy, *Analyze This*, is that it doesn't try too hard for laughs. Instead of force-feeding audiences stale, predictable jokes about mobsters and mayhem, Ramis is content to let the humor evolve naturally out of the situations postulated by the script and the performances of lead actors Robert De Niro and Billy Crystal. The resulting movie, while not consistently uproarious, is frequently funny and occasionally hilarious.

De Niro is the straight man to Billy Crystal's Ben Sobel, a psychiatrist who has unwittingly become a name on Vitti's payroll. Crystal finds the right tone for Sobel early in the proceedings — he's a witty individual, but he doesn't go overboard. Crystal manages to be funny without destroying the integrity of his character — a crucial achievement for the movie to work on any level.

Vitti is not a "happy, well-adjusted gangster." Once, he was able to kill and brutalize without compunction, but now the day-to-day activities of a made guy are wearing him down. He's suffering from panic attacks and sentimental TV commercials cause him to break down and cry. If he's going to survive in a world where the appearance of machismo is everything, he has to banish his weakness through the most expedient manner possible — therapy. Because Sobel had the misfortune of giving his business card to Vitti's stooge, Jelly (Joe Viterelli), he becomes the mobster's first candidate. Soon, like it or not, Sobel is on call — even if it means interrupting his wedding to a pretty Florida news reporter (Lisa Kudrow).

Analyze This is not a great comedy, but it offers a fairly good time by poking fun at mobsters and psychiatrists. Both Freud and *The Godfather* take a pounding, but the best-conceived comic sequence comes near the end, when Crystal's Sobel is placed in a situation where he has to impersonate a Mafioso, and finds that he can't even pronounce "consigliere." The film contains several other memorable moments, such as Vitti's reaction to a Merrill Lynch TV spot and a fender bender that causes a couple of gangsters a few anxious moments.

Harold Ramis, the director of *Groundhog Day* and co-writer of *Ghostbusters*, knows a thing or two about comic timing, and his skill in this arena is in evidence here. The basic storyline is pretty much a throwaway; what makes *Analyze This* work is the interplay between the actors and the manner in which comic vignettes are incorporated into the plot. For those who have grown weary of lame gangster parodies, *Analyze This* offers a more intelligent, better conceived alternative. **RECOMMENDED**

Anchorman: The Legend of Ron Burgundy [2004]

Starring: Will Ferrell, Christina Applegate, Paul Rudd, Steve Carell, David Koechner, Fred Willard, Chris Parnell, Vince Vaughn Director: Adam McKay Screenplay: Will Ferrell & Adam McKay Running Time: 1:31 Rated: PG-13 (Profanity, sex jokes, comic violence) Theatrical Aspect Ratio: 1.85:1

Anchorman is a very funny motion picture, but it also has a good sense of the time (the 1970s) and how the medium of TV news was changing. In addition, it explores how difficult a period it was for serious women journalists with on-air aspirations. Here, the Jessica Savitch–type is Veronica Corningstone (Christina Applegate), who encounters a wall of male chauvinism on her way to becoming KVWN's first female anchorperson. And the strongest opposition comes from Ron Burgundy (Will Ferrell), who, along with his cohorts, insists that news is a man's world.

As the movie opens, we are informed: "The following is based on actual events. Only the names, locations, and events have been changed." *Anchorman* then introduces Ron and the other members of the KVWN news team: sports reporter Champ Kind (David Koechner), weatherman Brick Tamland (Steve Carell), and on-the-spot reporter Brian Fantana (Paul Rudd). They represent the number-one news team in San Diego, but the arrival of Veronica Corningstone is about to stir the pot. At first, station manager Ed Harken (Fred Willard) gives her "puff pieces," but, when Ron is late for a broadcast one evening, she fills in and is such a hit that she and Ron are soon coanchors. To add fuel to the fire, they become romantically involved, then split when Ron views her career ambitions as a betrayal.

Farrell carries the movie on his broad shoulders, nailing the character perfectly. He becomes Ron: the shallow-but-photogenic anchorman whose backstage pettiness contradicts his on-air friendliness. And, even though Ron is a chauvinist, Farrell brings out his likability. Christina Applegate is an effective foil. There's just enough chemistry between her and Farrell to allow the love story to work. Effective support is provided by Paul Rudd as the station Lothario, David Koechner as a guy who doesn't know about much other than sports, and Steve Carell as a twit with an IQ of 40.

Anchorman's satirical bent makes the comedy seem richer. One of the areas where the film has fun is in choosing character names. We have great, theatrical-sounding monikers like Ron Burgundy, Veronica Corningstone, Brick Tamland, Champ Kind, and Wes Mantooth. It's hard to say whether *Anchorman* is the funniest movie of the year — it has enough offbeat and gut-busting moments to make it worth consideration in that category. And *Anchorman* would certainly make a great double feature with *Dodgeball*, another of 2004's most enjoyable comedies. RECOMMENDED

Anything Else [2003]

Starring: Jason Biggs, Christina Ricci, Woody Allen, Stockard Channing, Danny DeVito Director: Woody Allen Screenplay: Woody Allen Running Time: 1:50 Rated: R (Sexual situations, profanity, drug use) Theatrical Aspect Ratio: 2.35:1

With *Anything Else*, Woody Allen is attempting something that is simultaneously similar yet different from his past projects. The focal point of the movie is the relationship between two twenty-something characters, Jerry (Jason Biggs) and Amanda (Christina Ricci). Never before had Allen directed two protagonists this young, and over the course of his career he has more often dealt with May-December romances than those between adults of a comparable age. The

characters and their neuroses, however, are pure Allen. The actor/director is only on-screen in a supporting role, but he has overlaid his personality on Jerry.

The plot isn't groundbreaking. Most of it is lifted piecemeal from Allen's previous work, with the most obvious antecedent being *Annie Hall*. *Anything Else* autopsies the relationship of Jerry and Amanda, showing its development (through flashbacks) and its disintegration (in real time). One of the key differences between this and *Annie Hall* is that, in the earlier movie, we honestly believed that Alvy and Annie had a chance. In *Anything Else*, long-term for Jerry and Amanda would be about a year. Their relationship is doomed from the beginning.

The interaction between these characters is fascinating, and leads to two or three borderline remarkable scenes. Biggs, despite being saddled with the typical neurotic Allen personality, does a credible job. Ricci positively smolders. Not only does she perfectly inhabit her character, but she looks marvelous and Allen has no problem showing off her attributes (no nudity, but some very sexy stuff). Psychologically, Amanda's almost as big a mess as Jerry. We have all known someone like her — commitment-phobic, frightened of monogamy, incapable of telling the truth, and an expert at planning guilt trips for her partner. Yet, when she's being affectionate, she's so adorable that it makes everything seem worth it. Unfortunately for Jerry, she's not sleeping with him anymore (he reminds her of her father), and his problem is that he doesn't know how to end a relationship.

One of the reasons that *Anything Else* works more often than not is because Allen understands human sexual weaknesses. There's a lot of truth in the screenplay, and, combined with Ricci's top-notch, can't-take-your-eyes-off-her-when-she's-on-screen performance, this gives the movie a strong spine. Some of the subplots and secondary characters are weak, and there's almost too much angst for my taste, but on balance, the film is worth a look. For Allen, it's not a return to form, but it's a step in the right direction. RECOMMENDED

Bad Santa [2003]

Starring: Billy Bob Thornton, Bernie Mac, Lauren Graham, John Ritter, Tony Cox, Brett Kelly Director: Terry Zwigoff Screenplay: John Requa & Glenn Ficarra Running Time: 1:30 Rated: R (Profanity, vulgarity, sexual situations, violence) Theatrical Aspect Ratio: 1.85:1

Bad Santa's Willie (Billy Bob Thornton) is the kind of guy who makes Scrooge look like a generous, mild-mannered eccentric. With a character as thoroughly unlikable as this, you know immediately that *Bad Santa* is not going to be just another modern-day version of *A Christmas Carol*. It has two modes — dark, and darker — and dares to do some things with the Christmas motif that haven't been done since Norman Rene's *Reckless*. Realistically, however, what else would you expect from a movie directed by Terry Zwigoff (*Crumb, Ghost World*) and executive-produced by the Coen brothers?

The film's central figure is Willie, a loser who has adopted just about every vice known to man. The only reason he doesn't smoke more is because it would interfere with his drinking. Every Christmas, he and his partner, a dwarf (Tony Cox), get a job in a mall department store as Santa and his elf. Then, on Christmas Eve, after the mall has closed, they use their insider knowledge of the security system to disable the alarms. Willie, who has a background in safecracking, gets them enough loot so that they can live comfortably for the next year. Except this time, things are different.

Thurman (Brett Kelly) is an eight-year old dweeb who is constantly bullied, has no friends, and lives by himself (actually, he lives with his senile grandmother, but that's as good as alone). In need of someone to believe in, he inexplicably chooses Willie, whom he constantly refers to as "Santa," even when Willie's drunk, out of costume, or humping "Mrs. Santa's sister" (Lauren Graham as a woman with a serious Santa fixation). At first, Willie is annoyed with Thurman for hanging around him, but upon figuring out how he can use the kid, he has a change of heart. Soon, he's living in Thurman's house as he prepares for his next robbery.

Some will call this movie "mean-spirited," and they're probably right. But it is designed to shock. Early in the film, we see Santa urinating in his suit, and the contempt in which he holds the kids is unsettling. The movie doesn't cop out by reforming Willie, either. That might be the perfect approach for a film that contains an ounce of holiday cheer, but it's not *Bad Santa*. Yet, for all its darkness — or perhaps because of it — *Bad Santa* is sometimes laugh-aloud hilarious. The humor is offbeat and unconventional, but much of it is funny. The fact that they're laughing through this movie will make some people feel distinctly uncomfortable. *Bad Santa* is definitely not for everyone. If you appreciate movies that don't compromise on their comedic journey into the heart of

darkness, this is for you. But if you're expecting something kinder and gentler, look elsewhere. Because "kind" and "gentle" are two words no one is ever going to use to describe *Bad Santa*. RECOMMENDED

Being John Malkovich [1999]

Starring: John Cusack, Cameron Diaz, Catherine Keener, John Malkovich Director: **Spike Jonze** Screenplay: **Charlie Kaufman**
Running Time: 1:52 Rated: R (profanity, sexual situations) Theatrical Aspect Ratio: 2.35:1

These days, critics (and non-critics, for that matter) are fond of complaining about how multiplexes are populated by cookie-cutter motion pictures that follow safe, formula-derived patterns designed to please audiences who want a different version of a story they have already seen dozens of times. And, while there's some truth to the maxim that "there's nothing new under the sun," *Being John Malkovich* tries hard to be the exception. Admittedly, the themes addressed by the movie — those of identity, celebrity, and manipulation — are familiar, but the manner in which director Spike Jonze and writer Charlie Kaufman address them is fresh and inventive.

The premise is as intriguing and offbeat as it is difficult to adequately describe in a few sentences. Craig Schwartz (John Cusack) is a master puppeteer, but, after being out of work for a while, he is becoming restless, so his wife, Lotte (Cameron Diaz), suggests that he swallow his pride and get a job — any job. Since he has nimble fingers, he decides to apply for a position as a filing clerk. The job in question is on the 7½th story of a New York City office building — a floor that is 4 feet from carpet to ceiling ("low overhead") and can only be reached by stopping the elevator between the 7th and 8th stories and prying open the door with a crow bar. After a successful interview with the firm's sex-obsessed, carrot juice-drinking, 105-year-old boss, Dr. Lester (Orson Bean), Craig gets the job and meets his co-workers, including Floris (Mary Kay Place), the hearing-impaired secretary, and Maxine (Catherine Keener), a sexy brunette.

One day, while searching for a lost file behind a cabinet in his office, Craig discovers a hidden door. Venturing through it, he is sucked into a portal that lands him inside the brain of John Malkovich, where Craig can look out the actor's eyes and experience what he feels. It's the ultimate in voyeurism, but it doesn't last for long. Fifteen minutes after Craig enters Malkovich, the portal spits him out, dropping him from the sky and landing him alongside the New

Jersey Turnpike. He returns home and tells his wife, who wants to try the portal for herself. He also reveals the secret to Maxine, and, while he ponders "the metaphysical can of worms" the portal unleashes, she sees it as an opportunity to sell tickets: $200 a pop to be John Malkovich for 15 minutes.

The movie is surreal precisely because Jonze plays everything straight. The characters are not aware that they're in some kind of distorted reality, gazing through the looking glass darkly. This approach aids in the willing suspension of disbelief, drawing us into the story rather than distancing us and forcing us to gaze at the proceedings from the outside, looking for seams in the plot. *Being John Malkovich* is one of those rare cinematic experiences that works on one level or another for nearly everyone who sees it. It is a triumphant debut for Spike Jonze. **HIGHLY RECOMMENDED**

Best in Show [2000]

Starring: Christopher Guest, Eugene Levy, Michael McKean, Catherine O'Hara, Parker Posey, Fred Willard Director: Christopher Guest
Screenplay: Christopher Guest & Eugene Levy Running Time: 1:30
Rated: PG-13 (Profanity, sexual themes) Theatrical Aspect Ratio: 1.85:1

Arguably the King of the Mockumentary, Christopher Guest goes that route again with his latest endeavor, using the familiar format of *This Is Spinal Tap* (which he co-wrote and in which he co-starred) and *Waiting for Guffman* (which he wrote, directed, and appeared in) and applying it to the unlikely subject of dog shows. As with *Guffman,* Guest's satire is pointed and occasionally hilarious, but it is not mean-spirited. The film is a parody, but it displays knowledge and understanding of the subject it is satirizing, and it never takes cheap shots.

The story is simple, as befits a movie of this sort. By using "interviews" and manufactured documentary-style footage, *Best In Show* follows the travels and travails of several groups as they converge upon Philadelphia for the Mayflower Kennel Club's annual dog show. We meet Hamilton and Meg Swan (Michael Hitchcock and Parker Posey), a yuppie couple who met at a Starbucks and share a love of J. Crew and L.L. Bean catalogues; Gerry and Cookie Fleck (*SCTV* vets Eugene Levy and Catherine O'Hara), a mild-mannered businessman and his wife, whose "loose" reputation precedes her; gay couple Scott Donlan (John Michael Higgins) and Stefan Vanderhoof (Michael McKean), who pamper their dog incessantly; North Carolina native Harlan Pepper (Guest), who runs a shop called The Fishin' Hole and hits the road in his RV with his bloodhound; and Sherri Ann Ward Cabot

(Jennifer Coolidge), who shares a love of soup and snow peas with her rich, old husband, and is carrying on a lesbian affair with the handler of her dog.

The screenplay for *Best In Show* is funny in both subtle and overt ways. Some of the humor is sly; some is in-your-face. It's hard to imagine anyone sitting through this movie and not laughing on a fairly consistent basis. As in all of Guest's films, we come to care about the characters — perhaps not to the same degree that we might in a well-constructed melodrama or tearjerker, but, during the short span of 90 minutes, they become surprisingly real. And, while there's not a lot of tension surrounding the question of who eventually wins the "Best In Show" competition, Guest keeps us guessing, and rewards us with an unexpected twist or two. It's not great drama, but it prevents the story from dissolving into a series of loosely-connected comedy sketches. This is one rare occasion when we can be glad that the film industry is going to the dogs. **RECOMMENDED**

The Best Man [1999]

Starring: Taye Diggs, Nia Long, Morris Chestnut, Harold Perrineau Jr., Terrence Dashon Howard Director: Malcolm D. Lee Screenplay: Malcolm D. Lee Running Time: 1:58 Rated: R (profanity, sexual situations, violence, brief nudity) Theatrical Aspect Ratio: 1.85:1

The Best Man is not what it initially seems to be. Despite starting out with all the earmarks of a fairly ordinary romantic comedy, the project develops into a surprisingly effective look at a man's quest for rebirth after events topple him from a pedestal of arrogance. And, while there are plenty of laughs to be had, *The Best Man* functions better as a light drama than a straight comedy, with several scenes packing a punch because they're played straight. The film is the directorial debut of Malcolm D. Lee (Spike's cousin), who may have gotten this chance because of family connections but shows enough promise to earn further opportunities on his own.

The central character is, as one might anticipate from the title, scheduled to be the best man at a friend's wedding. Harper (Taye Diggs) is a Chicago-based writer who has just finished a novel called *Unfinished Business.* Although not yet published, it is described as a page turner, and Oprah has selected it for an upcoming book of the month. Like many good authors, Harper has filled his chapters with characters and events out of his past. And, just as a promising career is beginning to unfold before him, his girlfriend of 2 years, Robin (Sanaa Lathan), starts hinting that she wants a commitment that Harper is unwilling to give. He says he loves her, but he isn't ready for marriage.

Leaving Robin behind for a few days, Harper boards a New York-bound plane to participate in his best friend's wedding. There, he meets up with some old buddies. Much to Harper's dismay, just about everyone has read his book, even though it hasn't been published, and there are more than a few bruised feelings.

One cultural inequity that Lee dwells upon is the sexual double standard. Lance, the football gladiator, is essentially a throwback to the Stone Age. He believes that Mia should forgive him for his countless indiscretions; however, the thought that she might have slept with one other man fills him with a bubbling rage. Lee doesn't preach about this issue, but it's never far from the surface. Instead of applauding or condemning Lance's chauvinist perspective, he presents it neutrally and lets audience members draw their own conclusions. **RECOMMENDED**

The Big Lebowski [1998]

Starring: Jeff Bridges, John Goodman, Steve Buscemi, Julianne Moore Director: Joel Coen Screenplay: Joel & Ethan Coen Running Time: 1:55 Rated: R (Profanity, violence, nudity, drugs) Theatrical Aspect Ratio: 1.85:1

In a word, *The Big Lebowski* is a mess. But what a glorious, wonderfully-entertaining mess it is. Its single weakness, and what amounts to little more than a minor distraction, is that it doesn't have much of a plot, and what there is contains the kind of gaping holes that even the most obtuse viewer can identify.

The Coen Brothers begin by introducing us to their latest protagonist, The Dude (Jeff Bridges), a down-and-out, unemployed drifter who is still mentally mired in the '60s. Most of the time, The Dude is content to stay at home, which is why he's known as "the laziest man in Los Angeles County." That is, until a group of inept crooks confuse him with The Big Lebowski (David Huddleston), one of the city's richest businessmen.

It seems that Bunny Lebowski (Tara Reid), The Big Lebowski's ornamental wife, owes a great deal of money to porn producer Jackie Treehorn (Ben Gazzara). Treehorn's men mistake The Dude (whose real name is also Lebowski) for their quarry — and it takes them a while to realize their error (they're not Rhodes scholars). Irritated that his carpet has been ruined by the intruders, The Dude arranges a meeting with The Big Lebowski to extract compensation. But things don't go exactly as planned. Soon, The Dude finds himself on Lebowski's payroll as the bag man handling the ransom for his employer's kidnapped wife.

Much of the humor comes as a result of the sheer ineptitude of The Dude. This guy isn't a bad choice for handling the ransom drop in a kidnapping, he's the worst choice. He's a complete loser, and his friends (John Goodman, Steve Buscemi) aren't any better.

Problems with the plot notwithstanding, *The Big Lebowski* ranks as one of the most audacious comedies of recent years. The Coens keep the jokes coming, although some of them are so subtle they can easily be missed (for example, when The Dude writes a check for 69 cents). Profane, outrageous, and without inhibitions, *The Big Lebowski* further cements the Coens' reputation as *independent* film makers. **RECOMMENDED**

Big Trouble [2002]

Starring: Tim Allen, Rene Russo, Stanley Tucci, Omar Epps, Dennis Farina Director: Barry Sonnenfeld Screenplay: Robert Ramsey & Matthew Stone, based on the novel by Dave Barry Running Time: 1:22 Rated: PG-13 (Profanity, violence, brief nudity, sexual situations) Theatrical Aspect Ratio: 1.85:1

Big Trouble is a cinematic Rube Goldberg machine determined to prove the adage that the shortest distance between two points may be a straight line, but that is by no means the most interesting route. With a cast of characters so large that Robert Altman would feel at home, *Big Trouble* manages to do a lot of clever little things and generate quite a few big laughs without wearing out its welcome.

It's a mad, mad, mad world — a fact that Eliot Arnold (Tim Allen) is about to learn. A former Pulitzer Prize winning columnist for the Miami Herald, Eliot is currently stuck in a dead-end job running his own ad agency when destiny arrives in the form of a big metal suitcase containing a nuclear weapon that looks like a garbage disposal. With great rapidity, it changes hands. First, it's the property of a group of seedy Russian arms dealers. Then it's purchased by Arthur Herk (Stanley Tucci), a small-minded blackmailer with a foot fetish. Before Arthur has had a chance to become acquainted with his new property, it is stolen by the aptly named Snake (Tom Sizemore), who thinks it must be worth something. Eliot and Snake end up thrown together by circumstances, struggling with each other on a hijacked plane while the red digital display on the bomb counts down to zero. Thrown into the mix are Arthur's blond wife, Anna (Rene Russo); a hippie who's addicted to Fritos (Jason Lee); a couple of mismatched cops (Janeane

Garofalo, Patrick Warburton); a frustrated hit man (Dennis Farina); and a young couple (Ben Foster, Zooey Descanel) whose idea of a good time is shooting each other with water pistols. If all of this doesn't make any sense to you now, don't worry — it still might not after you have watched the movie.

Big Trouble's director is Barry Sonnenfeld, who is probably best known for *Men in Black*. Sonnenfeld's fondness for the warped and wacky is very much in evidence here. The high energy level and refusal to quit on the jokes reminded me of *Airplane*, and, although the movie primarily features stupid characters, *Big Trouble* plays well to a smart audience.

RECOMMENDED

The Birdcage [1996]

Starring: Robin Williams, Nathan Lane, Gene Hackman, Dianne Wiest, Dan Futterman, Calista Flockhart   Director: Mike Nichols   Screenplay: Elaine May, based on *La Cage aux Folles*   Running Time: 1:57   Rated: R (profanity, mature themes)   Theatrical Aspect Ratio: 1.85:1

Mike Nichols, the director of such well-received films as *The Graduate* and *Working Girl*, has taken the outrageous 1978 French farce, *La Cage aux Folles*, and, by tweaking, updating, and Americanizing it, come up with a huge winner. *The Birdcage*, as it's called, is one of those rare motion pictures with side-splitting laughs where the humor never stays dormant for long.

For some 20 years, Armand (Robin Williams) and Albert (Nathan Lane) have lived together as husband and wife (so to speak). Both are openly gay, and comfortable with their sexuality. They are partners in business as well as out of it — Armand operates a drag nightclub where Albert is the star performer. They have a son, Val (Dan Futterman), the product of Armand's one-night tryst 21 years ago with big-time executive Katherine Archer (Christine Baranski). As far as his upbringing is concerned, Val is as much Albert's son as Armand's, and he's not ashamed of his unusual family situation — at least not in the normal course of things.

But things are no longer normal. Val is engaged to the 18-year-old daughter of Senator Keeley (Gene Hackman), the co-founder of the Coalition for Moral Order. Since there's no way that Keeley would sanction a marriage between his daughter and the son of a gay couple, Val pleads with his father to pretend to be straight, if only for one night. The result of this, as might be expected, is a hilarious disaster.

Although most of the jokes come from Elaine May's screenplay, it's the performances that make them funny. Robin Williams, despite his reputation for unfettered mania, is surprisingly restrained throughout most of *The Birdcage*, doing a little serious acting along the way. Nathan Lane, playing the effeminate Albert, is the real star, whether he's trying to swagger like John Wayne (to act manly) or costumed like a housewife. Williams and Lane work well as a couple, feeding off one another in the fashion of all great comedy twosomes.

The structure of *The Birdcage* is designed to show us that there isn't much difference between conservatives and liberals or straight and gay people. Nichols' picture preaches tolerance and understanding, but neatly camouflages such themes beneath gaudy sets, colorful costumes, and unrestrained humor. The script has a few lulls, and there are times when it doesn't make a lot of sense, but there are few better ways to spend an evening than peering through the bars of *The Birdcage*. **HIGHLY RECOMMENDED**

Blast from the Past [1999]

Starring: Brendan Fraser, Alicia Silverstone, Christopher Walken, Sissy Spacek   Director: Hugh Wilson   Screenplay: Bill Kelly & Hugh Wilson   Running Time: 1:46   Rated: PG-13 (Sexual themes, profanity)   Theatrical Aspect Ratio: 2.35:1

Blast from the Past opens in 1962, when the Cold War is at its chilliest. Calvin and Helen Webber (Christopher Walken and Sissy Spacek) are regarded as eccentrics by their friends and neighbors. In a paranoid era when many affluent Americans are constructing their own personal fallout shelters, Calvin has taken things to an extreme. He has replicated his entire house underground. On the fateful night during the Cuban Missile Crisis, Calvin and Helen elect to play it safe and spend some time in their underground habitat. At the precise moment when they enter the shelter, a small plane falls out of the sky and crashes into their house. Convinced that a nuclear holocaust has begun, Calvin seals himself and his pregnant wife in. The locks on the shelter will not open for 35 years — the time Calvin has calculated that it will take for the surface to become habitable again.

Those 3½ decades pass quickly, and, by the late 1990s, Adam Webber, Calvin and Helen's grown son, is ready to venture forth into the world and find a wife. Considering his sheltered upbringing, he is ill-prepared for the pitfalls of making his way around present-day Los Angeles, but, when he hooks up with a young woman named Eve (Alicia Silverstone), he believes that not only has he found a guide and companion, but possibly a mate as well. Eve, who is being paid to help Adam, views things differently.

While it's possible to see *Blast from the Past* as a fairly traditional romantic comedy, the film is really more than that. It's a slick, clever satire of American culture, both as it exists today and as it was more than 3 decades ago. Director Hugh Wilson invested a great deal of thought and consideration into designing the look of the fallout shelter and the portion of 1998 Los Angeles into which Adam first emerges. For those who care to notice, there are numerous background sight gags. And the relationship between Adam and Eve is a little more substantial than just boy-meets-girl; it's about finding the middle ground between two radically different cultures.

Blast from the Past is arguably a little too ambitious. A subplot involving a religious cult isn't well-realized and a segment featuring a social worker is poorly integrated. Those are relatively minor hiccups in an otherwise frothy and enchanting motion picture. **RECOMMENDED**

Bowfinger [1999]

Starring: Steve Martin, Eddie Murphy, Heather Graham, Christine Baranski, Terence Stamp Director: Frank Oz Screenplay: Steve Martin Running Time: 1:37 Rated: PG-13 (Profanity, sexual situations) Theatrical Aspect Ratio: 1.85:1

Over the years, there have been a number of good films about the process of making a bad movie. *Bowfinger* is the latest entry into this semi-elite group. Powered by a hilarious, high-octane performance by Eddie Murphy and a witty, boisterous script by his co-star, Steve Martin, *Bowfinger* offers 90-plus minutes of solid entertainment. It's a comic oasis in the midst of the mid-August desert of motion picture mediocrity, and contains some of the biggest laughs of the year.

When Bobby Bowfinger (Martin) reads the script for *Chubby Rain* and decides that this is *the* movie he has been waiting for, Bowfinger is already in dire financial straits, but he manages to round up a group of performers, "borrow" the necessary equipment, and acquire the green light from high-power producer Jerry Renfro (Robert Downey Jr.). There's only one catch — for Renfro to back the movie's distribution, Bowfinger has to land action mega-star Kit Ramsey (Eddie Murphy) as his lead. And, when Kit sees the script, his immediate reaction is an emphatic "NO!" But that's only a minor bump in the road for Bowfinger. He forges ahead, using a hidden camera to photograph Kit as his actors come up to the star on the sidewalk and in restaurants saying their lines.

Soon Kit, paranoid at the best of times, is convinced that aliens are out to get him. And, when he disappears, Bowfinger must hire a lookalike replacement.

Bowfinger does what all good comedies do — it builds comic momentum as the film unfolds. This isn't just a series of gags strung together; it's a carefully orchestrated composition that delivers bigger and bigger laughs the longer it runs.

Bowfinger saves the best for last. The concluding series of scenes (excerpts from another Bowfinger masterpiece) are worth the price of admission in their own right. They're funny not just because they're madcap and silly (which they are), but because they display a knowledge of the subtleties of movie-making and utilize this know-how to create an unforgettable send-up of chop-socky action sequences. Not since Keenan Ivory Wayans' *I'm Gonna Git You Sucka* has a fight scene been done with this many winks at the audience. (None of the hero's punches or karate chops comes anywhere close to the bad guys). With all of the ingredients blended effectively together, director Franak Oz, Martin, and Murphy can be credited for supplying a deliciously amusing confection. **HIGHLY RECOMMENDED**

Bridget Jones' Diary [United Kingdom/ United States, 2001]

Starring: Renee Zellweger, Colin Firth, Hugh Grant Director: Sharon Maguire Screenplay: Richard Curtis, Andrew Davies, based on the novel by Helen Fielding Running Time: 1:35 Rated: R (Sex, profanity, violence) Theatrical Aspect Ratio: 2.35:1

The film tells the story of a year in the life of an average, single, 30-something British woman, who, armed with only her wits and charm (and a diary), goes in search of the ever-elusive Mr. Right. Unlucky-in-love Bridget (Renee Zellweger) has two candidates: the fun and sexy Daniel Cleaver (Hugh Grant) and the dour Mark Darcy (Colin Firth), whom she overhears calling her a "verbally incontinent spinster" when they first meet at a party. Not surprisingly, she goes for Daniel, but he turns out to be a less-than-perfect catch. Then, just when her interest in Mark begins to emerge, he hooks up with man-eating lawyer Natasha (Embeth Davidtz), who is determined to marry him. Meanwhile, her parents' marriage is on the rocks and she embarks upon a career in television news.

In England, the casting of American Renee Zellweger was initially greeted with much resistance by the press and the public. It was argued that not only was Zellweger an American, but she was too skinny to play the chubby Bridget. Well, some time between casting and shooting, Zellweger put on a few pounds and worked hard to perfect a British accent. These qualities, coupled with her natural charm and screen presence, make her a flawless choice for the lead. Zellweger embodies Bridget, and is a huge reason why the movie works.

Those who have read Jane Austen's *Pride and Prejudice* will find some familiar characters and elements in *Bridget Jones's Diary*. It doesn't take much deduction to determine that Helen Fielding is an Austen admirer, and that all of the nods to *Pride and Prejudice* are intentional. While it would be unfair to call *Bridget Jones's Diary* a 20th-century re-interpretation of *Pride and Prejudice,* there are some parallels — at least one of which the filmmakers have decided to emphasize.

The casting of Colin Firth as Mark Darcy is inspired. Firth, who essayed Mr. Darcy in the hugely popular 1995 BBC/A&E television production of *Pride and Prejudice,* plays this part exactly as he played the earlier role, making it evident that the two Darcys are essentially the same.

Bridget Jones's Diary is filled with moments of truth and flashes of humor (sometimes the two are the same). The direction, by newcomer Sharon Maguire, shows the deftness of a veteran. The energy level is consistently high and the characters (especially Bridget) don't take long to endear themselves to the audience. Congratulations to all involved. *Bridget Jones's Diary* is a triumph. **HIGHLY RECOMMENDED**

The Brothers McMullen [1995]

Starring: Mike McGlone, Edward Burns, Jack Mulcahy, Connie Britton, Shari Albert, Maxine Bahns Director: Edward Burns
Screenplay: Edward Burns Running Time: 1:37 Rated: R (Profanity, sex)
Theatrical Aspect Ratio: 1.85:1

Love, passion, and Irish Catholicism collide in *The Brothers McMullen,* writer/director Edward Burns' feature debut. Although it generally stays true to the clichés and plot turns of the genre, *The Brothers McMullen* is smart and honest rather than manipulative. Instead of resorting to hard-to-swallow story complications, this film stays on-target from its opening moments. Along the way, the empty dialogue too often incipient in this sort of picture is replaced by intelligent, insightful conversations.

One of *The Brothers McMullen*'s top assets is the brothers themselves. Despite their flaws (and each has a reasonably obvious one), Patrick (Mike McGlone), Jack (Jack Mulcahy), and Barry (Edward Burns) are likeable guys. They drink beer together, reminisce none-too-fondly about their dead father, and discuss topics ranging from true love to whether there's a hell.

Patrick, the youngest, has just graduated from college and is getting cold feet about the prospect of spending the rest of his life with his Jewish girlfriend, Susan (Shari Albert). Jack, the oldest, is happily married to Molly (Connie Britton), the love of his life. But, as her maternal instincts assert themselves, Jack's eye begins to roam. Barry, the middle brother, is the most cynical of the three. ("Being a pessimist," he says, "makes it easier to deal with my inevitable failure.") A screenwriter on the verge of a big breakthrough, Barry goes from relationship to relationship without ever finding love. Then he meets Audrey (Maxine Bahns), and suddenly nothing is quite so clear-cut.

If this film was only about the 3 men and their relationships, it would be enjoyable, but not particularly noteworthy. However, Burns has given his characters a slew of interesting things to say, and he hasn't reduced the women to pawns in male-centered romantic fantasies. In fact, in *The Brothers McMullen,* the female halves of the relationships are often smarter and hipper than their male counterparts. When one of the brothers thinks he's putting something over on his wife/girlfriend/lover, he's more likely just fooling himself.

Despite its occasional forays into weighty matters, *The Brothers McMullen* largely stays on the light side, where all good romantic comedies reside. The tone is upbeat and the script is laced with wit and, upon occasion, there are moments guaranteed to cause deeper, louder laughter. You don't have to be Catholic, or Irish, or even American, to "get it." Burns' language, despite originating on Long Island, is universal in appeal and meaning. **HIGHLY RECOMMENDED**

Bullets Over Broadway [1994]

Starring: John Cusack, Dianne Wiest, Chazz Palminteri, Jennifer Tilly, Mary-Louise Parker Director: Woody Allen Screenplay: Woody Allen & Douglas McGrath Running Time: 1:38 Rated: R (Violence, mature themes, language) Theatrical Aspect Ratio: 1.85:1

Bullets Over Broadway is the most insightful and deliciously droll look at show business since Robert Altman skewered Hollywood in 1992's *The Player*. The film questions what real art is. Just because a play is compromised, does that make it a less valid expression of ideas? And is it possible to get anything made without giving in on some element of artistic integrity? Woody Allen toys with those issues, taking playful jabs at his audience, himself, and the entertainment industry as a whole.

David Shayne (John Cusack as Allen's alter-ego) is a playwright with a brilliant script that no one wants to produce. Since it's "art," the belief is that it's destined for obscurity. ("If the common people don't understand your work, you're a genius.") Then, along comes a gangster (Joe Viterelli) looking for a role for his manifestly untalented actress girlfriend Olive (Jennifer Tilly). For the price of including her in the play, David can have all the money he needs. Despite a pricking conscience and the warnings of his girlfriend (Mary-Louise Parker), he agrees.

To round out the cast, David chooses as his leading lady Helen "Don't Speak" Sinclair (a wonderfully over-the-top Dianne Wiest), a star with an ego to match her mammoth reputation, and as his leading man, British thespian Warner Purcell (the always-reliable Jim Broadbent), a food addict who falls off the dieting wagon whenever he gets nervous.

With its legitimate issues couched in laughter, *Bullets Over Broadway* is a delight to experience. Solid performances, a clever script (which contains at least one truly outrageous twist), and a jaunty soundtrack of '20s songs keep this movie a notch above many of Allen's recent films. And good Woody Allen is always a sure bet for entertainment. **HIGHLY RECOMMENDED**

Bulworth [United States, 1998]

Starring: Warren Beatty, Halle Berry, Oliver Platt, Don Cheadle
Director: Warren Beatty Screenplay: Warren Beatty & Jeremy Pikser
Running Time: 1:48 Rated: R (Profanity) Theatrical Aspect Ratio: 1.85:1

In one sense, the film, put out by Warner Beatty with little concern for whose toes might get stepped on, can be summed up as an attack on the growing conservatism of the Democratic party, which is becoming increasingly more difficult to distinguish from its Republican rival. *Bulworth* is unrepentantly cynical in its view that all politicians are in the back pockets of big business and that every elected official, whether Democrat or Republican, is a member of an exclusive club. Hypocrisy, self-interest, and greed are the 3 forces that drive every campaign, and Senator Jay Billington Bulworth (Beatty) has had enough.

It's mid-March 1996, and Bulworth, an incumbent Senator from California, is running for re-election. However, he has reached the breaking point. After taking out a $10 million life insurance policy with his 17-year-old daughter as the sole beneficiary, he puts out a contract on his own life, then goes on the warpath against special interest groups. Suddenly,

Bulworth's "tell it like it is" philosophy is a national sensation, attracting the attention of millions, including a young black woman named Nina (Halle Berry), who is determined to show the Senator what life is like for those who live in South Central L.A. Right in the middle of everything, Bulworth suddenly decides that he wants to live, but learns that calling off a hit isn't as easy as setting one up.

Bulworth's only real weakness (and it's more in the nature of a minor inconvenience than a significant flaw) is the backstory, which, with its disguised hit men, car chases, and bungled assassination attempts, takes up a little too much time. The political satire, on the other hand, is brilliant. Not only is it honed to a viciously sharp edge, but it's frequently hilarious. Beatty manages to lampoon controversial issues, like kids selling drugs for dealers because they're too young to go to prison, while simultaneously making serious points. In addition to the political material, there are other targets, including the easy marks of tabloid reporters and TV news programs.

Bulworth is an angry movie, but Beatty is savvy enough to recognize that people respond better to comedies than serious "issue films," so he has camouflaged his message beneath the surface of this original, incisive satire. The movie has a take-no-prisoners attitude, and in today's climate of suffocating political correctness, that's a welcome trait.
HIGHLY RECOMMENDED

The Castle [Australia, 1997]

Starring: Michael Caton, Anne Tenney, Stephen Curry, Anthony Simcoe, Sophie Lee Director: Rob Sitch Screenplay: Santo Cilauro, Tom Gleisner, Jane Kennedy, Rob Sitch Running Time: 1:27 Rated: R (Profanity) Theatrical Aspect Ratio: 1.85:1

Fans of quirky Australian fare will appreciate *The Castle*'s offbeat sense of humor. The movie will probably not generate many belly laughs (although there are at least two hilarious sequences), but it will have all but the most die-hard curmudgeons smiling frequently. The feature debut of director Rob Sitch, *The Castle* represents a pleasant blend of gentle satire and feel-good comedy.

Michael Caton plays Darryl Kerrigan, the happiest homeowner in Australia. His abode at 3 Highview Crescent is his pride and joy, even though it's next door to an airport on one side and a high voltage tower on the other. Darryl lives in the ramshackle little house with his beloved wife, Sal (Anne Tenney), who makes the best meals of any woman on the face of the planet, and his two sons, narrator Dale

(Stephen Curry) and "idea man" Steve (Anthony Simcoe). A third son, Wayne (Wayne Hope) is in jail, and a daughter, Tracy (Sophie Lee), has recently entered a life of wedded bliss. For the eternally optimistic Darryl, life couldn't be better. But storm clouds are on the horizon.

The airport wants to expand, and, under an agreement with the government, they demand the compulsory acquisition of Darryl's home. Instead of accepting their generous offer and moving, he and a few neighbors decide to fight back. They hire a lawyer, Dennis Denuto (Tiriel Mora), to challenge the constitutionality of the airport's case. Unfortunately, Dennis isn't a very good attorney — he can't even get his copier to work — and he botches things up. All is not lost, however. The venerable Lawrence Hammill (Charles 'Bud' Tingwell) takes an interest in Darryl's seemingly lost cause, and intends to pursue the matter to the highest court in the land.

Although *The Castle* is a comedy, it's not entirely without themes and serious ideas. The central conflict is a classic David vs. Goliath (big business infringing on personal liberties) — something that almost everyone (except Fortune 500 CEOs) can relate to. Also, the concept of a "home" is presented as a deeply personal thing. One individual's shanty might be another's dream house. It's not just a case of bricks and mortar, but the whole package: memories, feelings, and other associations (both good and bad). Buildings do not have identities, but homes do. We don't just exist in them, we live there. *The Castle* is not an overly ambitious motion picture, but it has a point to make, and does so in an undeniably entertaining manner. RECOMMENDED

Children of the Revolution [Australia, 1996]

Starring: Richard Roxburgh, Judy Davis, Sam Neill, Geoffrey Rush, Rachel Griffiths, F. Murray Abraham Director: Peter Duncan
Screenplay: Peter Duncan Running Time: 1:40 Rated: R (Profanity, sex)
Theatrical Aspect Ratio: 1.85:1

Children of the Revolution opens in 1951 Sydney, where die-hard communist Joan Fraser (Judy Davis) is drumming up support to defeat a ballot referendum that would outlaw the party. Joan's mantra, which she utters at every possible opportunity, is taken directly from Marx: "From each according to his capacity to each according to his means." One of her fellow communists, a conventional fellow named Zachary Welch (Geoffrey Rush), proposes marriage, but Joan refuses, claiming that she's not in love with him.

Every week, she writes a new letter to her hero, Joseph Stalin (F. Murray Abraham). When the dictator finally gets around to reading her missives, he is so touched by her enthusiasm that he arranges for her to visit Moscow for the 1952 Communist Party Conference. There, on the night that Stalin dies, she sleeps with both him and an Australian/Russian double agent (or perhaps triple agent) named David Hoyle. Nine months later, when Joan is back in Sydney and married to Zachary, she gives birth to a baby boy. But is the child, Joe Welch (played by Ben McIver as a youngster; Richard Roxburgh as an adult), the offspring of Stalin or Hoyle?

Smartly written and adroitly developed, *Children of the Revolution* fires verbal and visual volleys at multiple bullseyes, from communism and Stalin to the news media and McDonalds. Not all of the satirical jabs hit their mark, but there are so many of them that most of the misses go unnoticed. And several that do work are just short of brilliant. One of the more absurd scenes, which calls to mind Mel Brooks' "Springtime for Hitler" (from *The Producers*), has Stalin singing and dancing to "I Get a Kick Out of You." There's also a sequence that details a "macabre and barbaric" means of breaking a hunger strike: blow the scent of sizzling bacon into the cell of the striking prisoner. *Children of the Revolution* uses a fresh approach to take aim at a broad range of targets, and the result is both decisive and incisive. RECOMMENDED

Citizen Ruth [1996]

Starring: Laura Dern, Swoosie Kurtz, Kurtwood Smith, Mary Kay Place
Director: Alexander Payne Screenplay: Alexander Payne & Jim Taylor
Running Time: 1:46 Rated: R (Profanity, mature themes) Theatrical
Aspect Ratio: 1.85:1

The average movie about the abortion debate tends to be preachy, melodramatic, and unbearably solemn. So, it comes as something of a shock that the latest venture to the front line of the pro-life/pro-choice battle is actually a *comedy*. Director/co-writer Alexander Payne has taken the slogans, name-calling, and behind-the-scenes tactics, and created a vicious satire that skewers (and probably offends) those on both sides of the issue. There's a serious message here, as well — that in a war between ideologies, it's too easy to lose sight of the individual.

Laura Dern (*Rambling Rose*) is Ruth Stoops, a glue-sniffing, alcoholic drifter who has been arrested 16 times for "hazardous vapor inhalation." She has given birth to 4 children, all of whom have been taken away from her by the government. Her family and friends have disowned or abandoned her. Now, after being jailed for getting high on patio sealant, she learns that she's pregnant again. The judge decides to allow charges of felony criminal endangerment of the fetus, but tells Ruth that if she gets an abortion, he'll reconsider. Suddenly, Ruth's case becomes a lightning rod for local activists. The struggle for Ruth's conscience pits the Baby Savers, run by an evangelical husband-and-wife team (played by Kurtwood Smith and Mary Kay Place), against a pro-choice organization headed by a lesbian feminist (Swoosie Kurtz). The situation rapidly develops into a war where the weapons are coercion and bribery, and the last thing anyone seems to care about is Ruth.

Laura Dern gives an excellent performance, allowing herself to be photographed in an extremely unattractive fashion, with no makeup, dark circles under her eyes, and lank, unwashed hair hanging below her shoulders. She plays Ruth as a selfish, but very human, character who only cares about the pro-life and pro-choice movements in relation to how she can benefit from them (preferably financially).

Citizen Ruth has its share of bitingly funny moments, and some of the comedy is quite inventive. By structuring the film as a satire, Payne is able to make statements about the abortion issue that no straight film would likely attempt, and, as is often the case, there's a great deal of truth buried in the humor. In fact, *Citizen Ruth*'s weakest moments occur not when it's savaging social causes and political concerns, but when it attempts to inject conventional drama into its exaggerated, outrageous milieu. RECOMMENDED

Clerks [1994]

Starring: Brian O'Halloran, Jeff Anderson Director: Kevin Smith Screenplay: Kevin Smith Running Time: 1:37 Rated: R (Graphic language, mature themes) Theatrical Aspect Ratio: 1.85:1

The comedy found in *Clerks* is raw and ribald, varying from somewhat off-color to truly tasteless. Nothing, no matter how outrageous, is beyond director Kevin Smith, and his willingness to flaunt cinematic taboos is one of the reasons why *Clerks* is such a unqualified success. The dialogue accurately captures the street language common in the part of the country where the movie was filmed. There are a few lines that come across as scripted, but this is often the result of the manner in which they're delivered (the actors are good, but not seasoned). As far as the level of profanity is concerned, anyone spending time on a Monmouth County (New Jersey) street won't be shocked, but those who are offended by such language should beware.

By Smith's own admission, there isn't much of a plot — just a loose framework to hold together a series of scenes featuring odd personalities in bizarre situations. The main characters are Dante (Brian O'Halloran), a Quik Stop clerk who does his best to cater to his customers, and Randal (Jeff Anderson), the man behind the counter at a local video store who spends his time insulting and offending every potential renter. Also wandering in and out of the story are a local drug-dealer, Jay (Jason Mewes), and his sidekick, Silent Bob (Kevin Smith), as well as Dante's current girlfriend, Veronica (Marilyn Ghiglotti), and his ex, Caitlin (Lisa Spoonhauer).

It's rare for a motion picture to maintain the level of irreverence and humor of *Clerks* for its full running length. In his first outing behind the camera, Kevin Smith has given his audience the kind of film at which veteran film makers often fail. As the final credits roll with the promise that "Jay and Silent Bob will return in *Dogma*," we can be thankful that this isn't the last we'll see of Smith or his cast of offbeat characters. HIGHLY RECOMMENDED

Clockwatchers [1997]

Starring: Toni Collette, Parker Posey, Lisa Kudrow, Alanna Ubach Director: Jill Sprecher Screenplay: Jill Sprecher, Karen Specher Running Time: 1:36 Rated: PG-13 (Profanity) Theatrical Aspect Ratio: 1.85:1

Clockwatchers opens with a brilliant scene that is repeated daily, all across the country, in hundreds of work places. A secretarial temp, Iris (Toni Collette), arrives to start a new assignment with Global Credit. She gets there a few minutes early and is ignored by the receptionist, who doesn't go on duty until the clock strikes 9. Then, she is shown into the office complex, where she is told to wait until someone comes to tell her what to do. Two hours later, she's still waiting. During all that time, no one has shown the slightest interest in her; she's a temp, and, therefore, beneath notice. In terms of the office food chain, she's plankton.

Four temps work for Global Credit, filing papers, making copies, and stuffing envelopes. In addition to the meek, mousy Iris, there's Margaret (Parker Posey), a rebel who doesn't mind raising eyebrows by speaking her mind; Paula (Lisa Kudrow), an airheaded blond with acting aspirations; and Jane (Alanna Ubach), a woman with low self-esteem who is willing to marry an insensitive fiancé just to get out of the corporate rat race. For its first 50 minutes, *Clock-watchers* explores the developing friendship among these 4 as their common employment status forms a natural bond. Then, during the film's second half, Sprecher investigates how the existence of an office kleptomaniac fosters distrust and paranoia, elevating the level of tension and fragmenting friendships.

The thing I liked best about *Clockwatchers* is its understanding and subtly satirical presentation of life in a rigidly conservative office, where anything other than strict conformance is regarded with a frown. Many employees have so little work that, in Margaret's words, "The . . . real challenge is trying to look busy when there's nothing to do." One man guards his stash of pencils, pens, and rubber bands like they are precious jewels. Meanwhile, everyone counts down the minutes remaining until quitting time.

Clockwatchers is billed as a comedy, and, in many ways, it is one. But there's also a lot of drama here, and, as the film moves along, there are fewer and fewer laughs. Essentially, this is an autopsy of a lifestyle, and, while a lot about it seems funny at first, the more we get to know the characters and understand the futility of their lives, the more disheartening it becomes. With *Clockwatchers,* director Jill Sprecher has created a setting that may be bizarre to those unfamiliar with the world of office temping, but will seem on-target for anyone who has endured a foray into this lifestyle. *Clockwatchers* offers a perspective of the American corporate office that is both viciously satirical and depressingly accurate. RECOMMENDED

Cold Comfort Farm [United Kingdom, 1996]

Starring: Kate Beckinsale, Eileen Atkins, Rufus Sewell, Ivan Kaye, Ian McKellan Director: John Schlesinger Screenplay: Malcolm Bradbury, based on the novel by Stella Gibbons Running Time: 1:44 Rated: PG-13 (Sexual situations) Theatrical Aspect Ratio: 1.66:1

Using an almost-apologetically gentle satire, *Cold Comfort Farm* parodies Merchant-Ivory films and their ilk. Transpiring in the 1920s, the movie takes us to the dilapidated rural estate of Cold Comfort Farm, where recently-orphaned Flora Poste (Kate Beckinsale) has come to stay with distant relatives. In some way, the Starkadders, who inhabit Cold Comfort, owe a debt to her father, but, while no one will say what it is, they agree to give her free room and board. For her part, Flora intends to organize the untidy farm, as well as the lives of everyone who call it home.

The residents of Cold Comfort Farm are a strange lot. There's Judith Starkadder (Eileen Atkins), a middle-aged widow who continually prophesies dis-aster for her family. There are her sons, Seth (Rufus Sewell), who loves movies, and Reuben (Ivan Kaye), who loves farming. Judith's brother, Amos (Ian McKellan), is a fire-and-brimstone preacher. Her mother, Ada Doom (Sheila Burrell), the Cold Comfort matriarch, remains locked in her room. Also living in the house are Elfine (Maria Miles), a beautiful-but-flighty young woman who wants to marry a member of the gentry, and Adamsbreath (Freddie Jones), the family's faithful retainer.

With comic efficiency, Flora sets to work giving each member of the Starkadder clan what they want. There are no real characters here — each member of the cast plays a certain period piece type to good effect. We sympathize with the men and women of Cold Comfort Farm largely because of strong performances, not because they're written with any depth or breadth. As is often true of satire, the people don't matter as much as the situations they're placed in.

Cold Comfort Farm is not a vicious lampoon. The script cares about its characters and doesn't want to distance the audience. Some of the best satire comes near the end, while the various subplots are reaching happy conclusions. Schlesinger uses "Tara's Theme" from *Gone with the Wind* to put the hilarious punctuation on a very funny scene. This sequence, the movie's comic highlight, had me nearly doubled over with laughter. There may not be intellectual enrichment forthcoming, but there's undeniable pleasure to be gained from watching Flora bring warmth to *Cold Comfort Farm*. RECOMMENDED

Commandments [1997]

Starring: Aidan Quinn, Courteney Cox, Anthony LaPaglia Director: Daniel Taplitz Screenplay: Daniel Taplitz Running Time: 1:26 Rated: R (Profanity, sex, mature themes) Theatrical Aspect Ratio: 1.85:1

Commandments, the first major feature from writer/director Daniel Taplitz, is a satire of faith, religion, and hypocrisy. Strangely enough, it's also the most offbeat disaster movie to come along in years (note: that's "disaster movie" *not* "movie disaster"). In fact, for the price of admission, we're treated to 3 different manifestations of Mother Nature's wrath: a tornado, a violent thunderstorm (with associated lightning strike), and a hurricane.

Taplitz obviously intended this to be a black comedy, and, viewed as such, it's reasonably successful. It is also potentially offensive to anyone who considers himself (or herself) a deeply religious person. *Commandments* dares to call God "a raging psychotic" (and mean it) and postulates that the reason he allows suffering is that he's either a fraud or malevolent. A few of the theological questions posed here are ones that fundamentalists tend to sidestep or talk around because they raise disturbing possibilities. And some of the satire is as vicious as it is risky, which may alienate mainstream viewers.

The main character, Seth Warner (Aidan Quinn), was a nice, well-adjusted True Believer — until God chose him to live a '90s remake of the Book of Job. Within a short time, he lost his wife and unborn child, his home, and his job. When he demands an answer from the Almighty, he gets struck by lightning and ends up in the hospital. While convalescing there, he comes up with an audacious scheme to show his contempt for God. He's going to break every one of the Ten Commandments. When he confesses the plan to his brother-in-law, Harry (Anthony LaPaglia), it doesn't provoke much of a reaction. It seems that Harry routinely breaks 5 or 6 commandments a day without much thought. "Get back to me when you start breaking some really serious ones," he says. Meanwhile, Harry's wife, Rachel (Courteney Cox), is far more sympathetic to Seth's circumstances, and it doesn't take long before she becomes his primary target for Commandment #7 ("Thou shalt not commit adultery").

Although the script isn't a masterpiece of twists and surprises, not everything goes as expected, and the audience isn't quite as far ahead of the characters as it initially thinks. For anyone who isn't easily offended and doesn't mind forthright irreverence, *Commandments* is worth checking out — at least you haven't already seen 5 movies like it already this year. **RECOMMENDED**

The Cook, the Thief, His Wife and Her Lover
[United Kingdom/France, 1989]

Starring: Richard Bohringer, Michael Gambon, Helen Mirren, Alan Howard, Tim Roth Director: Peter Greenaway Screenplay: Peter Greenaway Running Time: 2:05 Rated: NC-17 (Sex, nudity, violence, profanity, rotting fish and meat) Theatrical Aspect Ratio: 2.35:1

If there's anything disgusting or grotesque that *The Cook, the Thief, His Wife, and Her Lover* doesn't dabble in, I'm at a loss to figure out what it is. This film, a wildly exuberant, bitingly satirical examination of excess, bad taste, and great acting, is the kind of over-the-top experience that will have timid movie-goers running (not just walking) for the exits. Taboos? If director Peter Greenaway has any, you can't tell by this film.

Roughly ⅔ of the film takes place inside the fine French restaurant, Le Hollandais. With a dungeon-like kitchen that looks like it was snatched out of Terry Gilliam's *Brazil*, this is a fantastically bizarre place to eat dinner. The chef, Richard (French actor Richard Bohringer), is a gastronomical genius who cares as much for the artistry of a meal as for its taste. Le Hollandais' owner, an uncouth rogue by the name of Albert (Michael Gambon), visits the restaurant nightly in the company of his wife, Georgina (Helen Mirren), and a flock of toadies. There, sitting in the center of Le Hollandais' dining room, at the biggest table, Albert holds court, spouting often-absurd discourses about any subject he can think of. But, while he's talking, his neglected wife catches the eye of a nearby diner (Alan Howard), and soon those two sneak away for a tryst in the Ladies' Room.

The Cook, the Thief, His Wife, and Her Lover is well-written, with dark humor and irony peppering nearly every conversation and monologue. Set design is top notch. Le Hollandais is a surreal place. This is also a movie of vivid colors: reds for the dining room, pinks for the rest rooms, and greens for the kitchen. *The Cook* is always visually interesting, even on those rare occasions when other aspects of the production aren't as arresting.

One message that Greenaway clearly conveys is the association between two of life's most obvious sensual pleasures: eating and sex. He litters this picture with the brutal and the grotesque — including murder, covering someone with excrement, and cannibalism. *The Cook* is always as visceral as it is visual, with Gambon on hand to provide acid commentary for everything (he never seems to stop talking). Then there's the ending, which contradicts the saying that revenge is a dish best served cold. In this case, it's warm, and very, very appropriate. **HIGHLY RECOMMENDED**

Cookie's Fortune [1999]

Starring: Glenn Close, Julianne Moore, Liv Tyler, Chris O'Donnell, Charles Dutton, Patricia Neal Director: Robert Altman Screenplay: Anne Rapp Running Time: 1:58 Rated: PG-13 (Sensuality, suicide) Theatrical Aspect Ratio: 1.85:1

Cookie's Fortune deserves to be appreciated on its own terms. A less-ambitious outing from veteran director Robert Altman, this movie delivers agreeable performances and a charming, amusing story that offers little in the way of substance. The movie is set in the deep South. Actually, let me amend that — it's set is a world that is a gentle caricature of the deep South, a place which is manufactured from a combination of reality and the outsider's preconceptions.

As is often Altman's method, *Cookie's Fortune* was developed as an ensemble piece. The title character, played by Patricia Neal, is a Southern matriarch in her waning years. She's an odd but likable old lady who has an easy rapport with her close friend, confidante, and odd-jobs man, Willis (Charles S. Dutton). In addition to being fond of Willis, Cookie has a soft spot in her heart for Emma (Liv Tyler), the young daughter of her dim, gullible niece, Cora (Julianne Moore). Cookie also has another niece, the intolerant, image-conscious Camille (Glenn Close), who thinks of herself as the most important person in Holly Spring.

After spending some time introducing the characters and defining their relationships, *Cookie's Fortune* shifts into high gear with a change in tone. While the early portions of the film set us up for a lighthearted melodrama, Altman eventually guides his picture into the realm of farce and dark comedy. Despondent about her failing health, Cookie resolves to take her own life. When Camille finds the body, she decides to fake a burglary and murder, because "suicide is undignified." After eating Cookie's suicide note, she enlists Cora's aid in concocting a complicated cover-up that fools the local police.

The result of all this is a madcap plot that involves jailhouse trysts, paternity revelations, and all sorts of other intrigue. With a sly, clever script (by Anne Rapp) that consistently ratchets up the comic momentum and even throws in a little genuine suspense, *Cookie's Fortune* builds to a delightfully funny climax. Some of the best moments are provided by small, aside jokes, such as when one character literally gets caught with her hand in the cookie jar. And, while *Cookie's Fortune* never devolves to the level of mindless comedy offered by the many lowbrow films populating multiplex screens, this isn't intellectual humor, either. It's entirely accessible to anyone willing to invest 2 hours. **RECOMMENDED**

Cradle Will Rock [1999]

Starring: Emily Watson, John Turturro, John Cusack, Joan Cusack, Hank Azaria, Angus MacFadyen, Susan Sarandon Director: Tim Robbins Screenplay: Tim Robbins Running Time: 2:15 Rated: R (Nudity, profanity, mature themes) Theatrical Aspect Ratio: 2.35:1

Cradle Will Rock is Tim Robbins' most challenging feature to date. A combination screwball comedy and period piece drama, the film makes us laugh while presenting themes that are as relevant today as they were 6 decades ago. Intertwining the stories of more than a dozen characters and using a style that variously recalls the work of Preston Sturges, Orson Welles, and Robert Altman, Robbins generates a pace that is often frantic.

Cradle Will Rock is, according to the film, (mostly) based on a true tale. Actually, it's more like 5 episodes that are thematically and, at times, narratively, linked. The primary story tells of the efforts of director Orson Welles (Angus MacFadyen), producer John Houseman (Cary Elwes), writer Marc Blitzstein (Hank Azaria), and their cast to put on the pro-Union play "The Cradle Will Rock" despite attempts by the U.S. government to close it down. Folded into this tale are the struggles of Hallie Flanagan (Cherry Jones) to keep the Dies Committee from cutting financial support to the WPA (which funded the Federal Theater program) because of alleged pro-Communist propaganda in the plays. Meanwhile, Nelson Rockerfeller (John Cusack) hires artist Diego Rivera (Ruben Blades) to paint a mural in the lobby of Rockerfeller Center, then balks when he sees the final product. Steel magnate Gray Mathers (Philip Baker Hall) flirts with Mussolini's mistress, Margherita Sarfatti (Susan Sarandon), while his flighty wife, the Countess (Vanessa Redgrave), pursues social causes. And an alcoholic ventriloquist (Bill Murray) believes that communists are infiltrating vaudeville, but his attempts to do something about them alienate him from everyone he knows.

Cradle Will Rock treads into fascinating territory with some of its meatier issues. How far does freedom of expression go? Does the government have the right to arbitrarily determine what "art" it will fund, or is that censorship? And, when a person owns a piece of art, does he or she have the right to determine when or how it is displayed, or whether it can be changed, defaced, or destroyed? None of these questions have easy answers, and *Cradle Will Rock* doesn't pretend they do, but it addresses all of them during its 135-minute running time. **RECOMMENDED**

Crocodile Dundee [Australia, 1986]

Starring: Paul Hogan, Linda Kozlowski, John Meillon, David Gulpilil, Mark Blum Director: Peter Faiman Screenplay: John Cornell, Ken Shadie, Paul Hogan Running Time: 1:33 Rated: PG-13 (Profanity, mild violence, sexual innuendo) Theatrical Aspect Ratio: 2.35:1

Crocodile Dundee is a breezy, fun affair — a trifle that is extremely pleasant to sample and leaves no bitter aftertaste. It's a fantasy that's part romantic comedy and part fish-out-of-water, and, while most of the elements are familiar in a different context, *Crocodile Dundee*'s method of merging them is unconventional enough that the film seems as fresh and unsullied as the Australian bush in which the first half of the movie transpires.

The film opens with New York journalist Sue Charlton (Linda Kozlowski) hunting down the legendary Michael J. 'Crocodile' Dundee (Hogan) in the small rural Australian town of Walkabout Creek. She makes contact with Walter Reilly (the late John Meillon), the co-proprietor of "Never Never Safari Tours," who promises to send her on a 3-day, 2-night trip with Mick. Local myth states that Mick survived a one-on-one encounter with a crocodile, then, after having half his leg bitten off, he crawled back home. Sue wants to see where it happened so she can prepare a feature on Mick and his ordeal. After spending about 48 hours together in the bush, Mick and Sue have bonded, and she invites him to come back to New York with her. So, for the first time in his life, Mick leaves Australia for the wilds of Manhattan, where he encounters a stranger breed than anything found in the bush.

Crocodile Dundee is peppered with memorable moments, most of which occur during the second half, while Mick is navigating the ins-and-outs of New York City. In addition to his encounter with a mugger with a knife, he also plays the gallant gentlemen to a pair of hookers, and comes up with an infallible (if untactful) way of determining whether a woman is really a woman, or just a man dressed in drag. All the while, he and Sue have time to fall in love, which leads to the grand fairy tale ending in the subway station.

The movie works entirely because of Hogan. It's not hard to understand why American movie-goers reacted so positively to him; his Mick Dundee has a natural, unforced charm that is hard for even the best actor to artificially generate. Mick is the kind of guy all men would like to have for a buddy and all women would like to have for something a little more.

Many years after its initial release, *Crocodile Dundee* is still as fresh and enjoyable as ever. Little in the film seems dated, and Hogan's affability shines through. What the storyline lacks in ambition, it makes up for in sheer, unfettered likability.
RECOMMENDED

Deconstructing Harry [1997]

Starring: Woody Allen, Judy Davis, Elizabeth Shue, Kirstie Alley, Bob Balaban Director: Woody Allen Screenplay: Woody Allen Running Time: 1:38 Rated: R (Profanity, mature themes, sexual situations, nudity) Theatrical Aspect Ratio: 1.85:1

How much of Woody Allen is there in Harry Block? This is undoubtedly one of the questions likely to be foremost in any viewer's mind after watching Allen's 1997 feature, *Deconstructing Harry*. It's also the question most often asked of the director in interviews about the film. Allen has been understandably evasive, stating repeatedly that, while there may be some similarities between Harry and himself, the movie is a work of fiction and Harry is nothing more than a character.

So who is Harry Block? He is, by some accounts, one of the most unpleasant men alive. Since he's played by Woody Allen, he's also an insecure and self-absorbed individual, as well. Professionally, he's a world-famous, bestselling author who writes thinly-veiled autobiographical tales about his relationships with his 3 ex-wives. Personally, he's a wretch — a pill-popping, alcoholic lout who has few friends and can't stay faithful to one woman. Ostensibly, the film is about Harry's trip to upstate New York, where a college that expelled him as an undergraduate now wants to honor him as a distinguished alumnus. At the same time, he's looking to overcome a severe case of writer's block. Along with Cookie (Hazelle Goodman), a hooker he hired for the day; Richard (Bob Balaban), a friend with a bad heart; and Hilly (Eric Lloyd), his son, Harry heads north.

Allen's script isn't linear, but it isn't difficult to piece together. The intent is to amuse, not to confuse. However, aside from piquing the viewer's curiosity about how much of Allen is in Harry, there's not a whole lot of depth to *Deconstructing Harry*. It's a movie of moments, some of which are side-splittingly funny. Arguably, this is the most uproarious comedy that Allen has ever done. The dialogue is almost always as brilliant and witty as it is profane. Then there's Robin Williams, who, in a cameo, has never been so delightfully out of focus.

Deconstructing Harry is an uneven piece of work, but the high level of comedy covers up many of the rough spots. We may never know how much of this film is pure fiction and how much is self-analysis, but one thing is for sure — once the laughter has subsided and the end credits have rolled, audience members will begin deconstructing Woody. **RECOMMENDED**

Dodgeball [2004]

Starring: Vince Vaughn, Ben Stiller, Christine Taylor, Rip Torn, Justin Long, Stephen Root, Joel David Moore, Chris Williams, Alan Tudyk Director: Rawson Marshall Thurber Screenplay: Rawson Marshall Thurber Running Time: 1:32 Rated: PG-13 (Sexual innuendo, profanity, cartoon violence) Theatrical Aspect Ratio: 2.35:1

Of course, *Dodgeball* isn't a true underdog anything, but that's all part of the joke. A blistering satire of feel-good sports movies, this film makes its mark via the most direct route: It lampoons by adopting the tried-and-true "straight" formula and tweaking it a little. The approach works because many sports dramas are borderline unintentional parodies with less tension than a flaccid cable; all the filmmakers of *Dodgeball* had to do was to follow the plot-by-numbers approach, incorporate some obviously comedic material, and toss in a huge dose of over-the-top earnestness. The resulting product offers about 90 minutes of laughter (although the movie runs out of steam during its final third).

The showdown that *Dodgeball* builds to is the ultimate David-Goliath battle, with the "Average Joe's Gym" team facing the "Globo Gym" pros. And it's all being televised on ESPN 8 ("The Ocho"). On the one side, we have straight-shooting Peter La Fleur (Vince Vaughn), who's competing to get the $50,000 that will keep the bank from foreclosing on his gym. He is joined by five of his clients, an attractive ex-bank employee (Christine Taylor), and legendary dodgeball player-turned-coach, Patches O'Houlihan (Rip Torn). On the other side is a group of mean monsters assembled by Globo tycoon White Goodman (Ben Stiller), who wants to acquire Average Joe's so he can tear it down and erect a parking garage. No points for guessing who wins, who gets kissed, or whose luck runs out.

Although *Dodgeball* is built on a foundation of satire, there's plenty of conventional humor, varying from the not-too-silly to the absolutely ridiculous. Some of the one-off gags, such as White pumping himself up in preparation for an encounter with a woman, are hilarious. Others lose their effect through repetition — seeing someone get nailed by a volley of hard-thrown balls is only funny the first time or two. Few satires are capable of sustaining their comedic momentum for the length of a full-feature film, and *Dodgeball* is no exception. The film starts out slowly, hits its stride fifteen minutes in, then starts flagging around the two-thirds point. By the time *Dodgeball* reaches its obligatory conclusion, all of the potential for humor has been burned up. Of course, comedy is subjective, and there are those who will be less than enamored with *Dodgeball*'s sophomoric and occasionally vulgar brand of humor. For me, however, it was a pleasant diversion. **RECOMMENDED**

Election [1999]

Starring: Matthew Broderick, Reese Witherspoon, Chris Klein, Jessica Campbell Director: Alexander Payne Screenplay: Alexander Payne & Jim Taylor Running Time: 1:44 Rated: R (Sexual themes & situations, profanity) Theatrical Aspect Ratio: 2.35:1

Reese Witherspoon plays Tracy Flick, a model student who is running unopposed for the highest student office. She's an overachiever's overachiever. Witherspoon, who has shown her range in a variety of roles, presents Tracy as all seemingly-perfect students should be presented: superficially good-natured and perky, but a real bitch underneath. Teacher Jim McAllister (Matthew Broderick) doesn't like Tracy (she was the "victim" in a sex scandal that led to the firing of his best friend), so he decides to encourage another student to run against her in the election. His choice is Paul Metzler (Chris Klein), one of the best-loved and most sincere students at Carver. He's also a football star with a broken leg, and his intelligence is on the level expected from a jock. Paul is popular, but he runs an inept campaign. His idea of addressing the student body is reading a speech as a single run-on sentence, delivered in a monotone. There's also a surprise entrant into the election: Paul's sister, Tammy (Jessica Campbell), an angry lesbian whose view of student elections is that they're "pathetic charades." The race turns into a tight tug-of-war with Paul remaining completely honest, Tammy seeming not to care, and Tracy resorting to unethical stunts. Meanwhile, McAlliester, unable to remain a spectator, begins to harbor sexual fantasies about Tracy even as he works to orchestrate her downfall.

Election is the sharpest satire of any teen movie made in years. Like the best lampoons, it attacks by exaggerating reality ever-so-slightly and targeting a broad range of subjects. There are no cheap shots and no grotesquely distorted performances. Those who have been involved in school elections will recognize the accuracy of director Alexander Payne's portrayal. Actually, it's not just school elections that Payne is taking a swipe at, but elections in general.

Election doesn't pull any punches. Its frank view of sexuality is in stark contrast with the cute or crude versions presented in most teen stories. The film is frequently funny, but, as with all dark comedies, our laughter isn't always comfortable. The use of multiple narrators allows the viewer to understand the different perspectives. The ending is laced with the perfect touch of irony. *Election* may not present the most flattering portrait of today's teenager, but there's a lot of truth in the picture it paints. **HIGHLY RECOMMENDED**

Fierce Creatures [1997]

Starring: John Cleese, Jamie Lee Curtis, Kevin Kline, Michael Palin
Directors: Robert M. Young and Fred Schepisi Screenplay: John Cleese
& Iain Johnstone Running Time: 1:33 Rated: PG-13 (Profanity, sexual
situations) Theatrical Aspect Ratio: 2.35:1

After the unexpected success of 1988's *A Fish Called Wanda,* John Cleese began planning a movie that would reunite the entire cast. After flirting with the concept of a direct sequel, he decided instead to invent new characters for the actors to play. Now, 8 years later, Cleese's idea has finally reached screens, and, while it's not quite as bold, funny, or endearing as *Wanda*, it's still good for numerous hearty laughs, which is more than can be said for most comedies these days.

Cleese's script (co-written with Iain Johnstone) reads like a series of skits loosely connected by a flimsy storyline. The chief pleasure here is that several of the individual sketches are gut-bustingly funny. One of Cleese's fortes has always been humor based on mistaken assumptions, and *Fierce Creatures* features quite a lot of these. There's also enough crude (but still effective) sexual innuendo that an "R" rating wouldn't have been out of the question (although the MPAA granted a "PG-13"). Only the flatulence bits don't really work.

The rather convoluted storyline starts in Atlanta, where Willa Weston (Jamie Lee Curtis) arrives for work in her new post with Octopus Inc. to find out that multi-billionaire Rod McCain (Kevin Kline) has changed her job description. Now, along with his bumbling son, Vince (Kline again), she's supposed to go to England to take over management of the Marwood Zoo, which has to boost its profits by 20% or face closure. Meanwhile, the current zoo manager, Rollo Lee (John Cleese), has decided that the best way to increase revenue is to promote violence ("Sylvester Stallone did not get where he is today by playing in Jane Austen," he says). As a result, only fierce creatures are to be retained in captivity. Much to the consternation of the various animal keepers (Michael Palin, Cynthia Cleese, Ronnie Corbett, ex-Bond girl Carey Lowell), Lee decides that all the tame, cuddly animals must be eliminated — one way or the other.

Even when *Fierce Creatures* doesn't have you doubled over with laughter, it's still amusing. There are plenty of moments that, while not worth laughing aloud at, are capable of bringing a smile to the face. This isn't a great movie — the comedy is uneven and the connecting storyline is weak — but it's still a lot of fun, and I welcome any film that keeps me entertained for nearly the entire running length.
RECOMMENDED

A Fish Called Wanda [1988]

Starring: John Cleese, Jamie Lee Curtis, Kevin Kline, Michael Palin
Director: Charles Crichton Screenplay: John Cleese Running Time: 1:48
Rated: R (Profanity, sexual situations, brief nudity, violence) Theatrical
Aspect Ratio: 1.85:1

A Fish Called Wanda represents the high point of John Cleese's motion picture career. The film, which sprang from his pen and was directed by Charles Crichton, not only highlights Cleese's comic aptitude, but also that of co-stars Michael Palin, Jamie Lee Curtis, and Kevin Kline (who won a Best Supporting Actor Oscar for the part). The script contains enough hilarious moments to allow each member of the cast to have a chance to shine while the audience is kept in stitches.

The story centers around a quartet of jewelry store robbers. George (Tom Georgeson) is the ringleader, the man who has masterminded the theft. He is assisted by his stuttering, animal-loving friend, Ken (Michael Palin), and his girlfriend, Wanda (Jamie Lee Curtis). But Wanda wants the loot all to herself, and, to aid her in getting it away from George, she brings her psychotic, Nietzche-reading lover, Otto (Kevin Kline), into the gang. After the heist is successfully completed, Wanda and Otto place an anonymous call to the cops, and George is arrested. But, before he's hauled off to prison, he hides the jewels where Wanda and Otto can't find them.

In order to reduce his sentence if he's found guilty, George hints that he might be willing to turn over the location of the jewels to his barrister, Archie Leach (Cleese). As a result, the next step in Wanda's plan is to seduce Archie, a mild-mannered lawyer looking for a little romance and excitement. Soon, he's embroiled in the hilarious caper, and, as the situation grows progressively more convoluted, he learns that stolen jewels can make for very strange bedfellows.

Nothing is sacred to Cleese, who flouts every possible definition of political correctness by satirizing homosexuals, the British, the Americans, and stutterers. And, just to prove that he's got nothing to hide, Cleese does one of the most side-splitting stripteases ever to appear on screen. It's not erotic, but what happens immediately afterwards will have you doubled over with laughter. Despite the non-stop zaniness, Cleese manages to fashion his screen personae into a likable hero. We quickly come to sympathize with Archie, an appealing loser who's finally getting a chance to break out of the constrictive shell that has held him back all his life.

A Fish Called Wanda is one of the best-constructed, funniest, and most clever comedies to grace motion picture screens in recent years. It's outrageous, offensive, and even a little sick — and all the more enjoyable because of it. John Cleese has spent his entire career rejecting conventional comedy, and, on this occasion, there's no denying that he has hit paydirt. **MUST SEE**

Flirting with Disaster [1996]

Starring: Ben Stiller, Patricia Arquette, Tea Leoni, Mary Tyler Moore, George Segal, Alan Alda, Lily Tomlin Director: David O. Russell Screenplay: David O. Russell Running Time: 1:32 Rated: R (Sex, profanity, mature themes) Theatrical Aspect Ratio: 1.85:1

Ben Stiller's neurotic Mel Copland is going through a mid-life crisis long before mid-life. A control freak no longer in control, Mel, who was adopted as a baby, is on a quest for his biological parents. In fact, he's so hung up on the issue of his "true identity" that he hasn't been able to name his 4-month old son. Mel's long-suffering wife, Nancy (Patricia Arquette), is trying to be supportive, but, as Mel's obsession deepens, it becomes more difficult. Finally, one day, the adoption agency locates Mel's mother: a middle-aged woman living in San Diego. With Tina Kalb (Tia Leoni), a leggy counselor-in-training from the agency, in tow, Mel and Nancy head west. And that's where the disasters, which start with a mistaken identity and end with a flight across the border into Mexico, begin. Before it's all over, Mel will have become acquainted with 4 parents, 2 gay federal officers, and a brother who tries to send him on a bad acid trip. All the while, he'll be trying to figure out who he is, whether he wants Tina or Nancy, and why he bothered searching for his roots in the first place.

Director David O. Russell takes the traditional road picture and does some really strange things with it. With a view of middle America that David Lynch would applaud, Russell peels back the layers of normalcy to reveal the twisted and absurd things that go on underneath. However, where Lynch makes his case through violence and mysticism, Russell uses outrageous humor and parody. The results are no less telling, however.

Each new port of call offers a surprise. If it's not a false lead, it likely involves some time in handcuffs. Russell delights in stringing us along with Mel as his search becomes increasingly more surreal — he is trapped by circumstances beyond his control. But if there's one lesson he learns, it's that sometimes it's better to appreciate what you have instead of yearning for what you don't. To be sure, Mel grows from his experience, but if he had it to do over again, he'd probably stay home.

Russell has paced his film perfectly, gradually building from the relatively normal to the extremely strange, and heightening the humor with each new twist. *Flirting with Disaster* has its tongue firmly planted in its cheek the entire way; there's no opportunity for serious introspection. By the time the ninety-minute film has expired, you'll be glad you joined Mel and company on this hilariously eccentric journey. **HIGHLY RECOMMENDED**

Four Weddings and a Funeral [United Kingdom, 1994]

Starring: Hugh Grant, Andie MacDowell, Kristin Scott Thomas, Simon Callow, John Hannah Director: Mike Newell Screenplay: Richard Curtis Running Time: 1:57 Rated: R (Language, sexual situations, mature themes) Theatrical Aspect Ratio: 1.66:1

The simplest and most honest expression of praise that I can offer Mike Newell's movie is that it represents 2 hours of solid movie magic. *Four Weddings and a Funeral* possesses the rare ability to make an audience laugh (and laugh hard) and cry, without ever seeming manipulative or going hopelessly over-the-top.

Charles (Hugh Grant), now in his 4th decade of life, is a "serial monogamist" — someone who moves from girlfriend to girlfriend without ever falling in love. His friends have started down the matrimonial road, but not Charles. Thoughts of spending the rest of his life with someone never enter his head, until one day at a wedding when he encounters Carrie (Andie MacDowell), an American fashion editor. And, although the two enjoy a brief tryst at an inn, Charles' typical British reticence kicks in, and Carrie is on her way back to America before he realizes he should have said something.

Four Weddings and a Funeral is about, well, 4 weddings and a funeral (actually, if you want to be picky, it's about 3 weddings, a funeral, and another wedding). While the central story of this charming motion picture is fairly common romantic comedy fare, it is framed by a plot filled with little twists and turns, lots of laughs, and a frothy, intoxicating atmosphere.

Four Weddings and a Funeral is a modern comedy with a very traditional theme. It blends good breeding and bad language; laughter and tears; and marriage and friendship into a thoroughly enjoyable whole. Mike Newell knows what his viewers want, but appreciates them enough not to give it in a predictable or obvious manner — and that is the greatest pleasure of all in watching this movie. **HIGHLY RECOMMENDED**

Good Bye, Lenin! [GERMANY, 2003]

Starring: Daniel Brühl, Kathrin Sass, Chulpan Khamatova, Maria Simon, Florian Lukas, Alexander Beyer, Burghard Klaussner Director: Wolfgang Becker Screenplay: Wolfgang Becker, Hendrik Handloegten, Bernd Lichtenberg, Christoph Silber, Achim von Borries Running Time: 2:00 Rated: R (Profanity, brief nudity) Theatrical Aspect Ratio: 1.85:1 In German with subtitles

It's 1989, and Berlin is in turmoil. Hoenicker's iron fist, gloved by the Stasi, is beginning to lose its grip. East Berliners are heading West in droves, bleeding out through Hungary. Alex Kerner (Daniel Brühl) is the loyal and obedient son of Christiane Kerner (Kathrin Sass), an activist who believes in the virtues of Socialism. When she sees her son marching in an antigovernment protest, she suffers a heart attack and ends up in a coma. It's mid-1990 before she awakens, and much has changed. Her daughter, Ariane (Maria Simon) has a new boyfriend, Rainer (Alexander Beyer), and Alex has fallen in love with Lara (Chulpan Khamatova), one of Christiane's nurses. But those small human dramas are insignificant compared to what has happened outside: the Wall is down, and the wound dividing East from West is healing.

Christiane has a weak heart, and her doctor warns that any shock could kill her. Alex decides that he has to hide the fall of the Wall from his mother, so he concocts a fake world in which Hoenicker is still in power and Socialism remains potent. With the help of a would-be filmmaker friend, Denis (Florian Lukas), he creates mock newscasts. The deeper Alex gets into his fictional world, the more convinced his girlfriend and sister are that he's doing the wrong thing, but Alex will not be dissuaded. He believes that his actions are saving his mother. But what happens when she is well enough to get out of bed and begin to explore the world outside of her room?

What Alex does for Christiane is not the only example of reality manipulation. Another character has also promulgated a big lie. When this is revealed, it touches a number of lives and feeds into Alex's fantasy world. Of course, one wonders from the beginning whether Christiane suspects her son is up to

something, but since she is weak and bedridden, she has no choice but to trust him. What we have to determine is whether or not his actions are betraying her trust. Does she have the right to know, even if it kills her?

Lest I make the movie sound too somber, I should mention that Becker directs with a deft touch. *Good Bye, Lenin!* is filled with many lightly comedic moments and, in its development of the tender relationship between Alex and Lara, offers a portion of romance. The actors all do fine jobs, especially Daniel Brühl, who exhibits escalating pent-up stress as Alex's fabricated world spins out of control, and Kathrin Sass, whose Christiane hides a secret or two.

Perhaps most interesting to the non-German viewer is the exposure Becker provides of the social and political currents that were in force during that period. It is not a step-by-step chronicle of German reunification, but it gives a perspective of the time. It's a bonus that this comes as part of an engrossing and well-told story. **RECOMMENDED**

Gridlock'd [1997]

Starring: Tim Roth, Tupac Shakur, Thandie Newton, Vondie Curtis Hall, Bokeem Woodbine Director: Vondie Curtis Hall Screenplay: Vondie Curtis Hall Running Time: 1:31 Rated: R (Profanity, violence, drug use, nudity) Theatrical Aspect Ratio: 1.85:1

Gridlock'd is about people caught in one of life's most absurd traffic jams, and the lengths that they'll go to in order to get moving again. It's a darkly humorous, vicious satire, and, like all the best satires, it works because so much of what transpires on screen not only could happen, but does happen — every day in every major urban area across the country. First time writer/director Vondie Curtis Hall sees the comedy in the situation and uses it to deliver a blistering attack on the social system and its attendant bureaucracy.

Spoon (Tupac Shakur) and Stretch (Tim Roth) are a '90s odd couple. Spoon is a mature, even-tempered black man; Stretch is a childish, borderline-manic white guy. Yet, even though their personalities are 180 degrees apart, they're as close as brothers. They work together, live together, get high together, and, when they decide to free themselves from drugs, they try to kick the habit together.

The occasion for this momentous decision is an overdose by Cookie (Thandie Newton), Spoon's lover and the third member of their performance art group. While she lies in a coma at a nearby hospital, Spoon and Stretch come to grips with the precariousness of their lives. "I don't want to go out like that," laments Spoon (his words eerie in retrospect, considering the fate of the actor speaking them), "Lately, I've been feeling like my luck's running out." Getting into a detox program, however, proves to be next-to-impossible. Spoon and Stretch spend one long day racing from social service locale to locale, taking blood tests, filling out forms, waiting on lines, and being chased by both cops and drug dealers — all in a hopeless attempt to get a little help to "kick it."

Gridlock'd is refreshing because it's different. The subject matter isn't new, but the approach and tone are. For Vondie Curtis Hall, this is the promising beginning of what will hopefully be a long and fulfilling career. For Tim Roth, it's another fine performance to add to his ever-growing resume. And for Tupac Shakur, who displays genuine talent here, it's a fitting epitaph. Hopefully, *Gridlock'd* won't get lost in the traffic jam of low-quality, mid-winter releases that surround it. **RECOMMENDED**

Groundhog Day [1993]

Starring: Bill Murray, Andie MacDowell, Chris Elliot Director: Harold Ramis Screenplay: Danny Rubin & Harold Ramis Running Time: 1:41 Rated: PG (Little offensive) Theatrical Aspect Ratio: 1.85:1

The date is February 2 and the place is Punxsutawney, Pennsylvania. Pittsburgh weatherman Phil Connors (Bill Murray), on hand to cover the Groundhog Day ceremony, is having one of the most unpleasant experiences of his life. It's one of those days when Murphy's Law seems to be in full effect. But Phil soon discovers that things are worse than they first seemed, because for him, and him alone, time has stopped. Now, he's trapped in a bizarre time loop that forces him to re-live Groundhog Day over and over, with no hope of reprieve or release, and no way of explaining the situation to anyone else since he's the only one who realizes what's happening.

It's déjà vu gone mad. *Groundhog Day* is one of the most original comedies to grace the screen in months. With as much repetition as there is, it would be easy for the film to get bogged down. Solid directing, combined with judicious editing, eliminate the problem. The only time we see a scene repeated is when there's something new added, and even then we are re-shown little more than what's necessary for the effect.

The humor is of a higher caliber than that found in most so-called comedies. *Groundhog Day* finds its humor in situations and characters. Making use of Bill Murray's talent as a comedian, the film encourages him to play off of the more serious Andie MacDowell. While the chemistry between them isn't smouldering, they work well together. Their characters' romance is credible because it's low-key.

Groundhog Day isn't a science fiction or fantasy film, so it's not interested in answering the technical questions of how the time loop came about, or what might happen if Phil stayed up all night. Instead, it presents the situation to the audience on a take-it-or-leave-it basis. I'll wager that there are few who will choose the latter option.

With all of the formula-driven, painfully unfunny comedies available today, it's a pleasure to uncover something as unique as *Groundhog Day*, especially in the month of February, which isn't known for strong releases. This movie has all the qualities necessary to be a crowd-pleaser: likable characters, charismatic performers, a strong, capably-executed premise, and lots of laughs. **HIGHLY RECOMMENDED**

Grumpy Old Men [1993]

Starring: Jack Lemmon, Walter Matthau, Ann-Margret, Burgess Meredith, Ossie Davis Director: Donald Petrie Screenplay: Mark Steven Johnson Running Time: 1:43 Rated: PG-13 (Language, mature themes) Theatrical Aspect Ratio: 1.85:1

John Gustafson (Jack Lemmon) and Max Goldman (Walter Matthau) have been neighbors since they were kids, and the feud between them has lasted almost as long. A state of uneasy coexistence is in place, with namecalling and practical jokes being the most heated their exchanges get. Their rivalry turns more serious, however, when both of them become interested in the new neighbor across the street. Ariel (Ann-Margret) is vivacious, beautiful, and alluring, and both John and Max are smitten.

While not without its problems (some of which are readily apparent), *Grumpy Old Men* works more often than not. It's an example of a frothy, good-natured holiday picture that adults can relax and enjoy. As a comedy, the movie contains enough fresh humor to keep the laughs coming. Dramatically, however, it's rather feeble. There are formulas at work here, and anyone admitting to be surprised by the "plot twists" should hang his or her head in shame.

Lemmon and Matthau are perfect for their roles as lifelong sparring partners. Of course, these two are no strangers to this sort of interplay, having done it several times before, most memorably in *The Odd Couple*. This is an example of perfect casting, as is the choice of Burgess Meredith as the tough-talking, dirty-minded patriarch of the Gustafson family.

Fortunately, drama always plays second fiddle to comedy, and this is a consistently funny motion picture. There's everything from slapstick to puns, with a lot of clever references and gags. Witness Jack Lemmon and Walter Matthau's "performances" to the song "I'm too Sexy," Lemmon's send-up of Macaulay Culkin's aftershave scream from *Home Alone,* and the little dance number Lemmon does in his underwear. The end credit outtakes are perhaps the comic highlight of the movie. Most attending a showing of *Grumpy Old Men* will leave the theater with a smile, and that's basically what the movie is aiming for.
RECOMMENDED

Happy, Texas [1999]

Starring: Jeremy Northam, Steve Zahn, William H. Macy, Ally Walker, Illeana Douglas Director: Mark Illsley Screenplay: Ed Stone, Mark Illsley & Phil Reeves Running Time: 1:44 Rated: PG-13 (Profanity, sexual content, violence, mature themes) Theatrical Aspect Ratio: 1.85:1

Happy, Texas doesn't exactly shatter expectations by breaking new cinematic ground, but that's part of its charm. We're on a road that has to conclude with a happy ending; the fun is in the trip, not at the destination. A pair of escaped cons, the laconic Harry Sawyer (Jeremy Northam) and the dimmest bulb in the pack, Wayne Wayne Wayne Jr. (Steve Zahn), are looking for a place to lie low while the police are scouring the countryside for them. When they arrive in the small hamlet of Happy, Texas ("the town without a frown") in a stolen Winnebago, they are mistaken for the pair of gay beauty pageant consultants who have been hired to help the little girls of Happy win the 18th annual "Little Miss Fresh Squeezed" talent contest. Since this kind of impersonation seems like a great way to steer clear of the cops, the pair decides to play along with the town's enthusiastic residents. So, while Wayne, under the watchful eye of the local school teacher, Ms. Schaefer (Illeana Douglas), ineptly tries to instruct his charges on the finer points of winning a pageant, Harry plans a robbery of the local bank. But there are two complications — he is falling for the bank president, Josephine McLintock (Ally Walker), while being courted by the sheriff, Chappy Dent (William H. Macy), who thinks he finally has found a soul mate.

Jeremy Northam, as suave as always even out of period costume, gives a low-key rendering of Harry — he's the prototypical "likable crook" because, deep inside, he has a heart of gold, no matter how much he likes to pretend otherwise. With Northam playing the straight man, that leaves it up to Steve Zahn to generate most of the laughs — a task for which he is eminently suited. The only actor who stands a chance of upstaging Zahn is William H. Macy. For most of the film, Macy's reserved sheriff is content to remain in the background, but, as events shift into high gear, he emerges from the closet to add a dash of pathos to the proceedings.

If there's a down side to *Happy, Texas*, it's that the ending doesn't deliver the expected comic punch line — instead, it gets stuck incorporating a little too much action. That's really a minor quibble, however. The real pleasure of this film isn't that many of the jokes work, but that Illsley's affection for the characters carries over to the audience. **RECOMMENDED**

High Fidelity [2000]

Starring: John Cusack, Jack Black, Lisa Bonet, Joan Cusack, Iben Hjejle Director: Stephen Frears Screenplay: D.V. DeVincentis, Steve Pink, John Cusack & Scott Michael Rosenberg, based on the novel by Nick Hornby Running Time: 1:50 Rated: R (Profanity, sex) Theatrical Aspect Ratio: 1.85:1

Based on the novel by Nick Hornby, *High Fidelity* is a quirky comedy that explores the romantic misfortunes of the main character. Rob is the owner of "Championship Vinyl," a music store that specializes in LP's. Along with his assistants, belligerent Barry (Jack Black) and meek Dick (Todd Louiso), Rob does his best to keep his shop afloat, even though it's barely making enough for him to keep him off welfare. Rob is a neurotic, and he obsesses over his lackluster romantic history. Fond of making Top 5 lists, Rob has recently composed his "Top 5 all-time breakups," and he re-lives each of them in his head, from a high-school sweetheart he kissed under the bleachers to the beautiful Charlie (Catherine Zeta-Jones), who is even more self-absorbed than Rob. His latest loss, however, has hit Rob the hardest, because he belatedly realized she may have been "the one." Her name is Laura (Iben Hjejle), and, after growing weary of Rob's general listlessness and unwillingness to commit, she decided to leave him and move in with a former neighbor, new wave guru Ian (Tim Robbins).

As far as the plot goes, there really isn't one — *High Fidelity* is a movie driven by characters (Rob's in particular) and situational comedy. A significant portion of the film takes place in the record store, and it's there that *High Fidelity* shines, with Barry verbally abusing ignorant customers and Dick shyly making advances towards a girl (Sara Gilbert) he finds attractive. For the most part, Rob stays in the background during these scenes, watching bemusedly as his two cohorts conduct business. He comments that he can't fire them because he "hired [them] for 3 days a week, then they started showing up every morning — that was 4 years ago."

There's no deep meaning to *High Fidelity*, although it occasionally toys with the importance of pop music to a person's psychological development. At one point early in the film, Rob muses, "Did I listen to pop music because I was miserable, or was I miserable because I listened to pop music?" There's more than a hint of Woody Allen in the project, from the neuroses of the main character to the *Annie Hall*-type dissection of a failed romance, but without the stigma that some movie-goers attach to anything Allen does. Because of its quirky characters, smart dialogue, and occasional bursts of penetrating humor, *High Fidelity* stands out as a "small" motion picture that deserves wide exposure. **RECOMMENDED**

House of Angels [Sweden/Norway/Denmark, 1992]
Starring: Helena Bergstrom, Rikard Wolff, Sven Wollter, Viveka Seldahl
Director: Colin Nutley Screenplay: Susan Falck Running Time: 1:59
Rated: R (Language, nudity) Theatrical Aspect Ratio: 1.85:1 In Swedish with subtitles

House of Angels begins in a small farming community somewhere in Sweden, where a local citizen is about to meet his death in an automobile accident. At his funeral, his sole surviving relative arrives — a long-lost granddaughter named Fanny (Helena Bergstrom). She is accompanied by a gay companion, Zac (Rikard Wolff), who's the perfect picture of a biker: leather jacket, sunglasses, and five o'clock shadow. The pair are from Berlin, and have big city customs that don't fit in the small town setting, so when they move into the dead man's house, the residents of the village become uneasy. The women are afraid that Fanny will steal away their menfolk, and the men are uncertain what to make of their new neighbor. Only one person has a clear goal. Axel (Sven Wollter), the local bigshot, wants Fanny out so he can buy up her land.

Things aren't always what they seem — a point that *House of Angels* is adept at illustrating. Fanny and Zac look like the wild, drug-addicted deviants that the townspeople believe them to be, but few are willing to get to know the pair well enough to test their preconceived convictions. Once the label is affixed, nothing Fanny can do will remove it. Eventually, she decides to give people what they expect, but this leads to her own disillusionment.

The small town/big city conflict is played out with conformity as the principal weapon. Too many of the villagers don't want something new or different in their midst, and so are threatened by what Fanny and Zac represent. Rather than concede the potential value in diversity, they attempt to squash it.

House of Angels is an excellent example of how lighthearted film can be used to probe deeper, more intense issues without becoming preachy or overbearing. There's a priest in this film, but the movie isn't given to sermonizing. The picture's sense of fun rarely flags, nor does the inner core of drama that underlies each scene. *House of Angels* has a lot to say, and the best thing is that the audience enjoys every word that's spoken. **HIGHLY RECOMMENDED**

The House of Yes [1997]
Starring: Parker Posey, Josh Hamilton, Tori Spelling, Freddie Prinze Jr., Genevieve Bujold Director: Mark Waters Screenplay: Mark Waters, based on the play by Wendy MacLeod Running Time: 1:25 Rated: R (Sex, profanity, mature themes) Theatrical Aspect Ratio: 1.85:1

Going home to meet your fiance's family seems like the normal thing to do. Intimidating, perhaps, but normal. And Lesly (Tori Spelling) is a *very* normal girl, albeit not a particularly bright one. In fact, that's why Marty Pascal (Josh Hamilton) is attracted to her — he has a craving for normalcy, something that he never got from his family. His twin sister, Jackie-O (Parker Posey), is obsessed with the former First Lady, even going so far as to dress up as her and stage re-creations of JFK's final moments. And the relationship between Marty and Jackie-O isn't a typical sibling connection; it's more like a brother/sister affair. Mom (Genevieve Bujold) and little brother Anthony (Freddie Prinze Jr.) are aware of the situation, but, in the best interests of all involved, they turn a blind eye.

Then, on Thanksgiving Day in 1983, Marty shows up at his Washington D.C. home in the midst of a hurricane. He's not alone — Lesly, the proud bearer of a new engagement ring, is with him. Jackie-O's reaction upon learning that her beloved brother is no longer all hers is to let out a piercing scream. Mom is a little more reserved. On her way back into the kitchen, she calmly notes, "I'm going to go baste the turkey and hide the kitchen knives." Over the next 24 hours, Lesly will learn all there is to know about Marty and Jackie-O while capturing Anthony's affection and earning Mom's enmity.

Although *The House of Yes* is dark, bleak, and occasionally disturbing, it is subversively funny — and I mean laugh-aloud funny. Admittedly, most of the humor is warped (how else could you describe a comedy with central themes of incest and an obsession with JFK's assassination), but it would take an exceedingly bland viewer not to find at least a few amusing elements in the film. Consider, for example, the delightfully matter-of-fact manner in which Genevieve Bujold delivers her biting dialogue. Or the wonderfully off-the-wall way in which Parker Posey brings Jackie-O to demented life.

The House of Yes is what happens when a film takes the dysfunctional family melodrama to its farthest reaches. It's a bold, gutsy movie that's definitely not for everyone. But, for those who are always looking for the next daring motion picture and who aren't offended by off-color humor, *The House of Yes* offers 90 minutes of solid entertainment. Not every chance taken by Mark Waters works, but enough are successful to produce some memorable motion picture moments. **RECOMMENDED**

The Hudsucker Proxy [1994]

Starring: Tim Robbins, Jennifer Jason Leigh, Paul Newman, Charles Durning Director: Joel Coen Screenplay: Joel & Ethan Coen and Sam Raimi Running Time: 1:52 Rated: PG (Mature themes) Theatrical Aspect Ratio: 1.85:1

When he wanders into Hudsucker Industries for a job in the mail room, Norville Barnes (Tim Robbins) is an imbecile from Muncie with a single idea for a children's toy. Coincidentally, as Barnes is going in, the president of the company, Waring Hudsucker, is on his way out — through the window of the board room on the 44th floor (not counting the Mezzanine). Hudsucker's death sets off a panic; company rules state that since he died without having a will or living relatives, his majority share must be sold on the open market. Determined to devalue the stock so that the current board members can afford to buy it, Chief exec Sidney J. Mussberger (Paul Newman) devises a scheme to destroy the Hudsucker reputation by choosing a complete incompetent for the top seat. At that moment, he meets Norville Barnes . . .

From the opening sequence, soaring through the snow over the benighted building tops of New York, it's apparent that *The Hudsucker Proxy* is going to be a awe-inspiring visual experience. Given that the producer/director pairing is brothers Joel and Ethan Coen, who headed such projects as *Blood Simple, Miller's Crossing,* and *Barton Fink,* the emphasis on set design, artwork, and innovative cinematography (by Roger Deakins), shouldn't come as a surprise.

The Hudsucker Proxy skewers big business on the same shaft that Robert Altman ran Hollywood through with *The Player.* From the *Brazil*-like scenes in the cavernous mail room to the convoluted machinations in the board room, this film is pure satire of the nastiest and most enjoyable sort. In this surreal world of 1958 can be found many of the issues confronting large corporations in the 1990s, all twisted to match the filmmakers' vision.

The dialogue crackles, with one-liners and double entendres peppering the character exchanges. A Hula Hoop is referred to as an "Extruded Plastic Dingus," and a very un-Wim Wenders-like angel makes an appearance singing "She'll Be Comin' Round the Mountain." With its refined wit and glorious vision, *The Hudsucker Proxy* is certainly deserving of a wide audience. **HIGHLY RECOMMENDED**

An Ideal Husband [United Kingdom/United States, 1999]

Starring: Rupert Everett, Julianne Moore, Jeremy Northam, Cate Blanchett, Minnie Driver Director: Oliver Parker Screenplay: Oliver Parker, based on a play by Oscar Wilde Running Time: 1:36 Rated: PG-13 (Sensuality, brief nudity) Theatrical Aspect Ratio: 1.85:1

An Ideal Husband is a delightful parfait — an irresistible concoction of brilliant dialogue, sumptuous set design, top-notch acting, and a plot littered with Machiavellian twists. Possessing a light tone tinged with an acerbic accent, *An Ideal Husband* represents about the best that the motion picture industry can offer. It's an exquisitely crafted movie that can be appreciated from start to finish. Writer/director Oliver Parker has taken Oscar Wilde's play and tweaked it in such a way that the playwright's best lines remain intact while the setting has been opened up to offer a fresh perspective.

The film begins by taking us to England at the end of the 19th century. There, we are introduced to Lord Arthur Goring, played with panache by the underrated Rupert Everett. Goring is described by friends as "the idlest man in London"; his favorite pastimes are engaging in slothful activities, flirting with Mabel Chiltern (Minnie Driver), and avoiding being pushed into marriage by his stodgy father, the Earl of Caversham (John Wood).

Lord Goring's closest friends are Sir Robert Chiltern (Jeremy Northam) and his wife, Lady Gertrude (Cate Blanchett). Robert is an upright man of impeccable reputation and his wife, an independent-minded woman, is devoted to him. Several days before Robert is to speak before Parliament to denounce potential British support for an act to cut a canal through Argentina, he is approached by the devious Mrs. Laura Cheveley (Julianne Moore), who has just returned to London from Vienna. She offers him money to support the canal, and when he refuses, she comments that every man has his price. Her next action is to blackmail him — unless he capitulates, she will ruin his career and wreck his marriage by revealing the secret of how he acquired his wealth.

The plot has all the twists and turns of a David Mamet effort, yet remains surprisingly easy to follow. And it's a good thing, because unnecessary concentration on the mechanics of the story would take away from our ability to savor Wilde's dialogue, which never flags. Although the film's tone is primarily playful, there are serious moments, and it's during these that we gain genuine insight into the characters. Actually, some of the best interaction has less to do with words than with actions.

These days, with flashy action/adventure films and big budget science fiction flicks claiming the lion's share of the box office, it's easy to forget the simple, undeniable pleasure of watching a movie like *An Ideal Husband*, where dialogue, performances, and story construction combine to perfect the experience. **HIGHLY RECOMMENDED**

Igby Goes Down [2002]

Starring: Kieran Culkin, Susan Sarandon, Jeff Goldblum, Claire Danes, Ryan Phillippe Director: Burr Steers Screenplay: Burr Steers Running Time: 1:37 Rated: R (Profanity, sex, nudity, drugs, violence) Theatrical Aspect Ratio: 2.35:1

Igby (Culkin) hasn't had the greatest childhood. His father, Jason (Bill Pullman), is in a mental institution after suffering a breakdown while Igby was in grade school. His pill-popping mother, Mimi (Susan Sarandon) is cold, unfeeling, and more concerned about how Igby's frequent failures will reflect upon her reputation. His Young Republican brother, Oliver (Ryan Phillippe), appears embarrassed to be related to his undisciplined sibling. The only one Igby can rely upon is his open-minded, wealthy godfather, D.H. Baines (Jeff Goldblum), who views Igby's upbringing as his personal charity.

Igby fails at school because of his indifference. He has been expelled from one private institution after another until he finally ends up in military school. He doesn't last there, and ends up in rehab. Soon, he's hanging out in New York, acting like a bohemian. He lives in the same flat as D.H.'s artist mistress, Rachel (Amanda Peet), with whom his relationship quickly evolves from a platonic liaison to a sexual one. He gains an older girlfriend, the improbably-named

Sookie Sapperstein (Claire Danes), who stays with Igby until someone better comes along — namely his brother, Oliver. Meanwhile, Igby is hiding out from his detested mother and trying to figure out what to do with his existence. Despite his glib tongue and bravado, he is deeply insecure about the future. His major in life may be attitude, but on more than one occasion, he admits to being scared.

Igby Goes Down is one of those films where the whole is more than a sum of the pieces. There isn't much of a plot — this is basically just a series of episodes that, when strung together, present a patchwork tapestry of whom the main character is and how he got to be that person. With a less deft script, this could have been a thuddingly dull motion picture, but Steers finds the right balance between irony and pathos. Despite some heavy drama, things never become overly somber. As a first-time director, Steers is adequate — where he really shines is as a writer.

Igby Goes Down ends pretty much where it begins, with the majority of the story being told in flashback. For the most part, *Igby Goes Down* is lightweight, although it exhibits enough heft for us to develop an emotional connection with the main character. I have always appreciated a smartly written motion picture, and, whatever flaws *Igby Goes Down* may possess, it is undeniably that. **RECOMMENDED**

The Impostors [1998]

Starring: Oliver Platt, Stanley Tucci, Alfred Molina, Lili Taylor, Tony Shalhoub Director: Stanley Tucci Screenplay: Stanley Tucci Running Time: 1:41 Rated: R (Profanity, sexual comedy) Theatrical Aspect Ratio: 1.85:1

The Impostors is retro in almost every sense of the word. The only thing '90s about the movie are the actors, and the fact that the film stock is in color. The script and style hearken back to the early days of the motion picture industry. Savvy film-goers will recognize more than a little of the Marx Brothers, Charlie Chaplin, and Buster Keaton in the director's sophomore effort. This is the first screwball comedy in years that actually works, and that's mainly because Tucci hasn't tried to update the genre for a "modern" audience. Instead, he has crafted this film exactly as it might have been made 50 years ago. And, for those who want to look even further back into motion picture history, the opening sequence, which is done entirely without sound, is the director's homage to the great silent farces of the '20s.

The Impostors doesn't have much in the way of a plot. It's about the exploits of two Depression-era, unemployed actors, Arthur (Tucci) and Maurice (Oliver Platt), a likable Laurel and Hardy duo who would rather con people out of money and food than work for a living. After getting involved in a scrape with a famous Shakespearean actor, the absolutely awful Jeremy Burtrom (Alfred Molina), they end up as stowaways on a cruise ship bound from New York to Paris. They spend the rest of the film trying to avoid Burtrom, who's also on board, while unearthing a plot to blow up the ship.

Tucci pursues laughter with relish. An uncredited cameo by Woody Allen is only the tip of the iceberg. In the best tradition of the screwball comedy, there are role reversals and gender benders (look for Oliver Platt in drag). And, as the title implies, almost no one is who they seem to be, and much of the fun results from the various impostors being unmasked. No, there aren't any surprises for the audience, but it's entertaining to observe how the characters react to these revelations.

The goal of *The Impostors* is to tickle the funny bone, and it achieves that aim. Although I recognize that the appreciation of comedy is extremely subjective, it's hard to imagine anyone sitting through this film and not being captured by its infectious energy.
RECOMMENDED

In and Out [United Kingdom/United States, 1997]
Starring: Kevin Kline, Tom Selleck, Joan Cusack, Matt Dillon, Debbie Reynolds Director: Frank Oz Screenplay: Paul Rudnick Running Time: 1:30 Rated: R (Profanity, mature themes) Theatrical Aspect Ratio: 1.85:1

From the very first scene, you know that *In and Out* has struck a rich satirical vein. The movie opens in Greenleaf, Indiana, a conservative, family values-oriented town in middle America that seems to be stuck in the '50s. Director Frank Oz has photographed Greenleaf as a place with a gauzy, fairy tale-like quality that, along with some very pointed dialogue, gently pokes fun at cherished, *Leave it to Beaver* impressions of the "ideal" community. Unlike David Lynch, who has repeatedly attacked this image in his films, Oz and Rudnick are content to have a little affectionate fun with it.

We are introduced to Howard Brackett (Kevin Kline), one of the local high school's most popular teachers. Day-in and day-out, Howard attempts to stir the minds of his young charges to embrace Shakespeare and other forms of English literature. And, while the kids appreciate Howard's teaching methods, they're more interested in his recollections

of Cameron Drake (Matt Dillon), a pupil from several years ago who has gone on to become a teen heartthrob and the odds-on favorite to win this year's Best Actor Oscar. Howard is less interested in whether Cameron wins, however, than he is in planning his upcoming wedding to a fellow teacher, Emily Montgomery (Joan Cusack), with whom he has been engaged for 3 years. No one is more excited about the wedding than Howard's mother (Debbie Reynolds), who sees the ceremony as the culmination of a lifelong dream.

Then comes the bombshell. During his internationally-televised acceptance speech for the Academy Award, Cameron goes out of his way to thank "Howard Brackett," adding, rather unexpectedly, that "He's a gay teacher." Everyone, including Howard, is shocked by the statement. The next day, reporters converge on Greenleaf, looking for a story. One of them, Peter Malloy (Tom Selleck), manages to confront Howard alone, and what he reveals causes the confused teacher to question his own sexuality.

In and Out has a thinking person's script, and, as such, works on several levels. It can be seen as a light comedy, a biting satire, and/or a morality play that uses humor to examine society's approach to sexual identities. *In and Out* definitely isn't a pointless comedy of the *Dumb and Dumber* variety — it deals with issues in a shrewd manner, using a creative and well-written script to camouflage with wit any preaching. Regardless of your opinion of the gay community, *In and Out* is more than worth an evening's admission — provided, of course, that you like to laugh.
HIGHLY RECOMMENDED

Jeffrey [1995]
Starring: Steven Weber, Michael T. Weiss, Patrick Stewart, Bryan Batt, Sigourney Weaver Director: Christopher Ashley Screenplay: Paul Rudnick Running Time: 1:32 Rated: R (Profanity, sexual candor) Theatrical Aspect Ratio: 1.85:1

Jeffrey is a gay romantic comedy with a very impressive laugh-to-running time ratio. Written by *Addams Family* scribe Paul Rudnick (based on his play of the same name), this film is about as eccentric and quirky as they get. Rudnick throws everything at the viewer except the kitchen sink, and if he'd been able to find a way to get that in, he probably would have included it. And, despite all the mirth and mayhem, deep within *Jeffrey*'s core is a message everyone can relate to, regardless of their sexual orientation.

Jeffrey (Steven Weber) is a sexually compulsive, young, gay man. After a number of bizarre in-bed experiences, he decides to give up sex cold turkey. It's not an easy decision to begin with, but it becomes almost impossible when he meets Steve (Michael T. Weiss) at a gym. Jeffrey is immediately attracted to Steve, but his current celibate state makes a relationship difficult. However, Steve is patient, and it doesn't take long before Jeffrey starts to weaken. Then the bombshell is dropped — Steve is HIV+. At first, Jeffrey says it doesn't matter, but he's lying, and the moment he cancels a dinner date, Steve knows too.

Jeffrey never attempts to simulate real life. It's filled with asides to the audience, strange interludes (including a faux game show and a ghostly hospital encounter), and parodies of parodies. One hilarious segment has Sigourney Weaver playing "the nation's hottest post-modern evangelist." Another has Jeffrey talking frankly about sex to his mother and father. Then there's Nathan Lane as a randy priest who tries to seduce Jeffrey before breaking into a chorus of "Everything's Coming Up Roses." If nothing else, Rudnick and director Christopher Ashley know how to keep the audience off balance and in stitches.

You don't have to dig too deeply to find *Jeffrey*'s simple message, which is essentially the same as the one put forth by 1992's *Strictly Ballroom*: "A life lived in fear is a life half-lived." The AIDS epidemic has scared Jeffrey, and now he's not only hiding from his own sexuality, but from life in general. Darius, despite being mortally ill, describes Jeffrey as the saddest person he's ever known and offers this advice: "Hate AIDS, Jeffrey, not life." Ultimately, this is the point of *Jeffrey,* and it's what makes this film more than just a laugh-a-minute riot. RECOMMENDED

Joe Versus the Volcano [1990]
Starring: Tom Hanks, Meg Ryan, Lloyd Bridges Director: John Patrick Shanley Screenplay: John Patrick Shanley Running Time: 1:37 Rated: PG (Profanity) Theatrical Aspect Ratio: 2.35:1

The great god Big Woo, lord of the orange-soda swilling natives of Waponi Woo, demands a sacrifice. Big Woo is a volcano, and, unless someone jumps into its maw, the unappeased god will sink the island under the Pacific, drowning the Waponis. So along comes Joe (Tom Hanks), a man worn down by a drab life and a dead-end job. Joe has lost his self-respect — he lacks the courage even to ask out the boss' mousy secretary (Meg Ryan). Then, one day, Joe learns that he is afflicted with a terminal condition called a "brain cloud." Suddenly free from the constraint of worrying about his mortality, he accepts the offer of a

wealthy tycoon (Lloyd Bridges) to live out his last days "like a man," then die like a hero. In his case, being heroic means offering himself to Big Woo.

John Patrick Shanley's script can best be described as "quirky." Stretches of *Joe Versus the Volcano* are nearly perfect. On the other hand, the ending really doesn't work. In fact, the whole last act has problems. Once Joe and his love interest, Patricia (Ryan), reach Waponi Woo, things start to unravel. Shanley's attempts to have fun with the Waponi culture don't succeed. The satire isn't well-focused and the humor is flat. It's a shame, because this segment seems ripe with promise, all of which is wasted. Shanley never finds the right tone.

In fact, the second half of the film suffers from a mild case of split personality. On one hand, Shanley wants to continue the offbeat, delicious rhythm initiated with the opening credits, but, on the other hand, he wants to explore the romance between soul-sick Patricia and life-weary Joe. While the two motives aren't necessarily in conflict, each leeches time away from the other. Ultimately, the real reason we care about the pairing of Patricia and Joe has less to do with the script than with the appeal and charisma of the two leads, Tom Hanks and Meg Ryan.

Joe Versus the Volcano is difficult to review because some parts are fresh, inventive, and entertaining, while others are near-misses or even complete failures. On balance, however, I readily admit liking this movie, although the second half pales in comparison to the first. But, if only for the pleasure of its best moments, or the enjoyment of savoring Hanks and Ryan's chemistry (pre-*Sleepless in Seattle*), *Joe Versus the Volcano* is worth the price of a rental. RECOMMENDED

The Ladykillers [2004]
Starring: Tom Hanks, Irma P. Hall, Marlon Wayans, J. K. Simmons, Tzi Ma, Ryan Hurst, Diane Delano Director: Joel Coen & Ethan Coen Screenplay: Joel Coen & Ethan Coen, based on *The Ladykillers,* by William Rose Running Time: 1:44 Rated: R (Profanity) Theatrical Aspect Ratio: 1.85:1

The Ladykillers is an interesting concoction — a faithful update of the original Ealing comedy cooked in a vat of the Coen brothers' seasoning. Even though this is based on the 1955 British film of the same name, those unfamiliar with *The Ladykillers*' pedigree might mistake it for an original. It's an understandable error — *The Ladykillers* is at home with certain other Coen brothers titles, namely *Raising Arizona, The Hudsucker Proxy, The Big Lebowski,* and *Intolerable Cruelty.* Although the plot closely tracks that of Alexander Mackendrick's original, many of the nuances, not to mention the funniest jokes, are pure Joel and Ethan Coen.

The setting has been transplanted from London to the tiny southern town of Saucier, a lazy locale that plays host to a riverboat casino. Silver-tongued, Poe-quoting Professor G. H. Dorr (Hanks) arrives in Saucier with the express purpose of robbing that casino. He has assembled a diverse gang that includes Garth Pancake (J. K. Simmons), an explosives expert with a bad case of irritable bowel syndrome; Gawain MacSam (Marlon Wayans), the "inside man" who works as a janitor on the boat; The General (Tzi Ma), a cold, conscienceless killer who says little; and Lump Hudson (Ryan Hurst), the "muscle." For their base of operation, the professor chooses the house of an elderly widow named Marva Munson (Irma P. Hall), who has a room to rent. He claims that he and his friends will be practicing sacred music in her root cellar, when, in fact, they are digging a long tunnel.

The Ladykillers is divided into three easily recognizable parts. The first introduces the characters. The Professor, a living portrait of the perfect Southern gentleman, moves into Marva's house. For Gawain, it's another day on the job. The General foils a would-be hold-up at his convenience store. Garth's special effects work on a TV commercial goes awry (he kills the canine star of a dog food spot). And Lump has an unspectacular outing on the football field (all of which is shown from his point of view). The second act concerns the caper, which is straightforward and played primarily for laughs. (*The Ladykillers* should not be confused with a traditional crime movie). Finally, the third half hour represents the meat of the story, and relates what happens *after* the deed has been done.

Is appreciation of *The Ladykillers* relegated to those who enjoy the Coens' nontraditional approach to movies? Perhaps — the comedy is at times too dark and edgy for multiplex viewers in search of something frothy and romantic. And Tom Hanks isn't playing the nicest guy on Earth. I suspect that mainstream audiences will find plenty of things to take pleasure in, even though some viewers may be bewildered by what the Coens do. **HIGHLY RECOMMENDED**

Life [1999]

Starring: Eddie Murphy, Martin Lawrence Director: Ted Demme
Screenplay: Robert Ramsey & Matthew Stone Running Time: 1:40
Rated: R (Profanity, crude humor) Theatrical Aspect Ratio: 1.85:1

Most of *Life* takes place in a Mississippi State prison that could only exist in the movies. Of course, this is a comedy, so it wouldn't do to set up a grim, ugly locale where every day is worse (or at least no better) than the last. Consequently, director Ted Demme fashions a cozy prison that bears little resemblance to reality, and, for the most part (as long as you're not looking for realism), it works.

One of *Life*'s weaknesses is the lengthy and cumbersome setup necessary to get New Yorkers Ray (Murphy) and Claude (Lawrence) arrested for murder in Mississippi and sentenced to life. The film follows the turbulent relationship of Ray and Claude across the span of 65 years. Demme uses an episodic approach, first checking in with the pair in the 1930s, then returning in the 1940s, the 1970s, and the 1990s. Thanks to a reasonably convincing job by Hollywood makeup specialist Rick Baker, Murphy and Lawrence (as well as Obba Babatundé, who plays a fellow prisoner, and functions as the narrator) look like old men rather than younger men wearing multiple layers of latex. Through the years, Ray and Claude maintain a lively verbal repartee that hides a deep friendship.

Life moves along at a breezy clip, but there's a little more going on here than the sophomoric hijinks that characterize most Murphy films. Demme utilizes humor to tackle a serious issue as Ray and Claude are refused service in a whites-only diner. The point is made without preaching, because we're too busy laughing. *Life* also has its sentimental moments, especially as the years move by and many of Ray and Claude's longtime companions pass into the prison cemetery. Demme doesn't give us any death scenes — he merely has the characters fade away.

For those in search of a "true" Eddie Murphy picture, *Life* fills the bill. It has its share of flatulence jokes, homophobic double entendres, and gross-out moments, but there's enough going on here beyond that base level of comedy to allow acceptance and enjoyment by a more mainstream audience. Those who are turned off by Murphy's humor probably won't find a whole lot to like about *Life*, but, for everyone else, the movie represents a charming diversion that re-affirms the likability and comic aptitude of both co-stars. **RECOMMENDED**

Living in Oblivion [1994]

Starring: Steve Buscemi, Catherine Keener, Dermot Mulroney, James LeGros Director: Tom DiCillo Screenplay: Tom DiCillo Running Time: 1:31 Rated: R (Profanity, sexual situations, brief nudity)
Theatrical Aspect Ratio: 1.85:1

Living in Oblivion details one day in the life of director Nick Reve (Steve Buscemi), who is trying to put together an independent film on a shoestring budget. This particular morning, he's due to shoot scene 6. Little does he know that Murphy's Law is in full force. Nightmares — real, figurative, and cinematic — will plague the production, and what eventually emerges will be nothing like what anyone envisioned.

Reve's leading lady, Nicole (played by a shining Catherine Keener), is fraught with angst about her career choice. Does she belong in front of the camera or behind the counter at some greasy dive? The male lead, a stuck-up star by the name of Chad Palomino (James LeGros), has no worries about his ability. With an ego too big for the tiny set, Chad spends most of his time complaining to Reve and flashing smiles at the assistant director (Danielle Von Zerneck) and script girl (Hilary Gilford). The cinematographer (Dermot Mulroney), an eye-patched character who looks like Rambo but has the emotional sensitivity of Alan Alda, rarely lets a take go by without arguing the choice of shot.

The mishaps of scene 6 provide 90 minutes of unbridled fun. There are missed shots, booms in frame, exploding smoke machines, actors with bad breath, a vomiting camera operator, a senile mother on the set, and an irate dwarf in a red room (an obvious poke at David Lynch and *Twin Peaks*). Life imitates art, art imitates life imitating art, and all this happens in switches from black-and-white to color.

Living in Oblivion is packed with laughs and twists, and comes to an end far too soon. It's rare that a movie rolls the credits too early, but when this film fades to black, we're still longing for at least one more scene with Reve, his cast, and crew. While it's true that we don't get much sense of these people off the set, they're so wonderful in and around the camera that it doesn't matter. Best of all, *Living in Oblivion* doesn't demand that the viewer be a film buff — just that he or she enjoys laughing. **HIGHLY RECOMMENDED**

Love and Death on Long Island
[Canada/United Kingdom, 1997]

Starring: John Hurt, Jason Priestley Director: Richard Kwietniowski Screenplay: Richard Kwietniowski, based on the novel by Gilbert Adam Running Time: 1:33 Rated: PG-13 (Infrequent but extreme profanity, non-explicit sexual content) Theatrical Aspect Ratio: 1.85:1

Everyone knows someone like Giles De'Ath: stuffy, arrogant, set in his ways, and at war with anything that could in any way be associated with "progress." This

is the kind of role that could easily be turned into a flat stereotype, but John Hurt, in what is certainly his best performance in a decade and possibly the most impressive of his long and distinguished career, turns "erstwhile fogy" Giles into a three-dimensional human being. Giles, who is a widower and a recluse, does not frequent the cinema, but when he learns that an E. M. Forster film is playing at the local theater, he screws up his courage and decides to go. What he doesn't realize is that the movie house is showing 2 films: the Forster adaptation and a teen exploitation flick called *Hotpants College II*. A nonplused Giles ends up sitting in a darkened room watching buff male and female bodies in various states of undress. Just as Giles is about to leave, however, he notices Ronnie Bostock (Jason Priestley), and, suddenly, it's love at first sight. Giles is enraptured, and the moment *Hotpants College II* is over, he begins to scour stores for Bostock memorabilia, including teen magazines and video tapes. (In order to watch those tapes, Giles must buy a VCR, but he initially doesn't realize that he needs a TV to use the VCR.)

Eventually, not satisfied with being the world's foremost authority on Bostock, Giles boards a plane and travels to Long Island, where his idol's home is located. Bostock is away when Giles arrives, but the wily Englishman manages to befriend Ronnie's supermodel girlfriend, Audrey (Fiona Loewi). Eventually, the actor arrives home and, impressed with Giles' demeanor and intelligence, he begins to rely on the older man's advice. But, while Giles' affection runs deep, Ronnie's feelings are less constant.

Love and Death on Long Island is many things wrapped into one: a social commentary (it tackles the thorny issue of film as pure art versus film as mindless entertainment), a buddy picture/love story (Ronnie and Giles have one of the most interesting relationships found anywhere on a movie screen these days), and a "fish out of water" tale (Victorian relic Giles forced into the modern world). Yet, despite the many laughs *Love and Death* offers, it never takes cheap shots. It has a vibrant, beating heart — and that makes the comedy all the more worthwhile. **RECOMMMENDED**

Lovely and Amazing [2001]

Starring: Catherine.Keener, Brenda Blethyn, Emily Mortimer, Raven Goodwin Director: Nicole Holofcener Screenplay: Nicole Holofcener Running Time: 1:30 Rated: R (Profanity, nudity) Theatrical Aspect Ratio: 1.85:1

Somewhere between the whimsy of a fluffy romance and the grit of an uncompromising character study lies the realm of *Lovely & Amazing,* a dramatic comedy from Nicole Holofcener that tells the tale of a mother and her 3 children. *Lovely & Amazing* is the kind of motion picture that can make you laugh one moment and cry the next. It is at times serious and at times very funny. But it is always perceptive, and that quality, more than any other, is what makes it worth a recommendation.

At first glance, there couldn't be 4 more different people than Jane (Brenda Blethyn) and her daughters, Michelle (Catherine Keener), Elizabeth (Emily Mortimer), and Annie (Raven Goodwin). Jane is a good-natured, caring, middle-aged women. Michelle is trapped in an unhappy marriage while working an unfulfilling job at a photograph development shop. Elizabeth is a mostly unsuccessful actress who is questioning her career and her choice in men. And Annie, an adolescent African-American girl adopted by Jane, is struggling with the rigors of puberty. Yet there is a common thread that connects these women: insecurity about their personalities and bodies. Jane is undergoing liposuction to lose inches around her waist. Michelle, aware that her husband is unfaithful, contemplates dallying with an underage boy who finds her attractive. Elizabeth worries that she's not sexy enough to get the right roles. And Annie's answer to problems is to pig out on McDonald's food, even though everyone comments that she's getting fat.

It's Holofcener's insight into the female psyche that makes *Lovely & Amazing* such an engrossing motion picture. The director has recruited a talented cast to bring these characters to life. Brenda Blethyn, Emily Mortimer, and Catherine Keener are all good. On the male side, we are treated to appearances by James LeGros (as Elizabeth's emotionally detached lover), Jake Gyllenhaal (as the teenage object of Michelle's fantasies), and Dermot Mulroney (as a big-time Hollywood actor).

Holofcener crafts each of her characters carefully, showing their creativity and neuroses. And, while there's plenty of humor to be found in this 90-minute feature, there's never an occasion when we're laughing at the characters. We come to like these people, warts and all. **RECOMMMENDED**

The Man Who Knew Too Little [1997]

Starring: Bill Murray, Joanne Whalley, Alfred Molina, Peter Gallagher Director: Jon Amiel Screenplay: Robert Farrar & Howard Franklin, based on the novel "Watch That Man" by Robert Farrar Running Time: 1:33 Rated: PG (Sexual innuendo, cartoon violence, mild profanity) Theatrical Aspect Ratio: 1.85:1

With a title like *The Man Who Knew Too Little,* one might reasonably assume that actor Bill Murray's latest endeavor is a parody of Hitchcock's twice-made film, *The Man Who Knew Too Much.* In fact, although the movie takes a few stabs at mocking Hitchcockian plot twists, it's mainly a satire of the James Bond pictures. Unlike many similar productions, this one has a smart, knowing script that understands just how to play up all the tricks and contrivances of the secret agent genre to their best comic effect. It's a breezy, fun film that offers more than a few solid laughs.

Murray plays Wallace Richie, an American from Des Moines who decides to celebrate his birthday by purchasing a plane ticket and flying to see his brother, James (Peter Gallagher), and sister-in-law, Barbara (Anna Chancellor), in London. And, while James is delighted to see Wallace, the visit comes at an inopportune time — he is on the verge of closing a big deal with some German businessmen and he needs an quiet, conservative dinner party without a wild card like Wallace around to disturb things. So, for a birthday present, James gives Wallace an evening's participation in the "Theater of Life," an experimental form of entertainment that allows normal people to act out their fantasies. Only, instead of becoming involved in this "Theater of Life," Wallace accidentally intercepts a phone call intended for a real hit man, and, as a result, he becomes embroiled in a web of espionage, attempted assassinations, and a would-be terrorist attack at the signing of a peace treaty between Russia and England.

It's virtually impossible for the premise of a mistaken identity to sustain an entire motion picture, but *The Man Who Knew Too Little* employs enough variations that, until the very end, proceedings remain surprisingly lively. Of course, it could be argued that the situation in this film is so outrageous that it's as much a "fish out of water" scenario as a "mistaken identity" one. Wallace is, after all an "innocent" American thrown into the midst of a European game of murder, mayhem, and blackmail.

Despite a floundering ending, *The Man Who Knew Too Little* leaves a favorable impression. Although *The Man Who Knew Too Little* is less audacious than

Austin Powers and lacks all of the '70s references, it's frequently as enjoyable, if not more so, and that makes it a worthy choice for a frothy, funny evening. **RECOMMMENDED**

Manhattan Murder Mystery [1993]
Starring: Woody Allen, Diane Keaton, Alan Alda, Anjelica Houston, Jerry Adler Director: Woody Allen Screenplay: Woody Allen & Marshall Brickman Running Time: 1:48 Rated: PG (Mature themes)
Theatrical Aspect Ratio: 1.85:1

Carol Lipton (Diane Keaton) and her husband Larry (Woody Allen) are caught in a routine, commonplace marriage — until Carol turns into Nancy Drew following the death of a neighbor. It all seems like a open-and-shut case of a heart attack, and the police aren't thinking foul play, but Carol becomes suspicious when the widower of the dead woman (Jerry Adler) doesn't mourn "enough" ("What should he do," asks Larry, "walk down the street sobbing?"). With the help of Ted (Alan Alda), a close friend who encourages her sleuthing, she begins to assemble "clues" to fit her pet theory of a murder. But the evidence is weak, and Larry becomes concerned that his wife is obsessed with a macabre fantasy. He tries to be the voice of reason, but when no one listens to him, he ends up playing along.

Part of the fun of *Manhattan Murder Mystery* is guessing whether or not Lillian House was murdered, as Carol believes, or simply died of a heart attack. In a sense, that's the mystery of the film, and Woody Allen brings across the solution with his characteristic mix of madcap comedy and on-target realism.

Film buffs will find the usual number of references to look for, although these are perhaps more explicit than in many Allen movies, and include *Double Indemnity, Rear Window,* and *The Lady from Shanghi.* There certainly may be others, as Allen has a habit of putting more into his films than anyone can hope to get in one sitting.

Woody Allen is rarely a big commercial draw, and whether his off-screen antics will boost his box-office take remains to be seen, but *Manhattan Murder Mystery* may be his most accessible film since *Hannah and Her Sisters.* This movie is still pure Allen, but the humor is broad-based, and the "quirkiness" often associated with the director is kept to a minimum. Frankly, it's been years since I've enjoyed the director's work this much. **HIGHLY RECOMMENDED**

Me, Myself & Irene [2000]
Starring: Jim Carrey, Renee Zellweger, Chris Cooper, Robert Forster Directors: Bobby Farrelly, Peter Farrelly Screenplay: Peter Farrelly, Mike Cerrone & Bobby Farrelly Running Time: 1:55 Rated: R (Profanity, vulgarity, sexual situations, brief nudity, violence)
Theatrical Aspect Ratio: 1.85:1

Me, Myself & Irene highlights the continuing evolution of Jim Carrey as an actor (as opposed to a comic phenomenon). This is Carrey's second outing for the Farrellys, and his work here is by far the better of the two. Unlike in the previous film (*Dumb and Dumber*), which was essentially a group of thinly-connected dumb jokes, Carrey's comic energy is effectively focused. He's not trying so hard to be funny that he becomes irritating.

Carrey is Charlie and Hank, two faces of the same man. Charlie is meek, kind, and ineffectual. Hank, on the other hand, is aggressive and dumb, with an attitude and voice to match Dirty Harry. Charlie is one of the best liked members of the Rhode Island State Police Force, but, when he loses control of his mind and body and Hank emerges to go on a rampage, his career is in jeopardy. His captain (Robert Forster) sends him to deliver a female prisoner, Irene (Renee Zellweger), to an upstate New York police station. After that, he is supposed to take a little R&R. However, it turns out that Irene, the head groundskeeper at a golf course that was a front for criminal activity, may have seen something she shouldn't have, and, as a result, she has been marked for death by some crooked cops (Chris Cooper and Richard Jenkins). So, accompanied by an albino serial killer named Whitey (Michael Bowman), Charlie and Irene go on the lam.

As with the Farrellys' previous directorial outings, the plot is the least important aspect of the proceedings. It's there to move things along and provide a clothesline upon which the various comic situations can be hung. Thinking about it or pondering its coherence is not a good approach, because it doesn't make a lot of sense. In fact, things are so convoluted that a voiceover narrator is needed to keep audiences from becoming lost. And, for such a weak plot, there's too much of it. The movie runs nearly 2 hours, which is easily 20 to 30 minutes too long. The laugh quotient is down significantly during the final half-hour as the Farrellys make the mistake of concentrating a little too much on the story.

Ultimately, *Me, Myself & Irene* is a comedy, and it works because it does its job of making viewers laugh. It is perhaps a slight notch below *There's Some-*

thing About Mary on the Farrelly entertainment scale, but it's a significant improvement over either *Dumb and Dumber*. The film is less successful as a romance, primarily because of the weakness in Irene's character. Those who are offended by vulgar material certainly won't embrace this movie, but fans of the Farrellys, Carrey, and humor in the worst possible taste will find plenty to enjoy. **RECOMMENDED**

A Midwinter's Tale [United Kingdom, 1995]

Starring: Michael Maloney, Richard Briers, Julia Sawalha, John Sessions Director: Kenneth Branagh Screenplay: Kenneth Branagh Running Time: 1:38 Rated: R (Profanity, mature themes) Theatrical Aspect Ratio: 1.66:1

A Midwinter's Tale is loaded with allusions, both cinematic and literary. The most obvious are those from Shakespeare, which understandably permeate the film. Not only are the characters attempting to perform *Hamlet*, but certain scenes from the play hit a little too close to home for several of them. Director Kenneth Branagh also simultaneously pays homage to and pokes fun at one of the most respected British filmmakers of all time: Sir Laurence Olivier. Elements of *A Midwinter's Tale*'s presentation recall the work of Woody Allen, and the ensemble cast is the kind that Allen usually gathers — although Branagh uses British names while Allen typically assembles Americans.

With all of Branagh's energy focused on directing (he never appears on screen), *A Midwinter's Tale* is almost always on-target. Most of the so-called dramatic aspects of this film are subtle parodies of traditional Hollywood cliches: the struggling actor choosing love over fame, a reconciliation between a long-separated father and son, and a man finally earning his mother's approval after a lifetime of failure. Branagh handles these themes deftly, treating each with enough respect to create emotional arcs for the characters, but making sure the audience knows he's fully aware of how overused the material is.

The main character is actor/director Joe Harper (Michael Maloney, whose acting style echoes Branagh's), who, during a slow time in his career, risks bankruptcy to stage an experimental Christmas-time production of *Hamlet* in his home town of Hope. Unfortunately, auditions don't go well — all the respected theatrical talent is involved in one production or another of *A Christmas Carol* — and Joe finds only 6 willing participants. Since the text necessitates 24 roles, everyone is forced to play multiple

parts. Thus, Hamlet's Ghost, Claudius, and the Player King all bear a strong resemblance to one another, Laertes is moonlighting as about 5 other people, and Rosencrantz and Guildenstern are one. Gertrude is played by a drag queen (John Sessions), Ophelia is essayed by an amazingly nearsighted actress (Julia Sawahla), and Horatio is a drunk (Gerard Horan).

Branagh has fun with his material, weaving a tale likely to generate guffaws even for those with little knowledge of the play upon which it is based. No current film maker appears to love and understand Shakespeare as well as Branagh, and never has his affection for the Bard been more apparent than here. This picture succeeds as a comedy, a satire, and even, to a certain extent, as a mild melodrama about choosing between a paycheck and the nourishment of the soul. **HIGHLY RECOMMENDED**

Mighty Aphrodite [1995]

Starring: Woody Allen, Mira Sorvino, Helena Bonham Carter, Peter Weller, Michael Rapaport Director: Woody Allen Screenplay: Woody Allen Running Time: 1:38 Rated: R (Sexual situations, mature themes, profanity) Theatrical Aspect Ratio: 1.85:1

The film opens in an amphitheater in Greece, with an appropriately-garbed Greek chorus chanting of the deeds of Achilles and Oedipus. Suddenly, unexpectedly, the masked men and women decide to switch to the tale of Lenny Weinrib (Woody Allen) — definitely *not* a name known from mythology. And, as things go from slightly absurd to completely ridiculous, the Chorus, led by F. Murray Abraham, say things like "Oh cursed fate! Some thoughts are better left unthunk!" and breaking into verses of "When You're Smiling." And all this is accomplished with an appropriate level of pomposity.

The story starts out with Lenny and his wife, Amanda (Helena Bonham Carter), discussing adoption. Lenny doesn't want a child, but Amanda does, although she isn't willing to sacrifice a year of her life to have one the normal, biological way. Eventually, Lenny gives in and the couple gets a healthy male infant, whom they name Max. As the child grows and Amanda becomes more wrapped up in her attempts to procure her own art studio, Lenny fights a growing curiosity to learn more about his son's natural mother. Eventually, he sneaks a peek at the adoption agency's records. This leads to a meeting with Linda Ash (Mira Sorvino), the woman who gave birth to Max. Much to Lenny's dismay, she turns out to be a statuesque blond with a helium voice and little in the way of intelligence. Worse still is how she makes her living — her dual career involves starring in porn films and turning $200 tricks for a bald-headed, homicidal pimp.

The most original element of *Mighty Aphrodite* is the use of the Greek Chorus. However, what starts out as a clever, innovative device quickly becomes tedious through overuse. The Chorus seems always to be on hand to make pithy remarks, and their presence becomes intrusive. At times, it's as if Woody Allen is attempting to take a page out of the *Monty Python* book, and those two very different styles of humor do not mix well.

While not up to the level of many of Allen's recent films, *Mighty Aphrodite* is nevertheless an entertaining diversion. The comedy, most of which is light and easily accessible, is worthy of some laughs, and the movie has a good sense of irony. *Mighty Aphrodite* is far from a tour de force, and some Woody Allen diehards may be disappointed, but there's enough in this picture to recommend it. RECOMMENDED

A Mighty Wind [2003]
Starring: Christopher Guest, Michael McKean, Harry Shearer, Eugene Levy, Catherine O'Hara, Bob Balaban, Jane Lynch, Parker Posey, Larry Miller, Fred Willard Director: Christopher Guest Screenplay: Christopher Guest & Eugene Levy Running Time: 1:30 Rated: PG-13 (Sex-related humor) Theatrical Aspect Ratio: 1.85:1

When it comes to mockumentary parodies, no one does it better than Christopher Guest. The topic this time around is folk music — a genre that reached its zenith of popularity during the late 60s. Like Western movies, however, it has become something of a relic. Occasionally, some aging star will come out with a new album, but for the most part, folk music went out of vogue long before vinyl ceased to be the medium of choice for music lovers. Of course, there's still a limited audience for this sort of music, but Guest's movie is no more aimed at them than *Best in Show* is targeted at dog show participants. The comedy here is pretty universal. You don't have to like folk music to appreciate *A Mighty Wind*.

The film is a fake documentary that chronicles a reunion concert featuring three once-popular folk music bands. Organized as a tribute to recently deceased music producer Irving Steinbloom by his son (Bob Balaban), the concert is headlined by three of acts from the 60s: The Folksmen, a trio (Christopher Guest, Michael McKean, and Harry Shearer) whose lone hit is more than thirty years old; The New Main Street Singers, a "neuftette" of nine whose image is

pure Pat Boone even though one of their members (Jane Lynch) is an ex–porn star; and Mitch and Mickey (Eugene Levy and Catherine O'Hara), fondly remembered but no longer America's sweethearts. The concert is to occur live at New York City's Town Hall and be broadcast nationwide on Public Broadcasting (no doubt during a membership drive). Of course, not everything goes smoothly.

For the most part, the comedy in *A Mighty Wind* is more amusing than hilarious. The movie provokes a lot of smiles and chuckles, but few belly laughs. Some of the movie's funniest sequences feature Fred Willard as a promoter who is so full of himself that he always has to be at the center of attention. Eugene Levy is delightful as the burned-out Mitch, who walks around in a daze. And it comes as a bit of a surprise to learn that some of the squeaky-clean New Main Street Singers don't worship Jesus but are "Witches of Nature's Colors." Those with an appreciation of Guest's previous work — *This Is Spinal Tap, Waiting for Guffman*, and *Best In Show* — will likely enjoy *A Mighty Wind*. Although Guest rarely descends into the realm of lowbrow humor, neither does he inhabit a plane of intellectual snobbery. *A Mighty Wind* is another affectionate parody — one that delights in gently poking fun at its subject rather than tearing it to pieces — with plenty of amusing moments and one-liners that vary from lily white to off-color. RECOMMENDED

Mother [1996]
Starring: Albert Brooks, Debbie Reynolds, Rob Morrow Director: Albert Brooks Screenplay: Albert Brooks & Monica Johnson Running Time: 1:45 Rated: PG-13 (Mature themes, mild profanity) Theatrical Aspect Ratio: 1.85:1

In the formula-laden playground of modern comedies, *Mother* comes as a breath of fresh air. The film relies on smart humor rather than slapstick, puns, and dumb jokes with quick payoffs. Albert Brooks doesn't use the *Airplane* approach to comedy. His films aren't loaded with hit-and-miss gags. The director/writer strives for quality over quantity, and when he wants the audience to laugh, they generally do so.

Brooks plays John Henderson, a 40-year-old B-grade science fiction writer (his published books include *Planet Seven* and *Planet Eight*) who is going through his second divorce. For John, this is only the latest in a long line of failed relationships. In the words of a friend he meets at a bar (John C. McGinley), "You've gotta know what you're looking for [in a woman], and you don't have a clue." After a great deal of soul-searching, John decides that to better understand women, he needs to investigate his strained relationship with his mother, Beatrice (Debbie Reynolds). So, much to the surprise of his friends and his younger brother, Jeff (Rob Morrow), he decides to move back into his childhood home in Sausalito and live with her. Thus begins an odyssey of mother/son bonding that not even John is prepared for.

It would have been easy for Brooks' script (co-written by Monica Johnson) to treat Mrs. Henderson as a caricature. Most comedies would have opted for that route, I think. The result might have been funny, but it wouldn't have been as meaningful. As the film progresses, Beatrice is allowed to fill out into a full-fledged character, complete with her own desires, dashed hopes, and simmering dreams. We, like John, gradually recognize why she reacts to him the way she does.

Although *Mother* boasts a host of hilarious one-liners, the best moments are the extended episodes that delve into everyday life. One features John's attempt to start an intelligent conversation with a vacuous date (*Friends'* Lisa Kudrow). There are also the scenes with Mom: a trip to the grocery store, an excursion through the mall, and an afternoon at the zoo. All of these sequences could have been short, but Brooks allows them to develop and play out naturally, letting the comedy bubble to the surface rather than escape in one sudden, contrived explosion. RECOMMENDED

Mr. 3000 [2004]

Starring: Bernie Mac, Angela Bassett, Michael Rispoli, Brian J. White, Ian Anthony Dale, Paul Sorvino, Chris Noth Director: Charles Stone III
Screenplay: Eric Champnella & Keith Mitchell and Howard Michael Gould Running Time: 1:44 Rated: PG-13 (Sexual situations, profanity)
Theatrical Aspect Ratio: 1.85:1

Mr. 3000 understands baseball and the men who play it, and, for a film about the sport, that's half the battle. The other half is crafting an entertaining story with engaging characters, and although *Mr. 3000* isn't quite as successful in that arena, it is enjoyable enough to warrant a recommendation. The film's chief asset is Bernie Mac. Despite being a well-known comedian, this is the first time Mac has had the opportunity to play a leading man in a major motion picture. Perhaps surprisingly, Mac's most apparent strength in this part is not his comedic ability, but his dramatic one. He plays Stan like a real person. That's not to say that he doesn't get laughs, but his character is only larger than life in the way that players like Barry Bonds

and Gary Sheffield are larger than life. Mac has a lot of charisma, and he's not afraid to use it.

The movie opens with a prologue in 1995. Stan Ross, a superstar with the Milwaukee Brewers, has just gotten his 3,000th hit, capping off a stellar career. In typical "me first" fashion, he charges into the stands to grab the ball from the kid who caught it, pisses off the media during the post-game interview, and decides on the spot to quit baseball, leaving his team foundering in the middle of a pennant race. But for "Mr. 3000," it's okay because he has gotten what he wants. Nine years later, his election to the Hall of Fame seems to be a foregone conclusion until a careful review of his statistics reveals that three of his hits were counted twice. In reality, he only has 2997. And since "Mr. 2997" doesn't have as good a ring to it as "Mr. 3000," Stan decides to return to the game. The Brewers, seeing a chance to increase their attendance, welcome back the 47-year-old with open arms. The players aren't as overjoyed, viewing the addition of "Grandpa" to the expanded September roster as a publicity stunt (which it is). But a surprising thing happens. In his quest to get three more hits, Stan discovers the concept of "team" and imparts some wisdom to the Brewers' next potential superstar, T-Rex Pennebaker (Brian J. White). He also earns the respect of his teammates and rekindles a romance with ESPN reporter Mo Simmons (Angela Bassett). But his batting average remains horrible (around .030) and hit #3000 is elusive.

Mr. 3000 offers plenty of laughs, but the humor doesn't obscure its legitimate points. Some of the jokes are abrasive, but what else would one expect from Mac? Certainly not soft lobs. And he's a good enough actor that he doesn't have take refuge in a caricature constructed out of gags, puns, and pratfalls. By transforming Stan from a self-absorbed, arrogant jerk into someone who sees the error of his ways, Mac allows us to get in Stan's corner and root for him. We want him to get #3000, come through for his team, and connect with Mo. I don't know whether the role of Stan Ross was written with Mac in mind, but it's hard to imagine a more perfect fit. *Mr. 3000* is a feel-good movie with a little edge. No, this isn't the cinematic equivalent of a home run, but at the very least, it's a solid base hit. RECOMMENDED

Muriel's Wedding [Australia, 1994]

Starring: Toni Collette, Rachel Griffiths Director: P.J. Hogan
Screenplay: P.J. Hogan Running Time: 1:46 Rated: R (Language, sexual candor, mature themes) Theatrical Aspect Ratio: 1.66:1

Muriel Heslop (the vibrant, energetic Toni Collette) is a hopeless romantic. She spends her days locked in her bedroom, listening to ABBA songs and dreaming of the day she'll be able to put on a wedding dress. Her walls are covered with momentos of her two favorite things in life: posters of the singing group and pictures of brides-to-be. Part of her reason for living in a fantasy world is that her family life is so depressing. Her brothers and sisters spend all day lounging in front of the television. Her mother (Jeane Drynan) is oblivious to the goings-on around her, and her father (Bill Hunter) doesn't miss any opportunity to brand Muriel as "useless." In fact, he derides her as the *most* useless of his children. On top of that, her bitchy friends call her an embarrassment and announce that they don't want her accompanying them on a vacation.'

Muriel takes all this to heart and decides that the only way to change her life is to leave the town of Porpoise Spit and find a man. To this end, she follows her friends to the resort of Hibiscus Island. Once there, she encounters Rhonda (Rachel Griffiths), an old school chum. In this wild party girl, Muriel discovers something she has never before had — a *real* friend, someone who actually cares about her.

One of the most pleasant aspects of *Muriel's Wedding* is the distinctly unconventional third act. No one seeing this movie will confuse it with a Hollywood picture, as it continually flouts the "feel good" formulas that typically characterize this sort of romantic comedy. The ending is far-from-perfect, but it's a great deal better than several obvious alternatives.

Nevertheless, parts of *Muriel's Wedding* are heavy-handed and, as a result, needlessly uncomfortable to view. There are times when Hogan almost seems to enjoy belittling and degrading Muriel. While it's necessary to understand her low self-image, the director goes to excessive, almost-sadistic, lengths to get his point across. Balancing these moments are some high-energy scenes, including a wonderful lip-synch of ABBA's "Waterloo" by Muriel and Rachel, Muriel trying on wedding dresses to the tune of "Dancing Queen," and an almost-sex scene featuring sofa cushions being unzipped instead of skirts.

Muriel's Wedding isn't a perfect comedy, tragedy, or drama, but it contains enough original elements of each to make it worth a look. Ultimately, however, individual enjoyment of this picture may be in direct proportion to a viewer's ability to tolerate ABBA's omnipresent music. RECOMMENDED

My Big Fat Greek Wedding [2002]

Starring: Nia Vardalos, John Corbett, Michael Constantine, Lainie Kazan Director: Joel Zwick Screenplay: Nia Vardalos Running Time: 1:34 Rated: PG (Mild profanity, sexual situations) Theatrical Aspect Ratio: 1.85:1

My Big Fat Greek Wedding starts out as a modern day Cinderella story and culminates with the traditional end to most fairy tale romances — the wedding, with all of its associated complexities and mishaps. There's a significant element of cultures clashing here, as well. The 3 primary rules of life for a young Greek woman are to (1) marry a Greek boy, (2) make Greek babies, and (3) feed everyone for the rest of your life. So, when Toula Portokalos (Nia Vardalos) becomes involved with the not-at-all-Greek Ian Miller (John Corbett), she's set to create a family uproar.

When the film opens, Toula is a seating hostess at her father's downtown Chicago Greek restaurant, "Dancing Zorba's." At age 30, Toula has pretty much given up hopes of romance and marriage, as indicated by her frumpy appearance. Then Toula decides to embark upon a course of self-improvement, the first step of which is taking computer classes at a local college. Then she meets Ian.

Actually, the two had previously met, albeit briefly, when Ian stopped in for a bite to eat at "Dancing Zorba's." On that occasion, Toula was struck dumb by Ian's handsome visage. This time, the attraction is mutual. Soon, they are dating, then sleeping together, then are engaged. And that's when things get tricky. Toula's father, who was unhappy to learn that she was dating a non-Greek, nearly has an apoplexy when his daughter breaks the news to him that she intends to marry someone whose parents are as "white bread" as they come.

My Big Fat Greek Wedding is more in the nature of an embrace and celebration of Greek culture than it is a lampoon. Sure, there are times when it pokes fun, but, on those occasions, it is gentle and kind-hearted, not nasty or sarcastic. The movie is consistently funny without ever going over the top — a rarity in movies. While some of the comedy is more witty than sidesplitting, there are plenty of opportunities for belly laughs. And, in the process of boosting the laugh quotient, *My Big Fat Greek Wedding* does not lose sight of the characters. That's an important quality for any movie that wants to keep its audience invested in the eventual outcome. The result is an appealing blend of laughter, romance, and ethnic flavoring — an independent production to be appreciated for its likability and humor. RECOMMENDED

Mystery Men [1999]

Starring: Ben Stiller, William H. Macy, Hank Azaria, Geoffrey Rush, Janeane Garofalo, Greg Kinnear Director: Kinka Usher Screenplay: Neil Cuthbert, based on the comic book created by Bob Burden Running Time: 1:57 Rated: PG-13 (Violence, profanity, innuendo) Theatrical Aspect Ratio: 1.85:1

Mystery Men isn't just clever — it's genuinely funny, as well. Comic book and superhero fans will be pleased that *Mystery Men* isn't just a parody, but an homage. The film introduces us to a bunch of blue-collar superheroes. In Champion City, a stylized metropolis that looks like a cross between the futuristic world of *The Fifth Element* and *Batman*'s Gotham City, Captain Amazing (Greg Kinnear) is every little boy's idol. Children revere this Superman clone, and why not? He has singlehandedly cleaned up the city. But there's more to being a superhero than simply restoring law and order. During his period of fighting evil-doers, Captain Amazing has hired a publicist and earned sponsors. Now times are getting a little difficult. Without any supervillains to defeat, Captain Amazing's shining star is dimming, so he decides to help engineer the parole of his arch nemesis, Cassanova Frankenstein (Geoffrey Rush), so that he'll have someone to save the city from. Unfortunately, Cassanova proves to be smarter than Captain Amazing, and soon Champion City's #1 champion is nowhere to be found.

Enter the Mystery Men — 3 ordinary guys who want to be superheroes. Their powers are less than astonishing. Mr. Furious (Ben Stiller) supposedly shows amazing strength when he gets mad, but the depth of his abilities is exaggerated. The Blue Raja (Hank Azaria) is an "effete British superhero" who can do some impressive things with forks and spoons. And the Shoveler (William H. Macy) calls a spade a spade, then clanks people over the head with it. Unfortunately, these three aren't too successful in battle, and, when it comes to rescuing Captain Amazing, they're in over their heads — and they know it. So they do a little recruiting. Soon, their group has expanded, and, armed with some really cool weapons, they decide to storm Cassanova's castle and save Captain Amazing and the city.

Mystery Men offers a broad base of humor with something for everyone. There are puns, sight gags, fairly sophisticated satire, lowbrow humor, and fart jokes. The best scene in the film is arguably the one in which Mr. Furious, the Blue Raja, and the Shoveler interview new candidates. Some of the rejected wannabe superheroes have names like Ballerina Man, Pencil Man, and PMS Avenger. Another candidate for the most memorable moment is when the Mystery Men attempt to rescue Captain Amazing — with unexpected results. **RECOMMENDED**

Napoleon Dynamite [2004]

Starring: Jon Heder, Efren Ramirez, Jon Gries, Aaron Ruell, Tina Majorino, Haylie Duff Director: Jared Hess Screenplay: Jared Hess & Jerusha Hess Running Time: 1:26 Rated: PG-13 (Mature themes) Theatrical Aspect Ratio: 1.85:1

Napoleon Dynamite should be required therapy for anyone with a self-image problem. No matter how much of a loser a person believes himself to be, he couldn't possibly be in worse shape than the protagonist of Jared Hess's wickedly funny high school comedy. With a low-key sense of humor and without the slightest whiff of sentimentality, Hess delivers a film about geeks that makes *Revenge of the Nerds* look like the Hollywood tripe that it is. *Napoleon Dynamite* isn't about a cute, cuddly, inoffensive movie nerd; the main character is morose, antisocial, and has a working understanding of what happened at Columbine. There's plenty of humor in the film, but the movie is often a little uncomfortable to watch, and Napoleon is not an easy guy to like. Rooting for him takes effort.

John Heder plays Napoleon like a teenager who doesn't quite fit into his long, lanky body. The performance is dead-on. I don't know if Heder was a nerd in real life, but he certainly makes us believe. He subsists on a farm with his Uncle Rico (Jon Gries), a 30-something ex-jock who lives in the past, and his freaky older brother, Kip (Aaron Ruell), who spends most of his waking hours in Internet chat rooms. Despite looking like he's old enough to have completed college, Napoleon is still in high school, where he occupies the lowest rung of the social pecking order (getting slammed into a locker by someone bigger and more self-assured is a daily occurrence). Napoleon's only friend is Pedro (Efren Ramirez), the "new kid." Napoleon doesn't have a girlfriend, but he has his eye on Deb (Tina Majorino) — until Pedro beats him to the punch by asking her to the upcoming dance. So Napoleon has to settle for going with the daughter of one of his uncle's clients.

Not much happens during the course of *Napoleon Dynamite*. This is essentially a meet-and-greet movie, where we spend about 85 minutes getting to know the smart, sullen, socially maladjusted Napoleon. The biggest events are the dance and the school election, in which Napoleon becomes Pedro's campaign manager. And, as in all movies about losers, there's a chance for a measure of redemption, and *Napoleon Dynamite* shows its good heart by allowing for a ray of hope at the end. Although Napoleon Dynamite may not be the most immediately endearing protagonist, there's something memorable about him and the motion picture that bears his name. RECOMMENDED

Nurse Betty [2000]

Starring: Renée Zellweger, Morgan Freeman, Chris Rock, Greg Kinnear, Aaron Eckhart Director: Neil LaBute Screenplay: John Richards and James Flamberg Running Time: 1:48 Rated: R (Profanity, violence, sex) Theatrical Aspect Ratio: 1.85:1

Nurse Betty's two hallmarks are originality and star quality, both of which combine to draw the viewer through the film's occasional rough spots. Neil LaBute has put together an offbeat production that combines elements of fantasy, drama, satire, and black humor. It has an unusual tone that successfully encourages the willing suspension of disbelief and allows one to become involved in a story that, at least from the outside, is patently absurd.

Betty is a part-time housewife/part-time waitress living in a small, dead-end Kansas town. She's sweet, oblivious, and innocent, and allows herself to be taken advantage of by everyone around her, especially her philandering husband, Del (Aaron Eckhart). Because her own life is so empty, Betty is a fervent fan of the soap opera *A Reason To Love,* where her favorite character is Dr. David Ravell (Greg Kinnear). However, aside from getting her daily soap fix, making dinner for her husband, and serving coffee to regulars like the local sheriff (Pruitt Taylor Vince) and the town's only reporter (Crispin Glover), Betty doesn't have much to do.

Then, one day, a couple of strangers named Charlie (Morgan Freeman) and Wesley (Chris Rock) arrive at Del's Used Car lot, looking to do business with him. The end up back at his house for drinks, but things get ugly and Del doesn't survive. Unbeknownst to Charlie and Wesley, Betty sees the entire incident. Post traumatic stress from witnessing the murder pushes her into a half-fantasy world where she suddenly believes that characters from *A Reason To Love* are real people, and that she was once engaged to David Ravell. Armed only with her shaky sanity, she heads for Los Angeles, where her lost love "lives." Meanwhile, Charlie and Wesley, convinced that Betty could be a threat to them, start to search for her.

The best part of *Nurse Betty* is the climax, which gains a comic momentum of its own. Without revealing any details, I can say that a few unexpected things happen during this sequence, which also offers the most overtly humorous moments of the film. LaBute ends on a high note, which is a credit to him, his cast, and screenwriters John Richards & James Flamberg. Once again, the director has distinguished him as that rare Hollywood commodity: someone who is willing to take a chance on an unconventional project and turn it into something enjoyable. RECOMMENDED

The Object of My Affection [1998]

Starring: Jennifer Aniston, Paul Rudd, John Pankow, Timothy Daly Director: Nicholas Hytner Screenplay: Wendy Wasserstein, based on the novel by Stephen McCauley Running Time: 1:50 Rated: R (Sexual themes, profanity) Theatrical Aspect Ratio: 1.85:1

The Object of My Affection, based on the novel of the same name by Stephen McCauley, is a pleasant romantic comedy that asks (and tries to answer) questions about the nature of love, sex, family, and friendship. And, while some of the solutions are a little facile, the film nevertheless succeeds, due in large part to a luminous performance by Jennifer Aniston and the effectively-developed central relationship between Aniston's Nina Borowski, a pregnant twentysomething heterosexual, and George Hanson (Paul Rudd), a gay man in the same age range.

In most movies, friendships are the equivalent of cinematic side orders. Especially in contemporary productions, almost every main character has to have a best friend. This facilitates character development and allows secondary interaction. Rarely, however, is friendship the *point* of a movie. That's not the case in *The Object of My Affection,* which, although it is a little about sex and love, is much more about the undemanding, casual affection that builds between real friends. The chemistry between Aniston and Rudd is perfect in establishing this relationship. They have a real camaraderie which is only occasionally spiced up by a hint of sexual tension.

George and Nina meet at a dinner party that neither of them is enjoying. They soon discover that they have a great deal in common, and the fact that she's straight and he's gay makes them ideal candidates for roommates. Once George's current relationship with a egotistical doctor (Timothy Daly) comes to an end, George moves into a bedroom in Nina's Brooklyn apartment. The two quickly become best friends, with a closeness that is so extreme that, when Nina becomes pregnant by her boyfriend, Vince (*Mad About You*'s Ira, John Pankow), she tells George first.

Problems arise, however, when Nina begins to fall for George while he simultaneously becomes interested in a young actor (Amo Gulinello).

This is apparently director Nicholas Hytner's push to make a mainstream Hollywood movie. Although many of the secondary relationships are sketchily-developed and occasionally hard-to-swallow, the connection between George and Nina is so strong and believable that it draws us into their world and allows us to root for the seemingly-improbable happy ending. **RECOMMENDED**

The Opposite of Sex [1998]

Starring: Christina Ricci, Martin Donovan, Lisa Kudrow Director: Don Roos Screenplay: Don Roos Running Time: 1:45 Rated: R (Sexual themes, profanity, violence) Theatrical Aspect Ratio: 1.85:1

Christina Ricci's performance is only one reason why Don Roos' *The Opposite of Sex* is a success. This is the kind of daring feature that doesn't open every Friday at the local multiplex; its frank, sometimes politically incorrect approach towards the act and politics of sex is refreshing. And, in addition to dealing with intrinsically provocative material, first-time director Roos uses the unique approach of satirizing the conventions of road pictures and dysfunctional family dramas to tell his story. In particular, he has a lot of fun with the voice-over. The glib narrator, Deedee Truitt (Ricci), is aware that she's speaking to a movie audience, and, as a result, can't resist the opportunity to have some fun at the viewer's expense.

Although Deedee is the narrator, she's not the film's central character. That role belongs to her half-brother, Bill (Martin Donovan), "the definition of a softy." Bill, a gay high school teacher, has been leading a peaceful existence until his pregnant sister runs away from home and comes to him for shelter. He lets Deedee stay, and she repays his kindness by seducing his live-in lover, Matt (Ivan Sergei), who, after his fling with Deedee, decides that he's not really a homosexual — he's a bisexual. Another constant presence in Bill's life is the always-miserable Lucia (Lisa Kudrow), the sister of his dead true love. Then there are Jason (Johnny Galecki), who falsely tells the police that Bill molested him, and Sheriff Carl Tippett (Lyle Lovett), the genial cop who investigates the boy's claims.

As comedies go, *The Opposite of Sex* is consistently funny. Of course, humor is subjective, and I'm known for being a little warped in that area, so Roos' flamboyant, out-on-a-limb approach is perfect for some-

one like me. The dialogue is crisp and distinctive, occasionally invoking the spirit of something written by Kevin Smith. However, it's obvious to Roos (and to us) that this kind of slick, unconventional style can have trouble sustaining a feature-length movie. So the writer/director changes gears during the second half. Although *The Opposite of Sex* never completely loses its satirical, self-mocking edge, the final 50 minutes are more serious than what precedes them, and the humor is leavened by a couple of earnest, surprisingly-effective messages.

The tag line for *The Opposite of Sex* is: "You'll laugh, you'll cry, you'll be offended." While that's perhaps overstating the movie's impact, it's not completely off-base. The film manages to mix a portion of successful drama into its primarily-comic foundation, and conservative movie-goers will likely be turned off by the no-punches pulled, occasionally raunchy look at sex. However, with its memorable dialogue, solid performances, and idiosyncratic style, *The Opposite of Sex* is sure to be appreciated by those who aren't frightened away by the cinematic equivalent of hot chili. **HIGHLY RECOMMENDED**

The Original Kings of Comedy [2000]

Starring: Steve Harvey, D.L. Hughley, Cedric the Entertainer, Bernie Mac Director: Spike Lee Running Time: 1:53 Rated: R (Profanity, Sex related humor) Theatrical Aspect Ratio: 1.85:1

Concert films, regardless of whether they're music shows or comedy acts, run the gamut from excellent to unwatchable. The key to such a movie's success is its ability to capture the "you are there" feeling — a task that *The Original Kings of Comedy* is largely effective at. Admittedly, there's no way that sitting in a motion picture auditorium can duplicate the experience of being live, but, by using digital sound, uncomplicated shots that don't call attention to the camerawork, and simple editing techniques, Lee draws the viewer in.

The Kings of Comedy road tour showcased the talents of 4 of black America's hottest male comedians: Steve Harvey (the host of *It's Showtime at the Apollo* and the star of TV's *The Steve Harvey Show*), D.L. Hughley (of TV's *The Hughleys*), Cedric the Entertainer (also of *The Steve Harvey Show*), and Bernie Mac (of TV's *Moesha*). During the course of the movie/show, each has approximately 30 minutes of stage time, and, while their styles are different, there's enough synergy between them to make the program seem like a cohesive whole rather than a series of unrelated segments (a frequent drawback to many comedy club shows). The 4 men complement each other, and each seems to have just about the right amount of time to forward his comic cause.

The material is frequently ribald, often racy, and always laced with profanity. Those who are offended by the use of four-letter words in comedy will be openly horrified by what transpires here. No apologies are offered or needed, however, because the movie is consistently funny — often side-splittingly so. *The Original Kings of Comedy* only features a few dead patches, none of which last very long. And, while I found certain of the entertainers to be more enjoyable than others (Hughley being the most consistently humorous and Harvey getting the biggest laugh with his rap sketch), none of them are duds.

The stage personalities of Harvey, Hughley, Cedric, and Mac come across unfettered and bigger-than-life. Lee's 3 or 4 attempts to take us backstage slow things down for a few minutes, but they aren't long enough to kill the momentum. Overall, Lee takes a step back, allowing *The Original Kings of Comedy* to be about the Kings, not the filmmaker — and that's the way it should be, because these men are more than capable of holding anyone's attention for the nearly 2-hour running length. RECOMMENDED

Planes, Trains and Automobiles [1987]

Starring: **Steve Martin, John Candy, Laila Robins** Director: **John Hughes** Screenplay: **John Hughes** Running Time: **1:33** Rated: **R** (Profanity, mature themes) Theatrical Aspect Ratio: **1.85:1**

Planes, Trains, and Automobiles is a Murphy's Law story. For salesman Neal Page (Steve Martin), everything that can possibly go wrong is about to do so. This is like Martin Scorsese's *After Hours* on a grander, less psychotic scale. It all starts in New York City, 2 days before Thanksgiving. Neal is eager to get home into the bosom of his family so he can enjoy the holiday. But bad weather intervenes. His flight from LaGuardia to O'Hare is diverted to Wichita, Kansas after a snowstorm hits Chicago. What makes the trip even longer is that Neal is stuck next to one of those good-natured, annoying talkers who won't shut up. The man's name is Del Griffith (John Candy), and he's a shower curtain ring salesman armed with an endless supply of dumb jokes and pointless anecdotes. This isn't the first time Neal has run into him, either. Earlier in the day, when Neal was trying to get to the airport, Del stole his cab, getting their relationship off to a rocky start.

In the time-honored tradition of the buddy comedy, *Planes, Trains, and Automobiles* throws these two mismatched individuals together and allows them to suffer all sorts of bizarre misfortunes as they try to get home before the turkey is served. They spend a night in a cramped hotel room sleeping in the same bed, endure the blatant incompetence of uncaring rental car clerks, suffer through transportation breakdowns, and watch one of their last hopes literally go up in smoke. We know they're eventually going to reach the Windy City, so the fun is watching their slow, reluctant bonding as they take planes, trains, automobiles, and tractor trailers to get there.

Planes, Trains, and Automobiles is one of those rare movies that manages to mingle outrageous comedy and light drama in such a way that we aren't repulsed or offended by its simplicity and occasional mawkishness. It's a fine cinematic treat that doesn't demand much from a viewer, but gives back a lot, both in terms of laughter and good feeling. RECOMMENDED

Private Parts [1997]

Starring: **Howard Stern, Mary McCormack, Robin Quivers** Director: **Betty Thomas** Screenplay: **Michael Kalesniko & Len Blum,** based on the book by Howard Stern Running Time: **1:49** Rated: **R** (Profanity, vulgarity, nudity) Theatrical Aspect Ratio: **1.85:1**

Will the real Howard Stern please stand up? For, in truth, the man who haunts the airwaves of nearly three-dozen radio stations each morning seems vastly different from the kinder, milder version who graces the screen in Betty Thomas' sweet, often-hilarious biopic. Based on the bestselling book of the same name, *Private Parts* relates some of the details of Stern's life — his romance with his wife, Alison (Mary McCormack), his early radio failures, his development into America's foremost "shock jock," and his vitriolic war with NBC's top brass. Along the way, we get to know Howard as a tender, intelligent, affable guy who just happens to do an "offensive . . . obnoxious . . . disgusting" radio show.

The film begins when Howard is a child and traces his life to the present. His sidekicks are accounted for — Fred Norris, whom he met while working in Hartford during the late '70s; Robin Quivers, who started as a newswoman in Washington D.C. before becoming his friend; joke writer Jackie Martling; producer Gary Dell'Abate; and even Stuttering John Melendez, who pops up for an unforgettable cameo. Much of *Private Parts* details Howard's always-loving, occasionally-rocky marriage to Alison, who's played with warmth and charm by *Murder One*'s Mary Mc-Cormack. The battles with the FCC have been relegated to a minor annoyance, although the ongoing feud with a WNBC program director takes center stage during the film's final ⅓.

It will probably come as no surprise to Stern fans to learn that their hero has an undeniable screen presence. Unlike many personalities-turned-actors, he never seems awkward or out-of-place. Stern's surprisingly subdued portrayal of himself may open a few eyes, however. He's never out-of-control, and the only time he plays a "sexist, racist pig" is when he's on the air.

Private Parts is aimed primarily at a mainstream audience. The humor here is racy, but also universal, and many of the jokes will cause viewers to double over with laughter. And, as bizarre as it may sound, Stern is the kind of guy you can't help pulling for. Most who take a chance, regardless of what prejudices they harbor against WXRK's top personality, will find themselves rewarded by a surprisingly pleasant two hours. **RECOMMENDED**

Pumpkin [2002]

Starring: Christina Ricci, Hank Harris, Brenda Blethyn, Dominique Swain Directors: Anthony Abrams, Adam Larson Broder Screenplay: **Adam Larson Broder** Running Time: 1:55 Rated: R (Profanity, sexual situations, mature themes, brief nudity) Theatrical Aspect Ratio: 1.85:1

For approximately ¾ of its nearly 2-hour running time, *Pumpkin* finds the right balance between satire, black comedy, and offbeat drama. However, the quirky independent film loses its focus on its way to the finish line, stumbling through several "false endings" and ultimately concluding with a whimper. The film's last act problems do not obscure *Pumpkin*'s two greatest strengths: the majority of the film is original and engaging, and Christina Ricci turns in another fine performance. This pair of assets alone is worth the price of admission.

Carolyn McDuffy (Ricci) is the ideal sorority sister. The right-hand woman of Alpha Omega Pi's leader, Julie (Marisa Coughlan), Carolyn is as vacuous and peppy as any of the members of the rival house, Tri-Omega. As in the past, this year, Alpha Omega Pi and Tri-Omega are locked in a heated battle for the coveted title of "Southern California State University Sorority of the Year," and Julie is determined to win. To aid the cause, she decides that the sisters are going to perform mentorship duties for a group of physi-

cally and mentally handicapped individuals preparing for the "Challenge Games" (think Special Olympics). Carolyn's charge is a young man named Pumpkin (Hank Harris), who doesn't talk much and can only get out of his wheelchair for a few moments at a time. He is immediately smitten by Carolyn, and, after only a session with her, begins to show enough determination to improve his physical condition that his mother (Brenda Blethyn) notices. Meanwhile, Carolyn is freaked out by working with Pumpkin, and considers quitting. But she can't, and, despite having the "perfect" boyfriend, tennis star Kent Woodlands (Sam Ball), she finds herself increasingly attracted to Pumpkin.

There's a little of the satirical tone of *Bring It On* and *Legally Blonde* in *Pumpkin*'s approach, but, in this movie, it is better integrated into the overall story. *Pumpkin* is straightforward in choosing its targets — the "Stepford wife" mentality of sorority sisters, the lack of tolerance amongst supposedly-liberal college students, and society's views of the handicapped as second-rate citizens. The primary target of the screenplay's scorn, at least early in the film, is Carolyn, who represents all of these things. As her personality changes, and she becomes more "real," the movie develops a dramatic arc. Ultimately, while the relationship between Carolyn and Pumpkin is never played entirely straight, it makes for an effective motion picture romance. This particular *Pumpkin* deserves to be picked, not left out on the vine to wither away. **RECOMMENDED**

The Real Blonde [1998]

Starring: Matthew Modine, Catherine Keener, Maxwell Caulfield, Bridgette Wilson Director: Tom DiCillo Screenplay: Tom DiCillo Running Time: 1:30 Rated: R (profanity, sexual situations) Theatrical Aspect Ratio: 1.85:1

The Real Blonde examines the difference between illusion and reality, and satirizes the acting industry. Although the seams in the plot are visible (the movie plays best as a series of loosely-connected comic vignettes), there's enough light substance and lighter humor to warrant a recommendation.

The principals are Joe (Matthew Modine) and Bob (Maxwell Caulfield), a pair of out-of-work actors who are making a living waiting tables for the ever-stern Ernst (Christopher Lloyd). Joe believes in the purity of his craft — the only kinds of acting jobs he's interested in are "serious" ones. His resolve is tested, however, when Bob gets a plum role on the soap opera *Passion*

Crest. There's nothing remotely respectable about the part, but it offers Bob a regular income of $3,600 per week and turns him into an overnight heartthrob. Suddenly, a jealous Joe, with some prodding from his live-in girlfriend, Mary (Catherine Keener), decides that if he's going to be an actor, he's going to have to compromise his values. So he goes to his agent (Kathleen Turner) and tells her he's willing to do anything — even a TV commercial or a music video.

The title comes from an obsession of Bob's — for him, Ms. Right has to be a "real blonde." His on-again, off-again girlfriend, insecure supermodel Sahara (Bridgette Wilson), is a sweet, gorgeous girl, but she's got a dye job. Bob finds what he thinks he wants in Kelly (Daryl Hannah), his leading lady on the soap. He soon learns, however, that just because a woman really has blond hair doesn't mean that there's nothing artificial about her personality.

One aspect of American culture that *The Real Blonde* successful captures (and skewers) is the hollowness of what we're exposed to through the media. Image and fantasy are everything; reality is valueless. Bob is obsessed with a "real blonde" because he's tired of fake women — the irony is that he's just as artificial as any of the girls he goes out with. What's authentic in an industry of make-believe?

The Real Blonde would have been even more satisfying if it had seemed like a coherent whole rather than a batch of skits loosely connected by DiCillo's story arc of a struggling actor trying to remain true to both his calling and the woman he loves. Nevertheless, in part because of Catherine Keener's appeal and in part because DiCillo gets his point across with a successful portion of humor, *The Real Blonde* is enjoyable and inviting. **RECOMMENDED**

Romy and Michele's High School Reunion [1997]

Starring: Mira Sorvino, Lisa Kudrow, Janeane Garofalo, Alan Cumming Director: David Mirkin Screenplay: Robin Schiff Running Time: 1:31 Rated: R (Profanity, mature themes) Theatrical Aspect Ratio: 1.85:1

The title characters (played by Mira Sorvino and Lisa Kudrow) are blond Southern California babes who have been rooming together since they moved to the L.A. area after graduating from high school. They have been friends for a lot longer — two inseparable peas in a pod who have never fit in with the hip crowd and have never cared that they're outsiders. Now, a decade after brushing the dust of Tucson, Arizona from their heels, the receive word that the Sagebrush High School Class of '87 is holding a 10-year reunion.

So, armed with lies about how they have become successful business women, they head east to impress the classmates who used to taunt and ridicule them.

Although I smiled frequently during the film, I didn't laugh too often. Perhaps surprisingly, a lot of the humor is low-key, and there are very few truly hilarious moments. Another problem is that the script unsuccessfully attempts to inject a little lame drama with a moral ("be true to yourself") into the mix. I have no problem with ambitious comedies introducing dramatic elements into the storyline, but those aspects should be less banal than the ones pulled off the "stock plot device" shelf for this movie. *Romy and Michele* is at its best when it's being lighthearted and at its weakest when it takes a halfhearted stab at semi-seriousness.

Romy and Michele's High School Reunion is one of those pleasant movie-going experiences that doesn't offend, excite, or challenge anyone. There are all sorts of likable things about it — Sorvino and Kudrow, accessible humor, and an '80s soundtrack that's the most definitive survey of the decade in pop music since *Peter's Friends*. First-time director David Mirkin brings a lot of energy to the production, always keeping things moving. And, perhaps most intriguingly, anyone who has ever gone to a reunion will recognize a kernel of truth lurking under all of *Romy and Michele*'s blond and brainless icing. **RECOMMENDED**

The Royal Tenenbaums [2001]

Starring: Gene Hackman, Anjelica Huston, Ben Stiller, Gwyneth Paltrow, Luke Wilson Director: Wes Anderson Screenplay: Wes Anderson & Owen Wilson Running Time: 1:46 Rated: R (Profanity, brief nudity, sexual situations, mature themes) Theatrical Aspect Ratio: 2.35:1

For those who enjoy skewed, deadpan humor, *The Royal Tenenbaums* has enough to sate the appetite. The movie is a twisted satire on the feel-good genre in which an estranged family member returns to the fold and redeems himself. It's Frank Capra crossed with David Lynch, with a little Monty Python thrown in on the side. The movie is rarely (if ever) side-splittingly funny, but there are so many clever moments that nasty chuckles and devilish smiles come at frequent intervals. The movie doesn't have more heart than Anderson's vastly overrated *Rushmore,* but it's a smarter, more sophisticated endeavor — a clear indication that the filmmaker has grown.

The Tenenbaums are dysfunctional in only a way a movie family can be dysfunctional. Royal Tenenbaum (Gene Hackman), the patriarch, is not a good father. Although he and his wife, Etheline (Anjelica Huston), have raised 3 gifted children, all of them have grown up to be burnt-out neurotics with "issues." Chas (Ben Stiller), a real estate wheeler-dealer in high school, is afraid of his own shadow. Margot, a promising playwright (and the adopted daughter), is trapped in a loveless marriage with a much older man (Bill Murray). And Richie, a former U.S. Open tennis champion who had the biggest meltdown in the history of the sport, pines for his true love — his sister. Royal, meanwhile, has left the family home to live in a hotel. Although he has never officially divorced Etheline, he has not seen her or his children for 3 years. Then comes the news that Etheline is considering the marriage proposal of Henry Sherman (Danny Glover), and Royal decides he wants to win her back. So, faking a terminal illness, he returns to the Tenenbaum home — at about the same time that Chas, Margot, and Richie all show up. Suddenly, all the members of this none-too-happy clan are back together under the same roof. The Waltons, they aren't.

Anderson doesn't seem to mind breaking movie taboos. Not only does he have a lot of fun with the incestuous relationship of Richie and Margot, but he does something no director seems willing to do these days: kill a pet dog. Much of the humor is sly and dry, not outrageously flamboyant. Dramatically, *The Royal Tenenbaums* is on uncertain ground. Anderson wants the characters to grow on us, and seems to believe that Royal's Scrooge-like transformation should have some meaning, but it doesn't really work. Lovers of *Rushmore* will probably be delighted, but *The Royal Tenenbaums* contains enough that even those who were put off by the earlier movie may find something here worth savoring. **RECOMMENDED**

The Rules of Attraction [2002]

Starring: James Van Der Beek, Shannyn Sossamon, Ian Somerhalder
Director: Roger Avary Screenplay: Roger Avary, based on the novel by Bret Easton Ellis Running Time: 1:52 Rated: R (Sexual situations, profanity, nudity, drug use, violence) Theatrical Aspect Ratio: 1.85:1

Once you get past all of the wild camera tricks and visual gimmickry, you arrive at the core of *The Rules of Attraction* and find out that it's really *about* something other than replicating the party life at a New England college. Working from his own screenplay, which has its roots in the Bret Easton Ellis novel, writer/director Roger Avary spins a yarn about the pain of unrequited love that is at times darkly funny and at other times depressingly tragic. It's safe to say there aren't any movies out there quite like this one.

It is possible to consider *The Rules of Attraction* to be an anti-romantic comedy. The Hollywood convention is that, whenever a boy meets a girl, love will follow as quickly as the clichés allow. In real life, sex and romance are less perfect, and, in not giving in to the "love conquers all" mentality, Avary's film uncovers an important truth about male/female relationships — that attraction isn't always mutual, and, even when it is, happily-ever-after is frequently not the result. Each of the 3 protagonists in this movie is in love (or lust, or whatever), but none of them finds their feelings reciprocated to the same degree.

James Van Der Beek plays Sean Bateman, a student at Camden College who spends most of his time dealing drugs and sleeping with women. Sean is attracted to Lauren (Shannyn Sossamon), and is convinced that she has been leaving anonymous love letters in his mailbox. Meanwhile, although Lauren isn't indifferent to Sean, she has given her heart to her bum of a boyfriend, Victor (Kip Pardue), who has taken off to spend some time wandering around Europe. It is her intention to lose her virginity to him. (She spends her spare time studying pictures of the effects of STDs in an effort to keep her hormones under control.) Then there's Paul (Ian Somerhalder), who used to date Lauren but is currently exploring his bisexual side and has developed a huge crush on Sean. Sean, being self-centered and strictly hetero, is oblivious to Paul's feelings.

As with *Killing Zoe*, Avary has decided to focus upon a group of nihilistic, self-absorbed, drugged out individuals. Avary's view of his characters is cynical and unsympathetic, sometimes to the point of cruelty. *The Rules of Attraction* is not mainstream fare, but it is quirky and interesting, and worth a look for those who don't mind movies where you end up despising just about everyone who has a speaking part. **RECOMMENDED**

Scary Movie [2000]

Starring: Anna Faris, Shawn Wayans, Marlon Wayans, Cheri Oteri, Shannon Elizabeth Director: Keenen Ivory Wayans Screenplay: Keenen Ivory Wayans, Marlon Wayans, Shawn Wayans, Phil Beauman, Jason Friedberg, Buddy Johnson, Aaron Seltzer Running Time: 1:22 Rated: R (Profanity, explicit sexual language & images, nudity, violence) Theatrical Aspect Ratio: 2.35:1

Offended by gay and anti-gay humor? Avoid *Scary Movie*. Shocked by the sight of an erect (albeit prosthetic) penis? Avoid *Scary Movie*. Horrified by the thought of seeing grandma take a header down the stairs then get run over by a piano? Avoid *Scary Movie*.

Put off by the concept of a character so stoned that when he gets shot in the lung, smoke puffs out of the hole? Avoid *Scary Movie*. Embarrassed to laugh at some admittedly juvenile humor? Avoid *Scary Movie*. But if all those things are your cup of tea, you might think this is among the funniest movies around.

Only about 30-40% of the jokes in *Scary Movie* work. There are a lot of clunkers, and some that are simply too dumb to generate a response. However, considering the sheer quantity of material that is thrown at us, even a failure rate of more than 50% represents a lot of laughs.

The central target of the Wayans' wit is *Scream*. It's certainly not the only movie to be skewered by *Scary Movie*, but it's the most obvious. The film opens with bodacious high school student Drew Becker (Carmen Electra, who cheerfully toys with her image) making popcorn when the phone rings. A voice on the other end inquires what her favorite scary movie is and she immediately replies, "*Kazaam!*" Soon, she's running through sprinklers in her underwear with a masked man in pusuit. The next day, her murder is big news at the local high school, and pushy reporter Gale Hailstorm (Cheri Oteri) is on hand to get the story. Meanwhile, cute and innocent Cindy (Anna Faris) begins to worry that the murder might have something to do with a man she and her friends accidentally killed last Halloween. Her closest pals, Buffy the bimbo (Shannon Elizabeth) and Brenda (Regina Hall), and her boyfriend, Bobby (Jon Abrahams), try to convince her otherwise. But the killer is soon stalking her, and not even the efforts of Deputy Dufy (Dave Sheridan) can save the day.

One inherent problem with this type of motion picture is a tendency to lose comic momentum, and *Scary Movie* suffers from the malaise. The film has a significantly higher laugh quotient at the beginning than near the end, and there are several noticeable dead spots during the final half-hour. A shorter, tighter version of *Scary Movie* probably would have been better, but the film's lean running length of 82 minutes is already on the low side of what will play in a multiplex. Nevertheless, the material generates so much laughter that the overriding post-viewing impression is of an uneven film that's definitely worth the time investment. RECOMMENDED

Secretary [2002]

Starring: James Spader, Maggie Gyllenhaal Director: Steven Shainberg Screenplay: Erin Cressida Wilson, based on the short story by Mary Gaitskill Running Time: 1:45 Rated: R (Sexual situations, S&M, nudity, profanity) Theatrical Aspect Ratio: 1.85:1

Secretary is just your regular, garden-variety romantic comedy with heavy doses of S&M/B&D. The movie enters a realm where few non-porn films venture, and comes across as darkly funny, energetic, and surprisingly gentle. Part of the reason that *Secretary* succeeds is that it doesn't treat S&M relationships only as the butt of jokes or purely for their shock value — when we laugh, it's because the director intended us to laugh, not because we're uncomfortable or being exposed to a dirty little secret. While being aware of the absurdity of an S&M relationship, filmmaker Steven Shainberg recognizes that there are legitimate psychological reasons why people engage in this behavior. He is also careful not to make the actions of the characters too extreme.

The film opens by introducing the protagonist, Lee Holloway (Maggie Gyllenhaal). Lee has just been released from a mental institution where she was treated for her self-mutilation tendencies. Whenever the stress in her life becomes unbearable, she removes a sharp object from a small bag she carries and opens a wound on her thigh. No sooner has Lee emerged from treatment than her father's drinking binge veers her back towards the edge. In an attempt to fend off her condition, she decides to look for a job, and finds employment for a stern, emotionally closed-off lawyer, E. Edward Grey (James Spader).

At first, Lee's job entails little more than the daily rigors expected of a secretary — answering the phones, typing letters, and so forth. Gradually, however, Edward becomes more domineering in reprimanding Lee for typos, and, on one occasion, when his anger at her errors results in a spanking session, both Lee and Edward realize they have stumbled upon a taboo desire that fulfills them both. However, while Lee relishes her part as the submissive, Edward is tormented by his inability to give up his addiction to domination. Only when Lee begins to express genuine feelings for Edward does he become frightened enough to put an end to the non-business aspects of their relationship. Lee is crushed — and realizes that she loves Edward.

Secretary is less about sex than it is about human interaction outside of what society deems normal. Tone is critical, and that's where Shainberg hits pay dirt. *Secretary* has enough genuine laughs to eliminate the potential twitters and snickers, and it treats Edward and Lee as people. Some of the credit must go to Spader, who is his usual solid self, and Gyllenhaal, who is amazing, but the director knows exactly where he wants his characters to go, and successfully takes them there. *Secretary* is a romantic comedy for those who go into sugar shock from the usual entries into the genre. **HIGHLY RECOMMENDED**

Sideways [2004]

Starring: Paul Giamatti, Thomas Hayden Church, Virginia Madsen, Sandra Oh Director: Alexander Payne Screenplay: Alexander Payne & Jim Taylor, based on the novel by Rex Pickett Running Time: 2:03 Rated: R (Profanity, sexual situations, nudity) Theatrical Aspect Ratio: 1.85:1

Sideways is from Alexander Payne (*Election, About Schmidt*), whose films simultaneously satirize and observe life in America. Unlike David Lynch, who uses saws and butcher knives to dissect the American dream, Payne prefers a scalpel. Lynch often ridicules his characters, but it's clear that Payne likes the individuals he uses to populate his films, even though they're not always the nicest of people. *Sideways* looks at one of the oldest and oddest of "civilized" conventions: the bachelor party. Using this as a springboard, the movie becomes about friendship, love, sex, and wine.

There are no big, A-list stars, although the quality of the acting is of the highest caliber. The leads are played by character actors Paul Giamatti (as Miles) and Thomas Hayden Church (as Jack). These two are best friends who take a one-week road trip to California's wine country to celebrate Jack's upcoming wedding. Their plans are to spend their days tasting wine and playing golf. But an itch in Jack's pants gets in the way. He wants to have a last fling, and he targets the feisty Stephanie (Sandra Oh) — except he neglects to mention that he's not looking for a long-term commitment. While Jack is romping with Stephanie, Miles tentatively tries to set something up with her friend, Maya (Virginia Madsen), a waitress with whom he has had prior contact.

This is really Miles's story. He's a sad-sack loser who has written an unpublishable novel, mourns his failed marriage, and has obvious self-esteem problems. Despite the man's party-pooping attitude, a lot of us will see something of ourselves in Miles, and that's what makes it oh so easy to identify with him. He embodies many of the flaws of the human experience, but he is also capable of kindness and honesty, and one gets the sense that he's a survivor. Giamatti is great in the part. He has the face and the mannerisms down pat. His supporting cast — Church, Madsen, and Oh — are equally well selected.

In *Sideways*, Payne holds true to the form he displayed in his previous movies. The drama is leavened nicely with humor. There are plenty of so-called "big laugh" moments. None of the comedy seems forced or ill-timed, which is a key to material being fun in a picture like this. The real strengths of *Sideways* are the characters it develops, the road trip it takes us on, and the laughs with which it provides along the way. In my opinion, this is Payne's finest movie to-date. It is a little on the long side (slightly over two hours), but the minutes fly by. **HIGHLY RECOMMENDED**

Sliding Doors [United Kingdom, 1998]

Starring: Gwyneth Paltrow, John Lynch, John Hannah, Jeanne Tripplehorn Director: Peter Howitt Screenplay: Peter Howitt Running Time: 1:45 Rated: R (Sex, profanity) Theatrical Aspect Ratio: 1.85:1

Film makers are no less fascinated by issues of destiny than anyone else, and that's why there's no shortage of movies about this subject. While this approach has been the fodder for several notable dramatic films, *Sliding Doors* is the first romantic comedy to plumb its depths. The "road not taken" approach isn't just a plot device, either. Writer/director Peter Howitt expands upon both possible fates of a character after she just misses/catches a train. The audience watches, with ever-growing fascination, how this one event impacts upon every aspect of her life: her future career, where she lives, whom she loves, and whether she has a family. As her separate destinies diverge and then re-converge, she becomes two completely different individuals.

That woman is Helen, played by Gwyneth Paltrow as a long, dark-haired Brit. One day, after losing her job as an advertising executive, she decides to return home in the middle of the day. The scene of the pivotal moment is a train platform. In scenario #1, she just slips through the sliding doors before the train pulls out of the station. On board, she meets the cheerful, talkative James (John Hannah), a *Monty Python* fan who is taken with her beauty. Minutes later, in her flat, she walks in on her lover, Gerry (John Lynch), in bed with another woman (Jeanne Tripplehorn). In scenario #2, she misses the train and, shortly thereafter, is the victim of an attempted mugging. She doesn't meet James and fails to make it home in time to discover Gerry's infidelity. Juxtaposed one against the other, while sharing many places, cues, and characters, the two stories proceed in parallel from there.

On one level, for viewers who enjoy pondering the workings of fate, *Sliding Doors* can be viewed as a deep and wonderful experience. But, for those who just appreciate a romantic comedy characterized by solid acting, a script with a few twists, and a great deal of genuinely funny material, *Sliding Doors* still fits the bill. One of its most obvious strengths is that it can satisfy many different types of audiences — those who demand something substantial from their motion pictures, and those who couldn't care less.

HIGHLY RECOMMENDED

Slums of Beverly Hills [1998]

Starring: Natasha Lyonne, Alan Arkin, Marisa Tomei, Kevin Corrigan Director: Tamara Jenkins Screenplay: Tamara Jenkins Running Time: **1:31** Rated: R (Sex, nudity, profanity, drugs) Theatrical Aspect Ratio: **1.85:1**

Our guide through the *Slums of Beverly Hills* is Vivian Abramowitz, who is played by Natasha Lyonne in a star-making performance. Lyonne makes Vivian instantly likable. She's a tough-talking girl whose uncertainty about her own sexuality and her developing body reveals an inner innocence and vulnerability. Her uncertain lifestyle doesn't make it easy to deal with the effects of hormones racing out of control. Her father and mother are divorced, and she lives with her dad, Murray (Alan Arkin), and her two male siblings. Consequently, there is no woman around to shepherd her through experiences like her first period. So, when her perpetually-stoned cousin, Rita (the always energetic Marisa Tomei), comes to stay, Vivian is suddenly on the fast track to learning about sex.

The Abramowitzes are nomads. They don't have much money, so they move from cheap apartment to cheap apartment, often skipping out in the middle of the night to avoid paying the rent. They stay just within the limits of Beverly Hills because of the schools. As Murray states, "Furniture is temporary, education is forever." When Rita comes to live with them, however, her rich father (Carl Reiner) pays Murray enough money that he and his family can afford to move into a ritzy place. While there, Vivian meets and falls for a gentle-but-strange neighbor, Eliot (Kevin Corrigan), who is fixated with Charles Manson.

Slums of Beverly Hills is by turns funny and poignant, and it effectively expresses the various traumas of young womanhood. However, although Vivian is at the center of Jenkins' movie, the other characters are not ignored. Murray in particular is fleshed out, due in no small part to the contribution of veteran actor Arkin, who injects the right amount of wit into an otherwise straight performance. Murray is not the perfect father, but he loves his children and is trying to provide the best life he can for them.

First-time writer/director Jenkins has admitted in interviews that *Slums of Beverly Hills* contains a high quotient of autobiographical material. The truth of this shows in the insight she brings to Vivian's experiences. The character's struggles with the pitfalls of adolescent development may be particular to women, but many of the emotional ramifications will strike a chord of familiarity for men, as well. It's the differences in addition to the similarities that make all coming-of-age stories compelling to members of both sexes, and *Slums of Beverly Hills* is an example of how engaging one such tale can be. **RECOMMENDED**

The Snapper [United Kingdom/Ireland, 1993]

Starring: Colm Meaney, Tina Kellegher, Ruth McCabe Director: Stephen Frears Screenplay: Roddy Doyle Running Time: **1:34** Rated: R (Language, mature themes) Theatrical Aspect Ratio: **1.85:1**

In the Curley household, unwed motherhood isn't the disaster it might be elsewhere. When 20-year-old Sharon (Tina Kellegher) informs her father, Desi (Colm Meaney), and mother, Kay (Ruth McCabe), that she's "up the pole," they aren't thrilled, but there's no display of histrionics. After asking who the father is (and not being told), Desi invites his daughter out to the local pub for a drink. Sharon's friends are as interested as her family in the father's identity, but she resolutely keeps mum about the truth until an event in the neighborhood brings it into the open.

The Snapper is a very funny production, and it gets funnier as the movie progresses. Some of the humor has a distinctly Irish flavor, and it takes a while to get used to the ebb and flow of certain jokes. The biggest obstacle to laughter in *The Snapper* may be getting past the heavy accents. Wisely, however, Miramax has decided against subtitles, which would have ruined the subtlety of many of the wittier moments.

Those who think this is just another "unmarried girl gets pregnant" motion picture are in for a surprise. Rarely has a movie honestly, yet humorously, shown how the pressures of pregnancy can tear at the fabric of a close-knit, working-class family. The relationship between Sharon and her dad is more intimate than that of most daughter/father pairings, and the things these two have to admit to one another are often heartrendingly difficult to say.

In fact, the dramatic elements of *The Snapper* hold the humor in check. It's hard to let loose with unrestrained laughter when you recognize the pain underlying a scene. There are several sequences that move from laughter to tears back to laughter, bringing the audience along on the roller coaster ride. This structure doesn't always work, and that occasionally leads to an unsettled feeling.

It's refreshing to see an old subject dealt with in the open and original manner that *The Snapper* handles pregnancy. The marriage of humor and drama is admittedly imperfect, but it works well enough to occasionally spawn laughter and touch the heart, and there's a crucial scene between Colm Meaney and Tina Kellegher that is beautifully written, acted, and directed. Even those who have trouble understanding the accents will find that once the language barrier is broken and the slang deciphered, *The Snapper* has a surprising amount of depth. **RECOMMENDED**

Starsky and Hutch [2004]

Starring: Ben Stiller, Owen Wilson, Vince Vaughn, Juliette Lewis, Snoop Dogg, Chris Penn, Terry Crews, Will Ferrell Director: Todd Phillips Screenplay: John O'Brien and Todd Phillips & Scot Armstrong, based on characters created by William Blinn Running Time: 1:35 Rated: PG-13 (Profanity, drug use, partial nudity, violence) Theatrical Aspect Ratio: 1.85:1

The mining of old television shows continues, and, while one wouldn't expect much from a movie version of the late-1970s TV cop series *Starsky and Hutch*, this is one time when the filmmakers have uncovered some surprisingly rich ore. The key to the film's success is that it uses the burned-out premise as the springboard for a comedy, not an action flick. All the elements of the TV series are in evidence. Dave Starsky (Ben Stiller) and Ken "Hutch" Hutchinson (Owen Wilson) are the Felix and Oscar of undercover police work in Bay City. Where Starsky is buttoned-down, straight-laced, and by-the-book, Hutch tends to view rules more as guidelines. Roaming the streets in a red 1974 Ford Torino, the pair gets help from their reliable snitch, Huggy Bear (Snoop Dogg), as they seek to bring down drug kingpin Reese Feldman (Vince Vaughn), a seemingly civic-minded family man who has developed a strain of cocaine that foils normal detection methods.

The nuts and bolts of the plot don't much matter; the story is just an excuse for Stiller and Wilson to lampoon the one-time TV icons and have fun splashing around in their lagoon of 70s excess. The satire is gentle and genial, but unmistakable, with lots of affection for the television version. Starsky faces off in a disco dance-off with a John Travolta wannabe. Hutch croons "Don't Give Up On Us, Baby," which was a number one pop song in 1977 when sung by David Soul (the TV Hutch). We gets lots of 70s songs and shtick, and nearly all of it works to good comedic effect. Even the usually annoying Vince Vaughn (as the bad guy) and Juliette Lewis (as his vacuous wife) aren't tiresome in this setting.

Stiller and Wilson have fun playing the two detectives. Each employs a different style (as befits the characters). Stiller's approach is to overplay everything, while Wilson comes across as relaxed. The contrast is effective. The original Starsky and Hutch, Paul Michael Glaser and David Soul, have brief cameos. Going into the film, I was of the opinion that, of all the 70s TV shows I might like to see on the big screen, *Starsky and Hutch* wasn't on the list. A laugh-filled hour and a half later, I was happy that the film had proven me wrong. **RECOMMENDED**

State and Main [2000]

Starring: Alec Baldwin, Charles Durning, Philip Seymour Hoffman, William H. Macy Director: David Mamet Screenplay: David Mamet Running Time: 1:45 Rated: R (Profanity) Theatrical Aspect Ratio: 1.85:1

State and Main chronicles the trials and tribulations of a production crew trying to make a movie on-location in the small town of Waterford, Vermont. Although this is a farce, one has to wonder how many of the incidents related in the film represent episodes from director David Mamet's experience. The characters are a mix of Hollywood big shots and small town types. Arriving in Waterford are Walt Price (William H. Macy), the director; Marty Rossen (David Paymer), the producer; Bob Barrenger (Alec Baldwin), the male lead with a penchant for underage girls; Claire Wellesley (Sarah Jessica Parker), the female lead; and Joseph Turner White (Philip Seymour Hoffman), the sensitive writer. Greeting the movie-makers are the likes of Waterford's mayor, George Bailey (Charles Durning); the mayor's domineering wife, Sherry (Patti LuPone); the local bookseller, Ann Black (Rebecca Pidgeon); and the young and flirtatious Carla (Julia Stiles).

Problems crop up almost immediately. The town's historical old mill, where much of the film's action was to have taken place, burned down more than 30 years ago. Barrenger's notorious appetites get him in trouble the minute he meets Carla. Claire wants an additional $800,000 to appear topless (despite the fact that the American public can "draw her [breasts] from memory"). Rossen is pushing the product placement of bazoomer.com, even though the movie is a period piece set in 1895. And White falls for local girl Ann, enraging her lawyer/fiancé.

State and Main is not consistently funny, but it contains a number of winning scenes and barbed one-liners. Mamet's talent for writing shines through with comments like: "It's not a lie, it's a gift for fiction," "An associate producer credit is what you give your secretary instead of a raise," and "The better part of valor is to step away, or you, your kids, and your grandkids will die in poverty." There's a brief-but-timely exchange on how absurd the American electoral process is (ironically, the film was made long before the current Presidential situation). And, while Mamet's view of Hollywood types is sharp and cynical, it isn't nearly as nasty as what was portrayed in Robert Altman's *The Player*.

Mamet has a reputation for creating daring and powerful motion pictures. *State and Main* is neither daring nor powerful, but its lightness and lack of complexity should not necessarily be viewed as a negative. It's highly watchable, and, at times, humorously compelling. The film probably doesn't deserve the large crowds and long lines it generated at film festivals, but, in the more comfortable venue of a local theater, it offers 2 hours' diverting entertainment. **RECOMMENDED**

Strictly Ballroom [Australia, 1992]

Starring: Paul Mercurio, Tara Morice, Gia Carides Director: Baz Luhrmann Screenplay: Baz Luhrmann & Andrew Bovell Running Time: 1:34 Rated: PG (mature themes) Theatrical Aspect Ratio: 1.85:1

Scott Hastings (Paul Mercurio), one of Australia's best ballroom dancers, is targetted for a number of championships until he abandons the Dance Federation's rigid steps in favor of his own moves. Horrified by his unorthodox behavior, his partner, Liz (Gia Carides), leaves him, and Scott is forced to take up with an amateur. Fran (Tara Morice) matches Scott's zest for life, but one question hangs over them as they teach each other about life, love, and dancing: can they win by rejecting tradition?

Strictly Ballroom, based on an Australian play of the same name, was one of that country's biggest 1992 screen hits. It's easy to see why. The movie is funny, energetic, and enjoyable — the perfect film for a night or an afternoon out, regardless of what mood you're in. While the plot and characters don't boast any special depth, there's enough freshness to hold just about anyone's interest.

The movie possesses an inventive sense of humor that becomes apparent in the riotously funny opening scenes. Although *Strictly Ballroom* never recaptures the brilliantly offbeat quality of its beginning, there are still numerous laughs peppered throughout, and its upbeat sense of fun is infectious. *Strictly Ballroom* is filled with energy and color. The dance numbers are splendidly choreographed and the soundtrack is vibrant and varied. The romantic elements, while skillfully downplayed, are relegated to the background.

Like *Dead Poets' Society, Strictly Ballroom*'s motto might be "Seize the day!" When Scott is dancing to satisfy everyone else's expectations, he isn't happy, but when he takes a chance and does his own thing, he finds fulfillment, and, with Fran, love. In a world where winning means everything, Scott learns how hollow victory can be if the price is stifling creativity. His own father, as it turns out, is a living example of this.

Strictly Ballroom represents the best in light entertainment, and, apart from a slight fall-off during the second half, there aren't many flaws. The movie has wit, style, and a special brand of irreverence that allows it to work as a love story, a comedy of manners, and a satire. **HIGHLY RECOMMENDED**

Sweet and Lowdown [1999]

Starring: Sean Penn, Samantha Morton, Uma Thurman Director: Woody Allen Screenplay: Woody Allen Running Time: 1:35 Rated: PG-13 (Sexual situations, drug use) Theatrical Aspect Ratio: 1.85:1

Presented as if it's the bio-pic of a real person, *Sweet and Lowdown* mixes reminiscences with legends and "facts" to present a fragmented portrait of the lead character. As essayed by Sean Penn, Ray is a brilliant but egotistical and erratic artist whose personality traits included an inferiority complex to a French gypsy guitarist named Django Reinhardt, a mild case of kleptomania, and a tendency to show up "late, drunk, or not at all" for shows. Ray comes alive through a series of episodic vignettes, many of which are more in the nature of tall tales than historically believable recreations. (In one instance, we're even offered a multiple choice resolution for one of Ray's "legendary" escapades.) Along with various jazz authorities who appear in "talking head" segments,

Allen provides some of the linking narration between episodes; other than that, the director is absent from the screen.

Sweet and Lowdown is arguably the least ambitious and most atypical entry into Allen's '90s canon. Perhaps ironically, it is all the more pleasant for those qualities. The shift back in time and the lack of an obvious Allen-like central figure help things immeasurably — we don't spend the movie on the lookout for self-referential insights about the man behind the camera. The movie looks great, and, as one might expect from this sort of production, there's a top-notch jazz score. Ultimately, *Sweet and Lowdown* isn't a monumental event, but it represents an enjoyable diversion. **RECOMMENDED**

Tadpole [2002]
Starring: Sigourney Weaver, Aaron Stanford, John Ritter, Bebe Neuwirth Director: Gary Winick Screenplay: Heather McGowan and Niels Mueller Running Time: 1:15 Rated: R (Sexual situations, profanity) Theatrical Aspect Ratio: 1.85:1

Oscar Grubman (Aaron Stanford) is not an average 15-year-old high school sophomore. Aside from the fact that he attends an exclusive prep school, he reads (and quotes) Voltaire, is more interested in a woman's hands than any other physical assets, and makes shocking statements to the effect that life "isn't all about getting laid." According to his best friend, Charlie (Robert Iler, Tony Jr. from "The Sopranos"), he's like a 40-year old trapped in a 15-year-old's body. And, indeed, Oscar's taste in women runs to those who are decades his senior. He is hopelessly infatuated with his step-mother, Eve (Sigourney Weaver), and endlessly plots how to reveal his feelings. He is convinced that her marriage to his father, Stanley (John Ritter), has left her unfulfilled and has a vague notion that he might be able to fill the vacuum. Then, when he's home in Manhattan for Thanksgiving, he makes the mistake of getting drunk, then compounds that error by sleeping with Eve's best friend, Diane (Bebe Neuwirth). He then spends the rest of the vacation trying to hide his indiscretion from his parents while subtly wooing Eve.

The script, credited to Heather McGowan and Niels Mueller, is smart, witty, and occasionally very funny. The top-notch cast brings the story to life with aplomb. As the man-eating (or should that be "boy-eating") Diane, Bebe Neuwirth displays impeccable comic timing. She's the main reason why one of *Tadpole*'s standout scenes, a quiet little restaurant dinner, delivers as many laughs as it does. Newcomer Aaron Stanford makes a solid feature debut, although no one is going to mistake the 25-year old for someone 10 years his junior. Maybe one of the reasons this movie doesn't make us squirm as it flirts with pedophilia is that Stanford's Oscar looks like he's legally an adult.

Tadpole captures not the ebb and flow of average teenage relationship angst, but the currents that direct Oscar's atypical life. Of course, it's far off the beaten path for a high school student to lust after his step-mother and consummate a relationship with her best friend, but I find that to be a little more stimulating than watching Freddie Prinze Jr. and Sarah Michelle Gellar figuring out who's going to the prom with whom. As is astutely observed by Charlie, Oscar's life has the potential to become a Greek tragedy, but Winick keeps things light enough that it resolutely stays a comedy. **RECOMMENDED**

The Terminal [2004]
Starring: Tom Hanks, Catherine Zeta-Jones, Stanley Tucci, Chi McBride, Diego Luna, Zoe Saldana Director: Steven Spielberg Screenplay: Sacha Gervasi, Jeff Nathanson Running Time: 2:05 Rated: PG-13 (Profanity, mature themes) Theatrical Aspect Ratio: 1.85:1

Viktor Navorski (Tom Hanks) is a native of the Slavic country of Krakozhia, a fictitious neighbor of Russia. While he is en route from his homeland to JFK Airport, a military coup takes place, and when Victor arrives in the United States, he learns that his visa has been canceled. And because the United States has not recognized the new government of Krakozhia, he cannot be deported. So, in bureaucratic terms, he does not exist. The head of the airport, Frank Dixon (Stanley Tucci), decides to allow Viktor free reign of the international terminal, provided he does not attempt to leave the airport. So Viktor begins to set up a life for himself, getting to know the people who work in the terminal and developing an interest in a pretty stewardess, Amelia (Catherine Zeta-Jones), who comes across his path on more than one occasion.

When *The Terminal* is content to follow Viktor's everyday activities, it's a source of entertainment and fascination. We see him interact with a janitor, play poker for lost-and-found items, learn how to make money without engaging in illegal activities, visit the same INS agent (Zoe Saldana) every day, and make a deal with a food service delivery man to keep his belly full. He tries to contact home and get a job. He is tempted to walk out the door into New York City. And he finds himself falling in love with a woman who describes herself as poison to men. When he first arrives in New York, he can hardly speak English, but by studying volumes bought from the airport book store and listening to television news reports, he gains a working knowledge of the language. And, putting his carpentry skills to work, he constructs a bedroom of sorts at a disused gate.

The Terminal has a light tone that veers between comedy and drama. It is marginally more successful in the former arena; some of the scenes are very funny. Timing is critical anytime a movie wants to make an audience laugh, and Spielberg knows how to deliver each punch line. Hanks, who can veer effortlessly from heavy to breezy material, has no difficulty making Viktor believable and likable. It's the big moments — the ones inspired by a Capra-esque desire for grand, feel-good scenes — where Spielberg is on shaky ground. During these instances we can sense the manipulation, turning what's transpiring on screen into something false and forced. The negatives are not enough to drag *The Terminal* down. It's still a fine, enjoyable, uplifting fantasy that's suitable for viewing by all members of the family. (It's a "soft" PG-13, with only a few mild swear words keeping it from a PG.) RECOMMENDED

There's Something About Mary [1998]

Starring: Ben Stiller, Cameron Diaz, Matt Dillon Directors: Peter Farrelly & Bobby Farrelly Screenplay: Ed Decter & John J. Strauss and Peter Farrelly & Bobby Farrelly Running Time: 1:57 Rated: R (Profanity, gross-out jokes, fake nudity, cruelty to animals and human beings) Theatrical Aspect Ratio: 1.85:1

When we first meet the narrator of the story, Ted (Ben Stiller), it's 1985 in the small town of Cumberland, Rhode Island. The occasion is Ted's Senior Prom, and he is about to attend it with Mary (Cameron Diaz), the girl of his dreams. Ted can't believe this is really happening, but Mary, after breaking up with a long-time boyfriend, took a liking to Ted when he stood up for her mentally handicapped brother, Warren (W. Earl Brown). Things are going along perfectly for Ted until he makes a pit stop in Mary's bathroom while she's upstairs changing. Failure to tuck himself in properly before zipping up leads to one of the film's most painful comedy sequences and ruins Ted's chance for a date with Mary.

Cut to 1998. Ted, now a moderately successful writer, still carries the torch for Mary. On the advice of his best friend, Dom (Chris Elliott), he hires Pat Healy

(Matt Dillon), a sleazy private investigator, to track down Mary, who now lives in Florida. Pat finds and falls for his quarry, then lies to Ted about her whereabouts so he can pursue her on his own. But Ted, unconvinced by Pat's information, decides to check things out on his own, and soon finds himself in the middle of a bizarre romantic pentagon that also involves a British architect (Lee Evans) and a famous NFL quarterback.

Perhaps the most surprising thing about *There's Something about Mary* is that, while the film relies heavily on crude humor, it's also unexpectedly effective as a sweet, albeit offbeat, romantic comedy. Granted, if you're not at least open to laughing at the kinds of gags that the Farrellys bombard their audience with, it's doubtful that this aspect of the film will save it. But, for those who embrace the humor in all of its perversity, the effectiveness of the romance is a distinct plus.

To be fair to the Farrellys, not every joke in this film centers on genitals, breasts, bodily fluids, or an assortment of other, tasteless subjects. Granted, this isn't subtle or intellectual humor (two words that don't apply to any Farrelly Brothers production), but it is less earthy than their usual material. The Farrellys couldn't care less whether viewers are affronted by their material. In fact, they probably set out with the intention of offending at least 99% of the audience. RECOMMENDED

To Die For [1995]

Starring: Nicole Kidman, Matt Dillon, Joaquin Phoenix, Casey Affleck Director: Gus Van Sant Jr. Screenplay: Buck Henry, based on the novel by Joyce Maynard Running Time: 1:43 Rated: R (Profanity, sex, violence) Theatrical Aspect Ratio: 1.85:1

Told in an effectively disorganized fashion that jumps back and forth in time and includes pseudo-interviews and pieces of "actual" story, *To Die For* gradually unravels the tale of TV weatherperson Suzanne Stone (Nicole Kidman), who gains national notoriety as the result of a murder conspiracy rap that she beats. Her face and story are everywhere — *Donahue, USA Today,* and smaller talk shows across the country. For someone with Suzanne's vapid philosophy that "You're not anyone in America unless you're on TV," this is paradise.

More than a year before the end of the film (which is also the beginning), Suzanne is a single young woman in the town of Little Hope, New Hampshire. She has the looks, but not much intelligence to go with them. Despite that (or perhaps because of it), she catches the eye of local hunk Larry Maretto (Matt Dillon), an all-around nice guy and the son of a reputed mobster. Larry falls head-over-heels, and there are soon nuptials, with Suzanne wearing an exact replica of Maria Shriver's wedding veil. Not long after that, Larry has been transformed from "Van Halen to Jerry Vale" and is beginning to bore Suzanne with his desire to become a father, especially now that her career is taking off with a daily job as the weathergirl at a local cable station.

Van Sant, whose previous efforts include *Drug Store Cowboy* and *My Private Idaho,* is not an accomplished satirist, but his screenwriter, Buck Henry (adapting from a book by Joyce Maynard), is. The humor in this film is more often intellectually tantalizing than laugh-aloud funny. Suzanne is the embodiment of the extreme celebrity worship that has made the O.J. Simpson circus into the biggest TV event of all time. In the main, Van Sant and Henry know just how to exploit that element of their film.

To Die For has its share of truly delicious sequences, and some biting dialogue worth killing for. The best moments occur during a taped interview with Suzanne where she discusses her frighteningly shallow theories about life, death, television, and keeping her maiden name for on-air work. In the end, however, *To Die For* doesn't go quite far enough — there are times when Van Sant stays a little too conventional, and this causes the picture to have only teeth when it could have had fangs. **RECOMMENDED**

Twelfth Night [United Kingdom/United States, 1996]

Starring: Helena Bonham Carter, Imogen Stubbs, Nigel Hawthorne, Richard E. Grant, Ben Kingsley Director: Trevor Nunn Screenplay: Trevor Nunn, based on the play by William Shakespeare Running Time: 2:14 Rated: PG (Mature themes) Theatrical Aspect Ratio: 1.85:1

Twelfth Night opens with a scene alluded to, but never presented in Shakespeare's original text. Twin siblings, Viola (Imogen Stubbs) and Sebastian (Steven Mackintosh), are aboard a ship that is wrecked off the coast of the imaginary country of Illyria. Although both characters escape the disaster, they are separated, and each believes the other to be dead. In order to survive more easily in a "man's world," Viola cuts her hair, glues on a fake mustache, and dresses in men's clothing. Going by the name of Cesario, she enters the service of a local Duke, Orsino (Toby Stephens). Orsino is madly in love with a young countess, Olivia (Helena Bonham Carter), who steadfastly refuses his ad-

vances. Orsino sends Viola to woo Olivia in his name. Olivia immediately falls for Viola/Cesario, while, at the same time, Viola realizes that she is in love with Orsino. And so the triangle is established.

A secondary story concerns the goings-on in Olivia's household, where the countess' frequently drunk uncle, Sir Toby Belch (Mel Smith); her maid, Maria (Imelda Staunton); a foppish noble, Sir Andrew Aguecheek (Richard E. Grant); and an itinerant entertainer, Feste (Ben Kingsley), plot the downfall of Olivia's bad-tempered steward, Malvolio (Nigel Hawthorne).

Twelfth Night is chiefly about the similarities and differences between the sexes. By dressing Viola as a man, Shakespeare establishes an opportunity to explore through one character the different manners in which men and women approach the same situation, especially if it involves love. The play also addresses the deceptiveness of judging by appearance. After all, appearance, especially as it relates to identity, is an important aspect of *Twelfth Night*.

With *Twelfth Night,* as with any of the Bard's comedies, there's always a question of how well the humor will translate to a modern audience. Fortunately, in large part due to a wonderful comic turn by Nigel Hawthorne, the film offers plenty to laugh at. The finale, where all the mistaken identities are unraveled, is an example of how perfect timing can accentuate comedy.

Shakespeare aficionados will probably be pleased that so much of the written word has made it to the screen, but the 2+- hour running length is a bit burdensome. Nevertheless, the slow spots are worth sitting through, because, as a whole, this is solid entertainment. **RECOMMENDED**

Undercover Brother [2002]

Starring: Eddie Griffin, Chris Kattan, Denise Richards, David Chappelle Director: Malcolm D. Lee Screenplay: John Ridley & Michael McClullers Running Time: 1:23 Rated: PG-13 (Profanity, sexual situations, cartoon violence) Theatrical Aspect Ratio: 1.85:1

The filmmakers atop *Undercover Brother* understand that parody, no matter how inherently witty, cannot last for 90 minutes. Repetition will give birth to boredom. Thus, to keep the audience's interest, the film changes tone and focus on a fairly regular basis. By re-inventing itself every 20 minutes or so, *Undercover Brother* plays more like a series of thinly-connected skits than a coherent motion picture; however, for this kind of production, that's not a detriment. Also, director Malcolm D. Lee (cousin of Spike Lee) and his cast understand the meaning of the term "comedic timing." Because of that, jokes work here that might not have worked in other, similar endeavors.

Anton Jackson (Eddie Griffin) is Undercover Brother, a very conspicuous guy whose wardrobe and appearance are stuck in the '70s, and who is devoted to the cause of the Black Man. One day, Undercover Brother's path inadvertently crosses that of B.R.O.T.H.E.R.H.O.O.D., an organization dedicated to opposing the schemes of The (White) Man and his assistant, Mr. Feather (Chris Kattan), whose goal is to promote racial divisiveness. When the Chief of B.R.O.T.H.E.R.H.O.O.D. (Chi McBride) is impressed by Undercover Brother's moves, he offers the ultra-cool guy with the mega-afro a position in B.R.O.T.H.E.R.H.O.O.D.'s inner circle, joining the likes of Sista Girl (Aunjanue Ellis), Conspiracy Brother (David Chappelle), Smart Brother (Gary Anthony Williams), and Lance (Neil Patrick Harris), the white, affirmative action intern. Undercover Brother's first assignment: go undercover playing the black sellout in a white corporation and discover how Mr. Feather has managed to force a Colin Powell-type Presidential candidate (Billy Dee Williams) to abandon politics in favor of opening a fried chicken fast food chain.

The most consistently funny parts of *Undercover Brother* — and there are surprisingly quite a few to choose from — involve Undercover Brother losing himself in white corporate America. The movie uses humor to make its points, but it does so gently, not stridently, and with a smile, rather than an angry grimace. Of course, *Undercover Brother* is more interested in getting laughs and appealing to a wide audience than in making a social statement. Consequently, it takes equal jabs at black and white culture.

Undercover Brother needn't be a guilty pleasure — it's made with enough savvy to be appreciated on its own terms. There are laughs aplenty, and, as a bonus, viewers don't have to worry about being subjected to farts, urine, feces, semen, or any of the other foul substances that have overrun modern-day comedies. **RECOMMENDED**

Wag the Dog [1997]

Starring: Robert De Niro, Dustin Hoffman, Anne Heche, Woody Harrelson Director: Barry Levinson Screenplay: David Mamet & Hilary Henkin, based on the book by Larry Beinhart Running Time: 1:35 Rated: R (Profanity, mature themes) Theatrical Aspect Ratio: 1.85:1

Hollywood and Presidential politics — perfect together. Anyone who doubts this simple maxim will face a challenge to their opinion when they see *Wag the Dog*, the hilarious satire from director Barry Levinson. For, although this film is one of the funniest comedies out there, it also carries a serious, thought-provoking message about the relationship between politics and mass-market entertainment. This is one of Levinson's best films, and the screenplay, co-penned by noted writer David Mamet (along with Hilary Henkin), is brilliantly on-target.

The premise is relatively simple. Only 2 weeks before election day, a sitting president is hit by a sex scandal. A brief dalliance with a Firefly Girl becomes public knowledge, and now his 17% lead is about to plummet. Winifred Ames (Anne Heche), one of the President's top aides, calls in spin doctor extraordinary, Conrad Bream (Robert De Niro). Conrad goes to work immediately, deciding that the best way to get the public's mind off the Firefly Girl is to give them something bigger to think about. "Change the story, change the lead" is his motto, so he decides to manufacture a war against Albania. Why Albania? Because the name sounds sinister and no one in the United States knows anything about the country.

Conrad decides that he and Winifred can't do it alone. They need help, so they go to big-time Hollywood producer Stanley Motss (Dustin Hoffman). He has never won an Academy Award, but he's more than willing to help stage the war. They'll need slogans, a theme song, merchandising links, and sympathetic characters. Soon, carefully-controlled leaks to the press make it to the evening news, and everyone is reporting about the outbreak of hostilities between the United States and Albania, even though no troops have been moved and no shots have been fired. Actual battles don't matter, however, because, if it's on television, it must be real.

To avoid making *Wag the Dog* sound too much like an intellectual challenge, let me make this clarification: the movie is intelligent, but it's also a lot of fun. This is the kind of film that you can laugh and think your way through. I look forward to seeing *Wag the Dog* another time, and I think I'll enjoy it as much, if not more. No matter what your political persuasion is, or how cynically you regard the goings-on in Washington, you will be entertained. Let's just hope *Wag the Dog* isn't *too* close to the mark in its depiction of specific events. **HIGHLY RECOMMENDED**

Waiting for Guffman [1996]

Starring: Christopher Guest, Eugene Levy, Catherine O'Hara, Fred Willard, Parker Posey Director: Christopher Guest
Screenplay: Christopher Guest & Eugene Levy Running Time: 1:24
Rated: R (Profanity, mature themes) Theatrical Aspect Ratio: 1.85:1

Because the title sounds like *Waiting for Godot,* some viewers may be fooled into expecting highbrow entertainment from *Waiting for Guffman.* They are in for a huge surprise, for, although Christopher Guest's film is exceptionally perceptive, there's nothing remotely artsy or pretentious about it. This "documentary," which chronicles the production of an amateur play to celebrate the sesquicentennial of the fictitious town of Blaine, Missouri, offers one laugh after another.

Blaine has two claims to fame — it's the "stool capital of the United States" and it was visited by a UFO before Roswell was ever heard of. In fact, when the aliens landed in Blaine, they invited the residents on board their ship for a pot luck dinner, and when they took off, they left behind a circular landing site within which the weather never changes (67 degrees with a 40% chance of rain). Now, Blaine is 150 years old, and, to celebrate the occasion, the town council has decided on a number of special events, all to culminate with the play "Red, White, and Blaine," which is to be produced at the local high school.

Directing this play is off-off-off-off-Broadway exile Corky St. Claire (Christopher Guest), the man who attempted to turn *Backdraft* into a stage production. Corky is ably assisted by his music director, Lloyd Miller (Bob Balaban), and has a fine cast of 6. They are the husband-and-wife team of Ron and Sheila Albertson (Fred Willard and Catherine O'Hara), Blaine's travel agents (who have never been outside of Blaine), local dentist Allan Pearl (Eugene Levy), Dairy Queen waitress Libby Mae Brown (Parker Posey), auto mechanic Johnny Savage (Matt Keeslar), and an old coot by the name of Clifford Wooley (Lewis Arquette). Abandoning their day jobs, they come together to breathe life into a musical version of Blaine's history.

There are numerous reasons why *Waiting for Guffman* works. In the first place, it has intimate knowledge of the objects of its satire. Anyone who has ever participated in a high school play will be struck with an eerie sense of familiarity. And those who have lived in communities like Blaine will immediately recognize the acuteness of Guest's perception. Secondly, *Waiting for Guffman* doesn't go for cheap laughs. The play comes off much as it might in real life. And, perhaps unsurprisingly, there's the same kind of charm about "Red, White, and Blaine" that there is about any amateur production where the players substitute enthusiasm for talent.

There is such a thing as comic momentum, and Guest has a good sense of what that means. Comic momentum doesn't refer to nonstop jokes, but to an atmosphere that is always ripe for humor. By utilizing accomplished performers and crisp editing, the director achieves this. **HIGHLY RECOMMENDED**

Waking Ned Devine [Ireland, 1998]

Starring: Ian Bannen, David Kelly, Fionnula Flanagan, Susan Lynch, James Nesbitt Director: Kirk Jones Screenplay: Kirk Jones Running Time: 1:35 Rated: PG (Nudity, mature themes) Theatrical Aspect Ratio: 2.35:1

Ned Devine is dead. The news that he was holding a lottery ticket worth over 6.8 million pounds was too much for old Ned's heart. Now, the tiny Irish village of Tullymore has a decision to make: do they bury Ned's ticket along with him or do they choose one of their own to impersonate Ned and collect the money, then split it 52 ways? Although the answer to this question may not be surprising, the smoothly entertaining manner of the storytelling is.

Waking Ned Devine is an unabashed excursion into feel good territory. Director Kirk Jones, making his feature debut, revels in the film's lightheartedness. And, although his movie is not entirely without substance (themes about religion, morality, and spirituality abound, as one can guess from the title character's name), it's basically designed to allow the audience to have fun. The two main characters, Jackie O'Shea (played by veteran Irish actor Ian Bannen) and Michael O'Sullivan (David Kelly, best known as O'Reilly in John Cleese's *Fawlty Towers*), are as likable as any screen pair, and, even though they're committing a crime, we're with them all the way.

The crime in question is fraud — defrauding the lottery, to be specific. After Jackie and Michael learn that someone from Tullymore is holding the lucky ticket, they set out to discover who it is. Their intention is to "find the winner and make sure we're their best friends when they cash the check." Ultimately, the search leads to the very dead Ned Devine. Rather than let the money go unclaimed, they decide that Michael will pose as Ned, and, when the lottery officials arrive, the rest of the townspeople confirm his identity. Everyone is in agreement, except one disgruntled woman, who claims she can get more money by turning in the population of Tullymore than by participating in the scam.

Waking Ned Devine is filled with wonderful, magical moments and excursions into humor guaranteed to provoke laughter. Who can miss the comedy inherent in the sight of a buck-naked old man zipping along the roads around Tullymore on a motor scooter? Then there's the scene where Jackie and Michael are replac-

ing dead Ned's dentures. For the most part, the humor in *Waking Ned Devine* is innocent, although there are a few biting gems in the dialogue.

Jones has fashioned a visually lush motion picture that captivates with its images of the rolling hills and steep cliffs of a coastal Irish village. Combined, these elements make *Waking Ned Devine* a delightful 95-minute excursion in the company of people who are worth spending the time with. RECOMMENDED

Documentary

4 Little Girls [1997]

Director: **Spike Lee** Running Time: **1:42** Rated: **No MPAA Rating**
(Violence, mature themes) Theatrical Aspect Ratio: **1.66:1**

Basically, there are two types of documentaries: those set in the present or the near-past that feature numerous video images to support their thesis, and those based in a time that's decades or centuries ago, for which only paintings or still photos remain. *4 Little Girls,* feature director Spike Lee's first foray into the documentary realm, is in the time period of the former, but uses the techniques of the latter. Although the central event of the film — the bombing of the Sixteenth Street Baptist Church in Birmingham, Alabama where 4 little girls were killed — took place on September 15, 1963, the only surviving records of the victims exist as a series of black-and-white photographs.

4 Little Girls begins on the morning of September 15, 1963, with the atrocity that brutally killed 11-year-old Denise McNair, 14-year-old Carole Robertson, 14-year-old Cynthia Wesley, and 14-year-old Addie Mae Collins. In the absence of live footage to display the event, Lee must rely upon photographs taken in the aftermath. Intercut with them are pictures of the girls superimposed upon images of their tombstones. Through it all, we can hear the voice of Joan Baez singing "Birmingham Sunday," a song that recounts the tragedy.

During the 90 minutes that follow the stirring opening, Lee takes pains not only to detail the political climate in which this occurred, but, more importantly, to give us a sense of who the girls were and what their loss meant to the community. The words of Rev. Jesse Jackson, Coretta Scott King, Rev. Reggie White, and Walter Cronkite establish the girls' place in history; the words of Maxine McNair, Chris McNair, and Alpha Robertson express the crushing impact of the event in personal terms. It is a pain that, even after 3 decades, has not fully healed. As the sister of one of the victims explains, "You may not remember the details, but know how you felt [at the time]."

4 Little Girls therefore works on several levels, and that's the true nature of its mastery. Not only is it an excellent piece of historical research, but it's also a solid piece of drama. It's one thing to hear a talking head drone on about the importance of this event to the future of civil rights, but another thing altogether to hear the tearful, heartwrenching account of a mother as she tries to describe the depth of her loss.

HIGHLY RECOMMENDED

42 Up [United Kingdom, 2000]

Director: **Michael Apted** Running Time: **2:15** Rated: **PG** (Mature themes) Theatrical Aspect Ratio: **1.66:1**

42 Up is the latest, and perhaps final, installment in Michael Apted's long-running *Up* series. When the filmmaker began this project in 1964, he came armed with a simple concept: interview 14 British children, all age 7, representing a wide range of classes and backgrounds. Then, every 7 years for the remainder of the century, he would seek out those same 14 people and spend a day catching up with them. Those who have seen the other *Up* movies will recognize that the series really starts to get interesting with

21 Up, the 1978 entry. Each succeeding segment has grown progressively more engrossing as we see Apted's subjects mature before our eyes. *42 Up* represents the best of the movies to date.

Of the 14 original interviewees, 11 continue to co-operate, with 3 having elected to drop off. Between *35 Up* and *42 Up*, there has been one defection — Peter, who is curiously not mentioned during the movie, even though Charles and John, who haven't participated in a long time, are accorded screen time. Of the other 11, some seem more reluctant than others to dredge up older memories and recap recent occurrences. Watching *42 Up*, you get the sense that if Apted makes a *49 Up*, he might lose another participant or two. Then again, several of his subjects would probably stay with the project to their dying day.

The men and women of *42 Up* represent a reasonably comprehensive cross-section of British society, although not all of them still live in the United Kingdom. Nick, an engineering professor, has moved to the United States, and Paul resides in Australia. Most of the interviewees have been married, several are divorced, and only two don't have children. Nearly everyone in *42 Up* has been forced to cope with the loss of their parents. A good sampling of the class system and economic spectrum is presented — from the homeless Neil (who is getting his life together after bottoming out around the time of *35 Up*) to the comfortably situated Andrew.

There's something incredibly simple yet profound about what Apted has done with this series. It's an amazing achievement — not only is it a sociological masterpiece, but it's a fine example of how real-life drama can often be more compelling than fiction. We feel a kinship with these men and women because, in a very real sense, we have watched them grow up. These days, web cams allow us to enter the homes and lives of a wide variety of individuals, but such short-term, voyeuristic views are only appetizers to the kind of multi-course meal that the *Up* series offers. **HIGHLY RECOMMENDED**

American Movie [1999]

Director: **Chris Smith** Running Time: **1:47** Rated: **R** (Profanity, fake gore) Theatrical Aspect Ratio: **1.66:1**

To succeed in the independent film industry, a director must possess 3 critical attributes: luck, drive, and talent. The absence of any one of those characteristics can be fatal. *American Movie* is the story of Wis-consin filmmaker Mark Borchardt, a man with plenty of drive, but not much talent, and even less luck. He is one of those directors who invests his heart, soul, and sweat into a product that few will see and even fewer will appreciate.

In addition to being an examination of the genesis and development of a low-budget, independent film, *American Movie* is also a study of one average guy and his dream. Making movies is Borchardt's passion; it's the thing that keeps him going. Sure, he wants the expensive car and the big house, but one senses that these things are secondary. For Borchardt, obtaining the dream is not as important as pursuing it. In one way or another, this is something we can all relate to, even if our dream is vastly different. Crafting movies imparts meaning to Borchardt's life and gives him something to strive for. His enthusiasm is the one thing that differentiates him from everyone else in the film. They're reactive; he is proactive.

Directed by Chris Smith, who almost never intrudes himself or his camera into the action but allows it to play out in front of him, *American Movie* chronicles nearly 2 years in Borchardt's life. Ultimately, this film runs a little too long. Judicious trimming of about 15 to 20 minutes would have eliminated some of the slow spots and evened out the pacing. Nevertheless, even on those occasions when it drags, *American Movie* never fails to fascinate. Not only does it offer a worthwhile portrait of an individual who embodies aspirations and desires that we can all identify with, but it shows him doing something about them. *American Movie* may seem to be about filmmaking (and, to a degree, it is), but it's actually much more about the man behind the camera, and all that he represents. **RECOMMENDED**

Anne Frank Remembered [United Kingdom, 1995]

Director: **Jon Blair** Running Time: **2:02** Rated: **PG** (Mature themes) Theatrical Aspect Ratio: **1.66:1**

Those who have read the diary are aware of Anne's indomitable spirit, but, in terms of an historical perspective, her writings cover only 2 years. Blair's film fills in factual gaps, providing previously-unrevealed tidbits about the Frank family. More importantly, however, the movie extends the tale beyond August 1944, when the last journal entry was made. During the second half of this film, we follow the ultimately-fatal journey that took Anne from her family's hiding place in Amsterdam to Gestapo headquarters to Auschwitz and, finally, Bergen-Belsen, where she died in February 1945 of typhus (one month before the camp was liberated by advancing allied troops). Of the 7 who went into hiding with Anne, only one survived the war — her father, Otto Frank, who devoted the rest of his life to keeping his young daughter's memory alive.

Anne Frank Remembered interviews a number of people who knew Anne, either before or after she was sent to the concentration camps. Miep Gies, one of the quartet who concealed the Frank family from the Nazis in Amsterdam for over a year, offers extensive recollections of Anne, her father, and the war. Anne's lone surviving relative, Bernd Elias, expresses his feelings about his cousin. Excerpts from 1976 and 1979 interviews with Otto Frank (who died in 1980) are included. Together with many other testimonials, these form a compelling picture of events not covered by Anne's diary.

Perhaps the most remarkable piece of archival footage presented in this film is a small, one-second film clip of Anne on a balcony — the only known moving picture ever taken of her. It represents a tenuous link to a girl who is known to so many people through her diary. Even Otto Frank admitted that he never really knew his daughter until he read what she had written.

Anne Frank Remembered is as important for what it will preserve for posterity as for the story it tells today. The message emerging from the Holocaust has always been "Never Forget," and films of this quality make it impossible not to remember. If the story of each of Hitler's victims was told with the sensitivity and power of *Anne Frank Remembered,* there would not be enough buckets in the world to hold all the tears. **HIGHLY RECOMMENDED**

Bowling for Columbine [2002]

Director: **Michael Moore** Running Time: 2:00 Rated: **R** (Violence, profanity) Theatrical Aspect Ratio: **1.85:1**

While there will always be a debate about the authenticity of Michael Moore's documentary techniques, there's no arguing that *Bowling for Columbine* succeeds equally well as a provocative essay on gun violence in America and an opportunity for the writer/director to engage in some heavy self-promotion. Whether you like him or hate him, it's impossible to deny Moore's charisma and persuasiveness as a showman. He takes a thesis and runs with it, and, while some of his conclusions may be a little farfetched, his probing often pays unexpected dividends.

Regardless of how dubious its documentary tactics may be, *Bowling for Columbine* is powerful, thought-provoking, and, upon occasion, bitingly funny. Moore's easygoing tone never makes the viewer feel threatened — just as his rumpled personal appearance puts his victims and adversaries at ease. He's a predator in disguise. The movie offers something for everyone. Even those who disagree with Moore's politics will find themselves *thinking* during and after the movie. Whether you agree with the director's conclusions isn't the issue — it's that you recognize the problem.

The point of the film is to determine why gun violence, especially that of children on children, is rampant in this country. At first, Moore is guided by the precept that easy access to guns is the cause. And, despite being a card-carrying NRA member, he is more than willing to point the finger at Heston and his cronies. But, along the way, Moore makes a discovery — there are more guns per household in Canada than in the United States, yet the death toll, even when adjusted to consider the unequal populations, is much lower. This forces Moore to conclude that, while the ready availability of firearms in the United States may be a contributing factor to the high number of gun-related homicides, it's not the primary reason. Eventually, after conducting various interviews and hopping around the country (and out of it), Moore suggests that fear, enhanced by the media's obsession with death and violent crime, may be the root cause of America's death-by-gun problem.

I can predict with a large degree of certainty that *Bowling for Columbine* will outrage viewers whose political leanings are conservative. The film is at times laugh-aloud, viciously funny (provided you aren't among Moore's targets). But, above all, no matter how much you love or despise the messenger and his means, there's no denying that the message bears consideration and rumination. Imperfect as it may be, *Bowling for Columbine* is riveting stuff. **HIGHLY RECOMMENDED**

Capturing the Friedmans [2003]

Director: **Andrew Jarecki** Running Time: 1:47 Rated: **No Rating** (Profanity, mature themes) Theatrical Aspect Ratio: **1.85:1**

Various publications have labeled *Capturing the Friedmans* as a narrative documentary, a crime investigation, a meditation upon the nature of truth, and an exposé of the failings of the United States judicial system. First and foremost, however, it is an

American tragedy — a look inside a criminal case that shines a light into the dark, ugly corners of suburbia, then turns that same light on various other aspects of crime and punishment. The facts, as laid out by the media when the case broke in 1987, were apparently straightforward. A respected Long Island teacher, Arnold Friedman, was arrested on charges of child molestation when investigators learned that participants in a computer class he conducted in his home claimed to have been sexually abused. The shadow of doubt spread, falling on Arnold's youngest son, 18-year-old Jesse, who was ultimately accused of more than 200 criminal counts ranging from sodomy to child endangerment. Both men pled guilty and were sentenced to prison. Arnold died behind bars. Jesse was released after 13 years.

Capturing the Friedmans, directed by first-time filmmaker Andrew Jarecki, delves beneath the headlines to try for deeper understanding. What he finds is confusion and contradiction. Employing interviews with David and Jesse Friedman, and their mother, Elaine, as well as home movies and video taken during the course of the investigation, Jarecki has assembled a compelling documentary that questions both the investigative process and the results. Most viewers will leave the theater with more questions than they arrived with. *Capturing the Friedmans* doesn't offer many answers. Even Jarecki, who viewed hundreds of hours' worth of material not in the film, admits to not knowing the truth.

One curious thing about the film is that the Friedmans had this much video footage to make available to Jarecki. Seemingly every family argument after Arnold's arrest was captured on videotape. There's something a little creepy and voyeuristic about watching some of the material, because it is so candid. Nothing in the homemade video clarifies the questions of guilt or innocence. Arnold is evasive, Jesse is dazed, and Elaine spends most of the time yelling.

There is humor in *Capturing the Friedmans,* but even that, like everything else in the film, is underpinned by a sense of profound sadness. The film is as powerful as any narrative motion picture in telling a story that rips at the emotions. As facts are revealed, we find our sympathies switching from one individual to another. In the end, while Jarecki may not be able to answer our most basic questions about the guilt or innocence of the Friedmans, he makes a profound statement that, in a situation like this, no one can be completely innocent and everyone is a victim. **HIGHLY RECOMMENDED**

The Celluloid Closet [1996]

Directors: **Rob Epstein and Jeffrey Friedman** Running Time: 1:40
Rated: R (Mature themes, sexual situations, nudity, profanity)
Theatrical Aspect Ratio: 1.85:1

The thesis of Rob Epstein and Jeffrey Friedman's film, *The Celluloid Closet,* can be summarized by a line from the production: "Hollywood, that great maker of myths, taught straight people what to think about gay people, and gay people what to think about themselves." Unfortunately, most of those lessons have been negative. *The Celluloid Closet* presents a fairly comprehensive overview of how the gay/lesbian community has been portrayed in American films. Clips from dozens of motion pictures are included — everything from 1912's *Algie, the Miner* to 1993's *Philadelphia.* Well-known gay and straight personalities are on hand to offer opinions and observations. These include Tom Hanks, Whoopi Goldberg, Susan Sarandon, Tony Curtis, and Harvey Fierstein.

In the silent era, gay characters were used for comic relief. With exaggeratedly effeminate gestures, these thinly-drawn caricatures were foils for numerous silent stars, including Charlie Chaplin, who kissed a cross-dresser in *Behind the Screen.* With the arrival of the talkies, "the sissy," Hollywood's first stock gay character, arrived. This clichéd image of the gay man could be found in such films as *The Gay Divorcée* and *Call Her Savage.* In the 1930s, Hollywood decided to begin censoring its own films. The result was the infamous, and largely ineffective, Hays Code. While the Code didn't eliminate the presence of gay characters in films, they became less obvious. It wasn't until the late '60s when a few films appeared that dealt intelligently and sympathetically with homosexuality. With the 1968 British film, *The Detective,* and 1970's *The Boys in the Band,* a slow change was initiated. The attitude shift took a long time to grow roots, however, as the '70s and '80s saw many more films with gays as victimizers than as genuine characters.

The Celluloid Closet is one of the most fascinating documentaries to put Hollywood under the microscope. In about 100 minutes, this film convincingly defends its thesis. *The Celluloid Closet* is top-notch entertainment, not only because it's enjoyable, but because it argues its case with an effectiveness that would impress even a first class, homophobic attorney. **HIGHLY RECOMMENDED**

Crumb [1994]

Director: **Terry Zwigoff** Running Time: **1:59** Rated: **R** (Profanity, sexual candor, mature themes) Theatrical Aspect Ratio: **1.85:1**

Upon viewing the completed version of this film, cartoonist Robert Crumb, whose story it tells, informed director Terry Zwigoff, "After I saw it I had to go for a walk in the woods, just to clear my head. I took my favorite hat off, this hat that I've had for 25 years, and I threw it off a cliff. I don't want to be R. Crumb anymore." Considering the material, the reaction is understandable. This is the sort of movie capable of prompting a viewer to question and evaluate a great deal more than the inner workings of a single man. In addition to presenting one of the most compelling filmed documentary character studies of all time, *Crumb* asks a lot of pointed questions about life and art that no one can possibly answer, least of all the misanthropic genius at the center of the portrait.

Crumb's claim to fame is founding the underground comics movement in 1967, when issue #1 of his "Zap Comix" was released. Crumb is also the creator of the "Keep on Truckin'" logo, the artist for the LP cover of Big Brother and the Holding Company's *Cheap Thrills,* and the originator of Fritz the Cat, which Ralph Bakshi turned into the first X-rated animated feature (a film that Crumb hates).

Is Crumb a misogynist? Probably, since, in his own words, he harbors inner hostility towards women. But there's more than that to his work. Is Crumb obsessed with sex? No doubt. Apparently, there was a time when he masturbated 4 to 5 times each day, and everyone seems to agree that he finds his own work sexually stimulating. Is Crumb disgusted with popular culture and fame? In his own words, "As a teenager . . . I realized I was an outcast, I became a critic, and I've been disgusted with American culture from the time I was a kid. I started out by rejecting all the things that the people who rejected me liked, then over the years I developed a deeper analysis of these things."

Whatever opinion a viewer has of Crumb at the end of this film, an apathetic reaction is unthinkable. Empathy, fascination, disgust, or anger are all likely, but not disinterest. R. Crumb is the sort of person it's impossible to ignore, and Zwigoff's film creates such an honest portrayal of him that some sort of response is demanded. **MUST SEE**

The Endurance [United States/United Kingdom, 2001]

Director: **George Butler** Running Time: **1:33** Rated: **No MPAA Rating** (Mature themes) Theatrical Aspect Ratio: **1.85:1**

Sir Ernest Shackleton, a veteran explorer who visited Antarctica on several occasions (once almost becoming the first man to reach the South Pole), began planning a cross-continent expedition in late 1913. To obtain a crew, he used the following advertisement: "Notice: Men wanted for hazardous journey. Bitter cold. Small wages. Long months of complete darkness. Constant danger. Safe return doubtful. Honour and recognition in case of success." From the thousands of respondents, Shackleton hand-picked a crew of 28 (including himself and several men he had previously worked with). The endeavor that followed, which is chronicled in George Butler's documentary, *The Endurance,* was equal parts disaster and tragedy, and illustrated why Shackleton has since come to be regarded as one of the greatest leaders ever to tread the paths of humanity.

For those who go into the movie knowing the fate of *The Endurance* and the 28 men aboard, this motion picture represents a fascinating inspection of what happened every step of the way. For those who see *The Endurance* without previous knowledge of anything about Shackleton or his trips to Antarctica, the movie represents a rousing adventure film filled with high suspense. Butler is careful not to give away the ending too early; the words spoken by Liam Neeson in the running voiceover narration reveal things only when appropriate to the movie's internal chronology.

Unlike "talking head" documentaries, which stay on a airy, philosophical plane, *The Endurance* draws you into the story. The characters, especially Shackleton, are rich and the setting is vivid. The means by which Butler brings all of this together is perfect for the story. We do not have to sit through scene after scene of Polar Exploration scholars discussing Shackleton's importance to history (there is one of these individuals, but his comments are limited). Instead, Butler's new footage shows us the terrible beauty of Antarctica, the relatives' contributions further humanize the participants, and the stock images crystallize everything. *The Endurance* is many things, including a compelling adventure saga. However, above all, it is a testimony to the triumph of the human spirit, and a reminder that, under the right leadership, humankind is capable of virtually anything. In Shackleton's own words: "We have seen God and his splendors, heard the text that nature renders. We have reached the naked soul of man." You will leave the theater uplifted, exhilarated, and perhaps a little chilly. **HIGHLY RECOMMENDED**

Fast, Cheap & Out of Control [1997]
Director: **Errol Morris** Running Time: 1:22 Rated: PG (Nothing offensive) Theatrical Aspect Ratio: 1.85:1

Fast, Cheap & Out of Control isn't much like any of Errol Morris' other well-known films — *Gates of Heaven* (about a pet cemetery), *The Thin Blue Line* (about a murder), and *A Brief History of Time* (about science, space, and infinity). In fact, at first glance, this movie appears startlingly unambitious by comparison. But there's more to *Fast, Cheap & Out of Control* than initially meets the eye. Not only is there a great deal of craft involved in the film's production, but its underlying themes are compelling and universal.

The basic framework for *Fast, Cheap & Out of Control* has Morris interviewing 4 men with unique, but not terribly interesting, professions. Dave Hoover is a wild animal trainer who works with lions and tigers in the circus ring. George Mendonca is the topiary gardener (the person who sculpts hedges into lifelike shapes) for Green Animals' Gardens. Ray Mendez is a mole-rat specialist (mole-rats are hairless mammals that live in insect-like colonies). And Rodney Brooks is a robot scientist who works in an artificial intelligence lab at M.I.T. All 4 of these individuals are among the best in their respective fields, and it's their passion for their jobs, rather than anything especially startling or hypnotic about the work itself, that piques our interest.

As we watch, however, we become aware that, by structuring *Fast, Cheap & Out of Control* as he does, Morris is doing far more than merely presenting a series of talking-head interviews. By piecing the film together with fast cuts and sequences where the soundtrack of one interview overlaps images depicting the activities of another of the subjects, Morris explores at least two intriguing, interrelated themes: the evolution of humankind and our never-ending attempt to control our environment.

One thing that never changes, however, is man's desire to regulate everything around him. Brooks speaks of his robots being the forerunners of a new breed of silicon-based life form that may eventually render our species extinct. Despite his assertion that he is only an observer, Mendez takes an important role in shaping the existence of his mole-rats, hoping

to learn more about himself through their actions. Hoover's entire livelihood is based on mastering creatures that are more powerful and dangerous than himself. And even the mild-mannered Mendonca alters the course of nature by twisting and shaping bushes into works of art. In one way or another, all 4 are playing god. **HIGHLY RECOMMENDED**

The Fog of War [2003]
Director: **Errol Morris** Running Time: 1:46 Rated: PG (Mature themes) Theatrical Aspect Ratio: 1.85:1

Robert S. McNamara, the Secretary of Defense for Presidents John F. Kennedy and Lyndon Johnson, has been an observer of and participant in many of the key events of the 20th century. History has not been more kind to him than his critics have been, so McNamara has used this opportunity — a 106-minute edit of several interviews given to documentarian Errol Morris — to set the record straight and expound upon his role in firebombing Japan during World War II, the Cuban Missile Crisis, and Vietnam. The product of this collaboration between McNamara and Morris represents an engrossing piece of cinema that may offer a surprise or two to even the most learned scholars of recent American history.

The Fog of War looks at several crucial incidents that have occurred during the last 60 years. Since McNamara's name is often viewed synonymously with the Vietnam War, more than a third of the film is devoted to a detailed explanation of the hows and whys of our involvement. Much of this material is familiar, but some is new (or at least not widely known). Not only do we come to understand McNamara's feelings about the war, but we recognize that he may not have been as responsible as the rumblings of posterity lead us to believe. McNamara doesn't back away from accepting a degree of culpability, but he makes it clear that there were times when he urged the president (in this case, Johnson) to pull out the troops. In fact, the division of opinion between the two men led to McNamara's ouster from his cabinet position in early 1968. And, to this day, he believes that, had Kennedy lived, events in Vietnam would have been different. It was Kennedy's stated policy that the United States should withdraw from Vietnam by the end of 1965. Instead, under Johnson, we committed more than 175,000 men by that date.

McNamara has a reputation for being intelligent and belligerent. *The Fog of War* validates the former characteristic, but not necessarily the latter. He never loses his temper, although there are several times when he comes close to breaking down (such as when remembering Kennedy's assassination). At the age of 86 (when the film was shot), he remains vital and energetic. He speaks candidly about nearly every subject Morris raises, except toward the end of the film, when he refuses to discuss why he did not speak out against the Vietnam War after he left office.

Although *The Fog of War* incorporates archival footage, Oval Office tapes of conversations, and still photographs, most of the movie is McNamara sitting and talking to the camera, and he keeps us riveted. No flashy postproduction elements are needed. By asking the right questions and guiding the interview into compelling territory, Morris has produced one of 2003's most memorable documentaries. **HIGHLY RECOMMENDED**

The Girl Next Door [1999]

Director: **Christine Fugate** Running Time: 1:24 Rated: No MPAA Rating (Sex, frequent frontal nudity, profanity, graphic plastic surgical procedures) Theatrical Aspect Ratio: 1.85:1

Her stage name is "Stacy Valentine," and her list of credits list more than 65 adult movies, including a number of popular titles. She has been working in the porn industry since 1995, when she escaped from an abusive marriage in Oklahoma and surfaced in Hollywood. It was there that documentary filmmaker Fulgate made contact with her, and the result is a fascinating chronicle of 2 years in Stacy's life, including highs and lows. Stacy gives Fulgate surprisingly candid access, allowing the director to film her during some of the darkest moments of this period.

Although *The Girl Next Door*'s primary goal is to offer a well-rounded cinematic representation of Stacy The Person (not just Stacy The Porn Star), the cameras also reveal something about the world around her. Without being judgmental, Fulgate gives us an unvarnished look into the heart of the porn industry. *The Girl Next Door* isn't an expose, nor is it intended to be — the movie doesn't dwell on drugs, violence, and sleaze. Instead, it depicts the hollowness of this lifestyle. All that glitters is not gold, and, in this case, the glamour is all artificial and the adoration is skin deep.

Just as nothing about the industry is real, nothing about "Stacy Valentine" is either — not her name or her body. Fulgate's job is to peel away the porn star personality worn like a gaudy garment by Stacy Baker and reveal the naked character of the girl under-

neath. Stacy Valentine is a product of her environment — her breasts have been augmented more than once, her thighs and legs have been liposuctioned, and her lips have been injected with fat removed from her hips. On one occasion, she mentions that she hardly recognizes herself when she looks in the mirror.

Fans who have bought into the fantasy image of Stacy Valentine may find *The Girl Next Door* to be a disillusioning experience. After seeing this film, it is impossible to objectify her; she has become a real person. For Fulgate, *The Girl Next Door* represents nearly 4 years worth of effort — 2 years to find her subject and another 2 years to film her. For Stacy Baker/Valentine, it's an opportunity to open up before the camera and bare her soul in a more explicit manner than she has ever displayed her body. For the viewer, this is a rare chance to voyeuristically experience the life of a woman who occupies the fascinating position of being one of the adult entertainment industry's top draws. **RECOMMENDED**

Home Page [1998]

Director: **Doug Block** Running Time: 1:42 Rated: No MPAA Rating (profanity, nudity, sexual themes) Theatrical Aspect Ratio: 1.33:1

The function of *Home Page*, a documentary by Doug Block is not to present some sort of all-encompassing overview of the Internet, but to offer a sampling of viewpoints and personalities, with a heavy dosage of high-level pop psychology and sociology. In the end, we get as much from inferring how Block's topics relate to our own lives as from observing what's on the screen.

Watching *Home Page* is like surfing the Web. There is a trajectory of sorts, but it's a strange, rambling one, filled with stops, starts, dead-ends, odd tangents, and abrupt leaps. By the end, we feel like we have gone on a journey, although it's not entirely clear what sort. Block introduces us to a number of colorful Web eccentrics and celebrities (Justin Hall, Harold Rheingold, Jaime Levy, Julie Petersen, Carl Steadman), offering glimpses into their often dysfunctional real lives. And, in a way, *Home Page* represents a tour of self-discovery for Block. He starts out like any other indie documentary maker, then ends up creating his own home page, exploring a new world, and reconnecting with his wife.

One of the issues addressed by *Home Page* is what underlies the growing trend of on-line exhibitionism — men and women who place the most intimate details of their life on the Web (either via tell-all journals or the ever-popular cams, which often leave nothing to the imagination). Different theories are espoused, but the most convincing is that people do this because they crave the attention that making shocking revelations will earn them. They want their 15 minutes of fame, and outrageous content on a home page offers that opportunity. Another theme Block explores is how the growing sense of alienation in society has given birth to a generation that is becoming more comfortable with the anonymous, faceless communication of the Internet than with the face-to-face rigors of interpersonal interaction. Real-life communities are being replaced by virtual ones.

Home Page is probably more intriguing and interesting than it is compelling. Block doesn't offer any astounding revelations and his techniques are a little rough around the edges — this is not slick, accomplished filmmaking, but, considering the low budget, it works. **RECOMMENDED**

Hoop Dreams [1994]

Director: **Steve James** Running Time: 2:51 Rated: PG-13 (Mature themes, language) Theatrical Aspect Ratio: 1.33:1

Hoop Dreams, the tale of two high school basketball players, is less a story about the sport than it is a chronicle of life in the inner city and of following Aldous Huxley's advice that "a man's reach should exceed his grasp." *Hoop Dreams* follows two Chicago youths, William Gates and Arthur Agee, from their Freshman year of high school to their first year of college. In addition to documenting the inevitable on-court maturation process, the movie illustrates the difficulties of balancing sports with scholastic and family pressures. Neither William nor Arthur are advanced academically, and both suffer through a variety of away-from-school crises.

At the start of *Hoop Dreams,* when William and Arthur are 14, each appears to be a solid prospect for recruiting by "white" suburban basketball powerhouse St. Joseph High School and its legendary coach, Gene Pingatore. Arthur has the quickest step one talent scout has seen in 5 years, and William looks like the "next Isiah Thomas." One point explored by this film is that no matter how "can't miss" a prospect is, and regardless of their level of talent and enthusiasm, most of them, in fact, fail. Being the star of a high school team does not guarantee a trip to the NBA, and realizing this represents a rude awakening for William and Arthur.

While William quickly becomes Coach Pingatore's "go-to-guy" on the varsity squad, Arthur's slow development as a player allows him to be dropped from the Freshman team. When his parents can no longer afford St. Joseph's tuition, Arthur is cut loose and sent back to public school. His home life is further disrupted by financial struggles and the departure of his father. William, on the other hand, suffers a series of knee injuries that erode his confidence, and the unexpected arrival of a baby daughter throws his personal life into further turmoil.

The rich texture of *Hoop Dreams'* drama is its greatest asset. This is a film that goes beyond the verisimilitude of something to come from the pen of Spike Lee or John Singleton, into the realm of real life. The shattered illusions of William and Arthur are all the more poignant because these are not the dividends of a screenwriter's fertile imagination. And the drug deals depicted are chilling for exactly the same reason. If any single line sums up the lessons learned by the two protagonists, it comes late in the movie, and is spoken by William in his Marquette University dorm room: "People always say to me, 'When you get to the NBA, don't forget me.' Well, if I don't get to the NBA, *you* don't forget about *me.*" **HIGHLY RECOMMENDED**

The Last Days [1998]

Director: **James Moll** Running Time: 1:28 Rated: No MPAA Rating (Holocaust images) Theatrical Aspect Ratio: 1.85:1

When it comes to 20th-century events, few have generated more unforgettable documentary footage than the Holocaust. For those who normally avoid this sort of production, *The Last Days* offers a compelling reason to make an exception. Like all filmed Holocaust essays, it is disturbing and wrenching, but there is also an undercurrent of inspiration and optimism in the portraits painted by film maker James Moll. At its core, *The Last Days* is more about lives rebuilt than lives destroyed. It is a testimony to the resiliency of the human spirit.

For *The Last Days,* Moll has interviewed 5 survivors of Hitler's "Final Solution," all of whom currently live in the United States. He accompanies these Hungarian Jews as they return to the land of their birth, searching for closure and catharsis. Seeking solutions to unanswerable questions, they also visit the locations of their most nightmarish recollections —

the remains of Auschwitz and Berkenow. And they bring their children and grandchildren with them, entrusting memories of their experiences to future generations.

The most prominent of the 5 subjects interviewed in Moll's film is U.S. Congressman Tom Lantos, who was part of the Jewish underground in Hungary. He, along with many others, worked to provide fake Swedish passports for Jews seeking to escape from a homeland that had turned rank and deadly. Bill Basch was also a member of the Resistance. His most telling memory is of the day the Americans liberated the camp — how the former prisoners literally tore some of their captors to pieces. Alice Lok Cahana, an artist who paints as a way to memorialize the dead, returns to Europe to make peace with her ghosts. Renee Firestone goes back to Auschwitz to uncover details about her sister's death, even going so far as to question Dr. Hans Munch, the doctor in charge of the section of the camp where her sister was held. Finally, Irene Zisblatt tells a moving tale about the diamonds she now wears on a tear-shaped pendant. They are the only tangible momento she has of a mother who did not survive the ordeal.

While much of the archival footage presented in *The Last Days* is new, the substance is familiar. These are the kinds of images that no Holocaust film can ignore, because they drive home the horror of what transpired 5 decades ago, half a world away. For added impact, Moll interviews a handful of American servicemen who participated in the liberation of Dachow. What they saw and experienced there, they will never forget. The same will be true of those who view this film. **HIGHLY RECOMMENDED**

Looking for Richard [1996]

Director: Al Pacino Running Time: 1:52 Rated: R (Violence, profanity)
Theatrical Aspect Ratio: **1.85:1**

Any traditional version of Shakespeare's *Richard III* will open with "Now's the winter of our discontent made summer by this son of York," the first line of one of the Bard's best-known soliloquies. It's a telling point, therefore, that *Looking for Richard* starts with a stentorian voice declaring: "Our revels now are ended." This movie, a labor of love for Al Pacino, who makes his directorial debut, does not intend to present a complete, unabridged version of the text. Like all film makers who take on Shakespeare, Pacino's goal is to give life to his own passion for the plays. His

methods are decidedly unconventional. *Looking for Richard* is a condensed version of *Richard III* wrapped in a stream-of-consciousness documentary.

Pacino begins the film as a documentary investigating what modern day audiences think of Shakespeare's works. The answers he gets during person-on-the-street interviews are predictable: "it sucks," "it's boring," "huh?" The director's motivation for making the movie is stated up front: "It has always been a dream of mine to communicate how I feel about Shakespeare to others." After this lengthy introduction, Pacino moves on to the play. We glimpse the casting process and are given an impromptu history lesson about the War of the Roses. The second half of *Looking for Richard* concentrates on performing select scenes from the play.

A number of familiar faces fill roles here. Pacino, of course, is Richard, complete with faux hunchback and limp. Alec Baldwin plays Clarence, and Harris Yulin is King Edward. Penelope Allen is Queen Elizabeth, Kevin Spacey is Buckingham, Aidan Quinn is Richmond, and Winona Ryder is Lady Anne.

Looking for Richard is a fascinating piece of film making, but I don't think it does anything so revolutionary that non-believers will be suddenly converted. Pacino's passion is obvious, but it's not universally contagious. However, those who enjoy Shakespeare, or are at least open-minded, will find much to appreciate here. **RECOMMENDED**

Mr. Death: The Rise and Fall of Fred A. Leuchter Jr. [1999]

Director: **Errol Morris** Running Time: 1:36 Rated: PG-13 (Mature themes) Theatrical Aspect Ratio: **1.85:1**

To begin with, who is Fred Leuchter, and why has a filmmaker of Morris' caliber used him as the subject of a major documentary? By his own admission, Leuchter is an "execution technologist," who, from an early age, has harbored a fascination with death. As he grew older and became an engineer, Leuchter used his knowledge to design new, "more humane" (his words, not mine) electric chairs intended to eliminate the kind of horror stories that are often told and occasionally shown about electrocutions. This goal of this new approach was to make electrocution a safer, cheaper, and less horrific means of state-mandated killing. And, after achieving success with the electric chair, Leuchter was asked to stretch his scientific know-how to design a lethal injection machine for the state of New Jersey. At one point, he comments, "I sleep well at night — people executed by my machines have dignified, painless deaths."

Eventually, Leuchter's reputation as an "execution technologist" was eclipsed by another aspect of his life. This happened a decade ago when he became a key witness in the trial of Ernst Zundel. Zundel, a neo-Nazi, selected Leuchter as an expert witness to corroborate his assertion that the Holocaust was a hoax. On his 1988 honeymoon, Leuchter could be found poking around the ruins of Auschwitz, taking samples and evaluating the evidence. His conclusion: the so-called "showers" could not have been used as gas chambers without killing everyone in the camp (including the Nazis). Further studies led Leuchter to believe that Zundel was correct: 6 million Jews were not killed in death camps. In his opinion, it was not scientifically feasible. And, at least on the surface, his arguments *sound* persuasive.

It would be easy to label Leuchter as a hate-monger and an anti-Semite, but, as the film illustrates, he is neither. The man does not hate Jews, nor is he a neo-Nazi supporter. Leuchter, who lacks an imposing physical presence, is motivated by scientific principles. The problem is, his methods are flawed. He developed a hypothesis, but, in gathering the evidence to support it, he ignored facts that pointed to another conclusion. He cannot see another possibility because he isn't looking for one. He disproved the existence of the Holocaust based on a faulty premise and through an investigation that was riddled with inaccuracies. By presenting Leuchter sympathetically, Morris disallows us the comfort of simply labeling the man as "evil" and moving on to another target. *Mr. Death* is a compelling film because it paints Leuchter in three dimensions. HIGHLY RECOMMENDED

Super Size Me [2004]

Director: **Morgan Spurlock** Running Time: 1:38 Rated: No Rating (Profanity, occasionally disgusting images) Theatrical Aspect Ratio: 1.85:1

Is Morgan Spurlock's *Super Size Me* an attack on McDonald's? Not directly, although it's certainly not a Valentine. Rather, it's a look at the deleterious effects that modern fast-food culture is having upon our society. The movie's "hook" is that Spurlock performs an experiment upon himself to see how he would fare if he ate nothing but McDonald's food for 30 days. However, one could see that as tangential to the film's central themes, which advocate personal responsibility, decry corporate deniability, and emphasize

that people aren't getting the message that fast food can be bad for those who eat it with regularity.

The experiment is the most interesting, but not necessarily the most informative, aspect of *Super Size Me*. Spurlock goes on a one-month McDonald's spree in which he eats three gluttonous meals per day. He plays by a few rules: Everything he eats has to be on the McDonald's menu, he must sample every food choice at least once, and he only super sizes when asked by a cashier. Over the course of his study, he gains 25 pounds; experiences an extreme increase in cholesterol; suffers sexual dysfunction, headaches, and nausea; and shows signs of addiction. It's not a pretty picture, and while the extremity of Spurlock's reactions are in part a result of his excessive indulgence (5,000 calories per day), it illustrates a point about the unhealthiness of fast-food eating.

Alongside telling his personal tale, Spurlock interviews a variety of talking heads and spends some time investigating why fast-food entrées are replacing healthier choices in elementary and high schools. He also looks into the link between fast-food advertising aimed at children and the increase in obesity in the underage population. The evidence is all anecdotal, but it's pretty convincing, especially since it doesn't take a genius to make the connection between the increased availability of convenient fast food and the expanding national waist size. Little of what Spurlock presents in *Super Size Me* is new or revolutionary, but he packages it in an entertaining and easily digestible manner. It's one thing to know that fast food is bad for you. It's another to see that "badness" demonstrated.

In the end, it's pretty clear that Spurlock's goal is not to convince everyone in his viewing audience to stay away from McDonald's. (The experiment hasn't turned him into a vegetarian, although he avoids admitting whether he plans to eat any fast food in the near future.) Instead, he wants us to have a concrete understanding of *what* we're eating. The issue may be serious, but the tone is lighthearted, and that, more than anything else, makes *Super Size Me* a palatable cinematic entrée. Especially when enjoyed with a big carton of buttered popcorn and a double-sized cup of Coke. RECOMMENDED

Touching the Void [UNITED KINGDOM, 2003]

Director: **Kevin Macdonald** Running Time: 1:46 Rated: R (Profanity) Theatrical Aspect Ratio: 1.85:1

Truth, they say, is stranger than fiction . . . and also potentially more nail biting and harder to believe.

Touching the Void is an extreme example of this: a man versus nature epic so amazing that, if it was presented in a strictly narrative format, viewers would doubt its veracity. To capture this story in a way that would do it justice, British filmmaker Kevin Macdonald has blended elements of docudrama and documentary into a satisfying whole that will keep even the most stoic moviegoer gripping the armrest throughout.

The tale of Joe Simpson and Simon Yates is about as inspirational as stories come — an exhibition of human courage and the ability to endure in the most extreme circumstances. In June of 1985, Joe and Simon were cocky 20-somethings in search of adventure. The challenge they eventually settled on was to climb the previously unscaled western face of Siula Grande, a 21,000-foot peak in the Peruvian Andes. With the two tied together, the trip to the top took three days and passed mostly without incident. But on the way down, Joe lost his footing, fell, and shattered his leg, breaking the fibula and driving it up through his kneecap. For a while, Simon attempted to stay with Joe, lowering him in 300-foot increments by using two 150-foot ropes tied together. When a series of misfortunes convinced Simon that Joe might be dead and that he might soon follow, he was forced to cut the rope that was the injured man's lifeline. Incredibly, both men made it alive to the bottom.

Watching *Touching the Void* is an exhausting experience. The stunning photography at first overwhelms us with the enormity of the challenge facing the two men, then displays the ferocity of Mother Nature at her cruelest as zero-visibility snowstorms drive the temperatures to bone-chilling levels. But the story and pacing are what make this a white-knuckle experience, ratcheting up the tension degree by degree as the men relate their innermost thoughts. The suspense isn't about *whether* Joe and Simon survive, but about *how* they do it.

Few films can legitimately be considered "experiences," and in that select population, even fewer are rooted in reality. Admittedly, *Touching the Void* would not have been as engrossing had Joe and Simon not been people we could see and hear. As we watch their odyssey unfold, the same question will occur to nearly everyone: In their position, could I do what they did? Hopefully, none of us will have to find out. But for Joe and Simon, the love of climbing overcame their horrific memories. Two years and six operations after breaking his leg, Joe was once again back doing

what he loves most and, in his own words, "lives for."

HIGHLY RECOMMENDED

Unzipped [1995]

Director: **Douglas Keeve** Running Time: **1:13** Rated: **R** (Profanity)
Theatrical Aspect Ratio: **1.66:1**

Unzipped is a cinematic portrait of Isaac Mizrahi, an artist whose palette is fabric. Ostensibly, the film is a documentary, but use of that term requires stretching its meaning. Many scenes appear staged, and a great deal of cutting-and-pasting has been done in the editing room. The cinema verité effect is a conceit — genuine spontaneity is at a premium, and everyone is aware of and playing to the camera (especially would-be actresses like Cindy Crawford). Director Douglas Keeve (who was Mizrahi's lover at the time) freely admits that he "couldn't care less about the truth" but was more interested in capturing "the spirit and love in Isaac and in fashion."

Despite violating nearly every rule of "legitimate" documentary film making, however, *Unzipped* is a remarkably enjoyable piece of entertainment. While it sheds only a little light on the behind-the-scenes world of the fashion industry, it presents a fascinating, if incomplete, picture of designer Mizrahi. This man is the perfect subject for this kind of study — he's funny, energetic, and eminently quotable. He has unusual views on just about everything, from fashion ("It's about women not wanting to look like cows.") to Mary Tyler Moore ("Between her and Jackie Kennedy, they shaped this country.") to style ("It's almost impossible to have style nowadays without the right dogs.").

Unzipped also gives a glimpse into the creative process by which Mizrahi turns an idea into a dress. It's almost certainly different that anyone would imagine. The designer draws on a variety of sources for his look, including *Nanook of the North* and old Bette Davis movies, then enlists the aid of a Ouija board to help form the collection. In particular, *Unzipped* traces Mizrahi's development of his Fall 1994 line from its inception in the Spring to the final fashion show, which highlights a number of prominent models, including Cindy Crawford, Naomi Campbell, Kate Bush, and Linda Evangelista.

While *Unzipped* isn't an expose on the fashion industry per se, Keeve has enough clips of petulant models to make the viewer realize how tame Robert Altman was with *Ready to Wear*. Overall, however, this movie is far more about Mizrahi than anything else, and only when viewed from that perspective does *Unzipped* succeed. When the designer declares that "everything is frustrating except designing clothes — that's beautiful and liberating," it fits perfectly with the image of him that *Unzipped* has constructed. RECOMMENDED

The War Room [1993]

Directors: **D. A. Pennebaker and Chris Hegedus** Running Time: **1:36** Rated: **No MPAA Rating (Language)** Theatrical Aspect Ratio: **1:66:1**

The War Room is the story of James Carville and George Stephanopoulos, and their efforts on behalf of Bill Clinton throughout the 1992 Presidential campaign. From the New Hampshire primary to election night, *The War Room* depicts Carville and Stephanopoulos' backroom strategy sessions and public moves as they catapulted their man from a virtual unknown to President Elect.

This is not Bill Clinton's story, nor is it an account of how he beat the odds to become the first Democratic President in 12 years. Rather, *The War Room* is an examination of two of the men instrumental in the victory: James Carville, the "Ragin' Cajun," and, to a lesser extent, the yuppiesque George Stephanopoulos.

Carville, with his buoyant personality and glib one-liners, naturally steals every scene from the soft-spoken Stephanopoulos. Without Carville, this could have been yet another dry documentary on the behind-the-scenes political process. Stephanopoulos is intelligent, but he's not particularly interesting. Carville, on the other hand, is magnetic, not only because of his keen intellect, but because everything he does is suffused with a sense of sincerity.

While most of the movie focuses on Carville's professional activities as he heads the efforts to defuse the Gennifer Flowers situation, prepares a television commercial, and leads the attack on the Republicans, we are given a glimpse into his personal life. His girl-friend, Mary Matalin, appears several times — albeit doing her job as President Bush's campaign strategist.

Clinton, Bush, and Perot have peripheral roles in this film that concentrates its attention on the people behind the Democratic campaign strategies. While elements of the tactics used by the members of the so-called "War Room" are revealed (including a fascinating discussion of the relative importance of the colors of Clinton/Gore signs at the Democratic Convention), the movie is less concerned with political maneuvering than with the maneuverers. RECOMMENDED

When We Were Kings [1996]

Director: **Leon Gast** Running Time: **1:28** Rated: **No MPAA Rating (Boxing action)** Theatrical Aspect Ratio: **1:85:1**

When We Were Kings, a documentary about the Muhammad Ali/George Forman heavyweight "Rumble in the Jungle" boxing match, is a wonderfully nostalgic, and occasionally insightful, window into the recent past. While *When We Were Kings* is not a biography of Ali, it offers a great deal of insight into why the boxer was equally beloved and despised during his heyday. It's easy to forget how controversial a figure Ali was in the '60s and '70s, when he constantly proclaimed himself "the greatest," refused to register for the draft, and said things like "Damn America. I live in America, but Africa's my home." Age and Parkinson's Disease have softened the man's image, and, as Spike Lee comments, it's shocking to realize how few young people understand who Muhammed Ali was.

From the early press conferences to the aftermath, *When We Were Kings* chronicles the meeting of these two titans. At times, the structure is uneven, especially when the film goes on a tangent detailing the start of Don King's career, but the bulk of the material is engrossing. Since most of the footage was shot in 1974 (with the exception of "talking head" interviews with Spike Lee, Norman Mailer, and George Plimpton), watching this film is like taking a little time trip. Ali and Forman appear on-screen, but only as they did around the time of the fight. No retrospective interviews with either are presented.

When We Were Kings has several high points, including footage of Ali's press conference and coverage of the "Black Woodstock" event that was supposed to precede the fight (the music festival went off as scheduled, but the fight was postponed for more than a month). Unsurprisingly, however, the most involving portion of the film is the coverage of the match, which details exactly how Ali was able to use the now-famous "Rope-a-Dope" tactic to pull off what is probably boxing's greatest upset. This match, which took place at 4 a.m. local time on October 30, 1974 in Kinshasa, Zaire, marked the point at which Ali's image began to change from that of anti-hero to that of hero. For sheer dramatic impact, "The Rumble in the Jungle" exceeds even the best fictional boxing stories, including *Rocky*.

To use the old cliché, you don't have to be a sports fan to enjoy this motion picture. All you need is an appreciation of recent history and a desire to learn more about an event that had far more importance in the world's eyes than any other heavyweight bout in the history of boxing. RECOMMENDED

Winged Migration [FRANCE/ITALY/GERMANY/SPAIN/ SWITZERLAND, 2002]
Director: Jacques Perrin Running Time: 1:38 Rated: G Theatrical Aspect Ratio: 1.85:1

Winged Migration is a singular achievement — a documentary that took four years to produce using more than a dozen cinematographers filming on every continent of the planet. From Antarctica to the Arctic Circle, *Winged Migration* follows dozens of species of birds as they make their annual trek from warmer climates to cooler ones and back again. The cameras capture nature in all of its grandeur (mighty glaciers collapsing into the seas, avalanches, and fierce storms), and the birds in all of their magnificence, whether a single crane fishing for food or flocks of thousands rising up from the land and filling the sky.

To make *Winged Migration,* Jacques Perrin used every tool at his disposal, sending cameras airborne in balloons and using lightweight, motorless planes so he could get bird's-eye, "you are there" shots alongside a flock. *Winged Migration* gets closer to birds in flight than any previous cinematic outing has achieved.

The film moves along snappily, rarely pausing for more than a few minutes with any particular species, since there are so many places to visit and so many birds to talk about. The voice-over narration, delivered by Perrin with an obvious French accent, is bare-bones. In some ways, this is unfortunate, since numerous questions are left unanswered and many sequences could have benefited from some exposition. The sound is almost as impressive as the visuals, except that there are times when Perrin becomes overly enamored with the musical compositions of his collaborators when the cawing and trilling of his subjects would have been more compelling.

Winged Migration is a fascinating motion picture. It certainly isn't the ultimate documentary about birds and their migratory habits (any more than *Microcosmos* was the ultimate documentary about insects), but it's an excellent surface-level introduction that delivers some of the most amazing images of any movie in recent history. At its opening, *Winged Migration* informs us that no special effects were used in composing the film. It's good to know that, because some of the visuals offered by *Winged Migration* are more impressive than the most complex digital shot in *The Matrix Reloaded.* RECOMMENDED

Drama

8 Mile [2002]

Starring: Eminem, Kim Basinger, Brittany Murphy Director: Curtis Hanson Screenplay: Scott Silver Running Time: 1:50 Rated: R (Profanity, violence, sex, brief nudity) Theatrical Aspect Ratio: 2.35:1

At its heart, *8 Mile* is a very conventional motion picture. By applying the traditional sports formula to hip-hop music, it manages to extend a familiar plot structure into a new arena. So, instead of the climactic struggle taking place in a boxing ring or on a baseball field, it takes place in a club where two rappers battle it out to see who takes home the crown. And, as is usually the case with a well-made sports movie, you don't have to appreciate the particular sport in order to enjoy the movie. *8 Mile* has not been made solely with fans of hip-hop music in mind.

8 Mile has a grim, gritty feel. The camera captures the seedier quarters of Detroit in a way that will do nothing for the city's tourist industry. There aren't many smiles, either, or, for that matter, many reasons to smile. The people in this film are impoverished and struggling to make ends meet. In order to pay the rent, they have to hope that they win at bingo. Sex isn't about love; it's about surcease and forgetting, if only for a moment.

The controversial and high-profile rap artist Eminem plays Jimmy "B-Rabbit" Smith Jr., a worker at an automobile factory whose real passion is hip-hop. He's a master rhymer, but, upon entering a competition, he is overcome by stage fright. One day, he hopes to earn enough money to make a demo tape, but that day seems far off. In the meantime, he struggles through his daily life, living in a trailer with his mother (Kim Basinger) and stealing the occasional moment with his trampy girlfriend, Alex (Brittany Murphy). Then, one day, B-Rabbit gets a chance at redemption by taking on the current champion in a rap contest. It is an opportunity he cannot pass up.

Formulaic movies can work if they are well-made, and *8 Mile* qualifies. The movie's generally downbeat tone is relieved by the failsafe of a triumphant ending, but, along the way, the filmmakers aren't afraid of showing blue-collar life as it really is. Also, in an intriguing switch, the black/white racial division works in reverse. *8 Mile* is about a white guy trying to make it in a world dominated by African Americans. B-Rabbit's audience is black, making skin color the first obstacle he has to overcome. We have seen this theme explored before, but not from this angle. RECOMMENDED

21 Grams [2003]

Starring: Sean Penn, Benicio Del Toro, Naomi Watts, Charlotte Gainsbourg, Danny Huston, Clea DuVall, Marc Musso Director: Alejandro González Inárritu Screenplay: Guillermo Arriago Running Time: 2:05 Rated: R (Violence, profanity, nudity, sexual situations) Theatrical Aspect Ratio: 2.35:1

21 Grams is a stunning kaleidoscope of a motion picture — a mosaic of images that gradually resolves itself into a powerful tale of tragedy and redemption. This is not only one of 2003's most compelling motion pictures but, in terms of structure, it's also one of the most intriguing and unique. Not since *Memento* has a movie so successfully employed a nonlinear chronology. The jigsaw puzzle approach used by director Alejandro González Inárritu keeps us far more intrigued than a conventional vision of identical material would.

It's difficult to provide any kind of plot summary that doesn't give away crucial details, so I'll stick to the bare facts. *21 Grams* centers around three main characters whose fates intersect at a crucial moment. Paul (Sean Penn) is a math professor with a bad heart. His marriage to Mary (Charlotte Gainsbourg) seems as doomed as he is, but she refuses to leave him in his terminal state. She wants to have his child via artificial insemination, but without a heart transplant, he will not live long enough to see his offspring. Jack (Benicio Del Toro) is an ex-con who has reformed his life through devotion to Jesus. But there are times, especially in his home life, when glimpses of his past personality shine through. Christine (Naomi Watts) is a happily married woman with a loving husband and three delightful daughters. She is content with her daily routine until events send her life spinning out of control, impelling her back into the drug-induced haze from which her marriage rescued her.

At first, the movie is confusing. It's as if the filmmakers assembled about 50 scenes, all two to four minutes in length, and randomly edited them together. *21 Grams* moves backward and forward in time and jumps from character to character with dizzying frequency. But, out of what initially seems to be a maddeningly random approach, a pattern emerges. It becomes clear that Inárritu is paving a narrative path in a spiral that curves ever closer to a series of key moments. Past, future, and present are all converging. It takes a little while, but a picture begins to emerge from the fog. Then, it's just a matter of putting the pieces in the right places.

Visually, the film is dark and grainy, with a desaturated palette of colors. The music is slow and moody. All of this is appropriate to Inárritu's overall stylistic intent. Although the tone is brooding and somber, *21 Grams* offers a nugget of hope through one of its themes — that of redemption, which is clearly something the director believes in. In some ways, this is similar to Inárritu's recent outing, *Amores Perros*, which also reveled in the darkness of human nature and used a nonlinear narrative. However, despite its multiple tragedies, *21 Grams* is fundamentally more optimistic, because the characters are sympathetic. They're certainly not all saints, but we feel for them. I give this film my highest recommendation. **MUST SEE**

25th Hour [2002]

Starring: Edward Norton, Philip Seymour Hoffman, Barry Pepper, Rosario Dawson, Anna Paquin, Brian Cox Director: Spike Lee
Screenplay: David Benioff, based on his novel Running Time: 2:14
Rated: R (Profanity, sexual situations) Theatrical Aspect Ratio: 2.35:1

Spike Lee's *25th Hour* puts a new spin on an old question: what would you do if you knew you had less than 24 hours to live? In this case, the protagonist, Monty Brogan (Edward Norton), isn't headed for the embrace of the Grim Reaper, but he's getting the next best thing. Convicted on a major drugs charge (possession of more than one kilo with intent to distribute), he is headed for an overcrowded, maximum security prison where he will serve a 7-year sentence. He has less than a full day of freedom before he must present himself at the penitentiary (*why* he is free is never explained). In that time, he tries to tie up as many loose ends in his life as he can, spending time with his two close friends — insecure Jakob (Philip Seymour Hoffman), a high school teacher, and fiery Frank (Barry Pepper), a Wall Street broker; his girlfriend, Naturelle (Rosario Dawson); one of Jakob's students, Mary (Anna Paquin); and his father (Brian Cox).

Going to prison isn't Monty's only choice. A three-pronged fork in the road looms ahead. One branch takes him behind bars. Another branch takes him on the run, fleeing to some nameless town to spend the rest of his life in obscurity. The final branch involves putting a bullet through his brain. Don't expect to get a definitive answer to which path Monty chooses. *25th Hour* is deliberately (and, some might argue, maddeningly) open-ended, although it offers a tantalizing glimpse of one possibility.

25th Hour moves slowly — it's an unhurried, talky affair that consists primarily of members of the small group of characters interacting, while flashbacks reveal how and why Monty is in his current predicament. The movie seems largely detached from reality, although the tableau is more of a nightmarescape than a dreamscape. There's a sense of time (with the relentless clock ticking away) and place (a cold, inhospitable, post-9/11 New York City). Lee's decision to use digital video and desaturate the color enhance the gloomy atmosphere. *25th Hour* is not a happy experience, and there are times when it seems to drag, but there's no denying that it lingers in the mind long after the impressions left by other movies have evaporated. **RECOMMENDED**

About a Boy [United Kingdom/United States, 2002]

Starring: Hugh Grant, Toni Collette, Rachel Weisz, Nicholas Hoult
Directors: Chris Weitz, Paul Weitz Screenplay: Peter Hedges and Chris
Weitz & Paul Weitz, based on the novel by Nick Hornby Running
Time: 1:40 Rated: PG-13 (Profanity, sexual situations) Theatrical
Aspect Ratio: 2.35:1

Will Freeman (Hugh Grant) is the ultimate slacker. Living off the royalties of his one-hit-wonder father's Christmastime jingle "Santa's Supersleigh," Will is proud of never having had a job or, indeed, having done much of anything. He's not interested in a serious relationship — casual sex and one-night stands are his forté. Then he makes a mistake. On the prowl for easy female prey, he ventures into a single parents' group meeting, creating a fictitious son for himself. Soon, he is dating a woman who is babysitting for her friend's son, Marcus (Nicholas Hoult). This wouldn't mean much to Will, except that Marcus takes a liking to him and decides that Will might be the perfect match for his emotionally disturbed mother, Fiona (Toni Collette). Then the strangest thing happens — Will and Marcus strike up an unusual friendship. But complications ensue when Will falls for another single mother (Rachel Weisz) and wants Marcus to pretend to be his son.

Even though they use a stock plot, *About a Boy* injects enough fresh attitude to provide an enjoyable 100 minutes. There's nothing terribly challenging or original about the production, but it boasts nicely rounded, amiable characters, a fairly consistent sense of self-deprecating wit, and the occasional belly laugh. We grow to care about the protagonists, and the Weitzes manage the difficult task of making the big climax satisfying while, at the same time, they avoid pushing it over the top to the point where it becomes overly sentimental claptrap. We get to see Will move from his state of perpetual adolescence. His interaction with Marcus gives him a perspective on life that he never had. Suddenly, his insular lifestyle seems shallow and superficial, and, even though it's "hard work to be wonderful all the time," it's worth the sacrifice.

The key to the movie's success is the slightly irreverent tone adopted by the directors. The Weitzes know when to wink at the audience, and they employ internal monologues (for Will and Marcus) to provide biting commentary on what's going on. It is smart enough to avoid sit-com and movie-of-the-week situations. Hugh Grant is in rare form, toeing the line between his "aw shucks" good guy and the cad from *Bridget Jones's Diary*. In Will, Grant gives us a charac-

ter whose obvious flaws are a primary reason for his appeal. Meanwhile, Nicholas Hoult shows legitimate screen presence, and he and Grant generate some chemistry.

About a Boy is not a daring film, but it is immensely likable. Every once in a while, a movie comes along that, despite traversing familiar terrain, is made with enough all-around skill that it overcomes its clichéd origins. *About a Boy* is such a movie. RECOMMENDED

About Schmidt [2002]

Starring: Jack Nicholson, Hope Davis, Kathy Bates Director: Alexander
Payne Screenplay: Alexander Payne & Jim Taylor, based on the novel
by Louis Begley Running Time: 2:04 Rated: R (Profanity, nudity)
Theatrical Aspect Ratio: 1.85:1

Until recently, Warren Schmidt (Jack Nicholson) was like so many millions of American workers, leading a life bounded by conformity and routine. Now, at age 66, he has been forced to leave behind his assistant vice president job at a Nebraska-based insurance company, and amble into the great unknown of retirement. Suddenly, life seems to be closing in on Warren. Helen (June Squibb), his wife of 42 years, is getting on his nerves, he despises the man (Dermot Mulroney) about to marry his beloved daughter, Jeannie (Hope Davis), and, most importantly, when he looks back at his 6+ decades of life, he can't see any way that he has made a difference. So, after watching a television infomercial, he writes out a check to a "Save the Children" organization and "adopts" a 6-year-old Tanzanian boy named Ndugu. Then, unexpectedly, Helen dies and Warren finds himself alone. So he packs his bags, climbs into the spacious RV sitting in his driveway, and heads off to visit his daughter — after making a few stops along the way.

About Schmidt is an unsentimental yet effective portrait of a character struggling with the essential questions of life. Although it has moments of cynicism, this is not a cynical film. Although it contains instances of humor, it is not a comedy. And, although it contains elements of the road trip genre, it is not a road trip movie. Instead, this is an opportunity to spend 2 hours in the company of a fairly ordinary man who no longer understands the point of anything.

One thing that is rock-solid throughout is the performance of Jack Nicholson. Nicholson carries the movie, and does so by not just being Jack, but by using an understated approach to playing Warren. This isn't a flamboyant, over-the-top individual, but a sad, quiet man who looks at the world though lenses tinted with despair. This is one of Nicholson's best acting assignments in years.

About Schmidt is on the long side. Some of the road trip detours drag a little and there are perhaps a few too many "colorful" characters. The catharsis at the end hits the right note, giving the viewer a sense of closure without betraying the character or cheapening what has gone before. On balance, I recommend the movie both for Nicholson's performance and for the opportunity to spend some time with the kind of man that we often meet in real life, but rarely see on screen. **RECOMMENDED**

The Accompanist [France, 1993]

Starring: **Romane Bohringer, Richard Bohringer, Elena Safonova**
Director: **Claude Miller** Screenplay: **Claude Miller and Luc Beraud**
Running Time: **1:50** Rated: **PG (Mature themes)** In French with subtitles

It is 1942-43 in German-occupied France. Charles Brice (Richard Bohringer), a French businessman, is regarded as a collaborator because he's making money with the Germans in charge. His wife, singer Irene Brice (Elena Safonova), is beloved by both French nationals and the occupying power. Into this world of wealth and privilege comes a talented young pianist by the name of Sophie Vasseur (Romane Bohringer), who auditions to be Irene's accompanist. Irene, amazed by the young woman's remarkable ability, hires her, but Sophie soon learns that working with the singer demands more sacrifices than she could have dreamed possible.

The Accompanist is told in 3 parts. The first, which takes place in France, focuses on Sophie, exploring her life, feelings, and the love/hate relationship that develops between her and Irene. The second part, the journey from France to England, is more the singer's story, while the third segment, in England, concentrates on Charles and the demons of insecurity and jealousy that haunt him.

Despite the varying emphases of the different portions of *The Accompanist*, the central character is always Sophie, although she is rarely more of an observer. She has given up her own life to follow Irene, and off-stage as well as on, she is always in the background. Even as Sophie is obsessed with a woman whom she both despises and is jealous of, so Irene comes to depend on the young woman who plays the piano for her.

The third member of the trio is Charles, who at first appears to be a supremely confident, smug man whose business acumen has made him a force to be reckoned with. It isn't until Sophie has begun living under the Brices' roof that she learns how thin that veneer is. Charles is far more dependent upon his wife than Irene is on him, and this forms the backdrop for *The Accompanist*'s final scenes.

All three principal actors, as well as the members of the supporting cast, give fine performances. Romane Bohringer, who won the 1992 Cesar Award as Most Promising New Actress, is exceptional, bringing a silent expressiveness to the role of Sophie that would be beyond many veterans of the screen. Ms. Bohringer's rapport with her father Richard is evident in their many scenes together.

Ultimately, *The Accompanist* holds the viewer's attention through the power of its depiction of the bonds that develop between the singer, her husband, and her pianist. The story that conveys this relationship is neither original nor exceptional, but writer/director Claude Miller's presentation of the intricate and conflicting emotions makes this an experience that is always absorbing, and occasionally wrenching. **HIGHLY RECOMMENDED**

The Adventures of Sebastian Cole [1999]

Starring: **Adrian Grenier, Clark Gregg, Aleksa Palladino, Margaret Colin, John Shea, Marni Lustig, Gabriel Macht** Director: **Tod Williams**
Screenplay: **Tod Williams** Running Time: **1:39** Rated: **R (Profanity, sexual situations, drug use)** Theatrical Aspect Ratio: **1.85:1**

It's June 1983 in Dutchess County, New York. The Cole family, which consists of 16-year-old Sebastian, his older sister, Jessica (Marni Lustig); his mother, Joan (Margaret Colin); and his stepfather, Hank (Clark Gregg), is a relatively normal, stable unit until Hank makes a startling pronouncement — he's going to undergo a sex-change operation. Shortly thereafter, Sebastian is on his way to London with his mother, who has decided that life in a lesbian relationship isn't for her. But Sebastian doesn't fare well in England, and, in time for the next school year, he is back in New York, living with Hank (who now goes by the name of Henrietta). Sebastian's confused relationship with Hank/Henrietta impacts every aspect of his life, including his ability to function in school and the way he treats his girlfriend, Mary (Aleska Palladino).

For the most part, this is a serious motion picture about the common traumas encountered during the teenage years — alienation from the family, the need to rebel, the difficulties of love and sex, and the confusion of planning for the future — as well as at least one unusual one — relating to a parent undergoing a gender identity crisis.

The relationship between Hank/Henrietta and Sebastian is well realized and poignantly real. Although we never learn much about the factors that drive Hank/Henrietta to need the operation, his interaction with his step-son is effectively presented. The same is true of many of the other individuals — they are carefully developed when they enter Sebastian's orbit, but sketchy and incomplete outside of it. This approach serves to make Sebastian the most rounded character in the film. It's not difficult to understand what motivates his disruptive and occasionally self-destructive actions.

The Adventures of Sebastian Cole, which premiered in competition during the 1999 Sundance Film Festival, is a little more on the fringe than the bulk of its cinematic kin. Instead of offering the common delinquency/redemption cycle encompassed by most coming-of-age movies, it offers a fragmented slice of life with minimal closure. The protagonist does not sink to the depths reached by many central figures in films like this nor does he ever set his feet on the path to leading a productive life. *The Adventures of Sebastian Cole* isn't about telling a complete story; it's about giving the audience an opportunity to spend 90 minutes observing an interesting character during a critical period of his life. **RECOMMENDED**

The Advocate [United Kingdom, 1993]

Starring: Colin Firth, Ian Holm, Nicol Williamson, Amina Annabi, Donald Pleasance, Jim Carter, Lysette Anthony Director: Leslie Magahey Screenplay: Leslie Magahey Running Time: 1:50 Rated: R (Sex, violence, nudity, mature themes, language)

In the Middle Ages in France, the laws of the time applied not only to humans, but to some very unlikely subjects. Since it was the common belief that everything was created by God, all things — including animals, inanimate objects, and natural phenomena — could be held accountable for crimes.

The main character in this tale is Richard Courtois (Colin Firth), a young advocate who has abandoned Paris for the 1452 French countryside. There, he expects to find relative peace marred by only occasional land disputes and petty quarrels. Instead, he enters a hotbed of murder, rape, beastiality, and sorcery. People — and animals — are being tried and hanged for the most heinous crimes.

Joining Firth is a supporting cast of stellar quality. Donald Pleasance (attempting to shine up an image tarnished by four *Halloween* films) plays Pincheon, the local prosecutor, who has little difficulty attempting to convict a pig for the murder of two young Jewish boys. Ian Holm is Albertus, a Catholic priest whose personal beliefs fail to match those he publicly espouses. Nicol Williamson is a merchant-come-seigneur who freely and willfully abuses his considerable power. Together, they make a jab or two at the legal profession, raise serious questions about the nature of justice, and present a case against bigotry ant intolerance.

Leslie Magahey has penned an insightful and witty script whose underlying themes and currents are as valid today as they were 500 years ago in another part of the world. The deepest indictment in *The Advocate* is not of the practitioners of law, but of the system itself, and how easy it is to pervert the course of justice. Legal trickery is as old as the courts, and those who make the laws are easily motivated by self-interest. Few have the moral fiber to pass a law that hurts themselves, regardless of how many others it benefits.

Then there's *The Advocate*'s non-sermonizing approach to racial prejudice. Amina Annabi plays a dark-skinned gypsy who fascinates Courtois. Hers is the pig in danger, but the men and women of Abbeville view the woman as little better than the jailed animal. By sleeping with her, the advocate opens himself to a charge of bestiality — engaging in sexual activity with someone viewed as less-than-human.

Despite the rather dreary mystery subplot, the case for *The Advocate* is a strong one. Leslie Megahey's picture contains enough successful elements that it's possible to push aside those that don't work while concentrating on the ones that do. Taken at face value, this movie presents a view of a Medieval village caught in the grip of fear. Below that surface, however, can be found the themes and convictions which give this film its true victory. **RECOMMENDED**

An Affair of Love [France/Belgium, 1999]

Starring: Nathalie Baye, Sergi Lopez Director: Frederic Fonteyne Screenplay: Philippe Blasband Running Time: 1:20 Rated: R (Sex, nudity) Theatrical Aspect Ratio: 2.35:1 In French with subtitles

Meticulously crafted by director Frederic Fonteyne (in his second feature outing) and flawlessly acted by leads Nathalie Baye and Sergi Lopez, *An Affair of Love* offers the kind of deeply reasoned and rewarding romance that is almost never presented in traditional motion pictures (such as the slicker, high-profile American productions that dominate the world market).

The underlying premise represents a fairly typical

foundation for a motion picture romance — two individuals, initially drawn to each other for purely sexual reasons, fall in love. The mechanism of their first encounter is a personal ad that the woman (Baye) places in a magazine. The man (Lopez) answers, the two arrange a meeting, then, after a short introduction, they retire to a room in a hotel. We never learn exactly what they do behind the closed door of that room, but both acknowledge that it's out-of-the-ordinary. After their first encounter, they meet weekly for trysts, until, eventually, they decide they want to try making love "normally." Following this, they begin to realize that they have come to regard each other as more than sexual objects. Even though they don't know each other's names, ages, or professions, there is a deep connection. They feel comfortable and relaxed with each other. While sex is still an important part of their relationship, it is no longer the *only* part: they have fallen in love. Yet neither knows how to handle the unexpected turn of events.

Fonteyne is methodical in his approach to the subject matter; he chronicles the affair from start to finish — from the nervous uncertainty of the first meeting to the sad, final encounter. Intercut with scenes featuring the two unnamed characters conversing with each other in Paris cafes and discussing life and love in a hotel room are clips from faux interviews conducted with them an unspecified time after the end of their affair. In addition to providing some important background information, the interview segments offer a sense of closure — from the earliest moments in the film, we know that these characters will not end up together in some fairytale, happily ever after state, but that they will move on with their lives.

Ultimately, miscommunication and a fear of intimacy doom the relationship, but Fonteyne builds slowly to the inevitable break-up, allowing us to explore every stage in the couple's interaction. Baye and Lopez are on equal footing, each matching the other's performances scene-for-scene, fully inhabiting the skins of their characters. We learn almost nothing about these two as far as their lives apart from each other are concerned, but we come to know them through this relationship. We discover them as they discover each other. **HIGHLY RECOMMENDED**

Affliction [1998]

Starring: Nick Nolte, Sissy Spacek, James Coburn, Jim True, Holmes Osborne, Willem Dafoe, Mary Beth Hurt, Brigid Tierney Director: Paul Schrader Screenplay: Paul Schrader based on the novel by Russell Banks Running Time: **1:54** Rated: R (Profanity, violence) Theatrical Aspect Ratio: **1.85:1**

Wade Whitehouse (Nick Nolte) sees the world a little differently from everyone else. Alienated from his pre-teen daughter, Jill (Brigid Tierney) and unhappily divorced from his wife Lilllian (Mary Beth Hurt), he thinks he can get a lawyer and restructure his custody agreement. Likewise, when his best friend, Jack Hewitt (Jim True), accompanies a man on a hunting expedition, and the man accidentally shoots and kills himself, Wade begins to suspect a conspiracy, despite a lack of evidence. Unwilling to accept Jack's story of a simple, tragic mishap, Wade wonders about mob involvement, cover-ups, and hit men.

As a child, Wade was brutalized by an unloving father (James Coburn). The experience left profound scars, and old wounds are re-opened every time he visits his parents, who still live in the area. Fortunately for Wade, there is one stablizing influence in his life — Maggie Fogg (Sissy Spacek), a local waitress who genuinely cares for him and is willing to sacrifice her personal comfort to ensure that he has a chance at happiness.

All of these elements are woven together in a tapestry that is part drama, part mystery, and part psychological exploration of a compelling character. The glue that holds everything together, and the driving reason to see *Affliction*, is Nick Nolte. Nolte has always been regarded as a good actor, but, during his long and successful career, rarely has he poured himself into a part the way he does here. His portrayal of Wade is riveting. With his eyes, his voice, and his every body movement, he forces us to understand what it means to live in Wade's tortured skin. On an intellectual level, we realize that Wade is headed for a meltdown, but that doesn't lessen the connection between the character and the audience — a connection that Nolte is instrumental in forming. By the time the end credits roll, we know Wade inside out. We understand the forces that drive him, and recognize the inevitability of what transpires. In fact, the way Schrader chooses to present it, Wade's "criminal behavior" is almost an epilogue. *Affliction* is not about the crimes; it's about what leads up to them.

Affliction successfully and effectively navigates treacherous and complex psychological territory without ever missing a beat. Although many of the plot details can be found in any dysfunctional family drama, the vividness of Wade's character is what makes this film especially compelling. Presentation is everything, and this is far more powerful than any TV movie of the week about the effects of child abuse. *Affliction* is for anyone willing to take the journey into the heart and soul of a troubled man on the edge. **HIGHLY RECOMMENDED**

After Life [Japan, 1998]
Starring: **Arata**. **Erika Oda, Taketoshi Naito, Susumu Terajima, Takashi Naito** Director: **Hirokazu Kore-eda** Screenplay: **Hirokazu Kore-eda** Running Time: **1:58** Rated: **No MPAA Rating (Mature themes)** Theatrical Aspect Ratio: **1.85:1** In Japanese with subtitles

What happens after death? Director Hirokazu Kore-eda's vision, as shown in *After Life*, is that when someone dies, they go to a spiritual halfway house that looks like a country lodge. There is no heaven or hell, no god or religion. The dead stay at this place for exactly one week. During that time, they must choose the one memory from their life that they want to keep; the rest will all be erased. That memory is then re-created and filmed, and it becomes their constant and sole companion as they pass into the afterlife.

Kore-eda uses this premise as a springboard for numerous interwoven tales, telling us stories both of those who are passing through the way station on their way to the sweet hereafter and those who "live" and work there. There's one simple requirement for becoming a counselor at the halfway house: refuse to choose a memory. No one can pass on until they do.

After Life is intellectually satisfying, but emotionally cool. There are too many characters, and little time is accorded to any of them. The only three given more than token screen time are Ichiro Watanabe (Taketoshi Naito), a 70-year old businessman who died in the wake of an unhappy life of drudgery, and his afterlife case workers, Takashi Mochizuki (Arata) and Shiori Satonaka (Erika Oda). As Watanabe views videotapes of his life in order to select a memory, Takashi and Shiori are drawn into his drama, breaking the cardinal rule of not becoming involved. When it becomes apparent to Takashi that he and the old man share a past, he removes himself from the case. His subsequent decision causes a crisis of confidence for Shiori.

It's interesting to consider some of the memories most cherished by the characters. One man, who speaks ceaselessly about his sexual conquests, eventually chooses his daughter's wedding day. A teenage girl rhapsodizes about a trip to Disneyland, then, after learning that it's a common choice for children her age, decides on something more personal. There are as many memories as there are people — memories for everyone except the few who intentionally shun them.

Kore-eda's film also expends time exploring the world where the counselors reside, and the kind of existences they lead. The way station is virtually identical to a segment of modern-day Japan, complete with a city where people hustle to their destinations, traffic jams during rush hour, and stores decorate for the Christmas season. In many ways, it's the ordinariness of Kore-eda's limbo and of those who inhabit it that make this vision of the afterlife so fascinating. With Kore-eda's skillful hand behind both the camera and the pen, the result is a rewarding cinematic experience. **RECOMMENDED**

Afterglow [1997]
Starring: **Nick Nolte, Julie Christie, Lara Flynn Boyle, Jonny Lee Miller** Director: **Alan Rudolph** Screenplay: **Alan Rudolph** Running Time: **1:54** Rated: **R (Profanity, sex, brief nudity)** Theatrical Aspect Ratio: **1.85:1**

Afterglow introduces you to two unhappily married couples. Jeffrey Byron (Jonny Lee Miller) is a cold, seemingly-heartless businessman who is sexually indifferent to his young wife, Marianne (Lara Flynn Boyle). For her part, Marianne is so obsessed with having a baby that she never attempts to interact with her husband on a human level. All she's interested in is seducing him during those few days when she's ovulating. After he refuses to make love, she decides to find someone else to play the role of sperm donor.

The other couple, Lucky (Nick Nolte) and Phyllis Mann (Julie Christie), are an older pair, but they're no more content than Jeffrey and Marianne. A mysterious fracture in their past relationship has driven them apart. They remain married as a matter of convenience, but they have an unspoken agreement whereby Lucky can fool around as much as he wants. The landscape of emotional pain between them is palpable.

The four characters begin interacting when Marianne hires Lucky as a handyman to fix up the inside of the apartment she shares with Jeffrey. The two of them are immediately attracted to one another, and it doesn't take long before they're lounging together, naked, in her pool. Meanwhile, Jeffrey, who is captivated by older women, runs into Phyllis in a hotel bar, is smitten, and invites her to accompany him on a weekend retreat to the mountains.

The romantic couplings of the characters are

interesting in that they illustrate the multiple faces of love. Sex means something different to everyone — to Jeffrey, it's an unpleasant chore, a loss of control; to Marianne, it's a means to a maternal end. Ultimately, none of these characters appears to love anyone else as much as they love themselves.

The greatest strength of the film lies not in the script, but in the performances. The clear standout, however, is Julie Christie, who is nothing short of delicious as the world-weary Phyllis. Her often wry, occasionally cutting asides are the source of much of the film's humor, and there's hardly ever a moment when she doesn't steal the spotlight from her co-stars.

I don't know if *Afterglow* is the film to convert Rudolph-detractors, but it seems that this movie is a little more accessible than some of the director's earlier productions. Enough of his trademark style remains, however, to reassure his supporters. *Afterglow* is basically a four-pronged character study. The plot is not especially compelling, but the character interaction is, and that's the real reason to see this motion picture. Rudolph has painted an able picture of the non-romantic side of love — the one that has more to do with tolerance and familiarity than with affection and attraction. RECOMMENDED

The Age of Innocence [1993]

Starring: Daniel Day-Lewis, Winona Ryder, Michelle Pfeiffer, Miriam Margoyles, Richard E. Grant, Geraldine Chaplin Director: Martin Scorsese Screenplay: Martin Scorsese and Jay Cocks, based on the novel by Edith Wharton Running Time: 2:13 Rated: PG (Mature themes) Theatrical Aspect Ratio: 2.35:1

It's New York City in the 1870s, a society ruled by expectations and propriety, where a hint of immorality can bring scandal and ruin. Into this world arrives Countess Ellen Olenska (Michelle Pfeiffer), a woman who has spent much of her life in Europe and is now escaping from a disastrous marriage. Her initial adult meeting with Newland Archer (Daniel Day-Lewis) is sedate — he is engaged to her cousin May (Winona Ryder) — but there is a subtle fire smouldering from the first glance. From that point on, Archer's dilemma becomes painfully clear — marry the rather vapid May, or allow his heart and passions to carry him far from the realm of what is conventionally acceptable.

Martin Scorsese has made a reputation from making movies that show a profound perceptiveness of human nature through their images of toughness and violence. Scorsese has placed his indelible stamp on this picture, not only through the camerawork, but in the potent tension that builds between the main characters. For while blood has often been Scorsese's method, the characters, and what exists between and within them, have always been his ends.

Adapting from the 1921 Pulitzer Prize-winning novel by Edith Wharton, Scorsese and Jay Cocks have successfully incorporated the conflict of emotion against societal pressures that lie at the heart of *The Age of Innocence*. It is a sumptuous motion picture, a feast for the senses. The colors are vivid, from the red and yellow of roses to the flashes of crimson and white that transition scenes. The powerful score moves along with the story, in perfect counterpoint to the visuals — never intrusive, but always effective.

Daniel Day-Lewis never fails to impress, even when he appears in a poor film. Here, Day-Lewis immerses himself in the character of Newland Archer, and it's no great stretch for the audience to accept him. I have never subscribed to the widely held belief that Michelle Pfeiffer is a ravishing beauty. In fact, in *The Age of Innocence*, she looks rather plain (an impression that, in my opinion, heightened the impact of the story). Ellen is exotic, certainly, but beautiful? Nevertheless, there is no denying the stirring, heartfelt passion of Pfeiffer's performance. Outstripping anything she has done in the past, the role of Ellen can be considered a pinnacle.

There are few films this year that I recommend as heartily as *The Age of Innocence*, which has the rare distinction of being more of a cinematic experience than a simple movie. Something that transcends the medium like this shouldn't be set aside for viewing on the small screen. For those who expect more from their films than a lot of bangs and flashes, *The Age of Innocence* is not to be missed. MUST SEE

Ali [2001]

Starring: Will Smith, Jamie Foxx, Jon Voight, Mario Van Peebles Director: Michael Mann Screenplay: Stephen J. Rivele & Christopher Wilkinson and Eric Roth & Michael Mann Running Time: 2:35 Rated: PG-13 (Profanity, violence, sexual situations) Theatrical Aspect Ratio: 2.35:1

Ali, Michael Mann's attempt to chronicle 10 pivotal years in the life of former heavyweight boxing champion Muhammed Ali, suffers from the most common ailment of motion picture biographies — trying to do too much in a limited time. During the height of his career, Ali was reviled by much of white America — he was seen as a rebellious and divisive figure. Two decades later, the majority view of Ali has softened considerably. Age and Parkinson's have leached away much of the perceived arrogance that irritated many of Ali's critics. Consequently, the aging pugilist is now a revered figure. Ali's faults tend to be glossed over (we don't learn about his frequent philandering until the movie is almost over), while his praiseworthy tendencies are overemphasized. Even considering those flaws, *Ali* still manages to deliver. Every time the movie threatens to bog down, Mann takes us into the ring and re-invigorates the film with his fantastic boxing sequences.

Little blame for *Ali*'s weaknesses can be laid at the feet of actor Will Smith, who put his whole heart and mind into the performance. The actor bears only a passing physical resemblance to Ali, but Smith proves that great acting can overcome the need to look like a twin. This portrayal is at times passionate and fiery, and at others, quiet and thoughtful. Smith's Ali is a portrait of a man who was a fighter both inside and out of the ring. His work here will force those who doubted his selection to eat their words.

Smith casts such a long shadow that no one else appearing in the film can be considered as anything more significant than a supporting player. Jamie Foxx, who, like Smith, is better known for comedy than drama, offers an effective representation of Bundini, Ali's cornerman (he created, "Float like a butterfly, sting like a bee"). Then there's Jon Voight's interpretation of legendary sportscaster Howard Cosell, whose on-screen verbal sparring and off-screen friendship with "the champ" would mark a cornerstone of Ali's public life. Unrecognizable under layers of garish makeup, Voight at times looks like a moving, talking waxwork. But the voice and inflection are perfect, and, every time Voight opens his mouth, he becomes Cosell.

There's no debating that *Ali* could have been a far more impressive motion picture than what Mann has brought to the screen. It fails to deliver the hoped-for knockout, but also avoids the pitfalls of an early round collapse. *Ali* tells an involving story of individual heroism, and does so in a manner that keeps the audience engaged. In the genre of boxing movies, *Ali* falls short of the likes of *Raging Bull* and *The Hurricane,* but, just because this movie doesn't connect with every punch should not disqualify it from consideration as a way to spend a Saturday night. **RECOMMENDED**

All About My Mother (Todo Sobre mi Madre)
[Spain, 1999]
Starring: Cecilia Roth, Eloy Azorín, Marisa Paredes, Penelope Cruz
Director: Pedro Almodovar Screenplay: Pedro Almodovar Running

Time: **1:45** Rated: **R** (Sex, nudity, profanity, drug use) Theatrical Aspect Ratio: **2.35:1** In Spanish with subtitles

On the cusp of his 17th birthday in Madrid, Esteban (Eloy Azorín) is blossoming into an accomplished writer. He jots down in his journal that he wishes his mother, Manuela (Cecilia Roth), would tell him the story of his father, whom he has never met. After Esteban makes his feelings known to her, Manuela promises to tell him, but tragedy strikes before she has an opportunity. While running after a taxi to get the autograph of a star he admires, Esteban is struck and killed by a car. A grieving Manuela then decides to travel from Madrid to Barcelona, where Esteban was conceived, to find her ex-husband and inform him that the son he never knew about is dead.

Arriving in Barcelona, Manuela runs into her old friend, Agrado (Antonia San Juan), a transvestite prostitute, who informs her that her former husband, who goes by the name of Lola, has vanished. Together, Manuela and Agrado visit Rosa (Penelope Cruz), the young nun who last saw Lola. Although Rosa does not know Lola's current location, she is anxious to find him. While she was shepherding him through a drug detox program, Rosa became sexually involved with Lola, and she now carries his child. Meanwhile, Manuela takes time out of her schedule to see the Tennessee Williams play *A Streetcar Named Desire*. While there, she meets Huma Rojo (Marisa Paredes), the actress whose autograph Esteban was pursuing when he was killed.

As the title implies, *All About My Mother* is about mothers and their relationships with their natural or surrogate children. It's also about the other roles that women occupy when they're not caring for their sons and daughters. There are no significant male characters in the film. Esteban dies early and Agardo, while born a male (and still possessing male genitalia), thinks and behaves like a woman. The absence of men allows Almodovar to explore interpersonal interaction without being concerned about testosterone interference. This results in a thoughtful and emotionally rich tapestry.

For his principals, the director has mined the best of Spain's talent. Penelope Cruz and Marisa Paredes, both veterans of Almodovar's past work, breathe life into their characters. Cruz, as usual, is extremely likable, and Paredes brings a mixture of toughness and world weariness to the part of Huma. There's a particularly poignant scene in which she recognizes that though she may be successful, after you've had success for a while, you no longer notice it. The center-piece of *All About My Mother* is Cecilia Roth. Almodovar has used her several times before, but never has she been as vibrant as she is here. For Almodovar, this picture represents the latest high point in a lively career. **HIGHLY RECOMMENDED**

All the Real Girls [2003]

Starring: Zooey Deschanel, Paul Schneider, Patricia Clarkson, Shea Whigham Director: David Gordon Green Screenplay: David Gordon Green Running Time: 1:48 Rated: R (Sexual situations, profanity) Theatrical Aspect Ratio: 2.35:1

All the Real Girls is an anti-Hollywood romance; a tonic for all those weary of the usual cinematic over-glamorization of love. Anchored deep in the bowels of reality, this movie proves that love can be just as affecting and effectively realized when it is between two well-drawn, well-grounded characters as when it occurs in the fantasy realm inhabited by 90 percent of the romances (whether dramas or comedies) available on the market. *All the Real Girls* is slow moving and low-key and, when the final credits roll, you feel like you have spent nearly two hours in the company of a few real people, not constructs of a writer's imagination.

The film opens with a quiet scene between Noel (Zooey Deschanel) and Paul (Paul Schneider), who are in the opening stages of a relationship. She asks him why he hasn't tried to kiss her, and he replies that he wants to be able to answer truthfully that hasn't done so if the question arises. The issue is that Tip knows Paul's reputation for having meaningless sex with any willing girl, and he doesn't want his baby sister, newly returned home from boarding school, to become another notch in Paul's belt. However, that doesn't stop Noel and Paul's relationship from progressing through the expected states, Paul from growing up and learning what it means to love someone, and Noel from understanding the pitfalls of sex.

As the sexually curious Noel, Zooey Deschanel is mesmerizing. With expressive features and captivating eyes, she proves more than capable of succeeding in a lead role. (Previously, she was used as a supporting performer in movies like *Almost Famous* and *The Good Girl*.) Deschanel alternately shows strength and vulnerability, the kind of variation one expects to see in a teenage girl. Her costar, Paul Schneider, isn't as gifted, and there are times when an expression, action, or line of dialogue rings false. More importantly, however, there is chemistry between the actors, and on those occasions when Schneider stumbles, Deschanel is usually on hand to carry the load on her own.

Aside from a protracted conclusion, in which Green seems a little uncertain in precisely how he wants to wrap things up, there are few notable flaws. *All the Real Girls* is a love story for those who don't like Hollywood love stories. It never forces itself upon viewers and it steers clear of anything that remotely resembles manipulation. This is a low-profile gem that will endear itself to anyone who appreciates what Green is trying to do. **RECOMMENDED**

Almost Famous [2000]

Starring: Patrick Fugit, Kate Hudson, Billy Crudup, Frances McDormand, Jason Lee, Phillip Seymour Hoffman, Anna Paquin, Fairuza Balk, Noah Taylor Director: Cameron Crowe Screenplay: Cameron Crowe Running Time: 2:05 Rated: R (Profanity, sexual situations, drug use, brief nudity) Theatrical Aspect Ratio: 1.85:1

Almost Famous looks back at the world of rock 'n roll as it existed in the early 1970s. Fifteen-year-old William Miller (Patrick Fugit), a San Diego high school senior who skipped 2 grades in elementary school, gets to spend a few weeks on the road with his favorite band, Stillwater, and write an article about them for *Rolling Stone* magazine. His mentor, *Creem* rock critic Lester Bangs (Phillip Seymour Hoffman), gives him one key piece of advice: "You cannot make friends with the rock stars." William, however, allows himself to be seduced into the lifestyle by the group's guitarist, Russell Hammond (Billy Crudup). He also falls in love with one of Stillwater's groupies, Penny Lane (Kate Hudson), who has a "thing" going on with Russell. Back home, William's mother (Frances McDormand), does her best to keep tabs on her son's whereabouts by calling the hotels where he's staying, leaving one clear message: "Don't use drugs!"

Almost Famous isn't really about the '70s or the music scene. These are little more than background elements to William's coming-of-age story. The movie's central element is its depiction of how the socially immature William comes to grips with who he is, what he wants to do, and who he will become. For him, the trip with the band is about exploring his sexuality and learning how to live outside of his mother's protective umbrella. In the process, he loses his virginity, rejects the drug scene, forms a few lasting friendships, and saves a life.

Almost Famous contains a number of memorable characters: William, the ordinary young man who provides our portal into the movie, is effectively underplayed by actor Patrick Fugit. Kate Hudson (*Desert Blue*) gives a luminous star turn as Penny Lane, the girl who is at the center of the movie's romantic triangle. As William's mother, Oscar-winner Frances McDormand not only has some of the best scenes, but represents the movie's only truly unique character — a mother who is struggling to find the right balance between smothering her children and giving them their freedom. Phillip Seymour Hoffman has a wonderful turn as Lester Bangs (he gives a great speech about the benefits of being "uncool"), and Billy Crudup and Jason Lee are solid in their rolls as rock stars.

Almost Famous will be hard to top for its sheer exuberance and high feel-good quotient. The film's ecstatic atmosphere is only briefly interrupted by the sense of longing that is associated with first love and the pain that accompanies the inevitable separation between a child and a parent. Crowe's fourth feature represents another master stroke for the director, who has yet to have a bad outing. *Almost Famous* is an unqualified success. **HIGHLY RECOMMENDED**

Amelie [France, 2001]

Starring: **Audrey Tautou, Mathieu Kassovitz, Rufus, Dominique Pinon, Isabelle Nanty, Serge Merlin** Director: **Jean-Pierre Jeunet** Screenplay: **Jean-Pierre Jeunet, Guillaume Laurant** Running Time: 2:00 Rated: R (Sexual content, brief nudity) Theatrical Aspect Ratio: 2.35:1 In French with subtitles

Amelie is Amelie Poulain (brought to life with a delightful mix of shyness, energy, and mischievousness by Audrey Tatou), a young woman who has spent most of her life existing in the background. As a child, she was discouraged from having friends by her neurotic mother and emotionally distant father. As an adult, she has no boyfriend, no confidantes, and no real sense of purpose in life. That all changes with one small event — the discovery of a box of old snapshots and toys in a hidden compartment in her apartment. She sets out to find the owner of the box, and her quest eventually leads him to reconcile with his son. Emboldened by her success, Amelie decides to become a force for good in her small corner of the world, helping others around her. In the process, she encounters Nino Quincampoix (Mathieu Kassovitz), who may be her soulmate — if she can ever find the courage to talk to him face-to-face and admit her feelings for him.

Mathieu Kassovitz (the director of *Hate*) makes Nino an effective match for Amelie. Kassovitz underplays the part perfectly, showing that Nino, like Amelie, is shy about their relationship, but he is determined to pursue it. Since she never approaches him directly, but is content to leave him clues and anonymous messages, he is forced into the role of detective and pursuer. Other supporting performers include Jeunet regular Dominique Pinon as a disgruntled customer at the café where Amelie works, and Serge Merlin as Amelie's painter neighbor, who gives her advice on life and love.

One of the most intriguing aspects of the film, aside from its visual vivaciousness, is the manner in which Amelie chooses to help others. Rather than going about things in a straightforward manner, she devises stratagems, the complexities of which are analogous to the workings of a Rube Goldberg project. Her father has a hidden desire to travel, so, in order to bring his interest to the surface, Amelie kidnaps his garden gnome and has it photographed in front of various geographical landmarks around the world. For a neighbor who cherishes old love letters from her dead husband, Amelie fakes one that was "recently found." Throughout this movie, Jeunet keeps us guessing whom Amelie will help next, and how she will choose to do so.

By shooting all around Paris, Jeunet uses the city as more of a character than a mere backdrop, although the director's surreal and timeless vision should not be confused with the place seen by tourists (or even ordinary citizens). This is Jeunet's city, where magic abounds in the strangest places, where fate and predestination lurk around every corner, where photographs talk, and where one sprightly young woman can orchestrate small miracles. **HIGHLY RECOMMENDED**

American Beauty [1999]

Starring: **Kevin Spacey, Annette Bening, Thora Birch, Wes Bentley, Mena Suvari** Director: **Sam Mendes** Screenplay: **Alan Ball** Running Time: 2:00 Rated: R (Profanity, nudity, sexual situations, drugs, violence) Theatrical Aspect Ratio: 2.35:1

Most teenagers think their parents are strange, but, in the case of Jane Burnham (Thora Birch), this is as much a state of reality as it is a state of mind. Her father, Lester (Kevin Spacey), is suffering through a mid-life crisis. At the age of 42, he has become apathetic to everything. Jane's mother, Carolyn (Annette Bening), places such value on status that she has turned into a "bloodless, money-grubbing freak" who has no time for any form of intimacy. She and Lester continue in their dead marriage for their daughter's sake and so they'll look normal to the outside world. In a moment of clarity, Lester admits, "Our marriage is just for show — a commercial for how normal we are, when we're anything but."

We see how these characters grow, and the catalysts that break them out of their near-catatonic existences. Happiness, the goal of youth, is replaced by the desire for the artificial comfort that comes through the numbing sameness of repetition. Loveless marriages like Lester and Carolyn's exist because neither partner possesses the willingness to break the cycle. And the children they think they're protecting by staying together are often the biggest victims of their sham.

Lester's awakening is prompted by two events, the first being that he might lose his job. Lester faces this possibility with dread. But as he dissects the situation in his mind, he sees how liberating it can be. Then there's Jane's best friend, Angela (Mena Suvari), an attractive teenager who captures his attention and arouses his sexual interest. Lester's desire to have this girl reawakens his long-dead libido. While Lester goes through a complete reconstruction of his outlook on life, Carolyn's perspective is also changing. Frustrated by her relationship with her husband, she begins an affair with a fellow real estate agent who calls himself "The King" (Peter Gallagher).

Then there's sullen Jane, who's caught between the two of them. Displeased with her physical appearance, she is saving up for breast augmentation surgery (something she *clearly* does not need). She also develops an unusual relationship with Ricky Fitts (Wes Bentley), the boy next door. Ricky has his own problems — his mother (Allison Janney) is virtually withdrawn from life and his father (Chris Cooper) is an ex-Marine neo-Nazi who submits his son's urine for drug testing every 6 months. Meanwhile, Jane also has to deal with Angela's growing fascination with the possibility of sleeping with Lester.

American Beauty is emotionally satisfying. While it's not a groundbreaking movie, its presentation of vivid characters in interesting situations makes the story seem fresh. There's a sense of poignancy at the end, but also the feeling that we have been on an incredible trip through the lives and souls of three perfectly-realized characters. **HIGHLY RECOMMENDED**

American Buffalo [1996]

Starring: Dustin Hoffman, Dennis Franz, Sean Nelson Director: Michael Corrente Screenplay: David Mamet Based on a David Mamet play Running Time: 1:28 Rated: R (Profanity, mature themes) Theatrical Aspect Ratio: 1.85:1

American Buffalo starts out torturously slowly, with lots of cryptic dialogue about not confusing business with pleasure, a "broken toaster," and some kind of "job" that a couple of down-on-their-luck guys are preparing to pull. Those men are Don (Dennis Franz), the owner of a New York junk shop, and Teach (Dustin Hoffman), a '90s version of *Midnight Cowboy*'s Ratso Rizzo. The third character in the story is a teenage boy named Bobby (Sean Nelson) who wants to help in the upcoming job, but the two adults are reluctant to get him involved.

The film improves considerably after the unpromising opening. Don and Teach are planning to rob some rich guy's coin collection (the title, *American Buffalo*, refers to the pre-Jefferson nickel), but they don't have a plan or a clear sense of what they're doing. Teach, a take-things-as-they-come person, wants to get down to the action. Don, a more careful man, wants everything planned out in advance. This conflict leads to a fascinating scene where the two men sitting in the back of Teach's car, discussing the psychology of home safes.

Like a well-written musical composition, *American Buffalo* builds to a crescendo. The climax features a three-way confrontation between Teach, Don, and Bobby, and raises the specter that one or more might be double-dealing and committing a betrayal. The sense of paranoid claustrophobia makes the tension almost unbearable.

Dustin Hoffman plays Teach with caged energy. He's all mannerisms and nervous tics — the waiting is unbearable; he wants to *act*. He's the consummate failure who never gives up hoping for that one big score. But, by harkening back to *Midnight Cowboy* and resurrecting aspects of the long-dormant Ratso Rizzo, Hoffman makes this role his own.

Dennis Franz, an Emmy winner for *NYPD Blue*, holds his own opposite Hoffman. His Don is the picture of a man wracked by uncertainty. Should he do the job or not? Does he need the money badly enough to put up with all this aggravation? Meanwhile, Sean Nelson brings an enigmatic mixture of hardness and innocence to his portrayal of Bobby, keeping us unsure of his character's motives. Unfortunately, he doesn't quite have the screen presence to stand toe-to-toe with his experienced co-stars.

American Buffalo is an intense, but flawed, piece of drama. The ending winds the tension so tautly that everything feels ready to snap. To reach that point, it's necessary to plod through a murky beginning. Mamet's play may be 20 years old, but the themes of loyalty, betrayal, and ruthlessness are as applicable to the current social and economic environment as they were in the '70s. And that's a compelling reason why, if you don't mind the initial discomfort, it's worth staying for the entire film. RECOMMENDED

American History X [1998]

Starring: Edward Norton, Edward Furlong, Beverly D'Angelo, Avery Brooks, Stacy Keach, Fairuza Balk Director: Tony Kaye Screenplay: - David McKenna Running Time: 1:57 Rated: R (Profanity, violence, sex) Theatrical Aspect Ratio: 1.85:1

In the world of the skinhead neo-Nazi, slogans replace thought, fueling a mindless hatred that is startling in its intensity. Derek Vinyard (Edward Norton) is one of the most fervent members of the Venice Beach White Supremacist movement. An avowed hater of everyone who is not a white Protestant, he has risen to the top of a ragged group of hate-mongers. Derek is the disciple of Cameron (Stacy Keach), who stays behind the scenes to keep his record clean. Derek's followers include his younger brother, Danny (Edward Furlong), who worships him; and his girlfriend, Stacey (Fairuza Balk), who thoughtlessly parrots his words. Derek's mother, Doris (Beverly D'Angelo), and sister, Davin (Jennifer Lien), are frightened of and for him. On one fateful night, Derek uses deadly force to stop a pair of black youths from stealing his car. He ends up in prison for 3 years. While on the inside, he learns some hard truths about life from a fellow inmate (Guy Torry) and from the principal of his old high school (Avery Brooks). When Derek emerges with a desire to change attitudes, he finds that words are not enough.

American History X is in no way a comprehensive look at racism, hatred, or inner city violence. Instead, it examines the various ways these elements tear at the fabric of a family. The film emphasizes that actions have consequences, and that attaining redemption isn't as easy as saying "I'm sorry." The price for a change of heart can be, and often is, brutal. The final sequence in the film is shocking not because it's unexpected, but because it illustrates this truth.

The chief weakness in *American History X* is that we're presented with only one truly three-dimensional character. As portrayed by Edward Norton (who gained 30 pounds for the role), Derek is a fully-developed individual. We see the subtle elements that prime Derek for racist attitudes, follow the events that push him over the edge, then watch the trajectory of his life as his hatred spirals out of control before being reined in. Unfortunately, no one else in the movie comes close to being as real as Derek. Actors like Edward Furlong, Beverly D'Angelo, Fairuza Balk, and Avery Brooks do the best they can with lean material, but it falls on Norton's shoulders to carry the film.

The director, Tony Kaye, imbues *American History X* with a relentlessly ominous tone, especially during the final half hour, when we're expecting something grim to occur. Not all of Kaye's moves work — it seems unnecessarily showy for all of the "past" sequences to be in black-and-white, while the "current" ones are in color — but, on balance, Kaye displays ability in the motion picture arena. *American History X* may be flawed, but it's not easily forgotten. RECOMMENDED

American Me [1992]

Starring: Edward James Olmos, William Forsythe, Pepe Serna, Evelina Fernandez Director: Edward James Olmos Screenplay: Floyd Mutrux and Desmond Nakano Running Time: 2:04 Rated: R (Violence, profanity, nudity, mature themes)

Gut-wrenching, brutal, and powerful, *American Me* is not enjoyable in the conventional sense, but stands out as one of the most impressive purely dramatic offerings of 1992. It's a story of violence and its dehumanizing consequences that is reminiscent of *The Godfather*, with characters that echo those from the Puzo/Ford-Coppella epic. Director Edward James Olmos fearlessly takes aim at the culture of machismo which has enveloped so many inner city youths. This is an unrelenting, unallayed condemnation of that lifestyle, a portrait of the sort of brutality that violence begets.

The story centers around Santana (Olmos), a small time hood on the outside who becomes a big time prison gang leader on the inside. Santana supposedly organizes his fellow prisoners in an attempt to improve their conditions, but what he's really after is power. Once he has tasted it, he can't get enough. Those who stand against him are ruthlessly trodden underfoot, often ending up in the morgue.

As powerful as this film is, it has a few drawbacks, the most notable of which is the acting. Many of the players don't have much range. Olmos, the most-accomplished of them, tries to portray his character over a span of nearly 20 years without ever seeming to age. As a 40-year-old, he's believable, but no amount of makeup can make him look 25. There are times when Olmos' appearance detracts from his fine performance, and suspension of disbelief is difficult in a picture so well grounded in a cruel reality.

Olmos isn't especially interested in giving the audience characters they can sympathize with, and this may be a mistake, since it limits the force of the climactic scenes and eventual resolution. That's not to say that the characters aren't three-dimensional, because they generally are. There simply isn't any emotional empathy created between them and the audience. Difficult as this may be to accomplish, it can be done — numerous other films have succeeded (Quentin Tarantino's *Reservoir Dogs*). Here, however, Olmos doesn't try.

American Me is definitely not for everyone. This isn't escapist entertainment. It carries out its agenda with little concern for eliminating the "comfort barrier" that exists between the screen and the audience. Those daring to see the movie should be prepared to be disturbed. HIGHLY RECOMMENDED

An American Rhapsody [United States/Hungary, 2001]

Starring: Nastassja Kinski, Scarlett Johansson, Tony Goldwyn
Director: Eva Gardos Screenplay: Eva Gardos Running Time: 1:44
Rated: PG-13 (Mature themes, profanity) Theatrical Aspect Ratio: 1.85:1
In English and Hungarian with subtitles

An American Rhapsody opens in 1965, with American-raised teenager Suzanne (Johansson) standing on the Chain Bridge in Budapest and saying in a voiceover, "I was 15 and my life was already falling apart, so I came back to Hungary, where it all began." With those words, the film transports us through time to the beginning, via an extended flashback. Suzanne is a baby and her mother, Margit (Kinski), and father, Peter (Goldwyn), facing persecution and arrest, decide to flee the country. But circumstances conspire to keep Suzanne in Hungary, where she grows up as the daughter of foster parents. Meanwhile, in Los Angeles, Margit and Peter begin to make a life for themselves, all the while planning ways to get Suzanne to join them.

The opportunity arrives when Suzanne is 6 years old (and played by Kelly Endresz-Banlaki). She is whisked away from her foster parents, placed on a plane, and flown to the United States. There, the confused little girl is re-united with the family she does not remember. Her adjustment to her new life is not easy — she misses her mama and papa, and can't think of what to call Margit other than "lady." Events

skip forward 10 years, to an older Suzanne who can't figure out where she belongs. In an attempt to answer her questions, she returns to Hungary.

Gardos looks back on her life through an unfogged lens — she views all of the characters sympathetically. The only villain is the faceless totalitarian system of government which forces the separation of Suzanne from her birth family. The movie is exceptional in the way it presents the various characters' mindsets. Margit and Peter miss their daughter desperately and try everything possible to get her back — a process that takes 6 years. And Suzanne is bewildered and frightened by the sudden shift in her life, as her home is replaced by something altogether different.

The film stars Scarlett Johansson, one of today's finest young actresses. She presents Suzanne as a child-woman struggling with all the usual problems of girls her age (boys, curfews, overly restrictive parents) while suffering through an identity crisis. Her sense of frustration, and, later, of loss, is palpable. Nastassja Kinski and Tony Goldwyn offer Johansson effective support and hold the movie together during the early scenes when she is not on screen.

If there's a problem with the movie, it occurs at the very end, when Gardos rushes an emotional catharsis that feels forced and artificial. Perhaps it's difficult to conclude a film like this, but the ease with which everything is neatly wrapped via a short conversation feels too much like a cheat. That's only a few minutes, however. Everything that comes before it is as perceptive as it is involving and touching. RECOMMENDED

Amistad [1997]

Starring: Djimon Hounsou, Matthew McConaughey, Morgan Freeman,
Anthony Hopkins, Nigel Hawthorne Director: Steven Spielberg
Screenplay: David Franzoni Running Time: 2:37 Rated: R (Violence,
mature themes, nudity) Theatrical Aspect Ratio: 1.85:1

One stormy night during the summer of 1839, the 53 men imprisoned on the Spanish slave ship *La Amistad* escape. Led by the lion-hearted Cinque (Djimon Hounsou), they take control of the vessel, killing most of the crew. Adrift somewhere off the coast of Cuba and uncertain how to make their way back to Africa, they rely on the two surviving Spaniards to navigate the eastward journey. They are tricked, however, and the *La Amistad* is eventually captured by an American naval ship near Connecticut. The kidnapped Africans are shackled and thrown into prison, charged with murder and piracy.

The first men to come to the Africans' defense are

abolitionists Theodore Joadson (Morgan Freeman) and Lewis Tappan (Stellan Skarsgård). They are soon joined by Roger Baldwin (Matthew McConaughey), a property attorney of little repute. Baldwin proves a more persuasive orator than anyone gave him credit for, and his central argument — that the prisoners were illegally kidnapped free men, not property — convinces the judge. But powerful forces have aligned against Baldwin's cause. Current President Martin Van Buren (Nigel Hawthorne), eager to please Southern voters and 11-year-old Queen Isabella of Spain (Anna Paquin), begins pulling strings behind-the-scenes to ensure that none of the Africans goes free.

At its heart, *Amistad* is a tale of human courage. Cinque is a heroic figure whose spirit remains unbreakable regardless of the pain and indignity he is subjected to. Effectively portrayed by Djimon Hounsou, Cinque is the key to viewers seeing the *Amistad* Africans as more than symbols in a battle of ideologies. They are individuals, and our ability to make that distinction is crucial to the movie's success. To amplify this point, Spielberg presents many scenes from the Africans' point-of-view, detailing their occasionally-humorous observations about some of the white man's seemingly-strange "rituals."

Matthew McConaughey successfully overcomes his "pretty boy" image to become Baldwin, but the lawyer is never particularly well-defined outside of his role in the *La Amistad* case. Likewise, while Morgan Freeman and Stellan Skarsgård are effective as Joadson and Tappan, they are never anything more than "abolitionists." Nigel Hawthorne, who played the title character in *The Madness of King George*, presents Martin Van Buren as a spineless sycophant to whom justice means far less than winning an election. Finally, there's Anthony Hopkins, whose towering portrayal of John Quincy Adams is as compelling as anything the great actor has done.

Amistad is thematically rich, impeccably crafted, and intellectually stimulating. *La Amistad* is a part of American social and legal fabric. It is an important American film. **HIGHLY RECOMMENDED**

. . . And Justice for All [1979]

Starring: Al Pacino, John Forsythe, Jack Warden Director: Norman Jewison Screenplay: Barry Levinson and Valerie Curtin Running Time: 2:00 Rated: R (Profanity, mature themes) Theatrical Aspect Ratio: 1.85:1

Al Pacino plays Arthur Kirkland, a defense attorney who has been in practice for 12 years. His caseload is heavy; however, Kirkland isn't in the game for money, prestige, or power. He's one of those rare lawyers who believes in the judicial system and wants to help people. He'll spend a night in jail for contempt of court rather than let a judge ignore a crucial piece of evidence. Yet all of Kirkland's principles are about to be called into question when he is asked to defend a hard-line justice, Judge Fleming (John Forsythe), who is accused of rape. Kirkland's dislike of Fleming runs deep, but circumstances force the lawyer to take this case.

The more you consider . . . *And Justice for All*'s message, and the means by which it is delivered, the more aware you become of how uncompromising director Norman Jewison's attack is on the legal system. Insane and corrupt judges dole out life-and-death sentences with as much thought as a butcher would give to carving a side of beef. Attorneys view the courtroom as an arena where they can grapple with an opponent without concern for the cost in human pain and tears. And those who genuinely care about their clients are foiled at every turn by the deeply-rooted hypocrisy and cynicism that defines American law.

Pacino earned an Academy Award nomination for his work in . . . *And Justice for All*. However, of all his Oscar nominations, this is probably the least-deserved. Of the supporting performers, John Forsythe and Jack Warden leave the strongest impressions. Forsythe, known best at the time for being the faceless Charlie of *Charlie's Angels*, is the perfect picture of cold, controlled arrogance. There's nothing vaguely human about him except his capacity for vice. Whether guilty or innocent of rape, he's still a villain. Warden plays a suicidal, borderline-lunatic judge whose continued presence on the bench makes a mockery of every trial he presides over. Jeffrey Tambor is a lawyer who undergoes a crisis of conscience when a man whose acquittal he facilitated commits a double murder.

. . . *And Justice for All* ends with the kind of bravura outburst by Pacino that one might easily assume is designed to entice cheers and applause from the audience. Here, the actor's words radiate real outrage, and what he says caps the film's central ethical dilemma about a lawyer defending a man he knows to be guilty. This is a powerful, cathartic moment that's neither exhilarating nor uplifting. Like most of what precedes it, the climax of . . . *And Justice for All* underscores Jewison's message about how hollow and diseased the process of law has become. We need look no further than the fiasco of the O.J. Simpson trial to understand everything that this film is trying to say. **HIGHLY RECOMMENDED**

Angela's Ashes [United Kingdom/United States, 1999]
Starring: Emily Watson, Robert Carlyle, Joe Breen, Ciaran Owens, Michael Legge Director: Alan Parker Screenplay: Laura Jones and Alan Parker, based on the novel by Frank McCourt Running Time: 2:25 Rated: R (Profanity, nudity, sex, violence, mature themes) Theatrical Aspect Ratio: 1.85:1

Angela's Ashes is based on the memoirs of Frank McCourt. The film follows roughly 10 years in Frank's life, beginning when he's 5 years old (going on 6), and ending some time shortly after his 16th birthday. During the course of the movie, he is played by 3 different actors: Joe Breen (the young Frank), Ciaran Owens (the middle Frank), and Michael Legge (the older Frank). Breen, Owens, and Legge are all capable performers, and their physical appearances are similar enough that the changes are not jarring.

The film opens in 1935 Brooklyn, where Frank's family is struggling to ward off poverty and disease. Frank's father, Malachy McCourt (Robert Carlyle), is unemployed and his mother, Angela (Emily Watson), has just given birth to a baby girl — the 5th child in the family. But the new addition doesn't live long, and, after her death, the family decides to return to Ireland. Things, unfortunately, are even worse across the Atlantic. The house into which Frank's family moves is damp. Due to its proximity to the community privy, there's a permanent stench. When it rains, which is almost all the time, the first floor floods. In quick succession, Frank's two youngest brothers fall ill and die. Meanwhile, every scrap of money that Malachy earns goes to buying a pint or two at the pub. He comes home drunk at night and spends his days in a fruitless search for a new job. Through all of this, Frank faces the usual traumas of youth: peer pressure, learning about sexuality, and enduring the necessary Catholic rites of passage — especially the First Confession and First Communion.

Despite having first billing, Emily Watson plays a supporting character. This is Frank's story. His mother occupies a critical role, but she is rarely the focal point of the tale. Her performance is quiet, subdued, and powerful. Like Watson, Robert Carlyle does not seek the spotlight. His part is that of the flawed-but-loving father who cares for his family, but also

carries a great burden of guilt. Carlyle shows that he, like Watson, is capable of underplaying a part.

Angela's Ashes is a deftly realized and beautifully filmed story of a boy coming of age during the 1930s and 1940s in the Catholic portion of Ireland. There have been movies of this sort before, and most of them end in an ideological clash between the Irish Catholics and their Protestant counterparts. Here, the primary foe is not religious intolerance. It is one of the oldest enemies of humanity: poverty and hunger. Yet, while the film contains lengthy stretches in which the characters are subjected to ever more demeaning spates of pain and abject misery, the movie as a whole turns out to be a quietly triumphant experience — a testimony to the fortitude of the human spirit under even the worst circumstances. **HIGHLY RECOMMENDED**

Angels and Insects [United Kingdom/United States, 1995]
Starring: Mark Rylance, Patsy Kensit, Kristin Scott Thomas Director: Philip Haas Screenplay: Philip Haas and Belinda Haas based on the novella *Morpho Eugenia* by A.S. Byatt Running Time: 1:57 Rated: R (Sex, nudity, mature themes) Theatrical Aspect Ratio: 1.85:1

Angels and Insects, based on A.S. Byatt's novella *Morpho Eugenia*, opens in Victorian England with the arrival of naturalist William Adamson (Mark Rylance) at the demesne of the Alabaster family. William was recently shipwrecked on his return journey from South America. Reverend Alabaster (Jerermy Kemp), keen to have an educated scientist help with a book he is writing, invites William to live in his house. Once there, he becomes infatuated with the serenely beautiful-but-cold Eugenia (Patsy Kensit), the eldest daughter of the Alabasters. Although not hopeful that a match is likely, William nevertheless courts Eugenia, and is greatly surprised when she accepts his marriage proposal. But a dark secret in her past cannot stay buried forever.

In many ways, this film is a study in contrasts: the passionate abandon of the South American natives to the structured restraint of England's Victorian aristocrats, butterflies to ants, and beauty to intelligence. Philip Haas wants us not only to understand the rigidity of life on the Alabaster estate, but to see the decadence that bubbles just beneath the surface. Eugenia's apparent physical perfection — which enthralls William — hides a dead, ravaged soul.

Haas has elected not to reveal the horror of Eugenia's situation in one melodramatic moment of discovery. Instead, he gradually unfolds the truth, feeding it to the audience bit-by-bit, clue-by-clue, so that when the generally oblivious William finally learns his wife's secret, we are already cognizant of it. The entire narrative of *Angels and Insects* is fashioned like this, with slow, steady revelations.

If Eugenia is the butterfly — beautiful, fragile, and as vapid as "colored air" — then Matty Crompton (Kristin Scott Thomas), an educated woman living with the Alabasters, is the ant: plain, resourceful, and intelligent. It doesn't take William long to learn that he has married the wrong woman. Matty is his perfect companion, but he recognizes too late how little value should be placed on physical appearance.

The drawback of *Angels and Insects* is a combination of lackluster characterization and mediocre acting. None of the men or women populating this film grab our sympathy. In the case of someone as shallow as Eugenia, this is entirely appropriate, but William remains strangely distant, in part because of a bland performance by Mark Rylance. This leads us to watch him with interest, but never become emotionally engaged in his travails.

The reason to see *Angels and Insects* is for its keen and intricate explorations of human sexual and social interaction. In the world of insects, there is only one layer, but men and women hide truth beneath many facades. Yet perhaps the most striking similarity is how members of both species are capable of stinging without remorse, unconcerned about the consequences. That's an uncomfortable message that everyone can relate to. **RECOMMENDED**

The Anniversary Party [2001]

Starring: Alan Cumming, Jennifer Jason Leigh, Kevin Kline, Phoebe Cates, Jane Adams, John C. Reilly, Jennifer Beals, Denis O'Hare, Mina Badie, Gwyneth Paltrow, Michael Panes, Parker Posey Directors: Alan Cumming, Jennifer Jason Leigh Screenplay: Alan Cumming, Jennifer Jason Leigh Running Time: 1:55 Rated: R (Profanity, drug use, nudity, sexual situations) Theatrical Aspect Ratio: 1.85:1

Jennifer Jason Leigh and Alan Cumming first decided that they wanted to do a movie together when they shared the stage for a recent revival of *Cabaret* (she playing Sally Bowles and he playing the Master of Ceremonies). At the time, neither was aware that their intended collaboration would force them to wear so many hats: co-writer, co-producer, co-director, and co-star. And, even though there was very little money and a short shooting schedule (4 weeks), they were able to use their clout in the business to line up an impressive cast, including the likes of the husband-and-wife pair of Kevin Kline and Phoebe

Cates, indie icons John C. Reilly and Parker Posey, and Gwyneth Paltrow, who seems willing to try just about anything at least once.

There isn't much of a plot. This is an actors-and-their-characters piece, and, to that extent, it's almost like a filmed play. Joe (Cumming) and Sally (Leigh) are celebrating the 6th anniversary of their stormy marriage by inviting a few friends over for a party. Joe is an author who is about to try his hand at directing and Sally is a once-hot actress on the downside of her career. Among the guests are Cal and Sophie Gold (Kline and Cates), a fading screen icon and his ex-actress spouse, who gave up the business to raise their children; a well-regarded director (Reilly) and his neurotic wife (Jane Adams); a sexy photographer (Jennifer Beals); a likable guy (Michael Panes); two sourpuss neighbors (Denis O'Hare and Mina Badie); and high-salaried actress Skye Davidson (Paltrow), who is set to make $4 million for starring in Joe's upcoming film.

The most riveting scene is a vicious shouting match between Joe and Sally during which each exposes the other to a few cold, cruel facts. Filmed starkly, with no camera tricks, this represents an intense 5 minutes of acting by Cumming and Leigh. After it's finished, things kind of fizzle out. By then, the story has essentially been told and the end credits are not far away. Along the way to this sequence, there are some other nice moments, and almost every member of the large ensemble cast gets an opportunity to shine. Yet, while Cumming and Leigh don't hog the spotlight, in the end, their work is what we remember.

There's an almost voyeuristic appeal to this sort of film, and that aspect of *The Anniversary Party* is emphasized by the setting — a house that seems to be made entirely of glass. There's hardly any privacy. Because so many of the actors are playing variations of their public images, it adds a layer of verisimilitude. And the acting is what makes this picture worth framing. **RECOMMENDED**

Antonia's Line [Netherlands/Belgium/United Kingdom, 1995]

Starring: Willeke Van Ammelrooy, Jan Decleir, Els Dottermans, Thyrza Ravesteijn, Dora Van Der Groen, Marina De Graaf Director: Marleen Gorris Screenplay: Marleen Gorris Running Time: 1:42 Rated: No MPAA Rating (Nudity, sex, profanity, mature themes, violence) Theatrical Aspect Ratio: 1.85:1 In Dutch with subtitles

Opening shortly after the end of World War II and continuing for over 40 years, *Antonia's Line* introduces us to 4 generations of women — Antonia (Willeke Van Ammelrooy), her daughter Danielle (Els Dottermans), her granddaughter Therese, and her great-granddaughter Sarah. The film begins in the post-war Netherlands with Antonia returning to the village of her birth. In her company is her young daughter, whose initial impression of the town is that it's an unpromising place. Antonia, who left 20 years ago, has come back to bury her mother and take over running her inherited farm.

The movie progresses by highlighting various episodes in the lives of the characters. Aside from Antonia's family, we're introduced to many of the town's other residents: Farmer Bas, who carries a torch for Antonia; Crooked Finger, a student of Schopenhauer and Nietzsche; retarded Deedee, who is raped by her own brother; Mad Madonna, who bays at the full moon; and many others. Together, these misfits and outcasts form Antonia's tight-knit community — those friends and neighbors who are always ready to support one of their own, regardless of the circumstances.

Gorris imbues each of her characters with a sense of uniqueness, and we come to care about them, whether they're around for the entire film or just a small portion of it. The story flows smoothly from event to event, balancing such disparate elements as madcap humor (Danielle's vision of her grandmother rising from a coffin and breaking into a chorus of "My Blue Heaven") and shocking violence (two rapes). The only obvious flaw in the structure of *Antonia's Line* is its over-reliance upon a voiceover narrative; there are times when the plot is too easily advanced by telling instead of showing.

Antonia's Line is a thematically rich motion picture, with a visual style similar to that of Dennis Potter's work (*Pennies from Heaven*, *The Singing Detective*). In addition to the evident message about the importance of community, the film challenges different philosophies about death, from those of Schopenhauer to those of the Catholic church. It condemns the hypocrisies of organized religion while endorsing the concept of "church" as a gathering place. And it gently advances the director's feminist agenda, illustrating that women can thrive (not just survive) without men. Antonia doesn't want a husband and Danielle's lover is a lesbian.

The final lines of *Antonia's Line* are: "And, as this long chronicle draws to a conclusion, nothing has ended." Such is often the case for life stories brought to the screen with heartfelt realism. Aided by a fine cast giving unaffected performances, Gorris has fashioned a rare and wonderful world capable of provoking both laughter and tears — sometimes at the same time. **HIGHLY RECOMMENDED**

Antwone Fisher [2002]

Starring: Derek Luke. Joy Bryant, Denzel Washington Director: Denzel Washington Screenplay: Antwone Fisher Running Time: 1:57 Rated: PG-13 (Mature themes, mild profanity, violence) Theatrical Aspect Ratio: 2.35:1

For his directorial debut, Denzel Washington has used basic filmmaking techniques to tell a story that, although conventional, is at times deeply moving. The autobiography of Antwone Fisher (Derek Luke), who wrote the screenplay, is an inspirational tale that uses themes of family, courage, and the will to overcome as its building blocks. One could easily argue that Washington's relatively simple approach (he uses traditional camera placement, uncomplicated shots, and, from a storytelling perspective, doesn't do anything more radical than employ frequent flashbacks) is perfect for the material. The result speaks for itself.

When we first meet Antwone, he is an enlisted man in the U.S. Navy who is prone to uncontrollable outbursts of anger. One such incident earns him a reduction in rank and a visit to psychiatrist Jerome Davenport (Denzel Washington), who must determine whether Antwone is fit to continue serving his country. At first, Antwone and Jerome have a frosty relationship. Eventually, however, the doctor's non-confrontational attitude breaks through Antwone's silence, and he begins relating details about his past. Born in prison to a convict mother who abandoned him, Antwone spent the first 2 years of his life in an orphanage. He then moved in with a foster family and was physically, emotionally, and sexually abused until a bout of willfulness got him thrown out of the house. After a stint in reform school and a short period of life on the streets, he joined the Navy.

In short order, Jerome becomes a surrogate father to Antwone, whose biological male parent died before he was born. The young man also begins to cultivate a tentative relationship with Cheryl (Joy Bryant), a girl he has been attracted to for some time. Eventually, Jerome advises that Antwone search for his blood relatives. He reasons that only by locating them can Antwone free himself so he can go on with his life.

There are a few occasions when *Antwone Fisher* crosses the line to become too syrupy. (One such instance occurs during the speech used to conclude the movie.) For the most part, however, the production radiates emotional honesty. Some of the events of Fisher's real-life story may have been fictionalized in the name of producing a better narrative, but there's little doubt that this tale of genuine human courage will find favor with nearly everyone who sees it. **RECOMMENDED**

Anywhere But Here [1999]

Starring: Susan Sarandon, Natalie Portman, Eileen Ryan, Ray Baker, John Diehl, Shawn Hatosy, Bonnie Bedelia Director: Wayne Wang Screenplay: Alvin Sargent, based on the novel by Mona Simpson Running Time: 1:54 Rated: PG-13 (Profanity, sexual content) Theatrical Aspect Ratio: 2.35:1

When we first meet Adele August (Susan Sarandon) and Ann (Natalie Portman) they are loading up the car to leave Bay City, Wisconsin. Adele is anxious to get on the road, but Ann is heartbroken about leaving behind her friends and stepfather. The mother/daughter cross-country sojourn to Beverly Hills does not get off on the right foot. At first, it appears that Adele's motives are selfish. She's restless and being stifled by life in a small town. Her main motivation — which we don't recognize until later in the proceedings — is every parent's goal: to offer her child a better life. Adele thinks she knows what's best for Ann when she may not, and the thought of consulting her daughter on the matter never occurs to her. So, she heads to California with the intention of getting a job as a teacher and starting up Ann's acting career. But there's a problem — Ann wants to go to college and has no interest in entering show business.

The mother/daughter interaction is a tempestuous tug of war. In emotional terms, something of a role reversal is in play, with Ann being the sensible, responsible one and Adele needing grounding. Ann wants stability and normalcy, but Adele is incapable of providing either. She views her mother as irresponsible, impractical, and tyrannical, but Ann also catches enough glimpses beneath Adele's façade to recognize the loneliness and uncertainty hidden there. Adele does not live for herself — she lives for her daughter, and the thought of losing Ann is her greatest fear.

One of the best sequences in the film comes when Ann and Adele return to Bay City for a visit. For Ann, what should be a homecoming of sorts turns out to be a strange experience. Her relationships with her friends have cooled and she begins to recognize what Adele saw when she decided to hit the road. In her voiceover, Ann remarks, "The streets didn't seem as wide, the trees seemed lower and the houses smaller."

And someone else remarks to her, "I think if you would have stayed, you'd be just like your mom — always wanting to go away."

There are times when *Anywhere But Here* becomes uncomfortable because of the rawness of emotions it churns up. On one occasion, Adele butts her way into an audition she has forced Ann to take, and sees her daughter performing a cruel mimicry of her. At another time, Adele misconstrues a night of casual sex for something more meaningful, with painful and embarrassing results. For the most part, Wang keeps the movie's tone light and playful, but, in moments such as these, he allows the audience to feel the characters' discomfort. Although men cannot have first-hand experience with the mother/daughter bond, they should not dismiss the movie — well-made pictures like this cross the boundaries between sexes. **RECOMMENDED**

The Apostle [1997]

Starring: Robert Duvall, Miranda Richardson, Farrah Fawcett, John Beasley, Walter Goggins, Rick Dial, Billy Joe Shaver, Billy Bob Thornton Director: Robert Duvall Screenplay: Robert Duvall Running Time: 2:12 Rated: PG-13 (Mature themes, mild profanity, brief violence) Theatrical Aspect Ratio: 1.85:1

A relatively simple tale about a far-from-simple character, *The Apostle* never falters in its portrayal of Euliss "Sonny" Dewey (Robert Duvall) as a real, flesh-and-blood human being. *The Apostle* is a character study, and, like all motion pictures of this sort, its ultimate success depends upon how compelling the protagonist is. As essayed by Duvall, arguably one of America's ten-best living actors, Sonny is the kind of complex individual we could watch for hours on end without ever losing interest.

The film opens with a brief prologue in 1939 Texas that shows Sonny, as a boy, at a Pentecostal church service. *The Apostle* then fast-forwards nearly 6 decades. Now, Sonny is an aging preacher who spends most of his time on the road, leading revivals all across the deep South. His long-suffering wife, Jessie (Farrah Fawcett), grows tired of his never being home, and wants a divorce. The already-uncomfortable situation is further exacerbated when Jessie and her lover, a young minister named Horace (Todd Allen), use church by-laws to steal Sonny's congregation away from him. In a moment of jealous rage, Sonny attacks Horace, and the result of that confrontation forces him to flee his home state and change his identity. Bearing the name and title of "The Apostle E.F.," he soon re-surfaces in a small bayou community in

Louisiana with the intention of starting a Pentecostal ministry. His enthusiasm is so great that a respected, local black pastor (John Beasley) agrees to help him.

Like many flawed heroes, Sonny is a good man who is haunted by one tragic mistake. His entire life becomes devoted to redemption and atonement. He cannot take back what he did, but he is determined to act in a manner that will bring good into the lives of everyone he meets. Sonny has moments of weakness, but his sincerity never wavers, even when his ministry flourishes and the temptation for self-aggrandizement grows. He is a powerful, charismatic figure with a real gift for preaching. Watching Sonny lead revivals, it's easy to understand the appeal of an energetic preacher, and how some of the most popular achieve a status not unlike that of a rock star.

To enhance *The Apostle*'s verisimilitude, Duvall relied primarily on non-professional church-goers and evangelists (rather than experienced actors) in supporting roles. For the picture's style, he admits to being inspired by the near-documentary quality of Ken Loach's films. As a result, *The Apostle* possesses a truer and more intimate feel than it would have with slick camerawork. Sonny's character shines through clearly as he struggles to find a path that has meaning. *The Apostle* is not the kind of movie that provokes a profound change in the viewer, but it offers a balanced portrait of a unique personality. RECOMMENDED

Auto Focus [2002]

Starring: Greg Kinnear, Willem Dafoe, Maria Bello, Rita Wilson
Director: Paul Schrader Screenplay: Michael Gerbosi, based on the book *The Murder of Bob Crane* by Robert Graysmith Running Time: 1:47 Rated: R (Sex, nudity, violence, profanity) Theatrical Aspect Ratio: 1.85:1

Auto Focus is the story of the rise and fall of actor Bob Crane. Just about everyone in America is familiar with Crane, or, more precisely, with his television alter-ego, Col. Hogan of *Hogan's Heroes*. If every actor has a defining role, Crane's was unquestionably that of Hogan. The series opened on CBS during the 1965-66 TV season and was an immediate success. *Hogan's Heroes* lasted for 6 years before taking its 180-plus episodes into syndication, where it continues to play on cable stations to this day — 24 years after the tragic, unsolved murder of its lead actor.

When the film begins, Crane (Greg Kinnear) is a disc jockey for KNX radio. He seems happy — he has been married for 15 years to his childhood sweetheart, has a delightful family, and attends church regularly. Then his agent brings him the script for *Hogan's Heroes* and Crane's life changes almost overnight. Fame is a heady tonic, but Crane is able to keep on an even keel until he meets audio/video salesman John Carpenter (Willem Dafoe), a seedy individual who befriends Crane and introduces him to late-night sex parties, the swinging circuit, and provides him with the equipment to videotape his sexual exploits. For a while, Crane is able to lead a double life — nice guy in public, sex addict in private. Eventually, however, things spiral out of control. His wife, Annie (Rita Wilson), leaves him. And, once *Hogan's Heroes* is cancelled, he can't get another job because his reputation is badly soiled. His sole friend remains Carpenter, who has leeched onto Crane like a parasite — in large part because of an unconsummated homosexual longing on Carpenter's part.

Auto Focus is loaded with sex and nudity, as might be expected from a film with this subject matter, but Schrader manages to keep things at a level where we never sense a whiff of exploitation. There's as much here (no more, no less) as is necessary for the story to be properly told. The result is a compelling motion picture that illustrates an American tragedy and shows the transformation of a decent family man into someone whose struggles with addiction and association with the wrong man bring him to an untimely end, with no hope of retribution. RECOMMENDED

Autumn Tale (Conte d'automne) [France, 1998]

Starring: Marie Rivière, Béatrice Romand, Alain Libolt, Didier Sandre, Alexia Portal Director: Eric Rohmer Screenplay: Eric Rohmer Running Time: 1:50 Rated: none (Mature themes, sexuality) Theatrical Aspect Ratio: 1.66:1 In French with subtitles

Eric Rohmer has been taking his time turning out his Tales of Four Seasons cycle. The final chapter is *Autumn Tale* (*Conte d'automne*), which, in many ways, is the sunniest of the quartet. The picture is both penetrating and effervescent — a joyous romantic comedy filled with subtle humor and stunning performances. Unlike many directors, Rohmer allows his actors to take center stage as they chew on the lines he has given them; he never upstages them with scenery or visual gimmicks, and he never cuts away from scenes too quickly.

Autumn Tale centers on a middle-aged woman's quest for love. Magali (Béatrice Romand), the widowed owner of a vineyard and the mother of 2 grown children, is lonely for a romance. But, in her words, "At my age, it's easier to find buried treasure" than a man. Her best friend, Isabelle (Marie Rivière), who suggests that she place a Lonely Hearts ad.

When Magali rejects the idea, Isabelle does it for her, then carefully interviews Gerald (Alain Libolt), who answers the ad. Soon, Isabelle has contrived a meeting between Magali and Gerald. However, she isn't the only one playing matchmaker. Rosine (Alexia Portal), Magali's son's girlfriend, decides to introduce Magali to a former flame of hers, Etienne (Didier Sandre). Complications arise when the men selected by Isabelle and Rosine both arrive to meet Magali in the same place at the same time. The result is a farcical scene of great warmth and intelligence, and one of the most overtly humorous sequences ever to appear in a Rohmer movie. With *Autumn Tale,* the director uses common romantic comedy plot elements, such as the mistaken identity, in new and thoroughly enjoyable ways.

It goes without saying that the acting is superlative across the board. Béatrice Romand and Marie Rivière don't just play their characters; they inhabit them. By the end of the film, we are convinced we have spent 2 hours with a group of likable, familiar friends. Romand is vivacious and attractive, but we can feel her loneliness and despair that late middle age may have robbed her of a last chance at romance. Also impressive is the supporting cast, which features Alain Libolt as the solid, reliable Gerald and Didier Sandre as Etienne, a stuffy professor still pining for lovely Alexia Portal's Rosine.

Autumn Tale isn't Rohmer's most impressive work; in fact, it's not even the best of the Tales of Four Seasons group (that honor belongs to *A Winter's Tale*), but it's a solidly entertaining effort — the kind of movie that can be enjoyed by anyone who appreciates discerning comedy. There are a few minor missteps, but those don't significantly detract from the viewing experience. The characters, their relationships, and the things they say to one another are the highlights of *Autumn Tale*. **HIGHLY RECOMMENDED**

The Aviator [2004]

Starring: Leonardo DiCaprio, Cate Blanchett, John C. Reilly, Kate Beckinsale, Adam Scott, Alec Baldwin, Ian Holm, Alan Alda Director: Martin Scorsese Screenplay: John Logan Running Time: 2:48 Rated: PG-13 (Profanity, sexual situations, nudity) Theatrical Aspect Ratio: 2.35:1

The Aviator is a good, but not great, filmed biography, and continues Martin Scorsese's recent flirtation with mediocrity. The movie skims across roughly two decades in Howard Hughes's life, from the late 1920s until the late 1940s. The film opens with the millionaire sinking huge sums of money into his Hollywood dream epic, *Hell's Angels* (which would garner him more critical and public acclaim than anything else he did in the movie business). It ends with his getting the "Spruce Goose," an aircraft capable of carrying 700 people, into the air despite a 320-foot wingspan and a 400,000-pound weight. In between, he makes more movies, become the primary stockholder in TWA, is nearly killed while test-piloting the XF-11 spy plane, sets various aviation records, and enters into pitched battles with Maine Senator Ralph Owen Brewster (Alan Alda) and Pan-Am president Juan Trippe (Alec Baldwin).

The movie also details, to one degree or another, some of Hughes's most publicized romances. The one that is presented best is his dalliance with Katharine Hepburn (Cate Blanchett), which is depicted from witty beginning to acrimonious end (when she leaves Hughes for Spencer Tracy). Less satisfying glimpses are provided of his liaisons with actresses Ava Gardner (Kate Beckinsale) and Faith Domergue (Kelli Garner). *The Aviator* also spends perhaps too much time showing Hughes's battles with obsessive compulsive disorder and other mental disorders, including a lengthy sequence in which he is sitting naked in a "germ-free" zone watching movies.

The Aviator's first of three hours is engrossing. After exploring the tribulations faced by Hughes in making the most expensive motion picture to-date ($3.8 million), it moves on to chronicle his romance with Hepburn. Cate Blanchett's whirlwind performance, easily the best by a supporting actress this year, enlivens the film for about 40 minutes. She energizes *The Aviator,* and we're hardly aware of the passage of time. Then she's gone and there's still more than 90 minutes of footage to wade through. The second half of the film is unevenly paced and has a tendency to drag, although proceedings are enlivened by a terrifying plane crash. Story-wise, there are also some missteps (although these could be the result of cuts made to reduce the running length). Hughes's affairs with Ava Gardner and Faith Domergue are poorly developed, and Gardner's "rescue" of Hughes from a mental sinkhole is badly motivated and not credible.

Even if the subject had more appeal to mainstream audiences, the nearly three-hour length would cap the interest. Tighter editing is needed. Instead of incorporating half-told secondary stories (such as Hughes's liaison with Domergue), these could have been cut to better streamline the central narrative.

The color they add is not worth the havoc the wreak upon the overall plot. For those with an interest in Hughes and/or the era in which he operated, *The Aviator* represents a flawed but entertaining (and perhaps informative) tale. Others, unfortunately, will likely be more bored than engrossed once the first hour has passed. RECOMMENDED

The Barbarian Invasions [CANADA/FRANCE, 2003]
Starring: Rémy Girard, Stéphane Rosseau, Marie-Josée Croze, Marina Hands, Dorothée Berryman, Johanne Marie Tremblay, Piere Curzi, Yves Jacques, Louise Portal, Dominique Michel Director: Denys Arcand Screenplay: Denys Arcand Running Time: 1:39 Rated: R (Profanity, sexual language, drug use) Theatrical Aspect Ratio: 2.35:1 In French with subtitles

The Barbarian Invasions is a follow-up to director Denys Arcand's 1986 international art house hit, *The Decline of the American Empire*. Obviously, after the decline and fall, the barbarians arrive. Where the earlier movie was about sex and vitality, *The Barbarian Invasions* deals with an equally universal topic: mortality. However, although the specter of death hovers over the entire film, it is neither a grim nor a depressing experience. Arcand has injected a great deal of wit into the movie, and it meshes perfectly with the anticipated pathos. And one could easily make the argument that *The Barbarian Invasions* is as much about life as it is about death, and considering how intertwined the subjects are, it's hard to form a counterargument.

The film opens with one of the protagonists from *The Decline of the American Empire*, Rémy (Rémy Girard), facing death. Before Rémy's days are done, his ex-wife, Louise (Dorothée Berryman), persuades the dying man's estranged son, Sébastien (Stéphane Rousseau), to make the transatlantic journey from London to Montreal for a reconciliation. Their initial meetings are not promising, but a thaw begins with Sébastian recruiting many of Rémy's old friends to join him at his bedside. In addition, there is one newcomer — the deeply troubled Nathalie (Marie-Josée Croze), who is recruited by Stéphane to provide heroin used to dull Rémy's pain. However, as a drug addict, not only is she unreliable, but the potential for an overdose may mean that she has less time to live than Rémy.

The film starts out slowly, and for a while it looks like it might be just another movie about a fractured family coming to grips with its dysfunction. Indeed, the underlying material of *The Barbarian Invasions* could easily have been used to develop a soap opera,

so Arcand must be given credit for detouring the story line off the main track and onto a road that, while moving on a parallel trajectory, is less melodramatic and more intellectually satisfying. In the end, our tears are because we identify with these characters, not because the script has inelegantly manipulated our emotions.

This is a movie in which words and interaction take precedence over plot and action — a so-called "character piece." It's a film in which friends gather to meditate upon history, philosophy, and their shared pasts. In many ways, Rémy's death is the kind of passing we might all wish for. He does not suffer for long, goes out on his own terms and, at the end, is surrounded by his friends and loved ones. He is also given the opportunity to heal old wounds and speak his mind. Who could ask for anything more? HIGHLY RECOMMENDED

The Basketball Diaries [1995]
Starring: Leonardo DiCaprio, Mark Wahlberg, James Madio, Patrick McGaw, Lorraine Bracco Director: Scott Kalvert Screenplay: Bryan Goluboff based on the novel by Jim Carroll Running Time: 1:42 Rated: R (Drug use, profanity, sexual themes, violence)

The best anti-drug movies are the ones that eschew sermons. Nothing turns off an audience faster than a film that becomes pedantic. However, when a production gets the message across through a story that lacks even a trace of artifice, its effectiveness is indisputable. Such is the case with *The Basketball Diaries*, film maker Scott Kalvert's updating of Jim Caroll's autobiographical novel. The tale related here isn't all that original, but the honest presentation lends impact to a wrenching scenario.

Jimmy Carroll (Leonardo DiCaprio) is a star basketball player on his New York City Catholic school team. Fellow roundballers Mickey (Mark Wahlberg) and Neutron (Patrick McGaw) and unofficial cheerleader Pedro (James Madio) are Jimmy's closest friends, and whenever trouble stalks one, it invariably affects them all. So, when the drug cycle starts, it quickly spreads to each of the 4 corners of the friendship. What begins as casual use first becomes a weekend habit, then an everyday obsession. Grades plummet, on-court performance becomes unreliable, and crime looms as the only means to pay for a seemingly-endless supply of uppers, downers, cocaine, and heroin.

There have been quite a few addiction movies, but most are surface melodramas, concerned with busting the bad guys or facilitating a Hollywood-style transformation from user to productive member of society. Films like with *The Basketball Diaries*, which paint a stark, ugly portrait of drug abuse, are rare. This is not the type of picture likely to draw big at the box office. Much of what's shown is simply too raw for audiences out for a couple hours' entertainment.

In Collard's *This Boy's Life,* Leonardo DiCaprio played a young man coming of age in the Pacific Northwest. Here, though his character undergoes a far different change, the actor's performance is equally on-target. Because it demands so much range, the role of Jimmy Carroll requires more effort, but DiCaprio doesn't miss a beat.

The decay of the individual always makes for powerful drama. Such was the case with Cyril Collard's *Savage Nights,* and it is no less true here. The teen years — an age of rebellion and uncertainty in the best of circumstances — can be devastating when an individual loses control. *The Basketball Diaries* captures this with brutal effectiveness. Facile escapes are rejected, and the resolution is acceptable because we can believe it. In fact, that's the reason this film works as well as it does: credibility. You won't need many fingers to count the times when scenes ring false. By another name, call this *Hoop Nightmares.*
HIGHLY RECOMMENDED

A Beautiful Mind [2001]
Starring: Russell Crowe, Ed Harris, Jennifer Connelly, Christopher Plummer Director: Ron Howard Screenplay: Akiva Goldsman, based on the book by Sylvia Nasar Running Time: 2:12 Rated: PG-13 (Profanity, sexual situations, violence) Theatrical Aspect Ratio: 1.85:1

Affecting without being overtly manipulative, *A Beautiful Mind* tells the life story of John Nash, a Nobel prize winner who struggled through most of his adult life with schizophrenia. As directed by Ron Howard, this becomes a tale not only of one man's battle to overcome his own disability, but of the overreaching power of love.

While the gross facts may be accurate, one must expect embellishment of the details. Narrative features are not constrained by the same rules that limit documentaries. We first meet Nash as a student at Princeton in 1947. He is brilliant but erratic — a mathematical genius who lacks social skills. Years later, following an astounding breakthrough that revolutionizes economics, John is teaching at M.I.T. and doing code-breaking work for a shady government agent, William Parcher (Ed Harris). It's at this time that John meets, falls in love with, and marries Alicia (Jennifer Connelly). But his happy world soon starts

to crumble. John is afflicted with paranoid hallucinations; by the time he is taken to a mental hospital under the care of the mysterious Dr. Rosen (Christopher Plummer), he is diagnosed as having an advanced case of schizophrenia.

For Russell Crowe, this is another opportunity to broaden his range. Crowe successfully buries his personality beneath Nash's, allowing the character to come to the fore. And, when it comes to the sequences depicting Nash battling his demons, Crowe's performance is utterly convincing. Meanwhile, Jennifer Connelly is luminous as Alicia. Although the showier performance belongs to Crowe, it is Connelly's complex work, depicting a woman torn by love for and fear of the same man, that elevates the film to a higher level.

A viewer certainly doesn't have to be a mathematical expert to appreciate what *A Beautiful Mind* offers, although those with a strong left-brain component may relate better to John Nash than right-brainers. The movie tosses mathematical theories and theorems in the audience's direction, but explains them simply and lucidly; no one is going to become lost or bored. *A Beautiful Mind* isn't about mathematics except as a symbol. It's about human frailty and the ability to triumph over it. Nash could just as easily be a doctor, a lawyer, or a construction worker and the essence of the story would not change.

The strength of the writing and production values elevate it far above "disease of the week movie" quality. At the core of the picture lies the relationship between John and Alicia, and the tribulations that the strength of their bond allows them to overcome. *A Beautiful Mind* defies the conventional Hollywood wisdom that love is passion and romance. For John and Alicia, it is painful, heartbreaking work. And, while hearts and flowers are great for a fantasy, this is the kind of expression of emotion that touches a deeper chord. **HIGHLY RECOMMENDED**

Beautiful People [United Kingdom, 1999]
Starring: Charlotte Coleman, Charles Kay, Rosalind Ayres Director: Jasmin Dizdar Screenplay: Jasmin Dizdar Running Time: 1:47 Rated: R (Violence, drug use) Theatrical Aspect Ratio: 1.85:1

In what can only be viewed as a change-of-pace for movies about Bosnia and Bosnians, *Beautiful People* has a generally upbeat perspective. While recognizing the tragedy inherent in the current conflict, Jasmin Dizdar chooses not to dwell upon it. Instead, he focuses on the absurdities and ironies that the civil war has created, and how the situation has allowed some people to find the strength and courage to live a better life. *Beautiful People* is about men and women of different cultures coming together.

The film has an ambitious agenda. It tells 6 stories that are often separate, but occasionally intersect, merge, or break apart. Each of these tales has at least one connection to the people or events currently transpiring in war-torn Bosnia. Some are richer and more substantive than others, but Dizdar works hard to ensure that they all hold our interest. The only problem with his approach is that it necessitates the passing of roughly 1/3 of the film before the viewer has become immersed in Dizdar's world.

Beautiful People opens by introducing us to a Serb (Dado Jehan) and a Croat (Faruk Prutti) who encounter each other on a London bus. Fisticuffs break out, and the two end up brawling their way through the city's streets, eventually ending up in the same hospital room, recovering from their wounds. Meanwhile, another former Yugoslavian, ex-basketball player Pero (Edin Dzandzanovic), is brought to the hospital after being struck by a car. A nurse, Portia (Charlotte Coleman), falls in love with him, and, after his release, brings him home to meet her upper crusty family. A doctor (Nicholas Farrell) is distressed over the break-up of his marriage and the likelihood that his wife will take away his 2 children. Despite that, he does his best to help a pregnant woman and her husband come to grips with the harsh reality that the child she is about to give birth to is the product of a rape that happened before they left Bosnia.

It's worth noting that the perspective embraced by *Beautiful People* offers North American viewers an opportunity to see events from a closer vantage point. In this part of the world, Bosnia is a remote place, separated from us not only by differences in culture but by half a globe's distance. However, in London, the travel time is not as great and the circumstances are far less remote. Although, as Dizdar points out on more than one occasion, there are members of British society who would prefer to ignore the existence of any problems associated with the former Yugoslavia.

The most impressive thing about this film is the accessibility of the humor. While *Beautiful People* is best described as a black comedy, it is funny, not merely grimly amusing. This makes *Beautiful People* a very intriguing and thought-provoking comedy.

RECOMMENDED

Beautiful Thing [United Kingdom, 1996]
Starring: Glen Berry, Scott Neal, Linda Henry, Tameka Empson, Ben Daniels Director: Hettie Macdonald Screenplay: Jonathan Harvey Running Time: **1:30** Rated: **R** (Profanity, mature themes) Theatrical Aspect Ratio: **1.66:1**

Beautiful Thing tells of two teenage boys, Jamie (Glen Berry) and Ste (Scott Neal), who live next door to each other in southeast London's Thamesmead Estate. When Ste's chronically abusive father and older brother apply a fresh beating to him, he goes to Jamie's mother, Sandra (Linda Henry), for sanctuary. Ste ends up spending several nights in Jamie's room, and, as the days pass, the boys recognize a burgeoning attraction. However, each of them is apprehensive not only about acting upon it, but about even admitting it. Nevertheless, as others begin to notice the changing dynamic in their relationship, Jamie, the less popular of the two, becomes the target of his schoolmates' derision.

The central story is handled with warmth and intelligence by Hettie Macdonald, who is directing from a script adapted by Jonathan Harvey from his play. The relationship between Jamie and Ste comes across as surprisingly heartfelt yet unsentimental. There's all the angst and uncertainty one would expect from boys struggling with a foreign sexual identity, recognizing that if they choose what comes naturally, they will face society's contempt. But this is also a case of first love for both of the principals, each of whom, in addition to facing their homosexuality, must struggle with the distress and rapture of a passionate adolescent infatuation. Macdonald manages to capture the nuances of the situation, exploring the emotional complexity of the circumstances without resorting to melodrama.

Unfortunately, *Beautiful Thing* has a plethora of subplots, none of which comes close to the main story in terms of richness or sensitivity. Jamie's stormy relationship with his mother represents the kind of dysfunctional family situation that has become a motion picture cliche. The same is true for Ste's interaction with his father and brother. A neighborhood girl, Leah (Tameka Empson), initially looks like she might play an important part in the film, but she ends up in a supporting role, offering occasional comic relief and providing much of the soundtrack as a result of her obsession with Mama Cass (of the Mamas and Papas). Despite having the potential to be *Beautiful Thing*'s most interesting character, she remains severely underdeveloped and underused.

Beautiful Thing uses numerous conventions of urban dramas and forbidden love stories in its framework, but, because Macdonald keeps the focus intimately on Jamie and Ste, the result is still satisfying. Only the ending, which gives a false sense of closure to an otherwise well-balanced narrative, feels wrong. Otherwise, *Beautiful Thing* represents a keen, personal look at the difficulties of growing up gay in a heterosexual world. **RECOMMENDED**

Before and After [1996]

Starring: **Meryl Streep, Liam Neeson, Edward Furlong, Julia Weldon, Alfred Molina** Director: **Barbet Schroeder** Screenplay: **Ted Tally** based on the novel by **Rosellen Brown** Running Time: **1:48** Rated: **PG-13** (Violence, profanity) Theatrical Aspect Ratio: **1.85:1**

As an indictment of American Law, director Barbet Schroeder's *Before and After* has little new to offer. Numerous films over the years, from *Twelve Angry Men* to *Eye for an Eye*, have voiced various views about what's right and wrong with the U.S. criminal justice system. This particular film has the perspective that "truth" is relative and has little to do with whether someone is convicted or not. Trials are all about credibility, and doubt is the defendant's greatest ally.

However, as an examination of family dynamics, *Before and After* presents an incisive and stirring picture. And, ultimately, this movie is less about culpability than how a family copes with the realization that one of them may be a murderer. To what lengths should they go to protect him? And which is more important — faith in his innocence or practical action in case he's guilty?

Schroeder forges this tale about a family bound by love, yet torn apart by uncertainty. Jacob (Edward Furlong), the 16-year-old son of Carolyn (Meryl Streep) and Ben Ryan (Liam Neeson), is suspected of murdering his girlfriend, Martha (Alison Folland). Her body was found in the snow near where she and Jacob had been seen together in his car. Now, Jacob has disappeared and the police want to question him. When Ben conducts a cursory examination of Jacob's car, he finds gloves and a car jack, both covered with blood. He burns the gloves and washes the jack, deciding that protecting his son is more important than destroying evidence.

For those who want a little mystery, the truth about Martha's death isn't revealed until past the film's midpoint. The majority of the film is structured around Jacob's attempts to cope with the situation, his mother's faith, his father's steadfast refusal to abandon him, and the town's need for retribution. The central relationship is between Jacob and his father. Ben goes to great lengths to prove his love and, consequently, Jacob's actions and reactions are designed not to let this man down.

A degree of *Before and After*'s success must be ascribed to the performers. Meryl Streep and Liam Neeson are in fine form, as is the much younger Edward Furlong. Julia Weldon is Jacob's younger sister, Judith, and Alfred Molina has an energetic turn as a defense attorney who cares more about what's on his sandwich than whether his client is innocent. John Heard and Ann Magnuson both make cameo appearances.

Despite an overly-melodramatic climax, *Before and After* is, in large part, an affecting study of a family under pressure. It's easy to love when things are going well, but far more difficult in a crisis, especially when the difference between right and wrong isn't clear-cut. **RECOMMENDED**

Before Night Falls [2000]

Starring: **Javier Bardem, Olivier Martinez, Andrea Di Stefano, Sean Penn, Johnny Depp, Michael Wincott** Director: **Julian Schnabel** Screenplay: **Cunningham O'Keefe, Lazaro Gomez Carriles, Julian Schnabel** Running Time: **2:13** Rated: **R** (Sexual situations, violence, nudity) Theatrical Aspect Ratio: **1.85:1**

For the director, who is world-renowned for his painting, the appeal of a man like Reinaldo Arenas (the central character of *Before Night Falls*) is not difficult to understand. The outstanding question is not whether Schnabel is fascinated by his subjects, but whether he can make them as compelling on film to an audience as they are in real life to him.

The somewhat disjointed narrative manages to cover episodes throughout Arenas' life, although they are often disconnected. While Schnabel clarifies the time periods by employing captions, some of the fast-forwards are jarring. The first incident we see is Arenas' birth in 1943 rural Cuba. Following glimpses of his poverty-stricken childhood, the scene switches to Holguin in 1958, where Arenas becomes a revolutionary; by 1964, his status as a homosexual, an intellectual, and a writer has made him anathema to Castro's regime. For the next 15 years, he shuttles back and forth between jail and freedom, finally going into exile in New York City in 1981. Ten years later, at the age of 47, Arenas dies of AIDS.

In many ways, it's hard to fault Schnabel's storytelling choices. Since it's impossible to represent a man's complete life in 133 minutes, the filmmaker is content to hit as many highlights as he can. Although the result may leave us wondering a little about what happened during the interim between some scenes, *Before Night Falls* successfully paints a picture depicting the influences behind Arenas' writing: his difficult childhood, his conflicted feelings for his mother, coming to terms with his sexuality, the revolution in Cuba, and the pain of being an outcast in his own country. Arenas' writing is poignant, lucid, and intelligent — three characteristics that can easily be ascribed to the man who penned it.

At the center of *Before Night Falls* is actor Javier Bardem. With the film moving rapidly through the years and from location to location, Arenas becomes the only constant character, so it is up to Bardem to hold the film together. He gets some help from an effective supporting cast, including the likes of Sean Penn and Johnny Depp, but this is Bardem's show, and Schnabel's ability to recreate Arenas' life rests squarely on his shoulders. The Spanish-born actor is up to the challenge. This is a startlingly real and believable performance, with Bardem being credible as Arenas from his early twenties through his late forties.

Before Night Falls received its world premiere at the 2000 Venice Film Festival and its North American premiere at the 2000 Toronto Film Festival. It was lauded with critical praise at both venues, taking a number of top prizes in Venice. It is an intriguing and sporadically powerful motion picture with a stellar central performance. RECOMMENDED

Bend It Like Beckham [UNITED STATES/UNITED KINGDOM/ GERMANY, 2003]

Starring: Parminder K. Nagra, Keira Knightley, Jonathan Rhys-Meyers, Anupam Kher, Archie Kher, Shaheen Khan, Ameet Chana Director: Gurinder Chadha Screenplay: Gurinder Chadha, Paul Mayeda Berges, Guljit Bindra Running Time: 1:52 Rated: PG-13 (Sexual situations) Theatrical Aspect Ratio: 1.85:1

Jess (Parminder Nagra) is the British-born daughter of orthodox Hindu parents. She is also a fairly typical teenager and, as is true of nearly every teenager across the globe, feels the need to rebel. Her source of rebellion is to play soccer/football, and she dreams of one day being on the field with her hero, David Beckham, and kicking the ball in for the winning goal. However, although her parents tolerated her sports passion when she was young, they now believe she should become serious about her life and prepare for the future. That means giving up "children's games" for cooking lessons, marriage, and university studies. The edict to stop playing soccer comes just as Jess has been offered the opportunity to play for a semi-pro, all-girls team. One of the players, Juliette (Keira

Knightley), has seen Jess play and invites her to audition for the coach, Joe (Jonathan Rhys-Meyers), who thinks she's brilliant. So, what's a teenager to do? Sneak out of the house and lie about her whereabouts, of course.

Bend It Like Beckham touches on some serious issues like cultural assimilation, but doesn't go into any great depth. This is, after all, intended to be more light entertainment than a "message movie." In addition to the main story line — Jess trying to break free of her family's restrictions and find herself without irretrievably damaging her relationship with her parents — there are some subplots. One finds Jess falling for Joe, whose affection is also coveted by Juliette. Thus, we have a time-honored romantic triangle. Jess's best friend, Tony (Ameet Chana), has a secret he's afraid to tell his mother. Then there's the question of whether Jess can lead her team to the championship and get the chance to fly to America and be paid to play. So, of course, we get the big sports movie moment.

The leads are energetic and likable, especially Parminder Nagra and Kiera Knightley, both of whom bring a lot of spirit to their instantly likable characters. *Bend It Like Beckham* delivers a positive message that doesn't tax viewers in the delivery. It's frothy and undemanding, and proud of it. *Bend It Like Beckham* is enjoyable enough that the sprinkles of artificial sweetness in the mix don't do lasting or irreparable damage. RECOMMENDED

Better Luck Tomorrow [2003]

Starring: Parry Shen, Jason J. Tobin, Sung Kang, Roger Fan, John Cho, Karin Anna Cheung Director: Justin Lin Screenplay: Justin Lin, Ernesto Foronda, Fabian Marquez Running Time: 1:38 Rated: R (Violence, profanity, sexual situations, nudity, drug use) Theatrical Aspect Ratio: 1.85:1

Better Luck Tomorrow is a rarity indeed — a movie about high school teenagers that does not fall into one of the two most popular categories: the formula romantic comedy, or the angst-filled soap opera. Instead, Justin Lin's sophomore feature keeps things real. Lin obviously understands what it means to be a high school outsider; he develops his characters as genuine individuals with legitimate personalities, abandoning caricatures along the way.

Ben (Parry Shen) is an ideal student whose sole goal in life is to get into the best college possible. His grades are all A's, his SATs are nearly perfect (to correct the "nearly" portion, he studies one new word each day), and his after-school life is packed with extracurricular activities. He's even on the basketball team, albeit in the role of the "token Asian benchwarmer." Ben lacks a girlfriend, but that doesn't mean there isn't someone he wants to fill that role. She is Stephanie Vandergosh (Karin Anna Cheung), his biology lab partner. Ben is desperately infatuated with her, but he lacks the courage to tell her, and she is involved with a bad-boy named Steve (John Cho), who is, of course, cheating on her.

In the company of his friends Virgil (Jason J. Tobin), Han (Sung Kang), and Daric (Roger Fan), Ben is a member of the school's most notorious clique. They sell cheat sheets for exams, steal computer parts from stores, and are willing to participate in almost every imaginable scam, as long as it's profitable. Eventually, they graduate from petty crimes to drug dealing. That's when the first guns appear, and things start to get dangerous. Ultimately, while the money is a factor, greed is not the real reason Ben and his friends engage in these activities. They do it because it adds spice to an otherwise routine existence. Steve, who is not a member of the clique, talks about the need for a "wake-up call," and it's clear that Ben understands exactly what he's referring to.

Better Luck Tomorrow is noteworthy in that it is the first motion picture of this sort to deal with Asian-American teenagers. The Orange County high school has a diverse population, but Lin focuses exclusively on the Asian-descended students. One of the strongest points that this approach drives home is the universality of the many problems and issues. Most of the obstacles that Ben faces (boredom, peer pressure, drug addiction, sexual frustration) are unrelated to his race and upbringing. Typically, movies aimed at teenage audiences have little concern for things like intelligent scripts, credible characters, and meaningful dialogue. *Better Luck Tomorrow* contains all three, making it a hugely rewarding experience for anyone who goes to see it. **HIGHLY RECOMMENDED**

Beyond Silence (Jenseits der Stille) [Germany, 1996]

Starring: Sylvie Testud, Tatjana Trieb, Howie Seago, Emmanuelle Laborit Director: Caroline Link Screenplay: Caroline Link, Beth Serlin Running Time: 1:50 Rated: R (Nudity, sex) Theatrical Aspect Ratio: **1.85:1** In German and DGS (German Sign Language) with subtitles

Beyond Silence has the capacity to appeal to a broad range of audiences, because the subject material is so rich and multi-layered. The protagonist is Lara, the sprightly and gifted daughter of a deaf man, Martin (Howie Seago), and a deaf woman, Kai (Emmanuelle Laborit). When we first meet her, Lara is a precocious 8-year-old child (played by Tatjana Trieb) who is wise beyond her years. She is devoted to her parents, and uses her ability to sign (their language) and speak (society's) to translate for them in business meetings. She is the bridge between their realm of silence and the noisy world outside. Lara idolizes her musician-aunt, Clarissa (Sybille Canonica), a red-headed clarinet player who is engaged in a long-standing sibling feud with Martin. When Clarissa presents Lara with a clarinet, the little girl is enthralled, and immediately sets about learning how to play. Martin is angry, in part because of Lara's infatuation with something he cannot understand or participate in, and in part because he is jealous that the childless Clarissa is attempting to steal his daughter. Kai advises patience, however, warning that if Martin does not treat Lara gently, he risks losing her.

Flash-forward 10 years. Lara (Sylvie Testud) is now a young woman and an accomplished clarinet player. She is so good that both Clarissa and her music teacher encourage her to study professionally at a renowned German conservatory. Martin opposes the idea, but, with a little prompting from Kai, he allows Lara to spend the summer with Clarissa and her husband, Gregory (Matthias Habich), in Berlin, where she can prepare for the entrance exam. While there, she meets Tom (Hansa Czpionka), a teacher of deaf children, and falls in love. But tragedy is about to strike.

The most impressive portrayal is split between Sylvie Testud and Tatjana Trieb, both of whom play Lara. Not only are the actresses singularly effective, but they fit together so well that the viewer never loses sight of the character, not even for a moment, when the changeover occurs. Mannerisms, facial expressions, and even vocal inflections transfer from one actress to the other. Testud and Trieb immerse themselves in this role with astonishing results. Apparently, several hundred girls auditioned before Link settled on Trieb, who is making her feature debut. Testud, a theatrically-trained French actress, is appearing in her second film.

Beyond Silence has the capacity to appeal to a broad range of audiences, because the subject material is so rich and multi-layered. It truly involves the viewer; the characters and situations become so immediate and real that you feel like dancing or weeping with Lara as she grows into being her own person. **MUST SEE**

The Big Kahuna [1999]

Starring: Kevin Spacey, Danny DeVito, Peter Facinelli Director: John Swanbeck Screenplay: Roger Rueff, based on his play, "The Hospitality Suite" Running Time: 1:30 Rated: R (Profanity) Theatrical Aspect Ratio: 1.66:1

The Big Kahuna is driven entirely by character development and dialogue. There's a setup, but no story to speak of. Three salesmen for Lodestar Laboratories are operating a hospitality suite on the top floor of a hotel in Wichita, Kansas. Their goal is to attract the attention of "The Big Kahuna" — a corporation president who may have interest in buying Lodestar's industrial lubricants. But, as the evening wears on, it becomes clear that these 3 men may have different agendas.

Performances dominate this intimate piece. Bob, the youngest member of the Lodestar trio, is played by Peter Facinelli. Facinelli does an effective job conveying Bob's sense of arrogant superiority. He's a deeply religious man who never questions his beliefs and has a tendency to view others with a hint of condescension. Kevin Spacey (who also helped produce this film) plays Larry, the most driven of the 3 — someone who sees his entire future with the company married to this potential sale. Finally, there's Danny DeVito's Phil, a man on the far side of middle age who is beginning to view life from an existential perspective. Although Spacey's performance is the most dynamic and showy, DeVito's introspective turn as Phil represents *The Big Kahuna*'s best work.

From early in the evening until well past midnight, we see these characters trading jabs, exchanging stories, and reflecting on what is meaningful to them. Each represents a distinct stage in life. Bob is the callow youth — brimming with self-confidence and certain that his path is the right one. Larry is more mature in his outlook, but he is no less driven than Bob. However, while the younger man's motivator is religious zeal, Larry's impetus is a need to land the client. Because they are so alike in many ways, a clash is inevitable. Finally, there's Phil, who was once much like Larry, but now is growing older and weary. By default, he becomes the referee in the philosophical struggle between Bob and Larry. When it comes to an outlook on life, the men span the spectrum: Bob is an idealist, Larry is a cynic, and Phil is a pragmatist.

The Big Kahuna starts brilliantly and ends brilliantly, but there is a bit of a sag in the middle. With a few minor exceptions, the entire movie unfolds in one room, and the production's theatrical origins are evident. Director John Swanbeck, making his big-screen debut, and cinematographer Anastas Michos do their best to make the experience visually interesting, but there are limits to what can be accomplished in such a confined locale. *The Big Kahuna* is not the most visually dynamic motion picture. Then again, odd camera angles and other such trickery would have detracted from the performances, which are the movie's foundation. **RECOMMENDED**

Big Night [1996]

Starring: Stanley Tucci, Tony Shalhoub, Isabella Rossellini, Ian Holm, Minnie Driver Directors: Campbell Scott and Stanley Tucci Screenplay: Joseph Tropiano and Stanley Tucci Running Time: 1:55 Rated: R (Profanity, mature themes) Theatrical Aspect Ratio: 1.85:1

During the 1950s in the seaside resort of Keyport, New Jersey, two brothers — master chef, Primo Pilaggi (Tony Shalhoub) and his maitre d' brother, Secondo (Stanley Tucci) — open an authentic Italian restaurant called the Paradise. Not many customers frequent this small establishment, however — there aren't free side orders of pasta, the lovingly-prepared food takes too long to reach the tables, and there's no live performer. Across the street is Pascal's Italian Grotto, which nightly draws full houses for its cheap, plentiful, familiar Italian fare. In fact, many evenings after closing the Paradise, Secondo stops by to have a drink with his friend, the exuberant Pascal (Ian Holm, in a deliciously over-the-top role).

Not surprisingly, the Paradise is in financial trouble. Foreclosure is imminent. Secondo wants to make a few changes to broaden the restaurant's popularity, but Primo is against capitulating to "Philistines" who can't recognize good food from "the rape of cuisine" that is available at the Italian Grotto. For Primo, an uncompromising purist, "to eat good food is to be close to God."

Pascal, who respects both Primo and Secondo, offers his help. He assures the brothers that when famous singer Louis Prima is in town next week, he will invite him and his band to dine at the Paradise. To celebrate the event, Primo and Secondo prepare the feast of a lifetime, aware that if everything doesn't go right, this one expensive evening could turn out the be their Last Supper.

The centerpiece of *Big Night* is, obviously, the big night — everything from the preparation to the serving of the dishes comprising the multi-course dinner. For everyone, it's an evening to remember as Primo finds himself, Secondo wonders what he really wants from life, and the two brothers rediscover something they've known all along: that food, like love, is an unspoken, universal means of communication. This realization is cemented the next morning, when, in an unbroken 5-minute take, Secondo prepares an omelet that he and his brother wordlessly share.

While Primo and Secondo anchor the film, the guests at the party add flavor and color to the night's festivities. They include Pascal's mistress, the sensuous Gabriella (Isabella Rossellini); Secondo's earthy, charming girlfriend, Phyllis (Minnie Driver); and Primo's would-be flame, Ann (Allison Janney).

The cast is wonderful, as is the direction by Scott and Tucci. The bond between brothers is developed in a believable way, with the usual mix of friction and wordless affection. In addition to their deft skill with light drama, the directors understand well-placed humor, and throw just the right amount of comedy into the mix to make *Big Night* fun without turning it into an outright farce. When it comes to seeing *Big Night*, two words say it all: *Bon appetit!*

HIGHLY RECOMMENDED

Billy Elliot [United Kingdom, 2000]

Starring: Jamie Bell, Gary Lewis, Julie Walters, Jamie Draven
Director: Stephen Daldry Screenplay: Lee Hall Running Time: 1:50
Rated: R (Profanity) Theatrical Aspect Ratio: 1.85:1

In Margaret Thatcher's United Kingdom, the coal miners are on strike and the police are mobilized daily to put down potential riots. Scabs who cross picket lines are in bodily danger, and only the presence of numerous armed officers keeps the conflagration from exploding. Billy Elliot (Jamie Bell) is an 11-year old boy whose life has been turned upside down by the strike, since both his father, Jackie (Gary Lewis), and his brother, Tony (Jamie Draven), are among those currently not bringing home a paycheck. While they're out manning the picket lines, Billy is left home to care for his senile grandmother. His own mother is recently deceased and Billy, who visits her grave regularly, misses her more deeply than he is willing to admit.

Billy Elliot begins in much the same manner as many movies about amateur boxing providing a valuable outlet for youthful aggressions. But Billy is inept in the ring, and he soon finds his attention wandering to a ballet class that is being taught within the walls of the same gym. At first, Billy simply watches as the teacher, Mrs. Wilkinson (Julie Walters), puts her students through the moves, but it isn't long before he's paying 50 pence per lesson and learning that he may have the raw ability to succeed

in an audition for the Royal Ballet School. Unfortunately, while dancing may be Billy's dream for himself, it's not his father's. When Jackie finds out what his son has been up to, he explodes with the expected testosterone-induced reaction: "Lads do football, boxing, or wrestling — not friggin' ballet!" He questions Billy's sexuality and demands that he immediately cease having anything to do with Mrs. Wilkinson and her classes.

The acting is of consistently high quality, and is one of the reasons why the movie is as effective as it is. *Billy Elliot* wins over viewers because of its characters, not its plot, and these individuals are imbued with life by the actors inhabiting their skins. Newcomer Jamie Bell infuses Billy with boundless enthusiasm. He's a raw talent, but it's impossible not to be impressed by the way he throws himself into the role. Gary Lewis brings a quiet dignity to his passionate portrayal of Jackie, the man who would be the film's villain if he wasn't so human. And screen veteran Julie Walters lends her support as solid, determined Mrs. Wilkinson, who will not allow Billy's talent to go wasted and unrecognized.

With an audition that recalls Jennifer Beals' in *Flashdance*, *Billy Elliot* moves out of the tricky, murky waters of family dynamics and into the realm of formula plot development. Then there's a brief epilogue which, while not adding anything new to the story, provides a satisfactory sense of closure. *Billy Elliot* ends on a high note that will have many movie-goers smiling as they leave the theater. **RECOMMENDED**

Three Colors: Blue [France/Poland/Switzerland, 1993]

Starring: Juliette Binoche, Benoit Regent, Florence Pernel, Charlotte
Very Director: Krzysztof Kieslowski Screenplay: Krzysztof Kieslowski
and Krzysztof Piesiewicz Running Time: 1:38 Rated: No MPAA Rating
(Sexual situations, mature themes, nudity) Theatrical Aspect
Ratio: 1.85:1 In French with subtitles

One moment, Julie (Juliette Binoche) had everything; the next, her husband and daughter have been killed in a car accident and her own face is a patchwork of lacerations. The physical recovery proves less difficult than the emotional one, and Julie ends up selling her house, burning her late composer-husband's compositions, putting her mother in a home, and running off to live in relative anonymity, with "no memories, no love, no children." Life, however, is intent on forcing Julie to confront certain elements of her past that she might rather not face.

Juliette Binoche, in what amounts to a one-woman show, manages to bring an element of humanity and sympathy to a potentially unsympathetic character. There is little in Julie, as written, for the audience to latch onto, but Binoche provides the emotional link to the story. In *Blue*, we delve deeply into the psyche of Julie and perhaps examine our own perspectives on life, loneliness, and liberty as we watch her cope with her new, and dramatically different, existence. We are also reminded that control is often an illusion.

Along with director of photography Slawomir Idziak, Krzysztof Kieslowski has created one of the most technically impressive productions in recent years, rivaling Martin Scorsese's *The Age of Innocence* for sheer visual impact. Kieslowski uses light and shadow like a painter uses his palette, and even some of the most simple images — such as a sugar cube absorbing coffee — are memorable. Then there's the use of color — and one color in particular. In addition to blue filters and blue lighting, any number of objects are blue — a foil balloon, a tinted window, awnings, a folder, the walls of a room, coats, skirts, scarves, blouses, jeans, shirts, trash bags, crystals, a lollypop and its wrapper, binders, graffiti, a pool, a van, and a pen. Each use of the title color underlines the central messages.

Coping with loss and trying to build life anew is certainly not a unique theme, but the manner in which *Blue* portrays one woman's journey along this path is fresh and eye-opening. As rich in emotional impact as in style, this motion picture sets a high standard that we as viewers can only hope the other two chapters of the trilogy will match.

HIGHLY RECOMMENDED

Blue Chips [1994]

Starring: Nick Nolte, Mary McDowell, J.T. Walsh, Alfre Woodard, Shaquille O'Neal, Anfernee Hardaway Director: William Friedkin Screenplay: Ron Shelton Running Time: 1:47 Rated: PG-13 (Language) Theatrical Aspect Ratio: 1.85:1

Coach Pete Bell of Western University (Nick Nolte) is going through a nightmare season. After a decade of winning, his team is about to finish with a sub-.500 record for the first time in his tenure. The Western University Dolphins are thin on talent, so getting several blue chip prospects becomes the driving motivation for the off-season. Coach Bell singles out 3 (Shaquille O'Neal, Anfernee Hardaway, and Matt Nover). They all like Western U, but two are demanding a little something "under the table," which goes against Coach Bell's principles. Nevertheless, he is forced to consider that cars and cash might not be the worst price to pay.

Perhaps the best decision made by writer Ron Shelton and director William Friedkin was to focus on the off-court politics of recruiting rather than on the team's wins and losses. In the end, that's what makes *Blue Chips* different from so many other, similarly-marketed movies. There is a big showdown at the end, but the basketball game becomes peripheral to a more important crisis. It is a catalyst, not a conclusion.

Those who expect Shaquille O'Neal to dominate the film will be disappointed. While the NBA star has his share of scenes, the acting required is limited. From start to finish, this is Nick Nolte's picture, with his energetic performance approaching the point of frenzy. It doesn't take long to discern that Coach Bell is modeled after Indiana's Bobby Knight (who, along with numerous other basketball luminaries, makes an appearance).

The central moral dilemma facing Coach Bell is whether or not to pay off players with alumni money. While this goes against everything he believes in, it becomes apparent that it may not be possible to field a winning team without breaking the rules. There's a good dose of reality in this story, even if the script occasionally becomes too preachy. The end sequences especially could have been toned down.

Blue Chips is peppered with subtle humor and in jokes. One prime example is former UNLV coach Jerry Tarkanian (who was constantly accused of recruiting violations by the NCAA) expressing genuine concern about whether a prospective college player has the grades to stay academically eligible. The film's conclusion also features a droll parody of the "what happened to our characters after this movie ends . . ." messages that reality-based dramas often scroll across the screen.

Blue Chips will obviously appeal more to basketball aficionados than to those who are indifferent to the sport. Despite an advertising blitz of slam-dunks and crisp passes, this film has a story to tell that doesn't require much on-court savvy. The theme, which involves facing the consequences of one's actions, is universal, even if the attraction of "the Shaq" isn't. **RECOMMENDED**

Body Shots [1999]

Starring: Sean Patrick Flanery, Jerry O'Connell, Amanda Peet, Tara Reid Director: Michael Cristofer Screenplay: David McKenna Running Time: 1:42 Rated: R (profanity, graphic sex-related dialogue, sex, nudity, drug use, violence) Theatrical Aspect Ratio: 2.35:1

Body Shots is a graphic and sporadically compelling motion picture that uses equal parts comedy, introspection, and tragedy to offer a measure of social commentary about the confusion and frustration faced by superficial 20-somethings as they navigate a treacherous sexual road map. It's an edgy movie that doesn't pull any punches, and, despite some of the most frank discussions about oral sex in any multiplex-bound film, *Body Shots* managed to avoid the NC-17 kiss of death.

Filmmaker Michael Cristofer refuses to adhere to traditional narrative methods. His characters frequently address the camera directly, as if they are answering questions for a documentary interview. Add to that a lively camera that prefers odd angles, unusual visual effects such as filming at 6 frames per second to make objects appear to move fast, and a pulsing soundtrack, and *Body Shots* never lets the energy level dip.

The characters in *Body Shots* are all looking for human contact. They'll take sex, but they want love. In addition to exploring the difference between lust and love, *Body Shots* takes time out to give tips on oral sex and explain why nice guys are boring. Much of the film's second half deals with the controversial issue of what constitutes date rape. As has been illustrated repeatedly in the courts, a line that should be clear often becomes blurred, especially when alcohol and low self-esteem are involved.

There are 4 girls and 4 guys — all physically attractive, all immature and self-obsessed, and all with a lot of money to burn. The women are Jane (Amanda Peet), Sara (Tara Reid), Whitney (Emily Procter), and Emma (Sybil Temchen). The men are Rick (Sean Patrick Flanery), Michael (Jerry O'Connell), Trent (Ron Livingston), and Shawn (Brad Rowe). These two quartets meet at a club, where most of them get drunk, then pair off for the night. Jane goes with Rick, and Sara leaves with football player Michael, even though she has been dating nice guy Shawn. Distressed at seeing his girlfriend depart with another man, Shawn proves he's not all that nice when he corners Emma in an alley for a hot encounter. Meanwhile, Trent learns that Whitney has some kinky sexual preferences.

Late at night, a bleeding and disheveled Sara arrives at Jane's door, claiming to have been raped by Michael. Two versions of events — his and hers — are depicted, and it's clear that more than just a misinterpretation of words and gestures has taken place.

Someone is lying. And the question isn't just "Who?" but "Why?" The resolution isn't likely to satisfy anyone, and is a case of filmmakers taking the easy way out. This movie is designed to stir up controversy and fuel discussions outside of the theater, and it certainly has the content and capacity to fulfill that goal.
RECOMMENDED

Bogus [1996]
Starring: Whoopi Goldberg, Gerard Depardieu, Haley Joel Osment
Director: Norman Jewison Screenplay: Alvin Sargent Running
Time: 1:51 Rated: PG (Mild profanity) Theatrical Aspect Ratio: 1.85:1

Bogus is a lightly-dramatic fantasy and is sentimental without being mawkish. Only at the very end is there a brief, and largely inoffensive, slip into melodrama. As the film opens, we're introduced to Lorraine Franklin (Nancy Travis), a bubbly single mom with a delightful, 7-year-old son, Albert (Haley Joel Osment). Lorraine is part of the Circus Phantastique, a traveling band of performers currently based in Las Vegas. Albert has formed an attachment with the group's magician, Antoine (Denis Mercier), who acts as a substitute father. When Lorraine is killed in a traffic accident, Albert finds himself alone in the world. Antoine helps him with his grief, but he cannot be a full-time caretaker, and the young boy faces becoming a ward of the state.

To avoid that eventuality, Lorraine had drafted a will of sorts that names her one-time foster-sister, Harriet (Whoopi Goldberg), as Albert's guardian. Reluctantly, Harriet agrees to take the boy in, even though, by her own admission, she doesn't have a "motherly bone" in her body. Indeed, Harriet is not a good parent, and, to compensate for her inadequacies and fill a void in his life, Albert invents a good-natured, invisible friend named Bogus (Gerard Depardieu). Harriet, of course, doesn't believe in Bogus' existence, but a series of events makes her question her views of reality.

It's said that many intelligent, creative children invent imaginary friends. Considering that Albert has just lost his mother and surrogate family, and has been forced to move to Newark, New Jersey (ugh!), he has plenty of reasons to dream up Bogus. As the movie unfolds, we learn that, despite the weighty subject matter, *Bogus* isn't a downer. It's a magical excursion into the worlds of imagination and potential. Lorraine's death is just the starting point — the real story is about how Albert and Harriet grow close and learn that neither of them is so different from the other after all.

Whoopi Goldberg, who seems determined to act here rather than just rely on her goofy personality, turns in a sympathetic and multi-layered performance. Gerard Depardieu has finally found a solid English-language role to place aside his numerous critically-acclaimed French parts. His ability to mix light comedy with pathos makes Bogus more than just a cardboard character. Then there's Haley Joel Osment, who has as much charisma and screen presence as any under-10 performer.

Bogus is a well-crafted and moving motion picture. The film asks, but doesn't answer, the question of whether the process of growing up is worth the sacrifice of innocence and trust. The director doesn't attempt too much, and his weaving of several themes into one is masterfully handled. Children and adults of all ages will be enchanted by this movie, which is the exact opposite of its title. **RECOMMENDED**

Boogie Nights [1997]

Starring: Mark Wahlberg, Burt Reynolds, Julianne Moore, Don Cheadle, Heather Graham, John C. Reilly Director: Paul Thomas Anderson Screenplay: Paul Thomas Anderson Running Time: 2:28 Rated: R (Sex, nudity, profanity, violence) Theatrical Aspect Ratio: 2.35:1

Boogie Nights isn't an exposé of the porn industry — it's a provocative and involving character study. One of the movie's greatest, and most immediately obvious assets is its ability to capture the feel and mood of the late '70s and early '80s. At different times throughout the film, Anderson uses long, single takes where the camera pans from one character to another, putting the viewer in the midst of a swirl of activity. The director also has a talent for picking just the right songs for each scene, making the soundtrack an integral part of the movie rather than just a jumbled collection of old disco hits. Add to that the hairdos, clothing, decor, and attitudes of the era, and you have an effective re-creation of recent history.

At *Boogie Nights'* center is Eddie Adams (Mark Wahlberg), a waiter at a San Fernando Valley night club who is "discovered" by idealistic porn movie producer/director Jack Horner (Burt Reynolds). Jack's dream is to make a movie that is "true, and right, and dramatic," and his vision excites Eddie, who changes his name to Dirk Diggler and quickly becomes the hottest young stud in the industry. Together, the director and his star seek to elevate the Adult Film to the next level.

Dirk isn't the only one under Jack's wing. There's Amber Waves (Julianne Moore), a top female star who has lost custody of her son because of her involvement with Jack. Rollergirl (Heather Graham) is an airheaded young starlet who drops out of high school to be in the movies. Buck Swope (Don Cheadle) is one of Jack's veterans, but his dream is to have a wife, a family, and his own hi-fi equipment store. Reed Rothchild (John C. Reilly) is a hanger-on who becomes close friends with Dirk. And Little Bill (William H. Macy) is a behind-the-scenes worker who never feels comfortable with the kind of movies that he's involved in. His resolution to this dilemma leads to *Boogie Nights'* change of direction.

Although Mark Wahlberg has the starring role, he is easily overshadowed by two more impressive portrayals. Burt Reynolds, doing his best motion picture work in recent memory, develops Jack into a three-dimensional individual who really believes in his job until disillusionment hits. Matching Reynolds' performance step-by-step is Julianne Moore, who can add her role in *Boogie Nights* to an ever-increasing list of interesting and challenging characters. Meanwhile, Heather Graham, Don Cheadle, and William H. Macy are impressive in smaller parts. And porn icon Nina Hartley gets some mainstream exposure, and even a few lines, as Little Bill's wife.

Boogie Nights is a dramatically rich and visually arresting motion picture that has earned (and is deserving of) comparisons to the films of Robert Altman. Anderson takes risks with this movie, few of which fall short. The result is a memorably penetrating motion picture. **HIGHLY RECOMMENDED**

The Borrowers [United Kingdom/United States, 1998]

Starring: John Goodman, Jim Broadbent, Mark Williams, Hugh Laurie Director: Peter Hewitt Screenplay: Gavin Scott and John Kamps based on the books by Mary Norton Running Time: 1:23 Rated: PG (Cartoon violence) Theatrical Aspect Ratio: 1.85:1

A missing cufflink. A misplaced watch. A lost set of keys. In general, we attribute these absences to a faulty memory, but could there be another explanation? They live under the floorboards of our houses, and only emerge when the coast is clear to do their "borrowing," then are gone before any human can see them. That's the premise of *The Borrowers*, a new family film from director Peter Hewitt based on the series of children's books by Mary Norton.

In *The Borrowers*, the viewer isn't forced to identify with an animatronic rodent or an irritating child actor. Instead, we have Pod Clock (Jim Broadbent); his wife, Homily (Celia Imire); and their children, teenager Arrietty (Flora Newbigin), and 9-year-old

Peagreen (Tom Felton). Then there's Pete Lender (Bradley Pierce), the human boy who befriends the borrower family. The villain is the nefarious Ocious P. Potter (John Goodman).

Pete's family is being forced to move out of their house because the unscrupulous Potter has stolen the will that leaves the property to them. The house is to be torn down to make way for apartment buildings. Pete informs his new friends that they have to depart. However, in transit to the new house, the borrower children become separated from their parents. Arrietty and Peagreen return to the old dwelling in time to learn that Potter has cheated Pete's family out of their rightful property. So the two young borrowers set out to rectify matters.

Much of the violence found in *The Borrowers* is of the live-action cartoon variety — that is to say, it's wildly exaggerated and no one really gets hurt. Overall, it's not as mean-spirited as we've come to expect from this sort of movie. Aside from a massive electrical shock, nothing horrible happens to anyone. No irons fall on people's heads, no one tumbles out of a third-story window, and no one gets tarred and feathered.

One of the nicest surprises about *The Borrowers* is that it's not only charming, but genuinely funny. Granted, there aren't many belly laughs, but the screenplay offers plenty of opportunities for smiles and chuckles, and there's nothing here that kids need to be shielded from. Likewise, *The Borrowers* stays at a high enough level to involve adults. From time-to-time, some offbeat bit of humor coupled with the creative set design generates a distant echo of Terry Gilliam's brilliant *Brazil*. Best of all, however, is that *The Borrowers* doesn't limit its capacity for pleasure to any particular age group. It's a most delightful family film. **RECOMMENDED**

The Boxer [Ireland, 1997]

Starring: Daniel Day-Lewis, Emily Watson, Brian Cox, Ken Stott, Gerard McSorley, Ciaran Fitzgerald Director: Jim Sheridan
Screenplay: Jim Sheridan & Terry George Running Time: 1:48 Rated: R (Violence, profanity) Theatrical Aspect Ratio: 1.85:1

Although it takes place in Belfast, *The Boxer*'s themes are universal. This is a meditation on hatred and intolerance, and upon the "kill or be killed" mentality that fuels many conflicts. Director Jim Sheridan (*In the Name of the Father*) refuses to demonize or lionize the IRA, exposing the deep fissures within the organization that crack open in the wake of a cease-fire. To one group, peace means an end to the brutal cycle of violence. To others, inured to bloodshed and all-too-willing to continue it, peace means selling out to the English and betraying the memories of hundreds of dead IRA "soldiers."

At the center of all the turmoil is Danny Flynn (Daniel Day-Lewis), a boxer by trade and a Catholic native of Belfast by birth. After serving 14 years in prison for terrorist activities, Danny has just been released because of good behavior. At age 18, he was a staunch soldier in the IRA, and, when he was captured, he refused to name his co-conspirators. Now, free again at age 32, he wants nothing more to do with his former associates. In his view, they have stolen the best years of his life. He wants to rebuild the community, and, with the help of his old trainer, Ike Weir (Ken Stott), he intends to re-open the Holy Family Boxing Club — a non-sectarian training center where Catholics and Protestants can practice together.

The IRA in Belfast is split. The main branch, headed by Joe Hamill (Brian Cox), is negotiating with the British government to establish a peace treaty. A group of mavericks, led by an embittered man (Gerard McSorley) whose only child perished as a result of a British military action, threaten to break the cease-fire. Danny, a high profile figure, is caught in the middle. And he's not the only one. His one-time girlfriend, Maggie (Emily Watson), whose husband is in prison, becomes another central figure in the power struggle. It's only a matter of time before the bubbling tension and hatred boil over.

The Boxer's story is presented with a sense of overwhelming pathos and sadness, and it's not hard to empathize with the characters' despair. When members of the younger generation are drawn into the struggle, Danny realizes that something — anything — must be done to change the situation.

The film is not without weaknesses, chief of which is an erratic pace. The beginning is slow and murky, and the end seems rushed and incomplete. *The Boxer* doesn't offer more than a token sense of closure, but that's in keeping with the current situation in Ireland, which is anything but stable. The symbolism — especially the relationship between boxing and politics — is at times a little too obvious. The same is true of the parallels between the physical and emotional barriers within Belfast. **RECOMMENDED**

Boys Don't Cry [1999]

Starring: Hilary Swank, Chloë Sevigny, Peter Sarsgaard, Brendan Sexton III Director: Kimberly Peirce Screenplay: Kimberly Peirce, Andy Bienen Running Time: 1:56 Rated: R (Violence, rape, nudity, sex, profanity, mature themes) Theatrical Aspect Ratio: 1.85:1

On December 30, 1993 in Falls City, Nebraska, two men, John Lotter and Tom Nissen, shot and killed 21-year-old Brandon Teena. Brandon, a young woman who was actually born as Teena Brandon, had been living as a man in preparation for an eventual sex change operation, and had presented himself as such to Lotter and Nissen, with whom he became friendly. When they learned the truth, they reacted violently, humiliating Brandon in front of his girlfriend, Lana, then kidnapping and raping him. After Brandon reported the incident to the police, Lotter and Nissen resorted to murder. Because of the lurid details surrounding the case (sex, lesbianism, a woman masquerading as a man), the "Brandon Teena murder" fed national news headlines.

Most of the action takes place in the small town of Falls City. For a while, Brandon has both acceptance and friendship, but that all changes very quickly. The violence of his so-called friends' reactions makes a horrific statement about the deep-seated vein of homophobia that characterizes many rural, Midwestern communities. Lotter and Nissen are the only convicted killers, but they are aided and abetted by Lana's mother, the local sheriff (who treats Brandon, the victim, like some kind of sick, twisted criminal), and most of the other "good" citizens of Falls City.

The cast, which is comprised primarily of actors who have made their marks in small, low-budget features, is nearly perfect. The lion's share of the praise goes to Hilary Swank, who, with her hair cut short and her chest wrapped, bears a remarkable resemblance to the real Brandon Teena. This is raw, courageous work that draws the audience in. We feel Brandon's confusion, uncertainty, and alienation.

Chloë Sevigny (*The Last Days of Disco*) plays Lana, an affection-starved young woman with such a low sense of self-esteem that she deludes herself into believing that Brandon is actually a man, even after a sexual encounter. She provides the counterbalance to the tide of hatred that drowns the last act of the film. Even after Lana is forced to confront the truth, she will not abandon her lover. Peter Sarsgaard and Brendan Sexton III play Lotter and Nissen as typical redneck, "good ole boys." The most chilling thing about these two characters is that some people in this country regard them as heroes.

Sitting in a theater watching *Boys Don't Cry* is like observing a speeding train rushing headlong towards a certain crash. The ending, a matter of recent historical record, assures that there will be no room for an upbeat twist. We view events with a growing sense of discomfort as the inevitable catastrophe looms nearer. Ultimately, Pierce tells a story of great human tragedy — one that has happened before and is almost certain to be repeated more than once in the years to come. What human beings do not understand, they destroy. **HIGHLY RECOMMENDED**

The Breakfast Club [1985]

Starring: Emilio Estevez, Anthony Michael Hall, Judd Nelson, Molly Ringwald, Ally Sheedy Director: John Hughes Screenplay: John Hughes Running Time: 1:37 Rated: R (Profanity, mature themes) Theatrical Aspect Ratio: 1.85:1

The Breakfast Club is a small group of high school students, who, during the course of a 9-hour Saturday detention, are transformed from complete strangers to confidantes. For each of them, it is an unforgettable day, and, while the friendships they form between 7 a.m. and 4 p.m. may disintegrate once they get back into the real world, feelings are explored and emotions unearthed that give them insights into their own lives and the forces that drive the others. These are the kinds of realizations which, if more high school students understood them, might make grades 9 through 12 a little less traumatic.

The characters trapped in detention are all very different individuals. Hughes sets them up as traditional stereotypes, then delights in slowly peeling back the layers, showing how each suffers from surprisingly similar problems. There's the jock, wrestling star Andrew Clark (Emilio Estevez); the most popular girl in school, Claire Standish (Molly Ringwald); the all-brains, no-brawn geek, Brian Johnson (Anthony Michael Hall); the rebel without a cause, John Bender (Judd Nelson); and the outcast, Allison Reynolds (Ally Sheedy). It turns out that none of them communicates well with their parents, all are under tremendous pressure from their peers, and each is beset by angst about the future.

John Hughes has assembled a unique and singularly effective cast. Emilio Estevez, although a little too old to play a high school teenager (he was 22 at the time of filming), does a good job presenting the human side of the athlete on a pedestal. Judd Nelson is believable as the James Dean-type who is looking for some kind of acceptance and uses his pugnaciousness as a defense mechanism. Molly Ringwald, the star of 3 Hughes films (the other 2 being *Sixteen Candles* and *Pretty in Pink*), gives the strongest performance by showing the ugly, shallow side of being Ms. Popularity. Ally Sheedy is suitably weird as a compulsive liar and thief who takes a long time to open up. Anthony Michael Hall looks the part of the geek, but, of the 5 lead actors, his is the least impressive portrayal; Brian has trouble escaping from the stereotypical sinkhole in which he begins the movie.

Few will argue that *The Breakfast Club* is a great film, but it has a candor that is unexpected and refreshing in a sea of too-often generic teen-themed films. The material is a little talky, but it's hard not to be drawn into the world of these characters. The depiction of high school is evocative because it's so accurate (an actual suburban Illinois high school was used as the filming location). Unlike many teen films, which seem to transpire in some kid's dirty imagination, this picture, despite its occasional flights of fancy, is grounded in reality. In *The Breakfast Club,* Hughes has created a surprisingly enduring motion picture. **RECOMMENDED**

Breaking the Waves [Denmark/France, 1996]

Starring: Emily Watson, Stellan Skarsgård, Katrin Cartlidge, Jean-Marc Barr, Adrian Rawlins, Udo Kier Director: Lars von Trier
Screenplay: Lars von Trier Running Time: 2:39 Rated: R (Violence, sex, nudity, profanity) Theatrical Aspect Ratio: 2.35:1

According to writer/director Lars von Trier, *Breaking the Waves* is "a simple love story," but "simple" hardly begins to describe this deeply disturbing, multi-layered drama. In fact, nowhere is the picture's complexity more evident than in its study of contrasts — it is highly spiritual yet anti-religious, triumphant yet tragic, and personal yet universal.

This epic-length film is divided into 9 sections: a prologue, 7 "chapters," and an epilogue. Most of the action occurs in a closed village with deeply-rooted fundamentalist Christian beliefs. According to the elders who rule with an iron fist, life isn't for enjoyment; it's for serving God. Outsiders aren't welcome; they're consigned to hell. So when meek, kind-hearted Bess (Emily Watson) announces that she intends to marry oil-rig worker Jan (Stellan Skarsgard), an unbeliever, the entire community is stunned.

Despite the stern disapproval of all the elders, the marriage goes ahead, and Bess finds herself happier than she ever could have imagined. But heartbreak looms ahead. Jan returns to his rig, leaving a lonely Bess behind. Even her best friend and sister-in-law, Dorothy (Katrin Cartlidge), can't lift her out of her profound depression, but when a local doctor (Adrian Rawlins) is called in to evaluate her mental state, he proclaims her sane. Then tragedy strikes as a freak work accident renders Jan paralyzed from the neck down.

Central to the narrative is Bess' relationship with God. For most of the movie, von Trier keeps it ambiguous whether she is psychotic or truly involved in some kind of special communion with the Almighty. Does she really hear God's voice, or is she exhibiting signs of a split personality? Is she His instrument of salvation, or is she merely experiencing potentially self-destructive delusions? Unfortunately, in a late scene, von Trier tips the balance in favor of one interpretation, and this dilutes the film's overall impact.

As the deeply disturbed Bess, British stage actress Emily Watson turns in an award-worthy performance. Since Bess must endure a number of physically and mentally degrading events while her volatile personality veers from emotional calm to complete hysteria, Watson's task of creating a believable character becomes more difficult as the movie progresses. To her credit, she never falters. The supporting players, including Stellan Skarsgård and Katrin Cartlidge, do fine jobs, but none captures the lens the way Watson does.

There's no denying that *Breaking the Waves* is a difficult motion picture to endure. Excepting the chapter breaks, there isn't a wasted moment. And, if not for a somewhat forced catharsis during the epilogue (the weakest segment of the movie), *Breaking the Waves* would have been more wrenching than it is. This achievement announces that von Trier's aptitude for fashioning characters equals, if not exceeds, that which he has previously displayed for images. **HIGHLY RECOMMENDED**

The Bridges of Madison County [1995]

Starring: Clint Eastwood, Meryl Streep Director: Clint Eastwood
Screenplay: Richard LaGravenese based on the novel by Robert James Waller Running Time: 2:15 Rated: PG-13 (Mature themes, brief nudity) Theatrical Aspect Ratio: 1.85:1

Clint Eastwood plays Robert Kincaid, the male protagonist in the motion picture adaptation of Robert James Waller's *The Bridges of Madison County.* Kincaid is a sensitive loner, and while the actor is certainly known for his portrayal of independently-minded individuals, one would be hard pressed to describe Dirty Harry as a model of sensitivity. Nevertheless, this is not the first time Eastwood has successfully stretched his range.

As good as Eastwood is, however, it's his co-star, Meryl Streep, who really shines. After taking a break from drama, she returns to the kind of role that made her famous, and gives perhaps her best performance since *Sophie's Choice*. Streep is Francesca Johnson, a lonely housewife whose eyes and heart are opened to true love when Robert arrives in Iowa to take pictures of Madison County's covered bridges.

Francesca's husband and 2 children are away for 4 days at the Illinois State Fair, leaving her home alone when Robert stops for directions to the Roseman Bridge. Since the roads are unmarked, she guides him there in person, and the pair end up spending the rest of the day — into the evening — together. They start as friends with an endless capacity for conversation, but less than 24 hours later, they are in love.

The Bridges of Madison County is a beautiful film, not only in the way it was photographed, but for the manner through which the characters are revealed to us. Eastwood will not be hurried, choosing a relaxed pace for the unfolding of this romance. There's a lot of dialogue — some mundane and some touching on the quintessential aspects of the human experience. The Bridges of Madison County presents a richly-textured emotional tapestry.

In the book, Francesca is not an especially strong character — things happen around her and she's swept up in the current. Richard LaGravenese's screenplay rectifies this, creating a dynamic personality for Streep to work with. In fact, the actress commented that she was "blind to the book's power" but thought the script was "beautifully crafted."

There aren't many intelligent motion picture romances. But here, there is a profound sense of inevitability permeating the atmosphere, a realization that this magical time must come to an end — and soon. *In The Bridges of Madison County,* we know the conclusion before we learn the beginning and this lends an air of poignancy to the proceedings.

It's easy to believe that Francesca and Robert's love is deep and special, but perhaps the real test of the film's power is whether the statements, situations, and characters transcend the screen to leave a lasting impression. Not many pictures are created with the necessary skill to challenge our perceptions and beliefs, but *The Bridges of Madison County* is a rare exception. **HIGHLY RECOMMENDED**

Bringing Out the Dead [1999]

Starring: Nicolas Cage, Patricia Arquette, John Goodman, Ving Rhames, Tom Sizemore Director: Martin Scorsese Screenplay: Paul Schrader, based on the novel by Joe Connelly Running Time: 2:00 Rated: R (profanity, violence, drug use) Theatrical Aspect Ratio: 2.35:1

Nicolas Cage is Frank Pierce, a NYC Emergency Medical Technician ambulance driver. He and one of his partners, Larry (John Goodman), Marcus (Ving Rhames), or Tom (Tom Sizemore), respond to 911 emergencies barked across the ambulance's two way radio. Lately, Frank has been in a rut. His patients are all dying on him; he hasn't saved anyone in months. The frantic lifestyle is taking its toll on him. He rarely eats, surviving instead on an unhealthy mixture of booze and caffeine. His eyes are hollow and red-rimmed, but nightmares deprive him of sleep. And he has begun to see the ghosts of the many men and women he has lost.

Frank needs redemption, and he spends the entire film trying to find it. We first meet him on a Thursday, when he and Larry are called to help a man who has collapsed from a heart attack and is apparently dead. The man's daughter, Mary (Patricia Arquette), is in hysterics by his side as Frank goes to work with CPR. He revives the patient, then transports him to the hospital, where he remains in a coma. For the next 2 days, nearly every time Frank brings someone in, Mary is there, waiting and wondering if her father will ever get better. Soon, she and Frank realize that they have much in common.

Frank remains something of an enigma. We're aware of who he is here and now, and, in part because of Cage's voiceovers, we know what he's thinking, but his past and his relationships with his co-workers are shrouded in mystery. We get clues, but nothing more — he was married, his parents are still alive, his close working relationship with Tom fell apart, and he was once one of the best ambulance drivers in New York. But we never see where he lives, nor do we meet anyone that could be considered close to him. Perhaps there is no one. Even his developing relationship with Mary is uncertain and tentative.

Patricia Arquette plays the only other genuine character in *Bringing Out the Dead*. Everyone besides Frank and Mary functions as little more than a catalyst or a mouthpiece for bits of philosophy. Arquette draws on a wellspring of pain and darkness for this portrayal; the sultry vixen she often essays is completely sublimated. Mary is just another wretch in need of some sort of solace, and she doesn't care how that relief comes. Like Frank, we learn little about

Mary's past, except that she was heavily into the sex-and-drug scene, has been clean for 2 years, and is estranged from her dying father.

This is not one of Martin Scorsese's best films. Despite the lack of energy and the lethargic pace, there's something darkly compelling about *Bringing Out the Dead*. It's an uncomfortable excursion, sort of like a ride in a hearse to a funeral. See this film if you appreciate bleak character portraits that do not feel the need to let a little sunshine in. **RECOMMENDED**

Broken Wings [ISRAEL, 2002]

Starring: Orly Silbersatz Banai, Maya Maron, Nitai Gaviratz, Daniel Magon, Eliana Magon, Vladimir Friedman Director: Nir Bergman Screenplay: Nir Bergman Running Time: 1:24 Rated: R (Mature themes, profanity, brief nudity, drug use) Theatrical Aspect Ratio: 1.66:1 In Hebrew with subtitles

The death of a family member has often provided grist for a filmmaker's mill, and the resulting productions, both good and bad, have dotted the cinematic landscape for years. *Broken Wings*, from first-time Israeli director Nir Bergman, addresses this deeply painful subject. This film is an autopsy of a family that has been sundered by the death of the father and primary caregiver.

Broken Wings opens nine months after the death of a middle-aged husband and father of four. His unexpected demise has left a trail of emotional wreckage in its wake. His wife, Dafna (Orly Silbersatz Banai), emerged from a three-month state of near-catatonia to begin working every waking hour in an effort to make ends meet. Grief and economic necessity have transformed her into a terrible mother. She has no time for her children and, even if she did have it, she is so emotionally closed off that they couldn't reach her. The eldest daughter, Maya (Maya Maron), has been prematurely forced into the role of protector and nurturer because of her mother's state of mind. Resentment percolates within her. A teenager, she dreams of having a career in music, but her hopes are stymied by her need to care for her siblings. Yair (Nitai Gaviratz), only a year or two younger than Maya, has become distant and uncommunicative. Instead of studying and playing basketball, he has dropped out of school to take a menial job and he ruminates on death and the meaninglessness of life. Ido (Daniel Magon) has reacted to his father's death by becoming surly and contemplating what would happen if he jumped off a diving board into an empty pool. And little Bahr (Eliana Magon), who most needs her mother's affection, is left to fend for herself, encountering challenges that a child of her age would normally be shepherded through.

The point of the film is to examine how these five individuals begin to assemble the shards of their lives and move forward. Bergman chronicles the characters' struggles with personal demons without passing judgment. Despite having been filmed in Israel with an Israeli cast and crew, no mention is made of the current Middle East political situation. In fact, the cultural and religious struggles of the region are expressly ignored. To me, this is an appropriate approach, since it italicizes the universality of the feelings and experiences undergone by the characters. Race, religion, and culture are not boundaries against grief and guilt. Bergman's film is an affecting, character-based drama that ends not with tears, but on a note of optimism. **RECOMMENDED**

A Bronx Tale [1993]

Cast: Robert De Niro, Chazz Palminteri, Lillo Brancato, Francis Capra, Taral Hicks Director: Robert De Niro Screenplay: Chazz Palminteri based on his play Running Time: 2:01 Rated: R (Violence, language) Theatrical Aspect Ratio: 2.35:1

It's New York City in 1960 — the Fordham neighborhood. Living at East 187th Street is the family of Calogero (played at age 9 by Francis Capra and at age 17 by Lillo Brancato). Calogero's father Lorenzo (Robert De Niro) believes that a man should work hard for a living, and thus refuses to be involved in anything that has illegal overtones, such as working for Sonny (Chazz Palminteri), the local "boss." Calogero has different views, however. He idolizes Sonny, and, given a chance to help the "boss" beat a murder rap, Calogero takes it. A grateful Sonny brings the 9-year old under his wing and, despite the protestations of Lorenzo, a bond develops. Soon, Calogero has two fathers — each giving different advice and neither respecting what the other has to say.

Robert De Niro has appeared in some of the greatest gangster films of the past 2 decades, working for directors such as Francis Ford Coppola (*The Godfather 2*), Brian DePalma (*The Untouchables*), and, of course, Martin Scorsese (*Goodfellas*). As a result, it shouldn't come as a surprise to anyone that De Niro has chosen this genre for his first behind-the-camera motion picture.

A Bronx Tale covers little new ground, but the material's presentation is anything but ordinary. On the surface, it's another gangster movie, but the story, like the deeply-realized characters, is multi-layered.

It could be accused of tackling too much, and perhaps its few failures are because of an overly-ambitious scope, but the film has impressive vision and packs a legitimate emotional punch.

While there is violence in *A Bronx Tale*, it isn't a focal point. Most of the violent scenes are fairly "clean" — graphic beatings, but little blood). Instead, as they should be, the characters are kept at the center. The three principles — Calogero, Sonny, and Lorenzo — are all well-realized. This is as much a credit to the writing of Chazz Palminteri and the direction of Robert De Niro as to the quartet of fine actors essaying the characters.

If the movie takes a wrong turn, it's in trying to incorporate an anti-racist theme by having Calogero fall for Jane, a black girl. Today, mixed race relationships are subject to various tensions and pressures, but that's nothing compared to how it was in 1968. This isn't as successful putting these issues in perspective as when it deals with the complex relationship of Calogero and his "two fathers."

De Niro successfully varies the tone, keeping it light and playful at times, dark and somber at others. *A Bronx Tale* is his triumph, and a testimony that all those years of watching the best in the business have borne fruit. If what is yet to come has any of the promise shown by this debut, we may be witnessing the birth of yet another directing talent.

HIGHLY RECOMMENDED

Buffalo Soldiers [United States/United Kingdom/Germany, 2001]

Starring: Joaquin Phoenix, Ed Harris, Scott Glenn, Anna Paquin, Elizabeth McGovern, Michael Pena, Leon Robinson, Dean Stockwell Director: Gregor Jordan Screenplay: Robert O'Connor and Eric Axel Weiss & Nora Maccoby, based on the book by O'Connor Running Time: 1:38 Rated: R (Violence, profanity, sex, drug use) Theatrical Aspect Ratio: 2.35:1

Buffalo Soldiers takes place at the time of the fall of the Berlin War, when the Cold War was coming to an end. The events center around a group of American soldiers on duty in West Germany, who have little more to do than kill time. Special Fourth Class soldier Elwood (Joaquin Phoenix) is the local king of the black market. He has the slow-witted base commander, Colonel Berman (Ed Harris), wrapped around his finger, and he can get away with anything he wants — including having sex with Berman's wife (Elizabeth McGovern). There are three things Elwood loves about Germany: his car, the lack of a speed limit on the autobahn, and "a black market for anything [he]

can get [his] hands on." Along with his cohorts, Garcia (Michael Pena) and Stoney (Leon Robinson), he comes upon a cache of abandoned weapons that he sees as his ticket to wealth. But there's a problem: The new Top Sergeant, the no-nonsense Robert K. Lee (Scott Glenn), won't play ball and won't take a bribe. So Elwood has to find a way around him — and what better way than by dating his daughter, Robyn (Anna Paquin)? The plan, of course, blows up in his face — but irony steps in to save the day.

Buffalo Soldiers is not intended to be an exposé of how American soldiers spent their days and hours during peacetime, nor is it intended to be an attack on the U.S. military. It's not a cautionary tale or a morality play. Instead, it's a biting, black satire that takes full advantage of the absurdity of the situation. Without the draft, many of the people stuck in Germany were there as an alterative to spending time in jail. The unit depicted in *Buffalo Soldiers* isn't made up of gung-ho heroes, but of men whose lives are all about finding distractions.

Buffalo Soldiers represents a nice slice-of-life movie about some of the things that may or may not have happened 15 years ago in Western Europe. Certainly, black marketeering has always gone hand-in-hand with the military, and it's easy to see how a group of largely uneducated men could find allure in making a quick buck, both to line their pockets and to alleviate the boredom. Director Gregor Jordan sees *Buffalo Soldiers* as a comedy, and it comes across as such. The movie is frequently funny, sometimes in the most unexpected of places. It's an enjoyable and occasionally thought-provoking motion picture whose viewership should not be diminished by the unfortunate and inaccurate "anti-American" label it has been given in some quarters. **RECOMMENDED**

Bully [2001]

Starring: Brad Renfro, Rachel Miner, Nick Stahl, Bijou Phillips, Leo Fitzpatrick Director: Larry Clark Screenplay: Zachary Long, Roger Pullis, based on the book by Jim Schutze Running Time: 1:52 Rated: No MPAA Rating (Nudity, sex, violence, profanity, drug use) Theatrical Aspect Ratio: 1.85:1

Nearly every neighborhood has a bully, and some are worse than others. In the Hollywood, Florida suburb where Marty Puccio (Brad Rendfro) and his family live, that bully is Marty's "best friend," Bobby Kent (Nick Stahl). Bobby is a smart boy with a bright future — he gets good grades and is college-bound. But he has a dark side. He constantly abuses and humiliates Marty, and often displays an unchecked penchant for sexual violence. He likes rough sex, and has acquired a taste for rape. He's the kind of person who used to be known as a "bad seed."

Individually, none of the characters arrayed against Bobby would be capable of a homicidal act. Marty has spent so much time enduring Bobby's taunts and torments that it has become second nature to him. Lisa (Rachel Miner), Marty's girlfriend, has self-esteem problems. Lisa's pal, Ali (Bijou Phillips), is into kinky sex, and her friends, Donny (Michael Pitt) and Heather (Kelli Garner), are in constant pursuit of a drug-related high. Finally, there's Derek (Daniel Franzese), Lisa's neighbor and "protector," who spends most of his free time playing video games. All 6 are harmless on their own, but, when put together with a common goal — to kill Bobby — they become lethal.

These are teenagers who, instead of acting to better themselves, are content to be carried by the inertia of their wasted lives. When the idea of killing Bobby is broached, Lisa, Marty, and the others are galvanized. The murder, as viewed from afar, gives them the opportunity to break the monotony of their existences. They mark the approaching event much as they would a holiday — with excitement and anticipation.

Clark's brutal style is mostly successful, although there are some minor miscues along the way. In one scene, he puts the camera in the midst of a group of characters and rotates it for a needlessly long period of time, creating a dizzying effect. This is as close as I have ever come to being motion sick in a movie theater. *Bully* does not shy from shocking scenes — there is a lot of graphic simulated sex, full frontal nudity, and unvarnished violence. Had the movie been submitted to the MPAA for classification (which it was not), there's no doubt it would have received an NC-17.

Bully is one of those films that stays with you long after you have left the theater. It isn't a perfect motion picture, but it is a powerful one, and leaves a lasting impression. Adapted from Jim Schutze's "true crime" novel, *Bully* takes a seemingly straightforward tale of revenge and turns it into a cautionary narrative offering a few dark psychological insights. For those who can stomach its bleak vantage point, it is not to be missed. **HIGHLY RECOMMENDED**

The Butcher Boy [Ireland/United States, 1998]

Starring: Eamonn Owens, Stephen Rea, Fiona Shaw, Alan Boyle
Director: **Neil Jordan** Screenplay: Patrick McCabe and Neil Jordan
based on the novel by Patrick McCabe Running Time: 1:48 Rated: R
(Violence, profanity) Theatrical Aspect Ratio: **1.85:1**

The Butcher Boy takes place during the early 1960s, when the fear of atomic obliteration was on everyone's mind, even the denizens of out-of-the-way villages like the one pictured here. Twelve-year-old Francie Brady (Eamonn Owens) is the local bully. He and his best friend, Joe (Alan Boyle), delight in tormenting other kids, especially the shy Philip (Andrew Fullerton), whose mother, Mrs. Nugent (Fiona Shaw), is Francie's personal nemesis. According to him, everything that's bad in the world can be traced back to her. Meanwhile, Francie's home life is less-than-ideal. His mother (Aisling O'Sullivan) is on the verge of a breakdown, and his father (Stephen Rea), "the best drinker in the town," is frequently drunk and abusive.

At first, we view Francie as a fairly typical product of a dysfunctional home, but it soon becomes apparent that his problems run much deeper. This isn't the story of a prankster who finds redemption in a Dickensian fashion — it's a darker, more ominous tale about a boy whose hostile surroundings feed his inner anger and paranoia and turn him into an amoral monster. Most coming-of-age films are about kids triumphing by overcoming adversity. *The Butcher Boy* shows what happens when a child fights back not by bettering himself, but by lashing out at others.

Neil Jordan presents *The Butcher Boy* as more of a black comedy than a tragedy. Francie's internal monologues (the film is infected with the dreaded voiceover narrative) are sometimes corrosively funny, especially his descriptions of certain characters. He shows contempt for just about everyone except his best friend, Joe, and, at times, his mother and father. By playing up the most absurd aspect of almost every situation, Jordan manages to find the humor in even the most horrific sequences.

Without a doubt, Jordan has a good sense of time and place, and uses it to the film's advantage. This is a world where people go about their daily work under the constant threat of nuclear annihilation (the Cuban missile crisis occurs during the course of the film). The accepted treatment for psychiatric patients is shock therapy. And the influence of Catholicism is all-pervasive.

Jordan's occasional use of preposterous images and magic realism are designed to draw us into Francie's world. In reality, however, they accomplish the opposite by erecting an artificial barrier between the audience and the character. There's no debating that Francie is a fascinating individual, or that newcomer Eamonn Owens gives an amazing performance, but this boy doesn't burrow under our skin in the same way that the two girls from *Heavenly Creatures* (a not entirely dissimilar film) do. We see Francie's explosive rage clinically, from a distance. We do not experience or participate in it, and that keeps *The Butcher Boy* from being a truly memorable motion picture. **RECOMMENDED**

Camera Buff (Amator) [Poland, 1979]

Starring: Jerzy Stuhr, Malgorzata Zabkowska, Ewa Pokas, Stefan Czyzewski Director: Krzysztof Kieslowski Screenplay: Krzysztof Kieslowski and Jerzy Stuhr Running Time: 1:52 Rated: No MPAA Rating (Mature themes, sex) Theatrical Aspect Ratio: 1.33:1 In Polish with subtitles

Call *Camera Buff* a case of art imitating life. Although director Krzysztof Kieslowski admitted that this film doesn't tell his own story it will undoubtedly strike a responsive chord with many amateur and professional film makers. Although the film deals with serious themes: obsession, censorship, and the battle between artistic integrity and personal sacrifice, Kieslowski never allows the proceedings to grow maudlin or overly-introspective. The script is peppered with serio-comic incidents that leaven what could have been a staid, sober story.

The main character, Filip Mosz, is played by Jerzy Stuhr. In anticipation of his new baby's birth, Filip spends 2 months' pay on an 8mm camera to record of his child's first few years. But, from the moment he looks through the lens, Filip is hooked. He begins filming almost anything that moves. His boss at the factory (Stefan Czyzewski) appoints Filip as the establishment's official chronicler. At first, the manager is pleased with the films, and he allows Filip to proceed as he sees best. But, when the films begin to attract attention, winning amateur prizes and appearing on TV shows, the manager attempts to restrict Filip's work. Heedless of the personal cost (his wife leaves him) and risking his job, Filip pushes forward, only to stumble into a trap set for him by the factory's management. In the end, he faces a painful choice: destroy his own work or allow it to be used for a purpose he cannot condone.

All the dilemmas in *Camera Buff* center on Filip. He becomes so obsessed with film making that he neglects his family, eventually losing not only his wife, but his young daughter and unborn child. He also confronts censorship when his manager demands that scenes be edited out to make a film more complimentary to the factory. Eventually, when his employers attempt to suppress an entire movie and determine the content of another, Filip faces a crisis of conscience. Why does he make films? And do they mean anything if they are reduced to propaganda pieces instead of genuine depictions of the world as he sees it? When his immediate boss is fired because of a film's content, Filip finally sees how serious his "harmless" hobby has become.

This all sounds rather grim, but, perhaps surprisingly, *Camera Buff* may be the funniest of Kieslowski's features. None of the humor is excessive or intrusive, but there are moments of the absurd that maintain a relaxed tone, and Filip's enthusiasm is infectious. Kieslowski isn't attempting to bludgeon us with preachy morality lessons; his intent is to explore certain issues in an entertaining manner. And, while *Camera Buff* lacks some of the artistry evident in the director's later projects, it's worth seeing not only as an example of Kieslowski's early work, but as an important film in its own right. **HIGHLY RECOMMENDED**

Career Girls [United Kingdom, 1997]

Starring: Katrin Cartlidge, Lynda Steadman, Kate Byers, Mark Benton, Joe Tucker Director: Mike Leigh Screenplay: Mike Leigh Running Time: 1:28 Rated: R (Profanity, sexual situations, brief nudity) Theatrical Aspect Ratio: 1.66:1

Simplicity is *Career Girls*' greatest asset. Because the plot is so threadbare, it allows us to delve more deeply into the personalities of the two protagonists. They are Hannah (Katrin Cartlidge) and Annie (Lynda Steadman), a pair of 30-ish former university roommates-turned-business women who are spending a weekend together in London. Once, Hannah and Annie were inseparable, but, since completing their terms at college 6 years ago, they have become victims of the gulf that time and distance often build.

Mike Leigh uses the "fly on the wall" perspective to give us insights into the most mundane aspects of the women's weekend. We see them eating, drinking, and getting ready for bed. Their topics of conversation are often banal, but the intelligence of the writing keeps us involved even when the subject matter is stale. And, to give us a sense of perspective about Hannah and Annie's past, Leigh employs numerous flashbacks to allow us to share their memories.

The reunion is presented believably, with the initial awkwardness and tension giving way to the gradual recapturing of an easy familiarity. Reunions give us a chance to take a step back and examine how the years have altered our lives and those of others. This is the feeling that Leigh has captured here, by introducing not only Hannah and Annie, but 3 other important individuals from their past: the "idiot savant" Ricky (Mark Benton), the callous Adrian (Joe Tucker), and another former roommate, Claire (Kate Byers). Coincidence also plays a role in *Career Girls*, although Leigh seems a little self-conscious using this device, since he keeps mentioning it.

Career Girls is peppered with humor, although some of the comedy is underpinned by a bittersweet aura. The most memorable of this film's episodes has Hannah and Annie, who are looking at expensive condos without any intention of buying, encountering a sleazy owner who seems as interested in getting them into bed as in showing off his high-rise domicile.

Career Girls is a wonderful diversion — expert film making that's all the more effective because it seems so natural and effortless. The movie effectively transforms two strangers into people worth caring about, *Career Girls* can be regarded as nothing less than a success. **RECOMMENDED**

Carried Away [1996]

Starring: Dennis Hopper, Amy Locane, Amy Irving, Gary Busey, Hal Holbrook, Julie Harris Director: Bruno Barreto Screenplay: Ed Jones and Dale Herd based on the novel *Farmer* by Jim Harrison Running Time: 1:44 Rated: R (Nudity, sex, profanity) Theatrical Aspect Ratio: 1.85:1

It's difficult to say what *Carried Away* is primarily about, because it deals with so many issues: how we view sexuality, how love compares to lust, and how everyone — men and women — have a tendency to become stale and complacent with the approach of late middle age. Joseph Svenden (Dennis Hopper) knows about this latter issue first-hand. At age 47, he's dissatisfied with his life, but doesn't know what to do about it. He's engaged to a woman, Rosalee Henson (Amy Irving), whom he has loved since high school, but something lifeless in their relationship keeps him from actually tying the knot. He hasn't found anything that he's truly good at — he's a mediocre teacher and a worse farmer. He lives with his dying mother (Julie Harris) in the house where he has spent his entire life. Joseph is trapped, both in an infirm body, and in his village.

Relief — or at least a modicum of excitement — arrives in the person of Catherine Wheeler (Amy Locane), a sexually precocious 17-year old with a killer body. Her parents move into one of Joseph's neighboring houses, and she becomes his student at the small two-classroom school where he teaches. In her own way, Catherine feels as trapped as Joseph. Her mother is a drunk and her father is more interested in shooting pheasants than caring for her. So, looking for an escape, she discovers her teacher, whom she clumsily seduces. Joseph is quite willing, and, though he feels guilty at first, he gradually comes to view his relationship with Catherine as a liberating experience . . . until she begins to fantasize about marrying him.

In addition to Hopper's fine job, the principal supporting players are solid. Amy Irving bears all (literally and figuratively) in a performance of surprising emotional depth. Rosealee is a sad figure who, like Joseph, wants something that she doesn't understand and can't put into words. As Catherine, Amy Locane (*Blue Sky*) exudes not only sexuality, but vulnerability. Locane offers us glimpses of the hurt, confused child carefully concealed beneath the brazen exterior. Gary Busey, as Catherine's father, is uncharacteristically restrained, and Hal Holbrook provides most of the comic relief as a small town doctor.

Although Catherine is developed as a real character with real problems, *Carried Away* isn't as much about her as it is about Joseph's reaction to her. This is, after all, his story. Although these two profess to love one another, they are both lying, perhaps as much to themselves as to each other. Their reasons for having sex are far more complex than simple "love," and Barreto's film has the courage to examine those reasons. *Carried Away* is erotic, but it's also thoughtful and intelligent, and, coupled with Hopper's extraordinary performance, that's reason enough to be carried away by this motion picture. **HIGHLY RECOMMENDED**

Carrington [United Kingdom, 1995]

Starring: Emma Thompson, Jonathan Pryce, Steven Waddington, Samuel West, Rufus Sewell Director: Christopher Hampton Screenplay: Christopher Hampton based on the book *Lytton Strachey* by Michael Holroyd Running Time: 2:02 Rated: R (Mature themes, sex, violence, discreet nudity) Theatrical Aspect Ratio: 1.85:1

Screenwriter Christopher Hampton makes a successful directorial debut with this picture, an artistic and emotional examination of the 17-year liaison between Dora Carrington (Emma Thompson) and Lytton Strachey (Jonathan Pryce). *Carrington* is a special love story that challenges the intellect with as much vigor as it touches the heart. Hampton shows that it's possible to have souls in synch even when their sexuality is incompatible. Though Dora, a heterosexual woman who didn't lose her virginity until she was in her 20s, and Strachey, an avowed homosexual, each had an assortment of male bed partners, they were intensely devoted to each other with a passion that was "all absorbing" and "self-abasing." Even without a sexual element, their love was transcendent, majestic, and ultimately tragic, for one could not live without the other.

Lytton Strachey was born in 1880, 15 years before Dora Carrington. The two met shortly after the onset of World War I. At that point, he was a confirmed pacifist; she wanted nothing more than to be a man so that she could fight. The 1918 publication of *Eminent Victorians* cemented Strachey's literary reputation. Dora, on the other hand, remained a little-known talent during her lifetime, since she painted just for herself and Strachey, not to exhibit or sell.

Carrington is divided into 6 chapters, most named after the men who float in and out of the title character's life. Of course, Strachey is there all the time, a constant supportive and loving presence. In one segment, Dora loses her virginity to ardent suitor Mark Gertler (Rufus Sewell). In another, she marries Ralph Partridge (Steven Waddington), primarily because Strachey is attracted to him. This leads to a bizarre triangle where only one relationship is consummated.

The film is beautifully photographed, with each scene carefully composed. One of *Carrington*'s most poignant images is of Dora sitting outside of Ham Spray House at night. As she gazes in through lighted windows at the various couplings taking place, it's possible to feel her loneliness. The stunning sequence is made all the more impressive by the slow, deliberate manner in which it was filmed.

Thompson, as always, is a joy to behold. Here, with a Buster Brown haircut, the actress gives a carefully restrained, subtly nuanced performance. The versatile Jonathan Pryce is every bit Thompson's equal. It's a rare pleasure to watch two top-notch equals play off one another. There is tangible chemistry between them, although not of the conventional sort.

Carrington's tone is not one of restraint. Strachey and Dora don't have sex, but their love is definitely neither unrequited nor unacknowledged. This is a passionate, although never gratuitous, motion picture, with a clear view of how it wants to portray its

characters and their complex relationship. The result is a memorable portrait of two of history's most unique lovers. **HIGHLY RECOMMENDED**

Casino [1995]

Starring: Robert De Niro, Joe Pesci, Sharon Stone, Don Rickles, James Woods Director: Martin Scorsese Screenplay: Nicholas Pileggi & Martin Scorsese based on the book by Nicholas Pileggi Running Time: 2:58 Rated: R (Violence, profanity, drug use, sexual situations) Theatrical Aspect Ratio: 2.35:1

Casino opens with short sequence in 1983 before moving on to the meat of the story, which is related through flashbacks. Director Martin Scorsese makes heavy use of voiceovers, employing disembodied monologues by both lead actors — Robert De Niro and Joe Pesci — to fill in gaps. The sheer volume of words sporadically detracts from character development, but it is integrated successfully enough not to seem overly intrusive. While the intelligence and wit of the voiceovers makes them palatable, such nonstop talking isn't always the best way to convey a story — the temptation to *tell* something, rather than *show* it, is too great.

During its 3-hour running time, *Casino* tells the story of two men's intermingled lives. Sam "Ace" Rothstein (Robert De Niro) was a gambler who never lost. He researched all his bets carefully, and rarely made a bad pick. His winning tendencies gained him popularity and favor with the local mob, who used Nicky Santoro (Joe Pesci) to shadow and protect him. Now that Ace has moved to Vegas to manage the Tangiers Casino, Nicky isn't far behind. And, while the two gravitate to opposite sides of the law, with Ace keeping his fingers clean and Nicky taking over the local crime scene, their paths continue to cross, and their encounters become increasingly less friendly. Stirred into the mix is Ace's girlfriend, Ginger (Sharon Stone), an expert hustler who attracts men like flies. Although she agrees to marry Ace, she continues a liaison with her former pimp (James Woods) while encouraging Nicky's affections.

Supporting players include a restrained James Woods, comedian Don Rickles in a serious role, Alan King (also playing it straight), and Kevin Pollak. Scorsese's mother has a brief (and very funny) appearance as the no-nonsense parent of a bumbling, small-time gangster. And faces associated with Vegas, like Steve Allen, Frankie Avalon, Jayne Meadows, and Jerry Vale, have cameos.

Casino was filmed in Las Vegas, and this shows in

the splashiness and energy of nearly every scene. By using gaudy costumes and a '70s soundtrack, Scorsese takes us back some two decades. Starting with the vivid opening credits *Casino* sparkles like its fake diamond of a host city. The cinematography, which uses surprisingly few tricks other than freeze-framing to emphasize key moments, is crisp and clean.

By now, audiences have come to expect forceful films from Martin Scorsese. With *Casino,* he doesn't disappoint. The movie is long, but, with a fast-moving storyline, escalating tension, and surprisingly robust humor, the 3 hours move quickly. Several flaws, mostly minor, keep *Casino* on a plateau slightly below that of the director's best (*Mean Streets, Raging Bull, Taxi Driver, Goodfellas*), but this is worth making an effort to see. **HIGHLY RECOMMENDED**

The Cement Garden [France/Germany/United Kingdom, 1993]

Starring: Andrew Robertson, Charlotte Gainsbourg, Alice Coultard, Ned Birkin, Sinead Cusack   Director: Andrew Birkin
Screenplay: Andrew Birkin based on the novel by Ian McEwan
Running Time: 1:45   Rated: No MPAA Rating (Mature themes, nudity, sex, language)   Theatrical Aspect Ratio: 1.66:1

Considering the rancid, nightmarish quality of his books, it's somewhat amazing that a writer like British author Ian McEwan could have 3 of his works filmed by now. In addition to *The Cement Garden, The Comfort of Strangers* has been made into a movie (by Paul Schrader in 1991), and *The Innocent* (directed by John Schlesinger) is due to be released. The most controversial of these, however, is *The Cement Garden,* principally because of its subject matter: teenage incest.

An entire family is together at the outset of the film, but not for long. After the father collapses and dies of a heart attack, the mother (Sinead Cusack) becomes confined to bed, stricken by a mysterious and debilitating illness. This leaves the eldest sister and brother, Julie (Charlotte Gainsbourg) and Jack (Andrew Robertson), to care for their younger siblings, Sue (Alice Coultard) and Tom (Ned Birkin). These 4 are not what most people would define as "normal." Julie and Jack are drawn to each other by a forbidden sexual attraction that neither can deny, despite the obvious taboo.

The incest issue is dealt with in a straightforward and non-prurient fashion. Director Andrew Birkin is not attempting to shock his audience, but rather to candidly represent the factors that lead to this relationship. His style is sensitive, not exploitative, which makes all the difference to the success of *The Cement Garden.* The film works because the characters are alive, and morality is shown to be relative.

As dark as the subject matter is, Birkin still culls laughter from the audience. This isn't the nervous tittering of uncomfortable viewers, but a genuine reaction. Much of the humor is relatively harmless, although a few of the jokes are off-color.

The relationship between Jack and Julie holds the film together. This is a mutual seduction, and both play their parts. Julie has all the responsibility in the household, while Jack, on the other hand, gets away with doing as little as he can, preferring to spend his time masturbating in secret places or admiring himself in a mirror. Julie is a more likable character than her brother, but only because it's difficult to love a narcissist.

The Cement Garden makes no apologies. The quality of fascination is as much a credit to those producing the film as to the unorthodox — and grim — central theme. *The Cement Garden* is occasionally grotesque, frequently disturbing, and, at times, surprisingly humorous. No matter what else it may be, however, this movie is always thought-provoking, and it's hard to imagine anyone leaving without the strongest of opinions. **HIGHLY RECOMMENDED**

Central Station [Brazil, 1998]

Starring: Fernanda Montenegro, Vinicius de Oliveira, Marilia Pera, Soia Lira   Director: Walter Salles   Screenplay: Joao Emanuel Carneiro, Marcos Bernstein   Running Time: 1:46   Rated: PG-13 (Profanity, mature themes)   Theatrical Aspect Ratio: 2.35:1   In Portuguese with subtitles

Walter Salles' *Central Station* opens inside a large train station in Rio de Janeiro, where Dora (Fernanda Montenegro) is going about her daily job. At a dollar's price, she will write a letter for one of the many illiterate passers-by in the station, then seal it in an addressed envelope. When it comes to mailing the letters, however, Dora is not trustworthy. Based on an arbitrary criteria, she posts some letters, tears up others, and stashes a few in a drawer. Dora doesn't care when she betrays a trust; she has made the determination of what's best, and decides whether or not to send a letter based on that judgment. She stands aloof and uninvolved, making her assessments dispassionately. Until she meets Josue (Vinicius de Oliveira).

Josue is the 9-year-old son of a woman who dictates a letter to Dora. In it, she asks the boy's father if they can be reunited. When leaving the station afterwards, the woman is struck by a bus and killed. Josue, with nowhere to go, begins to loiter around the station, acting pugnacious and withdrawn. His plight stirs something in Dora, who brings him home, then sells him to an adoption agency. However, when her best friend notes that the organization may be a front for organ thieves, Dora kidnaps the boy from the agency, then goes on a journey with him, searching for his father.

Regardless of the political issues the film touches upon or its travelogue aspect, the real heart of *Central Station* is the relationship between Dora and Josue. As in the best of this sub-genre of movies, the two change each other in profound ways. Dora fills the maternal role left vacant in the boy's life by the unexpected demise of his mother. In turn, her cynicism melts away and she discovers that she still retains the capacity to love, to sacrifice. Salles develops the relationship perfectly. It is certainly a familiar story, but in this context, it seems fresh.

The two leads both do superlative work. Fernanda Montenegro believably conveys the changes in Dora as her relationship with Josue transforms her inner self. It's a finely-tuned portrayal that doesn't ask the audience to accept any sudden or hard-to-swallow shifts in behavior. Dora's rebirth is gradual. Newcomer Vinicius de Oliveira doesn't have as complex as role, but his performance as a young, lost boy touches the heart. Together, the two actors create a palpable, and very special, bond.

Central Station is both literate and emotionally-powerful — an increasingly rare combination. It does not rely upon camera tricks or overwrought performances to touch the viewer. There's manipulation going on here, but it's subtle and skillful, and, as a result, we don't feel like our heartstrings are being twisted and pulled by an unseen puppeteer. For that reason, *Central Station* is well worth seeing, especially if you're in the mood for an affecting drama.

RECOMMENDED

Character (Karakter) [Netherlands, 1997]

Starring: Fedja Van Huet, Jan Decleir, Betty Schuurman, Victor Low, Tamar van den Dop, Hans Kesting   Director: Mike van Diem
Screenplay: Mike van Diem, Laurens Geels, Ruud van Megen based on the novel by Ferdinand Bordewijk   Running Time: 2:00   Rated: R (Violence, sexuality)   Theatrical Aspect Ratio: 1.85:1   In Dutch with subtitles

Character is a fine motion picture about the relationships within a dysfunctional family in the Netherlands during the 1930s. The film tells the story of Katadreuffe (Fedja Van Huet), a young man who has made his mark in the world despite the conspiracy of numerous, diverse forces to keep him suppressed. As a child, he wasn't an orphan, but he might as well have been. His unmarried mother, Joba (Betty Schuurman), is a harsh, unloving woman who rarely speaks to her son. His father, Dreverhaven (Jan Decleir), is the city's most detested bailiff. After being rejected by Joba, Dreverhaven wants nothing to do with his son, and works actively to place obstacles in his path. The struggle between Katadreuffe and Dreverhaven turns into a personal war of attrition. This fuels Katadreuffe's single-minded goal to rise through the legal system, but costs him a chance at true happiness.

Through his entire life, Katadreuffe is impelled by a need to escape from the shame of his birth and upbringing. He uses Dreverhaven's contempt as a catalyst to push himself harder. Dr. De Gankelaar (Victor Low), a lawyer who represents Katadreuffe in a bankruptcy hearing, sees great potential in the young man, and takes him on as an assistant. From there, using money borrowed from Dreverhaven's bank, Katadreuffe applies himself exclusively to his studies in law.

Although Katadreuffe is *Character*'s protagonist, the most fascinating individual in the film is Dreverhaven, who is played with a combination of malice and world-weariness by veteran actor Jan Decleir (*Antonia's Line*). Dreverhaven's motives are far more complex than those of a typical villain. Underneath his cold, harsh exterior, he is tortured by inner demons. His feelings towards his son are unclear — a mixture of shame, anger, bitterness, and, curiously, perhaps even pride. He claims that his financial assault is designed to strengthen Katadreuffe's character, but it's really an attempt to assert control and prove his superiority. Despite all of his money and his respected position in society, Dreverhaven is filled with self-loathing and disgust with the odious process of living. He risks his life frequently, causing many to wonder whether he's brave or seeking his own death.

Dickensian elements abound, from the travails of the poverty-stricken masses to the struggles of an (almost) orphan. Director Mike van Diem has crafted the look of Rotterdam in the 1930s to resemble London of a century earlier. Politics play a small-but-important role in the film as Katadreuffe enjoys a brief flirtation with the communist movement, which stands in direct opposition to Dreverhaven and all that he stands for. Ultimately, everything comes down to the relationship between Katadreuffe and Dreverhaven, and the manner in which their constant power struggle shapes their futures.

RECOMMENDED

Chariots of Fire [United Kingdom, 1981]

Starring: Ben Cross, Ian Charleson, Nigel Havers, Nicholas Farrell, Ian Holm, John Gielgud Director: Hugh Hudson Screenplay: Colin Welland Running Time: 2:04 Rated: PG (Nothing offensive) Theatrical Aspect Ratio: 1.85:1

Chariots of Fire, the Oscar-winning 1981 film, transports us to the 1924 Olympics, and, in the process, highlights such commendable qualities as commitment, perseverance, and fraternity. That's not to say that winning isn't important to the competitors in Hugh Hudson's film. On the contrary, for British track stars Harold Abrahams (Ben Cross) and Eric Lidell (Ian Charleson), it's a paramount concern, but neither is so obsessed by their goal that they lose sight of the larger picture. Eric is a devout Christian who runs because he believes it glorifies God. Harold is a Jew who competes as a way of proving his worth. Both are driven by an inner fire, and have nothing but respect for their rivals.

Chariots of Fire tells the story of the British triumphs at the 1924 Olympics, where the UK representatives took a number of medals over the heavily-favored Americans. With Abrahams and Lidell leading the way, the British track team had one of their best-ever showings. This film traces the two principal athletes' paths to the Paris games, where their on-field successes form a surprisingly low-key climax. *Chariots of Fire* doesn't rely on worn-out sports film clichés; it's more interested in motivation and character development. Yes, it's important to know that Abrahams and Lidell win, but the real meat of the story is contained in what leads up to the races. Like in Sylvester Stallone's first *Rocky*, it's possible to claim victory before the competition begins — Lidell because he has holds fast to his beliefs and Abrahams because gives all he has to give.

There's barely a whiff of melodrama in *Chariots of Fire*, which makes the film-watching experience all the more effective — director Hugh Hudson shows respect for the integrity of his material and the intelligence of his audience. The absence of mawkish moments provides the narrative with a genuine quality that supports its factual background. Not only do we care about the characters, but we accept that they really existed. In fact, the entire production claims that same sense of verisimilitude. Most sports movies rely on nostalgia and adrenaline — *Chariots of Fire* stands on strong writing, direction, and acting. Appreciation of this picture doesn't demand a love of sports, merely an understanding of human nature.

HIGHLY RECOMMENDED

Children of Heaven (Bacheha-Ye aseman) [Iran, 1997]

Starring: Mohammad Amir Naji, Amir Farrokh Hashemian, Bahare Seddiqi Director: Majid Majidi Screenplay: Majid Majidi Running Time: 1:28 Rated: PG (Mild profanity) Theatrical Aspect Ratio: 1.85:1 In Farsi with subtitles

Children of Heaven opens in the poor quarter of an Iranian city. There we meet Ali (Mir Farrokh Hashemian), a 9-year-old boy going home with his sister's worn, pink shoes, which he has just taken to a cobbler for repairs. On the way, he stops at a fruit and vegetable stand to buy some potatoes. He puts the shoes down, and, while he's sorting through a bin, a rag picker mistakenly takes the shoes, thinking they're part of the stand owner's refuse. When Ali arrives home empty-handed, his 7-year-old sister, Zahra (Bahare Seddigi), is in tears. What will she wear to school?

Ali has a solution. She goes to school in the morning; he attends in the afternoon. They can share a pair of sneakers. Once her day is done, she can rush home and give the sneakers to him. Unfortunately, there's not enough time for the swap, and Ali arrives late to his first class. Meanwhile, on a day off, he accompanies his father (Amir Naji) to the city's wealthy section in search of work as a gardener — work that will pay enough to give the family a little extra money. And, at school, Ali discovers a possible solution to the shoe dilemma. Third place in a foot race is a pair of new sneakers (first and second prize are more lucrative, but Ali has no interest in them). All Ali has to do is beat out several hundred children and lose to only two, and his sister will be happy.

There are a number of reasons to like *Children of Heaven*, not the least of which is its inherent sweetness. Unlike many American movie kids, Ali and Zahara truly care for one another. Ali is deeply upset about losing the shoes, and the two siblings work together to find a solution without placing an additional financial burden upon their beleaguered parents. Seeing the film in North America also offers the fascination of looking through a window at a different culture and recognizing that it's not fundamentally different from our own.

The film's single weakness is the central conceit, which seems contrived. There's a sense of falseness in the way Ali loses his sister's shoes — a few too many coincidences occur for the viewer to miss the screenwriter's hand at work. Ironically, the awkwardness with which Majidi starts out his tale stands out only because the majority of the movie is so carefully constructed. In a big, flashy, Hollywood-style production, this kind of mistake wouldn't be noticed, but, in such a low-key picture, it calls attention to itself.

Children of Heaven isn't about Zahra's lost shoes, Dad's difficulty finding work, or Ali's placement in the race. It's about how those things define one family, and why the characters make worthwhile companions for 90 minutes of our time. There's certainly nothing epic about Majidi's narrative, but sometimes, as in *Children of Heaven,* an inconsequential and intimate story can provide a satisfying emotional payoff. **RECOMMENDED**

The Cider House Rules [1999]

Starring: Tobey Maguire, Charlize Theron, Delroy Lindo, Paul Rudd, Michael Caine Director: Lasse Hallström Screenplay: John Irving, based on his novel Running Time: 2:11 Rated: PG-13 (Sexual situations, violence) Theatrical Aspect Ratio: 2.35:1

Most of Lasse Hallström's *The Cider House Rules* transpires during the mid-1940s in an America that has added its strength to the Allied forces. Homer Wells (Tobey Maguire) is ineligible to join the military because of a bad heart. He has spent his entire life at an orphanage in St. Clouds, Maine as the special project of Dr. Wilbur Larch (Michael Caine), who sees great promise in the boy and imparts valuable medical knowledge to him. By the time he has reached adulthood, Homer is as good a doctor as Larch, albeit without a degree. There is also a moral divide between them: Larch will perform abortions (even though they're illegal), but Homer will not. Life changes for Homer with the arrival of Air Force officer Wally Worthington (Paul Rudd) and his girlfriend, Candy Kendall (Charlize Theron). She's at the orphanage for an abortion, and, after a brief stay, she is ready to go home. Homer chooses this moment to hitch a ride with them out of St. Clouds so he can see the world and establish a life for himself.

The script was written by John Irving and based on his novel of the same name. The impetus behind *The Cider House Rules* is Homer's search to find himself. During his time at St. Clouds, the course of his life has been mapped by the expectations of others. He is a big brother to the other orphans and a helper to Dr.

Larch, but, trapped within such an insular community, he has never had the opportunity to unlock the real Homer Wells. The arrival of Wally and Candy opens a door to the outside, and Homer rushes through it. Only after he has discovered himself can he chart his future.

The film addresses two serious issues: abortion and incest. There really aren't two sides to the latter subject, and *The Cider House Rules* doesn't pretend that there are. It shows the kind of emotional wreckage that can result from a twisted family relationship. Meanwhile, by having main characters on both sides of the abortion issue, *The Cider House Rules* manages to give the debate a reasonably balanced perspective, and the 1943 setting makes the proceedings seem more fresh than is often the case for films that tackle this subject. At first glance, it appears that Irving and Hallström may be short-changing the anti-abortion side, but, upon closer inspection, it becomes apparent that there's real sense of fairness to the film's approach. Impressively, the movie manages to make its points without resorting to sermonizing.

In a little over 2 hours, with a strong cast, an accomplished cinematographer, and a well-tuned script, Hallström has fashioned a motion picture of visual splendor and emotional depth. *The Cider House Rules* defies conventions as it successfully turns back the clock to the wartime years and tells a story that is unique, despite a number of familiar elements. Few films offer a more fulfilling experience than the one promised, and delivered, by *The Cider House Rules.* **MUST SEE**

Cinema Paradiso [Italy, 1988]

Starring: Philippe Noiret, Salvatore Cascio, Marco Leonardi, Jacques Perrin Director: Giuseppe Tornatore Screenplay: Giuseppe Tornatore Running Time (original): 2:03 Running Time (director's): 2:54 Rated: PG (Mature themes) Theatrical Aspect Ratio: 1.66:1 In Italian with subtitles

As a fatherless child, Salvatore (Salvatore Cascio) loved the movies. He would abscond with the milk money to buy admission to a matinee showing at the local theater, a small place called the Cinema Paradiso. The Paradiso became his home, and the movies, his parents. Eventually, he developed a friendship with the projectionist, Alfredo (Philippe Noiret), a lively middle-aged man who offered advice on life, romance, and how to run a movie theater. Salvatore worked as Alfredo's unpaid apprentice until the day the Paradiso burned down. When a new cinema was erected on the same site, an adolescent Salvatore (Marco Leonardi) became the projectionist.

But Alfredo, now blind because of injuries sustained in the fire, remained in the background, filling the role of confidante and mentor to the boy he loved like a son.

Once Salvatore has grown into his teens, *Cinema Paradiso* shifts from being a nostalgic celebration of movies to a traditional coming-of-age drama, complete with romantic disappointment and elation. Salvatore falls for a girl named Elena (Agnese Nano), but his deeply-felt passion isn't reciprocated. So he agonizes over the situation, seeks out Alfredo's advice, then makes a bold decision: he will stand outside of Elena's window every night until she relents. In the end, love wins out, but Salvatore's joy is eventually replaced by sadness as Elena vanishes forever from his life.

The Screen Kiss is important to *Cinema Paradiso*. Early in the film, the local priest previews each movie, using the power of his office to demand that all scenes of kissing be edited out. By the time the new Paradiso opens, however, things have changed. The priest no longer goes to the movies and kisses aren't censored. Much later, following the funeral near the end of *Cinema Paradiso*, Salvatore receives his bequest from Alfredo: a film reel containing all of the kisses removed from the movies shown at the Paradiso over the years. The deluge of concentrated ardor acts as a forceful reminder of the simple-yet-profound passion that has been absent from his life since he lost his one true love, Elena.

Thoughts about the "Director's Cut": When *Cinema Paradiso* was released in the late 1980s, the version seen by Italian movie-goers was much different than the cut shown to North American viewers. The truncated edition is still a stunning, masterful production, but it leaves the audience with a nagging question: What really happened to Elena? The answer is provided in a 35-minute sequence that never made it into the 1988 American release, but which has now been restored.

For lovers of *Cinema Paradiso*, this restored version is unquestionably a "must see." The magic and poetry of the original remain, but the added scenes fashion a different, more complete cinematic experience. For those who have never seen Tornatore's masterpiece, this is an excellent opportunity to view it for the first time. **MUST SEE**

Closer [2004]

Starring: Natalie Portman, Jude Law, Julia Roberts, Clive Owen
Director: Mike Nichols Screenplay: Patrick Marber, based on his play
Running Time: 1:40 Rated: R (Profanity, sexual situations, nudity)
Theatrical Aspect Ratio: 1.85:1

If you pay attention to Hollywood's romantic comedies, the interaction between men and women is all about love and companionship. If you instead rely upon the philosophy of *Closer*, it's all about power. *Closer* starts like a nice romantic drama, with a couple of "meet cutes" (as Roger Ebert calls them), then does a 180-degree turn and shows what happens when happily ever after rots from the inside out. It isn't just the relationships that curdle, but the characters. Their interaction becomes bitter and cynical. Sex is a tool used in power struggles and one-upmanship games. Although the word "love" is mentioned a few times, it has little place in this movie, where emotions are weaknesses to be exploited by others.

On the surface, *Closer* is the story of two couples whose infidelities rip them apart. Dan (Jude Law) and Alice (Natalie Portman) meet on the streets of London when she is hit by a car and he comes to her rescue. He takes her to a hospital, and the pair are soon living together. But Dan, an obituary writer who has penned a novel, finds himself obsessed with Anna (Julia Roberts), a photographer who takes the picture for his book jacket. He wants her, and tells her so, but she demurs when she learns he has a live-in girlfriend. "You're taken," she comments, as if that puts an end to things. Dan inadvertently introduces Larry (Clive Owen) to Anna when a practical joke (in which he pretends to be Anna in an Internet sex chat room) goes awry. The two start a romance, and are eventually married. But there's sexual chemistry between Dan and Anna, and, to a lesser extent, between Larry and Alice. Over the next four years, infidelities occur, betrayals are discovered, and all manner of ugliness ensues. From a physical standpoint, *Closer* is not a violent film. From an emotional one, it's brutal. Director Mike Nichols doesn't pull his punches. You leave the theater shaken.

In *Closer*, the actors get a chance to shine, and no one is brighter than Clive Owen. The ferocity with which Owen delivers his lines, and the restless energy he imparts to Larry, electrifies every scene that he's in. *Closer*'s two most riveting sequences involve Owen and Natalie Portman — one in an art gallery, where they first meet, and the other in a strip club, where he has all the money but she has the power, and uses it. Portman, in what has been called her first truly adult role (it's certainly nowhere close to Queen Amidala), is also very, very good. Like Owen, she must essay a character who undergoes a complete personality transformation — from vulnerable waif to ice queen seductress. There's a rawness and courage to her work.

Movies that look deeply into the human soul and uncover putrefaction are hard sells. But they are also some of the most fascinating films to be found. Are Nichols and Patrick Marber's characters too cynically drawn? Perhaps. Do they occasionally seem like marionettes manipulated by a clever writer? Yes. But those things don't diminish the film's compelling emotional qualities. *Closer* is powerful and disturbing stuff. It is not life affirming, and it's not for those who want to leave a movie theater uplifted and convinced that fairy tale endings can happen. **HIGHLY RECOMMENDED**

Cobb [1994]

Starring: Tommy Lee Jones, Robert Wuhl, Lolita Davidovich Director: Ron Shelton Screenplay: Ron Shelton based on *Cobb: A Biography* by Al Stump Running Time: 2:08 Rated: R (Violence, language, nudity) Theatrical Aspect Ratio: 2.35:1

A notorious drunkard, bigot, and womanizer, the "Georgia Peach" had few qualities to praise other than his ability to hit a baseball. He claimed to be misunderstood, but the sad truth is that he was understood too well. Described at various times as "difficult at best, psychotic at worst" and someone whose "brooding soul . . . bubbled with violence," Ty Cobb represented the kind of man who could be admired only from a distance — the farther the better.

In 1960, with death stalking him, Cobb (Tommy Lee Jones) decides that he wants his story told. To write this tale of a "prince among men," he recruits sportswriter Al Stump (Robert Wuhl) to do the typing. At first, Stump is ecstatic at the opportunity to spend days on end with the greatest baseball player of all time — until he meets him, that is. Cobb's poisonous personality quickly convinces him that little pleasure will be derived from the task. Yet, despite continual verbal and physical abuse, Stump stays with Cobb, and even drives him across country from his Nevada home to Cooperstown. Friendship is never the lure, however; Stump is seduced by the need to understand greatness. And, in the end, he compromises his principles to capture his own small measure of it.

With a lead character as abrasive as they come, *Cobb* is not always a pleasant movie. At times, it is

downright uncomfortable. The film is perhaps too long; much of the last half-hour feels excessive and redundant. Nevertheless, given such a forceful anti-hero, the viewer's horrified fascination lasts all 128 minutes, even to the end of the credits when Cobb declares, "Baseball is 100% of my life."

Jones' on-target portrayal of the dying athlete is mesmerizing. Robert Wuhl has considerably less screen presence, but this serves only to highlight Jones. Wuhl gives his co-star someone to play off of. There is a share of male bonding here, but not enough to turn *Cobb* into a cloying buddy picture. And, thankfully, the title character is never redeemed. Cobb remains detestable to the day of his death.

Image has little to do with reality. Tremendous statistics do not make for a tremendous person. When our heroes turn out to be less like Dale Murphy and more like Ty Cobb, we feel betrayed and slighted. On those occasions, we have only ourselves to blame because in our society, it's the .367 lifetime batting average that earns the reverence, regardless of how despicable the man holding the bat is. **RECOMMENDED**

Crooklyn [1994]

Starring: Alfre Woodard, Delroy Lindo, Zelda Harris, Carlton Williams, David Patrick Kelly Director: Spike Lee Screenplay: Joie Susannah Lee, Cinque Lee, and Spike Lee Running Time: 1:55 Rated: PG-13 (Language, mature themes)

From *Malcolm X* to *Crooklyn*, Spike Lee has moved from heavy, epic drama to something significantly more lighthearted. Instead of drifting back to the first half of this century, we're only going to 1973, a year when afros and bellbottoms were in fashion; when the Knicks won the basketball championship; and when there were enough pop tunes to fill a soundtrack.

Told from the point-of-view of 10-year-old Troy Carmichael (Zelda Harris), *Crooklyn* is the story of how one family struggles to survive and stay together. With Troy's musician dad Woody (Delroy Lindo) busy in the basement composing, the full burden of running the family and bringing home the money falls on Troy's mom, Carolyn (Alfre Woodard). This inevitably leads to tension between the two adults, and, when one particularly nasty fight explodes, Woody is out the door.

Producer/director Spike Lee has woven an evocative drama that has one major stumbling block. Two-thirds of the way through the movie, Troy goes south to visit a hyper-religious aunt. To emphasize how distorted the little girl's perception of this vacation is, Lee shoots this portion of the movie with an anamorphic lens, causing everything to seem elongated. While that's fine for short sequences, in this case it goes on for too long, becoming an annoying trick that nearly undermines the entire production.

Aside from this 20-minute detour, there aren't many overt flaws in *Crooklyn*. All but the most comic of urban violence has been removed, and we're left with a somewhat-idealized view of an early-'70s Brooklyn. Lee is as talented as any director is capturing an era, and some of the early scenes perfectly recall the mood of the time. The pop soundtrack may be a little too obvious, but it gets the job done.

Crooklyn comes to the screen with an upbeat tone and a lot of heart. The world of a child — especially one pushed all-too-soon into adulthood — is never easy, and this film captures the facets of Troy's odyssey. If Lee errs with his "Southern vacation" scenes, he recovers to fashion an ending that is both touching and hopeful. Beneath the surface of this deceptively simple motion picture lurks a keen insight. **RECOMMENDED**

The Crucible [1996]

Starring: Daniel Day-Lewis, Winona Ryder, Joan Allen, Paul Scofield
Director: Nicholas Hytner Screenplay: Arthur Miller based on his play
Running Time: 2:04 Rated: PG-13 (Mature themes, brief nudity)
Theatrical Aspect Ratio: 1.85:1

Arthur Miller's 1953 play, *The Crucible*, was written during Senator Joseph McCarthy's House Un-American Activities Committee hearings (for which Miller was called to testify in 1956). And, although the play is an historical allegory for the McCarthy period, its true power lies in its ability to be re-interpreted to fit any time period. Indeed, its fertile themes — the lure of power, the gullibility of those who believe they have a moral imperative, and the nature of truth — are universal in scope. Events such as those depicted in *The Crucible* have recurred with alarming predictability throughout human history.

The film opens with a seemingly-harmless event — Abigail Williams (Winona Ryder), Mary Warren (Karron Graves), Mercy Lewis (Kali Rocha), and several other Salem village girls attend a secret voodoo ritual in the woods. Tituba (Charlayne Woodard), a native of Barbados, presides over the ceremony, which involves drinking chicken blood, dancing naked, and casting charms to ensnare boys. However, when the local preacher, Reverend Parris (Bruce Davison),

stumbles upon the proceedings, witchcraft is suspected, and an expert in the field, Reverend Hale (Rob Campbell), is brought in to investigate.

To save themselves from the noose, which is the penalty for a witch who does not admit to consorting with the Devil, Abigail and her cohorts plead for their lives. However, they not only confess to performing witchcraft, but name other townspeople as servants of Satan. Soon, with the arrival of Judge John Danforth (Paul Scofield), the girls, now turned back to "the ways of God," are regarded as unimpeachable witnesses. Those whom they condemn are arrested, and the innocent who refuse to confess are hanged. Abigail's real reason for starting the charade is to eliminate Elizabeth Proctor (Joan Allen), the wife of John Proctor (Daniel Day Lewis), the man she loves. Although Abigail and John once had an affair, he will not abandon his wife for his former mistress, and his staunch defense of Elizabeth places him in jeopardy, especially when he accuses Danforth's court of "pulling down heaven and raising up a whore!"

In *The Crucible*, there are heroes and villains, but nothing is black and white. Shades of gray permeate every action. Abigail is the spark that ignites the inferno of mistrust; however, she is guided not by malice, but by a misplaced, obsessive love. John Proctor, the most upright man in the film, is an adulterer whose own actions indirectly lead to the tragedy. He is noble only to a point, and his character faults make him easy to identify with as a human being.

Whether on stage or on film, *The Crucible* is a powerful, thought-provoking production. This version illuminates the story's numerous strengths, resulting in a motion picture of surprising emotional and intellectual impact. **HIGHLY RECOMMENDED**

Cry, the Beloved Country [1995]

Starring: James Earl Jones, Richard Harris, Vusi Kunene, Charles
Dutton Director: Darrell James Roodt Screenplay: Ronald Harwood
based on the novel by Alan Paton Running Time: 1:48 Rated: PG-13
(Mature themes) Theatrical Aspect Ratio: 1.85:1

In the aftermath of World War II, South Africa is a divided country — a land of growing injustice where the white man prospers through the efforts of the black man, and where the majority of the wealth is in the hands of the racial minority. Whites live in beautifully-constructed mansions with immaculately-groomed gardens. Blacks are often forced to eke out an existence by turning to crime and living as squatters in a shantytown. The specter of fear looms large over everything. All men, black and white alike, feel its oppressive, pervasive influence.

In this climate, two very different men come to the city of Johannesburg. The first is a black pastor, Reverend Stephen Kumalo (James Earl Jones), who has left behind his poor community to make the journey in search of his son. The second is a white landowner, James Jarvis (Richard Harris), who has come to Johannesburg to bury his only child, Arthur, the victim of a shooting by 3 black youths, one of whom was Absalom Kumalo (Eric Miyeni), Stephen's son.

Arthur Jarvis was a well-known activist for native rights who devoted his life to improving circumstances for the blacks of Johannesburg. Whites did not understand him; blacks embraced him. Those at the Claremont African Boys Club, where he was president, loved him not only for the money he spent on the facility, but for the time he freely gave. In his writings, he spoke of South African whites as "tyrants, oppressors, and criminals."

The meat of *Cry, the Beloved Country* concerns how events in the wake of the shooting transform the lives of Stephen Kumalo and James Jarvis. Each is forced to abandon their naïveté and confront the grim truths of reality. For Stephen, this means a crisis of faith and a re-assessment of his role in the world. For James, it means coming to terms with the core of his son's beliefs and seeing his own bigotry for what it is. In the end, each gains more than he loses, yet the price of that new knowledge cuts deeply.

Rarely does a motion picture touch the heart so deeply, with no hint of artifice or manipulation. Producer Anant Singh has said he wanted to wait to film this version of *Cry, the Beloved Country* until after apartheid's death so that the new climate in South Africa could provide a more hopeful backdrop. *Cry, the Beloved Country* shows the path of tolerance and compassion that the leaders of South Africa have finally found. **MUST SEE**

Dance With Me [1998]

Starring: Vanessa L. Williams, Chayanne, Kris Kristofferson, Jane Krabowski, Beth Grant Director: Randa Haines Screenplay: Daryl Matthews Running Time: 2:06 Rated: PG (Mild profanity, mild sensuality) Theatrical Aspect Ratio: 1.85:1

Dance with Me isn't intended to be a deeply introspective look at the struggles of a man and woman to overcome their individual emotional troubles and find each other. Instead, it uses these familiar, lightweight plot elements as a foundation for the series of

colorful, energetic dance sequences that represent the real reason to see this movie. Vanessa Williams, the former Miss America-turned-singer-turned-actress, plays Ruby, a by-the-book professional dancer who's looking to win a World Latin Dancing Championship before she hangs up her shoes and costumes. Chayanne (the Latino sensation who isn't as well-known north of the Border as he is south of it) is Rafael, a free-spirited Cuban who has come to Texas in search of the father he never knew. Like Ruby, he's an accomplished dancer, but he's strictly an amateur. For him, what he does on the dance floor isn't a matter of pre-arranged moves; it's what the music tells him to do.

Ruby and Rafael fall in love. While the two stars strike a few sparks (as in the bathroom scene where Rafael is dressed only in a towel), theirs isn't a smoldering, hard-to-forget coupling. Both Williams and Chayanne are hot enough on their own, however, that the lack of palpable chemistry doesn't do irreparable harm. Anyone expecting to be swept away on the currents of a soaring love story may be a little disappointed.

Rafael is also struggling to communicate with the man he came to Texas to meet. John Burnett (Kris Kristofferson) is the father he never knew, but, while Rafael knows his sire's identity, John isn't even aware that he has a son. Meanwhile, Ruby is trying to get over the heartbreak caused by her breakup with her longtime partner, Julian (Rick Valenzuela, doing his best to outsneer Billy Zane's *Titanic* character), who also happens to be the father of her son.

The pedestrian narrative of *Dance with Me* is a necessary nuisance. One could argue that all it really succeeds in doing is taking away time from the dance sequences. The characters aren't well-developed and the drama, such as it is, is merely adequate. Fortunately, when it comes to choreography, Haines is aware of what the audience wants, and obliges with some breathtaking moments. The energy level is consistently high, and, even when we're forced to endure a painfully trite moment with John and Rafael bonding at the end of a fishing pier, we know that something delightful is just around the corner.

When I left *Dance with Me*, I was smiling. As far as feel-good movies go, this one works in spite of a bloated running length (over 2 hours) and a plot that could use an injection of originality. The dance sequences, which comprise roughly half of the screen time, have it all — great music, wonderful choreography, and attractive participants — and this makes up for many of the film's deficiencies. **RECOMMENDED**

Dancer In the Dark [Denmark/France/Sweden, 2000]
Starring: Björk, Catherine Deneuve, David Morse, Peter Stormare
Director: Lars von Trier   Screenplay: Lars von Trier   Running Time: 2:20
Rated: R (Violence, profanity)   Theatrical Aspect Ratio: 2.35:1

Dancer In the Dark takes place in Washington State during 1964. The characters all live in the same small town and many of them work at the local J. Anderson Tool Company. Selma (Björk) is a Czechoslovakian immigrant who came to the United States with her son, Gene (Vladica Kostic), to find a better life. She lives in a trailer on the property of a local policeman, Bill (David Morse), and his wife, Linda (Cara Seymour). Selma's best friend is Kathy (Catherine Deneuve), and she is courted by the shy, undemanding Jeff (Peter Stormare). When she's not working, Selma spends her time at the movies watching Hollywood musicals and practicing for a local production of *The Sound of Music*, in which she plays Maria.

Selma and Bill are close, and, late one night, they trade secrets. He is broke, and, unless he can find a way to make his mortgage payment, the bank will foreclose on his house. Not only will he lose his property, but he is sure that his materialistic wife will dump him as well. Selma, on the other hand, is going blind. She suffers from a hereditary, degenerative condition that she has passed on to Gene. There is an operation to cure it, but the procedure is expensive. Selma has been scraping together every dollar she can save so that Gene can have the surgery. When Bill hears this, he wonders if Selma's nest egg might prove to be the solution to his problem, but his plan to get the money has catastrophic consequences for everyone involved.

Lars von Trier fused in elements of an homage to old Hollywood musicals (including an overture). As a result, there are about 6 instances in which all the action stops so the characters can sing and dance their way through elaborate production numbers. Unfortunately, it doesn't always work, but it is consistently interesting. And it certainly takes a hell of a lot of guts to incorporate traditional musical elements into a dark, thought-provoking drama.

The acting standout is Björk. She is capably supported by fine performances from, in particular, David Morse as the decent-but-flawed Bill and an underused Catherine Deneuve as Kathy. For an actress of Deneuve's stature and ability, it's surprising that von Trier didn't offer her a meatier role. Cameo roles are filled by Stellan Skarsgård (whose career has gone into high gear since he appeared in *Breaking the Waves*), Udo Kier, and stage and screen veteran Joel Grey, who gets to participate in one of the song-and-dance numbers.

Lars von Trier's movies speak for themselves — loudly. The filmmaker is a talented risk-taker, and instances of failure in his features are often more invigorating than instances of success in the work of less ambitious directors. *Dancer In the Dark* does something almost inconceivable in the way it merges two disparate genres. The result represents a thought-provoking, emotionally resonant, and innovative cinematic experience. **HIGHLY RECOMMENDED**

Dangerous Beauty [1998]
Starring: Catherine McCormack, Rufus Sewell, Oliver Platt, Moira Kelly
Director: Marshall Herskovitz   Screenplay: Jeannine Dominy based on *The Honest Courtesan* by Margaret Rosenthal   Running Time: 1:51
Rated: R (Nudity, sex, profanity, violence)   Theatrical Aspect Ratio: 2.35:1

In 1583 Venice, women were regarded as little more than possessions. Education and willfulness were negative traits, reserved only for those who plied their bodies for money. Marriage had nothing to do with love — it was a contract made based exclusively on considerations of wealth and position. If a girl's family didn't have money, she had no hope of marrying an "important" man, no matter how deeply the two loved each other. In a situation like that, if she wanted him, her only hope was to become his mistress. And, if she was truly ambitious and skilled, she could become a courtesan, a mistress to dozens of men, all willing to pay for her services.

Such are the circumstances of Veronica Franco (Catherine McCormack), who is desperately smitten with Marco Vernier (Rufus Sewell) — and he with her. But the difference in their social position makes a legal relationship impossible. When Marco, not wanting to lead Veronica on, informs her of this harsh truth, she is devastated, and chooses to follow the advice of her mother (Jacqueline Bisset) and become a courtesan. Soon, she is the most prized prostitute in Venice, desired by everyone from the local bishop to the King of France. But, during the age of the Spanish Inquisition, power gained through "sinful" means can be a tenuous thing.

Against the backdrop of Veronica and Marco's tumultuous relationship, director Marshall Herskovitz explores the injustices visited upon women at a time when they were universally viewed as inferior to men. The obedient wives are presented as timid, uncertain creatures who dream of a better lot for their daughters while secretly envying Veronica's freedom. For her part, although Veronica uses every weapon at her disposal to hold her own in power struggles with men, she would give all that she has away for a life with Marco.

As is the case with too many melodramas designed to give the audience a triumphant rush, *Dangerous Beauty* goes over the top in its closing moments, offering speech-making and grandstanding that undercuts some of the film's drama. A "commercial" finale isn't the worst thing that could happen in a picture like this — it may be emotionally manipulative, but, on a certain level, it works. *Dangerous Beauty* isn't great art, but it is good entertainment. RECOMMENDED

Dead Man Walking [1995]

Starring: Susan Sarandon, Sean Penn, Raymond J. Barry, R. Lee Ermey Director: Tim Robbins Screenplay: Tim Robbins based on the nonfiction book by Sister Helen Prejean Running Time: 2:02 Rated: R (Profanity, violence, mature themes) Theatrical Aspect Ratio: 2.35:1

As a film about capital punishment, *Dead Man Walking* is effective, but the true brilliance of this picture is that it deals with so much more. Touching such universal themes as revenge and redemption, crime and punishment, and fear and salvation, the movie explores the relationship between Matthew Poncelet (Sean Penn), a convicted rapist/murderer on death row, and his spiritual advisor, Sister Helen Prejean (Susan Sarandon). The bond that develops between them is, paradoxically, both exceedingly complex and deceptively simple, and Robbins, with considerable help from his actors, captures it perfectly. *Dead Man Walking* could easily be manipulative or exploitative, but it's neither.

Sean Penn, in a remarkable performance, brings Matthew to life. There's never any doubt that Matthew was involved in the crime for which he is going to die, although he denies pulling the trigger. And *Dead Man Walking* doesn't attempt to portray him as a wrongly accused innocent man or someone misunderstood by society. He's a nasty piece of work — an arrogant, trash-talking racist. But, beneath all the bluster, he's lonely and frightened, as Helen discovers when she starts to probe.

Sarandon's Catholic nun is at the focal point of *Dead Man Walking* — and it's a performance to match her co-star's for aptness and intensity. Helen is the one we identify with, and the person around which all the moral and spiritual crises revolve. She is exposed to everyone's pain: Matthew's, his family's, and that of the victims' relatives. It's almost more than one woman can bear, but Helen is strong — strong enough to offer love to one of the most detestable human beings she has ever met.

Ultimately, the questions come back to capital punishment. They're all familiar. Is Matthew going to be executed because he was too poor to hire a fat-cat lawyer? Is there a moral difference when the State kills as opposed to an individual? Should justice be based on the "eye for an eye" edict or the one that says to "turn the other cheek"? Only in subtle details does it becomes clear that the director cannot condone the government taking a life.

I defy anyone to sit unaffected through *Dead Man Walking*. This is as powerful as motion pictures get, yet it doesn't descend into a valley of spiritual gloom. There are moments of comic relief, and, even if some of the humor is of the gallows variety, it keeps this 2-hour odyssey from becoming unbearably intense. Although this is only his second directorial outing, actor-turned-film maker Robbins has clearly mastered his craft. There's no sophomore jinx here.

Dead Man Walking refers to what the people on death row are called as they take that final walk towards their execution. It's ironic that a film with this title should be among the most vital, alive, and challenging cinema experiences of the year. MUST SEE

Decalogue [Poland, 1988]

Starring: (Part 1): Henryk Baranowski, Wojciech Klata, Maja Komorowska; (Part 2): Krystyna Janda, Aleksander Bardini; (Part 3): Daniel Olbrychski, Maria Pakulnis; (Part 4): Adrianna Biedrzynska, Janusz Gajos; (Part 5): Miroslaw Baka, Krzysztof Globisz; (Part 6): Grazyna Szapolowska, Olaf Lubaszenko; (Part 7): Anna Polony, Maja Barelkowska, Wladslaw Kowalski; (Part 8): Maria Koscialkowska, Teresa Marczewska; (Part 9): Ewa Blaszczyk, Piotr Machalica, Jan Jankowski; (Part 10): Jerzy Stuhr, Zbigniew Zamachowski Director: Krzysztof Kieslowski Screenplay: Krzysztof Kieslowski and Krzysztof Piesiewicz Running Time: 9:31 (in 10 parts) Rated: No MPAA Rating (Mature themes, violence) Theatrical Aspect Ratio: 1.33:1 In Polish with subtitles

Decalogue was initially produced as a series of 10 1-hour films for Polish television. Two of the episodes, parts 5 and 6, were expanded to full-length features released internationally under the titles of *A Short Film About Killing* and *A Short Film About Love*. Each segment of *Decalogue* ostensibly concentrates on one of the Ten Commandments.

Kieslowski first envisioned *Decalogue* as a project to give young Polish directors their first shots at film making. He and his writing partner, Krzysztof Piesiewicz (who also co-authored *No End, Veronique,* and *Three Colors*) scripted the episodes, intending for a different director to helm each one. However, when the screenplays were complete, Kieslowski realized they were too good to hand over to someone else. In the end, he directed all 10 — completing the entire series in under a year.

Anyone can make a movie about the Ten Commandments, but few such productions would share the subtlety and depth which characterize Kieslowski's vision. It isn't the subject matter per se that gives *Decalogue* its greatness — it's the manner in which the director handles his material. For part 5, those expecting to see a morality play about the evils of killing are in for a surprise. To be sure, this episode is about murder and its ramifications, but the issues examined are far more complex, and Kieslowski shuns absolutes of good and evil.

Each episode of *Decalogue* has a different tone. Part 1 starts out playful as we're introduced to a loving father and son. Part 2 is somber. And so on. Certainly, one of the many elements that makes *Decalogue* so powerful is that, among the dozens of primary actors, there are no inadequate performances. Every character is portrayed naturally, and each story unfolds without uneven acting creating a question of authenticity. For those familiar with other Kieslowski films, there are several recognizable faces. Zbigniew Zamachowski, who starred in *White*, plays a lead in part 10. Jerzy Stuhr, from *Camera Buff* and *White*, is also in the same segment. And Grazyna Szapolowska, Magda in part 6, also appeared in *No End*.

Throughout the history of film, there has been a select group of standout pictures — movies that, for technical or artistic reasons, have made an indelible imprint on viewers. Taken as one 10-hour exploration of the human experience, this is the product of a expert storyteller/filmmaker at the height of his craft, creating a masterwork the likes of which comes along only once in a great while. There is no other motion picture out there like *Decalogue*, which makes it more the pity how difficult it is to hunt down in North America. But, for those who take the trouble, the payoff is more than worth the effort. **MUST SEE**

Dolores Claiborne [2000]

Starring: Kathy Bates, Jennifer Jason Leigh, Christopher Plummer, David Strathairn Director: Taylor Hackford Screenplay: Tony Gilroy based on the book by Stephen King Running Time: 2:11 Rated: R (Mature themes, language) Theatrical Aspect Ratio: 2.35:1

Dolores Claiborne begins as a dark and dreary murder mystery set in the small town of Little Tall, Maine. The skies above this village are continually congested with clouds, the streets are slick with rain, and the sea is gray and angry. Yet this story, which starts out as an investigation of a suspicious death, soon takes on a more grim and disturbing tone. Memories crowd out the present as the narrative takes us back 18 years to expose the ugly roots of one family's dysfunction.

Two deaths lie at the center of *Dolores Claiborne* — Vera Donovan's (Judy Parfitt) in the present and Joe St. George's (David Strathairn) in the past. After Joe fell into a partially-concealed well during the total solar eclipse of 1975, his wife Dolores (Kathy Bates) was suspected, but never convicted, of murder. The death was eventually ruled as accidental, splotching the previously-perfect record of Detective John Mackey (Christopher Plummer). Now, Dolores stands accused of killing her invalid employer, and Mackey is determined to get a conviction.

Dolores' daughter Selena (Ellen Muth at age 13; Jennifer Jason Leigh at age 31), a reporter living in New York city, receives a fax of an article in a Bangor newspaper detailing her mother's suspected involvement in Vera's death. Haunted by her muddled recollections of her father's death, and driven by an unshakable conviction that her mother is guilty, she takes a brief leave-of-absence to go home. Once there, she is confronted not only by the unpleasantness of the present, but by the ghosts of the past.

The main characters, mother and daughter, are well-written and effectively portrayed. Dolores is a sad, lonely survivor who has, perhaps unjustly, endured a lifetime of misery. Secrets can be an oppressive burden, and Dolores has been worn down by them. Selena, on the other hand, has become an alcoholic and drug-abuser as the result of what she has repressed. Bates and Leigh are in peak form as they settle into the lonely isolation of their characters.

There's a lot to digest in *Dolores Claiborne*. The subtle visual effects, which mix digital animation and live-action, form an effective backdrop for a story teeming with emotional turmoil. With their unique method of delineating shifts in time, the flashbacks are invested with a degree of eerie immediacy.

Although the forced ending weakens the climactic catharsis, it doesn't diminish the naked honesty, which forms the foundation of *Dolores Claiborne*. **REC-OMMENDED**

Donnie Brasco [1997]

Starring: Al Pacino, Johnny Depp, Michael Madsen, Bruno Kirby, James Russo, Anne Heche Director: Mike Newell Screenplay: Paul Attanasio based on the book *Donnie Brasco: My Undercover Life in the Mafia* by Joseph Pistone with Richard Woodley Running Time: 2:06 Rated: R (Profanity, violence, mature themes) Theatrical Aspect Ratio: 2.35:1

Donnie Brasco is based on the true story of FBI agent Joe Pistone (Johnny Depp), who went undercover and infiltrated the New York City mob during the late 1970s. Joe, who went by the name of "Donnie Brasco," played his role so effectively that he rose to extraordinary heights within the organization, holding a place alongside his mentor, Lefty (Al Pacino), in the inner circle of boss Sonny Black (Michael Madsen). But, the more time he spent with members of the Mafia, the more like them he became. And, after a while, Joe could no longer tell where his true loyalties lay: to his wife (Anne Heche), family, and government, or to the wiseguys who had adopted him into their lifestyle.

Perhaps the most impressive thing that Newell has done with *Donnie Brasco* is to cull an atypically low-key and introspective performance from Al Pacino, an actor known for manic, scenery-chewing efforts. Lefty is a world-weary hit man with 26 kills under his belt and little to show for it. His dream is to buy a boat and sail far away from civilization, but he doesn't have the money or the gumption to chase that golden fantasy. Pacino presents Lefty as a tragic, and at times pathetic, character who earns our pity and understanding, if not our sympathy.

While not on Pacino's level, Johnny Depp is competent as the title character, a man who loses his perspective as he becomes seduced by the mobster's lifestyle. Depp lets us see the conflict within Joe as his friendship with Lefty grows into something real and as his wife and children become little more than distant images. Near the beginning of *Donnie Brasco*, Joe attempts to prevent a hit; by the end, he comes perilously close to taking part. If there are times when Joe's character doesn't seem whole, the blame lies more with the script's failure to provide the needed background or motivation than with Depp's performance.

Although *Donnie Brasco* is set against a backdrop of crime and violence, it, like many better gangster films, is really about family and relationships. Lefty and Joe have a surrogate father/son bond that gradually supersedes all other attachments in either of their lives. It's because *Donnie Brasco* focuses on characters and relationships that it makes for compelling viewing.

Although the film contains many of the usual mob clichés and stock secondary characters, these don't detract much from the viewer's enjoyment. The film has all the right little touches to be believable, such as Lefty's fascinating lesson to his protégé about how to dress, act, and speak to be respected in wiseguy circles. *Donnie Brasco* takes us into a world that the movies frequently open to us, but somehow this trip seems more real and less glamorized than most. The result is a satisfying film-going experience. **RECOMMENDED**

The Door in the Floor [2004]

Starring: Jeff Bridges, Kim Basinger, Jon Foster, Mimi Rogers, Bijou Phillips, Elle Fanning Director: Tod Williams Screenplay: Tod Williams, based on *A Window for One Year*, by John Irving Running Time: 1:50 Rated: R (Nudity, sex, profanity, mature themes) Theatrical Aspect Ratio: 2.35:1

As a character study that examines a pair of reprehensible individuals, *The Door in the Floor* does an excellent job. The problem with the film is simple: how many people want to spend nearly two hours in the company of such characters? The viewer's supposed surrogate in the film, a 16-year-old boy by the name of Eddie (Jon Foster), is so ineffectual as to be almost invisible. What starts out with the earmarks of a coming-of-age story turns into a tale of the disintegration of the marriage between two disagreeable personalities. If that's your kind of movie, you will find more here than unrelieved bleakness and boredom.

The two major characters personify nearly every unsavory characteristic inherent in human nature. Ted Cole (Jeff Bridges at his scraggliest), a well-known author of children's books, is living a dissolute life. A perpetual drunkard and debaser of women, he spends most of his waking hours wandering around his house in a bathrobe, playing racquetball in a converted barn, and painting nudes. His wife, Marion (Kim Basinger), is little better. She's a bad mother to her four-year old daughter, Ruth (Elle Fanning), is emotionally closed off, and ends up seducing an underage boy who bears a creepy resemblance to her dead teenage son. Her marriage to Ted is on the rocks. It has been unstable for some time, never having recovered from the tragic accident that claimed their sons, Tom and Tim.

Eddie enters this stinking stew of emotional wounds like a Christian being fed to the lions. He's a relative innocent — a 16-year-old virgin with few social skills but a burgeoning desire to write. He considers it a great honor to have been chosen by Ted as his assistant, but his attention soon switches to Marion. He develops an infatuation for her that she promptly exploits. Meanwhile, Ted calculates how to use his wife's indiscretion against her in a potential custody suit.

The film arrests our attention in the same way that a wreck does. Ted and Marion may have survived the accident that killed their sons, but their marriage did not. It has lain in ruins for years, and all it takes is one catalyst — the arrival of Eddie into the twisted dynamic that has become their interaction — to alter things permanently. As relationship autopsies go, this one is effective, although the scenes I thought worked the best are the ones where Ted mentors Eddie on writing — even if some of his advice is brutal. **RECOMMENDED**

Down In the Delta [1998]

Starring: **Alfre Woodard, Al Freeman Jr., Mary Alice, Esther Rolle, Loretta Devine, Wesley Snipes** Director: **Maya Angelou** Screenplay: **Myron Goble** Running Time: 1:51 Rated: PG-13 (Profanity, drug-related material) Theatrical Aspect Ratio: 1.85:1

Down in the Delta opens in Chicago, where one three-generation family is falling apart, despite the best efforts of the matriarch, Rosa Lynn (Mary Alice), to hold it together. Her daughter, Loretta (Alfre Woodard), is hooked on drugs and booze. Her grandson, Thomas (Mpho Koaho), makes money on the streets by selling polaroids to tourists for $5, and her granddaughter, Tracy (Kulani Hassan), is autistic. As a mother, Loretta is unfit. Her idea of keeping little Tracy happy is to fill her bottle with cola, and she's more interested in getting her next drink than in caring what her children are doing. Recognizing that her family's current path leads inevitably to disaster, Rosa Lynn calls her brother-in-law, Earl (Al Freeman Jr.), and arranges for Loretta and her children to spend a summer at his place on the Mississippi Delta. Loretta agrees to go, albeit reluctantly, and, with Thomas and Tracy in tow, she heads south. And, while the initial transition is difficult, she eventually finds herself, and connects with her family.

Down in the Delta suffers from some narrative hiccups. The most obvious of these is the quickness of Loretta's transformation from down-and-out loser to responsible mother and entrepreneur. The resolution is also a little too facile to be entirely believable. Fortunately, however, while Myron Goble's script may not be airtight, Angelou's cast is consistently reliable. Alfre Woodard becomes Loretta — there's not a moment when we doubt this performance. As the stubborn-but-wise uncle we all wish we had, Al Freeman Jr. is a commanding presence.

Down in the Delta doesn't just deal with healing through a change in locale, but regeneration through coming to grips with the past. As Loretta learns the history of "Nathan" (the name of a family heirloom — a candlestick holder passed down through the family from the time of slavery), she begins to understand that, by wasting her life, she is demeaning the sacrifices of those who came before her.

Maya Angelou is one of the most influential and powerful author/poets of the second half of the 20th century and this is her first stint as a director. While there's nothing groundbreaking in her approach, she does a highly credible job, and shows particular promise in handling actors.

Down in the Delta does not purport to offer an answer to the problem of inner city social decay. But, while the specifics of the film's solution are confined to this story, Angelou makes it clear that all healing must begin with self-respect, close-knit family connections, and an appreciation of personal history. Those are the life lessons Loretta must learn before she can move on, and, through her growth and development, Angelou teaches us without ever seeming preachy or didactic. With its rich characters and flawless performances, *Down in the Delta* is a fully-satisfying emotional experience that offers all we might expect from an individual of Angelou's accomplishments. **HIGHLY RECOMMENDED**

Drumline [2002]

Starring: **Nick Cannon, Zoe Saldana, Orlando Jones, Leonard Roberts** Director: **Charles Stone III** Screenplay: **Tina Gordon Chism and Shawn Schepps** Running Time: 1:58 Rated: PG-13 (Profanity, sexual innuendo) Theatrical Aspect Ratio: 2.35:1

Drumline introduces viewers to the competitive world of collegiate marching bands, for whom "half-time is game time." Devon (Nick Cannon) is a highly sought-after drummer who is attending Atlanta A&T on a full band scholarship. Devon is more cocky than the average freshman, wooing Laila (Zoe Saldana), an upperclass philosophy major with a passion for dance, and openly feuding with his section leader, Sean (Leonard Roberts). He also believes that the numbers chosen by the band leader, Dr. Lee (Orlando Jones), are outmoded and boring. His tendency towards flamboyancy makes him a controversial individual, but, when he is unable to repress his need for individual glory and live by Dr. Lee's motto of "one band, one sound," he finds himself on the sidelines heading into the BET Big Southern Classic band championship against A&T's arch-rival, Morris Brown University.

Drumline is a star vehicle for Nickelodeon staple Nick Cannon, who is making his first significant foray onto the big screen. Cannon carries himself well, coming across as self-confident and charismatic, without taking things to the level that would make him abrasive. He's more Will Smith than Martin Lawrence. If he chooses his roles wisely, there's no reason he can't find the same kind of mainstream success achieved by Smith. During the course of *Drumline,* he shows an affinity for both light drama and restrained comedy, having no difficulty with scenes that require pathos or intensity.

The soundtrack for *Drumline* — undoubtedly one of the film's selling points — is cross-generational, with the band playing more than just traditional marching tunes. But those performances are just color. At *Drumline*'s heart are the characters and the behind-the-scenes politicking that goes on whenever money is involved. (The leader of Morris Brown's band is eager to pull Devon away from Atlanta A&T — not only because he's a good drummer, but because of the insider information he can provide about what Dr. Lee is planning for the BET.) Director Charles Stone never strays too far from the familiar, but there are nice little twists that keep the production fresh. (Yes, Devon and Sean's relationship softens, but Dr. Lee never turns into Mr. Chips, and, in fact, he is forced to compromise his high values in order to keep his job.) Coming in the midst of so many high-profile, end-of-the-year motion picture, *Drumline* is a pleasant, and very welcome, surprise.

RECOMMENDED

Eat Drink Man Woman [Taiwan, 1994]

Starring: Sihung Lung, Kuei-Mei-Yang, Chien-Lien Wu, Yu-Wen Wang, Winston Chao Director: Ang Lee Screenplay: Ang Lee, James Schamus, and Hui-Ling Wang Running Time: 2:04 Rated: No MPAA Rating (Mature themes) In Mandarin with subtitles

Who said foreign films can't be fun? Ang Lee's followup to *The Wedding Banquet* is a delicious examination of the relationship between aging Chinese master chef Tao Chu (Sihung Lung) and his 3 daughters. The oldest, Jia-Jen (Kuei-Mei-Yang), is an unmarried school teacher in her late 20s. The middle daughter, Jia-Chen (Chien-Lien Wu), is a thriving corporate airline executive whose career comes before all else. The youngest, Jia-Ning (Yu-Wen Wang), is a 20-year-old romantic who works at a Wendy's fast food joint.

Eat Drink Man Woman is an accomplished motion picture. The comedy is spontaneous and relaxed, the drama is finely-tuned, and the plot is seasoned with unexpected little twists. The script delights in occasional forays just beyond the typical bounds of a screenplay.

Though filmed entirely in Taiwan, the themes of *Eat Drink Man Woman* are universal. The problems faced by the Chu family happen all around the world, and the difficulty of communicating across the generation gap is something almost everyone has experienced at one time or another. Love, especially that of Chu for his daughters, often goes unspoken, for to express emotion is to admit vulnerability.

With an ease that marks the true craftsman, Ang Lee develops a rapport between his characters and the audience. These people have a richness, texture, and depth that no stereotype could hope to match. The perfectly-proportioned measures of comedy and drama emerge through character interaction, not as a result of contrived situations and silly one-liners.

Food is as much a backdrop as a recurring symbol. Chu's failing taste buds parallel his loss for the zest for life. Jia-Chen's love of cooking harkens back to a frustrated childhood desire, and Jia-Ning's work at a Wendy's makes a statement about the infusion of Western culture into modern-day China. Nevertheless, *Eat Drink Man Woman* could perhaps be frustrating to any who view it on an empty stomach.

Eat Drink Man Woman is basted in its own wonderfully seasoned juices. Chu may have lost his taste, but writer/director Ang Lee has definitely not. A treat for those not scared off by subtitles, this movie provides one of the year's most sincere views of family dynamics. Dealing with subjects that could easily have emerged half-baked, Lee instead applies his talent and comes up with a dish cooked to perfection.

HIGHLY RECOMMENDED

Elizabeth [United Kingdom, 1998]

Starring: Cate Blanchett, Geoffrey Rush, Christopher Eccleston, Joseph Fiennes, Richard Attenborough, Fanny Ardant Director: Shekhar Kapur Screenplay: Michael Hirst Running Time: 2:01 Rated: R (Violence, sex, nudity) Theatrical Aspect Ratio: 1.85:1

In 1554, the Catholic Queen Mary (Kathy Burke), the daughter of Henry VIII, sat on the throne. Frightened that her younger half-sister, Elizabeth (Cate Blanchett), is involved in a plot to usurp her crown, Mary has her heir thrown into the Tower of London. Elizabeth survives the ordeal and, upon Mary's death, assumes the throne. Immediately, she is confronted by a legion of problems: a dry treasury, a weak army, the need to marry to secure the blood line, and a growing threat from Mary of Guise (Fanny Ardant), who is massing troops to move against England. There are also dangers within Elizabeth's court, the most notable of which comes from the dangerous Duke of Norfolk (Christopher Eccleston), who wants her dead. And, because Elizabeth is a Protestant, Pope Pius V (John Gielgud) declares her a heretic and issues a proclamation releasing all English Catholics from following her. To help her in her struggles, Elizabeth has 3 strong allies: the ever-faithful William Cecil (Richard Attenborough), the wily and dangerous Francis Walsingham (Geoffrey Rush), and the love of her life, Lord Robert Dudley (Joseph Fiennes).

From a general perspective, *Elizabeth* offers a reasonably accurate overview of the 16th century monarch's character and life. When it comes to specifics, however, the film is sorely lacking. Much of what happens in *Elizabeth* did not happen that way, and, if the plot occasionally seems unnecessarily convoluted and confusing, it's understandable, since writer Michael Hirst has chosen to compress many of the key events of Elizabeth's lengthy reign into a 5-year period. There are also several outright distortions of the historical record. In reality, for example, Mary of Guise's fate was significantly different than what the film depicts. Ultimately, however, all of this is, if not irrelevant, then inconsequential. Those who want a factual account of Elizabeth's reign can read a history book; *Elizabeth* does what it sets out to do: provide a solidly entertaining 2 hours.

One of the primary reasons *Elizabeth* works is because of the superlative performance of Cate Blanchett. Not only does Blanchett look like Elizabeth, but she acts the part of a fiery, determined young woman riddled by the uncertainty of a precarious position. She breathes life into the revered historical figure, transforming her from an old picture on an encyclopedia page to a flesh-and-blood individual whom an audience can root for and care about.

In addition to its factual inaccuracies, *Elizabeth*

possesses a few weaknesses. The movie's editing is uneven, a situation that can result in occasional bouts of confusion when trying to unravel the Byzantine plotting going on at court, and the ending seems a little too pat. **RECOMMENDED**

The Emperor's Club [2002]

Starring: Kevin Kline, Emile Hirsch, Embeth Davidtz Director: Michael Hoffman Screenplay: Neil Tolkin, based on the short story "The Palace Thief" by Ethan Canin Running Time: 1:49 Rated: PG-13 (Profanity, sexual situations) Theatrical Aspect Ratio: 1.85:1

The Emperor's Club starts out predictably, taking us back in time 25 years and introducing us to the reliable, enthusiastic, ethically unimpeachable Mr. William Hundert (Kevin Kline, in fine form), who educates the students at St. Benedict's School for Boys about the Greeks and the Romans while providing life lessons on the side. Enter the Troublemaker, Sedgewick Bell (Emile Hirsch), a stereotypical smart kid with a bad attitude. Mr. Hundert makes it his business to mold Sedgewick into the kind of person who realizes his potential and thereby makes a difference.

So far, so good. All of this is standard material culled from Screenwriting 101. But then comes the twist. Mr. Hundert fails with his pet project, and in a pretty big way. At first, it looks like Sedgewick has turned a corner, but then he shows his true colors. He falls from grace, backsliding all the way to the starting line. To exacerbate matters, Mr. Hundert has compromised his own ethics in his zeal to reform Sedgewick. And things get worse when we catch up with the characters in the modern time period. Mr. Hundert still believes in Sedgewick, even after so many disappointments, but the up-and-coming politician is as much a cheater and a manipulator as ever.

Ultimately, *The Emperor's Club* doesn't quite have the guts to follow this story to its natural, cynical conclusion. There are some feel-good elements thrown in that allow the movie to end on an upbeat note. The results of one scene convince Mr. Hundert that his career as an educator should be judged not by one failure, but by numerous successes. Nevertheless, the cheerful sheen can't obscure the fact that *The Emperor's Club* isn't business as usual for this sort of picture. It dares to be a little different, and that shading is what makes it worthwhile.

The Emperor's Club doesn't have a lot of heft. It's a relatively light-weight story that is carried more by the well-defined characters than by plot developments. In the end, we get a sense that it has all been worthwhile, not only for Mr. Hundert, but for those of us sitting in the audience. It helps, of course, that the movie confounds our expectations yet still delivers a positive message. There's still quite a bit of the essence of *Dead Poets Society* in *The Emperor's Club*. Thankfully, however, the level of schmaltz and manipulation has been greatly reduced. **RECOMMENDED**

The Emperor's New Clothes [Germany/Italy/United Kingdom, 2001]

Starring: Ian Holm, Iben Hjejle, Tim McInnerny, Tom Watson, Nigel Terry Director: Alan Taylor Screenplay: Kevin Molony, Alan Taylor, Herbie Wave, based on "The Death of Napoleon" by Simon Leys Running Time: 1:45 Rated: PG Theatrical Aspect Ratio: 1.85:1

According to the history books, Napoleon Bonaparte died in May 1821 on the island of St. Helena. According to Alan Taylor's *The Emperor's New Clothes*, it wasn't Napoleon who ended his days on St. Helena, but an imposter. Napoleon had previously escaped his captors and returned to France, where the news of his death made it difficult for him to be accepted as anything other than a melon seller with delusions of grandeur. Thus, Napoleon, once the most powerful man in the world, was forced to live as a commoner, and, in the process, understand that some things in life are more satisfying the power.

The movie begins on St. Helena, the island to which Napoleon (Ian Holm) was exiled following his defeat at Waterloo. He has a plan to escape — his aides have smuggled a lookalike, Eugene Lenormand, to the island. Eugene and Napoleon will switch places and he will make his way to Paris, pretending to be a deck hand. Once he is there, Eugene will announce himself to be a fraud, Napoleon will declare himself, and the people will rise up for their emperor. But, once Napoleon has returned home, he discovers that fate has conspired against him. Eugene likes playing the part of the emperor too much, and is unwilling to relinquish the fruits of the role. So Napoleon must live the life of a commoner, and, in the process, he has the good fortune to fall in love with a peasant woman, Pumpkin (Iben Hjejle), who does not believe that Eugene is *the* Napoleon, but will accept him as *her* Napoleon.

The Emperor's New Clothes is a lighthearted, feel-good film that embraces the time-honored truth that the most powerful thing in life is love. Granted, the real Napoleon never would have settled down to live with a common woman, but *this* Napoleon does, and, in the doing so gives us the moral of this story — acceptance of the changing world and our place in it

is the only way to keep time from passing us by. The film also toys with issues of identity.

Playing the dual role of Napoleon as Eugene and Eugene as Napoleon, Ian Holm turns in another fine performance. Quirks in mannerisms and body language easily differentiate the two individuals. This is actually the third time Holm has played Napoleon. He previously essayed the part in a mid-1970s mini-series called "Napoleon and Love," then again in *Time Bandits*. Iben Hjejle is affable as the unaffected Pumpkin, the woman who teaches Napoleon things he never knew about life when he was a world leader.

The film's director is Alan Taylor, whose primary experience is in television. Taylor's approach to this material — mixing occasional humor with undemanding drama — works well enough that we don't care about the logical inconsistencies and plot holes. To that end, *The Emperor's New Clothes* ends up as a pleasant diversion. **RECOMMENDED**

The End of the Affair [United States/United Kingdom, 1999]

Starring: Ralph Fiennes, Julianne Moore, Stephen Rea, Ian Hart, Sam Bould, Jason Isaacs Director: Neil Jordan Screenplay: Neil Jordan, based on the novel by Graham Greene Running Time: 1:44 Rated: R (Sex, nudity) Theatrical Aspect Ratio: 1.85:1

The End of the Affair takes place during the days and months following World War II. We meet the not-so-happily married couple of Sarah (Julianne Moore) and Henry Miles (Stephen Rea). Henry, a workaholic, admits to not having been much of a husband and never having been a true lover to his wife. During the summer of 1939, novelist Maurice Bendrix (Ralph Fiennes) and Sarah met and began a torrid affair. They professed undying love for one another, and, while Henry worked long hours on the war effort, Maurice and Sarah spent the time in Maurice's flat. But, on a night when Maurice was seriously wounded in a German air raid, the relationship abruptly ended. When Sarah left him, he was bitter and angry, and all of his love turned to rage and hatred. Sarah, on the other hand, believed in a pure love — a kind that would endure to her dying day, even if circumstances prevented her from ever seeing Maurice again.

Several years after the end of the affair, Maurice has a chance meeting with Henry, who confesses to his old friend that he believes Sarah is being unfaithful. The ugly specter of jealousy rears its head for Maurice — even though he has not seen Sarah in years, he cannot bear the thought of her being with someone else. Pretending to act on Henry's behalf, he hires a private investigator (Ian Hart) to follow Sarah and learn the identity of her new lover.

The End of the Affair is more satisfying on an intellectual level than it is on an emotional one. In addition to probing into the depth of the spiritual and physical components of love, Jordan explores the ways in which the vagaries of fate and/or the Hand of God shape people's destinies. In an attempt to maintain a balance between Sarah and Maurice's often contradictory perspectives, Jordan allows certain key scenes to be repeated twice — once from Sarah's point-of-view (using her words in a voiceover) and once from Maurice's (employing his words).

The End of the Affair is based on a semi-autobiographical novel by Graham Greene. Even with its flaws, it still possesses the quiet power to involve the viewer in a simple tale that is likely to invoke his or her own feelings about love, fate, and God.

RECOMMENDED

The English Patient [1996]

Starring: Ralph Fiennes, Kristin Scott Thomas, Juliette Binoche, Willem Dafoe, Colin Firth, Naveen Andrews Director: Anthony Minghella Screenplay: Anthony Minghella based on the novel by Michael Ondaatje Running Time: 2:40 Rated: R (Sex, nudity, violence, profanity) Theatrical Aspect Ratio: 1.85:1

For those who have forgotten the depth of romance and passion that the movies are capable of conveying, Anthony Minghella's *The English Patient* can remedy the situation. This well-crafted story, brought to the screen with great care by British playwright and director Anthony Minghella (*Truly, Madly, Deeply*) and based on the prize-winning novel by Michael Ondaatje, serves up the love of Almasy (Ralph Fiennes) and Katharine (Kristin Scott Thomas) in a way that is simultaneously epic and intimate.

The opening sequence, which takes place during World War II, shows a British plane being shot down over the North African desert. The pilot, a Hungarian count named Laszlo Almasy, is badly burned in the ensuing crash. Years later, in 1944 Italy, we meet him again. Although his outward injuries have healed, leaving his features scarred beyond recognition, he is dying. He has also supposedly lost his memory. Hana (Juliette Binoche), the Canadian nurse who cares for him, takes him to an isolated, abandoned church to allow him to die in peace. There, injecting him with morphine and reading to him from his beloved volume of Herodotus, Hana seeks to stimulate his memories. Meanwhile, others arrive at the church — a mysterious, crippled war veteran named Caravaggio (Willem Dafoe), and a pair of bomb experts, the British Sgt. Hardy (Kevin Whately) and his Sikh superior, Kip (Naveen Andrews), who becomes Hana's lover.

Eventually, through dreams and waking flashbacks, Almasy's memories come flooding back, although Caravaggio asserts that he hasn't really forgotten anything — he just *wants* to forget. The story then flip-flops between the present and a period during the late-'30s and early-'40s, when Almasy is part of a British map-making effort surveying the Sahara. It's then that he meets Katharine Clifton, the wife of a good-natured pilot (Colin Firth) who is helping with the project. Almasy and Katharine fall for each other, and the stage is set for a classic exploration of love and betrayal set against the dangerous background of Nazi aggression.

Ralph Fiennes gives us an Almasy who seems loosely based on *Casablanca*'s Rick — strong and silent until the right woman releases all of his pent-up passion. Kristen Scott Thomas is luminous as Katharine, effortlessly conveying to the audience the energy and zest for life that Almasy finds irresistible. Together, these two are hotter than the desert heat that simmers around them.

The English Patient is the sort of intelligent, epic love story that seems so rare these days. There's something about this film that lingers long after the end credits have rolled — a desire to re-experience all the feelings generated by the movie, perhaps. One of the reasons for *The English Patient*'s power is that it strikes universal chords. **HIGHLY RECOMMENDED**

Evelyn [Ireland, 2001]

Starring: Pierce Brosnan, Aidan Quinn, Julianna Margulies, Stephen Rea Director: Bruce Beresford Screenplay: Paul Pender Running Time: 1:34 Rated: PG-13 (Mature themes, profanity) Theatrical Aspect Ratio: 2.35:1

Evelyn is a shamelessly uplifting motion picture that attains its feel-good status by forging a deep emotional connection between the undertrodden protagonist and the audience. The bulk of the film transpires during 1954 in Dublin, and concerns a court case that resulted in sweeping changes being made to Irish custody laws. *Evelyn* bears the "based on a true story" label, but, considering the flow of the narrative, my guess is that only the bare-bones facts remain. I don't mind when a screenwriter takes a fair amount of artistic license with the historical record, and the strength of Paul Pender's script argues that he and Beresford made the right choices.

Desmond Doyle (Pierce Brosnan) is an average working-class Irishman, who happens to be out of work at the moment because of an employment shortage. His wife chooses this moment to run off with her wealthy lover, leaving Desmond alone to support his two young sons and his only daughter, Evelyn (Sophie Vavasseur). However, because Desmond has no job, the courts take his children away from him, placing his sons in a Catholic Boys' Home and Evelyn in a convent. Eventually, Desmond rights his financial situation, but discovers that he cannot regain custody of his children without his wife's consent — and she is nowhere to be found. So he rounds up a legal team comprised of 3 local lawyers (Aidan Quinn, Stephen Rea, and Alan Bates) with the intention of fighting the church and the government. With the support of those 3 men and a local woman, Bernadette (Julianna Margulies), he goes to battle to retrieve Evelyn and her brothers. (There is a romantic rivalry between Quinn's character and Desmond for Bernadette. Fortunately, the contest is friendly and free of the usual bickering and squabbling that often accompanies this kind of subplot.)

The film's root theme — a father's love for his children — is a proven cinematic favorite, and Beresford develops it perfectly. *Evelyn* offers plenty of light-hearted humor and gently manipulative melodrama, but the climactic moment seems to come from the heart. The performances of Brosnan and Vavasseur are on the mark, and the tactic of using a sports commentator to provide a running "play-by-play" of the courtroom action is a nice twist. It's easy to view this kind of movie with cynicism, but, as long as you're not too jaded, the film's ample good will should draw you in. I believe that virtually everyone who sees this motion picture will enjoy it. **RECOMMENDED**

Eve's Bayou [1997]

Starring: Samuel L. Jackson, Lynn Whitfield, Jurnee Smollett, Meagan Good Director: Kasi Lemmons Screenplay: Kasi Lemmons Running Time: 1:49 Rated: R (Profanity, sex, mature themes) Theatrical Aspect Ratio: 1.85:1

Eve's Bayou takes us to the Tennessee Williams country of the deep south and introduces us to the rarest of motion picture institutions: an affluent black family. Ultimately, however, this film is not about skin color, but about the deeply-rooted bonds that join women together, which not even the most tragic of mistakes can obliterate. The setting — a small town in Louisiana during the 1950s — serves its purpose, but the themes broached by the writer/director are anything but parochial in nature.

The focus of the film is on the 5-member Batiste family. There's Louis (Samuel L. Jackson), a prominent and respected doctor; Roz (Lynn Whitfield), the beautiful, elegant mother of a son and two daughters; and their children — 14-year-old Cisely (Meagan Good), 10-year-old Eve (Jurnee Smollett), and 9-year-old Poe (Jake Smollett). Members of the extended family, particularly Louis' mother (Ethel Ayler) and sister, Mozelle (Debbi Morgan), are never far away. On the surface, Louis is the perfect husband and father, but he doesn't pay much attention to his marriage vows. When his daughter Eve catches him in the act, the issue becomes a festering sore in the family's stability. The situation is further exacerbated when Cisely's near-worshipful affection for her father threatens to cross a forbidden barrier.

Louis pays both an emotional and a tangible price for his many affairs. Cisely's clouding of the truth has its own unfortunate result. And an ill-considered yet passionate decision on Eve's part has devastating ramifications. The film also makes a point of showing that everything is not as it seems, especially in the tangled web of family relationships.

The strongest element of *Eve's Bayou* is the character interaction. Every member of the family (except young Poe) is developed into a unique individual, and all of the relationships are well-defined. What family doesn't go through an upheaval when secrets come into the open? The low-key plot, with its elements of voodoo and spiritual sight, allows us the opportunity to get to know the Batistes. Lemmons' fine writing is complimented by a series of strong performances. Samuel L. Jackson is as solid as ever in a role that requires a less flamboyant portrayal than we have become accustomed to. Lynn Whitfield radiates cool beauty while Debbi Morgan emanates sensual heat. Jurnee Smollett and Meagan Good, the young actors playing Eve and Cisely, are both believable as sisters with close ties and hidden jealousies.

A subtle picture that treads a delicate line between drama and psychological thriller, *Eve's Bayou* is refreshing. Rather than perpetuating racial stereotypes, *Eve's Bayou* defies them, creating several well-rounded characters and placing them in a deceptively complex story that builds to a forceful conclusion. It's a movie like no other on the market today, and deserves to find its audience. **RECOMMENDED**

Exotica [Canada, 1994]

Starring: Bruce Greenwood, Mia Kirshner, Elias Koteas, Don McKellar, Arsinee Khanijian, Sarah Polley Director: Atom Egoyan Screenplay: Atom Egoyan Running Time: 1:43 Rated: R (Sex, nudity, language, mature themes) Theatrical Aspect Ratio: 1.85:1

The Exotica is a strip club in Toronto, where men go to watch, but not touch, a variety of unclothed women who strut their stuff to the pulsing sounds of a rich and varied soundtrack. Christina (Mia Kirshner) is a sultry brunette who comes on stage in a school girl costume and is introduced by the deejay Eric (Elias Koteas) as a "sassy bit of jailbait." Her gyrations as she unbuttons her white blouse give the illusion of corrupted innocence — a fantasy with its basis in reality. Mia Kirshner, with her combination of sensuality and thinly-veiled pain, arrests the viewer's attention.

One of the club's regulars is Francis (Bruce Greenwood), a lonely government auditor who spends hours paying out money for Christina to dance privately for him. The bond between these two is more profound than that of a normal dancer and client. When Francis utters his refrain of "How could anyone hurt you?" to Christina, we're not aware of all the layers inherent in his words.

Paralleling Francis' story is that of Thomas (Don McKellar), a gay pet shop owner who runs a lucrative smuggling operation. Currently, his business is being investigated by Francis, and this forms the narrative link by which everything is eventually tied together. Thomas is the shy, nerdy sort who doesn't know how to go about picking up men, until fate deals him a pair of opera tickets and a means by which to find a seemingly-limitless supply of partners. But for Thomas, filling that aching void of the soul involves paying a hefty material price.

On the surface, *Exotica* might seem to be about sex and lust. Nothing could be further from the truth. Those elements are a slick sheen of polish over the real core. While it's true that strip joints normally reek of excess, Egoyan's story seeks a more fundamental emotional level. This film is driven by the grief and isolation of the characters. The interpersonal connections made in *Exotica* are often obscure, and the reasons underlying otherwise-inexplicable actions are complex.

Everyone deals differently with loss, but Francis' problem is that he can't accept the tragedy which has defined his life. The effects are too devastating, so he huddles behind a curtain of illusion spun by Christina, trying to reduce his crushing despair to something more bearable. It's easy to mistake Francis for a dirty-minded middle-aged voyeur until you begin to understand what *Exotica* is saying. And it's not until the final credits roll that the last word of that litany is spoken. Very little about this picture is either predictable or conventional.

As movies go, this one is painful — painful because it exposes so much truth. *Exotica* becomes a journey of self-discovery. As the mysteries underlying the actions of Francis, Christina, Eric, and Thomas are slowly unwrapped, we learn as much about ourselves as we do about Egoyan's characters. When any motion picture succeeds at that, it deserves recognition as nothing less than a profound cinematic experience. **MUST SEE**

The Family Man [2000]

Starring: Nicolas Cage, Tea Leoni, Jeremy Piven, Don Cheadle, Harve Presnell Director: Brett Ratner Screenplay: David Diamond & David Weissman Running Time: 2:02 Rated: PG-13 (Nudity, sexual situations, profanity) Theatrical Aspect Ratio: 1.85:1

The Family Man proves to be an effective, if not truly impressive, look at the road not taken. Nicolas Cage plays Jack Campbell, a wheeler-dealer who's the toast of Manhattan and "a credit to capitalism." He is willing to do anything to close a deal, including forcing his entire team to work late on Christmas Eve then come in for a "strategy session" on Christmas Day. Family has no meaning for Jack. Then, on his way home after work late on Christmas Eve, he encounters a street hustler (Don Cheadle) who turns out to be an angel of sorts. When Jack claims that he has everything in life that he needs, the angel decides to prove that's not the case, and transports Jack into an alternate universe where he has been married for 13 years to Kate (Téa Leoni), his college girlfriend. He is no longer rich, he works at a tire dealership, he has 2 kids, and he lives in a small house in Teaneck, New Jersey. Jack is initially horrified, but, in true *It's a Wonderful Life* fashion, he begins to connect with this lifestyle, which focuses on people and relationships rather than money and possessions.

Boiled down to its essence, *The Family Man* is a romantic comedy dressed up with a lot of intriguing philosophical side issues. At the core of the film is the relationship between Jack and Kate, and how her love (and the affection of his children) redeems him and proves the old-fashioned ideal that true wealth comes from having a family, not a 10-figure bank account. For the most part, this relationship works. Neither Cage nor Leoni does groundbreaking work here, but they're both effective and likable, and, when together, they click. And, although Cage is not recognized as an actor with great range, he capably handles Jack's transition from self-centered bachelor to giving husband and father.

The Family Man is not a flawless exploration of this scenario. At a little over 2 hours in length, the movie wears out its welcome. Director Brett Ratner has a tendency to include redundant scenes, especially late in the film as Jack is coming to the realization that he likes his "new" life. Ratner seems unsure how much the audience needs to buy Jack's conversion, and he ends up belaboring the point. The conclusion is lame, as if the filmmakers couldn't decide how to wrap things up and went with a "you can have your cake and eat it" option. For a story that is in large part about sacrifice, this doesn't work.

Overall, however, *The Family Man* is a pleasant motion picture. Despite its flaws, the screenplay is effective enough to get us thinking about a few philosophical issues while it tells a worthwhile story. RECOMMENDED

A Family Thing [1996]

Starring: Robert Duvall, James Earl Jones, Michael Beach, Irma P. Hall, David Keith Director: Richard Pearce Screenplay: Billy Bob Thornton and Tom Epperson Running Time: 1:49 Rated: PG-13 (Violence, profanity, mature themes) Theatrical Aspect Ratio: 2.35:1

Richard Pearce's *A Family Thing* is a pleasant, if not especially groundbreaking, motion picture that takes the "buddy movie" concept a step forward by introducing themes of race relations and kinship. All the topics presented on an intimate level are equally applicable to society as a whole, which has become more sensitive to issues of skin color than those of basic humanity.

A Family Thing's premise is that Duvall's character, Earl Pilcher, has been raised as the son of white parents, even though his real mother was black. After the death of the woman he called "Mom," Earl learns about his true heritage, and heads north to Chicago to meet his half-brother, Raymond (Jones). However, Ray is less than pleased to see Earl, because he associates his white sibling with tragedy. His mother died giving birth to Earl, and Ray has nursed this bitterness for more than 60 years.

For Earl, the challenge is putting aside the bigotry bred into him by his rural Arkansas environment. Learning the truth about his mother forces him to abandon his black-and-white perceptions. As *A Family Thing* chronicles one man's gradual acceptance of himself, it reminds us that skin color is an artificial, not a natural, barrier. After meeting Ray, Earl realizes that intolerance is the product of ignorance, and, when it comes down to it, he and his black brother aren't fundamentally very different.

One character central to bringing Earl and Ray together is their blind aunt, played brilliantly by scene-stealing Irma P. Hall. In Aunt T's words, she doesn't "have the blessing of being able to separate people by looking at them." So what if Earl's skin is lighter than Ray's — that doesn't change their shared parentage. She recognizes that the rift between the brothers is carved out of pride and stubbornness, and decides that it's her job to bridge it. To that end, she forces Ray to stop blaming Earl for his mother's death while encouraging Earl to embrace his heritage. Gradually for both men, stereotyping gives way to understanding, and understanding to brotherhood.

Most of *A Family Thing* is devoted to Earl and Ray's struggles to reach common ground. The usual "mismatched buddy" film conventions are present: initial resentment and dislike that leads to a physical confrontation, followed by bonding and grudging admiration that grows into genuine affection. With actors of Duvall and Jones' caliber, however, such formulas attain a higher-than-ordinary level.

Overall, this film is an agreeable exploration of what it means to be part of a family. *A Family Thing* isn't just about accepting one's circumstances, but embracing them. The actors, playing characters it's easy to sympathize with, bring the story alive. Because Duvall and Jones establish a successful rapport, it has an unexpectedly strong emotional resonance, and that's a key reason why viewers are likely to leave this movie satisfied. RECOMMENDED

Far from Heaven [2002]

Starring: Julianne Moore, Dennis Quaid, Dennis Haysbert Director: Todd Haynes Screenplay: Todd Haynes Running Time: 1:47 Rated: PG-13 (Mature themes, brief profanity & violence) Theatrical Aspect Ratio: 1.85:1

Welcome to the world of "Father Knows Best," white picket fences, and brilliant fall colors. Todd Haynes' *Far From Heaven* takes us to Hartford, Connecticut, circa 1957. However, unlike most traditional period piece dramas, the intention here isn't just to replicate an American community as it was a half-century ago, but to emulate that community as it would have been portrayed in a movie of the era. One of Haynes' goals in crafting *Far From Heaven* is to emulate the so-called "women's films" of Douglas Sirk. In terms of style, visual approach, and general thematic content, Haynes has come as close as it's possible to in re-creating a '50s domestic melodrama for '00s consumption.

Cathy Whitaker (Julianne Moore) has a seemingly perfect life. Her husband, Frank (Dennis), is a recognized TV salesman. As per the American dream, she has two children and a comfortable home. She is content with the way things are, until Frank inadvertently provides a shock to her system. One night, when he is supposedly working late, Cathy hand-delivers him dinner, only to find him in a torrid embrace with another man. Afterwards, Frank confesses that he has always had homosexual feelings and promises to seek out a doctor to help him "beat this thing." While Frank is struggling with his sexuality, Cathy finds herself drawn to the quiet, kind gardener, Raymond (Dennis Haysbert). Raymond is black, and, on an occasion when he and Cathy are seen in public, a firestorm of nasty rumors begins. Raymond's idealistic belief that color should not be a social barrier is soon put to the test, and Cathy finds that her platonic relationship with Raymond is as much of a danger to her family as is Frank's homosexuality.

Haynes' style and approach draw the viewer in gently, but firmly. Once we are established in the seemingly-perfect world of Cathy and Frank, he allows their marriage and their lives to unravel before our eyes. *Far From Heaven* is not "realistic" in the traditional sense of the word (Haynes calls it "hyper-realistic"), but the emotions of the characters are genuine, and we feel for them and with them. In the end, *Far From Heaven* tells a simple story, but there's nothing remotely simple about the impact it has upon the viewer. **HIGHLY RECOMMENDED**

Felicia's Journey [Canada/United Kingdom/United States, 1999]

Starring: Bob Hoskins, Elaine Cassidy, Arsinée Khanjian, Peter McDonald Director: Atom Egoyan Running Time: 1:56
Screenplay: Atom Egoyan, based on the novel by William Trevor
Rated: PG-13 (Mature themes) Theatrical Aspect Ratio: 2.35:1

Felicia's Journey concentrates on two characters, switching between them, choosing transition points that italicize their similarities and differences while never causing the narrative to lose momentum. The first person we meet is Joe Hilditch (Bob Hoskins), who is introduced at the end of the opening credits. Hilditch is an old-fashioned man. His house is filled with things of the past: rotary phones, antique appliances, and a small, black-and-white TV.

Meanwhile, the title character (Eileen Cassidy), a teenager from Ireland, has arrived in England searching for her boyfriend. She comes from a Catholic, Republican family and has been disowned for literally sleeping with the enemy. But she's a stranger with nothing more than a vague sense of geography to go on until she meets Hilditch, who offers her aid and advice. Soon, he has agreed to help her find her beloved Johnny, but we begin to suspect his motives, especially when we realize he has been videotaping his interaction with Felicia, and this isn't the first time he has offered a kind, sympathetic ear to a lonely, young girl.

Felicia's Journey grows more fascinating with every frame, as each of the characters comes into clearer focus and the narrative intensity builds. We begin to understand what motivates Hilditch and Felicia, and why they are the way they are. Yet, the deeper we get into the story, the more disquieting it becomes. Emotionally and spiritually, these people are not whole. The grim reality is that any kind of relationship between them, whether platonic or not, will lead inevitably to disaster.

A simplistic label like "villain" does not apply to Hilditch. Even as we despise his actions, we feel pity for him. Bob Hoskins' gestures, vocal mannerisms, and body language make Hilditch into a real person rather than a mere writer's construct inhabited by an adept performer. Hoskins is a recognizable face, but he submerges himself so effectively beneath the character's skin that we lose sight of the actor. And, on those occasions when the camera looks into Hilditch's haunted features and catches a glimpse of hell, one can only marvel at the intensity of Hoskins' work.

Elaine Cassidy exhibits expert poise and ability in a role that requires great range and subtlety. She displays the necessary mix of naiveté, vulnerability, and emotional toughness that one would expect from someone like Felicia, who has defied her family in a moment of passion and now finds herself alone in a strange country.

Admittedly, *Felicia's Journey* can be a troubling and difficult film to sit through, and there is a contrivance near the end that fails to convince 100%, but the production's overall ability to leave a lasting impression is undeniable. This is not the kind of facile motion picture that is easy to shake off after leaving the theater; it lingers and ripens in the mind for days afterwards. Once again, Atom Egoyan has boldly stepped forward, deepening and broadening his reputation as one of the world's best living filmmakers.

HIGHLY RECOMMENDED

Fearless [1993]

Starring: Jeff Bridges, Isabella Rossellini, Rosie Perez, Tom Hulce, John Turturro Director: Peter Weir Screenplay: Rafael Yglesias based on his novel Running Time: 2:04 Rated: R (Mature themes, language, charred bodies) Theatrical Aspect Ratio: 1.85:1

Fearless opens with Max Klein (Jeff Bridges) striding purposefully through a head-high field of corn, a baby in his arms and a young boy by his side. These three are among the survivors of a brutal plane wreck which has strewn death and debris all over a southern California corn field. After delivering the boy to the authorities and the baby to its tearful mother, Max walks away from the scene of the accident and heads to Los Angeles, where he holes up in a motel, not even calling his wife Laura (Isabella Rossellini) to let her know that he's alive. Eventually, he is forcibly brought back to his San Francisco home, where his family finds him a changed man. Eventually, Max is introduced to another survivor, Carla Rodrigo (Rosie Perez), a young woman who lost her son in the crash. Perhaps not unexpectedly, the two embark upon an unusual, deeply emotional friendship.

Jeff Bridges, who tends to play his roles with more stoicism than emotion, finds the right balance. He gives us a Max that we aren't likely to identify with, but who doesn't promote audience apathy, either. Isabella Rossellini is not as effective as Laura, but her part doesn't demand the same level of intensity. Best of the 3 principles is Rosie Perez, whose portrayal of a grief-stricken mother unable to deal with the death of her son, comes across with stark believability. For the most part, Perez's acting is understated, which makes sudden bursts of emotion all the more forceful.

The theatrical trailers for this movie would lead you to believe that it's an uplifting experience. Nothing could be further from the truth. While there are a few moments of emotional exultation, most of the movie explores darker elements of human nature. The tangible presence of the Grim Reaper hangs above *Fearless* from start to finish.

While the relationship between Max and Carla is developed to perfection, there are a few offshoots of the main story that are never plumbed satisfactorily. Great care is taken to show the hero worship exhibited by the boy who followed Max out of the plane, but beyond the setup, little is done. There are indications of the stress that this places on Max's relationship with his own son, but the situation is given perfunctory treatment. Director Peter Weir fails to draw upon the possibilities of one of *Fearless*'s most emotionally-wrenching scenes: a group therapy session where survivors relate their memories of the crash.

Fearless is still an impressive film, even considering the untapped potential. The interactions of the 3 main characters are potent without being shocking or sensationalistic and the import of the questions raised isn't diminished because of the lack of firm answers. **HIGHLY RECOMMENDED**

Finding Forrester [2000]

Starring: Sean Connery, Rob Brown, F. Murray Abraham, Anna Paquin Director: Gus Van Sant Screenplay: Mike Rich Running Time: 2:18 Rated: PG-13 (Profanity, mature themes) Theatrical Aspect Ratio: 2.35:1

In Gus Van Sant's *Finding Forrester*, newcomer Rob Brown plays Jamal Wallace, a Bronx high schooler whose stunning achievement test scores and standout performance on the basketball court earn him the notice of officials at the exclusive Mailor-Callow Prep School, where he is offered a full scholarship as a junior. Jamal's mother (April Grace) and brother (Busta Rhymes) are thrilled by the offer, and, realizing that going to Mailor will allow him to advance his prospects, Jamal agrees to attend. Although his streetwise background makes him a social outsider amidst a sea of rich, pampered kids, Jamal's performance on the court and in the classroom earns him the respect of many of his teachers and peers, including Claire (Anna Paquin), the pretty daughter of the head of Mailor's board of directors.

Jamal inadvertently discovers the whereabouts of the reclusive author William Forrester (Sean Connery), a former Pulitzer Prize winner who disappeared from the public eye after writing "the Great 20th Century Novel," *Avalon Landing*. Forrester owns an apartment overlooking the blacktop where Jamal and his friends play pickup games, and, one day, after making a brazen statement, Jamal is forced to back up his words by sneaking into Forrester's apartment to steal something. He is caught in the act and accidentally leaves behind his backpack, which contains his journals. Forrester writes comments in the notebooks and returns the backpack. Thus begins a peculiar mentor/student relationship, with Jamal agreeing not to reveal Forrester's whereabouts in return for Forrester's instruction in the craft of writing.

At the core of *Finding Forrester* is a familiar "buddy story" — about how a brilliant, outcast youngster simultaneously learns from and teaches life lessons to a weary old-timer. Forrester tutors Jamal about how to be an author; Jamal encourages Forrester to shake off his fear of the outside world.

As Jamal, Rob Brown displays a natural, unforced charisma. There isn't a hint of artifice in his performance, and it's easy to understand why the filmmakers chose him instead of a better established actor. For his part, the eternally watchable Connery doesn't test the limits of his acting ability to play the curmudgeonly Forrester. This is a case when an actor's reputation works in the character's favor. As written, Forrester is an irascible, unpleasant fellow, but audiences are so used to liking Connery that it's impossible to accept that there isn't a heart of gold hidden beneath the aging author's thick skin.

With *Finding Forrester,* Van Sant appears to have put an exclamation mark on his intention to move into mainstream filmmaking. Viewers unaware of Van Sant's history will not be clued into it by anything found on-screen in this movie. *Finding Forrester* is well made but conventional, and, depending on your mood, that represents either its greatest strength or its most telling weakness. **RECOMMENDED**

Finding Neverland [United Kingdom/United States, 2004]

Starring: Johnny Depp, Kate Winslet, Julie Christie, Nick Roud, Radha Mitchell, Joe Prospero, Freddie Highmore, Dustin Hoffman, Luke Spill, Kelly Macdonald Director: Marc Foster Screenplay: David Magee, based on the play by Allan Knee Running Time: 1:41 Rated: PG (Mature themes) Theatrical Aspect Ratio: 1.85:1

Finding Neverland uses strands of historical fact to weave a story that is largely fictional. Yes, J. M. Barrie did write *Peter Pan*, and yes, many of the characters in the film existed, but this is predominantly a softball approach to the inspiration that led Barrie to write his most famous play. Still, even considering the liberties taken with the known record, the end result is compelling and life affirming.

The story is a nice mixture of drama, fantasy, romance, and tragedy, with no hints of some of the ugliness that marred the real J. M. Barrie's reputation. Barrie (Johnny Depp) is at the nadir of his creative powers, having just bombed with his latest play, when he encounters Sylvia Llewelyn Davies (Kate Winslet) and her four boys: Peter (Freddie Highmore), George

(Nick Roud), Jack (Joe Prospero), and Michael (Luke Spill). Barrie strikes up a quick friendship with the Davies family, and soon is viewed by the boys as a favorite uncle. Suspicious of his new relationship with the children and their mother are Barrie's wife, Mary (Radha Mitchell), and Sylvia's mother, Mrs. Du Maurier (Julie Christie). This association frees the block on Barrie's creativity, and he begins to develop *Peter Pan,* which would be his most successful stage production.

Finding Neverland contains some stock elements, but almost all of them are done well. There's the platonic relationship between Barrie and Sylvia — something that, under different circumstances, might have developed into a deeper interaction. There's the give-and-take between Barrie and the boys (Peter in particular) as they release his creative energy and he gives them lessons in living. And there's the bitchy Mrs. Du Maurier, whose intense dislike of Barrie allows her to come as close as the film has to having a villain. She wants the writer out of her daughter's and grandchildren's lives.

Finding Neverland is best described as a "safe" movie. It does what it sets out to do, but never attempts anything risky. It is by turns tender, humorous, and touching, but it never attempts anything that would elevate it to the next level. This is solid but unspectacular entertainment, and most who see it will leave theaters satisfied, although not overwhelmed. *Finding Neverland* deserves a recommendation because it works on an emotional and, to a lesser degree, intellectual level. **RECOMMENDED**

The Five Senses [Canada, 1999]

Starring: Mary-Louise Parker, Nadia Litz, Daniel MacIvor, Molly Parker, Gabrielle Rose Director: Jeremy Podeswa Screenplay: Jeremy Podeswa Running Time: 1:45 Rated: R (Profanity, nudity, sex) Theatrical Aspect Ratio: 1.85:1

The central conceit embraced by *The Five Senses* is that each of the primary characters represents a sense. Cake baker Rona (Mary-Louise Parker) is taste; sulky, voyeuristic teenager Rachel (Nadia Litz) is sight; Richard (Philippe Volter), an eye doctor losing the use of his ears, is hearing; cleaning man Robert (Daniel MacIvor), who has an odd habit of sniffing people's odors, is smell; and masseuse Ruth (Gabrielle Rose) is touch. The central connecting event is the disappearance of a 3-year-old child while in Rachel's care. The mother, Anna (Molly Parker), makes a public plea for help and the case becomes the central focus of the Toronto news scene.

Rona is involved with an Italian boyfriend with

whom she can't communicate (he speaks Italian; she speaks English). Her bisexual best friend, Robert, is looking up old boyfriends and girlfriends to see whether any of those relationships can be resurrected. Richard silently broods about his loss of hearing and makes up a list of sounds he wants to experience one last time before the chance is gone forever. He desperately misses his estranged wife and daughter, and seeks solace from a prostitute who has a deaf child. Ruth feels intense guilt for the young girl's disappearance because Rachel is her daughter. And Rachel dissociates herself from the entire incident, seeking comfort in the company of a boy her age who is also one of society's outcasts.

The characters in *The Five Senses* radiate a strong, almost overpowering sense of loneliness. It is their constant companion, and the lesson that each must learn (and not everyone does) is that genuine intimacy requires the use of all 5 senses, not just 1 or 2. Admittedly, the idea underlying the movie sounds pretentious, but the execution is not.

Each character is looking for something. Those who can define it, like Robert, are no closer to attaining it than those who are groping in the dark. A mother and daughter, both sharing a loss, have become strangers. To one degree or another, these are problems we are all familiar with. Rona's relationship with her Italian boyfriend is symbolic of this malaise of the soul — they have sex and eat, but, because of the language gap, they cannot engage in a meaningful conversation.

Underlying *The Five Senses* is a sharp understanding of the natures of grief, loneliness, and communication. As the film progresses, the importance of the individual senses is downplayed. The movie is not so much about the five senses as it is about how we process the information they provide. **RECOMMENDED**

Focus [2001]

Starring: William H. Macy, Laura Dern, David Paymer, Meat Loaf Aday
Director: Neal Slavin Screenplay: Kendrew Lascelles, based on the novel by Arthur Miller Running Time: 1:47 Rated: PG-13 (Mature themes, violence) Theatrical Aspect Ratio: **1.85:1**

It's a little disconcerting to watch something as timely and eerily prescient as Neal Slavin's *Focus*, which touches on many current "hot button" issues. The film is based on a 1945 novel by playwright Arthur Miller — a fact that illustrates the sad truth that, no matter how hatred and bigotry metamorphose, they remain constants of the human experience — dark, shadowy companions during our sojourn in this life.

Lawrence Newman (William H. Macy) lives in a quiet, middle-class neighborhood with his mother (Kay Hawtrey). Lawrence is a bit of a recluse. He'll politely greet his neighbors if he sees them on the street, but he rarely goes out of his way to start a conversation. His next-door neighbor, Fred (Meat Loaf Aday), is wary of Lawrence, failing to understand why an upstanding Protestant man avoids coming to a series of "neighborhood meetings" designed to discuss what to do about the unwanted presence of a local Jewish shopkeeper, Finkelstein (David Paymer). Then, Lawrence gets spectacles, and suddenly people begin to notice that he looks Jewish. When he meets, then marries, Gertrude (Laura Dern), suspicions deepen because, like Lawrence, Gertrude "looks" Jewish. Suddenly, these two Protestants have been blacklisted as Jews and are subject to the same persecution being visited upon Finkelstein.

Focus is an examination of the pervasive and uncompromising nature of hatred. The central irony is, of course, that neither of the main characters is a member of the race being singled out for vilification. Because of this, Slavin is able to show how truly irrational any form of group-specific hatred is. *Focus* also makes a statement about the fear of involvement. Lawrence believes the creed "see no evil, hear no evil, speak no evil." Little does he realize that it's only a matter of time before he becomes an outsider and everyone in the neighborhood turns a blind eye to his plight.

A secondary theme in *Focus*, and perhaps one of more immediate interest, is that of the resolve to stand firm in the face of terrorist threats. Both Lawrence and Finkelstein grow increasingly isolated and threatened. One option that is repeatedly suggested to them is that they move away, but they refuse to budge. This is their home and fear will not drive them from it. They stand resolute, regardless of how ugly circumstances become.

Few things, when taken to extremes, have positive results. *Focus* shows what can happen when patriotism and religious zeal turn sour. Hatred has no justification, but it always seeks an excuse, and, in the reactionary politics and misguided advocacy of a close-minded preacher, it finds one. *Focus* explores how acts of hatred begin small, then snowball out of control. Slavin's film is not without its faults, but, especially in today's climate, it's a fascinating motion picture, and its diverse-yet-interrelated subject matter can provide fodder for lengthy post-movie discussions. **RECOMMENDED**

For Love of the Game [1999]

Starring: Kevin Costner, Kelly Preston, John C. Reilly, Jena Malone Director: **Sam Raimi** Screenplay: Dana Stevens, based on the novel by Michael Shaara Running Time: 2:17 Rated: PG-13 (Profanity, sexual situations) Theatrical Aspect Ratio: 2.35:1

For Love of the Game is appropriately named. Crafted with respect for the game and an eye towards accuracy, the best scenes are some of the most true-to-life baseball moments ever presented in a non-documentary form on celluloid. The rest of the film tells a rather corny love story that is occasionally hamstrung by ripe dialogue. The romantic angle is necessary to the overall plot because it provides a sense of balance in the main character's life, but it is not written or developed as well as the baseball aspect.

Kevin Costner plays Billy Chapel, a pitcher who has thrown every major league pitch in his 19-year career for the Detroit Tigers. When the team won the World Series in 1984, Chapel was a big part of the victory. This has not been a good year, and the baseball gods haven't been kind to him — his record is a lackluster 8-11. Now, the team's owner has informed him that if he doesn't retire after today's game, the season finale against the Yankees in New York, he will be traded.

Weary in body, Billy takes the mound and gives it everything he has. As the innings go by, his mind drifts back through the last 5 years, recalling the only love of his life besides baseball. She is Jane Aubrey (Kelly Preston), and she has just broken things off with him so she can go to England to advance her career. Billy remembers key moments in their relationship — the first time they met, the time she surprised him at Spring Training when he was with another woman, and the night he rescued her teenage daughter (Jena Malone). Then, as the number of outs remaining drops into the single digits, everyone in the stadium, from the beer-guzzling fans in the stands to the announcers in the booth (Vin Scully and Steve Lyons), recognizes that Billy has a chance to pitch a perfect game. For 7 innings, no one has gotten on base. But, as anyone who watches baseball knows, the last 6 outs are always the hardest.

The film's structure — cutting back and forth between the final game of the season and the flashback highlights of Billy and Jane's romance — works. The problem is that the script isn't as smart or insightful when it deals with a man's love for a woman as it is when it concentrates on that same man's love for baseball.

In many ways, *For Love of the Game* is an old fashioned motion picture. Although it acknowledges the state of the game today, it views the sport with the respect it once had when it was America's Pastime. Today, winning has become everything. No one seems to care about the simple rhythm of 9 innings. As baseball movies go, this one isn't a home run — it's more of a single or a double. But, as any fan knows, that's still a hit, and it can generate some excitement. **RECOMMENDED**

Forrest Gump [1994]

Starring: Tom Hanks, Robin Wright Penn, Gary Sinise, Mykelti Williamson, Sally Field Director: Robert Zemeckis Screenplay: Eric Roth based on the novel by Winston Groom Running Time: 2:22 Rated: PG-13 (Mature themes, implied sex, discreet nudity, language, violence) Theatrical Aspect Ratio: 2.35:1

Passionate and magical, *Forrest Gump* is a tonic for the weary of spirit. For those who feel that being set adrift in a season of action movies is like wandering into a desert, the oasis lies ahead. In *Forrest Gump*, the main character remains a child in heart and spirit, even as his body grows to maturity.

Forrest Gump (Hanks), named after a civil war hero, grows up in Greenbow, Alabama, where his mother (Sally Field) runs a boarding house. Although Forrest is a little "slow" (his IQ is 75, 5 below the state's definition of "normal"), his mental impairment doesn't seem to bother him, his mother, or his best (and only) friend, Jenny Curran (played as an adult by Robin Wright Penn). In fact, the naïveté that comes through a limited understanding of the world around him gives Forrest a uniquely positive perspective of life.

During the next 30 years, Forrest becomes a star football player, a war hero, a successful businessman, and something of a pop icon. Through it all, however, there is one defining element in his life: his love for Jenny. She is never far from his thoughts, no matter what he's doing or where he is.

A trio of assets lift *Forrest Gump* above the average "lifestory" drama: its optimism, freshness, and emotional honesty. Though the movie does not seek to reduce every member of the audience to tears, it has moments whose power comes from their simplicity. Equally as important is laughter, and *Forrest Gump* has moments of humor strewn throughout.

Through the miracle of visual effects, Forrest meets

his fair share of famous people — George Wallace, Presidents Kennedy, Johnson, and Nixon, and John Lennon. While mixing the real footage of these notables with new images featuring Hanks is not a seamless process, the result is nevertheless effective.

Tom Hanks won an Academy Award for *Philadelphia*, but his performance here is more impressive. The Alabama accent may seem a little awkward at first, but it doesn't take long for the acting to dwarf the twang. Hanks has no difficulty creating a totally human character who is free of guile and deceit, and barely able to comprehend a concept like evil. Looking and seeming like a younger Jessica Lange, Robin Wright Penn is believable as the object of Forrest's undying affection. The real scene-stealer, however, is Gary Sinise. In this movie, his Lieutenant Dan Taylor is riveting. The passion and pain he brings to the middle portions of *Forrest Gump* hold together some of the film's weaker moments.

This is a marvelous motion picture — a mint julep on a hot summer's afternoon. MUST SEE

Fresh [United States, 1994]

Starring: Sean Nelson, Giancarlo Esposito, Samuel L. Jackson, Cheryl Freeman, N'Bushe Wright Director: Boaz Yakin Screenplay: Boaz Yakin Running Time: 1:54 Rated: R (Violence, language, drugs) Theatrical Aspect Ratio: 1.85:1

Never has chess been a more apt metaphor for life than in Boaz Yakin's feature debut, *Fresh*. Samuel L. Jackson sits in New York's Washington Square playing speed chess and dispensing valuable lessons about life. (As a trivia note, the chess advisor for this film was Bruce Pandolfini, whose real-life character was portrayed by Ben Kingsley in *Searching for Bobby Fischer*.) His son Michael (played with astonishing ability by Sean Nelson) eats up those lessons and promptly applies them to a far more dangerous game than the one in the park.

Michael, nicknamed Fresh by the drug lords who use him as a runner, has had the grisly misfortune of watching 2 children gunned down in cold blood. He knows the killer, and decides that if he orchestrates his revenge cleverly, he may be able to get both himself and his sister Nichole (N'Bushe Wright) out of the cycle of poverty and drugs they're trapped in. To succeed, however, he must play the perfect match. A false move means death at the hands of his mentor, Esteban (Giancarlo Esposito), the local smack distributor.

Fresh takes the setting and tone of *Boyz 'N the Hood* and *Menace II Society* and applies it to a thriller. Gone

is the documentary-like quality of filmmaking as well as the gritty sense of immediacy. *Fresh* uses higher-quality film stock and a more traditional cinematographic style to distance the audience ever-so-slightly from the characters. This way, it's easier to appreciate the complexity of Michael's plan and the manner in which he arranges his masterful scheme of manipulation.

With a script as smart as the title character, *Fresh* keeps its viewers guessing. Having a 6th grader as the protagonist is a stroke of genius that adds a further layer of tension to an already taut storyline. Thirteen-year-old Sean Nelson's performance would make many older actors envious. Without a hint of awkwardness, he conveys the sharp intelligence behind Michael's wide-eyed, seemingly innocent looks.

Samuel L. Jackson is a scene-stealer as Michael's near-vagrant speed chess playing father. The role isn't large, but this is an example of an actor at his most focused. Michael's father advises him that any piece on the chess board can be sacrificed to get the king. It is a lesson he takes to heart. Everyone becomes an expendable pawn in the high-stakes game, and there are casualties. The price of winning at all costs is depicted in the film's final shot. That's just one of the images that marks *Fresh* as an atypical thriller — a film that succeeds because it defies many conventions of its genre. HIGHLY RECOMMENDED

Friday Night Lights [2004]

Starring: Billy Bob Thornton, Lucas Black, Garrett Hedlund, Derek Luke, Jay Hernandez, Lee Jackson, Lee Thomspson Young, Tim McGraw Director: Peter Berg Screenplay: David Aaron Cohen and Peter Berg, based on *Friday Night Lights: A Town, a Team, and a Dream* by Buzz Bissinger Running Time: 1:57 Rated: PG-13 (Violence, profanity, sexual situations) Theatrical Aspect Ratio: 2.35:1

Friday Night Lights, which is based on true events as related in Buzz Bissinger's best-selling book, *Friday Night Lights: A Town, a Team, and a Dream*, follows the 1988 football season of the Odessa-Permian Panthers, one of the elite high school clubs of West Texas. This is die-hard football country, where stores close so everyone in town can attend the game. Sunday morning is for church. Friday night is for football. There are hopes for an undefeated season. The state championship is almost a given. With a player as talented as James "Boobie" Miles (Derek Luke), the concept of a loss is inconceivable — until Boobie goes down with a severe knee injury in the first game. Suddenly, his supporting cast, including quarterback Mike Winchell (Lucas Black) and running backs Don

Billingsley (Garrett Hedlund) and Chris Comer (Lee Thompson Young) must step up. The team's coach, Gary Gaines (Billy Bob Thornton), alternately endures the bile and the praise of the town. When the Panthers are winning, he can do no wrong. But when the Panthers are losing, he is persona non grata.

All of the Panthers are dogged by high expectations. Most sports movies are about the underdog coming out of nowhere to achieve a victory. *Friday Night Lights* is about the pressure to win. Boobie gets a painful life lesson when he sees a promising future vanish in an instant. This teenager, who had always imagined that his talent would take him to the NFL, stares resignedly at a group of garbage men making their morning rounds. Mike, a natural mama's boy, must shake his natural reticence and become a leader. Win or lose, he must learn to grow up. And Don has to resolve the love-hate relationship he has with his drunken father (Tim McGraw), who savored a measure of success two decades ago as a member of a champion Panthers team, and wants the same for his son.

Two things lend *Friday Night Lights* an aura of verisimilitude: the choice of actors and the manner in which Berg and cinematographer Tobias A. Schliessler have chosen to present the narrative. The film's style is documentary-like. *Friday Night Lights* has been hailed by some critics as the best sports movie ever made. While I think that is hyperbole, Berg's picture is certainly an above-average effort that provides a solid emotional punch. The difference between this film and many of those that have come before it is one of perspective. In most sports pictures, the big game at the end is the point. Here, the game is just a means by which what really matters comes into focus. And that's sufficient to set apart *Friday Night Lights*. RECOMMENDED

Fried Green Tomatoes [1991]
Starring: Mary Stuart Masterson, Mary-Louise Parker, Kathy Bates, Jessica Tandy Director: Jon Avnet Screenplay: Fannie Flag and Carol Sobieski based on the book *Fried Green Tomatoes at the Whistlestop Café* by Fannie Flag Running Time: 2:19 Rated: PG-13 (language, mature themes)

Fried Green Tomatoes is a thoroughly enjoyable movie-going experience, replete with laughter, tears, triumph, and tragedy. Unfortunately, it has been sanitized and "Hollywoodized," with the relationship between the two 1930 female leads left ambiguous, and a few too many scenes going over-the-top to manipulate an emotional reaction. So, while providing 2+ hours worth of solid entertainment, director Jon Avnet's picture lacks the crucial ingredient which would have lifted it above the level of a tearjerker to that of the extraordinary.

The acting can easily be counted among *Fried Green Tomatoes*' strengths. Especially noteworthy are the performances by Mary Stuart Masterson (as Idgie) and Mary-Louise Parker (as Ruth), who make their characters' improbable friendship come alive. Oscar-winners Kathy Bates and Jessica Tandy are fine, although their characters aren't as compelling, nor does their relationship have the same dynamics.

Some viewers have labeled this film a "woman's movie," which it is in the sense that the 4 protagonists are female. The themes and plot are universal, as male audience members who aren't afraid of sentiment will discover. *Fried Green Tomatoes* is 2 stories in one, both of which ultimately work as well as they can, given what the film is trying to do. It should be noted that the present-day scenes aren't as involving as those that take place in the 1930s. The structure is unusual, with the modern day scenes "framing" the flashbacks. Because the differences in the time periods are so marked, this may have not been the best way to handle the dual storylines. There are some awkward moments when the 1930s/1990s parallelism seems forced.

The greatest flaw of this movie is that Avnet tries relentlessly to get his viewers to reach for the box of tissues. A little manipulation is expected in any melodrama, but *Fried Green Tomatoes* goes overboard. That's not to say that the audience is likely to be weeping through the entire film, but Avnet isn't particularly subtle about what he's trying to do.

Because of its strong sense of character development, *Fried Green Tomatoes* touches a plethora of emotional chords. At times, it is gritty and inspirational, while still maintaining enough comedy to offset the less-comfortable instances of emotional upheaval. For mystery-lovers, there's even a murder thrown in. The film isn't perfect, but it has enough going for it to make it worthy entertainment. HIGHLY RECOMMENDED

The Full Monty [United Kingdom, 1997]
Starring: Robert Carlyle, Tom Wilkinson, Mark Addy, Steve Huison, Paul Barber, Hugo Speer Director: Peter Cattaneo Screenplay: Simon Beaufoy Running Time: 1:30 Rated: R (Profanity, nudity) Theatrical Aspect Ratio: 1.85:1

The Full Monty combines humor with light drama to explore the manner in which a group of men cope with the emotional and financial toll of being "force adjusted." The movie opens in Sheffield, England, a major steel working city whose central industry has been modernized and mechanized. Productivity is up, but the victims of the automation are the workers, many of whom have been laid off. *The Full Monty* focuses on one such man, Gaz (Robert Carlyle), who is hundreds of pounds behind on child support payments to his ex-wife, Mandy (Emily Woof). Gaz's best friend, Dave (Mark Addy), and his former boss, Gerald (Tom Wilkinson), are also unemployed. Their collective inability to find work is eating into their self-esteem. Gaz's son doesn't want to spend time at his dad's house because it's always cold, Gerald is frightened to tell his credit card-obsessed wife that he doesn't have a job, and Dave loses his ability to perform sexually.

Things change when the Chippendales arrive in Sheffield to perform a show. The tremendous crowds that turn out for the event give Gaz an idea. If male strippers who don't take it all off can rake in the money, what about those who are willing to show "the full monty"? In short order, Gaz has recruited an unlikely group of dancers: a sad loner (Steve Huison), an aging black man with rhythm and a bad hip (Paul Barber), and a cheerful, well-endowed young man (Hugo Speer) who has the body but not the moves. Drawing upon Gaz's enthusiasm and Gerald's experience as a ballroom dancer, the band of 6 develop a routine, dancing with and without clothes to the songs of Donna Summer, Gary Glitter, and Tom Jones.

The Full Monty throws pretended eroticism out the window. There isn't a sexually provocative moment in the film. The nudity is discretely handled, although the actors did in fact perform a live strip show in front of 400 extras in a sequence that was, according to the director, "a one-take deal." This lends a degree of spontaneity to *The Full Monty* that makes the movie's climactic scenes more believable and enjoyable.

The 6 members of the group relate well to each other and engage our sympathy. Robert Carlyle plays Gaz with the right mix of pathos and energy. Tom Wilkinson (*Sense and Sensibility*) has the "stuck up bastard with a good heart" role down pat. And, as the overweight Dave, Mark Addy brings to the fore feelings of insecurity that almost anyone can relate to.

The Full Monty is basically about overcoming adversity and succeeding is spite of certain perceived shortcomings. What *The Full Monty* lacks in depth, it makes up for in good will and likeability. This isn't a great movie, but it's breezy, enjoyable, and easy to sit through. And sometimes, even when dealing with a serious issue like unemployment, that can be the perfect tone to drive home a message. RECOMMENDED

Get On the Bus [1996]

Starring: Charles Dutton, Ossie Davis, Thomas Jefferson Byrd, Andre Braugher Director: Spike Lee Screenplay: Reggie Rock Bythewood Running Time: 2:00 Rated: R (Profanity, mature themes) Theatrical Aspect Ratio: 1.85:1

The Million Man March, which took place on October 16, 1995, was arguably the most important display of male black solidarity since the '60s. As depicted in *Get on the Bus*, it was about unity, self-discovery, and taking responsibility. *Get on the Bus* investigates the spirit and meaning of the March as seen through the eyes of a group of diverse men taking the long bus trip from Los Angeles to Washington D.C. for the event. Unfortunately, many of the bus riders are just variations of stock characters. Neither Lee nor screenwriter Reggie Rock Bythewood crafts more than one or two well-realized personalities.

The men who board the "Spotted Owl" bus in South Central L.A. are certainly not all cut from the same mold. There's Gary (Roger Guenveur Smith), a half-white cop who's insecure about his "blackness." Evan (Thomas Jefferson Byrd) and his son, Junior (De'aundre Bonds), are shackled together by court order. "Dog," as Junior calls him, is trying to make up for years of absent parenting by taking his reluctant, delinquent offspring to this historic event. Two homosexual lovers, Kyle (Isaiah Washington) and Randall (Harry J. Lennix), are in the midst of a breakup. An up-and-coming actor, Flip (Andre Braugher), is waiting to hear whether he'll get the co-starring role in a new Denzel Washington movie. Also along for the ride are Xavier (Hill Harper), an aspiring film student; and Jeremiah (Ossie Davis, in a standout performance), the aging voice of wisdom and experience.

There isn't enough screen time to develop these stories more than fitfully. Some get better exposure than others. The struggle of the homosexuals to attain acceptance is handled in a superficial manner. The battle lines between gay rights supporters and homophobes are clearly established on the bus, with each side mouthing the requisite slogans. Lee doesn't really offer anything new as far as the plight of the gay black man is concerned, and appears to have included this pair primarily as a means of illustrating diversity within the community.

The melodramatic ending, which includes a sermon on unity, is excessively manipulative. And there are several instances throughout when Lee uses contrived events to advance the plot. Still, all things considered, *Get on the Bus* presents an involving, intimate portrait of a group of men gathered for a common purpose. Artificial plot devices don't divert our attention from the strong, heartfelt performances.

Some moments in *Get on the Bus* cut to the heart of what the Million Man March symbolized. One such occasion has the characters singing an improvised "Roll Call," introducing themselves to each other in song. Another is an intense confrontation between Gary and Jamal about street violence, a topic that has a deep, personal meaning for each of them. Scenes like these, ripe with genuine emotion, are the most compelling reason to take this trip with director Spike Lee and his talented cast. **RECOMMENDED**

Ghost World [2001]

Starring: **Thora Birch, Scarlett Johansson, Steve Buscemi, Brad Renfro** Director: **Terry Zwigoff** Screenplay: **Daniel Clowes & Terry Zwigoff,** based on the comic book by Daniel Clowes Running Time: 1:51 Rated: R (Profanity, sexual situations) Theatrical Aspect Ratio: 1.85:1

Ghost World could easily be considered an "anti-Hollywood coming of age story." It is based on the comic book of the same name, which was devised by Daniel Clowes. In addition to co-writing the screenplay, he was available to help director Terry Zwigoff in a consultant capacity. *Ghost World* is being marketed as a comedy, and while that's technically correct, it should be noted that this is a bleak comedy.

The movie opens at a high school graduation. Best friends Enid (Thora Birch) and Rebecca (Scarlett Johansson) are preparing to venture into the "real world" together. They intend to get jobs, then rent an apartment together. College isn't in the cards for either of them. However, despite being inseparable during high school, Enid and Rebecca begin to drift apart as their maturing life goals take them in different directions. Rebecca is embracing conventionality — a steady job (at a coffee shop), a "regular" apartment, and plans for the future. Enid, on the other hand, is wandering aimlessly, entering into a semi-romantic relationship with a much older, timid jazz-lover, Seymour (Steve Buscemi), failing to hold down a job for more than a day, taking a remedial art class, and continuing to live in her father's house. The more the rift between Enid and Rebecca widens, the less likely it is that they will be able to bridge it.

The real strength of *Ghost World* are the characters. Enid in particular, who has the most screen time, de-

velops into a well-rounded individual. She has her rough edges (she's not the easiest person to get along with), but it doesn't take long for us to be rooting for her. In portraying Enid, Birch weds quirkiness with an underlying sense of melancholy and ennui.

Scarlett Johansson, provides an appealing Rebecca, although her role is a little underwritten (especially in comparison with Birch's). Meanwhile, indie favorite Steve Buscemi has the opportunity to play a kind of part he is rarely accorded — a romantic lead. Of course, Seymour doesn't represent the typical male half of a romantic pairing — he's emotionally withdrawn, painfully shy, and inexperienced with women — in short, a traditional dork. Seymour's relationship with Enid represents a non-traditional May/December pairing, although the manner in which their interaction is handled rings true.

Ghost World offers interesting characters, smart dialogue, biting satire (the concept of "high art" gets shredded), and dark comedy. Zwigoff, who brought us the brilliant portrait of cartoonist R. Crumb in the documentary *Crumb*, clearly feels at home in this territory. **RECOMMENDED**

Ghosts of Mississippi [1996]

Starring: **Alec Baldwin, Whoopi Goldberg, James Woods, Craig T. Nelson, Diane Ladd, Bonnie Bartlet, Bill Cobbs, William H. Macy** Director: **Rob Reiner** Screenplay: **Lewis Collick** Running Time: 2:10 Rated: R (Mature themes, profanity, violence) Theatrical Aspect Ratio: 1.85:1

Shortly after midnight on a steamy June evening in 1963, civil rights activist Medgar Evers was shot to death outside his home in Jackson, Mississippi. One shot, fired from a high-powered rifle, exploded through his chest, ripped through the nearby wall of his house, ricocheted off a refrigerator, and broke a coffee pot. The assassin was white supremacist Byron De La Beckwith, a man with such an intimidating personality that even the KKK feared him. De La Beckwith was captured, but, after two trials ended in hung juries, he went free. When, 30 years later, at the behest of Evers' widow, Myrlie, Assistant DA Bobby DeLaughter re-opened the case, he had no idea of the difficulties he would face in obtaining a new indictment. Evidence was missing, witnesses had died, and even the official court transcripts of the original trials could not be located. On top of that, the new trial reopened old wounds in the community. DeLaughter's life was threatened, and many people — including his own wife — turned against him. Undaunted, he pursued the case, determined to see it through to the end.

As a courtroom drama, *Ghosts of Mississippi* is reasonably successful. The trial, which carefully follows the actual transcript from 1994, avoids the contrived, theatrical twists that mar many similar films. There are no surprise witnesses or unexpected moves by either the prosecution or the defense. Each side presents its case, then leaves the final decision in the hands of the jury. As a result of this verisimilitude, the courtroom aspects of *Ghosts of Mississippi* are intelligent rather than over-the-top. We care about the characters and what happens to them.

As an examination of how the Civil Rights movement has changed lifestyles and attitudes in Mississippi (and, by extension, across the entire country) during the last 30 years, *Ghosts of Mississippi* is less effective. Reiner investigates two prevalent, albeit contradictory, views of how the Civil Rights movement has changed the nation. Either we are making slow progress, step by step, to a better future, or, "emotionally, we will always be segregated." DeLaughter's conscience becomes the battleground for these viewpoints. But, although the script is tightly-written for the most part, there are times when it lapses into sermonizing (such as when DeLaughter tries to explain to his young children why Evers was a great man).

At times, *Ghosts of Mississippi* resembles nothing more lofty than a toned-down, historically-grounded version of *A Time to Kill*. (A white man in the "new" South faces racism and personal danger for defending the "black" perspective.) So, although I recommend *Ghosts of Mississippi* and believe that it deserves to find a wide audience, I am cognizant that this is not a perfect motion picture. It is occasionally thought-provoking, but rarely haunting. RECOMMENDED

Girl, Interrupted [1999]

Starring: Winona Ryder, Angelina Jolie, Clea DuVall, Brittany Murphy Director: James Mangold Screenplay: James Mangold and Lisa Loomer and Anna Hamilton Phelan, based on the book by Susanna Kaysen Running Time: 2:07 Rated: R (Profanity, sexual situations, violence) Theatrical Aspect Ratio: 1.85:1

When it comes to sexual promiscuity in America, is there a double-standard? Of course, and it was even more evident during the mid-to-late-1960s, the era in which *Girl, Interrupted* is set. As Susanna (played by Winona Ryder), the lead character, puts it, "How many girls would a 17-year-old boy have to [sleep with] to earn the label 'compulsively promiscuous'? And how many boys for 17-year-old girls?" The answer is telling. A teenage boy with multiple partners

would be considered "virile" or would be viewed good-naturedly as "sowing his wild oats." At best, a girl who approached sex with a similar vigor would be called a "slut." At worst, as was Susanna's case, she would be classified as having a "borderline personality disorder."

Of course, enjoying sex isn't Susanna's only problem — she also occasionally hallucinates, and, after attempting suicide, she is encouraged to check into Claymoore, a suburban Boston mental hospital that's more like a country club than an asylum. Only after signing the admission papers does she learn that she can't just walk out — the hospital has to release her. So Susanna is stuck for the long haul, which turns out to be nearly 2 years.

Susanna's time in Claymoore is a period of self-discovery. At first, she is angry and antisocial, and gravitates naturally towards Lisa, (Angelina Jolie) the ward's most consistent troublemaker. Eventually, however, she learns that Lisa's cruel streak has a vicious edge that she doesn't want to be associated with. So she concentrates on writing in her journal and making a conscious effort to rehabilitate.

For the most part, the film manages to avoid seeming like a rip-off of *One Flew Over the Cuckoo's Nest* with women. Director Mangold ably mines the talent of his cast. Winona Ryder brings Susanna to life in a low-key, subtly powerful performance that allows Susanna to seem strangely normal compared to her fellow inmates. Give the film credit for having the courage to run with a protagonist who isn't entirely likeable: in addition to suffering delusions, Susanna is presented as spoiled, selfish, and occasionally unkind. Compared to Lisa, however, she's an angel. In *Girl, Interrupted*'s most visible role, Angelia Jolie shines like a supernova, radiating flamboyance. It's an electric performance that energizes every scene in which she appears, recalling but not imitating Jack Nicolson's turn as Randle P. McMurphy in *Cuckoo's Nest*.

Marred (not fatally) by a somewhat pat ending, *Girl, Interruped* is a fine film about relationships and self-discovery. While the movie may not entirely capture the tone and spirit of the book, it stands solidly on its own, separate yet never entirely divorced from its source material. RECOMMENDED

Girl with a Pearl Earring [United Kingdom/Luxembourg, 2003]

Starring: Scarlett Johansson, Colin Firth, Tom Wilkinson, Judy Parfitt, Cillian Murphy, Essie Director: Peter Webber Screenplay: Olivia

Hetreed, based on the novel by Tracy Chevalier Running Time: 1:35 Rated: PG-13 (Sensuality, sexual situations) Theatrical Aspect Ratio: 2.35:1

Girl with a Pearl Earring is the first feature for director Peter Webber. Most freshman filmmakers don't come close to Webber's level of accomplishment, and some of the credit must certainly be parceled out to the cast and the cinematographer, Eduardo Serra. *Girl with a Pearl Earring* offers sumptuous visuals and compelling drama effectively intermingled in a pleasing, satisfying production. The director has crafted the film with great care, composing each frame like a painting with respect to color, light, camera placement, and texture. *Girl with a Pearl Earring* could be silent and it would still be an amazing achievement. Indeed, the dialogue is sparse, which forces the performers to do most of their acting with expressions and body language — something Scarlett Johansson (*Lost in Translation*) excels at. By reading her eyes and face, we understand her thoughts. The movie purports to tell the story behind the creation of Vermeer's 1665 painting *Girl with a Pearl Earring*. Since historical records are sketchy at best, most of the screenplay (based on Tracy Chevalier's book) is conjecture. The film does not carry a "based on real events" label. Nevertheless, the postulated tale is both credible and dramatically solid, thus forming the spine of a sensitive, intelligent motion picture.

Griet (Johansson) goes to work in the household of Johannes Vermeer when she's a teenager. Forced into service because her parents can no longer support her, she must endure difficult conditions in order to remain employed. The Vermeers are not easy to work for. The head of the household (Colin Firth) is a moody individual, and spends long hours locked away in his vast studio. His perpetually pregnant wife, Catharina (Essie Davis), is resentful and jealous of Griet's youth and beauty. His mother-in-law, Maria (Judy Parfitt), is a strict disciplinarian. His children don't like Griet, and his patron, van Ruijven (Tom Wilkinson), likes her too much. Eventually, van Ruijven's attraction for Griet leads him to commission a painting of her. Maid posing for master leads to a variety of tensions, both domestic and erotic. The result of this, however, is *Girl with a Pearl Earring*.

Johansson's sublime performance is ably supported by those of her better-known costars. Colin Firth gives us a brooding, dour Vermeer who only shows passion while painting. Judy Parfitt is her usual excellent, acid-tongued self. Tom Wilkinson gives

himself to debauched abandon. And Essie Davis plays her part as a grown-up spoiled brat to the hilt. We have come to anticipate top-notch acting in British productions, and our expectations are not disappointed here. *Girl with a Pearl Earring* is one of those films that does many things right. It's a cut above the usual BBC costume drama. **RECOMMENDED**

Girlfight [2000]

Starring: Michelle Rodriguez, Jaime Tirelli, Paul Calderon, Santiago Douglas, Ray Santiago Director: Karyn Kusama Screenplay: Karyn Kusama Running Time: 1:50 Rated: R (Profanity, sex, violence) Theatrical Aspect Ratio: 1.66:1

The focal point of one of the 2000 Sundance Film Festival's more serious bidding wars, first-time director Karyn Kusama's *Girlfight* is a well crafted and emotionally satisfying debut — a fine drama about self-discovery and female empowerment. It's about taking charge of one's own life when it appears to be hurtling out of control towards disaster.

Girlfight tells the story of a would-be girl boxer. Diana Guzman (Michelle Rodriguez in a coming-out performance that is equal parts fire and luminosity) is a frequent troublemaker at school, where she's just a few months shy of graduation. However, her propensity for getting into fights has her one demerit away from expulsion. She has no boyfriend, and her few girlfriends are wary of her volatile nature. Her home life isn't much better. Her mother has been dead for years and there's a slow-burning, mutual antagonism between Diana and her father (Paul Calderon). The only one she seems to care for is her geeky brother, Tiny (Ray Santiago). One day, after dropping something off at the Brooklyn Athletic Club, Diana decides that she wants to take boxing lessons. She coaxes one of the trainers, Hector (Jaime Tirelli), into teaching her for $10 a session. Soon, she is channeling her hostility and energy into the sport and is becoming less disruptive at school. At home, however, her relationship with her father edges closer to an explosion of physical violence.

These days, boxing mostly gets a bad rap; thugs dominate the ring and crooks manage them. Though once a Hollywood staple, boxing movies that show a positive aspect to the sport — getting fighters off the street and giving them a focal point for pent-up adolescent angst and anger — are now rare. Rarer still is *Girlfight*'s finely modulated sense of drama, in a genre prone to sensationalism and fervent sermonizing. And, unlike in most sports movies where the underdog must inevitably triumph at the end, the victor's identity in *Girlfight* is very much in doubt, partly because the outcome of the "big bout" isn't all that important. This picture is much more about Diana's succeeding in life than it is about her winning in the ring.

Girlfight has a hard side, because it's about characters who have been dealt a bad hand by life, but it is ultimately emotionally satisfying because it explores the way they fight and struggle to right themselves. **HIGHLY RECOMMENDED**

Gods and Monsters [1998]

Starring: Ian McKellen, Brendan Fraser, Lynn Redgrave, Lolita Davidovich Director: Bill Condon Screenplay: Bill Condon based on the novel *Father of Frankenstein* by Christopher Bram Running Time: 1:45 Rated: R (Homosexual themes, nudity, mild profanity) Theatrical Aspect Ratio: 1.85:1

Frankenstein. The Old Dark House. The Invisible Man. The Bride of Frankenstein. Show Boat. Although this may sound like a "which one of these things doesn't belong" game, there is a common element to all 5 of these '30s motion pictures — they are the enduring legacy of director James Whale. Whale, an Englishman who started on the British stage, came to Hollywood in 1930, and, with the release of *Frankenstein* in 1931, established himself as a premiere horror film maker. Whale's career spanned the '30s, but, after the spectacular failure of 1937's *The Road Back* (a picture on which he claims to have lost creative control), his star dimmed. By the mid-'40s, he was out of the motion picture industry and had turned his attention to painting. In 1957, following a stroke that left him in a state of constant mental deterioration, he drowned himself in a swimming pool. *Gods and Monsters* presents a fictionalized account of the last month of Whale's life, and is replete with flashbacks to his boyhood, his time in the trenches during World War I, and his movie-making heyday.

The film explores the relationship between Whale (Ian McKellen) and his lawn cutter, Clay Boone (Brendan Fraser). Although Whale is homosexual, Clay is not, so their connection is strictly platonic. In Clay, Whale finds a willing audience for his stories, and a means to work through a painful event from his past. In Whale, Clay finds a sympathetic figure to replace the cold, harsh father who never understood him. While the primary focus of *Gods and Monsters* is their relationship, the movie also has a great deal to say about the process of filmmaking. We see a flashback to the creation of a classic scene from *The Bride*

of Frankenstein (actress Rosalind Ayres bears a striking resemblance to Elsa Lanchaster), experience a lavish Hollywood party given by George Cukor (the director of *The Philadelphia Story* and *A Star Is Born*), and listen with rapt attention as Whale tells stories of his triumphs and tragedies behind the camera. The "gods and monsters" of the title have many meanings in this story, but the most apparent is the one relating to the film maker and his creations. Throughout this movie, we wonder whether Whale is shaping Clay into his final monster.

Most of us know James Whale's monsters — the stiff Karloff creature (whose appearance was suggested by Whale), the bizarrely beautiful Bride of Frankenstein, and Claude Rains' Invisible Man — but we know little of the individual who gave them life, and faced his own private demons on a daily basis. *Gods and Monsters* is a rich, multi-layered portrait of a director from Hollywood's Golden Age whose own life was as interesting as any of his movies. **RECOMMENDED**

Going All the Way [1997]

Starring: Jeremy Davies, Ben Affleck, Amy Locane, Rachel Weisz, Rose McGowan, Jill Clayburgh, Lesley Ann Warren Director: Mark Pellington Screenplay: Dan Wakefield based on his novel Running Time: 1:43 Rated: R (Sexual situations, nudity, profanity, violence) Theatrical Aspect Ratio: 1.85:1

Going All the Way, based on Dan Wakefield's 1970 bestselling novel of the same name, is a coming of age story with characters who are a little older than usual in this genre. While most stories about the rituals of entering adulthood are set in high schools, *Going All the Way* looks at two 20-something men who, having served during the Korean War, are fresh out of the army and trying to find their place in the world. And, since the movie is set in 1954, it addresses the roles of religion and sex in the rites of passage — this is, after all, an era when the latter was taboo and the former was de rigueur.

Sonny (Jeremy Davies) and Gunner (Ben Affleck) are an unusual pair of close friends. Although both attended the same high school and each joined the army after graduation, that's where the similarity ends. Sonny is a shy, alienated young man who comes from a deeply conservative family and who gets tongue-tied around pretty girls. His war experience was limited to guarding the home front from Kansas City. Gunner, on the other hand, is an ex-jock who spent time in Korea and Japan. He's popular, well-liked, and can get any girl he wants. His mother (Lesley Ann

Warren), a swinging bachelorette, treats him more like a boyfriend than a son. Yet, despite the differences in their personalities and backgrounds, Sonny and Gunner have very similar concerns and questions about the mysteries of life, love, and the future.

Women are, of course, the great unsolved (and perhaps unsolvable) mystery. Gunner falls for a sexy art student named Marty (Rachel Weisz, sporting an unbelievably irritating faux American accent), while Sonny is looking for a way out of a dead-end relationship with his high school sweetheart, the loyal-but-uninteresting Buddy (Amy Locane). He finds his escape in Gale (Rose McGowan), but learns the hard way that dream girls are sometimes better left in dreams.

The movie, adapted by Wakefield and directed by MTV alum and first time feature filmmaker Mark Pellington, is at times uneven. *Going All the Way* contains elements of comedy ranging from subtle humor to blatant satire (most of the latter involve a scathing view of religion and conservatism in the '50s). Not all of these blend seamlessly with the movie's more dramatic elements, and several of the comic-to-serious transitions are jarring (such as the tragedy that follows closely upon Sonny's surreal trip into a fundamentalist church where he asks directions to a whore house).

Going All the Way is a pleasant way to spend an evening, and the characters are fashioned with enough detail for us to care about them, but this is in no way a seminal or transforming movie. The only thing that sets it apart from so many forgettable period piece coming-of-age stories is that it has been put together with a degree of care and skill.

RECOMMENDED

The Good Girl [2002]

Starring: Jennifer Aniston, Jake Gyllenhaal, John C. Reilly
Director: Miguel Arteta Screenplay: Mike White Running Time: 1:33
Rated: R (Sexual situations, profanity, violence) Theatrical Aspect
Ratio: 1.85:1

For Justine Last (Jennifer Aniston), the comfort of routine has crippled her. By her own admission, she feels like she's in a prison on death row. She has a job, a husband, and a home, but none of those things mean anything, except to offer the bland assurance that they were there yesterday, are there today, and will be there tomorrow. She's a retail clerk at a place called Retail Rodeo, an establishment that makes Wal-Mart look upscale. Her husband, Phil (John C. Reilly) is a house painter who spends his days working and his

evenings sitting in front of the TV and smoking pot with his best friend, Bubba (Tim Blake Nelson). Then along comes Holden Worther (Jake Gyllenhaal), a 22-year old who joins the Retail Rodeo staff. He keeps to himself and reads *Catcher in the Rye* during his lunch breaks. Holden is a lost soul. Like Justine, he is dissatisfied with the routine of his life. She is drawn to him, and he becomes obsessed by her. Soon, they have embarked upon the kind of explosive affair that can only result when two people are drowning in desperation.

For Jennifer Aniston, this is clearly an attempt to escape the *Friends* typecasting. Her performance is forceful and effective — she effortlessly submerges herself into the role, and, after only a moment's hesitation, Aniston has vanished and all that's left is lonely, trapped Justine. Many actors, especially those who are identified with one particular role, bring a great deal of baggage with them to any part. That's not the case here. Meanwhile, John C. Reilly plays Phil as a dullard without ambition, and Jake Gyllenhaal is creepy as the too-intense Holden.

Some Aniston fans may be disappointed — this isn't the kind of lighthearted, throw-away film she has done in the past. It's a work of some substance that requires an investment of attention and effort on the part of the viewer. *The Good Girl* is not mainstream fare. It does not have happy ending (instead, it has a *fitting* one) and ignores the traditional formulas. Instead, *The Good Girl* offers nothing more spectacular than a character study. And, although *The Good Girl*'s protagonist may be trapped by routine, that's one claim that can never be made about the movie.

RECOMMENDED

Good Will Hunting [1997]

Starring: Matt Damon, Robin Williams, Ben Affleck, Stellan Skarsgård,
Minnie Driver, Casey Affleck, Cole Hauser Director: Gus Van Sant
Screenplay: Matt Damon and Ben Affleck Running Time: 2:06 Rated: R
(Profanity, mature themes, violence) Theatrical Aspect Ratio: 1.85:1

Will Hunting is a troubled young man. As a child, he was the frequent victim of abuse. An orphan, he was in and out of foster homes on a regular basis. Now, not yet 21 years old, he has accumulated an impressive rap sheet. He has a short temper and any little incident can set him off like a spark in a tinder box. But he's a mathematical genius with a photographic memory and the ability to conceive simple solutions to complex problems. While working as a janitor at MIT, he delights in anonymously proving theorems on the math building's hall blackboards. Then, one evening, his anonymity is shattered when Professor

Lambeau (Stellan Skarsgård) catches him at work. Will flees, but Lambeau tracks him down. Unfortunately, by the time the professor finds him, Will is in jail for assaulting a police offer.

The judge agrees to release Will under two conditions: that he spend one day a week meeting with Lambeau and that he spend one day a week meeting with a therapist. Eventually, once several psychologists have rejected the belligerent young man, Sean McGuire, a teacher at Bunker Hill Community College, agrees to take the case. After a rocky start, the two develop a rapport and Will begins to explore issues and emotions he had walled up behind impregnable armor. And, as Will advances his self-awareness in sessions with Sean, he also learns about friendship from his buddy, Chuckie (Ben Affleck), and love from a Harvard co-ed named Skylar (Minnie Driver).

Director Gus Van Sant (*Drugstore Cowboy, To Die For, Finding Forrester*) culls genuine emotion from his actors, and this results in several affecting and powerful scenes. There's an edginess to some of the Sean/Will therapy sessions, and the offscreen chemistry between Matt Damon and Minnie Driver (who became romantically linked while making this film) translates effectively to the movie — the Will/Skylar relationship is electric. Likewise, the companionability of Damon and Affleck is apparent in the easygoing nature of Will and Chuckie's friendship. The outstanding performance of the film, however, belongs to Robin Williams, whose Sean is sad and wise, funny and somber. This is arguably the best dramatic work in the actor's career, alongside *The Fisher King*.

Good Will Hunting is an ordinary story told well. Taken as a whole, there's little that's special about this tale — it follows a traditional narrative path, leaves the audience with a warm, fuzzy feeling, and never really challenges or surprises us. But it's intelligently written (with dialogue that is occasionally brilliant), strongly directed, and nicely acted. **RECOMMENDED**

Goodfellas [1990]

Starring: Robert De Niro, Ray Liotta, Joe Pesci, Lorraine Bracco, Paul Sorvino Director: **Martin Scorsese** Screenplay: Nicholas Pileggi & Martin Scorsese, based on "Wiseguy" by Pileggi Running Time: 2:26 Rated: R (Graphic violence, profanity, drug use) Theatrical Aspect Ratio: 1.85:1

There are two kinds of Mafia movies: those that romanticize the life, and those that show its brutality and squalor. The best known and most accomplished of these films, *The Godfather*, towers above the first camp. *Goodfellas* stands atop the other. Both pictures are epic in scope, but Coppola's *Godfather* embraces the mythos of the gangster, while Scorsese's exploration is more pragmatic. Violence is a key component of each, but it is a more brutal companion in *Goodfellas* than in *The Godfather*.

Written by Scorcese and Nicholas Pileggi, *Goodfellas* is based on a true story originally recounted in Pileggi's book *Wiseguy*, a rich and multi-layered study of three characters and the culture that shaped their lives. It's a fascinating exploration of a lifestyle that has beguiled Americans for most of this century, whether in movies, in novels, or on television.

The story opens by introducing us to 13-year-old Henry Hill (played by Christopher Serrone as a youngster and by Ray Liotta as an adult), our narrator. It's the '50s in New York City, and becoming a member of the mob looks like one of the coolest employment opportunities around. "As far back as I can remember," Henry recollects, "I wanted to be a gangster." And no wonder — to a kid just entering his second decade of life, these men have everything: friends, girls, cars, cash, and, most importantly, respect. Henry pursues his goal and soon has become a gofer for the brother of Paul Cicero (Paul Sorvino), the neighborhood boss. His first taste of the life is a heady experience. "At 13, I was making more money than most of the adults in the neighborhood."

The story, which spans a quarter of a century, has an epic feel despite its intimate perspective. The first 40 minutes, which detail Henry's childhood and his acceptance into mob life, is presented almost as a fairy tale, using the same kind of romanticized approach embraced by *The Godfather*. The purpose of this segment is to forge a bond between the audience and the main character while he is still relatively innocent. Henry does not grow up to be a nice man, but, because of the way Scorsese has structured the early portions of the film, we remain sympathetic to him throughout.

Goodfellas begins calmly, but, by the time the final credits roll, there has been a great deal of blood shed. Some of the violence is sudden, shocking, and visceral. One death in particular comes as a total surprise, and leaves the viewer momentarily stunned and disoriented. Even after I have seen the film numerous times, this scene remains unsettling. *Goodfellas* does not rely on plot twists to hold the viewer's attention, but one of the film's strongest traits is the sense of uncertainty that hangs over every frame. Scorsese's tactic of using two narrators even leaves open the possibility that Henry might not survive the film.

Film critics will argue over which represents Scorsese at his best — *Taxi Driver, Raging Bull,* or *Goodfellas*. Taken together, these 3 films offer insight into the themes and ideas that are closest to Scorsese's heart. Taken individually, each represents an amazing motion picture accomplishment, with *Goodfellas* standing alongside *The Godfather* as the two greatest mob stories told on film. MUST SEE

Gosford Park [2001]

Starring: Emily Watson, Derek Jacobi, Maggie Smith, Kristin Scott Thomas, Kelly Macdonald, Clive Owen, Stephen Fry, Ryan Phillippe, Jeremy Northam, Helen Mirren, Michael Gambon Director: Robert Altman Screenplay: Julian Fellowes Running Time: 2:18 Rated: R (Violence, profanity, mature themes) Theatrical Aspect Ratio: 2.35:1

Gosford Park is an ensemble movie, with perhaps the largest and most distinguished group of actors director Robert Altman has ever worked with. The cast list reads like a who's who of British cinema, including Derek Jacobi, Emily Watson, Michael Gambon, Maggie Smith, Kristin Scott Thomas, Stephen Fry, Helen Mirren, Jeremy Northam, and Clive Owen. Thrown in for good measure are a Scottish lass (Kelly Macdonald) and two Americans (Ryan Phillippe, who doesn't seem out of his depth, and Bob Balaban). With such a roster, two things are never in doubt: (1) the film features some of the best acting in any 2001 feature, and (2) nearly everyone is underused.

Gosford Park takes place in November 1932 during a shooting party at the rural estate of Gosford Park, the home of Sir William and Lady Sylvia McCordle (Michael Gambon and Kristin Scott-Thomas). Their guests include other members of the local nobility, such as Lord Stockbridge (Charles Dance), the Honorable Freddie Nesbitt (James Wilby), and the Countess of Trentham (Maggie Smith), and some members of the movie-making community: actors Ivor Novello (Jeremy Northam) and Henry Denton (Ryan Phillippe), and producer Morris Weissman (Bob Balaban). As the story progresses, we become privy to the friction generated by old romances and new rivalries. Even more is going on below the stairs, where the servants live and work. The head of the household, Mrs. Wilson (Helen Mirren), is harboring a long-buried secret that is clawing its way from the grave. Housemaid Elsie (Emily Watson) is secretly carrying on an affair with Sir William. Probert (Derek Jacobi), Sir William's valet, is constantly jumping to fill his master's unusual requests. Into this mix are

thrown Mary (Kelly Macdonald), the Countess' maid, and Robert Parks (Clive Owen), Lord Stockbridge's valet, both of whom are new at service. Things are proceeding as smoothly as possible until the unthinkable occurs — a murder. And, with no shortage of suspects both upstairs and downstairs, a top-notch detective is needed to solve the crime. Unfortunately, Inspector Thompson (Stephen Fry) is assigned to the case, and he's more concerned about people mispronouncing his name than about gathering physical evidence.

Altman is widely regarded as a master of the ensemble film, but in *Gosford Park* he seems unable to wrap his arms completely around the large and talented cast. This is a hugely ambitious undertaking, and it's a pleasure to see so many accomplished actors on screen in one film. But perhaps Altman tries to cram a little too much into his 138-minute running length. Things go by too fast and there's little opportunity to identify with anyone in a more than perfunctory manner. Nevertheless, overshooting the mark is infinitely preferable to undershooting it, which is the failing of far too many films. *Gosford Park* is not an uncontested triumph, but it is thoroughly enjoyable. RECOMMENDED

The Governess [United Kingdom, 1998]

Starring: Minnie Driver, Tom Wilkinson, Florence Hoath, Jonathan Rhys-Meyers Director: Sandra Goldbacher Screenplay: Sandra Goldbacher Running Time: 1:54 Rated: R (Sex, nudity) Theatrical Aspect Ratio: 2.35:1

Before seeing *The Governess,* I never thought of Minnie Driver as a sex symbol. A good actress with charismatic screen presence, yes . . . but a sex symbol? In her previous films her characters have been more cute and bubbly than sexy. That has changed with *The Governess,* a period drama set in 19th century Great Britain.

Driver plays Rosina, a 20-something Jewish girl living in London who has eschewed marriage so that she can pursue a career as an actress. When her father is murdered, her family is left in heavy debt and she must either marry a rich man or seek employment. Unwilling to sell herself into a loveless union, she applies for a position as the governess of a girl living on the Isle of Skye in Scotland. And, because a woman of solid Christian values is sought, she assumes the pseudonym of Mary Blackchurch, and uses her acting skills to disguise herself as a "Gentile and a gentlewoman." Her application is readily accepted.

Rosina soon finds herself in a strange land, surrounded by people with bizarre customs. Not only do the Gentiles make her uneasy, but she finds the green, wide-open spaces of Scotland disconcerting. "I long for cities and chimneys," she remarks in a voiceover narration. Her employers are the Cavendishes. Mrs. Cavendish (Harriet Walter) is a relentlessly proper woman whose chief characteristics are prudishness and humorlessness. In Rosina's words, she's seems like "she has a lemon up her posterior." Mr. Cavendish (Tom Wilkinson) is a mysterious man who spends nearly all of his waking hours working on a project in his laboratory. Rosina's charge, 13-year-old Clementina (Florence Hoath), is a "rodent in lace" who is quickly subdued by a few pointed threats. Then there's Clementina's older brother, Henry (Jonathan Rhys-Meyers), who is almost immediately infatuated by the governess.

Rosina's natural curiosity leads her to explore Cavendish's laboratory. There she finds that he is experimenting with a new process called photography. Soon, the two are working as a team to find the critical agent that will allow the images captured by the camera to remain permanent. Initially, he resists taking a picture of Rosina, but eventually she wears him down, and, the more she bares herself to the camera, the more deeply Cavendish falls under her spell, even though he resists his own feelings every step of the way.

The Governess is solidly entertaining material with enough substance to lift it above the traditional period drama. Goldbacher's script takes the time to develop each of the major characters, which allows the climax and denouement to have greater impact. In addition to flawless acting by Driver and Wilkinson, the film is highlighted by Ashley Rowe's sumptuous photography. *The Governess* is far more absorbing than one might guess from the accurate, if plain, title. **RECOMMENDED**

Great Expectations [1998]

Starring: Ethan Hawke, Gwyneth Paltrow, Anne Bancroft, Robert DeNiro Director: Alfonso Cuaron Screenplay: Mitch Glazer based on the novel by Charles Dickens Running Time: 1:51 Rated: R (Sex, nudity, profanity) Theatrical Aspect Ratio: 2.35:1

You have to give a film maker credit for having the chutzpah to take one of the most beloved classics in the English language and transform it into a modern-day morality play/romance. *Great Expectations* is considered by many to be Dickens' finest novel; it is

certainly among his darkest. With the setting changed from 19th century England to contemporary Florida and New York, the social minefield of Dickensian England has lost some of its menace. Surprisingly, however, the story survived the transition relatively unscathed.

Even as the setting has changed, so have the names and occupations of many of the characters. The lead is no longer Pip; he's now called Finn, and is played by Ethan Hawke (with an assist from Jeremy Kissner as a 10-year-old). Estella, the love of Finn's life, is still Estella, and she is portrayed by a radiant-yet-restrained Gwyneth Paltrow (and Raquel Beaudene at a younger age). Mad Miss Havisham has become the equally deranged Miss Dinsmore, who spends her days in a ruined house mourning a wedding that never took place. With Anne Bancroft in this part, it's easy to imagine that Nora Dinsmore could be Mrs. Robinson gone bonkers, 30 years later. The criminal Magwich has become Lustig, an escaped death row inmate, and is played by Robert DeNiro. Finally, Chris Cooper (*Lone Star*) plays Finn's "uncle," Joe Gargery (no name change), and Hank Azaria is Walter Plane, Finn's rival for Estella.

Finn first meets Estella in the late 1970s, when both are 10 years old. Neither has any parents. Finn lives with his sister and her boyfriend; Estella has been adopted by Miss Dinsmore, who (though crazy) is one of the richest women in Florida. Despite a warning from the old lady that Estella will break his heart, Finn falls for the golden-haired girl, but their relationship never progresses beyond wet kisses at a water fountain. Finn is in earnest, but Estella likes to tease. More than a decade later, they meet in New York City. He's there to break into the Manhattan art scene (and earn enough money to impress her), while she's contemplating marriage to a man named Walter Plane, who has commitment problems. And, hidden beneath the love story, there's a mystery. Someone is bankrolling Finn's success. He assumes it's Miss Dinsmore, but is the truth perhaps less obvious?

The actors do admirable jobs, and all of the performances feed into the essence of *Great Expectations*, with its elements of unrequited love, broken class barriers, and unexpected revelations. Any missteps here are not so much the result of shifting the novel in time and place, but of condensing it to feature-length. Nevertheless, while *Great Expectations* falls short of being the definitive interpretation of the novel (for that, see David Lean's 1946 version) it still offers an entertaining 2 hours. **RECOMMENDED**

The Green Mile [1999]

Starring: Tom Hanks, David Morse, Bonnie Hunt, Michael Clarke Duncan, James Cromwell, Michael Jeter, Graham Greene, Doug Hutchison, Sam Rockwell, Barry Pepper, Jeffrey DeMunn, Patricia Clarkson Director: Frank Darabont Screenplay: Frank Darabont, based on the novel by Stephen King Running Time: 3:08 Rated: R (Violence, profanity, sex-related material) Theatrical Aspect Ratio: 2.35:1

Stephen King stories generally come in two flavors — the kind that top level directors fashion into powerful motion pictures (*Stand By Me*, *The Shining*, *The Shawshank Redemption*, *Dolores Claiborne*, etc.) and more schlocky, exploitative fare. Generally speaking, *The Green Mile* falls into the first category.

"The Green Mile" is the nickname given to the Coal Mountain Louisiana State Penitentiary's death row. The year is 1935, and narrator and main character Paul Edgecomb (Hanks), is head guard of The Green Mile. Four others work with him — his best friend, Brutus Howell (David Morse); the handsome and somewhat impetuous Dean Stanton (Barry Pepper); the veteran Harry Terwilleger (Jeffrey DeMunn); and the newcomer, a sadist and coward named Percy Wetmore (Doug Hutchison). Percy has a promotion to a desk job at a mental institution waiting for him — he's only on the Mile so he can see an execution. Paul would dearly like to get rid of him, but Percy has highly placed connections and cannot be transferred until he submits a request.

A new inmate, John Coffey (Michael Clarke Duncan), has come to The Green Mile, joining the two who are already awaiting signed death warrants. They are a Cajun named Eduard Delacroix (Michael Jeter) and a Native American, Arlen Bitterbuck (Graham Greene). John is a giant of a man, but he is quiet, simpleminded, and surprisingly docile: surprising considering the shocking crime he was arrested for — the brutal murder of two little girls. While Percy delights in tormenting the prisoners, both new and old, Paul and the other guards form tentative bonds with them. And, because of that, Paul makes a remarkable discovery about John, and realizes that something extremely unusual may be at work on The Green Mile.

With 3 hours to work with, it's no surprise that Darabont does an excellent job of character development. Realistically, however, the film probably would have been as effective at about two-thirds that length. The film also includes a strong Judeo-Christian message, and at times the symbolism is laid on a little thickly. Problems aside, *The Green Mile* is at times a powerful motion picture. The characters are well-drawn and ably portrayed, with Tom Hanks filling the shoes of the likable protagonist as only he can, and Doug Hutchison doing a good job making us hate him. Sam Rockwell gets an opportunity to chew on the scenery as an out-of-control, bad-to-the-bone nutcase who is shut up in a cell. Bonnie Hunt, who gets better with every movie, is Paul's wife. But the real standout is Michael Clarke Duncan, who easily acts circles around Hanks — his portrayal of John is often touching and occasionally wrenching. **RECOMMENDED**

The Grey Zone [2001]

Starring: David Arquette, Daniel Benzali, David Chandler, Steve Buscemi, Harvey Keitel Director: Tim Blake Nelson Screenplay: Tim Blake Nelson Running Time: 1:33 Rated: R (Holocaust images, nudity, violence) Theatrical Aspect Ratio: 1.85:1

Auschwitz, 1944. One of the darkest times in one of the darkest places in recent human history. It is into this nightmarish world that director Tim Blake Nelson plunges us with *The Grey Zone*, a harrowing film about compromise, betrayal, and moral ambiguity that tells the tale of the 12th Sonderkommando at Auschwitz — the only group ever to lead an armed uprising at the death camp. (The term "Sonderkommando" was coined by the Germans to describe those Jews who agreed to collaborate with the Nazis.)

In the darkness of the death camp, an armed uprising is being planned by the Sonderkommandos, who have been stockpiling illicitly gained explosives and guns. While some of the organizers, such as the self-serving Abramowics (Steve Buscemi), plan to use this as an opportunity to escape, others, such as Hoffman (David Arquette), Rosenthal (David Chandler), and Schlermer (Daniel Benzali) are more pragmatic. Their intention is to blow up the crematoriums, then die fighting. They do not believe they will ever again see anything outside of the walls of Auschwitz. Thirsty for some form of redemption, these men leap to the aid of a 14-year-old girl (Kamelia Grigorova) who miraculously survives a gassing. They hide her, and, with the aid of Dr. Nyiszli (Allan Corduner), Mengele's Jewish assistant, bring her back to consciousness. Even when Muhsfeldt (Harvey Keitel), the

Nazi camp commander, learns of her presence, they stubbornly refuse to let her die, even when their actions endanger the uprising.

The Grey Zone is as powerful as it is grim. The film illustrates the darker side of the human instinct for survival — how men can be capable of things they never would have thought possible in the face of death. In order to spare their consciences, the members of the Sonderkommando display an amazing ability to lie to themselves, but, the more aware they become of their culpability in what is transpiring around them, the greater their need is for a taste of redemption.

With its numerous complex issues, the Holocaust has formed the backdrop for countless powerful, emotionally wrenching dramas. And, with so many stories to tell, redundancy does not seem to be a problem — each new motion picture puts a face on another previously anonymous body. *The Grey Zone* gives life and meaning to an event that is little more than a footnote in history books (if that). Like so many of its fellow Holocaust dramas, *The Grey Zone* seeks not to comfort audiences, but to remind them.
RECOMMENDED

Hamlet [United Kingdom/United States, 1996]
Starring: Kenneth Branagh, Derek Jacobi, Julie Christie, Richard Briers, Nicholas Farrell, Kate Winslet Director: Kenneth Branagh Screenplay: Kenneth Branagh based on the play by William Shakespeare Running Time: 4:02 Rated: PG-13 (Mature themes, brief nudity, sex, violence) Theatrical Aspect Ratio: 2.35:1

This is not only the best filmed version of *Hamlet*, but the best film of *any* of Shakespeare's plays I have ever seen. *Hamlet* has long been something of a private obsession for actor/director Kenneth Branagh; now that vision has been realized, and with every line from the original play intact, it takes approximately 4 hours to run. It is a well-spent 4 hours.

Part of the enduring appeal of *Hamlet* lies in its complex characterization and twisty, tragic plot. *Hamlet* deals with, among other things, madness and revenge, sex and love, and ghosts, both real and figurative. There is also a great deal of humor, and good old-fashioned adventure. *Hamlet* can literally make you laugh and cry, hiss and cheer. It contains a slew of the most famous lines in English lit, including "To thine own self be true," "Something is rotten in the state of Denmark," "Brevity is the soul of wit," "The play's the thing," "The lady doeth protest too much," and, of course, "To be, or not to be, that is the question."

The story takes place in 12th-century Denmark. Prince Hamlet (Branagh), is mourning the death of his beloved father (Brian Blessed) and the untimely (and according to custom, unseemly) wedding of his mother, Gertrude (Julie Christie), to his uncle, Claudius (Derek Jacobi). Hamlet sees his mother's hasty remarriage as a betrayal of her union with his father, but worse news is yet to come. An apparition of the dead King haunts Elsinore Castle, and when Hamlet confronts it the ghost claims Claudius poisoned him to claim both queen and crown for himself. Hamlet vows revenge, and thus begins either his slow spiral into madness or his carefully orchestrated act to appear insane.

Meanwhile, Fortinbras (Rufus Sewell), the nephew of the King of Norway, is massing armies to attack Denmark. Ophelia (Kate Winslet), Hamlet's lover, has been forbidden to have any further contact with the prince. A group of traveling actors has come to Elsinore. And two old school mates of Hamlet's have been employed by Claudius to betray their old friend.

Branagh has assembled a top-notch international cast. Well-known actors like Charlton Heston (as the Player King), John Gielgud (Priam), Judi Dench (Hecuba), and Robin Williams (Osric) fill small roles. The leads are all in peak form. Richard Briers adds layers of guile and intelligence to his interpretation of the fatuous Polonius. Brian Blessed makes us feel the power and malevolence of the ghost. Julie Christie's wonderful Gertrude allows us to understand why Claudius would resort to murder to win her. And Derek Jacobi's cultured, politically savvy, yet privately tortured Claudius is richly portrayed.

Then there's Kenneth Branagh, the film's undisputed star. For Hamlet's calmer, quieter scenes (such as the soliloquies), Branagh brings a contemplative and introspective quality to his performance. But for the emotionally rousing sequences, his interpretation is brash and forceful, drawing us into the pure drama of the situation. It's a marvelous portrayal that complements those of the many other cast members.

From the moment it was first announced that Branagh would attempt an unabridged *Hamlet*, I never doubted that it would be a worthy effort. I have seen dozens of versions of this play (either on screen or on stage), and none has ever held me in such a grip of awe. This may be Kenneth Branagh's dream, but it is our pleasure. **MUST SEE**

Happenstance [France, 2000]

Starring: Audrey Tautou, Faudel, Eric Savin, Eric Feldman, Lysaine Meis   Director: Laurent Firode   Screenplay: Laurent Firode   Running Time: 1:37   Rated: R (Nudity, sexual situations, profanity)   In French with subtitles

Chaos theory, that arcane branch of mathematics with the cool name, has been showing up in some surprising motion pictures (see *Jurassic Park*). And why not? It all has to do with cause-and-effect — a perfect film vehicle — and is the subject of French filmmaker Laurent Firode's debut, *Happenstance*.

The central character, Irene, is played by the luminous Audrey Tautou, star of *Amelie*. "Central" is perhaps a misleading term. Although Irene has more exposure than anyone else, and the story keeps returning to her, she's just one of many faces to populate the screen.

We first meet Irene on a subway train during her daily commute to work. When a woman reads Irene's horoscope out loud, Younes (Algerian singer Faudel) realizes it is his as well because he and Irene share the same birthday. The horoscope speaks of discovering one's true love on the day of the full moon, which happens to be that day. So, Younes spends the rest of his waking hours searching for Ms. Right. Irene, meanwhile, undergoes one mishap after another, until she finally decides to pack up her things, leave Paris, and go home to her mother. We meet others whose paths cross those of Irene and Younes: Richard (Eric Savin), a married man carrying on an affair with Elsa (Lysaine Meis); Luc (Eric Feldman), a charming liar who seems incapable of being truthful around women; Stephanie (Irene Ismailoff), whose reunion with an old lover turns into a nightmare; an old woman (Francoise Bertin), who tries to return a coffee maker to the store where she bought it; a pickpocket (Said Serrari), who chooses an unfortunate victim; and many others.

The film is openly interested in the vagaries of chance and fate. It's a delight to watch the plot unfold, and to become aware of how a small, random action by one person can impact the life of another. Does the film overplay its hand and rely too much on coincidence? Only to those who aren't fascinated by the idea. In some ways, Firode's effort works better on a second viewing, when the characters and their relationships to one another have been established; but whether seen once or multiple times, *Happenstance* is an intriguing meditation on the unseen forces that no one can escape. **RECOMMENDED**

Happiness [1998]

Starring: Jane Adams, Dylan Baker, Lara Flynn Boyle, Philip Seymour Hoffman, Cynthia Stevenson, Jared Harris, Ben Gazzara, Louise Lasser, Camryn Manheim   Director: Todd Solondz   Screenplay: Todd Solondz   Running Time: 2:12   Rated: No MPAA Rating (Graphic sexual situations, profanity, nudity)   Theatrical Aspect Ratio: 1.85:1

Happiness, director Todd Solondz's second feature, is an ensemble piece of several different stories, all of which revolve around the Jordan sisters. Trish (Cynthia Stevenson), the oldest, is apparently living the American dream: she has a beautiful house, a loving husband, and 3 children. Helen (Lara Flynn Boyle), a successful author, leads a life of wealth and glamour. Joy (Jane Adams) is alone and lonely, and the only men she attracts turn out to be losers, cheats, and degenerates. Trish and Helen both pay lip service to their concern for Joy, but, in reality, they're so wrapped up in their own lives that they could care less. Self-centeredness is the chief characteristic of nearly everyone in this film.

Helen feels that she's a fraud, and, tired of empty nights of sex with good-looking men, she's in search of something adventurous. She finds it through Allen (Philip Seymour Hoffman), a repressed computer geek who derives sexual fulfillment from making obscene phone calls.

Meanwhile, Trish's marriage hides a dark secret. Her proper and caring psychiatrist husband, Bill (Dylan Baker), is a pedophile, and, while he presents the facade of the perfect family man, his obsession is always lurking just beneath the surface. For a while, he is content with masturbating to pictures of good-looking teen idols, but, when the opportunity presents itself, he drugs and rapes the best friend of his adolescent son. With the genie out of the bottle, there is no stopping him.

Finally, there's Lenny and Mona (Ben Gazzara and Louise Lasser), the retired parents of Joy, Trish, and Helen. After 40 years of marriage, Lenny decides that he needs to be alone. He doesn't want a divorce, but he craves "more space."

Solondz's overriding message is that true happiness is a myth. There is no such thing. Some are pragmatic enough to accept that fact and live with it. Others delude themselves into believing that it might be possible, only to be slapped down when faced with the truth. In *Happiness*, the disconsolate Joy is no less cheerful than the perfectly-married Trish or the financially-assured Helen.

It took me more than one viewing of *Happiness*

and a lot of thought to clarify my feelings about this movie. One thing is for certain: *Happiness* is not for everyone. John Waters (director of *Pink Flamingos* and *Pecker*) has lavished praise upon Solondz and *Happiness*. The Farrelly Brothers (*There's Something about Mary*), on the other hand, were quoted in the New York Times Magazine as calling the picture "sick." Audience reaction for this audacious experiment is no less divided. Love it or hate it, however, *Happiness* is not easily forgotten. **HIGHLY RECOMMENDED**

He Got Game [1998]

Starring: **Denzel Washington, Ray Allen, Rosario Dawson, Milla Jovovich** Director: **Spike Lee** Screenplay: **Spike Lee** Running Time: 2:11 Rated: R (Profanity, nudity, sex, violence) Theatrical Aspect Ratio: 1.85:1

Writer/director Spike Lee is a huge basketball fan (specifically, a New York Knicks fan), and *He Got Game* has been called "Lee's basketball film." Such a label is misleading. *Hoosiers* is a basketball movie; *He Got Game* is a story about life, relationships, and the pressures of fame.

The story opens with Jake Shuttleworth (Denzel Washington) serving a lengthy sentence in Attica for killing his wife. Meanwhile, on the outside, his son, Jesus (Ray Allen), has become the top-rated high school basketball player in the country, and is being recruited by every major college. In the words of one expert, he's "the best thing to happen to the game since the tennis shoe was invented." The warden of Attica (Ned Beatty) comes to Jake with a deal: convince Jesus to go to the governor's alma mater, Big State, and Jake's sentence will be reduced or commuted. To allow Jake to make contact with his son, he is given one week of freedom. There's a problem, though — Jesus doesn't want to have anything to do with his father, and Jake's increasingly desperate attempts at a reconciliation run into a brick wall.

The other aspect of *He Got Game* is the high-pressure salesmanship designed to encourage Jesus to sign a letter of intent with a college or to hire an agent and go pro. While there's something vaguely comical about many of these scenes, Lee conveys the strain that highly-touted, young athletes are under. With surreptitious cash payments and all sorts of perks so readily available, it's understandable why some high-schoolers make the choices and mistakes that they do. In its depiction of this side of the sports business, *He Got Game* makes an effective companion piece to *Hoop Dreams* and *Blue Chips* (which explored college recruiting from the coach's perspective).

Beyond Washington and Allen, Lee has populated the film with a number of credible supporting performers. Zelda Harris (the lead in *Crooklyn*) is delightful as Jesus' little sister. Rosario Dawson is convincing as Lala, Jesus' sexy girlfriend. Bill Nunn and Hill Harper provide comic relief as Jesus' uncle and cousin, respectively. And Milla Jovovich, best known for her work in *The Fifth Element*, is surprisingly sympathetic as a down-on-her-luck prostitute who connects with Jake during his week out of prison. There are cameos from the likes of Charles Barkley, Larry Bird, Michael Jordan, Shaquille O'Neal, John Thompson, and Reggie Miller.

While the father/son reunion gives the film its emotional core, the basketball recruiting sequences provide a cynical edge. Stylistically, *He Got Game* is uneven. Narratively, the film is hurt by a contrived setup and a hokey, overly-sentimental final scene. It's the stuff in between that makes this a worthwhile experience, however, which it surely is. **RECOMMENDED**

Heavy [1995]

Starring: **Pruitt Taylor Vince, Liv Tyler, Deborah Harry, Shelley Winters** Director: **James Mangold** Screenplay: **James Mangold** Running Time: 1:45 Rated: No MPAA Rating (Profanity, mature themes) Theatrical Aspect Ratio: 1.85:1

The characters in James Mangold's debut feature, *Heavy*, are the flotsam and jetsam of life. They all wash up at Pete and Dolly's Restaurant, a Hudson Valley roadhouse where a smile is just about the last thing anyone expects to see.

The roadhouse is owned and run by Dolly Modino (Shelley Winters), an aging woman in failing health. Dolly spends much of her time reminiscing about the past when her husband was still alive. Delores (Deborah Harry) is a frumpy waitress who has engaged in a 15-year war of words with Dolly. Life-weary and looking for a little affection, Delores drifts from day-to-day, not seeming to care what comes next. Leo (Joe Grifasi) is Pete and Dolly's most loyal customer, a perpetually drunk loser who hangs around the roadhouse hoping that Delores will agree to take him home. Callie (Liv Tyler) is the new employee, a college dropout in need of money who is saddled with a loutish boyfriend and may or may not be pregnant.

Then there's Victor (Pruitt Taylor Vince), the film's protagonist. Painfully shy and convinced that his overweight condition makes him unattractive, Victor lives in the shadow of his mother, Dolly. He's the restaurant's cook and the object of Delores' affection. With the arrival of Callie, Victor finds something to brighten up his days. He is instantly smitten with her, and, when she has a few kind words for him and seems interested in a friendship, Victor is eager to oblige. Nevertheless, his feelings for Callie are clearly not reciprocated on the same level, and lead to inevitable heartbreak.

Dialogue is sparse in *Heavy,* so it's left up to the actors to form and develop their characters with mannerisms and facial expressions instead of scripted lines. Considering that the cast is not made up of "great" names, this is a daring move by Mangold. Fortunately, it pays off, largely due to a gargantuan performance by Pruitt Taylor Vince (*Nobody's Fool*), who creates a heartwrenchingly sympathetic man we can't help caring about. Deborah Harry is also good, giving us the kind of waitress who would have made *Frankie and Johnny* a memorable movie. Liv Tyler (*Stealing Beauty*) gets by more on looks than ability, but she has her moments. And Shelley Winters is refreshingly low-key.

Heavy is not the kind of film to view when you're looking for something upbeat. It's too real, and, as a result, potentially too painful. Mangold captures the nuances of life perfectly, and, by never cheapening his vision through facile resolutions, he fashions a memorable cinematic portrait. **HIGHLY RECOMMENDED**

Hideous Kinky [United Kingdom, 1998]

Starring: Kate Winslet, Said Taghmaoui, Bella Riza, Carrie Mullan
Director: Gillies MacKinnon Screenplay: Billy MacKinnon from the
novel by Esther Freud Running Time: 1:39 Rated: R (Sex, profanity,
brief nudity) Theatrical Aspect Ratio: 2.35:1

Gillies MacKinnon's *Hideous Kinky* is a road movie, but one of a very different sort. Set in 1972 Morocco, it follows the quest of a young British woman to discover herself and give her two daughters a taste of the world.

When her longtime lover and the father of her two children moves on to another woman, Julia (Kate Winslet) quits the gray sadness of London for the warm brightness of Marrakech. However, although Morocco offers the promise of spiritual enlightenment to the 25-year-old mother, a lack of financial resources limits her prospects. She wants to travel to Algeria, where one of the great mystics resides, but, with barely enough money to live off of, the possibility of moving on seems remote. And, while 6-year-old Lucy (Carrie Mulligan) is happy in this new, strange country, 8-year-old Bea (Bella Riza) wants nothing more than to return to a "normal" life. One day, Julia's goals and priorities are re-arranged when she meets

Bilal (Said Taghmaoui), a charming acrobat who quickly insinuates himself into the vagabond family as Julia's lover and Lucy and Bea's father figure. Soon, the quartet is off on a short vacation to Bilal's home village, but that trip turns into a more revealing sojourn than anyone expected.

MacKinnon (*Regeneration*), directing from a script written by his brother and based on the novel by Esther Freud, captures time and place perfectly. The camera captures the stark beauty of the desert (complete with at least one memorable sunset) and a riot of colors marking the bustling city streets.

Kate Winslet, whose performance is top-notch, shows here that she's more interested in advancing her craft than in basking in publicity and trying to get a big paycheck.

Opposite Winslet is Said Taghmaoui (*Hate*), whose infectious charisma makes him a perfect choice for the part of the likable, roguish Bilal. As Julia's children, both Bella Riza and Carrie Mullan are making their feature debuts. Each displays natural talent; rarely is there even the barest hint of artifice in either performance. Also in the cast is veteran French actor Pierre Clementi, who plays a European who opens his villa to Julia and her daughters.

For all that *Hideous Kinky* introduces us to an unusual culture and takes us on a whirlwind trip of Morocco, the central feature of the film is the human element. It's the sacrifices Julia must ultimately make for her children that makes *Hideous Kinky* more than just a lush travelogue. MacKinnon has not allowed the glorious setting to overwhelm the characters. Through everything, Winslet's Julia remains the rock upon which the story is founded and developed. **RECOMMENDED**

Hilary and Jackie [United Kingdom, 1998]

Starring: Emily Watson, Rachel Griffiths, James Frain, David
Morrissey, Charles Dance, Celia Imrie, Auriol Evans, Keeley Flanders
Director: Anand Tucker Screenplay: Frank Cottrell Boyce, based on "A
Genius in the Family" by Hilary and Piers du Pré Running Time: 2:00
Rated: R (Sex, profanity, debilitating disease) Theatrical Aspect
Ratio: 2.35:1

The story of celebrated cellist Jacqueline du Pré is too good not to have been made into a movie. Add the best female performance of 1998, a glorious soundtrack, and vibrant cinematography, and *Hilary and Jackie* stands as a towering achievement for Director Anand Tucker.

Jaqueline du Pré (Emily Watson) was one of classical music's brightest stars during the 1960s and early '70s.

After making her professional debut as a teenager, she became one of the most in-demand cellists of her time, and was known not only for her peerless technique, but for the passion she exhibited by swaying to the music as she played. In 1973, while at the height of her popularity, Jacqueline was diagnosed with Multiple Sclerosis. The disease put an end to her career, and, following a 15-year battle, her life.

As the title makes clear, this film isn't just about the life of Jacqueline du Pré, but about her tempestuous relationship with her sister, Hilary (Rachel Griffiths). When they were both children they were inseparable soul-mates. Hilary, a flutist, was considered the greater talent. She was invited to play with orchestras and make special appearances. Through practice and hard work, however, Jackie elevated herself to her sister's level, then beyond. Hilary came to resent Jackie's success as her own musical aspirations floundered, and as an adult, Hilary all but gave up the flute in favor of marriage and a family, while Jacqueline chose fame. The price Jackie paid was a desperate yearning to have the stability and happiness that Hilary possessed. Then, when MS ended her career and left her alone and dependent, she had to cope with the loss of the music that defined her, unaccustomed powerlessness, and death.

As Jackie, Emily Watson gives a stunning performance. Watson, who earned an Oscar nomination for her courageous work in *Breaking the Waves*, is even better here, capturing every nuance of a character trapped between genius and madness, whose playing defines her existence. ("When you play, everyone loves you. When you stop, you're alone.")

Despite being in Watson's shadow, Rachel Griffiths acquits herself nicely. In fact, the relationship between the two sisters works because Griffiths is able to rise to Watson's level, and, on those occasions when the film focuses on Hilary, Griffiths' performance holds our attention.

Stylistically, the film is a success. The music is used extraordinarily effectively, especially when the Elgar Concerto (in a recording by Jackie) is played over the closing sequence. It's a poignant piece that plays as if composed just for that scene. *Hilary and Jackie* tells a heartbreaking tale of vividly-developed characters. It is a triumph. **MUST SEE**

Hollow Reed [United Kingdom, 1997]

Starring: Martin Donovan, Joely Richardson, Sam Bould, Jason Flemyng, Ian Hart Director: Angela Pope Screenplay: Paula Milne

Running Time: 1:46 Rated: No MPAA Rating (Violence, sex, mature themes) Theatrical Aspect Ratio: 1.66:1

Angela Pope's *Hollow Reed* can be extremely difficult to watch. In examining how the physical abuse of a child affects an already broken family, the film doesn't pull any punches, literally or figuratively. Yet, *Hollow Reed*'s real subject matter is the hypocrisy of a legal system that would rather let a child live in danger than grant custody to his gay father. Lawyers and judges can mouth PC platitudes, but when it comes to handing over a child into the custody of a gay household, the deep-rooted ugliness of homophobia rears its head.

Part of the reason that *Hollow Reed* is so punishing is that it's told from a child's point-of-view. That child is Oliver (Sam Bould), a quiet, introverted boy who seems to be the perfect son and student. He's a *Star Wars* fan, and spends hours in his room playing with Luke Skywalker action figures and remote-controlled cars. His parents are divorced, and their relationship is far from amicable. Oliver lives with his mother, Hannah (Joely Richardson), and her boyfriend, Frank (Jason Flemyng). Meanwhile, Oliver's father, Martyn (Martin Donovan), an out-of-the-closet homosexual who shares a home with his lover, Tom (Ian Hart), has only the right of "reasonable access" to his son.

The film opens with Oliver arriving at his father's door late one evening with a bleeding, bruised face. Although Oliver claims that he was beaten up by a group of local thugs, Martyn has his doubts. Days later, when the boy shows up at school with a crushed hand, Martyn goes to the police, requesting that they investigate whether Frank has been abusing his son. He then instigates a custody lawsuit, with the intention of taking Oliver away from Hannah if she doesn't kick Frank out. And, as the case goes before a judge, all sorts of ugly truths about society's perception of homosexuals are unveiled.

Both Martin Donovan and Joely Richardson do fine jobs as Oliver's parents. Richardson (Disney's live-action *101 Dalmatians*) arguably has the more difficult role playing the torn woman who doesn't want to believe a horrible truth. Oliver's silence allows her to remain in blissful denial. Donovan portrays a man who, despite having the moral high ground, is powerless to save his son. The key to Donovan's performance is that it starts out low-key, so as the situation becomes increasingly desperate, he never seems over-the-top. However, all of the adults, including Richardson, Donovan, and the fine supporting cast, are outacted by young Sam Bould, who captures the essence of Oliver without a hint of the confusion and awkwardness that sometimes marks child performances.

This is not the sort of motion picture that's likely to find favor with the "feel good" crowd, but, if you aren't afraid of a movie that is capable of challenging convictions and wrenching emotions, *Hollow Reed* makes for an unforgettable 2 hours.

HIGHLY RECOMMENDED

Homage [1996]

Starring: Frank Whaley, Blythe Danner, Sheryl Lee, Danny Nucci, Bruce Davison   Director: Ross Kagan Marks   Screenplay: Mark Medoff   Running Time: 1:37   Rated: R (Violence, sex, profanity)   Theatrical Aspect Ratio: 1.85:1

An edgy, unsettling look at obsession and its potentially catastrophic results, *Homage* is a dramatic character study; and though it features a number of questionable creative choices, a trio of powerful performances makes this film worthwhile.

The most dubious decision regarding *Homage* was forcing it into a non-linear chronological structure. The film begins at the end, with TV star Lucy Samuel (Sheryl Lee, in the best performance of her career) being gunned down by psychotic fan Archie Landrum (Frank Whaley), while her mother, Katherine (Blythe Danner), looks on in horror. So much for any suspense about how things are going to be resolved. From that point, the narrative alternates between the present and the past, using flashbacks and a contrived pseudo-documentary style to chronicle events leading up to the shooting, while giving us glimpses of an imprisoned Archie in the aftermath, and detailing the tactics employed by his public defender (Bruce Davison) to beat the charges. Along the way, director Marks also takes an occasional detour to shish-kabob celebrity worship and paparazzi.

Frank Whaley's portrayal of Archie is chillingly effective. Archie has a Ph.D. in math, but, in his own words, is "an inept human being." Katherine sees him as lonely and harmless, not recognizing that his personality is dangerous. He's extremely intelligent, but lost, and the more Lucy rejects him, the more determined he becomes to win her — at all costs. This is the obsession of someone with no sense of self-worth. The only way to validate his own existence is to become part of Lucy's life, and she thinks he's a creep. It's disturbing to watch the seemingly-normal Archie come completely unglued.

Meanwhile, Sheryl Lee returns to familiar territory

with Lucy — a character who is idolized in her home town while secretly battling addictions to drugs and booze. She keeps a private diary, and, in the end (or should I say, the beginning), is murdered. Lee's career started as Laura Palmer in David Lynch's *Twin Peaks,* and there are numerous similarities here. The marked difference is in the performance, however. When she appeared in *Peaks* (and reprised the role in the big-screen's *Fire, Walk with Me*), Lee was new at her craft. Here, she displays a depth and maturity that Lynch never captured.

The third member of the trio, Blythe Danner, is no less impressive than her co-stars, although her performance is more low-key. Nevertheless, it is only through Katherine's agonized reaction to her daughter's death that *Homage*'s most compelling tragedy becomes apparent.

There's something haunting and forceful about *Homage,* but I attribute that power more to what Whaley, Lee, and Danner do with the material than with the material itself. **RECOMMENDED**

Hoodlum [1997]

Starring: Laurence Fishburne, Tim Roth, Andy Garcia, Vanessa L. Williams, Chi McBride, Clarence Williams III   Director: Bill Duke   Screenplay: Chris Brancato   Running Time: 2:10   Rated: R (Violence, profanity, brief nudity)   Theatrical Aspect Ratio: 1.85:1

Hoodlum is a period-piece gangster film, harkening back to Depression-era Harlem. While Al Capone was king in Chicago, Lucky Luciano (Andy Garcia) ruled New York, parceling out the city to members of his "Sicilian Syndicate." The 1930s were the mob's heyday, when no cop, special prosecutor, or judge was too expensive to buy, and when the only real law was the one laid down by Luciano or one of his many "associates." Of course, in a place as big as New York, there were bound to be wild cards. One was Dutch Schultz (Tim Roth), a former partner of Luciano's whose forays into the uptown numbers racket put him on a collision course with the Queen of Harlem, Stephanie St. Clair (Cicely Tyson), and her trustworthy friend and protector, Bumpy Johnson (Laurence Fishburne). The resulting turf war between Schultz and the St. Clair/Johnson camp littered the streets of Harlem with bodies, and threatened the mob's security in New York when the violence spread to downtown targets.

Hoodlum's storyline is similar to the one told in Francis Ford Coppola's 1984 feature, *The Cotton Club.* The setting is the same, many of the characters are the same, and certain aspects of the storylines intersect.

The perspective, however, is different. Unlike *The Cotton Club*, which focused on the lives of many of the "normal" people who frequented and played in the nightclub, *Hoodlum*, as Bumpy's story, is a relatively straightforward gangster yarn that melds fact with fiction to create a dramatically compelling 2 hours.

The acting is top notch. As Bumpy, Fishburne is mesmerizing, displaying his range as an actor by subtly and effectively presenting the variety of emotions that lurk just beneath Bumpy's seemingly-placid exterior. Tim Roth, the versatile British actor who has portrayed almost every kind of character imaginable during his career, brings a flamboyant mix of impatience and casual viciousness to Dutch Schultz. Andy Garcia, on the other hand, is low-key in his approach to Lucky Luciano, presenting the famed mobster as charismatic, urbane, and intelligent, with only a hint of the danger he represents. Of the supporting players, only Vanessa L. Williams seems off-key. Chi McBride (as Bumpy's cousin and right-hand man, Illinois) and Clarence Williams III (as one of Schultz's most dangerous henchmen) are memorable.

Overall, *Hoodlum* may be the best depression-era gangster film since Brian DePalma's *The Untouchables*. The movie's decision to take the point-of-view of several black characters lends a fresh angle to a fairly well-known historical account. *Hoodlum* may not be the definitive chronicle of New York mob activity during the 1930s, but it's a welcome contribution. **RECOMMENDED**

The Horse Whisperer [1998]

Starring: Robert Redford, Kristin Scott Thomas, Sam Neill, Scarlett Johansson Director: Robert Redford Screenplay: Richard LaGravenese, Eric Roth based on the novel by Nicholas Evans Running Time: 2:50 Rated: PG-13 (Accident scene) Theatrical Aspect Ratio: 1.85:1

The Horse Whisperer is a powerful and moving tale of love and loss that eschews melodramatic manipulation in its pursuit of a simple, honest tale.

The film opens peacefully enough, with two teenage girls leaving their houses in the early morning hours for a horseback ride. The sunrise is brilliant, and, as snow begins to fall later in the day, the fields and forest are turned into a winter wonderland of blues and silvers. Everything is picture perfect until tragedy strikes, brutally and without warning. One of the girls' mounts loses his footing on an icy hill and, suddenly, the two friends are in the path of a skidding 18-wheeler. One girl and her horse die. The other pair, Grace MacLean (Scarlett Johansson), and her beloved steed, Pilgrim, are badly injured. Grace loses the lower half of one leg. Pilgrim is driven mad, and everyone advises that he be put to sleep.

Grace's parents, Annie and Robert MacLean (Kristin Scott Thomas and Sam Neill), are ill-prepared to help their daughter cope with her physical disability and the mental scars of having seen her best friend run down by an out-of-control truck. Annie decides that Grace's recovery will be aided if she can find a way to heal Pilgrim (the film's only dubious contrivance). So, with her daughter and the horse in tow, Annie heads out to Montana, where a legendary "horse whisperer," Tom Booker (Robert Redford), lives and works on a ranch. After seeing Pilgrim, Tom agrees to try to help the horse, and so begins a long period of restoration for 4 souls: Pilgrim, Grace, Annie, and Tom.

Everyone in this film has their own demons to wrestle with. Grace, who retreats into a sullen cocoon after the accident, is raw on the inside, but won't let it out. She resents her mother's emotional distance and is frightened that the loss of her leg makes her useless and will doom her to a life alone. ("Nobody will want me like this!") Annie, who is used to being in charge, doesn't know how to cope with the situation, and, when she takes the time to examine her life, she recognizes how the pressures of her career have leached away her humanity. Meanwhile, Tom, who is basically at peace with himself, begins to re-discover what it means to love, something he had lost when his wife left him.

Emotionally, *The Horse Whisperer* finds the perfect pitch, and as a director, Redford has never shown greater mastery of his material. His presentation of Montana, with all of its glorious open spaces, is enough to make anyone in the theater think about heading west. He also manages to make the day-to-day activities of running a ranch and working with horses seem interesting. All in all, *The Horse Whisperer* is as rich in its emotional resonance as it is in its visual presentation. **HIGHLY RECOMMENDED**

Hotel Rwanda [Canada/Italy/United Kingdom/South Africa, 2004]

Starring: Don Cheadle, Sophie Okonedo, Nick Nolte, Joaquin Phoenix Director: Terry George Screenplay: Keir Pearson & Terry George Running Time: 1:50 Rated: PG-13 (Violence) Theatrical Aspect Ratio: 2.35:1

Hotel Rwanda introduces us to Paul Rusesabagina (Don Cheadle), the then-manager of the five-star Hotel Milles Collines in Kigali. When Hutu extremists took over the country in 1994, their first goal was to exterminate all of the Tutsi people (whom they call "cockroaches"). With the UN mired in red tape that rendered their peacekeepers ineffective and most of the world turning a blind eye, there was little to stop the Hutus from slaughtering the Tutsis. Paul, a Hutu married to a Tutsi (Sophie Okonedo), takes a stand, allowing Tutsi refugees to camp out at the hotel. Initially, he is able to employ bribery to keep the soldiers away, but when his stocks of wine and whiskey run dry, he finds the circumstances increasingly desperate and he must resort to extreme measures to save not only the refugees but his family.

Hotel Rwanda offers a stirring reminder of the kind of senseless horror that can result from race and/or religious hatred. What happened in Rwanda isn't an isolated example. Conflicts that are occurring now re-enforce the notion that mankind is incapable of learning from history. Of course, most people don't know much about Rwanda, and that's something director Terry George is attempting to change with this movie. *Hotel Rwanda* is brutal and shocking when it needs to be, but it also has great emotional scope and power. We find ourselves enmeshed in Paul's struggle, sharing his despair at the warfare tearing apart his country, his frustration and anger at the UN's inability to act and, eventually, his hope for a better tomorrow.

This role could represent a career performance for Cheadle, whose forceful and multidimensional portrayal keeps *Hotel Rwanda* at a consistently high level. Although Cheadle owns this movie, it would be unfair not to mention the supporting work of Sophie Okonedo, who brings depth and humanity to the part of Tatiana, Paul's wife. Nick Nolte plays the head of the UN peacekeeping forces with a phone-it-in acting job that isn't going to earn him many raves. Joaquin Phoenix has a small part.

Hotel Rwanda is an important film. Not only does it offer a rounded perspective on the Rwandan tragedy, but it introduces a modern hero who stands against tyranny and oppression at the risk of losing all that is dear to him. **HIGHLY RECOMMENDED**

The Hours [2002]

Starring: Meryl Streep, Nicole Kidman, Julianne Moore, Ed Harris Director: Stephen Daldry Screenplay: David Hare, based on the novel by Michael Cunningham Running Time: 1:54 Rated: PG-13 (Mature themes, brief profanity) Theatrical Aspect Ratio: 1.85:1

With superb acting and a complexly structured narrative, *The Hours* tells the story of three women living in different times and places. Thematically, as well as concretely, there are connections, but the fabric that binds them the most strongly is Virginia Woolf's fourth novel, *Mrs. Dalloway*. Nearly everything of importance that occurs in this film pertains to that book. The first segment transpires in 1923 (with brief flash-forwards to 1941) on the day that Woolf (Nicole Kidman) begins committing *Mrs. Dalloway* to paper. The second episode occurs in 1951 Los Angeles, where a lonely, depressed housewife, Laura Brown (Julianne Moore), begins to discover some things about herself and her life by reading *Mrs. Dalloway*. The third piece takes place in 2001 New York City, where a modern day Mrs. Dalloway, Clarissa Vaughn (Meryl Streep), arranges a party for her terminally ill ex-husband, Richard (Ed Harris).

The Hours contains some rather dense and weighty material, and will have the strongest appeal for those who are familiar with *Mrs. Dalloway*. The movie does not immediately exclude anyone unfamiliar with Woolf's first great novel, but their appreciation will be limited. My sense is that those who consider themselves to be fans of Woolf and her book will regard *The Hours* as a brilliant, literate motion picture. Those who don't know Woolf from Brontë will find Stephen Daldry's film to be pretentious and glacially paced.

The Hours is a triumph of acting. The portrayal most likely to garner notice is Nicole Kidman's — in large part because she undergoes a physical transformation that renders her nearly unrecognizable. Wearing a prosthetic nose and buried under layers of makeup that hide her beauty, she comes across as sickly, homely, and somewhat demented. However, although Kidman's acting is strong, she overshadows neither Julianne Moore nor Meryl Streep, both of whom give taut, tightly controlled performances. The most notable supporting work is provided by Ed Harris, whose character represents a thread connecting two of the episodes.

The Hours isn't the kind of film that's going to stir a lot of widespread enthusiasm. The film's emotional frigidity is offset by its literate and artistic qualities. I'm sure mainstream audiences will be baffled, but, for those with at least a minimal appreciation of Woolf and Clarissa Dalloway, *The Hours* represents two of those well spent. **RECOMMENDED**

House of Sand and Fog [2003]

Starring: Ben Kingsley, Jennifer Connelly, Ron Eldard, Shohreh Aghdashloo, Jonathan Ahdout, Frances Fisher Director: Vadim Perelman Screenplay: Vadim Perelman, based on the novel by Andre Dubus III Running Time: 2:06 Rated: R (Violence, nudity, sex, profanity) Theatrical Aspect Ratio: 1.85:1

Kathy Nicolo (Jennifer Connelly) is a recovering drug addict who has recently been dumped by her husband and left to fend for herself. All she has in the world is the house left to her by her father when he died, and now that is being taken away. A bureaucratic snafu has resulted in her being held liable for unpaid taxes that she doesn't owe. The county evicts her from her house and puts it up for auction. Things happen so quickly that she doesn't have time to hire a lawyer before the property has been sold at a fraction of the going market rate.

The buyer is Massoud Amir Behrani (Ben Kingsley), an immigrant who moved to the United States a number of years ago with his wife, Nadi (Shohreh Aghdashloo), and his son, Esmail (Jonathan Ahdout). In his native Iran, Massoud was a high-profile air force colonel who personally knew the shah. But, when the ruler was deposed, Massoud was forced to flee for his life. He ended up in California, eking out an existence, working two menial jobs to make ends meet. Buying Kathy's house gives him an opportunity to plan for the future. By making some improvements and reselling it at market value, he can raise the cash to buy another house and have enough left over to fund his son's college education.

The problem is, of course, that Massoud's opportunity comes at Kathy's expense. As far as he's concerned, he has legally purchased the house and is guilty of nothing other than trying to make a better life for his family. Kathy, however, has lost all that matters to her. She views Massoud as a thief and calls him that to his face. She finds comfort in the person of a sympathetic police offer, Lester Burton (Ron Eldard), who chooses to help her by harassing Massoud and threatening his family. Instead of resolving matters, this deepens the tensions.

House of Sand and Fog goes to great pains to impart a balanced portrayal. Neither protagonist is lionized or demonized. Both sides are presented sympathetically, and the characters are developed as real people, with all the virtues and faults one might expect in these circumstances. And, as the story unfolds, the house becomes not just a battleground between two people divided by an unsolvable ethical situation, but a struggle between two cultures — the natural-born citizen who is losing the last vestiges of her dream, and the immigrant who is struggling to get a grip on his own. However, as titanic as that symbolic battle may be, director Vadim Perelman never loses sight of the characters at the center of the tragic maelstrom.

I love movies in which there are no easy answers, where the circumstances demand that, in the end, someone will end up broken. The rhythms of the film are such that I did not see where it was going. This is a hard, challenging motion picture. It demands much from the audience, and repays that investment with powerful, engrossing drama that does not offer insulting, facile answers. *House of Sand and Fog* is gripping and unforgettable. **HIGHLY RECOMMENDED**

How Stella Got Her Groove Back [1998]

Starring: Angela Bassett, Taye Diggs, Whoopi Goldberg, Regina King, Suzzanne Douglas, Michael J. Pagan Director: Kevin Rodney Sullivan Screenplay: Ron Bass and Terry McMillan based on the novel by Terry McMillan Running Time: 2:05 Rated: R (Sex, profanity, nudity) Theatrical Aspect Ratio: 1.85:1

How Stella Got Her Groove Back is a surprisingly low-key romantic melodrama dealing with the issues that arise when a woman "of a certain age" defies convention and falls for a younger man.

The film (and the novel that inspired it) is loosely based on writer Terry McMillan's own experience of falling in love and setting up house with a Jamaican man young enough to be her son. Perhaps this semi-autobiographical background is the reason why the characters resonate with warmth and believability. They're easy to like, and even easier to root for, and *How Stella Got Her Groove Back* is a fresh, sassy source of entertainment.

Stella Payne, the main character and McMillan's alter ego, is brought to life through a superior performance by Angela Bassett. Not only is Bassett gorgeous at the age of 40, but she has a body to die for and the acting skills to make us believe that she is Stella. The film begins by introducing the title character as an independent woman who is raising a son by herself and doesn't crave the constant company of a man. However, when her high-pressure job as a San Francisco-based stock broker gets to be too much for her, Stella decides to take a vacation. Along with her best friend, Delilah (Whoopi Goldberg), she books a trip to Jamaica. While there, she begins flirting with a 20-year-old hunk improbably named Winston Shakespeare (Taye Diggs). Soon Stella, who embarked upon the vacation in an uptight and unsettled mood, is beginning to unwind and rediscover the part of her that had gotten lost under the business suits. Within a matter of days, she finds that her fling with Winston is becoming serious, and her feelings for him don't dissipate once she's back in the Bay Area.

While Bassett is clearly the film's star, she is surrounded by a fine cast. Fresh face Taye Diggs does exactly what's demanded of him for this part: he portrays the too-good-to-be-true Winston with perfect sincerity while showing off a very impressive physique. The supporting cast includes a pair of wonderfully amusing performances from Whoopi Goldberg as the obligatory Best Friend, and Regina King (Cuba Gooding Jr.'s wife in *Jerry Maguire*) as Stella's chatty sister, Vanessa. We expect Goldberg to be funny, but King's comic aptitude is a revelation.

How Stella Got Her Groove Back is aimed at the black female audience, but this movie can be enjoyed by members of both genders of any race. It isn't the kind of "chick flick" that will have men looking at their watches every 5 minutes. And the film has a thing or two to say about older women and younger men. As *Stella* shows, there are times when the vapid cuteness of a young nymph can't hold a candle to the practiced sensuality of a mature woman. RECOMMENDED

How To Make an American Quilt [1995]
Starring: Winona Ryder, Ann Bancroft, Ellen Burstyn, Maya Angelou Director: Jocelyn Moorhouse Screenplay: Jane Anderson based on the novel by Whitney Otto Running Time: 1:56 Rated: PG-13 (Mature themes, brief nudity, mild profanity) Theatrical Aspect Ratio: 1.85:1

American movies are filled with male bonding rituals; *How to Make an American Quilt* offers a feminine alternative. Here, 7 quilters imbue their creation with passion and vitality. The "quilting bee" consists of 7 members: sisters Gladys (Ann Bancroft) and Hy (Ellen Burstyn); Sophia (Lois Smith), a woman known for frightening children; Emma (Jean Simmons), the timid wife of a perpetually unfaithful man; Constance (Kate Nelligan), who has been having an affair with Emma's husband; Anna (Maya Angelou), the leader of the group; and Marianna (Alfre Woodard), Anna's daughter. The project they're busy with is the wedding quilt for Hy's granddaughter, Finn (Winona Ryder), who has just become engaged. She's spending the summer with Hy and Gladys, and away from her fiancé, to decide whether a lifelong commitment is really what she wants, and whether it's better to marry a friend or a lover.

There are probably too many characters. So, instead of really getting to know a few of them, we are presented with quick glimpses into a single defining event in each of their lives. We learn about the root of the smoldering resentment between Gladys and Hy, and are told the reasons why Emma stays with her husband and Sophia is so irascible. There are other episodes as well: the love of Anna's life, Marianna's soul mate, and a look at the reasons why Constance entered into an affair with her friend's husband. The sum total of these tales is meant to provide the framework for Finn's story: whether to go forward with her marriage or dally with a hunky stranger.

On the whole, *How to Make an American Quilt* is a nicely-understated drama that has a lot to say about love, passion, and monogamy in relationships. There is no emotional epiphany in the movie. The stories are all well-told, but it's difficult to really connect with the characters — their moments pass so quickly. Finn's segment is by far the most compelling, because she's the focal point: her actions are shaped by everyone else's experiences. The other patches of this American Quilt are successful only to varying degrees, but the privilege of seeing such a fine cast in top form allows a viewer to enjoy this picture even if the story is somewhat conventional. RECOMMENDED

Hurlyburly [1998]
Starring: Sean Penn, Kevin Spacey, Robin Wright Penn, Chazz Palminteri, Garry Shandling, Anna Paquin, Meg Ryan Director: Anthony Drazan Screenplay: David Rabe based on his play Running Time: 2:02 Rated: R (Profanity, drug use, sex, violence) Theatrical Aspect Ratio: 1.85:1

Hurlyburly is a talky film — the entire movie is constructed around lengthy sequences of dialogue where the characters talk and talk and talk, often saying nothing. But in Anthony Drazen's adaptation of the David Rabe play, that's the point. Because the vocal rhythms are so perfect, the words so well-chosen, and the performances so powerful, listening to this much talk is a pleasure, not a chore.

Eddie (Sean Penn), is a fast-talking, coke-sniffing Hollywood casting agent whose contempt for others is exceeded only by his contempt for himself. Eddie has surrounded himself with 3 equally degenerate friends: his housemate and business partner, Mickey (Kevin Spacey), a mindless thug named Phil (Chazz Palminteri), and a sycophantic writer, Artie (Gary Shandling). Women have no real place in this mens' world, except as sexual objects and punching bags. Three female characters drift through the movie: Darlene (Robin Wright Penn), the love of Eddie's life; Donna (Anna Paquin), a hitchhiker who trades sex for lodging; and Bonnie (Meg Ryan), a perpetually stoned stripper with an oral talent.

If this sounds misogynistic, it is, but it's the characters that display that trait, not the movie. These 4 men are among the least likable individuals you'd ever run across, and Drazan makes no attempt to hide their shortcomings. As one character notes, Eddie surrounds himself with losers so that no matter how far he falls, there will always be someone in his immediate circle who is lower.

Sean Penn gives a towering, intense performance as Eddie, getting into the character's skin and inhabiting him completely. It's an amazing turn and a frighteningly believable portrayal of an opportunist on the edge. Penn's 3 male co-stars — Chazz Palminteri as the talentless actor whose chief ability is to whack people (women in particular), Kevin Spacey as the amoral but amusing Mickey, who's never without a dry comeback, and Gary Shandling as the oily Artie — are capable of holding their own in scenes with him, which is a testament to the strength of their performances. Those who think of Meg Ryan as all sugar and spice will be surprised to see her in this role, where she radiates a slutty sexuality. And Anna Paquin is effective as a vapid, oversexed girl who trades her body for a bed. Actually, it's almost a shame that Ryan and Paquin are so good — they make us want to see more of their characters.

It's hard to say whether *Hurlyburly* is a black comedy or a tragedy. For, while the film contains its share of absurd and darkly comical moments, the overall portrait is a grim one. The characters are bottom-feeders — scum that prey off the weaknesses of others and revel in the bleakest aspects of the Hollywood culture. *Hurlyburly* would be easier to take if its portrayals weren't so dead-on. But the sheer pleasure of watching such virtuoso performances makes it worthwhile. RECOMMENDED

The Hurricane [1999]

Starring: Denzel Washington, Vicellous Reon Shannon, Liev Schreiber, Deborah Unger, John Hannah, Dan Hedaya Director: Norman Jewison Screenplay: Armyan Bernstein and Dan Gordon, based on *Lazarus and The Hurricane* by Sam Chaiton and Terry Swinton, and *The 16th Round* by Rubin 'Hurricane' Carter Running Time: 2:05 Rated: R (Violence, profanity) Theatrical Aspect Ratio: 1.85:1

"Hate put me in prison. Love's gonna bust me out." Those words, spoken by Rubin "Hurricane" Carter (Denzel Washington), form the thematic foundation of Norman Jewsion's film, *The Hurricane*. Alternatively tragic and triumphant, it is an exhilarating trip through the life and times of the title character, a championship boxer from Paterson, New Jersey, who spent 19 years behind bars for murders he did not commit. *The Hurricane* not only details the crime and the miscarriage of justice that followed, but shows how Carter survived the long, lonely years in prison, and how the devotion of a small group of Canadians led to his redemption.

It's difficult to state exactly where and when the movie begins, since, especially during its first half, it jumps around freely and frequently in time. There are numerous flashbacks, but the editing is clean and sharp, which keeps the potential for confusion to a minimum.

There are two primary time periods. The first begins in 1963, when The Hurricane defeats Emile Griffith for the World Welter Weight title, and continues through 1966, when he is arrested and tried for murder, then into the 1970s, when he is incarcerated at Trenton State Prison on a life sentence. The second time period occurs during the 1980s, when Lesra Martin (Vicellous Shannon), a Brooklyn teenager living in Canada, buys a copy of Carter's autobiography, *The 16th Round*, and develops a passion to meet Carter. Encouraged by the 3 older people he is living with — Sam (Liev Schreiber), Terry (John Hannah), and Lisa (Deborah Unger) — he opens a correspondence with Carter, then travels to New Jersey to visit him. Following the face-to-face meeting, Lesra becomes determined to free Carter, and enlists the aid of Sam, Terry, and Lisa in his struggle.

Many people became aware of Carter's plight as a result of Bob Dylan's mid-70s ballad, "The Hurricane" (which is featured on two separate occasions during the course of the film). Over the years, a number of celebrities have leant their support to Carter's cause, but none of the marches or protests had any effect. What made the difference was the commitment of the group from Toronto, who gave up their jobs, moved to New Jersey, and literally risked their lives to find the evidence to prove Carter's innocence and to bring to light the corruption of the Paterson police lieutenant (Dan Hedaya) who hunted The Hurricane like a dog. Their efforts turn *The Hurricane* into a story of victory rather than defeat. HIGHLY RECOMMENDED

I Shot Andy Warhol [1996]

Starring: Lili Taylor, Jared Harris, Stephen Dorff, Martha Plimpton, Lothaire Bluteau, Donovan Leitch, Tahnee Welch Director: Mary Harron Screenplay: Mary Harron and Daniel Minahan Running Time: 1:40 Rated: R (Profanity, sex, violence) Theatrical Aspect Ratio: 1.85:1

The script for *I Shot Andy Warhol* began life as a documentary before the producers convinced writer/director Mary Harron to transform it into a dramatic interpretation. The result is an impressive feature debut — a provocative look at Valerie Solanas, the intellectual, possibly psychotic prefeminist who shot Warhol in 1968.

Most of *I Shot Andy Warhol* takes place in New York City from 1966 to 1968, chronicling the period in Valerie Solanas' (Lili Taylor) life when she wrote her definitive work, *SCUM Manifesto,* was introduced to Andy Warhol (Jared Harris), became a fringe member of his circle, and eventually shot him. Valerie, who had a "pitiful childhood" characterized by abuse and molestation, is subversive and disturbed, but many of her theories, as outlandish as they initially seem, are consistent, logical, and thought-provoking.

SCUM, or the Society for Cutting Up Men, was the prefeminist organization formed by Valerie (she was also the only member). It was founded on a number of basic principles — the male is a biological accident, women are the naturally superior gender, the female function is to create a "magical world," and men are sex-obsessed machines. *The SCUM Manifesto* represents Valerie's legacy (it's still in print today).

Those offended by the "male bashing" aspect of *Thelma and Louise* may become apoplectic during *I Shot Andy Warhol.* Since the film is essentially a character study of Valerie, it gives an uncompromising presentation of her views and experiences. She despises "men, married women, and other degenerates," and makes no secret of her feelings. She's a "butch dyke," and proud of it, and the only time she has any sexual interaction with men is when she gets paid.

Lili Taylor, who, like Eric Stoltz, has gravitated towards independent features, gives a powerful, passionate portrayal, bringing out Valerie's anger and disgust with the world.

Jared Harris (the son of Richard Harris), manages to capture not only Warhol's strange magnetism, but his aloof, almost-shy nature. Stephen Dorff (*Backbeat*) plays Candy Darling, Valerie and Warhol's transvestite companion. Supporting roles are filled by Martha Plimpton (as Valerie's best friend), Lothaire Bluteau (as Maurice Girodius, the publisher who buys the rights to Valerie's writing), and Tahnee Welch (as a member of Warhol's circle).

I Shot Andy Warhol is a toned-down, nostalgic look at New York in the late 1960s as well as the subculture that took root around Warhol — the wild, bohemian lifestyle, the drugs and sex. Primarily, however, this is Valerie's story — an invitation to explore her theories and understand her motivation, even if you can't relate to such a disagreeable personality. **RECOMMENDED**

The Ice Storm [1997]

Starring: Kevin Kline, Sigourney Weaver, Joan Allen, Tobey Maguire, Christina Ricci, Jamey Sheridan, Elijah Wood Director: Ang Lee
Screenplay: James Schamus based on the novel by Rick Moody
Running Time: 1:52 Rated: R (Sexual situations, profanity) Theatrical
Aspect Ratio: 1.85:1

It is Thanksgiving week of 1973 in New Canaan, Connecticut. On the political front, the nation is bathed in the aftermath of Vietnam, and President Nixon's regime is beginning to crumble as the Watergate scandal escalates. With trust in the government giving way to cynicism and disillusionment, it is the end of an era — politically, socially, and culturally.

The Hood family is the poster household of the times: poised and perfect on the outside, riven by doubt and guilt within. Paul (Tobey Maguire) is an average 16-year old off at prep school learning about Dostoevsky in the classroom and the difficulties of romance outside of it. His younger sister, Wendy (Christina Ricci) is a restless 14-year old, intensely curious about sexual matters, and willing to explore them beyond the bounds of prudence. Paul and Wendy's parents, Ben and Elena (Kevin Kline and Joan Allen) appear at first glance to be the perfect mother and father. But their perfection is a sham, and while Ben dallies with a willing neighbor (Sigourney Weaver), Elena stews in her own loneliness. Sexually and socially, everyone in this film is groping for answers, whether their age is 14 or 40. More often than not, the children in *The Ice Storm* are open about what they want. The adults, on the other hand, feel the need to resort to deception and wife-swapping games to achieve the same ends.

Lee accurately captures the "feel" of the early '70s, which is ironic since, during the year when *The Ice Storm* transpires, he didn't speak English and hadn't yet set foot in America. However, for those of us who lived through that era, there are plenty of familiar images and items. Some, like the bellbottoms, wide collared shirts, and gas-guzzling cars, are expected. Others, like the bubble umbrella and the anti-pollution TV spot featuring a crying Native American, show that Lee was willing to take things to another level of detail. While it's true that *The Ice Storm* may not represent the reality of the '70s, it effectively fits our memories of the time.

The ice storm of the title is a presence throughout the film. It is crucial to the narrative resolution, but its vivid presentation makes it almost a character in its own right as it coats trees, power lines, and streets with ice and turns the world into a beautiful-but-deadly place.

The Ice Storm is at times funny, poignant, moving, and sensitive; it is perceptive about people, relationships, and human nature, and there's not a single moment in the entire 112 minute running length that rings false. **MUST SEE**

I'm Not Rappaport [1996]

Starring: Walter Matthau, Ossie Davis, Amy Irving, Boyd Gaines, Martha Plimpton, Craig T. Nelson Director: Herb Gardner
Screenplay: Herb Gardner based on his play Running Time: 2:15
Rated: PG-13 (Profanity, mature themes) Theatrical Aspect Ratio: 1.85:1

I'm Not Rappaport, Herb Gardner's production of his own 1986 Tony award winning play, revolves around the unlikely friendship of two 80-year-old men who, despite infirm bodies and failing eyesight, aren't ready to give up on life. Together, Nat (Matthau) and Midge (Davis) sit around on benches in New York's Central Park, argue with each other, discuss life and philosophy, reminisce about better days, argue some more, share a joint, and try to do their small part in righting the world's wrongs. And, while most of their efforts are ultimately ineffective, it isn't until the very end that we, like them, recognize that even apparent failures can be successes.

Several minor characters occasionally cross Nat and Midge's paths. Nat's daughter, Clara (Amy Irving), doesn't trust her father on his own and wants to put him in an old age home. Laurie (Martha Plimpton), an attractive artist, watches the pair from afar, sketching them. The Cowboy (Craig T. Nelson), a high-testosterone drug dealer, roams the park on business. Danforth (Boyd Gaines), the yuppy spokesman of the group that wants to fire Midge from his maintenance job, breaks the bad news only to have the situation unexpectedly blow up in his face. And a mugger (Guillermo Diaz) tries to extort protection money from Nat.

For the most part, the plot is incidental. What matters in *I'm Not Rappaport* are the characters and their dialogue. Over the 2+- hour running time, Nat and Midge touch on an amazing variety of subjects: unions and bosses ("their tactics haven't changed in one century"), age ("an old man like me, I could wander through the world like a ghost"), memories ("nostalgia kills more of us than heart disease"), and the

war between idealism and realism ("I got smarter — I fought in battles I thought I could win"). They talk and talk and talk, and they're always a delight to listen to, whether we're hearing Nat's tall stories or Midge's less fanciful reflections.

I'm Not Rappaport is the kind of movie that grows on you. It's obviously a play that has been adapted for the cinema, but that doesn't take anything away from the delicate magic that Gardner has conjured by his use of sly comedy and keen social insight. While it's true that this is essentially a buddy movie, it's a very special one. Nat and Midge's friendship reminds us of what bonding really is — and it doesn't have anything to do with dodging bullets or running away from exploding buildings. In the final analysis, this motion picture is far more about a rapport than a Rappaport. **HIGHLY RECOMMENDED**

In America [Ireland/United Kingdom, 2003]

Starring: Samantha Morton, Paddy Considine, Sarah Bolger, Emma Bolger, Djimon Hounsou Director: Jim Sheridan Screenplay: Jim Sheridan & Naomi Sheridan & Kirsten Sheridan Running Time: 1:43
Rated: PG-13 (Mature themes) Theatrical Aspect Ratio: 1.85:1

In America is a unique and moving look at the so-called "immigrant experience" that is as much about family dynamics as it is about the struggle to survive in an unfamiliar country. Directed, cowritten, and coproduced by Jim Sheridan, *In America* represents a balanced portrait of the highs and lows of life for those who have ventured beyond familiar terrain in the search of something new.

Johnny and Sarah (Paddy Considine and Samantha Morton), along with their two young daughters, Christie (Sarah Bolger) and Ariel (Emma Bolger), have arrived in the United States from Ireland via Canada. They have left behind not only everything they knew, but raw memories of a son whose tragic death still haunts them. With all of their worldly possessions in a station wagon, they arrive at a dilapidated New York City apartment that they struggle to make into a home. It isn't easy — nor is getting money to pay the rent. Johnny finds that rejection is a way of life for a would-be actor. Sarah becomes the family breadwinner by working as a waitress at a local ice-cream parlor. The unexpected friendship shown by the mysterious Mateo (Djimon Hounsou) represents a turning point in the family's attempts to cope with their new life and come to grips with the ghosts that still haunt them.

There are two key differences between *In America* and a "typical" film about immigrants living in America. In the first place, the setting is contemporary. Most movies contemplating this subject take us back to the early 1900s, when Ellis Island was brimming with optimistic newcomers. Secondly, the movie is not relentlessly depressing, as many immigrant stories are. Sheridan focuses on the push-pull forces that simultaneously bind Johnny and Sarah's family and threaten to tear them apart. *In America* is filled with small moments of tragedy and triumph — much as is the case in real life. Those in search of a depressing tale of crushed dreams will need to look elsewhere.

It's a pleasure to encounter a motion picture about immigration that doesn't have an overt political agenda. While there's a place for that sort of movie, there's also a place for something like *In America*, which focuses on characters and their interaction, and doesn't leave the viewer floundering in a whirlpool of unrelieved depression. Sheridan's overall approach is cautiously optimistic and, as a result, *In America* turns out to be uplifting, even though the sensitive viewer will find many opportunities to shed tears. RECOMMENDED

In the Bedroom [2001]

Starring: Tom Wilkinson, Sissy Spacek, Nick Stahl, Marisa Tomei, Deborah Derecktor, Veronica Cartwright Director: Todd Field
Screenplay: Robert Festinger, Todd Field, based on the short story by Andre Dubus Running Time: 2:16 Rated: R (Profanity, violence, mature themes) Theatrical Aspect Ratio: 2.35:1

The stunning feature debut of Todd Field, *In the Bedroom* deals with issues that are rarely approached with this degree of sensitivity on film. The movie, set in Maine, stars Tom Wilkinson and Sissy Spacek as Matt and Ruth Fowler, a seemingly perfect middle-aged couple. Their only son, Frank (Nick Stahl), is spending the summer working on a lobster boat before going off to an Ivy League school in the fall. His latest girlfriend, Natalie Strout (Marisa Tomei), is an older woman with two young children. These characters are bound together when a criminal act results in a tragedy.

The movie is close to flawless. The set-up is sympathetic and involving; the crime is shocking; and the aftermath has the inevitability of tragedy. *In the Bedroom* shows how the pressure of a tragedy can put strain on even the most solid marriage. For Matt and Ruth, their quiet camaraderie gradually dissolves into anger and recrimination. One explosive confrontation between them leads directly to an action that brings catharsis and closure to one while causing the other to engage in deeper soul-searching.

The movie also presents some of the most poignant reminders of the little things that often cause the greatest pain in the wake of a tragedy. The narrative gathers an unwavering momentum as it moves towards the climax. *In the Bedroom* also addresses the frustration and anguish of crime victims, especially in cases when the perpetrators of a crime appear beyond the reach of legal punishment. The tendency in motion pictures these days is to develop sympathy for the criminal; it is rare that a film addresses the other side of the equation with this degree of intelligence and sensitivity.

The performances are all astonishing. Wilkinson, perhaps best known for his work in *The Full Monty*, imbues Matt with a quiet dignity, a deep wellspring of grief, and a simmering fury. Sissy Spacek's Ruth is a volcano that lies dormant for a while before erupting. Nick Stahl brings depth and strength to a character that could have turned into a one-dimensional type. Marisa Tomei impresses in yet another supporting role far away from the Hollywood spotlight (although her inconsistent New England accent is a little distracting).

In the Bedroom is the kind of motion picture that it's almost impossible to forget. It epitomizes what an American independent film can be when the director is willing to abandon the safety net. MUST SEE

In the Mood For Love [Hong Kong, 2000]

Starring: Tony Leung, Maggie Cheung, Lai Chen, Rebecca Pan Director: Wong Kar-wai Screenplay: Wong Kar-wai Running Time: 1:38 Rated: PG (Mature themes) Theatrical Aspect Ratio: 1.85:1
In Cantonese and French with subtitles

Longing — it is one of the great motivators of the human experience. It has driven poets to write sonnets, painters to create artwork, and composers to fashion music to wrench the soul. Hong Kong filmmaker Wong Kar-wai understands longing and, the sublime *In the Mood for Love* brings it to life on the screen.

The plot is simple, and is really just a vehicle for the characters and their delicate ballet of hidden feelings and concealed emotions. The film takes place in 1962 Hong Kong, where Chow (Tony Leung) meets Li-zhen (Maggie Cheung) when they become next-door neighbors in an apartment building. He's a journalist with dreams of publishing pulp martial arts books; she's a secretary. After learning that Chow's wife is having an affair with Li-zhen's husband, the two become close friends, and the attachment between them grows into something deeper and more lasting than a casual liaison. But, because of cultural issues and feelings of guilt (the guilt of things considered in the mind but never committed in the body), they never act upon those impulses. They remain true to their marriage vows even though their respective spouses do not.

The tone is languorous, allowing the shadings of the characters to deepen as the storyline advances. The camera makes us more of a voyeur than usual, as Wong employs unusual shots to imprint upon the film a unique look. There are times during conversations between Chow and Li-zhen when the camera frames one in the shot without the other, or peeks at them from between objects. In addition, Wong limits the number of people and locales. Chow's and Li-zhen's spouses remain faceless entities — they never appear on-screen — and the majority of *In the Mood for Love*'s scenes take place indoors.

For his lead characters, Wong couldn't have selected two better-suited actors. Both Tony Leung (*Chungking Express*) and Maggie Cheung (*Irma Vep*) have international followings, and neither has been better than they are here.

The Hollywood version of this motion picture would have a radically different ending — one that would satisfy the standard romantic formula even as it betrays the material and the characters. Wong's film is as anti-Hollywood as a motion picture can be. It is slow, it does not pander, it allows the characters room to breathe, and, in the end, it has an impact. *In the Mood for Love* is a powerful study of longing that uses innovative camera techniques, evocative music (mournful violins), and strong performances to bathe the audience in the mood of the characters — one of poignant yearning for something that both desire but which neither can find the courage to express. **HIGHLY RECOMMENDED**

Infinity [1996]

Starring: Matthew Broderick, Patricia Arquette, Peter Riegert, Dori Brenner, Peter Michael Goetz, Zelijko Ivanek, James LeGros
Director: Matthew Broderick Screenplay: Patricia Broderick based on the books of Richard Feynman Running Time: 1:56 Rated: PG (Mature themes) Theatrical Aspect Ratio: 1.85:1

Infinity is a biographical look at the early life of Richard Feynman (Matthew Broderick), the noted speaker, writer, and Nobel Prize-winning physicist who died in 1988.

Infinity tells two stories: Feynman's relationship with his beloved first wife, Arline (Patricia Arquette), and his involvement in the Manhattan Project's development of the first atomic bomb. While the tales cannot be split, it's clear that the film has a much bet-

ter feel for Feynman's personal life than for his ethical struggles about unleashing a force of mass destruction. As background, the Los Alamos material is effective, but, on those occasions when it is thrust into the foreground, it pales in comparison to the love story.

The bulk of the film has nothing to do with Los Alamos or the bomb. Rather, it's about Richard and his intense, unwavering love for Arline. He meets her one day in 1934, when both are still in high school. He wanders into a room where she's singing and playing the piano, and is immediately smitten. The attraction is mutual, and, from that day forward, they are a couple.

In 1941, however, Arline falls ill, and the initial diagnosis is Hodgkin's Disease, a fatal ailment. Eventually, however, it turns out to be tuberculosis, the AIDS of the time. Over the protests of his family, who are afraid that he might contract the disease, Richard decides to marry Arline, then accept a government job so he can support her. Shortly after they elope, he moves to Los Alamos to join the Manhattan Project as a theoretical physicist, and the head of the project, J. Robert Oppenheimer, makes sure that Arline has a place in an Albuquerque sanitarium, where Richard can visit her each weekend. For two years, things continue like this, until Arline's illness reaches its crisis point just as victory is declared in Europe.

As told here, Arline and Richard's touching love story is devoid of sensationalism. Only in the end, when Richard fails to display any significant emotion following Arline's death, does *Infinity* strike a wrong chord. Feynman may have really given this rather clinical, dispassionate assessment: "Everybody dies. It doesn't stop the world." But it's tough to get an audience to accept that a loving husband could turn into such a cold fish.

Knowledge of physics and mathematics isn't necessary to enjoy the film. Arline is, after all, an artist, so Feynman has to explain his work in a manner that she, and the audience, will understand. *Infinity* represents a journey of emotional and scientific discovery. It's just unfortunate that the ending isn't more fundamentally satisfying. That single flaw keeps this from being a remarkable feature. **RECOMMENDED**

The Insider [1999]

Starring: Al Pacino, Russell Crowe, Christopher Plummer, Diane Venora, Philip Baker Hall Director: Michael Mann Screenplay: Eric Roth & Michael Mann, based on the *Vanity Fair* article "The Man Who Knew Too Much" by Marie Brenner Running Time: 2:37 Rated: PG-13 (Profanity) Theatrical Aspect Ratio: 2.35:1

The Insider tells the story of CBS News's blackest hour — a time when greed and bad judgment overcame journalistic integrity. A story for *60 Minutes* compiled by correspondent Mike Wallace (played in the film by Christopher Plummer) and producer Lowell Bergman (Al Pacino) was killed when a potential lawsuit by tobacco giant Brown & Williamson threatened a buyout of CBS that would make a number of high-placed corporate executives very rich. The story: an interview with Jeffrey Wigand (Russell Crowe), a fired B&W corporate V.P. who had decided to blow the whistle on his former boss' lies to congress.

As a scientist, Wigand was deeply disturbed by the results of a study he ran, which showed that the tobacco companies deliberately manipulate the levels of the drug in their product to promote addiction. He first met Bergman when the *60 Minutes* producer was looking for an expert to translate industry-specific technical jargon. As the two spent time together, Bergman realized that Wigand knew an explosive secret, but was constrained from talking by a confidentiality agreement he had signed upon leaving B&W (the terms of which guaranteed his severance pay and continued medical coverage). Bergman, believing he knew a way around a breach of contract, offered Wigand the opportunity to be subpoenaed to testify in a Mississippi wrongful death class action lawsuit against the tobacco companies. Once his testimony was a part of the public record, he could go on *60 Minutes* to state his case. Even before Wigand agreed, he and his family became the targets of terrorist threats from anonymous sources. After risking everything (including his marriage and the possibility of going to jail), Wigand learned that *60 Minutes* had decided to cut the interview, rendering his sacrifices moot. Wigand had been betrayed, Bergman had been hung out to dry, and the Court of Public Opinion would not hear the truth about the tobacco giants.

The Insider is arguably a little too long with a few too many minor subplots thrown in (such as one about the Unibomber). However, when the movie is on-target, which is most of the time, it is riveting. Mann generates tension without resorting to the boring stand-bys of shootouts and chase scenes. The actors play their roles as if there's something tangible on the line, and those performances heighten the level of suspense.

The result is a compelling and engaging motion picture that weds the tautness of a thriller with the depth and impact of a drama. **HIGHLY RECOMMENDED**

Inventing the Abbotts [1997]

Starring: Joaquin Phoenix, Billy Crudup, Liv Tyler, Joanna Going, Jennifer Connelly, Will Patton, Kathy Baker, Barbara Williams
Director: **Pat O'Connor** Screenplay: **Ken Hixon** Running Time: 1:50
Rated: R (Sex, profanity, brief nudity) Theatrical Aspect Ratio: 1.85:1

Inventing the Abbotts begins with a voiceover, "The end of my innocence and childhood began in 1957." Openings like this are not promising, usually heralding overwrought coming-of-age melodramas of the most unremarkable sort. But while no one is going to mistake this for groundbreaking cinema, for what it is, *Inventing the Abbotts* does a more-than-acceptable job.

The film centers around two brothers: The older is Jacey Holt (Billy Crudup, from *Sleepers*) and the younger is Billy (Joaquin Phoenix, from *To Die For*), our narrator. Through the superfluous voiceover, we're given a quick rundown on the boys. Jacey is hard-working, obstinate, and gets all the girls; Billy is less sure of himself or where his life is going. The Holt boys are devoted to their mother, Helen (Kathy Baker), who brought them up on her own — their father died before Billy was born.

Next door to the Holts live the upper-class Abbotts. There are three daughters: Alice (Joanna Going), the "good girl" eldest child; Eleanor (Jennifer Connelly), the "bad girl" middle child; and Pamela (Liv Tyler), the youngest, who describes herself as "the one who sort of gets off the hook." Jacey is madly in lust with Eleanor, but it's a match that the Abbott patriarch (Will Patton) regards with ill-disguised contempt. Billy is friends with Pam, but, although theirs is a platonic relationship, it's clear that Pam would like it to go further. Billy, however, is wary, telling us that "I witnessed enough of my brother's social agony early on to know that I would never let the Abbotts matter to me." We in the audience, having seen this all before, know better.

Inventing the Abbotts is a routine Hollywood drama, which is to say that it doesn't take any chances and adheres rigorously to certain time-honored romantic conventions. The boy and girl appear fated to get together, but not until the last reel, and only after all sorts of social and emotional roadblocks have been cleared. The main story — Billy's relationship with Pam — is arguably the least interesting aspect of the film. In fact, the most compelling characters aren't necessarily the central figures. Jennifer Connelly's confident portrayal of Eleanor crackles with open sexuality; it's a shame that the film discards her so quickly. Likewise, Billy Crudup's Jacey is far more complex than his rather bland brother.

Watching *Inventing the Abbotts* is a comfortable experience. It would have been a better movie without the voiceover, but that particular narrative contrivance aside, the film comes across a genial, undemanding tale of love and life in the late '50s. And, while it's hard to get worked up about such a low-key motion picture, that doesn't diminish the simple enjoyment that the movie is capable of offering.

RECOMMENDED

Iris [United Kingdom/United States, 2001]

Starring: Judi Dench. Jim Broadbent, Kate Winslet, Hugh Bonneville, Penelope Wilton, Juliet Aubrey Director: Richard Eyre
Screenplay: Charles Wood, Richard Eyre, based on *Iris: A Memoir and Elegy for Iris* by John Bayley Running Time: 1:30 Rated: R (Nudity, sex, profanity) Theatrical Aspect Ratio: 1.85:1

Those who have had a loved one fall prey to the ravages of Alzheimer's will see in *Iris* a depiction so lucid and accurate that it may be painful to watch. Based on the memoir of John Bayley, *Iris* tells of the first and last days of his relationship with his wife, philosopher and novelist Iris Murdoch. It's a powerful, affecting tale that uses scenes of the young couple's new love as a counterpoint to Iris' final days — memories of a brightest spring echoing in the darkest depths of winter.

Iris' main storyline unfolds in the early 1990s, when Iris (Judi Dench), regarded by some as the "foremost novelist of her generation" begins to experience the first stirrings of the disease that would eventually reduce her to a state of childlike helplessness. At first, she forgets things, and, for someone with a deep and abiding passion for words, her inability to recall the best one becomes a frustrating experience. Eventually, she loses more than just words. She can no longer write or even think coherently. The unknown frightens her. She sits in front of the television, watching shows designed for children. Her husband, John (Jim Broadbent), comfortable for 40 years being the "weaker" half of the union, is now thrust into the role of caregiver. There are times when he is found lacking, but his love for his wife ensures that he will not give up on her until the end.

Intercut with the '90s scenes are sequences from the '50s, when John (Hugh Bonneville) first meets and falls in love with the young, vivacious Iris (Kate Winslet), who loves nude swimming, fast biking, and no-strings-attached sex. Unaccountably, Iris is as drawn to John as he is to her, and it's not long before some of her free-spiritedness rubs off on him. They are a classic case of opposites attracting. She introduces him to sex and he shows her the rewards of simple, honest tenderness. It is in these flashback moments that *Iris* derives a measure of its power. Through them, we see Iris at her strongest, and understand the foundation of her relationship with John.

Lest *Iris* seem like too much of a downer, there are moments of light humor to go along with the poignancy. Iris and John's courtship is presented playfully, and Eyre's decision to sprinkle the flashbacks throughout the film (rather than present them in one long block) gives us moments of needed respite from the sadness that accompanies Iris' downward spiral. And, while this is a story about the effects and ramifications of a disease, it is also a tale of the unbreakable power of love. While Alzheimer's defeats Iris' intellect, it never sunders the bond that she and John have formed. **HIGHLY RECOMMENDED**

It Could Happen to You [1994]

Starring: Nicolas Cage, Bridget Fonda, Rosie Perez, Wendell Pierce, Isaac Hayes, Stanley Tucci Director: Andrew Bergman Screenplay: Jane Anderson Running Time: 1:51 Rated: PG (Language, mature themes)
Theatrical Aspect Ratio: 1.85:1

Those with a cynical bent will not enjoy *It Could Happen to You*. If you don't like happy endings, think Christmas is just for kids, and feel vaguely ill while watching *It's a Wonderful Life*, you would do well to stay away from this movie. On the other hand, if you're looking for a "feel good" romantic comedy, there aren't too many around more affable than this one.

Charlie Lang (Nicolas Cage) is a New York cop, and a genuinely nice guy — so nice, in fact, that when he doesn't have the change to tip his coffee shop waitress Yvonne (Bridget Fonda), he promises to split his winnings from a lottery ticket with her — if he wins, that is. Yvonne, who is having a bad day (she declared bankruptcy before coming to work), doesn't give the offer a second thought — until Charlie returns the next day with the news that he's $4 million richer. Despite the pleadings of his wife Muriel (Rosie Perez) to "stiff" the waitress, Charlie lets his conscience guide him, and sticks to his promise.

Love is in the air, as the old John Paul Young tune goes. You know from the beginning that Charlie and Yvonne are going to get together. If you can't figure that out, you've probably rented the wrong movie. The chemistry between Fonda and Cage is tangible — not the sultry, sexy kind that often characterizes boy-meets-girl stories, but something cuter and more fanciful.

Often, relationships in romantic comedies are contentious. Not so in *It Could Happen to You*. Charlie and Yvonne are two kind-hearted people who don't yell at each other. Instead, all scenes of conflict are reserved for vain, gold-digging Muriel, who begrudges Charlie every penny he gives away. She's the obvious villain of the piece, *It Could Happen to You*'s version of Mr. Potter.

I'm not sure if Rosie Perez does a great job of acting or not, but her character is really, really annoying. The word "shrill" doesn't begin to do her justice. Watching most of her scenes is like sitting in a classroom while someone scrapes their fingernails across the blackboard. Screeeeeeeeech!

It Could Happen to You is the most inoffensive of motion pictures, and that's precisely where the core of its charm lies. Other than a little suspension of disbelief, it doesn't demand a heavy investment from its audience. Of course, you have to enjoy this sort of movie to appreciate its appeal. If you do, *It Could Happen to You* will convince you that the magic of Frank Capra isn't dead in Hollywood after all. RECOMMENDED

Jack [1996]

Starring: Robin Williams, Diane Lane, Brian Kerwin, Jennifer Lopez, Adam Zolotin, Bill Cosby, Fran Drescher Director: Francis Ford Coppola Screenplay: James DeMonaco & Gary Nadeau Running Time: 1:53 Rated: PG-13 (Mature themes) Theatrical Aspect Ratio: 1.85:1

This feel-good motion picture is intelligently written and expertly directed: cross *Big* with *Forrest Gump*, and you get an idea of where *Jack*'s appeal lies.

The premise for *Jack*, although seemingly simple, is riddled with potential problems — nearly all of which the script not only addresses, but answers without a whiff of condescension. Jack is born when his mother is only 10 weeks pregnant. The doctors are immediately aware that something strange is going on. Eventually, they arrive at an explanation. The child has an internal clock that's ticking 4 times faster than usual. So, by the time Jack turns 10, he appears like a 40-year old man (Robin Williams).

Until the fall of his 11th year, Jack has been taught by a tutor (Bill Cosby). But, after careful consideration, his mother (Diane Lane) and father (Brian Kerwin) agree that he should give public school a try, despite children's' propensity for name-calling and finger-pointing. So, one morning, Jack ventures into Nathaniel Hawthorne Elementary School to meet his 5th grade teacher, Miss Marquez (Jennifer Lopez), and his classmates.

The film has an excellent grasp of what it's like to be in 5th grade. Jack endures all the painful isolation of a "different" child, but, gradually, as he makes friends (by dominating schoolground basketball games and offering to buy *Penthouse* magazines), he begins to fit in. It's perhaps an idealized vision of elementary school, but there are enough aspects of reality not to jolt our suspension of disbelief. *Jack* is rarely maudlin, and manages to be affecting without heavy-handed manipulation.

One of the most difficult issues *Jack* has to deal with is the title character's rapid aging. If he looks like he's 40 at 10, that means he'll be lucky to live past 20. When his teacher asks him what he wants to be when he grows up, Jack's answer is succinct and poignant: "Alive." Mr. Woodruff, Jack's tutor, describes him this way: "You're a shooting star amongst ordinary stars . . . A shooting star passes quickly, but, while it's here, it's the most beautiful thing you'll ever want to see." The movie never shies away from confronting Jack's mortality.

Robin Williams is entirely believable as a 10-year-old. He has all the mannerisms and vocal inflections perfected — whining when he doesn't get his way, pulling at his shirts, adjusting his pants, and so forth. It's almost as if he regressed back into childhood for the duration of filming. (Then again, has Williams ever really grown up?)

Jack has something to offer just about everyone. It's good-natured, funny, heartwarming, and capable of being viewed on more than one level. Children will relate to *Jack* differently than their parents, although, with its "soft" PG-13, the film isn't for the very young. RECOMMENDED

Jane Eyre [France/Italy/United Kingdom, 1995]

Starring: Charlotte Gainsbourg, William Hurt, Joan Plowright, Josephine Serre, Anna Paquin, Geraldine Chaplin, Elle Macpherson, Amanda Root Director: Franco Zeffirelli Screenplay: Hugh Whitemore and Franco Zeffirelli based on the novel by Charlotte Bronte Running Time: 1:57 Rated: PG (Mature themes) Theatrical Aspect Ratio: 1.85:1

One of the best-loved of all the Victorian novels, *Jane Eyre* combines social commentary with gothic romance. This film, directed by Franco Zeffirelli (best known for his 1968 Oscar-nominated *Romeo and Juliet*), remains faithful to the original narrative in general, if not in all the particulars.

We are introduced to 10-year-old Jane (Anna Paquin) in the early 1830s at Gateshead Hall, where she lives with her aunt and cousins. Orphaned at an early age, Jane has grown up unloved and unloving, and now her aunt has decided to send her to the Lowood Charity School, citing her as willful, obstinate, deceitful, and in need of a stern upbringing. At Lowood, Jane finds life difficult under the tutelage of the cold-hearted Mr. Brocklehurst (John Wood) and Miss Scatcherd (Geraldine Chaplin), but she forms a pair of solid friendships that help her through the hardest times.

After 10 years at Lowood, an older, wiser, but still-spirited Jane (now played by Charlotte Gainsbourg) accepts a position as governess for the young French ward of Edward Rochester (William Hurt), master of Thornfield Hall. Jane settles in quickly, forming solid relationships with her charge, Adele Varens (Josephine Serre), and Thornfield's housekeeper, Mrs. Fairfax (Joan Plowright). However, the master of the house makes the strongest impression on the young woman. From her first meeting with Edward, when she offers aid after he is thrown from a horse, she is infatuated, but his natural reticence keeps her from confessing her feelings. But there is something other than Edward for Jane to consider as she beomes established in her new situation, because Thornfield Hall hides a secret. Who, or what, lives in the attic, under the stern and watchful eye of the semi-vigilant Grace Poole (Billie Whitelaw)?

Jane Eyre is a love story, but, instead of the lighter romance and humor of Jane Austen's novels, this tale is marked by stark realism and a pervasive sense of misery. The meticulously accurate settings and beautiful-but-gloomy cinematography establish the atmosphere. Even the daytime scenes are drab and colorless, and many of the interior shots are so dark that it's difficult to see the characters' expressions.

Charlotte Gainsbourg (*The Cement Garden*) brings Jane to life, and, on those occasions when the script fumbles because it's painting the narrative in too-broad strokes, she holds our attention and captures our sympathy. Unfortunately, Gainsbourg's opposite, William Hurt, lacks presence. His is a passionless portrayal of a tragic figure.

For Bronte aficionados, lovers of Victorian romance, or those who simply appreciate literate love stories, *Jane Eyre* offers 2 hours of quality entertainment. **RECOMMENDED**

Japanese Story [Australia, 2003]

Starring: **Toni Collette, Gotaro Tsunashima** Director: **Sue Brooks**
Screenplay: **Alison Tilson** Running Time: **1:50** Rated: **R** (Profanity, sex, nudity) Theatrical Aspect Ratio: **2.35:1**

At first glance, Sue Brooks's *Japanese Story* appears to be an infusion of genre stories: man versus nature, a road trip, and a mismatched romance. However, while there are elements of each ingredient in the movie, Brooks and screenwriter Alison Tilson want the finished product to be a deeper and richer mixture than one might anticipate from considering its parts. In fact, this is not an outback adventure story, but a character piece. *Japanese Story* looks at isolation and the fragility of human relationships. It's a poignant, unsettling motion picture that will baffle those who have become used to Hollywood's compact, tidy endings.

The film is clearly divided into three acts. The first, which is mostly setup, introduces the protagonists. Sandy Edwards (Toni Collette) is a geologist who has been drafted by her partner to escort Japanese businessman Tachibana Hiromitsu (Gotaro Tsunashima) around the Western Australian desert. Tachibana's father is an investor in Sandy's company, so she can't refuse the request, but she approaches the job with a surly disposition that disconcerts her passenger, who is used to docile women. Act two takes the pair into the desert, where they become stranded when Sandy's rental car gets bogged down in the fine red sand. She unhelpfully informs Tachibana that "people die out here," and her words seem prophetic when dehydration and a lack of food become issues. The desolation is complete — there are no signs of other humans — and the vast range of temperatures (frigid at night; insufferably hot during the day) proves challenging. The third act explores the aftermath of Sandy and Tachibana's desert (mis)adventures and how both are forever changed by what occurs out there.

The relationship between Sandy and Tachibana is not easy to define. It does not fall into the tradition of a Hollywood romance. There's clearly something between these two, although it's more in the nature of sexual chemistry than love. Alone in unending emptiness of the desert, each finds something captivating in the other. Their communication is largely wordless; he understands some English, but is not fluent, yet they have no difficulty understanding each other once they overcome the initial hurdle of mutual antagonism. However, it's clear that whatever connection they form will not survive a return to civilization.

One could argue that the third act slows things down too much. Considering what the filmmakers are attempting, this is inevitable. The tone is of necessity at variance with that of everything that comes before it. During the final 30 minutes it's the details that matter. They represent the path that leads to genuine acceptance and understanding of what Sandy is experiencing. The journey of *Japanese Story* is not complete until the final slow, agonizing steps have been taken. **HIGHLY RECOMMENDED**

Jason's Lyric [1994]

Starring: Allen Payne, Jada Pinkett, Forest Whitaker, Anthony "Treach" Criss, Suzzanne Douglas, Bokeem Woodbine Director: Doug McHenry Screenplay: Bobby Smith Jr. Running Time: 1:59 Rated: R (Language, violence, nudity, sex, mature themes) Theatrical Aspect Ratio: 1.85:1

Doug McHenry's tale of life for an urban black family is an extraordinary achievement, filled with passion, romance, and complex tragedy. *Jason's Lyric* is not so much a poem as a saga, and there is no part of this motion picture that ever feels contrived or forced.

This film is about many kinds of love, and the rage and jealousy that often go hand-in-hand with them. Only the strongest of emotions can provoke a violent reaction, and this is a truth that *Jason's Lyric* illustrates. A common adage states that there's a fine line between love and hate. If that's true, the characters in this film cross over and back several times.

The setting is Houston. We are introduced to the two young sons of Gloria Alexander (Suzzanne Douglas): Jason (played as an adult by Allen Payne), the elder, and Joshua (played as an adult by Bokeem Woodbine), the younger. As children, the two are forced to defend their mother when their drunken father Maddog (Forest Whitaker) storms into the house in a rage.

A decade and a half later, Joshua has become a criminal and Jason is living life on the "straight-and-narrow." The two could not be more dissimilar, but the ties binding them are stronger than their differences. Until Jason falls in love, that is. The object of his affection is Lyric Greer (Jada Pinkett), the sister of a local drug kingpin (Anthony "Treach" Criss). As soon as Joshua recognizes that this woman could come between his brother and him, he develops a powerful dislike of her.

As rich a story as this is, it would never have attained such an impact without a spate of strong performances. From Bokeem Woodbine, who plays the haunted, angry Joshua, to Forest Whitaker, as a man whose soul was lost in Vietnam, to Suzzanne Douglas, the torn mother, there isn't an instance of weak or sub-par acting. Allen Payne and Jada Pinkett, playing the title characters, possess that rare chemistry that so many screen couples lack. Their interaction drives *Jason's Lyric* to its inevitable climax.

Whether love is healing or destructive, any giving of this emotion demands opening one's heart, and an open heart can easily be broken. *Jason's Lyric* is about consequences — those that come about as a result of trusting, loving, and even living. The result showcases the talent of all involved, and weaves a rare and unforgettable story. **HIGHLY RECOMMENDED**

Jefferson in Paris [United States/United Kingdom, 1995]

Starring: Nick Nolte, Greta Scacchi, Thandie Newton, Gwyneth Paltrow, Lambert Wilson, Simon Callow Director: James Ivory Screenplay: Ruth Prawer Jhabvala Running Time: 2:22 Rated: PG-13 (Mature themes)

The Bostonians. A Room With A View. Mr. and Mrs. Bridge. Howards End. The Remains of the Day. These represent the best of Merchant-Ivory — a category to which *Jefferson in Paris* does not belong.

Nick Nolte looks like Thomas Jefferson, and his reputation as a fine actor is wholly deserved. But Nolte is inexplicably flat in a part that seems to smother him. He's adequate, but no emoting is involved, and there are many sequences where Jefferson comes across as stiff and lifeless. Nolte never successfully forges a bond between his character and the audience.

Four principal storylines are developed throughout the movie. The first relates to Jefferson's burgeoning friendship/romance with painter Maria Cosway (Greta Scacchi). The second follows the changes in his relationship with one of his slaves, 15-year-old Sally Hemings (Thandie Newton). Another examines the jealous reactions of his daughter Patsy (Gwyneth Paltrow) to his mistresses. The final, and potentially most interesting, is an observation of the political events leading up to the French Revolution, and how Jefferson (who was the U.S. minister to France between 1784 and 1789) reacts to these.

In general, it's the secondary performers who are most impressive. Thandie Newton brings life and vibrancy to Sally (although there is one horribly over-the-top scene where she dances for Jefferson in the privacy of his bed chamber). Gwyneth Paltrow gives a multi-dimensionality to a character conflicted by love, commitment, and jealousy. Simon Callow (*Four Weddings and a Funeral*) has a delightful turn as the gay husband of Scacchi's Maria.

When it comes to issues, *Jefferson in Paris* is feeble and fumbling. After introducing the ironic hypocrisy of Jefferson's having written a document claiming that "all men are created equal" while nevertheless maintaining a significant contingent of slaves, little more of substance is presented on the subject. The conflicts and ideologies underlying the French Revolution are given equally short shrift. Aside from a few brief discussions filled with facile arguments, this particular element of the plot seems designed more as an historical backdrop than anything else.

Impressions of *Jefferson in Paris* are likely to be based largely upon expectations. Those anticipating something with the depth and breadth of a *Howards End* will be disappointed. Regardless, though it may be occasionally slow-moving and perhaps a half-hour too long, this film is put together with care and a mindfulness of quality. Little here is exceptional, but, fortunately, less is below par. In the end, *Jefferson in Paris* is just another *Masterpiece Theater*-style costume drama. RECOMMENDED

Jesus' Son [Canada/United States, 1999]

Starring: Billy Crudup, Samantha Morton, Denis Leary, Jack Black, Will Patton, Holly Hunter, Dennis Hopper Director: Alison Maclean Screenplay: Elizabeth Cuthrell, David Urrutia, and Oren Moverman, based on the novel by Denis Johnson Running Time: 1:48 Rated: R (Drug use, nudity, sex, profanity, violence) Theatrical Aspect Ratio: 2.35:1

It's neither new nor revolutionary for a motion picture to be presented from the point-of-view of someone who is perpetually stoned. However, unlike most movie spirals into the drug culture, Alison Maclean's *Jesus' Son* offers a perspective that embraces, not alienates, the audience. The film's protagonist, the appropriately named "Fuckhead" (played with wide-eyed innocence by Billy Crudup), is impossible not to like, even though, like an inverted King Midas, everything he touches turns to dross.

In its own peculiar way, *Jesus' Son* is a road movie. Fuckhead and his girlfriend, Michelle (Samantha Morton), are constantly on the move, usually in his VW Bug, crashing in cheap motels and rarely spending more than a few weeks in any one place. Along the way, they meet a number of odd characters — the ill-fated Wayne (Denis Leary), who offers Fuckhead a job even though the work messes with his high; Georgie (Jack Black), a hospital orderly who steals uppers and downers from medical cabinets; John Smith (Will Patton), who offers Michelle a better life; and Mira (Holly Hunter), whose husbands and boyfriends have a history of dying.

Jesus' Son is hard to classify. The film is surprisingly funny, and could almost be described as a dark comedy. The movie's structure is unusual — the story is presented as a series of narrated flashbacks that are often disconnected. For the most part, they're offered in chronological order, but not always. And, on one occasion, Fuckhead stops one flashback in the middle because he forgot to tell another story. So he goes back to the other incident before returning to where he left off.

The acting is superlative. Billy Crudup, who is not a big name despite a fairly lengthy resume, has the ability to disappear into his character — a trait that serves him well here. Matching Crudup beat-for-beat is Samantha Morton, who has the rare gift of being able to meld sweetness, vulnerability, and earthy sexuality into her portrayal. Other performers, such as Denis Leary, Dennis Hopper, Holly Hunter, and *High Fidelity*'s Jack Black, have small (but colorful) parts.

Addiction is one of the key themes explored by *Jesus' Son*, but it's not only the inescapable lure of heroin. Fuckhead is as addicted to Michelle as he is to drugs, and she proves to be a more difficult habit to shake than anything he can inject into his veins. The result is a film that is odd, engaging, often comedic, and sometimes even a little haunting. RECOMMENDED

The Joy Luck Club [1993]

Starring: Ming-Na Wen, Tamlyn Tomita, Lauren Tom, Rosalind Chao, Kieu Chinh, Tsai Chin, France Nuyen, Lisa Lu Director: Wayne Wang Screenplay: Amy Tan and Ronald Bass based on the novel by Amy Tan Running Time: 2:19 Rated: R (Language, mature themes, violence) Theatrical Aspect Ratio: 1.85:1

The Joy Luck Club is a collection of Chinese women bound together more by hope than joy or luck. The 4 women — Suyuan (Kieu Chinh), Lindo (Tsai Chin), Ying Ying (France Nuyen), and An Mei (Lisa Lu) — came to America many years ago to escape China's feudal society for promise of a better life. Now, however, Suyuan has died and the 3 surviving members of the club invite her daughter June (Ming-Na Wen) to take her place. June belongs to the "new" generation, those of Chinese heritage who grew up speaking English and learning American customs. Also of roughly the same age are Waverly (Tamlyn Tomita), Lindo's daughter; Lena (Lauren Tom), Ying Ying's daughter; and Rose (Rosalind Chao), An Mei's daughter. *The Joy Luck Club* tells of the varied difficulties and tragedies involved in these mother/daughter relationships.

Co-writer Ronald Bass (who, along with Amy Tan, adapted from Tan's novel) says that there are 16 separate stories in *The Joy Luck Club*. These vignettes explore common themes that give solid grounding and greater resonance to the overall film. As Bass comments, "I saw all the mothers' and daughters' stories as facets of the same experience. Put together, they formed a mosaic."

The Joy Luck Club is clearly — perhaps too clearly — an adaptation of a book. The dialogue is often too poetic to be real, and the story too clearly plotted to be acceptable as anything more than an imperfect reflection of the world we live in. The line between drama and melodrama is a fine one, and, while *The Joy Luck Club* most often successfully navigates the tightrope, there are times when it slips and comes across as heavy-handed.

The characters are the movie's real strength. Many are played by more than one actor (as children then adults, for example), but all transitions are smooth and seamless. It's as easy to accept both a little girl and the beautiful, sophisticated-looking Tamlyn Tomita as Waverly, and that's because the characters transcend the performers portraying them.

It's fascinating and satisfying the way the diverse threads are knitted together into a single tapestry. *The Joy Luck Club*'s message is one of hope — that catharsis and emotional fulfillment often come through tragedy. Sure, a lot of bad things happen during the course of this film, but at the end, the tears are of happiness and new beginnings, not loss. **RECOMMENDED**

Jude [United Kingdom/United States, 1996]

Starring: Christopher Eccleston, Kate Winslet, Liam Cunningham, Rachel Griffiths, June Whitfield Director: Michael Winterbottom Screenplay: Hossein Amini based on *Jude the Obscure* by Thomas Hardy Running Time: 2:02 Rated: R (Nudity, sex, animal slaughter, mature themes) Theatrical Aspect Ratio: 2.35:1

Jude is an ambitious, big-screen adaptation of Thomas Hardy's heartbreaking classic, *Jude the Obscure*. This is a film of tremendous scope and emotional depth that uncovers the soul of a novel and brings it to life on the screen.

In every way that matters, *Jude* is faithful to its print inspiration. The rhythm of some of the dialogue has been changed to make it sound more natural to contemporary viewers, and a number of minor characters have been deleted, but the story arc is rigorously true to Hardy's vision.

As the film opens, young Jude (James Daley) has accompanied his beloved school teacher, Phillotson (Liam Cunningham), to the top of a hill outside his town of Marygreen. Phillotson is traveling to Christminster to become a scholar, and, with Jude by his side to bid him farewell, he points out the distant place, shimmering and gleaming on the horizon like Camelot. This vision becomes a driving force in Jude's life. Though he grows up to be a stone mason by trade, his dream is of scholarship, so he spends long hours studying, hoping eventually to follow Phillotson.

Years later, in the wake of a failed marriage to a pig farmer's daughter (Rachel Griffiths), Jude (now played by Christopher Eccleston) finally journeys to Christminster. And, although he fails in his quest for admission to a university, he meets his beautiful, young cousin, Sue Bridehead (Kate Winslet), a modern woman who refuses to be governed by religious superstitions. As she and Jude spend time together, they fall hopelessly in love. But, because they can never marry, the pressures of society doom their relationship. (In fact, it was Hardy's harsh condemnation of society's intransigence, in addition to his sexual frankness, that caused such a stir when *Jude the Obscure* first reached the public.)

Jude couldn't have been more perfectly cast. Christopher Eccleston (*Shallow Grave*) develops Jude as a somewhat naive dreamer who is forever chasing an elusive image of happiness. For a while, that's the existence of a scholar, then, for the bulk of the film, it's a life with Sue. Eccleston gets us to care about Jude, a development that is critical to the film's success. His chemistry with his leading lady, Kate Winslet, is electric. When Phillotson says of Jude and Sue, "Sometimes I think [those] two are one person split in two," we believe him. Their initial sexual encounter is both funny and touching.

The emotional intensity of *Jude* rivals that of films like *Carrington* and *The Remains of the Day*. Top notch production values and strong performances help, but more important is the universality of the sad, unforgettable love story that Thomas Hardy first told, and Michael Winterbottom has so effectively reinterpreted. **HIGHLY RECOMMENDED**

K-PAX [2001]

Starring: Kevin Spacey, Jeff Bridges, Mary McCormack, Alfre Woodard, Brian Howe Director: Iain Softley Screenplay: Charles Leavitt, based on the novel by Gene Brewer Running Time: 2:04 Rated: PG-13 (Profanity, mature themes) Theatrical Aspect Ratio: 2.35:1

All movies require of their audience a "willing suspension of disbelief." Watching a movie like *K-PAX* demands an abandonment of cynicism, as well. Because the movie tends towards melodrama, more hardened viewers may tune out without bothering to look beneath *K-PAX*'s surface to discover that there are some interesting themes and issues lurking there.

The premise, although not original, is intriguing, and the overall impact is helped immeasurably by the competent performances of lead actors Kevin Spacey and Jeff Bridges.

Prot (Spacey) is the newest patient to be admitted to the Psychiatric Institute of Manhattan. He's a gentle, intelligent man who seems abnormally sane and lucid until he starts talking about his origins. According to Prot, he's not a resident of Earth, but merely a visitor. He hails from the planet of K-PAX, located 1,000 light years away in the constellation of Lyra. He traveled here on a beam of light with the intention of investigating the population of a "BA-3 planet" — a world in the early stages of evolution with an uncertain future. His doctor is Mark Powell (Bridges), the Chief of Clinical Psychiatry. Of course, Mark doesn't believe that Prot is from K-PAX, but he acknowledges that the man's delusions are more detailed than usual, and he is at a loss to explain how the patient knows things about star systems that only a few eminent astronomers are aware of and how he can make calculations on paper that those same scientists require a computer for. Instead, he believes that Prot has fashioned a fantasy cocoon as a result of a traumatic event in his life, and it's up to Mark to ferret out the truth of what happened.

Thematically, the movie is concerned with the importance of families and human contact in everyday existence. Mark is a workaholic who often neglects his wife (Mary McCormack) and children in favor of his latest patient. Working on Prot's case, however, Mark begins to realize how desolate it can be for a person to be alone in the universe, with no family or friends to turn to. When Mark makes an offhand comment about accompanying Prot back to K-PAX, Prot responds that he should explore more of his own planet first.

Of course, the mystery at the core of *K-PAX* is whether Prot is really an alien sojourning for a time in our corner of the galaxy or whether he's a man with a deeply troubled past. In the end, the truth about Prot is only pointed at; there is some wiggle room for varying interpretations. What is clear is that Prot represents something a little different to everyone who knows him: patient, friend, savior, simpleton, genius. With versatile character actor Kevin Spacey playing the part, there's never any difficulty accepting Prot as any of these things. RECOMMENDED

Kandahar [Iran, 2001]

Starring: Nelofer Pazira, Hassan Tantaï, Sadou Teymouri
Director: **Mohsen Makhmalbaf** Screenplay: **Mohsen Makhmalbaf**
Running Time: **1:25** Rated: **Unrated (Mature themes)** Theatrical Aspect Ratio: **1.85:1** In Farsi with subtitles

When *Kandahar* had the first of its two screenings at the 2001 Toronto International Film Festival on September 8, most of the Western world knew very little about the Taliban. One week later, at the time of *Kandahar*'s second Toronto screening, everything had changed.

Nafas (Nelofer Pazira) is a female journalist returning to her birthplace in Afghanistan for the first time in over a decade. When she fled the country for Canada, she was forced to leave behind a sister who had been maimed by a landmine. Now, that sister, despondent as a result of the Taliban's oppression, has decided to kill herself during the final solar eclipse of the second millennium. When Nafas learns of this, she decides to travel to Kandahar to prevent the suicide. But getting to the city, especially with time working against her, is not an easy task. Disguised under an all-concealing burka (the head-to-toe garment worn by fundamentalist Muslim women), she is accompanied by various others on this trek, including an American living in Afghanistan (Hassan Tantaï), a child seeking to make money, and a one-armed man trying to sell an artificial leg. She is Dorothy traveling a demented yellow brick road, but her destination is not Oz.

Kandahar's narrative is just a skeleton that Makhmalbaf can use to expose the social system of Afghanistan under the Taliban. It would be easy to mistake *Kandahar* for a grim fantasy or something set in a long-forgotten land. It's difficult to believe that any modern country could be this backward and unenlightened, but during the course of the movie, one character remarks, "weapons are the only modern thing in Afghanistan."

Many of the episodes in *Kandahar*, including the exchanges at the Red Cross tent where artificial legs are handed out, the way in which doctors examine female patients (through a sheet with a hole in it, so faces cannot be seen), and the wedding procession, are drawn from things Makhmalbaf encountered during a clandestine trip into Afghanistan while preparing for the film. No professional actors are used, and filming was done near the Iran/Afghanistan border, less than a mile outside of Taliban-controlled territory.

Kandahar's story — that of Nafas' episodic jour-

ney — will likely be quickly forgotten. As a character, she is not well-developed and her situation, while tragic, pales in comparison with what will linger: the portrait of Afghanistan that Makhmalbaf paints on this cinematic canvas. For better or for worse, the reign of the Taliban appears to be over. But, as *Kandahar* shows, the end of that government does not mean an end to Afghanistan's problems.
RECOMMENDED

Kids [1995]

Starring: Leo Fitzpatrick, Justin Pierce, Chloë Sevigny, Rosario Dawson, Yakira Peguero Director: Larry Clark Screenplay: Harmony Korine Running Time: 1:35 Rated: No MPAA Rating (Profanity, sex, violence, drugs) Theatrical Aspect Ratio: 1.85:1

The vision presented in Larry Clark's *Kids* is as bleak as things get — an ugly portrait of amoral youths who resort to drugs and sex not as a form of rebellion, but to fill the void of otherwise empty and meaningless lives.

On the outside, Telly (Leo Fitzpatrick) is the kind of clean-cut teenage boy any mother might let her daughter go out with. He looks "normal" — perhaps even a little nerdy — and can be polite and sincere when it suits him. But Telly is an inveterate liar. He will say or do anything to satisfy his addiction for de-flowering virgins. Sexually uninitiated girls present the greatest challenge and, as a bonus, are guaranteed disease-free. Not that he believes in AIDS anyway — condoms, in his opinion, are a waste of time.

Telly's best friend is Casper (Justin Pierce). While Casper also enjoys sex, his partners don't have to come with their hymens intact. And Casper's as much into drugs and drink as sleeping with girls. Like Telly, he's not concerned about the future or the consequences of his actions. He takes life as it comes, whether that means inhaling dope, raping a stoned girl, or beating someone half to death with a skateboard.

Then there's Jennie (Chloë Sevigny), who's only had sex once, but, without protection, that was enough to do irreparable damage. When her HIV test comes back positive, her life collapses around her. Nothing makes sense. Her best friend, Ruby (Rosario Dawson), has had sex with at least 8 guys, yet she's clean. And when Jennie rushes to stop another girl from sharing her fate, she arrives too late.

Kids is shot like a documentary and, in its uncompromising depiction of every aspect of the characters' social and sexual interactions, it seems almost too raw for fiction. Clark has meticulously designed this movie to blur the lines between reality and scripted story, hiring 20-year old Harmony Korine to write a screenplay that reflects what's really going on in the streets. The actors are all newcomers, and their unfamiliar faces and unpolished-yet-effective performances add to the documentary-like effect.

Kids shows what happens when children are set adrift in a heartless world, and warns us what happens — and is already happening — in the absence of love and guidance. If people lose their souls as children, what happens when they grow up? This is a tragedy without a last act — a wrenching experience that offers no catharsis. **HIGHLY RECOMMENDED**

King of the Hill [1993]

Starring: Jesse Bradford, Jeroen Krabbe, Lisa Eichhorn, Adrien Brody, Spalding Gray, Elizabeth McGovern, Karen Allen Director: Steven Soderbergh Screenplay: Steven Soderbergh based on the memoirs of A. E. Hotchner Running Time: 1:49 Rated: PG (Mature themes) Theatrical Aspect Ratio: 2.35:1

In St. Louis during the Great Depression, Aaron Kurlander's (Jesse Bradford) family is falling apart. His little brother has been shipped off to live with an uncle, his sick mother (Lisa Eichhorn) has been admitted to a sanitarium, and his father (Jeroen Krabbe) must go on the road to make money. So Aaron is left on his own in a fleabag hotel, with no money and few friends. Life becomes a struggle for the 12-year-old — the hotel wants to evict him and his meager supply of food is running dangerously low — and it's only through his remarkable resourcefulness that he manages to survive.

Writer-Director Steven Soderbergh brings 1933 St. Louis to life with uncompromising accuracy. Many period pieces give only token acknowledgment to the era in which they take place, but *King of the Hill* has the Great Depression woven inextricably throughout.

Jesse Bradford does an excellent job as Aaron. His performance is unforced, regardless of the complexity of emotions he is expected to show. Take, for example, the touching, bittersweet relationship that develops between Aaron and a lonely, epileptic girl living down the hall. These scenes have a remarkable resonance.

Soderbergh's style is frank, not quirky, and yields up a number of powerful images: a starving boy cutting out pictures of food and serving them on a plate, a homeless man waving hello, and a puddle of blood-tainted water seeping from underneath a closed door. With an accomplished director at the helm, *King of the Hill* becomes a remarkable odyssey about a resilient young hero who uses both his imagination and his sense of reality to survive. **HIGHLY RECOMMENDED**

Kinsey [2004]

Starring: Liam Neeson, Laura Linney, Chris O'Donnell, Peter Sarsgaard, Timothy Hutton, John Lithgow, Tim Curry, Oliver Platt, Dylan Baker Director: Bill Condon Screenplay: Bill Condon Running Time: 1:58 Rated: R (Graphic sexual images, nudity, sexual situations, profanity) Theatrical Aspect Ratio: 2.35:1

It's open to debate whether today's society should be considered "sexually enlightened," but, compared with the one in which Dr. Alfred Kinsey (Liam Neeson) worked little more than a half-century ago, there's no doubt that we have come a long way. Kinsey, a professor at Indiana University, became the first American scientist to study sexual behavior. He did it because it had not been done before, and he felt that some kind of "hard evidence" was needed to contradict the untruths and rumors about sex born of ignorance and religious zealotry. Kinsey's two landmark books arrived five years apart, with *Sexual Behavior in the Human Male* being published in 1948, and *Sexual Behavior in the Human Female* reaching the public in 1953. *Kinsey*, Bill Condon's mostly accurate biography of Kinsey, highlight's the doctor's life before, during, and after this period. Although some fictionalizations are used for dramatic purposes, most of those who knew Kinsey (he died in 1956), indicate that the film is true to the substance, if not all the details, of his life.

One of the elements that differentiates *Kinsey* from a traditional bio-pic is that this film is as interested in the social context in which it transpires as it is in the life of its central character. Certainly, director Bill Condon never loses sight of Kinsey, but there are times when he allows the doctor's research to absorb the spotlight. It's fascinating to understand how naive and confused people were about sex in the 1930s and 1940s. Misconceptions outnumbered accurate information. Masturbation, oral sex, and other "unusual" forms of sexual contact were thought of not only as "wrong" but as potentially harmful. On their wedding nights, some women had no idea they were expected to do something more than kiss. Into this darkness, Kinsey shed a light, and his work became some of the most controversial by any professor during the 20th century.

On the wedding night of Kinsey and his bride, Clara (Laura Linney), both are virgins. Their first attempt at sex is disastrous. Only after visiting a sex specialist are they able to comfortably consummate their marriage. After that, Kinsey's primary academic interest begins to stray from wasps to the human animal. His informal advice on sexual matters earns him the title of "the Sex Doctor," and when Indiana University decides to add a course about human sexuality to the curriculum, Kinsey is selected to teach it. His forthrightness startles and offends some members of the class, but others, such as Clyde Martin (Peter Sarsgaard), find it refreshing. When Kinsey begins conducting face-to-face interviews with volunteers to amass data for his "sex project," he uses Clyde and two others, Wardell Pomeroy (Chris O'Donnell) and Paul Gebhard (Timothy Hutton), to help. Condon has followed up his critically acclaimed *Gods and Monsters* with another film that will likely find much favor among reviewers and those who enjoy intellectually challenging movies. *Kinsey* is not as strong on character, but is just as rich in ideas. For those who aren't put off by a movie whose sexual frankness knows few boundaries, *Kinsey* has much to recommend itself. This is a fine motion picture with a couple of superlative performances. **RECOMMENDED**

Kitchen Stories [Norway/Sweden, 2003]

Starring: Joachim Calmeyer, Tomas Norström Director: Bent Hamer Screenplay: Jörgen Bergmark, Bent Hamer Running Time: 1:32 Rated: Unrated (Mature themes) Theatrical Aspect Ratio: 1.85:1 In Swedish and Norse with subtitles

Kitchen Stories is a quirky Norse/Swedish coproduction that functions equally effectively as a critique of common sociological methods of observation, a male bonding movie, and a satire of certain aspects of the countries where it transpires. The film, which takes place during the 1950s, introduces a Swedish scientist, Folke (Tomas Norström), who travels to Norway to observe how a volunteer, Isak (Joachim Calmeyer), functions in his kitchen. It is Folke's job to map Isak's every movement in the kitchen so the results can be used to determine how to engineer a kitchen to best meet a single man's needs.

Before beginning his work, Folke is given strict instructions not to interact with Isak. He is to sit in a high chair (one that looks a little like a lifeguard's perch) in a corner of the kitchen and watch. The theory is that Isak will go about his business as usual, oblivious to Folke's presence. The reality is that the presence of an observer — even a silent one — influences Isak's every action. This raises questions about how legitimate any study can be that relies upon supposedly impartial observation. Not only is it impossible for a human observer to be objective about a subject, but the subject will almost always act differently.

As one might readily anticipate from a movie of this sort, Folke and Isak, both of whom are loners, develop a friendship. It begins with a few innocuous questions and ends with Folke buying Isak a birthday cake and Isak letting Folke listen to the chatter of radio station broadcasts that can be heard coming through the silver fillings in his mouth. There are other characters in the movie, but they fill minor roles, adding a little color. For the most part, director Bent Hamer is interested in Folke and Isak. The nature of their interaction will be familiar to those who have seen any of the countless male bonding pictures available in video stores, although the acting and writing are of a higher caliber than what one typically discovers in Hollywood fare. **RECOMMENDED**

La Promesse [Belgium/France, 1996]

Starring: Jeremie Renier, Olivier Gourmet, Assita Ouedraogo, Rasmane Ouedraogo Directors: Jean-Pierre and Luc Dardenne Screenplay: Jean-Pierre and Luc Dardenne Running Time: 1:35 Rated: No MPAA Rating (Mature themes, violence) Theatrical Aspect Ratio: 1.66:1 In French with English subtitles

La Promesse, a rare import from Belgium, tells the story of 15-year-old Igor (Jeremie Renier), who is trapped into choosing between his father, Roger (Olivier Gourmet), and the demands of his conscience.

When the film opens, Igor is already wise beyond his years. He's an active participant in his father's shady, "immigration service" business. For exorbitant fees, they smuggle illegal immigrants into Belgium, forge false work permits for them, and set them up in slum-like apartments (with unreasonably high rents). Many of the immigrants also work at Roger's construction site, where they are paid a pittance for hard, dangerous work. Igor serves as his father's assistant, and has learned to lie, cheat, and steal just as well as his old man.

Roger has trained himself (and is training Igor) to objectify the men and women he smuggles into the country, adopting the same basic philosophy as the Belgian police: "Illegals don't exist." To Roger, the immigrants are a less-than-human source of income, and that is a philosophy he attempts to pass on. Dad's lessons are leaving an impression upon Igor until an event occurs that forces him to reevaluate what he has learned.

One of Roger's workers, Amidou (Rasmane Ouedraogo), falls from a scaffold and is critically injured. As he lies dying, he extracts a promise from Igor to care for his wife, Assita (Assita Ouedraogo), and infant boy. Rather than taking Amidou to a hospital (where all sorts of difficult questions would arise), Roger elects to let the man bleed to death, then buries him under a thick layer of cement. He encourages Igor to forget the incident, but the boy cannot, and his attempts to honor his promise to the dying Amidou generate friction between himself and his father. Worse still, Assita is often a grudging, if not openly unwilling, recipient of Igor's aid.

Essentially, *La Promesse* is a variation of that motion picture staple, the "coming of age" story. The difference here, however, is that the choices faced by Igor are more complex than usual. Becoming an adult does not mean, as his father asserts, learning how to drive and "getting laid" — it means assessing the value of his word and heeding the call of his conscience, regardless of the price. No matter what Igor does, he will betray someone — and he must decide which betrayal he can live with. *La Promesse* speaks volumes about how we treat other human beings and what it means to truly grow up. **HIGHLY RECOMMENDED**

The Last Castle [2001]

Starring: Robert Redford, James Gandolfini, Mark Ruffalo, Delroy Lindo, Steve Burton Director: Rod Lurie Screenplay: David Scarpa and Graham Yost Running Time: 2:10 Rated: R (Violence, profanity) Theatrical Aspect Ratio: 2.35:1

The Last Castle, from director Rod Lurie (*The Contender*), is a rousing adventure film that entertains despite a raft of plot implausibilities. With its themes of courage, honor, and redemption, it lands squarely in the ranks of old-style, flag-waving American cinema.

Robert Redford, taking a break from behind the camera to do some acting-only work, plays decorated 3-star general Eugene Irwin, who has been court martialed as a result of disobeying an Executive Order. For his crime, Irwin has been sent to the military prison "The Castle," where he will serve out his ten-year sentence. The warden, Colonel Winter (James Gandolfini), is a huge supporter of Irwin's; however, when Irwin voices his disapproval of Winter's methods of discipline, a power struggle ensues. Winter's attempts to break Irwin will backfire — the general's weathering of the warden's punishment earns him respect amongst his fellow prisoners. Soon, Irwin mounts a challenge to Winter's authority with the intent of removing the warden — even if it means taking over The Castle.

The struggle between Irwin and Winter plays out like a chess game between a Grand Master missing a few pieces and a lesser-skilled opponent with all of his intact. While Winter scores a few minor victories because of his initial superior position, Irwin sacrifices the occasional pawn in going after bigger prizes. The chess metaphor is apt (especially since the script mentions it on more than one occasion), but it is not meant to over-intellectualize the story. Lurie's film works because it generates suspense without going overboard. There are pyrotechnics, but they are not the sole point. The characters are developed with enough dimensions that they become more than cardboard figures moving through a plane of action. Even Winter, who is the clear villain, is given an understandable motive and a few redeeming qualities. And Irwin *is* guilty of the crime that landed him in prison; he's not someone wrongly condemned.

In the world of "chick flicks" and "guy flicks," *The Last Castle* falls in the latter camp. That's not to say that women won't enjoy the film — the emotions it generates are universal — but there will be a greater appeal to men. At 130 minutes, this is fairly lengthy, but Lurie keeps things moving so that the proceedings never bog down. *The Last Castle* is winning entertainment, a bold cinematic tapestry. **RECOMMENDED**

The Last Days of Disco [1998]

Starring: Chloë Sevigny, Kate Beckinsale, Christopher Eigeman, MacKenzie Astin, Matthew Keeslar, Robert Sean Leonard, Tara Subkoff, David Thornton, Jennifer Beals Director: Whit Stillman Screenplay: Whit Stillman Running Time: 1:55 Rated: R (Sexual themes and discussion, brief nudity, drug use) Theatrical Aspect Ratio: 1.85:1

Popular culture has an imponderable fascination with things 20 years past. With *The Last Days of Disco*, independent writer/director Whit Stillman chooses to view the early '80s through a lens coated with satire. There's the requisite disco soundtrack loaded with tunes from Sister Sledge, Donna Summer, and others, and there are plenty of scenes featuring oddly-attired young people dancing under the flashing light of a strobe, but this film is packed with Stillman characters, and, more importantly, Stillman dialogue. There are discourses about whether yuppies really exist, why VDs aren't all bad, how virginity is defined, and whether it's a good idea to follow Shakespeare's maxim, "To thine own self be true." Plus, there's a hilarious deconstruction of Disney's *Lady and the Tramp*, where one character claims the movie's function is to "program women to adore jerks."

The Last Days of Disco opens during "the very early 1980s" in Manhattan at a packed disco obviously inspired by Studio 54. There we meet the two main characters, a pair of recent college graduates named Alice (Chloë Sevigny) and Charlotte (Kate Beckinsale), who are out for a night of dancing. Since they're young and attractive, they're able to get into the club without having to stand in the ever-growing line. Inside, they meet some of the other regulars, including Jimmy (MacKenzie Astin), an advertising executive; Josh (Matthew Keeslar), an assistant D.A.; and Tom (Robert Sean Leonard), an environmental activist. The club's womanizing manager, Des (Christopher Eigeman), is also on hand. Having just dumped his latest girlfriend by telling her he's gay, he is on the prowl for a new catch.

Kate Beckinsale is impeccable as the bitchy Charlotte. With a perfect American accent and a demeanor that recalls Parker Posey, Beckinsale fashions her character as the picture of the shallow, vain party girl. Chloë Sevigny makes Alice a warm, sympathetic character in the midst of a soulless world. By forging an emotional connection with the audience; Sevigny becomes our way into the story. Stillman regular Christopher Eigeman is delightfully self-centered as the callous Des, and Robert Sean Leonard plays a seemingly-charming guy who turns out to be a cad.

There's nothing inherently brilliant about the movie or its theme of shallow hedonism in the early Reagan era, but the combination of sharply-realized dialogue and infectiously energetic dance sequences keeps *The Last Days of Disco* from losing steam. And when the "Love Train" rolls through the New York subway at the end of the movie, it's almost impossible to keep from smiling. **RECOMMENDED**

The Last Good Time [1995]

Starring: Armin Mueller-Stahl, Olivia D'Abo, Maureen Stapleton, Lionel Stander, Adrian Pasdar Director: Bob Balaban Screenplay: Bob Balaban and John McLauglin based on the novel by Richard Bausch Running Time: 1:29 Rated: R (Language, nudity, mature themes) Theatrical Aspect Ratio: 1.85:1

On any given day, you can walk down a street in New York City (or any other city, for that matter) and pass hundreds of people, most of whom will be gazing straight ahead, wrapped in their own thoughts. Take a moment to consider the untold story behind each face. Most of the time, it won't be anything flashy or exotic — just a normal tale of the minor ups and downs of day-to-day life. *The Last Good Time* chronicles one of those simple-yet-affecting stories.

Approached with less sensitivity and intelligence, this movie could have been exploitative. The subject — the relationship between an older gentleman and a much younger woman — is, by nature, delicate. However, there is nothing salacious about *The Last Good Time*; instead, it's an examination not so much of sexuality, but of friendship, need, and platonic love. The story opens where most of the scenes take place: in a small apartment rented by Joseph Kopple (Armin Mueller-Stahl), an over-70 widower living a lonely life governed by a regimented daily routine. Every morning, he wakes up at 7:10, takes the bus to visit his friend Howard (the late Lionel Stander) in a nursing home, eats a TV dinner, then goes to sleep. There's no variety, but the unceasing blandness gives him a measure of comfort.

Then, as is often the case, things change suddenly and dramatically. Charlotte Zwicki (Olivia D'Abo), one of Joseph's upstairs neighbors, has a violent fight with her boyfriend (Adrian Pasdar). When she needs a place to stay, circumstances bring her to Joseph's door. After a few days, the pair form an unusual and fragile bond. There is a certain degree of sexual tension in their relationship, but it's neither provocative nor gratuitous.

Veteran actor Mueller-Stahl shows tremendous range in a role that demands the expression — and repression — of a variety of emotions. Much of Joseph's inner self is conveyed to the audience through body language and facial expressions. Dialogue is used exclusively as a supplement.

Olivia D'Abo, while not given the opportunity to show the same breadth of character as her more experienced co-star, displays impressive depth. In what is by far her best screen performance to-date, D'Abo uses Charlotte's raw energy to ignite her scenes. This memorable performance is all the more surprising coming from an actress who hasn't previously shown such ability.

Supporting the fine performances and well-crafted script is the evocative and atmospheric cinematography of Claudia Raschke. Working with a palette of shadow and light, she uses contrast and camera angles to amplify the relationship between the two leads. The filmmakers' willingness to proceed with patience, allowing the drama to unfold naturally, affords the audience an opportunity to experience a marvelously complex, character-based study of two apparently dissimilar people who recover lost fragments of their selves through each other.

HIGHLY RECOMMENDED

Last Night [Canada, 1998]

Starring: Don McKellar, Sandra Oh, Callum Keith Rennie, David Cronenberg, Tracy Wright, Geneviève Bujold, Roberta Maxwell, Robin Gammell, Sarah Polley Director: Don McKellar Screenplay: Don McKellar Running Time: 1:33 Rated: R (Sex, nudity, profanity, mature themes) Theatrical Aspect Ratio: 1.85:1

Of all the movies about the end of the world, it is significant and ironic that the best is the one with both the lowest profile and the smallest budget. That's because Don McKellar's *Last Night* isn't concerned about the how and why of Armageddon. Instead, it focuses on far more interesting and existential questions. Rather than showing space shuttles blasting off to blow apart an asteroid, *Last Night* stays grounded on Earth, and depicts the final hours of a small group of characters as they struggle to come to grips with their mortality and what life meant, and means, to them. Sometimes movie characters don't have pasts; these men and women lack futures.

The story opens at 6 p.m. on December 31, 1999 — 6 hours before the earth's existence will wink out. (The film never explains the cause of the world's end. The only clues we have are that there wasn't much time for preparation, and that the sun now shines 24 hours a day.) Of the men and women introduced here, everyone has their own idea of what a perfect last night entails. For Patrick (McKellar), it's abandoning friends and family, going back to his apartment, and listening to music by himself. For Patrick's best friend, Craig (Callum Keith Rennie), the end is an opportunity for nonstop sex. Patrick's parents (Roberta Maxwell, Robin Gammell) spend their last hours at home together, while his sister, Jennifer (Sarah Polley), goes out partying. Meanwhile, one distraught woman, Sandra (Sandra Oh), is having trouble getting home to her husband (David Cronenberg). A series of misfortunes befalls her, and, with public transportation down and taxis ignoring fares, her chances of making her way across Toronto look bleak until she hooks up with Patrick.

The Canadian filmmaking community is a small and close one, so many of the participants in *Last Night* will be familiar to those who have seen a Canadian film or two in recent years. The writer/director/

actor, behind the camera for the first time, is Don McKellar, who was involved in scripting both *Thirty-two Short Films About Glenn Gould* and *The Red Violin*, and appeared in Atom Egoyan's *Exotica*.

Last Night succeeds where so many other films have failed because it concentrates on the element that its predecessors have ignored: the human factor. It's only mildly diverting to watch end-of-the-world pyrotechnics, but it's endlessly fascinating to observe how seemingly normal people react to a catastrophe of unimaginable proportions. While limiting its canvas to the lives of a few characters, *Last Night* manages to capture aspects of every possible reaction, from nihilism and anarchy to stoic acceptance. McKellar doesn't cheat his characters, and more importantly, doesn't cheat his audience. RECOMMENDED

The Last September [United Kingdom/Ireland, 1999]

Starring: Keeley Hawes, Maggie Smith, Michael Gambon, Jane Birkin, Fiona Shaw Director: Deborah Warner Screenplay: Deborah Warner, based on the novel by Elizabeth Bowen Running Time: 1:43 Rated: R (Nudity, sex, violence) Theatrical Aspect Ratio: 1.85:1

The time is the early 1920s, and the location is County Cork, Ireland. The hostilities between the Irish Republicans and the British are heating up. Caught in the middle are the so-called Anglo-Irish, those British citizens who moved to Ireland decades before to "oversee" the country, and who now consider themselves to be Irish. Many of the locals, however, still view them as foreigners. As a result, the Anglo-Irish find themselves in a difficult situation, not belonging fully to either side, and thus earning a measure of distrust from both. Halcyon days are past; darker seasons are coming.

Sir Richard and Lady Myra Naylor (Michael Gambon and Maggie Smith) are an affluent Anglo-Irish couple who live in County Cork during these troubled times. Also dwelling in their spacious house is the young and vivacious Lois Farquar (Keeley Hawes), Sir Richard's motherless niece, whose father is a world traveler. Lois is being courted by Captain Gerald Colthurst (David Tennant), a British officer stationed in the area. But, although she is friendly with the upright young man, her passion is stirred instead by a young Irish hothead, Peter Connolly (Gary Lydon), who is part of a terrorist gang roaming the countryside, killing English soldiers. Eventually, the violence will reach into their lives and their home. Yet Sir Richard and Lady Myra wear blinders, continuing to host tennis and dinner parties while a "war" rages

outside the borders of their property. One of their guests puts it best when he states, "When this house burns, we will all be so careful not to notice."

The Last September is really Lois' story — she is the fulcrum and the emotional centerpiece. She is so involved in her own drama of being torn between a Republican lover and a proper Englishman that she has little time to reflect on the nature of the larger conflict. For her, it's all very personal, and, like the overall struggle, it is destined to end tragically.

The Last September features several noteworthy performances. Maggie Smith and Michael Gambon are in top form, she blending tart humor with an upper-crusty seriousness, and he radiating a gentle, paternal wisdom. Fiona Shaw is a delight as a woman who speaks her mind regardless of the consequences. Keeley Hawes is an excellent find; she shines in a role that demands a complex spectrum of feelings and reactions. Lois is the romantic whose illusions are brutally shattered.

Despite occasional bursts of humor, the prevalent tone throughout the movie is somber. This is a film about the impending end of an era, and an autumnal sense of loss hangs over everything. RECOMMENDED

Leaving Las Vegas [1995]

Starring: Nicolas Cage, Elisabeth Shue, Julian Sands Director: Mike Figgis Screenplay: Mike Figgis based on the novel by John O'Brien Running Time: 1:52 Rated: R (Profanity, violence, sex, nudity) Theatrical Aspect Ratio: 1.85:1

Around the time that Mike Figgis began production of *Leaving Las Vegas,* John O'Brien, the author of the book upon which the film is based, shot himself in the head. This story, according to O'Brien's father, is his son's suicide note. And what an epitaph it is.

Leaving Las Vegas tells the story of Ben (Nicolas Cage), an unapologetic drunk, and Sera (Elisabeth Shue), a prostitute. After Ben loses his L.A. job, he takes his termination pay and heads to Vegas, that American mecca of glitz and greed where souls go to die. His intent is not to gamble, however, but to do something more certain: take a room in a flea-bag motel, buy as much booze as he can afford, and drink himself to death. By his estimation, that should take only a few weeks. But Ben is a lonely man and, even as his body craves alcohol, his heart yearns for companionship. So, when he sees Sera walking the streets, he offers her $500 for an hour. As it turns out, though, what he needs more than sex is a friendly ear. Thus begins the relationship that forms the film's core.

One of the reasons *Leaving Las Vegas* is so heart-breakingly haunting is that the unconditional love between Ben and Sera blossoms against a backdrop of desperation, loneliness, and self-destruction. Ben's only plea to Sera is that she never try to stop him from drinking. This is not a lesson movie like *When a Man Loves a Woman*, where the triumph over alcoholism forms the central dynamic. Instead, *Leaving Las Vegas* is about passion that flares brightly for a moment before being extinguished. The audience understands when Sera says, "We both realized that we didn't have that much time. I accepted him as he was and didn't expect him to change. He needed me. I loved him — I really loved him."

Leaving Las Vegas wouldn't be as difficult to sit through — equal parts transcendent beauty and un-bearable pain — if it weren't for a pair of magnificent performances. Nicolas Cage, who has a track record of immersing himself in parts, gives one of his most powerful acting turns, a complex, multi-layered por-trayal. Meanwhile, Elisabeth Shue, whose filmogra-phy is far less impressive, matches Cage scene-for-scene, emotion-for-emotion. There's no glamour in this role, but we still see the beauty that attracts Ben — tarnished and dulled, perhaps, but still obvi-ously there.

Leaving Las Vegas has no taboos. It doesn't moral-ize about its characters. Like great poetry where each verse strives for new highs and lows, *Leaving Las Ve-gas* draws its audience along a rarely-traveled path whose scope can only be fully appreciated in the si-lence of the aftermath. **HIGHLY RECOMMENDED**

The Legend of 1900 [Italy, 1998]

Starring: Tim Roth, Pruitt Taylor Vince, Mélanie Thierry, Bill Nunn, Peter Vaughan, Clarence Williams III Director: Giuseppe Tornatore Screenplay: Giuseppe Tornatore, based on the book by Alessandro Baricco Running Time: 2:04 Rated: R (Profanity) Theatrical Aspect Ratio: 2.35:1

The entire tale of *The Legend of 1900* takes place aboard a cruise ship during the early decades of the 20th century, but this is no *Titanic*. Told in flashback by a down-on-his luck trumpet player named Max (Pruitt Taylor Vince), the movie is presented as half-fable, half-melodrama. The main character, Danny Boodman T.D. Lemon 1900, or 1900 for short (played by Tim Roth), is found abandoned as a child on board the ocean liner *The Virginian* by an engine room worker (Bill Nunn), who keeps him and gives him his name (based on the year of his birth). 1900 grows up

to be an agoraphobe who never knows life outside the ship. He is a genius at the piano, and his reputa-tion spreads far and wide across the globe, but he never leaves *The Virginian* to claim the slice of fame that could be his. Even love cannot lure him from the open sea. On one occasion, he falls for a pretty pas-senger (Melanie Thierry), but lacks the courage to follow her into the city when the ship docks. *The Vir-ginian* was where he was born and where he intends to die

As characters go, 1900 is a little underdeveloped, and no one else gets enough screen exposure to func-tion as more than a secondary player. Tim Roth, as engaging as ever, brings 1900 to life, imbuing him with energy and charisma. Pruitt Taylor Vince plays an adequate second fiddle as 1900's best friend. Even though the movie is told from his point-of-view, how-ever, Max is not fleshed out as anything more sub-stantive than a narrator. Melanie Thierry offers view-ers (and 1900) a pretty face to look at, but nothing more. The film's standout supporting role belongs to Clarence Williams III, who plays real-life jazz pianist Jelly Roll Morton. In *The Legend of 1900*'s standout se-quence, Jelly Roll boards the ship to challenge 1900 to a piano duel. The smokin' results are pure magic.

Director Giuseppe Tornatore (who also made the great *Cinema Paradiso*) has a talent for developing stories that are pleasantly sentimental without turn-ing mawkish. The director has blended one part fan-tasy, one part whimsy, one part comedy, and one part drama into a whole that stirs the spirit. *The Legend of 1900* is an uplifting experience — the kind of movie that can make a hardened moviegoer laugh and cry at the same time. **RECOMMENDED**

Les Miserables [France, 1995]

Starring: Jean-Paul Belmondo, Michel Boujenah, Alessandra Martines, Salome Lelouch Director: Claude Lelouch Screenplay: Claude Lelouch, inspired by the novel by Victor Hugo Running Time: 2:54 Rated: R (Violence, mature themes) Theatrical Aspect Ratio: 2.35:1 In French with English subtitles

Les Miserables, Victor Hugo's sprawling epic of love, honor, fortitude and social injustice has been brought to the screen many times. In this version, Di-rector Claude Lelouch has retained the heart, guts and muscle of the story, but shed its 19th century skin by setting it in WW II-era France.

It is impossible to overstate what Lelouch has ac-complished here. No film that I'm familiar with has so ably intersected a classical novel with a modern tale.

It's been tried, most frequently with Shakespeare, but never has the result been such an unqualified success. This version of *Les Miserables* is a masterpiece precisely because it doesn't merely regurgitate Hugo's tale. It's something simultaneously new and timeless.

The film centers around 4 people whose lives are inextricably entwined. They come together, offer redemption and salvation to each other, then are ripped apart. The outsider is Henri Fortin (Jean-Paul Belmondo), a former middleweight boxing champion-turned-truck driver who has agreed to aid a Jewish family in their flight from Nazi occupied France to Switzerland. The refugees are Andre Ziman (Michel Boujenah), a renowned defense attorney; Elise Ziman (Alessandra Martines), a prima ballerina; and their young daughter, Salome (Salome Lelouch).

As Henri and his charges trundle across the French countryside, the illiterate driver requests that Andre read aloud to him from Victor Hugo's *Les Miserables*. As the story-within-the-story unfolds, Henri is enraptured, seeing parallels in his own life to both *Les Miserables'* Jean Valjean and Cosette. Like Valjean after meeting the little chimney sweep, Henri is determined to devote the rest of his life to the selfless aid of others.

The rest of the film follows Henri, Andre, Elise, and Salome as their paths diverge and converge. Like a master composer, Lelouch overlays elements of Hugo's novel on each of their stories. One recurring theme throughout *Les Miserables* is that there are really only two or three stories that continuously repeat themselves throughout history. What makes a story great, whatever the medium chosen for its telling, is that in it we see ourselves and people we know. Themes echo and resonate and events inevitably recur as Lelouch masterfully mixes tales from two different centuries.

Les Miserables is a story of the indomitable nature of the human spirit. Despite the title and its attendant images of misery, poverty, injustice, and oppression (all of which are present in one form or another), the movie is a decidedly uplifting experience, because its concentration is on the power to overcome. To be sure, there's much evil in this world, but there's good as well. For every Gestapo officer, there's a Henri Fortin or Jean Valjean willing to risk everything to save a small child. **MUST SEE**

Les Miserables [1998]

Starring: Liam Neeson, Geoffrey Rush, Uma Thurman, Claire Danes, Hans Matheson Director: Bille August Screenplay: Rafael Yglesias, based on the novel by Victor Hugo Running Time: 2:15 Rated: PG-13 (Mild violence, sexual situations) Theatrical Aspect Ratio: 2.35:1

If Claude Lelouch's 1995 *Les Miserables* is a brilliant re-imagining of Hugo's classic, this edition, by director Billie August, is a faithful and heartfelt rendering, true in its period setting and detail, and true, most importantly, to the characters of Jean Valjean, Javert, and Cosette.

Towering over the film is Liam Neeson, the Irish actor who seems at home in any kind of picture, whether set in contemporary America (*Nell*), World War II Germany (*Schindler's List*), or centuries-ago Scotland (*Rob Roy*). Here, the setting is France during the 1820s and 1830s. Using all of his considerable powers as an actor, Neeson buries himself in the role of Jean Valjean, a convicted thief, who, after serving 19 years in prison, is released on parole. Valjean is a bitter, dejected man who is headed back to a life of crime until a monsignor takes pity on him, and, through a simple act of kindness, causes Valjean to re-evaluate his life and dedicate himself to the betterment of others. As brought to the screen by Neeson, Valjean is not only a grand, heroic figure, but a distinctly human individual as well, with frailties aplenty.

Valjean's opposite is Inspector Javert, an inflexible man who pursues the former criminal in part because he sees much of himself in his quarry. The one thing that separates the two is that, while Valjean lives a life of love and kindness, Javert is consumed by a fear of transgressing the law that he clings to like a lifeline. Geoffrey Rush, as dislikable here as he was likable as David Helfgott in *Shine*, makes Javert a memorable villain, but he avoids the obvious temptation of turning the inspector into a cartoonish bad guy. As Valjean has his failings, so Javert has his virtues, and there are many times when we pity him more than hate him.

For the most part, *Les Miserables* is the story of Javert's attempts to track down and punish Valjean. It's an obsession that blinds Javert to all else, and consumes his entire life. Other characters enter and leave as the tale progresses. There is Fantine (Uma Thurman), a poor, sick prostitute who Valjean takes under his protection, and with whom he forms a powerful bond. Cosette (Mimi Newman and, later, Claire Danes) is Fantine's bastard daughter, who Valjean raises after her mother's death. And Marius (Hans Matheson) is a fiery revolutionary who captures

Cosette's heart even as he plans to restore the Republic to France.

While this version of *Les Miserables* lacks the cleverness and contemporary spin of Lelouch's, it ably demonstrates the great and satisfying virtues of the well-made period film. **RECOMMENDED**

Liam [Germany/United Kingdom/France, 2000]
Starring: Ian Hart, Claire Hackett, Anthony Borrows, David Hart, Megan Burns Director: **Stephen Frears** Screenplay: Jimmy McGovern Running Time: **1:30** Rated: **R (Nudity, profanity)** Theatrical Aspect Ratio: **1.85:1**

Throughout a long and varied career, Stephen Frears has proven to be one of those few, rare filmmakers who feels comfortable and has success working on both sides of the Atlantic. He has achieved artistic — if not always commercial — success with such films as *My Beautiful Laundrette, Prick Up Your Ears,* and *Dangerous Liaisons.*

Liam is set in depression era Liverpool, where jobs are hard to come by and the seemingly-omnipotent Catholic Church controls charity. Liam Sullivan (David Hart) is the school-age son of a proud father (Ian Hart) and a loving, determined mother (Claire Hackett). He also has an older brother and a sister, Theresa (Megan Burns), with whom he shares a close relationship. The story is told mostly through the naïve eyes of young Liam, who becomes our gateway into the streets of Liverpool. We see his father lose his job then struggle with his inability to find meaningful work. His mother pawns off clothing and jewelry to keep food on the table. And Theresa, who works as a maid in a Jewish household, becomes her family's sole provider, bringing home table scraps to go along with the coins she is paid. Meanwhile, unrest on the streets grows as anti-Semitic fascists clash with Communists. And Liam discovers the pervasive power of religion, as his pre-First Communion lessons convince him that, after seeing his mother naked, he is headed for hell.

If an impoverished, 1930s Liverpool is *Liam's* setting, the teachings of Catholicism function as its foundation. Frears does a better job than most directors of presenting the guilt and fear used by the Church to influence its members without demonizing the men and women who deliver the message. The film offers an honest representation of the teachings that are drummed into the hearts and minds of children: the stain of sin can only be wiped away by confession, failing to make a true confession is a sac-

rilege, and those who die without having their souls washed clean will burn forever in hellfire. The language of the priests and schoolteachers is persuasive; watching *Liam,* it's not difficult to understand the Church's power in a neighborhood where Catholicism is a way of life and where not attending Sunday mass will set tongues to wagging.

Liam is the kind of movie that leaves an impression. Its masterful depiction of time, place, and characters, and its willingness to tell a story unfettered by formulaic cliches set up an ending with a powerfully ironic, poignant turn of fate that illustrates how deeply the sword of hatred can cut. **HIGHLY RECOMMENDED**

Liberty Heights [1999]
Starring: Adrien Brody, Ben Foster, Orlando Jones, Bebe Neuwirth, Joe Mantegna, Rebekah Johnson Director: **Barry Levinson** Screenplay: **Barry Levinson** Running Time: **2:07** Rated: **R (Sexual situations, profanity)** Theatrical Aspect Ratio: **1.85:1**

Liberty Heights is the fourth installment (so far) in Barry Levinson's overstuffed "Baltimore Trilogy," joining *Diner, Tin Men,* and *Avalon.*

The movie begins in the Fall of 1954, and follows the lives of the Kurtzman family: our narrator, Ben (Ben Foster), his older brother, Van (Adrien Brody), and their father, Nate (Joe Mantegna). According to Ben, who relates the story as a reminiscence (with sparingly used voiceovers), his family lived in an all-Jewish neighborhood in northwest Baltimore. When he was young, he thought everyone was Jewish. It wasn't until he started attending public school that he recognized that there was "the other kind." By the time *Liberty Heights* takes place, Ben is a senior in high school, and his brother, Van, has already graduated. Nate is a wealthy man as a result of an illegal numbers racket he runs, and he uses his profits to take care of his wife, Ada (Bebe Neuwirth), and children. For the most part, the film is a series of tiny vignettes strung together to form a cohesive and likable whole, but three narrative strains eventually emerge — one for each of the male characters. Ben becomes attracted to Sylvia (Rebekah Johnson), the lone black girl in his home room, and, despite racial boundaries and parental objections on both sides, he attempts to build a relationship with her. Van is also involved in a romantic dilemma — he meets his "dream girl" (Carolyn Murphy) at a Halloween party and is so flummoxed that he forgets to ask her name. And, when he finally discovers who she is, it turns out that she's dating the son of one of Baltimore's wealthiest men. Meanwhile, Nate finds himself in trouble when a small-time drug dealer, Little Melvin (Orlando Jones), strikes it big on the numbers. Nate ends up owing Little Melvin more cash than he has in reserve, and the impatient winner wants his money.

The film doesn't shy away from difficult issues, like racial and religious prejudice, but it plays up the absurdities of such bigotry without becoming heavy-handed. For example, there's a scene in which a black and a Jew are discussing how their races are viewed by White America, and the conversation devolves into an argument about which group has been more oppressed. The moment could have been tense and angry, but Levinson keeps things light, resulting in a sequence that is genuinely funny, but, at the same time, makes a point.

Liberty Heights is smart in the way it views the adolescent years. Levinson may not have constructed this story specifically out of events from his own life, but the quality of the remembrances depicted here have an authentic feel. RECOMMENDED

Life as a House [2001]

Starring: Kevin Kline, Kristin Scott Thomas, Hayden Christensen, Jena Malone, Mary Steenburgen Director: Irwin Winkler Screenplay: Mark Andrus Running Time: 2:03 Rated: R (Profanity, sex, nudity) Theatrical Aspect Ratio: 2.35:1

Things are not going well for George (Kevin Kline). Divorced from his ex-wife, Robin (Kristin Scott Thomas), and estranged from his rebellious son, Sam (Hayden Christensen), he lives in a run-down shack overlooking the ocean. Things go from bad to worse when he loses his job, then learns that he has terminal cancer. Knowing that the best he can hope for is another 4 months to live, he decides to spend his last summer with his son, tearing down the shack and building his dream home. Sixteen-year-old Sam, needless to say, is unhappy about exchanging a wild summer of drinking and drugs for several months of working alongside the father he doesn't really like. Once living with George, Sam considers running away, but the pretty girl next-door, Alyssa (Jena Malone), gives him something to stick around for. As the summer wears on and the old house comes down, Robin begins stopping by, and, during the course of these visits, she and George re-connect.

Life as a House derives its strength from its performances. As George, Kevin Kline is in the limelight for most of the film, and his portrayal is effective. He presents George as a man in search of a catharsis and personal redemption. Knowing that his days are

numbered, George wants to make a difference to someone before he leaves this planet. It is important to him that Sam thinks of him as a father, not as a stranger. (It is also worth noting that, unlike many individuals in movies who look better as their terminal diseases progress, George actually looks like he's dying.) Yet, as good as Kline is, he is arguably out-acted by Kristen Scott-Thomas, who brings passion and humanity to her conflicted character. Scott-Thomas makes this role her own, elevating Robin beyond the constraints of the stereotyped "still-loved ex-wife." Hayden Christensen, soon-to-be Anakin Skywalker, does solid work, and up-and-coming Jena Malone (most recently seen in *Donnie Darko*) is delightful as the surprisingly mature Alyssa.

The script gets some of the relationships just right, and I was fascinated by some of the details surrounding the demolition of the old house and the erection of the new one. Unfortunately, a few scenes, including the last one, try too hard to wring emotion from the material, and end up being laughably absurd. This is a case of filmmakers not recognizing when they're taking things too far.

Overall, however, the movie gets us to feel about the characters, their relationships, and their circumstances, and that goes a long way towards allowing us to forgive the screenplays' occasional missteps and wrong turns. Like most houses, this one is far from perfect, but it's a pleasant place to visit for a couple of hours. RECOMMENDED

Life Is Beautiful (La Vita e Bella) [Italy, 1997]

Starring: Roberto Benigni, Nicoletta Braschi, Giustino Durano, Sergio Bini Bustric, Marisa Paredes, Horst Buchholz, Giorgio Cantarini Director: Roberto Benigni Screenplay: Roberto Benigni, Vincenzo Cerami Running Time: 1:54 Rated: PG-13 (Mature themes, off-screen violence) Theatrical Aspect Ratio: 1.85:1 In Italian with subtitles

For the first 45 minutes of *Life is Beautiful*, the Italian comedy star Roberto Begnini tricks us into believing that it's nothing more than a pleasant-but-uninspired romantic comedy set in Fascist Italy, with Guido (Benigni) seeking to woo a pretty girl, Dora (Nicoletta Braschi, Benigni's real-life spouse), away from her stuffy fiancé.

But 50 minutes into *Life is Beautiful*, there is a transition. The year is 1945, and Guido and Dora have a 5-year-old son, Giosue (Giorgio Cantarini). The second World War is in its final days, and Jewish Italian families like Guido's are the recipients of nonstop persecution. One day, the police break into Guido's home and take his family into custody. Soon after, they are herded like cattle into a train bound for a nameless concentration camp. It is a place of horror and death, where healthy men and women work all day long melting down metal for weapons while those who are too old, too infirm, or too young to endure hard labor are sent to the showers.

Guido is well aware of what is happening, and is determined to shield his son from the terrifying reality of the situation. So he carefully concocts a storyteller's web of fantasy around Giosue, informing the boy that this is all part of an elaborate game. The object is to get 1,000 points; the winner gets a real tank, not one of the toys Giosue is used to playing with. The rules constantly change, but they usually involve a lot of hide-and-seek, plenty of make-believe, and something called "silence." The police aren't really bad guys; they're just acting that way because that's how they win. Anyone complaining about not having enough food is disqualified and has to go home. By deflecting or laughing off his son's most serious concerns (such as a rumor that the camp prisoners are all going to be "cooked in the oven" to become "buttons and soap"), Guido manages to transform Giosue's ordeal into what seems like a vacation.

While I have no reservations about *Life is Beautiful*'s second hour, I'm less enthused about the breezy material that precedes it. Even though this portion of the movie accomplishes its aim of introducing the characters and setting up the background, it consumes too much screen time for its weaknesses to be ignored. And, as forceful as the rest of the movie is, the awkwardness of the first 50 minutes mutes its overall impact.

Nevertheless, by the time the end credits begin rolling, this is all a dim memory. The best part of *Life is Beautiful* redeems the rest with its utter assurance that people will do whatever is necessary to protect what is most dear to them. In its perspective on the Holocaust, Benigni's film is unique. But it's the depiction of the love and sacrifice of a father for a son that makes *Life is Beautiful* worthwhile. **RECOMMENDED**

The Life of David Gale [2003]

Starring: Kevin Spacey, Kate Winslet, Laura Linney, Gabriel Mann, Matt Craven, Rhona Mitra, Leon Rippy Director: Alan Parker Screenplay: Charles Randolph Running Time: 2:10 Rated: R (Nudity, violence, profanity, sexual situations) Theatrical Aspect Ratio: 2.35:1

The filmmakers behind *The Life of David Gale* manage a tricky task — to make a movie that's about the death penalty, yet not to use the opportunity to preach from the pulpit. The focus of the movie is not on the moral correctness or incorrectness of the death penalty, but on whether the American judicial system can be manipulated. The foundation of *The Life of David Gale* is plot, not politics. That being said, the movie is not airtight. In fact, its desire to provide the expected twists and turns audiences demand from this sort of movie represents one of its weaknesses. The ending is overwrought and inflated with unnecessarily melodramatic tension.

Although Charles Randoph's screenplay is original, it has the rhythms of something adapted from a long and complex detective novel. There are times when the movie has a rushed feel. It's necessary to pay careful attention, because nearly every detail, no matter how seemingly irrelevant, is important. I appreciate that the movie doesn't spell everything out in big, neon letters at the end. A little bit of deduction is necessary to sort everything out, although anyone following the story line should not have difficulty determining what has transpired.

The movie eschews a linear narrative, preferring instead to present most of its background information through flashbacks. Dr. David Gale (Kevin Spacey), an ex-philosophy professor at a major Texas university, is on death row for the 1994 rape and murder of a woman named Constance Hallaway (Laura Linney). Connie and David worked together for an anti–death penalty group, but his career took a spectacular nose-dive after one of his students (Rhona Mitra) had sex with him, then claimed that it was nonconsensual. When Connie was found dead, the evidence pointed to David and, thanks to the seeming ineptitude of his smarmy lawyer, Braxton Belyeu (Leon Rippy), he ended up with a date with a lethal cocktail. Three days before his last meal, he decides to meet with hotshot New York reporter Bitsey Bloom (Kate Winslet), who has a reputation of a "Mike Wallace with PMS." Over the course of three two-hour sessions, he tells her the entire story and, as his narrative progresses, she becomes convinced that he was framed. However, once David is done speaking with her, she and her intern, Zack (Gabriel Mann), have less than 24 hours in which to prove him innocent.

Director Alan Parker has a solid résumé, with movies like *The Commitments* and *Angela's Ashes* dotting it. He will not be ashamed to add *The Life of David Gale* to that filmography. The picture is neither flawless nor foolproof, but it's smart and tight enough to keep audiences off-balance and entertained for the running length. It doesn't hurt that it ponders the same questions that many people privately consider concerning the death penalty — and that it doesn't insult us by pretending to have a better answer than the one each of us has privately reached. RECOMMENDED

Little Odessa [1994]

Starring: Tim Roth, Edward Furlong, Moira Kelly, Vanessa Redgrave, Maximilian Schell Director: James Gray Screenplay: James Gray Running Time: 1:38 Rated: R (Sex, violence, brief nudity) Theatrical Aspect Ratio: 2.35:1

Because of the richness of the subject matter and the complexity of the characters, gangster movies, especially those with strong ethnic overtones, make excellent vehicles for social commentary. *Little Odessa* is a case in point.

Joshua Shapiro (Tim Roth), is a deeply-troubled, emotionally detached hit man who has come home to Brooklyn to commit an assassination. Although difficulties in his past make it dangerous for him to be seen near Brighton Beach, the real impediment to his return is his father, Arkady (Maximilian Schell). For, while Josh loves his dying mother, Irina (Vanessa Redgrave), and his younger brother, Reuben (Edward Furlong), there is nothing but antipathy between father and eldest son. Nevertheless, left without a choice, Josh ventures back to the Russian/Jewish community, and eventually encounters all the members of his family. While there, he also hooks up with an old girlfriend, Alla Shustervich (Moira Kelly), a young woman who is reluctantly attracted to the lonely killer.

At the opening of *Little Odessa,* Josh is in a hell of his own making. During the course of the film, there are opportunities for redemption and love, all of which are rejected. Josh has no emotional capacity; when he makes love to Alla, the act is passionless and mechanical. He is unable to respond to his brother's simple offer of devotion. He cannot cry when he faces his dying mother. Only his father provokes a reaction, and that is a decidedly negative one. By this performance, Tim Roth adds yet another impressive credit to his resume.

Equally complex is Josh's tormented, self-pitying father — a man who has lost all authority over his household and his existence. Assimilation to the American way of life is a continuing struggle for someone like him, born and raised on traditions and values that his children don't share. Arkady loathes Josh as much as he hates himself. He has a mistress, but feels guilty about not being with his dying wife. He is educated, yet is forced by economic circumstances to run a newsstand. He loves Reuben, yet his actions

seem always to hurt his younger son. Maximilian Schell, an accomplished actor who hasn't had much screen exposure in the past few years, encourages in viewers a mixture of resentment and sympathy.

The violence of *Little Odessa* is brutal, quick, and always shocking. Scenes of bloodshed are presented graphically, but never gratuitously. Director James Gray was only 24 when he made this film, yet with an emotional impact as strong as its intellectual appeal, *Little Odessa* can sit alongside some of the best gangster films of the last 20 years. HIGHLY RECOMMENDED

Little Voice [United Kingdom, 1998]

Starring: Brenda Blethyn, Jane Horrocks, Michael Caine, Jim Broadbent, Ewan McGregor, Annette Badland, Philip Jackson Director: Mark Herman Screenplay: Mark Herman based on the play "The Rise and Fall of Little Voice" by Jim Cartwright Running Time: 1:39 Rated: R (Profanity, brief nudity) Theatrical Aspect Ratio: 1.85:1

Mari Hoff (Brenda Blethyn) is a late middle-aged widow with two passions: drinking and sex. She lives with her daughter, Laura (Jane Horrocks), above the disused record store that her late husband ran. Laura, whose nickname is "Little Voice," is a shy, quiet young woman. She rarely speaks or leaves her tiny attic room where she spends her days and nights listening to her father's extensive collection of record albums and conversing with his ghost. She has become an expert at mimicking the vocal styles of Billie Holiday, Shirley Bassey, Judy Garland, Marilyn Monroe, Marlena Dietrich, and others. When she sings "Somewhere Over the Rainbow," a local nightclub owner (Jim Broadbent) who hears her from the street below her window swears that it's Garland.

Mari's latest boyfriend, failed talent agent Ray Say (Michael Caine), sees $$$$ when he hears Little Voice sing. He immediately begins planning her show biz debut, even though she is petrified of performing in public. Meanwhile, Laura meets and forms a fragile relationship with an introverted telephone repairman, Bill (Ewan McGregor), who raises homing pigeons.

The most flamboyant performance in *Little Voice* is given by Brenda Blethyn, who earned an Oscar nomination in 1997 for her work in *Secrets and Lies*. Here, she relishes the opportunity to create a larger-than-life character. However, while there's nothing subtle about Blethyn's work, it is not a thoughtless or cartoonish performance. Mari is the kind of woman who lives life to its fullest, and Blethyn invests this portrayal with enough humanity to keep her from coming across as a pure caricature. She is not a nice woman. She's vain, vapid, and motivated purely by self-interest, but it's hard not to feel pity for her in the film's later stages. Underneath all of her bluster, Mari is a sad, pathetic soul.

If Blethyn's Mari is all sound and fury, Jane Horrocks' Laura is the exact opposite. She's the typical shy wallflower who blossoms under the spotlight. The highlight of the movie is a sequence in which Laura performs a tribute to her father's favorite artists. The actress sings all of her own songs, and her ability to mimic great female singers is astounding. Hearing her belt out "That's Entertainment" or "Big Spender" will give you chills.

Little Voice is incontrovertible evidence of how superior acting can turn a good movie into a great movie. By offering opportunities to laugh, cry, and cheer, *Little Voice* satisfies in a big way.

HIGHLY RECOMMENDED

Little Women [1994]

Starring: Winona Ryder, Trini Alvarado, Claire Danes, Kirsten Dunst, Samantha Mathis, Susan Sarandon, Christian Bale, Gabriel Byrne, Eric Stoltz Director: Gillian Armstrong Screenplay: Robin Swicord based on the novel by Louisa May Alcott Running Time: 1:50 Rated: PG (Nothing offensive) Theatrical Aspect Ratio: 1.85:1

This third, and most recent, film adaptation of Louisa May Alcott's classic 1868 novel about family and crossing the barrier between girlhood and womanhood, is a treatment for today's audiences. As faithful to the original story as a 2-hour production is likely to be, *Little Women* is in ways similar and dissimilar to its two cinematic predecessors (released in 1933 and 1949).

This tale of 4 independent sisters of differing temperaments is undeniably melodramatic, but it's very good melodrama, with an accumulation of vitality and charm that elevates the movie to an unexpectedly high level. The basic plot of *Little Women* isn't terribly original or invigorating; it's the effective realization of several memorable characters that gives this film its strength.

For those not familiar with the novel, it centers around the March demesne of Orchard House in Concord, Mass. With her husband away fighting in the Civil War, Marmee (Susan Sarandon) is left alone to care for her 4 daughters: the volatile and imaginative Jo (Winona Ryder), the sophisticated Meg (Trini Alvarado), the compassionate Beth (Claire Danes), and the romantic Amy (Kirsten Dunst as a child and Samantha Mathis as an adult). The girls share a bond that no outsider can penetrate, although there are some willing to make the attempt —

most of whom are men. There's Laurie (Christian Bale), a neighbor with a passion for the piano who becomes a friend to all the Marches; John Brooke (Eric Stoltz), a poor tutor who is smitten with Meg; and Professor Bhaer (Gabriel Byrne), a German immigrant who develops a friendship with Jo.

With rich, colorful cinematography and a fine score by Thomas Newman, *Little Women* is technically accomplished. It's the performances, however, that make this movie special. Winona Ryder fashions a near-perfect Jo, Alcott's headstrong alter-ego in the fictional autobiography. Had it been demanded of her, the actress undoubtedly could have carried the entire film. However, this version allows the other sisters some development independent of Jo, and all the actresses hold their own. The only hiccup comes as a result of the change in the aging Amy from the energetic and charismatic Kirsten Dunst to the more sedate Samantha Mathis.

Christian Bale, after a couple of extremely weak performances (in *Newsies* and *Swing Kids*), finally displays some recognizable talent. In fact, Bale is so solid as Laurie that it's hard to credit this actor as the same one who joined Robert Sean Leonard in the streets of Nazi Germany.

Perhaps the greatest fault — and some may not see it as such — is that even the best-developed characters in *Little Women* display an alarming lack of character flaws. Rare are the moments when someone says something nasty or does something unsavory. So much niceness occasionally makes *Little Women* seem too sugary and scripted. Nevertheless, the tale is engrossing enough, and the film put together with such obvious affection, that it's not hard to dismiss those things as necessary elements of a beloved period piece. **RECOMMENDED**

Live Flesh (Carne trémula) [Spain, 1997]

Starring: Liberto Rabal, Francesca Neri, Javier Bardem, Angela Molina, Jose Sancho, Penelope Cruz Director: Pedro Almodovar Screenplay: Pedro Almodovar, Jorge Guerricaechevarria, Ray Loriga based on the novel by Ruth Rendell Running Time: 1:40 Rated: R (Sex, profanity, nudity, drugs) Theatrical Aspect Ratio: 1.85:1

Almodovar. To those familiar with his body of work, that name is more than just a way to identify one of today's premiere directors — it offers valuable insight into the scope and intent of a movie. Since his debut in 1980 with *Pepi, Luci, Bom*, Almodovar has been the "bad boy" of Spanish cinema. Now, however, there are indications that Almodovar is maturing. With *Live Flesh*, based loosely on a novel by Ruth Rendell,

Almodovar is back in fine form, yet signs of restraint are evident in nearly every frame of this movie. By toning down his visual flourishes and curbing his tendencies towards excess, Almodovar has created what might be the finest work of his career to date.

The 5 principals come together on one fateful night in 1992 Madrid. Victor (Liberto Rabal) has fallen for a woman, Elena (Francesca Neri), whom he had sex with a week ago. Elena, however, wants nothing more to do with Victor, and, when he shows up at her apartment, she uses a gun to scare him away. A shot is fired and the cops are called. Arriving at Elena's apartment are two partners, David (Javier Bardem) and Sancho (Jose Sancho), who are in the midst of a crisis in their friendship. Sancho believes that his wife, Clara (Angela Molina), is having an affair, and he suspects David of being Clara's lover. What happens when the police break down the door to Elena's apartment sets off a chain of events that reverberate through time to a period 4 years later, when circumstances bring the characters together once again.

Live Flesh is really a mystery, which is why I won't give a more detailed plot description. This isn't a crime thriller, however — it's an exploration of characters' motives, secrets, and true emotions. They are all wrapped in a web of consequences, with each one hurting the others multiple times, and the strands around them growing ever thicker. The ending is surprising, not because it doesn't fit, but because, knowing all that we do about the involved parties, it's the perfect way to offer closure to the tale.

With *Live Flesh*, Almodovar offers a controversial viewpoint that seemingly contradicts the romantic's first rule of true love being the glue in long-term relationships. Time and time again, *Live Flesh* shows that "true love" is overrated. The married couples in this film love each other, but they're hopelessly, helplessly trapped. Almodovar isn't denying the value of romance, but he's emphasizing the complexities of any love-based relationship and affirming that sex is far from irrelevant.

One of the most delicious aspects of *Live Flesh* is its keen sense of irony. There's also a fair amount of humor, some of which borders on the absurd. Yet there is never a time when Almodovar's appreciation of off-beat comedy endangers the integrity of the characters or the story. Like the gorgeous cinematography, this is all part of Almodovar's stylistic package. Never has it been more impressive than here, where everything (not just the flesh) is vibrant with life. **HIGHLY RECOMMENDED**

Live Nude Girls [1995]

Starring: Dana Delaney, Kim Cattrall, Cynthia Stevenson, Lora Zane, Laila Robins, Olivia D'Abo Director: Julianna Lavin Screenplay: Julianna Lavin Running Time: 1:32 Rated: R (Frank sexual dialogue, nudity) Theatrical Aspect Ratio: 1.85:1

It would be impossible to write a review of this film without discussing the title. How many viewers will see Julianna Lavin's feature debut because it's called *Live Nude Girls*? And how many will avoid it for the same reason? There's little doubt that the title was chosen for its provocative value, because, although the movie deals with live girls, they're mostly clothed. The nakedness in this picture is of the emotional, not the physical, variety.

In essence, *Live Nude Girls* features 5 women in their early-30s hanging out and talking. It's 90 minutes of simple, pleasant conversation. Nothing earth-shattering occurs, and no one attempts to answer, or even raise, any meaningful, philosophical questions. One-by-one, these characters open up to one another about relationships, love, and sex, while those of us in the audience are transformed into flies on the wall.

In movies, slumber parties have been used as settings for everything from teen sex comedies to soft porn. Here, writer/director Julianna Lavin resorts to this overused plot device one more time. The occasion for the slumber party is the approaching wedding of one of the women, Jamie (Kim Cattrall). Four of her friends — Georgiana (Lora Zane), Rachel (Laila Robins), Jill (Dana Delaney), and Marcy (Cynthia Stevenson) — have decided to hold a girls-only get-together on the night of the groom-to-be's bachelor party. Hanging around on the periphery of this group is Chris (Olivia D'Abo), Georgiana's lesbian lover.

The reason *Live Nude Girls* works is that all 6 major actresses give unaffected performances. Each of them (even Kim Cattrall, who isn't known for her acting ability) slides effortlessly into her role, and their interpersonal interaction is relaxed. Perhaps because it was written and directed by a woman, *Live Nude Girls* has a genuine "feel." Everything from the petty bickering of two sisters (Jill and Rachel) to the frank, raunchy discussions about sex has a ring of truth.

Live Nude Girls mixes humor with the drama. On one occasion, Jamie is obsessing about the reprehensible acts her fiance might be engaged in at his bachelor party. The scene then cuts to 4 guys sitting around a table at a bar, drinking beer and guessing how much money a nearby jukebox brings in on a weekly basis. It's not exactly the sex-crazed nightmare of Jamie's vision. Although it isn't hilarious, this sequence is cleverly-constructed, and there are several more like it throughout the film. Beneath the familiar plot contrivances, there's a core of honesty that delivers a satisfying motion picture experience. **RECOMMENDED**

Living Out Loud [1998]

Starring: Holly Hunter, Danny DeVito, Queen Latifah, Martin Donovan, Richard Schiff, Elias Koteas Director: Richard LaGravenese
Screenplay: Richard LaGravenese Running Time: 1:42 Rated: R (Profanity, drug content, sex) Theatrical Aspect Ratio: 2.35:1

The best thing about Richard LaGravenese's directorial debut, *Living Out Loud,* are the characters; the minimal plot is almost inconsequential. LaGravenese's strength is developing multidimensional, wholly believable protagonists. In this film, which draws its inspiration from the Anton Chekhov short stories "The Kiss" and "Misery," they are Judith (Holly Hunter) and Pat (Danny DeVito), two lonely, middle-aged New Yorkers who find a measure of comfort in each other's company.

As the movie opens, Judith and Pat are both picking through the wreckage of collapsed existences. Judith, a nurse who has been dumped by her wealthy doctor/husband of 16 years, doesn't seem to know what to do with her life, because, at least in part, her identity was defined by her husband. No matter what went wrong, she could always rely on saying, "At least I'm married. At least I'm safe." But no longer. Pat, the doorman at the apartment building where she lives, is at a similar dead-end junction. His marriage is over, his daughter has recently died, and he's up to his ears in gambling debts. Somehow, he and Judith connect, and what begins as a form of casual interplay blossoms into a friendship that offers comfort to both of them.

Pat gradually becomes infatuated with Judith, but her feelings towards him remain platonic. To her, he's a reliable companion but not a good partner — she's looking for something more spontaneous and romantic in a relationship. Then, one night at a jazz club, she encounters the unexpected when a mysterious stranger kisses her. The friendship at the core of *Living Out Loud* is never allowed to go too far too fast, and both of the characters are intensely sympathetic. Judith can unburden her soul to Pat, telling him her

secrets, and, although his feelings for her run deeper, he is content to fulfill that role.

LaGravenese manages to give *Living Out Loud* a light (and occasionally quirky) touch by mixing in frequent doses of comedy and fantasy. Both characters are capable of laughing at their own failings, and they sometimes find themselves in absurd situations. From time-to-time, we see events from two different perspectives — as they really are and as Judith dreams they might be. *Living Out Loud* is not a monumental motion picture. In fact, in many ways, it's quite the opposite — a quiet, unassuming story of friendship and love that uses richly-developed characters to charm its audience. **RECOMMENDED**

Local Hero [United Kingdom, 1983]

Starring: Burt Lancaster, Peter Riegert, Fulton Mackay, Denis Lawson, Norman Chancer, Peter Capaldi, Rikki Fulton, Jenny Seagrove
Director: Bill Forsyth Screenplay: Bill Forsyth Running Time: 1:51
Rated: PG (Mature themes) Theatrical Aspect Ratio: 1.66:1

Local Hero is a fragment of cinematic whimsy — a genial dramatic comedy that defies both our expectations and those of the characters. Director Bill Forsyth (*Gregory's Girl*) finds the perfect tone for this not-quite-a-fairy-tale set in a quaint seaside Scottish village named Ferness. By injecting a little (but not too much) magical realism into the mix, Forsyth leavens his pro-environmental message to the point that those not looking for it might not be conscious of its presence.

The film stars Peter Reigert as Mac MacIntyre, a deal-closer for Knox Oil who is picked by the corporate head, Felix Happer (Burt Lancaster), to travel to Scotland and buy up an entire fishing village where the company can build a refinery. MacIntyre is chosen because of his name, even though he does not, in fact, have any Scottish ancestry. And, before he leaves, his boss gives him a secondary duty, which, in some ways, seems more important to Mr. Happer than the primary job: MacIntyre is to keep his eyes on the night sky, watching for new, previously-undiscovered comets. Huppert has decided that the best way to immortalize his name is to get it attached to a celestial body.

Once in Scotland, MacIntyre meets his local liaison, Danny Oldsen (Peter Capaldi), who turns out to be a likable twit. Together, the two make the trip to their destination, where they encounter the colorful locals: their landlord (who also happens to be the town's only accountant), Gordon Urquhart (Denis

Lawson); the hermit who owns the beach, Ben Knox (Fulton Mackay); the local priest, Reverend Macpherson (Christopher Asante), who came to Scotland on a mission from Africa and stayed; the appropriately named Marina, a marine biologist with certain mermaid-like characteristics (Jenny Seagrove); and others. It is MacIntyre's job to get everyone to agree to give up their homes in exchange for a cash payment.

Local Hero is suffused with the kind of almost magical color that typically characterizes comedies set in Scotland, Ireland (*Waking Ned Devine*), and Wales (*The Englishman Who Went Up a Hill But Came Down a Mountain*). For films like *Local Hero,* the setting is often as important a character as any being played by a human being. Indeed, in this film, it isn't the veteran Lancaster or the bewitching Seagrove who steals the most scenes, but the village and its surroundings. This is the best kind of light fare: a motion picture that offers a helping of substance to go along with an otherwise frothy and undemanding main course. **HIGHLY RECOMMENDED**

Lolita [United States/France, 1997]
Starring: Jeremy Irons, Dominique Swain, Melanie Griffith, Frank Langella Director: Adrian Lyne Screenplay: Stephen Schiff based on the novel by Vladimir Nabokov Running Time: 2:17 Rated: R (Sex with a minor, nudity, profanity, violence, mature themes) Theatrical Aspect Ratio: 1.85:1

Adrian Lyne's *Lolita* is a stately, non-gratuitous adaptation of Nabokov's controversial novel. It does not titillate or exploit; the only scenes of a nude girl are shadowy and indistinct. Despite that, the subject matter alone — pedophilia — was enough to scare off nearly every major American distributor. Interestingly, in many ways, the concept underlying *Lolita* is more provocative than the actual material, which tends to be a bit long-winded.

The pedophile is Humbert Humbert, brought to life by Jeremy Irons, an actor who enjoys playing deranged characters (he won an Oscar for his portrayal of Claus von Bülow in 1990's *Reversal of Fortune*). Humbert is not presented as a soulless monster or an evil predator, as most motion picture pedophiles are. Instead, *Lolita* attempts to understand Humbert, and allows us to sympathize with him without condoning his actions. He may be a deviant, but he is still a man. He recognizes that his obsession is unhealthy, but he cannot stop himself. Heedless of the fact that he is destroying three lives, he plunges on recklessly, letting an infatuation develop into a taboo physical relationship.

Dolores "Lolita" Haze (Dominique Swain) is the "nymphet" who becomes the object of Humbert's desire. At the tender age of 14, she's a character of contradictions — vixen and virgin at the same time. It's clear from the beginning that she knows the effect she's having on Humbert, and revels in the way a flash of her legs or the touch of a bare foot on his skin arouses him. Yet, despite her apparent sexual maturity, she's still a child in many ways, and, by responding to her teasing, Humbert turns her into a schemer and a whore.

Humbert first meets Lolita in 1947, after he travels across the Atlantic to New England, where he's to become a college professor. While lodging in the house of Charlotte Haze (Melanie Griffith), he falls for her daughter, whom he sees as a substitute for a lost love of his youth. Eventually, Humbert marries Charlotte to avoid losing Lolita, but his new wife finds out about his illicit desires. Before she can confront her daughter, however, she is killed in a car accident, and Humbert finds himself as Lolita's guardian. Together, the two begin a road trip that takes them to random destinations across America. As they travel, their relationship develops from playful to sexual to strained. Then another man, a sinister pedophile named Clare Quilty (Frank Langella), enters the picture, and draws Lolita away from Humbert. It is a rejection he cannot endure.

Lolita is not a sex film; it's about characters, relationships, and the consequences of imprudent actions. And those who seek to brand the picture as immoral have missed the point. Both Humbert and Lolita are eventually destroyed — what could be more moral? The only real controversy I can see surrounding this film is why there was ever a controversy in the first place. **RECOMMENDED**

Lone Star [1996]
Starring: Chris Cooper, Elizabeth Pena, Joe Morton, Ron Canada, Miriam Colon, Clifton James, Kris Kristofferson, Matthew McConaughey Director: John Sayles Screenplay: John Sayles Running Time: 2:15 Rated: R (Mature themes, profanity, violence, sexual situations) Theatrical Aspect Ratio: 2.35:1

In *Lone Star,* writer/director John Sayles (*City of Hope, Passion Fish*) cannily blends drama, romance, mystery, and social observation into a satisfying, if slightly overlong, whole. In the hands of a lesser film maker, this material could easily have degenerated into routine melodrama, but Sayles keeps it on a consistently high level.

Lone Star opens in the present time frame, and

most of the narrative takes place there, with the exception of several, seamlessly-interwoven flashbacks to 1957 and 1973. These are necessary to breathe life into the film's mystery and love stories, and Sayles gives us just enough to satisfy the script's dramatic needs.

In 1996, the sheriff of Rio County is Sam Deeds (Chris Cooper). He's been on the job for 2 years, and he's filling huge footsteps. His late lawman father, Buddy (Matthew McConaughey), is a local legend, and Sam won election more because of his last name than because voters respected his talents. For a variety of reasons, Sam's image of Buddy is far more tarnished than the one endorsed by the community, and, when the corpse of a bigoted ex-sheriff (Kris Kristofferson) is found on an abandoned rifle range, Sam tries his best to pin the 40-year-old murder on his father.

Several other stories occur in parallel with Sam's investigation. One involves the sheriff's old flame, Pilar (Elizabeth Pena), trying to explain to concerned parents why she's teaching high school history with a nontraditional slant. Instead of relying on the accepted anglo-approved text, she's attempting to show how "cultures come together in both negative and positive ways." In the meantime, she's wrestling with her feelings for Sam and coping with an unruly teenage son.

We also get to know Colonel Del Payne (Joe Morton), the new commanding officer of Fort McKenzie, which is due to close. Del's father, Otis (Ron Canada), lives in the area. He and his son haven't spoken for decades, but, while Del is bitter about the estrangement, it's impossible for the two men to avoid each other.

Lone Star contains a number of "escape hatches" — points when the story could have moved in a safe, predictable direction, but Sayles uses few of these. The weakest aspect of the movie is the mystery, but it's also the least important. *Lone Star* is most intimately concerned with how different cultures and generations mix, match, and interact. Sayles explores the bipolar issues of racial divisiveness and tolerance, both as they exist today and as they were nearly 40 years ago, and does so without ever losing sight of the characters. With its numerous strengths and few weaknesses, *Lone Star* is an example of why Sayles' films are so engrossing despite lengths which consistently exceed 2 hours. **HIGHLY RECOMMENDED**

Lorenzo's Oil [1992]

Starring: Nick Nolte, Susan Sarandon, Peter Ustinov, Zack O'Malley Greenburg Director: George Miller Screenplay: George Miller and Nick Enright Running Time: 2:15 Rated: PG-13 (Mature themes) Theatrical Aspect Ratio: 1.85:1

Lorenzo's Oil is based on the true story of Augusto Odone (Nick Nolte) and his wife, Michaela (Susan Sarandon), as they fight to save the life and sanity of their son, Lorenzo (Zack O'Malley Greenburg). Lorenzo, diagnosed in early 1984 as a victim of ALD, an incurable degeneration of the brain, is beyond the help of conventional medicine. His parents, unwilling to give up the struggle even after participating in several failed therapies, begin their own investigation of the disease. *Lorenzo's Oil* follows the triumphs and tragedies of this search.

The film is unique in that it avoids the obvious trap of becoming a melodramatic, tear-jerking soap opera. Instead of focusing primarily on a family being torn apart by guilt and pain, *Lorenzo's Oil* follows Augusto and Michaela's attempts to understand their son's disease and discover a method of treatment. This search is fascinating — a unique odyssey of discovery. Even though it delves into medical terminology that few laymen will grasp, simple metaphors, such as those of a kitchen sink and a chain of paper clips, are used to clearly and concisely explain the causes and effects of ALD. Comprehension is necessary to the success of the film, and *Lorenzo's Oil* easily overcomes what might seem a troublesome barrier.

Lorenzo's Oil is at its weakest when it steers away from the investigation to present "character moments." Most of these scenes are of the hit-and-miss variety. The only example of overacting in the film comes in one of these instances, when Nolte's Augusto slides down a flight of stairs, howling in agony. His pain is telegraphed with all the subtlety of a jackhammer.

Much of *Lorenzo's Oil* is based on true events, but there are at least a few moments when Hollywood intrudes, creating occasional leaps of exultation that are contrived (such as what happens when the results of Lorenzo's Oil are revealed to a group of ALD parents). Fortunately, the director/writer team of George Miller and Nick Enright have curbed excesses in this area. In the final analysis, when *Lorenzo's Oil* is stripped to the bare story, it's about the war for knowledge and the victory of hope through perseverance. And, for more than 2 hours, audience members are brought along to witness each battle. **RECOMMENDED**

The Loss of Sexual Innocence [1998]

Starring: Julian Sands, Saffron Burrows, Stefano Dionisi, Kelly MacDonald, Gina McKee Director: Mike Figgis Screenplay: Mike Figgis Running Time: 1:46 Rated: R (nudity, sexual situations, profanity, violence) Theatrical Aspect Ratio: 1.85:1

The Loss of Sexual Innocence is from the director of *Leaving Las Vegas*, Mike Figgis, and as the title implies, the film deals with the issue of sexual identity. *The Loss of Sexual Innocence* follows the life of Nic, a film ethnographer (played as a teenager by Jonathan Rhys-Meyers and as an adult by Julian Sands), through different periods in his life — as a young boy growing up in Kenya, as an adolescent coping with his first sexual encounters, and as a grown man involved in a stale marriage. Other tales are interwoven with Nic's, most notably those of twins (both played by Saffron Burrows) who were separated at birth but fleetingly encounter each other in an airport. There's also a stylized re-telling of Adam and Eve's expulsion from Paradise that takes a vicious jab at organized religion.

While there's nothing prurient to be found in *The Loss of Sexual Innocence* (in fact, considering the title, it's a relatively chaste film, although the "R" rating is deserved), a key theme relates to the importance of sex to the human experience. The characters are defined, at least in part, by their sexual activities. The central event of the film (which happens in the closing few minutes) occurs because of a sexual indiscretion on Nic's part — an impropriety that is built up to by his entire sexual history. Likewise, Figgis' version of the forbidden fruit is sex, and that's what causes Adam and Eve's fall.

More interesting than the film's thematic content, however, is the manner in which it is presented. Linear storytelling is out the window. *The Loss of Sexual Innocence* refuses to stay anchored in one time period, presenting disjointed pieces of a story without offering many clues about how they should be put together (although Figgis' use of amber filters helps a little). The production rejects the traditional narrative form, preferring instead to try something experimental. The result is curiously satisfying, because, while it leaves countless unanswered questions and loose ends, it demands thought and intellectual participation.

When asked his reasons for presenting the film in this manner, Figgis denounced the way the 3-act structure has become the filmmaker's Bible, then went on to attack the manner in which commercialism has destroyed the artistic elements of film. *The Loss of Sexual Innocence* is his attempt to restore art to the medium, and to prove that an involving, compelling experience can result from a fragmented narrative that relies more on music and images than dialogue. For the most part, *The Loss of Sexual Innocence* proves Figgis' point. **RECOMMENDED**

Love & Basketball [2000]

Starring: Sanaa Lathan, Omar Epps, Alfre Woodard, Dennis Haysbert, Debbi Morgan Director: Gina Prince-Bythewood Screenplay: Gina Prince-Bythewood Running Time: 2:04 Rated: PG-13 (Profanity, sex) Theatrical Aspect Ratio: 1.85:1

Love & Basketball is, as one can infer from the title, about love and basketball. The film follows the lives of two next-door neighbors, one male and one female, from their first meeting on the court at the age of 11 until a fateful night a dozen years in the future. Through all this time, their passion for basketball is equaled only by their passion for each other, but it's never clear for either of them which takes precedence — the game or the relationship. In the final analysis, the feature debut of writer/director Gina Prince-Bythewood (backed by producer Spike Lee) succeeds better as a sports movie than as a romance. While the sports clichés are kept to a minimum in favor of a *Hoop Dreams*-type view of basketball, the love story follows a familiar trajectory.

The two protagonists are Monica Wright (Sanaa Latham) and Quincy McCall (Omar Epps). She is determined to become the first woman ever to enter the NBA; he is driven by the need to better the accomplishments of his father, Zeke (Dennis Haysbert), a star for the Los Angeles Clippers. *Love & Basketball* is divided into "quarters" like a basketball game, with each segment chronicling a different period in Monica and Quincy's lives. The first quarter, set in 1981, details their meeting and their brief relationship as an 11-year-old "couple." The second quarter skips ahead seven years to high school, where both Monica and Quincy are stars. However, since he's a male and she's a female, his future in the sport appears to be set while hers is uncertain. When it comes to choosing a college, she has to wait anxiously to hear from a recruiter while he plans a press conference to announce his choice. Quarter number 3 transpires during the pair's freshman year at college, when she faces pressure from a demanding coach and he struggles with salacious revelations about his father. Finally, in the fourth quarter, the film shows the degree to which Monica and Quincy's dreams are realized both on and off the court.

Even though every major cast member of *Love & Basketball* is black, the film is essentially color-blind.

However, while race is a non-issue, gender is not. The film illustrates, among other things, the vast gulf of inequality that exists between male and female athletes. By dramatizing Monica and Quincy's lives in parallel, Pince-Bythewood is able to explore the inequities. Despite having the same drive, ambition, and passion, they cannot reach the same peak, nor are the plateaus along the way on the same level. Although not a slam-dunk, it's a satisfying lay-up. **RECOMMENDED**

A Love Song for Bobby Long [2004]

Starring: John Travolta, Scarlett Johansson, Gabriel Macht, Deborah Kara Unger Director: Shainee Gabel Screenplay: Shainee Gabel, based on *Off Magazine Street*, by Ronald Everett Capps Running Time: 1:54 Rated: PG-13 (Profanity, implied violence, brief nudity) Theatrical Aspect Ratio: 2.35:1

A Love Song for Bobby Long offers a case study of how a single performance can elevate a motion picture. The story is unremarkable — a soap opera filled with clichés — and the direction (by first-time feature filmmaker Shainee Gabel) is uninspired. Yet the acting by Scarlett Johansson is so raw and sincere that the film leaves an impact despite its deficiencies. The actress's work in *A Love Song for Bobby Long* re-enforces my opinion that Johansson is one of the brightest stars of her generation, and she is hands down the best thing about this movie.

The A-list star of *A Love Song for Bobby Long* is John Travolta, who appears greatly aged as a result of makeup and white hair, but there is no moment in which Travolta manages to steal the spotlight from Johansson. He, as well as costar Gabriel Macht (*The Recruit*), is reduced to a footnote in the production. The plot requires him to be there, but we hardly notice him. On every level that matters, we identify with Johansson's Pursy Will, and that has more to do with the actress's portrayal than with Gabel's writing or direction.

Pursy comes home when she learns that her estranged mother has died. She arrives too late for the funeral, and discovers that her mother's house is inhabited by two men: the rude and obnoxious Bobby Long (Travolta), and his younger, gentler protégé, Lawson Pines (Gabriel Macht). They lie to Pursy, telling her that her mother willed them each one third of the property (when, in fact, Pursy inherited the whole thing). Despite their presence, Pursy decides to stay in the house. After a rocky start, the three begin to develop an uneasy bond and, by inches, they open up to one another.

Pursy changes — the bitterness that fills her soul is gradually replaced by regret, then a sense of belonging. By the time the film concludes, she no longer defines herself as the girl who was abandoned by her mother. Instead, she has come to believe in herself and to find something to live for rather than just waking up the next morning. The film's "surprise" plot twist will not be unexpected for many viewers; it's a weak and obvious attempt by the filmmakers to ratchet up *A Love Song for Bobby Long*'s emotional impact. Nevertheless, despite this and other flaws, the characters remain interesting throughout, and Johansson's acting covers a multitude of sins. In the end, this song has enough of a tune to involve a majority of those in the audience. **RECOMMENDED**

Lucas [1986]

Starring: Corey Haim, Kerri Green, Charlie Sheen, Courtney Thorne-Smith, Winona Ryder Director: David Seltzer Screenplay: David Seltzer Running Time: 1:40 Rated: PG-13 (mature themes) Theatrical Aspect Ratio: 1.85:1

In the decade of the 1980s, when the teen movie was redefined as either a juvenile sex comedy or a bloody slasher movie, *Lucas* became one of the few exceptions to try a different approach. Even today, *Lucas* remains one of the best films to tackle the themes of first crushes and the adolescent angst of not fitting in. It's a poignant and effective character study that manages not only to explore important teenage issues without condescending to the audience, but to offer an upbeat ending without descending into mawkishness.

Lucas (Corey Haim) is a misfit, but he's not a misanthrope. A 14-year-old accelerated high school student with far more intelligence than common sense, he is the prototypical nerd. Like most children who are all brains and little brawn, Lucas is an outcast at school — he is relegated to a clique of others like him, whose scholastic aptitude overshadows their social maturity. Although Lucas has friends, he is pretty much a loner. His home life is not a happy one, and, rather than spend time in the trailer where he lives with his alcoholic father, he prefers to be outside, catching insects in a net or earning a few dollars cutting lawns. Being with other people is not Lucas' style — until he meets Maggie (Kerri Green).

Maggie's new in town and doesn't yet have any friends. The fact that she's 2 years older than him doesn't mean much to Lucas, and he cheerfully takes on the task of being Maggie's constant companion. It's the middle of the summer, and they spend a few idyllic weeks together sharing a variety of experiences. For a short period, they are in a magical world all their own until reality, in the form of school, intrudes. As Maggie meets other people and becomes increasingly popular, the green-eyed monster of jealousy begins to grip Lucas. His emotional crisis reaches a pinnacle when Maggie starts dating Cappie (Charlie Sheen), a football player. Cappie is the only jock at school to treat Lucas with respect, but that doesn't mean much to the younger boy when he sees his special relationship with Maggie slipping away. And it also doesn't matter to Lucas that Maggie never saw him as more than a friend, or that there's another girl at school who is desperate to be his girlfriend.

Lucas is fiction, but it touches the heart like real life, and the title character is so strongly drawn that it's hard to identify with him as nothing more than an artifact of a writer's imagination. In the end, *Lucas* manages to be touching, sad, thoughtful, funny, and joyous — it's a nearly-perfect portrait of the incredible highs and lows that accompany the high school journey of a square peg who doesn't fit into a round hole. **HIGHLY RECOMMENDED**

The Luzhin Defence [United Kingdom/France, 2000]

Starring: John Turturro, Emily Watson, Geraldine James, Stuart Wilson Director: Marleen Gorris Screenplay: Peter Berry, based on the novel by Vladimir Nabokov Running Time: 1:48 Rated: PG-13 (Sensuality, mature themes) Theatrical Aspect Ratio: 1.66:1

The Luzhin Defence is a motion picture from feminist director Marleen Gorris, whose past cinematic efforts have included *Antonia's Line* and *Mrs. Dalloway*. Based loosely on the novel by Vladimir Nobokov (who is perhaps best known for penning the controversial *Lolita*), this movie tells the unlikely story of a socially inept Chess Grand Master who finds love just as he is about to face the most pressure-packed challenge of his life.

Luzhin (John Turturro) is recognized as one of the greatest chess players of his era (which happens to be the late 1920s). Since the age of 10, his entire life has been devoted to chess. It has been an obsession and an addiction. It's the only thing he is good at and the only thing that has meaning for him. Until, while in Italy to play a match against his chief rival, he meets Natalia (Emily Watson), an elegant beauty who instantly captures his heart. He, in turn, despite his awkward manner and social ineptitude, touches her deeply — so much so that she describes him as the most "fascinating, enigmatic, and attractive man" she has ever met — much to the horror of her mother (Geraldine James), who wants her to marry someone

better. But, even as Luzhin is finding a life outside of chess with Natalia, forces are conspiring against him. His old teacher (Stuart Wilson) wants to see him lose the match, and has taken steps to increase the pressure on Luzhin to the point where he will crack.

While one might initially suspect that a movie about chess would inherently be dull (the game itself not necessarily being the best spectator sport), *The Luzhin Defence* is actually an involving and compelling tale. The story is presented in two pieces: events unfolding in the film's present and flashbacks that illuminate how Luzhin became the person he is today. Both timelines converge at the end, when the movie reaches its powerful climax. Gorris frequently toys with symbolism concerning how Luzhin's life replicates the game he plays, but the film never becomes overbearing or bogged down in making such parallels.

With its sumptuous photography and deeply realized characters, *The Luzhin Defence* offers everything one could ask from a period piece, including an emotional release at the end that lacks the artifice associated with manipulative melodramas. This is a fine, thoughtful motion picture that effectively combines the maneuvers of the chessboard with the unfathomable intricacies of the human heart. **RECOMMENDED**

Ma Vie en Rose (My Life in Pink) [France/Belgium/United Kingdom, 1997]

Starring: Georges Du Fresne, Michele Laroque, Jean-Philippe Ecoffey, Helene Vincent Director: Alain Berliner Screenplay: Chris Vander Stappen, Alain Berliner Running Time: 1:30 Rated: R (Profanity, mature themes) Theatrical Aspect Ratio: 1.85:1 In French with subtitles

Equal parts fantasy, satire, and pathos, *Ma Vie en Rose* investigates the role of sexual stereotypes in today's culture, and shows how the more conservative elements of society encourage conformity and stifle diversity. In terms of both its style and story, this is one of 1997's few unique motion pictures.

Pierre (Jean-Philippe Ecoffey) and Hanna (Michele Laroque), along with their 4 children, have just moved into a nice house in a suburban Paris neighborhood. Three of the kids are normal and well-adjusted, but the fourth, Ludovic (Georges Du Fresne), a 7-year-old boy, is showing "alarming" tendencies. His favorite toys are Barbie-like dolls, he expresses a desire to marry a male classmate when he "grows up and becomes a girl," and he shows up at a party dressed like a pink princess. His mother, convinced that this is a harmless phase, tries to be as supportive as possible, but, when pressure from unsympathetic and close-minded neighbors mounts, she begins to turn on Ludovic. Meanwhile, Pierre doesn't know how best to cope with his son's tendencies, and Ludovic's sometimes-embarrassing displays of femininity threaten to derail his career.

Ludovic can't understand what the fuss is about. After all, everything seems clear to him. When God was giving out chromosomes, his second "X" (of the "XX" pair that signifies a female) was lost in the trash and he somehow got stuck with a "Y" instead (for the male "XY" pair). As a result, he's a "girlboy," but, when he grows up, he's convinced that he'll be a woman. So why shouldn't he wear makeup and dresses, and play with dolls? And why is it wrong if he arranges a mock marriage with a boy in his class? When his parents and his schoolmates react angrily, he doesn't understand their surprise, discomfort, and rage. He just wants to do what feels right, yet everyone hates him for it. Those who assume that he's gay have missed the point entirely — sexuality isn't even an issue, at least not at this young age. *Ma Vie en Rose* isn't concerned with Ludovic's eventual sexual orientation.

Although the most memorable element of *Ma Vie en Rose* is the forceful visual style, the director proves himself to be an apt student of human nature. The film works because we understand the central characters and their tribulations. When Ludovic is teased and tormented, it's easy to remember how much unthinking cruelty there is in this world, whether the setting is Paris or next door. But, when all is said and done, *Ma Vie en Rose* is more of a fantasy than a straight drama, and Berliner's lighthearted touch keeps the film buoyant when it could easily turn grim. **RECOMMENDED**

Ma Saison Préferée (My Favorite Season)
[France, 1993]

Starring: Catherine Deneuve, Daniel Auteuil, Marthe Villalonga, Jean-Pierre Bouvier, Chiara Mastroianni, Anthony Prada Director: André Téchiné Screenplay: Andre Téchiné Running Time: 2:04 Rated: No MPAA Rating (Nudity, mature themes, profanity) Theatrical Aspect Ratio: 2.35:1 In French with subtitles

Ma Saison Préferée is about relationships and communication. It's about sacrifice and misunderstandings. And, above all, it's about the ties of family and how the passage of time constantly distorts and re-invents our relationships with those we are closest to. André Téchiné's masterful story probes these issues, constantly digging deeper to uncover hidden motivations. In the process, a pair of multi-dimensional, completely believable personalities are created. These characters get under our skin and stay there.

Ma Saison Préferée features international film icon Catherine Deneuve as Emilie and French star Daniel Auteuil (*Jean de Florette, Un Coeur en Hiver*) as her estranged brother, Antoine. The rift between these two has existed for 3 years, a time during which they haven't spoken. When their mother, Berthe (Marthe Villalonga), suffers a stroke, Emilie brings the older woman to her house to live. Bruno (Jean-Pierre Bouvier), Emilie's husband, resents Berthe's presence, and is even less pleased when Emilie breaks the silence with Antoine and invites him to Christmas dinner. On that night, with the snow falling outside, the tangled skein of Emilie and Antoine's relationship begins to untangle, causing Emilie to leave her husband and reach a new understanding with her brother.

When *Ma Saison Préferée* begins, none of the characters are happy with themselves, their lives, their relationships, or each other. As time passes, however, and Emilie and Antoine re-discover the closeness they once shared, they uncover their lost humanity. But how deep is this new understanding, and what level of sacrifice can it survive? Téchiné goes to great pains to illustrate that there are no easy answers to life's most difficult questions, and that no aspect of human interaction can avoid change.

A varied and intriguing group of supporting characters populate this film. The most important is Berthe, whose circumstances and actions impel change in Emilie and Antoine's relationship. We also meet Emilie's troublesome adopted son, Lucien (Anthony Prada), and her daughter, Anne (Chiara Mastroianni, the real-life offspring of Deneuve and actor Marcello Mastroianni), who feels unloved and neglected. These two members of the younger generation have their own stories, pieces of which we see when they intersect aspects of Techine's main narrative.

Ma Saison Préferée is the sort of intelligent, sensitive drama that we need more of. It engages the intellect without ignoring the emotions. **HIGHLY RECOMMENDED**

Maborosi [Japan, 1995]

Starring: Makiko Esumi, Takashi Naitoh, Tadanobu Asano Director: Hirokazu Kore-eda Screenplay: Yoshihisa Ogita based on the short story by Teru Miyamoto Running Time: 1:50 Rated: No MPAA Rating (Mature themes, brief nudity) Theatrical Aspect Ratio: 1.66:1 In Japanese with subtitles

In an era when MTV-inspired film making techniques have begun to dominate motion pictures, its refreshing to see something with the simple, unhurried style of Japanese director Hirokazu Kore-eda's feature debut, *Maborosi*. This film, which is really little more than a series of images connected by a bare-bones plot, explores the evolution of one woman's emotion as she ponders the unexplained (and seemingly inexplicable) death of her first husband.

The film opens with a brief prologue during which a young Japanese girl watches her beloved grandmother leave home, never to return. On that same day, she meets the boy who will eventually become her husband. When we next encounter her, Yumiko (Makiko Esumi) is 20 years older. She's married to Ikuo (Tadanobu Asano) and has a 3-month old son. She is content, and her happiness is shown through a playfulness that permeates every action. Then, one night, everything changes. Ikuo commits suicide by walking in front of a train. Yumiko is plunged into an extended period of mourning from which she only begins to emerge when she re-marries, this time to a widower named Tamio (Takashi Naitoh). To be with Tamio, Yumiko leaves the city of Osaka to live in a tiny fishing village. But she is a haunted woman, and her fear of intimacy keeps her emotionally isolated from her new husband.

Kore-eda has chosen not to illustrate Yumiko's emotions through traditionally melodramatic methods. In fact, it's rare that she sheds a tear, although the face of model-turned-actress Makiko Esumi is certainly capable of expressing a surprising range of feeling. Instead of relying on the character, however, Kore-eda uses Yumiko's surroundings. When she's on the way to the police station to identify her husband's body, the weather weeps for her, streaking the car windows with rain. After Ikuo's death, the director, much like Ingmar Bergman, uses spatial relationships to highlight her emotional isolation. She is often distanced from others, frequently appearing alone and shrouded by shadow. Towards the end of *Maborosi*, there is a memorable sequence when Yumiko, depicted in silhouette, is set far apart from everyone else. Kore-eda also uses certain sounds to contribute to the sense of solitude — the crashing of the waves and the roar of the wind, in particular.

Maborosi is a worthwhile movie experience not because it ventures into virgin territory, but because its presentation is so precise and unique. This is a haunting cinematic portrait, where the almost-poetic visual images and their associated emotional meaning hold the viewer enraptured. **HIGHLY RECOMMENDED**

The Madness of King George [United Kingdom, 1994]

Starring: Nigel Hawthorne, Helen Mirren, Ian Holm, Amanda Donohoe, Rupert Graves, Rupert Everett Director: Nicholas Hytner Screenplay: Alan Bennett based on his stage play "The Madness of George III" Running Time: 1:50 Rated: No MPAA Rating (Mature themes) Theatrical Aspect Ratio: 1.85:1

Opening in 1788, more than 5 years after England lost her North American colonies, *The Madness of King George* relates a dark episode in the king's reign. Bothered by increasingly painful abdominal pains, George (Nigel Hawthorne) begins to act irrationally and belligerently. The doctors — mostly a bunch of jumped-up quacks — do nothing for him. His eldest son and heir, the Prince of Wales (Rupert Everett) is eager to see his father declared mad so he can take over as regent. Ministers, retainers, and others at court begin to scheme how to get the most out of the king's indisposition. At last, when all appears lost, Prime Minister Pitt (Julian Wadham), aided by Queen Charlotte (Helen Mirren); her Mistress of the Robes, Lady Pembroke (Amanda Donohoe); and Greville (Rupert Graves), one of the king's aides; sends for Dr. Willis (Ian Holm), a doctor of the mind with a reputation for curing dementia.

The Madness of King George is much more than a simple study of one man's descent into insanity. With a style that's more tongue-in-cheek than melodramatic, the film is always witty and occasionally satirical. The characterizations are flawless (as well as historically accurate), and the political wrangling of the Tories and Whigs (led by PM Pitt and Charles Fox, respectively) provide a deliciously complex backdrop.

Medical historians are generally agreed that the cause of George's madness was something called porphyria, an acute, intermittent, hereditary disease that is physical (rather than mental) in nature. The king's symptoms, including blue urine and gastric crises, match those of porphyria, although some have postulated that there may have been a secondary affliction, such as manic-depression, involved. Whatever the case, as this film illustrates, it's clear that there were times when George was unfit to rule.

Despite allusions to *King Lear*, this movie's strength is in its story breadth, not its depth. A lot happens here, but few of the themes take root beyond their surface meaning. Adapted from Alan Bennett's play *The Madness of George III*, the film trims copious portions of dialogue, leaving behind a tightly-paced picture that has the feel of something created for the screen rather than for the stage. Certain subplots are watered down or eliminated, but what survives is more than enough to keep *King George* a source of solid entertainment. **HIGHLY RECOMMENDED**

The Magdelene Sisters [United Kingdom/Ireland, 2002]
Starring: Geraldine McEwan, Ann-Marie Duff, Nora-Jane Noone, Dorothy Duffy, Eileen Walsh Director: Peter Mullan Screenplay: Peter Mullan Running Time: 1:59 Rated: R (Violence, nudity, profanity) Theatrical Aspect Ratio: **1.85:1**

Despite shadings of an anti-Catholic bias, the story told by *The Magdalene Sisters* is powerful and disturbing — an example of how fundamentalist religions of all types often marginalize and brutalize women. The Catholic Church has largely moved beyond the attitudes and activities displayed in this film, but there are plenty of oppressors out there who continue to perpetuate such practices. It's also a historical fact that places like the Magdalene Sanctuary existed in Ireland. By making this movie, director Peter Mullan has opened eyes to circumstances that many around the world may be unaware of. *The Magdalene Sisters* tells the stories of three girls who, for a variety of reasons, are placed in the "care" of a group of nuns and priests whose duty is to put their bodies through suffering in order to save their souls. The girls in the Magdalene Sanctuary have three things in common: They have either been abandoned by their families or have no families; they are viewed as "impure" (due to a real or perceived sexual transgression); and they are completely under the thumb of the church. The Magdalene Sanctuary is like a prison. Escape is virtually unthinkable and, for those who do consider it, difficult to accomplish.

Margaret (Ann-Marie Duff) has been disowned by her family after she was raped by her cousin and had the temerity to accuse him of the wrongdoing. The sin was laid at her feet, and her payment was to be packed off to the sanctuary. Bernadette (Nora-Jane Noone) lived in an orphanage until her frequent saucy conversations with neighborhood boys resulted in her being given into the care of the nuns. Rose (Dorothy Duffy) had a baby out of wedlock, which she was forced to give up for adoption. The shame created by that misstep was enough to cause her mother and father to turn their backs on her. *The Magdalene Sisters* presents the stories of these girls, as well as that of the simpleminded Crispina (Eileen Walsh), who has been at the Sanctuary for some time.

The film might have been more compelling had Mullan allowed the head nun to exhibit as much compassion as sadism. Nevertheless, even considering the demonization of the authority figures, *The Magdalene Sisters* is a disturbing and compelling motion picture that depicts the forces that try to suppress the human spirit, and the strength of these girls in overcoming it. Issues surrounding Mullan's precise adherence to historical fact are a red herring. This is a worthwhile movie because it is well made and encourages viewers to think and feel. **RECOMMENDED**

Magnolia [1999]
Starring: Jason Robards, Philip Baker Hall, Tom Cruise, John C. Reilly, Melora Walters, Julianne Moore, William H. Macy, Philip Seymour Hoffman Director: Paul Thomas Anderson Screenplay: Paul Thomas Anderson Running Time: 3:05 Rated: R (Profanity, violence, sex) Theatrical Aspect Ratio: **2.35:1**

With *Magnolia*, director Paul Thomas Anderson has created a fascinating and worthwhile motion picture that manages to keep viewers interested in the plights of 10 different characters for nearly its full 3-hour length — right up to and through the improbable climax.

In order to get a sense of where *Magnolia* is going, it is necessary to introduce the various characters. At the center of events is Earl Partridge (Jason Robards), a television producer who, stricken by cancer, lies on his deathbed. His young wife, Linda (Julianne Moore), is desolate with grief and guilt, and has trouble coping with her impending loss. His estranged son, Frank Mackey (Tom Cruise), the charismatic guru of the "Seduce and Destroy" lifestyle, has worked hard to sever all connections with Earl. His nurse, Phil Parma (Philip Seymour Hoffman), seeks to fulfill his employer's dying wish and reunite him with Frank. Meanwhile, Jimmy Gator (Philip Baker Hall), who is the host of Earl's most popular TV show, the long-running "What Do Kids Know?," also has terminal cancer. Like Earl and Frank, a rift exists between him and his child. When he attempts a reconciliation with Claudia (Melora Walters), she rebuffs him. Later, she embarks on a strange relationship with a gentle but ineffectual police officer, Jim Kurring (John C. Reilly). And Jimmy must explain to his wife, Rose (Melinda Dillon), why Claudia hates him so intensely. At the same time, Stanley Spector (Jeremy Blackman), a child genius on Jimmy's show, finds that the only way to get his father's attention is to win money. And, as Stanley continues to answer questions right, a former quiz show star, Donnie Smith (William H. Macy), watches the remains of his life go up in smoke. Together, these characters make up the leaves and branches of this tree.

Like Robert Altman's *Short Cuts*, *Magnolia* is a

finely-tuned ensemble piece. Yet a direct comparison between the two films would be somewhat misleading. Thematically, at least when considering the role played by chance, there are similarities, but Altman used a different, more languid style than Anderson does. *Magnolia* is a kinetic picture that doesn't stop moving and rarely stays with one story for more than a couple of minutes before moving to the next. This approach allows us to get to know the principals quickly, and keeps us engaged by all of the storylines. *Magnolia* is admittedly not for everyone, but those who "get" the film are in for something that ranks as more of a cinematic experience than a mere movie.

HIGHLY RECOMMENDED

The Majestic [2001]

Starring: Jim Carrey, Martin Landau, Laurie Holden, Bob Balaban
Director: Frank Darabont Screenplay: Michael Sloane Running
Time: 2:32 Rated: PG (Mature themes, profanity) Theatrical Aspect
Ratio: 1.85:1

Once in a while, a movie arrives on the scene that immediately causes critics far and wide to compare it to the work of a legendary director, such as Hitchcock, Wilder, or Welles. In this case, it's Frank Capra. Typically, an effort associated with Capra will fall into the feel-good category, may engage in shameless manipulation, and will bring to mind words like "wholesome" and "sentimental." *The Majestic* has all the elements to be a crowd-pleaser. The only potential negatives are its languorous pace and long running time, which may cause some MTV-bred viewers to squirm in their seats.

The Majestic takes place in the early 1950s. The Cold War is well underway and Sen. Joseph McCarthy's anti-Communist fervor is at its peak. No one is safe from government bullying — especially in Hollywood, long viewed as a hotbed of seditious activity. Screenwriter Peter Appleton (Jim Carrey), whose movie, *Sand Pirates of the Sahara*, has just reached screens, is no exception. Years ago in college, he attended a pro-Communist meeting to impress a girl. Now, that simple action has come back to haunt him, as he finds himself blacklisted and called to testify in front of Congress. The night when Peter learns that his life will never be the same, he drinks himself into a stupor, then crashes his car into a river. He wakes up on a beach with no memory of who he is. But the citizens of the small, nearby town have no such uncertainty — he is Luke Trimble, a war hero who was reported missing in action 9½ years earlier.

Luke is welcomed home by everyone, including his aging father, Harry (Martin Landau), the mayor (Jeffrey DeMunn), and the love of his life, Adele Stanton (Laurie Holden). With the help of the townsfolk, Luke and Harry set to work restoring the local movie theater, The Majestic, to its former glory. But not everyone believes in the miracle of Luke's return, and the government is looking for Peter Appleton.

Most people will leave *The Majestic* with a smile reflecting the warm glow within. The film is unashamed of its feel-good intentions and, in that, is a throwback. There's no sex or violence, and very little in the way of profanity. Had *The Majestic* been made in black-and-white with a less high-profile cast, one might have assumed it to be the product of Hollywood during a kinder, gentler era. For those craving a large helping of nostalgia with a topping of crowd-pleasing patriotism, there are few choices better than *The Majestic*. **RECOMMENDED**

Malena [Italy/United States, 2000]

Starring: Monica Bellucci, Giuseppe Sulfaro, Luciano Federico, Matilde
Piana Director: Giuseppe Tornatore Screenplay: Giuseppe Tornatore,
based on a story by Luciano Vincenzoni Running Time: 1:32 Rated: R
(Nudity, sexual situations, violence) Theatrical Aspect Ratio: 2.35:1
In Italian with subtitles

Malena is a curious mix of whimsy and tragedy. Director Giuseppe Tornatore's blending of the divergent tones is not entirely successful — there are several jarring moments — but, on the whole, *Malena* works as an affecting coming-of-age story set against the backdrop of Fascist Italy and filtered through the memories of the narrator. Along the way, Tornatore sticks to the same basic style that served him well in his 1989 international hit, *Cinema Paradiso*, by employing equal parts nostalgia, comedy, and drama.

The year is 1940 and the place is the picturesque (and fictional) town of Castelcuta, Sicily. 13-year-old Renato Amoroso (Giuseppe Sulfaro) is about to experience his first major adolescent crush when he catches a glimpse of Malena Scordia (Monica Bellucci). Malena, the daughter of Latin teacher Professor Bonsignore (Pietro Notarianni), has come to Castelcuta to care for her father while her husband is away at war. As Malena walks by, every man's head turns and women's tongues wag with scathing gossip. Then Malena's husband is killed in the war and she becomes free to pursue and be pursued by Castelcuta's male population. Meanwhile, Renato, whose infatuation develops into an obsession, begins spying on Malena and, in the process, learns that the "real" Malena is much different than his idealized portrait of her.

Malena begins as a lighthearted drama that recalls one of Federico Fellini's best-known works, *Amarcord*. Tornatore does not have Fellini's deft hand, however, and the story eventually takes a dark turn, with some of its themes and ideas recalling the late Krzysztof Kieslowski's *A Short Film About Love,* in which a young voyeur has his fantasy picture of a woman brutally shattered by an encounter with her.

One of the most powerful elements of *Malena* is the music, by frequent Tornatore collaborator and legendary composer, Ennio Morricone. Combined with cinematographer Lajos Koltai's sweeping camera work and beautifully photographed vistas, the music gives *Malena* a glorious backdrop against which the story can unfold. This is not the writer/director's most accomplished feature, but it offers a strong central character, an interesting historical subtext, and a coming-of-age narrative that most people will be able to relate to on one level or another. RECOMMENDED

A Man of No Importance
[Ireland/United Kingdom, 1994]
Starring: Albert Finney, Brenda Fricker, Rufus Sewell, Tara Fitzgerald, Michael Gambon Director: Suri Krishnamma Screenplay: Barry Devlin Running Time: 1:38 Rated: R (Mature themes, sex, nudity, violence)

As it turns out, the only thing of real importance in *A Man of No Importance* is Albert Finney's performance. His turn as bus conductor Alfie Byrne is yet another extraordinary credit to add to an already-impressive resume. The man who played Tom Jones in the 1960s matured into of the best character actors of the 1990s, with memorable appearances in such films as *The Playboys, Rich in Love,* and *The Browning Version.* Even when these movies had little to offer, Finney's presence was a saving grace.

When he's not entertaining his regular passengers with readings of Oscar Wilde, Alfie is a would-be director who delights in putting on not-so-successful amateur productions. In the past, he has been known for doing *The Importance of Being Earnest,* but this time around, Alfie has chosen to attempt *Salome.* This decision is crystalized when he finds the perfect choice for the title role — an enchanting young woman named Adele (Tara Fitzgerald) who wanders on his bus one day.

But Alfie's personal life isn't nearly as joyful as his public personae might lead others to believe. Despite attempts by his sister (Brenda Fricker) to find him a wife, Alfie steadfastly resists the idea, primarily because women don't interest him. However, the only one to whom he has openly admitted his homosexuality (or "the love that dare not speak its name," as Wilde called it) is himself. In Alfie's world of 1963 Dublin, tolerance for gays is in short supply.

If *A Man of No Importance* is anything other than a nicely-detailed portrait of one unfulfilled middle-aged Dubliner, it's about the value of friendship. Although Alfie never finds the love for which he so desperately searches, he discovers a far more valuable commodity. In Adele, he uncovers someone else who hides a secret. The two are kindred spirits and there are times when their interaction has a closeness that lovers often strive for. Then there's the driver of Alfie's bus, a young man named Robbie (Rufus Sewell), to whom Alfie is attracted. Because Robbie is straight, Alfie never reveals his feelings, choosing instead to pursue a platonic friendship.

"The only way to get rid of temptation is to yield to it," wrote Oscar Wilde, but when Alfie tries to apply this lesson, the results are — to put it mildly — unfortunate. That life cannot be lived without risk and failure is certainly one of *A Man of No Importance*'s more emphatic messages. RECOMMENDED

Man on the Moon [1999]
Starring: Jim Carrey, Danny DeVito, Paul Giamatti, Courtney Love, Jerry Lawler Director: Milos Forman Screenplay: Scott Alexander & Larry Karaszewski Running Time: 1:59 Rated: R (Profanity, sexual situations, nudity) Theatrical Aspect Ratio: 2.35:1

During his lifetime, Andy Kaufman was regarded by fans as a comic genius and by detractors as an out-of-control lunatic. Most of the American public simply didn't understand him, and the numerous outrageous antics of his later life alienated many of those who had initially enjoyed him in the role of Latka Gravas in the TV series *Taxi.*

In telling its story of Kaufman's rise to fame and fall out of favor, *Man on the Moon* briefly visits him as a young boy, then zooms ahead to the mid-'70s, when he is starting his career as a stand-up comedian in improv clubs. One night, agent George Shapiro (Danny DeVito) sees him perform and decides that he wants to represent him. When the two later meet, Kaufman confides to Shapiro that he considers himself to be a song & dance man, not a comedian. "I don't do jokes. I don't even know what's funny." Following his signing with Shapiro, Kaufman makes an appearance as a "musical guest" on the first episode of *Saturday Night Live,* then goes on to star in *Taxi.* Along with his writing partner, Bob Zmuda (Paul Giamatti), he pens a prime time special that ABC executives nix, calling it bizarre and unfunny. Meanwhile, Kaufman is living a double life — his alter ego is an offensive and thoroughly untalented lounge singer named Tony Clifton.

Once he has the spotlight, Kaufman is unwilling to become creatively apathetic. He enjoys playing with his mercurial image and toying with the lines between fantasy and reality. So he sets himself up as a sexist wrestler who will only wrestle women. His first public "bout" occurs on the Merv Griffin show, where he defeats a woman named Lynn Marguiles (Courtney Love), with whom he later falls in love. Other matches follow, until Kaufman is challenged to go one-on-one with the King of Wrestling, Jerry Lawler.

Kaufman becomes so adept at the art of deception and illusion that, when he discovers he has terminal cancer, no one believes him. His family views it as the latest in a series of cruel practical jokes and believes that his doctor is a paid actor. Like the boy who has cried wolf once too often, Kaufman must struggle to convince those around him that, for once, he is serious.

Man on the Moon does not whitewash its lead character, but he is presented as a likable, albeit strange, protagonist. And, as a side benefit, we are given the opportunity to peer behind the scenes at some of the goings-on in Kaufman's projects. There are many reasons to see *Man on the Moon,* but the two most compelling are to appreciate the way the movie works on many levels and to experience what has the potential to be the crowning performance of Jim Carrey's career. **HIGHLY RECOMMENDED**

The Man without a Past [Finland, 2002]

Starring: Markku Peltola, Kati Outinen, Juhani Niemelä, Kaija Pakarinen, Sakari Kuosmanen Director: Aki Kaurismaki Screenplay: Aki Kaurismaki Running Time: 1:37 Rated: PG-13 (Violence) Theatrical Aspect Ratio: 1.66:1 In Finnish with subtitles

Amnesia is a common movie plot device — it probably occurs about 1,000 times more often on-screen than in real life. Some of the best thrillers use this as a lynchpin, but, while *The Man Without a Past* starts out looking like a noir Hitchcock homage, it's really nothing of the sort. Instead of using the main character's amnesia as a means of generating mystery and suspense, director Aki Kaurismaki employs it as a cat-

alyst for rebirth. *The Man Without a Past* is about starting over, and how the absence of memory allows an individual to wipe clean the slate of his life and begin afresh. This gives new meaning to the term "born again."

The film begins with an unnamed man (Markku Peltola) being robbed and brutally beaten at a train station. He is brought to a nearby hospital, where, after being pronounced dead, he unexpectedly awakens from a coma with no memory. After a period of convalescence, during which his injuries heal, he emerges into the local community — an economically depressed area where families live in disused tractor trailers — with the intention of making a difference. After attracting the attention of Irma (Kati Outinen), a female Salvation Army worker, he begins working with her. Eventually, the two embark upon a tentative romance, but it is complicated by the man's inability to remember anything about his past, including whether he is already married.

The Man Without a Past is a simple, gently told story that relies primarily upon mood. There is a plot, but the film is not plot-centric. The film is peppered with slyly comedic moments, few of which are uproarious, but many of which are droll. If there's a meaning to *The Man Without a Past,* it's about the value of fitting into a community. The man starts the film alone, broken, and bleeding. At the end, he is surrounded by the group of people who have become his friends and neighbors. He has learned to forget the past and move on — even when he remembers something. In its own strange way, *The Man Without a Past* is a modern fairy tale. It certainly is divorced from reality. Despite this — or perhaps because of it — it's a satisfying motion picture.
RECOMMENDED

Manny & Lo [1996]

Starring: Scarlett Johansson, Aleksa Palladino, Mary Kay Place Director: Lisa Krueger Screenplay: Lisa Krueger Running Time: 1:25 Rated: R (Profanity, sex, mature themes) Theatrical Aspect Ratio: 1.85:1

Manny & Lo, the debut feature from writer/director Lisa Krueger, is a wonderfully-textured comic fantasy about family life. With only a few missteps along the way, this film takes us on a deceptively complex journey of discovery into a world that is similar, yet different, from the one we travel through every day. For, although Krueger presents her characters as the human flotsam of modern-day life, there is a timeless, placeless quality to this story. Ultimately, it doesn't matter *when* or *where Manny & Lo* takes place, but *how* the characters' trajectories bring them together at their final destination.

Eleven-year old Amanda (or Manny, played by Scarlett Johansson) and 16-year-old Laurel (or Lo, played by Aleksa Palladino) are sisters on-the-run. After the death of their mother, they were placed in separate foster homes, only to be reunited after Lo ran away and "so-called kidnapped" Manny from her substitute family. Together, the pair live life on the road, watching out for state troopers who may have their description, stealing food from small convenience stores, sleeping in model homes, and checking the milk cartons to make sure that their pictures aren't on the "missing" panels.

Their unorthodox lifestyle is seriously disrupted, however, when Lo becomes pregnant. By the time she acknowledges that it's not just a few extra pounds, she's too far advanced for an abortion. Unwilling to turn herself in for medical care, but recognizing that she needs help, Lo decides to kidnap Elaine (Mary Kay Place), a "baby expert." With Manny's help, Lo uses a shotgun to encourage Elaine to accompany her to a deserted mountain cabin retreat. There, the 3 of them, captors and captive, await the baby's arrival while growing into a strange pseudo-family.

The best parts of *Manny & Lo* are the quiet, character-driven scenes, when it's just the 3 women alone, exploring their new relationship and contemplating the future. A subplot involving the cabin's owner (Paul Guilfoyle) shows us something about how desperately Elaine wants to be part of Manny and Lo's life, but there are aspects of this sequence that strain the film's delicately-struck balance between reality and fantasy.

There's something magical about the way Lisa Krueger's film transports us to its unique reality. There have been many films about family and belonging, but none with quite the same perspective as this one. *Manny & Lo* is always pleasant, never confrontational, and comes to a conclusion that is emotionally true. With its carefully-modulated combination of light comedy and drama, the film casts a gentle spell. **HIGHLY RECOMMENDED**

Mansfield Park [United Kingdom/United States, 1999]

Starring: Frances O'Connor, Jonny Lee Miller, Embeth Davidtz, Alessandro Nivola, Harold Pinter Director: Patricia Rozema
Screenplay: Patricia Rozema, based on Jane Austen's novel *Mansfield Park*, her letters and early journals Running Time: 1:50 Rated: PG-13 (Sex, nudity, mature themes) Theatrical Aspect Ratio: 1.78:1

There are 3 primary problems associated with filming Jane Austen's most confounding novel, *Mansfield Park*. In the first place, the text is long (this is Austen's second most verbose novel). Secondly, it's a deeply introspective work, with much of the "action" taking place inside the heroine's head. Finally, that heroine, Fanny Price, is passive and difficult to like. To put her on screen the way she is on the written page would risk driving viewers away. Canadian director Patricia Rozema's innovative (and possibly controversial) solution has been to change the text. In streamlining the plot, scenes and characters have been eliminated. Rozema also allows Fanny Price to address the camera, reducing the use of the voiceover narrative. And, most importantly, the director has altered Fanny's personality by injecting a great deal of Austen into her. The result is a hybrid of author and creation.

The film begins just after the turn of the 18th century. Young Fanny Price (played by Hannah Taylor Gordon as a child and Frances O'Connor as an adult) is shipped off from her squalid home in Portsmouth to live with wealthy relatives in the country estate of Mansfield Park. Because of her inferior social class, she is treated as an outcast by most of the family: Sir Thomas Bertram (Harold Pinter), Lady Bertram (Lindsay Duncan), and cousins Tom, Maria, and Julia. Only Edmund (Philip Sarson as a child, Jonny Lee Miller as an adult), the Bertrams' second son, is kind and open. He takes an interest in Fanny's writings, and, over the years, they become friends — and perhaps a little more. Although Edmund is seemingly oblivious to it, Fanny has fallen in love with him, and her affection is more than that of one cousin for another.

The scene shifts ahead several years, and life at Mansfield Park is considerably shaken by the appearance of Henry and Mary Crawford (Alessandro Nivola and Embeth Davidtz), a cosmopolitan brother and sister who arrive from London in search of marriageable prey. Much to Fanny's dismay, Mary sets her sights on Edmund, and he appears receptive to her overtures. Meanwhile, although Henry initially flirts with all the eligible young women at Mansfield Park, his attention eventually focuses on Fanny. He likes a challenge, and she provides it. Her reluctance only fuels his desire, but she does not trust him and she is distracted and dismayed by the growing bond between Edmund and Mary.

Of all the Austen novels to reach the big or small screen during the '90s, this one makes the most departures from its source material. From a technical standpoint, *Mansfield Park* is gorgeously composed, with standout production design and stunning cinematography. The screenplay achieves the difficult goal of making *Mansfield Park* both accessible to and engaging for a modern audience. Overall, this is a fine addition to the filmed Austen canon. Rozema's *Mansfield Park* should slake nearly every movie-goer's thirst for the most beloved female author of the pre-Victorian 1800s. RECOMMENDED

Me Without You [United Kingdom, 2001]

Starring: Michelle Williams, Anna Friel, Kyle MacLachlan
Director: Sandra Goldbacher Screenplay: Sandra Goldbacher,
Laurence Coriat Running Time: 1:47 Rated: R (Profanity, sexual
situations, drug use, nudity) Theatrical Aspect Ratio: 2.35:1

The movie opens in 1973 London, where best friends Holly (Ella Jones) and Marina (Anna Popplewell) are finding ways to spend the long summer days. Despite their differences, Holly and Marina are inseparable. Holly is the "clever" one, whose looks and self-confidence don't match the strength of her mind. Marina, on the other hand, is pretty, uninhibited, and not Holly's intellectual equal. Despite her wildness, however, she's actually vulnerable, with her outward boldness hiding a deep insecurity. Marina is clearly the dominant one in the relationship; Holly follows along, at times almost in awe.

The scene shifts to 1978. Both girls are now in their late teens and into the punk rock scene. Holly (now played by Michelle Williams) is as much of a wallflower as ever, and Marina (Anna Friel) is even more brash and outgoing. One night at a party, while Marina is doing heroin, Holly loses her virginity to Marina's older brother, Nat (Oliver Milburn). This creates a rift between the friends. Four years later, while at college, they both have affairs with the same professor (Kyle MacLachlan). Each is hurt to learn of the other's "betrayal" of sleeping with "her" man. Meanwhile, Nat makes an appearance, and it's clear that he's as besotted with Holly as she is with him. But a jealous Marina pushes them away from each other, and Nat goes to France to patch things up with his actress girlfriend.

The relationship between Holly and Marina starts as a typical teenage friendship before developing into something dark and unhealthy. In the early years, the two share everything and are as necessary to one another as oxygen. As they grow older and Marina's dominance strengthens, the downward spiral begins. Jealousy gradually poisons what exists between them. By the time the movie has reached its third act in the late '80s, these two women are together simply because they have been close for so long that the idea of splitting up seems unthinkable. Yet their friendship is dysfunctional. The bonds between them are rotten, and the situation has become suffocating.

Too few dramas these days have an arc such as the one traversed by *Me Without You*. The story works because it's about ordinary people — women you wouldn't look at twice if you passed them on the sidewalk. *Me Without You* offers more insight into the experience of female bonding that dozens of Hollywood features about the same subject. Touching and sincere, this film deserves to be seen by anyone who is searching for a movie about compelling characters in real circumstances. RECOMMENDED

Mean Creek [2004]

Starring: Rory Culkin, Trevor Morgan, Scott Mechlowicz, Carly
Schroeder, Ryan Kelley, Josh Peck Director: Jacob Aaron Estes
Screenplay: Jacob Aaron Estes Running Time: 1:29 Rated: R (Violence,
profanity) Theatrical Aspect Ratio: 1.85:1

It's an axiom that if a group of teenagers ventures into the woods during the course of a motion picture, something bad is going to happen. *Mean Creek* is evidence that there are times when even the most uninspired clichés can result in compelling stories.

Sam (Rory Culkin) is a perfect target for bullies: He's a loner with a small frame and a large intellect who would rather harbor his resentment than act upon it. That makes him an ideal punching bag for George (Josh Peck), whose abuse of Sam goes beyond verbal taunts to physical brutality. One day, when Sam comes home from school with some telltale bruises, his older brother, Rocky (Trevor Morgan), decides that the time has come to teach George a lesson. Sam will only go along with the plan if Rocky promises that George will be "hurt without really being hurt." With the help of his friends, Marty (Scott Mechlowicz) and Clyde (Ryan Kelley), Rocky comes up with the perfect scheme involving a seemingly innocent boat ride on a nearby river.

Getting George to come is an easy task. Sam pretends that he wants to mend bridges, so he invites George to his "birthday party." Also in the boat along with Sam, Rocky, George, Marty, and Clyde is Sam's sort-of-girlfriend, Millie (Carly Schroeder). But an unusual thing happens during the course of the journey: Sam and Rocky discover that George isn't really a bad guy. He's uncouth and socially immature, but all he really wants is to have a few friends. Were he to possess a scrawny frame rather than a bloated one, he would likely be the target of bullying rather than the bully. Sam and Rocky decide they want to call off the practical joke, and Millie and Clyde agree. But Marty, who is being victimized by his older brother, wants this taste of revenge, even if it's only through a surrogate. His determination to move forward leads to a predictable tragedy.

If, by reading this review, you can guess what happens on the river, *Mean Creek* will not be spoiled. This is not a thriller, and there aren't a lot of surprises. It is a character piece that examines how teenagers face their first true moral dilemma. The test of principles isn't a simple quandary like whether it's wrong to steal food in the absence of money, but something far more substantive — the kind of test that would strain the ethics of even the most upright adult. When does inaction become culpability? And to what degree can the promptings of a guilt-ridden conscience be ignored?

With *Mean Creek*, director Jacob Aaron Estes has provided a keenly honed view of human psychology. We would all like to think we would do "the right thing" in the face of a tragedy, but how many of us really know? Each of the characters reacts differently, and we're never left wondering about the reasons underpinning the reaction. By entering such fertile, intellectually stimulating, and psychologically rich territory, Estes provides us with a feature that is far beyond the generic coming-of-age tale *Mean Creek* initially seems to be. HIGHLY RECOMMENDED

Message in a Bottle [1999]

Starring: Kevin Costner, Robin Wright Penn, Paul Newman, Illeana Douglas, Robby Coltrane Director: Luis Mandoki Screenplay: Gerald DiPego, based on the novel by Nicholas Sparks Running Time: 2:10 Rated: PG-13 (Sexual themes, mild profanity) Theatrical Aspect Ratio: 2.35:1

In addition to being a beautifully-photographed motion picture with a solid (albeit melodramatic) storyline and good acting, *Message in a Bottle* was also Kevin Costner's bid to once again be taken seriously in the wake of several unfortunate career choices (capped off by the disastrous *The Postman*).

Message in a Bottle starts out with single mom Theresa Osborne (Robin Wright Penn), leaving her young son, Jason (Jesse James), in the care of his father, with whom he's visiting for a few weeks. After that, she takes a stroll along a New England beach, where she finds a bottle with a message in it. The note is addressed to someone named Catherine, and appears to be a heartfelt letter of love and loss. The

writer calls the woman his "true North," expresses how much she means to him, and laments her loss. Theresa is deeply touched, and, when she returns home to Chicago, she shows the missive to her friends and co-workers at the Tribune. The next day, the letter is printed in the paper, and the resulting reader response is overwhelming. Contained in the stacks of mail delivered to the Tribune are two other messages, both found in bottles, that appear to be from the same source. Using her investigative instincts, Theresa tracks down the writer, a North Carolina ship repairman named Garret Blake (Kevin Coster), and, without revealing her profession, she strikes up a friendship with him. It turns out that Garret is still grieving for his dead wife, Catherine, and his life has been an empty shell for the past 2 years. But, through his interaction with Theresa, he begins to shake off some of the cobwebs of loneliness and pain.

The movie's premise promises more than the rather standard grief-assuaged-by-new-love story that's ultimately delivered. The first half-hour of *Message in a Bottle* is engrossing because it appears to be going in a completely new direction. After that, things fall into familiar patterns. Once the initial 30 minutes are over, the best part of *Message in a Bottle* is the character interaction.

Working from a script by Gerald DiPego (based on Nicholas Sparks' novel), director Luis Mandoki has fashioned one of his most complete films to date. Credit both the actors and the material for making *Message in a Bottle* a worthwhile 2 hours. It's not a great film, but it succeeds in being both tender and cathartic, and, unlike *Patch Adams* and *Stepmom*, it isn't unbearably cloying in the process. RECOMMENDED

Michael Collins [United Kingdom/United States, 1996]

Starring: Liam Neeson, Aidan Quinn, Julia Roberts, Alan Rickman, Stephen Rea, Ian Hart, Brendan Gleeson Director: Neil Jordan Screenplay: Neil Jordan Running Time: 2:12 Rated: R (Violence, profanity) Theatrical Aspect Ratio: 1.85:1

Neil Jordan's *Michael Collins* is a biopic of the man who co-founded the IRA and signed the 1921 treaty that partitioned Ireland and provoked the 1922 civil war. Even before its release, the film fanned passions in the United Kingdom, where is was tagged with such diverse labels as "ammunition for IRA recruiting sergeants and fund-raisers" (Ruth Dudley Edwards) and "as important a film as ever to be made in Ireland about Ireland" (Art Cosgrove).

While its clear that *Michael Collins* does distort elements of history, most of the changes and compressions are dramatically effective. Certain characters are combined, a few deaths happen differently from what history records, and events have been streamlined. This aside, however, viewers are left with an expertly-directed and well-acted historical epic that disappoints only in its shallow perspective of the Irish/British and Irish/Irish conflicts.

Michael Collins opens in 1916 Dublin, with the infamous Easter Rising, where the better-organized British troops rout the Irish Volunteers. From there, the movie progresses rapidly through the next 2 turbulent years, tracking Collins' rise in power and popularity and De Valera's ascension to the head of Sinn Fein. Then, while De Valera is in America drumming up support for an independent Ireland, Collins' campaign of urban guerrilla warfare against the British proves to be a spectacular success. Rejecting conventional tactics, he uses an "invisible army" that strikes unexpectedly with whatever means are available. Informers are shot and England's Irish intelligence operation is brought to its knees. By late 1921, Churchill and Lloyd George are willing to talk peace, and De Valera sends Collins as the Irish representative. The resulting controversial treaty, the best Collins felt he could get at the time, fuels the drama of *Michael Collins*' final act. Because the agreement still requires that the Irish pay fealty to England's king and because it divides the country in two, De Valera rejects it, labeling it as a betrayal. Civil war ensues, and, on August 22, 1922, Collins is assassinated while in his home district of Cork.

In tone and spirit, if not in time and place, this film shares a great deal with Oscar-winning *Braveheart*. Michael Collins, like William Wallace, fought for independence, and, in the end, was its victim. Neil Jordan felt that this story was so important that he nurtured the script for 13 years until he had the clout to command the actors and budget he wanted. The ultimate result may not quite match his ambitions, but it was one of 1996's most talked-about motion pictures. **HIGHLY RECOMMENDED**

Midnight in the Garden of Good and Evil [1997]

Starring: John Cusack, Kevin Spacey, Jack Thompson, Lady Chablis, Alison Eastwood, Irma P. Hall Director: Clint Eastwood
Screenplay: John Lee Hancock based on the novel by John Berendt
Running Time: 2:35 Rated: R (Mature themes, profanity, violence)
Theatrical Aspect Ratio: 1.85:1

Clint Eastwood's *Midnight in the Garden of Good and Evil* is a compelling but meandering tale of lust, murder, sex, voodoo, and betrayal. Despite the presence of so many titillating elements, the film's nearly somnambulant pace makes it easy for a viewer to lose his or her concentration.

Midnight in the Garden is the story of New York journalist John Kelso (John Cusack), who travels to Savannah when *Town and Country* magazine hires him to write a story about the much-ballyhooed annual Christmas bash held by millionaire Jim Williams (Kevin Spacey). After a brief discussion with Jim's football-loving lawyer, Sonny Seiler (Jack Thompson), John meets Jim, who turns out to be a suave, appealing gentleman with extravagant tastes. The writer is given a brief tour of Jim's opulent house, which was built by the grandfather of songwriter Johnny Mercer. Over the course of the next twenty-four hours, as he waits for the party to begin, John meets some of the locals: a man who walks an imaginary dog, a sexy young woman named Mandy (Alison Eastwood), an attorney-turned-housesitter (Joe Odom), and the brash, cocky Billy Hanson (Jude Law), who is Jim's lover. Then, suddenly, after the party, when John is getting ready to go home, *Midnight in the Garden* turns into a murder story. Jim shoots and kills Billy under mysterious circumstances, and the question of his innocence is put before a jury. John, seeing the potential to expand his short article into a full-length book, begins his own investigation of the incident, and his detective work leads him to two more unusual citizens of Savannah: transvestite Lady Chablis (playing herself) and Minerva (Irma P. Hall), a voodoo priestess.

Midnight in the Garden demands a certain temperament to enjoy a long, unhurried experience like this. And, while the movie doesn't succeed in effectively developing all of the subplots and secondary themes in its complex tapestry, its main point — that morality is a relative, not an absolute, quantity — is presented in a striking fashion. With *Midnight in the Garden of Good and Evil*, Eastwood has captured a peculiar yet involving slice of life. **RECOMMENDED**

Mifune [Denmark/Sweden, 1999]

Starring: Iben Hjejle, Anders W. Berthelsen, Jesper Asholt, Emil Tarding, Anders Hove, Sofie Gråbøl Director: Søren Kragh-Jacobsen
Screenplay: Søren Kragh-Jacobsen, Anders Thomas Jensen Running Time: 1:38 Rated: R (Profanity, sexual situations, violence) Theatrical Aspect Ratio: 1.66:1 In Danish with subtitles

It's refreshing to see a movie in which there are no special effects, no camera tricks, and no incidental music to strum on a viewer's emotional strings. These are some (but certainly not all) of the tenets of Dogma 95, the much-ballyhooed "cinematic vow of chastity" taken by four Danish directors, one of whom, Søren Kragh-Jacobsen, is responsible for this film.

Mifune takes its title from the name of the legendary Japanese actor Toshiro Mifune, who starred in many of Akira Kurosowa's films, including the classic *The Seven Samurai*. Mifune died around the time that this movie, then simply called *Dogma 3*, was going into production. Director Kragh-Jacobson decided that he wanted to find a way to honor Mifune's memory, and so was born a storyline in which one character dresses up as a Samurai named "Mifune" in order to please his mentally retarded brother. That's how a Danish film came to be named after a Japanese icon.

Mifune opens with a wedding. Kresten (Anders W. Berthelsen) is marrying Claire (Sofie Gråbøl), a domineering woman who happens to be the daughter of Kresten's boss. The two haven't been united in marital bliss for long when Kresten receives a phone call: his father has died and he has to return home to care for his brother, Rud (Jesper Asholt), and to prepare the funeral. All of this comes as a great surprise to Claire, who didn't realize that her husband had any surviving family. She offers to accompany him, but Kresten doesn't want her meeting Rud (whom he views as an embarrassment) or seeing the seedy, run-down farm where he grew up and from which he fled. When he arrives, the place is in a mess, as is his brother. Looking for someone to help clean up as well as to babysit Rud, Kresten places a newspaper ad for a housekeeper. The only one who responds is Liva (Iben Hjejle), a young, attractive blond who is running from demons of her own. She is a prostitute who is fed up with selling her body just to keep her ungrateful brother, Bjarke (Emil Tarding), in boarding school.

Some have argued that the tenets embraced by Dogma 95 amount to little more than a marketing tool — an attempt by a group of underappreciated Danish directors to obtain wider distribution for low-budget motion pictures. And, while there may be some truth to those charges, there's no denying the artistic and entertainment value of a movie like *Mifune*. RECOMMENDED

Million Dollar Baby [2004]

Starring: Clint Eastwood, Hilary Swank, Morgan Freeman Director: Clint Eastwood Screenplay: Paul Haggis, based on stories from *Rope Burns*, by F. X. Toole Running Time: 2:17 Rated: PG-13 (Violence, mature themes) Theatrical Aspect Ratio: 2.35:1

Three strong performances highlight *Million Dollar Baby*. Clint Eastwood and Morgan Freeman are their usual, reliable selves. Each approaches the material with the practiced ease of a veteran, and the result is a pair of three-dimensional characters. But, in many ways, they're just supporting Hilary Swank. Since her Oscar-winning turn in 1999's *Boys Don't Cry*, Swank has appeared in a number of less-than-memorable films. Eastwood has drawn another great performance out of her, proving that the talent is there for a director who understands how to tap it.

Swank plays Maggie Fitzgerald, a 31-year-old woman who wants to box professionally. She approaches Frankie Dunn (Eastwood), hoping that he will train her. His response is curt: He doesn't teach girls, and even if he did, she's too old. But Maggie is relentless, and she gains an ally: Eddie Dupris (Freeman), Frankie's longtime friend and cohort. When Frankie loses his job managing a potential heavyweight contender, he finds himself at loose ends and, in a moment of sympathy, he agrees to help Maggie. Soon, under his tutelage, she finds herself on the fast track to a championship bout.

For a while, the film plays like a version of *Rocky* or *Girlfight*, with equal focus on the trainer and the trainee. There's also less glamorization of the ring activity than often occurs in boxing movies. For Maggie, winning isn't about fame and making money — it's about loyalty and earning respect. According to the voice-over monologue, "she grew up knowing one thing: She was trash." Boxing is her way to escape her past. And she remains true to her gruff coach, who spends his free time learning Gaelic and reading Yeats, and attends Mass every day. When a hotshot manager offers to take over her career and help her into the big time, she politely turns him down to remain with Frankie. One of the most impressive aspects of *Million Dollar Baby* is its scope, and the way it manages to pack so much into 2¼ hours. The story never seems rushed; Eastwood allows the characters and circumstances to breathe by including subplots featuring a mentally retarded would-be fighter (Jay Baruchel), Maggie's ungrateful and rapacious family, and Frankie's guilt-ridden past.

I deem a movie to be worthwhile if I need time to

recover after seeing it. *Million Dollar Baby* is such a film. It does not easily release the viewer, and it demands a time of reflection and contemplation afterward. It is a rich and challenging motion picture that both affirms life and emphasizes its fragility. Eastwood touches our hearts and energizes our minds without resorting to overt manipulation. *Million Dollar Baby* is refreshingly free of the kind of tear-wringing melodrama that has become seemingly obligatory for this kind of story. You don't have to be a boxing fan to appreciate what Eastwood has wrought. This is a movie with the ability to win over all comers. HIGHLY RECOMMENDED

Mona Lisa [United Kingdom, 1986]

Starring: Bob Hoskins, Cathy Tyson, Michael Caine, Robbie Coltrane, Sammi Davis Director: Neil Jordan Screenplay: Neil Jordan, David Leland Running Time: 1:44 Rated: R (Sexual themes, violence, profanity, nudity) Theatrical Aspect Ratio: 1.85:1

Although Cathy Tyson's character, the prostitute Simone, is the representation of the Mona Lisa in Neil Jordan's *Mona Lisa*, the central character is an everyman named George, played by Bob Hoskins. It is George's obsession for Simone that validates the title. For him, she is the Mona Lisa — beautiful, mysterious, and unattainable. From his limited contact with her, and based on the stories she tells him (some true, some not), he concocts an image of the woman he wants her to be. In the end, when he discovers that the reality is nothing like his fantasy, he is stunned and hurt.

Jordan has skillfully developed this story not only to examine George's fascination for Simone, but to dissect their relationship. Although Simone does not return George's feelings, she is attuned to them, and uses them to her own ends. But she does not think harshly of George. He is kind towards her, and she appreciates that. Both of them need each other, albeit in different ways, so, in a sense, the relationship is mutually beneficial. But, in the end, once Simone has gotten what she wants, George realizes that he can never have what he hoped for.

The story takes place in the seedier parts of London. George has just been released from a lengthy term in prison. His first stop is to visit his old home. Initially, his daughter doesn't seem to recognize him, but his ex-wife does, and she throws him out. At that point, an old friend of George's, Tommy (Robbie Coltrane), shows up and offers his mate a place to sleep. On the way back to Tommy's, George stops in

at a bar to find Mortwell (Michael Caine). It seems that his prison term was in some way connected to this man, and he feels that he is owed something. Mortwell's henchman gives George work as the driver for Simone (Cathy Tyson), a local prostitute.

The initial meeting between George and Simone is not promising. By virtue of her profession, George sees her as somewhere below him on the social scale, and is contemptuous of being ordered around by her. His coarse manner irritates Simone, and his careless approach to dressing offends her sensibilities (for her, a high priced call girl, clothes are everything). But Simone immediately recognizes something in George that can satisfy a need she has, and she sets about trying to win his confidence, first by buying him expensive suits, and then by telling him her life's story. George responds as she knows he will — by offering to help her. He soon learns that Simone is in trouble. An ex-pimp is anxious to cut her face, and Mortwell is somehow involved.

In an era when movies about love almost always invariably devolve into formulaic affairs, Neil Jordan's *Mona Lisa* stands out as an often-surprising, multi-layered achievement. By offering a rumination on a wide variety of love — real, imagined, romantic, sexual, and platonic — *Mona Lisa* defies easy categorization and offers a complex and superior 100 minutes for all who view it. MUST SEE

Monsoon Wedding [India/United States/Italy/France, 2001]

Starring: Naseeruddin Shah, Lillete Dubey, Shefali Shetty, Vijay Raaz, Tilotama Shom Director: Mira Nair Screenplay: Sabrina Dhawan Running Time: 1:54 Rated: R (Mature themes, profanity) Theatrical Aspect Ratio: 1.85:1

Monsoon Wedding, an infectious celebration of life and love, is an effort from Indian director Mira Nair (*Salaam Bombay!, Mississippi Masala, Kama Sutra*). Throwing caution to the wind with an invitation to the hedonist in us all, Nair has constructed this motion picture in such a way that even the most cynical curmudgeon with find himself or herself smiling at one time or another.

The primary story concerns the impending nuptials of Aditi (Vasundhara Das) and Hemant (Parvin Dabas), a couple who are getting to know one another after agreeing to participate in an arranged marriage. Aditi is a lively young woman who is trying to conclude a dead-end relationship with her boss. Hemant is an engineer who lives in Houston, Texas and is interested in finding a bride who shares his roots and heritage. As Aditi and Hemant are forging a fragile bond, Aditi's boss predatorily moves back into the picture and threatens both the marriage and Aditi's future happiness.

Complementing Aditi's story are a pair of other tales — one dark and one light. The wedding coordinator, Dubey (Vijay Raaz), suddenly and unexpectedly falls for the shy and insecure Alice (Tilotama Shome), Aditi's maid. Their gentle, tentative courtship is presented with a mixture of humor and tenderness. Meanwhile, Aditi's cousin, Ria (Shefali Shetty), reveals a malignant secret she has kept for nearly 2 decades about how she was sexually abused as a child by a family member who may be attempting to repeat the offense with another young girl.

Most of *Monsoon Wedding* is frothy and enjoyable, with the lush, varied music of Mychael Danna heightening the delicious sense of celebration. (Nair's film borrows from the Bollywood tradition of incorporating vivid musical numbers into the main story.) Visually, the film also tantalizes the senses, with nearly every scene offering a riot of color. Ria's story provides the dramatic glue that keeps the film grounded — the theme of sexual abuse is treated sensitively, but nothing can hold this irrepressible motion picture down for long.

The actors all do fine jobs, especially lovely Vasundhara Das as Aditi. But the real star of this movie is its director, who, in cooperation with screenwriter Sabrina Dhawan, has crafted the kind of motion picture that represents 2 hours of pure, unfettered joy. Typically, movies that offer this much fun do so because they are mindless and inconsequential. Nothing could be further from the truth where *Monsoon Wedding* is concerned. This film manages to be delightful without insulting the characters or the audience. RECOMMENDED

Monster [2003]

Starring: Charlize Theron, Christina Ricci, Bruce Dern Director: Patty Jenkins Screenplay: Steven Bernstein Running Time: 1:45 Rated: R (Violence, sex, nudity, profanity) Theatrical Aspect Ratio: 1.85:1

An understanding of how society uses — and, more importantly, misuses — the term "monster" offers crucial insight into the intentions of first-time filmmaker Patty Jenkins. Without offering justifications or excuses, Jenkins seeks to provide some understanding of the underlying motivation of serial killer Aileen Wuornos, a prostitute who murdered seven

men during 1989. She was subsequently tried, found guilty, and executed in 2002. By exploring details primarily from Wuornos's viewpoint, *Monster* eschews the easy path of transforming her into a one-dimensional psycho. Instead, without diminishing the horror of her actions, the picture humanizes Wuornos, developing a three-dimensional character where one might not normally expect to find one.

Aside from the movie's unique approach to a story involving a serial killer (no one will think of it as a slasher film), there is another persuasive reason to see *Monster*. It displays one of the most impressive examples of acting by a woman in the last ten years. The process that transforms the glamorous Charlize Theron into the haggard, homely Wuornos is nothing short of astounding. In addition to gaining 25 pounds and letting her well-toned body sag in some unflattering areas, she perfectly adapts the attitude and mannerisms of a white trash prostitute. Theron's presence and physical appearance have been overwritten by Wuornos's.

The movie introduces us to Aileen Wuornos before she kills anyone. She already has a gun, but plans to take only one life — her own. Before committing suicide, however, she wants a drink, and fate leads her into a gay bar, where she encounters Selby (Christina Ricci), a painfully shy lesbian who is looking for a friend. Improbably, Aileen and Selby form a bond. For Aileen, who is craving some form of affection to give meaning to a barren life, Selby is her salvation. But, as is often the case when it comes to mad love, the brief burst of redemption gives way to a clinging codependency. After the first murder, Selby becomes Aileen's enabler — initially unknowing, then with a gradual recognition (and perhaps perverse enjoyment) of her power. What we initially mistake for love turns into something dark and unhealthy.

Jenkins presents the murders in a straightforward manner. Although we understand Aileen's reasoning, we neither sympathize nor empathize with her. *Monster* asks for a measure of comprehension, not identification. It wants us to understand what led Aileen to kill and kill again, not to absolve her of the responsibility for her crimes. And it demands that we consider what role (if any) society may have played in the murders. That approach, more than any other, defuses charges of exploitation and moral indifference, marking this as a compelling, thought-provoking, and unsettling drama. RECOMMENDED

Monster's Ball [2001]

Starring: Billy Bob Thornton, Halle Berry, Peter Boyle, Heath Ledger, Sean Combs, Coronji Calhoun Director: Marc Forster Screenplay: Milo Addica & Will Rokos Running Time: 1:51 Rated: R (Sex, nudity, profanity) Theatrical Aspect Ratio: 2.35:1

Monster's Ball is a powerful and poignant motion picture not about racism and redemption, as one might initially suppose, but about one of the most urgent and universal of human needs — that of finding solace for pain and loneliness. Though it has some of the trappings of an interracial romance, *Monster's Ball* is not that, either. The sex in this movie is not a precursor to love; it is a means by which two people can find temporary refuge from their otherwise bleak existences. An orgasm is an effective way to wipe away everything else, if only for a few moments.

Coincidence forms the fulcrum of *Monster's Ball's* storyline. The principle male character is Hank Grotowski (Billy Bob Thornton), a corrections officer who is greatly respected at work, but whose home life is a disaster. It's hard to say whether he has a worse relationship with his surly, racist father (Peter Boyle) or his soft-hearted son (Heath Ledger). Hank is charged with supervising the execution of death-row inmate Lawrence Musgrove (Sean Combs), a cop killer who has exhausted 11 years' worth of appeals. Lawrence has a son, Tyrell (Coronji Calhoun), who idolizes him, and a wife, Leticia (Halle Berry), who can't stand him. Following the execution, both Hank and Leticia suffer shocking, unexpected tragedies, and, in the wake of one of these, they are thrown together. And, because they happen to be there, they turn to each other.

This is a brave movie requiring courageous performances. With this role, Halle Berry sheds years of lightweight baggage and a deserved Oscar win. Billy Bob Thornton matches her intensity pace-for-pace. These two radiate neediness and anguish. We can see their inner torment mirrored in their eyes and faces. The hand of Job is upon them both.

Hank is, in many ways, an ugly individual. He is a racist who has inherited his feelings from his father. As the film wears on, his tolerance for blacks grows. This is not the result of some sudden enlightenment, but because the passion necessary to sustain prejudice has drained out of him. Leticia, too, is no angel, either. She abuses her son, both verbally and physically, because he eats too much. She has trouble keeping her job and is on the verge of being evicted from her home.

This is the second feature from director Marc Forster, whose debut, *Everything Put Together,* was never widely seen outside of the film festival circuit. Thus, *Monster's Ball* has become Forster's calling card, and it makes a bold statement. **HIGHLY RECOMMENDED**

The Motorcycle Diaries [United States/United Kingdom/Argentina/Germany, 2004]

Starring: Gael Garcia Bernal, Rodrigo De la Serna, Mia Maestro, Jorge Chiarella Director: Walter Salles Screenplay: Jose Rivera, based on books by Ernesto Guevara and Alberto Granado Running Time: 2:08 Rated: R (Profanity) Theatrical Aspect Ratio: 1.85:1 In Spanish with subtitles

Before he became the leader of the Cuban Revolution, Che Guevara (Gael Garcia Bernal) was an introverted medical student living a sheltered life in Buenos Aires. His life changed in 1952, when, despite almost being done with his degree, he decided to take a break from his studies and join his friend, Alberto Granado (Rodrigo De la Serna), on a trip through South America. Their journey, begun on an old motorcycle and completed on foot, by hitchhiking, and on a raft, took more than seven months and covered 7,500 miles. By the time it concluded in Caracas, Guevara was not the same man who had started on the odyssey. *The Motorcycle Diaries,* which is based on Guevara's journals and a book written by Granado, is the story of that trek.

Brazilian director Walter Salles (*Central Station*) avoids the easy path of politicizing Guevara's life and turning him into a symbol or an icon. As portrayed by Gael Garcia Bernal, he is an ordinary 23-year-old whose exposure to the realities of poverty and disease causes a monumental spiritual upheaval. The transformation is presented slowly and subtly and, although it is pretty much complete by the time the end credits roll, only those who are aware of Guevara's role in history will understand what comes next.

Throughout *The Motorcycle Diaries,* Salles uses the beauty of the countryside as a counterpoint to the ugliness of human conditions. In making the film, Salles took his cast and crew along the exact route described by Guevara and Granado in their accounts. In many ways, this is the ultimate in on-location filming, and it functions almost as effectively as a travelogue as a drama. Plus, to keep things from becoming too somber, Salles interjects occasional moments of humor, such as when Guevara fails to recognize mambo music and starts dancing the tango.

The way Salles has chosen to present the material establishes *The Motorcycle Diaries* as more of a character drama and an offbeat road adventure than a bio-pic. If you aren't aware that it's a true story, you probably won't make the connection. In the end, *The Motorcycle Diaries* tells a very personal tale with a central theme we can all relate to: the loss of innocence. And therein lies the universality of Salles's film, and the reason why you don't have to share Guevara's politics to appreciate this telling of a key chapter from his life. RECOMMENDED

Mr. Holland's Opus [1995]

Starring: Richard Dreyfuss, Glenne Headly, Olympia Dukakis, W.H. Macy, Jay Thomas, Alicia Witt, Jean Louisa Kelly Director: Stephen Herek Screenplay: Patrick Duncan Running Time: 2:22 Rated: PG (Mild language) Theatrical Aspect Ratio: 2.35:1

Mr. Holland's Opus, a Capra-esque motion picture in its sentimentality, persuades its audience that no life spent in a worthy pursuit is ever wasted. However it doesn't stoop to heavy-handed proselytizing.

Mr. Holland's Opus spans 31 years in the life of a high school music teacher. When Glenn Holland (Richard Dreyfuss) first comes to the newly-dedicated JFK High School in 1964, he has a dream of spending a few years teaching to accumulate a nest egg, then returning to his true passion: composing. His loving wife, Iris (Glenne Headly) is completely supportive — until she becomes pregnant. After that unexpected event, teaching is no longer just Glenn's "fall back position." It has become his means to provide for his family.

Yet Glenn finds that instructing students in music appreciation has its rewards. When lectures and text assignments don't fire his pupils' passion for the subject, Glenn tries unique ways of encouraging an understanding that "playing music is supposed to be fun — it's about heart . . . not notes on a page." Repeatedly during his 3 decades of teaching, Glenn chooses boys and girls with special skills to nurture and encourage. In the process, he creates a deep loyalty among JFK's student body while straining the harmony of his home life. His wife and son wonder if Glenn cares more about his pupils than about them.

The musical metaphors in *Mr. Holland's Opus* are rather obvious, and the soundtrack is an effective mix of pop tunes, classical compositions, and Michael Kamen's score.

In recent years, it has become common practice for movie studios to release at least one emotionally stirring drama around the holiday season. Flaws aside, one common element in these films is that each focuses on the triumph of the human spirit, using a story that seeks to touch the heart. *Mr. Holland's Opus* deserves a place in their ranks. It's a symphony of solid storytelling and good feeling that pays tribute to Hollywood's rarely-seen, gentler side. HIGHLY RECOMMENDED

Mrs. Brown [United Kingdom, 1997]

Starring: Judi Dench, Billy Connolly, Geoffrey Palmer, Richard Pasco, Anthony Sher Director: John Madden Screenplay: Jeremy Brock Running Time: 1:43 Rated: PG (Mature themes, violence) Theatrical Aspect Ratio: 1.85:1

Mrs. Brown is a love story much in the same vein as *Carrington* in that it deals with platonic affection that runs deeper and truer than that of the motion picture staple romantic variety. These days, it seems that whenever we see a male/female friendship on screen, it's just a setup for the inevitable moment when the two realize that they're fated to be lovers. Not so with *Mrs. Brown.* It shows, amongst other things, that it's possible to love completely and with unflagging devotion without sex ever becoming an issue.

Queen Victoria was born on May 24, 1819 and died nearly 82 years later, in the first month of 1901. Her reign as England's monarch, which began in 1837, lasted more than 6 decades and left such an indelible impression upon the country that, upon hearing of her death, author Henry James wrote, "We all feel a bit motherless today." *Mrs. Brown,* which is based on actual events and uses historical figures, transpires during one of the darkest periods of Victoria's reign — a 4-year segment from 1864 to 1868 (with a brief epilogue in 1883). Still mourning the death of her beloved husband, Prince Albert, who died over 2 years earlier, the Queen (Judi Dench) is in virtual seclusion at Windsor. She sees no one outside of her servants and her immediate family, rarely goes out, and has no taste for politics. In the words of her loyal secretary, Henry Posonby (Geoffrey Palmer), they are all "prisoners of the queen's grief." So, in an attempt to revive Victoria, Posonby summons John Brown (Billy Connolly), the highlander who runs the queen's Scottish retreat of Balmoral, to Windsor. It's Posonby's hope that Brown will "appeal to the queen's sentimental belief that all highlanders are good for the health."

Brown arrives and proves to be a breath of fresh air. Before he enters Windsor, the castle is a place of icy silence and solitude. Director John Madden so effectively conveys this atmosphere that we become keenly aware of such things as a ticking clock and a cleared throat. Brown's attitude of speaking what he thinks, regardless of the consequences, horrifies the servants and family. But, after initially being annoyed, Victoria warms to his methods, and it isn't long before the two develop a unshakable friendship. They become so close, in fact, that wags begin calling the Queen "Mrs. Brown." The Prince of Wales, wary of Brown's growing influence over his mother, seeks to have the highlander sent back to Scotland. And the Prime Minister, Disraeli, wonders whether Brown is more likely to be a valuable ally or a dangerous enemy.

Perhaps the best thing of all about *Mrs. Brown* is that it doesn't offer any hokey, Hollywood-type moments. *Mrs. Brown* is a fascinating character study, a wonderful love story, and a brilliant period piece that will delight and touch any viewer who seeks it out.

HIGHLY RECOMMENDED

Mrs. Dalloway [United Kingdom, 1997]

Starring: Vanessa Redgrave, Natascha McElhone, Rupert Graves, Michael Kitchen, John Standing Director: Marleen Gorris
Screenplay: Eileen Atkins based on the novel by Virginia Woolf
Running Time: 1:37 Rated: PG-13 (Mature themes, brief nudity)
Theatrical Aspect Ratio: 1.85:1

In 1996, director Marleen Gorris, who hails from the Netherlands, entered the international spotlight when her 1995 feature, *Antonia's Line*, won the Best Foreign Film Oscar. Two years later, Gorris' follow-up to that much-lauded effort arrived in the form of *Mrs. Dalloway*, an adaptation of Virginia Woolf's classic novel. Because of its strong leading character and female-oriented themes, it's easy to understand why the film held such appeal for an avowed feminist like Gorris. In conjunction with Vanessa Redgrave, the director paints a probing-but-flawed portrait of a thoughtful woman.

Mrs. Dalloway is a "day in the life" motion picture that uses flashbacks to broaden the time span from a single day in June 1923 to a lifetime. The film begins by introducing viewers to Clarissa Dalloway, the upper class wife of Richard Dalloway (John Standing), a wealthy Member of Parliament. Clarissa, who lives a life that is safe, isolated, and dull, is planning a gala party for the evening. Clarissa is well-known for her parties, and they have become social events in London society. Then something happens to shatter the stillness of Mrs. Dalloway's life — a man named Peter Walsh (Michael Kitchen), an old flame from 30 years ago, shows up on her doorstep. This leads Clarissa to think back to the choices she made during the summer of 1890, and how they shaped the rest of her life.

Juxtaposed with Mrs. Dalloway's story is that of a young, shell-shocked soldier, Septimus Warren-Smith (Rupert Graves), who has never recovered from his experiences in World War I. This material, although thematically relevant to the main plot, causes unwanted interruptions in the narrative that threaten to derail the picture. Graves plays the part effectively, and the story of the young man's loss of identity is tragic, but I found the Warren-Smith scenes to be more of a distraction than a crucial subplot.

Not surprisingly, the acting is top-notch. Redgrave shines, whether she's gazing back through the mists of the past or, in the film's best sequence, making pithy asides to expose the true nature of the guests at her party. Michael Kitchen and John Standing are solid as the two men who were once rivals for Clarissa's affections, and who have changed very little over time. In flashbacks, Natascha McElhone (*Surviving Picasso*) brings a sparkle to the young Clarissa, and Alan Cox cuts a dashing figure as Peter. The 1890 scenes also feature Lena Headley as Clarissa's best friend, and there are hints of a subtle lesbian attraction.

Mrs. Dalloway will probably appeal most strongly to those who appreciate Merchant-Ivory's unhurried pace. The story, which is more of a character study than a plot-oriented narrative, moves slowly and deliberately, giving us a crystal-clear picture of the many faces of Clarissa Dalloway — who she was, who she might have been, and who she has become.

RECOMMENDED

Mrs. Parker and the Vicious Circle [1994]

Starring: Jennifer Jason Leigh, Campbell Scott, Matthew Broderick, Gwyneth Paltrow Director: Alan Rudolph Screenplay: Alan Rudolph and Randy Sue Coburn Running Time: 2:04 Rated: R (Sex, nudity, language, mature themes) Theatrical Aspect Ratio: 2.35:1

Mrs. Parker and the Vicious Circle is set primarily against the backdrop of the roaring '20s, with critic/poet/writer Dorothy Parker (Jennifer Jason Leigh) as the centerpiece. Parker was by far the best known female member of the famed Algonquin Round Table — a collection of journalists, actors, writers, and other artists who gathered daily for lunch at a 44th Street Manhattan hotel. Also included in the membership of this exclusive circle were Robert Benchley (Campbell Scott), Harold Ross (Sam Robards), and Charles MacArthur (Matthew Broderick). Among their successes, the Algonquin clique could claim Pulitzer Prizes, Oscars, successful stage shows, and bestselling books. To the outside world, they were celebrities; to some on the inside, they were "just a bunch of loudmouths showing off."

Dorothy Parker is perhaps best remembered for her tart sayings and pithy turns of phrase, and that's the tone that this movie initially adopts — playful and clipped. However, as the screenplay delves beneath the surface of its lead character's personality, a grim, more serious mood becomes pervasive, turning Dorothy's witticisms into self-contemptuous jabs or cries for help.

Arguments can be made about the historical accuracy of the film. Many of the events related herein are based on Parker's own statements, and she was notorious for exaggerating — if not outright lying — about her past. Regardless of how faithfully it records its title character's life, however, *Mrs. Parker and the Vicious Circle* is a top-notch movie. Everything is in place — a striking lead performance from Jennifer Jason Leigh, solid supporting players, a well-written script, and, above all, expert direction to merge the ingredients. In a case like this, "truth" may not be the most important factor to consider in the overall evaluation. **HIGHLY RECOMMENDED**

Murder in the First [1995]

Starring: Christian Slater, Kevin Bacon, Gary Oldman, R. Lee Ermey, Embeth Davidtz Director: Marc Rocco Screenplay: Dan Gordon Running Time: 2:01 Rated: R (Violence, torture, mature themes, language) Theatrical Aspect Ratio: Not Given

Murder in the First is another example of a movie that strays from historical reality to create a more dramatically-appealing product. And, regardless of how this version raises the hackles of Alcatraz aficionados, Marc Rocco's movie is a solid and affecting example of film making.

It's March 25, 1938, and an escape attempt from the maximum security federal penitentiary at Alcatraz has failed. Two of the 4 escapees are dead, a third — the informant — is returned to his cell, and the fourth — a 25-year-old named Henri Young (Kevin Bacon) — is placed into a dark, grimy cubicle deep beneath the ground. There, for 3 interminable years, his only respite from loneliness are the frequent visits of guards and Associate Warden Glenn (Gary Oldman), and the beatings they administer.

When his long stint in solitary confinement ends and Young is re-integrated into normal prison society, revenge consumes him — a need to lash out against the man who blew the whistle on the escape. This he does, driving a spoon through the victim's throat, tearing away his life. With no regard for the barbaric treatment which turned a petty thief into a killer, the government tries Young for first-degree murder — a crime that carries a death sentence. Assigned to defend him is an up-and-coming member of the public defender's office named James Stamphill (Christian Slater), perhaps the only man to believe in his client's innocence.

Murder in the First is as much an indictment of the penal system as an account of one man's fight against a first degree murder rap, and that's where the picture's strength lies. The events leading to Young's actions are graphically rendered, and little doubt remains about where the responsibility lies. The questions that arise are whether Stamphill can prove it and, in the process, how much of his personal security he's willing to sacrifice.

Unlike *The Shawshank Redemption,* this movie isn't about triumph behind prison bars. Instead, *Murder in the First* is an unrelenting look at the dehumanizing effects of prison life, and what can happen when power is abused. Some scenes may be too graphic for audience members to view comfortably, but "comfort" isn't on director Rocco's agenda. Little that occurs towards the end to affect a false sense of dramatic closure reduces the power of bearing witness to the exposure of Henri Young's soul — or what's left after Glenn and Alcatraz have finished with it. **RECOMMENDED**

My Family [1995]

Starring: Jimmy Smits, Eduardo Lopez Rojas, Jenny Gago, Edward James Olmos, Esai Morales Director: Gregory Nava Screenplay: Gregory Nava and Anna Thomas Running Time: 2:07 Rated: R (Violence, profanity, sex, nudity) Theatrical Aspect Ratio: 1.85:1 In English with Spanish subtitles

My Family, a portrait of a Mexican-American family living in East Los Angeles, boasts a series of distinguished thematic antecedents, including Francis Ford Coppola's *The Godfather* and Zhang Yimou's *To Live.* Here, as in the 1972 gangster saga, the significance of family is a central issue, although each movie chooses to explore this differently.

My Family opens in 1926 Mexico, as Jose Sanchez heads north to California to find a long-lost relative.

Once there, he meets and marries Maria, who bears him a son and daughter. She is pregnant with their third child when immigration officials illegally deport her. The rest of this segment concentrates on her attempts to return to her husband and family.

The 1958 and 1980s episodes present the fortunes of two of the Sanchez children: Chucho (Esai Morales) and Jimmy (Jimmy Smits). Chucho is a brash youth who leads a gang, incurs the wrath of his father when he sells marijuana, and is constantly skirting trouble with the police. Jimmy idolizes his older brother and eventually follows in his footsteps, but the underlying pain of one shared, tragic moment haunts Jimmy's future. It is only during a watershed scene, when the anger and grief are released, that Jimmy is able to agree that "tomorrow matters."

My Family is amazingly rich, with themes that are topical-yet-timeless, a solidly constructed story to give them vitality, and superlative production values. Cinematographer Edward Lachman has photographed all three eras differently, and his visual flair adds another layer to this production. *My Family* gives us culture shock and class distinctions, metaphors involving owls and bridges, and the struggle between traditional values and modern ethics. It never dwells on gang violence, crime, or racism; but ignores none of these three. Above all, however, it is faithful to its title, presenting the newest portrait of an ancient truth — of all the ties that bind humans to each other, none is more lasting than that of birth and blood. **HIGHLY RECOMMENDED**

My Life So Far [United Kingdom, 1999]

Starring: Robbie Norman, Colin Firth, Rosemary Harris, Irène Jacob, Tchéky Karyo, Mary Elizabeth Mastrantonio, Malcolm McDowell Director: Hugh Hudson Screenplay: Simon Donald, based on *Son of Adam* by Sir Denis Forman Running Time: 1:33 Rated: PG-13 (Mature themes, brief nudity, animal sex) Theatrical Aspect Ratio: 1.85:1

My Life So Far is a pleasantly nostalgic look at a few transformative months in the life of a 10-year-old Scottish boy. *My Life So Far* provides 90 minutes of solid entertainment that runs the gamut from outright hilarity to melodrama. The film doesn't offer many surprises or deep insights into human nature, but it possesses an easygoing charm and likability that overcomes such potential deficiencies.

The place is Argyll, Scotland. The time is the late-1920s, a "safe" era in Europe when the horrors of the Great War are receding into the past and Hitler's proclamations are not yet shaking the firmament. Fraser Pettigrew (Robbie Norman) is an average child growing up in a somewhat abnormal household. He lives with his family on the estate of Kiloran, a vast, sprawling piece of the countryside that houses The Pettigrew Sphagnum Moss Factory. Fraser's father, Edward (Colin Firth), is an unsuccessful inventor with two passions: Beethoven and the Bible. He has a deep and abiding love for his children, and shares a special bond with Fraser. Also living in Kiloran Castle are Edward's wife, Moira (Mary Elizabeth Mastrantonio), and his mother-in-law, Gamma Macintosh (Rosemary Harris), who owns the land. Moira's brother, Morris (Malcolm McDowell), is a frequent visitor. His relationship with Edward is stormy but he gets along well with his nephews. The catalyst for change is the arrival of Morris' finacée, a French cellist named Heloise (Irène Jacob), who is half her intended husband's age. Fraser develops a childlike crush on the beautiful, soft-spoken woman, but Edward's infatuation is of a more adult, and potentially damaging, nature.

During the course of *My Life So Far*, Fraser learns truths about hypocrisy, death, and sex. He spends quite a bit of time in an attic, looking at pictures of naked women and reading through an "Encyclopedia of Ethics" that elaborates subjects he doesn't always understand. His incomplete comprehension of the activities performed by a prostitute leads to an uproarious scene that is as funny as anything this side of *American Pie*. Fraser also enjoys bath time, because it gives him an opportunity to peek down the dress of the maid who bathes him, an experience he describes as being "better than looking at the pictures."

My Life So Far features many beautiful shots of the Scottish countryside as it tells the story of a group of generally well-detailed characters traipsing through a series of anecdotes. The film doesn't so much unravel a traditional narrative as it allows us to roam around for a short while in a different time and place. The difference between success and failure for a picture of this sort is whether the filmmakers engage the audience's attention and sympathy, and provoke an emotional response. With *My Life So Far*, Hudson's ability to meet those criteria makes this a rewarding movie-going experience. **RECOMMENDED**

My Name Is Joe [United Kingdom, 1998]

Starring: Peter Mullan, Louise Goodall, David McKay, Anne-Marie Kennedy, David Hayman, Gary Lewis Director: Ken Loach Screenplay: Paul Laverty Running Time: 1:45 Rated: R (Extreme profanity, drug use, brief nudity) Theatrical Aspect Ratio: 1.85:1

Movie-goers attend Ken Loach movies for a variety of reasons, but one of them is not to have a "feel good" experience. The reason? Loach consistently looks at believable characters in realistic situations. His pictures are not escapist; they're frequently grim and sometimes downright depressing. They're about the trials and tribulations of those who engage in back-breaking labor on a daily basis trying to scrape enough together to put bread on the table. They're about men and women trapped by poverty and a social system that doesn't care whether they live or die. And they're about the sometimes-tragic consequences of the actions some people take in a vain attempt to liberate themselves from their circumstances. (A few titles: *Riff-Raff, Raining Stones, Ladybird Ladybird,* and *Land and Freedom.*)

My Name Is Joe is perhaps in some way Ken Loach's most accessible film. As the title suggests, the name of the main character is Joe — Joe Kavanagh, to be precise. Joe is a recovering alcoholic who has been on the wagon for 10 months. A believer in the 12-step program, he attends AA meetings regularly where he speaks his mantra: "My name is Joe and I'm an alcoholic." Actor Peter Mullan, who plays Joe, gives a tremendously natural, Oscar-caliber performance. His Joe is a boisterous, likable fellow — the kind of guy we all wish could be our neighbor.

Joe is the coach of a perennially inept soccer team, and, although he acts as a father-figure to all of the young men, he has taken a special interest in Liam (David McKay), a former drug dealer who is trying to walk the straight-and-narrow. Liam has a heroin-addicted wife, Sabine (Anne-Marie Kennedy), and a 4-year-old son, and his financial situation is hopeless. Sabine's habit has put him deep in debt to a local mobster, McGowan (David Hayman), and, if he can't pay, he has two choices: let McGowan pimp Sabine or get both of his legs broken. Meanwhile, Joe has become involved with Liam and Sabine's health visitor, Sarah (Louise Goodall). Although she resists his initial advances, Joe's reckless charm eventually wins her over, but dark times loom ahead.

Although addiction is a key element of *My Name Is Joe,* the movie is not as much about substance abuse as it is about accepting the consequences of one's actions. The greatest strength of *My Name Is Joe* is the sense of stark reality. The humor and tragedy are presented without a whiff of melodrama, and the movie will leave almost any viewer with a sense of disquiet. If the definition of a great film is a picture with two memorable scenes and no bad ones, then *My Name Is Joe* unquestionably makes the cut. **HIGHLY RECOMMENDED**

The Myth of Fingerprints [1996]

Starring: Noah Wyle, Julianne Moore, Roy Scheider, Blythe Danner, Michael Vartan, Laurel Holloman, Hope Davis Director: Bart Freundlich Screenplay: Bart Freundlich Running Time: 1:33 Rated: R (Sex, profanity, mature themes) Theatrical Aspect Ratio: 1.85:1

With *The Myth of Fingerprints,* writer/director Bart Freundlich has scored a coup: he has created a low-key holiday drama that's refreshing not only because it lacks the big discovery melodrama of most similar movies but because it's entirely believable.

The Myth of Fingerprints begins with the familiar process of the family re-assembling at Mom and Dad's New England house during Thanksgiving week. The only one who still lives with her parents (who are ably portrayed by Roy Scheider and Blythe Danner) is Leigh (Laurel Holloman), the sprightly youngest child who has a boundless well of enthusiasm and good cheer. The same cannot be said of most of the returning children. There's Warren (Noah Wyle) who hasn't been home in 3 years since breaking up with his high-school sweetheart (Arija Bareikis). The perpetually-cranky Mia (Julianne Moore) arrives with her latest significant other, therapist Elliot (Brian Kerwin), in tow. Their relationship is clearly on the rocks, and Mia's fascination with an old grade school pal (James LeGros) doesn't help matters. Jake (Michael Vartan) shows up with his flighty girlfriend, Margaret (Hope Davis), who amuses Jake's Mom by insisting that she and her boyfriend share the same bed.

At its best, *The Myth of Fingerprints* is a sensitive, intelligent examination of the dynamics of a dysfunctional family (note: families in movies like this must always be dysfunctional, otherwise there wouldn't be much of a story). At its worst, which isn't often, Freundlich's feature debut runs into difficulties with cliches: the overbearing father who has left his "fingerprints" on the lives of each of his offspring, the search by various couples to rekindle the old flame, etc.

The Myth of Fingerprints contains a number of noteworthy scenes, including some strangely quiet dinners and awkward moments between estranged siblings. But the best sequence occurs early in the film, on the night when everyone has finally assembled under one roof. One-by-one, the various couples begin to make love, and the concert of moans, thumps, and squeaks creates an atmosphere that is both poignant and funny, especially as we observe Warren's reaction to all the noise around him.

Nothing much happens during *The Myth of Fingerprints,* but that's the point. For 90 minutes, Freundlich opens a window into the lives of a few characters, and our perspective is so clear that we feel we get to know them. So, although the material is not especially challenging, the results are among the best for an American film of this genre. For those who appreciate this sort of simple drama, *The Myth of Fingerprints* is worth a trip to the theater. **RECOMMENDED**

Naked [United Kingdom, 1993]
Starring: David Thewlis, Lesley Sharp, Katrin Cartlidge, Greg Cruttwell, Claire Skinner, Peter Wight Director: Mike Leigh Screenplay: Mike Leigh Running Time: 2:12 Rated: No MPAA Rating (Violence, sexual violence, language, sex, nudity) Theatrical Aspect Ratio: 1.66:1

Mike Leigh has always been known as a creator of exceptional, insightful character studies. Often, his films do little more than trace activities in the life of a person or persons over a several-day period. However, whereas comedies such as *Life is Sweet* and *High Hopes* showed Leigh's whimsical side, *Naked* is anything but charming. This movie is brutal and raw, and its sense of humor comes with a serrated edge.

We meet Johnny (David Thewlis) on the benighted streets of Manchester, pinning a woman against a building as he rapes her. Then, threatened with bodily harm, Johnny heads for London to find his old girlfriend, Louise (Lesley Sharp). Their reunion is less-than-affectionate, and propels Johnny into a violent and self-destructive sexual relationship with Louise's flatmate, Sophie (Katrin Cartlidge). Not long after, Johnny starts to feel trapped by his new lover's unexpected dependence, and he takes to the streets, wandering through the backways and alleys of the city's underprivileged districts (where a rat is always less than 30 feet away), meeting an assortment of people even more bizarre than himself.

There are so many thought-provoking themes and issues addressed by *Naked* that it's impossible to mention them all, let alone do them justice, in the space of a movie review. Johnny, despite having the appearance of a tramp, has the heart and mind of a philosopher, and isn't afraid to express his views. In line after line of energetic, dazzling dialogue delivered at a rapid-fire pace, we are exposed to the lead character's views on why everyone is bored, the importance of cliches, the interrelationship between the past, present, and future, the Apocalypse, evolution, God's relationship to man, and life in general.

He's not particularly choosey about his listeners, entering into conversations with the vacuous Sophie, a middle-class guard named Brian (Peter Wight), a lonely woman who he initially observes from afar through a window, and a man putting up posters.

David Thewlis didn't get his deserved Oscar nomination, but his work here is extraordinary, and possibly better than that of any of the 5 nominees (including Anthony Hopkins). Thewlis creates an amazing character — someone with a keen intellect and ugly appetites, who can be reviled, understood, and respected.

Naked is one of those rare motion pictures that refuses to slip easily from memory. Its images and themes linger long after the viewer has left the theater. Those in search of escapism should not look to this motion picture, but anyone willing to assume the risk of facing the ugliness of Johnny's world will find a startling, gut-wrenching, eye-opening experience. **HIGHLY RECOMMENDED**

The Navigators [United Kingdom, 2001]
Starring: Dean Andrews, Tom Craig, Joe Duttine, Steve Huison, Venn Tracey, Andy Swallow, Sean Glenn, Charlie Brown Director: Ken Loach Screenplay: Rob Dawber Running Time: 1:32 Rated: R (Profanity, sexual situations) Theatrical Aspect Ratio: 1.85:1

Ken Loach's *The Navigators* is a hard-as-nails drama that, instead of offering viewers an escape from reality, forces them to face some of the colder facts about living in today's world. Loach's subject isn't terrorism, but something equally destructive and far more insidious: the way big businesses routinely discard faithful employees, rewarding long-term loyalty with a few weeks' severance pay and a cheerful good-bye. This is the kind of subject matter that will strike home painfully for many men and women in today's workforce. And, while Loach includes occasional flashes of humor, this is predominantly a grim motion picture.

The movie deals specifically with the privatization of British Rail, which transpired during the mid-1990s, but the themes explored by Loach apply to countless other industries in today's world. The idea of company loyalty died with the 80s. Today, it's every man (or woman) for himself (or herself), as prized employees bounce from company to company, depending upon who offers the best salary and benefits. Meanwhile, "generic" workers often find themselves turned loose for no reason whatsoever, their job inexplicably "eliminated."

In 1995, British Rail left government control and

the portion of the company in South Yorkshire became East Midland Infrastructure. The employees were subjected to new buzzwords and theories. Customer satisfaction replaced safety and efficiency as the number one priority. A "mission statement" was developed. And employees were subjected to demeaning and pedantic training films. Soon, workers found themselves facing uncertain futures with jobs that could be eliminated any day. High quality became a victim of the obsessive need to cut costs. Loach allows us to see the shortsightedness of these management policies without ever launching into a didactic sermon. He doesn't have to — we instinctively believe everything we see on-screen because many of us have experienced this in our everyday work environment.

As is typically the case, Loach coaxes effective performance out of unknown actors. This is one way he keeps the films more real and immediate, believing that familiar faces can distort the gritty, near-documentary style he prefers. *The Navigators* would have been a more powerful feature had we developed a stronger emotional connection with one or more of the characters (we see occasional snapshots of their home lives, but nothing substantive), but, nevertheless, it is a worthwhile motion picture whose central topic will resonate with many who see it. **RECOMMENDED**

Nell [1994]

Starring: Jodie Foster, Liam Neeson, Natasha Richardson, Richard Libertini, Nick Searcy Director: Michael Apted Screenplay: William Nicholson and Mark Handley based on the play "Idioglossia" by Mark Handley Running Time: 1:52 Rated: PG-13 (Nudity, language) Theatrical Aspect Ratio: 2.35:1

In *Nell*, a lush, green world of rolling hills and crystal pools, technology is an unwelcome intruder; civilization, a threatening monster. Both are slaves to the avaricious. *Nell* is about the importance of communication and interaction, about how the events of childhood shape a life, and about the difficulty — and rewards — of reaching out to others.

Nell (Foster) has lived her entire life alone in the woods with an aging mother. She is eventually discovered by a local doctor, Jerome Lovell (Liam Neeson), who comes to her secluded, ramshackle hut after her mother's death. Nell's panicked and hostile response to strangers forces Jerome to travel to nearby Charlotte to recruit the expert assistance of Dr. Paula Olsen (Natasha Richardson). After meeting the young woman, Paula's impression is that Nell

should be committed. Jerome, horrified by this possibility, obtains a court order to stop it. The two opposing sides eventually argue the case before a judge. Deferring his verdict for 3 months, the judge gives the two doctors that time to observe their subject, learn her language, and present him with enough evidence to make an informed decision.

Jodie Foster's Oscars are no fluke, as her simple-yet-profound performance in *Nell* illustrates. She is one of only a few actors capable of so fully immersing herself in a character that it's possible to forget the star behind the performance. With Jack Nicholson or Al Pacino, you watch a variation of the same personality; with Jodie Foster, you see a new individual.

Nell is an almost-childlike woman who speaks her own fractured form of English, hides inside her house by day, and takes moonlight swims in a nearby lake. In Jerome and Paula, she finds a substitute father and mother, and together, these three attempt to breach the non-physical walls between them. This, the real meat of *Nell*, is where the film attains its depth and richness.

It is difficult to deny *Nell*'s intelligence and sensitivity. We approach this story with the same fascination that Nell faces each day, seeing, if only for a short time, how different the world — and people — *can* be. It is this impression more than any other that stays with the viewer after the drama has been played out and the final credits roll. **RECOMMENDED**

Nicholas Nickleby [United States/United Kingdom, 2002]

Starring: Charlie Hunnam, Jamie Bell, Christopher Plummer, Jim Broadbent, Anne Hathaway, Romola Garai Director: Douglas McGrath Screenplay: Douglas McGrath, based on the novel by Charles Dickens Running Time: 2:12 Rated: PG (Mature themes) Theatrical Aspect Ratio: 1.85:1

Writer/director Douglas McGrath has successfully condensed Charles Dickens' *Nicholas Nickleby* to the point where it can fit into a time span of less than 2¼ hours without doing irreparable damage to the story's essence. The narrative shows occasional hiccups, but, considering how it has been shoehorned, it is reasonably clear. This still *feels* like Dickens, perhaps because the best things about *Nicholas Nickleby* remain, including the uniquely Dickensian setting (19th century England) and characters.

The title character is played by British TV actor Charlie Hunnam, whose good looks prove not to be a detriment to his ability to play the 19-year old only son of a recently deceased country gentleman. When

Nicholas' father dies, leaving behind a legacy of debt, the young man is forced to travel with his mother and sister, Kate (Romola Garai), to London to seek the assistance of Nicholas' uncle, Ralph (Christopher Plummer). A notorious miser with little concern for his poorer relations, Ralph nevertheless appears to show signs of humanity by securing a position for Nicholas as the assistant headmaster at a rural boys' school, working for Wackford Squeers (Jim Broadbent). Soon, however, Nicholas learns that his uncle has given him an unbearably odious job — Squeers is a sadist who delights in punishing the children in his charge. One day, when Squeers is beating the crippled boy Smike (Jamie Bell), Nicholas loses patience with the headmaster and turns the cane on him. He then departs, taking Smike with him. This action enrages Ralph, exacerbating his already prickly relationship with Nicholas and encouraging Ralph to take revenge upon Kate, who is under his "protection."

McGrath's *Nicholas Nickleby* is set up as a struggle of good, as personified by Nicholas, against evil, as represented by Ralph. Each of these characters has various allies, but the final struggle is between the two of them. The progression of the story is somewhat episodic, as is characteristic of many of Dickens' tales. Purists and die-hard aficionados of the novel may be dismayed by the manner in which it has been adapted, with all of the fat trimmed off (and, as I'm sure some will comment, some of the meat and bone with it), but, for a general movie-going audience, *Nicholas Nickleby* works. This is the engaging story of an upright man's quest to protect his family, find love, and see justice done. As a means to bring a classic novel to the attention of a modern audience, McGrath's *Nicholas Nickleby* is a success. **RECOMMENDED**

Night Falls on Manhattan [1997]

Starring: Andy Garcia, Ian Holm, Richard Dreyfuss, Lena Olin, James Gandolfini Director: Sidney Lumet Screenplay: Sidney Lumet based on the novel *Tainted Evidence* by Robert Daley Running Time: 1:55 Rated: R (Profanity, violence, mature themes) Theatrical Aspect Ratio: 1.85:1

With *Night Falls on Manhattan*, which is based on a fact-inspired novel by New York writer Robert Daley, director Sidney Lumet is in top form. The basic framework is familiar: corrupt cops, tainted evidence, and a big trial that will make or break the hotshot lawyer protagonist. But, if you think you've seen this story already, be prepared for more than one surprise.

Sean Casey (Andy Garcia) is an earnest young lawyer fresh out of school. A former cop, he's one of the few in his profession who still cares about the importance of justice. He goes to work as an assistant district attorney not because he views it as a stepping stone to the next plateau of his career, but because he cares about the cases. The situation becomes personal when his police detective father, Liam (Ian Holm), is shot in a drug bust gone bad. Liam is the lucky one — 3 of his fellow officers are dead. The suspect, a drug kingpin (Shiek Mahmud-Bey), turns himself in via a media circus that's carefully orchestrated by his attorney, Sam Vigoda (Richard Dreyfuss).

For the D.A., Morgenstern (Ron Leibman), it's an election year, and he decides on a risky strategy that, if it works, could give him a publicity edge. He chooses Sean to prosecute the case, with Liam as the star witness. The media goes wild with the story, Sean sees this as his big chance, and Liam is bursting with pride. But there's an obstacle — Vigoda is a brilliant lawyer, and he has an ax to grind. From the moment the defense attorney presents his opening argument, it's clear that his tactic will involve putting the entire N.Y.P.D. on trial.

Night Falls on Manhattan is savvy about a number of things. Not only does it have a good feel for both sides of the police corruption issue, but it's aware of the political rivalries and behind-the-scenes dealmaking that keeps a city running. The script is smart, and the characters are better realized than their counterparts in countless similar-yet-inferior motion pictures. Sean may be the knight in shining armor trying to stay afloat in a sea of corruption, but it doesn't take long for him to recognize that survival demands compromise.

Sidney Lumet has done something that I wasn't sure was possible in this age of instant, formulaic gratification: make a riveting cop movie without a car chase and a courtroom thriller without cheap theatrics. *Night Falls on Manhattan* isn't about the trappings of these situations; it's about their inner workings, their underlying issues, and the men and women who keep things moving. **HIGHLY RECOMMENDED**

Nixon [1995]

Starring: Anthony Hopkins, James Woods, Paul Sorvino, Joan Allen, Powers Boothe, Ed Harris Director: Oliver Stone Screenplay: Oliver Stone, Stephen J. Rivele, and Christopher Wilkinson Running Time: 3:10 Rated: R (Language, mature themes) Theatrical Aspect Ratio: 2.35:1

It's always a tricky proposition to make a motion picture based on recent history — and the more public the episode, the more difficult it is for the film maker to balance drama with accuracy. This is especially true when that film maker is Oliver Stone, a director known more for self-aggrandizement than for the thoughtful handling of difficult issues. Under Stone, *JFK*, for instance, turned into a 3-hour paranoid ordeal with a conspiracy theory 10 times less plausible than the Warren Commission's "one bullet" hypothesis.

It's entirely because of Stone's reputation that the even-handedness of *Nixon* is such a surprise. While not an unassailable portrait of the late president, this movie at least attempts to present Nixon as a human being, with all the failings and greatness inherent in a man of his stature. Nixon is portrayed as neither demonic nor angelic.

Nixon is not a simple regurgitation of historical events. In fact, history is used primarily as the backdrop against which this character study takes place. Less a biography than an impressionist's vision, the film may disappoint those expecting a vitriolic attack on someone who is surely not among Stone's heroes. But the lead persona, as realized by Anthony Hopkins, isn't reduced to an unthinking, unfeeling caricature. While Nixon is depicted as a paranoid, borderline-megalomaniac, he's also shown to have deep moral convictions, a strong sense of loyalty, and a love of his country. The drama plays out in a Shakespearean fashion, with Nixon's tragic flaw of hubris clearly in evidence. Hopkins is not heavily made up — and therefore doesn't really look like his character — but his mannerisms are perfect and he is allowed a full range of facial expressions (unlike Robert Duvall in *Stalin*). Hopkins does far more with acting than fake jowls could ever accomplish.

The film's structure is disjointed, especially during the first hour, as the narrative skips back and forth through time from Watergate to 1960 to the 1920s and 30s. Stone is giving us a snapshot of Nixon's life, but it comes in such a random and haphazard fashion that it dims the dramatic impact and dilutes early character development. It's not until the film's second hour, as Nixon faces the dilemma of how to end the Vietnam War, that Hopkins' character starts to click.

Nixon really doesn't offer any surprising insights, nor does it break new ground for the director. This is a dynamic — if flawed — look at the man who, for better and for worse, changed America's place in the world and its perception of itself. There are few who do not have an opinion of Nixon. In this motion picture, Oliver Stone presents his vision of the forces that drove and motivated the late President. And, factual or not, there's no denying that *Nixon* has moments when it is nothing short of compelling. RECOMMENDED

No End [Poland, 1984]

Starring: Grazyna Szapolowska, Maria Pakulnis, Aleksander Bardini, Jerzy Radziwillowicz, Artur Barcis Director: Krzysztof Kieslowski Screenplay: Krzysztof Kieslowski and Krzysztof Piesiewicz Running Time: 1:47 Rated: No MPAA Rating (Mature themes, sex, nudity) Theatrical Aspect Ratio: 1.66:1 In Polish with subtitles

No End, the first collaboration between writer-director Krzysztof Kieslowski and lawyer-turned-screenwriter Krzysztof Piesiewicz, takes place in a Poland that is under the cloud of martial law. More than any of the director's other internationally-screened features, this one requires some (however rudimentary) knowledge of the political situation in Poland during the early-to-mid-'80s. Martial law was declared in late 1981, and, in the resulting climate of uncertainty and tension, the courts began to pass 2–3 year sentences on anyone caught painting graffiti, found in possession of an underground newspaper, breaking curfew, or participating in strikes or other resistance activities. One of Kieslowski's objectives in *No End* was to explore potential ramifications of this situation from a noncritical perspective.

No End is really three stories in one, all of which revolve around people connected to a lawyer, Antoni Zyro (Jerzy Radziwillowicz), who dies just before the film begins. There's Ulla (Grazyna Szapolowska, who later appeared in *Decalogue 6, A Short Film About Love*), the lawyer's widow. Only after his death does she realize how much she loved her husband and how little meaning her life has without him. Then there's Dariusz (Artur Barcis), Antoni's client, who has been jailed for leading a labor strike. After Antoni's death, Dariusz is forced to employ an older, more cautious lawyer (Aleksander Bardini), who believes in compromising with the state to obtain a lenient sentence. Finally, there's the ghost of Antoni, who silently haunts his friends and family, watching as they continue their lives.

The three motifs of *No End* frequently cross and occasionally entwine. Kieslowski doesn't always handle these interconnections well; in fact, there are times when the different stories mesh clumsily. Nevertheless, the film is so packed with ideas that there's never any shortage of material worth pondering, and Ulla's emotional torment touches the heart. Looking back on the full body of Kieslowski's films, *No End* can be viewed as an important entry, because, despite its flaws, we can observe embryonic forms of several themes that the director explored more fully in *Decalogue* and *Three Colors*. Thus, *No End* functions both as a compliment and a precursor to the director's most lasting works. **HIGHLY RECOMMENDED**

Nobody's Fool [1995]

Starring: Paul Newman, Dylan Walsh, Jessica Tandy, Melanie Griffith, Bruce Willis Director: Robert Benton Screenplay: Robert Benton based on the novel by Richard Russo Running Time: 1:52 Rated: R (Profanity, brief nudity) Theatrical Aspect Ratio: 1:85:1

Nobody's Fool is about as sublime a motion picture as is likely to come out of Hollywood. With a structure that contravenes the norm, this film concentrates on character first, letting the plot fall naturally into place. Situations are forced on neither the film's inhabitants nor the audience. It's rare to sit through a drama and not feel manipulated, but the feelings generated by Robert Benton's movie are entirely natural, and likely to bring a smile to the heart.

Paul Newman gives an unforgettable performance as Donald Sullivan (or Sully), a cantankerous, aging man living in the small, snowbound town of North Bath, New York. With the spirit of a mischievous teenager but the body of a 60-year-old, Sully has the kind of infectious presence that, in his own words, "grows on you." He delights in flirting with women half his age, and engages in a game of theft where he and his sometimes-boss, Carl Roebuck (Bruce Willis), take turns devising creative means by which to steal a snow blower from one another.

Nobody's Fool is as much about regrets as about choices made; as much about the road not taken as the one travelled. It's about families broken apart, and parent/child relationships mended. Sully's father was a ruthless, violent drunk whom he never forgave, and that is perhaps why he was such a poor father to his own son, Peter (Dylan Walsh). Now, decades later, the abandoning father is trying to make amends — not only to his son, but to his grandchildren as well.

Offering the best in easygoing, unconfrontational drama, the story is told with wry, intelligent humor. For Melanie Griffith, this is the best acting she has done in a long time. After a string of lackluster comedies (the last one of which was *Milk Money*) and ineffective thrillers (*Shining Through*, *A Stranger Among Us*), *Nobody's Fool* offers a role for which she is suited. Playing the dowdy wife of a perpetual womanizer, she finds the right mixture of strength and pathos.

Also holding his own is Bruce Willis, here in his second consecutive solid performance (on the heels of

Pulp Fiction). Jessica Tandy, to whom the film is dedicated, is as effective as ever. Of course, no one can quite match Newman, who shows a chameleon-like ability to shed his star image and don a most atypical personality. This is the sort of part normally associated with a character actor of Albert Finney's status.

Quiet and enchanting in its simplicity, *Nobody's Fool* is a joy. Admittedly, it meanders a bit, but that's part of its charm. The intelligent sensitivity of the script, coupled with Newman's powerfully understated performance, make this motion picture special. There aren't many of them like this out there. **HIGHLY RECOMMENDED**

Normal Life [1996]

Starring: Ashley Judd, Luke Perry Director: John McNaughton Screenplay: Peg Haller and Bob Schneider Running Time: 1:42 Rated: R (Profanity, nudity, sex, violence) Theatrical Aspect Ratio: 1:85:1

Fine Line Features, *Normal Life*'s distributor, elected not to release the film in theaters, opting instead for a run on HBO. This infuriated director John McNaughton (*Henry: Portrait of a Serial Killer*), who claimed that he never would have directed the movie had he been aware of Fine Line's intentions. Now, *Normal Life* is out on video cassette, and its availability should generate a wider audience.

Normal Life is a character study loosely based on a true-life crime spree that occurred in Chicago's western suburbs. It is compelling because of the characters' twisted, co-dependent relationship, and not because it falls into the often-sordid category of having its narrative built around a real criminal case.

Those characters are the husband-and-wife team of Chris and Pam Anderson (Luke Perry and Ashley Judd), and *Normal Life* tells their story over a 2-year period. The two meet in a bar one night when Pam has a fight with her boyfriend and cuts her hand on a broken glass. Chris comes to the rescue, bandages the wound, then asks her to dance. Soon thereafter, they are married, and that's when the trouble begins.

Despite her cheerleader looks, Pam is not the perfect wife. Sexually, she's frigid; emotionally, she's unstable, and has self-destructive tendencies. Yet, through all of this, her husband sticks by her. There's something about Pam that holds him in thrall.

When Chris loses his job, Pam's profligate spending traps the couple in an ever-widening vortex of debt. To save them, Chris robs a bank. Then another. Then another. It appears he's good at it. Soon, he and Pam have moved into an upscale townhouse. Then, by chance, Pam finds out about her husband's new source of income. The idea excites her. She joins him in a robbery and, afterwards, experiences her first-ever orgasm during sex. But the pattern of self-destruction returns, and the resolution is inevitable.

Normal Life isn't really about whether Pam and Chris get away with their crimes — they don't, and that point is never in doubt. Rather, it's about how they relate to each other, and how Pam's manic-depressive behavior destroys not only her own life, but Chris's as well. Why would someone stay with a woman like this? Watching Ashley Judd's wrenching, uninhibited portrayal of Pam, it's easy to understand the reasons. Buried beneath the madness, there's a sweetness and vulnerability that cries out for protection and nurturing. Luke Perry, giving the most convincing performance of his career to date, makes it clear how desperately, hopelessly smitten Chris is by his wild, troubled wife.

I have watched *Normal Life* twice now, and I don't understand Fine Line's decision regarding the movie's distribution. By depicting the sham of "normality," *Normal Life* reminds us how fictitious and unattainable the "American dream" can be. **RECOMMENDED**

O [2001]

Starring: Mekhi Phifer, Josh Hartnett, Julia Stiles, Elden Henson, Andrew Keegan, Rain Phoenix, John Heard, Anthony Johnson, Martin Sheen Director: Tim Blake Nelson Screenplay: Brad Kaaya, based on "Othello" by William Shakespeare Running Time: 1:35 Rated: R (Violence, profanity, sexual situations, drug use) Theatrical Aspect Ratio: 1.85:1

There are two ways to adapt Shakespeare into a contemporary setting. The first is to take the story and dialogue and dump them wholesale into modern times. The second is to extract the essence of the material and re-work it for our era. Tim Blake Nelson's *O*, based on *Othello*, takes the latter route, and the result is a stirring and affecting piece of drama.

O re-locates the story into a United States high school circa 2000, and in keeping with the violent nature of Shakespeare, doesn't shy away from bloodshed. A simple emotion (in this case, it's jealousy), unchecked and stoked, forms the foundation of this violence. Mixed with the rampant hormones of the teen years, *O* demonstrates this combination to be as explosive and unstable as nitroglycerine.

The Othello of *O* is Odin James (Mekhi Phifer), the god of the Palmetto Grove basketball team. He's the lone black student in an all-white prep school, but he has a good heart, is smart, and is unstoppable on the court. He has won the love of the dean's daughter, Desi (Julia Stiles in the Desdemona role), and the respect of his teammates — all except one. Hugo (Josh Hartnett as Iago) is keenly jealous of Odin because Hugo's own father (Martin Sheen), the coach of the basketball team, considers Odin to be more of a true son than Hugo. This breeds resentment and hatred, and Hugo puts a plan in place to destroy Odin by sowing seeds of doubt about the legitimacy of Desi's love and fidelity. Odin, who is on some level insecure, reluctantly takes the bait.

The single most memorable aspect of any Shakespeare play is the dialogue. Yet, in *O*, where all of those lines have been stripped away, the strength and universality of the play's themes come to the fore. The intent of director Tim Blake Nelson (*Eye of God*) is to fashion a dramatic milieu that approximates high school in the '00s. He is not looking for a hard-core, gritty reality.

In the wake of the Columbine tragedy, Miramax Films, the company that owned the rights to *O* at the time, shelved it because they feared controversy. Obviously they ignored the fact that this picture has a message that is thought-provoking rather than exploitative. Eventually, Lions Gate picked up the rights and the movie was able to see the light of day. And that's a good thing for everyone who appreciates Shakespeare or a serious examination of the volatile issue of school violence. **RECOMMENDED**

October Sky [1999]

Starring: Jake Gyllenhaal, Chris Cooper, Chris Owen, William Lee Scott, Chad Lindberg, Laura Dern, Natalie Canerday Director: Joe Johnston Screenplay: Lewis Colick, based on the book "Rocket Boys" by Homer H. Hickam Jr. Running Time: 1:43 Rated: PG (Mature themes, mild profanity) Theatrical Aspect Ratio: 1.85:1

There has always been a distinction between high school nerds and jocks. Those in the former category are on the chess club, play Dungeons & Dragons, and participate in academic contests, while those in the latter are guided by testosterone, muscles, and not much else. Jocks look forward to winning the big championship game and being scouted by college coaches. Nerds hope to score a 1600 on their SATs or take first prize at a national science fair, thereby attracting a university's attention. There's always been a social dividing line between the grunts and the geeks, and it's very much in evidence here.

October Sky is based on the book by Homer Hickam, and relates the true story of 4 boys who experimented with home made rockets during the autumn of 1957, the year that the Soviet satellite Sputnik blasted into orbit. Set in the coal mining town of Coalwood, West Virginia, this movie is about one boy's struggles to escape from a lifestyle that he views as an unsafe and unhealthy prison.

Homer (Jake Gyllenhaal), along with his 3 friends, Quentin (Chris Owen), Roy Lee (William Lee Scott), and O'Dell (Chad Lindberg), is determined to make a rocket that will soar. His primary adult ally in this endeavor is his teacher, Miss Riley (Laura Dern), who supports and encourages his dream. But his father, John (Chris Cooper), who runs the local coalmine, dismisses his son's avocation as foolish. Football and mining are acceptable; hoping to get into college by winning a national science fair is a waste of time and effort. Indeed, for a while, it looks like all of Homer's efforts are doomed to failure as rocket after rocket explodes on the launch pad, but, when the 4 boys discover the secret to success, they become local celebrities — until one of their rockets is suspected of starting a forest fire. And, when an accident at the mine threatens to ruin Homer's family, the idealist must choose between preserving his dream and working to allow his parents to keep their home.

There are a lot of reasons to like *October Sky,* but the most compelling is the multi-faceted, complex relationship between Homer and John. This isn't the kind of one-dimensional interaction we have come to expect from movie fathers and sons; it's characterized on both sides by anger, jealousy, resentment, bitterness, respect, pride, and love. While at first it appears that the rocket building lies at the movie's heart, we gradually realize that the connection between Homer and his father is more important.

October Sky gets a lot of the details right. With its use of period costumes and accessories, the film has the proper look for the late-1950s, and the soundtrack contains numerous pop hits from the time. Believable, subtle, and consistently intelligent.

HIGHLY RECOMMENDED

Oleanna [1994]

Starring: William H. Macy, Debra Eisenstadt Director: David Mamet
Screenplay: David Mamet based on his play Running Time: 1:30
Rated: R (Mature themes, violence, language) Theatrical Aspect
Ratio: 1.66:1

Two people approach an intersection from different vantage points. When an accident occurs, they both observe the same facts, yet afterwards their versions of events differ considerably. Neither is lying; rather,

the subjective element of their experience accounts for this gap in perception. This sort of difference of perspectives (albeit in other circumstances) is one theme explored by writer/director David Mamet in *Oleanna.*

Sexual harassment is certainly an issue of some importance in today's society. Ultimately, perhaps the question in *Oleanna* is not whether sexual harassment has been committed, but exactly who is persecuting whom. *Oleanna* also examines the significance of today's college education. Is it more important to go through the expected routines — taking notes, reading texts, and passing exams — than it is to have one's intellect stimulated and one's interests awakened? To use Mamet's words, "Is higher education useful?"

Faithfully adapted by the director from his own play, *Oleanna* is a two-character piece. For the most part, the dynamics are played out in a series of rooms on an unnamed northeastern college campus. The only two speaking parts belong to William H. Macy as a middle-aged professor and Debra Eisenstadt as Carol, a student who comes to him to discuss why she's failing his course. Needless to say, these characters are central to Mamet's presentation of certain themes. Their relationship is developed through 3 acts, each showing a new phase of their interaction. In some ways, the progression of *Oleanna* is more like that of a psychological thriller than a drama. The film spirals in on itself, twisting from sanity and reason to primal emotion.

As is always the case, Mamet's dialogue has a rhythm and cadence all its own. Early in the film, this, combined with a sluggish tone, causes *Oleanna* to seem staged and unnatural. Later, however, as the pace builds, the strengths of what the actors are saying — and how they're saying it — outstrip the weaknesses. By photographing *Oleanna* using dim lighting frequently designed to hood the eyes, motives, and feelings of the characters, cinematographer Andrezej Sekula (*Reservoir Dogs, Pulp Fiction*) enhances the sense of claustrophobia created by Mamet's restrictive setting. By the end of the movie, we in the audience feel as trapped as the characters on screen.

Oleanna probes deeply into some of the darker facets of human interaction, and anything with this keen an edge will cause discomfort. This film has been made for those willing to look beneath the surface to see a taut, intellectual sparring match where

there is no absolute truth. For such an audience, this picture will leave an indelible imprint.
HIGHLY RECOMMENDED

Once Upon a Time . . . When We Were Colored
[1996]
Starring: Charles Earl Taylor Jr., Willis Norwood Jr., Damon Hines, Al Freeman Jr. Director: Tim Reid Screenplay: Paul W. Cooper based on the novel by Clifton Taulbert Rated: PG (Violence, mature themes) Theatrical Aspect Ratio: 1.85:1

In a time when intelligent family pictures are at a premium, intelligent African American family pictures are virtually nonexistent. Filling this void is *Once Upon a Time . . . When We Were Colored*, Tim Reid's feature adaptation of Clifton Taulbert's memoirs. Blending sepia-toned nostalgia with harder-hitting, passionate themes, Reid has crafted a portrait of growing up in the middle-of-the-century South the likes of which is rarely found in any medium.

In *Once Upon a Time*, a sense of quiet dignity has replaced the rage that often typifies films targeted for black audiences. Yet this movie is no less emotive or potent because of it. Issues of equality, fairness, and self-respect form the cornerstones of the subtext for this coming-of-age story. Although *Once Upon a Time* is rooted in a setting that will have greater resonance for black Americans, much of what this film says has universal scope and intent.

Once Upon a Time . . . When We Were Colored opens in 1946, in Colored Town, the black companion community to Glen Allen, Mississippi — the year and place of Clifton Taulbert's birth. The film traces his first 16 years, ending in 1962 when Cliff decides to leave his home and family, and go to work in the cotton fields for the promise of the North. Although *Once Upon a Time* is occasionally disjointed, and some of the transitions are abrupt, it nevertheless offers a compelling chronicle of one man's growth into adulthood during volatile times, when courageous men and women began challenging an unjust system.

Once Upon a Time . . . When We Were Colored is about growing up and breaking free, both as an individual and as a community. It's about standing up for denied rights and not backing down in the face of pressure. Moreover, it's an intimate odyssey through the kind of childhood that is forever lost in the not-so-distant-past, when, despite the plague of legal racism throughout the South, the closeness of a community still offered support, comfort, and love. In

Cliff's words, "All that I am or ever will be comes from growing up with my extended family in . . . Colored Town." That simple statement embodies the core of the film's message to viewers of all races and generations. **HIGHLY RECOMMENDED**

Once Were Warriors [New Zealand, 1994]
Starring: Rena Owen, Temuera Morrison, Mamaengaroa Kerr-Bell, Julian Arahanga, Taungaroa Emile, Cliff Curtis Director: Lee Tamahori Screenplay: Riwia Brown based on the novel by Alan Duff Running Time: 1:39 Rated: R (Violence, rape, language) Theatrical Aspect Ratio: 1.85:1

Once Were Warriors is centered upon the touchy yet timely topic of domestic violence. It is not, however, merely another "domestic violence motion picture." With its complex cultural backdrop and its stark view of this societal cancer, *Once Were Warriors* attains a level where it is equally painful and potent.

The critical themes of this movie are universal, even though there is a great deal of background that only a New Zealander can appreciate. Nevertheless, though many elements of the subtext may be lost to outside viewers, the key issue — the brutal cycle of violence and denial within a family — is brought to the fore in a manner that necessitates no special awareness.

Equality is not a basic tenant of the Maori lifestyle (Maoris are the Polynesian warrior-race who settled New Zealand some 1,000 years ago), at least as depicted in this film. However, alcoholism and unemployment are. It's the lot of the woman to work, while the man — the "protector" — spends all day at the local pub getting drunk. Wife-beating, while distasteful, is acceptable behavior, especially if the woman has the audacity to talk back to her husband.

Once Were Warriors takes place in an urbanized area of south Auckland, where Beth and Jake Heke (Rena Owen and New Zealand soap stud Temuera Morrison) live in a small house with 4 of their 5 children. The fifth, Nig (Julian Arahanga), has moved out to join a local gang. At first glance, Beth and Jake seem to have a solid marriage. But when Jake is drunk (which is frequently), his temper is easily ignited, and when one of Beth's barbs pushes him too far, the bloody and violent results are terrible to behold. Many films have depicted wife-beatings. Few have been as graphic and difficult to watch.

The acting throughout *Once Were Warriors* is uniformly strong, with leading and supporting actors turning in performances that range from credible to electric. The musical score, by Murray McNabb, is evocative, and a perfect match for the drab, dreary colors suffusing Stuart Dryburgh's camerawork. Great pains have been taken to emphasize that everyone in this film is trapped by one thing or another — if not their circumstances, then their personality. The only moment of serenity — the opening scene depicting a pastoral setting — turns out to be an illusion: a billboard in the midst of a gray city.

By anchoring *Once Were Warriors* in the turmoil of a Maori family, director Lee Tamahori takes full advantage of an opportunity not only to dissect the forces that lead to domestic violence, but also to focus on the clash between Maori traditions and modern values. The snares laid for men and women are not the only concepts put forth to ponder. *Once Were Warriors* works, to some degree, on 3 levels: the visceral, the emotional, and the intellectual, and it is the amalgamation of these that makes this a memorable film. **HIGHLY RECOMMENDED**

One True Thing [1998]

Starring: Meryl Streep, Renée Zellweger, William Hurt, Tom Everett Scott Director: Carl Franklin Screenplay: Karen Croner based on the novel by Anna Quindlen Running Time: 2:07 Rated: R (Language, sexual situations, mature themes) Theatrical Aspect Ratio: 1.85:1

Sometimes, the performance of one actor can elevate a mediocre script to the level of solid entertainment. This is a phenomenon we see again and again, and *One True Thing* is a good example of this. Perhaps surprisingly, however, that performance does *not* come from veteran screen presence Meryl Streep, who plays a woman dying of cancer. Streep is good in the role, but, frankly, this is the kind of part she could play in her sleep. Likewise, Oscar winner William Hurt is solid, but not spectacular. The one who rivets our attention with her pouty expression and subtle demonstrations of pain is Renée Zellweger.

Zellweger is Ellen Gulden, an ambitious young writer working for a New York-based magazine. When the film opens, it's 1988, and Ellen is being questioned in connection with the death of her mother. Kate Gulden (Streep), beloved member of a small upper New York state community, died in her sleep at the age of 48. At the time, she was suffering from advanced, terminal cancer, but the cause of death was a morphine overdose. Also under suspicion is Kate's husband, George (Hurt), a local college professor.

The story gradually evolves in flashback, showing Ellen's sometimes-contentious relationship with her mother and her unswerving devotion to her father.

When Kate's condition is diagnosed, George pleads with Ellen to quit her job and come home to help around the house. Somewhat resentfully, Ellen agrees to return to the nest. Soon, she finds herself losing her own identity as her mother's lifestyle swallows her up.

Director Carl Franklin (*Devil in a Blue Dress*) has chosen to model the movie as a tearjerker, albeit a superior one. There are plenty of moments of sentimental melodrama, but there are also instances of surprisingly keen character insight. Although George, Kate, and Ellen start out as stereotypes, they quickly evolve beyond that baseline level. The relationships between these individuals are suitably complex; there are no clear-cut boundaries separating love, admiration, and resentment. And the issue of euthanasia is handled sensitively and intelligently, without the filmmakers getting on a pulpit to preach down to us.

One True Thing will undoubtedly be pigeonholed as a "chick flick," and it's not an unreasonable classification. Like *Terms of Endearment*, the movie deals with the two issues most likely to draw raves from the average female viewer: a well-defined mother/daughter relationship and a slow death. However, I would argue that *One True Thing* is a little less overt than *Terms* in its approach to these issues, and that makes it a less cloying experience. There's no denying that *One True Thing* is affecting, and, although the plot rarely excels, the actors bring enough to their roles to transform this motion picture into a satisfying weeper. **RECOMMENDED**

Osama [Afghanistan/Japan/Ireland, 2003]

Starring: Marina Golbahari, Arif Herati, Zubaida Sahar Director: Siddiq Barmak Screenplay: Siddiq Barmak Running Time: 1:22 Rated: PG-13 (Mature themes) Theatrical Aspect Ratio: 1.85:1 In Dari with subtitles

It's fair to say that *Osama* may offer the most honest and straightforward cinematic portrayal of life in Afghanistan during the rule of the Taliban. The film's authenticity derives from its having been shot in Kabul (post-Taliban), so there's no need for another country to act as a stand-in. Director Siddiq Barmak recruited his nonprofessional cast, including impressive lead actress Marina Golbahari, from orphanages and refugee camps, further adding to the "you are there" feeling that pervades the production.

The story is simple, yet painfully tragic. Golbhari plays the 12-year old daughter of a widowed Afghan doctor (Zubaida Sahar) who is forced to stop working when the Taliban comes into power. Left without a means of income, the mother dresses up her daughter as a boy and sends her out to work. Renamed "Osama," the child, on the cusp of puberty, ends up being pressed into a military training school, where she is ruthlessly bullied by the boys because of her feminine features. Yet Osama cannot reveal the truth about herself, since the punishment for impersonating a boy could be death.

Osama is less of a story than it is a record — a record of a time and place that most of us cannot fathom existed in this modern era. The attitudes and living conditions presented in the film look like something out of the dark ages. Were it not for the presence of a few mechanized vehicles and advanced guns, one could easily assume that the events in *Osama* occur during the 15th or 16th century, not the 21st. Without a word of preaching, Barmak provides a stinging condemnation of the kind of social and cultural stagnation that can arise when religious fanaticism becomes the law.

Osama brings to mind a real-world consideration. The United States attacked Afghanistan and brought down the Taliban because of its complicity in the 9/11/01 attacks. Had those events not occurred, it is likely that the Taliban would still be in power, and the massive human rights violations depicted in this film would be ongoing. So, although it's possible to argue about the motive in the case of the military action, it's difficult to disagree with the result. This is clearly an occasion when the end justifies the means. Anyone doubting this need only watch *Osama*. In most ways that count, it's as true as any documentary.
RECOMMENDED

Oscar and Lucinda [Australia/United States, 1997]
Starring: Ralph Fiennes, Cate Blanchett, Ciaran Hinds, Tom Wilkinson, Richard Roxburgh Director: Gillian Armstrong Screenplay: Laura Jones based on the novel by Peter Carey Running Time: 2:10 Rated: R (Violence, sex, mature themes) Theatrical Aspect Ratio: 2.35:1

Oscar and Lucinda opens in the mid-1800s, with parallel story lines in New South Wales, Australia, and Devon, England. As the narrative voice of Geoffrey Rush informs us, Lucinda Leplastrier (Cate Blanchett) is a headstrong young woman being raised in the Australian outback. Meanwhile, half the world away, Oscar Hopkins (Fiennes) has broken with his puritanical father over religious issues, and has gone away to school to study to be an Anglican priest. Lucinda is fascinated with glass; Oscar is obsessed with theology. Lucinda is rich; Oscar is poor. Lucinda is forward and self-assured; Oscar is timid and uncertain of himself. Yet one characteristic

unites these two diverse individuals — the compulsion to gamble, whether it's on horses, dogs, cards, or the flip of a coin. And fate has decreed that they will one day meet.

That day doesn't occur until 45 minutes into the film, when Oscar boards a ship bound for Sydney, Australia, where he hopes to change his life and minister to anyone in need of his help. Another of the passengers is Lucinda, who is returning from England where she has been shopping for machinery to equip her newly-acquired glassworks factory. At first, their relationship is that of a reverend and a confessor, but it doesn't take long for both of them to recognize a kindred spirit in the other. A friendship is born, and, once they reach Australia, it develops into something more potent. But Oscar is uncertain of Lucinda's affection, and feels he must do something to prove himself worthy of her.

Oscar and Lucinda isn't beyond a little manipulation to get the desired emotional response, and there are times when the story line curves in preposterous directions. On more than one occasion, it's apparent that events are occurring specifically to funnel the characters into a position where there is only one possible route. Coincidence is a crucial plot device; without it, this movie can't go anywhere. The voice-over narration is also too verbose and breaks into the story at undesirable moments.

There's a real magic in the way director Gillian Armstrong develops the story, keeping things moving in unexpected directions without lingering too long on any one moment or sequence. With the skill of a consummate storyteller, she weaves romance, friendship, passion, humor, and tragedy together into a complete package. The characters, with all of their human foibles and neuroses, are wonderfully developed by Fiennes and Blanchett. So who cares if the storyline is a little ripe and unwieldy? *Oscar and Lucinda* still offers abundant pleasures to reward the viewer. **RECOMMENDED**

Othello [United Kingdom/United States, 1995]
Starring: Laurence Fishburne, Irene Jacob, Kenneth Branagh, Nathaniel Parker, Michael Maloney Director: Oliver Parker Screenplay: Oliver Parker based on the play by William Shakespeare Running Time: 2:04 Rated: R (Nudity, sex, violence) Theatrical Aspect Ratio: 1.85:1

To condense *Othello* into a reasonable, 2-hour running time, writer/director Oliver Parker has lopped approximately 50% of Shakespeare's original text from the screenplay. Yet, even with so much gone, the movie remains faithful to the play's central themes and conflicts, and the streamlined narrative is surprisingly easy to follow. For sheer impact, this *Othello* can stand side-by-side with the versions brought to the screen by Orson Welles (as restored in 1992) and Lawrence Olivier.

Laurence Fishburne plays the Moor Othello, a gifted general who is commissioned to confront a Turkish army at Cyprus. Always by Othello's side are his two right-hand men: Cassio (Nathaniel Parker) and Iago (Kenneth Branagh). However, for reasons that are never fully explained, Iago is not the faithful retainer Othello believes him to be. In fact, hatred bubbles just beneath Iago's cool, rational exterior, and he has put a plan into action by which he intends to cause Othello's downfall and shatter the relationship between the Moor and his devoted wife, Desdemona (Irene Jacob).

Laurence Fishburne, a black actor playing the black title role (in some of his various other film incarnations, Othello has been essayed by the likes of Orson Welles, Lawrence Olivier, and Anthony Hopkins — none of whom are black), gives a stirring and powerful interpretation of a man haunted by uncertainty about his wife's faithfulness. Irene Jacob (*The Double Life of Veronique, Red*) imbues Desdemona with far more vitality than she has had in any other movie version. Kenneth Branagh, perhaps better focused since he's only acting in this piece, makes Iago a chillingly rational character whose acerbic asides to the camera draw the audience into his plot almost as an accomplice.

Certain Shakespeare purists will probably dismiss Parker's *Othello* because of the sex scenes and liberal cuts. Such a reaction might be a mistake, however, since this director's view of Othello's tragedy has an unusual slant. Parker is careful to play up the love affair between the title character and his wife so that when the inevitable occurs, it has a more profound impact. When Othello declares, "My life upon [Desdemona's] faith," you believe him.

With this version of *Othello,* Parker wanted to create a Shakespearean film that anyone could see, relate to, and enjoy. In large part, he has accomplished this. *Othello* has never been one of my favorites of the Bard's plays, but, at times, I found myself engrossed by this adaptation. Using the visual aspects of film to enhance certain story elements, Parker has crafted a fine motion picture. RECOMMENDED

Outside Providence [1999]

Starring: Shawn Hatosy, Alec Baldwin, Amy Smart, Jon Abrahams, George Wendt Director: Michael Corrente Screenplay: Peter Farrelly & Michael Corrente & Bobby Farrelly Running Time: 1:30 Rated: R (Profanity, drug use, sexual situations) Theatrical Aspect Ratio: 1.85:1

Outside Providence is a simple coming of age story, a nostalgia-soaked trip back to the mid-'70s when the social fabric of the American youth was stitched together by sex, drugs, and rock music. The film, despite never venturing into uncharted territory, is funny, warm, and endearing, and features a protagonist who grows on the audience. Because the themes are universal (first love, rebellion against restrictive authority, generational friction), nearly everyone, regardless of their age or gender, should be able to relate to the experiences of Timothy "Dildo" Dunphy.

The film opens in Pawtucket, Rhode Island during the summer of 1974. Timothy Dunphy (Shawn Hatosy), or Dunph, as his friends call him, has nothing better to do than to while away the days smoking dope and hanging out with friends with names like Drugs Delaney (Jon Abrahams). One evening, however, while stoned, Dunph gets into an accident with a parked cop car. His father (Alec Baldwin) is furious, and promptly pulls a few strings to get Dunph sent off to the Cornwall Academy, an exclusive prep school that has a reputation for academic excellence and discipline.

Cornwall has a seemingly endless list of rules, but the three most important are no drugs, no alcohol, and no sex. Dunph, of course, manages to break all three on numerous occasions. The game is to avoid being caught. During his time at Cornwall, Dunph falls in love with an "unattainable" girl, wins her affections in return, becomes serious about studying, and turns his life around. The material is standard fare for this kind of motion picture, but the script handles the familiar situations well and presents us with several likable characters. The voiceover narration is kept to a minimum, although Corrente relies on a few too many montages to convey advances in relationships.

Outside Providence effectively treads the line between comedy and drama, providing us with an enjoyable confection that's neither too leaden nor too airy. As a coming of age story, it's comfortable and effective; it hits all the high points and follows the expected general structure. There are serious moments, such as when Joey makes a surprising confession, or when Dunph learns a lesson about mortality. But, as one would expect from a Farrelly Brothers screenplay, there are quite a few laughs to be had, as well — and some of them are pretty big. But none of the jokes are as over-the-top or outrageous as we have come to expect. Instead of bodily fluid hair gel, we have verbal ripostes and modern-day proverbs ("Sex is like a Chinese dinner — it ain't over till you both get your cookies"). Overall, while *Outside Providence* isn't the kind of movie that challenges an audience, it is likely to cause most viewers to leave the theater with a warm, pleasant feeling inside. **RECOMMENDED**

The Paper [1994]

Starring: **Michael Keaton, Glenn Close, Robert Duvall, Marisa Tomei, Randy Quaid** Director: **Ron Howard** Screenplay: **Stephen and David Koepp** Running Time: **1:51** Rated: **R (Profanity, mature themes)** Theatrical Aspect Ratio: **1.85:1**

Ron Howard has a history of making entertaining films with weak conclusions. For something that starts out as a boisterous, amusing, potentially-incisive look at the newspaper business and the people who run it, *The Paper* finishes with a relative whimper.

Henry Hackett (Michael Keaton) is at a watershed, and the next 24 hours are going to determine a lot — perhaps more than he could imagine. Caught in a dilemma between two jobs — his current one at the tabloid-like *New York Sun* and an offer from the prestigious *New York Sentinel* — Henry must make a decision. On one hand, there are factors that argue for the career change: his pregnant wife Martha (Marisa Tomei) wants security, and his bitter feud with his boss Alicia Clark (Glenn Close) is getting nastier by the moment. On the other hand, Henry doesn't want to leave the friendly chaos of *The Sun* and the friends he has made while there.

No viewer is likely to be bored by *The Paper*. The film moves along quickly, using mobile cameras and rapid cuts to keep the energy level high and the pacing crisp. This is especially true in the newsroom scenes, as director Ron Howard attempts to convey the spirit and atmosphere of the disorganized-but-productive work environment. His eye for detail is evident.

Away from the paper's offices, the movie is less successful. The personal lives of Henry and his co-workers aren't all that interesting, and seem scripted rather than real. This is especially true during the drawn-out melodrama that characterizes the last 15 minutes. There are also several out-of-place scenes with Robert Duvall and Jason Alexander commiserating at a bar. The contrivance used to incorporate these into the overall plot is a little too obvious.

But there's a lot in *The Paper* that works. Although most of the characters are types, the actors portray them with sympathy and understanding. Three-dimensionality may not be achieved, but attempts are made to give the men and women in this film some depth, and the freshness of the performances helps a great deal.

The Paper is a crowd pleaser, and, regardless of any viewer's experience (or lack thereof) with the behind-the-scenes wrangling that goes on in newspaper offices, the story is affable and entertaining. While there are no startling revelations, the film's atmosphere contains enough strength of realism that more than one viewer may momentarily think of the goings-on at *The Sun* as they sit down with their morning cup of coffee and look at the day's headlines. **RECOMMENDED**

The Passion of the Christ [2004]

Starring: **James Caviezel, Maia Morgenstern, Monica Bellucci, Hristo Jivkov, Hristo Naumov Shopov, Mattia Sbragia** Director: **Mel Gibson** Screenplay: **Benedict Fitzgerald and Mel Gibson** Running Time: **2:07** Rated: **R (Graphic violence)** Theatrical Aspect Ratio: **2.35:1 In Aramaic and Latin with subtitles**

There are so many ancillary issues surrounding the release of Mel Gibson's *The Passion of the Christ* that they threaten to dwarf the 127-minute movie that lies at the maelstrom's epicenter. So let me cut to the chase: *The Passion of the Christ* is a gripping, powerful motion picture — arguably the most forceful depiction of Jesus' death ever to be committed to film. It leaves an indelible imprint on the psyche; viewers of this movie may never look at a crucifix in quite the same way.

The violence in the film is as necessary as it is disconcerting. There's no question that Gibson is pushing the envelope, going as far as he can without emptying the auditorium. It's easy to be desensitized by extreme, graphic violence in a cartoon-like setting, but that's not what we're getting here. The torture of Jesus is presented in such a brutal, unflinching manner that it's almost impossible not to look away as chunks of flesh are ripped out by a scourge, and the bloody, mangled skin is shredded to appear like a grotesque parody of ground meat. This is tough stuff, capable of unsettling adults and potentially traumatizing young viewers.

For the most part, *The Passion of the Christ* follows Jesus (James Caviezel) during the final 12 hours of his life — from Gethsemane to Golgotha, with stops along the way for a hearing before Ciaphas (Mattia Sbragia) and the Sanhedrin, the scourging under the auspices of Pilate (Hristo Naumov Shopov), the court of Herod, Pilate's eventual condemnation, and the final, torturous journey with the cross, as Mary (Maia Morgenstern), Mary Magdalene (Monica Bellucci), and John of Zebedee (Hristo Jivkov) follow behind. There are occasional, brief flashbacks to the Last Supper, the Sermon on the Mount, and the Triumphal Entry into Jerusalem (Palm Sunday) interspersed throughout, but nearly all of the action unfolds chronologically. And, as one would expect, the movie ends on a note of hope: a short, understated shot of the resurrected Christ.

Watching *The Passion of the Christ* is an immersive experience, at least after the first 30 minutes. It takes a little while for the movie to find its feet — some of the early scenes are awkwardly paced, with uneven performances by secondary actors. Once Jesus is first brought before Pilate, however, the film's grip inexorably tightens. The toughest scene to watch is the scourging — more difficult, even, than watching nails being driven through Jesus' hands and feet, because Gibson allows it to go on for so long. What transpires after is not easier, but it at least will not exceed the threshold of those who have come this far.

In making *The Passion of the Christ*, Gibson set himself up to fail. His goal — to take one of the best-known stories in all of human history and transform it into something new, vital, and emotionally potent — was audacious to the point of foolhardiness. Yet, somehow, against all odds, he succeeded. Understanding Christian doctrine — that this suffering was necessary to save sinners from damnation — adds an additional layer of meaning to the narrative. You don't have to be a believer to "get it" — good movies work on their own terms, and that's what happens with *The Passion of the Christ*.
HIGHLY RECOMMENDED

The People vs. Larry Flynt [1996]

Starring: Woody Harrelson, Courtney Love, Edward Norton, James Cromwell Director: Milos Forman Screenplay: Scott Alexander and Larry Karaszewski Running Time: 2:09 Rated: R (Nudity, sex, profanity, mature themes) Theatrical Aspect Ratio: 2.35:1

Larry Flynt, the self-proclaimed king of smut, as an American hero? Unlikely as it may seem, that's the scenario set up and successfully pursued by Milos Forman's (*One Flew Over the Cuckoos Nest, Amadeus*) *The People vs. Larry Flynt*. While this movie doesn't say anything that we haven't learned in high school civics classes, it gives names and faces to the subjects. Instead of "righteous" men stepped upon by the sys-

tem, we're presented with a person who has been demonized not only by the religious right, but by the mainstream press. Nevertheless, when Larry Flynt won his case before the Supreme Court in 1987, we all emerged victorious. His wasn't just a fight for his own rights, but a battle for everyone who cherishes the freedoms afforded by the First Amendment.

The People vs. Larry Flynt picks up Flynt's story in 1972, when he's trying to drum up business for his "Hustler" go-go clubs. His solution: start a "newsletter" with lots of pictures of naked women. Soon, *Hustler* is a nationwide publication, but poor sales threaten to financially ruin its publisher. Then Flynt manages an amazing coup. The *Hustler* issue featuring pictures of a naked Jacqueline Kennedy Onassis sells in excess of 2,000,000 copies and puts the magazine in the big leagues. Suddenly, Flynt becomes the target of obscenity and pandering law suits, with big guns like Charles Keating (James Cromwell) and Jerry Falwell (Richard Paul) lined up against him.

Perhaps the most obvious flaw in *The People vs. Larry Flynt* is making the central figure too likable. He's played by Woody Harrelson, an actor who has been synonymous with good-naturedness since his days on *Cheers*. And, with the real Flynt taking a bit part (an unsympathetic judge who presides over the first trial), and his lawyer, Alan Isaacman, acting as consultant, it's reasonable to wonder how much the publishing magnate's image has been smoothed over to make him more palatable to an unbiased viewing audience. It's no great stretch to assume that Flynt wasn't the civil rights advocate he comes across as being, since, by his own admission, he was "just trying to make an honest buck."

Why is *The People vs. Larry Flynt* entertaining? Probably because the lead character is so much bigger than life, and perhaps because, by making him into a sympathetic man, we're spared the darkest portions of his personality. There's no doubt that Flynt is a compelling figure, but his crusade for personal freedom is only part of the reason. Sex undoubtedly sells, and Forman doesn't skimp on it here. Ultimately, it doesn't matter much how true-to-life everything on screen is. What's important is that *The People vs. Larry Flynt* tells a good, intelligent story that keeps us interested and involved. Since that's what happens, the verdict is clear: see the movie. You don't have to like the man to support his struggles and enjoy this dramatization of them. **HIGHLY RECOMMENDED**

A Perfect World [1993]

Starring: Kevin Costner, T. J. Lowther, Clint Eastwood, Laura Dern
Director: Clint Eastwood Screenplay: John Lee Hancock Running
Time: 2:18 Rated: PG-13 (Language, violence, sexual situations,
mature themes) Theatrical Aspect Ratio: 2.35:1

Upon cursory examination, *A Perfect World* may seem like a buddy movie crossed with a road picture, but the film's surprising emotional depth transcends that which is normally found in either genre.

Halloween, 1963 is just another day for 8-year-old Phillip Perry (T. J. Lowther), since his mother, a devout Jehovah's Witness, refuses to let him go trick-or-treating. In fact, that's not the only thing on the boy's "forbidden" list. He can't celebrate Christmas, has never eaten cotton candy, and hasn't ridden a roller coaster. For Phillip, life is dull until Butch Haynes (Kevin Costner) bursts into his kitchen. Recently escaped from prison, Butch is in need of a hostage, and Phillip happens to be in the wrong place at the wrong time. Strangely, the boy instinctively trusts Butch, and accompanies him meekly. The ride starts out a little bumpy, with Butch's sadistic fellow escapee attempting to molest the hostage — a situation that Butch corrects. Then, when it's only the two of them, Butch and Philip head across Texas with Police chief Red Garnett (Clint Eastwood) and his band of Rangers in pursuit.

Those who understand the psychology of hostage situations are aware of the bond that develops between captive and captor. The case presented in *A Perfect World,* however, is far from normal, even for these circumstances. The connection between Kevin Costner's Butch and T. J. Lowther's Phillip isn't something nebulous, but a father-and-son-like relationship that profoundly affects them both. Once they're together, neither of them can be the same — not spiritually, physically, or morally.

Like his star, Kevin Costner, Clint Eastwood is a better director than actor. In *A Perfect World,* he again wears both hats, although his on-screen appearances are limited. Eastwood the actor has two modes — the cynical tough guy and the sensitive tough guy, both of which are present here (the former more often than the latter). He's in fine form, but it's his behind-the-scenes work that really deserves the credit. There are moments when *A Perfect World* manipulates, but they are masterfully subtle.

A Perfect World is evidence that Hollywood is still capable of producing the kinds of moving, intelligent movies that have increasingly become the province of independent filmmakers. The characters here have depth and breadth, and the themes and relationships are complex. Clint Eastwood won an Oscar for directing *Unforgiven,* and *A Perfect World* shows that the wellspring of talent is still bubbling energetically. May it never run dry. **HIGHLY RECOMMENDED**

Permanent Midnight [1998]

Starring: Ben Stiller, Elizabeth Hurley, Maria Bello, Janeane Garofalo,
Owen Wilson Director: David Veloz Screenplay: David Veloz based on
the book by Jerry Stahl Running Time: 1:25 Rated: R (Drug use,
profanity, sex) Theatrical Aspect Ratio: 1.85:1

If the progress of one man's descent into drug abuse in *Permanent Midnight* looks familiar, that's because the patterns of addiction are universal. It doesn't matter what an individual's demon is — alcohol, speed, cocaine, gambling, sex, or one of a hundred other vices. In this case, David Veloz's adaptation of Jerry Stahl's autobiography, the substance is heroin. The resulting spiral into dependence, debauchery, degradation, and disaster is as predictable as it is sad. And, for every lucky man like Stahl who manages to recover after hitting bottom, there are numerous nameless, faceless statistics who never again rise from the depths to which they have sunk.

Back in the 1980s, Jerry Stahl was a highly-successful TV sitcom writer (his best-known credit was *Alf*). Every week, he pulled in $5,000. The problem was, he had a smack habit that was costing him $1,000 more than that. What began as a minor recreational activity developed into an all-consuming obsession. Stahl couldn't function without heroin, but, after sticking a needle in a vein, he was "a real stud." Eventually, after being caught high while driving a car with his own baby in the passenger seat, Stahl straightened out his life.

As gritty as most of *Permanent Midnight* is, it doesn't wallow in unrelieved depression. The script injects a fair amount of black humor into the situation. The dialogue is smart and the narrative voiceover is riddled with cynical, self-deprecating observations. Because the film is structured as an extended series of flashbacks after Stahl has successfully made it through rehab, we know that he's going to be all right in the end, so that allows us to laugh at the jokes while still recognizing the seriousness of the situation.

Ben Stiller portrays a man on the edge, driven by forces he loses control of. There's one scene in particular that stands out in my memory. Unable to find a vein in his arm for the heroin injection, Stahl plunges the needle into his neck. On another occasion, we see him rooting through a trash bin in search of the residue of someone else's fix. Through all of this difficult material, Stiller is entirely convincing.

Permanent Midnight doesn't offer much in the way of surprises or revelations. It is largely what you expect it to be — the story of a man ruining his life because of his endless, desperate quest to inject a dangerous fluid into his bloodstream. Nevertheless, as familiar as the material may be, Veloz and Stiller invigorate it, making *Permanent Midnight* a more compelling and effective motion picture than one might normally anticipate from an entry into what has become a crowded field. RECOMMENDED

Philadelphia [1993]
Starring: Tom Hanks, Denzel Washington, Jason Robards, Mary Steenburgen, Antonio Banderas Director: Jonathan Demme
Screenplay: Edward Saxon and Jonathan Demme Running Time: 2:05
Rated: PG-13 (Mature themes, language, brief nudity) Theatrical Aspect Ratio: 1.85:1

Some will argue that a film, being essentially a means of entertainment, can do little to change a national consciousness. Others, citing the power of the medium, will claim that motion pictures possess this rare and extraordinary ability. In Jonathan Demme's *Philadelphia*, the question is not whether we sympathize with Tom Hanks' AIDS-afflicted, gay character, but whether that sympathy opens up a different perspective on the victims of the disease in the real world.

Andrew Beckett (Tom Hanks), a hotshot law graduate from Penn, has a promising career ahead of him when he discovers that he has AIDS. Choosing not to tell his mentor at the firm, Charles Wheeler (Jason Robards), of either his disease or his sexual orientation, Andrew moves forward with his caseload as a senior associate. But the partners learn of his affliction, and while their dismissal is couched in terms of incompetence, Andrew knows that his AIDS and homosexuality are the root cause. He takes his case to a number of lawyers, including ambulance-chaser Joe Miller (Denzel Washington), none of whom is willing to represent him — until Miller has a change of heart, recognizing a hint of familiar discrimination in the way Andrew is being treated.

Tom Hanks gives what has rightly been called "the performance of his career," lending humanity and vibrancy to the victim. We feel for Andrew Beckett because he seems to be a genuine human being, not

because the script and production have twisted circumstances to manipulate our emotions.

The work of Denzel Washington, while less obvious, is as impressive. Washington plays the "everyman," the on-screen representation of those in the audience who harbor homophobic tendencies. He, like many viewers, is forced to examine his bigotry and reassess his feelings about the gay community as he comes to know them as people rather than symbols and caricatures.

Symbolism is crucial to the story; the most obvious example is the role of physical space between Beckett and Miller. Before the AIDS revelation, they are shoulder-to-shoulder, two lawyers on opposite sides. Then Beckett drops his bombshell, and Miller moves to the other side of the room. As the film progresses, they grow gradually closer, sitting across a table at a library, then side-by-side in court. Finally, past the moment of Miller's crisis of conscience, he drops all barriers by lifting an oxygen mask to Andrew's face, momentarily touching flesh to flesh.

Even as it stands, with its faults, *Philadelphia* is still a remarkable expression of honesty and openness. Miller's court statements about this country's fear of homosexuals are frank and to-the-point. The story is timely and powerful, and the performances of Hanks and Washington assure that the characters will not immediately vanish into obscurity. And as long as people remember, there's a chance they can change. HIGHLY RECOMMENDED

The Pianist [United Kingdom/France/Germany/Poland/ Netherlands, 2002]
Starring: Adrien Brody, Thomas Kretschmann Director: Roman Polanski Screenplay: Ronald Harwood, based on the book by Wladyslaw Szpilman Running Time: 2:28 Rated: R (Violence, profanity) Theatrical Aspect Ratio: 1.85:1

To lump *The Pianist* in with all of the other Holocaust stories brought to the screen does a great disservice to this powerful, compelling motion picture. Crafted without a whiff of melodrama, this motion picture takes a steady, unflinching look at the plight of Jews in Warsaw during the years when Poland was occupied by the Nazis. For director Roman Polanski, this represents his most effective film in nearly 3 decades. Not since 1974's *Chinatown* has Polanski reached such dramatic heights.

How is *The Pianist* different from an "average" Holocaust drama (if there can be said to be such a thing)? To begin with, there are no concentration camp scenes. In addition, Polanski does not flinch from showing the naked horrors perpetrated by Nazis on Jews. There is no attempt to sugar-coat this bitter pill — we see frequent gunshots to the head, torture, and the effects of starvation. The tone and style of the film are documentary-like — Polanski observes from a detached perspective, detailing atrocities without manipulating his audience. The result is bleak and powerful, and may overcome more sensitive viewers.

The Pianist opens in 1939 Warsaw, shortly after Poland's defeat to Germany. The film's protagonist is celebrated Jewish pianist Wladyslaw Szpilman (Adrien Brody), who, along with his family, is forced to watch as the restrictions against Jews become increasingly more odious. Initially, Jews are forbidden from eating in certain establishments, walking in public parks, or sitting on public benches. Soon, they must wear distinguishing armbands, bow to Nazis passed in the streets, and walk in the gutters. Eventually, all Jews in Warsaw — approximately 500,000 — are moved into a ghetto, where whole families are crammed into single small rooms. After the Nazis begin implementing their "Final Solution," most of the Jews in Warsaw are shipped to the concentration camps to be exterminated. Only those capable of labor are allowed to remain behind. Wladyslaw is separated from his family at this point. He remains behind as part of a work force, while his family is herded into a cattle car. Eventually, with the help of the underground, Wladyslaw escapes into hiding, where he battles starvation, disease, and cold until the arrival of the Soviets.

With *The Pianist*, Roman Polanski has not only given us the most recent motion picture to remind future generations of what happened under Hitler's regime, but he has also provided us with hope that his own career, after numerous dead-ends, may finally be back on track. **HIGHLY RECOMMENDED**

The Piano [Australia/New Zealand/France, 1993]

Starring: Holly Hunter, Harvey Keitel, Sam Neill, Anna Paquin
Director: Jane Campion Screenplay: Jane Campion Running Time: 2:01
Rated: R (Nudity, sex, violence, mature themes) Theatrical Aspect
Ratio: 1.85:1

The Piano is about passion, the most basic and primal element of human nature. No matter how thick the veneer of civilization is, or how deeply-buried beneath layers of social repression those latent emotions are, passion ultimately cannot be denied. This is something that the 3 principals of this movie learn in various, often unpleasant, ways.

In the mid-1800s, Ada (Holly Hunter) arrives on the stormy shores of New Zealand, a mute bride sold by her father to a British emigrant named Stewart (Sam Neill). In addition to a normal assortment of baggage, Ada brings with her 8-year-old Flora (Anna Paquin), her illegitimate daughter, and a piano. Initially, Stewart declares that the piano is too bulky to move from the beach, and resists bringing it to his house despite Ada's wordless pleadings. Next, he sells it to fellow Englishman Baines (Harvey Keitel), a man who has embraced the local Maori ways. In addition to the piano, Baines wants a reluctant Ada as his teacher. When he offers her a deal to get the instrument back, she is unprepared for the price she must ultimately pay.

Jane Campion's story is often stirring and occasionally gut-wrenching; the latter perhaps to a fault. There is a single visceral scene in this movie which becomes the most stark and enduring image taken from the theater. While definitely an expression of passion, this is perhaps not intended as the single defining moment of *The Piano*, although it may be remembered as such.

As affecting as Campion's basic story is, both characterization and technical presentation are lacking. Taken in tandem, these flaws prevent *The Piano* from attaining its full potential. The editing is choppy, at times causing the narrative to become disjointed or confusing. More than one transition is jarringly abrupt.

While Ada is as fully-rounded as she can be, the others all have elements missing from their personalities. Stewart never attains three-dimensionality, despite Sam Neill's best attempts, and Baines is occasionally little more than a sounding board for Ada's emotions to reverberate off of. Flora's personality undergoes a radical shift that, at best, is only partially-motivated by what we see on screen.

The Piano is a solid motion picture with a universal message and occasional splashes of genius, but it is remarkable only as Holly Hunter's performance is concerned. **RECOMMENDED**

Picture Bride [United States/Japan, 1995]

Starring: Youki Kudoh, Akira Takayama, Tamlyn Tomita, Cary-Hiroyuki Tagawa, Toshiro Mifune Director: Kayo Hatta Screenplay: Kayo Hatta and Mari Hatta based on a story by Kayo Hatta, Mari Hatta, and Diana Mei Lin Mark Running Time: 1:30 Rated: PG-13 (Mature themes, brief nudity) Theatrical Aspect Ratio: 1.85:1 In English and Japanese with subtitles

At the beginning of the 20th century, Hawaii's economy was dominated by the output of its sugar cane plantations. To boost production, plantation owners imported workers from China, Japan, Korea, the Philippines, and other countries. Men arrived in droves, with illusions of getting rich. Reality, of course, was far from the dream, and the immigrant workers had little choice but to accept their lot and limit their expectations. So, instead of wealth, they sought the comfort and stability of a family. Attaining even this modest goal proved difficult, however, as Hawaii lacked an abundance of available women. The eventual solution was the concept of the "photo marriage" — arranged matches established through photographs and letters sent between the plantation workers and their prospective partners across the sea.

Writer/director Kayo Hatta spent 5 years researching stories of the picture brides, and at one point considered producing a documentary rather than a feature. In the end, however, she blended real-life anecdotes with historical facts to form what is, in essence, a simple love story. Hatta tells her tale with a heartfelt sincerity that comes across on the screen, and the Hawaii of the early 1900s is realistically portrayed. *Picture Bride* has its faults, but artifice and melodrama are not among them.

The title character is Riyo (Youki Kudoh), a 16-year-old girl from Yokohama who has come to Hawaii to escape her past and begin a new future with Matsuji (Akira Takayama). When she first meets her husband-to-be, she is shocked: the aging plantation worker barely resembles the young man in her photograph. Somewhat shamefacedly, Matsuji admits that he didn't have a good recent likeness, so he sent one taken a long time ago.

The marriage starts on shaky ground. Riyo will not sleep with Matsuji, and thinks of nothing but earning the money to return to Japan. With wages of about $11 a month, however, raising the necessary $300 seems an impossible task. And, as Matsuji informs her, "After a while you think of the homeland less and less. Going back to Japan becomes an old dream." Kana (Tamlyn Tomita), a veteran worker of the cane fields who also came to Hawaii as a picture bride, befriends Riyo and attempts to bring a little harmony to her unsettled marriage.

Picture Bride depicts the struggle of a strong-willed, female Asian American protagonist. As an attempt to re-create a segment of Hawaii's colorful history, this film is extremely effective. As a love story, it is only marginally less so. Through much of *Picture*

Bride, we feel like we're viewing the story rather than experiencing it. We understand the motives of Riyo, Matsuji, and Kana, but moments of intimate identification are rare. For Kayo Hatta, *Picture Bride* represents a satisfying culmination to a labor of love.
RECOMMENDED

Pieces of April [2003]

Starring: Katie Holmes, Derek Luke, Patricia Clarkson, Oliver Platt, John Gallagher, Jr., Alison Pill, Alice Drummond, Sean Hayes
Director: Peter Hedges Screenplay: Peter Hedges Running Time: 1:20
Rated: R (Profanity, sex, violence) Theatrical Aspect Ratio: 1.85:1

As human beings, we have an amazing thirst for closure. Thus, when an estranged family member dies without a reconciliation, the gaping sore can be especially painful for the ones left behind. There are countless stories of deathbed peacemaking sessions between fathers and sons, mothers and daughters, sisters and brothers. But what of all those missed opportunities? This subject is very much in the forefront of director Peter Hedges's feature debut, *Pieces of April*. However, despite its themes of terminal illness, dysfunctional families, and the need to heal old wounds, the film spends as much time provoking laughter as tears.

The story concerns twenty-something April Burns (Katie Holmes), the proverbial black sheep of the family, who moved out of the family house to a dismal Lower East Side apartment as soon as the opportunity arose. Now, learning that her domineering mother (Patricia Clarkson) is dying from cancer, and prodded by her new boyfriend, Bobby (Derek Luke), to re-open contact, April extends the olive branch and invites the family to Thanksgiving dinner at her place. So the entire Burns clan bundles into the car to make the trip into the city: Mom, Dad (Oliver Platt), pothead brother Timmy (John Gallagher, Jr.), stuck-up sister Beth (Alison Pill), and senile Grandma (Alice Drummond). Meanwhile, as she's getting ready to put the turkey in the oven, April has an uninvited guest: Murphy, whose law declares that anything that can go wrong will go wrong.

Pieces of April plays like the intersection of two road pictures. The first is almost conventional, with the Burns family making the trek through the woods and over the river to April's apartment. April's "road trip" is a little less usual — it takes her from apartment to apartment within her building as she searches for a working stove after hers gives up the ghost. Meanwhile, Bobby is out looking for some cool threads, while someone named Tyrone is trying to contact him. Except Bobby doesn't know any "Tyrone."

The ending of *Pieces of April* is conventional, but satisfying, and there's enough delightful weirdness up to the final moments that it's hard to fault Hedges for taking the easy way out. The digital video isn't the most polished medium in which to have made the movie (there are several occasions when bright lights wash out everything), but one could argue that it adds a certain grittiness to the proceedings. Perhaps because this is such a personal story, it's affecting and effective, and represents a solid first effort.
RECOMMENDED

Playing by Heart [1998]

Starring: Sean Connery, Gena Rowlands, Gillian Anderson, Madeleine Stowe, Angelina Jolie, Dennis Quaid Director: Willard Carroll
Screenplay: Willard Carroll Running Time: 2:01 Rated: R (Profanity, sexual situations, mature themes) Theatrical Aspect Ratio: 2.35:1

Playing by Heart is an ensemble dramatic comedy about the many faces of love: romance, longing, loss, sex, and lust. Set in modern-day L.A., the film tells 6 seemingly-unrelated tales about men and women finding each other, losing each other, unearthing long-buried secrets, and discovering things about themselves and others. Nothing in *Playing by Heart* is groundbreaking. In fact, one could argue that every one of the stories is unremarkable to the point of being trite. But the movie is consistently well-acted and features a gallery of characters so affable that it's difficult to actively dislike any of them, or, for that matter, the film as a whole.

The biggest name in the cast is undoubtedly Sean Connery, who plays Paul, a robust man afflicted with a brain tumor. Paul is dying, but you'd never know it to look at him. Connery is in fine form, with a mischievous twinkle in his eye and not a hint of James Bond in his performance. It's a pleasure to see the actor in a low-profile role like this. Paul is married to Hannah (the always-reliable Gena Rowlands), the host of a successful TV cooking show. After 40 years of marriage, the two think they know everything about each other — until Hannah's discovery of a 25-year-old photograph forces Paul to reveal several long-buried secrets.

Shaking her popular TV image, Gillian Anderson plays Meredith, a lonely young woman whose disastrous romantic history has caused her to give up on love. Madeleine Stowe is Gracie, a woman who engages in frequent affairs to plug the void in her sexually-unfulfilling marriage. Dennis Quaid is Hugh, an individual whose personality and life story changes from night to night. Ellen Burstyn and Jay Mohr are Mildred and Mark, a mother and son coming to grips with the latter's impending death from AIDS complications. And Angelina Jolie, who gives the film's standout performance, is luminous as the sassy, self-confident Joan, a Generation X-er in search of Mr. Right. Also in the cast are Jon Stewart, Anthony Edwards, Nastassja Kinski, and Ryan Phillippe as partners for the various main characters.

Love is an emotion that everyone experiences at one time or another. For that reason, at least one of the stories in *Playing by Heart* is likely to touch each viewer to some degree. Cynics may balk at the audience-friendly disposition of the film, but that's usually only a bad thing when melodrama suffocates intelligence, which only happens here on rare occasions. On the surface, the title doesn't mean much but, after seeing the film, it seems to fit the mood. *Playing by Heart* will not make many Top 10 lists, but, as a way to spend a January afternoon or evening, it's an enjoyable diversion. **RECOMMENDED**

Ponette [France, 1996]

Starring: Victoire Thivisol, Matiaz Bureau, Delphine Schiltz, Xavier Beauvois, Claire Nebout Director: Jacques Doillon
Screenplay: Jacques Doillon Running Time: 1:37 Rated: No MPAA Rating (Mature themes) Theatrical Aspect Ratio: 1.66:1 In French with English subtitles

Few of us who call ourselves "adults" truly remember the experience of childhood, except as a dim and distant illusion. Oh, we can recall what we did as a child, and often our memories of that period are among our most precious, but, looking back, we view things through the haze of maturity. Every once in a while, however, something comes along that breaks through that filter — a movie, a scene on television, a page in a book, or a moment in real life. Jacques Doillon's *Ponette* is one such catalyst. By presenting the world through the eyes of a grieving 4-year-old, *Ponette* manages to do what few motion pictures can — regress an audience into childhood.

Ponette works in large part because of its simplicity and realism. The plot is minimal — just enough to give us a reason to stay with the tiny protagonist for ninety minutes. Ponette has recently lost her mother in a car accident. Her father, a somber, emotionally-detached man, informs her that "Mommy was broken," then disappears for a while, leaving his daughter in the care of her aunt. So, with the aid of two cousins and, later, a group of other school children, Ponette must grapple with confusing religious issues while trying to understand the meaning of life and death.

The film effortlessly takes us into the magical world of a 4-year-old, where stuffed animals have extraordinary powers, dolls are more than inanimate objects, and God is someone you can talk to and expect an answer from. Some of the most memorable moments in *Ponette* center around the innocent conversations of children — how Catholics are different from Jews, what it means to be "single," and how eating a certain candy can make you fall in love forever.

For more than 80 minutes, *Ponette* continues strongly, but, in the end, writer/director Jacques Doillon seems at a loss how to end the movie. His choice, while admittedly cathartic, feels like a cheat. The pseudo-realistic, almost-documentary quality of the film evaporates; *Ponette*'s final scenes jar us out of the fragile reverie generated by what preceded them. Fortunately, the contrived ending does little to dampen my enthusiasm for the picture as a whole. When I recall *Ponette*, the first thing I think of is the heartbreakingly pure performance of young Victoire Thivisol.

From start to finish, Thivisol is nothing short of amazing. This is the kind of portrayal that would be labeled as a standout from an actor of any age, but, from someone who's only four, it's astonishing. A share of the credit must be lavished upon Doillon — it takes a masterful filmmaker to elicit this kind of unforced performance from a child. Had Thivisol shown a hint of artifice, *Ponette* would not have worked. The strength and consistency of her acting keeps this film on a high level. RECOMMENDED

The Portrait of a Lady [United Kingdom/United States, 1996]

Starring: Nicole Kidman, John Malkovich, Barbara Hershey, Martin Donovan, Mary-Louise Parker Director: Jane Campion
Screenplay: Laura Jones based on the novel by Henry James Running Time: 2:25 Rated: PG-13 (Mature themes, brief nudity) Theatrical Aspect Ratio: 2.35:1

The Portrait of a Lady, the first motion picture adaptation of Henry James' beloved classic, presents a stark contrast to the light-and-sunny Jane Austen movies. Although it examines some of the same issues as *Pride and Prejudice, Sense and Sensibility*, and *Emma*, the perspective is much darker. Those expecting a light romance from *The Portrait of a Lady* are in for a rude awakening.

Kidman plays Isabel Archer, a headstrong-but-naive young woman who, as the story opens in 1872, has recently arrived in England from America. While there, she's staying at the estate of her aunt (Shelly Winters) and uncle (John Gielgud). Her closest companion and confidante is her cousin, Ralph Touchett (Martin Donovan), a consumptive who encourages his father to will a large sum of money to Isabel. She is also pursued by two suitors: the rich and unexciting Lord Warburton (Richard E. Grant) and the dashing Caspar Goodwood (Viggo Mortensen). She rejects both, saying "I don't want to be a mere sheep in the flock. I shall probably never marry." Her desire is to explore the world and forge her own way in it.

When her uncle dies, leaving her a fortune of 70,000 pounds, she has the financial means to do so. She begins to travel, spending a great deal of time in Italy. But her naïveté enables her to be led astray by the sinister Madame Serena Merle (Barbara Hershey), whom she falsely believes to be her friend. Madame Merle contrives a meeting between Isabel and the dangerous Gilbert Osmond (John Malkovich). Soon, Isabel, seduced by Osmond's promises of love, agrees to marry him. Too late, she recognizes Osmond's true nature.

Those familiar with Jane Campion's previous effort, *The Piano*, will not be surprised by the dismal tone of *The Portrait of a Lady*, which, if anything, is even grimmer than that of the novel. Campion films over half of the scenes in dim light, making effective use of contrast to highlight character attributes. Isabel is frequently shown standing in patches of light while Madame Merle and Osmond keep to the shadows. Occasionally, Campion gets a little too artsy, as in a surreal, black-and-white dream sequence where Isabel's subconscious wrestles with Osmond's declaration of love.

The Portrait of a Lady is a difficult story to film, and Jane Campion and screenwriter Laura Jones have done an admirable job with this adaptation. The motifs of love, betrayal, and accepting the consequences of one's actions are well-established. The movie does not attain the emotional depth of Michael Winterbottom's *Jude*, but there are definite thematic and tonal similarities. The result is a fascinating portrait not only of a lady, but of the society and marriage that entrap, then attempt to destroy, her. RECOMMENDED

The Postman (Il Postino) [Italy, 1995]

Starring: Massimo Troisi, Philippe Noiret, Maria Grazia Cucinotta, Linda Moretti Director: Michael Radford Screenplay: Anna Pavignano, Michael Radford, Furio Scarpelli, and Massimo Troisi based on the

novel *Burning Patience* by Antonio Skarmeta Running Time: **1:55**
Rated: **PG (Mature themes)** Theatrical Aspect Ratio: **1.85:1** In Italian
with subtitles

The Postman, an Italian film from British director Michael Radford, is a charming piece of cinema that takes several comfortable formulas and expands upon them in ingenious and emotionally-satisfying ways. There's a little of everything here: poetry, politics, humor, love, and heartbreak. Best of all, these elements flow together seamlessly in a production characterized by solid acting, balanced pacing, and eye-catching cinematography.

Mario (played by the late Italian writer/director/actor Massimo Troisi) is a postman in a fishing village on a small island off the coast of Italy. Arriving there in 1953 is famed Chilean poet Pablo Neruda (Philippe Noiret), exiled from his native country for espousing communist doctrine. Mario is curious about this new resident who, despite his advancing age, has a seemingly magical power over women. Eventually, after delivering Neruda's mail for a while, he gets up the courage to engage the poet in a conversation about writing. This begins an unusual collaboration, with Mario providing a sounding board for Neruda's ideas and Neruda teaching Mario about poetry and its relationship to life.

In the final performance of a great career, Massimo Troisi (who died at the age of 41, shortly after completing this picture) gives us a memorable character. Hesitant, shy, and uncultured, Mario has the heart of a poet, but little talent with words. In this post-*Forrest Gump* era, it would be easy to compare him to the Tom Hanks character, but Mario is really a more complex individual. He occasionally makes some startlingly insightful observations, such as "the whole world is a metaphor for something," often without realizing how thought-provoking his comments are. *The Postman* is about Mario, and Troisi imbues him with a captivating humanity.

Philipe Noiret's Pablo Neruda is the perfect foil for Mario — a kindred spirit with all the experience and talent that the postman lacks. Noiret plays Neruda as part father-figure, part dreamer, and part realist. When Mario asks him how to become a poet, the older man responds by advising his "pupil" to take a walk along the island's shoreline and see what images come to mind. After Mario has fallen for the stunning Beatrice (Maria Grazia Cucinotta), Neruda tells him about the many women of that name to have inspired poets.

For 2 hours, it's possible to fall under *The Postman*'s spell and be completely enchanted. There is more vitality and genuine passion here than in any ten big-budget extravaganzas. This movie about words and images will delight not just because it entertains, but because it takes the motion picture experience one step further, and fulfills. **MUST SEE**

The Princess and the Warrior [Germany, 2000]
Starring: **Franka Potente, Benno Furmann, Joachim Król, Marita Breuer**
Director: **Tom Tykwer** Screenplay: **Tom Tykwer** Running Time: **2:09**
Rated: **R (Violence, profanity, sexual situations)** Theatrical Aspect
Ratio: **2.35:1** In German with subtitles

German filmmaker Tom Tykwer first gained a measure of international recognition in 1997, when his second feature, *Winter Sleepers* received attention outside of his native Germany. Then came the 1998 Toronto Film Festival and the debut of *Run Lola Run,* which became one of the hottest and most talked about properties in Toronto that year.

Although Tykwer uses many of the same flourishes that made *Lola*'s style unique, the tone and pacing of *The Princess and the Warrior* are much different. *Lola* was an explosion of riotous color and kinetic energy; this movie is more restrained and thoughtful. It also has greater thematic depth and resonance.

Franka Potente, who has traded in her bright red hair from *Lola* for blond tresses, plays Sissi, a meek nurse at a psychiatric hospital whose daily life represents a sea of monotony. One day, her path crosses that of Bodo (Beno Furmann), an ex-army officer who can't hold down a stable job. Because of something Bodo does, Sissi is struck by a truck while crossing a street. Unaware that he was the cause of the accident, Bodo slips underneath the stopped truck to escape the policemen who are pursuing him. There he finds Sissi, immobilized and struggling to breathe. Acting quickly, Bodo saves her life, then vanishes. Two months later, once her recovery is complete, Sissi seeks out her savior, only to find a bitter individual who wants nothing to do with her. But his rejection is not enough for Sissi, who believes that destiny brought them together, so she continues to pursue Bodo — only to have fate throw another curve ball in her direction.

Thematically, *The Princess and the Warrior* has a lot going on. One of Tykwer's pet issues — that of fate and coincidence guiding our lives — is in play here, as it was in both *Winter Sleepers* and *Run Lola Run.* The film also explores ideas about life, death, guilt, salvation, and male anger towards women. Tykwer finds a way to blend everything together into a production that challenges as much as it entertains.

Often, a director's follow-up to an acclaimed work results in a letdown. Thankfully, *The Princess and the Warrior* represents a step forward for Tykwer, not a step backward. Those who like stories with clean, unambiguous resolutions will probably not appreciate (or understand) the freedom and latitude offered by *The Princess and the Warrior*'s conclusion. But for anyone who esteems the experience of participating in a movie rather than being a passive observer, this film comes with a "Do Not Miss" label. It is the reason I review movies. **MUST SEE**

Proof [Australia, 1991]

Starring: Hugo Weaving, Geneviève Picot, Russell Crowe
Director: Jocelyn Moorhouse Screenplay: Jocelyn Moorhouse
Running Time: 1:30 Rated: R (Sex, nudity, profanity) Theatrical Aspect Ratio: 1.85:1

Proof is a delightful and dark dramatic comedy that can be hilarious one moment and poignant the next. The script is intelligent, the acting is brilliant, and the overall result is fabulously entertaining.

For Martin (Hugo Weaving), trusting has never been easy. He has been blind his entire life, and, as a boy, he believed his mother lied to him when she described the sights around him. Why? Because she could. Martin was sure that his mother never loved him, but merely put up with him out of a sense of responsibility. When she died at a young age, he thought it was all a ruse so she could get away from him. Those beliefs followed him into adulthood, where he became a recluse, unwilling to let anyone into his life or his heart beyond what was absolutely necessary. Martin has an interesting pastime for a blind man — he's a photographer. He takes pictures, then has someone describe them to him. In his words, the photographs are proof that what he senses is what others see.

Martin has a housekeeper, a 30-year-old woman named Celia (Geneviève Picot). She's in love with him to the point of obsession. Like Martin, Celia dabbles in photography, but she only has one subject — him. The walls and tables of her home are covered with pictures of Martin. But theirs is not a cordial relationship. Celia torments Martin and, in response, he humiliates her. Celia wants Martin's trust and respect, but those are things he is unwilling to part with, especially to her. So they continue in a state of unhealthy co-dependency, where each needs something from the other, and both are unhappy.

Enter Andy (Russell Crowe in an early role), the outsider who impels the relationship between Martin and Celia out of its stasis. Andy is a waiter at a local restaurant who befriends Martin, and, after a short while, becomes his regular describer of photographs. When Andy meets Celia, he is immediately smitten, but all she sees in Andy is a rival for Martin. So Celia concocts a plan designed to discredit Andy and finally give her what she wants — Martin, all to herself.

The soundtrack of *Proof* is remarkable in the way it amplifies the blind man's perspective. We hear bracelets jingling, rain pattering on ceilings, cats purring, dogs panting, truck breaks squeaking, distant phones ringing, the hum of fluorescent lights, footsteps, wine being poured into glasses, and a china teacup rattling on a saucer. Moorhouse makes us aware of sounds in a way that most directors don't. It isn't necessary to the plot, but it's one of those touches that elevates the movie's impact. *Proof* would have been a fine feature without such details and subtleties. With them, it's a tour de force for a first-time director, and the kind of motion picture that deserves to be playing in VCRs, not sitting untouched on video store shelves. **HIGHLY RECOMMENDED**

The Quiet American [United States/Germany/Australia, 2002]

Starring: Michael Caine, Brendan Fraser, Do Thi Hai Yen Director: Phillip Noyce Screenplay: Christopher Hampton and Robert Schenkkan, based on the novel by Graham Greene Running Time: 1:41 Rated: R (Violence, sexual situations) Theatrical Aspect Ratio: 2.35:1

It's 1952 Saigon, and British journalist Thomas Fowler (Michael Caine) is about to find his comfortable life upset by the arrival of a fresh-faced, self-effacing American medical aid worker. Alden Pyle (Brendan Fraser) at first seems to be nothing more than an idealistic young doctor, but his activities cause Thomas to wonder whether he has an alternate agenda. Meanwhile, Alden falls for Thomas's beautiful young Vietnamese mistress, Phuong (Do Thi Hai Yen). Because Alden is unattached, while Thomas is married to a woman in London who will not give him a divorce, Alden can offer Phuong one thing that Thomas cannot: a wedding ring.

At the time when the movie takes place, Vietnam is being torn being torn apart by the rival Communists and the French, who still considered Indochina to be their colony. Into this mix comes a third faction — that of General Thé (Quang Hai), a egotistical megalomaniac who is revered by a segment of the population and backed by an invisible financial institution with deep pockets. General Thé organizes terrorist actions against Vietnamese citizens, then blames the Communists in order to curry international sympathy for his side. As the story unfolds, Thomas recognizes that Alden has unexpected influence where General Thé is concerned.

The screenplay, by Christopher Hampton and Robert Schenkkan, downplays the heavy allegorical aspects of Graham Greene's source novel in favor of the romantic triangle. *The Quiet American* is primarily a tragic love story set against the backdrop of the beginnings of the turbulent conflict that would devastate much of the small Asian country. We see the roots of the Vietnam War, and have no trouble understanding that the United States' rabid win-at-all-costs struggle against the devil of Communism led to bad alliances and shortsighted determinations.

From a dramatic standpoint, I have a quibble with *The Quiet American*'s structure. The movie begins at the end, telling most of the story in flashback. Unfortunately, this means that we know from the start how the love triangle is going to be resolved, and which character will die. While this approach heightens the movie's allegorical elements, it diminishes the dramatic and romantic tension. Director Phillip Noyce obviously felt comfortable about the trade-off, but I'm not sure it works in the film's favor. However, all things considered, Noyce has wrought an often-compelling tale of life, love, and jealousy played out under the gathering storm clouds of war. **RECOMMENDED**

Quills [2000]

Starring: Geoffrey Rush, Kate Winslet, Joaquin Phoenix, Michael Caine, Amelia Warner Director: Philip Kaufman Screenplay: Doug Wright, based on his play Running Time: 2:03 Rated: R (Sexual situations, sex-related dialogue, nudity, profanity, violence) Theatrical Aspect Ratio: 1.85:1

Two assumptions can readily be made about any motion picture centered around the Marquis de Sade. The first is that the material will be of a sexual nature. The second is that the movie will not be a light-hearted romp. Both of these presumptions are true in the case of Philip Kaufman's *Quills*, arguably the most provocative and best historical melodrama of 2000.

Count Donatien-Alphonse-François de Sade, better known as the Marquis de Sade, lived from 1740 until 1814, although his infamous reputation has survived for nearly 2 centuries since his remains were scattered. For most of his adult life, the Marquis was in and out of prison, as his penchant for deviant sex-

ual behavior (which typically included torture) continually put him at odds with the law. Following the French Revolution and the storming of the Bastille, he was incarcerated in the Charenton Asylum for the Insane, where he resided for a year. After his release, he spent approximately a decade writing scandalous manuscripts and putting on plays before his activities once again landed him at Charenton, where he spent the rest of his life.

Quills, although a fictionalized account of the Marquis' last years, is moderately faithful to the historical record. The characterization of the title character, despite being softened to make the man bearable to a mainstream audience, captures some of Sade's essence. As portrayed by the energetic Geoffrey Rush in a brilliant turn that avoids the easy path of caricaturization, Sade is a shrewd, dangerous man with an intelligence that is matched in magnitude by his perverse sexual desires.

Kate Winslet plays Madeleine, a chambermaid at the asylum who is engaged in a clandestine (albeit platonic) relationship with the Marquis. His writing fascinates her, and she smuggles his manuscripts out of Charenton so that they can be published. Winslet's performance, while generally low key, is so strong that she is able to stand toe-to-toe with the more flamboyant Rush. Joaquin Phoenix turns in solid work as a priest who conceals romantic feelings for Madeleine. Finally, Michael Caine's portrayal of Dr. Royer-Collard, the "man of science" sent by Napoleon to oversee Charenton, results in a memorably detestable villain.

For those who aren't offended by the idea of a movie that presents the Marquis de Sade as a multi-dimensional character rather than a cartoon-like pervert, *Quills* has much to offer. It is based on a play by Doug Wright, and, while the dialogue has the intelligence and crispness of something originally designed for the stage, Wright and Kaufman have done an excellent job of opening up the setting. Employing the talents of a top-flight cast and working from a screenplay that uses the historical backdrop as a means to deal with issues of contemporary import, *Quills* offers a thoroughly compelling 2 hours. **HIGHLY RECOMMENDED**

Quiz Show [1994]

Starring: Ralph Fiennes, Rob Morrow, John Turturro, Paul Scofield, David Paymer Director: Robert Redford Screenplay: Paul Attanasio based on *Remembering America: A Voice from the Sixties* by Richard N. Goodwin Running Time: 2:13 Rated: PG-13 (Profanity, mature themes) Theatrical Aspect Ratio: 1.85:1

1958. Television quiz shows like "Twenty-One" are ratings hits. Americans tune in every week to root for the charming, erudite Charles Van Doren (Ralph Fiennes) in his quest to vanquish new challengers. Following his defeat of the previous champion, Herbie Stempel (John Turturro), Van Doren, the son of the well-known poet Mark Van Doren (Paul Schofield), has become a national celebrity, sending sales of Geritol, the sponsor of "Twenty-One," through the roof. But all is not well behind the scenes. Van Doren's victories are cheats, the results of pre-supplied answers guaranteed to keep him on the air. When a bitter Stempel decides to go public, and Congressional investigator Dick Goodwin (Rob Morrow) listens to him, a national scandal erupts.

The clearest message of *Quiz Show* is a cynical truth: the entertainment industry is a business where ethics are meaningless when it comes to winning a ratings war. This is hardly a revelation, of course. No American in 1994 is naïve enough to blindly accept anything they see on television. "Twenty-One," however, is where that disillusionment started.

One of the reasons that *Quiz Show* is so extraordinary is because it spins a story as compelling on the personal level as on the national one. Ralph Fiennes' Charles Van Doren is a fascinating individual, equally seduced and repelled by greed. Desperate to escape his father's shadow, he wallows in public adulation until it begins to stink from his own hypocrisy. On the other side of the father/son conflict is Paul Scofield's character. Masterfully rendered, Mark Van Doren is far more than the usual stern, disapproving patriarch. He is a man with keen insight and sensitivity who looks sadly upon the track of his son's ambitions.

John Turturro is exceptional as the uncharismatic Herbie Stempel, a man so petty and dislikable that it's impossible to sympathize with him even when he's presented as a victim. Rob Morrow is good enough not to be completely overshadowed by his co-stars, although his forced accent could have been toned down. Mira Sorvino provides a spark as Goodwin's wife.

Towards the end of the movie, David Paymer's Dan Enright comments that the sham of "Twenty-One" created a situation in which nobody lost — not the sponsor, NBC, the public, or the contestants. Viewers of *Quiz Show*, however, are likely to form the opposite impression — that, in the end, there were no winners. **HIGHLY RECOMMENDED**

Raise the Red Lantern [China, 1991]

Starring: Gong Li, Cao Cuifen, He Caifei, Jin Shuyuan, Kong Lin, Ma Jingwu, Zhao Qi Director: Zhang Yimou Screenplay: Ni Zhen based on the novel *Wives and Concubines* by Su Tong Running Time: 2:05 Rated: No MPAA Rating (Mature themes) Theatrical Aspect Ratio: 1.85:1 In Mandarin with subtitles

Raise the Red Lantern is one of those all-too-rare motion pictures capable of enthralling an audience while they're watching it, then haunting them for hours (or days) thereafter. With its simple story and complex themes and emotions, *Raise the Red Lantern* hints at the kind of film a great director like Ingmar Bergman might have made had he attempted a story set in mainland China.

The difference between Songlian (Gong Li), the fourth wife of a rich landowner, and the other three spouses, is that she is educated, and has been married (by her mother) against her will. Now, her whole world is reduced to one small compound, and the only people she sees are her husband, his family, and their servants. She is given a maid (Kong Lin) that she doesn't get along with, and finds her new home to be a cheerless place, despite all the bright colors that adorn the inside walls.

It's the master's tradition to light lanterns outside the house of the wife he intends to join for the night. Since Songlian is new to the compound, it is expected that he will spend much of his time with her. However, on their first night together, the master is called away to soothe his pampered third wife (He Caifei), who complains of an ailment. From then on, Songlian realizes that she'll have to resort to deceit and manipulation to retain her husband's interest. And, while she doesn't necessarily appreciate his attentions, she realizes that her status in the household is directly proportional to how highly she is favored.

Within days of her arrival, Songlian's relationships with her "sisters" are established. The first wife (Jin Shuyuan), an aging woman with a grown son, does her best to ignore Songlian's presence. She is tolerant — no more, no less. The third concubine, a beautiful ex-opera singer, is fiercely jealous of Songlian, worried that the master will find his new, educated bride more enticing. However, the second concubine (Cao Cuifen) offers friendship and kindness to the newest member of the family — or so it initially seems.

The film is beautifully photographed using a process that captures the vividness of the many colors employed by the director. *Raise the Red Lantern* is visually stunning, and the appeal to the eye only heightens the movie's emotional power. The fullness of reds, oranges, and yellows is unlike anything that has been seen in an American film for years. Zhang clearly understands at least one of the fundamental rules of film making: that a great-looking picture will enhance a superior story.

Songlian's ultimate fate is wrenching, and the closing scene represents a sad epilogue to a unique motion picture experience. I don't think I've ever seen a movie quite like *Raise the Red Lantern,* and, since I consider it to be a defining example of Chinese movie-making and one of the best films of the '90s, I doubt that I ever will again. **MUST SEE**

Raising Victor Vargas [2002]

Starring: Victor Rasuk, Judy Marte, Melonie Diaz, Altagracia Guzman, Silvestre Rasuk, Krystal Rodriguez, Kevin Rivera, Wilfree Vasquez
Director: Peter Sollett Screenplay: Peter Sollett Running Time: 1:28
Rated: R (Profanity, sexual situations) Theatrical Aspect Ratio: 1.85:1

Raising Victor Vargas is the latest in a series of independent films to depict life as it really is for teenagers. Hollywood has decreed that a teen romantic comedy must follow a certain formula and contain two-dimensional, instantly recognizable protagonists. *Raising Victor Vargas* breaks those rules and is all the more worthwhile as a result. This is a teen romance where the characters have not been whitewashed and the circumstances sanitized. *Raising Victor Vargas* has been made with heart and passion — two qualities that are almost never evident in a Hollywood movie where the leads are of high school age.

Raising Victor Vargas takes place on New York's Lower East Side, in a rough-and-tumble neighborhood where the usual trappings of an urban story — drugs and gang violence — are absent. Victor (Victor Rasnuk) is a 16-year old Romeo who pretends to be a lot more experienced with girls than he actually is. When gossip starts circulating about him trying to lose his virginity to the aptly named "Fat Donna," his reputation takes a big hit. To repair it, Victor decides to go after "Juicy Judy" (Judy Marte), an untouchable beauty who routinely fends off raunchy proposals from guys. Meanwhile, Victor's best buddy, Harold (Kevin Rivera), hones in on Judy's plain-Jane friend, Melonie (Melonie Diaz). Initially, Judy has no more interest in Victor than she has in any other boys. But he is persistent and, eventually, she relents, agreeing to pretend to be "his girl" in order to keep other guys from asking her out. Melonie believes she should give Victor a chance, and Victor slowly learns that it takes more than false bravado and fake charm to woo someone like Judy.

The film also spends time developing Victor's home life. He lives in a cramped, two-bedroom apartment with his strict Catholic grandmother (Altagracia Guzman); his younger brother, Nino (Silvestre Rasuk, Victor's real-life sibling), who idolizes him; and his pudgy kid sister, Vicki (Krystal Rodriguez), who spends most of her life sitting on the couch. Grandma is suspicious of Victor — she believes his life to be a hotbed of sinful activity, and fears that his influence on Nino and Vicki will lead them astray.

The movie was written and directed by Peter Sollett, who developed the story from a short he made featuring the same actors. None of the players are professionals, but they are accomplished, and we never doubt the characters they are bringing to life or the situations they are in. Likewise, Sollett's camera work looks appropriately low-budget, but the effect is to add to the movie's pseudo-realism, not to detract from our enjoyment of the story. He is not a flashy director, but he understands his craft. The result is a satisfying motion picture that wins its audience over because the characters are allowed to be themselves. **RECOMMENDED**

Real Women Have Curves [2002]

Starring: America Ferrera, Lupe Ontiveros, Ingrid Oliu, George Lopez
Director: Patricia Cardoso Screenplay: George LaVoo and Josephina Lopez Running Time: 1:30 Rated: PG-13 (Profanity, sexual situations)
Theatrical Aspect Ratio: 1.85:1

Ana (America Ferrera) is an 18-year-old second generation Mexican American living in Los Angeles. She's an excellent student — good enough, in fact, that her English teacher, Mr. Guzman (George Lopez), believes that she has a chance for a scholarship to a good college. But Ana's mother, Carmen (Lupe Ontiveros), is against Ana continuing her education — she wants her youngest daughter to work at a dress-making shop run by her eldest daughter, Estela (Ingrid Oliu). Ana agrees, albeit reluctantly and petulantly. She still dreams of college and freedom from her mother — dreams that grow stronger when she begins a fling with an Anglo classmate, Jimmy (Brian Sites).

Real Women Have Curves does little to hide its primary, female-empowerment theme: that a woman should be judged by the quality of her mind and thoughts, not by how closely her body matches the so-called "ideal." Certainly, it's a laudable stance for a movie to take, but director Patricia Cardoso and writer Josephina Lopez become too strident in their advocacy of it.

At the core of the movie is Ana's tempestuous relationship with her mother. Carmen, who sees any form of "progress" as evil, wants her daughter to follow in her footsteps: find a man, get married, and have children. She criticizes Ana's weight because she believes that a fat girl won't be able to catch a husband. She is adamantly opposed to further education for Ana because that would take the girl away from home. There's also probably some sublimated jealousy here, with Carmen being envious of all of Ana's opportunities — opportunities she never had.

For Ana's part, living with her mother is stifling her. She recognizes that Carmen manipulates her life, and is resentful of it. She sees a college education as the way to broaden her horizons — a sentiment that is shared by her father, grandfather, and teachers. Once it becomes clear that Carmen will not change, Ana comes to the sad conclusion that she may be forced to chose between her mother and her future. One of the reasons the film resonates is that the final break of independence is something every individual must face, regardless of the family relationship. **RECOMMENDED**

Three Colors: Red [France/Switzerland/Poland, 1994]
Starring: Irene Jacob, Jean-Louis Trintignant, Frederique Feder, Jean-Pierre Lorit Director: Krzysztof Kieslowski Screenplay: Krzysztof Kieslowski and Krzysztof Piesiewicz Running Time: 1:40 Rated: R (Mature themes, sexual situations, nudity) Theatrical Aspect Ratio: 1.85:1 In French with subtitles

Red, the final chapter of Krzysztof Kieslowski's *Three Colors* trilogy, is a subtle masterpiece. With its satisfying exploration of such complex and diverse themes as destiny and platonic love, *Red* is not only a self-contained motion picture, but also a fitting conclusion to the series. Through one brief-but-important scene, this movie adds closure to both *Blue* and *White*, tying both to each other and to *Red*, and thereby reinforcing the commonality of ideas threaded through all three.

This time around, the protagonists are a young woman named Valentine (Irene Jacob, who starred in Kieslowski's *The Double Life of Veronique*) and a crotchety retired judge, Joseph Kern (Jean-Louis Trintignant). Valentine, a fashion model, meets the judge after running down his dog in the street and taking the injured animal to the address listed on the collar. Kern is initially indifferent to his pet's predicament, telling Valentine to keep the dog if that's what she wants. She does; however, the animal eventually runs away and finds its way back to the judge. When Valentine goes searching, she inadvertently learns Kern's secret — he enjoys spying on people by illegally tapping into their phone conversations.

Told in parallel with the chronicle of the unusual friendship between Valentine and the judge is the story of two lovers that Kern spies upon. Auguste (Jean-Pierre Lorit) and Karin (Frederique Feder), seem devoted to each other, but fate has already cast its die against them. For Auguste's life is eerily similar to that of Kern 30 years ago and, like the older man, he is drawn by forces beyond his control towards Valentine.

Thematically, *Red* is the strongest of the three films. Its construction allows hardly a moment to pass when the viewer isn't considering how fate manipulates the lives of Valentine, Auguste, Kern, and Karin. Then there's the meaning of platonic love (or "fraternity") — friendship completely divorced from sexual overtones. Kieslowski shows exactly how multi-faceted any relationship can be, and what occasionally must be sacrificed to the basic human need of finding a kindred spirit.

Red virtually demands more than one viewing for an appreciation of the picture's ambitious scope. It's a tragedy that this movie was not eligible for the Best Foreign Film Oscar (Switzerland, the country of origin, decided to reject *Red* because of its strong French and Polish production elements), but the lack of official recognition does not alter the fact that this is one of 1994's exceptional motion pictures. **MUST SEE**

The Red Violin (Le Violon Rouge) [Canada, 1998]
Starring: Samuel L. Jackson, Don McKellar, Carlo Cecchi, Irene Grazioli, Jean-Luc Bideau Director: François Girard Screenplay: François Girard, Don McKellar Running Time: 2:11 Rated: R (Nudity, sex, mature themes) Theatrical Aspect Ratio: 1.85:1 In English, French, German, Mandarin, and Italian with subtitles

What do the following people have in common: a 17th century fiddle-maker in Cremona, Italy; a young orphan with a prodigious musical talent in 18th century Vienna; a famous British Lord performing during the reign of King George III; a lover of Western music struggling through the Chinese Cultural Revolution; and a musicologist in modern-day Montreal? The answer: the Red Violin. Not only is that the name of the instrument that lies at the center of François Girard's new film, it's the movie's title, as well. Appropriately, the picture relates the story of the violin from its genesis in 1681 to its sale at auction in 1997.

Girard has assembled a huge international cast to present 5 key episodes in the violin's history. In the first, the creator, Nicolo Bussotti (Carlo Cecchi) labors on the instrument as a present for his unborn child. Meanwhile, his wife, Anna (Irene Grazioli), uncertain about the stability of her pregnancy, seeks advice on the future from a fortune-teller. A century later, the violin has become the property of an orphanage outside of Vienna. It is there that Georges Poussin (Jean-Luc Bideau) discovers it in the possession of an amazing prodigy, young Kaspar Weiss (Christoph Koncz), whom he intends to instruct himself. Soon afterwards, Lord Frederick Pope (Jason Flemyng), a popular concert violinist, takes possession of the fiddle and makes it his instrument of choice. But, as his career flourishes, his personal life is thrown into turmoil when his beloved mistress, Victoria (Greta Scacchi), leaves him behind to take a trip to Russia. By the early 20th century, the violin has come into the possession of Xiang Pei (Sylvia Chang) in Shanghai, but she must hide it or face punishment from an establishment that deems all Western instruments to be a corrupting influence. When the violin re-surfaces in 1997 Montreal, Charles Morritz (Samuel L. Jackson) and Evan Williams (Don McKellar) work to restore the instrument so it can bring a huge price at auction.

Movies that follow objects rather than characters are always difficult to craft, and the central item often ends up being little more than a gimmick used to tie together unrelated narratives. Girard and McKellar avoid that trap, which is one reason why *The Red Violin* works. Another is that the film offers a wonderful trip through three centuries and across several countries. *The Red Violin* may not succeed on every level, but it's still a pleasing and fascinating excursion.

RECOMMENDED

The Remains of the Day [United States/United Kingdom, 1993]

Starring: Anthony Hopkins, Emma Thompson, James Fox, Christopher Reeve Director: James Ivory Screenplay: Ruth Prawer Jhabvala based on the novel by Kazuo Ishiguro Running Time: 2:14 Rated: PG (Mature themes) Theatrical Aspect Ratio: 2.35:1

Most of *The Remains of the Day* is presented as a series of flashbacks, with a 1950s James Stevens (Anthony Hopkins) recalling his days of service under the late Lord Darlington (James Fox), especially during the years leading up to the second world war. However, at the center of the tale is Stevens' never-defined relationship with the head housekeeper, Sally Kenton (Emma Thompson). They love each other, but that love remains unvoiced, for no matter how hard Miss Kenton tries to draw him out, Mr. Stevens can not admit his feelings, not even to himself.

This relationship is explored under the shadow of the Nazis' rise to power in Germany. Lord Darlington, a German sympathizer who believes that the Treaty of Versailles was cruel, is determined to fight for peace, no matter what the cost. Some of those that he invites to stay under his roof are not as enthusiastic, including U. S. Congressman Lewis (Christopher Reeve), who warns Darlington that he is an amateur playing a game best left to professionals. The warning is prophetic, but its consequences are not explored as fully as they might have been.

Anthony Hopkins has the central role, and he portrays Stevens to perfection. Hopkins is forced to employ a great deal of subtlety to exhibit the turmoil beneath the surface. Stevens is tortured by his love, but the need to express his feelings cannot overcome his deep reserve. Emma Thompson does her usual solid job with her part, but the role of Ms. Kenton lacks the substance of the actress' character in *Howards End*.

Christopher Reeve is a perfect choice to play the "typical American." No one would confuse Congressman Lewis with a real character, but it doesn't seem that James Ivory was interested in presenting more than a stereotype. Lewis is involved for two reasons, and once both aims are accomplished, there's no real reason for him to be in the story at all. He serves his purpose, and that's good enough.

The Remains of the Day is an engaging and powerful motion picture, every bit the equal of Merchant-Ivory's best work, and certainly the most emotionally-wrenching tale they have brought to the screen. Tragic love stories often hit with the hardest impact, and few are better-crafted and more intelligently presented than that of Mr. Stevens and Miss Kenton.

HIGHLY RECOMMENDED

Remember the Titans [2000]

Starring: Denzel Washington, Will Patton, Wood Harris, Ryan Hurst, Ethan Suplee, Hayden Panettiere Director: Boaz Yakin Screenplay: Gregory Allen Howard Running Time: 1:53 Rated: PG (Mature themes, mild violence) Theatrical Aspect Ratio: 2.35:1

If viewed as a crowd-pleasing, feel-good sports movie, *Remember the Titans* is an unqualified success. However, if seen as a socially conscious retrospective on race relations in the South during the early 1970s, it can best be described as timid and unexceptional. In soft-peddling the theme of intolerance, the picture refuses to take even the smallest chance. From the beginning, we are meant to know that the events portrayed in *Remember the Titans* have their roots in historical fact, as if the "based on a true story" caption lends added credibility to the story.

With the exception of a pair of bookend scenes transpiring in 1981, the film takes place a decade earlier in the town of Alexandria, Virginia, where the T.C. Williams High School has just been integrated. This means that not only will whites and blacks be mingling in the halls, but on the football field as well. And, in a place like Alexandria, the composition of the T.C. Williams Titans is a serious matter, as is the identity of the coach. So, when the eminently qualified local choice, Bill Yoast (Will Patton), is passed over in favor of an out-of-towner named Herman Boone (Washington), the citizens are in an uproar, especially since they believe Boone has been selected based not on his qualifications but because of his race. The commonly held opinion is that school board hopes the presence of a black coach might be able to calm the tensions that are threatening to turn Alexandria into another Watts.

Boone is initially uncomfortable with his reasons for getting the job, but he vows to be color-blind in his treatment of his players. He invites Yoast to be his defensive coordinator — an offer that is reluctantly accepted. Then, over the course of a grueling, late-summer boot camp for would-be football players, he concentrates on destroying the preconceptions of all of his charges, both black and white. In the process, some of the players become fast friends, and Boone and Yoast develop a bond. But the team's new-found internal harmony does not necessarily reflect that of the outside world, which regards the racially integrated team with mistrust and, at times, disdain.

As sports films go, *Remember the Titans* is a notch above the average entry in part because its social message creates a richer fabric than the usual cloth from which this kind of movie is cut. The film's racial slant gives the football games a little more meaning and energy, and the characters come across as more sincere and less self-centered. Still, when compared to a high school sports classic like *Hoosiers*, which contained many of the same elements, *Remember the Titans* shows a few flaws. Fortunately, they aren't serious enough to lower the film's broad-based appeal or to diminish its quotient of feel-good moments. **RECOMMENDED**

Requiem for Dream [2000]

Starring: Ellen Burstyn, Jared Leto, Jennifer Connelly, Marlon Wayans Director: Darren Aronofsky Screenplay: Darren Aronofsky, based on the novel by Hubert Selby Jr. Running Time: 1:42 Rated: Unrated (Drug use, sex, nudity, violence, profanity) Theatrical Aspect Ratio: 1.85:1

Requiem for a Dream presents the darkest take imaginable on a story of hopes and dreams shattered by drug addiction. There's no preaching or sermonizing here, just an almost-clinical depiction of lives laid to waste. This is not a film for the weak of mind or soul. It is a force to be reckoned with.

The movie starts slowly, introducing each of the characters and establishing their relationships. Visually, Aronofsky tries for something a little different here, employing a split-screen approach that neither enhances nor detracts from the narrative. (It isn't around long enough to become distracting.) The central figure is Harry (Jared Leto), a young man who lives hand-to-mouth because nearly every cent he saves, earns, or steals goes towards buying something he can inject into his veins. His best friend and business partner is Tyrone (Marlon Wayans, playing it straight and doing so effectively), who shares many of Harry's aspirations. His girlfriend is Marion (Connelly), who, like Harry and Tyrone, is an addict. The fourth significant player is Harry's widowed mother, Sara (Ellen Burstyn), who is as addicted to television as Harry is to drugs. When she learns that a marketing company may be able to offer her a spot in the studio audience of a live TV broadcast, she decides to lose weight. Following a visit to the doctor's, she is on her way to dropping 30 pounds and becoming hooked on the uppers and downers that comprise her diet.

For these characters, drugs gradually take the place of everything else — food, sex, aspirations, and even the day-to-day impulse to live. They become the sole sources of pain and pleasure. They form the core of relationships. Would these people have anything to do with one another if they weren't bound by the ceremony of the injection? Perhaps it's not that way in the beginning, but the life-destroying power of drugs is insidious and undeniable, and the spiral of all-consuming addiction is what Aronofsky has captured with unnerving effectiveness.

Requiem for a Dream certainly isn't the first recent motion picture to offer an unpleasant picture of what happens when an individual becomes hooked on drugs, but its quadruple character study is unsparing.

This is in large part because of the brilliant final fifteen minutes, which is a tour de force of direction and editing. Employing hundreds of cuts, Aronofsky careens back and forth between his 4 main players, showing their increasingly dire circumstances and allowing those to escalate to a brutal climax. Don't be fooled by the passively poetic title; there's nothing serene or restful about this motion picture. *Requiem for a Dream* gets under your skin and stays there. **MUST SEE**

Restoration [United Kingdom/United States, 1995]

Starring: Robert Downey Jr., Sam Neill, Meg Ryan, Ian McKellan, Hugh Grant Director: Michael Hoffman Screenplay: Rupert Walters based on the novel by Rose Tremain Running Time: 1:57 Rated: R (Sex, nudity, plague) Theatrical Aspect Ratio: 1.85:1

The setting for *Restoration* — England in the 1660s — represents one of the most interesting eras in European history. Following the death of Oliver Cromwell, Charles II returned from exile to reclaim the throne for the Stuart family. His coronation heralded the Restoration — a time of great enlightenment and debauchery. Then, in 1665, the Great Plague struck, and in 1666, London burned. The film *Restoration* attempts to incorporate all of these events into its 2-hour story. Those hoping for historical accuracy will be sorely disappointed, however. The 1660s serve as little more than a backdrop for the action. The costumes and sets are authentic-looking, but little else has more than a flavor of the period. Even the dialogue is frequently anachronistic.

Historical authenticity aside, *Restoration* is still a worthy source of entertainment. The narrative has numerous dramatic hiccups — most caused by trying to cram too much into too little time — but, overall, it tells an engrossing tale. The film, which opens in 1663 London, follows the rise and fall of Robert Merivel (Robert Downey Jr.), a reluctant physician. Despite his undeniable medical gifts, he would rather spend time drinking and whoring. When King Charles II (Sam Neill) needs someone unconventional to heal his ailing dog, he sends for Merivel. The animal's recovery assures the doctor a place at court, where he is gradually transformed from physician to fool.

One of the most unusual services demanded of Merivel by the King is that he marry the royal Mistress, Celia Clemence (Polly Walker). The doctor is told in no uncertain terms that the marriage is never to be consummated — it is in name only ("I need a man far too enamored of women in general to love one in partic-ular," Charles tells Merivel). Unfortunately for his status at court, Merivel falls for Celia, and when the King learns of this, he dispatches Merivel from his service. The now-penniless physician ends up in a Quaker community with an old friend (David Thewlis). It is there that he discovers the true nature of his talents.

Restoration is developed as a series of episodes which combine to form a story arc taking Merivel's character from debauchery to poverty to redemption. Flaws aside, the film is a sumptuous, affecting tale about the most roguish of men making good. And, despite assorted tragedies along the way, the tone and intent are decidedly upbeat.

As a well-developed, fast-paced movie that tells a "feel good" story, *Restoration* is a welcome entry. As a history lesson, it's a failure. The British are famous for their period pieces, and, while *Restoration* isn't among the best (all of Jane Austen's adapted novels are superior), it's still solid entertainment. **RECOMMENDED**

Richard III [United Kingdom/United States, 1995]

Starring: Ian McKellan, Jim Broadbent, Annette Bening, Kristin Scott-Thomas Director: Richard Loncraine Screenplay: Ian McKellan and Richard Loncraine based on the play by William Shakespeare as adapted for the stage production by Richard Eyre Running Time: 1:45 Rated: R (Violence, sexual candor, brief nudity) Theatrical Aspect Ratio: 2.35:1

Opening in a 1930's England war room with a tank crashing through a wall, one is immediately struck by the realization that, whatever else *Richard III* is doing, it certainly isn't preserving the story's original time frame. However, while the sets and costumes have been moved to a mythical, Nazi-like pre-WWII England, the dialogue, characters, actions, and themes remain unchanged from the original text by Shakespeare. While this curious clash between a near-modern setting and the much older source material might seem confounding, it actually serves to energize the play, as well as making it more palatable to present-day audiences.

Richard III is the last in the series of Shakespeare histories to chronicle England's tribulations during the period before the Tudors took the throne (an event which occurs at the end of *Richard III*, when Henry VII, the first of the Tudors and grandfather to Shakespeare's Queen Elizabeth, becomes King). This play tells of the machinations of Richard (Ian McKellan), a royal prince with a twisted spine and grotesque physical appearance, to place himself in power. Richard is a spiteful person who kills without compunction and, in the process, earns nothing but enmity from all around him. There are 4 bodies that impede his march to the crown: two of his brothers — Clarence and King Edward — and the king's two young sons. One-by-one, Richard has them removed, caring only that he should one-day rule England.

Does Richard have a conscience? Can evil such as his triumph completely, with no recompense expected on this side of the grave? Can the British monarchy exist without venom and corruption filtering up to the highest levels? These are a few of the more cogent questions addressed by *Richard III*, and McKellan and director Richard Loncraine make sure that they remain intact in the final version of the film.

In its own bloody way, *Richard III* is as enjoyable to watch as any recent screen production of Shakespeare, and the shift to the 1930's with its attendant Nazi imagery (parallels between Richard III and Hitler abound) gives the film a twist that conventional productions do not have. If there's a flaw to the movie, it's that this is one of Shakespeare's least ambitious and less thematically rich plays. Nevertheless, since the only memorable motion picture version is Lawrence Olivier's 1956 version, *Richard III* doesn't suffer from overexposure, and this interpretation offers an unconventional — and easily accessible — perspective. **RECOMMENDED**

Ridicule [France, 1996]

Starring: Charles Berling, Jean Rochefort, Fanny Ardant, Judith Godreche Director: Patrice Leconte Screenplay: Remi Waterhouse Running Time: 1:42 Rated: R (Nudity, mature themes) Theatrical Aspect Ratio: 1.85:1 In French with subtitles

In Patrice Leconte's *Ridicule*, the pen — or rather the word — is truly mightier than the sword. In late 18th century France, before the advent of the guillotine, wit was used as often for pain and humiliation as it was for pleasure. Those who had mastered the art of ridicule could, with one turn of phrase, strip a less adept opponent of pride and position, hurling him from the pampered confines of Louis XVI's court into the hostile world beyond, where indignities and possibly death awaited.

Ridicule is not meant to be taken as a rigorous historical account, but, as with all French movies, the period detail is impeccable. The general atmosphere, if not the specifics, reflects 1783 Versailles, where a witty conversationalist was greatly prized as a source of entertainment, and where those with a gift for bon mots could attain a position of importance at the king's court.

Gregoire Ponceludon de Malavoy (Charles Berling), a baron from the rural province of Dombes, comes to Versailles to obtain money for an ambitious engineering scheme that would drain southwest France's swamps to reduce disease and pestilence. Ponceludon entertains a hope that the king, known to be intrigued by science, might take an interest in the project and offer to fund it. However, what he discovers at Versailles disheartens him. Gaining an audience with the king has more to do with one's ancestors, bedpartners, and verbal agility than with the merits of one's proposal.

Undeterred, Ponceludon finds a local sponsor, Bellegarde (Jean Rochefort), who sees promise in the idealistic newcomer and offers lessons of how to survive in Versailles ("Don't laugh with your mouth open," "We call puns the death of wit," "The soul of wit is to know one's place"). While the young nobleman is learning the rules of acceptable court behavior, he falls for Bellegarde's beautiful, young daughter, Mathilde (Judith Godreche). But, when Ponceludon's would-be romance with Mathilde flounders because of her impending marriage, he seeks the sexual (and political) favors of Madame de Blayac (Fanny Ardant), a fixture at court who consorts with all the finest wits. Ponceludon then becomes involved in a series of contests with the appropriately-named Vilecourt (Bernard Giraudeau) to see whose wit is the most corrosive.

Leconte's film is tightly-plotted and well-paced, with few wasted or unnecessary scenes. The script does have lapses, such as a sequence that uses a conventional duel to generate unnecessary tension and uncertainty, but, on the whole, the writing is *Ridicule*'s greatest asset. The carefully-rendered French-to-English subtitles do justice to the sparkling dialogue, making the verbal matches between Ponceludon, Madame de Blayac, and Vilecourt one of *Ridicule*'s highlights. For those who appreciate movies with a bite, *Ridicule* shows its teeth early and keeps them razor-sharp throughout. **RECOMMENDED**

Rocky [1976]

Starring: Sylvester Stallone, Talia Shire, Burt Young, Carl Weathers, Burgess Meredith Director: John G. Avildsen Screenplay: Sylvester Stallone Running Time: 1:59 Rated: PG (Violence) Theatrical Aspect Ratio: 1.85:1

There are essentially 3 kinds of boxing movies: those that offer a grim, tell-it-as-it-is perspective of life in the ring, those that focus (often in an exaggerated fashion) on the business aspects of things, and those that seek to uplift through a rags-to-riches story. *Rocky*, the 1977 Best Picture Oscar winner, belongs unabashedly in the third category. Although the movie contains realistic elements and is set in a believable arena, it is essentially a fairy tale about a down-and-out pugilist who gets a chance at the fight of a lifetime, and, at the same time, wins the girl. Since 1976, nearly every film featuring a big sports comeback and triumph has been inspired by and/or compared to *Rocky*, regardless of whether it involves boxing or not.

Rocky is as much a tender love story as it is about ring action. Rocky Balboa (Stallone) is a boxing bottomfeeder — someone who will fight anyone for a $50 purse. His lone ambition is to stay afloat. He lives in a one-room apartment with two turtles and a fish, and spends his days working as a collector for a South Philly loan shark. Mickey (Burgess Meredith), the crusty manager at the boxing club where he works out, is disgusted with Rocky, because he had the natural ability to become a great fighter, but threw it all away. When Rocky's attention isn't on fighting or his job, it's on wooing Adrian (Talia Shire), the painfully shy sister of his best friend, Paulie (Burt Young). Rocky is in love with her, but his inarticulate attempts to ask Adrian out frighten her off.

Rocky's fortunes change when Apollo Creed (Carl Weathers), the World Heavyweight Champion, hand picks him as an opponent. A fight scheduled for January 1, 1976 (and dubbed the "Bicentennial Match") was to feature Creed against his #1 challenger, but injuries to the opponent cause him to back out 5 weeks before the event. In an attempt to salvage something, Creed decides to give a local Philadelphia fighter a chance, and Rocky's nickname of the "Itallion Stallion" catches his attention. As a result, a boxer with no apparent future suddenly has a chance at the World Championship title. From Rocky's perspective, however, winning is secondary. He wants one thing out of the fight with Apollo: the self-respect he can earn by going the distance. Even more than that, however, he wants to win Adrian's heart.

Considering what the *Rocky* series became — popcorn action films with little heart, less intelligence, and a lot of testosterone — it's somewhat refreshing experience to go back and re-connect with the original, which offers a lot more substance than the sequels. *Rocky* is not a flawless motion picture, but it is a feel-good classic, and well worth another look. The basic storyline has been done to death over the years; this is still one of the most effective and successful applications of the formula. **HIGHLY RECOMMENDED**

The Rookie [2002]

Starring: Dennis Quaid, Rachel Griffiths, Brian Cox, Trevor Morgan, Beth Grant, Jay Hernandez Director: John Lee Hancock
Screenplay: Mike Rich, based on the book by Jim Morris and Joel Engel Running Time: 2:08 Rated: PG Theatrical Aspect Ratio: 2.35:1

A good baseball movie embraces the magic of baseball, and uses the game as a metaphor for life. Such is the case with *The Rookie*, and, while this outing will not challenge the likes of *The Natural* for the title of the best baseball movie ever made, it's a solid effort in its own right.

Jim Morris is a southpaw who spent parts of two seasons in the bullpen for the Tampa Bay Devil Rays. His career statistics — a 4.80 ERA, 15 IP, 13 K, and 9 BB — are hardly the stuff of which legends are made. Yet, in spite of that, Morris is the subject of Disney's *The Rookie* — not because of what he did once he reached The Show, but because he reached there in the first place. The unlikeliest of heroes, Morris became the second-oldest rookie ever to play Major League baseball when he stepped on the mound at the age of 35. A longer-than-long-shot with a story to inspire the most blasé individual, Morris' tale is a testament to the age-old saying that dreams can come true if you fight hard enough for them.

The Rookie starts out in the 1970s, as a young Jimmy Morris (Trevor Morgan) arrives in the small town of Big Lake, Texas. Jimmy's a baseball fan, but football, not baseball, is king in Big Lake. Flash forward to 1999: Jim (Dennis Quaid) is now married and has 3 kids. He's the coach for the local high school baseball team, the Big Lake Owls — a post he took after an arm injury ended his quest to break into Major League Baseball. However, while Jimmy is throwing batting practice, his players notice that his fastballs have a lot of zip on them, so they make a deal with him — if they win the district, he'll attend a big league tryout. Sure enough, when the season is over, the Owls have fulfilled their part of the bargain, so Jim throws in front of some scouts for the Tampa Bay Devil Rays. When his velocity reaches 98 mph on the radar, Jim suddenly becomes the hottest prospect around — even at age 35.

As inspirational stories go, this one is top-notch. It satisfies without becoming cloying or going over-the-top. From a technical perspective, the film's baseball sequences are virtually flawless. This doesn't guarantee a good movie, but it helps. More important than the film's verisimilitude, however, is its structure. It manages to be uplifting without forcing us to endure a 9th-inning, come-from-behind victory. Because, when it comes down to it, *The Rookie* isn't as much about wining in a game as it is about winning in life.

RECOMMENDED

Rosewood [1997]

Starring: Jon Voight, Ving Rhames, Don Cheadle, Bruce McGill, Loren Dean Director: John Singleton Screenplay: Gregory Poirier Running Time: 2:22 Rated: R (Violence, profanity, mature themes) Theatrical Aspect Ratio: 2.35:1

Rosewood, central Florida, 1923. The town's population numbered about 120, mostly black. It was a prosperous, happy community until a January day when one woman's lie set off a chain of events that would have devastating results. That woman was Fanny Taylor, and her false claim to have been assaulted by a black man resulted in the formation of a lynch mob that headed for Rosewood with arson and murder on their minds. Before the week was over, blood was shed and the town was in ashes.

If Singleton takes liberties with the historical account of what happened at Rosewood (and that account is murky at best — the death count differs greatly depending on which source is being consulted), it's in the name of dramatic license, and it works. This is a deeply affecting tale about the naked emotional and physical devastation that can be wrought by racial hatred. But it is also a story of hope that highlights the indomitable nature of the human spirit and the fraternity that can bind together two apparently different people. *Rosewood* does not glamorize evil, but neither does it demonize those who practice it. Singleton is careful to present a balanced and believable picture of the participants on both sides. The result presents a forceful message without ever preaching.

While *Rosewood* must be seen as a cohesive whole to be fully appreciated, there are isolated moments that stand out because of their haunting power. One of the most startling depicts white folk picnicking and frolicking while Rosewood burns in the background. In another scene, McGill's character carefully teaches his son how to make a noose for a lynching — one of the essential lessons he must learn to become a man. There are, in fact, times when *Rosewood* is reminiscent of *Schindler's List*. There's a kernel of truth that both films have in common — the theme

of the duality of human nature: the capacity for great good and great evil, boundless love and infinite hatred. And, while this film is not as well-paced or tightly-structured as Spielberg's Holocaust drama, it evokes many of the same feelings and emotions. It is an important film that should not be missed.

HIGHLY RECOMMENDED

The Run of the Country [Ireland, 1995]

Starring: Albert Finney, Matthew Keeslar, Victoria Smurfit, Anthony Brophy Director: Peter Yates Screenplay: Shane Connaughton Running Time: 1:49 Rated: R (Sex, nudity, violence, profanity) Theatrical Aspect Ratio: 2.35:1

Albert Finney is one of today's best character actors, yet Finney's character is not the focus of *The Run of the Country*. His is a supporting role, presenting an opportunity for conflict with his teenage son, Danny (Matthew Keeslar). This is Danny's story — how, coping with the recent death of his beloved mother, he struggles to find independence from an overbearing father. Part of this process is moving out of his childhood home and in with his friend, Prunty (Anthony Brophy). Another part is falling in love. The object of his affection is Annagh (Victoria Smurfit), a girl from just north of the border separating Catholic South Ireland from the Protestant North.

Though it takes place in contemporary Ireland, the way in which people live — many in ramshackle huts with little evidence of modern "conveniences" — gives the story a timeless quality. Likewise, the characters would probably be equally at home in the 19th century as in the 20th. Danny and Annagh are both virgins well into their teens and Danny's father is opposed to any sort of contraceptive. Religion is a powerful force, and the penalties for premarital sex are terrible to contemplate.

The best-crafted element of the film is the love story. Director Peter Yates brings real feeling and tenderness to the interactions between Danny and Annagh, from their first furtive glances at each other to Danny's faltering attempts to address her in conversation. Annagh is somewhat more world-wise than Danny, which makes it amusing to watch her nonplussed reactions to some of his unintentional double entendres.

The relationship between Danny and his father, although of equal importance to the romance, is less developed. Drawn with broad strokes, this conflict always seems more peripheral than central, which robs a cathartic scene of emotional power. Finney does all he can with the material, creating a mild character always on the brink of an emotional eruption, but Matthew Keeslar can't keep up with him. In fact, Keeslar, who is at times flat, isn't the equal of any of his co-stars. Both Victoria Smurfit and Anthony Brophy have impressive debuts.

The script has a fair number of affecting sequences, and manages to deftly mix humor and serious issues. While the political situation and the possible involvement of the IRA are kept in the background, they are not ignored. More crucial to the story, however, are the boundaries created by religion, education, and class. Every conflict in this film has its roots in one of these three causes. So, although *The Run of the Country* has its weak spots, it nevertheless gives us a more original coming-of-age story than that which typically graces American screens.
RECOMMENDED

The Scent of a Woman [1992]

Starring: Al Pacino, Chris O'Donnell Director: Martin Brest
Screenplay: Bo Goldman Running Time: 2:36 Rated: R (Language, mature themes) Theatrical Aspect Ratio: 1.85:1

Scent of a Woman is about Charles Simms (Chris O'Donnell), a Boston prep school senior, and the Thanksgiving weekend he spends working as the aide and companion of Lt. Colonel Frank Slade (Al Pacino), an embittered, lonely, blind veteran. The job, which begins as an onerous task performed principally for money, becomes a tour of self-discovery when Slade decides to make an unexpected visit to New York City. There, amidst all the holiday hoopla, the lieutenant's actions force Charlie into making an emotionally painful — and potentially physically dangerous — decision.

There are certain actors that, when they appear in a film, are almost invariably indicators that the production is of high quality. They are an elite few, with names like Nicholson, Hoffman, Hackman, and Pacino. Considering some of the roles that Al Pacino has played during his celebrated career (in *The Godfather* trilogy, for example), it would be hyperbole to say that he gives the "performance of a lifetime" in *Scent of a Woman* . . . or would it? For 2 hours, he brings Frank Slade to life in a way that few others in Hollywood could. As portrayed by Pacino, there's far more to this man that a rancorous outlook on life and a couple of hearty "hoo-ha"s.

Chris O'Donnell is solid, if somewhat obscured in the more experienced man's shadow. Although the role of Charlie is understated by O'Donnell, he nev-

ertheless manages to fashion a rapport with the audience. This is necessary for the film to succeed, since it's through his eyes that the story unfolds.

In essence, *Scent of a Woman* is another in a never-ending series of bonding pictures where each person has something unique to offer to the other. If there's anything special about the film, it's that on this occasion, the emotional realism of the characters, especially Slade, is heartwrenchingly believable. His relationship with Charlie works because Pacino won't let it fail.

Unfortunately, considering how sound the bulk of the picture is, the final moments, with their overt pandering to a Hollywood-style ending, are a severe liability. Certainly, such "triumphs" are fun to watch, but they cheapen *Scent of a Woman*. Would it have cost the production team that much to inject a little realism into the film's last reel?

The movie is as long as its storyline demands. It doesn't seem like 2½ hours, and less time with these characters would have cheated the audience. Aided by an emotive score from Thomas Newman, the picture has opportunities to soar. Hampered by the script's limitations, however, *Scent of a Woman* falls short of being a masterful production.
RECOMMENDED

Schindler's List [1993]

Starring: Liam Neeson, Ben Kingsley, Ralph Fiennes, Caroline Goodall, Embeth Davidtz Director: Steven Spielberg Screenplay: Steven Zaillian based on the novel by Thomas Keneally Running Time: 3:15 Rated: R (Violence, Holocaust images, nudity, profanity) Theatrical Aspect Ratio: 1.85:1

Schindler's List opens in September of 1939 in Krakow, Poland, with the Jewish community under increasing pressure from the Nazis. Into this tumult comes Oskar Schindler (Liam Neeson), a Nazi businessman interested in obtaining Jewish backing for a factory he wishes to build. He makes contact with Itzhak Stern (Ben Kingsley), an accountant, to arrange financial matters.

March 1941. The Krakow Jewish community has been forced to live in "the Ghetto," where money no longer has any meaning. Several elders agree to invest in Schindler's factory and the DEF (Deutsche Emailwarenfabrik) is born — a place where large quantities of pots are manufactured. To do the work, Schindler hires Jews (because they're cheaper than Poles), and the German army becomes his biggest customer.

March 1943. Germany's intentions towards the

Jews are no longer a secret. The Ghetto is "liquidated," with the survivors being herded into the Plaszow Forced Labor Camp. During this time, Schindler has managed to ingratiate himself with the local commander, Amon Goeth (Ralph Fiennes), a Nazi who kills Jews for sport. Using his relationship with Goeth, Schindler begins to secretly campaign to help the Jews, saving men, women, and children from certain death.

Schindler's List gives us 3 major stories and a host of minor ones. First and foremost, it tells the tale of the Holocaust, presenting new images of old horrors. Spielberg emphasizes the brutality of the situation by not pulling punches when it comes to gore. The blood, inky rather than crimson in stark black-and-white, fountains when men and women are shot in the head or through the neck.

The second story is that of Oskar Schindler, the Nazi businessman who saved 1,200 Jews from death. Schindler starts out as a self-centered manufacturer, concerned only about making money. He hires Jews because they're cheap, not because he likes them. But his perspective changes, and he risks losing everything to save as many lives as he can. His eventual lament that he couldn't save more is heartbreaking.

The third story belongs to Amon Goeth, the Nazi commander of Krakow, a man who teeters on the brink of madness. Despite his intense hatred for Jews, he is inexplicably attracted to his Jewish housekeeper, Helen Hirsch (Embeth Davidtz). Disgusted by his feelings, he lashes out at her with a display of violence that is almost Scorsese-like in its blunt presentation. Spielberg works carefully to show unexpected depth and complexity to his character.

Despite the grisly subject matter, this movie is essentially about uncovering a kernel of hope and dignity in the midst of a monstrous tragedy. The story of Oskar Schindler's sacrifices for the Jews sets this apart from other Holocaust dramas. *Schindler's List* offers a clear view of human nature laid bare: hatred, greed, lust, envy, anger, and, most important of all, empathy and love. Because this film touches us so deeply, the catharsis has a power that few — if any — other moments in film history can match. **MUST SEE**

The Sea Inside [Spain/France/Italy, 2004]

Starring: Javier Bardem, Belén Rueda, Lola Dueñas, Mabel Rivera, Celso Bugallo Director: Alejandro Amenábar Screenplay: Mateo Gil, Alejandro Amenábar Running Time: 2:05 Rated: PG-13 (Mature themes) Theatrical Aspect Ratio: 2.35:1 In Spanish with subtitles

At the age of 26, Ramon Sampedro misjudged the depth of water he was diving into and he broke his neck. For the next 29 years he lived the life of a quadriplegic — one that he considered not worth living. Despite having lost the use of his body below the neck, he still had a voice and a mind, and he put both of those to use, waging a one-man war for the right to die: *his* right to die. In the late 1990s, as Ramon's case made its way through the Spanish courts, he became not only a national celebrity, but one whose story reached beyond the shores of Spain. But it was after his death that the controversy exploded, especially when his "open letter" to the legal, political, and religious authorities in Spain was made public. In it, he made the following damning accusation: "It is not that my conscience finds itself trapped in the deformity of my atrophied and numb body; but in the deformity, atrophy, and insensitivity of your consciences." Now, albeit with a few fictionalizations, Ramon's story has been transformed into one of the best movies of 2004.

The Sea Inside is so far from a typical "euthanasia" movie that it's startling. Whenever Hollywood tackles this subject (which doesn't happen often — this isn't a topic that packs in the crowds), the melodrama and manipulation go into overdrive. Not here. Director Alejandro Amenábar maintains a low-key approach that preserves the film's emotional integrity while still making a powerful statement. And, because Ramon is such a forceful presence and positive influence, there are times when *The Sea Inside* is uplifting. This is a movie that may cause viewers to both laugh and cry.

When the story opens, Ramon (Javier Bardem, in a titanic and moving performance) has been confined to his bed for 28 years. During all his time as a quadriplegic he has been fighting for the right to die because he believes that his existence has become "a life without dignity." Now, as he faces the culmination of his court battles, he writes a book with his new lawyer, Julia (Belen Rueda), with whom he has fallen in love. But even this new spark of emotion does not change Ramon's mind, and with or without the court's consent, Julia expresses a willingness to make the ultimate sacrifice and help him. Other key figures in Ramon's life are his sister-in-law, Manuela (Mabel Rivera), who cares for him and sympathizes with him; his brother, José (Celso Bugallo), who refuses to acknowledge Ramon's pleas for death; and Rosa (Lola Dueñas), a local DJ who opens her heart and life to Ramon.

For a movie about a man battling for the right to die (an inherently somber subject), *The Sea Inside* contains a fair amount of humor. Especially memorable is the exchange between Ramon and a quadriplegic priest that involves an intermediary running up and down stairs. Then there are the dual romances (Ramon and Julia, Ramon and Rosa), each of which has its own tone and nature, yet both of which are heartfelt and radiate longing. Like the rest of Amenabar's most mature film to-date, they are sublime. **HIGHLY RECOMMENDED**

Seabiscuit [2003]

Starring: Jeff Bridges, Chris Cooper, Tobey Maguire, William H. Macy, Elizabeth Banks, Gary Stevens Director: Gary Ross Screenplay: Gary Ross, based on the book by Laura Hillenbrand Running Time: 2:25 Rated: PG-13 (Mature themes, sexual situations) Theatrical Aspect Ratio: 2.35:1

Seabiscuit is the kind of inspirational drama that generally plays well 12 months a year. The movie follows a time-honored, easily predictable path to victory and redemption. The script is perhaps more high-minded than the material deserves, but director Gary Ross understands how to *compose* a motion picture and, even though *Seabiscuit* is a little on the long side, it works more often than not. The movie generally follows the outline of Laura Hillenbrand's book of the same name, which chronicles the story of the racing horse Seabiscuit (one of the great sports success stories of Depression-era America). Everyone loves an underdog, and this movie has a quartet of them. There's businessman Charles Howard (Jeff Bridges), who made a fortune by selling cars in the Roaring Twenties, then lost his zest for life when his son died in an accident and his first wife left him. Tom Smith (Chris Cooper) is a horse trainer who believes in caring for, not killing, lame animals. Most "reputable" racers view him as a fringe lunatic. Red Pollard (Tobey Maguire) is a failed boxer and too-tall jockey who has spent much of his life on the streets and bus-stop benches. And Seabiscuit has been a disappointment to nearly everyone who has owned him. Despite a good pedigree, he has turned into a consistent loser.

After remarrying, Charles turns his interest from cars to horses. Having little knowledge about animals, he hires Tom as his horse whisperer. Tom in turn discovers Seabiscuit. He likes the horse's spirit, and thinks he can be a winner. Tom also brings Red on board, believing that he, like Seabiscuit, can be reclaimed. After retraining the animal to abandon his loser's mindset, Charles enters him in a race at Santa Anita Park. Soon, the underdog is winning races and setting records. At that point, Charles sets his sights on a bigger target: He wants to race (and beat) War Admiral, a Triple Crown winner. After much wrangling, the one-on-one match finally takes place, in November 1938, at Pimlico (War Admiral's "home track").

Seabiscuit is *Rocky* in a saddle, with Hollywood-enhanced feel-good impulses oozing from every frame. That's not a bad thing, especially if you're a sucker for underdog-triumphant sports movies. Don't be fooled into thinking *Seabiscuit* is a history lesson — it plays fast and loose with some of the facts, but one could argue that the changes make for better drama. The intent of the movie is to show the parallelism between Charles, Tom, Red, and Seabiscuit, but it overplays its hand. The connections are too obvious (such as a scene in which both Red and the horse have similar-looking casts on their legs). A little subtlety would have been more rewarding. Eventually, *Seabiscuit* settles into a nice rhythm and, as it enters the stretch, it exhibits all the necessary elements of a good sports movie. Like the horse it's named after, *Seabiscuit* has a lot of heart and, in the end, that's what won me over. **RECOMMENDED**

Searching for Bobby Fischer [1993]

Starring: Max Pomeranc, Joe Mantegna, Joan Allen, Ben Kingsley, Laurence Fishburne Director: Steven Zaillian Screenplay: Steven Zaillian based on the book by Fred Waitzkin Running Time: 1:50 Rated: PG (Mild profanity) Theatrical Aspect Ratio: 1.85:1

At the tender age of 7, Josh Waitzkin (Max Pomeranc) becomes fascinated by the game of chess. Without giving up little league baseball, he learns how to play, hanging out with Vinnie (Laurence Fishburne) and a group of speed chess hustlers who occupy nearby Washington Square. It isn't long before Josh is able to beat them all. His father, looking to take him to the next level, employs ex-chess master Bruce Pandolfini (Ben Kingsley) as a teacher. Under Pandolfini, Josh matures as a player, and, for the first time, he starts to fear losing.

Searching for Bobby Fischer is based on the true life story of Josh Waitzkin who, at the age of 16, became the highest-ranked American player under 18. It isn't just Josh's tale, however. The name and image of the mysterious chess genius Bobby Fischer infiltrate this movie. Fischer is as much an icon to this game as Babe Ruth is to baseball.

How important are games to the American way of life? Have they become so crucial that we lose sight of the people playing them? And at what point does the need to win become so important that the game ceases to be fun? These are some of the questions that *Searching for Bobby Fischer* probes. It certainly can't answer them, but the film offers fodder for thought as it explores Josh's early career and examines the relationship between the young chess master and his sports writer father, Frank Waitzkin (Joe Mantegna).

Josh starts playing chess because it fascinates him. As soon as Frank recognizes his son's gift, however, he begins to apply subtle pressure. Winning becomes important — perhaps too important — and Josh is afraid that to fail at the game is to risk losing his father's love. It's then that chess becomes a burden and he stops enjoying it.

Searching for Bobby Fischer is an intensely fascinating movie capable of involving those who are ignorant about chess as well as those who love it. The focus of the film is less on the actual game than it is on the people, emotions, and pressures surrounding Josh. It is a tale of human trials and triumph, not a sports movie that panders to a certain segment of the population. Chess may not be the most exciting activity to watch, but *Searching for Bobby Fischer* makes for engaging entertainment. **RECOMMENDED**

The Secret of Roan Inish [1994]

Starring: Jeni Courtney, Mick Lally, Richard Sheridan, Eileen Colgan, John Lynch Director: John Sayles Screenplay: John Sayles based on *The Secret of the Ron Mor Skerry* by Rosalie K. Fry Running Time: 1:43 Rated: PG Theatrical Aspect Ratio: 1.85:1

In content, setting, and cast choice, *The Secret of Roan Inish* is a departure for writer/director John Sayles. The creative force behind such memorable and diverse films as *Matewan, City of Hope, Eight Men Out,* and *Passion Fish,* has taken pen and camera across the Atlantic to Ireland, a land steeped in mystery and legend.

The Secret of Roan Inish is the story of 10-year old Fiona Coneelly (Jeni Courtney), a motherless girl living in the city who is sent to stay with her grandparents (Mick Lally and Eileen Colgan) when her father determines that his poor lifestyle is not suitable for raising a daughter. Fiona's grandparents live in a small fishing village across the waters from Roan Inish ("seal island"), the island where the Coneellys had thrived for generations until tragic circumstances forced them to the mainland. Now, however, legends about the family's connection to Roan Inish abound. Is Fiona's little brother, who drifted out to sea in a storm years ago, really dead, or have the seals nur-

tured and protected him? Is there any truth to the story that in Fiona's veins runs the blood of a selkie, a seal who became a woman? And what will it take to restore the ways of the past, something which inspires equal portions of longing and dread?

Geographically, Sayles may be in unfamiliar territory with *The Secret of Roan Inish,* but his inimitable style has been imprinted on this movie. Two of the director's trademarks — the ability to tell an engrossing story and the development of strong, three-dimensional characters — are in evidence. With *Roan Inish,* Sayles has found the perfect balance between the mystical and the concrete. The result is exuberant and compelling.

There's no doubt that *The Secret of Roan Inish* is a most atypical motion picture, but in many ways, this is the best kind of movie — one that takes us to a land where magic is real, and where a little girl can strive to find a lost brother and bring happiness to an entire family. The story, although straightforward, is by no means simple, and there's enough in *The Secret of Roan Inish* to delight both children and adults.

HIGHLY RECOMMENDED

Secrets and Lies [United Kingdom/France, 1996]

Starring: Brenda Blethyn, Marianne Jean-Baptiste, Timothy Spall, Phyllis Logan, Claire Rushbrook Director: Mike Leigh Screenplay: Mike Leigh Running Time: 2:22 Rated: No MPAA Rating (Mature themes, profanity) Theatrical Aspect Ratio: 1.66:1

By wedding comedy with tragedy in intricate, realistic unions, Mike Leigh has become one of the foremost film making voices for the British working class. Yet, even though his movies bring a certain social viewpoint to the screen, this in no way limits the universality of Leigh's themes. *Secrets and Lies,* 1996's Palme D'Or winner at Cannes, represents the director at his best — unsentimental yet powerful, funny and poignant, and, in the end, undeniably satisfying.

Secrets and Lies opens with a funeral, then quickly switches to a wedding. During the former ceremony, Hortense (Marianne Jean-Baptiste), a 27-year-old black optometrist, is burying her mother. In the next scene, we meet Maurice (Timothy Spall), a 38-year-old white photographer who's taking pictures of a nervous bride. It takes nearly the entire movie before these two characters come face-to-face, but what happens during that meeting represents the climax of Leigh's beautifully-realized film. Hortense and Maurice are crucial to unraveling the entire sequence of secrets and lies.

Hortense was adopted. She has known this since

she was 7 years old, but it's not until both of her parents are dead that she feels compelled to seek out her birth mother. Despite being warned by a social worker to anticipate unpleasantness or disappointment, Hortense is shocked to learn that her mother is white. Her name is Cynthia (Brenda Blethyn), and she's a 42-year-old neurotic living in a dark, gloomy rowhouse with her 21-year-old daughter, Roxanne (Claire Rushbrook). Cynthia is disliked by just about everyone who knows her, except perhaps her brother, Maurice.

Secrets and Lies chronicles Hortense's initial approach to Cynthia, their first meeting, and the development of a tentative bond. Each offers something unique to the other: Cynthia has lost her "real" daughter's love and respect, and is desperate to find a surrogate. Hortense, on the other hand, feels rootless now that the two people who brought her up are dead, and, while she doesn't look to Cynthia for parenting, she is curious about, and, ultimately, sympathetic with the disappointments that have defined her biological mother's life. There are no recriminations, at least not on Hortense's part.

Secrets and Lies exhibits the kind of breathtaking power that can be unearthed in a simple story. There's no sensationalism — Leigh has ignored stereotypes in carefully developing the situation (wealthy black professional; underprivileged, uneducated whites) to dispel racial tension. This allows the dysfunctional family dynamics to be the sole focus. What the director has accomplished with this picture is to fashion an amazingly-textured story that grips us with unexpected force on the first viewing, and is sure to reveal a new aspect each time we come back. Without a doubt, *Secrets and Lies* is worth more than one trip to the theater. **MUST SEE**

Selena [1997]

Starring: Jennifer Lopez, Edward James Olmos, Jon Seda, Constance Marie Director: Gregory Nava Screenplay: Gregory Nava Running Time: 2:05 Rated: PG (Mild profanity, mature themes) Theatrical Aspect Ratio: 1.85:1

Going into *Selena*, I didn't know or care much about the life of the late Tex-Mex singer, whose death in 1995 came just as she was attempting to break into the mainstream American pop market. As far as I was aware, Selena's tragic end was just another minor footnote in music history — I hadn't heard of her before and I didn't expect to hear of her again. Then along came this movie, and, sitting in a darkened theater, watching Selena's story unfold, my perceptions

changed. I not only cared, but understood a measure of the tragedy that had stricken her fans.

It would have been easy to trivialize Selena's story, turning it into a sudsy, made-for-TV type motion picture. The details for something lurid and exploitative are there, but that was never an approach considered by writer/director Gregory Nava. It's not an original tale — movies like this abound — but Nava's point-of-view is fresh.

This is a multigenerational story, exploring not only Selena's realization of her dreams, but the importance of her father's vision to all that she accomplished. It was his belief in her that prodded her to follow her own path, and his support that convinced her that she could succeed in a field where every other Mexican American woman had failed.

Jennifer Lopez is radiant as the title character, conveying the boundless energy and enthusiasm that exemplified Selena, while effectively copying not only her look, but her mannerisms. I wonder if Selena's family, upon watching this performance, felt an eerie sense of déjà vu. It's apparent from the clips of the real performer shown at the movie's conclusion that Lopez has done a masterful job of re-creating a personality.

Nava's film flows beautifully, and the concert sequences effectively capture the electricity of such events. *Selena* achieves the perfect emotional pitch for the subject, and, though this is a celebration of life, youth, and family, our awareness of the inevitable end lends a sense of poignancy to the proceedings. It's impossible to watch Selena's triumphant Astrodome concert without remembering that her life would be snuffed out less than a month later.

Fame often follows tragedy, especially when the victim is cut down in the prime of life. James Dean. Buddy Holly. Roberto Clemente. These are just a few names in a long, long list. Now, Selena has joined that roster. This movie will serve to further elevate her name and advance her legend. *Selena* is a shining story. **HIGHLY RECOMMENDED**

A Self-Made Hero [France, 1996]

Starring: Mathieu Kassovitz, Anouk Grinberg, Sandrine Kiberlain, Albert Dupontel Director: Jacques Audiard Screenplay: Alain Le Henry and Jacques Audiard from the book by Jean-Francois Deniau Running Time: 1:45 Rated: No MPAA Rating (Mature themes, profanity, sex, brief nudity) Theatrical Aspect Ratio: 1.66:1 In French with subtitles

Have you ever wished that you could become someone else? That, without regard for the consequences, you could shed your current personality like an old shirt and slip into something more comfortable? If so, then you'll be intrigued by the premise of *A Self-Made Hero*, director Jacques Audiard's smart, fascinating, satirical meditation on the flexibility of identity.

The film opens in modern-day France, with an unseen interviewer asking questions of a seventy-something man named Albert Dehousse (Jean-Louis Trintignant). As Albert begins to talk about his past, we see it unfold on screen — his childhood in rural, pre-World War II France, his life during the German occupation, and, finally, how he rose to prominence in the wake of the Allied liberation. And, while *A Self-Made Hero*'s narrative traces Albert's life during the 1940s, a pseudo-documentary overlay offers occasional commentary and observations from those who once knew Albert.

In Lambersart, France during 1944, 26-year-old Albert (Mathieu Kassovitz) lives his life as if no war is under progress. He is content to marry a pretty blond (Sandrine Kiberlain), take a job as a salesman, and stay out of the Germans' way. Then, after the Liberation, he learns that his father-in-law was an important member of the Resistance, and, feeling overwhelmed by inadequacy, Albert flees Lambersart for Paris, where, with the help of a mysterious friend named "The Captain" (Albert Dupontel), he reinvents himself as a high-ranking member of the Resistance. Through a combination of hard work, good fortune, and brashness, Albert makes the right connections and ends up as an important player in the post-war order. But, when he falls in love with the vivacious Servane (Anouk Grinberg), he wonders about the psychological penalty of keeping the truth from her.

A Self-Made Hero has an extraordinarily perceptive script that asks a lot of complex questions but doesn't insult its audience by offering simple answers. Audiard has designed this film as part-drama, part satire, and there are times when the movie's pointed comedy is worth more than a perfunctory chuckle. And the often-ironic "documentary interview" segments, which add a layer of verisimilitude to the project, open a window onto how modern-day Parisians view their history of fifty years ago.

At the heart of *A Self-Made Hero* is a simple question: Who am I, and can I be a different person? The Captain indicates that there's no such thing as a fixed identity — losers can successfully disguise themselves as winners, cowards as heroes, and devils as saints. Albert notes that "the best lives are invented," and goes on to prove his words by actions. *A Self-Made Hero* offers an ambitious portrait of one man who used an alternative path to realize his dreams only to discover that the richest fiction can never truly supplant reality. **HIGHLY RECOMMENDED**

Seventh Heaven [France, 1997]

Starring: Sandrine Kiberlain, Vincent Lindon, Francois Berleand, Francine Berge, Leo Le Bevillon Director: Benoît Jacquot
Screenplay: Jérôme Beaujour, Benoît Jacquot Running Time: 1:31
Rated: No MPAA Rating (Mature themes, sexual situations, nudity)
Theatrical Aspect Ratio: 2.35:1 In French with subtitles

Seventh Heaven introduces us to Mathilde (Sandrine Kimberlain) and Nico (Vincent Lindon), a dysfunctional couple. Mathilde is not well. In addition to having kleptomaniac tendencies, she is prone to fainting spells. She wanders around with a distracted, dazed expression on her face. Her husband, who is involved in a sexual relationship with his assistant at work, cares for Mathilde as he would for a child. When he sleeps with her, he appears pleased by her passivity and lack of passion. Then Mathilde meets a mysterious hypnotist (Francois Berleand), who puts her under his influence, regresses her back to childhood, and cures her malaise. Suddenly, she is emotionally, mentally, and sexually whole. The next time she and Nico have sex, she experiences an orgasm. Oddly, this disturbs him, because his simple, well-defined home life has now been turned upside down.

At first glance, it seems that Jacquot may be going in one of two directions: exploring the power and potential for abuse inherent in hypnotism, or examining the impact of repressed memories. In reality, however, these are only red herrings — minor ideas in a tapestry whose main focus is the shifting dynamics of a marriage. Before her awakening, Mathilde is trapped in a sterile union. Her husband is more of a caregiver than a friend or a lover. He is content with the arrangement, which makes her more like a pet or a servant than an equal. She cooks his meals, cleans the house, and helps care for their child. They do not engage in lengthy conversations and their sexual relationship is limited to a few minutes of rigorous activity in the dark while he satisfies himself. Once Mathilde has shaken off her emotional lethargy, Nico feels threatened and frightened. He does not know this woman, and he isn't sure that he wants to. His most sincere desire is for things to go back to the way they were.

Jacquot is a meticulous director who relies heavily

upon the performances of his actors. During one sequence in the hypnotist's office, when Mathilde is relating a childhood memory, Jacquot keeps the camera on her face, rather than yielding to the temptation of inserting a flashback. Were Kiberlain less accomplished, this could have been an unfortunate move, but the actress is capable of handling the approach. Jacquot also uses a few minor photographic tricks to emphasize the thrust of his narrative. The film opens with a freeze-frame shot of an out-of-focus Mathilde. It closes with Nico groping in the dark. Yet, as confused as the characters' needs may sometimes be, the hand of the director is never anything less than sure, and his vision is always crystal clear. **RECOMMENDED**

Shanghai Triad [Hong Kong, 1995]

Starring: Gong Li, Li Baotian, Wang Xiaoxiao, Sun Chun, Fu Biao, Li Xuejian Director: Zhang Yimou Screenplay: Bi Feiyu Running Time: 1:48 Rated: R (Violence, mature themes) Theatrical Aspect Ratio: 1.85:1 In Mandarin with subtitles

Throughout the 1990s, Zhang Yimou, one of the most internationally acclaimed of all the so-called "Fifth Generation" Chinese film makers, made a series of visually striking, narratively compelling pictures, including *Raise the Red Lantern* and *To Live*. In *Shanghai Triad*, Zhang delves deeply into the workings of Shanghai's gangland during the 1930s. Reminiscent of Prohibition-era Chicago — and therefore depicting the universality of organized crime — *Shanghai Triad* is a fascinating, though imperfect, look at the lure and power of greed to corrupt and destroy.

The story is told from the point-of-view of 14-year-old Shuisheng (Wang Xiaoxiao), a country "innocent" brought by his uncle (Li Xuejian) to Shanghai to work for Boss Tang (Li Baotian). Zhang uses Shuisheng to represent the audience; everything that takes place is seen through the young boy's eyes. In fact, there are several effective first person camera shots where we see events unfold as if from Shuisheng's perspective. Like those of us watching the film, Shuisheng has no knowledge about what it means to live in Tang's circle, and his education is ours.

Shuisheng's first job for the Boss is to serve his mistress, the petulant, controlling Bijou (Gong Li). Like Shuisheng, Bijou was born and bred in the country, but, unlike her new servant, she has allowed the bright lights, easy money, and fast life of Shanghai to corrupt her innocence. A singer in the Boss' nightclub and lover to both him and one of his top men, she is trapped in a situation that is out of control.

There are times when she recognizes the futility of her existence and lashes out in mingled pain and despair.

Shanghai Triad takes place over an 8-day period that chronicles Shuisheng's arrival to work for the Boss, his conflicted emotions for Bijou, a bloody attempt to kill Tang, and the subsequent flight to an island safe house. There is plenty of action, but the primary focus is on relationships and internal conflicts. The interaction between Shuisheng, Bijou, and Tang forms the central dynamic, and those three characters represent this movie's true "Shanghai triad."

With its underworld violence and straightforward narrative, *Shanghai Triad* is one of Zhang's most accessible films. It is not, however, his best work, having neither the epic scope of *To Live* nor the quiet emotional power of *Raise the Red Lantern*. Yet there is still much to like about *Shanghai Triad*, not the least of which is the production's gorgeous look (credit the director and his cinematographer, Li Xiao). *Shanghai Triad* overflows with memorable imagery and atmosphere. And, as this film verifies, a weak entry by Zhang is often far more engrossing than a strong entry by many other directors. **RECOMMENDED**

The Shape of Things [2003]

Starring: Paul Rudd, Rachel Weisz, Gretchen Mol, Frederick Weller Director: Neil LaBute Screenplay: Neil LaBute, based on his play Running Time: 1:36 Rated: R (Profanity, sexual situations) Theatrical Aspect Ratio: 2.35:1

If Neil LaBute's views about love and human relationships are represented by what appears in his motion pictures, then to call him a cynic would be an understatement. *The Shape of Things* offers a twisted love story about manipulation, the loss of innocence, and the brutality of betrayal. What starts out as a talky, modern-day re-interpretation of *Pygmalion* (Henry Higgins is explicitly mentioned) turns into something heart-wrenchingly bleak. If this is the potential price of opening oneself up to tender feelings, why would anyone bother?

The Shape of Things skims a lot of issues — the nature and importance of art, the value that society places upon the superficiality of physical beauty, and the ease with which one who surrenders to love can be emotionally wrecked. The latter is the aspect most likely to preoccupy viewers as they depart the theater. Don't let the surprisingly light and airy beginning fool you — this film gets very dark before the end credits roll. If you're not prepared to inhale a devastatingly negative view of human nature, this film isn't for you. There is no catharsis worth mentioning.

Adam (Rudd) is a shy, nerdy college student moonlighting as a museum guard when he first meets Eveyln (Weisz). She's an artist who is about to deface a statue of Zeus as an act of protest. Sparks fly between the two, and they're soon an item. Adam's engaged friends — quiet Jenny (Mol) and domineering Phillip (Weller) — are at a loss to understand the attraction, since Adam and Evelyn are complete opposites. Jenny is wary of Evelyn, but for Phillip, it's hate at first sight. Gradually, as he spends more time with Evelyn, Adam begins to change — he loses weight, turns in his glasses in favor of contacts, gets a haircut, starts wearing hip clothing, and agrees to a nose job. And, in addition to reshaping his appearance, Evelyn gradually insinuates some of her own ideas and characteristics into Adam's personality. The consequences of this, especially as they involve Jenny and Phillip, are not entirely what Evelyn expects.

Four solid performances help to overcome some of the film's shortcomings, and LaBute delivers a knockout final punch that will impact even those who see it coming. *The Shape of Things* is imperfect, but the flaws don't detract much from what is a singularly effective, grim perspective of contemporary romance. **RECOMMENDED**

Shattered Glass [2003]

Starring: Hayden Christensen, Peter Sarsgaard, Chloë Sevigny, Steve Zahn, Melanie Lynskey, Hank Azaria, Rosario Dawson Director: Billy Ray Screenplay: Billy Ray, based on the article by H. G. Bissinger Running Time: 1:35 Rated: PG-13 (Profanity, drug use) Theatrical Aspect Ratio: 2.35:1

In the late 1990s, as the stock market boomed and a president argued that fellatio wasn't really sex, ethics and morality had become terms that corporate America viewed as quaint relics of the past. This was the New Market. You did what was necessary to get ahead, and if it meant "bending" the established rules, would anyone find out? Journalist Stephen Glass (played here by Hayden Christensen) didn't think so. After starting out as a hungry, promising journalist for the *New Republic* (the "in-flight magazine of Air Force One"), Glass discovered that he could make a bigger splash with less effort if he faked facts and sources. Soon, he was making up entire stories, and there was a big enough hole in the *New Republic*'s fact-checking process that he was able to get away with it. Twenty-seven of the 41 stories he wrote for the magazine were partially or entirely false, and

Glass was only caught by accident, when an online magazine tried to check his sources and figured out that they didn't exist.

It's difficult to tell from the movie whether Glass is a good journalist. He certainly has the capacity to schmooze and mingle, which are more important than ethical considerations in many aspects of today's corporate world. Hayden Christensen provides an unsettling portrayal of Glass. He presents the character as a wide-eyed and seemingly naive kid, with a lot of childish mannerisms, and an almost pathological need to be liked. Hank Azaria plays Glass's first editor, Michael Kelly, who demanded the highest level of journalistic honesty from his writers.

Integrity is one of the cornerstones upon which reliable journalism is based, and when it is called into question, we begin to doubt everything we read in newspapers and magazines and see on television. The recent Jayson Blair/*New York Times* incident has re-enforced the idea that, while most members of the media are forthright and hardworking, there are exceptions. Glass was not the first, nor will he be the last, but he was caught in a very public way, and his trial in the media represented the first such Internet-fueled scourging of a journalist. *Shattered Glass* may be light when it comes to psychological questions, but its detailed accounting of Glass's actions makes for fascinating viewing. Most importantly, however, it raises questions about how much reliability we should place in our everyday sources of news if faking stories is so simple. **RECOMMENDED**

The Shawshank Redemption [1994]

Starring: Tim Robbins, Morgan Freeman, Bob Gunton, William Sadler, Clancy Brown, Gil Bellows Director: Frank Darabont Screenplay: Frank Darabont based on "Rita Hayworth and the Shawshank Redemption" by Stephen King Running Time: 2:22 Rated: R (Violence, language, mature themes) Theatrical Aspect Ratio: 1.85:1

With a legion of titles like *Pet Sematary, Firewalker,* and *Children of the Corn*, it's reasonable not to expect much from Stephen King-inspired motion pictures. Adaptations of the prolific author's work typically vary from mildly entertaining to virtually unwatchable. There are a few notable exceptions, however; two of which (*Stand by Me, Misery*) were crafted by widely-respected director Rob Reiner. While *The Shawshank Redemption* is not a Reiner movie per se, it is a production of Castle Rock Pictures (Reiner's film company).

Spanning the years from 1947 through 1966, *The Shawshank Redemption* takes the "innocent man in prison" theme and bends it at a different angle. Instead of focusing on crusades for freedom, the movie ventures down the less-traveled road of concentrating on the personal cost of adapting to prison life and how some convicts, once they conform, lose the ability to survive beyond the barbed wire and iron bars. As one of the characters puts it: "These [prison] walls are funny. First you hate them, then you get used to them, then you start to depend on them."

Filmed on location in a disused Ohio prison, *The Shawshank Redemption* is set in a place of perpetual dreariness. What little color there is, is drab and lifeless (lots of grays and muted greens and blues), and there are times when the film is a shade away from black-and-white (give credit to cinematographer Roger Deakins, a longtime Cohen brothers collaborator). It's ironic, therefore, that the central messages are of hope, redemption, and salvation.

Tim Robbins, as Andrew Dufresne, plays the wrongly convicted man with quiet dignity. Andy's ire is internal; he doesn't rant about his situation or the corruptness of the system that has imprisoned him. Ellis Boyd Redding (Morgan Freeman), or "Red" as his friends call him, is the self-proclaimed "Sears and Roebuck" of the Shawshank Prison (for a price, he can get just about anything from the outside). His is the narrative voice and, for once, the disembodied words aid, rather than intrude upon, the story. Gil Bellows, in a small-but-crucial role (that was originally intended for Brad Pitt), brings the poise of a veteran to his portrayal of Tommy Williams, Andy's protege. Ultimately, the standout actor is the venerable James Whitmore. Whitmore's Brooks is a brilliantly-realized character, and the scenes with him attempting to cope with life outside of Shawshank represents one of the film's most moving — and effective — sequences.

Prison movies often focus on the violence and hopelessness of a life behind bars. While this film includes those elements, it makes them peripheral. *The Shawshank Redemption* is all about hope and, because of that, watching it is both uplifting and cathartic. **HIGHLY RECOMMENDED**

She's So Lovely [1997]

Starring: Sean Penn, Robin Wright Penn, John Travolta, Gena Rowlands Director: Nick Cassavetes Screenplay: John Cassavetes Running Time: 1:38 Rated: R (Profanity, violence) Theatrical Aspect Ratio: 2.35:1

The director of *She's So Lovely* is Nick Cassavetes, the son of John and actress Gena Rowlands. And, since Rowlands appears in *She's So Lovely*, this is, in a sense, a family production. The younger Cassavetes' approach to directing is different from his father's. Nick is more of a polished, traditional film maker. John relied upon improvisations from both his actors and his cinematographer; Nick scripts and choreographs everything beforehand. He may be following in his father's footsteps, but he is not attempting to copy him.

Real-life couple Sean Penn and Robin Wright Penn play Eddie and Maureen, a husband and wife who are very much in love. When we first meet them, it's the late 1970s, although only the music, hairstyles, and clothing seem to differentiate the time period from today. Both Eddie and Maureen exhibit streaks of violent, self-destructive behavior. But, although Eddie carries a gun and isn't unwilling to use his fists, he never strikes Maureen. She and the child she carries are his reason for living. Neither husband nor wife is entirely sane, and when Eddie loses it in public and shoots a mental health care worker, he is sent away to an institution for the criminally insane.

A decade passes before Eddie is given his release, but the world he returns to is far different from the one he left. His best friend, Shorty (Harry Dean Stanton), is still the same, but his wife is not. During the last 10 years, Maureen has cleaned herself up, divorced Eddie, and married a prosperous businessman named Joey (John Travolta). She lives in a big house with a swimming pool out back, and has 3 daughters (the oldest is a product of her troubled marriage to Eddie). It's an idyllic situation, yet when she learns of Eddie's release, Maureen feels the tug of long-buried feelings, and their re-emergence threatens not only her family's stability, but her own tenuous grip on sanity.

She's So Lovely is uncomfortable because it challenges our perceptions about love and family. Maureen and Joey have the American dream, but does it really mean anything? And is true love just another form of insanity? Some viewers will undoubtedly be dismayed by the film's abrupt ending but, by the time the end credits roll, we know all that we need to know to guess how things will probably turn out. *She's So Lovely* isn't a flawless production, but it's a fitting tribute to John Cassavetes, and a reminder of the many ways that a woman can be under the influence. **RECOMMENDED**

Shine [Australian, 1996]

Starring: Geoffrey Rush, Armin Mueller-Stahl, Noah Taylor, Lynn Redgrave Director: Scott Hicks Screenplay: Jan Sardi based on a story by Scott Hicks Running Time: 1:45 Rated: PG-13 (Mature themes, brief nudity) Theatrical Aspect Ratio: 1.85:1

Shine is a deceptively simple title for an amazingly powerful motion picture. Based on the life story of Australian pianist David Helfgott, director Scott Hicks' film touches on themes as diverse as the nature of genius, the triumph over adversity, and the destructive power of love.

Shine has its roots in 1986, when director Scott Hicks read a newspaper story about David Helfgott, a pianist who performed a flawless classical repertoire at a Perth restaurant. Hicks' interest was piqued, and he arranged to see Helfgott in concert. For the better part of the next year, he worked to earn the man's trust with the goal of presenting his story in a motion picture. That odyssey, which is admittedly fictionalized to some degree in Jan Sardi's wonderful screenplay, became *Shine*, one of 1996's most stirring and inspirational tales.

To fully comprehend David Helfgott's story, it is necessary to understand his father, Peter Helfgott (powerfully portrayed by Armin Mueller-Stahl), a Polish Jew who settled in Australia after surviving Hitler's purge. He's a soul-sick man whose ongoing battle with private demons makes his personality erratic and his actions unpredictable. He lost his parents and sisters-in-law to the Holocaust, and the anguish of those losses impels him to keep his family together at all costs. When we first encounter him during the 1950s, he is still rebelling against his long-dead father's influence. Peter's drive to teach his children to play instruments is a direct reaction to his own father's dislike of music.

Shine follows David's life from childhood (Alex Rafalowicz), through adolescence (Noah Taylor), to adulthood (Geoffrey Rush). When we first meet him, he's performing at a school recital. There, a music teacher, Ben Rosen (Nicholas Bell), notices his obvious talent, and offers to teach him. Eventually, after winning several competitions, David is invited to study music in the United States. His father, determined not to "let anyone destroy this family," refuses to let him go. Soon after, David's talent begins to languish as his musical progress stagnates. When he receives a scholarship to the Royal College of Music in London, an elderly writer friend (Googie Withers) encourages him to take the offer, whether his father objects or not. In following that advice, David sunders his relationship with Peter.

In London, he studies under the guidance of Cecil Parkes (John Gielgud), attempting to reach his potential. But, on the night of his crowning glory, when he plays a perfect rendition of Rachmaninoff's Third Piano Concerto, the cumulative pressure overwhelms David, and he suffers a nervous breakdown. The next time we see him, more than 10 years older, he's a pathetic, jittery individual given to incoherent, babbling monologues. Public piano performances are long behind him . . . until he enters a small restaurant.

This is unbelievably rich material, and I can say without reservation that Scott Hicks' work deserves the highest recognition. *Shine* truly does what its name says. **MUST SEE**

Short Cuts [1993]

Starring: Andie MacDowell, Bruce Davison, Jack Lemmon, Julianne Moore, Matthew Modine Director: Robert Altman Screenplay: Robert Altman and Frank Barhydt based on the writings of Raymond Carver Running Time: 3:09 Rated: R (Frontal nudity, mature themes, language) Theatrical Aspect Ratio: 2.35:1

Helicopters thunder through the air over Los Angeles, raining malathion on the city in an attempt to end the dreaded Medfly invasion. Below, in each house and apartment, an individual drama is being played out. As in any human settlement at any time in history, there is joy, sadness, jealousy, fear, reconciliation, pain, and death. With *Short Cuts*, a film by director Robert Altman based on 9 short stories and one poem by the late Raymond Carver, the audience is given a glimpse into several of those dramas.

Infidelity mars two marriages, while a tragic accident to another couple's son brings their lives to an abrupt halt. A trio of fishing buddies find a dead girl's body floating near their campsite. Another marriage is troubled by a husband's uncertainty about his wife's career choice — running a phone sex business. A man decides to teach his estranged wife a little something about the real meaning of "dividing things up," and a mother and daughter discover the pain that can come from not communicating.

Twenty-two characters and 10 tales — it would take a master to interweave all of these into a seamless whole. There are few directors who would tackle the challenge, and fewer still who could succeed. Not only has Robert Altman faced the Herculean task, but he has emerged victorious. *Short Cuts* is a magnificent triumph, an example that dramas can still be found that don't make use of the time-honored tactics of manipulation and oversentimentalization.

What is impressive about *Short Cuts* is not only that it presents so many diverse personalities and situations, but that it manages to interconnect them in a manner that doesn't leave the viewer shaking his or her head in confusion. Fans of Carver, however, should check their expectations at the door — these are not strict adaptations (as the change of setting from the Pacific Northwest to angst-riddled L.A. indicates). Altman admits that *Short Cuts* is "not a verbatim retelling of Carver's works, but rather a cinematic interpretation of their essence."

It's a genuine pleasure to find a movie with such a deep and intelligent portrayal of simple human lives, with all their minor triumphs and tragedies. *Short Cuts* is an example of a highly-respected modern director in top form. **HIGHLY RECOMMENDED**

A Short Film about Killing [Poland, 1987]

Starring: Miroslaw Baka, Krzysztof Globisz, Jan Tesarz
Director: Krzysztof Kieslowski Screenplay: Krzysztof Kieslowski and
Krzysztof Piesiewicz Running Time: 1:25 Rated: No MPAA Rating
(Violence) Theatrical Aspect Ratio: 1.66:1 In Polish with subtitles

A Short Film About Killing, Krzysztof Kieslowski's powerful examination of the nature of murder, was a stunning success at the 1988 Cannes Film Festival, taking home the Jury prize. In the same year, the film also captured Europe's coveted Felix award. An extended version of *Decalogue 5, A Short Film About Killing* was one of two features to spring from Kieslowski's 10-part television drama about applying the Ten Commandments to modern-day life (the other being *A Short Film About Love*).

Wrenching in its uncompromising indictment of capital punishment, *A Short Film About Killing* doesn't pull punches. Sitting through this film is the emotional equivalent of going through a grinder. Everything about the production is dark — from its themes and characters to the manner in which Kieslowski and cinematographer Slawomir Idiak chose to shoot the picture. Bleaker even than *Blue*, *A Short Film About Killing* captures the perfect tone for an autopsy of its subject matter.

The movie follows the activities of 20-year-old Jacek (Miroslaw Baka), a seemingly-normal young man with a sadistic streak. He goes through a day, wandering around town but rarely interacting with anyone. Then, suddenly, in a seemingly-unprovoked action, he murders a cab driver (Jan Tesarz) by gar-

roting him then beating him to a bloody pulp with a rock. Jacek is captured and tried. Despite the best efforts of a newly-practicing, idealistic lawyer named Piotr (Krzysztof Globisz), Jacek is sentenced to die. Before the execution, the condemned man spends some time in a cell with his attorney, telling fragments of a tragic life's story and expressing his final request — to be buried in a plot alongside his father and beloved sister.

A Short Film About Killing is as grim as a motion picture gets, but the intelligence and insight applied to its themes will keep the viewer riveted despite the pervasive gloom. Whether an individual agrees or disagrees with Kieslowski's position on the issue of capital punishment, there is no denying that his case against it is powerfully made. And, while the director cannot answer the question of why men kill, his scrutiny of murder offers a bloody portrait worth repeated study. **HIGHLY RECOMMENDED**

A Short Film about Love [Poland, 1988]

Starring: Grazyna Szapolowska, Olaf Lubaszenko, Stefina Iwinska
Director: Krzysztof Kieslowski Screenplay: Krzysztof Kieslowski and
Krzysztof Piesiewicz Running Time: 1:26 Rated: No MPAA Rating (Sex,
mature themes) Theatrical Aspect Ratio: 1.66:1 In Polish with subtitles

A Short Film About Love, the second of Krzysztof Kieslowski's *Decalogue* episodes to be transformed into a feature film (the other being *A Short Film about Killing*), takes a unique look at the emotional latticework that interconnects love, lust, and sexual obsession. Hypnotically engrossing, this picture delves deep into the psyches of its two main characters, employing irony, humor, and drama to weave a masterful tale of human interaction that will leave an indelible imprint on all who view it.

The story begins with 19-year-old Tomek (Olaf Lubaszenko) training a telescope on the windows of an apartment opposite his. Inside, a beautiful, older woman, Magda (Grazyna Szapolowska), is undressing. Initially, we assume that Tomek is watching for the titillation value, but, as we observe him night after night, it becomes clear that he's more interested in Magda when she's fully clothed and engaged in some mundane activity than when her actions turn sexual. In fact, when she goes to bed with a man, Tomek trains the telescope away.

As his obsession deepens, Tomek is no longer content with merely watching. He begins to make phone calls and pilfer letters, then eventually works up the courage to meet Magda face-to-face. In a guilty, rushed confession, he tells all. At first, Magda is furious and seeks her own form of revenge, but eventually she finds herself drawn to the young man. One night, after the two go out on a relatively harmless date, she invites him into her apartment and proceeds to shatter his illusions. A brief, unsatisfying sexual encounter rips away Tomek's innocence and sends him fleeing Magda's apartment. Once home, he slits his wrists.

Tomek survives the suicide attempt, but while he's in the hospital, Magda is riddled with guilt. She begins to obsess over him, trying to find out everything she can about his life and friends. She uses a pair of binoculars to watch his apartment, waiting for his return. She turns away her lover, unwilling (or unable) to engage in sex while Tomek is away.

Love is probably the most commonly presented theme in all motion pictures. Most of the time, it is used as a plot device, so rarely is there a thoughtful examination of the dynamics of the emotion. *A Short Film About Love* is the exception, and what a magnificent exception it is. With actors that give finely-tuned performances and a script that is richly detailed, the movie is nothing short of a masterpiece. There is more real feeling in this brief feature than in a hundred full-length Hollywood romantic comedies. **MUST SEE**

Show Me Love (a.k.a. Fucking Amal) [Sweden, 1998]

Starring: Alexandra Dahlström, Rebecka Liljeberg, Mathias Rust, Erica Carlson Director: Lukas Moodysson Screenplay: Lukas Moodysson
Running Time: 1:29 Rated: No MPAA Rating (Profanity, mature themes) Theatrical Aspect Ratio: 1.66:1 In Swedish with subtitles

Show Me Love, the feature debut of Swedish filmmaker Lukas Moodysson, is not bound by the constraints of most Hollywood-produced teen movies, with their manufactured, formulaic plots and characterizations. It's a powerful, deeply affecting depiction of the tribulations of two teenage girls who are struggling with their sexuality and identities.

Sixteen-year-old Agnes (Rebecka Liljeberg) is a loner living in the small, dead-end town of Amal. Perhaps the worst place on Earth, and certainly the most boring (or so many of the underage inhabitants believe), Amal is a backwards hamlet that always seems to be a step behind the rest of the world. Despite having attended the school in Amal for the nearly 2 years since her family moved there, Agnes has no friends. Although attractive, she does little to care for her appearance, and rumors are making their way through the classrooms and hallways that she likes girls. However, while the nature of Agnes' sexuality has yet to

fully emerge, she has a deep crush on a fellow female student, the pretty and popular Elin (Alexandra Dahlström). And, like Agnes, Elin despises Amal. One night, prodded by her older sister, Jessica (Erica Carlson), Elin plays a practical joke on Agnes by kissing her on the lips. Giggling, Jessica and Elin race away, leaving a stunned and hurt Agnes behind. Later that evening, however, Elin feels remorse, and returns to Agnes' house to apologize. She arrives just as Agnes is making a halfhearted attempt to slit her wrists. The two end up spending most of the night together, talking and sharing their innermost thoughts, and their unplanned "date" ends with a real kiss. The next day, frightened by her feelings for Agnes and determined to assert her heterosexuality, Elin nabs the willing Johan (Mathias Rust) as a boyfriend and ignores Agnes, who is understandably devastated.

Show Me Love is an emotional roller-coaster ride for viewers of both genders and all sexual orientations, because the feelings it uncovers are universal in nature. No matter how far removed an individual is from high school, this film has the ability to strip away the years. And, although Moodysson is obviously sympathetic towards both of his protagonists, he does not hesitate to show the mean and selfish sides of their natures. The adults (chiefly Agnes' parents) are not presented as boorish clods; they are helpful and sensitive to the needs of their children. The script's perceptiveness provides us with a fresh, non-manufactured perspective on what it means to be a bored teenager. And it gets the details right.

Not only is this a highly dramatically sound depiction of the life struggles of adolescent girls, but it is one of the most honest and heartfelt teen dramas ever to grace the screen. **HIGHLY RECOMMENDED**

Sidewalks of New York [2001]

Starring: Edward Burns, Rosario Dawson, Dennis Farina, Heather Graham, David Krumholtz, Brittany Murphy, Stanley Tucci
Director: Edward Burns Screenplay: Edward Burns Running Time: 1:47
Rated: R (Profanity, sexual situations) Theatrical Aspect Ratio: 1.85:1

Sidewalks of New York feels so strongly like a Woody Allen film that the sensation couldn't be coincidental. From the setting (Manhattan, where Allen lives and breathes) to the use of hand-held cameras to the focus on a group of neurotic characters who use humor to mask their insecurities, *Sidewalks of New York* obviously owes a strong debt to New York's most famous jazz-loving movie-maker. While nothing in *Sidewalks of New York* reaches the lofty heights of an *Annie Hall* or *Manhattan,* there are plenty of moments in this film that would slide comfortably into some of Allen's less acclaimed efforts.

The 6 characters in *Sidewalks of New York* are trapped in a romantic maze of their own making. Using faux documentary interview segments with the principals to frame the narrative segments, Edward Burns seeks to make these stories seem more real and immediate. The gimmick works, primarily because there's an improvisational quality to these scenes (although I'm sure everything was carefully scripted and the guy in the background giving the finger was instructed to do so). Plus, it helps that most of the unseen interviewer's questions are about sex — a subject that few viewers will be bored by.

One practically needs a scorecard to keep all the entanglements straight. Tommy (Burns) is a 32-year-old TV show producer who has just been thrown out of his apartment by an irate girlfriend. He is immediately attracted to two women — Maria (Rosario Dawson), a school teacher, and Annie (Heather Graham), a realtor. Maria has just gotten her life together after going through a divorce, but her ex-husband, Ben (David Krumholtz), has begun stalking her, wondering if ending the marriage was a mistake. Although still hung up on his ex-wife, Ben is also attracted to Ashley (Brittany Murphy), a 19-year-old waitress at the coffee shop he frequents. He asks her out, but she rebuffs him because she's involved with Griffin (Stanley Tucci), a middle-aged man with whom she's having an affair. Griffin, meanwhile, is married to Annie.

Once fertile territory for American independent films, this sort of ensemble relationship movie has fallen out of favor of late — even Allen isn't making these any more. Despite a few easily identifiable flaws, *Sidewalks of New York* is a breezy, enjoyable motion picture that manages to be smart without demanding our undivided attention. And, during a time when New York is in need of positive portrayals, this movie functions as a postcard to the city whose skyline has changed but whose essential character has not. **RECOMMENDED**

Silver City [2004]

Starring: Danny Huston, Chris Cooper, Richard Dreyfuss, Maria Bello, Daryl Hannah, Billy Zane, Kris Kristofferson, Michael Murphy, Sal Lopez, James Gammon, Tim Roth Director: John Sayles Screenplay: John Sayles Running Time: 2:10 Rated: R (Profanity, sexual situations, violence) Theatrical Aspect Ratio: 1.85:1

John Sayles has always made political films; they are his bread-and-butter. Yet none, not even *Matewan* or

City of Hope, has been more openly partisan than *Silver City*, which rips into the anti-environmental policies of the current administration, shows the pointlessness of fighting the alliance of big business and bigger government, and presents a scathing caricature of our current president in the person of Dickie Pilager (Chris Cooper), the man who would be governor of Colorado. Pilager is all smiles and charm, yet, beneath the polished surface, there's nothing.

Silver City takes us into the 2004 Colorado gubernatorial race. The odds-on favorite to win is Dickie Pilager (not the most subtle last name for an anti-environmentalist), the son of popular Senator Judd Pilager (Michael Murphy). Dickie looks the part and, as long as he sticks to the text of a prepared speech, he sounds like he knows what he's talking about, even if he does promise something for everyone. But if circumstances force him to talk extemporaneously, he becomes a stammering, incoherent idiot. "Don't ever let yourself get caught out in the open like that again," cautions his campaign manager, Chuck Raven (Richard Dreyfuss), after one such incident.

When the appearance of a dead body at one of Dickie's speaking engagements threatens to embarrass the candidate, Raven hires private investigator Danny O'Brien (Danny Huston) to do some detective work. Danny, who has a checkered past (he was fired from the *Denver Monitor* for fabricating a story, when, in reality, he was set up), starts digging deeper than his employers want him to, and his investigation leads him to Dickie's sister (Daryl Hannah) and a gangster type who "imports" illegal migrant workers. He also ends up mucking around in an abandoned silver mine that holds a few buried secrets. And his path crosses with old flame Nora (Maria Bello), who is currently engaged to a materialistic lobbyist (Billy Zane).

Silver City offers a bitter antidote to feel-good, "true" stories like *A Civil Action* and *Erin Brockovich*, in which ordinary citizens go up against big businesses and win. *Silver City* illustrates that those are exceptions to the rule. Sayles never lets us forget where the real power exists in this country. Although there's a lot of politics in *Silver City*, this is first and foremost a detective story. Danny's investigation is all about procedure, and peeling back the layers of corruption to reveal deeper secrets. There are no real shocks; dead people don't suddenly turn up alive, and any smoking gun has long since rusted under the waters that have flooded most of the silver mines. *Sil-*

ver City may startle some viewers because it doesn't pull punches. It doesn't pretend that politics and business are decoupled, that the little guy can pull off the upset, or that the bottom line is anything other than money. It's refreshing, albeit grim, to see a movie that's not afraid of telling these truths.
HIGHLY RECOMMENDED

Sleepers [1996]

Starring: Jason Patric, Brad Pitt, Ron Eldard, Billy Crudup, Robert DeNiro, Joseph Perrino, Brad Renfro, Kevin Bacon, Minnie Driver, Dustin Hoffman Director: Barry Levinson Screenplay: Barry Levinson based on the novel by Lorenzo Carcaterra Running Time: 2:32 Rated: R (Violence, rape, mature themes, profanity, brief nudity) Theatrical Aspect Ratio: 2.35:1

Sleepers is a movie about revenge and redemption, and how, in America's darkest social corridors and backalleys, the two can be inextricably linked. It's also a condemnation of a criminal justice system that allows innocence to be callously destroyed. Yet, even though *Sleepers* is basically a vigilante motion picture, there's little thrill in watching the vengeance extracted by the protagonists of this film because *Sleepers* approaches its subject with a conscience. The movie's moral compass is Robert DeNiro's Father Bobby, a Catholic priest who recognizes that friendship and loyalty can require sacrifices of the soul.

Sleepers spans 15 years. Much of the action transpires in New York's Hell's Kitchen. During the film's era, the neighborhood was ruled by two vastly different powers: the mob (represented by gangster King Benny, played by Vittorio Gassman) and the Catholic Church (represented by Father Bobby). Every child learned to respect both, and live by a simple creed: never commit a crime against someone else in the neighborhood.

The film opens in 1966 by introducing us to four inseparable friends: Lorenzo (Joseph Perrino), Michael (Brad Renfro), John (Geoffrey Wigdor), and Tommy (Jonathan Tucker). Like most boys, they're curious about sex, enjoy playing stickball, and have an appetite for pranks. One such practical joke, gone horribly wrong, changes their lives. When their theft of a hot dog vendor's cart nearly causes a man's death, Lorenzo and his friends are found guilty of reckless endangerment and sent to the Wilkinson Reform School. There, under the watchful eye of a sadistic guard named Sean Nokes (Kevin Bacon), they are subjected to mental, physical, and sexual abuse.

Although their sentences are only for a year, those 12 months fundamentally alter their personalities. When we next meet them, in 1981, their lives have moved on, but the submerged hatred lingers. Lorenzo (now played by Jason Patric) is an aspiring reporter working for the *New York Daily News*. Michael (Brad Pitt) is an attorney in the D.A.'s office. John (Ron Eldard) and Tommy (Billy Crudup) are hardened criminals. All 4 are forced to confront their shared past when John and Tommy encounter Nokes in a restaurant. Their actions provide the catalyst for a plan that Michael devises to bring the entire Wilkinson experience into the open. So, with the help of Lorenzo; John's lover, Carol (Minnie Driver); and a burned-out lawyer (Dustin Hoffman), Michael strives to attain redemption and revenge for them all.

There has been some controversy as to whether or not *Sleepers* is based on a true story. Ultimately, however, it doesn't make much difference whether the events of *Sleepers* happened or not. The themes and messages are no less valid either way, and, even if it isn't a true story, events like these *could have* transpired. Fact or fiction, this is a memorable motion picture. **HIGHLY RECOMMENDED**

Sling Blade [1996]

Starring: Billy Bob Thornton, Lucas Black, Dwight Yoakam, Natalie Canderday, John Ritter, Robert Duvall Director: Billy Bob Thornton Screenplay: Billy Bob Thornton Running Time: 2:15 Rated: R (Violence, profanity) Theatrical Aspect Ratio: 1.85:1

Sling Blade is a fascinating examination of a damaged man's quest to make restitution for his past crimes. To a lesser extent, it also offers an atypical vision of the concept of "family" in modern society. Thornton has developed *Sling Blade* as a slowly-paced character study. Nearly every scene is designed to reveal something about one of characters rather than advance the minimalist story. The narrative is little more than a flimsy envelope — it's the men and women who are sealed within that make *Sling Blade* worth watching.

The best acting in the entire motion picture is by Thornton himself. He plays Karl Childers, a "mentally challenged" man who has been incarcerated in the Arkansas State Hospital for the criminally insane since the age of 9, when he butchered his mother and her lover with a sling blade. As the film opens, Karl is being released from the hospital. According to the doctors, he has been cured. By Karl's own admission, he doesn't reckon he's got a reason to kill anyone else. But we in the audience aren't so sure. His rough, gravely voice is intimidating, and his nervous mannerisms — constantly rubbing his hands together, uttering "uh-huh"s every few words, and never meeting anyone else's gaze — do not inspire confidence. Is he still dangerous, or just the "gentle, simple man" others see him to be?

Once Karl is out of the hospital, he goes to work as a mechanic in the small town where he was born (and where he committed his crime). He befriends a fatherless young boy, Frank Wheatley (Lucas Black), and, after meeting Frank's mother, Linda (Natalie Canderday), is invited to live in their garage. Frank is glad to have Karl around, not just because he yearns for a father-figure, but because he's afraid of Linda's often-drunk, abusive boyfriend, Doyle (Dwight Yoakam), and believes that Karl's presence will keep Doyle in line. Meanwhile, Linda's friend and boss, Vaughan Cunningham (John Ritter), is concerned about a stranger living with Frank and Linda, and decides to keep an eye on the newcomer.

It could be argued that the ending is predictable, but I think "inevitable" is a better word. The audience sees the resolution long before any of *Sling Blade*'s characters do, but that's because we're more removed from the situation than they are. The film builds to a perfectly-fitting, climactic moment. The key scene is not overplayed, nor are the ramifications.

Sling Blade runs for a little longer than it needs to, and there are a few scenes that border on being too cute (such as one where Karl's "date" from the previous evening gives him flowers), but, in general, it's a fine motion picture. Karl is sufficiently interesting to hold our attention for more than 2 hours, and, if the resolution of his dilemma is obvious, watching him arrive at it makes *Sling Blade* worthwhile. **RECOMMENDED**

The Slingshot [Denmark/Sweden, 1993]

Starring: Jesper Salen, Stellan Skarsgård, Basia Frydman, Niclas Olund Director: Ake Sandgren Running Time: 1:42 Rated: R (Violence, mature themes) Screenplay: Ake Sandgren based on the novel by Roland Schutt In Swedish with subtitles

It's interesting how almost every film out of Sweden evokes, in one way or another, impressions of Ingmar Bergman's work. *The Slingshot* is certainly not a Bergman-derivative — it's almost too lighthearted for that — but there are moments here and there when one could imagine something similar from the great director.

The Slingshot is set in the 1920s, and it explores some of the difficult realities of growing up as a boy in Sweden, especially for someone like Roland (Jesper Salen), whose mother, Zipa (Basia Frydman), is a Jew and whose father, Fritiof (Stellan Skarsgård), is devout socialist. Roland is often the target of bullying and name-calling, but the resilient lad always bounces back from whatever problems beset him, often in the most unexpected of ways. On one occasion when he needs money, Roland fashions slingshots out of scrap metal and condoms, then sells them to his schoolmates. Then there's the time when he has some fun with a few lice . . .

The Slingshot successfully navigates the turbulent waters of Roland's boyhood adventures as they turn from absurd to heartwrenching. It is a wonderful mix of tragedy, humor, and triumph. Writer/director Ake Sandgren creates a series of rich screen personalities who could easily slip into comfortable stereotypes, but don't. Take Fritiof, for example. At first, this man seems to be the typical "Swedish father figure" — someone who is stern, demanding, and distanced from his children. As *The Slingshot* progresses, however, we learn that there's a lot more to Fritiof than is initially evident.

With a trio of formidable performances (by Salen, Skarsgård, and Frydman), *The Slingshot* offers a moving, intriguing look at the difficulties faced by one child set adrift in a sea of bigotry where his own resourcefulness is the key to survival. There's more to this film than is suggested by its apparently-simple story, and it's a tribute to the ability of Ake Sandgren and his cast that so much is effectively realized.

HIGHLY RECOMMENDED

Smoke Signals [1998]

Starring: Adam Beach, Evan Adams, Irene Bedard, Gary Farmer, Tantoo Cardinal Director: Chris Eyre Screenplay: Sherman Alexie based on his book "The Lone Ranger and Tonto Fistfight in Heaven" Running Time: 1:28 Rated: PG-13 (Mature themes) Theatrical Aspect Ratio: 1.85:1

Chris Eyres' *Smoke Signals*, the winner of both the Audience Award and the Filmmakers Trophy at the 1998 Sundance Film Festival, is, in essence, a road movie/buddy story. What differentiates this effort from so many others are the characters and the subtext. *Smoke Signals* is a motion picture about Native Americans made by a Native American who doesn't have an ax to grind. Sure, he deals with concerns particular to his people, but he doesn't do it from a pulpit, spewing fire and brimstone at uncomfortable audience members. The movie also features two well-rounded, interesting protagonists whose conversation is a little more memorable than the banal banter that comprises the dialogue often found in this kind of genre picture. As a result, *Smoke Signals*, while not a pillar of originality, is enjoyable and, at times, engrossing.

The movie has all the necessary ingredients of a road movie: the trip from point A to point B that turns into as much of a philosophical journey as a physical one, the oddball characters encountered along the way, and the crowd-pleasing finale. But the foundation of *Smoke Signals* isn't the plot (which, frankly, is pretty ordinary), but the central figures of Victor Joseph (Adam Beach) and Thomas Builds-the-Fire (Evan Adams), two natives of the Coeur D'Alene Reservation in Idaho. Victor and Thomas aren't friends, but they have known each other since childhood, and they share a link. On a night in 1976, Arnold Joseph (Gary Farmer), Victor's father, saved the infant Thomas from a fire that killed his parents. Now, more than 20 years later, Arnold, who abandoned his wife, Arlene (Tantoo Cardinal), and son for a life in Phoenix, has died, and Victor must make the trip to claim his ashes. Thomas, who is supplying the money for the journey, accompanies him.

While *Smoke Signals* probably wasn't the best choice to win at 1998's Sundance Film Festival, it was one of the most sincere films shown there. It doesn't manipulate, rely on contrivances, or devolve into sudsy melodrama. At a time when almost everything coming out of Hollywood seems to be getting bigger and dumber, movies like *Smoke Signals*, which are made with care and craftsmanship, are always welcome. **RECOMMENDED**

Snow Falling on Cedars [1999]

Starring: Ethan Hawke, James Cromwell, Richard Jenkins, James Rebhorn, Sam Shepard Director: Scott Hicks Screenplay: Ronald Bass, Scott Hicks based on the novel by David Guterson Running Time: 2:06 Rated: PG-13 (Violence, profanity, sex) Theatrical Aspect Ratio: 2.35:1

Seeking to do justice to the complexity of the best-selling novel by David Guterson on which *Snow Falling on Cedars* is based, Scott Hicks employs a non-linear, multi-layered structure in the movie that is characterized by flashbacks and flashbacks-within-flashbacks. Events are presented non-chronologically, with frequent, repeated jumps through time to flesh out the characters' backgrounds and reveal the truth of the mystery that lies at the film's core. This is apparently an approach that Hicks feels comfortable with — he used something similar (albeit less convoluted) in his previous movie, *Shine*. Despite the intricacy of the structure, it's not difficult to follow the progression of events. Changes in actors (characters as children versus adults), hairstyles, lighting, and

weather all serve to tip us off about which era any particular scene is transpiring in.

The movie is framed as a courtroom mystery in the Pacific Northwest during the early 1950s, with a local Japanese fisherman named Kazuo Miyamoto (Rick Yune) being tried for the murder of another man, Carl Heine (Eric Thal). One foggy night, while Carl was out on his boat, the *Susan Marie*, something happened. (Only at the end of the movie do we discover what.) The next morning, he was found dead, tangled in his own fishing nets with a nasty gash on his head. Ishmael Chambers (Ethan Hawke), a reporter for the local newspaper, watches impassively as events unfold in the courtroom. Gradually, we learn that Ishmael's first and only true love is Hatsue (Youki Kodoh), the wife of the man on trial. As he begins to research background information, he discovers facts that neither the prosecutor (James Rebhorn) nor the defense attorney (Max von Sydow) are bringing out in court. But the bitterness he feels towards Hatsue for inexplicably ending their relationship years ago keeps him silent. At the same time, memories of his dead father, Arthur (Sam Shepard), one of the most respected men in the community and a pillar of integrity, haunt his thoughts.

Throughout much of the film, Ishamael is obsessed by facts. He insists that his profession, that of a reporter, is all about uncovering the truth. Not until the end does he understand what his father meant by arguing that "journalism is making choices." Indeed, only once Ishmael makes those choices — to give up his obsession for Hatsue and to embrace his father's values — is he able to find peace. Viewers who go on this excursion with him will find their time well rewarded. **HIGHLY RECOMMENDED**

A Soldier's Daughter Never Cries [1998]

Starring: Kris Kristofferson, Barbara Hershey, Leelee Sobieski, Jesse Bradford Director: James Ivory Screenplay: James Ivory, Ruth Prawer Jhabvala based on the novel by Kaylie Jones Running Time: 2:04 Rated: PG-13 (Sex, profanity, mature themes) Theatrical Aspect Ratio: 1.85:1

Merchant-Ivory (the film making team comprised of Ismail Merchant and James Ivory) is probably best known for their somewhat austere tales of life in England. One could be forgiven for the assumption that every Merchant-Ivory film features Helena Bonham Carter (*A Room with a View, Howards End*), Emma Thompson (*Howards End, The Remains of the Day*), and/or Anthony Hopkins (*Howards End, The Remains of the Day, Surviving Picasso*). As it happens, *A*

Soldier's Daughter Never Cries features none of these fine actors.

These days, most movies about families deal with deep dysfunctions and hidden secrets — parents who are alienated from their children, brothers and sisters who don't get along, incestuous relationships, etc. For those looking for a change-of-pace, *A Soldier's Daughter Never Cries* offers the opportunity. This film is about a loving, united family that endures good times and hardships together. It's not an overbearing, saccharine story, but a realistic portrait of characters who are bound together by affection, respect, and shared experiences. What's even more amazing is that it transpires during the period between 1964 and 1973, when social upheaval was tearing many families apart. But not the Willis', an expatriate American clan living in Paris. In addition to adults Bill (Kris Kristofferson) and Marcella (Barbara Hershey), there are two children: Channe (short for "Charlotte Anne," and played by Luisa Conlon at an early age and Leelee Sobieski later), the couple's biological daughter, and Billy (Samuel Gruen turning into Jesse Bradford), their adopted son.

When we first meet Channe, the movie's emotional center, she's a 4th-grader who can't spell "gym." Like many foreigners who spend nearly their entire life caught between two cultures, she isn't sure whether she's French or American. The same is true of Billy, who is more introverted than his sister. We follow these two as they grow up, with the innocence of childhood giving way to the awkwardness of adolescence. When Bill's health begins to fail, he moves his family to Long Island, where he intends to live out his final years. There, in their new school, Channe and Billy are treated as outsiders. She starts having indiscriminate sex with boys because she can't make friends. He is taunted and teased, and, instead of developing a social life, he spends his free time vegetating in front of the television.

Someone once said that the reason there are so many movies about dysfunctional families is because those are the only kinds of families capable of holding an audience's attention. *A Soldier's Daughter Never Cries* disproves that theory. It doesn't tell of anything big or earthshaking, but, in its careful portrayal of life, it offers something equally precious — an insight into the human experience.

HIGHLY RECOMMENDED

Some Mother's Son [Ireland, 1996]

Starring: Helen Mirren, Fionnula Flanagan, Aidan Gillen, David O'Hara, John Lynch Director: Terry George Screenplay: Jim Sheridan and Terry George Running Time: 1:52 Rated: R (Violence, profanity) Theatrical Aspect Ratio: 1.85:1

In 1979, when Margaret Thatcher assumed the role of England's Prime Minister, one of her stated aims was to crush the IRA and its associated "terrorism." Her "Northern Ireland Solution," as it became known, included three principles: Isolation, Criminalization, and Demoralization. Those members of the IRA captured for terrorist acts were to be treated as criminals, not soldiers. Prisons were to be used to break morale, not create martyrs.

On March 1, 1981, IRA prisoner Bobby Sands began a hunger strike which would earn him worldwide notoriety. Sands laid out 5 demands that, if met by the British government, would end the strike. Chief among these was the requirement that imprisoned IRA members would be recognized as "prisoners of war" (not common criminals), and, as such, would be allowed to wear their own clothing (instead of prison uniforms). Thatcher's government refused to negotiate, even when, on April 9, Sands was elected as the Member of Parliament from Fermanagh and South Tyrone. Sixty-six days after it began, Sands' protest ended with his death. Others followed his example, and, by the time the strike ended on October 3, ten of the more than 300 IRA prisoners in Long Kesh prison's H-Blocks had perished.

The story of Sands' hunger strike forms the background of Terry George's directorial debut, *Some Mother's Son*. However, while there is a great deal of information in the film about Sinn Fein, the IRA, and the political situation in Ireland during the early 1980s (some of which is fictionalized), this is principally a tale of sacrifice and family relationships. It's about a mother being forced to confront the very real fear that her son may die for convictions that she does not share, and that it could ultimately be her responsibility to choose life or death for him.

Make no mistake: while the core story of *Some Mother's Son* is universal in theme and deeply personal in scope, the narrative nevertheless shows evidence of a pro-Republican bias. Although the movie is arguably more balanced than Sheridan's powerful and riveting *In the Name of the Father,* the British still come off as faceless villains. Margaret Thatcher's mouthpiece is a caricature of vicious, heartless clichés. For those with an interest in the ongoing conflict in Northern Ireland, *Some Mother's Son* makes an excellent companion piece to Neil Jordan's *Michael Collins*. But, regardless of your political leanings, Terry George's picture is well worth seeing because of its intelligence and emotional depth, not to mention Helen Mirren's Oscar-caliber performance. **HIGHLY RECOMMENDED**

Sommersby [1993]

Starring: Richard Gere, Jodie Foster, Bill Pullman, James Earl Jones, Lanny Flaherty Director: John Amiel Screenplay: Nicholas Meyer and Sarah Kernochan Running Time: 1:53 Rated: PG-13 (Mature themes, sexual situations) Theatrical Aspect Ratio: 2.35:1

The United States Civil War has ended, and Jack Sommersby (Richard Gere) is returning home to a farm in ruins and a wife (Jodie Foster) who wishes he was dead. It's up to Jack to prove is that he's no longer the person he was 6 years ago when he left. Gone is the man who gambled and beat his wife, newly replaced by someone of a giving and caring nature. Yet, even as Jack begins to assemble a new beginning, questions about his identity arise. Could Jack Sommersby change this much, or is this really him at all?

Sommersby is based on the 1982 French film *The Return of Martin Guerre*, and is one of those rare remakes that does not tarnish the image of its inspiration. While *Sommersby* owes much to its predecessor, it is not a direct copy. There are differences, not only in setting, but in scripting. With the exception of a few early scenes lifted almost directly from *Martin Guerre*, only the general trajectory of the movies remains the same. The transition from 16th century France to 19th century America works effectively, and allows a few surprises for those who are familiar with *Martin Guerre*.

First and foremost, *Sommersby* is a love story. Much screen time is devoted to the relationship between Jack and Laurel. The movie takes its time with its characters; there are no sudden epiphanies. Love, and its realization, comes slowly, with a look and a touch. In many ways, this film goes against the grain of a typical Hollywood film. It has a slow, leisurely pace, and is almost (but not quite — there is one fight scene) devoid of action.

In *Sommersby*, Richard Gere gives one of his most energetic performances in recent years. Jodie Foster outdoes her Oscar-winning *Silence of the Lambs* performance, playing Laurel with equal parts strength and vulnerability. Often in period pieces such as this, forceful female characters seem anachronistic. *Sommersby* shows that, with good scripting and even better acting, that problem can easily be overcome.

Technically, *Sommersby* is a superior production. Period details abound, and the cinematography is consistently strong, and occasionally breathtaking. Virginia is shown to its best advantage. Composer Danny Elfman, best known for his *Batman* score, delivers something refreshingly different. Occasionally, the music is imperfectly matched to the scenes, but the typical Elfman repetition is absent.

Sommersby should equally entertain those who have seen *The Return of Martin Guerre* and those who have not. From start to finish, it is a well-crafted film: part love story, part mystery, and all drama. The most painful and obvious of Hollywood's contrivances are nowhere to be found. With respect to *Martin Guerre* — the spirit of the original remains intact, which is perhaps the most satisfying aspect of this production. **HIGHLY RECOMMENDED**

The Son's Room [Italy/France, 2001]

Starring: Nanni Moretti, Laura Morante, Jasmine Trinca, Giuseppe Sanfelice, Sofia Vigliar Director: Nanni Moretti Screenplay: Nanni Moretti Running Time: 1:38 Rated: R (Mature themes, sexual situations, nudity) Theatrical Aspect Ratio: 1.66:1 In Italian with subtitles

The average, mainstream American feature deals with grief by employing a mixture of histrionics and melodramatic manipulation. In order to find a motion picture that offers a sensitive, intelligent examination of grief and the guilt that often accompanies it, one has to look beyond the multiplexes, to the realm of foreign and independent movies.

The Son's Room, winner of the Palm D'Or at the 2001 Cannes Film Festival, is a film from celebrated Italian director Nanni Moretti, who, at one time during his career, was known at the "Italian Woody Allen." Although he shed that moniker early last decade, Moretti still shares traits with Manhattan's best-known filmmaker. Like Allen, Moretti writes, produces, and stars in his movies, which often feature autobiographical threads and mix humor and pathos. *The Son's Room* is a departure for Moretti in many ways. It is a more straightforward drama than his other work, it is not filmed in Rome, and Moretti's character lacks the numerous neuroses that he has become known for.

The film introduces us to something very rare: a happy, well-balanced family without a hint of dysfunction. Giovanni (Moretti) is a psychiatrist who practices out of his home. He has a loving relationship with his wife, Paola (Laura Morante), and is liked and respected by his two teenage children: son Andrea (Giuseppe Sanfelice) and daughter Irene (Jasmine Trinca). For about 30 minutes, Moretti carefully develops a picture of familial bliss, keeping us uncertain where the film is going until the tragedy occurs. Once that happens, the movie moves along a more somber trajectory. Andrea dies in a diving accident, and his grieving family is left trying to pick up the pieces.

For the most part, *The Son's Room* stands as a powerful portrait of what real (as opposed to Hollywood) families go through in the wake of the loss of one of their members. There's nothing out-of-the-ordinary about Giovanni, Paola, or Irene. The difficulties they have coping with Andrea's death are easy to empathize with.

If the film has a minor weakness, it's that an outside presence is needed to bring about the necessary catharsis. It's not exactly a contrivance, but it feels less natural than all that precedes it. Moretti, perhaps aware of this flaw, provides enough of a justification in the script for us to accept things as they are. In all other areas, however, this is a superior motion picture — an example of the pleasant surprise that can result when a skilled director departs from his usual style. By daring to be honest and unsparing, *The Son's Room* is meaningful. **HIGHLY RECOMMENDED**

Soul Food [1997]

Starring: **Vanessa L. Williams, Vivica Fox, Nia Long, Michael Beach, Mekhi Phifer, Irma P. Hall** Director: **George Tillman Jr.**
Screenplay: **George Tillman Jr.** Running Time: **1:55** Rated: **R** (Profanity, sexual situations, brief violence) Theatrical Aspect Ratio: **2.35:1**

When it comes to "food" movies, you know the titles: *Babette's Feast, Eat Drink Man Woman, Big Night.* You also know the advice: eat before coming to the theater or suffer a grumbling stomach for 90-plus minutes followed by a mad dash to the nearest restaurant once the end credits start to roll. And, while *Soul Food,* the first major release from director George Tillman Jr., isn't on the same level as the previously-mentioned motion pictures, there's at least one scene that's a literal feast for the eyes.

Soul Food tells the story of the trials of the Joseph family when their beloved matriarch, Mama Joe (Irma P. Hall), slips into a diabetes-induced coma. Without Mama Joe's ritual Sunday dinners to keep everyone together, the family begins to drift apart, with gaps widening between sisters and spouses. The film essentially follows the lives of Mama Joe's 3 daughters. Terri (Vanessa L. Williams), the eldest, is a driven lawyer who puts work above her neglected husband, Miles (Michael Beach). Miles is tempted away from his steady, well-paying job by the lure of his true love, music, and away from his wife by the proffered charms of Terri's cousin, Faith (Gina Ravera). Maxine (Vivica Fox) is happily married to Kenny (Jeffrey D. Sams), and spends her days caring for her husband and three children. Bird (Nia Long) is newly hitched to ex-con Lem (Mekhi Phifer), an intense, caring man whose volatile temper often proves to be his undoing.

Soul Food is told from the point-of-view of young Ahmed (Brandon Hammond), Maxine and Kenny's son. While a few of his observations are insightful, most of his voiceover narrative is superfluous and even irritating. Seventy-five percent of what he says is either needless exposition or useless trivia. Simply put, the kid won't shut up. It's one thing to open and close a film with a voiceover, but Ahmed's voice can be heard throughout, dispensing pearls of wisdom that we could have easily done without.

With a uniformly attractive cast, *Soul Food* isn't hard on the eyes. Everyone (including Vanessa Williams, who isn't known as a stellar actress) acquits themselves admirably, although it's worth noting that none of the roles are terribly complex, so there's little need for anyone to stretch their range. And, while the meals don't take on the same importance as in certain other food movies, we still get an eyeful: deep-fried catfish, chicken and dumplings, cornbread, cakes, and other assorted dishes. *Soul Food* contains enough diverse cinematic ingredients to add a little zest and flavor to the pleasant-but-familiar cinematic fare of an African American family drama. **RECOMMENDED**

Spanglish [2004]

Starring: **Adam Sandler, Téa Leoni, Paz Vega, Cloris Leachman, Sarah Steele, Shelbie Bruce, Ian Hyland** Director: **James L. Brooks**
Screenplay: **James L. Brooks** Running Time: **2:08** Rated: **PG-13** (Sexual situations, brief profanity) Theatrical Aspect Ratio: **1.85:1**

The strength of *Spanglish* lies in the characters, not the plot. In fact, there isn't much of a story line — it's a lightly dramatic "slice of life" that gives the men, women, and children populating it a chance to interact. There's some comedy, but for a film starring wacky man Adam Sandler, it's surprisingly low-key. As world-renowned chef John Clasky, Sandler is restrained, perhaps heralding a new era in his career. Lately, he has been moving away from the kinds of films that please his core audience.

John is trapped between two forces of nature. The first is his wife, Deborah (Téa Leoni), an uptight woman who has become increasingly erratic since being downsized. Stripped of her center, Deborah is stumbling around, groping for something to give her life meaning. Her actions are often destructive, but she is no monster. She causes pain nearly everywhere she turns, but is ignorant of how hurtful she has become — until one act brings her face-to-face with dire consequences. The other woman in John's life is his Mexican housekeeper, Flor (Paz Vega). A quiet, sensitive woman who only works for the Claskys so she can support her daughter, Cristine (Shelbie Bruce), Flor initially tries to remain aloof from the everyday dramas of her employers. Eventually, however, she is sucked in, and the distance of separation diminishes when the Claskys go on vacation and bring Flor and Cristine with them. As the situation between John and Deborah worsens, the chef and his maid find themselves increasingly drawn to each other, even though each is aware of the impossibility of any significant relationship.

The relationship between John and Flor is nicely developed. It occurs naturally, building slowly and tentatively, and is punctuated by stolen glances and late-night conversations. The sexual tension and chemistry between these two is powerful, although some may find its culmination anticlimactic. I have problems with the resolution of John and Flor's dance of seduction (although not with its ultimate conclusion, which is inevitable) — it fits the tone of a "take few risks" film and feels artificial. Brooks seems unwilling to cross a line that should be crossed for fear of alienating portions of his audience. Many aspects of *Spanglish* are tragic; he wants to avoid the *entire* film being a downer.

Since the film is told through Cristine's eyes, elements of the story are left hanging. The most important relationships — John and Flor; Flor and Cristine — unfold completely. The film concludes with a moving scene between mother and daughter that emphasizes the universal fears of all parents (not just immigrants) concerning their children's futures. It is one of *Spanglish*'s strongest moments, and one of many why I recommend this unassuming yet effective motion picture. **RECOMMENDED**

Spring Summer Fall Winter . . . and Spring

[South Korea/Germany, 2003]
Starring: Oh Young-Soo, Kim Jong-ho, Seo Jae-kyeong, Kim Young-min, Kim Ki-duk, Ha Yeo-jin Director: Kim Ki-duk Screenplay: Kim Ki-duk Running Time: 1:43 Rated: R (Sex) Theatrical Aspect Ratio: 1.85:1 In Korean with subtitles

Spring Summer Fall Winter . . . and Spring is a gorgeous motion picture. Using perfectly composed shots to amplify an emotionally resonant story, the film successfully argues that "artistic" films do not have to be boring. Although few in the audience are likely to identify intimately with the characters (Buddhist monks who live in virtual isolation), the movie's themes about the mutability of life and the desire for peace and atonement have universal implications. One can be a New York City stockbroker or a Salt Lake City teacher and still understand the points being made by Kim Ki-duk's film.

Spring Summer Fall Winter . . . and Spring uses the changing of seasons as a metaphor for life. It's not an original idea, but it is handled deftly. As the film opens, it is spring in South Korea, and the two inhabitants of a floating monastery (located in the middle of a lake) are going about their daily routine. They are a teacher (Oh Young-Soo) and his very young apprentice (Kim Jong-ho). The boy is not yet 10 years old, but he is learning the ways of Buddhism. And, during this segment, he learns an especially forceful lesson. Skip ahead ten years to summer. A sick girl (Ha Yeo-jin) has come to the monastery to heal. While there, she and the apprentice (now a teenager, played by Seo Jae-kyeong) fall in love. Lured from the calmness of his ascetic lifestyle by the promise of carnal pleasure, he abandons his master and accompanies the girl back to the "real world." His master's warning — that lust leads to possession, and possession to murder — is prophetic. Ten years later, in the fall, the apprentice (Kim Young-min) returns to the monastery, this time as a fugitive from the law. Through his master, he learns the path to redemption — just as the police arrive to arrest him. Finally, a decade later in winter, the apprentice (Kim Ki-duk) returns for a final time, content now to accept the role of master (the old monk has died), make the monastery his home, and take on an apprentice of his own.

The film raises questions about how we live our lives and how our actions, like ripples in the waters of time, can have unexpected consequences years later. By depicting the life of one unnamed individual in ten-year snapshots over the course of his development from boyhood to maturity, Kim provides us with insight and an uncommon perspective. Idealism is supplanted by a yearning for physical satisfaction. Romance turns to tragedy. Repentance leads to understanding. These things happen quickly on-screen, with the years elapsing in a heartbeat. We mourn for lost innocence and appreciate the accumulation of wisdom. By the end of the film, even though we do not know the main character's name, we feel that we have taken a long and rewarding journey at his side. **HIGHLY RECOMMENDED**

The Star Maker [Italy, 1995]

Starring: **Sergio Castellitto, Tiziana Lodato, Franco Scaldati**
Director: **Giuseppe Tornatore** Screenplay: **Giuseppe Tornatore and Fabio Rinaudo** Running Time: **1:48** Rated: **R** (Nudity, sex, violence, profanity) Theatrical Aspect Ratio: **2.35:1** In Italian with subtitles

The Star Maker is a cynical, often-grim look at cupidity and its tragic consequences. In tone, it's more like *Lamerica* than *The Postman*, and, even though director Giuseppe Tornatore previously made *Cinema Paradiso*, *The Star Maker* has little of that film's warm sense of nostalgia. This movie is designed to be disturbing, not exhilarating, and it's extremely effective at that.

Tornatore has structured his film in a most atypical fashion. *The Star Maker* starts out as a light comedy with dark undertones. Sergio Castellitto is Joe Morelli, an itinerant talent scout who is making his way across Sicily, advertising that, for 1,500 lire, anyone can film a screen test. He dangles fame and fortune before all comers, most of whom can't really afford the fee. There are numerous comic anecdotes as men and women do their own, often-absurd interpretations of Rhett and Scarlett from *Gone With the Wind,* but, lurking beneath the surface humor is a sense of growing desperation. It doesn't take long to recognize that Morelli is a con man, and his promises are as empty as the purses of those who entrust their dreams to him.

As the film progresses, Morelli becomes more reprehensible. Men and women come to him as if he was a priest, with heartfelt confessions of their past and hopes for a brighter future, but Morelli doesn't hear or care about their words — all he wants is payment, either in coin or in trade (he accepts sexual favors from one woman who doesn't have any money). He's a cruel, self-absorbed man who scavenges through life's wreckage in the small, bombed-out towns of post-World War II Sicily.

In the village of Scordizzi, a girl named Beata (Tiziana Lodato) is enraptured by Morelli and his lifestyle. To obtain the 1,500 lire for a screen test, she strips naked in front of a local bigwig, then, when Morelli leaves her town, she stows away in his van, offering him her body when he discovers her. Beata is hopelessly in the star maker's thrall, but, as usual, Morelli cares only about himself.

With *The Star Maker*, Tornatore has fashioned a powerful motion picture whose impact comes through legitimate drama, not cheap manipulation. The primary actors, Castellitto and Lodato, are both excellent, and the film's unhurried pace allows the audience to gradually understand how much subtle damage Morelli is doing. Historically, *The Star Maker* reminds us of the deep divisions in Italy after Mussolini's fall, and how isolated Sicily is from the rest of the country. Ultimately, however, this is a study of the baser elements of human nature, and a reminder that any person's actions can have unexpectedly painful ramifications for others. **HIGHLY RECOMMENDED**

The Story of Us [1999]

Starring: **Bruce Willis, Michelle Pfeiffer, Rob Reiner, Rita Wilson**
Director: **Rob Reiner** Screenplay: **Alan Zweibel & Jessie Nelson**
Running Time: **1:35** Rated: **R** (Profanity, sexual themes) Theatrical Aspect Ratio: **2.35:1**

The Story of Us illustrates what happens when the fissure of minor differences in a marriage widens into a seemingly unbridgeable chasm. Although peppered with occasional contrivances, the film is insightful and intelligent more often than not, and paints a convincing portrait of the disintegration of a family — until the final 10 minutes, when director Rob Reiner cheats with an implausible ending.

Ben and Katie Jordan (Bruce Willis and Michelle Pfeiffer) could be Harry and Sally after the magic is gone. He's a freespirit; she's anal. She thinks he's irresponsible; he believes she should be more spontaneous. They have become incompatible. Finally, after a year of increasingly loud and acrimonious quarrels, they decide to separate as a prelude to divorce. The hardest part is telling the kids. So, instead of getting it over with, they let their son and daughter go off to summer camp without knowing the truth. As those warm, childless days pass, they attempt to cope with their new distance. A despondent Ben spends time hanging out with his two best friends, one of whom is married (Rob Reiner) and one of whom is single (Paul Reiser). Meanwhile, Katie is consoled by her gal pals, Rachel (Rita Wilson) and Liza (Julie Hagerty), and begins flirting with a dentist (Tim Matheson).

There is no doubt that *The Story of Us* falls under

the "chick flick" umbrella. It is manipulative, but at least the manipulation is skillful, rather than sloppy and overwrought. For the most part, the characters are well developed and easy to sympathize with. And, even though the material is serious, Reiner keeps the tone light. There are no villains here; everyone is essentially likable.

While there are many things to appreciate about *The Story of Us,* there are problems as well. Too many of the arguments between Ben and Katie have a contrived feel. We can see them coming. While it's true that people fight about silly things in real life, rarely do they work so hard to twist each phrase into an intentional insult, and it's not this often that every minor slight is magnified into an incident of gargantuan proportions. Reiner also seems to have a problem with wringing convincing tears out of his actors.

I like the structure employed by *The Story of Us.* It ricochets back and forth between people, places, and time periods (via frequent flashbacks). Without slowing down the story, this approach allows us to get a good feeling for the various stages of Ben and Katie's marriage. We see them "meet cute," say their vows, raise their children, then drift apart. As lightweight comedy/dramas go, this one doesn't cover much new ground, but it is mostly effective as it canvasses the familiar material. *The Story of Us* is flawed, but not seriously enough to curtail its ability to function as unpretentious entertainment. **RECOMMENDED**

The Straight Story [United States/France, 1999]

Starring: Richard Farnsworth, Sissy Spacek, Jennifer Edwards, Barbara E. Robertson Director: David Lynch Screenplay: John Roach & Mary Sweeney Running Time: 1:51 Rated: G Theatrical Aspect Ratio: 2.35:1

David Lynch's body of work is surely one of the most recognizable of any living director. From the nightmarishness of his debut, *Eraserhead,* to the bleakness of *Blue Velvet* to the bizarrely compelling quality of his TV series, *Twin Peaks,* Lynch has defined himself as a filmmaker who relishes peeling back the façade of Americana and exposing the rot that lies beneath. *The Straight Story* is completely different from anything we have previously seen from Lynch. Here, Lynch does not attempt to dissect middle America — he celebrates it.

The Straight Story is based on a real event in the life of a real person — the kind of thing that often shows up during the final, "feel good" segment of the evening news. Veteran actor Richard Farnsworth (*The*

Grey Fox), in what is arguably the best performance of a long (and somewhat uneven) career, plays Alvin Straight, a 73-year-old man living in Laurens, Iowa with his daughter, Rose (Sissy Spacek). Alvin is not in the best of health — he has a bad hip that requires him to use two canes while walking and he has trouble with his vision. One day, Alvin receives a phone call from a family member informing him that his brother, Lyle (Harry Dean Stanton), whom he has not spoken to in 10 years, has suffered a stroke. Alvin decides that he must make the 320-mile trek to Mt. Zion, Wisconsin, and the only means of transportation available to him is his lawnmower. "I've got to go see Lyle, and I've got to make the trip on my own," he remarks. So, hitching a home-made trailer to a John Deere, he begins one of the most unusual road trips ever committed to celluloid.

The cross-state journey, which takes 6 weeks during the late summer and early fall, is chronicled episodically. Early in his trip, Alvin encounters a female hitchhiker who spends some time around a campfire with him. She has run away from home, but he gives her the following advice: "A warm bed in a house sounds a mite better than eating a hot dog on a stick with an old geezer traveling on a lawn mower." On another occasion, he encounters a woman who has just struck and killed a deer — her 13th such accident in the past 7 weeks. There's a lot of Lynchian comedy in this scene. And, while his transport is being repaired after a breakdown, he spends time reminiscing about World War II horrors with another veteran.

The Straight Story may lack the surreal, compelling quality that has defined the director's other features, but it is an example of an artist in peak form. **HIGHLY RECOMMENDED**

The Sum of Us [Australia, 1994]

Starring: Jack Thompson, Russell Crowe, John Polson, Deborah Kennedy Director: Geoff Burton and Kevin Dowling Screenplay: David Stevens based on his play Running Time: 1:40 Rated: No MPAA Rating (Mature themes, profanity)

Love is perhaps the most common theme explored by movies. It is also the most frequently misrepresented. Many Hollywood love affairs end up heavily over-romanticized, and the picture they paint is invariably far from reality. So it's refreshing to find a film like *The Sum of Us,* which is about love in all its genuine forms: sexual, platonic, and most important, familial. Given the honesty of the script, it should come as no surprise that America's film industry had nothing to do with the movie — this is yet another gem from Australia.

Not only are Harry (Jack Thompson) and Jeff (Russell Crowe) father and son, but they're best friends as well. Their relationship is relaxed and comfortable — they banter and kid around and, though they occasionally get under each other's skin, there's never any acrimony in their arguments. Harry is aware of his son's homosexual preferences and accepts them unquestioningly. The only thing he has to say on the subject is that he's disappointed Jeff will never have an opportunity to father a child. With so many dysfunctional family stories around, *The Sum of Us* serves as the perfect antidote.

Despite his good looks and outgoing personality, Jeff is actually somewhat shy, as becomes obvious when he's getting to know Greg (John Polson), a man he meets at a local gay pub. Greg is no more certain of himself than Jeff, and it's only after a lot of nervous conversation that the pair arrive at Jeff's home. No sooner have the two dimmed the lights, however, than Harry wanders into the room to greet his son's prospective lover, unintentionally but effectively dispelling the romantic atmosphere.

Meanwhile, Harry, who has been a widower for a number of years, is looking for female companionship. To that end, he enrolls in Desiree's Introduction Agency, and is set up with a middle-aged woman named Joyce (Deborah Kennedy). The two hit it off almost immediately, but, while both are interested in pursuing a serious relationship, it's unclear exactly how far each is willing to go.

The Sum of Us is delightful, by turns droll and serious. Yet even during its most dramatic moments, it retains a lighthearted tone that keeps things from becoming too grim. There's always a joke right around the corner, and none of the humor seems ill-suited to the situation.

The Sum of Us isn't exactly cutting-edge, but it takes a few chances. Jeff's homosexuality is a complete non-issue. There's nothing political or tragic in his situation. In fact, he and the other characters frequently joke about it. Also, no compromises are made to give the conclusion an extra lift, proving it's possible to have a happy ending without undermining the story's intelligence. It's production elements like this that make *The Sum of Us* such a worthwhile examination of what love is like for those whose lives don't follow traditional movie scripts.

HIGHLY RECOMMENDED

Summer of Sam [1999]

Starring: John Leguizamo, Adrien Brody, Mira Sorvino, Jennifer Esposito, Anthony LaPaglia Director: Spike Lee Screenplay: Victor Colicchio, Michael Imperioli, Spike Lee Running Time: 2:22 Rated: R (Extreme violence, sex, profanity, brief nudity) Theatrical Aspect Ratio: 1.85:1

Spike Lee's *Summer of Sam* is only tangentially about David Berkowitz, the man who, over a 4-month period, managed to paralyze New York City with terror. Actually, the movie is an exploration of '70s culture and how the paranoia fueled by the killing spree illuminated the worst aspects of human nature. Like *Boogie Nights,* this picture delves beneath the facade of glitz and glamour that was the disco era and uncovers a rotten, hollow shell. It is a dark, violent, sexually explicit motion picture that will surely offend timid viewers.

Summer of Sam focuses on a small group of Italian-American characters living in the Bronx. They aren't necessarily the most compelling individuals — Lee relies on a few too many clichés to develop them (especially those with supporting parts) — but they get the job done. There's Vinny (John Leguizamo), the slick, Travolta-like disco king who is married to the lovely Dionna (Mira Sorvino), but is constantly unfaithful. Ritchie (Adrien Brody) is Vinny's closest friend, but his punk hairdo and standoffish attitude have made him persona non grata in the old neighborhood. Other players include Luigi (Ben Gazarra), the local Mafioso; Detective Lou Petrocelli (Anthony LaPaglia), a cop investigating the Son of Sam killings; and Berkowitz himself (Michael Badalucco).

The movie begins and ends with a few brief narrative comments by *New York Post* columnist Jimmy Breslin. Soon, we're in Vinny's world, watching him light up the dance floor with Dionna on an April night. On the way home, the pair comes across a murder scene. When Vinny gets out of the car to investigate why the cops have cordoned off the area, he encounters the bodies of Valentina Suriani and Alexander Esau in the car where they were shot. They are the 4th and 5th murder victims of the ".44 Caliber Killer." Shaken, Vinny goes home, vowing to turn his life around and remain faithful to Dionna. Not surprisingly, he is unable to keep the oath.

Over the next several months, tensions run high in Vinny's neighborhood. Luigi believes that the police will be unable to prevent more murders, so he puts the word out on the streets for his boys to be on the lookout. This fosters an atmosphere in which vigilante justice takes root. After dark, people stay off the streets and out of the discos, and a July blackout results in chaos. And, for outsiders like Ritchie, who are viewed with suspicion by their neighbors, one wrong move can make them a suspect and a target for mob violence.

Although *Summer of Sam* prevails as a period piece, it works even better as an examination of how the need to assign blame can result in grave injustices. While this is one of Spike Lee's most ambitious motion pictures, it's not his angriest. Nevertheless, there's an edginess to the proceedings that makes watching the film an unsettling experience. *Summer of Sam* opens a window on the '70s that juxtaposes light pop cultural references with something dark and monstrous. The result, while not wholly successful, is compelling and disturbing. RECOMMENDED

Sunshine [Hungary/Germany/Canada/Austria, 1999]

Starring: Ralph Fiennes, Rosemary Harris, Jennifer Ehle, Rachel Weisz
Director: Istvan Szabo Screenplay: Istvan Szabo, Israel Horovitz
Running Time: 3:00 Rated: R (Violence, profanity, nudity, mature themes) Theatrical Aspect Ratio: 1.85:1

Istvan Szabo's *Sunshine* runs for an unapologetic 3 hours, and Szabo has lavished a great deal of time and attention on crafting a grand, beautifully shot motion picture that engages audiences for the full running length.

The film follows 3 generations of the Sonnenschein family, a close-knit clan of Hungarian Jews who live and struggle through two world wars and countless changes of government. *Sunshine* is loosely divided into 3 periods. The first spans the era from the late 1800s to the years just after World War I, and focuses on Ignatz Sonnenschein, a judge in the Austro-Hungarian Empire. The second picks up in the 1930s and concludes at the end of World War II. The central character during this segment is Ignatz's son, Adam, a fencer who represents Hungary at the 1936 Olympics, but faces persecution from the Nazis despite his fame when he refuses to live by the creed stating that "assimilation is the only possible way." Finally, the third period begins in the late 1940s and finishes around 1960. During that time frame, *Sunshine* focuses on Adam's son, Ivan, who contends with the various factions of Communism that dominate the post-World War II political climate. One of Szabo's unsubtle "tricks" is to have all 3 of the central protagonists (grandfather, father, and son) played by the same actor: the versatile Ralph Fiennes. Another character, Valerie (Jennifer Ehle as a young woman; Rosemary Harris in later years), survives virtually the entire movie, providing a glue that holds the story together.

On one level, *Sunshine* can be viewed as little more than an entertaining historical melodrama about the tribulations of a group of characters set against the backdrop of the century's most important historical events. But there's a deeper theme at work here, as well. It has to do with the repetitive cycle of history and how power inevitably corrupts, no matter who wields it. Throughout *Sunshine*, governments in Hungary rise and fall — a dictatorship, a Nazi regime, and more than one flavor of Communism — but, despite fundamental philosophical differences, they all bear remarkable similarities to each other. What begins with hope and freshness in each case quickly degenerates into something twisted and rotten. Each of the characters played by Fiennes has an opportunity to be both a hero and a criminal, depending on who is in power.

Over the course of one evening at the movies, Szabo effectively realizes more than 70 years of history, and, in the process, presents a gallery of interesting characters. Sub-themes and memorable moments abound. Ultimately, the director may have tackled a scope so vast that even 3 hours is not enough to contain it, but the result, while somewhat uneven and occasionally rushed, is still solidly entertaining and occasionally thought provoking. RECOMMENDED

The Sweet Hereafter [Canada, 1997]

Starring: Ian Holm, Sarah Polley, Bruce Greenwood, Tom McCamus
Director: Atom Egoyan Screenplay: Atom Egoyan based on the novel by Russell Banks Running Time: 1:50 Rated: R (Mature themes, sex, nudity, profanity) Theatrical Aspect Ratio: 2.35:1

The Sweet Hereafter is film making at its most powerful: drama capable of shaking the soul, yet free of even the slightest hint of manipulation, sentimentality, or mawkishness. Canadian director/writer/producer Atom Egoyan shows the effects of grief and anger on a community devastated by an unspeakable tragedy.

The central event of *The Sweet Hereafter* is a school bus accident that results in the death of fourteen children and the injury of many others. On a cold winter's day in the small town of Sam Dent, British Columbia, the driver loses control of the vehicle and it careens off the road onto a frozen lake which gives way beneath the weight. The scene of the bus sinking into the water — a stark, simple shot — is a painfully effective and disturbing sequence. Death has become such a cheap, bloody commodity in modern movies that viewing a scene like this is a revelation.

Since Egoyan eschews linear storytelling by allowing time to be fluid rather than fixed, we don't see the actual accident until midway through the movie. The opening scene introduces us to Mitchell Stephens (Ian Holm), an ambulance-chaser who has come to Sam Dent to persuade the victims' parents to join in a class action lawsuit. He promises financial compensation for their losses, claiming that while no one can offer an outlet for their grief, he can be the voice of their anger. But there is no clear culprit to sue for the bus accident, and Mitchell is groping for a villain who doesn't exist. Parents join him in the vain hope that money will soothe the pain or bring some sort of "closure," but the greed for compensation fractures the community.

Other players in the drama include Nicole Burnell (Sarah Polley), one of the accident survivors. She's a teenage, would-be rock star who loses the use of her legs because of the experience, and who becomes the corner stone of Mitchell's case. As the victim of incest, however, she is a damaged individual. Her parents, Sam (Tom McCamus) and Mary (Brooke Johnson), are among the lawyer's most eager clients. Two others involved in the suit are Wanda and Hartley Otto (Arsinee Khanjian and Earl Pastko), who lost an adopted child in the crash. Risa and Wendell Walker (Alberta Watson and Maury Chaykin), whose only son perished beneath the cold waters, have also signed with Mitchell. But Risa's lover, Billy Ansell (Bruce Greenwood), reject's Mitchell's advances. Having recently lost his wife, Billy is acquainted with grief, and this enables him to accept the death of his twin children, rather than wallow in denial. Finally, there's Dolores Driscoll (Gabrielle Rose), the longtime bus driver who must live with the weight of responsibility for what happened.

The most amazing thing about *The Sweet Hereafter* is not the style, the acting, or the cinematography (all of which are exceptional), but the way the film successfully juggles so many themes, persuading us to reflect upon them all before the 110-minute running time is up. This is truly a great film. **MUST SEE**

Sweet Sixteen [United Kingdom, 2002]

Starring: Martin Compston, Annmarie Fulton, William Ruane, Michelle Coulter, Gary McCormack Director: Ken Loach Screenplay: Paul Laverty Running Time: 1:46 Rated: R (Profanity, violence, mature themes) Theatrical Aspect Ratio: 1.85:1

Sweet Sixteen represents Ken Loach's most accomplished film since *My Name Is Joe*. It's an uncompromising movie that illustrates one of the most convincing personality transformations that I have seen in a recent motion picture. This change, from scrappy underdog to nearly conscienceless criminal, is achieved through small steps — a gradual eroding of morals and shifting of ethics. It's made all the more heartbreaking because the individual at the center of this transformation is a 15-year old boy.

Liam (Martin Compston) is bright, tough, and resourceful. While awaiting his mother's release from prison, he lives with his sister, a single mother, in a small flat. (This after being kicked out of an apartment he shared with his vulgar, nasty-minded grandfather and his mother's cruel boyfriend, Stan.) Liam's primary desire in life is to liberate his mother from Stan's pernicious influence, and he will do anything to achieve that goal. One day, he sees a trailer for sale and believes that if he can collect enough money to buy it, he and his mother can live there together when she gets out. But the trailer is expensive, and Liam will not earn enough to buy it by selling stolen cigarettes at cut-rate prices. So he decides to branch out — into drug dealing.

Liam is not a user, but he has no problem selling once he steals a stash from Stan and his grandfather. The life of a dealer is not an easy one — Liam has to defend himself from those interested in getting his product without paying for it, and as he becomes successful, he draws the attention of major drug dealers in the area, who are interesting in having Liam join their organization. In a way, the film plays out like a twisted Cinderella story, with Loach showing the relativistic morality that exists in the lower classes. Becoming a drug dealer is a way out of poverty — perhaps the only way out — and its seductive lure (that of fast cash) is impossible to resist for someone in Liam's position. He never considers the "evils" of drug use and addiction. Those are irrelevant. For him, selling drugs is like selling anything else.

Eschewing melodrama, Loach is able to present Liam's story in a frank, straightforward manner that shows how easily it is for someone in his position to become sucked into the criminal world. There's also a surprising amount of humor, especially during the first half. (One line, about the "definition of initiative" is laugh-aloud hilarious.) Yes, this is a political movie (at least it has a political viewpoint), but, more than that, it's a character study of an individual who will not easily be forgotten. RECOMMENDED

A Tale of Springtime [France, 1992]

Starring: Anne Teyssedre, Florence Darel, Hugues Quester
Director: Eric Rohmer Screenplay: Eric Rohmer Running Time: 1:47
Rated: PG Theatrical Aspect Ratio: 1.66:1 In French with subtitles

A Tale of Springtime is the first installment in French director Eric Rohmer's *Tale of Four Seasons* series. Rohmer's intention with these films is to "focus on attractive, intelligent, self-absorbed if not entirely self-aware young women who present their dilemmas with clarity and elegance and express their feelings in inspired and witty dialogue."

A Tale of Springtime tells of the budding friendship between a young woman and a girl 10 years her junior. It has a lot to say about the human condition, and does so through a small group of characters that we grow to know and care about. Occasionally, the film slips off-track with pretentious intellectual spiels on philosophy, but in general *A Tale of Springtime* progresses like real life, with superb characterization and deft acting as its hallmarks.

The film opens by introducing us to Jeanne (Anne Teyssedre), a 30ish woman with a penchant for order and a dislike of living alone in an apartment other than her own. Since her boyfriend is away on a trip, she has decided to temporarily move out of his place, but needs somewhere to go, having lent her own rooms to a cousin. Fate intervenes in the person of Natasha (Florence Darel), a college student that Jeanne meets at a party. The two take an immediate liking to one another, and Natasha invites Jeanne to spend the night. It doesn't take long for a friendship to spring up, and Natasha begins to weigh the possibility of manipulating a relationship between her father Igor (Hugues Quester) and Jeanne.

A Tale of Springtime is a slice of heaven for anyone who enjoys solid character dramas. Those looking for action, adventure, or plots that *move* will likely be bored to tears by Rohmer's picture. The storyline is merely a playing field for Jeanne, Natasha, and Florence — an arena in which Rohmer and his actors can explore the complexities of these individuals' personalities.

Aided by tremendously natural, unaffected performances from his lead actors, Rohmer has molded three real people and created a marvelous one-hundred seven minute film about philosophy and life. *A Tale of Springtime* presents a rare and wonderful opportunity to discover a trio of multidimensional cinematic characters. Once you've been introduced, you won't want to be parted from them, whether or not *Springtime* ends. HIGHLY RECOMMENDED

A Tale of Winter [France, 1992]

Starring: Charlotte Very, Frederic Van Dren Driessche, Michel Voletti
Director: Eric Rohmer Screenplay: Eric Rohmer Running Time: 1:53
Rated: No MPAA Rating (Nudity, sexual situations) Theatrical Aspect
Ratio: 1.66:1 In French with subtitles

A Tale of Winter is the second installment in French director Eric Rohmer's *Tale of Four Seasons* series. The theme of this film is love, and whatever form that love might take — friendship, companionship, passion, sex — *A Tale of Winter* examines it.

The movie opens with Felicie (Charlotte Very) engaging in a brief-but-intense "vacation affair" in the south of France with Charles (Frederic Van Dren Driessche), an itinerant chef who is on his way to America. As a result of a mistake in the address she gives him, Felicie loses touch with Charles, and is unable to contact him when she gives birth to Elise (Ava Loraschi), their daughter.

Five years later, it's winter in Paris, and even though Felicie is currently involved with two men — Maxence (Michel Voletti) and Loic (Herve Furic) — both of whom are madly in love with her, Felicie is unable to commit to a relationship with either because of a premonition that someday she will again find Charles, her one true love. Nevertheless, reality is a cruel taskmaster, and Felicie is finding it increasingly difficult to define exactly how she feels about Maxence and Loic.

A Tale of Winter is gripping and engaging, not only because of the mystery of whether Felicie will ever again encounter Charles, but in its carefully realistic portrayals of her relationships with Maxence (a beautician whom she finds physically attractive) and Loic (an "egghead" whom she finds intellectually stimulating). No matter who you are, you're likely to see some element of yourself in one of the three main characters.

As seems obligatory in any Rohmer movie, there are a number of highly-philosophical discussions, some of which run on a little long. Topics include the nature of intelligence, the relationship between the supernatural and religion, the meaning of love, and the existence of the soul. Some of these are engrossing; others are worthy of a yawn. For those to whom such intellectual interactions do not appeal, there is always the core story.

With *A Tale of Winter,* Eric Rohmer has given us a wonderful motion picture that deals with the complexities of apparently-simple themes, and utilizes genuine characters and uncontrived situations to work through them. **HIGHLY RECOMMENDED**

Talk to Her [Spain, 2002]

Starring: Javier Camara, Dario Grandinetti, Leonor Watling, Rosario Flores Director: Pedro Almodovar Screenplay: Pedro Almodovar Running Time: 1:52 Rated: R (Nudity, sexual content, profanity) Theatrical Aspect Ratio: 2.35:1 In Spanish with subtitles

Talk to Her uses the kind of offbeat premise we have come to expect from Pedro Almodovar, whose films all-but-guarantee an offbeat view of life, love, and relationships. This time, we have two men — nurse Benigno (Javier Camara) and journalist Marco (Dario Graninetti) — who spend a great deal of time in a private clinic, where the most important people in their lives are in comas. For Benigno, it's Alicia (Leonor Watling), a dancer he barely knew before she arrived at the clinic, but for whom he has unceasingly cared for years. Benigno is in love with her, and believes the feeling to be mutual. (At one point, speaking about the period during which he has nursed Alicia, he comments, "These last 4 years have been the richest of my life.") Meanwhile, Marco's girlfriend, Lydia (Rosario Flores), was a bullfighter before the fateful day when she was gored, trampled, and nearly killed. Now, she, like Alicia, lies in seeming repose, unlikely ever to awaken.

There are plenty of movies available about women talking to one another, but films that chronicle deep, meaningful conversations between men are a rarity. *Talk to Her* is one of these unusual films, with Benigno and Marco developing a powerful bond as a result of their common circumstances. They speak to their comatose women, but, with increasingly greater frequency, they begin to rely upon one another. There may be an element of homoeroticism here, at least on Benigno's part. He is a virgin and is unsure of his feelings. He is obsessed by Alicia, but there are times when his friendship with Marco seems unusually intense. Benigno is clearly a disturbed individual — he spent 20 years caring for a bedridden mother before switching his attention to Alicia. Some of the most telling scenes about him are the flashbacks, which show him spying upon the dancer from afar before working up the courage to approach her. Marco's past is less creepy, but has left deep emotional wounds.

Almodovar gets all the details right, from Alicia's dancing to Lydia's bullfighting to Benigno's nursing.

As is the director's trademark, he interweaves moments of humor (of a variety that occasionally borders on the absurd) into the dramatic tapestry. *Talk to Her* is a drama of great power, yet some members of the audience will leave the theater believing they have seen a comedy. **HIGHLY RECOMMENDED**

Tango [Spain/Argentina, 1998]

Starring: Miguel Angel Sola, Cecilia Narova, Mia Maestro, Juan Carlos Copes, Juan Luis Galiardo Director: Carlos Saura Screenplay: Carlos Saura Running Time: 1:54 Rated: PG-13 (Sexual themes) Theatrical Aspect Ratio: 2.35:1 In Spanish with subtitles

It's said that the tango is a dance of passion, and nowhere is that more ably demonstrated than in Carlos Saura's involving film, *Tango.* With only the thinnest of narrative threads linking scenes and moments together, this movie becomes a celebration of the dance from which it takes its name. Approximately ¾ of the nearly 2-hour running time is devoted to expertly-choreographed performances featuring dancers of exceptional skill, sensuality, and poise.

While the music is undeniably important, this is as much a celebration of visual splendor and diversity as it is an audio feast. Saura (*Carmen, Flamenco*) uses celluloid the way a master painter uses a canvas. *Tango* is an orgy of colors and images — an intense sensory experience that stands out as one of the most memorable I have seen. The contributions of veteran cinematographer Vittorio Storaro (*Apocalypse Now*) and composer Lalo Schifrin are as significant as those made by the actors and Saura himself.

Tango is not entirely without a plot, but that's definitely not the film's forte. The main character is Mario Suarez (Miguel Angel Sola), a film maker who is in the process of producing a musical in which various episodes of Argentinean history are presented via dances. From immigrants entering Buenos Aires around the turn of the century to Argentina's recent, repressive government, Mario's film ranges over a variety of themes and topics. The leading actress/dancer is Laura Fuentes (Cecilia Narova), Mario's ex-wife. Near the beginning of *Tango,* he still carries a torch for her, but, after an explosion of jealousy and desire, he is able to move forward romantically. He falls deeply in love with a young, lithe dancer named Elena (Mia Maestro), who, as luck would have it, is the girlfriend of the gangster who is funding Mario's project.

Like Sally Potter's far less compelling *The Tango Lesson,* *Tango* refuses to be bounded by conventional storytelling techniques, and those who crave a narrative will be disappointed. Saura boldly blurs the lines between Mario's reality, his dreams, and the film within the film. On more than one occasion (especially during the climactic tango), we're unsure whether what we're watching is happening around Mario or whether it is a manifestation of his imagination. One dance in particular, which features men and women being brutally tortured then dumped into mass graves, is as evocative as any filmed nightmare.

Working in concert, Saura and Storaro use a variety of methods to tantalize the eyes: silhouettes, shadows, reflections, and hues that span the spectrum from blood red to pastel violet. The result, a sumptuous and energetic example of filmed poetry, testifies to the success of Saura's approach. **RECOMMENDED**

Temptress Moon [China, 1996]

Starring: Leslie Cheung, Gong Li, Kevin Lin, He Saifei, Zhang Shi, Lin Lianqun, Ge Xiangting, Zhou Jie Director: Chen Kaige Screenplay: Shu Kei, based on the story by Chen Kaige and Wang Anyi Running Time: 1:55 Rated: R (Sex, mature themes) Theatrical Aspect Ratio: 1.85:1 In Mandarin with subtitles

Farewell My Concubine, director Chen Kaige's 1992 epic drama, told a tale about sex and friendship against a turbulent political backdrop. *Temptress Moon*, the film maker's 1996 followup (which premiered with much hoopla at that year's Cannes Film Festival) has similar intentions, but less successful results. Rather than existing as a deeply-moving exploration of characters and relationships, *Temptress Moon* plunges into a sudsy, melodramatic formula that it never quite manages to escape from. The film boasts many interesting elements, but, in comparison to *Concubine*, it's a disappointing effort.

Temptress Moon opens on the Pang estate in 1911 rural China, following a lengthy opening scroll (in English) which describes the current political situation. We are introduced to the three main characters — Zhongliang, Ruyi, and Duanwu — as children, before the film skips forward in time to the 1920s. In Shanghai, we encounter an older Zhongliang (played by Leslie Cheung), who is now in the employ of one of the city's many criminal bosses. Zhongliang's specialty is blackmail — he sleeps with a wealthy woman, then threatens to go to her husband if she doesn't pay up. He's very good at his job, and the boss treats him like a son.

Meanwhile, on the Pang estate, the opium-addicted Ruyi (Gong Li) has taken command following an unfortunate "accident" in which her older brother smoked arsenic instead of his usual poison. Ruyi's cousin, Duanwu (Kevin Lin), acts as her personal servant, kowtowing to her every whim. When Zhongliang arrives from Shanghai, sent to seduce Ruyi so the boss can gain her wealth, he becomes embroiled in a more intense relationship than he anticipated. Ruyi's passionate reaction to his advances discomfits the gangster and his cold-hearted composure is shaken.

Temptress Moon requires concentration, especially at the beginning, because, as scenes change and the story makes occasionally-jarring chronological jumps, it's easy to lose track of who the characters are and how they relate to each other. Miramax has attempted to ease the burden by supplying descriptive subtitles, but it's only a minor aid. Anyone who becomes lost early during *Temptress Moon* will have a difficult and frustrating time playing catch-up.

Although *Temptress Moon* falls short of the lofty perch upon which other Chinese classics like *Farewell My Concubine* and *Raise the Red Lantern* reside, there's still something compelling about the rhythm of this film, and the ending has its own brand of power. *Temptress Moon* is a flawed motion picture, but still makes for worthwhile viewing. **RECOMMENDED**

Thieves (Les Voleurs) [France, 1996]

Starring: Catherine Deneuve, Daniel Auteuil, Laurence Côte, Fabienne Babe Director: André Téchiné Screenplay: Michel Alexandre, Pascal Bonitzer, Gilles Taurand, André Téchiné Running Time: 1:57 Rated: R (Sex, nudity, profanity, violence, mature themes) Theatrical Aspect Ratio: 1.85:1 In French with subtitles

Thieves is André Téchiné's followup to his unexpectedly successful 1995 art-house entry, *Wild Reeds*. The film features riveting performances by French icons Catherine Deneuve and Daniel Auteuil as two points of a romantic triangle. The third component is essayed by the sexy Laurence Côte.

Auteuil plays Alex, a French cop with a chip on his shoulder and a penchant for keeping his emotions under lock and key. Auteuil, who does this kind of role so well (check out *Un Coeur en Hiver* for an example), is perfectly cast, and never for the briefest of moments does his portrayal ring false. Deneuve, the ageless star, is superlative as Marie, the fragile philosophy professor who falls in love often and easily. On the other hand, although Côte gives a strong performance, her character, Juliette, is more of a catalyst than a three-dimensional individual. Juliette's presence remains enigmatic and sketchily drawn, and is all-but-forgotten during the movie's final third.

The event that jump-starts *Thieves* is the murder of

Alex's criminal brother, Ivan (Didier Bezace), who was the head of a car-stealing ring. Juliette is somehow mixed up in the ring, but the situation is complicated because she's sleeping with Alex, who has been trying to gather enough evidence to put his brother behind bars. Marie, Juliette's other lover, becomes involved in the investigation when Juliette disappears and Alex approaches her to see whether she has been in touch with the young woman. Through a series of flashbacks presented from 4 different perspectives (Marie's, Juliette's, Alex's, and that of Alex's adolescent nephew, Justin), Téchiné develops both plot and characters.

Thieves' payoff occurs during the last ⅓, when Alex and Marie, ostensibly searching for Juliette, become entwined in each others' lives. This isn't love, at least not in the conventional sense, but something that is, paradoxically, less profound and more complex. As the two of them try to establish a sense of trust, the normally-open Marie finds herself shutting down while the emotionally-closeted Alex discovers, much to his surprise, that he is capable of developing feelings for a woman whom he initially treats with contempt.

Ultimately, the film's anchor is Alex, whose highest hope for life is not to feel pain, who never laughs and sees evil everywhere, and whose personality alters with brilliant-but-unmistakable subtlety. Téchiné's development of Alex and Marie is masterful; Auteuil and Deneuve keep our attention riveted to the screen whenever they're on. And, while the director doesn't succeed in plumbing the emotional depths reached by *Ma Saison Préférée*, there are elements of *Thieves* that touch us nearly as forcefully — those moments just aren't as plentiful. RECOMMENDED

Third Miracle [1999]
Starring: Ed Harris, Anne Heche, Armin Mueller-Stahl
Director: Agnieszka Holland Screenplay: John Romano, Richard Vetere
Running Time: 2:00 Rated: PG-13 (Mature themes, profanity) Theatrical
Aspect Ratio: 1.85:1

Polish director Agnieszka Holland is a practicing Catholic, and one of her motivations for making *Third Miracle* was to depict issues of faith and religion in a positive, but still dramatically compelling, manner. For the most part, she has succeeded. *Third Miracle* is not without flaws, however.

Holland doesn't whitewash the Church. This isn't a pro-Catholic cheerleading effort, but it treats the religion, its creeds, processes, and beliefs with fairness and respect. Nothing in *Third Miracle* could be

viewed by any reasonable person as an attack on the Church. One character, a crusty archbishop with calcified views on doctrine (played by veteran actor Armin Mueller-Stahl), comes across as an antagonist, but he's not a villain in the traditional sense of the word. His opinions, despite being intractable and outdated, are legitimate, and his motivation is not malicious. This is not a gross caricature or a stereotype. There are real people in the Church like this.

Ostensibly, *Third Miracle* is about the investigation of a Catholic priest, Father Frank Morris (Ed Harris in a strong performance) — into whether a deeply spiritual, recently departed woman named Helen O'Regan should be recommended for sainthood. Morris, an avowed skeptic, researches the supposed miracles associated with Helen and discovers that the typical causes for doubt do not apply. This is really just the surface story, however. The real meat of *Third Miracle* is the way it dissects Frank's faith (or lack thereof). He has fallen into what is theologically referred to as apostasy, and now must find his way back to redemption. By promoting Helen's cause, despite stern opposition from those in power within the Church, Frank discovers the path that may lead to spiritual restoration. Of course, there are temptations along the way, including the possibility of a sexual liaison with Helen's estranged daughter, Roxanne (Anne Heche), who is attracted to Frank.

Those who have seen *Stigmata* will find elements of *Third Miracle* to be eerily familiar (especially the opening 15 to 20 minutes). Consider the following . . . Both movies open with a statue of Mary weeping blood. Both focus on supposed miracles that have no rational explanation. And both feature a priest sent to investigate such occurrences, and who is in the midst of a crisis of faith, as the protagonist. However, despite the many similarities in the initial premise, the two films are very different in tone and intent. *Stigmata* is an over-the-top thriller, while *Third Miracle* is a restrained drama. RECOMMENDED

Thirteen [United States/United Kingdom, 2003]
Starring: Evan Rachel Wood, Nikki Reed, Holly Hunter, Jeremy Sisto, Brady Corbet, Deborah Kara Unger Director: Catherine Hardwicke
Screenplay: Catherine Hardwicke & Nikki Reed Running Time: 1:40
Rated: R (Profanity, drug use, sex, self-mutilation, nudity) Theatrical
Aspect Ratio: 1.85:1

Thirteen is a welcome exception to the rule: a smart movie that does not simplify or candy-coat the rigors of the teenage years. Instead, it amplifies them by dealing with characters who are less stable than "average" junior high schoolers. The film begins with a premise that has been utilized as the foundation for less ambitious outings — that of the introverted nerd who dreams of joining the popular crowd. Except, instead of developing this idea into a moralistic fairy tale or a black comedy, *Thirteen* descends into tragedy. In addition to being a fascinating and disturbing character study, Catherine Hardwicke's film examines the meltdown of an already dysfunctional family treading the razor's edge of collapse. Light the blue touch paper . . . and kaboom! That's what happens when popular bad girl Evie (Nikki Reed) enters the life of straight-A student Tracy (Evan Rachel Wood).

Tracy is every teacher's dream student: a quiet, serious young woman who is less concerned with her looks than with her grades. But, like most geeky girls on the ripe side of puberty, Tracy desperately wants to be liked and noticed, and not just by those in her clique. When an opportunity arises for her to jump the striations of the junior high school social circles by associating with Evie, every guy's wet dream, she takes advantage. Soon, the good girl and the bad girl are inseparable, and Evie has lured Tracy over to the dark side. Manipulative and conniving, Evie has driven a wedge between Tracy and her mother, Melanie (Holly Hunter), while at the same time insinuating herself into Tracy's home and school life. Tracy goes from earning A's to F's, from virginal reserve to wanton promiscuity, from sober to drunk, and from clean to strung out. It's a total transformation. Yet, while Evie is acting on a deeply buried need to *belong* and to find a perfect match to her own confused, uncertain soul, Tracy has embarked upon a path of self-loathing behavior that leads to a razor blade repeatedly slicing through the skin on her forearm.

Thirteen is tough because it has a raw energy and doesn't pull any punches. Hardwicke takes the viewers into the girls' psyches. Tracy is vulnerable because her father has walked out, leaving behind Mom's boyfriend, Brady (Jeremy Sisto), newly released from a halfway house, as her only male role model. Her mother tries to be more of a friend than a parent, further confusing the teenager. When Tracy falls under Evie's spell, she doesn't just absorb some of the other girl's bad habits. Instead, she becomes a sponge, soaking up everything. Yet Evie is not as self-assured as she first appears to be. She, too, is troubled, and her friendship with Tracy, which is overlaid with unmistakable lesbian tones, becomes an unhealthy exercise in codependency.

In opting to go with such an uncompromising approach, Hardwicke (who is making her directorial debut after toiling for years as a production designer) has placed *Thirteen* in a small category of tell-it-like-it-is teenage films. This movie has little in common with trite fare like *She's All That*. Instead, it belongs alongside Lukas Moodysson's *Show Me Love*, the Sichel sisters' *All Over Me*, and Jim McKay's *Girls Town*. Noteworthy company, indeed, but by virtue of the strength of its story and character development, *Thirteen* belongs there. **HIGHLY RECOMMENDED**

This Boy's Life [1993]

Starring: Leonardo DiCaprio, Robert DeNiro, Ellen Barkin
Director: **Michael Caton-Jones** Screenplay: Robert Getchell from the novel by Tobias Wolff Running Time: 1:59 Rated: R (Mature themes, language, sexual situations, violence) Theatrical Aspect Ratio: 2.35:1

This Boy's Life is based on the autobiographical book by Syracuse University professor Tobias Wolff. It tells of his early life in Salt Lake City, Seattle, and Concrete, Washington. Tobias (Leonardo DiCaprio) and his mother, Caroline (Ellen Barkin), travel from place-to-place, repeatedly trying to start anew. Because of the nomadic nature of their existence, Tobias never knows the stability of a traditional home life. Then he and his mother arrive in Seattle, where Caroline meets Dwight (Robert DeNiro). With his upstanding character and resolute moral fiber, Dwight seems like the perfect choice for a husband and father. However, when Tobias spends a few months alone with Dwight and his children in advance of the wedding, he experiences firsthand his stepfather-to-be's dark side.

There isn't much that can be said about the plot of a story based on a person's boyhood adventures. No one but Tobias Wolff knows how much dramatic license was used in writing his memoirs, but, on the whole, *This Boy's Life* has the ring of truth. Every boy who has grown up in America will surely recognize parts of himself, both good and bad, in Tobias. The film is well-paced and expertly edited, allowing scenes to flow naturally into one another.

Using Dwight as its subject, *This Boy's Life* explores domination as a means of compensating for emotional inadequacy and insecurity. Dwight believes in mastery through physical and psychological force. He will insult and abuse anyone to make it clear that he is in control. He *needs* to dominate — at one time or another, he asserts his power over everyone close to him: his children, his wife, and Tobias. Since Dwight doesn't know how to react with love or tenderness, he consistently resorts to violence.

Another motif present in this film mirrors an aspect of *The Crying Game*. One of the key lines in that movie is "It's in your nature." *This Boy's Life* deals with the question of what a person's nature is and whether or not it can be changed. Tobias is forever trying to make himself into a "better person," but it becomes clear as the movie unfolds that transforming one's basic character is not a simple matter.

Ultimately, *This Boy's Life* is effective because we get to know the characters, understand their circumstances, and empathize with their dreams. Certain individual scenes don't work (too overwrought or cliched), but the film as a whole stands up relatively well. Since *This Boy's Life* is a true story, there is a sense of incompleteness, but, as coming-of-age tales go, the realism of this one gives it an edge over many overly-sentimental contenders. **RECOMMENDED**

This Is My Father [United States/Ireland, 1999]

Starring: James Caan, Aidan Quinn, Moya Farrelly, Gina Moxley, Jacob Tierney Director: Paul Quinn Screenplay: Paul Quinn Running Time: 2:00 Rated: R (Sexual situations, mature themes) Theatrical Aspect Ratio: 1.85:1

Paul Quinn's *This Is My Father* is clearly a family affair. Paul writes and directs, his brother Aidan has one of the starring roles, and his other brother Declan serves as cinematographer. All three are listed as executive producers. If the final result wasn't as emotionally satisfying, Quinn's "keep it in the family" approach would be an easy target for criticism.

This Is My Father is hampered by an unnecessarily cumbersome structure. The action begins in modern-day America, where Kieran Johnson (James Caan), a self-confessed "lonely history teacher [living] in rural Illinois," begins to wonder about his father, a man he never knew. He finds evidence (an old photograph wrapped in newspaper) to suggest that his mother's story about his sire's identity might not be true. And, since a recent stroke has rendered her mute and apparently senseless, he has to go to Ireland's County Galway to seek his answers. Accompanied by his nephew, Jack, he travels there and finds an elderly woman (Moira Deady) who is willing to reveal the entire story.

Caan's scenes represent a bookend for the more involving and better realized flashback sequences, which tell of the tragic love between Kieran O'Day (Aidan Quinn), a penniless farmer, and Fiona Flynn (Moya Farrelly), the only daughter of a wealthy widow. It's the spring of 1939, and Fiona has just returned from boarding school. Although she and Kieran have known each other their whole lives, they have never been close. Now, they strike up a friendship. Kieran, a loner who has little knowledge about women, tries desperately to do everything right (and usually fails). For her part, Fiona finds his efforts endearing. During one magical night they spend together at the beach, they confess their love for one another. But "times were different" in 1939, and a match between the two is frowned upon for social and religious reasons. So, as factions within the town (headed by Fiona's mother and the local priest) try to rip them apart, the two lovers fight to stay together.

This Is My Father does not startle with plot twists and unexpected revelations, but that's part of its charm. The film is always true to its simple story, and does not attempt to stray in a sensationalistic direction just to mislead the audience. It's not all that difficult to guess how things are going to end long before the cinematic punctuation is placed on Fiona and Kieran's romance. For director Paul Quinn, this is a fine effort, and represents the kind of motion picture that lovers of well-constructed romances long for. **RECOMMENDED**

Three Seasons [United States/Vietnam, 1999]

Starring: Don Duong, Ngoc Hiep Nguyen, Manh Cuong Tran, Harvey Keitel, Zoe Bui Director: Tony Bui Screenplay: Tony Bui, Timothy Linh Bui Running Time: 1:53 Rated: PG-13 (Sexual themes) Theatrical Aspect Ratio: 1.85:1 In Vietnamese with subtitles

The accolades heaped upon *Three Seasons*, the debut feature of Vietnamese American film maker Tony Bui, at the 1999 Sundance Film Festival are a publicist's dream. Not only did director of photography Lisa Rinzler win the cinematography award, but Bui took home both the Best Dramatic Picture trophy and the Audience Award. *Three Seasons* is a solid and effective motion picture, however it lacks the depth and breadth one typically associates with an award winning effort.

The narrative is comprised of four different stories. One tells of the relationship between Kien An (Ngoc Hiep Nguyen), a young girl who harvests lotus flowers, and her employer, Teacher Dao (Manh Cuong Tran). He's a poet who has lost the ability to write due to the progressive degeneration of his body caused by leprosy. He lives in the past because he cannot bear the present and sees no future. Kien An, feeling pity for him (and perhaps an odd, creative kinship), agrees to function as his fingers if he will return to writing poetry. Meanwhile, in the city, a cyclo driver, Hai (Don Duong), has become infatuated with a prostitute, Lan (Zoe Bui). From the moment he first helps her out of a tight spot, he is smitten with her, but she regards his attentions as annoyances. Hai, however, is a patient man, and he saves up his money so he can afford to buy a night with her. His intention is to give her something that none of her other customers would think of offering. Elsewhere in the city, an American GI, James Hager (Harvey Keitel), has returned to Vietnam after a 30-year absence to find the daughter he fathered during the war. In his words, "It's time to find her and maybe make some kind of peace with this place." But, as he quickly discovers, tracking down one individual can be a daunting task. Finally, there's the boy Woody (Huu Duoc Nguyen), a street peddler who makes his living selling cheap watches, flashlights, chewing gum, and cigarettes to passersby in the street. When the case containing his wares is stolen, he must face the wrath of his father and seek to find a new way to earn money.

One criticism that can be leveled against *Three Seasons* is that its vision of Vietnam is too sunny (not literally — it's almost always raining). Indeed, with the exception of a few rare moments, we fail to glimpse anything dark or depressing. Prostitution and street solicitation are sanitized so they appear almost appealing. The country itself looks like the ideal place for a vacation. Nevertheless, it is unfair to charge the movie with being a slice of pro-Vietnamese propaganda, because it's much more than that. It's an accomplished and effective piece of film making that works on many levels. RECOMMENDED

Tin Cup [1996]

Starring: Kevin Costner, Rene Russo, Cheech Marin, Don Johnson, Linda Hart, Dennis Burkley Director: Ron Shelton Screenplay: John Norville and Ron Shelton Running Time: 2:10 Rated: R (Profanity, nudity, sex) Theatrical Aspect Ratio: 1.85:1

As far as sports movies go, *Tin Cup* turns in a respectable showing, injecting some intelligence and maturity into a story that easily could have succumbed to a flood of "struggling underdog" cliches. That's not to say that elements of the formula aren't here, but they rarely threaten to overwhelm *Tin Cup's* better aspects.

The story centers around Roy (Kevin Costner), an aging club pro who lives in a Winnebago in the lonely west Texas town of Salome. He spends his day in the company of his best friend, Romeo (Cheech Marin), working for $7 an hour at a deserted driving range. Once upon a time, Roy had a bright golfing future ahead of him, but he blew his cool on the links, went

for the trick shot instead of the smart one, and failed to qualify for the tour. Since then, he has been hiding out in obscurity, picking up cash where he can, and watching bitterly as his old college partner, Dave Simms (Don Johnson), "a rich, happy, soulless" man, rises through the PGA ranks.

One day, Roy's marginal existence is turned upside down by the arrival of a woman psychologist named Molly Griswold. She wants to take golf lessons to impress her boyfriend. To the men of Salome, the concept of a female doctor is a revelation, and, in one of the film's more slyly amusing scenes, they watch eagerly as Roy teaches her the basics of hitting a golf ball, wondering how "such a pretty girl can have such an ugly swing." It doesn't take long for Roy to fall in love with Molly, so it comes as a blow when she reveals that her boyfriend is none other than Dave Simms. Roy then decides that a grand gesture is needed to win her — something like qualifying for the U.S. Open and beating Dave in front of a national TV audience.

Although this may sound like a very familiar, traditional sports movie, don't worry — director Ron Shelton applies enough tweaks and twists to the formulaic story to keep us interested and a little unsure of the outcome. *Tin Cup* isn't concerned with blazing new trails — that's beyond its scope or ambition. Instead, it's content to offer a pleasantly likable, gently comic 2 hours of simple life lessons, with golf as the obvious metaphor.

As the saying goes, you don't have to appreciate the sport to enjoy the movie. *Tin Cup* has a broad enough appeal that intimate knowledge of the joys and frustrations of playing 18 holes isn't necessary. This movie ranks as better-than-par entertainment. RECOMMENDED

To Live [China, 1994]

Starring: Ge You, Gong Li, Niu Ben, Guo Tao, Jiang Wu, Liu Tian Chi, Zhang Lu Director: Zhang Yimou Screenplay: Yu Hua and Lu Wei based on the novel by Yu Hua Running Time: 2:13 Rated: No MPAA Rating (Mature themes, violence) In Mandarin with subtitles

To Live explores territory that is rapidly becoming familiar to those who view the works of China's so-called "Fifth Generation" film makers. The events of the middle decades of the twentieth century, including the Communist Civil War, the "Great Leap Forward," and the Cultural Revolution, represent fertile ground for grand stories of mingled tragedy and triumph. However, this marvelously-textured movie, which is by turns funny and touching, takes a different approach from pictures like *The Blue Kite* and

Farewell My Concubine. Instead of viewing the cultural changes on an epic scale, *To Live* gives a far more intimate, and affecting, perspective.

Fugui (Ge You), Jiazhen (Gong Li), and their 2 children are normal, hard-working Chinese citizens caught up in the chaotic changes transforming their country. Unlike many of their counterparts in other, similarly-themed films, they are not accused of acting against Mao Tse-tung's Red government, but their faithfulness to the new order doesn't keep tragedy from touching their lives. As one of the film's explanatory capsules states, few families in China were not affected by the Cultural Revolution.

Although *To Live* was banned in its country of origin because of a supposed negative portrayal of certain pro-Maoist historical events, Zhang's presentation of 3 turbulent decades of life in China seems reasonably balanced. Other films (most notably *Farewell My Concubine*) have more openly attacked the Communist Revolution and its aftermath.

The characters are powerfully developed and realized, representing some of the most "real" men and women to populate any of 1994's films. From the 1940s to the early 1970s, we follow Fugui's family through good times and bad. Zhang's skill is such that we become less a detached observer and more a passive participant. Gong and Ge (both of whom appeared in *Farewell My Concubine*), who imbue Fugui and Jiazhen with life and humanity, are perfect choices for the central characters.

Few films approach the level of honesty reached by *To Live*. This is a story whose underlying central theme is expressed in the through all the struggles, hardships, and moments of rare magic and joy, the characters continue their lives. As Jiazhen points out, no matter how bleak circumstances appear, the only choice is to go on.

With *To Live* Zhang has cemented his reputation as one of today's premier directors. It is an accolade not lightly accorded, but the filmmaker has earned it through his telling of rare stories brimming with humanity and unforced drama. **MUST SEE**

Together [China/South Korea, 2002]

Starring: Tang Yun, Liu Peigi, Chen Hong, Wang Zhiwen, Chen Kiage Director: **Chen Kiage** Screenplay: Chen Kiage and Xue Xiaolu Running Time: 1:58 Rated: **PG** Theatrical Aspect Ratio: 1.85:1 In Mandarin with subtitles

The story revolves around a 13-year old prodigy named Xiaochun (Tang Yun), who plays the violin with a passion and technical proficiency that few

adult masters can match. Accompanied by his peasant father, Liu Cheng (Liu Peigi), Xiaochun comes to Beijing to further his opportunities with his instrument. While his father works long hours, Xiaochun earns a little extra by playing music for an eccentric young woman, Lili (Chen Hong), who lives nearby. Meanwhile, due in large part to the persistence of his father, he becomes the pupil of Professor Jiang (Wang Zhiwen), a teacher who spends as much time wallowing in his own sorrow as instructing Xiaochun. Eventually, Liu recognizes that for his son to advance, he must have a more prominent teacher, so he secures the interest of Professor Yu (Chen Kiage), who accepts only the best and often takes them into the spotlight.

Together is in many ways about the price of being a prodigy. Everyone desires something from Xiaochun, even though many of those close to him genuinely care about his well-being. His father wants him to succeed at any price so that he can vicariously experience the thrill of standing onstage in front of enraptured crowds. Lili treats Xiaochun as a personal servant until circumstances force her to make a sacrifice. Professor Jiang sees in his pupil a chance to expiate past sins. And Professor Yu views Xiaochun as a can't-miss prospect whose career he can guide. For his part, Xiaochun must wade through the falseness surrounding him to find what's genuine, and determine what he really wants. Is it to play the violin, even at the cost of his soul?

Together is strangely edited, with several jarring cuts and times when entire sequences seem to be jumped over. It's possible that Chen, whose movies typically run long, may have clipped a little more from the final cut than he had initially intended, resulting in a film that occasionally lacks a smooth, polished feel. Despite its drawbacks, however, the movie is affecting and emotionally satisfying. Although not as ambitious as some of Chen's celebrated works (*Farewell My Concubine* and *The Emperor and the Assassin* come to mind), *Together* nevertheless contains moments of cinematic power, and by the end, almost everyone in the audience will care about Xiaochun and perhaps even the secondary characters. It's not a perfect film, but it's certainly worth a look.
RECOMMENDED

Topsy-Turvy [United Kingdom, 1999]

Starring: Jim Broadbent, Allan Corduner, Lesley Manville, Eleanor David, Ron Cook, Timothy Spall Director: **Mike Leigh** Screenplay: Mike Leigh Running Time: 2:40 Rated: **R** (Nudity, drug use) Theatrical Aspect Ratio: 1.85:1

Over the course of their famous partnership, which lasted from 1871 until 1896, the team of William Gilbert (librettist) and Arthur Sullivan (composer) produced 14 operettas, including such classics as "The Pirates of Penzance," "The Mikado," and "The Gondoliers." British filmmaker Mike Leigh (*Secrets & Lies*) has chosen to take a closer look at this duo, whose names will be forever linked. Instead of focusing on an entire quarter-century of sometimes turbulent collaboration, Leigh has limited his scope to a 14-month period between January 1884 and March 1885. *Topsy-Turvy* begins with the opening of "Princess Ida" and closes with the triumphant debut of "The Mikado." Along the way, we learn bits and pieces about Gilbert, Sullivan, and those who loved them and worked with them.

As a history lesson, *Topsy-Turvy* is on uncertain ground, making liberal use of what is commonly termed "dramatic licence." While there is more structure to this narrative than is typical for Leigh, there are a number of sequences that have little or nothing to do with what really happened backstage at the Savoy Theater. The film is essentially divided into two parts. The first concentrates on the personal lives and ambitions of Gilbert and Sullivan, and stakes out the territory that defines their relationship. The second explores the development of "The Mikado," from Gilbert's visit to a Japanese restaurant (where inspiration struck) to its opening night performance.

Topsy-Turvy's second half is unquestionably stronger than its first. Like John Turturro's *Illuminata,* this movie takes us behind the scenes of a theatrical production around the turn of the 20th century, but Leigh's scenario and characters are better realized. In detailing the transition of "The Mikado" from idea to reality, the director shows every aspect of the process: writing, casting, costuming, developing dance steps, acting rehearsals, and musical rehearsals. Some of these episodes are highly amusing, especially a ten-minute sequence in which Gilbert puts three of his actors through their paces. Because of scenes like this, *Topsy-Turvy*'s final 80 minutes fly by. Unfortunately, the same cannot be said of the other portion of the movie, which suffers from occasional spells of torpidity.

On a certain level, this is one of Mike Leigh's most challenging productions. Not only has he produced a narrative feature based on real events and historical figures, but he has elected to stage significant portions of Gilbert and Sullivan productions. In addition to four or five numbers from "The Mikado," we are treated to songs from "The Sorcerer" and "Princess Ida." Although there are times when this movie does not seem like a "Mike Leigh Film," it is a well crafted and solidly entertaining effort that illustrates how expert filmmakers can expand their ranges while still producing movies that are worth seeing. RECOMMENDED

Two Bits [1995]

Starring: Jerry Barrone, Mary Elizabeth Mastrantonio, Al Pacino, Andy Romano Director: James Foley Screenplay: Joseph Stefano Running Time: 1:25 Rated: PG-13 (Mature themes) Theatrical Aspect Ratio: 2.35:1

When you think of Al Pacino, the image that comes to mind is one of energy, intensity, and violence. Whether a cop (*Sea of Love, Serpico, Heat*) or a crook (*The Godfather, Scarface*), Pacino's characters are almost always hard-hitting, hyperactive portraits of caged fury. So it's more than a minor departure for the actor to appear in James Foley's *Two Bits* as Gitano Sabatoni, a dying, regretful old man. This is a small, understated role — character actor material — yet Pacino immerses himself so fully in the part that we forget about the performer the moment we see the performance.

Despite Pacino's presence in the cast, this isn't his movie. Nor does it belong to Mary Elizabeth Mastrantonio, who has a supporting role as Gitano's timid daughter. Instead, the focus is on Jerry Barrone, who plays 12-year-old Gennaro, the fictionalized childhood counterpart of screenwriter Joseph Stefano. This film, which Stefano first committed to paper in 1970, is autobiographical, recounting one crucial day in his life as a boy in South Philadelphia during the heat of a Depression era summer.

That day is August 26, 1933, when Gennaro first starts noticing life for what it is. It's a day of eye-opening experiences and tough lessons; of awareness, magic, and sadness. As Alec Baldwin states in his voiceover narration, it's the day La Paloma — the newest movie theater in the neighborhood — opens. Until 6 P.M., there's a special rate at the cinema: get in for only 25 cents. So Gennaro spends his time roaming the streets, looking for odd jobs that will pay enough for him to afford a matinee. This quest for two bits takes place against the backdrop of an America where the only thing more scarce than money is employment.

The story is simple, and the film's message is

equally as plain: never give up wanting and striving, no matter how unattainable the dream seems. For Gennaro in *Two Bits*, that goal is watching a movie in the air-conditioned confines of La Paloma. As the film progresses, this simple theater takes on a monumental symbolic importance.

The greatest failing of *Two Bits* is a tendency to ramble. Individual episodes work well on their own, but some of the connecting material is weak, and the voiceover is often more irritating than helpful. The film is also too self-conscious about getting across its theme.

Two Bits represents an undemanding form of entertainment — a period piece that lives on nostalgia and an elemental story. Perhaps the most successful aspect of this film is that it encourages us to connect events in Gennaro's life with moments in our own, thereby enriching the emotional impact. Credit director Foley (*Glengarry Glen Ross*) for a fine, character-based piece. **RECOMMENDED**

Un Air de Famille (Family Relations) [France, 1996]

Starring: Jean-Pierre Bacri, Agnes Jaoui, Jean-Pierre Darroussin, Catherine Frot Director: Cédric Klapisch Screenplay: Agnes Jaoui, Jean-Pierre Bacri & Cédric Klapisch Running Time: 1:47 Rated: No MPAA Rating (Mature themes) Theatrical Aspect Ratio: 2.35:1 In French with subtitles

Un Air de Famille, from French director Cédric Klapisch, is a study of a dysfunctional family on the verge of blowing apart. While this isn't exactly an original topic, Klapisch's approach is vastly different from what we have come to expect from this sort of motion picture. There's no overwrought melodrama, no sudden moment of great personal triumph, and no real catharsis. Instead, what *Un Air de Famille* offers is 110 minutes of discovery through dialogue, as the characters spar with each other, and, as the film wears on, gradually shed their carefully-erected disguises and allow their true selves to show.

The main characters are a trio of very different siblings. There's Philippe (Wladimir Yordanoff), the suave, successful one, who arrives at a family dinner immediately after finishing a television interview. The dinner, a birthday get-together for Philippe's insecure wife, Yolande (Catherine Frot), is being held at the restaurant managed by Philippe's brother, Henri (Jean-Pierre Bacri), a dour man whose wife has recently left him. Then there's Philippe and Henri's younger sister, Betty (Agnes Jaoui), whose leather jacket is just one sign of her ongoing rebellion against

convention. Also in attendance for the night's "festivities" are the siblings' domineering mother (Claire Maurier), and a bartender named Denis (Jean-Pierre Darroussin), who is secretly involved with Betty.

Things don't begin well, as Betty and Henri engage in a frosty conversation before Betty unceremoniously dumps Denis. When Philippe shows up, the evening's decline accelerates. Mother's arrival exacerbates tensions as the siblings begin sniping at each other and anyone else within verbal reach. As the film progresses, it becomes apparent that first impressions aren't always accurate, and that the supposedly-affable Philippe may be far less caring and humane than his sour-faced brother. Betty begins to realize this as we do, and her attitude gradually changes. The recognition that she has been wrong about her brothers all along gives her the impetus to truly defy her family for the first time.

All of the events of *Un Air de Famille* take place over a 4-hour period, meaning that the film unfolds almost in real time. It would be interesting to see how the characters react to each other in the future, since the events of this dinner demand changes in every relationship that is explored. By the time the closing credits unfold, each member of the family has learned something new about everyone else, and we, the viewers, have come to understand and appreciate the complexities that define their interaction. In that way, *Un Air de Famille* is a wonderfully rich and intelligent exploration of family dynamics. **HIGHLY RECOMMENDED**

Under the Sand [France, 2000]

Starring: Charlotte Rampling, Bruno Cremer, Jacques Nolot Director: François Ozon Screenplay: François Ozon, Emmanuelle Bernheim, Marcia Romano, Marina de Van Running Time: 1:30 Rated: No MPAA Rating (Sex, nudity, profanity) Theatrical Aspect Ratio: 1.85:1 In French with subtitles

Death: it is the lone certainty in life (forget the bit about taxes). Despite that, when the end comes to a loved one, even if expected, it can be difficult to process and handle. This is the province of *Under the Sand*, from internationally celebrated French director François Ozon, whose credits include *See the Sea* and *Water Drops on Burning Rocks*.

Charlotte Rampling plays Marie Drillon, an English-born college professor who lives in France with her beloved older husband, Jean (Bruno Cremer). One summer, as usual, the couple travels to a country house near the sea to take a vacation. While Marie is lying on the beach, sunning herself and dozing off,

Jean decides to take a swim. He never returns. Marie is left with a host of unanswered questions. Was Jean's death accidental or did he kill himself? Is he really dead or did he fake his death and disappear? Was there anything she could have done to prevent the tragedy? Instead of coping, she goes into deep denial, pretending that Jean is still alive and awaiting his daily return from work. Her friends worry as she continues to refer to her husband in the present tense. The one in the most difficult position is Marie's new lover, Vincent (Jacques Nolot), who knows Jean is dead and is disconcerted by Marie's seeming unwillingness to acknowledge this fact.

The film is resolutely and unflinchingly unsentimental in its depiction of Marie's situation, and this lack of melodrama is one of the most effective weapons in *Under the Sand*'s arsenal. It does not trivialize through manipulation. Instead, Ozon depicts discrete moments in Marie's life, and how they are impacted by her uncertainty: dinner with friends, dates with her lover, a teaching session with her class. When she arrives home, a specter-like Jean is there — a construct of her memories and imagination who listens quietly as she unburdens herself, only occasionally offering advice. Yet there are times when it's clear from Marie's face that she understands, at least on some level, that she is fooling herself. And, occasionally, she comes face-to-face with reality, such as when she enters Jean's home office and sees everything untouched, or when the police call to report that they may have found Jean's body.

Ozon's careful and detailed approach to the subject matter has resulted in a movie that is difficult to dismiss or forget, and is forceful in its simplicity. The ending is intentionally ambiguous, giving us the same lack of closure that defines Marie's existence. *Under the Sand* is an effective and moving account of the power of grief and denial. **HIGHLY RECOMMENDED**

Under the Skin [United Kingdom, 1997]

Starring: Samantha Morton, Claire Rushbrook, Rita Tushingham, Stuart Townsend Director: Carine Adler Screenplay: Carine Adler Running Time: 1:25 Rated: No MPAA Rating (Sex, frontal nudity, frank sexual discussion, profanity) Theatrical Aspect Ratio: 1.85:1

The subject matter of *Under the Skin*, while not inherently uninteresting, doesn't break barriers or attempt anything radical. The script, too, is solid and effective, but not extraordinary. The director, Carine Adler, shows promise but lacks polish, in part because her verite approach bears a resemblance to the

styles of Mike Leigh and Ken Loach. But all of these things pale into insignificance in the light of *Under the Skin*'s principal performance, a stunning debut by Samantha Morton.

The film is an examination of unresolved grief, and the way it can erode a person's identity. Iris (Morton) and Rose (Claire Rushbrook) are sisters. Iris is the younger, wilder child; Rose, who is 5 years older, is happily married and pregnant. The two of them are subtle rivals for the love and attention of their aging mother (Rita Tushingham), but, when Mum dies unexpectedly, it widens the gulf between the two girls rather than bringing them together. Rose reacts to the tragedy as one might expect — she is sad and cries, then gets on with her life. Iris, however, doesn't shed a tear and shows contempt for her sister's grief, but her personality starts to disintegrate. She begins a search for *something* (comfort? affection? attention?) that throws her into a downward moral spiral of sex-and-alcohol binges.

Morton makes Iris real. Every moment she's on screen, the actress forces us to accept Iris as a living, breathing individual. This is a raw, riveting performance — deeply moving and free of artifice. Morton handles the complete range of emotions expertly, from the subtle (watch the longing in her face as she observes a choir singing) to the overt (a wrenching breakdown). In committing herself totally to this portrayal, she gives Adler everything she has, allowing herself to be captured on camera in a state of both physical and emotional nakedness.

Adler's approach, which includes a lot of hand-held camera shots to achieve a documentary-like look, is effective in bringing out the best in Morton's performance. *Under the Skin* is emotionally potent; we are not left on the outside looking in. It's important to the director that viewers become absorbed in Iris' sordid world, and that we feel her despair and confusion. There's a note of hope at the end that keeps us from leaving the theater in a suicidal funk. *Under the Skin* is a fine movie, and features one of the best debut performances of 1997. **RECOMMENDED**

Unhook the Stars [1996]

Starring: Gena Rowlands, Marisa Tomei, Gerard Depardieu, Moira Kelly, Jake Lloyd Director: Nick Cassavetes Screenplay: Nick Cassavetes and Helen Caldwell Running Time: 1:44 Rated: R (Profanity, mature themes) Theatrical Aspect Ratio: 1.66:1

Unhook the Stars is the directorial debut of Nick Cassavetes, the son of acclaimed international director

John Cassavetes. It is a pleasantly unsentimental character study of one woman who has difficulty letting go. Although Cassavetes may want independence from his father's name and memory, this film won't earn it, for, although the style bears only a passing resemblance to the late film maker's, Nick not only uses several members of John's crew (notably Phedon Papamichael), but has cast his mother, Gena Rowlands, in the lead role. In addition, the script has a heavy autobiographical tinge — Cassavetes is using cinema to work out his ambiguous feelings towards his famous father.

For Mildred (Rowlands), a single mother (she was widowed many years ago), her last chick is about to fly the coop. Her oldest, a son (David Sherrill), has already left home. Now, her daughter, Annie (Moira Kelly), is on her way out. Their parting is less-than-amicable. Annie finds her mother to be a controlling and interfering influence, and wants to get away as soon as possible. Mildred watches her go sadly, wondering what happened to all the aspirations she harbored for her only female offspring. But Mildred isn't destined to be alone for long. Her new neighbor across the street, Monica Warren (Marisa Tomei), has thrown her husband (David Thornton) out following a particularly nasty quarrel. Now, she's alone with her young son, J.J. (Jake Lloyd), and doesn't have the money to pay a sitter when she goes to work. Mildred offers to help, gratis, and soon becomes J.J.'s surrogate mother.

One of the more striking aspects of *Unhook the Stars* is the script's openness and honesty. It doesn't try to trick and manipulate us with melodrama. Every action has a natural consequence — nothing ever feels forced or scripted. When Monica's husband returns to town, wanting to see his son, there's no shouting match or violence. When Annie eventually comes home, there's no big, tearful reunion. And, when Mildred begins to realize that her time with J.J. is coming to a close, we're spared an emotional scene. *Unhook the Stars* is consistently low-key, and, in the context of an intelligent script and strong acting, this represents a welcome change-of-pace from most American films.

Unhook the Stars is an engaging motion picture, mixing various flavors of comedy and drama into a satisfying whole. Admittedly, there are times when Cassavetes skims lightly over subject matter that is deserving of a fuller exploration, but the quality of the finished product allows us to overlook most of these incidents. *Unhook the Stars* is a movie of many special, small moments, that, combined together, make for a shining cinematic experience. **RECOMMENDED**

Unstrung Heroes [1995]

Starring: Andie MacDowell, John Turturro, Nathan Watt, Michael Richards, Maury Chaykin Director: Diane Keaton Screenplay: Richard LaGravenese based on the book by Franz Lidz Running Time: 1:33 Rated: PG (Mature themes) Theatrical Aspect Ratio: 1.85:1

Unstrung Heroes opens as another coming of age story set in the early '60s. Steven (Nathan Watt) and his sister Sandy (Kendra Krull) are the children of a happily married, if somewhat unusual, non-practicing Jewish couple. It's not long, however, before we learn that Selma (Andie MacDowell), the mother of this family, is terminally ill. Sid (John Turturro), the father, doesn't handle the situation well, so when Steven asks to spend the summer with his two oddball uncles, there are only token objections. While living with Danny and Arthur, Steven changes his name to Franz and learns the importance of his Jewish faith.

MacDowell, playing dying wife/mother Selma Lidz, does a solid job. John Turturro, too, fills the role of Selma's husband, scientist/experimenter Sid Lidz, with his usual aptitude. As Selma fades away, Turturro's face expresses Sid's unspeakable loss with heart-breaking poignancy. Also effective is Nathan Watt as Steven, the Lidz' young son, who is forced to cope with death before he really understands what living is. On hand to teach him life's lessons are two eccentric, "black sheep" uncles: paranoid Danny (Michael Richards) and packrat Arthur (Mary Chaykin). As Steven's home life becomes increasingly unstable, Danny and Arthur are there for him, dispensing their own variety of wisdom, which includes advice never to throw away memories — like dreams, they're easily lost, and an effort must be made to preserve them.

Director Diane Keaton is on certain ground chronicling the tragedy of Selma's illness and its inevitable conclusion. While the emotional impact of *Unstrung Heroes* isn't as potent as that of Richard Attenborough's similarly-themed *Shadowlands*, the scenes showing Selma, Sid, and their children coping with impending death are well-written and effectively conveyed. Thankfully, most of this is handled with refreshing subtlety — there is no obvious audience manipulation.

Less successful is the presentation of Uncles Danny and Arthur. There's a sense that these two exist simply to populate *Unstrung Heroes* with a pair of eccentrics, and they seem more like scripted characters than real people. Their ultimate function within the context of the story — life's castoffs teaching an impressionable boy secrets of how to stay afloat — is more than a little cliched.

There's nothing especially original about *Unstrung Heroes*, but the story is told with intelligence and sensitivity. In a time when so many movies are botching promising premises, it's refreshing to see something appealing done with a retreaded subject. This film isn't a masterpiece, but it offers another view of what makes family so important, and does so with an emotional honesty that many other movies don't approach. RECOMMENDED

Vanity Fair [United States/United Kingdom, 2004]

Starring: Reese Witherspoon, Romola Garai, James Purefoy, Rhys Ifans, Gabriel Byrne, Jonathan Rhys-Meyers, Bob Hoskins, Eileen Atkins, Jim Broadbent Director: Mira Nair Screenplay: Matthew Faulk, Julian Fellowes, Mark Skeet, based on the novel by William Makepeace Thackery Running Time: 2:20 Rated: PG-13 (Sensuality, brief nudity, brief violence) Theatrical Aspect Ratio: 2.35:1

There's always a risk inherent in adapting a lengthy classic novel, and pacing is often the first casualty. Such is the case with Mira Nair's version of William Thackery's *Vanity Fair*. Despite impeccable production values and some impressive supporting performances, the film suffers from choppiness and a sense that too much is being crammed into the two-hour, twenty-minute running time. One could argue that Nair did the best that's humanly possible with the story, considering the natural constraints of a motion picture, but although the film is entertaining and eminently watchable, one could easily argue that it does not do full justice to its source material.

To those who are students of English literature, the story is well known. It centers around perpetual schemer and social climber Becky Sharp (Reese Witherspoon), who spends the first third of the movie looking for a husband who can elevate her above the poverty and low social standing inherent in her position as an orphan and a governess. When she finds her match in Rawdon Crawley (James Purefoy), she does her best to ingratiate herself into the highest circles of English society. But Rawdon, who is dedicated to her, is also a gambling addict, and his losses at the tables bring financial ruin to himself and Becky. Only the intervention of the Marquis of Steyne (Gabriel Byrne), who has his own motives, saves them from losing everything. Meanwhile, Becky's lone friend, Amelia Sedley (Romola Garai), is unlucky in romance. She is in love with George Osborne (Jonathan Rhys-Meyers), the callow, self-centered son of businessman John Osborne (Jim Broadbent). Her eventual marriage to George is not happy, and she is oblivious to the devotion of her husband's fellow soldier, William Dobbin (a subdued Rhys Ifans).

Nair might at first seem to be an odd choice to helm the movie, but the Indian-born director, whose *Monsoon Wedding* was a major art house hit, breathes life into what could have been a stodgy, *Masterpiece Theater*–style costume drama. Nair's re-creation of England and Belgium during the early 19th century is sumptuous without going overboard. In scenes when a certain drabness is required, she keeps the colors earthy and muted. But, on occasions of gaiety, bright hues abound. In general, there are more things to like about *Vanity Fair* than there are to dislike, especially if you're not a Thackery purist. Despite its flaws, the movie is compulsively watchable, and few will be bored by it. RECOMMENDED

Vera Drake [United Kingdom/France/New Zealand, 2004]

Starring: Imelda Staunton, Phil Davis, Peter Wight, Daniel Mays, Alex Kelly, Eddie Marsan, Adrian Scarborough, Heather Craney, Jim Broadbent Director: Mike Leigh Screenplay: Mike Leigh Running Time: 2:05 Rated: R (Mature themes, rape) Theatrical Aspect Ratio: 1.85:1

Although *Vera Drake* is about the downfall of an abortionist working during a time when the law in England decreed that it was unlawful to perform an "unauthorized" operation, this isn't really an "abortion movie." That's the context, but the tale is a lot closer to a Greek tragedy than a sermon. As always, Mike Leigh keeps his camera firmly fixed on his central character. We see her, warts and all, at her best and worst, and her tragic flaw — that of willful obliviousness — is too obvious to miss.

For the first half of the film, we view the title character as a cliché come to life: a cheerful, always helpful, grandmotherly type of woman who's ready with a kind word or an offer to "put the kettle on." Imelda Staunton plays the part like everyone's beloved aunt or grandmother. She's a little eccentric, but no more than is to be expected of someone of her disposition — or so we initially think. Then we learn that, on the side, she has a secret: She performs abortions for women who can't afford to get them done "the right way." She is not a barbaric surgeon — she uses a syringe to pump a woman's womb full of soapy water, which results in a miscarriage. There are no coat hangers or other unpleasant instruments involved.

Vera does not view what she does as wrong, even though she is aware it's against the law. She doesn't use the word "abortion." Instead, she refers to herself as "helping women." Unfortunately, when one of the women she "helps" ends up in the hospital and nearly dies, a detective inspector (Peter Wight) is forced to interrupt a Drake family celebration to confront Vera with evidence of her crime. She immediately goes to pieces and, thereafter, little is left of the lively, good-natured woman who inhabited the body for the film's first hour. All that remains is a broken, whimpering shell.

It's tough to deny the film's emotional impact. It's probably the most complete and satisfying movie Leigh has made since *Secrets and Lies*. Regardless of your opinion of the woman's actions, it's impossible not to feel for Vera as we see her well-ordered, simple life fall apart suddenly and dramatically. There's a lot of improvisation, and all of the actors make contributions. The result is a sense of verisimilitude that many directors either don't aim for or fail to achieve. We believe that these characters and their circumstances are real. For those who don't like the low-key, "slice-of-life" approach (no melodrama), *Vera Drake*'s slow pace may be difficult to appreciate. But it's the unhurried vision that gives the movie its power. For those who have the patience to become absorbed in this kind of drama, *Vera Drake* offers a stunningly real character portrait whose image will linger long. **HIGHLY RECOMMENDED**

The Virgin Suicides [2000]

Starring: James Woods, Kathleen Turner, Kirsten Dunst, Josh Hartnett, Hanna Hall, Chelsea Swain Director: Sofia Coppola Screenplay: Sofia Coppola based on the novel by Jeffrey Eugenides Running Time: 1:36 Rated: R (Mature themes including suicide) Theatrical Aspect Ratio: 1.85:1

The Virgin Suicides is Sofia Coppola's directorial debut, and its effectiveness illustrates that she's better behind the camera than she is in front of it. (Most movie-goers will remember her ill-fated attempt to portray Michael Corleone's daughter in *The Godfather III*.) Tragic, haunting, and sometimes darkly comedic, this movie leaves a strong impression in its telling of a story about the destruction of innocence.

The time frame is the mid-'70s and the setting is an upper class suburban community in Michigan. The film tells the sad story of the 5 Lisbon sisters — Cecilia (age 13, played by Hanna Hall), Lux (age 14,

played by Kirsten Dunst), Bonnie (age 15, played by Chelsea Swain), Mary (age 16, played by A.J. Cook), and Therese (age 17, played by Leslie Hayman) — all of whom come to a bad end before finishing high school. Unhappy, neglected Cecilia is the first to give up on life — after surviving one suicide attempt, she is successful on the second try. In the wake of that event, the atmosphere surrounding the surviving sisters becomes grim, and their parents' overprotectiveness threatens to suffocate them. For most children, mothers and fathers set boundaries; for the Lisbons, it's iron bars.

The Virgin Suicides is filmed as a memory looking back through 25 years, and the point-of-view is that of a boy who was in love with one (or perhaps all) of the girls. As a result, the events recounted here offer a filtered perspective of the sisters and the complexities of their lives.

One of *The Virgin Suicides*' strengths is its ability to effectively capture the nuances of teenage life during the '70s. Coppola gets all of the little things right: the awkwardness of a chaperoned boy/girl party, the thrill of first love, and the nervousness of the pre-dance ritual (in this case, the homecoming dance, not the prom). The film also boasts a solid soundtrack featuring a few songs that haven't been endlessly recycled in other, recent, set-in-the-'70s features. In one key scene, music provides a link between the Lisbon girls and the outside world — it becomes their only viable means of communication and free expression.

By using occasional bursts of humor and setting up the film as a collage of reminiscences, Coppola establishes a mood that is wistful and sad, but not funereal. There are a few instances when the film gets a little heavy-handed, but, for the most part, the tone is well modulated. Although Coppola almost certainly gained more than a little help from her famous father in getting the production off the ground, the talent evident in her debut argues that this is not a case of unwarranted nepotism. The apple has not fallen far from the tree. **RECOMMENDED**

A Walk on the Moon [1999]

Starring: Diane Lane, Liev Schreiber, Viggo Mortensen, Anna Paquin, Victoria Barkof Director: Tony Goldwyn Screenplay: Pamela Gray Running Time: 1:45 Rated: R (Profanity, sex, brief nudity) Theatrical Aspect Ratio: 1.85:1

The year is 1969. The setting is a Jewish bungalow community in the Catskills. Unlike in *Dirty Dancing*, where Jerry Orbach played a rich patriarch who could afford to spend a vacation with his family, *A Walk on the Moon* looks at the lower middle class. Instead of staying in clean, well-maintained hotel rooms, the characters in this film spend their days and nights in a ramshackle little house where the youngest child sleeps on the floor in the kitchen. Since Marty (Liev Schreiber) can't afford to take a whole week off from his job as a TV repairman (especially with the moon walk coming up — everyone wants to have a working television), he can only join his family in the mountains on weekends. That leaves his wife, Pearl (Diane Lane), alone there with the kids and her mother-in-law for the rest of the week.

The typical rhythms of Pearl's camp life are interrupted by the arrival of the "Blouse Man" (Viggo Mortensen), an itinerant salesman who travels from resort to resort in a converted bus, hawking his wares at cheap prices to eager customers. The Blouse Man, whose real name is Walker Jerome, is affable and sexy. And, when it comes to inhibitions, he's the opposite of Pearl. She's a captive in her marriage — wedded at 17 because she was pregnant, she has seen every dream die over the years. It isn't that she doesn't love her husband, but that she yearns to see where her life might have gone had things worked out differently. When it becomes obvious that Walker is attracted to her, and she to him, she embarks on a reckless affair with him as a means of breaking free from the constraints of her ordered life. They make love in his bus, share a blissful day in the wilderness, and attend Woodstock together. However, when Pearl's mother-in-law senses what's happening, she warns her son that his marriage is in trouble.

It's easy to make a bad movie about a woman finding herself by cheating on her husband, but difficult to fashion one that hits most of the right notes. With a strong assist from Lane and Schreiber, Goldwyn has taken the nostalgia of 1969 and used it to good effect as background for a story that never loses sight of the characters. **RECOMMENDED**

Walking and Talking [1996]

Starring: Catherine Keener, Anne Heche, Liev Schreiber, Todd Field, Kevin Corrigan Director: Nicole Holofcener Screenplay: Nicole Holofcener Running Time: 1:30 Rated: R (Sex, profanity, mature themes) Theatrical Aspect Ratio: 1.85:1

Walking and Talking deftly portrays the dynamic of the relationship between a perpetually single young woman and her soon-to-be-wed soul-sister. By turns, it's funny, charming, and even a little touching. Director Nicole Holofcener has an ear for dialogue, and, as is often the case with the best character-centered

films, a chief pleasure is simply enjoying what the participants have to say to one another. The two leading ladies represent another asset. Anne Heche and Catherine Keener are effective in both comic and dramatic scenes. Each has mastered the knack of giving a completely unforced performance. Once they step into character, they never slip out.

Walking and Talking successfully navigates a minefield of familiar territory. The storyline, which is essentially a slice-of-life, doesn't attempt anything big, but it offers a number of small surprises. Just when you think you know how one romantic entanglement is going to turn out, Holofcener throws in a little twist. That's not to say that the plot is masterful (in fact, it's rather simple), but there's enough there to hold the viewer's interest.

While *Walking and Talking* is pretty light fare, it's not without substance, too. Both Amelia and Laura are confused about the future, albeit in different ways. They're afraid of change, even though they recognize it's inevitable, and each suffers from the typical Generation X lack of self-esteem. Amelia sits alone in her room, stroking her cancer-riddled cat and listening to "music to slit your wrists by," and Laura bemoans her career choice, saying that she's not a good therapist because she makes her patients worse. Even though these two don't need each other the way they once did, their mutual importance is still apparent.

Walking and Talking ends by giving us closure without wrapping everything up in a neat package. Because the main characters are both women, the writer/director is a woman, and the themes relate to female bonding, this will inevitably be pegged as a "chick flick." That's an unfortunate appellation, because *Walking and Talking* has universal appeal. Many of the issues it approaches have less to do with gender than with the simple condition of living in the '90s. **RECOMMENDED**

The War Zone [United Kingdom, 1999]

Starring: Ray Winstone, Tilda Swinton, Lara Belmont, Freddie Cunliffe Director: Tim Roth Screenplay: Alexander Stuart, based on his novel Running Time: 1:38 Rated: No MPAA Rating (Sex, nudity, graphic rape, profanity, mature themes) Theatrical Aspect Ratio: 2.35:1

Despite the title, this stunningly accomplished feature debut from Tim Roth has nothing to do with traditional battlefields, yet it is every bit as harrowing as the first 30 minutes of *Saving Private Ryan* or the whole of *Schindler's List*. The destruction presented in this film is as graphic and shocking as anything depicted in the most unsparing war movie, except that the victims are not soldiers trained for combat, but children placed in harm's way.

The film takes place in the rural Devon countryside, where a family of 4 has just moved from London. Events are related from the perspective of 15-year old Tom (Freddie Cunliffe), who is unhappy with life away from the city. His 18-year-old sister, Jessie (Lara Belmont), has apparently adjusted better than he has. His parents (Ray Winstone, Tilda Swinton) seem happy and comfortable in their new home, and his mother is on the verge of delivering her third child. Then, shortly after the baby is born, Tom's world is turned upside down when he spies a covert sexual encounter between Jessie and his father. Tom confronts Jessie about the incident, but she denies it, accusing him of having an overactive imagination. He is not convinced, however, and sets out to learn the facts. The truth he must face, and its ramifications upon every member of the family, form *The War Zone*'s core drama.

In his handling of the material, Roth shows more ability than many accomplished, veteran filmmakers. He paints Devon as a grim, rainy place where darkness and grayness are always enroaching upon the light. There is much ambiguity to be found here. While one key rape is graphically depicted, the depth of the father's depravity and the question of how much the mother knows are left up to the individual to determine. Roth freely admits that, with *The War Zone*, he has pushed the envelope as far as it can go — had he attempted more, the movie would have become too painful for anyone to watch. There is no comic relief and no happy ending (although there is a catharsis of sorts).

The War Zone is a devastating motion picture; it's the kind of movie that stuns an audience so absolutely that they remain paralyzed in their seats through the end credits. It does not deal in euphemisms nor does it hide the physical and emotional brutality of the act from viewers. In my lifetime, I have seen thousands of films, but none has been as unflinching in its approach to this issue as *The War Zone*. For his courage and ability, Tim Roth deserves praise and recognition. **MUST SEE**

Washington Square [1997]

Starring: Jennifer Jason Leigh, Albert Finney, Ben Chaplin, Maggie Smith Director: Agnieszka Holland Screenplay: Carol Doyle based on the novel by Henry James Running Time: 1:55 Rated: PG (Mature themes, mild profanity) Theatrical Aspect Ratio: 1.85:1

While most films are content to explore the lighter, romantic side of love, *Washington Square* takes a cold, hard look at the painful, destructive aspect of the same emotion.

Washington Square is actually the second film to be made from the James novel of the same name. The first, 1949's *The Heiress* (directed by William Wyler and starring Olivia De Havilland), was based on a stage play version of the book that eliminated many of the more subtle aspects of James' text. For this interpretation of *Washington Square*, director Agnieszka Holland and screenwriter Carol Doyle have returned to James' original story and created a quiet, thoughtful examination of the author's favorite theme: the difficulty of balancing love and money, and the pernicious influence of the latter upon the former.

As *Washington Square* opens, we are greeted with a tragic scene: a young woman lying dead in the aftermath of childbirth. Her husband, Austin Sloper (Albert Finney), barely looks at his newborn daughter, Catherine, as she is presented to him. Flashforward several years. Catherine, an awkward adolescent, is shown trying to please her father on his birthday. But, despite her best efforts, everything goes wrong, and she is forced to flee from his party in embarrassment. When we next meet Catherine (now played by Jennifer Jason Leigh), she is an adult, but is still slavishly trying to win her father's adoration. However, in his characteristically brusque manner, he finds fault with nearly everything she does.

The domestic tranquillity of the Sloper household changes dramatically on the day that Catherine meets Morris Townsend (Ben Chaplin), an adventurer and wanderer who has just returned to America from abroad. Catherine falls in love with him, and, although he apparently returns her feelings, Austin is suspicious of his motives. Morris is penniless and Catherine is wealthy, and all Austin sees in the young man is a fortune hunter. He refuses to sanction a marriage and indicates that if Catherine defies him, he will disown her.

Washington Square deftly draws us into the world of the characters and challenges us to understand them and question their views and motivations. The film is emotionally effective without going overboard. Director Agnieszka Holland (whose previous efforts include *Europa Europa* and *Olivier Olivier*) opts to avoid the temptation of reducing *Washington Square* to the level of a costume melodrama. Her careful, modulated handling of the material makes this resemble Merchant-Ivory's better work (like *The Remains of the Day*). *Washington Square* is faithful representation of James' text, and a moving and satisfying portrait of one woman's struggle for independence in a society where everything is defined by love, money, or both. **RECOMMENDED**

Welcome to the Dollhouse [1996]

Starring: Heather Matarazzo, Victoria Davis, Christina Brucato, Christina Vidal Director: Todd Solondz Screenplay: Todd Solondz Running Time: 1:27 Rated: R (Profanity, mature themes) Theatrical Aspect Ratio: 1.85:1

Welcome to the Dollhouse, which won the Grand Jury Prize at the 1996 Sundance Film Festival, is Todd Solondz' counterattack against the *Wonder Years* nostalgia that clouds movie memories of adolescence. After all, junior high school isn't the endless series of halcyon days that television and films would have us believe. Especially for those who aren't members of the "in" crowd, the pre-teen and early teen years can be an extremely painful time. In this impressive debut, Solondz doesn't pull any punches in conveying the side of junior high that *The Wonder Years* never depicted: the naked cruelty that some boys and girls suffer at the hands of their classmates, their teachers, and even members of their own family.

This is the story of Dawn Weiner (Heather Matarazzo), or "Dogface Weiner," as just about everyone at school calls her. Bespectacled and not blessed by perfect features or a good complexion, Dawn is not a popular girl. A loner by nature, she has only one friend — a sickly elementary school boy who is as much an object of derision as she is. At school, she is pelted by spitballs and epithets. When she asks a classmate "Why do you hate me?," the response is simple and succinct: "Because you're ugly." The teachers at Benjamin Franklin Junior High seem to go out of their way to humiliate Dawn, accusing her of grade-grubbing and forcing her to write essays about the meaning of dignity. At home, as the middle child, she is the most frequently neglected. Her older brother is a nerdy computer whiz and her younger sister is her parents' favorite. The only time Mom and Dad take notice of Dawn is when she does something wrong.

Despite its grim subject matter, *Welcome to the Dollhouse* isn't a complete downer. Dawn is resigned to her fate, and, though her dearest wish is to be popular, she's able to accept her lot. Solondz has injected a fair amount of natural humor into his script. Some of the audience's laughter will be in response to uneasy situations, but there are a few genuinely funny situations, such as when Dawn avenges herself against her fairy princess sister (who often appears on screen to the strains of "The Nutcracker") by taking a saw to a doll's neck.

Welcome to the Dollhouse is sort of like *Angus*, but without the false Hollywood sheen and forced happy ending. Solondz's perceptiveness is acute, and, at one time or another, it will make most viewers feel uncomfortable. It's not a perfect motion picture, but, as far as taking a cold look at an over-romanticized period of childhood, it's uncompromising. *Welcome to the Dollhouse* won't make you wistful for your lost junior high years; it will make you glad you grew up. **RECOMMENDED**

Whale Rider [New Zealand/Germany, 2003]

Starring: Keisha Castle-Hughes, Rawiri Paratene, Vicky Haughton, Cliff Curtis, Grant Roa, Mana Taumaunu, Rachel House Director: Niki Caro Screenplay: Niki Caro, based on the novel by Witi Ihimaera Running Time: 1:45 Rated: PG-13 (Mature themes, profanity) Theatrical Aspect Ratio: 2.35:1

The theme of *Whale Rider* — that of female empowerment — is not unique, but the context in which it is presented is. Like many tribal societies, the Maoris are patriarchal, and the concept of a female ruler, if not unthinkable, goes against tradition. *Whale Rider*, based on the novel by Maori author Witi Ihimaera, postulates what might happen if, in seeming contravention of religious custom, a girl appears to have been endowed with the mystical abilities of chieftain.

The Whangara people live in a village on the eastern coast of New Zealand — a place they have inhabited for more than a millennium. Legend says that their demigod ancestor, Paikea, arrived in New Zealand on the back of a whale. Since then, the firstborn son has always been the Whangara chieftain — until now. Pai is the lone survivor of a difficult birth that claims the lives of her mother and her twin brother. Her grief-stricken father, Porourangi (Cliff Curtis), flees the island for Europe, leaving his little daughter in the care of his father and mother, Koro (Rawiri Paratene) and Nanny Flowers (Vicky Haughton). Koro is bitterly disappointed since it appears that the bloodline of centuries has ended with his immediate family. He cannot bring himself to consider that Pai, the firstborn in Paikea's bloodline, might be the rightful chieftain — because she is not a male.

The majority of the story takes place when Pai (Keisha Castle-Hughes) is about 11 years old. She spends most of the film trying to prove herself to her grandfather, who stubbornly refuses to consider her as anything more than a disappointment. He begins to teach all the firstborn males in the village in the "old ways," hoping that one of them will show the courage, strength, and fortitude to take over the Whangaras' leadership. Ultimately, however, it is the whales — those animals that bore Paikea to New Zealand — who indirectly reveal the truth.

The story itself is richly rewarding and uplifting — the coming-of-age tale of a girl who must defy the odds to achieve her goals. There's plenty of humor to keep the overall tone light, although there are moments of deeper, heartfelt pathos. The characters and relationships are three-dimensional. The most rewarding of these is that of Pai and her grandfather. There is affection there, but, on Koro's side, a self-imposed distance. Especially early in the film, we see that he genuinely cares for his granddaughter, but his disappointment about her gender colors his actions and perspective. For her part, all she wants to do is earn his respect — a point that is heartbreakingly illustrated when she gives a speech dedicated to him. **RECOMMENDED**

What Dreams May Come [1998]

Starring: Robin Williams, Annabella Sciorra, Cuba Gooding Jr., Max von Sydow Director: Vincent Ward Screenplay: Ron Bass based on the novel by Richard Matheson Running Time: 1:48 Rated: PG-13 (Mature themes, images of hell, mild profanity) Theatrical Aspect Ratio: 2.35:1

If I wanted to be cynical about this film, I could say that the moral is not to get out of the car and help at the scene of an accident. That's what gets Chris Nielsen (Robin Williams) killed. Of course, I'm not giving anything away here, since this happens at the beginning of the movie, after a short prologue that offers glimpses of Chris' marriage to his wife, Annie (Annabella Sciorra). In more than a decade of bliss, there was only one dark period. Four years ago, Chris and Annie's two children, Marie (Jessica Brooks) and Ian (Josh Paddock), died in a car crash and now, tragically, Chris has joined them. One moment, he's trying to help someone trapped in a wreck; the next, he's making his way into the light.

As it turns out, the afterlife isn't what Chris expected. To begin with, he has a guide — an old mentor named Albert (Cuba Gooding Jr.). He spends some time wandering around on Earth — looking in at his funeral, checking on his grief-stricken wife, and generally seeing how the world is progressing without him. Eventually, when he realizes that his continued ghostly presence is causing Annie pain, he quits this realm and heads into heaven, a place of colors, light, and beauty. But Chris is not content. Even the realization that he can again meet with his children is not enough. Then an event occurs that threatens to sever his connection with Annie forever.

What Dreams May Come has the sensibilities of an art film placed into a big-budget feature with an A-list cast. A tear-jerker, its offbeat storyline, which has Chris relishing the serenity of heaven before taking a trip through hell, is compelling, even if the ending is a little too cute. Part of the reason the movie works is that the characters are likable. Most of us would love to have the kind of relationship that Chris and Annie enjoyed, so it's not hard to root for them to somehow find each other again, even with the chasm of death dividing them.

Many movies have offered representations of heaven and hell, but few with as much conviction and creativity as *What Dreams May Come*. The plot, which focuses on the sacrifices one man will make for true love, is neither complicated nor original, but, bolstered by the director's incredible visual sense, it becomes an affecting piece of drama. While not as sickly sweet as *Ghost*, *What Dreams May Come* shares an important trait with the Demi Moore/Patrick Swayze melodrama — namely, that love does not end with death. Those who embrace this belief and don't mind a somewhat artistic approach are likely to enjoy Vincent Ward's movie. **RECOMMENDED**

When a Man Loves a Woman [1994]

Starring: Meg Ryan, Andy Garcia, Tina Marjorino, Mae Whitman, Ellen Burstyn Director: Luis Mandoki Screenplay: Ronald Bass and Al Franken Running Time: 2:06 Rated: R (Profanity, mature themes) Theatrical Aspect Ratio: 1.85:1

Luis Mandoki's *When Man Loves a Woman* film succeeds not because it tackles alcoholism, but because it faces up to the trauma that eats away at the lives of the non-alcoholics in the family.

When a Man Loves a Woman centers on a seemingly-happily married couple. Michael Green (Andy Garcia) and his wife Alice (Meg Ryan) have, at first glance, the perfect relationship. But take a peek beneath the veneer, and there are problems. Alice is a habitual drinker, and her periods of sobriety are getting fewer and fewer. Meanwhile, Michael's duties as an airline pilot take him away from home for weeks at a time, keeping him ignorant of the extent of his wife's problem

Completing the family unit are Jess (Tina Marjorino), Alice's daughter by another man whom

Michael has adopted as his own, and Casey (Mae Whitman), the 4-year-old child of the Greens. The presence of these children, and their importance to the development of the story, is what elevates *When a Man Loves a Woman*. As potent as some of the scenes between Michael and Alice are, those featuring Jess or Casey invariably have greater impact. It helps that both young actresses are believable.

One failing of the script is that it assumes an unlikely level of ignorance from its audience. Alcoholism is such a pervasive social problem that it's hard to accept that anyone likely to see *When a Man Loves a Woman* wouldn't have a better understanding of the disease than the movie gives them credit for. After all, everything from high school health classes to *Oprah* have, at one point or another, addressed the issue. Unlike AIDS, alcoholism is not a new disease that the public needs to be educated about.

The ending is too facile, and *When a Man Loves a Woman* may take longer than necessary to arrive at its resolution. There are moments throughout when the script is apt to strike a raw nerve with some, as is often the case when a "real" issue is probed with any degree of sincerity. Whatever else it may do, this film does not play it safe, and the risks it takes keep the audience engaged by the drama.

When a Man Loves a Woman is about pain. This is not an original topic for a movie — especially one about alcoholism — but the script does a good enough job establishing the dynamics of the Green family that we never doubt that the story deserves to be told. The film's poignancy is its strength, even as occasional didactic tendencies are its weakness. In balance, the former by far outweighs the latter, making this a worthwhile picture. **RECOMMENDED**

Where the Heart Is [2000]

Starring: Natalie Portman, Ashley Judd, Stockard Channing, Joan Cusack, James Frain Director: Matt Williams Screenplay: Lowell Ganz & Babaloo Mandel, based on the novel by Billie Letts Running Time: 1:58 Rated: PG-13 (Profanity, mature themes, violence, sexual situations) Theatrical Aspect Ratio: 1.85:1

Natalie Portman isn't just the foundation upon which *Where the Heart Is* is built; she's the glue that holds it together. Portman plays Novalee Nation, a frightened, 7-month pregnant teenager on the road from Tennessee to California with her self-centered boyfriend, Willy Jack Pickens. When the couple stops at a Wal-Mart in Oklahoma so that Novalee can take a bathroom break, Willy Jack sees his chance to get away, so he abandons her with nothing more than a Polaroid

camera and $5.55 in change. Novalee, homeless and alone, begins to establish a life in the community of Sequoyah, befriending the open-hearted Sister Husband and spending time at the library, where she captures the attention of the librarian, Forney. From dusk till dawn, she hides out in Wal-Mart, carefully recording every dollar and cent that she owes the company for food, clothing, and bed materials. Then, one rainy night, she goes into labor, and, with the help of Forney (who arrives on the scene after following her), she gives birth to a healthy baby girl. When she wakes up, she's in the hospital, being cared for by a perky nurse, Lexie, who tells her that she's an instant celebrity: the mother of "the Wal-Mart baby."

Where the Heart Is is as obvious a "chick flick" as they come. All of the typical elements are in place: the strong-willed heroine dealt a bad hand by life, the abusive and selfish men, and the supportive women. However, by subduing the melodrama to a tolerable level, the filmmakers have crafted a motion picture that should appeal to members of both sexes.

Where the Heart Is is the story of someone who overcomes life's hardships despite overwhelming odds. She does not become famous, wealthy, or successful, but attains family and love — two things which were robbed from her as a child and which she has craved ever since. We spend 5 years in Novalee's company, but the time goes by quickly. *Where the Heart Is* is not perfect, but it works in almost every way that a character-based drama is supposed to. It is a simple pleasure. **RECOMMENDED**

Three Colors: White [France/Switzerland/Poland, 1994]

Starring: Zbigniew Zamachowski, Julie Delpy, Janusz Gajos, Jerzy Stuhr Director: Krzysztof Kieslowski Screenplay: Krzysztof Kieslowski and Krzysztof Piesiewicz Running Time: 1:32 Rated: R (Sexual situations, mature themes, violence) Theatrical Aspect Ratio: 1.85:1 In French and Polish with subtitles

White, the second chapter of Krzysztof Kieslowski's *Three Colors* trilogy, is different from *Blue* in more ways than the color it centers on and the ideals represented. Instead of the dark, somber tone adopted *Blue*, this film aims for something lighter. Additionally, while *White* possesses a sardonic quality never sought after by its predecessor, the emotional tapestry of this picture is not the other's equal.

Although *White* is self-contained, there is an intersection with *Blue*. In the previous film, the stars of this one, Julie Delpy and Zbigniew Zamachowski, make brief appearances; likewise, Juliette Binoche sticks her head through a courtroom door near the beginning of *White* (blink and you may miss her). Delpy, Zamachowski, and Binoche all turn up at the conclusion of *Red*, along with the featured performers of that movie, Jean-Louis Trintignant and Irene Jacob.

White begins in a Parisian courtroom with the arrival of a lonely, dejected Karol Karol (Zamachowski), clutching a summons and looking downtrodden. Shortly thereafter, his marriage has been dissolved by the court because of his inability to consummate the union, and his beautiful young wife Dominique (Delpy) has claimed that she no longer loves him. Karol is devastated, and decides to quit Paris for his native Poland.

To make matters worse, he has no passport and no money to obtain one, and after Dominique sets fire to a beauty shop that he and she owned together, the police want him for arson. Fate, however, is not entirely working against Karol, and he finds a friend in his fellow countryman Mikolaj (Janusz Gajos), who helps him back to Warsaw, where he begins rebuilding his life and planning revenge against the woman he still loves.

White focuses mainly on Karol's life, and that's one of its possible flaws. While we are presented with a well-rounded picture of the Polish hairdresser, we see so little of his wife that the eventual resolution falls a little flat. The few glimpses we are afforded of Dominique reveal an intensely interesting character who is quite simply never given enough screen time.

Kieslowski understands human nature, and his ability to breathe life into that understanding through these characters is what sets his films apart from those of many others. As *Blue* did for liberty, so *White* does for equality, giving a face to an abstract concept. **RECOMMENDED**

The White Balloon [Iran, 1995]

Starring: Aida Mohammadkhani, Moshen Kalifi, Fereshteh Sadr Orfani, Anna Bourkowska Director: Jafar Panahi Screenplay: Abbas Kiarostami Running Time: 1:25 Rated: No MPAA Rating (nothing offensive) Theatrical Aspect Ratio: 1.85:1 In Farsi with subtitles

The White Balloon, written by Abbas Kiarostami and directed by one of his protégés, Jafar Panahi, has the characteristic slow, stately tone that dominates Iranian efforts, but, at least in terms of its minimalist narrative, it's reminiscent of Vittorio De Sica's Italian classic, *The Bicycle Thief*.

The White Balloon is told in real time through the eyes of its 7-year-old, female protagonist, the feisty Razieh (Aida Mohammadkhani). Our impressions of other characters are filtered through Razieh, so we see them as she does, whether they're strange, frightening, indifferent, or helpful. All the facets of humanity are represented, from a generous-but-ineffectual old woman to a sinister soldier who tells lies to gain the young girl's confidence.

It's New Year's Day in Tehran, and, in 90 minutes, all the shops will close for a week-long holiday. Before that happens, Razieh desperately wants to buy a plump, white goldfish with elaborate fins. She has her heart set on this prize and refuses to give up even when her mother says "no." So, with the help of her brother (Moshen Kalifi), she eventually wears down all resistance, and, armed with her mother's last 500 tomans bill, heads into the marketplace on her own. Between home and the fish store, however, she loses the money down a street grate, where the metal bars keep it within sight, but out of reach.

In addition to its account of a girl's first venture into the adult world on her own, *The White Balloon* gives Western viewers a rare glimpse into the real Iran. Here, freed of political shading, we meet the genuine inhabitants of Tehran, and, unsurprisingly, find that they're not all that different from us. *The White Balloon* certainly isn't everyone's kind of film, but those with the patience to sit through all 85 minutes will uncover a sublime, unconventionally engrossing story. **RECOMMENDED**

The Whole Wide World [1996]

Starring: Vincent D'Onofrio, Renee Zellweger Director: Dan Ireland Screenplay: Michael Scott Myers based on the novel *One Who Walked Alone* by Novalyne Price Ellis Running Time: 1:45 Rated: PG (Mild profanity, mature themes) Theatrical Aspect Ratio: 2.35:1

During the course of his short, stormy life, Depression era writer Robert E. Howard created more than two dozen pulp heroes, and wrote hundreds of short stories. His best-known creation, Conan the Barbarian, became so popular during the 1970s and '80s that he spawned comic books, more than fifty original novels (far outstripping Howard's original output), and two motion pictures (*Conan the Barbarian* and *Conan the Destroyer*, both starring Arnold Schwarzenegger). It's said that the best way to know an author is to read his writing, and, as Dan Ireland's *The Whole Wide World* shows, Howard was a man who gave his all to his work.

During Conan's resurgence in the 1970s, a lot of things — many of them profoundly uncomplimentary — were written and said about the author, who had died some 40 years earlier from a self-inflicted gunshot wound. Novalyne Price Ellis, a woman who had enjoyed a special relationship with Howard, decided to set the record straight by revealing "the real Bob Howard." The result was *One Who Walked Alone,* which was published in 1985. This memoir became the basis of *The Whole Wide World.*

The film opens during 1933 in Brownwood, Texas, with the meeting of Novalyne (Renee Zellweger), a would-be author, and Robert (Vincent D'Onofrio). The two hit it off almost immediately, despite the difference in their life-views. Over the course of the next three years, their relationship ebbs and flows, with Novalyne falling for Robert in a way that is never reciprocated. It's clear that he cares for her, but he is emotionally unable to commit to a relationship.

There's nothing earthshaking about *The Whole Wide World,* a film that is, by the director's own admission, very small. Nevertheless, it successfully accomplishes what it sets out to do, and the result is affecting and involving. So, while it may be true that the best way to get into the mind of Robert E. Howard is to read his stories, seeing *The Whole Wide World* will give you an appreciation of a side of him that was never revealed in any Conan yarn. **HIGHLY RECOMMENDED**

Why Do Fools Fall in Love [1998]

Starring: Halle Berry, Vivica A. Fox, Lela Rochon, Larenz Tate, Paul Mazursky Director: Gregory Nava Screenplay: Tina Andrews Running Time: 1:55 Rated: R (Profanity, drug use, sex, violence) Theatrical Aspect Ratio: 1.85:1

It was in the mid-'50s when, at the tender age of 13, Frankie Lymon burst onto the pop music scene with the Top 10 hit, "Why Do Fools Fall in Love?" Frankie and the Teenagers, as the group was called, became an instant success story. Soon, prodded by an unscrupulous manager, Frankie went solo, and his fall from grace was as spectacular as his meteoric rise. By the age of 20, he was a washed-up has-been whose only gigs were nostalgia shows. Seven years later, he was dead of a drug overdose. But, even in death, Frankie Lymon's story continued. In 1981, Diana Ross' cover of "Why Do Fools Fall in Love?" became a financial success, and this led to an unusual court case over music rights. During his lifetime, Frankie had married 3 women, but he never divorced any of them. Now, they all wanted a piece of his legacy and the decision was left up to a court of law as to who was legally entitled to be called Mrs. Frankie Lymon.

These are the essential facts behind Gregory Nava's spotty-but-entertaining biopicture of the '50s singing star. Actually, while Frankie (played by Larenz Tate)

has more screen time than any other character, *Why Do Fools Fall in Love* is more about his wives, and the hardships they endured while with him, than about him. By the end of the film, we have a clearer picture of Zola Taylor (Halle Berry), Elizabeth Waters (Vivica A. Fox), and Emira Eagle (Lela Rochon) than we do of the self-destructive singer. Frankie may be at the center of the movie, but his wives represent its heart, soul, and funny bone.

Why Do Fools Fall in Love has a nearly 2-hour running length, but the manner in which Nava has structured it, with frequent leaps backward and forward through several decades, keeps the viewer involved for the entire time. The focus on the women and the different points-of-view used to piece together the story give *Why Do Fools Fall in Love* an edge. Despite employing the familiar motion picture elements of sex, greed, and music, this is not a run-of-the-mill biopic. **RECOMMENDED**

The Widow of St. Pierre [France, 2000]

Starring: Juliette Binoche, Daniel Auteuil, Emir Kusturica Director: Patrice Leconte Screenplay: Claude Faraldo Running Time: 1:52 Rated: R (Violence, sex, mature themes) Theatrical Aspect Ratio: 2.35:1 In French with subtitles

The Widow of St. Pierre is a costume drama with a distinct anti-death penalty flavor. Thankfully, its intent is not to preach but to demonstrate by example. *The Widow of Saint-Pierre* asks two complex questions: what does it take to redeem a murderer and which path should an individual choose when morality conflicts with the law?

To play out this tale, which transpires during the 1850s in the French territory of Saint-Pierre, an island off the coast of Newfoundland, Leconte has brought together two of his country's best-known actors. Juliette Binoche plays Madame La and Daniel Auteuil is her husband, the captain in charge of the French military stationed on the island. The third player in the drama is Neel Auguste (Yugoslavian director Emir Kusturica in his acting debut), a convicted killer. The court sentences Neel to death for his act, but there's a problem. French law demands execution by guillotine, and there isn't one on the island, nor is there an executioner. So, while the islanders of Saint-Pierre await the arrival of the instrument from Martinique (a several month delay), Neel is allowed a degree of freedom by the Captain and Madame La. A series of good deeds on his part make him a beloved member of the community, and, when the guillotine eventually arrives, no one is willing to wield it. Meanwhile, the Captain, having decided that it would be unjust to execute Neel given his reformed character, informs the local government that his troops will not aid in the beheading — a stance that places him in a dangerous, possibly treasonous position.

Leconte's point is that not all criminals are beyond rehabilitation and redemption. Neel commits a brutal, senseless crime, but his actions afterward prove that his transformation is one of the heart and soul. In truth, he believes that he deserves his sentence, and is unwilling to put others at risk to flee from it. *The Widow of Saint-Pierre* points out one of the key flaws inherent in the death penalty — the possibility that a man's nature can be re-shaped.

If there's a flaw in the film, it's Leconte's cool, detached perspective of the characters, which dissuades emotional involvement. It's as if the starkness of the film's setting has seeped into the heart of the production. Leconte's film will not be remembered alongside his masterworks, but it is nevertheless a worthy effort. RECOMMENDED

The Wings of the Dove [United Kingdom, 1997]
Starring: Helena Bonham Carter, Linus Roache, Alison Elliott, Charlotte Rampling Director: Iain Softley Screenplay: Hossein Amini Running Time: 1:48 Rated: R (Sexual situations, mature themes) Theatrical Aspect Ratio: 2.35:1

When adapting classic novels (such as *The Wings of the Dove*) into movies, there are generally two approaches that film makers consider. The first is a straightforward, literal translation that leaves the characters, narrative, and dialogue intact. The second is to opt for a more "free" adaptation that allows condensation, change, and, in some cases, "modernization." Sometimes it works (*Sense and Sensibility*), sometimes it doesn't (*Anna Karenina*). At any rate, the latter method is the one chosen by director Iain Softley and screenwriter Hossein Amini for *The Wings of the Dove*. While leaving the general storyline and basic themes of the novel intact, these 2 men elected to alter certain key aspects of James' book to make it more cinematic and to give it greater appeal for a contemporary audience.

As might be expected, the basic plot of the movie and the book is the same (although the time line has been shifted by 10 years to 1910 in the film). *The Wings of the Dove* opens with Kate Croy (Helena Bonham Carter) going to live with a wealthy, cultured aunt (Charlotte Rampling) shortly after the death of

her mother. Kate's aunt has every intention of setting up her niece in a comfortable, socially-acceptable marriage. But Kate, who has fallen in love with Merton Densher (Linus Roache), a poor journalist far below her social station, has other ideas. But when her aunt threatens to disinherit her if she doesn't break off the illicit relationship, Kate is faced with a moral dilemma. Her singular solution proves to be damaging to all involved.

Kate befriends a wealthy young American, Milly Theale, who has come to Europe for health reasons. Milly is seriously ill, and her state of health suggests a plan to Kate, who contrives for Milly to meet Merton. Soon, Milly is hopelessly in the thrall of the handsome journalist, and, with Kate's aid, Milly makes a play for him while all 3 are on a holiday in Venice. It is only then that Merton divines the nature of Kate's plot: that he should marry Milly for her money, then, upon her death when he would be rich, he could marry Kate.

Much as he did with his adaptation of Thomas Hardy's *Jude the Obscure*, screenwriter Amini focuses on the emotional aspects of the story, detailing how the consequences of each of the characters' actions tears at their psyches. Like *Jude*, *The Wings of the Dove* is not a happy tale, but it is a vivid and unforgettable one, featuring multi-dimensional characters, beautiful cinematography, impressive set design, and accomplished acting. *The Wings of the Dove* is an impressive motion picture adaptation of a classic novel. HIGHLY RECOMMENDED

The Winslow Boy [1999]
Starring: Nigel Hawthorne, Rebecca Pidgeon, Jeremy Northam, Gemma Jones Director: David Mamet Screenplay: David Mamet, based on the play by Terence Rattigan Running Time: 1:44 Rated: G Theatrical Aspect Ratio: 1.85:1

The Winslow Boy is set in the Edwardian era of pre-World War I England. It seems better suited to the style of Merchant-Ivory than to that of the man who is best-known for writing the 4-letter word tirades of *Glengarry Glen Ross* and *American Buffalo*. Yet the job David Mamet has done here should silence his critics. *The Winslow Boy* remains true to playwright Terence Rattigan's source material; at the same time, it retains an element of Mamet's singular style as a filmmaker — the characters frequently speak in clipped, staccato sentences.

Loosely based on a true event, *The Winslow Boy* tells the story of 14-year-old Ronnie Winslow (Guy

Edwards), a young cadet who was expelled from Britain's Osbourne Naval College in 1908, and his family's arduous struggle to exonerate him of theft and fraud charges. After being found guilty of forging another student's signature in order to steal a 5-shilling postal order, Ronnie is thrown out of the college and dejectedly returns home. His mother, Grace (Gemma Jones); older sister, Catherine (Rebecca Pidgeon); and brother, Dickie (Matthew Pidgeon) all express sympathy and support. His father, Arthur (Nigel Hawthorne), asks one question of his son: Did you steal this postal order? When Ronnie looks his father in the eyes are responds, "No," that's good enough for Arthur to begin a campaign to prove his son's innocence. Arthur's long battle drains his financial resources, saps his strength, and causes everyone in his family to sacrifice. Grace must give up her comfortable lifestyle. Dickie must leave Oxford and go to work. And Catherine loses her fiancé and is forced to contemplate a loveless marriage. Even Sir Robert Morton (Jeremy Northam), the famous lawyer hired by the Winslows to argue their case, turns down a prestigious honor to continue the fight.

The Winslow Boy asks two pointed questions. The first penetrates to the heart of human altruism by examining the point at which the quest for justice turns into an exercise in pride and self-interest. How much of Arthur's fight is really to remove the blight from his son's record and how much is because of his own stubbornness and intransigence? It's clear that Ronnie really doesn't care about the results and everyone else in the family is being hurt, yet Arthur doggedly pushes onward. The second question reiterates a common theme in legal dramas: how does what's right differ from what justice demands?

Despite a few failings, *The Winslow Boy* is a solidly engaging movie. What it lacks in emotional involvement, it makes up for in intelligence and, at times, wit. It's to Mamet's credit that he keeps the tone low-key; in another director's hands, the finale might have turned into the overblown melodrama of a *Scent of a Woman*. RECOMMENDED

The Winter Guest [United States/United Kingdom, 1997]

Starring: Phylida Law, Emma Thompson, Gary Hollywood, Arlene Cockburn, Sheila Reid Director: Alan Rickman Screenplay: Sharman Macdonald and Alan Rickman Running Time: 1:50 Rated: R (Profanity, mature themes, brief nudity) Theatrical Aspect Ratio: 1.85:1

The Winter Guest does not tell a traditional tale, nor does it ascribe to a conventional narrative structure — there is no real beginning or end. Instead, we are given an opportunity to observe one day in the lives of eight humans. They represent both sexes, multiple generations, and a variety of relationships — male and female; young, middle-aged, and elderly; friends, would-be lovers, and kin. We see expectations fulfilled and disappointed, emotional boundaries eroded, and truths unveiled.

The setting is a small town in Scotland on the coldest day of the year. It's so frigid that the sea has begun to freeze over. The onshore wind cuts like a knife and snow blankets the beach, giving the terrain an alien appearance. It is against this backdrop that the relationships of the film are captured. There are four pairings, and, although there is some interaction between the different twosomes, *The Winter Guest*'s focus is on the dynamics internal to each relationship.

The first, meatiest pairing is that of Elspeth (Phylida Law) and her recently-widowed daughter, Frances (Emma Thompson). These two have a stormy relationship. They love each other deeply, but both are stubborn and willful, and neither is willing to admit that they need the other. Much of their interaction is argumentative, but, during the course of a long walk to the frozen shoreline, they come to an unspoken understanding of how much each means to the other.

Frances' adult son, Alex (Gary Hollywood), is a lonely young man who has been caring for his mother since the death of his father. On this day, he meets a girl, Nita (Arlene Cockburn), who has secretly been spying on him for weeks. Although their first encounter is antagonistic, both quickly become aware of an undeniable attraction. Once they retire to a place where they can be alone, however, things don't go exactly as planned.

Lily (Sheila Reid) and Chloe (Sandra Voe) are a couple of old friends who are frequent funeral attendees. Death is a topic of endless fascination for them, perhaps because they are so close to it, and they spend their spare time scanning the obituaries, looking for the next funeral or cremation in the area. It doesn't matter whether or not they knew the deceased. It's the ceremony that they're interested in.

Sam (Douglas Murphy) and Tom (Sean Biggerstaff), a pair of schoolboy chums, are spending this cold February day cutting classes and hanging out at the beach, horsing around, building a small fire for warmth, and walking on the frozen water. Unlike Lily and Chloe, these two have their entire lives ahead of them. They are young enough to still believe in magic, but old enough to recognize that the process of crossing into adulthood robs life of the simple joy that only children can experience.

If you appreciate character studies, *The Winter Guest* is a solid effort with staying power. **RECOMMENDED**

Without Limits [1998]

Starring: Billy Crudup, Donald Sutherland, Monica Potter, Jeremy Sisto Director: Robert Towne Screenplay: Robert Towne, Kenny Moore Running Time: 1:57 Rated: PG-13 (Profanity, sexual situations) Theatrical Aspect Ratio: 235:1

During the late '60s and early '70s, Steve Prefontaine singlehandedly revitalized the sport of track, transforming it from a second-tier college activity to a major national interest. Prefontaine became something of a hero, the James Dean of running. His competitive spirit was so fierce that he could not accept being anything worst than first, and he refused to pace himself to allow a victory with anything less than a full effort. At one point, when asked how he could win against men who arguably possessed more pure talent, Prefontaine's response was, "I can endure more pain than anyone you've ever met." For him, each race was a work of art, which made his poor placing in the 1972 Olympic Games galling.

Munich was the culmination of Prefontaine's amateur track career. After setting countless American and collegiate records, Pre (as he was commonly known) was ready for the world stage. There, although the off-field murder of the Israeli athletes overshadowed any on-field activity, the race was held, with Prefontaine coming in a disappointing fourth. Following the loss, Pre went into an extended tailspin. He eventually recovered, and was preparing for the 1976 Olympics, when, at the age of 24 in 1975, he was killed in a single-car accident.

As far as true sports movies go, Prefontaine's story has all of the elements necessary for an engaging motion picture (except a happy ending), and Towne does the best he can with the material at his disposal. Consequently, *Without Limits* makes for an engrossing examination of the will to win, the importance of icons in American sports, and the interference of money in amateur athletics. Above all, however, this film is an effective character study of a figure who has attained an almost-mythical status among track-and-field followers. **RECOMMENDED**

Wonder Boys [2000]

Starring: Michael Douglas, Tobey Maguire, Frances McDormand, Katie Holmes, Robert Downey Jr. Director: Curtis Hanson Screenplay: Steve Kloves, based on the novel by Michael Chabon Running Time: 1:48 Rated: R (Profanity, drugs, homosexual themes) Theatrical Aspect Ratio: 2.35:1

Wonder Boys uses a standard premise — the older, wiser father figure who both teaches and learns from his protégé — as a starting-off point. While it's true that familiarity can breed contempt, and too many movies of this sort veer into overly-sentimental melodrama, *Wonder Boys* manages to keep audiences involved despite its less-than-original underlying idea. There are two obvious reasons for this. The first is tone — the film successfully shifts from comedy to poignancy without the awkwardness that often mars such transitions, and it never goes overboard in either category. The second is characters. The men and women inhabiting this film feel like real people, not recycled caricatures from other, similar motion pictures.

Grady Tripp (Michael Douglas, looking worn out and unkempt) is a celebrated English professor at a small university. Once upon a time, Grady was regarded as a literary luminary, but it has been seven years since his critically acclaimed *Arsonist's Daughter* was published. His editor, Terry Crabtree (Robert Downey Jr.) is itching to release the much anticipated follow-up, but the author keeps putting him off. It isn't that Grady is suffering from writer's block, but he can't figure out how to end his lastest novel — an epic endeavor that is at least twice the length of *War & Peace*. Meanwhile, Grady's personal life is a mess. His wife has left him. His married girlfriend, Sarah Gaskell (Frances McDormand), who also happens to be the college's chancellor, is pregnant with his child. And a student named Hannah (Katie Holmes), who rents a room in his house, has a huge crush on him. Then there's the strange case of James Leer (Tobey Maguire), a brooding young man with unlimited writing potential. Grady decides to take James under his wing and teach him a little about life. The experience turns out to be much different than Grady anticipated.

Wonder Boys is about the relationship between Grady and James, and the importance of storytelling to both of them. The film's other characters are secondary, and often serve little purpose beyond acting as catalysts. In fact, Grady's wife is so unimportant that she never makes an appearance in the flesh (although we do catch a glimpse of her in a photograph). *Wonder Boys* explores themes that most of us can relate to: chasing the dreams of youth, taking risks and making a commitment, and finding and pursuing something of meaning.

Wonder Boys is not as accomplished a feature as *L.A. Confidential,* but it's a strong follow-up for Hanson, especially since it shows that he is not afraid to broaden his horizons. With vivid characters, an ironic voice-over narrative, and a solidly written screenplay, *Wonder Boys* provides its share of small pleasures. **RECOMMENDED**

Wonderland [United Kingdom, 1999]
Starring: Shirley Henderson, Gina McKee, Molly Parker, Ian Hart, John Simm, Stuart Townsend Director: Michael Winterbottom Screenplay: Laurence Coriat Running Time: 1:48 Rated: R (Profanity, sex, nudity) Theatrical Aspect Ratio: 2.35:1

Wonderland covers 4 days (Thursday through Sunday) in the lives of several characters as their paths intersect, merge, and diverge. The film is not constructed using events of momentous dramatic importance — almost everything that transpires is the kind of everyday incident that a typical viewer can relate to. The circumstances and situations take on an added importance because of the bond that Winterbottom creates between the protagonists and the audience. Only a few scenes into the movie, we have a strong sense that these are real people and that everything they do matters, if not to anyone else, then at least to them (and, by extension, to us).

Wonderland's three primary characters are sisters: single mother Debbie (Shirley Henderson), whose 11-year-old son is spending the weekend with his dad; lonely Nadia (Gina McKee), whose quest for a worthwhile companion has led her to place an ad in the personals; and pregnant Molly (Molly Parker), who is only days away from giving birth. There are men here, too, although they play secondary roles. There's Molly's husband, Eddie (John Simm), who is becoming unnerved by the possibility of fatherhood. Debbie's ex, Dan (Ian Hart), uses a VCR to babysit his son while he goes out to the pub. And quiet Tim (Stuart Townsend) allows Nadia to believe that not all the men responding to her ad are creeps. Finally, to round out things out, we're given a look into the unhappy married existence of Eileen (Kika Markham) and Bill (Jack Shepherd), an older couple whose feelings for each other are as empty as the rooms in which their children once lived.

Watching *Wonderland* is like stripping away the public anonymity offered by the crowd, separating the individual from the vast human continuum that forms an ever-changing background. There's nothing extraordinary about any of the characters whose lives unfold during the course of Winterbottom's 108-minute film, so it's the essential truth of the material that makes *Wonderland* a compelling and rewarding experience. **RECOMMENDED**

Wonderland [2003]
Starring: Val Kilmer, Lisa Kudrow, Kate Bosworth, Dylan McDermott, Josh Lucas, Franky G, Time Blake Nelson, Eric Bogosian, Ted Levine, Christina Applegate, Natasha Gregson Wagner Director: Niki James Cox Screenplay: James Cox & Captain Mauzner and Todd Samovitz & D. Loriston Scott Running Time: 1:39 Rated: R (Strong violence, pervasive drug use, profanity, sexual situations) Theatrical Aspect Ratio: 1.85:1

There's no nudity whatsoever in James Cox's *Wonderland,* which is ironic, since it's about events from the life of the first big-time porn star, John Holmes (Val Kilmer). Unlike *Boogie Nights,* which was loosely based on the rise and fall of Holmes during his time in front of the camera, *Wonderland* takes a look at things "once the legend was over." By 1981, Holmes was no longer doing X-rated movies. His drug habit had forced him out of the industry and, with no money to spend, he was scrounging and borrowing, trying to scrape together enough to buy the next hit. He had moved out of the house he shared with his wife, Sharon (Lisa Kudrow), and was on the road with a teenage junkie named Dawn (Kate Bosworth). That's when events spun out of Holmes's control.

On July 1, four of the six members of a gang of drug dealers were brutally murdered in a house on Wonderland Avenue in Los Angeles. Holmes was tied in to the crime, as was gangster Eddie Nash (Eric Bogosian). The police brought in the only uninjured survivor of the massacre, David Lind (Dylan McDermott), for questioning, and his version of events was damning to Holmes. Unsurprisingly, the ex–porn star's account was radically different, leaving the police stuck in a web of contradictions. Unfortunately, since neither Holmes nor Lind could be considered a reliable witness, it was virtually impossible to reconstruct the truth.

There isn't a likable character in *Wonderland.* Even Dawn, who could have been portrayed as a victim, is shown to be less than innocent (in one scene, she allows herself to be pimped out to Nash so that the drug supply to Holmes isn't shut off). Everyone in this film is a bottom-feeder — individuals whose lives revolve around money, drugs, and violence. If there's no nudity in *Wonderland,* it's because sex doesn't enter the equation. These characters are much deeper in the muck. This is not one of those films where you're going to identify with a character. Some will find the experience of watching this picture to be an uncomfortable one. Others, like me, will be fascinated by the perversity of the characters and the intriguing way in which Cox has pieced together the story line. Cox uses different amounts of grain and various levels of color desaturation in an effort to make the film look more gritty and give it a stronger "you are there" feel. He is successful, although one could argue that this is the kind of world that viewers may want to distance themselves from. Once you leave *Wonderland*, you may feel like you need a shower, but while you're in the moment, it's a compelling journey into the depths of hell on earth. RECOMMENDED

The Woodsman [2004]

Starring: Kevin Bacon, Kyra Sedgwick, Benjamin Bratt, Mos Def
Director: Nicole Kassell Screenplay: Steven Fechter, Nicole Kassell
Running Time: 1:27 Rated: R (Sexual situations, nudity, profanity, mature themes) Theatrical Aspect Ratio: 1.85:1

For obvious reasons, there aren't many movies about pedophiles or pedophilia. To date, the best-known of these is, of course, Stanley Kubrick's *Lolita*. Since the 1960s, however, entries have been few and far between, and in most cases, the pedophile is depicted as a sinister caricature. Enter Philadelphian Nicole Kassell, who has decided to break through the taboos and make a movie about a pedophile who is developed as a character, not a stereotype. It's the kind of thing British director Ken Loach might do; indeed, the approach is a little Loach-like. For Kassell, this is a bold and perhaps foolhardy move, especially since it's her feature debut.

The impulse of the viewer is to be revolted by a pedophile, so Kassell does two things to curb this tendency. She gets the likable Bacon to play the character, and she doesn't explicitly reveal his infraction until a third of the way through the movie. This gives us time to get to know him before the hatred builds. Kassell does not ask us to like Bacon's Walter, nor does she expect us to sympathize with him. This is not a bleeding-heart "feel sorry for the criminal" movie. All Kassell is asking is that we try to understand Walter — and even that is a bigger step than some viewers will be able or willing to take. When we first meet Walter, he is an ex-con being re-introduced to society. He has a new apartment (improbably located across the street from an elementary school playground), a new job, and a new chance at life. His family has all but disowned him, with the lone exception of his brother-in-law (Benjamin Bratt). For the most part, he shuns his coworkers, preferring his own company during lunch and standing alone at the bus stop when the day is over. An affair with a forklift operator, Vickie (Kyra Sedgwick), leads Walter to admit his crime. Meanwhile, his old impulses are pulling at him, and his situation is exacerbated as the view through his window shows him what he believes to be another pedophile at work. Visits by a local cop (Mos Def) are intended to keep him on the straight and narrow, but they further erode his self-esteem, making his quest for redemption all the more difficult. It's clear from his conversations with his psychologist that he wants to be "normal," but something deep within him is pushing him away from that goal.

People rightly talk about the courage exhibited by Charlize Theron to play the convicted serial killer in *Monster*. But does it require less bravery for Kevin Bacon to take on this role? This is arguably the best performance in the actor's career. In every scene, we can sense monsters, demons, and compulsions lurking just beneath surface. It takes a confident actor to accept a role like this and to perform it to flawless perfection. As for Kassell, it will be interesting to see where she goes from here. Two paths lie open to her: She can either move into a more mainstream arena, or try something equally daring. RECOMMENDED

You Can Count On Me [2000]

Starring: Laura Linney, Mark Ruffalo, Rory Culkin, Matthew Broderick
Director: Kenneth Lonergan Screenplay: Kenneth Lonergan Running Time: 1:49 Rated: R (Profanity, drug use, sex) Theatrical Aspect Ratio: 1.85:1

Kenneth Lonergan's directorial debut, *You Can Count On Me,* is one of those movies that straddles a number of fences. It functions well as either a comedy or a drama. It tells a straightforward story, but does so in a slightly off-kilter manner. It's bold enough to appeal to aficionados of independent cinema, but conventional enough not to drive away mainstream audiences.

You Can Count On Me is a seemingly simple family drama that turns out not to be so simple. The film opens with a short sequence in 1982 that shows two young children attending the funeral of their parents, who were killed in a car accident. Fast forward 18 years. Sammy (Laura Linney) is now a single mother, trying to cope with raising a precocious 8-year old, Rudy (Rory Culkin), and holding down her job at the local bank. Brian (Matthew Broderick), the new manager, has come aboard with Gestapo-like tactics that are driving Sammy crazy. Out of the blue, Sammy's brother, Terry (Mark Ruffalo), decides to visit his sister. She is overjoyed, but he has an ulterior motive for coming home — he needs money. And his arrival in the small upstate New York town where he grew up causes a few minor waves.

In terms of broad plot, *You Can Count On Me* doesn't offer much that's new. The film uses some fairly standard building blocks: the brother/sister angle, the single mother struggling to raise a child on her own, and the contentious at-work relationship between two people who are simultaneously attracted to and repelled by one another. However, instead of relying exclusively on formulas, Lonergan gives his characters and their circumstances some room in which to breathe. He is also a talented screenwriter. The dialogue in this film is not written for a least-common-denominator audience, and there's plenty of humor (some of it laugh-aloud funny) peppered in between the dramatic episodes. Lonergan also brings religion into the mix in a way that is not condescending or preachy — a difficult thing for any filmmaker to accomplish.

On the whole, *You Can Count On Me* is a pleasant motion picture, offering a solid evening's worth of entertainment. The film probably wouldn't have suffered had a few minutes been trimmed from the running length — the final cut seems a little protracted. As far as dramatic comedies (or comedic dramas) go, this one offers everything one might expect from a successful entry into the genre, delivering laughs and some genuinely moving instances of character interaction. **RECOMMENDED**

Your Friends and Neighbors [1998]

Starring: Jason Patric, Ben Stiller, Catherine Keener, Aaron Eckhart, Amy Brenneman, Nastassja Kinski Director: Neil LaBute
Screenplay: Neil LaBute Running Time: 1:35 Rated: R (Sex, profanity)
Theatrical Aspect Ratio: 2.35:1

Those looking for something lightweight or feel-good need not bother with *Your Friends and Neighbors,* a slow-moving, often disturbing look at miscommunication between the sexes, dysfunctional personalities, and the disintegration of relationships. The film contains enough humor to qualify it as a black comedy, but, underneath all the dialogue, *Your Friends and Neighbors* offers a bleak message about life and love in an era of growing emotional isolation.

The characters in *Your Friends and Neighbors* are well-defined, but there isn't much growth. We know who they are, but not who they have been or who they will become. That's really the point, though, since *Your Friends and Neighbors* is designed as a voyeuristic peek behind the drapes and blinds of suburban bedrooms, not a drama with character arcs. With a sparse narrative that does little more than move the protagonists from situation to situation, the movie lives and dies on the basis of two primary characteristics: acting and dialogue. Both, fortunately, are strengths.

The first person we're introduced to is Cary (Jason Patric), an egotistical womanizer who uses sex as a weapon. Those who saw *In the Company of Men* will recognize similarities between Cary and that film's vicious protagonist, Chad. Cary doesn't really have women problems, because he never lets anyone get close to him. He sleeps with them, then discards them. On the other hand, Cary's two friends, Jerry (Ben Stiller) and Barry (Aaron Eckhart), are embroiled in problematic relationships. Jerry, a college drama professor, is having increasing difficulties with his girlfriend, Terri (Catherine Keener), who wants him to be quiet during sex. Barry is unable to perform with his wife, Mary (Amy Brenneman), leaving them both sexually frustrated. Meanwhile, there's the wild card, Cheri (Nastassja Kinski), an artist's assistant who, in her quest to have meaningful human contact, meets the other characters one-by-one as they stop by the gallery where she works.

There isn't one healthy male/female relationship in *Your Friends and Neighbors.* Jerry and Terri are at each other's throats from the beginning, and are cheating on one another before the movie is half over. Barry and Mary, despite having what looks to outsiders like the ideal marriage, are miserable because their attempts at sexual intimacy turn into sessions of ego-bruising failure. Then, when Mary tries to have an affair, the experience is an unmitigated disaster, destroying what little self-confidence she has about her ability in bed. As for the other two characters, Cary rejects the concept of intimacy, and Cheri craves it like a drug.

As was true for *In the Company of Men,* LaBute doesn't care if viewers are offended. Supported by a fine group of actors, he tells the story without compromises, and that gives us a refreshing alternative to multiplex fare. **RECOMMENDED**

Family

Babe [1995]

Starring: James Cromwell, Magda Szubanski, Christine Cavanaugh (voice) Director: Chris Noonan Screenplay: George Miller & Chris Noonan, based on Dick King-Smith's book, *Babe: The Gallant Pig* Running Time: 1:29 Rated: G Theatrical Aspect Ratio: 1.85:1

At first glance, a movie about the adventures of a piglet who thinks he's a sheepdog doesn't appear to be the perfect entertainment recipe for those beyond puberty. However, through a mixture of imaginative storytelling, impressive animatronics, and irresistible cuteness, *Babe* casts a spell over all viewers — young, old, or somewhere in between.

Babe is a small pig whose parents have gone to hog heaven. Abducted from the pork penitentiary, he ends up as the lone representative of his kind on the property of Farmer Hoggett (James Cromwell), a kindly man of few words who knows far more about sheep than pigs. On the farm, Babe makes a few enemies, but many more friends, including a talkative duck who wants to be a rooster and a dog willing to play the role of substitute mother. Unfortunately, one of those not in the pig's corner is Mrs. Hoggett (Magda Szubanski), who has visions of a roast pork Christmas dinner dancing in her head.

Babe is a new twist on the traditional story of the underachiever attaining greatness. It's a buddy film, about a man and his best friend (who, in this case, happens to be pink), and an adventure-comedy. Above all, it teaches the lesson of how easy it is to fall back on "comfortable" prejudices. Babe triumphs because his first thought is always of bridging gaps, not building walls. Unlike in George Orwell's *Animal Farm*, here the pig is the instrument of unity and mediation.

Babe's greatest asset (besides the pig) is director Chris Noonan, who finds the right tone for this modern fable. Most animal movies come across as unbelievably cloying or simply unbelievable, but Noonan makes his picture work. And, by using the talents of the men and women of Jim Henson's workshop, Noonan has assured that when the animals' lips move, they don't look like *Mr. Ed*. Thought was put into the adaptation of Dick King-Smith's book. Even the narrative voiceovers, laced with subtle irony and understated revelations, are effective in this context.

RECOMMENDED

Babe: Pig in the City [1998]

Starring: Magda Szubanski, James Cromwell, Mary Stein, Mickey Rooney, E.G. Daily (voice) Director: George Miller Screenplay: George Miller, Mark Campbell, Judy Morris, based on *The Sheep Pig* by Dick King-Smith Running Time: 1:32 Rated: G Theatrical Aspect Ratio: 1.85:1

Pig in the City has a slightly darker tone than *Babe*, but it's by no means grim or frightening. The G-rating is still deserved; only the smallest of children will be disturbed by some of the movie's most disconcerting images. *Pig in the City* has been designed with the goal of recapturing the enchanting feel of the original while taking the story in new and different directions. It succeeds at both aims, standing as a worthy sequel to one of the decade's most innovative family features.

Pig in the City opens on "a place just a little to the left of the 20th century" — the farm of "Boss" Arthur

Hoggett (James Cromwell), who has returned home triumphant with his world-renowned sheep-pig, Babe. However, Babe's time to bask in the glow of his fame is short-lived. After the farmer suffers an accident and is laid up in bed, his wife (Magda Szubanski), needing to raise money to keep the bank men at bay, takes the pig with her on a trip, hoping to get a generous appearance fee by showing up at a county fair. (Apparently, she's no longer obsessed with the thought of a pork dinner.) After missing a connecting flight, however, Mrs. Hoggett and Babe end up stranded in the unfamiliar land of the Big City, where a series of astounding adventures awaits them.

This is essentially a fractured fairy tale. The unnamed city is a fantasyland mixture of cultures, eras, and places — a visually tantalizing display of all that is grand and intimidating about the world's largest population centers. In the city's vast canyon of buildings can be found the "Hollywood" sign, the World Trade Center, the Space Needle, the Statue of Liberty, the Golden Gate Bridge, the Eiffel Tower, and dozens of other famous landmarks, all nestled together. Much of the action takes place in and around a quaint, old hotel in a section of the city that looks like a romanticized slice of Venice (canals, bridges, etc.).

George Miller, who co-wrote and co-produced *Babe,* takes over for Chris Noonan in the director's chair. The transition is relatively seamless. All the elements that made the first film successful are here — comedy, adventure, fantasy, and a happy ending. Even though the title character is adorable, *Pig in the City* is careful not to overdo the cuteness factor (at times, the tone seems almost gothic). The film's underlying sense of sophistication will satisfy adults, while the nearly nonstop adventure will grab kids' attention. RECOMMENDED

Black Beauty [1994]

Starring: Justin, Rat, Alan Cumming, David Thewlis, Andrew Knott, Peter Davison Director: Caroline Thompson Screenplay: Caroline Thompson, based on the book by Anna Sewell Running Time: 1:28 Rated: G Theatrical Aspect Ratio: 1.85:1

Even though it's eminently suitable for family viewing, the latest adaptation of Anna Sewell's *Black Beauty* could be a film in search of an audience. Adults may avoid this movie because it's G-rated, based on a children's book, and has actors speaking with British accents. Children, on the other hand, may stay away because there are no musical numbers with singing animals, no McDonald's Happy Meals, and the actors speak with British accents.

In many ways, *Black Beauty* is almost more of an adult movie than one for children. Restless kids are going to have difficulty sitting through several of the slower portions, and the overall tone is more somber than anything put out by Disney. Even *The Lion King,* with its Shakespearean leanings, is ultimately lighter than *Black Beauty*.

Not the first adaptation of the classic story, Caroline Thompson's is the most faithful. Told from the perspective of Black Beauty (played by the stallion Justin, with a voice supplied by Alan Cumming), the film follows the horse's adventures as he serves masters both kind and cruel. It's a tale of friendship, abuse, betrayal, and redemption. The setting moves from the verdant pastures of rural England to the crowded streets of 19th-century London.

Tremendous camerawork by Alex Thomson and an effective score from Danny Elfman (this sounds nothing like his *Batman* music) add to *Black Beauty's* luster. The film has the look and feel of something out of Dickens, with a theme to match.

Black Beauty has a lot more to offer than the typically available, brainless family entertainment. It's worth the price of admission (or a rental) even if you don't have a kid to bring with you. Entertainment of this sort knows no age limits. RECOMMENDED

Fly Away Home [1996]

Starring: Anna Paquin, Jeff Daniels, Dana Delany, Terry Kinney Director: Carroll Ballard Screenplay: Robert Rodat & Vince McKewin Running Time: 1:47 Rated: PG (Nothing offensive) Theatrical Aspect Ratio: 1.85:1

Fly Away Home starts with one of the most disconcerting scenes I've seen in a recent motion picture: a silent car accident that takes place during the opening credits while a soft, gentle melody plays in the background. The effect created by this juxtaposition of tragic and hopeful elements is sufficient to arrest anyone's attention. And, while the film never again attains this level of artistry, there are a few scenes that come close. Caleb Deschanel's photography is one of the movie's highlights.

The opening crash occurs in New Zealand, where Amy Alden (Anna Paquin) and her mother live. Amy's mother dies in the accident, and the 13-year-old is forced to move to Ontario, Canada, where her father, Thomas (Jeff Daniels), has a home. Thomas, a sculptor and wilderness conservation activist, doesn't understand his daughter, and his earnest attempts to get close to her are rebuffed. When asked why he didn't visit her more often when she was younger, he says that New Zealand is a long way off. Her response to that: "That's a lame excuse, Dad." And, of course, it is.

While Thomas is busy with his work, Amy plays mother to 16 goose eggs that she finds abandoned in their nest. After constructing a makeshift incubator, Amy awaits the big moment. One day, when she comes home from school, a brood of newly-hatched birds are waiting to greet her. The story then shifts to the question of how Amy, recognized by the geese as their mother, can teach them certain basic necessities of survival — namely, how to fly and migrate. Thomas comes up with the answer: instruct Amy to pilot an ultra-light plane, then accompany her in his own craft on a 600-mile, 4-day aerial flight to North Carolina, with the geese tagging along behind.

As a family film, *Fly Away Home* has something for members of every temperament and age group: adventure, pathos, technical detail about the design of the aircraft, cute animals, and human drama. There's a subplot involving attempts to clip the birds' wings, a look at how the media covers Amy's flight, and a sequence where Amy and Thomas' crafts are mistaken for UFOs by the U.S. military. There's also a pro-conservation message that, while laudable in intent, comes across as simplistic and heavy-handed (land developers = bad; geese = good). Ballard uses this as the backdrop for a warm drama that's more about love and trust between a father and daughter than inter-species connections. The result, even for geese-haters, is charming. **RECOMMENDED**

Harriet the Spy [1996]

Starring: **Michelle Trachtenberg, Vanessa Lee Chester, Gregory Smith** Director: **Bronwen Hughes** Screenplay: **Theresa Rebeck & Dogulas Petrie,** based on the novel by Louise Fitzhugh Running Time: 1:41 Rated: PG (Some potentially disturbing sequences) Theatrical Aspect Ratio: 1.85:1

Harriet the Spy, based on the popular novel by Louise Fitzhugh and directed by feature newcomer Bronwen Hughes, is the premiere theatrical film from the popular cable TV channel, Nickelodeon. Harriet Welsch (Michelle Trachtenberg) is an unusual 6th-grader. Instead of spending her time playing "tag" or "spin the bottle" with her schoolmates, she dons a yellow slicker, carries a notebook and pencil, and spies on people. From her vantage point in a tree, on a rooftop, outside a window, or even in a dumbwaiter, she watches, then jots down comments in her notebook about those she observes. There are even entries about her two best friends, Janie (Vanessa Lee

Chester), a budding chemist, and Sport (Gregory Smith), a motherless boy who lives just above the poverty line. Harriet has been raised by a nanny named Golly (Rosie O'Donnell), who encourages her creativity. However, when Golly leaves, Harriet feels lost. And things go from bad to worse when the most popular girl in Harriet's class, Marion (Charlotte Sullivan), finds the notebook and reads the most damning passages aloud. As a result, Harriet becomes a pariah, shunned by even her friends. She plots revenge, but learns that vengeance can have a bitter taste.

To heighten its appeal for the under-12 crowd, *Harriet the Spy* uses MTV-like camera movements. The cinematography is kinetic, almost to the point of being distracting, with strange angles and numerous quick cuts. This, however, is what children are used to, and, admittedly, it keeps the film's energy level high. But the subtlety absent from the picture's visual aspect is more than compensated for on an emotional plane. As Harriet travels the long road from isolation to bittersweet revenge to redemption, we can see and feel her every change in emotion. This is a real person acting believably as dictated by a script that remains low-key. The ending is a little saccharine, but, considering the target audience, it's reasonable.

Certainly, one of the reasons *Harriet* effectively captures our sympathy is the fine performance by Michelle Trachtenberg (Nickelodeon's *The Adventures of Pete & Pete*), who exhibits the charisma of a younger Christina Ricci. Trachtenberg is very good in the title role, embodying all of Harriet's traits from youthful exuberance to petulance. As the cliché goes, good things do indeed come in small packages. **RECOMMENDED**

Holes [2003]

Starring: **Sigourney Weaver, Jon Voight, Patricia Arquette, Shia LeBeouf, Tim Blake Nelson, Khleo Thomas, Siobhan Fallon, Henry Winkler, Dule Hill** Director: **Andrew Davis** Screenplay: **Louis Sachar,** based on his novel Running Time: 1:51 Rated: PG (Cartoon violence) Theatrical Aspect Ratio: 1.85:1

In the pantheon of authors writing for young readers, Louis Sachar may not have achieved the exalted status of J. K. Rowling, but he's at least a demigod. *Holes* has been read and enjoyed by millions of children (and more than a few adults), so it's no surprise that a movie adaptation has arrived. With a script penned by Sachar (that shoehorns most of the book's content into 111 minutes of screen time), the movie will likely please those who have spent long hours enjoying the written word, and offers two hours of solid entertainment for those who have never heard of Sachar.

The film follows the misadventures of teenager Stanley Yelnats (Shia LeBeouf), whose palindrome name is the least remarkable thing about him. One day, Stanley becomes the unexpected recipient of a pair of sneakers that fall from the sky. Unfortunately for Stanley, these are the footgear of baseball player Clyde Livingstone, who has donated them to a local orphanage. Accused, then convicted, of theft, Stanley is sentenced to spend 18 months at "Camp Green Lake"— a facility that isn't a camp, nor does it have a lake. There, under the watchful eye of Warden Walker (Sigourney Weaver) and her two stooges, Mr. Sir (Jon Voight) and Mr. Pendanski (Tim Blake Nelson), the boys are forced to dig one 5-foot-diameter, 5-foot-deep hole per day, pockmarking the flat, unpromising landscape. The camp's philosophy is simple: "You take a bad boy, make him dig holes all day long in the hot sun, it makes him a good boy." Stanley quickly learns what it takes to co-exist with the other boys, who are (for the most part) bigger and more stupid than he is, and he develops a close friendship with Zero (Khleo Thomas), who is the butt of everyone else's jokes. Eventually, Stanley determines that he and the other boys aren't just digging holes for the purpose of character building, but are looking for something. The question is: What?

Holes moves briskly, limiting character development. A nice rapport grows between Stanley and Zero, but the rest of the boys remain largely faceless. The adult authority figures — the warden and her henchmen — are portrayed as cartoon buffoons, rarely seriously menacing. The movie inhabits the semifantasy world in which many family films exist, divorced from some of the harsh realities of 21st-century America, in a place where magic is not a laughable conceit.

The litmus test for a creatively successful family film is whether a single adult can sit through a showing without becoming fidgety or feeling the urge to sneak into the theater next door. *Holes* passes that test with little difficulty. Children will be delighted, but no less so than the grateful parents who accompany their offspring to theaters. Like the hugely popular *Spy Kids* movies, *Holes* has something to offer to viewers of all ages — and that's a rare and prized quality. **RECOMMENDED**

How the Grinch Stole Christmas [2000]

Starring: Jim Carrey, Taylor Momsen, Jeffrey Tambor, Christine Baranski, Molly Shannon Director: Ron Howard Screenplay: Jeffrey Price & Peter S. Seaman, based on the book by Dr. Seuss Running Time: 1:38 Rated: PG (Nothing offensive) Theatrical Aspect Ratio: 1.85:1

For more than 3 decades, *How the Grinch Stole Christmas* has been a holiday season television staple. The 22-minute cartoon, based on the book by Dr. Seuss and narrated by Boris Karloff, has enchanted multiple generations of children (not to mention adults), and, even with its ready availability on video, it still draws a sizable viewing audience every time it is broadcast. With the possible exception of the Peanuts Christmas Special, no other seasonal program is as beloved and respected as this venerable classic. So, in deciding to transform it into a 90-minute, live action motion picture, director Ron Howard has taken a sizable risk. To Howard's credit, he has worked hard to keep the spirit of the animated *Grinch* intact. The text of the Dr. Seuss book is in place, although a great deal has been added to pad out the running time.

The movie opens with nearly one hour of background material about the Grinch and Whoville that was not in either Seuss' book or the TV special. We learn all sorts of interesting tidbits designed to fill in supposed "holes" in Grinch lore (not that anyone really noticed). We come to understand why the Grinch hates Christmas (it has more to do with bad childhood experiences than with a heart that's 2 sizes too small), why he has it in for the Mayor of Whoville, and why Little Cindy Lou-Who finds his soft spot so easily. Finally, at about the film's two-thirds point, the narrative switches over to following the book letter-for-letter, and we get a strikingly faithful re-creation of the cartoon. There is a difference in tone between the two portions of the film — the part that follows the book is smoother, has considerably more narration, and consistently rhymes, while the remainder has a "tacked on" feel. Children, however, won't notice, and the shift isn't glaring enough that it will bother most adults — even those who have sat through the TV special countless times.

Of course, *How the Grinch Stole Christmas'* big selling point isn't nostalgia or great production values — it's Jim Carrey. Buried beneath Rick Baker's flexible makeup, he's a dead ringer for the cartoon creature, but, although he isn't physically recognizable, there's no doubt who's under all of the green latex and hair. For Carrey, whose caged energy is released, this falls just short of a tour de force. He brings animation to the live action, and, surrounded by glittering, fantastical sets and computer-spun special effects, Carrey enables Ron Howard's version of the classic story to come across as more of a welcome endeavor than a pointless re-tread. RECOMMENDED

The Jungle Book [1994]

Starring: Jason Scott Lee, Cary Elwes, Lena Headey, Sam Neill, John Cleese Director: Stephen Sommers Screenplay: Stephen Sommers and Ronald Yanover; based on characters from *The Jungle Book* by Rudyard Kipling Running Time: 1:51 Rated: PG (Violence) Theatrical Aspect Ratio: 2.35:1

Beautifully photographed and tightly paced with a spate of solid performances, this latest Kipling-inspired motion picture is an enjoyable and exuberant film-going experience. Where Disney's animated *The Jungle Book* was a light-hearted affair, this rendition is more of a straightforward adventure. That's not to imply that it's in any way stodgy or somber; comic relief is provided by an orangutan called King Louie and a human named John Cleese.

Taking place in late 19th-century, British-occupied India, *The Jungle Book*'s story is uncomplicated: a human boy who has grown up in the jungle is lured back to civilization by the sight of a beautiful young woman. There, surrounded by a few who wish to help him and many whose motives are less pure, he learns to speak and act like a man. Eventually, his enemies, motivated by jealousy, ill-will, and greed, drive him back into the wild. Once there, the battle for life becomes a struggle of man's guns against the Law of the Jungle.

Those familiar with the animated feature will recognize some non-human characters, including King Louie, Baloo the bear, Bagheera the panther, and, of course, Shere Khan, the tiger king. Mowgli, the "wild boy" of the Black Jungle, is portrayed by Jason Scott Lee. This performance, while not of award-winning caliber, is characterized by a number of nice little "man/beast" touches. Lena Headey, as Katherine, is the object of Mowgli's love, but she's engaged to a British officer (Cary Elwes) who kills wild animals for sport. Sam Neill plays Katherine's father, and John Cleese is the kindly Dr. Julius Plumford.

There are moments when *The Jungle Book* may be too intense for small children. Animal maulings, while shown obliquely, occur on screen. Those old enough not to be disturbed by such things should enjoy this movie, regardless of whether they consider themselves adults, kids, or something in-between.

The Jungle Book doesn't offer any thought-provoking philosophical messages, and its view of good and evil is simplistic, but that lack of complexity is part of its charm. RECOMMENDED

Lemony Snicket's A Series of Unfortunate Events [2004]

Starring: Jim Carrey, Meryl Streep, Jude Law, Emily Browning, Liam Aiken, Kara and Shelby Hoffman, Billy Connolly, Timothy Spall, Catherine O'Hara Director: Brad Silberling Screenplay: Robert Gordon, based on *The Bad Beginning, The Reptile Room,* and *The Wide Window* by Daniel Handler Running Time: 1:50 Rated: PG (Scary situations, some violence) Theatrical Aspect Ratio: 1.85:1

As almost anyone in the age 8-to-14 age bracket will tell you, the *Lemony Snicket* books are second in popularity only to *Harry Potter* (and some would argue that they are more popular). For this first movie, the filmmakers have elected to cobble together elements from the first three *Lemony Snicket* tales (*The Bad Beginning, The Reptile Room,* and *The Wide Window*), resulting in a fast-paced but episodic motion picture. In case a sequel is warranted, there's still plenty of untapped material remaining. To date, there are eleven *Lemony Snicket* books, and writer Daniel Handler isn't done yet.

The title character is played by the ubiquitous Jude Law, whose only real contribution to the movie is to provide a voice-over narrative. The real star is Jim Carrey, who, as the nefarious Count Olaf, plays his most sinister character since the Grinch. The story relates Olaf's various, often elaborate attempts to get his hands on the fortune of the Baudelaire orphans: 14-year-old Violet (Emily Browning), preteen Klaus (Liam Aiken), and infant Sunny (Kara and Shelby Hoffman). These three are left on their own when a house fire claims the lives of their parents. Just when things seem their darkest, in steps Olaf, claiming to be either "a fourth cousin three times removed or a third cousin four times removed." Olaf thinks of the children's arrival as a godsend — free labor and access to a huge sum of money — until he learns that he can't legally touch the money unless the children die. But, before he can ensure their demise, he is stripped of guardianship. The orphans are given first to Uncle Monty (Billy Connolly), then to Aunt Josephine (Meryl Streep). All the while, however, Olaf is plotting to once again get his hands on the Baudelaires and their money.

A mention of Roald Dahl's possible influence is appropriate. Dahl wrote dark, warped stories that were ostensibly for children, and the *Lemony Snicket* books are in the same vein. As the movie warns in Mr. Snicket's clever opening monologue, this isn't a happy movie. Bad things happen. People die (and don't come back from the dead), and children are mistreated. The film is first and foremost a fantasy, but there are dark currents running just beneath the surface. I give Silberling credit for not allowing them to swallow the film. *Lemony Snicket's A Series of Unfortunate Events* manages to remain witty throughout. Coupled with its fast pace and occasional cliffhangers, that makes it a candidate for an easy recommendation, regardless of whether you have previous experience with the books or not.

RECOMMENDED

The Leopard Son [1996]

Director: **Hugo Van Lawick** Screenplay: **Michael Olmert** Running Time: **1:25** Rated: **G** Theatrical Aspect Ratio: **1.85:1**

Even frequent viewers of made-for-TV nature specials won't be fully prepared for the majesty of *The Leopard Son*. This is a singularly cinematic experience that will lose much when cropped for television viewing. And, because the cinematography is by far the most important aspect of this movie, the high aptitude level evidenced by directors of photography Hugo Van Lawick and Matthew Aeberhard makes this a rewarding motion picture experience.

Van Lawick is a Dutch photographer and naturalist who has spent most of his adult life living on the plains of the Serengeti. In his own words, "To be as close as possible to nature as I could — that was my dream." *The Leopard Son* is his filmed journal of 2 years in the life of a young male leopard. Van Lawick's camera first captures the cub when he's only a few weeks old, then follows him through youth and adolescence to adulthood. Along the way, we observe his relationship with his mother, his first attempts at hunting his own meals, and the harsh lessons that identify his place in the food chain. And, in a film which has a leopard as the central character, there are supporting appearances by all manner of other African wildlife, including baboons, elephants, giraffes, hyenas, rhinos, cheetahs, and lions. Some children may rightfully see this as a kind of live action *Lion King*.

What's unusual about *The Leopard Son* is that it's a nature film with characters and a plot. We are drawn into the drama of the title creature's life, and find ourselves rooting for him to hunt down a meal, redis-

cover his mother, make peace with his half-siblings, and, in the end, find a mate. As in any well-constructed motion picture, there's humor, pathos, passion, and danger. Unfortunately, however, we are subjected to an irritatingly repetitive and superfluous voiceover provided by Sir John Gielgud. This would have been a better film without it. *The Leopard Son* is so well-crafted visually that it doesn't need a narrator.

HIGHLY RECOMMENDED

The Little Princess [1995]

Starring: **Liesel Matthews, Eleanor Bron, Liam Cunningham, Vanessa Lee Chester** Director: **Alfonso Cuaron** Screenplay: **Richard LaGravanese and Elizabeth Chandler** based on the novel *Sara Crewe* by **Frances Hodgson Burnett** Running Time: **1:38** Rated: **G** Theatrical Aspect Ratio: **1.85:1**

The film is based on the popular 1888 children's book *Sara Crewe* by Frances Hodgson Burnett. This is the third filmed version, following 1917's *A Little Princess* with Mary Pickford and 1939's, which featured Shirley Temple. This new version can more than hold its own in a sea of overly-commercial attempts to grab children's hard-earned money. Unfortunately, since it actually takes the time to develop characters and a story while eschewing explosions, it's unlikely to garner much at the box office. Witness the performance of similar recent films if you doubt that.

The main character is Sara, played delightfully by newcomer Liesel Matthews. The motherless girl has grown up in India, a land where "the air is so hot you can taste it." In fact, the scenes there are filmed with warmth and color to emphasize the beauty as seen through Sara's eyes. The year is 1914, and World War I is in full swing. When Sara's father (played by Liam Cunningham), a British army captain, decides to rejoin his regiment, he deposits Sara in an exclusive girls' school in New York City. Run by the nasty Miss Minchin (Eleanor Bron), this is a place that stifles creativity in favor of etiquette and strict rules. Sara is immediately unhappy there, but her fortunes go from bad to worse when her father is declared dead in Europe and all his assets are seized by the Indian government. Sara is left penniless and forced to work as a servant to earn her keep.

A Little Princess is an engaging tale about self-respect and the importance of imagination. In India, Sara is told that "all girls are princesses," and this is a lesson she clings to when forced to mop floors and serve meals. Even dressed in rags and living in a bare attic room, she is special — and so are all the others around her, regardless of whether they're nice, snobbish, or bossy. Princess or pauper, there's no difference in Sara's eyes.

She also accepts magic. In her father's words, "Magic has to be believed — that's the only way it's real." Her stories about Princess Sita and Prince Rama not only enchant her schoolmates, but they give Sara an escape route once her father has been declared dead. She uses fantasy as a tonic for her bleak reality without ever losing sight of what's happening around her. Together with her friend Becky (Vanessa Lee Chester), she ventures to amazing places without leaving her room. **RECOMMENDED**

Madeline [United States/France, 1998]

Starring: Frances McDormand, Nigel Hawthorne, Hatty Jones, Ben Daniels Director: Daisy von Scherler Mayer Screenplay: Mark Levin & Jennifer Flackett based on the book "Madeline" by Ludwig Bemelmans Running Time: 1:35 Rated: PG (A few mildly scary moments) Theatrical Aspect Ratio: 1.85:1

Madeline is based on the popular series of illustrated children's books by Ludwig Bemelmans, whose first volume, *Madeline,* was written in 1939. The movie version of the tiny heroine's adventures, scripted by husband-and-wife Mark Levin and Jennifer Flackett, incorporates elements from four Madeline tales — "Madeline," "Madeline and the Bad Hat," "Madeline's Rescue," and "Madeline and the Gypsies" — into an entirely new story that is sure to please those familiar with Bemelmans' work and delight those for whom this is a first exposure.

Madeline transpires in Paris during the 1950s, where we're introduced to the sturdy, reliable Miss Clavel (Frances McDormand), a nun who runs a French school for girls. Madeline (Hatty Jones) is the smallest and most outspoken of the 12 children in Miss Clavel's care. Unlike her 11 friends, Madeline is not at the school merely to earn an education — she's an orphan, and Miss Clavel and her friends are the closest thing she has to a family. When the owner of the school, Lady Covington (Stephane Audran), dies, her bereaved husband, Lord Covington (Nigel Hawthorne), decides to sell the house where the girls live and learn. Madeline, unwilling to bear this nasty twist of fate passively, recruits the aide of a local boy troublemaker, Pepito (Kristian De La Osa), in her attempts to fight back.

Director Daisy von Scherler Mayer wisely develops the film in such a way that adults will observe things a little differently than children. For example, grown-ups will see Lord Covington as a sly caricature of British nobility; children will view him as a nasty man determined to take away Madeline's home. It's this kind of layering that makes a movie of this sort a true "family film" rather than 95 minutes with kids-only appeal. Of course, there are sequences, such as one in which Madeline and Pepito seek to foil a kidnapping, that are enjoyed by everyone for the same reason — they're fun and exciting. **RECOMMENDED**

Matilda [1996]

Starring: Mara Wilson, Danny DeVito, Rhea Perlman, Embeth Davidtz Director: Danny DeVito Screenplay: Nicholas Kaza & Robin Swicord, based on the book by Roald Dahl Running Time: 1:33 Rated: PG (Scary situations) Theatrical Aspect Ratio: 2.35:1

Matilda contains numerous elements of traditional fairy tales — a wicked step-aunt, a true friend with a pure heart, and more than a little magic — but "traditional" is about the last word that comes to mind when describing this quirky film. The basic material may seem odd for a family film, dealing as it does with issues of child neglect, abuse, and revenge. By removing the story from conventional reality, however, director Danny DeVito pulls it off. This is a world where adults (except two) are bad and children (except one) are good. It's a place where television is a force of mind-numbing evil and where books represent escape and solace. And, most importantly, empowerment is genuine, not just a slogan.

Matilda (Mara Wilson) is the youngest child, and only daughter, of Harry and Zinia Wormwood (Danny DeVito and Rhea Perlman), who are described as living "in a very nice neighborhood in a very nice house," but not being very nice people. Mr. Wormwood is a used car salesman with the police tracking his every move, and Mrs. Wormwood is obsessed with bingo parlors and television game shows. Both parents are extremely neglectful of their little 6½-year-old daughter, even though she shows signs of amazing intelligence and various remarkable powers.

Eventually, Mr. Wormwood notices his daughter long enough to send her off to Crunchem Hall, an elementary school lorded over by the ogre-like Miss Trunchbull (Pam Ferris), whose motto is "Use the rod, beat the child." She practices what she preaches, taking delight in punishing her charges and informing them mercilessly that her idea of a perfect school is one where there are no children. Fortunately for Matilda, her 1st grade teacher, Miss Honey (Embeth Davidtz), is kind and good-hearted, and immediately recognizes her new student's amazing gifts.

Matilda is not politically correct — it is, after all, a

pint-sized revenge fantasy — but, in this case, that's a definite plus. Besides, for those who want bland, "wholesome" family entertainment, there's always Disney. Children aren't likely to understand much of the black comedy and satire here, but they'll be so involved in the story that they won't notice that a lot is going over their heads. Hardly a moment of *Matilda* can be described as either juvenile or condescending, and, compared with many of this summer's so-called "mature" features, that makes for a delightfully refreshing change-of-pace. RECOMMENDED

The Mighty [1998]

Starring: Elden Henson, Kieran Culkin, Sharon Stone, Gena Rowlands, Harry Dean Stanton Director: Peter Chelsom Screenplay: Charles Leavitt, based on the book *Freak the Mighty* by Rodman Philbrick Running Time: 1:46 Rated: PG-13 (Mild violence, mild profanity) Theatrical Aspect Ratio: 1.85:1

The Mighty, which is based on the book *Freak The Mighty* by Rodman Philbrick, tells the story of two phenomenally mismatched children who complement each other so well that, together, they form one complete (not to mention formidable) individual. The film's narrator, Max Kane (Elden Henson), is a hulking 7th-grader who makes up for his limited intellectual prowess with an imposing physical presence. But, because Max is a gentle giant — slow to anger and even slower to retaliate — he has become the target of taunts and teasing. But that all changes when Kevin Dillon (Kieran Culkin) moves in next door. Kevin is Max's opposite: frail in form, but a giant in intelligence. Crippled by a disease that eats away at his body, Kevin has devoted himself to developing a powerful world of imagination where he is a knight in King Arthur's court and the braces on his legs do not affect his ability to do great deeds (slay dragons and save damsels). Now, in concert with Max, these things become possible in the real world, even if the dragons are just local bullies and the damsels are not maidens of virtue.

At the center of *The Mighty* is the friendship between Max and Kevin, two constant outsiders who discover the joy of finding someone else in the same predicament. Their relationship is presented with such insight and sensitivity that we feel the strength of their bond. The film is also a salute to the power of imagination and creativity. Kevin introduces Max to his magical world of the mind, and soon both boys are employing it as a refuge. They do not use it as a means of denying reality, but as a way to help them struggle through the most difficult times. Reassured

that they are Knights of the Round Table, and knowing that "a knight proves his worthiness through his deeds," each can face his most daunting opponent.

Although the list of good, live-action family features is small, the list of great ones is microscopic. *The Mighty* deserves a place on the exclusive roster of the latter. Seeing a film like this does more than simply entertain; it fills the viewer with optimism that the future of motion pictures might not be as bleak as it sometimes seems. If something like *The Mighty* can be produced, then the monsters haven't yet won, and the knights still have a chance. HIGHLY RECOMMENDED

Miracle [2004]

Starring: Kurt Russell, Eddie Cahill, Michael Mantenuto, Patrick O'Brien Demsey, Nathan West, Noah Emmerich, Patricia Clarkson Director: Gavin O'Connor Screenplay: Eric Guggenheim Running Time: 2:15 Rated: PG (Mature themes) Theatrical Aspect Ratio: 2.35:1

February 22, 1980. For hockey fans, that day will be forever remembered. "The Miracle on Ice," as it became commonly known, was to some a battle in the Cold War and to others the greatest upset in sports history. But to those who played in the game, it was validation and an opportunity to move on to win an Olympic gold medal. In the United States, hockey has always been the runt of the major sports litter, trailing football, baseball, and basketball in popularity. But, for a few days in Lake Placid, 24 years ago, it was suddenly, briefly bigger than all of its siblings.

Miracle is a reasonably straightforward retelling of how the team was assembled, polished, and pushed into battle under the relentless domination of its coach, Herb Brooks (Kurt Russell). The film ends with a 20-minute re-creation of the classic game, complete with audio excerpts of the original broadcast by Al Michaels (with his immortal call "Do you believe in miracles? Yes!" included). For the most part, Eric Guggenheim's screenplay is respectful of the historical record. He takes minimal artistic license, except during some of the quieter scenes when the participants are away from the rink.

Miracle is told from Brooks's perspective, and as a result, he's the only well-developed character. (The film is dedicated to the coach, who died shortly after primary photography completed.) He has a wife (Patricia Clarkson), a son and a daughter, and a burning desire to lead Team USA to an Olympic victory. Most of his players are either anonymous or identifiable only by a trait or two. They include goal tender Jim Craig (Eddie Cahill), who plays to honor his recently deceased mother; team captain Mike Eruzione

(Patrick O'Brien Demsey), who is in danger of being the last man cut from the squad; and hotshot Jack O'Callahan (Michael Mantenuto). Then there's assistant coach Craig Patrick (Noah Emmerich), who is torn between loyalty to Brooks and compassion for the boys. Brooks's tough-as-nails philosophy becomes apparent early. He believes two things: (1) if his players are in top physical condition, they can skate with anyone; and (2) their dislike of him will bind them together as a team. He is not their father or their friend; he's their general.

In recent years, Disney has scored a couple of big hits based on real-life sports stories, and there's no reason why *Miracle* can't succeed in the same way. The story is as crowd pleasing as it gets, with the only possible misstep being that the first half (which deals with the assembling of the team) occasionally seems to drag. There's no need to understand hockey to appreciate the film; it has universal appeal. *Miracle* is inspirational and uplifting — qualities we are as much in need of today as we were during the winter of 1980. **RECOMMENDED**

Peter Pan [2003]

Starring: Jeremy Sumpter, Rachel Hurd-Wood, Jason Isaacs, Lynn Redgrave, Richard Briers, Olivia Williams, Geoffrey Palmer, Harry Newell, Freddie Popplewell, Ludivine Sagnier Director: P. J. Hogan Screenplay: P. J. Hogan and Michael Goldenberg, based on the play by J. M. Barrie Running Time: 1:45 Rated: PG (Violence) Theatrical Aspect Ratio: 2.35:1

2003's *Peter Pan* is a marvelous movie to behold. The set design is colorful and imaginative, and could easily have come from the riotous imagination of Baz Luhrman. Nothing in this film is real — it's all highly stylized. Even London is a fantasy-city: the kind of place that only exists in idealized stories. The clouds are pink, the seas around Hook's ship surge and roil, and the fairies dance deep in the forest. Neverland is supposed to be a place of endless wonders, and that's the impression director P. J. Hogan conveys.

The story, for those who don't know it, involves the journey of Wendy Darling (Rachel Hurd-Wood) and her two younger brothers, John (Harry Newell) and Michael (Freddie Popplewell), to the land of Neverland. They are guided there by the eternally young flying boy, Peter Pan, (Jeremy Sumpter) and his petulant fairy, Tinkerbell (Ludivine Sagnier). Once in Neverland, they become enmeshed in Peter's war with his archenemy, the nefarious Captain Hook (Jason Isaacs). Meanwhile, in London, Wendy's parents (Olivia Williams and Jason Isaacs) and aunt (Lynn

Redgrave) worry and wonder whether their children will ever return home.

The cast is comprised of character actors and unknowns, and the lack of star power works to the film's advantage, since there's no one to steal the spotlight. The two children of real note are Jeremy Sumpter, and, making her screen debut, the luminous Rachel Hurd-Wood. Both are perfect for their roles. Sumpter plays Peter as a prepubescent boy who would rather ignore emotions than confront them, disturbing though they may be. Hurd-Wood's Wendy is a believer in love and romance, and sees Peter as a dashing hero. The light romantic chemistry between the two is on-target: playful without a hint of salaciousness. There's affection, but no sex.

The standout is Jason Isaacs, whose Captain Hook makes Lucius Malfoy (the role he played in *Harry Potter and the Chamber of Secrets*) look like a choirboy. Yet, despite all the sinister sneers, there's something human about Hook. Isaacs gives us occasional glimpses of the man beneath all the poisonous bile. For good measure, the actor takes on a second, milder role: that of Wendy's milquetoast father. Other players include French actress Ludivine Sagnier as the diminutive Tinkerbell, Olivia Williams as Mrs. Darling, Lynn Redgrave as Aunt Millicent, and Richard Briers as Hook's henchman, Smee. *Peter Pan* offers enough entertainment value to allow Mom, Dad, and the kids to have a good time. Plus, pirate movies are big these days, and this is one of the better ones. P. J. Hogan's *Peter Pan* proves that some concepts, like their characters, are ageless. **RECOMMENDED**

Secondhand Lions [2003]

Starring: Michael Caine, Robert Duvall, Haley Joel Osment, Kyra Sedgwick, Emmanuelle Vaugier, Josh Lucas Director: Tim McCanlies Screenplay: Tim McCanlies Running Time: 1:40 Rated: PG (Violence, mild profanity) Theatrical Aspect Ratio: 1.85:1

Simple and affecting, *Secondhand Lions* is a comedic fantasy with a big heart. Despite flaws that are (for the most part) easily overlooked, this film has enough charm and whimsy to capture the attention and imagination of children and parents alike. It's also a distinct change of pace for respected actors Michael Caine and Robert Duvall, who put aside their usual adult fare to star in Tim McCanlies's second feature.

The setup is simple, although the time line is a little confused. Most of the story, shown in flashbacks, takes place during the 1950s. There are flashbacks-within-flashbacks that transport us to North Africa between the world wars, and short, bookending "modern day" sequences that transpire around 1990. The main tale, set in America's heartland, features teenager Walter (Haley Joel Osment) being abandoned by his mother (Kyra Sedgwick) to the care of his two cantankerous uncles, Garth (Michael Caine) and Hub (Robert Duvall). She is determined to make something of herself or, failing that, find a rich guy to marry, but she can't do that with a kid in tow. So, even though Garth and Hub are only distant relatives, she never hesitates to impose upon them, and soon a very unhappy boy is stuck with two old codgers who don't own a television or a phone, and whose idea of entertainment is taking potshots at the door-to-door salesmen who drive up their road seeking to bilk them of some of the enormous sum of money they have stashed away.

Grudgingly, as one would expect from this kind of movie, Walter begins to bond with Garth and Hub. The former tells tales of the latter when he was in his prime — a valiant swashbuckler who defeated enemies by the dozens and won the love of the beautiful Princess Jasmine (Emmanuelle Vaugier). These days, Hub isn't the man he used to be, but he can still be pretty impressive in a fight, such as a barroom brawl in which he handily beats four punks. Then there's the lion who becomes Walter's pet and ends up living in the cornfield in Garth and Hub's yard.

Secondhand Lions never takes itself too seriously — there are moments of irreverent comedy sprinkled throughout — but it isn't so farcical that the characters become meaningless pawns of a jokester screenwriter/director. Quite the opposite, in fact. We come to care deeply about Garth, Hub, and Walter — so much so that the unnecessary epilogue isn't as bothersome as it might otherwise be. While it's true that McCanlies occasionally pokes fun at his characters, he also treats them with respect. Garth and Hub may start out as caricatures, but they quickly develop into much more.

The themes of *Secondhand Lions* will appeal to many parents since there aren't many movies out there that value faith (human beings need to believe things that may not be true) and true love. Adults will appreciate the light, tongue-in-cheek tone, and children will enjoy the action sequences and the coming-of-age perspective. *Secondhand Lions* isn't groundbreaking or astoundingly original, but it is enjoyable, and that earns it a recommendation. There's nothing secondhand about this movie. **RECOMMENDED**

The Secret Garden [United Kingdom/United States, 1993]

Starring: Kate Maberly, Heydon Prowse, Andrew Knott, Maggie Smith, John Lynch Director: Agnieszka Holland Screenplay: Caroline Thompson, based on the novel by Frances Hodgson Burnett Running Time: 1:39 Rated: G Theatrical Aspect Ratio: 1.85:1

Orphaned in India, where her transplanted English parents lived before falling victim to an earthquake, Mary Lennox (Kate Maberly) comes to the cold, aloof household of her uncle, the widower of her mother's twin sister. There, she is viewed as a meddlesome nuisance by the housekeeper, Mrs. Medlock (Maggie Smith), and is ordered to stay in her room. Mary doesn't obey, of course, and, during one of her unauthorized explorations, she discovers the room of her sickly cousin, Colin (Heydon Prowse). Outside, she finds something even more wondrous: the secret garden of her late aunt. With the help of Dickon (Andrew Knott), a local boy who can talk with animals, Mary sets to work reclaiming the garden from the weeds and brambles that had overrun it.

The Secret Garden is based on Frances Hodgson Burnett's 1911 novel, and director Agnieszka Holland has taken care that the screenplay follows the book. Holland is an avowed fan of the story, having read it over and over again as a child. The care and effort she poured into this, her first English-language effort, is proof enough of that, resulting in a picture that is magical for viewers of all ages.

The story is essentially about the redemption of two damaged children. Mary, while hale of body, is an emotional cripple. She grew up unloved in a household where her selfish parents handed her off to the servants. Colin is neither physically nor emotionally whole. His father, never having recovered from the death of his wife, rarely visits Colin in the sickroom, leaving the boy's care to the implacable and unaffectionate Mrs. Medlock. The secret garden is a place of rare and wondrous beauty, and it becomes the emotional balm that heals all wounds, both physical and psychological.

I'm not sure how younger viewers will react to this film. Many will miss the subtle nuances that Agnieszka Holland brings to the screen (which are aimed at adults), but the story, centering as it does around children, will captivate many. By any standard, this is an excellent family film for those willing to immerse themselves in its leisurely pace — the picture proceeds just fast enough to keep the audience's attention while exhibiting a great attention to detail. **RECOMMENDED**

Shiloh [1997]

Starring: Blake Heron, Michael Moriarty, Scott Wilson, Ann Dowd, J. Madison Wright, Rod Steiger Director: Dale Rosenbloom Screenplay: Dale Rosenbloom, based on the novel by Phyllis Reynolds Naylor Running Time: 1:33 Rated: PG (Mild violence) Theatrical Aspect Ratio: 1.85:1

I have never been a big fan of "animal in danger" tales, but *Shiloh* is far better than most. Not only does it show the animal, a 1-year-old beagle, being abused (although not graphically), but it doesn't turn the dog into some sort of living cartoon character. Likewise, the young protagonist, 11-year-old Marty Preston (Blake Heron), doesn't have all the answers and isn't constantly outsmarting his parents. And the film's villain, Judd Travers (Scott Wilson), isn't just inherently evil — there's a legitimate reason why he's so nasty, as Marty comes to find out during the movie's second half.

Shiloh takes place in the tiny town of Friendly, West Virginia. It's a lazy summer and Marty is wandering around town looking for odd jobs to earn a little cash. On his way home one day, he encounters a beagle with a cut over its eye. It follows him, and Marty, a loner by nature, develops an immediate attachment to the injured animal. He even gives it a name — Shiloh — after the bridge where he encountered it. His father (Michael Moriarty) recognizes Shiloh as the new hunting dog of the reclusive Judd Travers, and Marty reluctantly agrees to return it, even though he suspects Judd of mistreating the animal. Several days later, Shiloh again runs away from Judd, and this time, when the dog seeks him out, Marty decides not to tell his parents. So, with the help of his friend Samantha (J. Madison Wright), he hides the beagle in a fort and sneaks food to it every night. But it's only a matter of time before someone else learns his secret.

The strength of *Shiloh* is that it approaches its subject matter intelligently. There are no easy answers to Marty's dilemma — the Law is on Judd's side, but the boy believes his position is morally defensible. At one point, when his father accuses him of not doing the right thing, Marty's response is a simple question: "What's right?" Later, the kindhearted town doctor (played by Rod Steiger) tells him that if he wants to keep Shiloh, he may be forced to fight for the dog.

Shiloh, which is adapted from a Newberry Award winning book, fits nicely into the class of better animal-related family films, joining the ranks of *Lassie* and *Black Beauty*. And, while the primary target audience is undeniably children, few adults who sit through this motion picture will wish they had done otherwise. **RECOMMENDED**

Spy Kids [2001]

Starring: Antonio Banderas, Carla Gugino, Alexa Vega, Alan Cumming, Daryl Sabara Director: Robert Rodriguez Screenplay: Robert Rodriguez Running Time: 1:28 Rated: PG (Violence) Theatrical Aspect Ratio: 1.85:1

The storyline isn't terribly complex, and the movie develops in a cartoonish, tongue-in-cheek fashion that promises never to take anything too seriously. *Spy Kids* isn't exactly a parody, but it doesn't mind occasionally poking fun at staples of the espionage genre. Gregorio and Ingrid Cortez (Antonio Banderas and Carla Gugino) are retired spies who gave up their secret agent duties to act as "consultants" while raising two kids: Carmen (Alexa Vega) and Juni (Daryl Sabara). But Gregorio and Ingrid still have adventure in their blood, and, when a mission calls, they can't resist. Unfortunately, they're rusty, and end up being captured by the diabolical Fegan Floop (Alan Cumming), a children's TV show host who is planning to use an army of robot children to take over the world. So it's Carmen and Juni to the rescue. After paying their dour Uncle Machete (Danny Trejo) a visit, they load up on cool gadgets and head for Floop's castle to save their mom and dad.

One common failing of the generic family film is to make everyone over the age of 12 terminally stupid. Another is to make the child protagonists either (a) unbearably cute or (b) irritatingly obnoxious. These are pitfalls that Rodriguez consciously avoids. Carmen and Juni are cute, likable kids — but not too cute or cloyingly likable. And, although the adults are occasionally prone to doing dumb things, they are presented sympathetically. They're not all ogres with pea-sized brains, à la the crooks in *Home Alone*.

The film moves at a brisk pace that never threatens to bog down. In addition to the humor, which surfaces on a consistent basis, there's a lot of adventure and action. Several of the creatures living in Floop's castle look like refugees from the *Star Wars* cantina, and there is a race of human-sized thumbs that are, predictably, clumsy ("all thumbs"). Since the film was made on a modest budget, digital effects were used liberally to spruce up the look. Their incorporation is sometimes a little too obvious, but there are times when they work. There are also numerous neat gadgets — everything from a super-fast, single-passenger spy plane to bubble gum that packs a real punch.

For Robert Rodriguez, who began his career with great promise as the hotshot director of *El Mariachi*, it has been a while since he has been embraced by the critics or the public. *Spy Kids* proves that he can be as adept at the family genre as he is at making ultra-gory revenge and horror films. With this charming and unpretentious effort, Rodriguez has successfully put the "family" back into the term "family film." **RECOMMENDED**

Spy Kids 2: The Island of Lost Dreams [2002]

Starring: Antonio Banderas, Carla Gugino, Alexa Vega, Daryl Sabara, Steve Buscemi Director: Robert Rodriguez Screenplay: Robert Rodriguez Running Time: 1:38 Rated: PG (Cartoon violence, mild profanity) Theatrical Aspect Ratio: 1.85:1

With his tongue planted firmly in his cheek, Robert Rodriguez sets out to lampoon the spy genre while still providing a breezy, fast-paced ride full of bumps and jolts. The movie has the sensibility of a cartoon, with larger-than-life bad guys, a thoroughly implausible plot, and enough nifty gadgets and vehicles to impress Q.

Once again, our heroes are Carmen Cortez (Alexa Vega) and her younger brother, Juni (Daryl Sabara). They are the children of ace spies Gregorio and Ingrid Cortez (Antonio Banderas and Carla Gugino) and the grandchildren of two legendary agents (Ricardo Montalban and Holland Taylor). As the film begins, Carmen and Juni, now junior members of the OSS, are out to save the President's daughter, Alexandra (Taylor Momsen), who is in danger at an extreme amusement park. Rival spy kids Gary and Gerti Giggles (Matthew O'Leary and Emily — sister of Haley Joel — Osment) arrive in time to complicate the rescue. But this is only a prelude to the real adventure. Soon, all 4 kids end up on a mysterious island, fighting bizarre creatures while looking for the mysterious Romero (Steve Buscemi) and his dangerous creation, the "Transmooger Device," which can be used to control (or destroy) the world.

Boiled down to its basics, *Spy Kids 2* is just good, clean fun. It works as well for kids as it does for adults, due in large part to two things: (1) its refusal to talk down to the audience, and (2) an unflagging pace. There are opportunities for character expansion — Carmen has a "thing" for Gary, Juni develops a crush on the President's daughter, and Gregorio has to deal with insecurities regarding his in-laws and the consideration that his son may be outgrowing him. And, as a mad scientist creator, Romero finds himself asking surprisingly deep philosophical questions like, "Do you think God stays in heaven because he fears what he has created?"

Spy Kids 2 is a worthy successor to the original, and an enjoyable romp in its own right. **RECOMMENDED**

Stuart Little [United States, 1999]

Starring: Geena Davis, Hugh Laurie, Jonathan Lipnicki, Michael J. Fox (voice), Nathan Lane (voice) Director: Rob Minkoff Screenplay: Gregory J. Brooker and M. Night Shayamalan, based on the book by E.B. White Running Time: 1:20 Rated: PG (Mild profanity, mouse in danger) Theatrical Aspect Ratio: 1.85:1

Stuart Little has been inspired by E.B. White's book, a classic that almost every child is familiar with. The picture is quiet, gentle, and family-friendly — 3 qualities that rarely apply to the form of entertainment that kids crave. The story begins in a New York City orphanage, where Mr. And Mrs. Little (Hugh Laurie and Geena Davis) have come to adopt a baby brother for their only son, George (Jonathan Lipnicki). However, while observing the children at play, their attention is arrested by a mouse (voice of Michael J. Fox) who approaches them and offers tips about which girls and boys might make the best daughters or sons. When it comes time to make a choice, the Littles select the mouse and name him Stuart. George is at first unimpressed, but, after a few false starts, he bonds with his "brother." The only one displeased by the new arrival is the cat, Snowbell (voice of Nathan Lane), who is upset by the idea of being placed lower in the family pecking order than someone who should be below him on the food chain. So Snowbell enlists the aid of a pair of other felines: the hyperactive Monty (voice of Steve Zahn) and the dangerous Smokey (voice of Chazz Palminteri). Together, the 3 of them plan a way to "scratch" Stuart from the Little family album.

Stuart Little is not a film of great performances, but it is one of subtle-but-impressive special effects. Without a doubt, Stuart is the most real and sympathetic character in the film. From a visual standpoint, he is also consistently believable. Equally impressive are the cats. One of the reasons for this is that, at least most of the time, Snowbell, Monty, and Smokey are living, breathing animals, but the manipulation of their mouths (when they talk) is executed flawlessly.

The vocal talents fit into the category of "familiar, but not necessarily recognizable without a credits list." Another high-profile name involved with the project is M. Night Shyamalan, who co-wrote the screenplay. (Shyamalan is, of course, a suddenly hot property in the wake of the success of *The Sixth Sense*, which he wrote and directed.) Of course, all of this talent would mean little if the final product wasn't worthwhile, but, in the case of *Stuart Little*, the results are favorable. Hopefully, parents and children seeking theatrical fare will give this movie a chance before seeking out something that's louder, flashier, and lobotomized. **RECOMMENDED**

Stuart Little 2 [2002]

Starring: Geena Davis, Hugh Laurie, Jonathan Lipnicki, Michael J. Fox (voice), Nathan Lane (voice) Director: Rob Minkoff Screenplay: Bruce Joel Rubin Running Time: 1:16 Rated: PG (Mildly frightening images) Theatrical Aspect Ratio: 1.85:1

Stuart Little 2 brings back all of the elements that made its predecessor so successful, including most of the original cast (both live-action and computer generated) and director Rob Minkoff. The screenplay, freed from the constraints of having to introduce everyone, can go off in more interesting directions. In this case, the story involves a wounded bird befriended by Stuart and a dangerous falcon who is hunting her. There are also issues of sibling separation, or what happens when the older child outgrows the younger one and starts spending more time with his school friends. This is a theme that many children, and more than a few adults, will be able to relate to: the point at which the younger brother or sister ceases to be a playmate and starts to be a pest. (In this case, however, Stuart literally is a "pest," although no one refers to him in those terms.)

The talking animals are all back, and the digital technology that allows their lips to seemingly move is as effective as it was 3 years ago. Michael J. Fox picks up where he left off providing the voice of the lead character. Nathan Lane returns as the scene-stealing Snowball, the Littles' disgruntled cat. (About 90% of the best lines all go to Snowball, and Lane utters them with relish.) Newcomers include James Woods as the dangerous Falcon and Melanie Griffith as Margalo, Stuart's new flying friend. The live-action actors are Geena Davis and Hugh Laurie as Stuart's mom and dad, and Jonathan Lipnicki as George Little.

As was true of the first film, the special effects will have kids thinking Stuart and Margalo are real. Indeed, the computer animators went to great lengths to put a lot of the real actions of mice and birds into the way the characters look and act. Meanwhile, the humans are unreal, taking everything in with a cheerful seriousness that pokes gentle fun at old TV programs like *Father Knows Best* and *My Three Sons*. And no one thinks its odd that George's little brother is actually a mouse. Watching the blasé reactions of everyone to a talking mouse is worth a smile and a chuckle, but that's only one of many reasons to see, and enjoy, *Stuart Little 2*. **RECOMMENDED**

Tuck Everlasting [2002]

Starring: Jonathan Jackson, Alexis Bledel, Ben Kingsley, Sissy Spacek, William Hurt Director: Jay Russell Screenplay: Jeffrey Lieber & James V. Hart, based on the novel by Natalie Babbitt Running Time: 1:29 Rated: PG (Mature themes) Theatrical Aspect Ratio: 2.35:1

"Do you want to live forever?" That question has become a prominent "payoff" line for movies and television shows, but, underneath the flip tone in which it is often asked hides a query that expresses humankind's greatest longing — immortality. The first reaction of most people when asked that question would be to answer "yes." After all, immortality (with invulnerability and eternal youth thrown in at no extra charge) is a heady possibility. Unquestionably a blessing . . . or is it? Think about the price. It's not immediately apparent, but it is an unpleasant one. Never dying means *never*. Life will go on and on and on, until, inevitably, one is almost guaranteed to wish and hope and pray for some way to end it all.

No one asked the Tuck family if they wanted to live forever. In the early years of the 19th century, they came upon a small spring in the woods in upstate New York. Unbeknownst to them, it was the fountain of youth — the water for which Ponce de Leon had so aggressively sought. Drinking froze all 4 Tucks at their current ages. The parents, Mae and Angus (Sissy Spacek and William Hurt), remained middle-aged but spry. Miles (Scott Bairstow) was trapped in the prime of his life. And Jesse (Jonathan Jackson) was fated to exist through eternity in a 17-year-old body.

Nearly 100 years later, on the eve of the United States' entrance into the Great War, a teenage girl, Winnie Foster (Alexis Bledel), stumbles upon the Tucks' house while running away from home. After living with the Tucks for a while, Winnie learns their secret. Meanwhile, she and Jesse fall in love. Then she must face a choice — drink from the fountain and gain the promise of everlasting life and love with Jesse, or refuse and live for the normal span of human years.

The romantic aspect of *Tuck Everlasting*, which is clearly the element that will attract pre-teen and teenage girls, is nicely developed, although it follows the familiar arc of the overprotected rich girl falling for the poor, free-spirited boy. For younger viewers, the immortality question probably won't mean much, but, for those who have lived long enough, it represents the film's true strength. We know from early in the proceedings that Winnie will have to choose — and it won't be an easy choice.

Viewed on its own terms, this is a gently engaging and thought-provoking motion picture. *Tuck*

Everlasting is suitable for children, but the material is designed more for those with longer attention spans. The cartoonish buffoonery and mindless action of many family films is entirely absent. Disney's live-action division has a history of releasing cinematic flotsam, but this is one occasion when they have unearthed a rare gem. HIGHLY RECOMMENDED

Horror

28 Days Later [Netherlands/UK/USA, 2003]

Starring: Cillian Murphy, Naomie Harris, Noah Huntley, Brendan Gleeson, Megan Burns, Christopher Eccleston Director: Danny Boyle
Screenplay: Alex Garland Running Time: 1:52 Rated: R (Violence, gore, profanity, nudity) Theatrical Aspect Ratio: 2.35:1

Danny Boyle, the director of *Shallow Grave* and *Trainspotting*, has brought his off-center perspective to this story. Armed with a screenplay written by Alex Garland, Boyle's vision of humanity's twilight has mankind wiped out not by fire, brimstone, and nuclear fallout, but by disease. The living are divided into two categories: the infected, who are more like mindless zombies than human beings, and the survivalists, who eschew making plans, realizing that "staying alive is as good as it gets." The allegorical nature of the movie is impossible to miss. And Boyle touches upon such potentially weighty matters as the fundamental difference between man and beast, and whether human beings are natural killers.

The movie opens with a brief prologue that explains the start of the plague (a misguided group of animals' rights activists release contaminated monkeys), then jumps ahead 28 days to a drastically changed world. Jim (Cillian Murphy) awakens in an empty hospital where he has been laid up, unconscious, since before the calamity struck. Befuddled and disbelieving, he staggers into the streets and finds London to be deserted. When he is attacked by one of the infected — a slavering, red-eyed, feral human being whose only desire is to draw blood — his life is saved by Selena (Naomie Harris) and Mark (Noah Huntley). They inform him of what has happened, and after it sinks in, Jim decides to visit his parents' house. Selena and Mark accompany him. Soon, the humans are joined by a middle-aged man, Frank (Brendan Gleeson), and his teenage daughter, Hannah (Megan Burns), and they elect to seek out a group of soldiers, led by Major Henry West (Christopher Eccleston), who claim to have the answer to the infection.

When Boyle wants to shock us, he has no trouble doing so. There's a little of George A. Romero (*Night of the Living Dead*) here. Several scenes in which the infected attack are genuinely creepy. One sequence in particular — in which Jim and Frank race to change a tire while a band of infected relentlessly approach — generates as much tension as any other 2003 motion picture. This is followed in short order by an effective character building sequence in which the protagonists enjoy a picnic while ruminating about what, if anything, the future might hold. Suddenly, Jim and Selena have become aware that the mantra of "just survive" is not enough.

28 Days Later is dark, the video quality is dubious (it was shot on digital video to curtail cost and provide a grittier look), and the subject matter is familiar. But the filmmakers counter these questionable qualities with solid performances, an intelligent script, and sure-handed direction. The result is a movie that kept me involved from start to finish. RECOMMENDED

Army of Darkness [1993]

Starring: Bruce Campbell, Embeth Davidz, Marcus Gilbert
Director: Sam Raimi Screenplay: Sam & Ivan Raimi Running Time: 1:21
Rated: R (Violence, gore, language) Theatrical Aspect Ratio: 1.85:1

Ash (Bruce Campbell) is a housewares salesman at an S-Mart department store before a venture to the house from *Evil Dead 1* and *2* sends him through a time tunnel into the Middle Ages. Suddenly, as the "Promised One" of prophesy, he is expected to save the locals from an upsurge in evil. Armed with a chainsaw and a 12-gauge shotgun, Ash sets out to put down an army of skeletons and woo one of the locals (Sheila, played by Embeth Davidz), all the while trying to find a way back home.

Army of Darkness is openly campy — and proud of it — blending a unique mix of horror, swords-and-sorcery, and the Three Stooges. Bruce Campbell, returning after the two *Evil Dead* films, is in top form, delivering ridiculous lines with a deadpan seriousness that would make Leslie Nielsen take notice. As the reluctant hero, he's a walking anachronism who shoots up ghouls, turns his Chevy into a tank, and can't remember how to pronounce a series of magic words that pay homage to Robert Wise's *The Day the Earth Stood Still*.

There are some very memorable Three Stooges-type moments, complete with sound effects (pops, zings, and so forth). There's eye-poking, headshaking, and other slapstick standards. What makes these moments especially bizarre — and effective — is that most of the time, Larry, Curly, and Moe are represented by ghouls and animated skeletons. Every ounce of fat has been trimmed from this production. It's a comic book brought to life, with no time for characterization, exposition, or subplots. *Army of Darkness* moves with breakneck speed, but its direction is straight, so there's little chance of anyone getting lost on the way. Those who like this kind of thing — lots of action and gore, silly dialogue, over-the-top acting, and a self-mocking campiness that permeates all eighty-one minutes — will love this movie. Anyone who prefers a more "traditional" motion picture will probably do best to stay away. Then again, you never know . . . **RECOMMENDED**

Beloved [1998]

Starring: Oprah Winfrey, Danny Glover, Thandie Newton, Kimberly Elise Director: Jonathan Demme Screenplay: Adam Brooks, Akosua Busia, Richard LaGravanese, based on the novel by Toni Morrison Running Time: 2:55 Rated: R (Violence, sexual violence, frontal nudity, sex) Theatrical Aspect Ratio: 1.85:1

Beloved, Jonathan Demme's much-anticipated adaptation of Toni Morrison's novel, is a powerful and disturbing motion picture that is likely to leave many movie-goers unsettled as they file out of the theater.

Beloved is a ghost tale. It's about a woman's sins literally coming back to haunt her. The main story transpires in Ohio during 1865, but there are numerous flashbacks to pre-Civil War times. Like many other motion pictures set during this era, *Beloved* is about the pernicious influence of slavery, but the approach taken by Morrison's novel attains its uncommon power through originality. Some of what happens in *Beloved*, you will expect. Other things, you will not.

The film opens on a peaceful summer afternoon in Ohio, when a lonely traveler named Paul D (Danny Glover) arrives at the house at 124 Bluestone Road. Living there is Sethe (Oprah Winfrey), a woman Paul D knew many years ago when they were both slaves on a Kentucky farm named Sweet Home. ("It wasn't sweet and it wasn't home.") Sethe is not alone in her house. Her daughter, Denver (Kimberly Elise), a virtual shut-in, also lives there. However, her 2 sons have long since gone, scared away by the ghost of another child that haunts the premises. ("It ain't evil, just sad.") No sooner has Paul D arrived than he meets the spirit, and, in a struggle of wills, appears to dispel it. But Denver doubts his success, thinking that the dead baby is planning something.

Soon after, Paul D, now Sethe's lover, has moved in, and is setting his sights on winning Denver's trust. One afternoon, on the way back from a carnival, Denver and Sethe encounter a nearly-mute young woman (Thandie Newton) who has been overcome by heat exhaustion. They bring her home and revive her. The only name she gives them is "Beloved." Thereafter, Denver makes Beloved her special project, teaching her things about life, and how to speak. But, while Denver and Sethe are infatuated with this strange, wild woman, Paul D is suspicious. Something about Beloved strikes him as dangerous.

Beloved is one of those films that won't work for someone in search of light entertainment. The movie deals with difficult subjects without flinching or sugar-coating the truth. *Beloved* is for those who want substance from a movie, and don't mind facing uncomfortable truths in the process. **HIGHLY RECOMMENDED**

Below [2002]

Starring: Matt Davis, Bruce Greenwood, Holt McCallany, Olivia Williams Director: David Twohy Screenplay: Lucas Sussman, Darren Aranofsky and David Twohy Running Time: 2:55 Rated: R (Violence, profanity) Theatrical Aspect Ratio: 1.85:1

Although it's hard to imagine a better match than ghosts and submarines, this story has never previously been told. Consider all of the natural claustrophobia and tension inherent in a movie about men trapped in the bowels of a submerged sub, and add in the possibility that the boat might be haunted. The result would seem to be the formula for a superior horror/thriller. And, while director David Twohy arguably doesn't mine the premise for all it's worth, he gets enough out of it to make it an effective Halloween treat.

The film, which transpires during World War II, begins with a rescue mission, as the crew of the *Tiger Shark* brings on board 3 survivors of a torpedoed British hospital ship. All is not well aboard the *Tiger Shark*, however. Morale has been at a low ebb since the death of the captain. The current commander, Lt. Brice (Bruce Greenwood), seems unsure of his position. When the *Tiger Shark* is attacked soon after the British are brought on board, Brice reacts by accusing a female nurse, Claire (Olivia Williams), of being a collaborator. Ensign Douglas O'Dell (Matt Davis) watches all of this transpire with unease, sensing that Brice may know more about the captain's death than he is willing to acknowledge. Meanwhile, supernatural occurrences begin plaguing the boat, starting with a record player that turns itself on at will.

Twohy understands the importance of atmosphere, and allows it to suffuse *Below*. Nearly every scene is shot in dim lighting, and the camera moves in such a way that we think, but are not certain, that something out-of-the-ordinary is happening. There are a few "boo!" moments, but not as many as there could have been. Twohy uses sound to good effect, as the men trapped in the sub hear the eerie, expected echoes of whale songs and sonar pings, as well as some chilling noises that they cannot identify.

Below is a psychological horror movie that emphasizes tension over the macabre. And, in the end, the protagonists must determine whether they have more to fear from the spirits haunting the sub, the Germans prowling the waters above, or the men who will do almost anything to keep their secrets buried. **RECOMMENDED**

The Blair Witch Project [1999]

Starring: Heather Donahue, Michael Williams, Joshua Leonard
Directors: Eduardo Sanchez and Daniel Myrick Screenplay: Eduardo Sanchez & Daniel Myrick Running Time: 1:27 Rated: R (Profanity, terror) Theatrical Aspect Ratio: 1.33:1 & 1.66:1

The Blair Witch Project is, in a word, brilliant — and is even more impressive considering that it's the debut effort from filmmakers Eduardo Sanchez and Daniel Myrick. Watching this film is a harrowing experience because we accept the characters as completely real and become engaged in their ordeal. In one corner of my mind, I knew this was all fictional, but the verisimilitude is impressive, and results in an experience that is as fascinating as it is involving and creepy.

The Blair Witch Project is presented as a documentary within a documentary. Aspiring director Heather Donahue, a film student at Montgomery College, has decided to chronicle the legend of the supposed "Blair Witch" — a mythical figure that has supposedly haunted Maryland's Black Hills Forest since the late 18th century and is credited for numerous, heinous murders. Accompanying Heather are camera man Joshua Leonard and sound operator Michael Williams. In addition to making a 16mm black-and-white film, Heather is capturing virtually everything on High 8 video with the intention of assembling a behind-the-scenes look at how her movie, "The Blair Witch Project," was made.

The element that makes *The Blair Witch Project* unusually compelling is the atypical manner in which it is presented. Every scene is a point-of-view shot, shown exactly as one might expect from someone carrying around a video camera. The transitions are unexpected and often jarring — the kind of thing that would result from turning the camera off at one point, then turning it back on later. Some of the most chilling sequences occur at night, when the darkness foils the video. There are instances when the screen is black and all we have to rely on is the audio — the near-panicked voices of the protagonists in the foreground and strange, unearthly noises in the background. At other times, the action depicted is chaotic and difficult to piece together, often because the person doing the filming is running or unsure what to capture.

It's not hard to understand why these segments work so well — they rely on the imagination to fill in the pictures, and what our minds conjure up is always more horrifying than anything the filmmakers can put on screen. Also, this seemingly haphazard and "unprofessional" approach gives the audience a "you are there" feeling that draws them into the experience, making everything that transpires more shocking and immediate that it would seem in a conventional format. Sanchez and Myrick deserve credit not only for attempting something different, but for succeeding so brilliantly at it. **HIGHLY RECOMMENDED**

Bubba Ho-Tep [2002]

Starring: Bruce Campbell, Ossie Davis, Bob Ivy Director: Don Coscarelli
Screenplay: Don Coscarelli, based on the short story by Joe R. Lansdale
Running Time: 1:32 Rated: R (Violence, profanity) Theatrical Aspect
Ratio: 1.85:1

If you're tired of conventional horror movies, try *Bubba Ho-Tep*, a cinematic oddity from director Don Coscarelli. Based on indisputable facts, the film finally reveals what really happened to Elvis and why so many people are reluctant to admit that he's dead. In fact, the man buried in the King's grave is a fake. At one point, Elvis (Bruce Campbell) got tired of being the King, so he decided to perpetrate the biggest hoax in rock 'n' roll history by switching places with his best impersonator. When "Elvis" died, the real singer was trapped in a life of trailer parks and cheap concerts, until he broke his hip, fell into a coma, then ended up in an East Texas rest home. It's there that the 70-year-old Elvis must face his greatest challenge. Alongside a black JFK (Ossie Davis), he must confront the ancient evil of the soul-sucking mummy Bubba Ho-Tep (Bob Ivy).

Okay, so maybe the movie takes a little artistic license with the facts. The screenplay, written by Coscarelli, is based on a short story by Joe R. Lansdale. One of the most cool and tantalizingly bizarre flicks of 2003, this movie isn't afraid to try anything. Elvis has appeared in many movies, but this is the first time he has been cast as an aging action hero who fights an undead monster while hampered by his need to use a walker. Amidst all of the outrageousness and downright silliness, viewers might be surprised to know that, although there's quite a bit of caricature associated with this version of Elvis, an effort has been made to develop him into a sympathetic and multidimensional individual. On more than one occasion, he expresses sincere regret about abandoning his daughter, and he wonders whether Priscilla would take him back if she found out he was still alive.

As a satire and an off-the-wall comedy, *Bubba Ho-Tep* hits the bull's-eye. As a horror movie, it's less successful. Maybe we're too busy laughing to be scared, but the title character isn't that frightening, and we instinctively recognize that he's no match for Campbell's Elvis. Nevertheless, as I enjoyed this low-budget tale of a dead Egyptian let loose on today's world, I couldn't help but wonder how much better the recent big-budget Mummy movies could have been with Coscarelli at the helm. Without a doubt (and with virtually no budget), *Bubba Ho-Tep* blows them away. To the writer/director, I have only one thing to say: Thank you very much. **RECOMMENDED**

Dawn of the Dead [2004]

Starring: Sarah Polley, Ving Rhames, Jake Weber, Mekhi Phifer, Ty Burrell, Michael Kelly, Kevin Zegers, Lindy Booth Director: Zack Snyder Screenplay: James Gunn, based on the 1978 screenplay by George A. Romero Running Time: 1:40 Rated: R (Violence, profanity, sexual situations, brief nudity) Theatrical Aspect Ratio: 2.35:1

Calling this version of *Dawn of the Dead* a remake is applying a misnomer. It's more of a re-imagination. The premise and circumstances are similar to those of George Romero's picture, but the specifics are different. Having seen the 1978 movie doesn't mean that you will be able to predict the outcome of the 2004 version, since very few of the same things happen. The ending in particular is different — especially the unprecedented way in which director Zack Snyder arrives at it. Those who bolt from their seats the moment the closing credits begin will leave with a much different impression of the resolution than those who stay to the bitter end. Interspersed between screens filled with names are *Blair Witch Project*–style video clips that extend the story.

The movie transpires in the city of Everett, Wisconsin, where a mysterious epidemic is running rampant through the population. No one knows who the first victims are, or how the virus started, but anyone bitten by an infected individual dies, then is born again as a mindless ghoul. A group of five surviving humans — nurse Ana (Sarah Polley), cop Kenneth (Ving Rhames), ordinary guy Michael (Jake Weber), and expecting parents Andre (Mekhi Phifer) and Luda (Inna Korobkina) — seek refuge in a local mall. There, they encounter a pugnacious security guard, CJ (Michael Kelly), and his sidekicks, Terry (Kevin Zegers) and Bart (Michael Barry). Later, they spot a truck circling the mall parking lot and rescue the passengers, including smart-ass Steve (Ty Burrell), sexpot Monica (Kim Poirier), father and daughter Frank (Matt Frewer) and Nicole (Lindy Booth), tough-as-nails Norma (Jayne Eastwood), and ever-practical Tucker (Boyd Banks). Banding together, these people try to outrun and outgun their undead opponents. With so many characters, it's inevitable that most of them end up as one-dimensional throwaways whose sole purpose is to increase the body count. But there are exceptions. Ana, Kenneth, Michael, and Andre are developed to a point where we care about them. And several touching subplots are handled with a deft hand: Andre's concern about his unborn fetus, Frank's and Nicole's sad farewell, Kenneth's long-distance friendship with a man on the roof of a nearby gun shop, and Ana and Michael's halting attempts at intimacy. Of course, not many people go to a horror film looking for character development and drama, so there are plenty of good scares, and a moment or two of gut-wrenching terror. The movie even crosses the PC line and allows children to do demonic things.

The creatures in this film move a lot more quickly than those in the original, whose slow, staggering gait was ripe for parody. Here, their swiftness proves to be the undoing of more than one character. As zombie films go, this one is a small step beneath Danny Boyle's *28 Days Later,* which was darker and creepier, but it's still a respectable effort. Adherents of the original may be annoyed by some of the changes, but cameos by Tom Savini, Scott Reiniger, and Ken Foree (who once again makes the dire pronouncement "When there's no more room in hell, the dead will walk the earth.") should build some goodwill. For those who enjoy tight, tense, graphic horror, this movie offers an ample helping. RECOMMENDED

The Evil Dead [1982]

Starring: Bruce Campbell, Ellen Sandweiss, Hal Delrich, Betsy Baker, Sarah York Director: Sam Raimi Screenplay: Sam Raimi Running Time: 1:25 Rated: NC-17 (Extreme gore, violence, profanity, brief nudity) Theatrical Aspect Ratio: 1.85:1

Long before *Scream* came along to simultaneously parody the horror genre while participating in it, there was Sam Raimi's *Evil Dead* trilogy (the third entry into the series, *Army of Darkness,* was released in 1993). Equal parts suspense, camp, comedy, and over-the-top gore, the first two *Evil Dead* movies didn't take long to attain the status of cult classics. Today, while relatively few mainstream movie viewers have heard of these movies, they have garnered a small but loyal gathering of fans who can recite every one liner delivered by the ultra-cool hero, Ash.

The Evil Dead follows the ill-fated expedition of 5 20-somethings who decide to spend a weekend at an isolated cabin in the middle of the woods. They are Ash (Bruce Campbell); his girlfriend, Linda (Betsy Baker); his sister, Shelly (Sarah York); and his friends, Cheryl (Ellen Sandweiss) and Scotty (Hal Delrich). At the cabin, the 5 discover a strange book whose pages are made out of human skin and whose writing is done in human blood. This is the Necronomicon, or the "Book of the Dead," which "speaks of a spiritual presence — a thing of evil — that roams the forests and dark bowers of man's domain." It also includes incantations to raise demons — spells that are invoked when a tape recording of a man reading them is played. Soon, Ash and his compatriots are the unfortunate targets of an implacable force that lurks in and around their little cottage and, one-by-one, they are possessed or killed.

The Evil Dead is much more of a straightforward horror endeavor than its sequel, containing little in the way of overt comedy. Its humor comes through accentuating traditional elements of the thriller/horror genre, including drenching the screen in copious amounts of fake blood, allowing the actors to give over-the-top performances, and intentionally placing characters in positions where they do stupid things.

One of the most remarkable things about *The Evil Dead* is how much it was able to accomplish on such a small budget (reportedly around $50K). Of course, it could be argued that many of the best horror films, including *Halloween* and *The Blair Witch Project,* have come cheaply, with the lack of funding forcing the filmmakers to rely more on innovation than special effects. *The Evil Dead* is at times genuinely creepy, due in no small part to the imaginative camerawork devised by Raimi and cinematographer Tim Philo. Also, the evil force inhabiting the forest is never shown in *The Evil Dead,* leaving all the details to our imagination. RECOMMENDED

Evil Dead II [1987]

Starring: Bruce Campbell, Sarah Berry, Dan Hicks, Kassie Wesley, Denise Bixler Director: Sam Raimi Screenplay: Sam Raimi, Scott Spiegel Running Time: 1:25 Rated: R (Extreme gore, violence, profanity) Theatrical Aspect Ratio: 1.85:1

What do you get when you cross George Romero with The Three Stooges by way of the director of *A Simple Plan* and *The Gift*? Something offbeat, to be sure. Something grotesque, without a doubt. Something . . . groovy.

To say that the *Evil Dead* movies are not for everyone is an understatement. A strong stomach is required. If you can't take copious amounts of blood and gore, this is not your movie. Both *The Evil Dead* and *Evil Dead II* have enough vile colored liquids to fill a small swimming pool. Plus, there are assorted body parts (decapitated heads, bodiless hands, etc.). Of course, the extreme nature of the gore isn't beside the point — it *is* the point. Raimi goes so far over the top in presenting these displays that they take on a campy, almost humorous appearance. It's impossible to take all this blood seriously. So, instead of being sickened, we're strangely amused — and this is all intentional.

Evil Dead II can be seen as a sequel to *Evil Dead*, a remake, or a little of both. Rather than starting off where its predecessor finished, *Evil Dead II* goes back to the beginning — sort of. The first 10 minutes of the second film essentially recap what occurred in *The Evil Dead*. Ash heads up to the cabin, although, in this movie, his only companion is Linda (played here by Denise Bixler). The two discover the Necronomicon, and, in no time, Linda is a zombie and Ash is forced to chop her up to save himself. Before long, Ash is possessed, but he manages to fight off the demonic influence. He is joined by a group of 4 additional characters: Annie Knowby (Sarah Berry), whose father owns the cabin; her boyfriend, Ed (Richard Domeier); a redneck named Jake (Dan Hicks); and his girlfriend, Bobbie Joe (Kassie Wesley). Predictably, these characters are dispatched one-by-one, leaving Ash as the last one standing. The ending of *Evil Dead II* leads directly into *Army of Darkness*.

That brings us to the Three Stooges. Raimi is on record as being an avid Three Stooges fan, and his appreciation of the old-time comics shows clearly in a variety of slapstick homages that appear throughout both *Evil Dead II* and *Army of Darkness*. While the Stooges' routines might not seem to be ripe for incorporation in a horror movie, Raimi's use of this material works, primarily because the tapestry into which it is woven already has a highly satirical/comedic aspect. It's also interesting to note that, while the role of one of the Stooges is occasionally played by the human Ash, there are occasions when a zombie takes on the part of Larry, Curly, or Moe. **RECOMMENDED**

The Exorcist [1973]

Starring: Ellen Burstyn, Max von Sydow, Lee J. Cobb, Kitty Winn, Jack MacGowran Director: William Friedkin Screenplay: William Peter Blatty Running Time: 2:02 Rated: R (Violence, profanity, horror elements) Theatrical Aspect Ratio: 1.85:1

During the cold months of the winter of 1973-74, the release of a horror film called *The Exorcist* became a national phenomenon. Would-be viewers stood outside for hours in bad weather to get a ticket, and the lines in New York City were said to circle entire blocks. Although this kind of fervor was not unprecedented, it was unexpected. As recently as several months before the movie's release, Warner Brothers had been discussing shelving the entire project. The distributor's ultimate willingness to take a chance returned huge financial dividends and established one of the most frequently copied films about demonic possession.

The Exorcist's strength is that it places character development on the same level as the horror elements, but it is not a ground-breaking motion picture. It is also too long, with a setup that could have accomplished the job with equal effectiveness in about ⅔ the time. There are instances when the first hour of *The Exorcist* noticeably drags, and there will always be a debate about whether the prologue (featuring Max von Sydow's Father Merrin at an archeological dig in North Africa) is necessary (or even useful).

The story is based on a series of true events that occurred in 1949 and were later fictionalized by author William Peter Blatty in his novel. It tells of the demonic possession of 12-year-old Regan MacNeil (Linda Blair), the daughter of popular actress Chris MacNeil (Ellen Burstyn). When we first meet Regan, she seems like any happy, well-adjusted girl. Soon, however, she is hearing strange noises, uttering obscenities, and experiencing violent tantrums and seizures. As her condition worsens and she begins speaking in an inhuman voice (provided by Mercedes McCambridge), the army of attending doctors advises calling in spiritual help. So Chris consults a local priest (who also happens to be a psychiatrist), Father Damien Karras (Jason Miller). After examining Regan, he agrees to assist in an exorcism, which will be performed by the respected and mysterious globe-trotting priest, Father Merrin (von Sydow).

Friedkin has crafted an atmospheric motion picture that is creepy from its early scenes in Georgetown (one of which shows Chris casually walking home on a Halloween afternoon). The film includes one of the most evocative and memorable images in a modern horror film, with Father Merrin emerging from a taxi and standing, in silhouette, under a street lamp as he faces the house where his latest struggle with the Devil will transpire. Moments like these, peppered throughout the production, give *The Exorcist* an artistic edge. **RECOMMENDED**

From Dusk Till Dawn [1996]

Starring: George Clooney, Harvey Keitel, Quentin Tarantino, Juliette Lewis Director: Robert Rodriguez Screenplay: Quentin Tarantino Running Time: 1:48 Rated: R (Gore, violence, gore, profanity, gore, nudity, gore) Theatrical Aspect Ratio: 1.85:1

It's great fun, but certainly not great art. *From Dusk Till Dawn*, a special effects blood-and-gore extravaganza from director Robert Rodriguez (written by Quentin Tarantino), follows in the footsteps of such cult classics as Sam Raimi's *Evil Dead* series, thumbing its nose at conventional film expectations and gleefully embracing the campiness of the B-movie genre. With its palette of hideous monstrosities, decapitations, dismemberments, eviscerations, topless dancers, profane dialogue, and bare foot licking, this motion picture pushes the R-rating to the edge.

Yet the reason *From Dusk Till Dawn* entertains is because it never takes itself seriously. The film is steeped in wit, parody, and offbeat humor. There aren't any characters here — only caricatures. The movie has been designed as a burst of high energy, and that's exactly what it turns out to be. *From Dusk Till Dawn* will appeal to only a small portion of the cinema-visiting population, but for those who enjoy this kind of tongue-and-cheek horror story, the film has a lot to offer.

In *From Dusk Till Dawn,* the setup is as long as the main story. The film opens by introducing us to two bank robbers on the run — Seth Gecko (George Clooney) and his nutcase brother Richie (Tarantino). They're on their way to Mexico, but they need a cover to get across the border. So, to that end, they hijack the mobile home of ex-preacher Jacob Fuller (Harvey Keitel) and his two kids (Juliette Lewis and Ernest Lieu), and force them, at gunpoint, to help. Once in Mexico, the 5 stop at an all-night bar for a little R&R. Only one problem: the place is run by vampires, and, after a little topless dancing, it's feeding time.

The film isn't for everyone, but, if you're in the target audience, you'll get what you want: a stylish, ultra-hip twist to one of humanity's oldest, darkest legends. Vampires will never live this one down. **RECOMMENDED**

The Gift [2000]

Starring: Cate Blanchett, Katie Holmes, Keanu Reeves, Giovanni Ribisi, Greg Kinnear Director: Sam Raimi Screenplay: Billy Bob Thornton & Tom Epperson Running Time: 1:51 Rated: R (Violence, nudity, sex, profanity) Theatrical Aspect Ratio: 1.85:1

The Gift is an example of how superior craftsmanship can transform a ho-hum genre entry into a sporadically gripping thriller. On the surface, there's nothing special about this movie — it's a run-of-the-mill supernatural murder mystery with all of the elements one expects from this sort of a motion picture: ghostly apparitions, courtroom drama, red herrings, and an "unexpected" twist at the end. Yet, while the script, credited to Billy Bob Thornton and Tom Ep-

person, is strictly generic, the direction by Sam Raimi and the performances of a stellar cast are anything but that. As a result of their contributions, a film that might originally have been strictly palatable for late-night cable viewing has turned into something worthy of theatrical consumption.

The Gift tells the story of Annie Wilson (Cate Blanchett), a widowed psychic scraping out a meager living by telling fortunes. Having lost her husband a year ago, she must provide for herself and her 3 young boys. There are plenty of people in the backwater Southern town who don't approve of what Annie does — they think she's a fraud or in league with the devil. Chief among them is Donnie Barksdale (Keanu Reeves), the abusive husband of one of Annie's clients, Valerie (Hilary Swank). One of Annie's few defenders is Buddy Cole (Giovanni Ribisi), the emotionally disturbed owner of a local garage. And, although Annie isn't looking for romance, there's clearly a connection between her and clean-cut Wayne Collins (Greg Kinnear), the principal at her sons' school. But a relationship doesn't look likely — Wayne is set to marry Jessica King (Katie Holmes), whose father is one of the most respected men in town. Then, one night, Jessica turns up missing and Annie experiences visions that implicate Donnie in her murder. Unwilling to credit the genuine nature of Annie's talent, the police are reluctant to believe her, but when the investigation uncovers a body, Annie becomes a star witness in a sensational trial.

Cate Blanchett, who can play any part from the Queen of England to a denizen of J.R.R. Tolkien's Middle Earth, proves that a gritty, unglamorous role like that of Annie does not challenge her range. Blanchett is wonderful as the uncertain, tortured psychic, and her performance brings Annie's humanity to the surface in a manner that a less gifted actress might not be able to manage. Katie Holmes is suitably saucy and sassy (and exhibits in graphic terms that she is willing to take roles that require nudity), and Greg Kinnear is intentionally bland. Finally, there's Keanu Reeves, who surprises with the pure evil he radiates. Maybe it takes a tough role like this to bring out the actor in Hollywood's original bogus adventurer. **RECOMMENDED**

Halloween [1978]

Starring: Jamie Lee Curtis, Donald Pleasance, Nancy Loomis, P.J. Soles Director: John Carpenter Screenplay: Debra Hill & John Carpenter Running Time: 1:33 Rated: R (Violence, profanity, sex, brief nudity) Theatrical Aspect Ratio: 2.35:1

· Because of its title, *Halloween* has frequently been grouped together with all the other splatter films that populated theaters throughout the late-1970s and early-1980s. However, while *Halloween* is rightfully considered the father of the modern slasher genre, it is not a member. This is not a gruesome motion picture — there is surprisingly little graphic violence and almost *no* blood. *Halloween* is built on suspense, not gore, and initiated more than a few of today's common horror/thriller cliches. The ultimate success of the movie, however, encouraged other film makers to try their hand at this sort of enterprise, and it didn't take long for someone to decide that audiences wanted as many explicitly grisly scenes as the running length would allow.

The film opens with a long, single-shot prologue that takes place on Halloween night, 1963. A young Michael Myers watches as his older sister, Judith, sneaks upstairs for a quickie with a guy from school. After the boyfriend has departed, Michael takes a knife out of the kitchen drawer, ascends the staircase, and stabs Judith to death. The entire sequence employs the subjective point-of-view, an approach that writer/director John Carpenter returns to repeatedly throughout the movie. Only after the deed is done do we learn that Michael is only a grade-schooler.

The bulk of the movie takes place 15 years later. Michael, confined to an asylum for the criminally insane for more than 10 years, escapes on the night before Halloween. His doctor, Sam Loomis (Donald Pleasance), believing Michael to be the embodiment of evil, tracks the killer back to his hometown of Haddonfield. From there, it's a race against time as Loomis seeks to locate and stop Michael before he starts again where he left off in 1963.

The final body count in *Halloween* is surprisingly low, but the terror quotient is high. This is the kind of impeccably crafted motion picture that burrows deep into our psyche and connects with the dark, hidden terrors that lurk there. *Halloween* is not a perfect movie, but no recent horror film has attained this pinnacle (as evidenced by the plaudits heaped upon it in Wes Craven's recent *Scream*). Likewise, John Carpenter has never come close to recapturing *Halloween*'s artistic or commercial success, though he has tried many times. *Halloween* remains untouched — a modern classic of the most horrific kind. **MUST SEE**

Interview with the Vampire [1994]

Starring: Tom Cruise, Brad Pitt, Kirsten Dunst, Antonio Bandaras, Christian Slater Director: Neil Jordan Screenplay: Anne Rice Running Time: 2:02 Rated: R (Violence, gore, mature themes, nudity) Theatrical Aspect Ratio: 1.85:1

Interview with the Vampire, based on the hugely successful novel by Anne Rice, begins and ends in present-day San Francisco, with Louis (Brad Pitt), a 2-century old vampire, telling his story to a fascinated interviewer (Christian Slater). His tale opens in 1791 Louisiana, just south of New Orleans, where Louis falls victim to the vampire Lestat (Tom Cruise). Given a choice between death and eternal life as one of the undead, Louis chooses the latter, a decision he will forever regret.

Louis cannot kill with the impunity of Lestat, but, to sate his hunger, he must feed, and the blood of animals is not enough. Eventually, he pierces the neck of a grief-stricken young girl named Claudia (Kirsten Dunst), whom Lestat then curses with his unholy form of resurrection so that she can be a surrogate daughter to both himself and Louis. For a while, they are one "big, happy family." But all things end, and Claudia's growing resentment of Lestat fuels a bloody confrontation.

When *Interview with the Vampire* works, it's as compelling and engrossing a piece of entertainment as is available on film today. When it falters, the weaknesses seem magnified. Fortunately, under the care of director Neil Jordan, instances of the former are more frequent that those of the latter, although the film noticeably stumbles during two key sequences (a needlessly drawn-out exploration of life as a vampire in Paris and the illogical, dumb conclusion). Despite the ups and downs of the second half, however, the first hour is classic horror at its most grotesque. In the best tradition of the *Grand Guignol, Interview with the Vampire* revels in its graphic and horrifying bloodiness. **RECOMMENDED**

Mary Reilly [1996]

Starring: Julia Roberts, John Malkovich, George Cole, Glenn Close Director: Stephen Frears Screenplay: Christopher Hampton, based on the novel by Valerie Martin Running Time: 1:48 Rated: R (Violence, mature themes) Theatrical Aspect Ratio: 1.85:1

Mary Reilly, brought to the screen by *Dangerous Liaisons* director Stephen Frears and *Liaisons* screenwriter Christopher Hampton, may be the most thought-provoking, intelligent, and disturbing motion picture version of Robert Louis Stevenson's *The Strange Case of Dr. Jekyll and Mr. Hyde* ever to be produced. Telling the classic split-personality story from the point-of-view of Dr. Jekyll's (John Malkovich) maid, Mary Reilly (Julia Roberts), this movie is an engrossing examination of the elemental forces that define human nature.

Any serious film interpretation of *Dr. Jekyll and Mr. Hyde* must, first and foremost, explore the meaning of Jekyll's split personality. As *Mary Reilly* interprets it, this is not a classic conflict between good and evil — life isn't that simple. Hyde does not represent the distillation of pure evil, just as Jekyll is not a paragon of righteousness. Each has virtues and flaws, and only together do they represent a whole person. Hyde is raw emotion — the animal side of humanity. His passion, twisted though it may be, gives Jekyll the will to live. Through the dichotomy presented by these two characters, we are challenged to consider that perhaps it's the combination of good and evil, control and liberation, and restraint and passion that makes each of us who we are. *Mary Reilly* has the power to disturb because it forces us to look inside and recognize our own Jekylls and Hydes.

By using Mary as the main character, this film is also able to illustrate the transforming power of love. To be sure, *Mary Reilly* isn't a conventional romance, but it's a love story nevertheless. Mary loves Jekyll for his goodness, and Hyde for what she sees of herself mirrored in him. When Jekyll speaks of having a fractured soul, Mary understands his pain. Her own spirit has been crippled by her childhood torture at the hands of an abusive father (Michael Gambon). Moreover, Hyde's feelings for Mary prove to be his undoing. In the end, her gift to him is indescribably precious.

I suspect that many who see *Mary Reilly* will get a completely different movie than they're expecting. Instead of murder and mayhem (although both of these are evident), we are presented with a beautifully-textured motion picture tapestry that focuses on characters and themes rather than gory special effects. *Mary Reilly* is haunting, not only because of its foggy, shadowy settings, but because of the questions it encourages us to ask about ourselves and others. **HIGHLY RECOMMENDED**

A Nightmare on Elm Street [1984]

Starring: John Saxon, Ronee Blakley, Heather Langenkamp, Johnny Depp, Robert Englund Director: Wes Craven Screenplay: Wes Craven
Running Time: 1:31 Rated: R (Violence, gore, sexual situations)
Theatrical Aspect Ratio: 1.85:1

The primary element that elevates *A Nightmare on Elm Street* above many of its contemporaries is that the storyline invites intellectual participation. In addition to offering the visceral thrills that are necessary in a genre entry, Wes Craven's screenplay works on another level. He wants viewers to think about the division between dreams and waking, between fantasy and reality, between other worlds and this one. He also warps expectations — at times, we're aware that the characters are trapped in a dreamscape, but there are times when we're not. And there are occasions when we think they're dreaming and they're actually awake.

In the first *A Nightmare on Elm Street*, Freddy Krueger (Robert Englund) is the demon in the background. His popularity, however, mandated that subsequent sequels center increasingly upon his character. He has a backstory, only part of which is revealed in the first film, and many of the later *Elm Street* chapters focus on the events that led to Freddy's becoming the monster of dreams that he is. Unfortunately, the more we learn about Freddy, the less imposing he is, which is the reason the he's the most frightening in this installment, where he's a new, and entirely unknown, danger.

A Nightmare on Elm Street isn't principally about Freddy. It's about Nancy Thompson (Heather Langenkamp), a typical teenager with the usual teenage problems — divorced parents, gossipy friends, and a boyfriend who wants a little more than she's willing to offer. Nancy lives in an average house in an average middle America town. In keeping with the theme that sex equates to death in horror movies, the first one to fall victim to Freddy is Nancy's best friend, Tina (Amanda Wyss), who is ripped to shreds shortly after enjoying an athletic evening under the covers with her boyfriend, Rod (Nick Corri). In the wake of the massacre, Rod ends up in jail for murder, but Nancy isn't sure of his guilt. Freddy begins appearing in her nightmares and she becomes convinced that he, not Rod, is responsible for Tina's death. Shortly after that, Freddy strikes again, eliminating Rod. Nancy realizes that either she or her boyfriend, Glen (Johnny Depp), will be next, so she decides to take the offensive and attempt to bring Freddy out of the dream world.

A Nightmare on Elm Street is tailor made for those who like their gore leavened with thought-provoking ideas — something that is a rarity in this genre. Sequels dumbed down the series to a regrettable degree, but the first movie still stands on its own as an intriguing and chilling example of how horror works best when the characters and the audience don't have to be lobotomized. **HIGHLY RECOMMENDED**

Nosferatu the Vampyre [Germany, 1979]

Starring: Klaus Kinski, Isabelle Adjani, Bruno Ganz Director: Werner Herzog Screenplay: Werner Herzog, based on *Dracula* by Bram Stoker
Running Time: 1:47 Rated: PG (Ghoulish images, sexual innuendo)
Theatrical Aspect Ratio: 1.85:1

Werner Herzog approached *Nosferatu the Vampyre* with fewer preconceptions than many directors who tackle the tale of Count Dracula. The image of Dracula burned into his memory was of the gaunt, predatory Max Schreck. It's no surprise, therefore, that Schreck's appearance served as a blueprint for Klaus Kinski's count.

Kinski's Dracula is unlike any other interpretation of the character. Visually, he resembles Schreck, with a bald pate, pointed ears, rat-like fangs, clawed hands, and a stiff gait — but that's where the similarity ends. This version of the count is neither a cultured nobleman, a sadistic monster, nor a romantic lead. Instead, he is a twisted wretch — monstrous yet sad; indomitable yet tragic. He is undone not by hubris or carelessness, but by the yearning to steal a few moments extra pleasure in the arms of a woman.

That woman is the gorgeous Isabelle Adjani, who plays Lucy Harker, the object of the count's obsession. As in the original *Nosferatu*, Lucy and Dracula share a psychosexual connection, and he is drawn to her like a moth to a flame, with equally traumatic results.

The third member of the main acting trio is Bruno Ganz, who plays the unfortunate Jonathan Harker. The film opens with Harker leaving behind his young wife, Lucy, and venturing into the Carpathian Mountains on the way to Castle Dracula, where he is to finalize a real estate deal with the mysterious and elusive Count Dracula. Once there, he becomes the Count's prisoner. Later, after escaping from the castle, he races Dracula back to Wismar, but, by the time he arrives, brain fever has struck and he can no longer remember his friends, his wife, or his ordeal in Transylvania.

Unlike most vampire films, *Nosferatu the Vampyre* rejects the expected frantic tone in favor of a deliberate, relentless pace. Some find that the film moves too slowly, but Herzog's unwillingness to rush things allows the images and music to work their magic, building a powerful and foreboding sense of atmosphere. Jonathan's journey through the Borgo Pass is a perfect example of this. Another director might have edited this 10-minute sequence to a fraction of its running length, but, by keeping it intact, the striking visuals and haunting score heighten suspense and build anticipation.

Nosferatu the Vampyre will not be to everyone's taste. This film, like its silent inspiration, concentrates on tone and atmosphere. The result is a superior horror film that offers a greater sense of disquiet than any other Dracula motion picture. *Nosferatu the Vampyre* may not be scary in a traditional sense, but it is not easily forgotten. **HIGHLY RECOMMENDED**

Scream [1996]

Starring: Neve Campbell, Rose McGowan, Skeet Ulrich, Courteney Cox, David Arquette Director: Wes Craven Screenplay: Kevin Williamson Running Time: 1:50 Rated: R (Violence, gore, profanity)
Theatrical Aspect Ratio: 2.35:1

Scream is a rarity: a horror movie spoof that succeeds almost as well at provoking scares as laughs. That's because director Wes Craven, in addition to having a genuine affection for the genre, understands how wildly improbable and easy to lampoon it is. And, with *Scream,* he skewers it at every corner, using self-referential humor and a flood of in-jokes (some subtle, some obvious).

Scream opens with a 12-minute prologue that introduces us to Casey (Drew Barrymore), an all-American girl who's popping popcorn in preparation for watching a video. The phone rings, and there's a mysterious voice on the other end. He asks her what her favorite scary movie is, and she replies that it's *Halloween*. He then invites her to play a game, but she gets freaked out and hangs up. When he calls again and she demands to know what he wants, his response is simple and succinct: "To see your insides." The cat-and-mouse game continues until both Casey and her boyfriend (who has the misfortune to stop by) are gutted like fish.

This double murder is only the beginning, however. It appears that the killer's real target is Sidney Prescott (Neve Campbell, from TV's *Party of Five*), a high school girl with a troubled past. One year ago, Sidney's mother was raped and murdered in a highly-publicized case. Now, when Sidney is attacked by someone wearing a Grim Reaper mask and her boyfriend, Billy (Skeet Ulrich), is arrested, her life is turned upside down. From the bathrooms at school to a friend's house, the stalking continues. Meanwhile, an aggressive tabloid reporter (Courteney Cox) begins harassing Sidney for a story.

Scream never stops poking fun at itself. Craven and screenwriter Kevin Williamson allow their characters to make all sorts of disparaging remarks about the horror movie clichés they're living (and dying) through. Craven couldn't have made this movie if he didn't understand both his craft and what his fans expect. Of all the mainstream horror directors, he has been the one most willing to take chances. This is a horror film designed with movie-lovers in mind. Beneath all the gore and violence (and there's a lot of both), there's a keen sense of wit and intelligence which sophisticated viewers are likely to appreciate. And that makes this much more than a common slasher flick. Have fun, and remember that "movies don't create psychos; movies make psychos more creative." **RECOMMENDED**

Scream 2 [1997]

Starring: Neve Campbell, Courtney Cox, David Arquette, Jamie Kennedy, Liev Schreiber Director: Wes Craven Screenplay: Kevin Williamson Running Time: 2:00 Rated: R (Violence, gore, profanity) Theatrical Aspect Ratio: 2.35:1

Scream 2 isn't quite as clever as its predecessor, but it fills the gap with a cutting wit. Death — even gruesome, bloody death — can be funny if handled the right way. As stipulated by one of the "rules of sequels" uttered by a movie-obsessed character in the film, the body count in *Scream 2* is higher than that in the original. Paradoxically, there's a lot less gore. Craven has remembered that scares are more important that graphic displays of human insides and bodily fluids. A second strength of *Scream 2* is that it features a gallery of legitimate characters rather than a group of cardboard cut-out stereotypes lined up for slaughter.

Scream 2 opens approximately 2 years after the original. As in the first picture, there's a slick, self-mocking prologue. This time, the victims are Jada Pinkett and Omar Epps, whose characters are visiting a local theater for a preview screening of the movie *Stab* (which is based on the "true life" events of *Scream*).

Following the prologue, we are re-introduced to Sidney Prescott, who has left her sleepy hometown to go to Windsor College. Her friend Randy (Jamie Kennedy) is a student there as well, and he's just as knowledgeable about horror films as ever. Once the double murder at *Stab* becomes big news, the media converges on Windsor, looking to interview the original victim. At the head of the flock of vultures is Gale Weathers (Courtney Cox), who has a little surprise for Sidney. She has brought Cotton Weary (Liev Schreiber), the man Sidney falsely accused of murder, with her. Also arriving at the college is Deputy Dewey (David Arquette), who is there to act as a big brother to Sidney during this latest round of tribulations.

From the *Stab* scenes to lines like "Brothers don't last long in situations like this," Craven and Wil-

liamson are clearly having a lot of fun with *Scream 2*, and the movie is enjoyable, if overlong (the livelier first hour is better than the second). Their resolution to the obligatory "whodunit?" is less of a letdown than it could be, and knowingly offers a wink and nod at past unmasking scenes. One senses, however, that by the end of this picture, the overall concept of a hip, self-referential slasher film has been played out. **RECOMMENDED**

Shadow of the Vampire [United States/United Kingdom, 2000]

Starring: John Malkovich, Willem Dafoe, Cary Elwes, Eddie Izzard, Udo Kier Director: E. Elias Merhige Screenplay: Steven Katz Running Time: 1:30 Rated: R (Violence, sexual situations, brief nudity) Theatrical Aspect Ratio: 1.85:1

Nosferatu. For movie-lovers, that one-word title conjures a whirlwind of indelible images forever imprinted in the mind's eye, with none more stark than the harrowing sight of the gaunt, horrific Count Orlock. E. Elias Merhige's sophomore feature offers a compelling, fictionalized account of the filming of the seminal 1922 film. As Merhige and screenwriter Steven Katz have imagined things, the pointy-eared, bald star of *Nosferatu*, Max Schreck, didn't just play a vampire — he was one in real life.

John Malkovich gets top billing, being Murnau. However, the standout is an unrecognizable Willem Dafoe, whose eerie turn as the bloodthirsty Schreck should earn him an Oscar nomination. Dafoe is the spitting image of Schreck, from the unmistakable look to the mannerisms.

The simple story follows the movie's production history, which runs into trouble early when Bram Stoker's widow refuses Murnau the rights to *Dracula* and certain substitutions have to be made. The director also is forced to deal with a temperamental leading lady (played by Catherine McCormack). Then there's the casting of the mysterious Schreck as Count Orlock. Murnau introduces the reclusive performer to his co-workers as the ultimate method actor, and they all marvel at his dedication (staying in character all the time). Soon after, various cast and crew members inexplicably begin to fall ill. Murnau knows Schreck's nasty little secret — the two have made a pact — but his conscience is clear. He is willing to do almost anything in the name of making a great movie.

Based exclusively on the concept, one might easily assume that *Shadow of the Vampire* is a horror film, and, to a degree, it is. But Merhige's intention is not to scare the daylights out of his audience. The amount of comedy — good, genuinely funny comedy — to be found in this movie surprised me. Great one-liners abound, many of which are delivered by Dafoe's Schreck in a delightfully deadpan manner. And some of his bemused expressions are priceless. Obviously, those who have seen *Nosferatu* are going to get a lot more out of this movie than those who are unfamiliar with it, but *Shadow of the Vampire* stands up well enough on its own that viewers who haven't even heard of Murnau's original will not feel set adrift in an unfamiliar cinematic landscape. The idea of a real-life vampire playing one in a movie should appeal to wider crowd than silent movie buffs and film historians. **HIGHLY RECOMMENDED**

Shaun of the Dead [UK, [2004]

Starring: Simon Pegg, Kate Ashfield, Nick Frost, Lucy Davis, Dylan Moran, Penelope Wilton, Bill Nighy   Director: Edgar Wright
Screenplay: Simon Pegg, Edgar Wright   Running Time: 1:37   Rated: R (Violence, gore, profanity)   Theatrical Aspect Ratio: 2.35:1

Shaun of the Dead is a spoof, but at the same time, it's a semi-serious horror movie. It's also an homage to George Romero's *Dead* series (*Night of the Living Dead, Dawn of the Dead, Day of the Dead*) and a societal commentary. Admittedly, with so many choices on the menu, director Edgar Wright cooks some of them better than others. But the bottom line is simple: *Shaun of the Dead* may not be consistently scary (in fact, it's almost never scary), but it is consistently funny (if you have a slightly warped sense of humor) and never loses its audience.

Twenty-something Shaun (Simon Pegg) is stuck in a state of arrested development. His idea of a perfect evening is to get home from work and unwind at the local pub in the company of his girlfriend, Liz (Kate Ashfield), and his flat mate/best friend, Ed (Nick Frost). For Shaun and Ed, this is the good life. But Liz is fed up. She wants to do something *different,* and when Shaun messes up a dinner reservation and suggests going instead to the pub, she has had it with their relationship. Luckily for Shaun, his chance at redemption is just around the corner with the arrival of "Z-Day" (as in "Zombie Day"). Once the undead first appear, Shaun and Ed are so oblivious to what's going on, they don't realize anything is amiss. When a female zombie wanders into their back garden, they think she's drunk. Later, when it becomes clear that something is very wrong, they attempt to use old LPs like Frisbees to decapitate her. After this encounter, Shaun and Ed formulate a plan: collect Liz, and Shaun's mother, Barbara (Penelope Wilton), and then

hole up in the pub until it's all over. Along the way they collect a few other refugees: Liz's flat mates, David (Dylan Moran) and Dianne (Lucy Davis), and Barbara's husband, Philip (Bill Nighy). Philip has a nasty zombie bite, but he thinks it will be okay because he has run it under cold water.

There were times when, while watching George Romero's zombie movies, I had to stifle laughter. Cheesy moments abound, although diehards will deny this. Wright reproduces many of those instances here, but with a difference. In the *Dead* movies, we're laughing *at* the film. In *Shaun,* we're laughing *with* the director. I won't pretend that *Shaun of the Dead* is the be-all and end-all of horror comedies. It has plenty of problems, not the least of which is that the horror elements are largely unconvincing. While there are numerous opportunities to laugh, the movie doesn't always go for the easy joke. Wright wants us to like and identify with Shaun, and there are two things that facilitate this aim: a few surprisingly poignant scenes, and a solid "Everyman" performance by lead actor (and co-screenwriter) Simon Pegg that elevates Shaun above the level of a caricature. *Shaun of the Dead* is a movie that one might not expect to work at first glance, but for those who don't mind a little laughter with their zombies (or perhaps it should be the other way around), this is an unusual source of entertainment. **RECOMMENDED**

Stigmata [1999]

Starring: Patricia Arquette, Gabriel Byrne, Jonathan Pryce
Director: Rupert Wainwright   Screenplay: Tom Lazarus   Running Time: 1:42   Rated: R (Blood, mature themes, profanity, brief sex & nudity)   Theatrical Aspect Ratio: 2.35:1

Stigmata are bleeding injuries that represent the 5 wounds received by Jesus when he was crucified: nails through the wrists & feet, lashes on the back, scratches on the scalp from the crown of thorns, and a spear through the side. The phenomena of stigmata is neither well understood nor extensively studied, but those afflicted with it are invariably deeply religious and view their condition as a gift of God. Director Rupert Wainwright and screenwriter Tom Lazarus have chosen to use this as the jumping-off point for an unconventional thriller.

At the center of the story, providing a human perspective on issues with vast and far-reaching implications, are Frankie Page (Patricia Arquette), a 23-year-old Pittsburgh hairdresser who is a confessed athiest, and Father Andrew Kiernan (Gabriel Byrne), a Roman Catholic Priest who investigates (and disproves) miracles. When *Stigmata* begins, Frankie is just one of Pittsburgh's many anonymous citizens. That all changes when she receives a package from her globe-trotting mother, who has recently been vacationing in Brazil. Included in a box of odds and ends is an old rosary. Within 24 hours of touching the elegant circlet of black beads, Frankie is in the hospital with a deep puncture wound in each wrist — the first of the 5 stigmata. She receives the second, a crisscrossing of her back with the lashes of a whip, while on a subway train, and in plain view of a priest, who contacts Rome about the strange occurrence. Cardinal Houseman (Jonathan Pryce), the head of the Vatican's "Sacred Congregation for the Causes of Saints," sends Andrew Kiernan, his best investigator, to Pittsburgh to meet the woman and determine what's going on. What Andrew finds not only tests his own belief system, but threatens the authority of the modern church.

Stigmata is an unusually intelligent and original thriller. While it loosely resembles end-of-the-world efforts like *The Seventh Sign,* the plot is more thoughtful and restrained. *Stigmata* takes an unflinching look at the power of and the capability for corruption in organized religion. Yet *Stigmata* is not an attack; it does not hurl cruel or thoughtless barbs at Catholicism, and its view of religion in general and Christianity in particular is almost reverent. RECOMMENDED

Stir of Echoes [1999]

Starring: Kevin Bacon, Kathryn Erbe, Illeana Douglas, Kevin Dunn, Zachary David Cope Director: David Koepp Screenplay: David Koepp, based on the novel by Richard Matheson Running Time: 1:40 Rated: R (Violence, profanity, nudity, sex) Theatrical Aspect Ratio: 1.85:1

Stir of Echoes belongs to one of the oldest genres of horror films: the ghost story. And, unlike a multitude of subpar entries that have borne this appellation over the years, it's mostly effective. Like all good ghost stories, it understands that the intent is to build suspense through atmosphere and a strong narrative, not through a barrage of sudden shocks and copious gore.

The main characters are both normal, likable people — husband and wife Tom (Kevin Bacon) and Maggie (Kathryn Erbe). Both are hard workers, and, with their combined incomes, they can just about make ends meet for their family, which includes a 5-year-old boy named Jake (Zachary David Cope) and another baby on the way. One night, at a party, Tom allows himself to be hypnotized by Maggie's new-agey sister, Lisa (Illeana Douglas). While she's in

his mind, she leaves a suggestion for him to "open up." This results in Tom beginning to experience paranormal experiences, including seeing the ghost of a teenage girl (Jenny Morrison) in his living room. He becomes obsessed with initiating a second contact with the ghost, losing his job and neglecting his friends and family in the process. Only his son understands — because, like Tom, Jake also has strange visions of dead people.

Director David Koepp does an excellent job of creating atmosphere. *Stir of Echoes* is an eerie movie; Koepp gets us into Tom's unstable mindset through a series of tight closeups and distorted point-of-view shots. As a study of obsession, the film is first-rate. Tom's tunnel vision focuses on the ghost to the virtual exclusion of all else. Maggie desperately wants to support him, but, not being able to share the experience with him, she is unable to understand the forces that are driving him.

The film is intelligent, but not so talky or esoteric that it could be labeled as an art house attraction. And, while *Stir of Echoes* isn't as downright disturbing as some horror movies, it's still the kind of film that may give you pause the next time you walk into a dark room by yourself. RECOMMENDED

Wes Craven's New Nightmare [1994]

Starring: Heather Langenkamp, Robert Englund, Miko Hughes Director: Wes Craven Screenplay: Wes Craven Running Time: 1:52 Rated: R (Violence, gore, language) Theatrical Aspect Ratio: 1.85:1

Wes Craven's New Nightmare focuses on the lives of some of the actors who appeared in the 1984 original (Heather Langenkamp, Robert Englund, and John Saxon, all of whom play themselves). Langenkamp is having dreams about Freddy, and Englund is painting some very strange pictures. For his part, Craven (who also appears in the film) is writing a new script (which turns out to be the screenplay for *this* picture). All of them realize that something is very wrong.

Then, Langenkamp's young son, Dylan (Miko Hughes), starts having catatonic episodes where he speaks in Freddy's voice, and her husband, Chase (David Newsom), is involved in an accident that appears to involve razor-sharp claws. Freddy, according to Craven (who is called upon to provide an explanation for everything that's going on) is a being of mythical evil whose essence was captured by the *Nightmare* films. Now that the series is complete, he is seeking a gateway into the real world.

Whereas the other *Nightmare on Elm Street* films delighted in blurring the lines between waking and dreaming, this one adds another layer — that of pseudo-reality versus fantasy. Craven has given himself a wonderful new playground to fool around in, and he clearly relishes the opportunity. Those who can accept the basic premise are likely to have nearly as much fun. The only argument against Craven's vision is that he perhaps didn't push the envelope far enough.

Of course, the centerpiece of *Wes Craven's New Nightmare* is Freddy Krueger (once again played by Englund, even though the end credits ascribe Freddy's role to "himself"). This time around, the dream demon has been given a newer, meaner look and a set of nastier claws. The visual and gore effects, while not top-of-the-line, are believable and occasionally downright chilling. The entire production is steeped in an unsettling atmosphere. **RECOMMENDED**

The Wicker Man [United Kingdom, 1973]

Starring: **Edward Woodward, Christopher Lee, Diane Cilento, Britt Ekland** Director: **Robin Hardy** Screenplay: **Anthony Shaffer** Running Time: **1:40** Rated: **R (Nudity, sexual situations, violence)** Theatrical Aspect Ratio: **1.85:1**

The Wicker Man is an early '70s British export that criss-crosses genres as easily as it confounds audience expectations. A film that defies categorization, *The Wicker Man* can be considered to be a horror film, a psychological thriller, a musical, or a melodrama. In reality, since it includes elements of each of those types, it literally has something for just about everyone. And, because there's a richness and intelligence to the story that leads to an unexpected climax, few viewers leave *The Wicker Man* unshaken.

Edward Woodward has the lead role of Sergeant Howie, a humorless policeman whose devout religious views cause him to look dimly upon any kind of hea-

then activity. When Howie receives an anonymous letter informing him that a young girl is missing on the remote Scottish island of Summerisle, he flies out to investigate. What he discovers shocks him — a community of pagans who worship the old Celtic gods and have rejected Christianity. The leader of the island, Lord Summerisle (Christopher Lee), explains to Howie that the citizens of the island are not irreligious — they just worship different gods. And Howie's faith comes under assault when Willow (Britt Ekland), the sensual daughter of the local innkeeper, offers herself to him. But, under it all, there is the mystery of the missing girl, and, as Howie uncovers clues, he begins to suspect a terrifying possibility.

The Wicker Man places us in Howie's shoes, although his dour disposition and puritanical outlook on life makes it difficult to sympathize with him entirely. Like Howie, we suspect that there's something rotten at the core of the community, and, also like the dauntless police officer, we don't figure out what it is until it's far, far too late. The brilliance of the writing is such that we don't seen the twist coming until it's nearly upon us. And that's when *The Wicker Man*'s uneasy undertow turns into a riptide of roiling dread.

Woodward's approach to the final scenes is critical to their being as unsettling as they are. His broken cry of "Oh my God!" is unnerving. Hardy's meticulous approach to filming the final scenes leaves us more than a little shaken and disturbed. By a combination of careful planning and happenstance, he chooses all the right shots to send *The Wicker Man* out with a bang. The story is told, although there are questions than linger. **HIGHLY RECOMMENDED**

Musical

Chicago [2002]

Starring: **Renee Zellweger, Catherine Zeta-Jones, Richard Gere, John C. Reilly, Queen Latifah** Director: **Rob Marshall** Screenplay: **Bill Condon, based on the play by Fred Ebb & Bob Fosse** Running Time: **1:52** Rated: **PG-13 (Sensuality, profanity, violence)** Theatrical Aspect Ratio: **1.85:1**

Chicago represents good, solid entertainment. It's not nearly as rousing as the Broadway revival (then again, it's rare that the cinematic version of a musical comes close to the stage incarnation), but, for those unable or unwilling to see a live production, it represents a sparkling replacement. The film strikes a nice balance between the lavishly overproduced likes of Baz Luhrmann's *Moulin Rouge* and the less openly flamboyant movies from the '50s. The style, by intention, echoes that of the late, great choreographer Fosse.

The film's central characters are Roxie Hart (Renee Zellweger), a housewife who fantasizes becoming a vaudeville star, and Velma Kelly (Catherine Zeta-Jones), a chorus girl who dreams of greater fame than she currently has. Both women find themselves in the Cook County Jail on "Murderers' Row." Roxie shot her lover after discovering that he had lied to her about working to further her singing career. Velma eliminated her husband and sister after finding them together in bed. Both women are being represented by slick lawyer Billy Flynn (Richard Gere), who has never lost a case. His approach is to set up his clients as media darlings, then use that exposure to swing the trial in their favor. "In this town, murder's a form of entertainment," he comments. He refers to courtrooms as "three-ring circuses" and assures Roxie that justice can be blinded by the "razzle dazzle" he will employ.

Their notoriety sets up Roxie and Velma as rivals for the public spotlight. The lurid details of their lives and crimes make them instant celebrities. But neither stays on top for long, and it becomes a difficult task to recapture the interest of the public once another sensational crime has been committed. There's an insatiable appetite for fresh blood, and, unless Roxie and Velma can come up with new revelations to keep them on the front page, they will be quickly forgotten — not only by the general populace, but by their camera-loving lawyer, as well.

Even though the movie's original source material is 75 years old, the issues addressed by this film will be familiar to everyone in the audience, proving the point that technology may evolve, but human nature remains the same. The social commentary and attacks on the American system of jurisprudence are as stinging as they are valid. The 9 or 10 song-and-dance numbers allow us to enjoy *Chicago* on a less cerebral, more visceral level than might be the case if this was not a musical, but there's still a fair amount of substance to be considered. It's a pleasure to note that the return of the movie-adapted stage musical is such an unqualified success. **HIGHLY RECOMMENDED**

De-Lovely [USA/UK, 2004]

Starring: **Kevin Kline, Ashley Judd, Jonathan Pryce, Kevin McNally, Sandra Nelson, Allan Corduner, Peter Polycarpou, Keith Allen** Director: **Irwin Winkler** Screenplay: **Jay Cocks** Running Time: **2:05** Rated: **PG-13 (Sexual situations)** Theatrical Aspect Ratio: **2.35:1**

As a bio-pic, *De-Lovely* is pretty standard, run-of-the-mill stuff (albeit with an interesting framing device). However, as a "best-hits" collection of Cole Porter's music, it is unparalleled. With approximately two dozen of his tunes performed by artists as diverse as Robbie Williams, Elvis Costello, Alanis Morissette, Sheryl Crow, and Natalie Cole, this is a treasure trove of music and memories. It's that, rather than Irwin Winkler's unremarkable presentation of Porter's life, which makes *De-Lovely* worth seeing. That, and the de-lightful performance of Kevin Kline.

The story opens with an aged Porter (Kline) accompanying a musical stage director (Jonathan Pryce) to a theater where he is about to watch a re-enactment of his life. We're never told whether this is a dream or an after-death experience, but it doesn't much matter. Porter is taken on a literal trip down memory lane, with special attention paid to the one true love of his life: his wife, Linda (Ashley Judd). Interestingly enough, since Porter was gay, his relationship with Linda was largely platonic — their sexual encounters were few and unsatisfying, and they slept in separate bedrooms — but that did little to lessen the strength of their feelings for each other. She let him have as many male lovers as he needed, and he devoted his daylight hours to her.

The window into Cole's past opens in 1919 Paris, with the meeting between Cole and divorcée Linda. Soon, they are married, and Cole's career as a songwriter is taking off. While in Venice, he forms an important friendship with Irving Berlin (Keith Allen), and he is been requested to write a Broadway musical. So it's off to New York City for the Porters. After that, the bright beacon of Hollywood beckons. Although Cole is initially reluctant to move to the West Coast, he eventually yields to Linda's persuasion and becomes a workhorse for L. B. Mayer (Peter Polycarpou). While living in California, Cole's marriage begins to deteriorate and his promiscuity increases, but when tragedy strikes, Linda is again by his side.

At 125 minutes, *De-Lovely* seems a little long, and there are times when it moves slowly. On the whole, however, it's an enjoyable experience, with the level of enjoyment influenced by how much a viewer knows and enjoys Porter's music. The love story is touching, but not out of the ordinary. It's at least strong enough to hold our interest until the next musical number comes along — which is never more than a few minutes away. RECOMMENDED

Evita [1996]

Starring: Madonna, Antonio Banderas, Jonathan Pryce Director: Alan Parker Screenplay: Alan Parker and Oliver Stone Running Time: 2:14 Rated: PG (Minor violence) Theatrical Aspect Ratio: 2.35:1

As bold and dazzling a spectacle as *Evita* is, it's missing a soul. This brash, glitzy, energetic entertainment has the power to hold an audience enraptured, but, at the same time, there's a sense that what we're experiencing is just candy for the eyes and ears. In its own way, *Evita* is much like this past summer's blockbusters — lots of flash and pizzazz, but very little beneath the surface. Anyone expecting more than loud music and boisterous musical numbers will be disappointed. *Evita,* even more than the stage show upon which it is based, is light on characters and even lighter on historical facts.

Only the bare facts of Evita Peron's life have been retained for the film. As in the stage musical, she is represented as an heroic figure — sometimes vain and self-serving, but rarely harsh or manipulative. This doesn't necessarily agree with the historical record, but it makes for better cinema. Likewise, Jonathan Pryce's Juan Peron is played as far more amiable than the actual dictator who took control of Argentina during the mid-'40s.

Eva Duarte (or, as she was better known, Evita) was born in 1919, the bastard child of a man who perished when she was 7. Thirty-three years after her birth, Evita, then the wife of Argentina's President, Juan Peron, died of cancer. The film, which opens with a flash forward to Evita's funeral, takes us from the day in 1926 when she places flowers upon her father's casket to the time when thousands of mourners file past her own still form. In between, she uses an affair with a singer (Jimmy Nail) to enable a move from her family's rural home to Buenos Aires, where she eventually becomes Peron's wife. Once he takes over the country, she attempts to apply her newfound power to the task of bettering the lot of Argentina's women and lower classes.

Evita tells Evita's story almost entirely in song (spoken lines are few and far between), making it more of an opera than a traditional musical. There are several familiar tunes (most notably, "Don't Cry for Me, Argentina"), but much of the dialogue is delivered in recitatives, which occasionally seem awkward. Nevertheless, in those instances when *Evita* reaches its musical stride, with a full orchestra accompanying Madonna's strong, clear voice, this movie soars. Unfortunately, in the end, it always comes back to Earth. RECOMMENDED

Fiddler on the Roof [1971]

Starring: Topol, Norma Crane, Leonard Frey, Molly Picon, Paul Mann
Director: Norman Jewison Screenplay: Joseph Stein, adapted from his
stage play and based on "Tevye and His Daughters" by Sholom
Aleichem Running Time: 3:00 Rated: G Theatrical Aspect Ratio: 2.35:1

Fiddler on the Roof takes place around 1910 in a small Ukranian village. It is an uncertain time. Unrest grips the country — unrest caused by the Pogroms (when Jews were driven en masse from their homes), rising anti-Tsarist sentiment, and the approach of World War I. The historical realities of the time do not simply provide a colorful backdrop to this story; they are central to all that transpires. A central theme is how the old traditions are disintegrating under the pressure of a world culture that is being re-shaped by industrialization and mechanization.

One of those traditions is the means by which Jews have been married: a matchmaker chooses a wife for a man, the girl's father approves the match, and the ceremony is held. That's how Tevye (Topol) and his wife, Golde (Norma Crane), were united, and that's how the hard-working milkman believes his 5 daughters should find their husbands. But Tzeitel (Rosalind Harris) has other, modern ideas. She spurns Tevye's selection of a mate, the wealthy butcher Lazar Wolf (Paul Mann), in favor of her childhood sweetheart, the poor tailor Motel (Leonard Frey). Reluctantly, Tevye eventually assents to her choice, but, in doing so, he acknowledges the freedom of all his children. Subsequently, his second daughter, Hodel (Michele Marsh), decides to marry a young revolutionary, Perchik (Paul Michael Glaser). And Tzeitel and Hodel's younger sister, Chava (Neva Small), falls in love with a non-Jew by the name of Fyedka (Raymond Lovelock). This is one match that Tevye cannot countenance, and he warns of dire consequences if Chava goes through with the marriage.

As with any musical, the focus never strays far from the songs, and *Fiddler on the Roof* contains a number of instantly recognizable numbers, from the lively and uplifting "Tradition," "If I Were a Rich Man," and "To Life" to the delightful "Matchmaker" and the sublime "Sunrise, Sunset." In all, the film contains more than a dozen songs. Jewison does his best to incorporate them seamlessly into the storyline, which causes "Matchmaker" and "Sunrise, Sunset" to be more subdued than in many stage productions. However, those in search of a particularly rousing rendition need look no further than "If I Were a Rich Man."

Fiddler on the Roof is not a perfect motion picture — it is too long and there are times when it's obvious that the musical numbers have been pre-recorded then lip-synched — but it represents an enjoyable 3 hours. Jewison's attention to detail is undeniable, and it's obvious that he immersed himself in the material, creating an effective and enduring cinematic representation of a great play.

HIGHLY RECOMMENDED

Grease [1978]

Starring: John Travolta, Olivia Newton-John, Stockard Channing,
Jeff Conaway Director: Randal Kleiser Screenplay: Allan Carr,
Bronte Woodward based on the play by Warren Casey and
Jim Jacobs Running Time: 1:50 Rated: PG (Sexual innuendo,
mild profanity) Theatrical Aspect Ratio: 1.85:1

Grease boasts what all successful motion picture musicals have: likable stars, a simple but not trivial plot, and a lot of enjoyable music. Familiarity with the soundtrack is undoubtedly one of the reasons for the film's popularity — several of the songs have achieved pop hit status. Who can't recognize "Grease," "Hopelessly Devoted to You," "You're the One that I Want," "Greased Lightning," and "Summer Nights"? These may not represent great music, but they're a lot of fun to listen to, as their abiding appeal proves. (Incidentally, 3 of those, "Grease," "Hopelessly Devoted," and "You're the One" were penned specifically for the movie; the others are leftovers from the stage show.)

The plot, such as it is, opens during the summer of 1958 when, to the tune of "Love is a Many Splendored Thing," Danny (Travolta) and Sandy (Newton-John) fall in love. After pledging their undying affection, they go their separate ways, returning to the reality that every teenager must face after Labor Day — high school. The two are in for a surprise, however. Sandy has changed schools, and, unbeknownst to Danny or her, they are now both in Rydell High's Senior Class. Their eventual reunion, however, is anything but joyous. Although Danny is secretly delighted to see Sandy, he realizes that an overt display of joy will look bad in front of his tough friends, so he plays it cool. To Sandy, the reaction is like a slap in the face. The two then spend the rest of the movie dancing around each other, eventually getting together for the musical finale.

In addition to the songs, highlights of *Grease* include Travolta's daffy, limber performance as Danny, Newton-John's sexy-but-sweet Sandy, and a cast of adults trying vainly to pass themselves off as highschoolers. Despite all of the silliness and singing, the exuberance of youth lies at the core of *Grease*, and, although everything is greatly exaggerated here, the film brings back memories of what it was like to hang out in the school yard, take a date to a drive-in movie, and attend a prom. *Grease* works as a musical, a comedy, a light romance, and a gentle satire of teenage life during the '50s. RECOMMENDED

Hedwig and the Angry Inch [2000]

Starring: John Cameron Mitchell, Michael Pitt, Miriam Shor, Stephen Trask Director: John Cameron Mitchell Screenplay: John Cameron Mitchell, based on the play by John Cameron Mitchell and Stephen Trask Running Time: 1:35 Rated: R (Sexual situations, profanity, nudity) Theatrical Aspect Ratio: 2.35:1

In many ways, *Hedwig and the Angry Inch* is the most far afield of any recent musical. The subject matter is certainly edgy: a transvestite singer, who, as a result of a botched sex-change operation only has an "angry inch" left between his legs, strives for the same stardom accorded to his successful former gay lover and protégé. Hedwig (John Cameron Mitchell) grew up behind the wall in East Berlin. Living in a cramped apartment with an unloving mother, Hedwig (nee Hansel) led an unhappy childhood and, by late adolescence, he was confused about his sexuality. His chance for freedom arrived when a U.S. serviceman offered to marry him and take him to the United States — provided he obtained the sex-change operation. Eventually, Hedwig ended up alone and penniless in the U.S. midwest, where he met Tommy Gnosis (Michael Pitt), who became Hedwig's musical collaborator. After a rift developed between Tommy and Hedwig, the former hit paydirt and started playing in front of arena crowds while Hedwig and his band continued to toil in small clubs and bars. Now, shadowing Tommy on his U.S. tour, Hedwig is determined to get what he believes to be rightfully his — a piece of Tommy's action.

Although *Hedwig and the Angry Inch* features an array of over-the-top costumes and a strong central performance by writer/director/star John Cameron Mitchell, the movie's selling point is its music. While none of *Hedwig*'s half-dozen numbers are likely to become Top 40 radio hits, they aren't as outrageous as one might expect from a film with this title. A mix of rock and pop, there's nothing in any of these tunes that couldn't be ascribed to the likes of a Phil Collins or an Elton John (with the exception of one song that could have been written by the Sex Pistols). The musical numbers are gaudily presented and exhibit a lot of toe-tapping energy.

Hedwig deals with issues of duality and healing.

The aim of the film is to show how Hedwig became the confused, conflicted individual he is and to illustrate the healing process he undergoes to again become whole. At the movie's beginning, Hedwig believes he has already become a butterfly; we learn that he's still in the chrysalis. In addition to the high level of energy imparted by the musical numbers, *Hedwig* boasts a darkly funny screenplay that is littered with instances of self-deprecating humor. The film wants us to take something away from it, but it also doesn't want us to take it *too* seriously. RECOMMENDED

Jeanne and the Perfect Guy [France, 1998]

Starring: Virginie Ledoyen, Mathieu Demy Directors: Olivier Ducastel, Jacques Martineau Screenplay: Olivier Ducastel, Jacques Martineau Running Time: 1:38 Rated: Not rated (Sex, nudity, mature themes) Theatrical Aspect Ratio: 2.35:1 In French with subtitles

At first glance, *Jeanne and the Perfect Guy* appears to be a relatively traditional French melodrama — well acted and intelligently written, but nothing special. Then a group of janitors breaks into song and the cinematic landscape has changed. Approximately 50% of this movie is told through its music, with a significant portion of the dialogue being presented in the lyrics.

Jeanne (Virginie Ledoyen) is a sexually promiscuous young woman. By days, she toils as a receptionist at a travel agency; by nights, she plays musical beds with her many lovers, one of which is a supervisor at work (portrayed as a self-centered cad by Frédéric Gorny). Even her sister, Sophie (Valérie Bonneton), thinks she's a slut. But Jeanne is simply looking for Mr. Right — someone she's not sure really exists. Then, one Sunday morning on a train, she locks eyes with Olivier (Mathieu Demy), and it's love at first sight. The two are so drawn to each other that, once the car has emptied, they have sex there and then. Jeanne has found her perfect man, but there's a problem: Olivier is HIV+ (acquired from his days as a heroin user), and the AIDS virus is already taking its toll on his health. By entering into a relationship with him, Jeanne risks the inevitable pain of a permanent separation — but she is powerless to control her feelings for Olivier. And, although he feels terrible guilt for subjecting her to such an unfair ordeal, he cannot deny the strength of the attraction.

Presenting *Jeanne and the Perfect Guy* as a musical gives the film a fresh perspective (the story alone certainly isn't unique). Co-directors Olivier Ducastel and Jacques Martineau, making their motion picture debuts, sail smoothly through potentially treacherous waters. Done incorrectly, this movie could have turned into an awkward experience, but Ducastel and Martineau are in control of the material. The movie is also characterized by genuine emotional depth and the refreshingly open attitude that the French have towards sexuality. One of the best scenes features a naked Jeanne and Olivier in bed, singing heartfelt (and somewhat bittersweet) endearments to each other.

Jeanne and the Perfect Guy is not a perfect movie. The final cut is a little unpolished, but the compensation for this is a raw, infectious energy, and, as offbeat fare, it's difficult to beat. Even for those who don't consider themselves to be fans of musicals, there's plenty about this movie to applaud. **RECOMMENDED**

Little Shop of Horrors [1986]

Starring: Rick Moranis, Ellen Greene, Vincent Gardenia, Steve Martin Director: Frank Oz Screenplay: Howard Ashman, based on the screenplay by Charles B. Griffith Running Time: 1:34 Rated: PG (Cartoon violence, mild profanity) Theatrical Aspect Ratio: 1.85:1

The 1986 version of *Little Shop of Horrors* is a celebration of two beloved motion picture genres: the musical and the cheesy science fiction flick. Before making it to the screen in its final form during the '86 Christmas season, *Little Shop of Horrors* had a long and colorful history. It is based on an off-Broadway play that soared to popularity during the early '80s. That, in turn, was loosely adapted from Roger Corman's infamous 1960 B-grade monster movie of the same name

Little Shop of Horrors tells the story of a downtrodden nerd named Seymour Krelborn (Rick Moranis) who lives in the basement of his workplace, Mushnik's Flower Shop. Mr. Mushnik (the late Vincent Gardenia) treats Seymour like dirt, causing Seymour to bemoan his fate: "I keep askin' God what I'm for, And He tells me 'Gee, I'm not sure.'" The other employee at the "God — and customer — forsaken store" is the platinum blond bimbo Audrey (Ellen Greene, reprising the role she played on stage in New York and London), with whom Seymour is hopelessly in love. Audrey secretly fantasizes about living a life with Seymour as her husband, but doesn't reveal her dreams because her boyfriend, a sadistic dentist named Orin Scrivello, D.D.S (Steve Martin), wouldn't like it.

For Seymour, everything is about to change. A strange and exotic plant he recently bought is beginning to blossom into something the likes of which no one has ever before seen. It's a sickly thing, however, because it responds only to one kind of food: fresh blood. After draining himself on a daily basis via cuts in his fingers, Seymour is rewarded by a spurt of growth from Audrey II. Suddenly, the plant is the talk of the city, Seymour is famous, and Mushnik's Flower Shop is flooded with customers. But, when Seymour cannot keep up with the plant's insatiable appetite, Audrey II makes a suggestion (yes, it can talk, using the voice of the Four Tops' Levi Stubbs): ice the nasty, abusive Orin and use him as food.

Little Shop of Horrors is one of those musicals where it benefits the viewer to pay attention to the lyrics, because they're saturated with humor and in-jokes. This is the kind of charming motion picture that can be viewed repeatedly without ever wearing out its welcome. With several triumphant musical numbers, an original villain, a smart and witty script, a cute romance, and a new, upbeat ending, this *Little Shop of Horrors* offers countless delights during its 94-minute running time. **HIGHLY RECOMMENDED**

Love's Labour's Lost [United States/United Kingdom, 2000]

Starring: Kenneth Branagh, Alicia Silverstone, Alessandro Nivola, Natascha McElhone Director: Kenneth Branagh Screenplay: Kenneth Branagh, based on the play by William Shakespeare Running Time: 1:35 Rated: PG-13 (Sensuality) Theatrical Aspect Ratio: 2.35:1

Love's Labour's Lost is about $1/3$ Shakespeare, $1/3$ song-and-dance, and $1/3$ ribald slapstick. At times, the wedding of these elements is awkward, but the overall result is strangely appealing. Kenneth Branagh has envisioned the film as a romantic musical comedy, with an emphasis on the final two words of the term. Branagh has elected to liven up the story by including about 10 musical numbers, often replacing lengthy verse-laden soliloquys with elaborate production numbers. But there's a catch. The play has been time-shifted into the late-1930s, allowing Branagh to incorporate standards of the era. As a result, we hear such familiar tunes as "The Way You Look Tonight," "Cheek to Cheek," and "There's No Business Like Show Business."

The story is undoubtedly the movie's weakest point, and does not stand out as one of Shakespeare's high points. We are introduced to the 4 male leads: King Ferdinand of Navarre (Alessandro Nivola), and his 3 best friends, Berowne (Branagh), Longaville (Matthew Lillard), and Dumain (Adrian Lester). In concert, these 4 have agreed to sign a ridiculous pact: for 3 years while students at a university, they will fast, sleep only 3 hours per day, and forego women. Berowne warns that the oath is not one that any of them will be able to keep, and his words prove to be prophetic. When the Princess of France (Alicia Silverstone) arrives with her 3 lady attendants,

Rosaline (Natascha McElhone), Maria (Carmen Ejogo), and Katherine (Emily Mortimer), all of the men are smitten. But complications ensue when Berowne entrusts a love letter to the king's clown, Costard. At the same time, Don Adriano de Armado gives the fool a missive professing his love for a local wench, Jaquenetta (Stefania Rocca) — and Costard mixes the letters up.

Although *Love's Labour's Lost* does not score the kind of complete success that Branagh has achieved with his other Shakespeare adaptations, it is a welcome addition, not only because it represents the first time the play has been brought to the screen, but because it shows the lengths to which the director is willing to stretch the envelope. Flaws (most of which are minor) aside, *Love's Labour's Lost* is an enjoyable trifle, especially for those who don't take their Shakespeare *too* seriously and those who love the old Hollywood musicals as much as Branagh obviously does. **RECOMMENDED**

Madame Butterfly [France, 1995]
Starring: Ying Huang, Richard Troxell, Ning Liang, Richard Cowan, Jing-Ma Fan Director: Frederic Mitterrand Screenplay: Giuseppe Giacosa and Luiji Illica Running Time: 2:14 Rated: Not rated (Mature themes) Theatrical Aspect Ratio: 1.66:1 In Italian with subtitles

For his 1995 version of Puccini's *Madame Butterfly,* Frederic Mitterrand chose not to film a live performance or craft a set-bound, stagy motion picture. Instead, he took his cast and crew on location, giving this rendition of the opera a decidedly cinematic quality. From a technical standpoint, Mitterrand's approach to *Madame Butterfly* is unique, and it reaps dramatic dividends.

For those unfamiliar with the story, Puccini's opera tells of a self-absorbed American naval officer named Benjamin Franklin Pinkerton (Richard Troxell) who buys a 15-year-old geisha, Cio-Cio-San (a.k.a. "Butterfly," played by Ying Huang), to be his "Japanese wife." From the beginning, Pinkerton has no intention of staying with Butterfly — he is using her as temporary amusement, a bit of comfort in a foreign port. Despite being enchanted by her quiet, fragile beauty, he has no difficulty abandoning her at the first opportunity. Yet, even after Pinkerton has been gone for 3 years, Butterfly awaits his return, confident that he loves her as much as she loves him.

Madame Butterfly takes place in 1904 Japan, just outside of Nagasaki, and, in addition to being a tragedy of Shakespearean proportions, it also illustrates a common international perception of American imperialist attitudes. Pinkerton isn't just a good-looking, dislikable cad who abandons a young, innocent girl — he's a personification of his entire nation, and, by extension, Butterfly represents the countries that the United States ruthlessly plundered and left behind. Using archival footage of the time, Mitterrand brings home the film's historical perspective far better than a live version ever could.

For the most part, operas, like musicals, improve with familiarity. It's difficult to guess how Puccini diehards will react to some of Mitterrand's creative choices, but the result is a cinematic success — powerful, passionate, and memorable. It's a daring way for the director to present *Madame Butterfly,* and I applaud his decision to try something different than a traditional, formal version. I have little doubt that my appreciation will increase with successive viewings. **HIGHLY RECOMMENDED**

Moulin Rouge [United States/Australian, 2001]
Starring: Nicole Kidman, Ewan McGregor, John Leguizamo, Jim Broadbent, Richard Roxburgh Director: Baz Luhrmann Screenplay: Baz Luhrmann & Craig Pearce Running Time: 2:06 Rated: PG-13 (Mature themes, double entendres) Theatrical Aspect Ratio: 2.35:1

Moulin Rouge subjects its viewers to a sensory overload with gaudy, gloriously overproduced musical numbers that pay homage to the greats of the past while simultaneously outdoing them. When Ewan McGregor and Nicole Kidman are dancing on the clouds, they're doing so with digitally-created stardust falling all around them. Splashed with garish colors that span the spectrum, *Moulin Rouge* is bright, brash, and wildly entertaining. It modernizes the musical in a way that may give younger movie-lovers a sense of why this genre was once so popular. The production numbers are presented with so much energy and gusto that it's impossible not to be sucked in — and also impossible not to feel a moment's letdown on each occasion when one is over and it's time to get back to moving the paper-thin narrative forward.

The film's protagonist and narrator is Christian (Ewan McGregor), a penniless writer who hooks up with a group of bohemians putting together a play to be performed at the Moulin Rouge. His goal: "to write about truth, beauty, freedom, and love." When the group's leader, the dwarf Toulouse Lautrec (John Leguizamo), likes Christian's work, he decides to get him a one-on-one interview with the star of the Moulin Rouge's racy revue, the courtesan Satine

(Nicole Kidman, who keeps her clothes on throughout — much to the chagrin of male viewers). He is immediately smitten, and, to her surprise, so is she. But she is also being pursued by a wealthy duke (Richard Roxburgh), whose investment in the Moulin Rouge will make the club's owner, Zidler (Jim Broadbent, who keeps his clothes on throughout — much to the relief of all viewers), a wealthy man. And there's another factor — Satine is afflicted with tuberculosis (her fate is revealed in the film's first scene, but I won't give it away here).

Despite all of the bombastic musical numbers, or perhaps because of them, the love story in *Moulin Rouge* works. At times, it's even touching. Some of this has to do with the actors. Ewan McGregor plays his role with a puppydog likability and naïve romanticism, and Nicole Kidman positively smolders. Their voices are strong and clear (although occasionally drowned out by the instruments). Historical purists and those who enjoy only sedate films are likely to be infuriated by what Luhrmann has done here, but who cares? We live in an age of excess, and Lurhmann takes it to the hilt. RECOMMENDED

The Singing Detective [2003]

Starring: Robert Downey, Jr., Robin Wright Penn, Mel Gibson, Jeremy Northam, Katie Holmes, Adrien Brody, Jon Polito, Carla Gugino, Saul Rubinek, Alfre Woodard Director: Keith Gordon Screenplay: Dennis Potter Running Time: 1:49 Rated: R (Profanity, sexual situations, violence) Theatrical Aspect Ratio: 2.35:1

These days, it seems that nearly every television series ever devised for the small screen is getting a motion picture treatment. *The Singing Detective*, however, is a little different. In the first place, the original six-part BBC miniseries was not watched by tens of millions of people; it showed on PBS in the mid-1980s and garnered a small but passionate audience. Most mainstream viewers either had never heard of it, or tuned in and then quickly changed the channel when they discovered that it was "weird." In the second place, the movie adaptation is not intended to please mindless audiences. The film's screenplay was written by the late Dennis Potter, who created the miniseries, so there's no question of someone other than the original author taking over the property and ruining it.

Robert Downey, Jr., plays Dan Dark, a pulp fiction author who is flat on his back in a hospital, suffering from a debilitating skin condition. If anything, his mind is in worse shape than his body. As he slowly recovers, he imagines scenes from his first novel, *The Singing Detective*, with himself as the lead character,

a gumshoe who croons on the side. His ex-wife, Nicola (Robin Wright Penn), visits him at the hospital and plays a key part in his imaginings. He also has dreams and visions of his childhood, where he sees his mother (Carla Gugino) have an affair with his father's partner, Mark Binney (Jeremy Northam). His psychotherapist, Dr. Gibbon (Mel Gibson), believes that things he experienced as a child have led to his sudden outbursts of violent temper. It is Gibbon's job to heal Dan's mind in tandem with his recovering body. Other characters who float through Dan's real and imaginary worlds are pretty Nurse Mills (Katie Holmes) and a Laurel and Hardy–like pair of hoods (Adrian Brody, Jon Polito).

In order to present the story without alienating or confusing the viewer, director Keith Gordon has employed a different style for each aspect of the movie. The real-life hospital scenes are presented with a bright, antiseptic look. *The Singing Detective* scenes are very stylized, with lots of shadows and darkness. The dream/memories also have a somewhat "unreal" feel to them, but it's not as strong as the book sequences. Then there are the song-and-dance numbers, which aren't depicted as big-production numbers but employ stages and colored lights. Two of the most memorable are "At the Hop," where doctors bicker over how to treat Dan, and "Mr. Sandman," in which he imagines a sweet romance with Nurse Miles.

The Singing Detective works not primarily because it's a strange and original brew, but because it accomplishes its goals without seeming to force things. The blending of reality with dreams, memories, and imagination is done flawlessly, aided by the occasional appearance of a fictional character in the hospital, the way in which some individuals suddenly and unexpectedly break into song, or the use of actors to play multiple roles. Many of the real people in Dan's life have alter egos in his book. Ultimately, the film is about one man coming to grips with his demons and finding the path to redemption, but the process by which this is accomplished is much different from what one normally encounters in movies. RECOMMENDED

Stop Making Sense [1984]

Starring: David Byrne, Tina Weymouth, Chris Frantz, Jerry Harrison Director: Jonathan Demme Running Time: 1:28 Rated: Not Rated (Nothing offensive) Theatrical Aspect Ratio: 1.85:1

Upon its release in 1984, Jonathan Demme's *Stop Making Sense* was hailed by many critics as the "greatest concert film of all time." The picture, which captured a live concert performance given by the Talking Heads, used state-of-the-art direct-to-digital re-recording and non-intrusive camera positioning and movement to capture the kinetic energy of the experience and replicate it for nationwide theatrical viewing. Demme's greatest ally is simplicity. He understood that the Talking Heads put on a strong enough show that there was no need for the cameras to artificially enliven things. Consequently, we are not subjected to the barrage of irritating quick cuts that have become the norm in the MTV era of concert footage.

Despite being a concert film, *Stop Making Sense* possesses the skeleton of dramatic structure. It takes 6 numbers for the entire band to assemble in front of the audience. For the first song, "Psycho Killer," David Byrne takes the barren stage alone, using a boom box and acoustic guitar as his only accompaniments. Tina Weymouth joins Byrne for "Heaven," followed by Chris Frantz for "Thank You For Sending Me An Angel," Jerry Harrison for "Found A Job," and the supporting band members for "Slippery People." Not until "Burning Down the House" are all the pieces in place.

The Talking Heads capture their audience through music and shared energy, not through pyrotechnics and violent/sexual imagery. The set design is stark and the lighting simplistic. Sex might normally sell rock-and-roll, but not in this case. For the most part, the Talking Heads don't do love songs — they sing about simple things in life. In fact, David Byrne, with his herky-jerky movements that resemble a man undergoing electric shock treatment, is almost antisexual. He is also the consummate showman. At various times during the concert, he jogs in place, runs from one side of the stage to the other, appears ready to devour the microphone, bobs his head like a chicken, dances with a floor lamp, falls on his back and sings from a prone position, and seems to lose complete control of his body. This movie is pure fun and sheer exuberance transferred onto celluloid and perfectly re-created at the other end. Experiencing what Demme and the Talking Heads have crafted with this motion picture makes perfect sense. **MUST SEE**

The Umbrellas of Cherbourg [France, 1964]

Starring: Catherine Deneuve, Nino Castelnuovo, Anne Vernon, Marc Michel, Ellen Farner Director: Jacques Demy Screenplay: Jacques Demy Running Time: 1:27 Rated: Not Rated (Mature themes) Theatrical Aspect Ratio: **1.66:1** In French with subtitles

The Umbrellas of Cherbourg was initially released in 1964, and, amongst other things, helped catapult Catherine Deneuve to stardom. In filming *The Umbrellas of Cherbourg*, director Jacques Demy opted to sacrifice print longevity for vibrant color. The stock he used yielded brilliant hues, but degraded quickly. By the mid-'70s, the only remaining copies of the film were in terrible condition. But Demy, anticipating this problem from the outset, had archived multiple monochromatic negatives that, when properly combined with each other, allowed re-creation of the original color. With Demy's widow, Agnes Varda, supervising the re-mastering, *The Umbrellas of Cherbourg* was recently brought back to life, and is now available in its previous splendor.

As a musical, *The Umbrellas of Cherbourg* is unusual in several ways. First, unlike most big American productions of the time, there are no show-stopping production numbers. There's no dancing, no chorus, and no duets. Secondly, there are *no* spoken lines of dialogue — everything, from the mundane to the important, is sung. Finally, *The Umbrellas of Cherbourg* isn't a lightweight bon-bon with a happily-ever-after ending. While the film has its share of effervescent moments, there's also an element of undeniable poignancy.

The two main characters, 17-year-old Genevieve (Deneuve) and 20-year-old Guy (Nino Castelnuovo), are star-crossed lovers. Despite the stringent objections of Genevieve's mother (Anne Vernon), who thinks a gas station mechanic is beneath her daughter, the two continue their clandestine meetings, and eventually consummate their relationship. Soon after, Guy has to serve a stint away from France in the army. Following his departure, Genevieve learns that she is pregnant, and must decided whether to wait for Guy's uncertain return or marry the rich, cultured Roland Cassard (Marc Michel), who offers stability, undying love, and the promise of raising her child as his own. Genevieve's choice irrevocably alters the lives of at least four people.

Agnes Varda's recent reconstruction has done the film justice. The colors, which include bright pinks, reds, purples, and oranges, look great, and the cleaned-up soundtrack is better than ever. Although *The Umbrellas of Cherbourg* lacks song-and-dance numbers, there is one tune that recurs throughout. This song, beautifully composed by Michel Legrand, radiates longing and loss, and forms the movie's core.

It, like the film, is far more powerful than one would initially suppose. **HIGHLY RECOMMENDED**

West Side Story [1961]

Starring: Natalie Wood, Richard Beymer, Russ Tamblyn, Rita Moreno
Directors: Robert Wise & Jerome Robbins Screenplay: Ernest Lehman
based on the play by Arthur Laurents and Jerome Robbins Running
Time: 2:32 Rated: Not Rated (Mild violence) Theatrical Aspect
Ratio: 2.35:1

The movie transpires in New York's Upper West Side during the late 1950s. The feuding Montagues and Capulets are represented by rival gangs: the Jets and the Sharks. The former group is comprised of first-generation New Yorkers whose parents came across on boats during the early decades of the century. Their rivals are Puerto Rican immigrants who are newly arrived in the United States. The constant skirmishing of the Jets and the Sharks is primed to explode into an open war, but not before Tony (Richard Beymer), a founder of the Jets (who is no longer with the gang — he has gotten a job), falls in love with Maria (Natalie Wood), the sister of the Sharks' leader. In true *Romeo and Juliet* fashion, these two defy conventions and risk everything, including their lives, to be with one another. And, also as in Shakespeare's play, there are no happy endings.

To its credit, *West Side Story* does not shy away from difficult issues. It explores both the senselessness of gang strife and the prejudice faced by immigrants. Yet, by today's standards, its views on both seem a little naïve. However, the film's approach to violence is unique. *West Side Story* is almost bloodless — even the stabbing and gunshot scenes are sanitized. All the fights are highly stylized and divorced from reality. The characters dance around each other while in the process of stalking and attacking. Yet there's a real sense of menace to some of these scenes, due in large part to the choreography and Bernstein's dissonant score. We end up feeling the violence more than seeing it. It doesn't always work — the power of the scenes in which characters die is arguably lessened by this approach — but it enables a grittier story to be told within the musical framework.

Until Baz Luhrmann attempted a highly unusual take of *Romeo + Juliet* using snatches of Shakespeare's original dialogue in a radical setting, *West Side Story* remained the best known and most atypical modernization of the Bard's tale. And, even though the movie version of the stage production does not play quite as well today as it once did, it still represents a brave and effective fusion of serious and fantasy elements, and offers 2½ hours of solid entertainment. Admittedly, there are times when *West Side Story* strikes a campy or discordant note, but those instances are overbalanced by the more frequent moments when it offers its own brand of cinematic magic. **HIGHLY RECOMMENDED**

Romance

10 Things I Hate About You [1999]

Starring: Heath Ledger, Julia Stiles, Joseph-Gordon Levitt, Larisa Oleynik Director: Gil Junger Screenplay: Karen McCullah Lutz & Kirsten Smith Running Time: 1:38 Rated: PG-13 (Sexual themes, double entendres, profanity) Theatrical Aspect Ratio: 1.85:1

10 Things I Hate About You is a modern-day, souped-up version of William Shakespeare's *The Taming of the Shrew*. What sets this apart from its many competitors for teen dollars is that not only does the movie feature a surprisingly edgy and intelligent script, but it offers a group of characters capable of holding an audience's interest for more than 90 minutes.

Kat (Julia Stiles) and Bianca (Larisa Oleynik) are sisters, but, despite sharing the same parents, their personalities are polar opposites. Bianca, the younger, is pretty, popular, and shallow. Kat, the older one, is a rebel without a cause, a girl who is described kindly as being "incapable of human interaction." Kat and Bianca's father, Walter (Larry Miller), has one hard and fast rule for his daughters: Bianca cannot begin dating until her sister does. This represents a major problem for the socially-adept Bianca, since Kat shows no inclination whatsoever to date. As the prom approaches, Bianca finds herself as the object of two boys' affections: cool, vain Joey Donner (Andrew Keegan) and kind, somewhat shy Cameron James (Joseph Gordon-Levitt). Working as reluctant allies, Joey and Cameron pick out a potential date for Kat: Patrick Verona (Heath Ledger), the local bad boy. They reason that Kat might find him too great a challenge to refuse, and, once she starts going out with him, Bianca will be free to date one of them. But getting Kat and Patrick

together proves to be a difficult chore, and, when he realizes that he genuinely likes her, Patrick must go to extraordinary lengths to tame the shrew.

The dialogue in *10 Things I Hate About You* is peppered with sexual references and double entendres. Kat has all of the best lines, and Stiles utters them with relish. Smart, sharp dialogue may not be the foundation of a good movie, but it certainly is a key ingredient, and one of the reasons why *10 Things I Hate About You* succeeds. The comedy (and there's plenty of it) is of the hit-and-miss variety, sometimes trying too hard to get laughs instead of letting them come naturally. Some of it is genuinely funny, while other examples (the buffoonery of Kat and Bianca's father) miss the mark by a wide margin. The love stories are frothy, although the plot is littered with the debris of several unfortunate romantic comedy devices. However, if we accept that these elements are a necessary part of the genre, then *10 Things I Hate About You* ranks as one of the strongest entries in the recent wave of teen-oriented films — a pleasant blend of Shakespeare and John Hughes. **RECOMMENDED**

50 First Dates [2004]

Starring: Adam Sandler, Drew Barrymore, Sean Astin, Rob Schneider, Blake Clark Director: Peter Segal Screenplay: George Wing Running Time: 1:36 Rated: PG-13 (Sexual situations, crude humor, profanity, cartoon violence) Theatrical Aspect Ratio: 2.35:1

50 First Dates offers viewers a kinder, gentler Adam Sandler. Gone (at least for one movie) is the narcissistic adolescent caught in a perpetual state of arrested development. In his place is a likable goofball whose rough edges are worn off by a force more effective than sandpaper: falling in love. Although there are moments that will tickle the bellies of longtime Sandler fans, *50 First Dates* is sweet enough to capture the attention, and perhaps affection, of those who would not ordinarily see a movie headlined by this particular star. The fact is, *50 First Dates* is more of a romantic comedy than an Adam Sandler comedy.

If *Memento* represents the serious side of short-term memory loss, *50 First Dates* stands in for the comedic aspect. Henry Roth (Sandler) is a Hawaiian veterinarian who spends much of his free time seducing female tourists. One day, while at breakfast, he encounters Lucy Whitmore (Drew Barrymore). They strike up a conversation and, before they know it, morning has become afternoon. Lucy has to go, but she agrees to meet Henry the next day for breakfast. Twenty-four hours later, however, when he approaches her, she doesn't recognize him. The owner of the diner explains to him that, as the result of an accident, Lucy has lost her short-term memory. Every night when she goes to sleep, she forgets everything that happened to her the day before. Thus begins Henry's quest to win her heart, even though he has to try repeatedly, and never gets more than about 12 hours with her. In addition, he has to deal with her overprotective father (Blake Clark) and flaky brother (Sean Astin). The only one on his side is a pothead named Ula (frequent Sandler flunky Rob Schnieder).

There's an element of *Groundhog Day* in *50 First Dates*. Both films feature characters who repeatedly live the same day. Because of Lucy's memory loss, she awakens every morning and believes it to be a Sunday in October. Her father and brother are enablers, encouraging the fantasy in an effort to make her happy. For Henry to have any hope to be with Lucy, he has to find some way to help her connect with her recent past. That involves a video camera and a diary.

The script is far from watertight, but director Peter Segal does something truly shocking for this kind of movie: He gets us to care enough about the characters that the idiotic plot elements aren't all that off-putting. If there's a downside, it's that, aside from a few notable moments of outrageousness, the comedy is both low-key and limited in its ability to generate laughs. Perhaps the biggest surprise of all is that the film doesn't resort to an easy cheat at the end. It plays things straight and still manages to satisfy, making this one of Sandler's most appealing outings to-date. **RECOMMENDED**

Addicted to Love [1997]

Starring: Meg Ryan, Matthew Broderick, Kelly Preston, Tcheky Karyo
Director: Griffen Dunne Screenplay: Robert Gordon Running Time: 1:41
Rated: R (Sexual content) Theatrical Aspect Ratio: 1.85:1

Maggie (Meg Ryan) is a bad girl, although not quite as bad as she'd like everyone to believe. She wears her hair short and unkempt, travels around the streets of New York on a motorcycle, and prefers donning anything in black that exposes her navel. She talks tough and her eyes are hard little agates, except when she's alone and a softer side comes to the surface (Ryan does a good job showing this in mostly-subtle ways, such as the set of Maggie's shoulders). Why is she so abrasive? Because her currently mission in life is revenge — revenge against the ex-fiancée, Anton (Tcheky Karyo), who cast her aside when he found his latest paramour, Linda (Kelly Preston).

Linda happens to have been the lifelong love of small-town astronomer Sam (Matthew Broderick). When *Addicted to Love* opens, we're shown a slice of his idyllic life (complete with a number of irritating technical inaccuracies about the abilities of a telescope) — how he has a job he loves and a woman he adores. But Linda is restless, and she decides to take a 2-month trip to New York City. While there, she meets Anton, falls in love, and moves in with him. When Sam learns the truth via a "Dear John" letter, he gets on the next flight to the Big Apple.

In New York, he sets up home in abandoned building across the street from the apartment shared by Linda and Anton, and constructs a camera obscura to watch their every movement (his voyeurism recalls the likes of *Rear Window* and *Stakeout*). Soon, Maggie joins him in his "bohemian hellhole," bringing along bugging equipment so they can have sound in addition to video. Together, the two hatch a plan to break apart the new lovers — Sam, so he can win back Linda, and Maggie, so she can see Anton "in pain, hopeless, and finished off."

It's kind of fun seeing Meg Ryan suppress her usual mannerisms and do the grunge thing, but not nearly as enjoyable as it is immersing oneself in director Griffen Dunne's bizarre-yet-oddly-engaging romantic comedy about voyeurism, moldy strawberries, and monkeys wearing lipstick. *Addicted to Love* is for those who don't mind a world view that's a little askew, yet who can still accept that love conquers all. **RECOMMENDED**

As Good as It Gets [1997]

Starring: Jack Nicholson, Helen Hunt, Greg Kinnear, Cuba Gooding Jr.
Director: James L. Brooks Screenplay: Mark Andrus and James L.
Brooks Running Time: 2:18 Rated: PG-13 (Nudity, profanity, mature
themes, violence) Theatrical Aspect Ratio: 1.85:1

As Good as It Gets is really two related movies in one, which explains the surprisingly long running time. While 138 minutes is fine for an epic adventure or a weighty drama, it makes a lightweight effort like this seem a little bloated. The film is ambitious: it tries to wed the modern-day, non-supernatural *A Christmas Carol* with a traditional romantic comedy. Director James L. Brooks, who does these kinds of movies as well as anyone in Hollywood, has moderate success. *As Good as It Gets* is not a positive triumph, but it does bring a smile to the face and, perhaps in some cases, a tear to the eye.

Jack Nicholson plays Melvin, a successful author who lives the life of a recluse. He's a homophobic, anti-Semitic racist with an intense dislike of dogs and people. The neighbors in his Greenwich Village apartment building all avoid him, and the waitress at his favorite restaurant barely tolerates his presence. To make matters worse, Melvin is afflicted with an obsessive/compulsive disorder that makes his behavior seem even more strange.

Then something happens to change Melvin's life. One of his neighbors, a gay artist named Simon (Greg Kinnear), is beaten up by a group of robbers. Simon's dealer, Frank (Cuba Gooding Jr.), forces Melvin to care for Simon's dog. Gradually, Melvin comes to love the little animal, and, after discovering a previously-unsuspected wellspring of humanity deep within himself, he begins exercising it in other ways: paying a doctor to care for the sick son of his regular waitress, Carol (Helen Hunt), and offering Simon support when he comes home from the hospital.

Ultimately, it's the quirks and details of *As Good as It Gets*' script (by Brooks and co-writer Mark Andrus), rather than the broad strokes, which make the film enjoyable. Essentially, this is a formulaic, connect-the-dots tale which offers few, if any surprises. Fifteen minutes into the movie, you'll be able to guess exactly how it will all work out. As a result, the chief pleasure for the next 2 hours is watching the characters grow and interact as they traverse the familiar path. *As Good as It Gets* may not quite live up to its title, but it doesn't fall unacceptably short of the mark. **RECOMMENDED**

Before Sunrise [1995]

Starring: Ethan Hawke, Julie Delpy Director: Richard Linklater
Screenplay: Richard Linklater and Kim Krizan Running Time: 1:41
Rated: R (Mature themes, language) Running Time: 1:41 Theatrical
Aspect Ratio: 1.85:1

Richard Linklater has succeeded where many before him have failed — in fashioning a modern-day romance that is both original and enthralling. *Before Sunrise* is nothing short of movie magic. Even the best romantic comedy/dramas tend to be formula-driven, frequently relying more upon actor chemistry than plot. Surprises are about as foreign to this genre as a pacifist hero is to a shoot-'em-up. Somewhere along the way, a storyteller originated the basic love story structure. Film makers have religiously followed this roadmap, rarely taking more than an occasional minor detour. With *Before Sunrise,* however, Linklater not only travels an entirely different route, but heads for a new destination.

Jesse (Ethan Hawke) meets Celine (Julie Delpy) on a train traveling through Europe. His destination is Vienna, where a flight back to America awaits him the next morning. She's on her way to Paris, where she starts classes at the Sorbonne next week. From their first moment of eye contact, they're drawn to each other. They share a meal in the lounge car, savoring the conversation more than the food, and when they arrive in Vienna, Jesse persuades Celine to disembark with him and keep him company wandering the streets until the time comes for his plane to depart. Thus begins an unforgettable screen romance.

One of the first things to notice about *Before Sunrise* is how completely natural it all seems. Credit both director Linklater and his two leads. The rapport between Jesse and Celine is so lacking in artifice that at times the viewer feels like a voyeur. We are privy to everything, including the sort of "unimportant" dialogue that most films shy away from. Here, its inclusion is just one of many fresh elements. *Before Sunrise* is about life, romance, and love. It magnifies the little things, paying scrupulous attention to the subtleties and mannerisms of body language. There are moments of unforced humor, and times of bittersweet poignancy. *Before Sunrise* speaks as much to the mind as to the heart, and much of what it says is likely to strike a responsive chord — a rare and special accomplishment for any motion picture. **MUST SEE**

Before Sunset [2004]

Starring: Ethan Hawke, Julie Delpy Director: Richard Linklater
Screenplay: Richard Linklater, Ethan Hawke, Julie Delpy Running Time:
1:20 Rated: R (Profanity, sexual language) Theatrical Aspect Ratio:
1.66:1

The litmus test for whether a viewer is likely to appreciate *Before Sunset* is simple: Anyone who enjoyed *Before Sunrise* will react favorably to the new movie. Those who thought the 1995 film was dull, too talky, or too pretentious will find similar faults with *Before Sunset*. And, although this film can *theoretically* stand on its own, the experience is greatly enhanced by watching it only after being immersed in the earlier picture. The plot could best be called minimalist. Nine years ago, Jesse (Ethan Hawke) and Celine (Julie Delpy) bid each other an emotional farewell after having spent an intensely romantic day in Vienna. They promised to meet six months later. The rendezvous never occurred. Now, Jessie has recorded a slightly fictionalized account of his encounter with Celine in a book, *This Time,* and he is on the European leg of a book-signing tour. While in a small shop in Paris, he once again encounters Celine and, for both of them, the feelings come rushing back.

Before Sunset unspools in real time. Jesse has about 60 minutes before he must leave for the airport to catch a flight home, and he intends to spend every moment in Celine's company. Linklater's approach to their interaction is flawless. At first, their conversation is filled with awkward pauses and too-long silences. Gradually, as they again become comfortable with each other, the dialogue flows more naturally and the physical space between them narrows. We feel the unspoken tension as they try to break through a barricade and recapture at least a part of what they once had.

The movie is a love story (or, to be precise, the continuation of a love story), but it's more about regrets than romance. Jesse and Celine's story is one of lost opportunities. The topics of conversation, which range from the mundane (politics, having a meaningful job, and the nature of memory) to the intimate (sex), are not as interesting as they were in the first movie, but what fascinates in the interaction between Jesse and Celine is observing the way they react to each other — how much of themselves they choose to hold back and how much they elect to reveal. When the movie is over, you may not remember much of what they said, but you will remember *how* they said it.

Watching *Before Sunset* isn't like watching most movies. This is an almost interactive experience. We feel like we're spending time in the characters' company. We're in the moment *with* them. If I had to choose between the two movies, I would admit that the first film is the stronger of the two, but *Before Sunset* is a worthy follow-up, and a must-see motion picture for those who appreciate this kind of story. **HIGHLY RECOMMENDED**

Born Romantic [United Kingdom, 2000]

Starring: Craig Ferguson, Ian Hart, Jane Horrocks, Adrian Lester,
Catherine McCormack Director: David Kane Screenplay: David Kane
Running Time: 1:36 Rated: R (Profanity, sex) Theatrical Aspect
Ratio: 1.85:1

The light, frothy, and likeable *Born Romantic* is from theater and TV director David Kane (who has made motion pictures before, none of which have been released on this continent). He has gathered a reasonably high profile cast for this project, including such notable names as Craig Ferguson, Ian Hart, Jane Horrocks, Adrian Lester, Catherine McCormack, Olivia Williams, Jimi Mistry, and David Morrissey. *Born Romantic* essentially tells three loosely connected romantic stories set against the backdrop of a salsa club that is visited by all of the principals.

Fergus (Morrissey) is an ex-musician who is scouring London for his One True Love (Jane Horrocks), a woman he jilted 8 years ago. Eddie (Mistry), an inept thief, unexpectedly falls for shy Jocelyn (McCormack), who has a fetish for morbidity. And Frankie (Ferguson) is hot for the aloof Eleanor (Williams), who seems to have no interest in him whatsoever. In the background are a group of cab divers who act almost like a Greek chorus, offering differing opinions on such diverse subjects as life, love, and blowjobs.

Kane keeps things moving, and it doesn't hurt that there's a great deal of lively salsa music to elevate the energy level. All of the characters are affable; it's virtually impossible not to wish for them to hook up with their soul mates. The screenplay is a shade smarter than that of the average romantic comedy, and there are plenty of funny lines and scenes. And, unlike in many British films, Kane doesn't seek any dark tangents for his characters to explore. This is a straightforward film — enjoyable and fresh, but not terribly deep. **RECOMMENDED**

Bounce [2000]

Starring: **Ben Affleck, Gwyneth Paltrow** Director: **Don Roos**
Screenplay: **Don Roos** Running Time: **1:45** Rated: **PG-13** (Profanity, sensuality) Theatrical Aspect Ratio: **1.85:1**

Bounce is a solid romance with 3 things going for it. In the first place, Don Roos' dialogue is a cut above the norm. Secondly, stars Ben Affleck and Gwyneth Paltrow connect in a credible manner. Finally, the film touches on a few intriguing philosophical issues, such as the guilt an individual feels when someone close to him or her unexpectedly dies.

The setup is not complicated. It's a few days before Christmas and a group of strangers is stranded at a bar in Chicago's O'Hare Airport. Buddy (Ben Affleck), an ad man, has a first-class ticket back to Los Angeles. Mimi (Natasha Henstridge) has been forced to take a room at the airport hotel because her flight has been canceled. And Greg (Tony Goldwyn) has allowed himself to be bumped from an L.A.-bound flight in order to get 2 free round-trip tickets to anywhere in the U.S. plus $200. So he's waiting for a spot to open up on a later flight. However, when Mimi makes it clear to Buddy that she wouldn't mind it if he shared her hotel room, he gives his ticket to Greg. Hours later, Flight 82 from Chicago to Los Angeles has crashed and Greg is dead, leaving behind a wife, Abby (Gwyneth Paltrow) and two children (Alex D. Linz and David Dorfman).

It takes Buddy a year and a stay in an alcohol rehab clinic before he can overcome his feelings of guilt and re-emerge into the real world. One of his first actions is to seek out Abby. Even though he has never met her, he feels responsible for her circumstances and wants to make sure she's okay. She's working as a real estate agent and he pretends to be a client. After arranging for his company to buy an expensive property through her, Buddy believes he has paid his karmic debt. But Abby is attracted to him, and keeps contriving ways to meet him. Before long, Buddy finds himself falling in love — not only with Abby, but with her kids as well. And, as this relationship transforms him from a self-serving hotshot into a caring individual, he is aware that, sometime, somewhere, his secret must emerge.

Effective romances are difficult to craft. They must be sentimental and endearing without going overboard. Low-key love stories run the risk of coming across as cold and unemotional. Conversely, going too far in the other direction can result in a cloying, mawkish production. Roos has landed safely on the middle ground. He gives us characters worth caring about and a situation we can feel comfortable with.
RECOMMENDED

Brown Sugar [2002]

Starring: **Taye Diggs, Sanaa Lathan, Mos Def, Ralph E. Tresvant, Nicole Ari Parker** Director: **Rick Famuyiwa** Screenplay: **Michael Elliot and Rick Famuyiwa** Running Time: **1:48** Rated: **PG-13** (Sexual situations, profanity) Theatrical Aspect Ratio: **1.85:1**

Those looking for a concise description of *Brown Sugar* could refer to it as the "African American *When Harry Met Sally*." After all, it is a romantic comedy that asks the popular movie question of whether a man and woman can be platonic friends without sex becoming an issue.

Music producer Dre (Taye Diggs) and magazine editor Sidney (Sanaa Lathan) have known each other since childhood, when they became friends as a result of their mutual love for hip-hop music. That love led both of them to their respective careers. Dre makes records and Sidney reviews the music. Over the years, neither of them has seriously considered the other as a potential romantic partner, until something happens to upset the chemistry — Dre falls in love with the willowy Reese (Nicole Ari Parker), and decides to get married. Despite feigning delight, Sidney is less-than-happy with the prospect of her friend tying the knot, and, after she and Dre share a kiss on the night before his nuptials, he is left with his own doubts — doubts that are deepened when Sidney begins dating a star New Jersey Nets basketball player (Boris Kodjoe).

The backdrop of *Brown Sugar* is the world of hip-hop music, and rapper Mos Def has a role as an artist that Dre decides to back. The soundtrack is loaded with hip-hop numbers, and will prove to be a "must have" for fans. However, although hip-hop provides form, color, and a rather obvious metaphor (Dre and Sidney's love for music represents their love for one another), it is not *Brown Sugar*'s focal point. The key to unlocking the film's enchantment is to uncover the unforced romance. We know how this is going to play out, but, as in any worthwhile comedy about love, the pleasure is derived not from the destination, but from the road taken to get there.

Despite having an all-black cast, *Brown Sugar* is essentially color-blind. Or, to put it another way, the film's intrinsic appeal is not confined to African American audiences. There are undoubtedly some who will complain that *Brown Sugar*'s screenplay has been homogenized for mass-market consumption, but it doesn't seem to me that there's anything wrong with making a movie that can attract both black and white viewers. And, if you want edgy, looking to a romantic comedy to provide it is ill-advised. *Brown Sugar* is undemanding fun capable of providing 2 hours of entertainment for anyone who enjoys a smart story with plenty of romantic tension.

RECOMMENDED

Chasing Amy [1997]

Starring: Ben Affleck, Joey Lauren Adams, Jason Lee Director: Kevin Smith Screenplay: Kevin Smith Running Time: 1:55 Rated: R (Profanity, frank sexual discussion) Theatrical Aspect Ratio: 1.85:1

With *Chasing Amy*, it's easy to anticipate a certain degree of inventive humor, but what's a bit unexpected is the solid drama, effective romance, and strong characters. *Clerks* worked because the dialogue sparkled, but Smith has honed his screenwriting and film making skills since then. While *Chasing Amy* boasts the same keen interplay, that quality, along with first-rate character development, acts as a supplement to the smart, surprisingly original plot. The movie starts out as light as a feather, but it doesn't take long for us to realize that *Chasing Amy* isn't just another lark for Smith. This movie is *about* something, and the deeper we get into it, the more we realize how emotionally on-target the script is.

Holden McNeil (Ben Affleck) and Banky Edwards (Jason Lee) are comic book authors. Their *Bluntman & Chronic* magazine is a big-seller, and, when they attend a comic book convention in New York, they attract long lines for autograph signings. At that convention, Holden meets fellow comic writer/artist Alyssa Jones (Joey Lauren Adams). Alyssa's project is the less testosterone-oriented *Idiosyncratic Routine*. She and Holden hit it off almost immediately. They go out for a few drinks and play darts. Later, when talking to best friend Banky, he claims that he and Alyssa "shared a moment" and confesses that he has fallen for her. But, whether or not it's really love, Holden is in for a big surprise because Alyssa is a lesbian. So, while she wants to be friends and pal around with him, Holden finds himself helplessly, hopelessly smitten.

Smith clearly has his hand on the pulse of his generation ("X" marks the spot). His observations about comic books, video games, and other aspects of life in the '90s are as insightful as they often are scathing. But this is nothing new — it was evident in both *Clerks* and *Mallrats*. What's different here is that Smith has crafted a touching, nuanced romance. There are real human feelings and problems involved in Holden and Alyssa's relationship, and, every time the storyline threatens to devolve into a cliché, it somehow avoids the trap. There's also a rich subtext pertaining to the difficulty that many individuals face in attaining a level of comfort with their sexual identity. **HIGHLY RECOMMENDED**

City of Angels [1998]

Starring: Nicolas Cage, Meg Ryan, Denis Franz, Andre Braugher Director: Brad Silberling Screenplay: Dana Stevens based on *Wings of Desire* Running Time: 1:56 Rated: PG-13 (Occasional profanity, discreet sex, brief male nudity) Theatrical Aspect Ratio: 2.35:1

City of Angels is based, not unexpectedly, in Los Angeles, which here is a literal "City of Angels," with the invisible celestial agents sitting high atop billboards and skyscrapers. Dressed like Heaven's Men in Black, the angels are an odd bunch. They spend their days and nights observing and occasionally offering comfort to select humans. They cannot touch, taste, or smell. They are immortal and ethereal. They live in a library and spend time at the beach in a kind of wordless communion.

Seth (Nicolas Cage) is just one of many angels assigned to Los Angeles. But, unlike most of his brethren, he has a strong desire to experience what it's like to be human. He seems to share the sentiment of a comment that he relates to fellow angel Cassiel (Andre Braugher): "What good would wings be if you couldn't feel the wind on your face?" One day, Seth is in a hospital to guide a dying man to the next life. His attention is captured by the determination of a doctor, Maggie Rice (Meg Ryan), to save the patient's life. Later, he returns with the intention of soothing Maggie's distress, but it proves to be a difficult task. Soon, he is spending hours on end watching her, eventually revealing himself as a benevolent stranger. Seth has fallen in love with Maggie, but he thinks it's a doomed proposition until a angel-turned-human (Denis Franz) reveals that God gives all of his creations free will, and, if Seth wants it enough, he can shed his wings for a human body. But, just because Seth loves Maggie, there's no guarantee that she will reciprocate his feelings, and if he gives up his immortality for a romantic illusion, what then?

When it comes to heavenly matters, *City of Angels* doesn't offer any particular insights. The movie does not ponder the meaning of life; rather, it shamelessly celebrates the human experience by demonstrating the monotony of endless voyeurism. On a somewhat less-intellectual level, it's also about sacrifice. *City of Angels* is more romantic than profound, but Dana Stevens' script is thoughtful and intelligent, and I never felt insulted by what the characters said, did, or thought. It's a subdued motion picture, but the lack of overt melodrama makes for a moving and involving story. RECOMMENDED

The Closer You Get [Ireland, 2000]
Starring: Ian Hart, Sean McGinley, Niamh Cusack, Ruth McCabe
Director: Aileen Ritchie Screenplay: William Ivory, based on a story by Herbie Wave Running Time: 1:32 Rated: PG-13 (Occasional profanity, mild violence, sexual themes) Theatrical Aspect Ratio: 1.85:1

The Closer You Get, the feature debut of director Aileen Ritchie, is one of those feather-light romantic comedies that's pleasant to watch but not likely to stick in the mind long after the end credits have rolled. It's a welcome distraction, but not much more. The film takes place in Ireland, and some of its charm comes from the culture and countryside. Of course, all of the characters in this film are eccentrics, but that's only to be expected, since a movie featuring normal Irish folk wouldn't be as quirky.

The Closer You Get focuses on the romantic trials and tribulations of a group of young men living in a small, out-of-the-way village. They meet every night in the pub to bemoan the lack of attractive, eligible women in their town. Of course, this sort of talk doesn't go over well with the members of the opposite sex. Oddly, with the exception of the pub owner, no one seems to be married. In fact, the local priest, who is new to the district, has never performed a wedding. Eventually, bitten by the romance bug, the men take an action out of desperation. Led by their ring-leader, Kieran O'Donnagh (Ian Hart), who is said to have "the constitution of an ox and the wits to match," they decide to place an ad in a Miami newspaper trumpeting the assets of their village and its men for any adventurous American women who would like to cross the ocean and get married. Then, to the amusement of the local womenfolk, they sit back and await the arrival of their potential brides.

The romantic fantasy employed here is a common one — that we often miss true love because we're busy looking in the distance while it's right under our nose. That's where the title comes from: "The closer you get to something, the harder it is to see." With a single exception (the pub keeper), everyone in *The Closer You Get* is likable. Kieran may be a bit dense, but he's the kind of dullard who's easy to like. As was true of the characters in *The Full Monty,* we find our-

selves rooting for these men, even though they're not traditional hero material. While Irish films have yet to become a staple of American cinema, they are gradually gaining in popularity. RECOMMENDED

Cold Mountain [2003]
Starring: Jude Law, Nicole Kidman, Renée Zellweger, Kathy Baker, Aileen Atkins, Natalie Portman, Philip Seymour Hoffman, Giovanni Ribisi, Brendan Gleeson, Charlie Hunnam, Ray Winstone, Donald Sutherland Director: Anthony Minghella Screenplay: Anthony Mingella, based on the novel by Charles Frazier Running Time: 2:26 Rated: R (Violence, sex, nudity) Theatrical Aspect Ratio: 2.35:1

It's not often that, when the primary thread of a movie fails, the secondary story lines are compelling enough to make the overall experience a positive one. However, that occurs with *Cold Mountain,* a Civil War–era romance where the love affair fizzles but the episodic approach allows the narrative to breathe. The end result is that the film has more to offer than the tepid Nicole Kidman–Jude Law pairing. There are a lot of things to like about *Cold Mountain,* but those who expect director Anthony Minghella to recapture the tragic, romantic enchantment of *The English Patient* will be disappointed.

The movie opens in 1864, with the South well on its way to losing the Civil War. After recovering from a devastating injury, infantryman Inman (Law) decides to desert and make his way back to his home town of Cold Mountain, North Carolina, where he hopes to have a life with Ada (Kidman), the preacher's daughter. It has been three years since they last saw each other, and he doesn't know for sure whether she is waiting for him. They hardly know each other — their interaction was brief, but left a lasting impression. However, the trek back to Cold Mountain proves to be an arduous one. Along the way, Inman meets a number of odd people, some of whom are interested in helping, and others who see him only as a way to make a profit.

Meanwhile, Ada has been waiting. Following the death of her father (Donald Sutherland), she has let the farm lapse into disarray. Enter Ruby Thewes (Renée Zellweger), a plain-speaking free spirit who offers to help Ada rebuild the farm in exchange for meals and lodging. A bargain is struck, and the two begin a mutually beneficial partnership that develops into a friendship. But troubles lurk. The head of the local "home guards" (Ray Winstone, who does evil as well as anyone), a group empowered to kill deserters, wants Ada and her land, and Ruby's father (Brendan Gleeson) pays his daughter an unexpected visit.

Cold Mountain's strengths lie in its vignettes. Inman's and Ada's paths to their reunion are broken into various episodes. Some of these are quite good, and even the least impressive retains some degree of interest. It's fair to say in *Cold Mountain*'s case that the journey counts more than what happens once the destination is reached. In fact, one could make a legitimate argument that the quality that keeps this movie from greatness is the lack of fire in Inman and Ada's relationship. Give them the chemistry of Bogart and Bergman in *Casablanca* (or even Fiennes and Scott-Thomas in *The English Patient*) and this would have been an unforgettable motion picture.

Cold Mountain was adapted from the long, complex novel by Charles Frazier, and clearly proved to be a challenge for Minghella to capture on film. The movie has its share of structural problems, and may be a little longer than seems necessary, but it rarely lost my attention. I would not place this in the top echelon of motion pictures, but it's certainly a successful adaptation, features numerous memorable performances (mostly by the supporting players), and is worth an expenditure of time. RECOMMENDED

The Cutting Edge [1992]

Starring: D. B. Sweeney, Moira Kelly, Roy Dotrice, Terry O'Quinn
Director: **Paul M. Glaser** Screenplay: Tony Gilroy Running Time: **1:40**
Rated: PG (Mature themes, profanity) Theatrical Aspect Ratio: **1.85:1**

Romantic comedies are a dime-a-dozen, and most of them fail because they pursue slapstick while losing sight of the characters. Because *The Cutting Edge* doesn't fall into that trap, it results in an enjoyable lark. Despite a recycled plot, this appealing motion picture is likely to be embraced by everyone who enjoys a little romance.

It's "The Taming of the Shrew" on ice, even down to the name of the female lead. Kate Mosely (Moira Kelly) has been a pairs skater for most of her life, and her ultimate goal has always been an Olympic gold medal. But, despite her talent, she has an attitude problem that drives partner after partner away until even the least experienced skaters would rather "sleep with [a] cross and wear garlic" than join Kate on the ice. So, when her coach (Roy Dotrice) becomes desperate, he tries something unconventional — seeking out ex-Hockey star Doug Dorsey (D.B. Sweeney), who's spending his days working at his brother's sports bar while coming to grips with the reality that an eye injury has ended his professional dreams.

The Cutting Edge is not built on storyline. From the opening scene to the closing credits, there is not one new plot element in this entire movie. Zip. Nada. Zilch. We've seen it all before, whether in sports films or romantic comedies. Those looking for originality had best search somewhere else. However, there are some movies where plot has to play second string to characters, and this is one of them. Kate and Doug are refreshingly real and immensely likable. Their love/hate relationship is played out perfectly, recalling the Bruce Willis/Cybill Shepherd sparring matches of *Moonlighting*, albeit without all the teasing. It's the romantic tension, not the skating story, that holds *The Cutting Edge* together.

Anyone expecting a movie dominated by figure skating will be disappointed. *The Cutting Edge* concentrates on its characters, with the skating limited to a supporting role. This is not a movie for cynics, nor for those who don't occasionally like to sit back and enjoy an undemanding, "comfortable" film. For unadulterated fun, *The Cutting Edge* may not earn a gold medal, but it's worth at least a bronze. RECOMMENDED

Don Juan De Marco [1995]

Starring: Marlon Brando, Johnny Depp, Faye Dunaway, Rachel Ticotin
Director: **Jeremy Leven** Screenplay: **Jeremy Leven** Running Time: **1:37**
Rated: PG-13 (Mature themes, nudity, profanity) Theatrical Aspect Ratio: **1.85:1**

The title character, a modern day Don Juan (with the Italian last name of DeMarco), is played by Johnny Depp. At the age of 21, he claims to have made love to more than 1,500 women. He has been rejected only once, by the enchanting and innocent Ana (Geraldine Pailhas), but, as is so often the case, she was "the only one who really mattered." So, with no possibility of a life with his true love, Don Juan decides to kill himself. He climbs high atop a billboard and demands that the police send him the greatest living swordfighter so he can die in a duel. What he gets instead is Dr. Jack Mickler (Marlon Brando), a massively overweight, near-to-retirement psychiatrist who pretends to be Don Octavio de Flores and talks Don Juan down from his perch. Then, at Woodhaven State Hospital, where the young man is temporarily held, Jack petitions his boss (Bob Dishy) for the right to supervise the newcomer's treatment.

Don Juan DeMarco is a lighthearted, frothy fable about romance and the way a patient's fantasies affect his doctor's reality. Despite several astute lines which give the film an intellectual appeal, this is not an exceptionally deep movie. The playful, often humorous tone, coupled with Don Juan's accent, suggests *The Princess Bride*. Writer/director Jeremy Leven takes pleasure in clouding the division between what's real and what isn't, but he never stretches matters to such an extreme that *Don Juan DeMarco* is reduced to a mindless farce.

Don Juan DeMarco has a seductively sensual veneer, but the full complement of the title character's sexual conquests lacks the romance of the low-key relationship between Jack and his wife (Faye Dunaway). These two act like they've been married for 32 years, and her wonder at his sudden re-awakening is charmingly unaffected. There is proof here — as if any is really needed — that couples don't have to be under thirty to capture an audience's heart.

With so much blurring between reality and fantasy, there are bound to be a few missteps, but Leven keeps these to a minimum, and the film is mostly a success in its approach to its themes. Don Juan asks the four essential questions about existence: "What is sacred?," "Of what is the spirit made?," "What is worth living for?," and "What is worth dying for?" The proposed answer to all is "love," that singular emotion which pervades this disarming motion picture.
RECOMMENDED

Down with Love [2003]
Starring: Renée Zellweger, Ewan McGregor, David Hyde Pierce, Sarah Paulson, Tony Randall Director: Peyton Reed Screenplay: Eve Ahlert & Dennis Drake Running Time: 1:37 Rated: PG-13 (Sexual innuendo) Theatrical Aspect Ratio: 2.35:1

With *Down with Love*, director Peyton Reed has addressed the common complaint of old-time filmgoers that "they don't make movies the way they used to." This feature is intended to emulate early-1960s sex farces in every way imaginable. The intention is not to parody the genre but to affectionately re-create the kind of movie that was popularized by Doris Day. *Down with Love* shows the strong influence of 1959's *Pillow Talk* and 1961's *Lover Come Back*, both of which starred Day and Tony Randall, who has a small cameo in this movie.

The film introduces us to Barbara Novak (Renée Zellweger), a small-town girl who has come to New York City for the publication of her book, *Down with Love*. Barbara has written a how-to tome on female empowerment, which advocates three simple steps that women can use to achieve equality in both the bedroom and the workplace. The keys to success involve treating sex like a man does, and eating lots of chocolate. Peter MacMannus (David Hyde Pierce),

the editor of *Know* magazine, wants his star reporter, Catcher Block (Ewan McGregor), to interview Barbara for a story. Catcher initially blows off the assignment, but after the book becomes a huge best seller and changes the attitudes of women worldwide, he can't get an appointment with her. So, determined to prove her to be a fraud — someone interested only in "love and marriage like all women" — he creates the false personality of Major Zip Martin to seduce her. Predictably, Catcher's plan works too well — not only does Barbara fall for him, but he falls for her. But she has a trick or two up her sleeve.

Down with Love is light, funny, and clever. There are times when the film's seeming naïveté will cause viewers to chuckle, but this is a case in which the filmmakers expect the audience to laugh *at* their production, much as anyone watching those early-60s romantic comedies will be amused by their innocence. In addition, there's a fair amount of overt humor, such as a rat-a-tat exchange that comes across like a "Who's on first?" bit, and a split-screen phone conversation that uses odd body positions and double entendres to suggest a variety of sexual activities. This is as risqué as *Down with Love* gets. There's also a wonderful scene where Barbara has a single-shot, five-minute monologue during which she hardly takes a breath.

Those familiar with the era to which Reed aspires will sit through *Down with Love* enveloped by a feeling of fondness and affection. It's sort of like looking at old, yellowed snapshots after many years and dredging up only the good memories. **RECOMMENDED**

Emma [1996]
Starring: Gwyneth Paltrow, Toni Collette, Jeremy Northam, Alan Cumming, Ewan McGregor Director: Douglas McGrath Screenplay: Douglas McGrath based on the novel by Jane Austen Running Time: 2:01 Rated: PG (Nothing offensive) Theatrical Aspect Ratio: 1.85:1

It's the romantic buried inside each of us that responds to movies like *Emma*. Sure, the film, like the Jane Austen novel upon which it is based, is laced with wit and sophistication. And, although it contains enough social commentary and character development to lift it well above the plane of genre romances, *Emma* is still primarily about lovers finding each other during a simpler age (Austen published her novels in the early 19th century).

Emma details the matchmaking attempts of 21-year-old Emma Woodhouse (Gwyneth Paltrow), an incorrigible meddler who believes that "there is nothing more beautiful than a match well made." After successfully marrying her governess (Greta Scacchi) to a widower (James Cosmo), Emma sets her sights on pairing her plain, uncultured friend, Harriet Smith (Toni Collette), with the local vicar, Reverend Elton (Alan Cumming). Elton, however, has other ideas, as does Emma's closest male friend, Knightley (Jeremy Northam), who describes her activities as "vanity working on a weak mind [that] produces every kind of mischief." Emma herself is unattached, but, since this is a Jane Austen story, it's obvious that won't last for long. Indeed, before the 2 hours are up, the title character has become enmeshed in a number of romantic entanglements, and it doesn't take a genius to uncover the identity of Emma's true soul-mate.

Emma lacks the depth of passion present in the other Austen films, but, in large part because it's trying for something lighter and breezier, it's still fun. The film runs a little longer than seems necessary, and gets off to a slow, fitful start (Douglas McGrath's screenplay is not the equal of the other Austen adaptations), but Paltrow keeps us interested until the story's inherent romantic magic begins to weave its spell. **RECOMMENDED**

Ever After [1998]

Starring: Drew Barrymore, Dougray Scott, Anjelica Huston, Megan Dodds Director: Andy Tennant Screenplay: Susannah Grant and Andy Tennant & Rick Parks Running Time: 2:00 Rated: PG-13 (Mild violence, mild profanity) Theatrical Aspect Ratio: 1.85:1

Ever After's twist is that it's telling the "real" Cinderella story from which the Brothers Grimm fable was derived (the two famous fairy tale scribes make a brief appearance in a prologue that also features a cameo by the incomparable Jeanne Moreau). Consequently, there are no pumpkins, mice, magic spells, or fairy godmothers. The love story between a peasant girl and a prince is still at the core, although, in this case, "Cinderella" (whose name is Danielle), has the kind of progressive attitude that would be more at home in the 1990s than in the 1500s.

The broad strokes of the story are certainly familiar. After the tragic death of her father (Jeroen Krabbe), Danielle (played by Anna Maguire as a little girl, and Drew Barrymore thereafter) is consigned to a life of servitude for her cruel stepmother, Rodmilla (Anjelica Huston), and vain step-sister, Marguerite (Megan Dodds). Danielle has an ally in the household, her second step-sister, Jacqueline (Melanie Lynskey), but she's too meek to stand up to her mother. While Rod-

milla, Marguerite, and Jacqueline enjoy as much luxury as their farm house provides, Danielle (dubbed "Cinderella" by Marguerite for the cinders that always stain her clothing) is forced to scrub the floors, cook the meals, and feed the animals.

One day, when Danielle is picking apples, she spies a man stealing one of her step-mother's horses. It's actually Prince Henry (Dougray Scott), the heir to the throne of France, in the process of running away from his father because he is unwilling to be trapped in a loveless, arranged marriage. Mistaking Henry for a common thief, Danielle knocks him from the horse with a well-aimed apple. After she realizes who he is, she is apologetic, but the meeting leaves an impression on both of them. At the time of their next encounter, Danielle is posing as a countess in order to rescue a family retainer from debtors' prison. She engages the Prince in a spirited debate, and, although he thinks he recognizes her, he can't put a name to the face. Soon, he is scouring the countryside looking for her, and, although Danielle is attracted to him, she avoids contact, fearing that if he learns that she isn't a member of the nobility, he will shun her. Through all of this, there is a fairy godmother of sorts — Leonardo da Vinci (Patrick Godfrey), who uses science, not magic, to smooth the path of true love.

Tennant, who showed skill at the helm of a romance with *Fools Rush In*, has found the right tone for this effort. The love story is wrapped around interludes of comedy, adventure, and drama. It never seems to matter that we know the entire story from the beginning — the characters, not the plot, capture our attention. **RECOMMENDED**

Fools Rush In [1997]

Starring: Matthew Perry, Salma Hayek Director: Andy Tennant Screenplay: Katherine Reback from a story by Joan Taylor and Katherine Reback Running Time: 1:46 Rated: PG-13 (Mature themes, sex) Theatrical Aspect Ratio: 1.85:1

Done well, a romantic comedy can be an enchanting experience — something guaranteed to bring a smile to the lips of all but the most hardened cynic. Done poorly, a film in that genre can be sickening and unbearable. It's all a matter of style, tone, and chemistry. Some films have it; many don't. Fortunately for those who venture out to *Fools Rush In*, it's camped in the former category. If you want daring or original, *Fools Rush In* isn't the movie to see. Like 90% of all romantic comedies, it follows a time-honored formula that allows little room for variation. For those who don't know it, it goes something like this: boy meets girl, boy and girl fall in love, boy loses girl, boy goes after girl, boy and girl get together and live happily ever after.

The "boy" in this scenario is Alex Whitman (Matthew Perry), a WASP construction manager for a chain of nightclubs popping up all over the United States. His latest gig has landed him in Las Vegas, where he runs into the "girl." She's Isabel Fuentes (the radiant Salma Hayek), a strict Mexican American Catholic who has just broken off an engagement to longtime boyfriend Chuy (Carlos Gomez). She and Alex have a one night stand, then, 3 months later, she shows up at his home and tells him that she's pregnant. Twenty-four hours later, they're married, but it takes the rest of the movie before they attain wedded bliss.

Between falling in love and finding happiness come The Complications. Depending on the romantic comedy, these can be (guess the movie): deciding whether men and women can be just friends, claiming to be engaged to an unconscious man, trying to split up the winnings from a lottery ticket, arranging a meeting atop the Empire State Building, skating into the Olympics, and so on . . . In *Fools Rush In*, The Complications arrive in the form of a culture clash. Mexico-born Isabel and Connecticut-born Alex are from two different worlds, and the impending birth of a baby doesn't suddenly sweep away all differences. While *Fools Rush In* isn't going to win any awards, it should please most audiences, which is about the most anyone can ask for from this kind of effervescent, unambitious project. **RECOMMENDED**

Forces of Nature [1999]

Starring: Sandra Bullock, Ben Affleck, Maura Tierney, Steve Zahn
Director: Bronwen Hughes Screenplay: Marc Lawrence, Ian Bryce, Donna Roth Running Time: 1:46 Rated: PG-13 (Mild profanity, sexual themes) Theatrical Aspect Ratio: 1.85:1

Murphy's Law states that anything that can go wrong will go wrong, and that's exactly what happens to Ben Holmes (Affleck) with the approach of his wedding day. Ben, who earns his living by writing blurbs for book jackets, and his fiancée, Bridget (Maura Tierney), live in New York City, but the big event is being conducted in Savannah, Georgia. So, a couple days before he's due to tie the knot, Ben, who's terrified of flying, reluctantly boards a southern-bound plane at JFK. Shortly thereafter, the plane has crashed (actually, it never gets off the ground), and Ben is trying to find an alternative means of transportation to Savannah. Coming to his rescue is Sarah (Sandra Bullock),

an attractive freespirit he helped during the crash. She gets them both a ride in a rental car with a guy named Vic. It's only the first of many segments of a wild and unpredictable trip down the East Coast that includes planes, trains, and automobiles. Along the way, Ben starts to fall for Sarah, and is forced to examine whether he *really* wants to marry Bridget after all.

Affleck and Bullock share an effective chemistry that enhances their scenes. Although *Forces of Nature* isn't really about sex — it's more about love, romance, and taking chances — there's an element of eroticism in Ben and Sarah's interaction, and it's never overplayed. Affleck also connects with his other female co-star, Maura Tierney, in a palpable way, which makes it difficult to determine which lovely lady Ben will finish the film with. Because Affleck and Bullock spend the lion's share of the screen time in each other's company, it's only natural to root for them to end up together. On the other hand, there's a sense of genuine affection and tenderness between Ben and Bridget. This conflict heightens the limited dramatic aspect of *Forces of Nature*. There's a realization that, no matter what happens, someone is going to get hurt — if only a little bit.

In many ways, the romance is just a backdrop for a series of crazy misadventures. While *Forces of Nature* doesn't go for the all-out zaniness of *Planes, Trains, and Automobiles* (there are no pillows), the 1986 film is clearly an inspiration. During the course of their trek, Ben and Sarah are arrested, end up on a train going in the wrong direction, lose all their money (a necessary plot device), masquerade as a rich, married couple, are chased by the police, and are waylaid by a hurricane. Towards the end of the trip, as the couple watches a building go up in flames, Ben jokes, "Let's just sit here and wait for the locusts to come." *Forces of Nature* represents a pleasant movie-going experience — one that replaces cloying romance with something breezier while remaining true to the appeal of the leads. **RECOMMENDED**

The Girl Next Door [2004]

Starring: Emile Hirsch, Elisha Cuthbert, Nicholas Downs, Timothy Olyphant, Chris Marquette, Paul Dano, James Remar, Jacob Young
Director: Luke Greenfield Screenplay: Stuart Blumberg and David T. Wagner & Brent Goldberg Running Time: 1:48 Rated: R (Sexual situations, profanity, nudity, brief violence) Theatrical Aspect Ratio: 1.85:1

The Girl Next Door builds up enough goodwill during its successful first half that we're willing to forgive some of the strange and disappointing convolutions the plot takes us through during the final 45 minutes. The protagonist is high school senior Matthew (Emile Hirsch), a quiet, studious boy who has used his education thus far as a stepping-stone to the college of his choice, Georgetown. But when it comes time to write down a memory for the yearbook, he realizes he doesn't have one. Instead of living, he has played it safe while at Westport High School, hanging out with his two best friends, Eli (Chris Marquette) and Klitz (Paul Dano). That all changes when Danielle (Elisha Cuthbert) moves in next door. She's a blond bombshell running away from a porn star past and eager to start afresh.

One night, Matthew spies her undressing through her bedroom window. Transfixed, he forgets the first rule of voyeurism — turn out the light in your viewing space — and, as a result, he gets busted. Danielle takes him for a little ride in her car and demands tit for tat (so to speak). He saw her; now she gets to see him. So, in the middle of a suburban street, he strips down to nothing. Soon after, he's following her around like a lovestruck puppy. For her part, she finds something fresh and appealing about his innocence. But trouble arrives when her past becomes her present. A porn producer ex-boyfriend by the name of Kelly (Timothy Olyphant) arrives to bring her back to the business and to teach Matthew a few lessons from the school of hard knocks.

When the movie concentrates on the relationship between Matthew and Danielle, it's on firm ground, even when it ventures into Romantic Comedy 101 territory. The natural charisma and screen presence of the two stars has a good deal to do with this. Both Cuthbert and Hirsch have cut their teeth in television, but neither has trouble making the transition to the big screen.

The Girl Next Door runs into a few potholes during its second half, which requires the plot to go through all sorts of contortions to prevent Matthew and Danielle from finding happiness too early. So we get scenes with the creepy Kelly, the even creepier porn kingpin Hugo Posh (James Remar), Matthew's ecstasy-enhanced speech about "moral fiber" and sacrifice, and a prom night to remember. Some of this works, and some doesn't. And there are times, thanks to the filmmaker's overuse of slow-motion photography, when it feels like we're watching a sports movie. In a way, maybe that's what the pairing of these two is, because it's hard not to be rooting for Matthew and

Danielle to reach the finish line arm-in-arm, with hands clasped and lips locked. **RECOMMENDED**

Innocence [Australia, 2000]
Starring: Charles Tingwell, Julia Blake, Terry Norris Director: Paul Cox
Screenplay: Paul Cox Running Time: 1:38 Rated: R (Sex, nudity, profanity, mature themes) Theatrical Aspect Ratio: 1.85:1

Innocence is little more than a solid, old-fashioned romance. In essence, the movie doesn't do anything more ambitious than chronicle the ebb and flow of a romantic relationship between two characters. The emotions they feel are familiar to all of us — young and old, male and female, gay and heterosexual. The plot doesn't do anything extraordinary, and, if it's given to occasionally slipping into melodrama, we must forgive it — after all, that's a characteristic of even the best romances. And, if the dialogue occasionally becomes somewhat stilted and esoteric, we must forgive that, as well — better characters saying these kinds of things than spouting the dumbed-down lines that permeate big-budget features. To a degree, *Innocence* doesn't sound that far afield from many motion pictures that arrive in theaters every year, but there is one important difference: the lovers in this romance are both around 70 years of age, and have far less of their lives ahead of them than behind them.

Innocence tells of the affair between Andreas (Charles Tingwell), a widower, and Claire (Julia Blake), a woman trapped in a comfortable but loveless marriage. Fifty years ago, Andreas and Claire were deeply in love, but circumstances separated them. They both married, had children, and lived their lives. Now, in their twilight years, they have found each other again, and, even though their bodies have aged, their passion is as strong as it ever was. Of course, there are complications — Andreas is afflicted with terminal cancer and Claire's husband (Terry Norris) reacts in an expectedly negative manner to the news of his wife's late-life infidelity. But Paul Cox's script remains thought-provoking, even when it veers into melodrama.

Is *Innocence*'s appeal generation-based? While older viewers are more likely than younger ones to identify intimately with the characters, the central emotions are universal. There's nothing in *Innocence* that will confound or alienate an 18-year old. It has been suggested that the idea of depicting two 70-year olds having sex (the scenes are not graphic, but they are present) is somehow revolutionary, but that would imply that 70-year olds don't have sex — an idea that is ludicrous. The only thing *Innocence* has done is to face up to a fact of life that some people, for whatever reason, aren't comfortable acknowledging. In the end, *Innocence* speaks to the romantic in all of us, and it doesn't take long before we don't care about age. Cox works his magic on us, and we are drawn in. **RECOMMENDED**

Intolerable Cruelty [2003]

Starring: George Clooney, Catherine Zeta-Jones, Geoffrey Rush, Cedric the Entertainer, Edward Herrmann, Paul Adelstein, Richard Jenkins, Billy Bob Thornton, Julia Duffy Director: Joel Coen Screenplay: Robert Ramsey & Matthew Stone and Ethan Coen & Joel Coen Running Time: 1:40 Rated: R (Sexual situations, profanity, brief violence) Theatrical Aspect Ratio: 2.35:1

For those who like intelligent, quirky movies filled with big laughs, dry wit, and other small pleasures, it's difficult to beat Joel Coen's and Ethan Coen's humorous outings. *Intolerable Cruelty* is the most recent of these: a film that takes the traditional romantic comedy and tweaks it by way of *The War of the Roses*. Rarely has strife between the sexes been so ruthless, so civilized, and so funny.

The combatants are attorney Miles Massey (George Clooney) and fortune hunter Marylin Rexroth (Catherine Zeta-Jones). The only thing stronger than their attraction to each other is their need to win. Miles, who is already wealthy, is driven by the desire to savor "the ultimate destruction of [his] opponent." Marylin, on the other hand, is simply looking for "wealth, independence, and freedom." Their first skirmish occurs when Miles represents Marylin's philandering husband, Rex (Edward Herrmann), in a divorce action. It is not fated to be the last time these two will encounter each other, inside or outside of the courtroom and the bedroom.

Perfect casting is doubtlessly one of the reasons why *Intolerable Cruelty* succeeds as unconditionally as it does. It's hard to think of anyone better than charming George Clooney to play the smooth, preening Miles, who never passes up an opportunity to check on his smile in a mirror. As regal as she is classically beautiful, Catherine Zeta-Jones radiates a cool sensuality that's impossible to ignore. Marylin is constantly on low burn, but there are a couple of occasions when she ignites in Clooney's company. The dance these two do around each other makes the moves of an average screen couple appear clumsy and poorly choreographed.

As much fun as the Coens have with the conventions of the genre, and despite the great delight they take in flouting our expectations, they never venture too far from the familiar trail. *Intolerable Cruelty* maintains a jaunty tone throughout, even as the story line crisscrosses from con game to romance and back. The ending is satisfying on its own terms, which may not be the same ones under which more traditional romantic comedies operate. And, while there are similarities to Danny DeVito's *The War of the Roses*, *Intolerable Cruelty* lacks the earlier film's bleak, black attitude. By comparison, one could almost call the Coens' approach optimistic. **HIGHLY RECOMMENDED**

Italian for Beginners [Denmark, 2000]

Starring: Anders W. Berthelsen, Ann Eleonora Jørgensen, Anette Støvelbæk Director: Lone Scherfig Screenplay: Lone Scherfig Running Time: 1:52 Rated: R (Profanity) Theatrical Aspect Ratio: 1.66:1 In Danish with subtitles

Based on the title, one might mistakenly assume that *Italian for Beginners* is a saucy Italian romp; in point of fact, it comes from Denmark. It is a comedy, and there is romance involved, but the film also has a bit of an edge. There are several truly loathsome characters — an aging mother and father and a deposed pastor, to name a few — which keep the movie from turning light and frothy. And the film earns its R-rating simply because characters occasionally use profanity, not because of a litany of 4-letter words or the presence of explicit sex and/or violence.

Italian for Beginners is 3 romances bundled into one. The connecting thread is that all of the principals live in the same Danish town and, at one time or another, they all attend the same adult education night class: Italian for Beginners. Andreas (Anders W. Berthelsen) is the new pastor, and is desperately uncertain of himself. He becomes interested in shy, clumsy Olympia (Anette Støvelbæk), who works at a baker's shop and lives with a despot of a father. Because the former pastor has not yet vacated the living quarters, Andreas is forced to stay at a hotel. The desk manager there, Jorgen Mortensen (Peter Gantzler), befriends the minister. Jorgen, who hasn't had sex in 4 years, is beginning to despair that he'll ever find a woman who excites him, although there is an attraction between him and Giulia (Sara Indrio Jensen), a waitress at a local restaurant. The restaurant is managed by the sharp-tongued Halvfinn (Lars Kaalund), who also happens to be Jorgen's best friend. He is drawn to Karen (Ann Eleonora Jørgensen), who runs a hair-cutting salon. These characters engage in an elaborate courtship dance until, during a vacation they take together in Venice, each relationship is clarified — one way or another.

Director Lone Scherfig has the benefit of a well-written script (which she penned) that throws a few surprises the viewer's way and doesn't tie up all the loose ends to the degree that a Hollywood production might. She also has an expert cast portraying characters that are not lifted off of a stereotype shelf. There is far more going on than one might expect to see in a traditional romantic comedy, and *Italian for Beginners* is all the more rich for it. RECOMMENDED

Jerry Maguire [1996]

Starring: Tom Cruise, Cuba Gooding Jr., Renee Zellweger
Director: Cameron Crowe Screenplay: Cameron Crowe Running
Time: 2:18 Rated: R (Profanity, sexual situations, nudity) Theatrical
Aspect Ratio: 1.85:1

Jerry Maguire is magic on celluloid — fresh, funny, romantic, and upbeat. As the movie opens, super sports agent Jerry Maguire is facing a crisis of conscience (that he still possesses one after working in such a cynical, materialistic business is something of a miracle). He wonders what he has become — "Just another shark in a suit?" He realizes that he hates himself and his place in the world, and laments that, although he has a lot to say, no one will listen. So, late one night, he writes a Mission Statement called "The Things We Think and Do Not Say: The Future of Our Business." The essay attacks the sports agency business, advocating a more humane approach. The next day, a copy is distributed to everyone in the office. And, although Jerry's co-workers applaud his courage ("Somebody finally said what had to be said"), his bosses are offended, and he loses his job. Only one client, unremarkable Arizona Cardinals wide receiver Rod Tidwell (Cuba Gooding Jr.), elects to remain with Jerry as he strikes out on his own. Also joining him is a 26-year-old single mother, Dorothy Boyd (Renee Zellweger), who is so moved by Jerry's Mission Statement that she's willing to throw away a safe job to be part of his new venture.

Jerry Maguire is about redemption and love. It's about finding one's heart and soul in a business climate that attempts to rip both away. Writer/director Cameron Crowe brings both a strong sense of verisimilitude and a lively wit to his film. Even as *Jerry Maguire* reaches out to the heart, it tickles the funny bone. Not only does Crowe have a knack for creating multi-dimensional personalities for secondary characters with minimal screen time, but he uses traditional formulas in unique ways to serve his themes.

While the budding romance between Jerry and Dorothy is *Jerry Maguire*'s most enchanting element, the remainder of the film has the necessary appeal to keep our attention when Zellweger isn't around (Cruise, on the other hand, is in just about every scene). Crowe, who doesn't have a subpar entry on his short resume, has crafted another winner here. For anyone who has forgotten the feelings that a wonderful movie can trigger, *Jerry Maguire* provides a welcome reminder. HIGHLY RECOMMENDED

Kate & Leopold [2001]

Starring: Meg Ryan, Hugh Jackman, Liev Schreiber Director: James
Mangold Screenplay: James Mangold and Steven Rogers Running
Time: 2:00 Rated: PG-13 (Profanity) Theatrical Aspect Ratio: 1.85:1

In an attempt to add some freshness to the romance, *Kate & Leopold* throws a little science fiction flavoring into the cinematic stew. As it turns out, however, while this aspect of the film spices things up, it doesn't lead to anything ground-breaking. The Twilight Zone is kept at bay. It's more of a means to create a fish-out-of-water subplot than to investigate the paradoxes of time travel. Ultimately, however, the love story aspect works better than the science fiction one.

Leopold, the Duke of Albany (Hugh Jackman), lives a life of privilege in 1876 until the night when he spies a stranger in his uncle's house. He pursues the man and ends up in 2001 New York City, in the apartment of Stuart (Liev Schreiber), his great-great-grandson. When Stuart is involved in an elevator accident that lands him in the hospital before he can send Leopold back to 1876, the Duke comes under the care of Stuart's ex-girlfriend and downstairs neighbor, Kate (Meg Ryan), and her actor brother, Charlie (Breckin Meyer). Kate knows the truth about Leopold, but doesn't believe it, and she bears her obligation of looking after him like a burden — until she realizes that he would be the perfect spokesperson for an advertising campaign her marketing company is working on. Suddenly, hard-bitten, unromantic Kate and Leopold, the "psychotic escapee from a Renaissance Fair," are spending quite a bit of time together and falling in love. But there's an obvious problem in the form of a 125-year age gap.

One could argue that the dialogue in *Kate & Leopold* is a cut above that from many of Ryan's previous romantic comedies (except perhaps *When Harry Met Sally*), but if this film is relying on its occasional zingers and smart bits of conversation to get bodies in theater seats, it's in trouble. People will go to see Ryan, who's as cute at age 40 as she was in her late 20s, and Jackman, who continues to prove that his range extends beyond that of playing Wolverine in *X-Men*. The chemistry between these 2 bubbles pleasantly. There's no powerful sexual attraction, but this movie is more about innocent romance than passion, so it works. Like most of Ryan's films, *Kate & Leopold* succeeds as a diversion (although, at 2 hours in length, it's too long). It is cinematic cotton candy — insubstantial perhaps, but ultimately sweet and pleasant to the taste. **RECOMMENDED**

Kissing Jessica Stein [2002]

Starring: Jennifer Westfeldt, Heather Juergensen, Scott Cohen, Tovah Feldshuh Director: Charles Herman-Wurmfeld Screenplay: Heather Juergensen & Jennifer Westfeldt, based on their play "Lipschtick" Running Time: 1:34 Rated: R (Profanity, sexual situations) Theatrical Aspect Ratio: 1.85:1

Without resorting to hyperbole, I can state that *Kissing Jessica Stein* may be the best same-sex romance I have seen. The screenplay is written with a thinking audience in mind, the dialogue sparkles, the characters leap off the screen in full three-dimensionality, and the clichés are kept to a bare minimum. Plus, unlike the average romantic comedy, this one deals with thought provoking issues. To wit: if a person is not gay, but is in love with someone of the same sex, how do they display that emotion? Is it possible to have romantic love without a physical expression of it?

Neither of the 2 principles in this movie is a lesbian. Jessica (Jennifer Westfeldt) is straight. Her entire sexual history has been one of pairing with men, and the very thought of having a sexual relationship with another woman is . . . well . . . a little weird. Helen (Heather Juergensen), on the other hand, is bisexual. Her primary partners are men, but there are times when she feels in the mood for female companionship, and usually has no difficulty procuring it. When Jessica and Helen meet, Helen is on the prowl. The two do not immediately connect romantically, but there is a spark, and it doesn't take long for their new friendship to begin straying into the sexual realm. Jessica is nervous about sleeping with Helen, but Helen is patient. She knows that Jessica loves her, but that crossing the line is difficult. Meanwhile, at her office, where Jessica works as a proofreader, she has to deal with her ex-lover (Scott Cohen), whose frequent put-downs and pugnacious nature may hide feelings that he is unwilling to admit.

Kissing Jessica Stein has been called a "lesbian *Annie Hall*," and, while such a description is too facile, it's easy to understand its origins. Like Woody Allen's classic romantic comedy, this movie chronicles the entire arc of a relationship, not just the beginning. Both films effectively wed comedy and drama, never veering too much in one direction or another. Each is set in the shadow of the towering skyscrapers of Manhattan. Finally, *Annie Hall* and *Kissing Jessica Stein* display an understanding of human nature that far, far too many motion pictures ignore. The average romantic comedy relies almost exclusively on the chemistry between the leads; the plot is usually a throw-away. In this case, we are fortunate to have both an interesting storyline and actresses who interact with each other in a pleasant, unforced manner. **HIGHLY RECOMMENDED**

Loser [2000]

Starring: Jason Biggs, Mena Suvari, Greg Kinnear Director: Amy Heckerling Screenplay: Amy Heckerling Running Time: 1:35 Rated: PG-13 (Sexual situations, drug use, mild profanity) Theatrical Aspect Ratio: 1.85:1

Loser is a straightforward romantic comedy where the relationship between two unlikely friends develops into something deeper than a casual acquaintanceship. The film's romantic complications are restrained — they neither stretch the viewer's credulity nor make the characters seem airheaded, vindictive, or blind. Most importantly, the protagonists — a geek's geek named Paul (Jason Biggs) and a gothic grunge girl named Dora (Mena Suvari) — are presented as real people with genuine problems. These two seem less like the product of a writer's invention than the type of individuals one meets on a college campus. Of course, there are limits to the level of verisimilitude that can be employed, since a truly satisfying ending requires a heavy dollop of fantasy.

Paul is a hopeless loser, but he's also the nicest guy attending a prestigious New York City university. He won't accept money from his grandfather, is nice to his little sister, and willingly hangs out with his dad (a cameo appearance by Dan Aykroyd). However, in a city populated by cynics, he is viewed as a living caricature. His three party-animal roommates (played by Thomas Sadoski, Zak Orth, and Jimmi Simpson) find his presence so restricting that they have him kicked out of the dorm. The school relocates him to a small room in a local veterinary clinic. Meanwhile, Dora is trying to balance her financial difficulties with her studies and a torrid affair she's having with her European Lit professor, Edward Alcott (Greg Kinnear). She works nights as a waitress at a topless bar, but her commute is running her down. One night at a party held by Paul's ex-roommates in the veterinary clinic, someone slips something into her juice, and she wakes up in Paul's care.

Romantic comedies, especially those set in high schools and colleges, have suffered from overexposure in the past few years. Most have been cliché-riddled pabulum — endless, thinly-veiled reworkings of *Pygmalion* and *The Taming of the Shrew*. The danger is that *Loser* will suffer from guilt by association at the box office. That would be a shame, because Heckerling's movie is smarter and breezier than anything that has recently traveled this well-trodden path. While *Loser* never quite breaks free of the romantic comedy envelope, it occasionally tests the boundaries. With one exception, the film earns its laughs without turning its characters into buffoons or endangering their dignity. And it's a pleasure to watch a movie in which the protagonists speak and act like individuals who have more on their minds than who they're going to take to the big dance. **RECOMMENDED**

Lost in Translation [2003]

Starring: Bill Murray, Scarlett Johansson, Giovanni Ribisi, Anna Faris
Director: Sofia Coppola Screenplay: Sofia Coppola Running Time: 1:42
Rated: R (Profanity, mature themes, brief nudity) Theatrical Aspect Ratio: 1.85:1

Simply put, Sofia Coppola's *Lost in Translation* is an amazing motion picture. This study into the unfathomable depths of human relationships has more honesty than 95 percent of the movies made these days. Beautifully photographed with some amazing shots of nighttime Tokyo and a gorgeously composed scene of two characters reflected in a plate-glass window as they hold a conversation, this movie has a look to match its acting and content.

The film details the "accidental" relationship that develops between Bob (Bill Murray) and Charlotte (Scarlett Johansson). Bob, an internationally recognized actor on the downside of his career, is in Tokyo filming a series of ads for a whiskey company. Charlotte, a recent Yale graduate, is accompanying her photographer husband (Giovanni Ribisi) on a business trip. However, she spends most of the time alone. Bob and Charlotte's first few encounters are casual — on an elevator, in a bar. Gradually, however, they begin to seek out each other, and a bond develops. The two eventually spend nearly every waking hour together, holding deep conversations and finding ways to avoid the eventual parting that both know must occur.

Lost in Translation is smart and perceptive about how people interact on a personal level. It portrays the disorientation of the two main characters flawlessly. They are two normal individuals who might not offer each other more than a smile under ordinary circumstances, but, put together in a place where they don't understand the language or customs and have no one else to turn to, their attachment is potent. The closeness shared by Bob and Charlotte is likely not something that would survive in "the real world." Will it get a chance? The screenplay cleverly leaves the decision up to the viewer. The relationship between Bob and Charlotte remains at the film's core, and remains platonic despite strong sexual undercurrents. A deep bond of friendship takes root, which leads to something more sublime than what we normally see between male and female characters in movies. The romantic tension starts out subtle, but builds until every frame throbs with it. There never really is a release, but the last, perfectly pitched scene alleviates some of the pent-up pressure.

Lost in Translation requires a certain amount of patience, but it is by no means a slow or lugubrious endeavor. Director Coppola has done what any young director wants to accomplish: improve upon a successful first feature. As good as *The Virgin Suicides* is, *Lost in Translation* is superior in almost every way. **MUST SEE**

Love Actually [UK, 2003]

Starring: Hugh Grant, Colin Firth, Alan Rickman, Liam Neeson, Bill Nighy, Laura Linney, Martine McCutcheon, Keira Knightley, Emma Thompson, Billy Bob Thornton, Rowan Atkinson Director: Richard Curtis Screenplay: Richard Curtis Running Time: 2:09 Rated: R (Sex, nudity, profanity) Theatrical Aspect Ratio: 2.35:1

Love Actually doesn't have a cynical frame in its celluloid. It's for all those romantics who think there aren't enough happy endings. Richard Curtis's movie dips so deep into the well of feel-good sentiment that it will threaten to send some audience members into sugar shock. There are times when all of this goodwill feels a tad forced and artificial (such as at the ending), but, on balance, *Love Actually* is appealing and genial with plenty of solid laughs, and worthy of a recommendation for those who appreciate this kind of thing. Just don't expect material that's edgy, dark, or challenging.

The film is about love in its many forms and guises: love between siblings, love between parents and children, love between spouses, puppy love, platonic love, unrequited love, and (of course) sexual/romantic love. The last, unsurprisingly, gets the most screen time as Curtis delights in pairing off a number of his characters. The "central romance," if there can be considered one, is between the British prime minister (Hugh Grant) and a shapely assistant, Natalie (former U.K. soap star Martine McCutcheon). Other couplings involve writer Jamie (Colin Firth) and his Portuguese maid, Aurelia (Lucina Moniz); widower Daniel (Liam Neeson) and the mother of his stepson's classmate; the PM's sister, Karen (Emma Thompson), and her husband, Harry (Alan Rickman); and Harry's subordinate, Susan (Laura Linney), and a younger coworker, Carl (Rodrigo Santoro). Meanwhile, people like aging pop star Billy Mac (Bill Nighy) and a details-oriented department store clerk (Rowan Atkinson) are around to provide comic relief. The problem with *Love Actually,* as is often the case with large ensembles, is that we don't spend nearly enough time with the interesting characters. Half of the stories presented in the film are sufficiently engaging that they could warrant their own feature, and it becomes a little frustrating to get only the Cliff's Notes version. Character development is spotty, which pretty much goes with the territory when you divide 129 minutes by about 18 significant parts. How much can a writer do when he has an average of about seven minutes to work with for each individual? One often gets the sense that the state of love is more important to Curtis than the people he uses to examine it.

This is one of those times when a film's goodwill allows critics and viewers alike to overlook its most egregious flaws and enjoy it for what it's trying to be. This is Curtis's first outing behind a camera, but many potential moviegoers will be familiar with his work as a screenwriter, which includes *Bridget Jones's Diary, Notting Hill, Four Weddings and a Funeral,* and *The Tall Guy. Love Actually* fits very well into that group, and anyone who has enjoyed Curtis's past projects will probably like his latest one.
RECOMMENDED

Love and Sex [2000]

Starring: Famke Janssen, Jon Favreau Director: Valerie Breiman Screenplay: Valerie Breiman Running Time: 1:22 Rated: R (Sexual situations, profanity) Theatrical Aspect Ratio: 1.85:1

It is said that first-time filmmakers should stick to what they know, and that's one rule Breiman has taken to heart, jokingly referring to *Love and Sex* as "my sex life on screen." And, although Breiman's admission is designed more as a sound bite than anything else, there's probably some truth to it. Of course, there's a happy ending, but the route to get to

that point takes a few refreshing detours from the expected path.

Love and Sex's main character is Kate Welles (Janssen), a writer for *Monique* magazine, where she pens "happy, perky [pieces] on how to find and keep that perfect man." She spends the early part of the film ruminating over a number of failed relationships; in fact, like the female lead in every romantic comedy, she's looking for Mr. Right, but having a hard time finding him. In her words, "It hurts so much to be alone that we'd all rather blow up than be single" — a sentiment that explains her predilection for becoming involved with inappropriate men. Then Adam (Favreau), an artist who creates bizarre paintings, bulldozes his way into her life and heart. "We were instant best friends," Kate rhapsodizes as she recounts the early stages of their relationship — the so-called "honeymoon period" when love rules by day and sex by night. Unfortunately, no two people who remain together can stay in that wonderful place, and things settle down into a dull routine. "The more you're with someone, the more annoying they'll become." Eventually, Adam decides that he is bored with the relationship's stasis and wants to move on. Of course, it's only once the two have separated that they realize how right they were for each other.

In person, Breiman is a bundle of barely contained enthusiasm, and some of that energy comes across in her film. There's also a little Woody Allen at work here. Bits and pieces of *Love and Sex* may remind viewers of some of Allen's earlier, lighter work. It's a refreshing, unpretentious romantic comedy that works for what it is, and doesn't try to be more than it is capable of being. Favreau and Janssen both show themselves to be capable in the comedy arena, and, while there isn't much heat between them, they are playful and cute as a couple, and the fact that they were having a good time making the film shines through. **RECOMMENDED**

Love Jones [1997]

Starring: Larenz Tate, Nia Long, Isaiah Washington, Lisa Nicole Carson Director: Theodore Witcher Screenplay: Theodore Witcher Running Time: 1:48 Rated: R (Sex, profanity, brief nudity) Theatrical Aspect Ratio: 1.85:1

Love Jones' main characters are Darius Lovehall (Larenz Tate), a soulful poet with a roving eye, and Nina Mosley (Nia Long), a would-be photographer on the rebound from a long-term relationship. He has only once been with a woman for more than 6 months; she's through with love, saying that it's "played out like an 8-track." Needless to say, the two meet each other, sparks fly, and they end up in bed. And, even though the truth is obvious to their friends and everyone in the audience, they assert that they're not in love, they're "just kickin' it." So, when complications arise, as they must in any motion picture romance, the question (which in this sort of movie isn't that hard to answer) is whether their relationship can survive the stormy waters.

There are several reasons why this film works better than the common, garden-variety love story. To begin with, the setting and texture are much different than that of most mainstream romances. The culture, in which post-college African Americans mingle while pursuing careers and relationships, represents a signficiant change from what we're used to. The Sanctuary, the intimate Chicago nightclub where Darius and Nina meet, is rich in its eclectic, bluesy atmosphere. And *Love Jones'* dialogue is rarely trite. When the characters open their mouths, it usually because they have something intelligent to say, not because they're trying to fill up dead air with meaningless words.

Larenz Tate (*Dead Presidents*) and Nia Long (*Boyz 'N the Hood*) invest their portrayals with a great deal of energy. The chemistry between Darius and Nina alternately sizzles and smolders, resulting in a relationship that varies from playful to hot. While the romantic dynamic between these two is familiar, the performances add a refreshing dimension to the often-stale choreography of motion picture love affairs. And, in a surprising move, while Witcher ends the film on an upbeat note, there's no "happily ever after" promise. **RECOMMENDED**

Love Me if You Dare [France, [2003]

Starring: Guillaume Canet, Marion Cotillard, Thibault Verhaeghe, Joséphine Lebas-Joly, Gérard Watkins, Emmanuelle Grövold Director: **Yann Samuell** Screenplay: Jacky Cukier, Yann Samuell Running Time: 1:33 Rated: R (Sex, profanity) Theatrical Aspect Ratio: 1.85:1 In French with subtitles

Love Me if You Dare is a romantic comedy, but unlike most genre entries, this one explores love not as a redemptive force but as a potentially destructive one. Yet, even as the characters are humiliated and put through extreme anguish, we find opportunities for laughter, and the whimsical tone never devolves into something uncomfortable. *Love Me if You Dare* doesn't happen in a world anything like the one we live in, and its most memorable sequences are wreathed in fantasy. The film defies predictability:

the moment you think you know how things are going to go, they take a turn in a different direction.

Julien (played by Thibault Verhaeghe as a child and Guillaume Canet as an adult) and Sophie (Josephine Lebas-Joly, Marion Cotillard) have been friends since childhood, when Julien played a trick on a bus full of kids who were teasing Sophie. From that day, the two have engaged in an elaborate game of dares and counter-dares, with the objectives becoming increasingly outrageous as the protagonists grow to be teenagers, then adults. Although Julien and Sophie share a deep bond that goes beyond a conventional friendship, and it seems inevitable that they will one day end up together, obstacles continuously block their paths, and the sexual aspect of their relationship is not consummated. But still the dares continue, until they become so monumental that they inflict emotional pain and distress.

The performances by Canet and Cotillard are wonderful; these two make one of the most delightful screen couples in recent years. Cotillard is radiant, and Canet displays the suave insecurity that has, for many years, been Patrick Dempsey's trademark. With a smart script, superlative performances, and some of the most audacious and black-edged comedy of any romance, *Love Me if You Dare* deserves to be seen. If you like romantic movies but find Hollywood's increasingly sterile formulas to be a poisonous bore, *Love Me if You Dare* offers an antidote. **RECOMMENDED**

Lovers of the Arctic Circle [Spain, 1998]

Starring: **Najwa Nimri, Fele Martínez, Nacho Novo, Maru Valdivieso, Kristel Díaz** Director: **Julio Medem** Screenplay: Julio Medem Running Time: 1:54 Rated: R (Sex, nudity, profanity) Theatrical Aspect Ratio: 1.85:1 In Spanish with subtitles

The first hour of *Lovers of the Arctic Circle* comes close to being a perfect romance. The characters are meticulously developed as their relationship is explored, starting from their initial meeting as schoolmates to the clandestine sexual trysts they engage in behind their parents' backs. In many ways, Otto and Ana share the kind of love we all strive for. Yet, once fate has brought them together, it shows its fickle nature by seeking to tear them apart. For much of the weaker second half, Otto and Ana are seeking to find themselves (metaphorically) and each other (literally). *Lovers of the Arctic Circle* allows the lovers to be in close physical proximity (as when they sit nearly back-to-back in an outdoor café) without recognizing it. Of course, we know they'll meet once again in the end . . . or will they?

The script for *Lovers* relies heavily on coincidence. Writer/director Julio Medem gets around this by making fate a significant theme in the film. He sets the tone early, during the scene when Otto and Ana first meet. In a voiceover, Otto remarks that if a ball had been kicked straight, he wouldn't have chased it, and if he hadn't run after it, he never would have encountered Ana. Throughout the film, coincidence builds upon coincidence. By acknowledging it, however, Medem keeps us from shaking our heads and muttering, "Give me a break!"

Lovers of the Arctic Circle touches on several intriguing and potentially-controversial issues, but avoids the trap of becoming obvious or moralistic. One is incest — when Otto's father marries Ana's mother, the two become step-brother and step-sister. However, instead of circumstances cooling their ardor, things heat up. Now, the two teenagers are living under the same roof, just a bedroom apart. The ending is likely to polarize viewers. Some will hate it, and I admit that the impact is a little like being kicked in the stomach. Nevertheless, there's also something poetic about the cosmic irony of the resolution, and the way Medem elects to present it. *Lovers of the Arctic Circle* is a moving film that touches the heart without insulting the mind. **HIGHLY RECOMMENDED**

Much Ado About Nothing [United Kingdom/United States, 1993]

Starring: Kenneth Branagh, Emma Thompson, Denzel Washington, Robert Sean Leonard, Kate Beckinsale Director: Kenneth Branagh Screenplay: Kenneth Branagh based on the play by William Shakespeare Running Time: 1:51 Rated: PG-13 (Mature themes, nudity) Theatrical Aspect Ratio: 1.66:1

Much Ado about Nothing is Kenneth Branagh's adaptation of one of Shakespeare's better-known comedies. Centered around two romances — Hero (Kate Beckinsale) and Claudio (Robert Sean Leonard), and Benedick (Kenneth Branagh) and Beatrice (Emma Thompson) — the story follows these very different courtships. For Hero and Claudio, it's love at first sight and, as with any immediate attraction, they have a lot to learn about each other. Beatrice and Benedick, on the other hand, have known each other for quite some time and it takes a little none-too-subtle prodding from their friends to help them realize and admit their feelings.

For those who don't find Shakespeare's comedies funny, this is the film to see, because it's hilarious. It isn't just the lines that create laughter, but the manner in which they're set up and delivered. Expressions and actions often play a large part in the comedy, some of which is decidedly physical. These are the kinds of things that don't appear on the written page. The film also contains its share of drama, and the pathos and poignancy come as easily and naturally as humor.

The life and vitality of this production are amazing. Things move along with a breezy energy that makes it impossible not to get caught up in the experience. Cuts and edits to the unabridged play are partly responsible for the uptempo pace. However, while Branagh is not entirely faithful to the original text of *Much Ado about Nothing*, his film takes pains to capture the play's spirit. Only Shakespearean purists are likely to recongized what has been excised.

Much Ado about Nothing is a gem of a movie. Branagh has successfully used a mixed cast of "names" and "unknowns" to breathe life into this lavish production, and never has Shakespeare been more warmly received. I'm not sure if "feel good" has ever been used to describe a picture based on the Bard's work, but the expression fits. **MUST SEE**

My Best Friend's Wedding [1997]

Starring: Julia Roberts, Dermot Mulroney, Cameron Diaz, Rupert Everett Director: P.J. Hogan Screenplay: Ronald Bass Running Time: 1:45 Rated: PG-13 (Mature themes, profanity) Theatrical Aspect Ratio: 2.35:1

As in any romantic comedy, the two most important elements are in place: the couples and the complications. Couple #1 consists of the soon-to-be married groom, Michael O'Neal (Dermot Mulroney) and his perky bride, Kimmy (Cameron Diaz). Couple #2 comprises food critic Julianne Potter (Julia Roberts) and her gay editor, George Downes (Rupert Everett). They're not really together, but they pretend to be to make Michael jealous. Because, for the past 9 years, since they had a one-month fling in college, Julianne has carried a torch for Michael. They've been best friends, but only now, when she's about to lose him to another woman, does Julianne realize that she wants to be the bride. And, to get her man, she's willing to do almost anything, including play dirty. So, when Kimmy opens her arms to Julianne and offers her the position of maid of honor, Julianne accepts, all the while plotting the best way to break up the happy couple.

Because *My Best Friend's Wedding* features a smart script and deft direction, it manages to keep alive the mystery of who will end up with whom. Things aren't as clear-cut as they initially seem to be, and, with every passing minute, they get murkier. The film has a high energy level and features a number of stand-out scenes, some of which are designed to cull laughter from the audience, others which go for the tear ducts. The best is arguably a restaurant episode where an impromptu sing-along gets everyone in the place to join in. It's clever, irreverent, and fun.

Although *My Best Friend's Wedding* is intended to be relatively light entertainment, it briefly addresses some interesting, serious issues regarding the nature of friendship, jealousy, and love (real and idealized). There's a wonderfully evocative scene that suggests "a moment passing by," which will undoubtedly cause a portion of the audience to reflect on similar occasions in their own lives. In the final analysis, *My Best Friend's Wedding* represents 2 hours of fine entertainment not because it offers a feel-good love story but because the film makers understand that it's possible for a romantic comedy to appeal not only to the heart, but to the mind as well. RECOMMENDED

Paperback Romance [Australia, 1994]

Starring: Gia Carides, Anthony LaPaglia, Rebecca Gibney Director: Ben Lewin Screenplay: Ben Lewin Running Time: 1:27 Rated: R (Sexual situations, nudity) Theatrical Aspect Ratio: 1.66:1

The phrase "paperback romance" generates all sorts of vivid images: lusty, well-endowed women; men with "ruggedly handsome features" and "well-chiseled muscles"; exotic locations; and, most importantly, plenty of steamy sex. The purple prose of these so-called bodice-rippers is appreciated and admired by millions, yet, by its very nature, it's ripe for the kind of satire evident in *Paperback Romance*. This film can be considered a legitimate romantic comedy, although it's a little too quirky to be lumped in with most of the run-of-the-mill entries.

Our heroine is Sophie (played by the delightful Gia Carides), an author of romance novels. She's a dreamer who takes refuge in her writing; since her love life is barren, she kisses through her characters. One day at a library, as Sophie is reading aloud while she pens an erotic passage, her voice and words captivate Eddie (Anthony LaPaglia), a high-stakes jewel dealer who is browsing nearby. He is so taken with Sophie's beauty and charm that he asks her out on the spot, but she refuses. A childhood victim of polio,

Sophie cannot walk without a leg brace, and she doesn't want Eddie to see her disability. He leaves, convinced that she's the perfect woman. (Why? Because she rejected him.)

For Sophie, out of sight does not mean out of mind. Unable to dismiss Eddie from her thoughts, she finds out where he works, then goes to spy on him, watching him with his fiancée, Gloria (Rebecca Gibney). When she's afraid that Eddie is about to notice her, brace and all, Sophie hurries to get out of sight. In the process, she takes a nasty spill and breaks her leg. Now, with her stricken limb in a cast, she can pretend that she's normal and that the injury is the result of a skiing accident. Freed from her fear that Eddie will reject her because she's disabled, she is able to pursue a relationship with him — at least temporarily.

The tone of *Paperback Romance* is erratic; you can be laughing one minute and wincing the next. On at least two occasions, the slapstick, while admittedly funny in a sophomoric way, is so overblown that it seems out of place. In general, however, *Paperback Romance* manages to successfully navigate such choppy waters, and the result is a pleasant, if uneven, hour and a half. RECOMMENDED

Persuasion [United Kingdom, 1995]

Starring: Amanda Root, Ciaran Hinds, Sophie Thompson, Samuel West Director: Roger Michell Screenplay: Nick Dear based on the novel by Jane Austen Running Time: 1:44 Rated: PG (Mild language) Theatrical Aspect Ratio: 1.85:1

Persuasion, based on the Jane Austen novel, opens in early 19th century England (1814, to be precise), in the wake of war with France. Across the Channel, Napoleon has abdicated and been confined to Elba, and British servicemen are returning home. Among them is Captain Frederick Wentworth (Ciaran Hinds), a navy officer who has been away for more than 8 years since his marriage proposal to then-19-year-old Anne Elliot (Amanda Root) was refused. Now, almost a decade later, Anne lives in a state of constant regret, attempting to fill an empty life through her selfless devotion to family and friends. However, although she remains without either husband or suitors, circumstances have decreed that she has not seen the last of the one true love of her life.

Even though the subject material of the film might sound like the stuff of a Harlequin romance, *Persuasion* has far greater depth than any dime store soap opera. The movie offers not only keen insights on the lasting, and agonizing, effects of love, but explores the theme of consequences. While the hand of fate can be seen working throughout, the characters' circumstances are ultimately the result of their own choices and actions. Anne is responsible for her unhappiness, and, when an opportunity arises to redress her past error, she must seize it or lose Frederick forever. The barrier to overcome is the deep emotional scarring created by her decision of eight years ago.

To a lesser extent, *Persuasion* also works as a social commentary. The film takes aim at the pre-Victorian society in which it is set — a social structure that encouraged the empty words of sycophants over true expressions of friendship. Many of the characters are cloaked in artifice, and it's only as their real motives are uncovered that we learn of their duplicity and superciliousness. Michell uses some of this shallowness to comic effect through the fatuous presentation of characters like Anne's father (Corin Redgrave) and sister Elizabeth (Phoebe Nichols). It's men and women like this that draw our sympathy towards those who are honest and straightforward, like Anne and Frederick.

Like so many British costume dramas, this one boasts impeccable production values. Its faithfulness to the source material results in a few slow spots, but *Persuasion* is nevertheless fine entertainment. And, at a time when most love stories involve copious displays of skin, it's a rare pleasure to see so much emotion brought to the screen by a single kiss.
HIGHLY RECOMMENDED

The Pillow Book [United Kingdom, 1996]
Starring: Vivian Wu, Ewan McGregor Director: Peter Greenaway
Screenplay: Peter Greenaway Running Time: 2:06 Rated: Not Rated
(Nudity, sex, mature themes) Theatrical Aspect Ratio: 1.66:1 and 2.35:1

Calligraphy is one subject that not many movies have explored, and none has approached it in quite the way that British director Peter Greenaway does in *The Pillow Book*. To use the film's own words to describe it, this is about the "two things in life that are dependable: the delights of the flesh and the delights of literature" and how they can be melded into one. While there's nothing especially groundbreaking or difficult to grasp in *The Pillow Book*, Greenaway's experimentation here still has the power to alienate audiences who aren't prepared for what the film offers. As has been true in his past efforts, there are copious amounts of full frontal nudity, and it seems that lead actors Vivian Wu

and Ewan McGregor perform half of their scenes without any clothes on. Nevertheless, by keeping the audience at arm's length, Greenaway manages the impressive feat of de-eroticizing the nudity.

For the most part, the director seems more concerned about technique than narrative and character development. The plot functions more as a series of markers for Greenaway's stylistic riffs than a necessary aspect of the movie. Indeed, *The Pillow Book* is so visually arresting that it's capable of holding our attention for 2 hours largely on the strength of its images. The only character of any real importance in *The Pillow Book* is Nagiko (Vivian Wu), a Japanese-born fashion model with obsessions for calligraphy, physical pleasure, and revenge. When she was little, Nagiko's aunt would read her excerpts from the *Pillow Book of Sei Shonagon*, the 1,000-year old diary of a courtesan. In Hong Kong, Nagiko begins her own pillow book, but, instead of writing on paper, she uses the bodies of her lovers. They, in turn, utilize her flesh for their calligraphy. Nagiko's quest is for the perfect lover/calligrapher combination, but it becomes a difficult search. As she says, the older men are not interested in the pleasure she can provide, and the younger men are easily distracted. Then she meets Jerome (Ewan McGregor), an Englishman in Hong Kong, who proves not only to be her artistic match, but offers the means by which she can enact a long-dormant plan of vengeance against her father's publisher.

The great irony of this film, which is (at least on one level) about the power of writing, is that the words are of secondary importance to the overwhelming visual presentation. The camera, not the script, dominates our response to Greenaway's film. In the final analysis, *The Pillow Book* has much more to show than it has to say. **RECOMMENDED**

Polish Wedding [1998]
Starring: Lena Olin, Gabriel Byrne, Claire Danes, Adam Trese
Director: Theresa Connelly Screenplay: Theresa Connelly Running
Time: 1:48 Rated: PG-13 (Profanity, sex) Theatrical Aspect Ratio: 1.85:1

In an age during which the traditional family is disintegrating under the pressure of modern-day existence, Theresa Connelly's debut feature, *Polish Wedding*, illustrates that there are still some households in which blood-ties are the most important thing. The film opens a window into the ongoing chaos that marks the day-to-day activities of the Pzoniaks, a lower middle class Polish American clan living in

Detroit. The Pzoniaks all live together in two adjoining single-family units. The walls are paper thin and there's no privacy. Space is at such a premium that the 4 unmarried children (3 boys and 1 girl) must all sleep in the same room. The matriarch and patriarch of the clan are Jadzia (Lena Olin) and Bolek (Gabriel Byrne), who have been married for more than 20 years. Over the span of their union, they have had 5 children (4 boys), the oldest of which is now married and has his own son.

Jadzia and Bolek's only daughter is Chala (Claire Danes), a carefree and sensual teenager who finds subtle ways of rebelling. She's very close to her father, but there's an emotional gulf between her and her mother. This year, Chala has been selected to lead the annual procession for the Feast of the Virgin, an honor reserved for girls of the highest moral caliber. Ironically, it's around this time that Chala elects to lose her virginity with Russell (Adam Trese), a local policeman. The brief tryst, which begins with smoldering looks, results in a pregnancy.

Theresa Connelly, who clearly has a great deal of affinity for these characters, presents them in warts-and-all fashion, rightfully certain that we will sympathize with them in spite of (or perhaps because of) their faults. Connelly displays the skill of a veteran in the unforced manner in which she weds comedy and pathos throughout the film.

Certainly, the American film industry has produced a large number of first-and second-generation immigrant family stories. This is only natural, considering the ethnic diversity of our society. *Polish Wedding* uses the Pzoniaks' cultural heritage as more than a colorful backdrop — it's an integral part of the plot, and that's one of the things that makes the film enjoyable. By offering a slightly different flavor of the immigrant experience, *Polish Wedding* carves out its own small niche in a crowded genre, and manages to entertain in the process. **RECOMMENDED**

Possession [2002]

Starring: Gwyneth Paltrow, Aaron Eckhart, Jeremy Northam, Jennifer Ehle Director: Neil LaBute Screenplay: David Henry Hwang and Laura Jones and Neil LaBute, based on the novel by A.S. Byatt Running Time: 1:42 Rated: PG-13 (Sexual situations) Theatrical Aspect Ratio: 2.35:1

Roland Michell (Aaron Eckhart) is an American researcher who has come to London to further his investigations into the life of his favorite author, Randolph Henry Ash (Jeremy Northam), who once served as Queen Victoria's poet laureate. After discovering two previously unknown letters, Michell believes that Ash may have had contact with an obscure female poet named Christabel LaMotte (Jennifer Ehle). This discovery leads him to collaborate with England's foremost authority on Christabel, Maud Bailey (Gwyneth Paltrow), who is initially unimpressed by Michell's findings. However, as the two begin to delve more deeply into the potential Christabel/Ash connection, they learn that not only did the two know each other, but they may have been lovers. And, as they unravel the story of Christabel and Ash's relationship, Michell and Maud find their own interaction becoming increasingly intimate.

Neither romance in *Possession* represents a timeless love story (one could argue there's not enough tear-inducing melodrama for that), but, in large part because of credible performances and Neil LaBute's workmanlike helmsmanship, we come to care about the characters and their interactions. The relationships of the two couples are very different, even though one would not exist without the other. Ash and Christabel have a short-lived, fiery affair, preceded by a long period of written correspondence and succeeded by a series of personal tragedies. Michell and Maud are attracted to each other almost from the beginning, but both have erected heavy emotional barriers that have to be overcome, and their mutual fear of commitment nearly prevents them from getting together at all. Nevertheless, the more they learn about the connection between the 19th century lovers, the more they become open to possibilities that neither has been previously equipped to deal with. For a while, the progression of their relationship echoes the discoveries they unearth about Ash and Christabel.

Although LaBute goes to some lengths to emphasize the connections between the two love stories, he also stylistically italicizes the differences. It's interesting to note that the present-day romance is developed primarily through words while the past-tense one is defined though gestures and images (Northam and Ehle don't have many lines). Yet the words of those two poets, written more than 100 years earlier, resonate with the man and woman investigating their liaison. *Possession* is compelling material, especially for those who believe that the lives and loves of the dead can impact the trajectory of the existences of the living. **RECOMMENDED**

Prelude to a Kiss [1992]

Starring: Alec Baldwin, Meg Ryan, Sydney Walker Director: Norman
René Screenplay: Craig Lucas, based on his play Running Time: 1:45
Rated: PG-13 (Sexual situations, profanity) Theatrical Aspect
Ratio: 1.85:1

Prelude to a Kiss opens with one of the most delight-fully romantic half-hours of any recent motion pic-ture. Not only is the aura intoxicating, but it gives us an almost-immediate investment into the main char-acters and their relationship. René offers a striking portrait of the "psychotic bliss" of love's early stages. Bartender Rita Boyle (Ryan) and publishing executive Peter Hoskins (Baldwin) are attracted to each other from the moment they first meet at a party. Their romance progresses quickly, from dancing in a crowded room to a coy exploration of each other's feelings to uninhibited sex, all punctuated by smartly written dialogue. Eventually, despite their differences on key issues (he wants children; she doesn't), Peter asks Rita to marry him, and she accepts. Meanwhile, we are briefly introduced to Julius (Sydney Walker), an old man who spends most of his time vegitating in his bedroom. One morning, he dresses up in his best clothing and walks to the train station. There, he buys a ticket to Lake Forest. The next time we see him, he is wandering into Peter and Rita's wedding, an unin-vited but apparently unthreatening interloper. After the ceremony, Julius approaches Rita and asks to kiss her as a means of congratulations. She agrees, and, when their lips meet, a transference takes place. Sud-denly, Rita finds herself in the old man's body while his essence inhabits her form.

One can successfully argue that, in a strange way, *Prelude to a Kiss* follows the traditional pattern of a romance: the characters meet, fall in love, are torn apart by plot complications, then find their way back to each other in the end. The difference here is that the "plot complications" are far from the norm, and give the film a rich subtext that more conventional motion pictures lack. The intelligence of what the characters say also elevates the production. Like most plays-turned-into-movies, this one is a little talky, but that's not much of a problem, because what the characters have to say is absorbing.

I have always considered *Prelude to a Kiss* to be one of 1992's most underrated motion pictures. It was one of the most original romances to grace the screen that year, yet it was swallowed up in a summer season where audiences weren't interested in intelligent, penetrating dramas that ask provocative questions about substantive issues. The film doesn't have many holes and offers an ending that is satisfying, cathar-tic, and poignant. In the final analysis, it can be said that *Prelude to a Kiss* explores the issue of love in a way that will encourage many viewers to examine what the emotion means to them. Too few motion pictures cause us to think and feel this deeply. HIGHLY RECOMMENDED

The Promise [Germany, 1995]

Starring: Meret Becker, Corinna Harfouch, Anian Zollner, August Zimer
Director: Margarethe von Trotta Screenplay: Peter Schneider Running
Time: 1:59 Rated: R (Mature themes, sex, profanity) Theatrical Aspect
Ratio: 1.66:1 In German with subtitles

Sometimes lovers are separated by race. Other times, it's age. On still other occasions, it's religion. But in *The Promise*, Sophie and Konrad are the same na-tionality, the same age, and the same faith. What di-vides them is an ugly construct of stone and barbed wire that becomes a symbol of the cold war. In Berlin during the 1960s, nothing was more tragic than the reality of families, friends, and lovers kept apart by what became known simply as "the Wall."

The Berlin wall was erected in the summer of 1961. In the early days, a crossing was less difficult than it eventually would become. As *The Promise* opens, So-phie (Meret Becker), Konrad (Anian Zollner), and two friends have planned an escape to the West. When the time arrives to climb through a manhole and a passing guard troop passes dangerously near to the escape route, Konrad stays behind to cover the oth-ers' tracks. He promises to join his girlfriend and her pals later, but he never does. By 1968, Konrad has be-come a respected astronomer, and is allowed to travel to Prague for a seminar. After receiving his let-ter, Sophie meets him there. Shortly after Sophie becomes pregnant, however, events split the cou-ple, with Konrad again in the East and Sophie in the West.

Their next meeting occurs 12 years later. This time, the lead actors have been seamlessly switched (Corinna Harfouch now plays Sophie; August Zimer, Konrad). By now, Konrad is married and has a daugh-ter, and Sophie is living with someone. Their com-mon link is their son, Alexander, and Konrad, as a top-level scientist, is allowed visitation privileges. The final segment is in November 1989, at the fall of the Wall. Equally full of promise and poignancy, this sequence gives the film closure. *The Promise* ends on an ambiguous note, allowing the viewer to draw his or her own conclusions about what comes next.

Director Margarethe von Trotta effortlessly weaves history and personal events into a tapestry full of emotion and irony. Sophie and Konrad are likeable and we, as an involved audience, can't help but root for them to reach each other, even while recognizing that their different values and goals make a lasting union unlikely. Von Trotta doesn't cheat either side of her story, West or East. People and politics mix, but nothing is black or white in exploring one of many tales about the Wall. **HIGHLY RECOMMENDED**

Punch Drunk Love [2002]

Starring: Adam Sandler, Emily Watson Director: Paul Thomas Anderson Screenplay: Paul Thomas Anderson Running Time: 1:29 Rated: R (Profanity, sexual dialogue, violence) Theatrical Aspect Ratio: 2.35:1

Punch Drunk Love is quirky and stylish, but not in a manner that comes across as overly artsy or pretentious. Writer/director Paul Thomas Anderson, whose previous outings (*Boogie Nights* and *Magnolia*) were challenging, compelling, and deep, has not abandoned his affinity for trying new things, even though he's working in a vastly different genre.

In Anderson's crosshairs is Barry Egan (Sandler), a grown man with serious emotional issues. In addition to being socially retarded and borderline agoraphobic, he is subject to frequent emotional outbursts that can alternately result in an explosion of anger or an unrestrained bout of crying. Then he meets Lena (Emily Watson), the shy and secretive British friend of one of Barry's seven sisters. She is smitten with him, and he with her, and they begin a tentative relationship. When she goes to Hawaii on a business trip, Barry elects to follow her. Meanwhile, he is feuding with a phone sex girl whose services he once employed. She has decided to extort money from Barry, and, when he refuses to pay, she gets her boss (Philip Seymour Hoffman) to arrange to have him roughed up.

Some will probably trumpet *Punch Drunk Love* as an opportunity for Adam Sandler to show his range. And, while it's true that Sandler has unquestionably ventured into virgin territory, he's not doing things significantly different from what he usually does. Barry is the quintessential Sandler character — an angry man stuck in a state of arrested emotional and social development — with the humor siphoned off. This is Happy Gilmore or Billy Madison with the comedy button on mute. It's interesting to see how genuinely disturbed Sandler's screen alter-egos can

be when they are no longer viewed through the distorted lens of mirth.

In the end, *Punch Drunk Love*'s real strength is its willingness to take off on some unexpected tangents. Anderson has created the kind of unconventional "romantic comedy" we might expect from him. And, while it could be a disappointment to die-hard Sandler fans (who don't get even a sampling of their hero's usual lowbrow humor) and lovers of traditional romance, *Punch Drunk Love* offers a lot to those who appreciate motion pictures that embrace a journey into relatively new territory. **RECOMMENDED**

Return to Me [2000]

Starring: David Duchovny, Minnie Driver Director: Bonnie Hunt Screenplay: Bonnie Hunt & Don Lake Running Time: 1:55 Rated: PG-13 (Mature themes, profanity) Theatrical Aspect Ratio: 1.85:1

Return to Me is the cinematic child of actress-turned-filmmaker Bonnie Hunt. This is the directorial debut for Hunt, who has an affinity and aptitude for this kind of material, rarely striking a sour note even though there are plenty of opportunities to do so. Hunt manages the tricky task of balancing drama, comedy, and romance, and, as a result, avoids unnecessary silliness, lugubriousness, and moments of extreme sugar shock.

The film opens with parallel stories, both taking place in Chicago. In one, a happily-married couple, Bob and Liz Rueland (David Duchovny and Joely Richardson), are attending a fund-raiser being held for the Lincoln Park Zoo. In the other, a young woman, Grace (Minni Driver), is lying sick in a hospital bed awaiting a heart transplant while her sister, Megan (Hunt), looks on anxiously. What happens next is a tragic irony: Grace's life is saved when Liz is killed in an accident. Within months, she is at home, leading a normal life. The same cannot be said of Bob, whose entire world has crumbled around him.

Skip ahead a year. Grace is fully recovered from the operation and is working as a waitress at her grandfather's place, "O'Reilly's Italian Restaurant." Bob, trying to get his life back on track, goes there on a blind date, but loses interest in his companion when he spies Grace. The attraction between them is as mutual as it is immediate. Of course, neither realizes that Liz's heart beats in Grace's breast, and the question of how the characters will react when they learn this truth (as they surely must) provides a little suspense, since there's no uncertainty about whether these two will end up together. That is, after all, what the formula demands.

These days, an increasing number of romantic comedies feature teenagers, leaving a void for those who enjoy these kinds of stories with slightly older characters. *Return to Me* fills that breach, and does so with admirable restraint. There's enough emotion in the interaction of the characters that there's no need for a big, over-the-top finale or the inclusion of an old boyfriend or girlfriend to provide romantic complications. Watching *Return to Me* is not a trailblazing experience, nor is it intended to be, but Bonnie Hunt proves to be an expert tour guide through this familiar terrain. Despite sticking pretty much to the expected formula, *Return to Me* manages to disarm with its charm and delight with its bite. **RECOMMENDED**

The Road Home [China, 1999]

Starring: Zhang Ziyi, Sun Honglei, Zheng Hao, Zhao Yuelin Director: Zhang Yimou Screenplay: Bao Shi, based on his novel, *Remembrance* Running Time: 1:30 Rated: PG (Mature themes) Theatrical Aspect Ratio: 2.35:1 In Mandarin with subtitles

For celebrated Chinese director Zhang Yimou, *The Road Home* represents a short journey on a path not previously taken in his career. This simple love story, which is poignant, sensitive, and emotionally-satisfying, lacks Zhang's characteristic hard edge and political subtext. *The Road Home* is a chaste romantic melodrama that engages, but does not challenge, viewers. The movie features emotional intensity, but not breadth, and offers little in the way of subject matter that could be considered controversial. *The Road Home* works, but may not offer followers of Zhang's work the kind of experience they have come to expect from his outings.

The movie transpires in two eras. The framing story, which comprises *The Road Home*'s first 15 minutes and final 15 minutes, is presented in stark black-and-white and takes place in a modern-day village in north China. The bulk of the film occurs in the same village 40 years ago, and is photographed in color. In the bookends, Yusheng Luo (Sun Honglei), a successful businessman in his late-30s, returns to his native village to help his aging mother, Di (Zhao Yuelin), bury his recently deceased father. The extended flashback details the fairy-tale courtship of 18-year-old Di (Zhang Ziyi) and 20-year-old Yusheng Luo (Sun Honglei), who broke with tradition and married for love rather than based on an arrangement.

Zhang has developed *The Road Home* as a pure romantic fable. In the director's canon, this must be considered a lesser effort (especially when compared to some of his great movies, like *Raise the Red Lantern* and *To Live*). It's also very much a change-of-pace. However, in the hands of someone with Zhang's talent, even a minor motion picture can be fundamentally satisfying, warts and all. That is the case with *The Road Home*. It's certainly not perfect, but it is a nicely realized love story and will find an audience in those who appreciate Chinese cinema and the poetry of a simple, well-developed romance. **RECOMMENDED**

Romeo + Juliet [1996]

Starring: Leonardo DiCaprio, Claire Danes, Brian Dennehy, John Leguizamo Director: Baz Luhrmann Screenplay: Craig Pearce and Baz Luhrmann based on the play by William Shakespeare Running Time: 2:00 Rated: PG-13 (Mature themes, violence) Theatrical Aspect Ratio: 2.35:1

In *Looking for Richard*, actor/director Al Pacino expresses his great hope for his film — to extend his enthusiasm for the Bard's plays to a broader audience. In a very different way, that's what Baz Luhrmann (*Moulin Rouge*) is attempting to do with this radical approach to *Romeo and Juliet*. Luhrmann hasn't fashioned this motion picture with the stodgy, elitist Shakespeare "purist" in mind. Instead, by incorporating lively, modern imagery with a throbbing rock soundtrack and hip actors, he has taken aim at an audience that would normally regard Shakespeare as a chore to be endured in school, not a passionate drama to ignite the screen.

Make no mistake, this *Romeo + Juliet* isn't the match of Franco Zeffirelli's unforgettable 1968 classic. While Leonardo DiCaprio and Claire Danes make an effective couple, their romance doesn't burn with the white-hot intensity of Leonard Whiting and Olivia Hussey's. For those who aren't aware, *Romeo and Juliet* tells the tale of two "star-cross'd" teenage lovers who secretly fall for each other and marry. Their families, the Montagues and Capulets, have been fierce enemies for decades, and, even as Romeo and Juliet say their wedding vows, new violence breaks out between the clans. In the end, their love is doomed. When Romeo mistakenly believes Juliet is dead, he poisons himself. And, when Juliet discovers that he is dead, she too commits suicide.

Ultimately, no matter how many innovative and unconventional flourishes it applies, the success of any adaptation of a Shakespeare play is determined by two factors: the competence of the director and the ability of the main cast members. Luhrmann, Danes, and DiCaprio place this *Romeo + Juliet* in capable hands. And, while such a loud, brash interpretation may not go down in cinematic history as the definitive version of the play, hopefully it will open a few eyes and widen the audience willing to venture into any movie bearing the credit "based on the play by William Shakespeare." **RECOMMMENDED**

Sabrina [1995]

Starring: **Harrison Ford, Julia Ormond, Greg Kinnear** Director: **Sydney Pollack** Screenplay: **Barbara Benedek & David Rayfiel** Running Time: **2:07** Rated: **PG** (Sexual innuendo) Theatrical Aspect Ratio: **1.85:1**

In general, I approach romances with a great deal of skepticism, principally because it's so easy to mess up this kind of movie. Love is a difficult emotion to effectively capture on film, and, too often, screen romances look like two actors going through the motions. Happily, with *Sabrina*, that's not the case. Despite the unambitious, formula-driven plot, wonderful performances by Julia Ormond and, especially, Harrison Ford keep this remake afloat.

The title character, Sabrina Fairchild (Ormond), is the daughter of the Larrabee family's chauffeur (John Wood). Since she was little, Sabrina has had a crush on the youngest Larrabee son, David (Greg Kinnear), a dashing playboy. Unfortunately for her, David doesn't really know she exists. So, when Sabrina goes off to Paris to change her life (and appearance), she still harbors her passion in secret. When, after "finding herself" abroad, she returns home and dazzles David with her new glamour and self-possession, she sees a chance for her dreams to become real. But complications arise — David is engaged to a wealthy pediatrician (Lauren Holly), and the marriage will seal a major merger between the Larrabee Corporation and Tyson Electronics. David's older brother, Linus (Harrison Ford), the "living heart donor" head of the corporation, won't allow his brother's flirtation with Sabrina to endanger the deal, so, in the best interests of business, he makes a play for her. Unfortunately, Linus gets in over his head and the cold, calculating businessman discovers that he does indeed have a heart.

In 1954, Audrey Hepburn was Sabrina. While Julia Ormond is no Hepburn, she possesses the kind of luminous screen presence which allows us to accept her part in this modern-day fairy tale. Harrison Ford, taking over for Humphrey Bogart, is very good as Linus, carefully mixing pathos, cruelty, and compassion into a surprisingly complex personality. The weakest of the main performers is Greg Kinnear (in the William Holden part), who is more of a personality than an actor — and, at times, this shows. Of the supporting players, only veteran actor John Wood is

worthy of special note. The rest of the cast do adequate, but not noteworthy, jobs.

It's not really that difficult to defend *Sabrina*, despite its numerous faults. Even though it isn't as good as the original 1954 version, this movie, brought to the screen by director Sydney Pollack (*Out of Africa*), simply has too much romantic appeal and on-screen chemistry to be dismissed as "just another" in the ever-growing pool of remakes. **RECOMMMENDED**

Say Anything [1989]

Starring: **John Cusack, Ione Skye, John Mahoney** Director: **Cameron Crowe** Screenplay: **Cameron Crowe** Running Time: **1:40** Rated: **PG-13** (Profanity, sexual situations) Theatrical Aspect Ratio: **1.85:1**

Say Anything is one of the best in a long line of teen romance movies, if not *the* best. Unlike many of its fellow genre entries, it is not filled with crude sex jokes, nudity, a lobotomized population, and poorly-defined subplots. And, while the broad strokes of the storyline are familiar, the details are what make this movie special — smart, well-developed characters, believable situations, and a solid emotional investment for us in the film's people and circumstances

Lloyd Dobler (John Cusack) is an average high school senior. As *Say Anything* begins, he's getting ready for graduation, even though his future is wide open. His father wants him to join the army, but Lloyd doesn't think that's for him. The object of Lloyd's high school affection is Diane Court (Ione Skye), the class valedictorian. Lloyd has yearned for her from afar, but, after graduation, he finally works up the courage to ask her out. Much to his delight, she accepts, and he takes her to an all-night, post-graduation bash. She discovers that she genuinely likes Lloyd, even though he and she have virtually nothing in common.

Diane's parents are divorced, and she lives with her father, James (John Mahoney), a businessman who runs a nursing home. He loves his daughter dearly, and enjoys showering her with expensive gifts. His high expectations also place a great deal of pressure on Diane. He is also profoundly distrustful of Lloyd, especially when the young man describes his career aspirations as being "to spend as much time as possible with your daughter." Then, with the arrival of a pair of tax men at the door, James' entire world is turned upside down.

In one sense, *Say Anything* is a romantic comedy, but it's firmly grounded in reality (rather than the fantasy world of hearts and candies where many love stories exist). The film isn't overly-intellectual in its approach, but it is smart. It doesn't demand anything from its audience except a willingness for each viewer to turn over a couple of hours to these two characters and the special magic they weave while together. *Say Anything* hardly has a misstep, and, despite the passage of a decade since its release, it's just as hip today as it was at the time of its theatrical run. **HIGHLY RECOMMMENDED**

Sense and Sensibility [United Kingdom, 1995]

Starring: Emma Thompson, Kate Winslet, Alan Rickman, Hugh Grant Director: Ang Lee Screenplay: Emma Thompson based on the novel by Jane Austen Running Time: 2:15 Rated: PG (Nothing offensive) Theatrical Aspect Ratio: 1.85:1

Sense and Sensibility is a wonderful motion picture, even given the weaknesses of the source material. Emma Thompson's screenplay has remained faithful to the events and spirit of Jane Austen's novel, while somehow managing to plug a few holes and infuse the tale with more light humor than is evident in the original text. The resulting product is a little too long (135 minutes), but still represents a fine time at the movies, especially for those with a bent towards historical romantic melodramas.

We're introduced to the three Dashwood sisters: _Elinor (Emma Thompson), the eldest — a old maid past marriageable age who keeps her emotions bottled up in favor of a constant show of public decorum; Marianne (Kate Winslet), the middle child, who is Elinor's opposite in temperament and attitude; and Margaret (Emilie Francois), an 11-year-old who seems to be following in Marianne's uninhibited footsteps. The girls live with their mother (Gemma Jones) in a small country cottage to which they are "exiled" after their half-brother inherits their father's estate and decides there's not enough room for everyone.

During the course of *Sense and Sensibility,* three men come in and out of the Dashwoods' home: Edward Ferrars (Hugh Grant), a charming, if somewhat inept, young gentleman who captures Elinor's heart; Colonel Brandon (Alan Rickman), a gallant neighbor who is hopelessly smitten by Marianne; and the dashing Willoughby (Greg Wise), who is the living embodiment of Marianne's every fantasy. The story of who ends up with whom, and how they get that way, is told with deft skill and a pleasantly humorous romantic touch.

The novel's flaws guarantee that *Sense and Sensibility* cannot be a perfect motion picture, but it would be difficult, I think, to do much better with the material than Emma Thompson and director Ang Lee have here. **HIGHLY RECOMMMENDED**

Shakespeare in Love [United Kingdom/United States, 1998]

Starring: Gwyneth Paltrow, Joseph Fiennes, Geoffrey Rush, Colin Firth Director: John Madden Screenplay: Marc Norman and Tom Stoppard Running Time: 2:03 Rated: R (Sex, nudity, brief profanity) Theatrical Aspect Ratio: 2.35:1

At first glance, the film appears to be little more than a period piece romantic comedy. The main character, Will Shakespeare (Joseph Fiennes), is a struggling writer in 1593 England. Currently, he's having trouble with his latest play, a comedy called *Romeo and Ethel the Pirate's Daughter.* His problem is that he needs a muse to inspire him. He finds her in Viola (Gwyneth Paltrow), the daughter of a rich man. Viola, one of the few theater-goers who prefers Shakespeare to Christopher Marlowe, is equally smitten with Will, but she is engaged to the cold, loveless Lord Wessex, who wants her for her money. To fulfill a lifelong dream to be on stage, Viola dresses as a man and auditions for the role of Romeo, a part that she wins. With Viola's inspiration, Will begins writing a great play, which he retitles *Romeo and Juliet,* while simultaneously trying to find a way to make his impossible romance work.

Although *Shakespeare in Love* offers its share of belly laughs, most of the humor — and there is quite a bit of it — falls more into the "wit" category. For example, while the scene of Will undergoing a primitive form of psychoanalysis is amusing, it's not likely to cause anyone to roll in the aisles. The romance between Will and Viola is not one of the great pairings of the decade (or even of the year, for that matter), but there's enough chemistry between Paltrow and Fiennes to make it work. For admirers of Shakespeare, however, there's a great deal more to appreciate. Numerous aspects of the script are peppered with elements from the Bard's plays: mistaken identities, transvestites, ghosts, poetry, and significant chunks of dialogue from *Romeo and Juliet.*

Shakespeare in Love is about 10 minutes too long, but, for most of the 2-hour running length, Stoppard and Norman's script seamlessly blends comedy, romance, and light drama. An added bonus is that, unlike in most romantic comedies, the ending isn't a foregone conclusion. Plus, for those who like *Romeo and Juliet,* there's an opportunity to see how scenes from the play look with Gwyneth Paltrow alternately playing *both* of the title roles. *Shakespeare in Love* is not a great film, but it's an excuse to have an evening of pure enjoyment with a little culture painlessly mixed in. **RECOMMENDED**

Shall We Dance? [Japan, 1996]
Starring: Koji Yakusyo, Tamiyo Kusakari, Naoto Takenaka, Eriko Watanabe Director: Masayuki Suo Screenplay: Masayuki Suo Running Time: 2:06 Rated: PG-13 (Mature themes) Theatrical Aspect Ratio: 1.85:1 In Japanese with subtitles

In Japan, where public displays of affection between a husband and a wife is considered scandalous behavior, the concept of two unmarried people holding each other close in a dance is "beyond embarrassing." For that reason, ballroom dancing is not popular, and anyone caught engaging in it risks being labeled as depraved and lecherous. Nevertheless, for some men and women trapped in such a restrictive culture, dancing offers the seductive, forbidden allure of slipping the confining boundaries of what is socially acceptable and finding a measure of liberty.

Shohei Sugiyama (Koji Yakusyo) is a 42-year-old Japanese businessman who lives in a comfortable house with a loving wife and an adolescent daughter. But all is not right in his world. Now that he has attained his goals (a home, a family, and a successful career), his life feels empty. His wife notices his growing depression, commenting that "he really should get out and enjoy himself more often." One day, while riding the train home from work, Sugiyama spies the figure of a sad, beautiful woman (Tamiyo Kusakari) gazing out a dance school window. Day after day passes, with Sugiyama watching for this mysterious woman on each trip home. Eventually, he summons all his courage, exits the train at the stop nearest to the dance school, and enrolls for lessons. However, what begins as an attempt to get to know a pretty woman turns into the cure for Sugiyama's soul-sickness.

The parts of *Shall We Dance?* that are done well, are done *very* well, muting the negative impact of certain less successful elements. One of the most interesting aspects of the film for a Western viewer is that we're offered an opportunity to peer through an open window into Japanese society, especially as it addresses issues of intimacy. For those of us who are used to the idea that dancing is an integral part of the cultural fabric, understanding how the Japanese view this activity can cause a shift in perspective. The pleasant emotional aftereffects are a testimony to Suo's ability to fashion a story whose appeal reaches far beyond the shores of his native country. *Shall We Dance?* promises a convivial evening at the movies, and a rare chance to mix culture with pleasure. RECOMMENDED

Sleepless in Seattle [1993]
Starring: Tom Hanks, Meg Ryan Director: Nora Ephron Screenplay: Nora Ephron, David S. Ward, and Jeff Arch Running Time: 1:45 Rated: PG (Mature themes, language) Theatrical Aspect Ratio: 1.85:1

Eight-year-old Jonah Baldwin (Ross Malinger) misses his mother, who died from cancer 18 months ago. More than that, however, he recognizes that his father, Sam (Tom Hanks), is desperately lonely. So, on Christmas Eve, Jonah calls a radio talk-show psychologist and asks for help. Forced onto the phone by his son and identified as "Sleepless in Seattle," Sam reluctantly (at first) opens up and talks about his love for his dead wife and the things that made her special. Across the country in Baltimore, Annie Reed (Meg Ryan) is listening to the syndicated program, and Sam's testimonial of love brings tears to her eyes. Even though she is engaged to Walter (Bill Pullman), Annie begins to wonder what it would be like to meet Sam. She even becomes one of thousands to write a letter to him. But, when circumstances make an assignation possible, the question is whether either Sam or Annie will have the courage to follow through with it.

There are those who will claim that *Sleepless in Seattle* is too corny, with sugar-coated cuteness filling in for the lack of a strong plot. And, while they have a point, there's something that the cynics are missing — it's meant to be that way. By its own admission, this film is intended as a throwback to the screen romances of the past (*An Affair to Remember* in particular, which is cited numerous times, and borrowed from explicitly and implicitly). Anyone expecting a tale of stark modern life from *Sleepless in Seattle* has walked into the wrong theater. This is a dreamy, romantic fantasy whose mood falls somewhere between magic and reality.

Coincidence is the backbone of Nora Ephron's story, wending its way through the plot with uncanny repetitiveness. The concept of destiny is an important thematic element. At the beginning of the film, Annie is a realist who dismisses the idea of a supernatural sign as nothing more than a random occurrence. By the end of *Sleepless*, she has become a believer in fate. Considering the unusual nature of the bond she develops with Sam, how could she not? RECOMMENDED

A Summer's Tale [France, 1996]
Starring: Melvil Poupaud, Amanda Langlet, Gwenaëlle Simon, Aurelia Nolin Director: Eric Rohmer Screenplay: Eric Rohmer Running Time: 1:53 Rated: Not Rated (Mature themes) Theatrical Aspect Ratio: 1.66:1 In French with subtitles

With this outing, director Eric Rohmer once again proves something he has been doing for his entire career: movies don't have to be about momentous events or larger-than-life characters to be entirely absorbing. *A Summer's Tale* works because the characters are so real and their circumstances presented in such a natural, unforced manner that we cannot help but be drawn into their lives. When it comes to traditional plot development, very little happens during the course of *A Summer's Tale*. The film is all about characters interacting. What they say — and, in some cases, don't say — forms the framework of the story.

Gaspard (Melvil Poupaud) is a young mathematician/musician vacationing by the seaside in Brittany, France before starting a new job. The film covers roughly 3 weeks in his life and introduces us to the trio of women he encounters during that time. First is Margot (Amanda Langlet), a cheerful waitress who enjoys spending time with Gaspard, but isn't interested in more than a friendship. Solene (Gwenaëlle Simon) is more affectionate and sensual — she's willing to have a relationship with Gaspard if he will commit to only her. Then there's Lena (Aurelia Nolin), Gaspard's longtime semi-girlfriend whose ambiguous romantic attitude towards him keeps him in a state of constant consternation. As the summer wears on, Gaspard finds himself increasingly torn between the 3 women, finding each the most appealing when he's with her, and recognizing that the day is fast approaching when he will have to choose.

As is often the case with Rohmer, the director has chosen a completely natural group of young actors to portray his protagonists. Melvil Poupaud, who plays Gaspard, has a fairly long resume, stretching back to the mid-'80s. Amanda Langlet, who worked with Rohmer 13 years earlier as the title character in *Pauline At the Beach*, is flawless as Margot — it's impossible to see how any man wouldn't be mesmerized by her charm. Both Gwenaëlle Simon and Aurelia Nolin, making their feature debuts, show amazing poise for a first film.

Of the 4 films that comprise Rohmer's *Tale of Four Seasons*, *A Summer's Tale* is arguably the lightest. But, as is always true of the director's work, there's far more going on than is initially apparent. What might at first seem to be a pleasant-but-inconsequential motion picture conceals deep (but not dark) emotional currents. Rohmer has always enjoyed exploring the lighter side of the human psyche, with a special affinity for love. *A Summer's Tale* finds him plumbing that familiar well one more time with results that are likely to please anyone who isn't averse to a movie where character development and dialogue take precedence over plot contortions and mindless action. **HIGHLY RECOMMENDED**

The Tao of Steve [2000]

Starring: Donal Logue, Greer Goodman, Kimo Wills Director: Jenniphr Goodman Screenplay: Duncan North, Greer Goodman and Jennifphr Goodman Running Time: 1:27 Rated: R (Sexual situations, profanity, drug use) Theatrical Aspect Ratio: 1.85:1

So what is the Tao of Steve? Some ancient Buddhist practice that allows the practitioner to better confer with eternity? A means to come closer to god? Actually, it's a way to pick up babes. Just ask Dex (Donal Logue), whose entire sex life is defined by it. As Jack Palance once declared in a TV commercial (and as Dex would no doubt agree), "Confidence is sexy." In this philosophy, "Steve" isn't just a name, it's a state of mind. "Steve" represents the kind of man who never tries to impress a woman but ends up getting the girl in the end. Think Steve McGarrett (of *Hawaii 5-0*). Or Steve Austin (*The Six Million Dollar Man*). Or especially Steve McQueen, the "ultimate Steve." James Bond is a "Steve." And so is Dex.

Back in high school, Dex was voted most likely to succeed. By the time his 10-year reunion comes around, however, the only thing he has succeeded at is perfecting the life of a slacker. But, when it comes to women, he's a veritable babe magnet. No one, married or unmarried, can seemingly resist his dubious charm. Even someone like Dex can't hide forever from love, and he's smitten from the first time he sees Syd (co-writer Greer Goodman, the director's sister) playing drums for the band at the high school reunion. She remembers him — he was the smartest guy in her philosophy class — but he can't place her. Nevertheless, whatever he may have thought of her during their time together in school, he is definitely intrigued now. And, while his life has stagnated, she has moved on to become the set director for the Santa Fe opera. She has a boyfriend and a lifestyle she enjoys, and Dex's charisma seemingly has no effect upon her.

The most enjoyable romantic comedies focus on characters, ideas, and dialogue (plotting is never a big issue, due to obvious constraints). *The Tao of Steve* is strong in all three areas. Admittedly, the men and women populating this movie do not talk the way real people talk, but since what they have to say is so interesting, we're willing to forgive the cinematic conceit. *The Tao of Steve* will be remembered for its fresh, breezy approach and its easy mingling of pop culture and spiritualism. RECOMMENDED

Trick [1999]

Starring: Christian Campbell, John Paul Pitoc, Tori Spelling, Stephen Hayes Director: Jim Fall Screenplay: Jason Schafer Running Time: 1:30 Rated: R (Sexual situations, gay themes, nudity, profanity) Theatrical Aspect Ratio: 1.85:1

Trick is one of the few gay romantic comedies with the potential to be appreciated by a more diverse audience than those who typically explore this niche of the motion picture market. And the film's quintessential appeal is not diminished by the assertion of first-time director Jim Fall that he made the film with the primary intention of appealing to homosexual viewers. There is enough charm and tenderness on the screen that it's virtually impossible not to sympathize with the characters on some level. Unlike many gay-themed motion pictures, *Trick*'s central focus isn't sex. Sure, that's what it's superficially about, but it doesn't take much digging to determine that the movie is really concerned with issues of intimacy and commitment — and these will strike a chord with any viewer, regardless of his or her sexuality. That's where Fall's picture works, and the reason why it has crossover potential.

Gabe (Christian "brother of Neve" Campbell) is a would-be Broadway songwriter whose inability to pen believable lyrics can be traced to a lack of experience in meaningful relationships. After meeting Gabe, we are soon introduced to those who inhabit his inner circle of friends and acquaintances. There's his straight roommate, Rich (Brad Beyer), who often makes Gabe sleep in the hall so he can be alone with a girl. His best friend is Katherine (Tori Spelling), who isn't nearly as good a singer/actress as she thinks she is. And his #1 supporter is Perry (Stephen Hayes), a semi-successful member of his desired trade who spends his evenings playing tunes at a New York City piano bar. One night while passing his time at an all-males strip joint, Gabe catches the eye of Mark (John Paul Pitoc), and it's lust at first sight. Later, on the subway, the two meet again and, without preliminaries, Mark asks Gabe if he knows of a place where they can be alone. For the rest of the movie (and the rest of the night), Gabe and Mark undergo a series of comic misadventures as they pursue this goal.

Despite not being graphic in its depiction of certain acts, the movie is frank in the way it deals with the characters' sexuality. The dialogue is not brilliant, but it gets the job done. Once in a while, screenwriter Jason Schafer resorts to saccharine platitudes, but, for the most part, he sticks to well-written lines and occasionally hits paydirt. But the strength of the script is not in what the characters say nor in the way it throws contrived obstacles in their paths. Instead, it's in the believable nature of the central relationship — a key element that many big budget, mainstream romantic comedies lose sight of. This movie gets that trick (and a few others) right. RECOMMENDED

The Truth About Cats and Dogs [1996]

Starring: Janeane Garofalo, Uma Thurman, Ben Chaplin Director: Michael Lehmann Screenplay: Audrey Wells Running Time: 1:37 Rated: PG-13 (Profanity, phone sex) Theatrical Aspect Ratio: 1.85:1

Since Edmond Rostand first committed the play to paper in 1897, *Cyrano De Bergerac* has become a reliable romantic formula. With a standout performance by Janeane Garofalo, this loose reworking makes for solid, if feather-light, entertainment.

The story, which starts out as upbeat variation of *Cyrano* before moving in another direction, introduces Garofalo as radio pet doctor Abby Barnes. Her show, *The Truth About Cats and Dogs,* has made her a household voice, but, as is often true for radio personalities, her face is less familiar. One day, a British-accented photographer named Brian (Ben Chaplin) calls up with a problem: he has an angry dog on roller skates ruining his studio. Abby talks him through the process of pacifying the dog, and, in gratitude, Brian invites her out for a drink. She accepts, but, afflicted with low self-esteem, lies about her appearance. Although Abby is a 5' 1" brunette, she tells Brian to look for someone 5' 10," blond, and "hard to miss" — an exact description of her airhead actress/model neighbor, Noelle (Uma Thurman).

When Abby explains her deception to Noelle, the statuesque beauty agrees to help, but it doesn't take long for things to get out of hand. Inevitably, Noelle becomes attracted to Brian, and the two women vie for his attention — Noelle using her body and Abby, her voice. Brian doesn't realize that the face of his dreams isn't that of the woman with whom he has a 7-hour telephone conversation that culminates in phone sex.

Buying into the premise of *The Truth About Cats and Dogs* — that any man could mistake a ditz like Noelle for Abby — requires a huge suspension of disbelief, but, once you get past that stumbling block, the film is disarmingly charming, and even offers a few flashes of substance. Nothing in the screenplay is groundbreaking, but there are some observations about low self-confidence. Brian gets tongue-tied around women. Abby is unsure of herself because she thinks she's ugly. And Noelle has self-esteem problems because she believes herself to be stupid. The requisite chemistry between Chaplin and Garofalo is present, and the story follows an unthreateningly predictable route. RECOMMENDED

Two Family House [2000]

Starring: Michael Rispoli, Kelly MacDonald, Kathrine Narducci
Director: Raymond De Felitta Screenplay: Raymond De Felitta Running Time: 1:54 Rated: R (Profanity, sex) Theatrical Aspect Ratio: 1.85:1

The time is 1956. The place is Staten Island. Buddy Visalo (Michael Rispoli), his head bursting with grand plans of self-employment and wealth, has just bought a dilapidated two family house with the intention of turning the downstairs into a tavern and using the upstairs as an apartment for him and his shrewish wife, Estelle (Kathrine Narducci). There are a few complications, however. In the first place, Estelle hates the idea of her husband running a bar. Convinced that the venture will fail, she does everything in her power to accelerate that failure. In the second place, the upstairs is occupied by a belligerent, perpetually drunk Irishman (Kevin Conway) and his pregnant wife, Mary (Scottish actress Kelly MacDonald), who are unwilling to give up their tenancy and have the law on their side.

Things change when Mary gives birth, and the child turns out to have much darker skin than his supposed father. Mary's husband leaves her, and Buddy, pressured by his wife, evicts her. Feeling remorse, however, he rescues Mary from the dive where she is forced to go and sets her up in a cozy, low-rent apartment where she and the baby can live in relative peace. Finding Mary's company more pleasant than his wife's, Buddy becomes a regular visitor, and, although their friendship begins platonically, circumstances force them closer together until the inevitable happens.

Two Family House is thoroughly charming. The romantic relationship that forms the film's core is presented on a level that's a notch above what we usually see in movies. There are some serious cultural and social elements that De Felitta has to juggle, and he does so without sweeping them under the table. Mary is ostracized by almost every segment of society because her baby is biracial. The closer Buddy gets to her, the more he risks. He admires her strength and spirit and, most importantly, she supports and encourages his dreams while his wife is interested only in shooting them down.

One of the most refreshing aspects of *Two Family House* is that it doesn't feel the need to go through all of the obligatory (and predictable) plot contortions mandated by most romances. Buddy and Mary don't endure the Big Breakup caused by the Big Misunderstanding, which, in turn, is followed by the Bigger Reunion. Their relationship has its share of complications, but they're not the run-of-the-mill stumbling blocks that we see in 9 out of 10 mainstream films. That's only one of many reasons why *Two Family House* is worth seeing. RECOMMENDED

What Women Want [2000]

Starring: Mel Gibson, Helen Hunt, Marisa Tomei, Bette Midler
Director: Nancy Meyers Screenplay: Josh Goldsmith and Cathy Yuspa
Running Time: 2:05 Rated: PG-13 (Sexual humor, sexual situations, profanity) Theatrical Aspect Ratio: 1.85:1

Most of the credit for the film's success has to be laid at the feet of Mel Gibson, who exudes energy and oozes charm. Gibson's dynamic personality elevates the film. His co-star, Helen Hunt, seems content to remain largely in the background, although, during the course of her low-key performance, she does a nice job of developing her character into the semblance of a rounded individual.

What Women Want has a simple premise that it exploits to a point, although not to the fullest. Nick Marshall (Gibson) is a "man's man" — the kind of politically incorrect charmer whom women fall for instantly. But there's a drawback to all of that machismo. Despite being the most accomplished ad man at Chicago's Sloane Curtis agency, Nick is passed over for the job of Creative Director, a position everyone in the office assumed he would get — everyone except the boss, Dan Wanamaker (Alan Alda), who patiently explains that, with the increase in female buying power, Sloane Curtis needs someone who understands that "it's a woman's world out there." That person isn't Nick; it's Darcy Maguire (Helen Hunt), the queen of female-driven marketing. And the moment she gets the job, Nick is determined to unseat her at all costs.

Then, suddenly, the King of Testosterone gets an unexpected infusion of estrogen. A home accident gives him the unlikely ability to hear what women are thinking. At first, he believes it's a curse, but then a psychologist (Bette Midler in a cameo) convinces him that it's a gift. So he begins to employ his powers for personal gain, both in bed and at the office, where he shamelessly pilfers Darcy's ideas and passes them off as his own. But, along the way, two things start happening. First, Nick begins to actually empathize with women. Secondly, he develops feelings for Darcy.

A fair amount of the comedy, like the romance, works. Some of the humor is pretty raunchy, but there are enough solid laughs to make up for when things fall flat. When the film strays into dramatic territory, it's on less certain ground. Director Nancy Meyers has fashioned cinematic cotton candy — all sugar and air. She understands the essence of the formula, and applies it in a manner that is infectious. In an era of largely disposable and forgettable motion pictures, there are far worse ways to spend a couple of hours. RECOMMENDED

When Harry Met Sally [1989]
Starring: Billy Crystal, Meg Ryan, Carrie Fisher, Bruno Kirby
Director: Rob Reiner Screenplay: Nora Ephron Running Time: 1:36
Rated: R (Profanity, sexual situations) Theatrical Aspect Ratio: 1.85:1

The thing that *When Harry Met Sally* does best is to keep the focus firmly on the relationship between the two title characters, never wandering off on unwelcome tangents. There are subplots, to be sure, but even those are crucial to the evolution of Harry and Sally's friendship. And the film is not hamstrung by a litany of familiar romantic comedy clichés. *When Harry Met Sally* offers an often humorous, occasionally poignant view of men, women, sex, love, and friendship.

When Harry Burns (Billy Crystal) and Sally Albright (Meg Ryan) first meet, it's 1977. Both are leaving the University of Chicago for New York City, and they share the drive. Along the way, they discover that they have little in common. At one point, Harry makes a pass at Sally, but she demurs, saying that they'll have to settle for being friends. That's when he makes his famous comment. They part in Manhattan, and it's 5 years before they bump into each other again, this time in an airport. By then, Harry is engaged to be married and Sally is in the midst of a serious relationship. They spend some time together on a plane, then separate amicably when they reach their destination. Their next encounter occurs in the late-'80s. They are both newly single (Harry's wife has recently left him and Sally has broken off a long-term, dead-end affair), and this mutual bond of loss draws them into a close friendship. When events push their relationship over the sexual line, things don't go smoothly.

Ultimately, *When Harry Met Sally* works because it

dares to be *slightly* different from most romantic comedies. While there's nothing radical in the trajectory of Harry and Sally's romance, it's not entirely conventional, either. The two main characters are well-written, with both easily transcending the level of stereotyping they could have easily fallen into. The dialogue is smart and witty, offering numerous quotable passages. However, although the film poses some intriguing questions about the nature of male/female relationships, it never really answers them, instead using this material as little more than a jumping-off point for the interaction between Harry and Sally. For those who appreciate romantic comedies for both aspects of the genre (the "romance" and the "comedy"), *When Harry Met Sally* is a treat. HIGHLY RECOMMENDED

Wicker Park [2004]
Starring: Josh Hartnett, Rose Byrne, Matthew Lillard, Diane Kruger, Christopher Cousins, Jessica Paré Director: Paul McGuigan
Screenplay: Brandon Boyce, inspired by *L'Appartement*, by Gilles Mimouni Running Time: 1:55 Rated: PG-13 (Sexuality, profanity)
Theatrical Aspect Ratio: 1.85:1

Wicker Park's narrative is constructed as a puzzle, with each scene revealing more details about the characters and the unexpected ways in which their paths have crossed. The film works best if you go into it with no preconceived notions about what's going to happen. The film opens in the middle of the story. As things move forward, the past is unveiled by means of a series of flashbacks. Eventually, we are presented with the opportunity to see various situations from different points of view. By the end of the film we have a complete picture of nearly all of the events, and get to see that some of the "guilty" parties are not as culpable as they first appear to be.

Wicker Park reunites two of the female leads from *Troy*. Diane Kruger, who was rather stiff as the face that launched a thousand ships, appears much more relaxed and "in her element" as Lisa, the "one who got away" from male lead Matthew (Josh Hartnett). Rose Byrne, whose Briseis was one of the more sympathetic women in *Troy*, shows great emotional depth as Alex, who ends up romantically linked with both Matthew and his best friend, Luke (Matthew Lillard). Hartnett approaches Matthew in his usual low-key manner, avoiding the kind of melodramatic performance that could have sunk this movie. His "Everyman" method, while not always effective, works in this case.

One of the reasons I think *Wicker Park* works is because it tells a story that could be presented as a

thriller or in a straightforward, dramatic fashion. Instead of scares and moments of high tension, the film focuses on the characters and the motives that drive them. This film is genuinely interested in getting us inside the heads of its three leads (Matthew, Alex, and Lisa). It wants us to understand, although not necessarily sympathize with, all three of them. That's the bait that hooked me and held my attention. And, as the movie approached the end credits, I cared about what happened to these characters, and that made the coincidences and occasional missteps forgivable.
RECOMMENDED

Wimbledon [UK/France, 2004]

Starring: Kirsten Dunst, Peter Colt, Sam Neill, Jon Favreau, Bernard Hill, Eleanor Bron, Austin Nichols Director: Richard Loncraine
Screenplay: Adam Brooks and Jennifer Flackett & Mark Levin Running Time: 1:38 Rated: PG-13 (Sexual situations, profanity, partial nudity)
Theatrical Aspect Ratio: 2.35:1

Love in tennis doesn't have to be bad, as Richard Loncraine's *Wimbledon* shows. A formulaic motion picture that delights in spite of (or perhaps because of?) its reliance upon conventions, *Wimbledon* is the kind of movie that allows the noncynical moviegoer to sit back and relax in the presence of actors who work well with one another and a script whose familiarity is an asset. It's rare for any motion picture to successfully combine the clichés of the sports and romance genres while keeping a balance between them.

Peter Colt (Paul Bettany) is a 31-year-old tennis has-been. Actually, make that a never-was. His current world ranking of #119 is considerably below his position at #11 in 1996, but even in his heyday, he was never a household name. Now, he has decided to announce his retirement after one more try at Wimbledon, where he has garnered a wild-card bid. He first encounters up-and-coming American star Lizzie Bradbury (Kirsten Dunst) when he accidentally enters her hotel room and finds her in the shower. This mistake turns out to be the beginning of a whirlwind romance. For Peter, it's the best thing that could have happened to him — he's winning matches he was expected to lose and is advancing further into the tournament than anyone believed he could. The opposite is true for Lizzie, who is favored to reach the finals. She's losing her focus, and her play is becoming sloppy.

As I have said dozens of times, romantic movies are made or broken by how well the leads interact with each other. If an audience believes they are in love and wants them to be together, it's irrelevant how plain or convoluted the plot is. And, in this case, there's plenty of chemistry between Bettany and Dunst. Also, while both are convincing when playing the romantic aspects of their roles, they look good on the court as well. Although it's possible that the editing has something to do with it, Bettany and Dunst look like they know what to do with a racket.

Yes, *Wimbledon* is a crowd-pleaser, but it doesn't energize audiences by pandering to the least common denominator. The film has heart and spirit, and it does a lot of things well. There are plenty of other choices out there if you're looking for something surprising. *Wimbledon* has the feel of a comfortable bathrobe — you can sink into it and relax.
RECOMMENDED

You've Got Mail [1998]

Starring: Tom Hanks, Meg Ryan, Greg Kinnear Director: Nora Ephron
Screenplay: Nora Ephron & Delia Ephron Running Time: 1:57
Rated: PG (Mature themes, mild profanity) Theatrical Aspect Ratio: 1.85:1

Joe Fox (Tom Hanks), part owner of the Fox Books Superstore chain (a Barnes & Noble clone), is a cold businessman who puts the competition out of business without a second thought. As things develop, Joe's character follows a Scrooge-like arc. He isn't haunted by ghosts, but events gradually open his eyes to the evil of his ways, and he undergoes an attitude change. By the final reel, Joe gives us exactly the kind of Jimmy Stewart personality we expect from someone played by Hanks. Kathleen Kelly, on the other hand, is pure Meg Ryan, from her chirpy pep to the tilt of her head. And can anyone cry quite like Ryan? Kathleen, who owns a small children's bookstore called The Shop Around the Corner, finds herself in direct conflict with Joe, whose nearby superstore is stealing all of her customers. But that's not the whole story. To this standard rivals-who-fall-for-each-other tale, Ephron adds a great opening credits sequence (a view of "cyberManhattan") and a heavy dose of fate. For, while Joe and Kathleen are locking horns in business, their on-line alter-egos are falling in love.

You've Got Mail is appropriately rated PG, because, while Hanks and Ryan play well off of one another, there are no sparks. This film is about pure, old-fashioned romance, unsullied by things like lust and sex. *You've Got Mail* is peppered with Ephronisms (the kind of exchanges that characterized both *When Harry Met Sally* and *Sleepless in Seattle*). In *Sleepless,* the movie that embodied a woman's fantasies was *An Affair to Remember*; for men, it was *The Dirty Dozen*.

Here, the approach is the same, but the text is different. For Kathleen, *Pride and Prejudice* is the Bible. In Joe's case, *The Godfather* is "the sum of all wisdom." For the most part, the script, despite being predictable, is smart and quirky, although the final line of the film, delivered by Ryan to Hanks, is a miscalculation. The punctuation mark would have been there without the neon sign to point it out.

You've Got Mail has the virtue of delivering *exactly* what's expected from it. It's a feel-good movie that of-fers enough comedy and romance to warm the heart without risking a sentimental overdose. Fans of *Sleepless in Seattle* will almost certainly fall in love with the similar-yet-different nature of the production; only die-hard cynics will be turned off by all of the unabashed good will. If there are messages to be found here, they're that romance is still thriving in our technological era, and that well-written romantic comedies starring Hanks and Ryan don't represent much of a gamble for the financing studio. RECOMMENDED

Science Fiction/Fantasy

A.I. [2001]
Starring: Haley Joel Osment, Jude Law Director: Steven Spielberg
Screenplay: Steven Spielberg, based on the screen story by Ian
Watson Running Time: 2:25 Rated: PG-13 (Profanity, sexual situations)
Theatrical Aspect Ratio: 1.85:1

A.I. is a science fiction re-interpretation of *Pinocchio* (a story the film frequently references) crossed with *Frankenstein*. Events take place in a futuristic setting, where the rise of the oceans has swallowed up seaside cities like New York and Amsterdam, where New Jersey resembles an Amazon rain forest, and where the sin-and-sex center of the planet is a place called Rouge City, which resides across the Delaware from New Jersey. This future, as imagined by Spielberg and his set designers, is every bit as awe-inspiring as what Ridley Scott brought to the screen in *Blade Runner* and what Luc Besson crafted for *The Fifth Element*. Rouge City is stunning, and the waterlogged ruins of Manhattan are hauntingly beautiful.

The story centers around David (Haley Joel Osment), a child substitute "mecha" who represents the first of his type — a synthetic who can actually love. In this case, the object of his incompletely-understood emotion is his "mother," Monica Swinton (Frances O'Connor). Monica's husband, Henry (Sam Robards), who brought David home as a pilot project from his workplace, Cybertronics of New Jersey, is more wary of the robot child. And, when one of David's actions endangers Monica and Henry's natural son, Martin (Jake Thomas), Monica is forced to take David into the woods and "lose" him. He is quickly found by a group of anti-robot fanatics, and, while being held captive by them, he befriends

Gigolo Joe (Jude Law), who becomes an invaluable ally in his escape.

Like the real-life science surrounding the development of Artificial Intelligence, the movie is top-heavy with moral and ethical questions. What is life and where is the line that divides sentience from a programmed response? If a robot can genuinely love a person, what responsibility does that person bear in return? How can an immortal robot cope with outliving its organic creators? Writers from Mary Shelley to Isaac Asimov have been fascinated by these dilemmas. Perhaps Spielberg attempts too much with *A.I.* To some degree, by trying to tackle all of these issues, he fails to effectively present any of them.

A.I. is an ambitious film that, when it misses its mark, does so because it strives for so much. The script does not insult the audience's intelligence, and it gets us thinking about "big issues," such as love, life, god, and our place in the universe. It's unfortunate that as much thought didn't go into structuring the narrative as went into crafting the movie's thematic content. And those who have come to equate science fiction with action will be disappointed. *A.I.* is a drama with little in the way of adrenaline-boosting sequences. Spielberg has consciously slowed things down, relying on viewers' curiosity about the ideas and identification with the characters to keep them involved in the proceedings. **RECOMMENDED**

Alien [1979]
Starring: Tom Skerritt, Sigourney Weaver, Ian Holm, John Hurt
Director: Ridley Scott Screenplay: Dan O'Bannon Running Time: 1:56
Rated: R (Violence, gore, profanity) Theatrical Aspect Ratio: 2.35:1

In many ways, *Alien* was the first of a kind. True — it wasn't the first space movie to feature a homicidal monster, nor was it the first time a group of characters were hunted down one-by-one in dark, dank spaces. However, this "haunted house in space" film was one of the first to effectively cross-pollinate these two genres. In addition to blending graphic horror with science fiction, *Alien* has another distinction — it is one of the first films to feature a female action hero. Even today, on those rare occasions when a woman takes the lead in an action/adventure movie, she is typically measured up to Sigourney Weaver's Ellen Ripley.

Alien begins slowly and calmly by introducing us to the crew of the *Nostromo*, a commercial towing space vehicle on a return course for Earth. They number 7 — the relatively laid-back captain, Dallas (Skerritt); his second-in-command, Ripley (Weaver); Lambert (Veronica Cartwright), the ship's highly-strung navigator; science officer Ash (Ian Holm), who seems to have ice water for blood; Kane (John Hurt), who is possessed of a gallows humor; and grunts Brett (Harry Dean Stanton) and Parker (Yaphet Kotto), who spend their time grumbling about not getting full bonuses.

After receiving a possible distress signal from a seemingly uninhabited planet, Dallas, Kane, and Lambert head down to investigate. On the inhospitable surface, they come across what appears to be a downed space ship. Inside, they find a chamber full of egg-like objects. As Kane is examining one, it opens and a leathery creature emerges, launches itself at Kane, and forces a proboscis down his throat. Kane is taken to the medical lab, where Ash determines that it would be too dangerous for the life form to be removed from his face. Eventually, however, it falls off on its own, apparently dead. Kane returns to consciousness and all seems to be well. Then comes the fateful dinner. The normal mealtime chit-chat of the crew is interrupted when Kane begins gagging and choking. Before anyone can help him, a creature bursts through his chest and scampers into the air ducts, leaving behind Kane's bloody, dead husk. The rest of the crew mounts a search through the *Nostromo*'s dark, claustrophobic passageways, with the alien picking them off one-by-one. And, with each new victim, it grows larger and stronger.

Alien contains its fair share of genuine scares. These aren't mere "boo" moments, where something benign jumps out of the shadows accompanied by a loud noise and a musical crescendo, but legitimate shocks. The level of suspense during the film's final 30 minutes becomes almost unbearable. What started as a seemingly low-key motion picture turns into a real white-knuckler. *Alien* may not have been totally original in its approach, but the film's widespread acceptance made it a blueprint for an entire sub-genre.
HIGHLY RECOMMENDED

Aliens [1986]

Starring: **Sigourney Weaver, Carrie Henn, Michael Biehn, Paul Reiser**
Director: **James Cameron** Screenplay: **James Cameron** Running Time: **2:17** Rated: **R** (Violence, gore, profanity) Theatrical Aspect Ratio: **1.85:1**

Perhaps the best single word to describe James Cameron's *Aliens* is relentless. Tautly paced and expertly directed, this roller coaster ride of a motion picture offers a little bit of everything, all wrapped up in a tidy science fiction/action package. From the point when the opening half-hour of exposition ends and the real movie begins, Cameron barely gives viewers a chance to catch their breaths or ease their grips on their armrests as he plunges his characters from one dire situation to the next. This is one of those rare motion pictures that involves the audience so completely in the story that we're as worn out at the end as our on-screen counterparts.

Aliens takes place a half-century after the events in *Alien*. Ellen Ripley (Sigourney Weaver) has been in cryogenic sleep in outer space until a salvage ship discovers her and brings her back to Earth. There, she finds herself facing serious charges of official misconduct and her claims about the alien are greeted with skepticism. She is stripped of her pilot's license and left to cope on her own with life in the future. Then, all contact is suddenly lost with the terraforming colony on LV-426 — the planet on which Ripley's crew discovered the alien. A corporation executive, Carter Burke (Paul Reiser), approaches Ripley with a proposition: accompany a military team to LV-426 as an advisor and have her pilot's license restored. She agrees, but with a proviso: they are going there to destroy the aliens, not to harvest them or bring them back. Burke agrees.

Ripley's new companions are a tough-talking, hard-bitten bunch: Ground Troop Commander Apone (Al Williams), wisecracking Private Hudson (Bill Paxton), somber Corporal Hicks (Michael Biehn), unflappable Vasquez (Jenette Goldstein), quiet android Bishop (Lance Henricksen), and several others. Only Gorman (William Hope), the squadron commander, is cut from a different cloth — he's by-the-book and does not react well to unexpected developments, especially in combat. Of course, when faced with the plethora of aliens on LV-426, the others don't know what to do either, as the insect-like creatures decimate their ranks and trap them in an abandoned operations center. There, they encounter Newt (Carrie Henn), a young girl who is the only survivor of the aliens' attack on the colony. Newt is unconvinced that a small group of armed soldiers will be able to stop the ever-growing army of aliens. Soon, they are fighting the clock as well as the creatures, as the plant's nuclear reactor starts on a countdown to going critical.

For James Cameron, who would go on to direct two of the 1990s most memorable motion pictures (*Terminator 2* and *Titanic*), *The Terminator* may have been the movie to put him on the map, but *Aliens* announced him as a force to be reckoned with. When it comes to the logical marriage of action, adventure, and science fiction, few films are as effective or accomplished as *Aliens*. **MUST SEE**

The Arrival [1996]

Starring: Charlie Sheen, Lindsay Crouse, Teri Polo, Ron Silver
Director: David Twohy Screenplay: David Twohy Running Time: 1:55
Rated: PG-13 (Violence, mature themes) Theatrical Aspect Ratio: 1.85:1

When aliens can disguise themselves as humans, as in *The Arrival*, we're never sure who's a friend and who's a foe, and the best science fiction/horror films of this ilk continuously keep us guessing. Conspiracy lovers will have fun sorting through the layers of cover-up and treachery here. And those who crave scary-looking, otherworldly creatures will get their fill from the aliens in their natural forms.

The premise is rather simple. The aliens hail from a planet orbiting Wolf-336, an unstable star located 14.6 light years from Earth. A colonizing force has arrived here incognito with the goal of readying this world for inhabitation. That process involves accelerating the greenhouse effect — intentionally polluting the atmosphere so that the global temperature rises, causing the polar ice caps melt.

Zane (Charlie Sheen) and Calvin (Richard Schiff), a pair of SETI radio astronomers, intercept communications between Wolf-336 and Earth. When they report this to their boss, Phil Gordian (Ron Silver), Zane is fired and Calvin suffers an unfortunate accident. With the help of Kiki (Tony T. Johnson), a neighborhood boy, Zane begins investigating on his own, ignoring his girlfriend (Teri Polo) in his quest to determine who's out there. But Zane isn't the only one observing strange goings-on. A UCLA environmentalist (Lindsay Crouse) has noticed the alarming increase in global warming, and it's only a matter of time before she and Zane meet each other and compare notes.

The Arrival is low key, which is refreshing, and it's as much horror as pure science fiction. This is the kind of movie that a director like John Carpenter might have made during his late-70s/early-80s heyday. It's creepy and atmospheric, and, after a rather protracted opening 40 minutes, well-paced. **RECOMMENDED**

Big Fish [2003]

Starring: Ewan McGregor, Albert Finney, Billy Crudup, Jessica Lange, Alison Lohman, Helena Bonham Carter, Steve Buscemi, Danny DeVito, Matthew McGrory Director: Tim Burton Screenplay: John August, based on the novel by Daniel Wallace Running Time: 2:00
Rated: PG-13 (Nudity, mild profanity) Theatrical Aspect Ratio: 2.35:1

Big Fish is the tale of how a son, William Bloom (Billy Crudup), tries to piece together a picture of the life of his father, Edward (Albert Finney), based on the facts he can uncover; the accounts of his mother, Sandy (Jessica Lange); and the tall tales told by the old man. Edward is an inveterate storyteller, with a penchant for embellishing events from his own life. As William puts it, "In telling the story of my father's life, it's impossible to separate fact from fiction, the man from the myth." But now Edward is dying and William must come to terms with all aspects of his father — the real and the imaginary. In the process, he discovers that some of Edward's supposed fantasies aren't as outlandish as he supposed.

Large chunks of *Big Fish* dramatize Edward's most impressive stories: how, as a boy, he had the courage to approach a witch and ask to see his future; how his growth spurt led him to seek out "bigger things"; how, as a young man (Ewan McGregor), he discovered the secret town of Spectre, and later met the love of his life, Sandy (Alison Lohman), at a circus. There are other tales, too — of giants, lycanthropes, armed robberies that don't go as planned, secret missions, Siamese twins, and fishing expeditions. In addition to telling a wonderful fairy tale, Burton is lauding the importance of storytelling and emphasizing the need to keep some element of magic and mystery in a world that has become coldly cynical.

Unlike in many of Tim Burton's previous movies, there is no cynicism here, and hardly any darkness. The film retains the director's trademark quirkiness, which resides somewhere between Terry Gilliam and

David Lynch, but is entirely optimistic. Unless you count the disease that has numbered Edward's days or the antagonism that has developed between father and son, *Big Fish* has no villains, nor does it require any. And, although there is a bittersweet quality to the ending, it is ultimately uplifting and optimistic. Burton has grown with this film, but without really expanding the envelope too far.

Big Fish takes place in a fantasy realm with just enough connection to the real world that we feel a certain sense of comfortable familiarity with the settings. This is Alabama, not J.R.R. Tolkien's Middle Earth. Yet *Big Fish* goes far beyond what is commonly referred to as "magical realism" without quite reaching the level of the classic "tall tale" (although it comes close at times). It works. We smile at all the right moments — such as when time stops when Edward first sees his true love — and feel a sense of pathos when the truth behind Edward's "double life" is revealed. *Big Fish* is a clever, smart fantasy that targets the child inside every adult without insulting the intelligence of either. RECOMMENDED

The Butterfly Effect [2004]

Starring: Ashton Kutcher, Amy Smart, William Lee Scott, Elden Henson, John Patrick Amedori, Eric Stoltz, Logan Lerman Director: Eric Bress, J. Mackye Gruber Screenplay: J. Mackye Gruber & Eric Bress Running Time: 1:53 Rated: R (Violence, profanity, sexual situations, nudity) Theatrical Aspect Ratio: 1.85:1

The Butterfly Effect is a compelling and intriguing movie that toys with the powers of choice and chance in a way that is not overused. Sure, there are plot holes (some of which are quite substantial), but most of them don't become apparent until long after the end credits have rolled and the film is being analyzed in a post-screening discussion. The ending is a cheat, and Ashton Kutcher is perhaps not the best choice for the lead role. Nevertheless, despite these flaws, I don't hesitate to recommend the film.

Evan Treborn (Kutcher) is a 20-year-old college student with a bigger parcel of emotional baggage than most young Americans. Since age seven, he has been experiencing blackouts at moments of high emotional stress, such as when a friend of the family molested him, or when he and some friends became involved in a prank gone bad. Evan learns that, by concentrating on the words in a journal he composed while growing up, he can transport himself back in time and relive certain events. Sometimes he can make changes; sometimes he can't. When a childhood friend, Kayleigh Miller (Amy Smart), com-

mits suicide because of something Evan does, he becomes obsessed with reworking her life. And, when he does, he learns that he might have been better off not meddling with the complex formula of cause-and-effect.

Codirectors Eric Bress and J. Mackye Gruber (who also cowrote the screenplay) have fashioned a movie that not only entertains in its own right, but asks us to consider the consequences of our own actions. There's a little *Sliding Doors* in this film, although, unlike the earlier movie, *The Butterfly Effect* is not a romantic comedy, nor does it show us the parallel evolution of different universes. This film follows a single incarnation of Evan as he meddles in his own time stream, changing his future from grim to grimmer, even as he remembers all of the permutations he has been through.

The ending is weak, and may be the result of the filmmakers writing themselves into a corner and not wanting to conclude things in a burst of nihilistic excess. Yet, even though it's a cheat, it retains a degree of resonance, primarily because it doesn't seek to sabotage the dark tone. In many ways, *The Butterfly Effect* is about regrets, and the closing sequences emphasize this. The film is engrossing enough to minimize such misgivings, however; few who enjoy unconventional pictures and see *The Butterfly Effect* will regret the experience. RECOMMENDED

The City of Lost Children [France, 1995]

Starring: Daniel Emilfork, Ron Perlman, Judith Vittet, Dominique Pinon Directors: Jean-Pierre Jeunet and Marc Caro Screenplay: Jean-Pierre Jeunet, Marc Caro, Gilles Adrien Running Time: 1:52 Rated: R (Mature themes, profanity) Theatrical Aspect Ratio: 1.85:1 In French with subtitles

In *The City of Lost Children*, directors Jeunet and Caro have presented a gloomy world where "normal" life is no more. The film is saturated with atmosphere and features imaginative set construction. The picture works in part because the film makers have taken the time and effort to frame a strange land where all their quirky characters can live and operate. *The City of Lost Children* is characterized by dark, twisted humor, yet this movie is more of a fantasy than a macabre comedy.

The City of Lost Children relates dreams to creativity, youth, and wonder. The capacity to escape the rational world through imagination fuels not only the desire to continue living, but the need to make something out of one's life. In this film, we are introduced the brilliant-yet-warped mad scientist Krank (Daniel

Emilfork), who is aging prematurely because he cannot dream. In an effort to stay alive, he has begun capturing children to steal their dreams. One of the toddlers abducted by Krank is little Denree (Joseph Lucien), the brother of a simpleminded circus strongman named One (Ron Perlman). One is joined in his search for his brother by Miette (Judith Vittet), the 9-year-old, wise-beyond-her-years leader of an orphan gang. Together, One and Miette seek to penetrate Krank's fortress; elude his 6 cloned henchmen (all played by Dominque Pinon), the deadly Miss Bismuth (Mireille Mosse), Irvin the talking brain (voice of Jean-Louis Trintignant), and the scientist himself; and rescue Denree. It proves to be a difficult task.

While much of *The City of Lost Children* is surreal and strange, the film's emotional center — the relationship between One and Miette — is nurtured with care and genuine feeling. Miette sees in One and Denree the chance for the family she has never known, although there are times when her intentions towards the older, child-like man seem more romantic than sisterly. It's to Jeunet and Caro's credit that they are able to present the ambiguities of this relationship tenderly, without ever injecting a hint of the sordid or perverse. **HIGHLY RECOMMENDED**

Conan the Barbarian [1982]

Starring: Arnold Schwarzenegger, James Earl Jones, Max von Sydow, Sandahl Bergman Director: John Milius Screenplay: John Milius and Oliver Stone, based on the stories by Robert E. Howard Running Time: 2:08 Rated: R (Violence, nudity, sex) Theatrical Aspect Ratio: 2.35:1

The plot of *Conan the Barbarian* is broad and adventurous, with plenty of the elements that have made Conan popular: voluptuous women, brawny men, a vile wizard, grotesque monsters, faithful sidekicks, and plenty of violent, bloody battle action. Those who have an inherent distaste for this sort of entertainment will appreciate *Conan the Barbarian*'s impeccable production values without enjoying the story; most everyone else will be swept away by the film's spectacle. *Conan* is not designed to have broad appeal. It is a well-made motion picture, but it is constricted by the constraints of the genre.

As the movie opens, Conan (Jorge Sanz), is a boy learning the "Riddle of Steel" from his father. Shortly thereafter, the young barbarian is in chains, a prisoner of the wizard Thulsa Doom (James Earl Jones) and his henchman, Rexor (Ben Davidson), who have burned down his village and killed his parents. Co-

nan grows up as a slave, and, once he is an adult (now played by Arnold Schwarzenegger), he becomes a gladiator champion and is used to breed prime slave stock. Eventually, his owner, fearing Conan's physical prowess, sets him free. After stealing a sword from a crypt and picking up a thief sidekick named Subotai (Gerry Lopez), he heads for the riches of civilization. In the city of Zamora, he meets Valeria, Queen of the Thieves (Sandahl Bergman), and, with her help, robs the Tower of the Serpent. He and Valeria become lovers, but Conan is only temporarily sated by gold, drink, and sex. The flame of revenge burns within him, and he is given valuable information to find Thulsa Doom when King Osrik (Max von Sydow), the ruler of Zamora, summons him to the palace with a proposition.

To date, *Conan the Barbarian* has been one of the few successful Swords and Sorcery movies. The reasons for this film's effectiveness are not difficult to understand. It treats its characters and subject matter seriously without becoming lugubrious. There is some humor, but it is mostly underplayed, and Milius avoids any overt suggestions of camp. *Conan the Barbarian* is also adult in nature — the battles are bloody and the women take their clothes off. Instead of the slightly overblown epic aura of *Conan*, most other films adopt a jokey tone. Years after its release, *Conan the Barbarian* still weaves a spell capable of ensorcelling fans of fantasy adventure. **RECOMMENDED**

Contact [1997]

Starring: Jodie Foster, Matthew McConaughey, James Woods, Tom Skerritt Director: Robert Zemeckis Screenplay: James V. Hart and Michael Goldenberg based on a story by Carl Sagan and Ann Druyan Running Time: 2:30 Rated: PG-13 (Profanity, mature themes) Theatrical Aspect Ratio: 2.35:1

Contact opens with an unforgettable sequence that takes the viewer on a tour of the universe. After this eye-popping trek, we return to Earth during the early 1970s, where we meet 9-year-old Ellie Arroway (Jena Malone), a budding scientist with a fascination for short wave radio (she likes hearing messages from far away) and astronomy. Her father, Ted (David Morse), is an English teacher, and has schooled Ellie in the beauty of the stars. Following his sudden death, an event that leaves Ellie orphaned, she decides to devote her entire life to pursuing the mysteries that her father opened her eyes to.

When we next encounter Ellie (now played by Jodie Foster), she's a promising researcher for the SETI (Search for Extraterrestrial Intelligence) Institute, working on a giant radio telescope in Puerto Rico. Ellie's obsession is to find evidence of life on another planet. Despite the scorn of her colleagues, she spends hours on end listening for that proof. While in Puerto Rico, she becomes involved with a religious scholar, Palmer Joss (Matthew McConaughey). The two have a short, passionate affair that ends when Ellie's former mentor (and the President's national science advisor), David Drumlin (Tom Skerritt), pulls the plug on the SETI project in Puerto Rico. To maintain her work, Ellie is forced to seek private funding, which she receives from a multi-billionaire eccentric named S.R. Hadden (John Hurt). Armed with as much money as she needs, Ellie rents time on New Mexico's VLA (very large array) radio telescope range, and, while there, discovers a message from the star Vega that indicates intelligent life. Once the signal is confirmed, the VLA becomes the center of a media blitz, and, along with the reporters, National Security Advisor Michael Kitz (James Woods) arrives, ready to militarize the project and push Ellie out.

In its own unique way, *Contact* offers a little bit of almost everything: drama, romance, suspense, and science fiction. It touches the emotions and the intellect. There are glorious special effects, wonderful acting, and a couple of impressive pyrotechnic displays. The plot contains the most believable approach to this subject matter ever presented in a movie. In addition to the scientific aspect, there's the media feeding frenzy, the fierce in-fighting to gain control of the project, the international ramifications of the U.S. taking charge, and the religious implications of life on another planet. One of the key, recurring struggles presented in *Contact* is that of science versus religion, and how the conflict between these two seemingly-divergent disciplines reveals the importance of both faith and facts to human well-being. **MUST SEE**

Dark City [1998]

Starring: Rufus Sewell, Kiefer Sutherland, Jennifer Connelly
Director: Alex Proyas Screenplay: Alex Proyas and Lem Dobbs and David S. Goyer Running Time: 1:43 Rated: R (Violence, nudity, profanity) Theatrical Aspect Ratio: 2.35:1

No movie can ever have too much atmosphere, and *Dark City* exudes it from every frame of celluloid. Alex Proyas' world isn't just a playground for his characters to romp in — it's an ominous place where viewers can get lost. We don't just coolly observe the bizarre, ever-changing skyline; we plunge into the city's benighted depths, following the protagonist as he explores the secrets of this grim place where the sun never shines. *Dark City* has as stunning a visual texture as that of any movie that I've seen. Visually, this film isn't just impressive, it's a tour de force.

Dark City opens by immersing the audience in the midst of a fractured, nightmarish narrative. The protagonist, who later learns that his name is John Murdoch (Rufus Sewell), has amnesia. He begins his "new life" as a full-grown adult naked in a bath tub, uncertain of how he got there. His only company in the grungy hotel suite is the nude body of a dead prostitute. Did he kill her or not? He doesn't know. Suddenly, Murdoch receives a phone call from someone named Dr. Schreber (Kiefer Sutherland), who claims to have his best interests at heart. Schreber warns him to get out of the hotel immediately. Soon, without a clue about his identity, Murdoch is fleeing from corpse-like creatures with incredible mental powers. But it turns out that Murdoch is not defenseless against his enemies — his mind, like theirs, can shape reality, although he doesn't understand how to harness his abilities. Soon, his quest to unearth his past links him up with Emma (Jennifer Connelly), a woman who is supposedly his wife, and Police Inspector Bumstead (William Hurt), who believes Murdoch to be innocent of the prostitute's murder. But Murdoch's small group of allies offer little help when it comes to dealing with his powerful, ghoulish adversaries, the amoral Mr. Book (Ian Richardson) and Mr. Hand (Richard O'Brien).

Thankfully, *Dark City* doesn't have an "all style, no substance" problem, because there's a mind-challenging story to go along with the eye candy. Proyas hasn't written this film for the passive viewer. To become involved in *Dark City*, thinking is mandatory. Unless you're puzzling out the answers alongside Murdoch, you're going to miss more than one revelation. Very little is spelled out in this movie; the answers are all there, but you have to recognize them for what they are. How often do we get features like this, that don't pander to the least common denominator? **HIGHLY RECOMMENDED**

Donnie Darko [2000]

Starring: Jake Gyllenhaal, Jena Malone, Drew Barrymore
Director: Richard Kelly Screenplay: Richard Kelly Running Time: 2:00
Rated: R (Profanity, drug use, violence) Theatrical Aspect Ratio: 2.35:1

Donnie Darko, the debut feature from writer/director Richard Kelly, is part psychological thriller and part science fiction mystery. The title character (Jake Gyllenhaal), a teenager in his last year of high school, is suffering from all manner of delusions and hallucinations. He sees and does the bidding of a 6-foot high rabbit wearing an insect mask, and, at times, appears completely dissociated from his surroundings. He is visiting a therapist and taking medication, but neither solution is working. Donnie is getting worse, but is it because he's descending deeper into a web of mental instability or because he's really seeing and experiencing these things? These are questions that the movie leaves unanswered until the end.

For much of the running length, *Donnie Darko* focuses more on Donnie's relationships with his sisters, parents, and girlfriend than on the science fiction aspects. This is meant to humanize a non-traditional protagonist and make him more "accessible" to viewers. It also allows the climax to have an emotional component (in addition to explaining the storyline's assorted, convoluted weirdness). *Donnie Darko* has a slow, methodical pace that allows the narrative to breathe; unfortunately, there are times when Kelly falls prey to the easy trap of self-indulgence. Selective edits would have made *Donnie Darko* tighter and more gripping, and, as a result, a better motion picture. As it is, there's a little too much redundancy in what's on screen.

One aspect of *Donnie Darko*'s production that's definitely worth mentioning is the special effects. The movie was made on the kind of low budget typically associated with independent films, yet the visual effects are first-rate. *Donnie Darko* proves that it's possible to do science fiction with visual effects in the independent film arena. This is just another area where the line between mainstream and indie movie-making has become increasingly blurred. Perhaps the only remaining difference is that smaller efforts like *Donnie Darko* use effects in service of an interesting story, while too many Hollywood productions think of the plot as a bothersome adjunct to their CGI eye candy. **RECOMMENDED**

E.T.: The Extra-Terrestrial [1982]

Starring: Dee Wallace, Henry Thomas, Peter Coyote Director: Steven Spielberg Screenplay: Melissa Mathison Running Time: 1:57 Rated: PG (Mature themes, mild profanity) Theatrical Aspect Ratio: 2.35:1

Steven Spielberg has always harbored a more benevolent view of space aliens than most of his Hollywood brethren. In *E.T.*, he postulates what might happen if a cute-but-strange-looking alien is marooned on Earth. "E.T.," as he is dubbed, chances upon a boy named Elliot (Henry Thomas). After their initial encounter, in which they frighten one another, they meet again, and form a tentative bond. Elliot invites E.T. into his house and hides him in his closet. He tells his older brother, Michael (Robert MacNaughton), and his younger sister, Gertie (Drew Barrymore), about his new friend. But, under the influence of Earth's unfamiliar climate, E.T. begins to show symptoms of a wasting sickness. Using household items, the strange little alien builds a communication device that allows him to "phone home" by sending a signal into space. Elliot's mother, Mary (Dee Wallace), learns about E.T. when government operatives, led by agent Keys (Peter Coyote), arrive at her house and place it under quarantine. But E.T. is dying, and Elliot, who is psychically bonded to him, is seriously ill.

E.T. is a tear-jerker and a feel-good experience rolled into one. It plays best to the child inside all of us, and is most effective when fitted into the family film niche. Members of the under-10 crowd are guaranteed to fall under its spell, but there's enough intelligence in the story (written by Melissa Mathison) to enchant adults, as well. Strip away 20 years of hype, all the hyperbole and overblown praise, and *E.T.* comes across as a very pleasant diversion, but little more. The movie has (perhaps unfairly) been saddled with the mantle of "masterpiece," a title for which it is ill-suited. *E.T.* earned its reputation by capturing the imagination of movie-going audiences across the nation and holding it for an entire summer. Parents could take children. Teenagers could take dates. And older viewers were pleased to find a movie with old-fashioned values. Over the years, *E.T.*'s strengths have been magnified and its weaknesses diminished. In its latest re-release, it will draw crowds for the same reasons it did in 1982 (in addition to the nostalgia factor).

Even considering its mawkish tendencies and unsubtle manipulation, *E.T.* represents effective storytelling. It's a fairy tale with a heart, an allegory whose themes of peace and anti-prejudice will not be lost on those who don't recognize the allusions. For those who have previously seen *E.T.*, this is a chance to recapture something. And for those who haven't, this is an opportunity to see a movie that, at its best, is almost as special as its reputation indicates. **RECOMMENDED**

Eternal Sunshine of the Spotless Mind [2004]

Starring: Jim Carrey, Kate Winslet, Kirsten Dunst, Tom Wilkinson, Elijah Wood, Mark Ruffalo Director: Michel Gondry Screenplay: Charlie Kaufman Running Time: 1:50 Rated: R (Profanity, sexual situations, drug use) Theatrical Aspect Ratio: 2.35:1

A unique romantic comedy, unfettered by the normal expectations of the genre, is a rare and wondrous thing. That's precisely what director Michel Gondry, working from a screenplay by Charlie Kaufman (*Being John Malkovich, Adapatation*), delivers. Without being too offbeat or esoteric, *Eternal Sunshine of the Spotless Mind* nevertheless manages to convey romance without forcing the mind to shift into neutral or dragging the characters through a formulaic structure where chemistry becomes the most important asset.

That's not to say that there's no nonverbal connection between stars Jim Carrey and Kate Winslet; merely that the success of *Eternal Sunshine of the Spotless Mind* does not rely upon it. The writing is strong enough and the approach embodies ample originality for the effectiveness of the interaction to serve as an enhancement. Plus, this isn't a romance in the traditional sense of boy meets girl, boy loses girl, boy gets back girl. It's more of a Woody Allen kind of love affair, where the trajectory from beginning to end is bumpy and unpaved.

Joel Barish (Carrey) is a meek, unassuming man who discovers his perfect other half in uninhibited Clementine Kruczynski (Winslet). Their relationship ignites quickly, but the things that initially draw them together become hurdles and barriers. In the end, Clementine decides that Joel is too boring for her, and Joel concludes that Clementine is too needy. The breakup is abrupt and painful — so painful, in fact, that Clementine seeks the services of Dr. Howard Mierzqwiak (Tom Wilkinson), a specialist in memory erasure. For a fee, he and his associates Stan (Mark Ruffalo) and Patrick (Elijah Wood) will eliminate all of an individual's memories of another person. Once Clementine has undergone this procedure to forget Joel, he decides to follow her lead. But his memory proves to be a tricky place, because the past images of Clementine refuse to be cleanly expunged.

The story is told nonchronologically, with many of the more imaginative sequences being set deep in Joel's mind as he invades his own memories to keep them from slipping away. Somewhere along the way, he realizes that many of his recollections are too precious to give up, but by that time, he is already committed. Meanwhile, as all of this is going on in Joel's head, we follow Clementine as she tries to adjust to her new life, and get to know the people who are working on Joel, including Howard, Stan, Patrick, and their receptionist/nurse, Mary (Kirsten Dunst).

Memory loss has become an increasingly fertile ground for movies to plow. By using a slightly different approach to the subject than those films (but still staying in the Twilight Zone), *Eternal Sunshine of the Spotless Mind* carves out its own niche. This is unlike any other film I have seen. And, although I value originality in motion pictures, the primary reason I'm recommending *Eternal Sunshine of the Spotless Mind* with so much enthusiasm is because it's a great romance. It's willingness to flout conventions and eschew formulas is just one of many things to celebrate about this charmingly eccentric movie.

HIGHLY RECOMMENDED

Galaxy Quest [1999]

Starring: Tim Allen, Sigourney Weaver, Alan Rickman, Tony Shalhoub
Director: Dean Parisot Screenplay: Robert Gordon, David Howard
Running Time: 1:42 Rated: PG (Mild violence) Theatrical Aspect
Ratio: 1.85:1

Since its cancellation in 1982, *Galaxy Quest* has developed a loyal and fanatical following. However, none of the actors who appeared in the series have gone on to greater glory. Instead, they continue to earn a living by taking bit parts and appearing in costume at *Galaxy Quest* conventions. Jason Nesmith (Tim Allen), who played Commander Peter Quincy Taggart, seems to enjoy being associated with his character, but his opinion is not shared by his fellow cast members. Gwen DeMarco (Sigourney Weaver), Fred Kwan (Tony Shalhoub), and Tommy Webber (Daryl Mitchell) regard their lot in life with resignation, but Alexander Dane (Alan Rickman), who played the alien Dr. Lazarus, is resentful. Then, during one *Galaxy Quest* convention, Nesmith is approached by a group of fans dressed up (or so he thinks) as aliens. Their leader, Mathesar (Enrico Colantoni), explains that his people, the Thermians, need Commander Taggart's help. In short order, thinking they're going to some sort of low-level acting gig, Nesmith and his fellow actors find themselves transported to a space ship where they are expected to dispatch an intergalactic tyrant. It seems that the Thermians have picked up the *Galaxy Quest* TV show broadcasts and have mistaken the program for a series of "historical documents." So, believing Nesmith to be Taggart, they expect him to save the day.

In terms of parodying all things *Star Trek*, *Galaxy Quest* is often inventive, hitting both obvious and not-so-obvious targets. Fandom receives the sharpest edge of director Dean Parisot's satirical blade, although he and his screenwriters (Robert

Gordon and David Howard) are never overtly vicious or cruel in their thrusts. What we see of the *Galaxy Quest* TV show looks an awful lot like *Star Trek* — right down to the indoor planet sets with styrofoam rocks. Taggart is a Kirk clone, and there's more than a passing likeness between Dr. Lazarus and Spock. The tempestuous relationships among the *Galaxy Quest* actors also recall those of the *Trek* cast members. Nesmith's colossal ego is undoubtedly supposed to echo the personality trait for which Shatner became best known after the original program went off the air.

Galaxy Quest has a good time playing with different aspects of science fiction in general, and *Star Trek* in particular. And, although it isn't necessary to come armed with an encyclopedic knowledge of the original *Star Trek* TV series to enjoy this movie, the better you know *Galaxy Quest*'s inspiration, the more you will get out of this picture. **RECOMMENDED**

Gattaca [1997]

Starring: **Ethan Hawke, Uma Thurman, Alan Arkin, Jude Law**
Director: **Andrew Niccol** Screenplay: **Andrew Niccol** Running
Time: **1:52** Rated: **PG-13** (Violence, mature themes, profanity)
Theatrical Aspect Ratio: **2.35:1**

Welcome to the 21st Century, an era when things aren't that much different, but people are. No longer is standard procreation the accepted way to reproduce. While it would be unreasonable to outlaw sex for the purpose of producing offspring, be aware than any children so conceived are almost certain to be "in-valids" — genetically imperfect and ill-suited to be productive members of society. There is a better, more rational way. Let science do a little tinkering with the DNA.

Andrew Niccol's oppressive future, which contains more than an element of Orwell's "Big Brother is watching" mentality, isn't just a clever backdrop against which to set a thriller. Instead, it's an integral part of the story. While it's true that there is a murder mystery, that's just a subplot. The main focus of *Gattaca* is the struggle of a genetically inferior man, Vincent Freeman (Ethan Hawke), to survive and prosper in a world where his kind is routinely discriminated against.

Shortly after they were married, Vincent's parents decided to start a family the old-fashioned way, without any help from doctors and test tubes. The result was a boy who was diagnosed as 99% likely to have a serious heart defect. That rendered Vincent ineligible for all but the most menial of jobs. But his dream was to one day work at The Gattaca Aerospace Corpora-

tion and participate in the first-ever manned flight to the moons of Saturn. For most "in-valids," this would have remained a fantasy, but Vincent possessed the determination and drive to make it real.

With the help of a shady middle-man, Vincent locates Jerome Morrow (Jude Law), a genetically superior individual who was paralyzed as the result of an accident. He agees to sell Vincent his identity (including blood and urine on demand, fingerprints, hair and other body debris, etc.). So, equipped with Jerome's genetic resume, which guarantees him work anywhere, Vincent applies for a position at Gattaca. He is accepted and quickly proves his worth to everyone. But, a week before he is to attain his lifelong ambition of making a space flight, he becomes a suspect in a murder investigation and his carefully-guarded secret is in danger of being exposed.

One of the things that impressed me the most about *Gattaca* is its ability to keep the level of tension high without compromising the script's intelligence or integrity. First-time director Andrew Niccol, a New Zealander working in Los Angeles, displays a sure hand in his execution of the material.
HIGHLY RECOMMENDED

Godzilla 2000 [Japan, 1999]

Starring: **Takehiro Murata, Naomi Nishida, Mayu Suzuki**
Director: **Takao Okawara** Screenplay: **Hiroshi Kashiwabara, Wataru
Mimura** Running Time: **1:37** Rated: **PG** (Monster movie violence, mild
profanity) Theatrical Aspect Ratio: **2.35:1** Dubbed into English

Godzilla 2000 represents Toho's attempt to reclaim their most durable, bankable product and re-package it for a new series of movies whose special effects are sporadically good enough to stand toe-to-toe with the American version. As is typical of a Godzilla movie, the plot is extremely silly, but one sort of has to take that as a given and sit back to enjoy the film on its own terms. Seen in that light, *Godzilla 2000* represents solid, campy, escapist entertainment.

The basic story will sound pretty familiar to those familiar with any of the other Godzilla movies. The Not-So-Jolly Green Giant (who actually seems a little shorter in this version than in his previous incarnations) goes on a rampage, gleefully stomping a Japanese city while humans try in vain to stop him. Meanwhile, an alien spacecraft has surfaced after an extended period under the sea. It eventually comes into contact with Godzilla, which results in a short-but-sweet battle sequence. Later, after a half hour's worth of Godzilla-less exposition and action scenes, the spacecraft metamorphoses into an ugly monster of about Godzilla's size and engages our hero in a no-holds-barred grudge match. In the end, when one character philosophically wonders about why Godzilla always seems to help humanity, his conclusion (the last line in the movie) is enough to send even the most dour viewer into paroxysms of laughter.

Godzilla 2000 uses the Godzilla formula effectively. The human beings are rather inconsequential, the dubbed, Americanized dialogue is frequently hilarious, the battle sequences are impressive, and the expository/character building sequences are kept to a minimum. Godzilla is more majestic than ever (although he's still a guy in a monster suit). In fact, his introductory scene, where he chomps on a ship then menaces a car in a tunnel, is handled impressively. The special effects are a leap forward for Toho. Although there are still some cheesy instances when it's obvious that models are being used, there are enough impressive moments to counterbalance the sillier ones. As for Godzilla himself, he is presented as more of the force of nature he represented in the first movie than the champion of Earth he eventually turned into. This Godzilla isn't out to save humanity; he's trying to ensure his own survival. If you have enjoyed any of the previous Godzilla outings, it's a pretty good bet that *Godzilla 2000* will be up your ally. If not, this is one big green lizard to avoid. RECOMMENDED

Harry Potter and the Sorcerer's Stone [United States/United Kingdom, 2001]

Starring: Daniel Radcliffe, Rupert Grint, Emma Watson, Richard Harris, Robbie Coltrane Director: Chris Columbus Screenplay: Steve Kloves, based on the novel by J.K. Rowling Running Time: 2:32 Rated: PG (Mild violence) Theatrical Aspect Ratio: 2.35:1

The movie opens in modern-day England, where 11-year-old Harry Potter (Daniel Radcliffe) dwells with his aunt, uncle, and cousin. Harry has lived with his mother's sister's family since shortly after birth, when his parents were murdered by the evil wizard Voldemort. On his birthday, Harry is visited by the imposing Rubeus Hagrid (Robbie Coltrane), who has come to bring Harry to Hogwarts School of Witchcraft and Wizardry, where he will study to fulfill his true calling as a wizard. Once at Hogwarts, he meets classmates who will become close friends, such as red-haired Ron Weasley (Rupert Grint) and bossy Hermione Granger (Emma Watson), and antagonists, such as the arrogant Draco Malfoy (Tom Felton). Then there's the headmaster of Hogwarts, the venerable wizard Albus Dumbledore (Richard Harris), and his staff —

Professor Minerva McGonagall (Maggie Smith), who teaches Transfiguration; Professor Quirrell (Ian Hart), whose course is Defense Against the Dark Arts; Professor Flitwick (Warwick Davis), who teaches Charms; and Professor Snape (Alan Rickman), master of Potions. For Harry, however, there's more to attending Hogwarts than studying, as he begins to suspect one of the teachers of being in league with a dark force lurking in the forest.

Harry Potter and the Sorcerer's Stone is a rigorously faithful adaptation of the novel. With the exception of occasional details, short scenes, and a poltergeist, everything in the book is in the movie. For Harry Potter fans looking to see how their favorite scene appears on screen, this is a boon. But there's something almost workmanlike about Columbus' approach to the project. Movies and books are different media, and the best approach for adapting the latter into the former is not always an unvarnished translation. Columbus doesn't use any imagination beyond that which J.K. Rowling previously supplied for her book. There's no denying that the film is diverting, but it isn't *inspired*.

Harry Potter and the Sorcerer's Stone delivers as promised — a herd of colorful characters, fast-paced, inventive adventure, liberal doses of comedy, and even a little pathos. The film runs 2½ hours, but doesn't seem that long, and all but the youngest children should be able to sit through it without becoming restless. Just as the Harry Potter books have reached a wide audience, so too does the movie appeal to audience members of all ages. The film's spell may not be as potent as that of the book, but there's still some magic in what Columbus and his crew have wrought. RECOMMENDED

Harry Potter and the Chamber of Secrets
[United States/United Kingdom, 2002]

Starring: Daniel Radcliffe, Rupert Grint, Emma Watson, Richard Harris, Kenneth Branagh Director: Chris Columbus Screenplay: Steve Kloves, based on the novel by J.K. Rowling Running Time: 2:41 Rated: PG (Mild violence) Theatrical Aspect Ratio: 2.35:1

Harry Potter and the Chamber of Secrets opens up with Harry (Daniel Radcliffe) joining his friends, Hermione (Emma Watson) and Ron (Rupert Grint), and his nemesis, Draco (Tom Felton), as they prepare to begin their sophomore year at Hogwarts School for Witchcraft and Wizardry. Many of the old professors and administrators are back, including headmaster Albus Dumbledore (Richard Harris in his final role), the strict Professor McGonagall (Maggie Smith), and the dark, unwelcoming Professor Snape (Alan Rickman). There's also a newcomer — the charismatic, self-absorbed Gilderoy Lockhart (Kenneth Branagh), who is more concerned with answering fan mail than teaching how to defend against the dark arts. But all is not well at Hogwarts. A dark plot is brewing, with someone planning to break into the legendary "Chamber of Secrets" and unleash a monster that can petrify or kill with a look. It's up to Harry and his two friends to uncover the individual behind the plot and foil him or her before Hogwarts is closed.

All of the true inspiration underlying *Harry Potter and the Chamber of Secrets* lies in J.K. Rowling's writing. The Harry Potter books don't break new barriers, but they mix long-accepted fantasy formulas into a mélange that is fresh, easygoing, and infectious. Some of that comes across in the movies, but there are times when director Chris Columbus' pedestrian filmmaking lacks the spark that would truly ignite a movie. Columbus doesn't take a single chance. As a result, there are times when *Harry Potter and the Chamber of Secrets* seems more like a pre-packaged product than a living, breathing motion picture. It satisfies, but does not overwhelm.

The film's high octane second half is vastly better than the fitfully entertaining opening 75 minutes. All of the memorable scenes occur late in the movie, including an amazingly realized sequence featuring a bunch of large, unfriendly spiders and an equally eye-popping battle with a giant snake. As a companion piece to *Harry Potter and the Sorcerer's Stone*, *Harry Potter and the Chamber of Secrets* makes for effective viewing. The second film may be a little darker than the first, but the two pictures mesh perfectly — not surprising, considering that many of the same people were responsible for both. **RECOMMENDED**

Harry Potter and the Prisoner of Azkaban [2004]

Starring: Daniel Radcliffe, Rupert Grint, Emma Watson, Michael Gambon, Maggie Smith, Robbie Coltrane, David Thewlis, Alan Rickman, Gary Oldman, Emma Thompson, Tom Felton Director: Alfonso Cuarón Screenplay: Steve Kloves, based on the novel by J. K. Rowling Running Time: 2:22 Rated: PG (Scary images) Theatrical Aspect Ratio: 2.35:1

Although *Harry Potter and the Prisoner of Azkaban* stands well enough on its own, it has a "middle chapter" feeling. In other words, there's no real beginning or ending. Little is resolved, and the film's climax is low-key. The villain of the first two chapters and the

overall series, the dreaded Voldemort, is absent. His apparent replacement is Sirius Black (Gary Oldman), although appearances can be deceiving. All of this doesn't make *The Prisoner of Azkaban* inferior to its predecessors. The appeal is much the same, but the "feel" is a little different. The tone is darker and more claustrophobic.

If there's a theme to *The Prisoner of Azkaban*, it's "something wicked this way comes." Those lyrics rattle around in the brain even before they make an explicit appearance. There are plenty of candidates for who can fill the "wicked" role: the convicted killer Sirius Black, who apparently is determined to eliminate Harry Potter (Daniel Radcliffe); the vile Dementors, who are pursuing Black and look like Ghosts of Christmas Future; nasty Draco Malfoy (Tom Felton), the school bully; or Professor Snape (Alan Rickman), who dresses in black and sneers most wonderfully. For Harry, now in his third year at Hogwarts School for Witchcraft and Wizardry, it becomes increasingly difficult to tell friend from foe. While there are no questions about his best pals Ron (Rupert Grint) and Hermione (Emma Watson), or about Headmaster Dumbledore (Michael Gambon), what about the secretive new professor, Lupin (David Thewlis)? Or Sybil Trelawney (Emma Thomspon), who sees ominous things in crystal balls? For Harry, surviving his encounters with Sirius Black and the Dementors means unraveling the truth about whose betrayal of his parents led to their deaths.

There's no question that director Alfonso Cuarón has put his stamp on this movie. The return of so many familiar characters will keep viewers comfortable, but the stylistic changes make it seem as if this Harry Potter adventure is taking place in a different universe. The most obvious change is to Hogwarts. Although outwardly the same, the school is photographed and presented in a manner that makes it more ominous and less friendly than in the previous two installments.

The recent bankability of fantasy has resulted in a large number of copycat possibilities entering the production pipeline. With both *The Lord of the Rings* and the Harry Potter movies proving to be solid box office performers, there's little question that the genre is here to stay. Although Tolkien's story is done, J. K. Rowling's has at least four more installments to go (the final two of which haven't even been published). If the filmmakers continue to keep the quality level high, there will be plenty of pleasurable hours ahead. *Harry Potter and the Prisoner of Azkaban* proves that a new director with a different perspective can freshen a series that could otherwise resort to stale repetition.

RECOMMENDED

I, Robot [2004]

Starring: Will Smith, Bridget Moynahan, Alan Tudyk, James Cromwell, Bruce Greenwood, Adrian L. Ricard, Chi McBride Director: Alex Proyas Screenplay: Jeff Vintar and Akiva Goldsman, suggested by the book by Isaac Asimov Running Time: 1:55 Rated: PG-13 (Violence, profanity, brief nudity) Theatrical Aspect Ratio: 2.35:1

Directed by Alex Proyas — who previously imagined the strikingly noir cityscapes of *The Crow* and *Dark City* — *I, Robot* takes ideas (and a character) presented in Isaac Asimov's classic anthology of nine short stories and uses them as a jumping-off point for a thrilling action-adventure movie. Proper recognition goes to credited screenwriters Jeff Vintar and Akiva Goldsman (and uncredited Hillary Seitz) for remaining faithful to the essential themes of Asimov's writing while taking the story in a different, more cinematic direction. Asimov fans take note, however: This isn't close to a faithful adaptation. In fact, it's not really an adaptation at all.

I, Robot transpires some 30 years in the future, when robots are becoming as familiar an everyday household appliance as refrigerators or vacuum cleaners. But, on the eve of the rollout of the landmark NS5 series, trouble is brewing at U.S. Robotics. Dr. Alfred Lanning (James Cromwell), the head of robot and cybernetic research, has apparently committed suicide. Technophobe cop Del Spooner (Will Smith) has been called in to investigate, and his first suspicion is that Dr. Lanning didn't kill himself — a robot did it. His prime suspect is Sonny (Alan Tudyk), a robot with personality and who seems to have found a way around the Three Laws of Robotics. Dr. Susan Calvin (Bridget Moynahan), a robopsychologist who works for U.S. Robotics, and CEO Lawrence Robertson (Bruce Greenwood) are suspicious of Spooner's motives for blaming a robot and skeptical of his conclusions. But that doesn't stop Dr. Calvin from aiding the detective's investigation and Robertson, who has a lot of money on the line, from pulling out all the stops to end it.

The film's action sequences, which include chases and fights, are anything but generic. They are directed with flair, and that results in them being both tense and involving. The way the robots swarm after Spooner during one of *I, Robot*'s centerpiece scenes is reminiscent of the aliens' attack patterns in James Cameron's *Aliens*. The film carries a sense of the unpredictable; we're never sure exactly what's going to happen next, and there's no assurance that Spooner will be alive when the end-credits roll. These elements, not flashes and bangs, are what make action films suspenseful.

I, Robot tinkers with ideas that have always fascinated science fiction fans. At what point does a personality simulation become a personality? Where is the line that divides a machine from a living being? When does consciousness occur? And at what point does an entity achieve the ability to interpret the Three Laws as it sees fit, not as they were intended? There's plenty of thought-provoking material in *I, Robot* — certainly enough to keep a thinking viewer attuned to the plot while never slowing down the proceedings or dulling the action. *I, Robot* deserves to be called "smart." It earns that distinction during nearly every frame of its 115-minute running time.

HIGHLY RECOMMENDED

Jurassic Park [1993]

Starring: Sam Neill, Jeff Goldblum, Richard Attenborough, Laura Dern Director: Steven Spielberg Screenplay: Michael Crichton and David Koepp based on the book by Michael Crichton Running Time: 2:06 Rated: PG-13 (Violence) Theatrical Aspect Ratio: 1.85:1

On a small island off the coast of Costa Rica exists a most unusual animal preserve by the name of Jurassic Park. Operated by dinosaur lover John Hammond (Richard Attenborough), Jurassic Park is the first of its kind. Its population of creatures includes brachiosaurs, dilophosaurs, triceratops, velociraptors, and a Tyrannosaurus Rex, each of which has been cloned using the latest technology that takes DNA from dinosaur-biting prehistoric insects preserved in amber, and uses that DNA for the re-creation. When the consortium funding Jurassic Park become concerned that all is not as it should be, Hammond is forced to call in 3 experts: paleontologist Dr. Alan Grant (Sam Neill), his partner, paleo-botanist Dr. Ellie Sattler (Laura Dern), and the brilliant-but-cynical mathematician Dr. Ian Malcolm (Jeff Goldblum). When the trio arrives at Jurassic Park, they are astonished by what it represents. It doesn't take long, however, for astonishment to turn to horror.

The apparent realism of some of Crichton's pseudo-science imbues *Jurassic Park* with a grounding that is acceptable in our high-tech world. After all, to weave a dinosaur fable in this day and age, it helps if science, not fantasy, is the driving force. Of course, the special effects help immensely. They are so good, in fact, and the dinosaurs look so real, that I half expected to see "dinosaur trainer" during the closing credits. Instead, however, plaudits go to the creators of *Jurassic Park*'s primary screen presences (all apologies to the actors).

I doubt there are many who will go to *Jurassic Park* for its characters or story. Rightly so, viewers will see this movie so they can ooh and aah, jump in their seats, and root for the overmatched humans against the big, bad dinosaurs. Even those familiar with the written work can't help being drawn in to the pulse-pounding exhilaration of the chase as the Tyrannosaurus menaces two powerless electric cars and the trapped humans inside. In the end, *Jurassic Park* succeeds because it's good entertainment. **RECOMMENDED**

Jurassic Park: The Lost World [1997]
Starring: **Jeff Goldblum, Julianne Moore, Vince Vaughn**
Director: **Steven Spielberg** Screenplay: **David Koepp** based on the novel by **Michael Crichton** Running Time: **2:13** Rated: **PG-13** (Violence)
Theatrical Aspect Ratio: **1.85:1**

Like its predecessor, *The Lost World* is basically a big-budget monster movie of the sort that has been popular ever since the dawn of motion pictures. Unfortunately, like many entries into the genre, it falls into expected patterns. As a result, much of this movie seems like a retread of *Jurassic Park* (with a little *King Kong* thrown in at the end), not because director Steven Spielberg is intentionally copying himself, but because there's really not much more that he can do with the premise. If there's a third movie in the series, it will probably follow pretty much the same storyline as the first and second installments.

Returning from the first film is Jeff Goldblum as Dr. Ian Malcolm, a mathematician with an analytical mind and a wry sense of humor. This time, he has an adolescent daughter, Kelly (Vanessa Lee Chester), and a paleontologist girlfriend, Sarah Harding (Julianne Moore). Ian gets pulled back into the dinosaur game when Sarah joins an expedition to the island of Isla Sorna, which is populated by a wide variety of genetically-engineered extinct species. John Hammond (Richard Attenborough), older and wiser after his *Jurassic Park* experience, no longer intends to open an amusement park; he simply wants to study dinosaurs in a natural environment. So, a reluctant Ian, along with Sarah, a nature photographer named Nick Van Owen (Vince Vaughn), and a gadgets expert, Eddie Carr (Richard Schiff), begins a "look-but-don't-touch" foray. Little do they know, however, that Hammond's nephew (Arliss Howard) is on his way to the island with far less benevolent intentions. He wants to bring dinosaurs back to San Diego for a prehistoric zoo. Accompanying him is big game hunter Roland Tembo (Pete Postlethwaite), whose goal is to bag a male T-Rex.

The differences between *Jurassic Park* and *The Lost World* can be summed up relatively simply: more dinosaurs, fewer legitimate thrills. Although *The Lost World* has its share of problems, chief of which is the familiarity factor, it still offers a couple hours of glitzy, hi-tech fun. And that's just about all that anyone can reasonably expect from this kind of blockbuster.
RECOMMENDED

The Lord of the Rings: The Fellowship of the Ring
[New Zealand/United States, 2001]
Starring: **Elijah Wood, Ian McKellen, Viggo Mortensen, Sean Astin**
Director: **Peter Jackson** Screenplay: **Fran Walsh & Philippa Boyens & Peter Jackson**, based on the novel by **J.R.R. Tolkien** Running Time: **2:58**
Rated: **PG-13** (Violence, mature themes) Theatrical Aspect Ratio: **2.35:1**

The Fellowship of the Ring begins in the quiet countryside of the Shire, where Bilbo Baggins of Bag End (Ian Holm), a hobbit, is celebrating his 111th birthday. In attendance, among other people, are Bilbo's young heir, Frodo (Elijah Wood), and the wizard Gandalf (Ian McKellan). Gandalf informs Bilbo that the time has come for him to leave Bag End and go on a journey. To Frodo, he leaves his home and his most beloved possession, a magical ring that turns the wearer invisible. But this isn't just any magical ring — it is the One Ring, forged by the Dark Lord, Sauron, and capable of corrupting the wearer. Sauron's servants, the Ring Wraiths, are scouring Middle Earth for it, since, when it is returned to their master, nothing will be able to stop him. All of the world is about to be plunged into war, and the only way to stop the evil will be to destroy the ring by casting it into the fire where it was forged — in Mordor, on the Dark Lord's doorstep. That unenviable task falls to Frodo, the ring bearer.

Frodo starts his journey in the company of 3 other hobbits — his faithful servant, Sam (Sean Astin), and his cousins, Merry (Dominic Monaghan) and Pippin (Billy Boyd). Later, as the dangers mount and Frodo faces even greater challenges, others join his company: the humans Aragorn (Viggo Mortensen) and Boromir (Sean Bean), the wizard Gandalf, the elf

Legolas (Orlando Bloom), and the dwarf Gimli (John Rhys-Davies). Together, these 9 individuals must face Ring Wraiths, orcs, and worse; travel through strange lands and the dreaded mines of Moria; and face mistrust within their fellowship. And this is all just the first of 3 cinematic chapters . . .

Lord of the Rings devotees will be delighted to learn that the motion picture adaptation is as faithful as one could imagine possible. Jackson and his co-screenwriters (Fran Walsh & Philippa Boyens) do an excellent job condensing more than 500 pages of text into a script that never feels choppy, uneven, or rushed. *The Fellowship of the Ring* moves fluidly and, in the process, exhilarates. Certain scenes have been cut or condensed in the name of pacing, and the role of one character (Arwen) has been expanded to enhance a romantic angle, something that was largely absent from Tolkien's work.

First and foremost, *The Lord of the Rings* is an adventure, and, in that, it is relentlessly successful. One does not need to have read the books to appreciate the movie. The background is explained concisely in a voiceover prologue, and the action proceeds in a straightforward manner. As long as one enjoys a well-crafted adventure yarn set against the backdrop of a mythical clash between good and evil, *The Lord of the Rings* will satisfy. At last, someone has figured out how to do an epic fantasy justice on the big screen. **MUST SEE**

The Lord of the Rings: The Two Towers [United States/New Zealand, 2002]

Starring: Elijah Wood, Ian McKellen, Viggo Mortensen, Sean Astin
Director: Peter Jackson Screenplay: Fran Walsh & Philippa Boyens & Stephen Sinclair & Peter Jackson, based on the novel by J.R.R. Tolkien Running Time: 2:59 Rated: PG-13 (Violence, mature themes) Theatrical Aspect Ratio: 2.35:1

In nearly every way that counts, *The Two Towers* is *The Fellowship of the Ring*'s equal. In terms of tone, pacing, character development, plot advancement, and visual splendor, there is no drop-off. More importantly, the continuity is seamless, allowing a viewer familiar with the first movie to flow effortlessly into the second. Of course, therein lies a drawback, as well. *The Two Towers* cannot stand on its own. Familiarity with *The Fellowship of the Ring* is not just advisable, it is mandatory.

The Two Towers essentially picks up where *The Fellowship of the Ring* concludes, albeit following a short flashback to the battle between the wizard Gandalf (Ian McKellan) and the Balrog. In the wake of his victory over his foe, Gandalf is reborn as a white wizard, and returns to the world above to re-unite with his former companions. In the company of Aragorn (Viggo Mortensen), Legolas the elf (Orlando Bloom), and Gimli the dwarf (John Rhys-Davies), the wizard heads for the city of Rohan, where he hopes to convince the king, Theoden (Bernard Hill), that war is upon his kingdom. At the same time, the hobbits Merry (Dominic Monaghan) and Pippin (Billy Boyd), having escaped from their orc captors, flee into the forbidding Fanghorn Forest, where they encounter Treebeard the Ent (voice of John Rhys-Davies).

Meanwhile, to the East, Frodo (Elijah Wood) and Sam (Sean Astin) find themselves lost on their way to Mount Doom. And, in addition to suffering from the physical difficulties of such an arduous journey, Frodo is beginning to show the strain of bearing the ring, with the Dark Lord Sauron's baleful glare constantly seeking him. The creature Gollum (Andy Serkis), who has been following the hobbits, attempts to steal the ring from Frodo, but is subdued and captured. Thereafter, he reluctantly agrees to serve as Frodo and Sam's guide and take them to Mordor.

The stunning climax of *The Two Towers* is the battle of Helm's Deep — a 30-minute spectacle that features the siege of a seemingly impregnable stone fortress by an army of 10,000 creatures of Sauruman (Christopher Lee). Inside that fortress is a small force of several hundred humans and elves, led by Aragorn, Theoden, Legolas, and Gimli. While a huge special effects contribution is needed to make the battle such an awesome feast for the eyes, Jackson never lets the CGI work overwhelm the human element of what's going on.

The Two Towers starts out a little slowly, but the rousing second half, which gathers momentum like a boulder racing downhill, will leave audiences craving more when the end credits roll. Combined, *The Fellowship of the Ring* and *The Two Towers* represent one of the most engrossing and engaging six-hour segments of cinema I have ever enjoyed. Like its predecessor, *The Two Towers* is a great motion picture, and not to be missed by anyone who appreciates fantasy adventure. **MUST SEE**

The Lord of the Rings: The Return of the King [New Zealand/USA, 2003]

Starring: Elijah Wood, Ian McKellen, Viggo Mortensen, Sean Astin, John Rhys-Davies, Billy Boyd, Dominic Monaghan, Orlando Bloom, Miranda Otto, Bernard Hill, Andy Serkis, John Noble, Liv Tyler Director: Peter Jackson Screenplay: Fran Walsh & Philippa Boyens & Peter Jackson, based on the novel by J.R.R. Tolkien Running Time: 3:21 Rated: PG-13 (Violence, mature themes) Theatrical Aspect Ratio: 2.35:1

The Return of the King opens where *The Two Towers* ended, with hobbits Frodo (Elijah Wood) and Sam (Sean Astin), and the creature Gollum (Andy Serkis) approaching the dark land of Mordor. Meanwhile, the company of Gandalf the wizard (Ian McKellan), Aragorn the ranger (Viggo Mortensen), Legolas the elf (Orlando Bloom), and Gimli the dwarf (John Rhys-Davies) reunite with their hobbit friends Pippin (Billy Boyd) and Merry (Dominic Monaghan) in the wake of the battle of Isengard. From there, the film follows two branches. The first tracks Frodo's progress as the increasingly haunted and weary ringbearer attempts to make his way to Mount Doom. Along the way he is burdened by betrayal and paranoia, and must face a deadly giant spider called Shelob. Meanwhile, Gandalf and Pippin head to the city of Minas Tirith to warn them against a coming invasion, while Aragorn prepares to announce himself as Iseldur's heir, the returned king of Gondor.

The slowest portions of *The Return of the King* occur early in the proceedings, as director Peter Jackson re-establishes the characters. From there, it's a slow, steady buildup to a rousing climax. The experience is so immersive that I found myself in the middle of the Battle of the Pelennor Fields along with the heroes, rooting for them — even though I knew how things were going to turn out! Along the way there are moments of genuine pathos that draw a tear from the eye; times of triumph that cause the heart to soar; instances of overwhelming tension that cause the adrenaline to surge; and images of spectacle that make the jaw drop. The pace is unflagging — once Jackson has us, he doesn't let go. When the movie was over, I couldn't believe that 3¾ hours had passed. Although it's unfair to characterize the film as a collection of great moments — the character arcs and overall narrative are too strong for that — it is nevertheless impossible to deny the power of many individual scenes. One of Jackson's most notable contributions is that he directs the film with the intention that certain instances will raise nape hairs. It's the "wow" factor, and it is frequently repeated. Expectedly, the special effects set a new standard. The CGI participants of the major battles look more like real combatants than cartoonish computer creations. The locations, set design, and costumes are without flaw. By building many of the elaborate locales, Jackson achieves a sense of verisimilitude that he might not have attained by relying more heavily on computers. And composer Howard Shore's score is perfectly wed to the visuals, being alternately bombastic and delicate, as circumstances dictate.

The Lord of the Rings will go down in cinematic lore as a milestone. It has legitimatized fantasy like no other production and has shown that it is possible for studio executives to realize huge gains when taking huge risks. History will show the importance of *The Lord of the Rings*. The present illustrates its broad appeal and undeniable critical and commercial success. This is one time when the product is good enough to weather the storm of hype. This ring is golden. MUST SEE

The Matrix [1999]

Starring: Keanu Reeves, Laurence Fishburne, Carrie-Anne Moss, Joe Pantoliano, Hugo Weaving Directors: Andy Wachowski, Larry Wachowski Screenplay: Andy Wachowski, Larry Wachowski Running Time: 2:15 Rated: R (Violence) Theatrical Aspect Ratio: 2.35:1

Thomas Anderson (Keanu Reeves) is leading a double life. To most people, he's a hard-working computer programmer who holds down a 9-to-5 job for a major software corporation. But, in the privacy of his home, he's a hacker named Neo who is "guilty of virtually every computer crime [there's] a law for." Neo is dissatisfied with his existence, and, while he's groping for a meaning to it, he is contacted by a mysterious computer presence known as Morpheus. "Wake up Neo," a printout on his monitor screen reads. "The Matrix has you. Follow the white rabbit." And so begins an amazing odyssey for both Neo and the audience.

It turns out that Morpheus (Laurence Fishburne) is the captain of a small space ship, and he believes that Neo is a messianic figure. When the two finally meet, Morpheus explains to Neo that all is not as it seems. The reality he is used to is a fabrication, the product of a sinister race of intelligent machines that use human beings as power supplies, to be discarded at will. Neo is dubious, and Morpheus sets out to show him the truth. Soon, he is learning how to manipulate the Matrix: a computer-generated dreamworld built by the machines to control human minds. But danger lurks ahead for Morpheus and his small band of followers. The goal of the machines is to eliminate all free humans, and their most powerful weapons, the Sentient Agents (who look like Men in Black), are closing in. Led by Agent Smith (Hugo Weaving), their goal is to capture Morpheus and pry the secrets from his brain.

The Matrix offers a little something for everyone. The die-hard science fiction fan will discover a plot that mixes and matches both new and old conventions of the genre in a compelling fashion. Action aficionados will find that there's no shortage of electric excitement, whether it's in the form of hand-to-hand kung fu-type fights or shoot-outs with seemingly limitless ammunition. There's also betrayal, a little romance, some humor, and a moral dilemma or two, all wrapped into a well-produced package. The way in which the Wachowskis choose to resolve everything seems slightly contrived, but, in the overall scheme of things, that's a small price to pay for one of the most enjoyable science fiction thrillers to reach the screen in months. **HIGHLY RECOMMENDED**

Men in Black [1997]

Starring: Tommy Lee Jones, Will Smith, Linda Fiorentino
Director: Barry Sonnenfeld Screenplay: Ed Solomon based on the
comic book by Lowell Cunningham Running Time: 1:35 Rated: PG-13
(Violence, profanity) Theatrical Aspect Ratio: 1.85:1

As Jay, Will Smith is the latest recruit of the ultra-secret sixth division of the INS (the "Men in Black" of the title) — a group of government workers in charge of licensing and regulating the presence of non-Earth-born aliens. His partner, Kay (Tommy Lee Jones), is a venerable agent who knows the ropes and is willing to give lessons. Together, the pair go in search of an intergalactic assassin (played in human form by Vincent D'Onofrio) whose unauthorized activities on Earth could result in the planet's destruction.

Men in Black is a snappy, clever, often-funny motion picture that provides the perfect blend of science fiction-style action with comic dialogue. The screenplay, credited to Ed Solomon (and based on the Marvel comic book by Lowell Cunningham) has a sly, sophisticated edge that many blockbuster scripts lack. Sonnenfeld's direction is crisp and the editing is tight, resulting in a film that clocks in at a mere 95 minutes, which proves to be a nearly-perfect length.

The chief pleasure of *Men in Black* isn't being dazzled by the special effects, but enjoying the deadpan performances of Tommy Lee Jones (whose offhand attitude towards the most bizarre events would make Jack Webb proud) and Will Smith. This is a rare case when the multi-million dollar, computer-generated creatures don't upstage their real-life co-stars. Smith and Jones are a fine pair, and the film's focus on them never wavers.

Men in Black is an outright comedy, not a pastiche of worn sci-fi/adventure elements, and there's no big space battle to be found. In fact, from the opening credits to the closing ones, our heroes stay firmly rooted on terra firma. Those accepting *Men in Black*

for what it is will likely agree that this is a satisfying big-budget offering. **RECOMMENDED**

A Midsummer Night's Dream [1999]

Starring: Kevin Kline, Michelle Pfeiffer, Rupert Everett, Stanley Tucci
Director: Michael Hoffman Screenplay: Michael Hoffman, based on the
play by William Shakespeare Running Time: 1:58 Rated: PG-13
(Sensuality, nudity) Theatrical Aspect Ratio: 2.35:1

A Midsummer Night's Dream is arguably the best loved and most frequently performed of Shakespeare's comedies. The text shows its great versatility with each new interpretation — depending on the director's vision, *A Midsummer Night's Dream* can be a light fantasy, a dark nightmare, a slapstick comedy, or a semi-serious melodrama. One might understandably wonder whether there's a pressing reason for a new motion picture version. But director Michael Hoffman deflects such criticism by presenting a rendering that is sufficiently contemporary and fresh.

Hoffman has elected to shift the setting from 16th century Greece to Tuscany in the late 1800s. The bicycle — a relatively new invention at the time — becomes a key prop, allowing characters to pedal after each other instead of chasing around on foot. Understandably, the basic story has not changed, even though the locale and time period have. *A Midsummer Night's Dream* opens by introducing Duke Theseus (David Strathairn), who is preparing for his wedding to the reluctant Hippolyta (Sophie Marceau). Theseus is called in to resolve a dispute centering on the romantic inclinations of Hermia (Anna Friel), the daughter of Egeus (Bernard Hill). While the girl wants to marry the dashing Lysander (Dominic West), whom she loves, her father has betrothed her to Demetrius (Christian Bale). When Theseus' ruling goes against them, Hermia and Lysander resolve to elope. Meanwhile, Demetrius is being pursued by Helena (Calista Flockhart), who is willing to suffer any number of humiliations to be with him. These four, along with an actor named Bottom (Kevin Kline), end up in a nearby forest on a night when the nymphs, satyrs, and fairies are out and about. The King of the Fairies, Oberon (Rupert Everett), is quarrelling with his queen, Titania (Michelle Pfeiffer). To untangle matters, Oberon enlists his servant, Puck, to procure a love potion, of which he says, "The juice of it on sleeping eyelids laid will make or man or woman madly dote upon the next live creature that it sees." However, not everything goes according to plan, resulting in some unexpected romantic pairings.

Although set design and atmosphere are critical to Hoffman's vision of the play (and represent the primary cues by which this version can be differentiated from its predecessors), Shakespeare's text still lies at the movie's heart. In a fantasy setting such as this, the flowery language works exceptionally well. This thoroughly enjoyable piece of cinema does credit to its director, cast, and writer. **HIGHLY RECOMMENDED**

Mighty Joe Young [1998]

Starring: Charlize Theron, Bill Paxton, Rade Sherbedgia, Peter Firth Director: Ron Underwood Screenplay: Mark Rosenthal & Lawrence Konner Running Time: 1:50 Rated: PG (Violence, mild profanity) Theatrical Aspect Ratio: 1.85:1

Mighty Joe Young begins in Africa during the mid-1980s, when Jill Young (Mika Boorem) loses her mother (Linda Purl) to a gunshot fired by a ruthless big-game hunter, Strasser (Rade Sherbedgia). Strasser is a major player in the black market selling of endangered species, and he has come to Jill's part of Africa in search of new inventory. Another of his bullets finds a female gorilla, the mother of Jill's simian friend, Joe. Bonded by their mutual orphanage, the two become inseparable as they grow up together. But Joe is no ordinary gorilla — by the time he reaches adulthood, he's 15 feet tall and weighs 2000 pounds.

The next time we meet Joe and Jill (now played by Charlize Theron), it's 12 years later. Poachers are threatening Joe's existence and Gregg O'Hara (Bill Paxton), an adventurous zoologist who works for the California Animal Conservatory, has arrived with an offer of sanctuary for Joe if Jill is willing to bring him to a preserve in America. Reluctantly, she agrees. Soon, Joe is acclimating to his new home, but all is not well. The Conservatory, anxious to use their new attraction as a fund-raising tool, has put Joe in the media spotlight, and Strasser is eager to capture him. Eventually and inevitably, Joe escapes from the preserve and begins romping around Hollywood.

Plot-wise, there's not much going on here. *Mighty Joe Young* is like a low-rent *King Kong* with a little more emphasis on the humanity of the primate. In fact, a great deal of effort is undertaken to make Joe a likable character — he is shown to be intelligent, childlike, and gentle (except when provoked). Although Joe's size makes him a monster, his disposition makes him cuddly. The movie contains elements of comedy and romance (between Gregg and Jill, although Joe is jealous), but the silliest aspects of the original 1949 film have been eliminated. Despite not being daring in style or story, *Mighty Joe Young* is nevertheless a charming and enjoyable adventure, and a rare remake that's better than the original. **RECOMMENDED**

Minority Report [2002]

Starring: Tom Cruise, Max von Sydow, Colin Farrell, Samantha Morton Director: Steven Spielberg Screenplay: Scott Frank and Jon Cohen, based on the short story by Philip K. Dick Running Time: 2:31 Rated: PG-13 (Violence, mature themes, drug use) Theatrical Aspect Ratio: 2.35:1

For those that must classify *Minority Report*, the primary category is science fiction. But *Minority Report* can also be viewed as an action thriller or a futuristic film noir. It owes a debt to Dashiel Hammitt and Raymond Chandler. And *Minority Report* plays like a different film to different audiences. Those in the mood for the action and adrenaline rush will find something to their taste here. Yet there are richer rewards for viewers who are willing to engage their brains. Anyone who wants to think through the mysteries and paradoxes presented herein will discover a multi-course cinematic buffet that can keep the gray matter occupied for days to come.

The year is 2054. Washington D.C., once the murder capital of the union, is now the safest place to live — thanks in large part to the Department of Pre-Crime, an elite taskforce of law officers who, by using the predictive capabilities of 3 captive "precogs," know that a murder is going to happen before it takes place. Armed with that knowledge, they can arrest someone before he actually kills, saving the victim(s) and preventing the crime. The head of the Department is Director Burgess (Max von Sydow), a dispassionate man who has shepherded the group through eight years of growing pains and is now on the verge of losing control of it as the program goes national. His right hand man, Detective John Anderton (Tom Cruise), is in an equally precarious position.

The first part of the movie introduces us to the Pre-Crime squad and shows how they operate by illustrating their attempts to solve Case #1108 — a crime of passion in which a man discovers his wife's infidelity and kills both her and her lover. Once that is successfully wrapped up, *Minority Report* moves on to Case #1109 — the pre-meditated murder of a man by none other than Anderton. Within moments of recognizing that he has run afoul of the system he works for, Anderton is in full flight, certain that he is being set up by Detective Ed Witwer (Colin Farrell), a federal agent who is after his job. Anderton's belief in his own innocence is so strong that he even risks breaking into the Pre-Crime building and kidnapping Agatha (Samantha Morton), the most gifted of the 3 Precogs. He suspects that, with her help, he can clear himself.

Predestination or free will? It's a question that has obsessed philosophers and religious scholars throughout the years. Now, it is the underlying subject material of a major motion picture made not for deep thinkers but for a mass audience. Action fans have plenty to engage their attention. *Minority Report* features its share of shoot-outs, fights, and chase scenes, some of which are quite spectacular. And the special effects serve the ingenuity of the script, not the other way around. These days, many blockbusters offer eye candy without substance. Not so in here, where both are available in equal proportions. **MUST SEE**

Pitch Black [2000]

Starring: Vin Diesel, Radha Mitchell, Cole Hauser, Keith David
Director: David Twohy Screenplay: Jim Wheat & Ken Wheat and David Twohy Running Time: 1:47 Rated: R (Violence, gore, profanity, scary aliens, bad science) Theatrical Aspect Ratio: 2.35:1

Pitch Black can be viewed as a slick, stylish version of the kind of outer space creature feature that is typified best by the *Alien* movies. At its best (which is quite often), *Pitch Black* is an entertaining effort. On the down side, there are times when various largely anonymous characters wander around in the dark and do incredibly stupid things while being stalked by vicious alien creatures. As they get picked off one-by-one, the only question is who's going to be *next*.

The movie begins with the crash, a violent concussion that leaves most of the crew and passengers dead. Among the handful of survivors are Fry (Radha Mitchell), the pilot; Johns (Cole Hauser), a police officer; Riddick (Diesel), a convicted murderer who is being transported in chains; and Inam, a holy man (Keith David). The planet is an apparently lifeless wasteland — a desertscape where 3 suns assure that there is no night and possibly no water. Shortly after the rough landing, Riddick escapes, but, while the survivors are looking for him, they too are being hunted — by a species of alien that shuns the daylight but is lethal in the dark. Soon, with the realization that the world is about to be plunged into blackness by an inconvenient total eclipse, everyone must learn to trust Riddick, who can see in the dark, if they are to survive. Meanwhile, it's unclear whether Riddick's primary goal is self-preservation or redemption.

Pitch Black has a stylish look. The outdoor sequences, which are nearly monochromatic to emphasize the color-leaching power of the multiple suns, are effectively photographed. After the eclipse occurs, there are some genuinely creepy sequences featuring packs of aliens honing in on the protagonists, who are only able to keep them at bay by waving around lights. For the most part, the special effects are first-rate — I was impressed by the scene of a ringed planet sliding across the sky on its way to block out the sun. These strong visuals complement a workmanlike script, resulting in a consistently engaging science fiction/horror excursion. **RECOMMENDED**

Pleasantville [1998]

Starring: Tobey Maguire, Reese Witherspoon, Jeff Daniels, Joan Allen
Director: Gary Ross Screenplay: Gary Ross Running Time: 1:56
Rated: PG-13 (Mature themes, sexual situations, mild profanity)
Theatrical Aspect Ratio: 1.85:1

Pleasantville opens in the comfortable familiarity of the '90s, with a common '90s family — David (Tobey Maguire) and Jennifer (Reese Witherspoon) are the twin children of a broken marriage. They live with a mother who's never around. One night, a mysterious television repair man (Don Knotts) shows up at the door and gives David a "special" remote control for the set. Later, as he's settling down to watch a 24-hour marathon of his favorite show, *Pleasantville*, he and his sister struggle over the remote. In the process, something very strange happens.

Suddenly, they are no longer in their home. In fact, they're no longer in color. They have entered the black-and-white world of '50s television, where the temperature is always 72 degrees, it never rains, profanity is never spoken, sex is taboo, there are no toilets, and words like "swell," "gee-whiz," and "keen" are part of the regular vocabulary. David is thrilled with the change in events. After all, *Pleasantville* is his favorite program. Jennifer, on the other hand, is horrified ("I'm pasty!" she screams upon seeing her gray complexion). She wants to go back immediately. She doesn't like the idea of having a perfect Dad in George (William H. Macy) and a perfect Mom in Betty (Joan Allen). But the gateway the two teens entered appears to be one-way, so they have to make do with their new world. Soon, however, David and Jennifer's "radical" ideals are bringing about changes in their environment. Perfection begins slipping away. Colors start to dot the black-and-white vistas. Jealousy, anger, and passion make appearances. The stale utopia of family values begins evolving.

The most stunning thing about *Pleasantville* is the

film's look. Color is used purposefully and impressively; it's hard to describe the impact of seeing one red rose amidst the black and white, or one monochromatic person in a sea of green grass. Ross has a reason for every change in hue, and the way he gradually evolves the film from pure black and white to a vibrant cacophony of colors is stirring.

One of the things I liked best about *Pleasantville* is that, while it entertains with its quirky plot and stunning visuals, it also made me think. Too few movies manage to be both thought-provoking and thoroughly entertaining. *Pleasantville* is a tour de force — it's a magical, modern-day fairy tale that invites us to explore who we are, and, like *The Wizard of Oz* and *It's a Wonderful Life* (heady company indeed), it trumpets the messages that the individual can make a difference, and that life in an alternate reality isn't necessarily better, just different. Not only is *Pleasantville* a satire, a fantasy, and a visual marvel, but it's the best kind of feel-good movie. **HIGHLY RECOMMENDED**

Reign of Fire [2002]

Starring: Matthew McConaughey, Christian Bale, Izabella Scorupco
Director: Rob Bowman Screenplay: Gregg Chabot & Kevin Peterka and Matt Greenberg Running Time: 1:45 Rated: PG-13 (Violence) Theatrical Aspect Ratio: 2.35:1

The film begins with a short prologue in modern-day London, where a construction crew working underground awakens a huge fire-breathing dragon. Skip ahead to 2020, where most of civilization is a blackened cinder — reduced to ashes by a scourge of countless flying reptiles. The few remaining humans have banded together into small refugee camps, trying to eke out an existence while staying out of the way of the dragons, who, in their hunger, are starting to feed on one another. Quinn (Christian Bale) is the leader of one such settlement, and his world is turned upside down by the arrival of Van Zan (Matthew McConaughey), Alex (Izabella Scorupco), and their group of gung-ho American military men, who are hunting dragons. They have come all the way to England in search of the big prize — the lone male dragon, the most fearsome creature on Earth. Kill it, they reason, and the dragons will die out. With no means of fertilizing their eggs, they will disappear within a generation.

The dragons look much more impressive than any of their past kin in other films. Sleek, deadly, and lightning fast, they strike quickly, then move on. There are times when the dragons, especially the bull, are imposing enough to be a little frightening. This is an instance when a filmmaker uses CGI to good effect. The visuals are not the least bit cheesy, and the dragons blend in well enough with the live-action actors that suspending disbelief is not difficult.

To say that the casting is a bit unusual is to understate matters. Christian Bale, the British actor who has had a smattering of success on both sides of the Atlantic, and Matthew McConaughey do not fit the mold of traditional action heroes, yet they acquit themselves admirably. Both have bulked up and tossed aside their pretty-boy images in an effort to get down and dirty. With his shaved head, beefy physique, and wild gaze, the cigar-chomping McConaughey is virtually unrecognizable, and entirely believable as a madman who will play chicken with a dragon.

I certainly wouldn't want every movie to be like *Reign of Fire*, but this sort of picture has just as much of a place in theaters as an adaptation of a Henry James novel. The key to the success of either is for the production to be well done, which, in this case, it is. *Reign of Fire* has no pretentions (which is refreshing in a way). It's about kicking butt, killing big, ugly monsters, and saving the human race. Bowman believes in it, and, because of his conviction, so do we.
RECOMMENDED

Screamers [1996]

Starring: Peter Weller, Roy Dupuis, Jennifer Rubin Director: Christian Duguay Screenplay: Dan O'Bannon and Miguel Tejada-Flores Running Time: 1:47 Rated: R (Violence, profanity) Theatrical Aspect Ratio: 1.85:1

Screamers oozes atmosphere. It's a dark film that borrows heavily from the likes of the *Alien* films, *Dune*, *Blade Runner*, and John Carpenter's updated *The Thing*. From start to finish, *Screamers* is shot in a manner intended to convey paranoia and claustrophobia. Set design is always impressive, if bleak, and consists primarily of ruined buildings and underground bunkers. Matte paintings of wrecked bridges and smashed cities form an ominous backdrop to much of the movie's action.

The film opens with several paragraphs of background text. The year is 2078 and the place is Sirius 6B. Once a paradise, it has been reduced to a radioactive wasteland as the result of mining toxic Berynium (the "solution" to Earth's energy crisis) and a war that has lasted more than a decade. Peace may be close at hand, however, and it's up to Commander Hendricksson (Robocop himself, Peter Weller) to decide the legitimacy of his enemies' appeal for an armistice.

Along with fresh-out-of-training rookie Ace (Andy Lauer), Hendricksson heads into the wasteland, traveling to the opposition's control bunker. Along the way, he meets several other Sirius 6B survivors, all eking out a nomadic existence: bootlegger Jessica (Jennifer Rubin), a woman who wants nothing more than to go to Earth; Ross (Charles Powell), the sole survivor of a massacre; and Becker (Roy Dupuis), a hardened cynic who prefers killing to asking questions.

As these five trek across the surface of Sirius 6B, they encounter a new, deadly adversary: the screamers (so nicknamed because of the squeal they make when attacking). Originally created as "autonomous mobile swords" by Hendricksson's side, the electronic, buzz-saw-like creatures have evolved, shaking off the yoke of slavery. With the ability to form a human shape and mimic human behavior, little appears beyond their capabilities, including infiltrating Hendricksson's small group.

Screamers emphasizes that science fiction doesn't have to be upbeat to succeed. This "sci-fi noir" style has led to a crop of films that hopefully heralds a new trend in the industry. If nothing else, *Screamers* underlines an important truth: you don't need a big budget or big-name stars to make this sort of motion picture succeed. **RECOMMENDED**

Signs [2002]

Starring: Mel Gibson, Joaquin Phoenix, Rory Culkin, Abigail Breslin
Director: M. Night Shyamalan Screenplay: M. Night Shyamalan
Running Time: 1:48 Rated: PG-13 (Mature themes, profanity, violence)
Theatrical Aspect Ratio: 1.85:1

Mel Gibson, whose salary probably represents a significant portion of *Signs*' budget, plays Father Graham Hess, a widower who is caring for his two children, Morgan (Rory Culkin) and Bo (Abigain Breslin), on a Bucks County (Pennsylvania) farm. Following his wife's death 6 months ago, Graham has done his best to keep his family together. He is aided by his younger brother, Merrill (Joaquin Phoenix), who moved to the farm following the tragedy. But Graham has lost his faith in God and has renounced his vocation. Then, one morning, he awakens to an amazing discovery — crop circles in his fields. At first, he is inclined to believe it's all a hoax, but, as evidence mounts that this may not be the case, he and his family realize that what has happened in their fields may be the first signs that Earth is about to have a close encounter.

While much of Shyamalan's setup is familiar, the meat of the story has an exotic flavor. Taking a page from Steven Spielberg's *Jaws*, the director keeps the

aliens hidden from our view. We catch occasional, brief glimpses — a leg in the corn field, a hand under a door, and a flash of green on a television screen. With today's special effects being so convincing, it's unusual for a filmmaker to fall back on the old, tried-and-true technique of "less is more." In the case of *Signs*, it creates a level of tension that a full revelation would have spoiled.

Then there's the added mystery of whether the aliens are benevolent or aggressive. Shyamalan obscures their intentions for most of the movie, concentrating instead upon the fears and concerns of the characters when they don't know the truth. Graham gives a speech in which he talks about how some humans will view first contact as a miracle that gives them hope, while others will see it as a cause for anxiety and uncertainty. In other words, is Earth about to be subjected to a *Close Encounters* or an *Independence Day?* For quite some time, Shyamalan doesn't tip his hand, and, when he does so, it isn't in a predictable manner. **RECOMMENDED**

Sky Captain and the World of Tomorrow [2004]

Starring: Jude Law, Gwyneth Paltrow, Angelina Jolie, Giovanni Ribisi, Michael Gambon, Bai Ling, Omid Djalili, Sir Laurence Olivier Director: Kerry Conran Screenplay: Kerry Conran Running Time: 1:47 Rated: PG (Science fiction violence) Theatrical Aspect Ratio: 1.85:1

Sky Captain and the World of Tomorrow is about 70 percent style and 30 percent substance. It has a plot and characters, but those are almost beside the point. They are devices that function as hooks upon which first-time director Kerry Conran can hang his amazing visuals. The film transpires in a stylized version of the 1930s — an alternate reality where all the world's on a silver screen and the Great Depression never existed. In keeping with the nostalgic tone of the movie, Conran presents things in a gauzy brown-and-white with a thin sheen of color. It's like watching an old, nonrestored copy of *The Wizard of Oz,* or looking at an aged color photograph. Vibrant hues are not part of Conran's agenda. He's going for something that will take us back 70 years, to a time before television, when Saturday afternoon serials were one of the cinema's staples. In fact, *Sky Captain* is designed and scripted like one.

The characters are familiar types. Joe "Sky Captain" Sullivan (Jude Law) is a tough yet sensitive adventurer who comes to the rescue in his private plane whenever he is needed. Polly Perkins (Gwyneth Paltrow) is an intrepid reporter for the *Chronicle*, as well as a former flame of Joe's. Like Lois Lane, when she latches on to a story, she doesn't let go. Joe's sidekick is Dex Dearborn (Giovanni Ribisi), who's handier than MacGyver. Then there's Franky Cook (Angelina Jolie), the British airship captain who lends a hand to Joe when he most needs it (like Polly, she's a former lover). The villains are a mysterious Asian woman (Bai Ling) who could give Jackie Chan a fight he'd never forget, and the dangerous Dr. Totenkopf (the late Laurence Olivier), a megalomaniac who lives in seclusion.

The action starts when an army of giant robots invades Manhattan and starts stomping all over the place. (These look like they were lifted right out of 30s and 40s science fiction stories.) Enter Sky Captain, called in to save the day. It turns out that the invasion of the robots is connected with the disappearance of six prominent scientists — a story that Polly is researching. All of the clues point to Dr. Totenkopf, but his location is unknown and probably requires a trip to Napal and into the mystical land of Shangri-La. When Dex is captured, Joe decides to go after him, and plucky Polly won't be left behind. Saving the world becomes an almost secondary consideration to saving their friend.

The bottom line is that *Sky Captain and the World of Tomorrow* is fun to watch, even if you don't care about the visual style or Conran's affinity for old movies and serials. There's a *Raiders of the Lost Ark* quality to the action and cliffhangers, and in the way that humor is used to offset tension. Law and Paltrow have great chemistry and they play their roles like a pair of 30s stars. The whole package, a labor of love for the director, offers a lot to every viewer who takes a chance on a movie with such a kitschy title.

RECOMMENDED

Solaris [2002]

Starring: George Clooney, Natascha McElhone, Jeremy Davies, Viola Davis Director: Steven Soderbergh Screenplay: Steven Soderbergh, based on the novel by Stanislaw Lem Running Time: 1:38 Rated: PG-13 (Mature themes, sexual situations, brief nudity) Theatrical Aspect Ratio: 2.35:1

Solaris may be the first big budget science fiction motion picture that belongs in an art house rather than a multiplex. The movie bears a stronger resemblance to *2001: A Space Odyssey* than to *Star Wars*, with an emphasis on ideas over action. Those expecting to see space battles and bug-eyed aliens will be disappointed. There's nothing like that here. The experience of watching *Solaris* doesn't just invite thought and rumination; it demands it.

Solaris transpires at an unspecified time in the near future. Therapist Chris Kelvin (George Clooney) travels to a space station orbiting the distant planet of Solaris after a friend requests his help analyzing a problem that the crew of the station has encountered. When Chris arrives, he finds that his friend is among the dead, and there are only 2 survivors — the laid-back Snow (Jeremy Davies) and the paranoid Dr. Gordon (Viola Davis). Although neither Snow nor Gordon provides helpful information, Chris soon discovers on his own what's transpiring when he receives a visitation from his dead wife, Rhea (Natascha McElhone). Rhea does not appear to be a hallucination or a ghost, and that leaves Chris with a serious issue to resolve: Is she real or not, and, if she is, *what* is she?

Solaris examines weighty issues like the power of guilt, the nature of life, and the importance of memory. There are no traditional antagonists in this film; Chris' greatest enemy is a burden of conscience that he carries with him, the presence of which weighs down his soul and clouds his judgment. Initially, he doesn't believe his visitor is Rhea. Later, he no longer cares. The presence of someone who looks, feels, and sounds identical to his dead wife gives him an opportunity to assuage the pain of misplaced responsibility.

The number of "thinking" science fiction films is small, and most are produced on small budgets for start-up directors. The first-rate production values and A-list star make *Solaris* an exception — and a rewarding one, at that. This is the first film I have seen in a long time to make me feel some of the things I experienced while watching *2001*. *Solaris* is neither as effective nor as ambitious as Kubrick's masterpiece, but it's still a compelling cinematic experience for those who are willing to abandon themselves to the unforced, measured rhythms of an issues-based motion picture. **RECOMMENDED**

Star Trek: The Motion Picture — Director's Edition [2001]

Starring: William Shatner, Leonard Nimoy, DeForest Kelley Director: Robert Wise Screenplay: Alan Dean Foster and Harold Livingstone Running Time: 2:16 Rated: PG (Science Fiction action) Theatrical Aspect Ratio: 2.35:1

In 1979, the release of *Star Trek — The Motion Picture* represented the climax to every *Star Trek* fan's wet dream. The date, December 7, lived in infamy for the entire production crew. Paramount Pictures etched this date into their release calendar and informed everyone involved that the film *would* be ready on that day. Despite the Herculean effort by legendary director Robert Wise and his army of post-production assistants, the version of *Star Trek — The Motion Picture* that reached theaters was not complete. Now, more that 20 years later, Robert Wise has had the opportunity to return to the film and complete it in the manner he had originally envisioned.

The film opens with the destruction of three Klingon warships by a mysterious energy cloud that is on a direct heading for Earth. The newly redesigned *U.S.S. Enterprise* is the only ship available to intercept the cloud, and it hasn't undergone its shakedown cruise. Admiral James T. Kirk (William Shatner), restless after 2½ years behind a desk, uses the crises to once again take command of the *Enterprise,* forcing the ship's expected captain, Will Decker (Stephen Collins), into the role of Executive Officer. Most of the crew is re-united, including the irascible Dr. McCoy (the late DeForest Kelley) and the half-Vulcan Mr. Spock (Leonard Nimoy). Spock senses a kinship with the vast consciousness that exists at the heart of the cloud. Also on board are Chief Engineer Scotty (James Doohan), Security Chief Chekov (Walter Koenig), Helmsman Sulu (George Takei), Communications Officer Uhura (Nichelle Nichols), and a newcomer, Navigator Ilia (Persis Khambatta).

After battling several systems failures, including a malfunctioning transporter that kills two crewman and a propulsion system that becomes unstable and creates a wormhole, the *Enterprise* makes contact with the entity within the cloud, called V'ger. The journey to the center of the alien ship is a strange and bizarre one. Ilia is killed when a probe invades the *Enterprise* bridge, and V'ger later sends a second probe to the ship in the form of a mechanism that mimics Ilia's body and features. Kirk learns that V'ger is a living machine traveling to Earth to make contact with its "Creator." If this contact is not made, V'ger intends to wipe out all of the human beings "infesting" the planet. It is up to the crew of the *Enterprise* to prevent that eventuality.

Re-visiting *Star Trek — The Motion Picture* via this director's cut is like seeing a familiar story unfold in a new way. Wise's picture was an ambitious effort from the beginning, striving for a greatness that it never attained. In this new version, it still falls short, but not by as much. It has taken more than 20 years for Robert Wise to return to his chapter of the *Star Trek* saga and fulfill his vision. With no hesitation, I can say that it has been worth the wait. *Star Trek — The Motion Picture: Director's Edition* vaults this movie from a position as one of the weakest entries in the long-running film series to a perch as one of the strongest. **RECOMMENDED**

Star Trek II: The Wrath of Khan [1982]

Starring: William Shatner, Leonard Nimoy, DeForest Kelley, Ricardo Montalban Director: Nicholas Meyer Screenplay: Harve Bennett and Jack B. Sowards Running Time: 1:50 Rated: PG (Violence) Theatrical Aspect Ratio: 2.35:1

The film is a sequel to a first season episode of the series ("Space Seed"). Here, the evil genius Khan (Ricardo Montalban, in a deliciously over-the-top performance) and his followers have escaped from the barren planet where then-Captain Kirk (William Shatner) stranded them some 15 years ago. Khan, once a brilliant, charismatic leader, has become an embittered maniac, dedicated only to revenge. He blames Kirk for the death of his wife and the waste of his own life, and intends to extract payment — in blood. After hijacking a Federation starship, Khan steals Genesis, a potential doomsday weapon created by Kirk's son, David (Merritt Butrick), and ex-lover, Carol (Bibi Besch), and lures the *Enterprise* into a carefully-orchestrated trap.

The *Star Trek* regulars do what's expected of them. William Shatner, not generally regarded as a top-flight actor, fits comfortably into this role, mixing heroic arrogance with surprising vulnerability. Of the seven *Star Trek* features in which he has appeared, Shatner does his best work here. Leonard Nimoy, as usual, plays Spock with a touch of sardonic wit, and DeForest Kelley proves to be his perfect, illogical foil. Familiar faces James Doohan (Scotty), Walter Koenig (Chekov), George Takei (Sulu), and Nichelle Nichols (Uhura) are all on hand, although only Koenig has more than a few token scenes.

The Wrath of Khan is a top-notch, fast-paced adventure that can be enjoyed equally by fans of the series and those who have never seen an episode. There are several tense, well-executed battle sequences that feature impressive special effects and a soaring score by James Horner. The ending, which I won't reveal (although everyone probably knows it by now) is tender and poignant — proof that *Star Trek* can still touch the heart. *The Wrath of Khan* shows the potential inherent in the *Star Trek* concept as applied to the big screen. It's unfortunate that none of the other films in this long-running series have come close to the level achieved by this marvelous example of entertainment. **HIGHLY RECOMMENDED**

Star Trek III: The Search for Spock [1984]

Starring: **William Shatner, DeForest Kelley, Christopher Lloyd**
Director: **Leonard Nimoy** Screenplay: **Harve Bennett** Running
Time: **1:45** Rated: **PG** (Violence) Theatrical Aspect Ratio: **2.35:1**

With a title like *The Search for Spock*, did anyone really expect that they wouldn't find the erstwhile first officer? So, with the resolution never in doubt (especially considering that Leonard Nimoy was directing), the *real* question to ask is: Is the search fun? The answer, for the most part, is "yes," at least once the story kicks into high gear. *Star Trek III* takes nearly 40 minutes, much of which is filled with silly, mystical exposition about the current state of Spock's soul, before things start moving. The last 20 minutes are equally slow, but the stuff in between is quite enjoyable.

The Search for Spock opens where *The Wrath of Khan* left off — with Spock's death and funeral. Days later, the *Enterprise* is limping home, ready to be decommissioned, with the crew awaiting reassignment. Dr. McCoy (DeForest Kelley) is suffering from some sort of unexplainable trauma — he hides out in dark rooms speaking in Spock's voice and tries to hire a ship to take him back to the Genesis planet, which has been classified as "off limits" for all space travel. A visit by Spock's father (Mark Lenard) to Kirk (William Shatner) reveals that McCoy carries Spock's soul within him, and must be taken to Vulcan to have it exorcised. For the ritual, Kirk must also retrieve Spock's body from Genesis — a task impeded by Starfleet's policy regarding the new planet. Undaunted, the Admiral, accompanied by his crew, steals the soon-to-be-mothballed *Enterprise,* and heads into a confrontation with a ship of belligerent Klingons who are trying to steal "the secret of Genesis."

Like *Star Trek II, Star Trek III* is about sacrifice. In *The Wrath of Khan,* Spock gave his life for his shipmates. Here, Kirk loses just about everything except his life so that his friend can have a chance at a future. It's this sort of thing — placing characters and themes above battles and special effects — that has always distinguished *Star Trek*. While the absence of Spock leaves a vacuum in character interaction (there is none of the witty repartee that defines the Kirk/Spock/McCoy relationship), expectations about his return create a palpable sense of anticipation. So, while the sluggish beginning and ending mar this *Star Trek* outing somewhat, there's still enough here to please fans of the series, and, to a lesser extent, moviegoers in general. **RECOMMENDED**

Star Trek IV: The Voyage Home [1986]

Starring: **William Shatner, Leonard Nimoy, DeForest Kelley, Catherine Hicks** Director: **Leonard Nimoy** Screenplay: **Harve Bennett, Peter Krikes, Steve Meerson, and Nicholas Meyer** Running Time: **1:59** Rated: **PG** (Mild profanity) Theatrical Aspect Ratio: **2.35:1**

Star Trek IV picks up where *Star Trek III: The Search for Spock* left off, and forms the final segment of the motion picture trilogy begun in *Star Trek II: The Wrath of Khan*. The crew of the destroyed starship *Enterprise* has been in exile on Vulcan while their resurrected shipmate, Captain Spock (Leonard Nimoy), is re-trained in the ways of logic. Once Spock has recovered sufficiently to travel, Admiral Kirk (William Shatner) and his fellow officers must go back to Earth to answer a battery of charges leveled against them for stealing the *Enterprise* and nearly provoking a war with the Klingon Empire.

However, before Kirk and company can return home, a mysterious probe enters orbit around Earth and wreaks havoc on the planet's climate. Nothing seems capable of stopping the probe, and a planetary distress call is issued. Spock, analyzing the probe's transmissions, determines that they match the songs of humpback whales, an extinct species of ocean-dwelling life. For Earth to survive, the crew of the former *Enterprise* must travel back in time to 20th Century Earth, capture a humpback whale, confine it in their stolen Klingon spaceship, then return to the future. Soon, Kirk and his friends are wandering around 1986 San Francisco, every bit out-of-place as Crocodile Dundee was in New York City.

The tone of *The Voyage Home* is considerably lighter than that of its predecessors; in fact, this is as close as *Star Trek* gets to being a straight comedy. At times, the proceedings become overly silly to garner cheap laughs, and the characters suffer as a result. Kirk, McCoy, and especially Spock, flicker back and forth between resembling the heroic figures we know and acting like caricatures of themselves. There's a running gag about Spock's inability to master profanity that, while undeniably amusing, is a little too cute.

Star Trek IV: The Voyage Home marked the end of the "golden age" of *Star Trek* movies, such as it was (three straight quality outings). *Star Trek IV,* while not a superior effort, is an effective and enjoyable sample of entertainment — not good science fiction, but a lightweight piece of comic fantasy utilizing characters so familiar that they feel like old friends. **RECOMMENDED**

Star Trek: First Contact [1996]

Starring: Patrick Stewart, Jonathan Frakes, Brent Spiner, LeVar Burton
Director: Jonathan Frakes Screenplay: Rick Berman, Brannon Braga,
and Ronald D. Moore Running Time: 1:51 Rated: PG-13 (Violence,
profanity, sexual innuendo) Theatrical Aspect Ratio: 2.35:1

For the first time in the 17-year run of the successful *Star Trek* movie franchise, there is no Captain Kirk. *Star Trek: First Contact*, the 8th entry into the motion picture series, is the first to rely exclusively on the crew of *The Next Generation*. First time director Jonathan Frakes (who also plays Riker, the *Enterprise*'s second-in-command) injects some badly-needed energy and inventiveness into a series that, prior to this effort, was sinking under its own weight and boldly going nowhere.

The highlight of *First Contact* is the first reel, a recklessly-paced, dazzling display of special effects that is exhausting in its intensity. For the first time in eight films, there's no "getting to know you" period. Five minutes after the opening credits have ended, we're right in the middle of the action. And what action it is — the most spectacular space battle ever to grace the screen in a *Star Trek* film. It's clear that this sequence, with dozens of starships doing battle with the enemy — a cube-like Borg vessel — ate up a considerable portion of the budget.

The Borg, undoubtedly *The Next Generation*'s most popular foe, appeared in about a half-dozen TV episodes, but created a legacy that made them a natural choice for a big screen appearance. Half-organic, half-robot, the Borg all share one mind, and have proven to be the most difficult foe for the Federation to overcome. In *First Contact*, when an attack of Earth during the 24th century fails, the Borg travel back in time to change history. The *USS Enterprise-E*, helmed by Captain Jean-Luc Picard (Patrick Stewart), must follow them to the mid-21st century to save the future. But the Borg are on board the *Enterprise*, and a battle for control of the ship soon develops.

As a species, the Borg are effective, cinematic villains, although, on an individual level, their "queen" (played by Alice Krige) is probably the least menacing of them all. The Borg's natural implacability enhances their sinister aura. There's something eerie about creatures that kill matter-of-factly and don't make a sound when they're injured. The Borg's hive — actually the corridors of the *Enterprise*'s lower decks — bears more than a passing resemblance to the nest of the Alien queen in James Cameron's *Aliens*.

The script is cleverly written so that non-fans will be able to follow and enjoy the plot while aficionados will get all the little "in" references. *First Contact* effortlessly negotiates a number of potential problem areas (such as time travel), which is a credit to the screenwriting team of Brannon Braga, Ronald Moore, and producer Rick Berman. *First Contact* ensures that *Star Trek* continues to live long and prosper.

RECOMMENDED

Star Wars Episode I: The Phantom Menace [1999]

Starring: Liam Neeson, Ewan McGregor, Natalie Portman, Jake Lloyd
Director: George Lucas Screenplay: George Lucas Running Time: 2:15
Rated: PG (Mild violence) Theatrical Aspect Ratio: 2.35:1

Jedi Master Qui-Gon Jinn (Liam Neeson) and his apprentice, Obi-Wan Kenobi (Ewan McGregor), are on a diplomatic mission to the planet Naboo, where they hope to negotiate the end to a blockade of the planet organized by the Trade Federation. When they arrive, however, they find themselves caught in a trap sprung by the mysterious Darth Sidious (Ian McDiarmid), who is making a play to take control of the Galactic Republic. After surviving an attempt on their lives in a planet-orbiting space station, Qui-Gon and Obi-Wan end up on the ground in the midst of an invasion by an army of droids. After meeting the amphibious Jar Jar Binks (Ahmed Best), they move to save Naboo's teenage ruler, Queen Amidala, from possible execution. That involves taking her and her retinue (including her favorite squat droid, R2-D2) into space. From Naboo, the action moves to the desert planet of Tatooine, where the two Jedi encounter young Anakin Skywalker (Jake Lloyd), a slave child with amazing potential in the Force, then to the capital world of the Republic, and finally back to Naboo. Meanwhile, Darth Maul (Ray Park), Sidious' minion, is tracking the Jedi with dire intentions.

Plot-wise, the film borrows a lot, at least in terms of structure, from *Return of the Jedi*. After a rousing opening sequence, things slow down for a while. Then, on Tatooine, there's an amazing racing sequence featuring "pod" space ships. Finally, the film concludes with three separate, simultaneous story threads all building to a climax. The martial arts-influenced light saber duel between Darth Maul and Qui-Gon & Obi-Wan is the best that *The Phantom Menace* has to offer — a virtuoso action sequence directed with skill and understanding of what an audience craves from this sort of confrontation.

The *Star Wars* movies have always relied on the nobility of heroes and the nastiness of villains, and *The Phantom Menace* is no exception. As Qui-Gon, Liam Neeson brings an unforced nobility to his performance, while Ewan McGregor injects a sense of recklessness into his portrayal of Obi-Wan. On the other side of the Force is Ray Park's Darth Maul, who doesn't say much, but compensates with menacing stares and quick reflexes. Ian McDiarmid makes for a more chilling villain, even though his Darth Sidious stays in the shadows.

Plainly, this is not an actors' movie and the director, George Lucas, is not an actors' director. Lucas' forte is in creating worlds and pushing the special effects envelope, and, in both of those areas, *The Phantom Menace* doesn't just meet expectations — it exceeds them. For the most part, Lucas' vision isn't limited to putting spectacular visuals on screen for the purpose of creating a momentary sense of awe. His intention is to craft a wonderful, weird, vast universe that we can experience in a way that no other movie has been able to offer. **HIGHLY RECOMMENDED**

Star Wars Episode II: Attack of the Clones [2002]

Starring: Ewan McGregor, Natalie Portman, Hayden Christensen, Christopher Lee Director: George Lucas Screenplay: George Lucas and Jonathan Hales Running Time: 2:18 Rated: PG (Science fiction violence) Theatrical Aspect Ratio: 2.35:1

Middle episodes in trilogies have the potential to be fundamentally dissatisfying. Thankfully, George Lucas has managed to avoid that pitfall for Episode II of the *Star Wars* saga, *Attack of the Clones*. Admittedly, the primary purpose of this film is to advance the overall story, bridging the gap between the lightweight, heroic antics of *The Phantom Menace* and the overwhelming darkness of the as-yet unnamed *Episode III*. *Attack of the Clones* has a starting point and a stopping point, but no true beginning or end.

Attack of the Clones opens approximately 10 years after the events of *The Phantom Menace*. Anakin Skywalker (Hayden Christensen), having spent a decade under the tutelage of his mentor, Obi-Wan Kenobi (Ewan McGregor), is anxious to take the tests that will mark him as a full-fledged Jedi, although Obi-Wan advises patience. Senator Amidala (Natalie Portman), formerly the Queen of Naboo, has arrived on the planet of Coruscant, the Republic's capital, to let her voice be heard on the key issue of what to do with seceding systems. When an attempt is made on her life, Jedi Master Mace Windu (Samuel L. Jackson) assigns Obi-Wan and Anakin to protect her. This mission leads them in different directions — Obi-Wan pursues the assassin, a bounty hunter named Jango Fett (Temeura Morrison), while Anakin accompanies Amidala to Naboo. While there, the would-be Jedi

and the Senator fall in love. Soon after, Anakin and Amidala leave Naboo for Tatooine to discover what has become of Anakin's mother. Meanwhile, Obi-Wan begins to unravel a sinister plot that leads to the mysterious Count Dooku (Christopher Lee) and the Sith Lord Dark Sidious (Ian McDiarmid), who is manipulating everything from behind the scenes.

Episode II opens with a bang — literally. There are some early action scenes, including an impressive chase sequence through the air and streets of Coruscant, then exposition takes over. In fact, the middle section of *Attack of the Clones* is so bogged down with setting up current and future plotlines that the pace starts to flag. It's difficult to decide how Lucas could have done this differently, but the reality is that parts of the film border on being too talky. Nevertheless, from a dramatic standpoint, the screenplay holds up better than that of *The Phantom Menace*. The film's highlight is a rousing battle sequence that consumes the final 40 minutes and includes, among other things, a massive conflict between Jedi, clones, and battle androids; a two-on-one lightsaber duel; and our first opportunity to see why Yoda (Frank Oz) is considered the greatest of all Jedi. *Attack of the Clones* closes with a series of scenes that presage what will happen in Episode III. **HIGHLY RECOMMENDED**

Star Wars Episode IV: A New Hope [1977]

Starring: Mark Hamill, Harrison Ford, Carrie Fisher, Alec Guinness Director: George Lucas Screenplay: George Lucas Running Time: 2:09 Rated: PG (Science fiction violence) Theatrical Aspect Ratio: 2.35:1

When one examines the roster of the tens of thousands of motion pictures produced since the late 1800s, not many stand out as trailblazers. One of the few inarguable members of that select cadre is George Lucas' soaring 1977 space opera, *Star Wars* (or, as it has since become known, *Star Wars: A New Hope*). Not only is this film a rousing adventure, but, upon its initial release, it revived science fiction as a viable movie medium, and, most importantly, began a special effects revolution that is still going on

By now, the heroes — Luke Skywalker (Mark Hamill), Han Solo (Harrison Ford), Princess Leia (Carrie Fisher), Obi-Wan Kenobi (Alec Guinness), Chewbacca (Peter Mayhew), C-3P0 (Anthony Daniels), and R2-D2 (Kenny Baker) — are household names. Equally well-known are the villains — Governor Tarkin (Peter Cushing) and, of course, the Dark Lord of the Sith, Darth Vader (David Prowse; voice courtesy of the inimitable James Earl Jones). These characters, familiar types with enough unique personality traits to brand them as individuals, have become so universally recognized that the mere mention of their names almost anywhere in the world will spur a reaction.

At its heart, *Star Wars* is about Luke's quest to join the battle against evil. He doesn't want to be just another bystander while the struggle for freedom goes on all around him — he wants to be a participant. And, when two droids carrying a secret message from a beautiful rebel princess fall into his hands, his chance arrives. Amidst of the dunes of Luke's home planet of Tatooine, the young man meets the aging Jedi Knight, Obi-Wan Kenobi, who teaches of the mysterious Force, a mystical energy field that binds together all things in the universe. Obi-Wan convinces Luke to join the droids and him on a mission to rescue the princess. Accompanied by a cynical smuggler, Han Solo, and his first mate, the hairy Chewbacca, the odd little group blasts off into space with agents of the corrupt Galactic Empire in pursuit. Their destination: the dreaded Imperial Death Star, a confrontation with the evil Darth Vader, and motion picture immortality.

Since 1977, there have been many science fiction movies, but none has managed to equal *Star Wars'* blend of adventure, likable characters, and epic storytelling. Like some indefatigable King of the Hill, it stands alone and triumphant, regardless of the many imitators that assail its position. *Star Wars* will endure long after its creators are gone. And watching it today is like coming home after a long journey and finding everything just as you remember it — if not better. **MUST SEE**

Star Wars Episode V: The Empire Strikes Back
[1980]

Starring: Mark Hamill, Harrison Ford, Carrie Fisher, Billy Dee Williams
Director: Irvin Kershner Screenplay: Leigh Brackett and Lawrence Kasdan, based on a story by George Lucas Running Time: 2:06
Rated: PG (Science fiction violence) Theatrical Aspect Ratio: 2.35:1

Although it lacks the pioneering "newness" of *Star Wars, The Empire Strikes Back* is in many ways a superior motion picture. The storyline is more interesting and ambitious, the characters — little more than appealing types in the original — are allowed to grow and develop, the special effects are more mature, and the tone is deliciously dark and downbeat. It's the latter quality that has made *The Empire Strikes Back* the least favorite among young *Star Wars* fans — except-

ing Yoda, there's nothing cute to be found, and the film definitely doesn't leave viewers with a warm, fuzzy feeling. In the first film, good triumphed decisively over evil; here, it's almost the other way around.

The movie does not pick up where *Star Wars* left off. The Death Star's destruction is a thing of the past; Luke Skywalker (Mark Hamill) and Han Solo (Harrison Ford) have been with the Rebellion for quite some time. There's a love triangle involving the two friends and Princess Leia (Carrie Fisher), although Han, the perpetual scoundrel, has the upper hand. When an Imperial Probe Droid turns up on the ice world Hoth, where the current Rebel base is located, it's time for a quick evacuation. Darth Vader (David Prowse, voice of James Earl Jones) detects his quarry, Luke, there, and orchestrates a full-scale invasion. Suddenly, the Rebels are on the run, with Han taking the princess, Chewbacca (Peter Mayhew), and C-3P0 (Anthony Daniels) on board the *Falcon* and into an asteroid field to avoid pursuing TIE fighters. Meanwhile, Luke, along with the faithful R2-D2 (Kenny Baker), heads for the swamp planet of Dagobah to learn from the wizened Jedi Master, Yoda (Frank Oz).

The defining moment of *The Empire Strikes Back* occurs in the final 15 minutes, and, during screenings in 1980 (before the nature of the secret became public knowledge), one particular scene provoked collective gasps. In terms of the mythological antecedents that Lucas based much of his *Star Wars* trilogy on, there was nothing startling about Vader's origins, but, considering the darkness it would inevitably inject into the series, it was a bold stroke.

Seventeen years after its intial release, *The Empire Strikes Back* is still as thrilling and involving as ever. Because of the high quality of the original product, it doesn't show a hint of dating. Neither the first nor the third chapters (or, properly, the "fourth" and "sixth") of the *Star Wars* saga were able to match the narrative scope of *Empire*, which today remains one of the finest and most rousing science fiction tales ever committed to the screen. **MUST SEE**

Star Wars Episode VI: Return of the Jedi [1983]

Starring: Mark Hamill, Harrison Ford, Carrie Fisher, Billy Dee Williams, Ian McDiarmid Director: Richard Marquand Screenplay: Lawrence Kasdan and George Lucas, based on a story by George Lucas
Running Time: 2:15 Rated: PG (Science fiction violence) Theatrical Aspect Ratio: 2.35:1

There's an old saying that states something about leaving the best for last. George Lucas certainly didn't follow that adage when crafting the original *Star Wars* trilogy. *Return of the Jedi,* the final installment of the series, is easily the least innovative and most hokey of the three films. In fact, most of the enjoyment derived from this motion picture comes from the simple act of getting together with old friends and enemies one more time.

Cuteness is the watchword here. The dark, eerie atmosphere that oozed from every frame of *The Empire Strikes Back* is gone. Instead, for *Return of the Jedi,* we have good triumphing decisively over evil, a too-pat resolution to a love triangle, and walking teddy bears. Even Darth Vader doesn't seem very daunting this time around. With the arrival of the Emperor (a gaunt-looking Ian McDiarmid), Vader has turned into a second fiddle. It's decidedly unsatisfactory to watch him engage Luke in a civilized conversation.

Return of the Jedi picks up an unspecified time after the conclusion of *The Empire Strikes Back.* Luke (Mark Hamill), Leia (Carrie Fisher), Lando (Billy Dee Williams), Chewbacca (Peter Mayhew), and the droids (Anthony Daniels and Kenny Baker) are on a rescue mission to Luke's home planet of Tatooine. Their aim: to save Han (Harrison Ford) from the clutches of Jabba the Hutt. Once this goal is attained, it's back to outer space, where the Rebel alliance is about to face the Empire's newest threat: a second, more powerful Death Star, that, if activated, could spell doom for anyone who stands against the Emperor. So, while the fleet prepares for the final battle, Luke and company travel to the forest moon of Endor to knock out the shield that defends the Death Star against all attacks. There, they are befriended by the Ewoks, the teddy bear-like indigenous race, and Luke, fearing that his presence is endangering the group, turns himself over to Vader.

Return of the Jedi has some interesting elements. The Luke/Vader/Emperor scenes are suitably tense and well-acted, and, if the resolution isn't a complete surprise, at least it's a little more original that it could have been. From a technical point-of-view, the space battles are amazing, easily dwarfing anything depicted in the previous films. Not only are there many, many more ships, but their speed and range of movement have been dramatically improved. Despite its flaws, this is still *Star Wars,* and, as such, represents a couple of lightly-entertaining hours spent with characters we have gotten to know and love over the years. *Return of the Jedi* is easily the weakest of the series, but

its position as the conclusion makes it a must-see for anyone who has enjoyed its predecessors. **RECOMMENDED**

Starship Troopers [1997]

Starring: Casper Van Dien, Dina Meyer, Denise Richards, Jake Busey, Neil Patrick Harris   Director: Paul Verhoeven   Screenplay: Ed Neumeir based on the novel by Robert A. Heinlein   Running Time: 2:09   Rated: R (Extreme violence, profanity, nudity)   Theatrical Aspect Ratio: 1.85:1

Probably the best way to approach *Starship Troopers* is to divorce it from its intelligent and gripping pedigree. Many of the most intellectually stimulating aspects of the book have been stripped away, and those that remain are only shadows of their former selves. Nevertheless, taken on its own terms, the movie entity *Starship Troopers* offers an enjoyable 2 hours. At its best, the film recaptures the kind of taut, visceral thrills offered by James Cameron's *Aliens.* At its worst, it replicates the feel of a futuristic episode of TV's *Beverly Hills 90210.*

The story begins sometime in the future on Earth, where society has evolved into what producer Jon Davison calls a "fascist utopia." It's there, in the city of Buenos Aires, that we meet *Starship Troopers'* protagonist, Johnny Rico, played by relative newcomer Casper Van Dien. Rico, along with classmates Carmen Ibanez (Denise Richards), Carl Jenkins (Neil Patrick Harris, TV's Doogie Howser), and Dizzy Flores (Dina Meyer, from Dragonheart), is preparing for the future as high school graduation approaches. All 4 friends are considering joining the Federal Service — the futuristic equivalent of today's military. Carmen wants to be a pilot, Carl wants to enter the intelligence ranks, and Rico and Dizzy are headed for the infantry. To add a little spice to their interaction, a romantic triangle has developed between Rico, Carmen, and Dizzy.

While the early sequences of *Starship Troopers* can seem like a prime time soap opera, complete with cheesy dialogue and unconvincing character development, it's clear that Verhoeven knows what he's doing. None of this is played completely straight; at times, *Starship Troopers'* first half-hour treads a line between overblown melodrama and parody.

Eventually, we get to the action. Humanity is at war with a race of lethal bugs who hail from the planet Klandathu, located halfway across the galaxy. They nuke an Earth city and mankind retaliates by launching an invasion of their homeworld. Rico and Dizzy are members of the invading army, and Carmen pilots the ship taking them there, but the campaign turns into a debacle. The death toll is phenomenal and the enemy scores a clear victory. The war, however, is just beginning.

In the final analysis, *Starship Troopers* is flawed but fun. And, while the outline of Heinlein's story and many of the characters remain intact, only echoes of the rich and controversial political subtext have survived. If you want content, read the book. If you want a skillfully-directed, fast-paced ride through space and into war, see the movie. **RECOMMENDED**

Strange Days [1995]

Starring: Ralph Fiennes, Angela Bassett, Juliette Lewis, Tom Sizemore
Director: Kathryn Bigelow Screenplay: James Cameron and Jay Cocks
Running Time: 2:25 Rated: R (Violence, sex, nudity, profanity)
Theatrical Aspect Ratio: 2.35:1

December 30, 1999: the penultimate day of the penultimate year of the century (the 20th century doesn't officially end until the close of 2000). In Los Angeles, the "biggest party of all time" is already underway. Crime is flowing as freely through the streets as champagne at the high-class galas. Ex-cop Lenny Nero (Ralph Fiennes) is in his element: a world where his former colleagues are too busy with serious matters, like the roadside shooting of rapper/black activist Jeriko One (Glenn Plummer), to harass small-time dealers like him. What Nero sells, however, isn't traditional dope, although it's just as addictive and arguably more dangerous. He's the magic man, not the candy man, and his bag of goodies contains disks full of memories and experiences. Once plugged into the appropriate player, one disk allows the user to relive its contents, which could be something as innocent as taking a shower, something as raunchy as participating in an orgy, or something as grotesque as committing a murder.

This is the premise of James Cameron's script for *Strange Days,* the technologically slick action/thriller directed by his ex-wife, Kathryn Bigelow (*Point Break*). Where *Total Recall* underused a similar concept, *Strange Days* takes the subject matter and runs with it. The picture does not attempt to mix, mingle, or confuse fantasy and reality. Instead, it uses these ideas as a launching pad for a murder mystery conspiracy that involves a car chase, shoot-outs, and a fight-to-the-death climax — all the things expected from this sort of motion picture. One of the most fascinating elements of *Strange Days* is the subculture that has developed around Superconductor Quantum Interference Device (SQUID) users. Even though it's illegal to buy or own these machines, their availability has created a thriving black market for disks to run in them.

While *Strange Days* is accomplished in choreographed action, character development, pacing, and visual effects, it displays serious flaws as a murder mystery. Not only is the killer's identity telegraphed far too early, but one of the worst clichés of the genre is reproduced here: while holding the good guy at gun point, the bad guy describes his entire plan. Even the slight twist Cameron employs isn't enough to camouflage this contrivance. Overall, however, *Strange Days* is a thriller first and a mystery second. It's big, explosive entertainment and, although not directed by Cameron, is very much in the vein we've come to expect from him. **HIGHLY RECOMMENDED**

Superman [1978]

Starring: Marlon Brando, Gene Hackman, Christopher Reeve
Director: Richard Donner Screenplay: Mario Puzo and David Newman and Leslie Newman & Robert Benton Running Time: 2:23 Rated: PG (Violence, disaster sequences) Theatrical Aspect Ratio: 2.35:1

To date, the 1978 theatrical version of *Superman* remains the only motion picture based on a comic book to have a lush, epic feel. Developed by *Godfather* scribe Mario Puzo with reverence for the venerable superhero, *Superman* pays homage to the legend's mythology without losing sight of the character's essential humanity.

Superman opens in deep space on the planet Krypton, where respected citizen and elder Jor-El (Marlon Brando) warns that evidence indicates the world's destruction is at hand. The leaders, who disagree with his conclusions and are concerned about a widespread panic, extract a promise that he will keep silent and that neither he nor his wife, Lara (Susannah York), will leave Krypton. Nothing, however, is said about Jor-El's son, Kal-El, and, when the end begins, the child's parents bundle him into a small spacecraft bound for Earth. Once he crash-lands on Earth, he is adopted by the Kents (Glenn Ford and Phyllis Thaxter), who raise him as their own.

Clark (Jeff East as a teenager; Christopher Reeve as an adult) grows up as a clean-cut, all-American type boy, but he knows his origins are not of this planet. Following the death of his adopted father, he goes on a journey to the arctic circle to find himself. There, in a fortress of solitude made out of crystal and ice, he spends 13 years learning about the histories and cultures of Krypton and Earth. When he emerges, wearing the unmistakable blue spandex suit, Superman has been born.

However, even as Metropolis' first superhero makes his presence known, the man who will become his arch enemy is planning. Lex Luthor (Gene Hackman) has hatched a plan that will make him the wealthiest man in the world. By detonating a nuclear warhead in the San Andreas Fault, Luthor will cause California to sink into the ocean. While Luthor plots, Superman, using his secret identity as the mild-mannered Clark Kent, begins working as a reporter for Metropolis' largest newspaper, *The Daily Planet*. As Clark, he befriends co-worker Lois Lane (Margot Kidder). Unfortunately, she only has eyes for Superman. Thus begins one of the oddest romantic triangles ever to grace the screen.

Taking *Superman* as a whole, there's no doubt that it's a flawed movie, but it's one of the most wonderfully entertaining flawed movies made during the 1970s. It's exactly what comic book fans hoped it would be, and it never apologizes about its origins. There are numerous sly nods to many aspects of Superman lore — a young Clark Kent outracing a train, Clark stopping a speeding bullet, the race to find a place to change into the Superman costume when a telephone booth has been replaced by a kiosk, and the reference to "truth, justice, and the American way." Perhaps most heartening of all, however, is the message at the end of the credits announcing the impending arrival of *Superman II*. **HIGHLY RECOMMENDED**

Superman II [1980]

Starring: Gene Hackman, Christopher Reeve, Terence Stamp, Margot Kidder Director: Richard Lester Screenplay: Mario Puzo & David Newman & Leslie Newman Running Time: 2:07 Rated: PG (Mild profanity, violence) Theatrical Aspect Ratio: 2.35:1

Superman II opens with a visual recap of the first movie during the opening credits. This is intended to refresh the memories of those who saw *Superman,* not to provide a primer for those who did not. Almost all of the surviving characters from *Superman* are back, some for cameos and some for more substantive screen time. The comically villainous Lex Luthor (Gene Hackman) once again provides a thorn in Superman's side. The 3 villains from Krypton — General Zod (Terence Stamp), Ursa (Sarah Douglas), and Non (Jack O'Halloran) — have greatly expanded roles. Everyone on the Daily Planet staff has returned: Perry White (Jackie Cooper), Jimmy Olsen (Marc McClure), and, of course, Lois Lane (Margot Kidder).

The film opens with Superman (Christopher Reeve) flying to Paris to stop a group of terrorists from blowing up the Eiffel Tower with a hydrogen bomb. Hurling the device deep into space before it can explode, Superman saves the planet from nu-

clear devastation. Unbeknownst to him, however, he creates a bigger problem. Shock waves from the bomb rip open the "Phantom Zone" in which Jor-El had imprisoned Zod and his two cronies. Free, they make their way to Earth, intent upon conquest. Meanwhile, Clark and Lois end up in Niagara Falls doing a piece of investigative journalism. While there, things heat up between the two of them as Lois finally realizes that Clark and Superman are one and the same. Once she has confessed her love for him, and he for her, they fly to his Fortress of Solitude, where he uses a supposedly irreversible process to strip away his superpowers so he can share his life with a mortal. Unfortunately, after returning to the real world and getting a rude awakening about his new physical limitations, Clark learns that, without Superman, the world is doomed to be ruled by Zod, Ursa, Non, and perhaps Luthor (who only wants Australia). So, leaving Lois to return to Metropolis by herself, he heads back to the Fortress, hoping to find some way to resurrect his powers.

As with the original *Superman, Superman II* is a comic book come to life. It is a fantasy, and, as a result, the more deeply you apply rational thought to what's transpiring on screen, the more quickly everything will unravel. Fortunately, the rapid pacing and strong character identification makes suspension of disbelief a relatively easy task, even during the most preposterous of moments. *Superman II* delivers on the promise hinted at in *Superman. Superman* acquaints us with the characters and sets up the scenario; *Superman II* takes the plot threads introduced in the original and resolves them. Viewed together, the two movies tell the entire story and allow anyone to understand why Superman is the comic book superhero with the greatest longevity. **HIGHLY RECOMMENDED**

The Truman Show [1998]

Starring: Jim Carrey, Laura Linney, Ed Harris, Noah Emmerich, Natascha McElhone Director: Peter Weir Screenplay: Andrew Niccol Running Time: 1:43 Rated: PG (Mild profanity) Theatrical Aspect Ratio: 1.85:1

Truman Burbank (Jim Carrey) is the star of the most popular show in the history of television. For 10,909 days, it has been on the air, using 5,000 cameras to show every moment in every day of the life of one man. The public loves it — there are Truman addicts who go to sleep with the TV on and who have sets installed in the bathroom so they don't miss anything when they're taking a bath. Every individual in "The Truman Show" is an actor with one important exception: the lead character himself. For, while everyone around Truman is playing a part, he is cheerfully ignorant about the truth. He thinks this is all real, and his obliviousness to the situation gives the program its core appeal — that there's nothing counterfeit about Truman. One day, however, when a former member of the cast sneaks back onto the set with a warning for the star, Truman begins to suspect that appearances can be deceiving.

For Carrey detractors who are easily turned off by the comic's rubber-faced antics, *The Truman Show* proves to be an eye-opener. Not only does Carrey remain rigidly-controlled and reigned in, but it would be fair to call his performance both understated and effective. Exhibiting the charm and charisma of a Tom Hanks or even a young Jimmy Stewart, Carrey develops the sort of likable personae that a movie of this sort needs to succeed. He is ably supported by a cast that includes Laura Linney as Truman's TV wife, Natascha McElhone as his one true love, Noah Emmerich as his best friend, and Ed Harris as "God," the TV program's creator and director.

As an intriguing, well-written piece of entertainment and a mild social commentary, *The Truman Show* deserves high marks. Not everything in the film works, and the script isn't perhaps as deep or incisive as it would like us to believe, but there's enough here to mark *The Truman Show* as a worthwhile motion picture — an appealing, offbeat, one-hundred minute diversion for those who really are tired of monsters tearing down buildings and action heroes saving the world. RECOMMENDED

Twelve Monkeys [1995]

Starring: Bruce Willis, Madeleine Stowe, Brad Pitt, Christopher Plummer Director: Terry Gilliam Screenplay: David Peoples and Janet Peoples, inspired by the film *La Jetee* Running Time: 2:09 Rated: R (Violence, profanity, nudity) Theatrical Aspect Ratio: 1.85:1

On December 13, 1996, in Philadelphia, a malignant virus is let loose. Months later, 5 billion worldwide are dead. The few survivors are relegated to living underground in germ-free cellars and tunnels. On the surface, Earth is ruled by animals, insects, and vegetation. Mankind's legacy to the planet is its slowly-decaying cities.

James Cole (Bruce Willis) is a 21st century convict living in a hellhole prison sometime in the 2020s. In order to reduce his sentence, or even obtain a full pardon, he "volunteers" to travel back in time to the 1990s to obtain a pure sample of the virus so that

modern science can analyze it. Cole's trip takes him to 1990, where he is incarcerated in a Maryland asylum under the care of psychiatrist Kathryn Railly (Madeleine Stowe). One of Cole's fellow inmates is a totally off-the-wall nutcase named Jeffrey Goines (Brad Pitt), the son of renowned virologist Leland Goines (Christopher Plummer), a man whose name is featured prominently in future headlines.

Twelve Monkeys spans four time periods: 1917 in the trenches of World War One, 1990 in Maryland, 1996 in Maryland and Philadelphia, and the 2020s deep beneath Philadelphia. Like director Terry Gilliam's previous efforts *Brazil* and *Time Bandits*, this movie is saturated with atmosphere. The grim, gray film has two tones: somber and apocalyptic. For the most part, *Twelve Monkeys* is a maze of plot twists and turns. Yet, despite all the hiccuping through time, the story is neither exceptionally obtuse nor hard to follow. In fact, it's possible to make shrewd guesses about some of what's going to happen. Even a movie as complex as this doesn't want to lose its audience along the way — at least not for too long.

Although the movie as a whole is open to interpretation, certain elements of Gilliam's film are straightforward. *Twelve Monkeys* uses a rapier-sharp wit to skewer both sides of the animal rights' movement, as well as the general conscience of society. The scenes of wild animals running amok might recall *Jumanji* to some, but Gilliam's sense of style makes for more startling and lasting images. If anything, these sequences underline the ephemeral nature of humanity's supremacy on this planet. HIGHLY RECOMMENDED

Waterworld [1995]

Starring: Kevin Costner, Dennis Hopper, Jeanne Tripplehorn, Tina Majorino Director: Kevin Reynolds Screenplay: Peter Rader and David Twohy Running Time: 2:15 Rated: PG-13 (Violence, brief nudity) Theatrical Aspect Ratio: 1.85:1

It's an unspecified date in the future. As we're told in a quick voiceover intro, the polar ice caps have melted and Earth's continents are buried under water. Humanity has been relegated to a tenuous existence on shakily-constructed floating fortress-cities. There is no land, and pure water and dirt have become exceptionally valuable commodities. There are three kinds of survivors: those who try to live in orderly societies, nomads who roam the seas in their own vessels, and members of an outlaw band called the "Smokers." Headed by the larger-than-life Deacon (Dennis Hopper), these criminals amuse themselves by raping and pillaging while on a quest for the mythical Dryland — a paradise that no one has seen, yet everyone believes exists.

The Mariner (Kevin Costner) becomes one of the Smokers' targets when he rescues the girl Enola (Tina Majorino) from a raid on a fortress-city. She is no ordinary child — on her back is a tattoo which supposedly identifies the location of Dryland. The Mariner, a mutant man who has developed working gills and webbed feet, has little use for Enola or her older companion, Helen (Jeanne Tripplehorn), but he owes them his life and intends to pay the debt. Once the scales are even, however, they become expendable.

Waterworld follows two parallel paths. The first sets the Mariner's personality on a course of transformation from self-centered to heroic. The other is the more tangible search for Dryland, which we instinctively know is going to appear during the film's last act. After all, how often do movie quests go unfulfilled? The script doesn't do a great job with either the spiritual or the physical trek, but the spectacular action sequences occur with enough regularity that strong writing isn't necessary to keep *Waterworld* afloat. A little adrenaline can obscure quite a few holes. In the tradition of the old Westerns and Mel Gibson's Road Warrior flicks, this film provides good escapist fun. Everyone behind the scenes did their part with aplomb, and the result is a feast for the eyes and ears. **RECOMMENDED**

The X-Files [1998]

Starring: **David Duchovny, Gillian Anderson, Martin Landau, Blythe Danner** Director: **Rob Bowman** Screenplay: **Chris Carter** Running Time: **1:58** Rated: **PG-13** (Violence, gore, mature themes) Theatrical Aspect Ratio: **2.35:1**

In interviews, writer/producer/series creator Chris Carter has stated that his goal with *The X-Files* was to make a movie that could stand on its own. There's no question that he has succeeded. The script can be followed by someone with literally no previous knowledge of the characters or situations. FBI special agents Fox Mulder (David Duchovny) and Dana Scully (Gillian Anderson) are introduced as any film protagonists might be, and we're presented with bits and pieces of information about their background through cleverly constructed dialogue.

As the film opens, the X-Files special unit of the FBI has been disbanded. Mulder and Scully have exchanged their investigations of things paranormal and extraterrestrial for more mundane matters such as terrorism. But, when an Oklahoma City-like bomb explosion destroys a $45 million building in Dallas, Mulder and Scully appear to be the FBI's first choice for fall guys. Their research to clear their names reveals what could be the tip of a massive cover-up of alien activity on Earth. And, as their search stretches from Texas to Washington D.C. to Antarctica, they come face-to-face with the dark secret that endangers the future of the human species.

It's not hard to understand the appeal of Mulder and Scully. Both are competent, intelligent, and resourceful, and their different approaches to their jobs (he's a believer; she's a skeptic) enable them to complement one another. It also doesn't hurt that they're both likable and neither is hard on the eyes. Actors David Duchovny and Gillian Anderson are both accomplished and entirely believable in these roles.

Having seen the movie, it's easy for me to comprehend why so many people are enamored with the series. Although a lot of the material explored in *The X-Files* isn't new or revolutionary, the style of presentation and the quality of the writing set this above most other conspiracy theory/alien invasion pictures. **RECOMMENDED**

2 Days in the Valley [1996]

Starring: Danny Aiello, Greg Cruttwell, Jeff Daniels, Teri Hatcher
Director: John Herzfeld Screenplay: John Herzfeld Running Time: 1:47
Rated: R (Violence, sex, profanity, nudity) Theatrical Aspect
Ratio: 1.85:1

The film opens with two hitmen, Desmo (Danny Aiello), an old-timer who's washed up, and Lee (James Spader), a cool-as-a-cucumber sociopath, staking out the house where a notorious womanizer, Roy Foxx (Peter Horton), is making the moves on his ex-wife, Becky (Teri Hatcher). Desmo and Lee have a contract to kill Roy, but who's paying the bill? Meanwhile, a wealthy art dealer, Allan Hopper (Greg Cruttwell), suffering from an acute case of kidney stones, has to be rushed to the hospital. His personal assistant, Susan (Gleanne Headly), brings him home afterwards. Two vice cops, Alvin (Jeff Daniels) and Wes (Eric Stoltz) are staking out a Japanese massage parlor, intending to bust the employees for illegal sexual activities. However, when Wes goes inside to get a first-hand experience, he feels sorry for the girl who services him, and walks out without making an arrest. Finally, there's Teddy Peppers (Paul Mazursky), the Emmy-Award winning director of *Arthur's Last Hope*. But that was 4 years ago, and, since then, he's had nothing but bombs. His life is a wasteland and his finances are in disarray. So, after finding a woman (Marsha Mason) who's willing to take responsibility for locating a new home for his beloved dog, he decides to end it all with a gun. Fate intercedes, however — but not just in Teddy's life. In one way or another, the wheels of destiny bring nearly all of these characters together, although not always at the same time and in the same place.

2 Days in the Valley has a penchant for the outrageous, with generous helpings of dark and ironic humor. There are a number of laugh-aloud lines, but the film works best when the comedy is of the "wink-wink-nudge-nudge" variety. I enjoyed *2 Days in the Valley*. It's pure entertainment — nothing too serious, nothing too deep — with an artistic sensibility. It's rare for movies these days to recognize that their audience has an intelligence, and even more unusual for them not to talk down to us. *2 Days* does both. So, if you're looking for some smart fun, John Herzfeld's feature is a worthy choice. And you don't need 2 days — just 2 hours. RECOMMENDED

After the Sunset [2004]

Starring: Pierce Brosnan, Salma Hayek, Woody Harrelson, Don Cheadle, Naomie Harris Director: Brett Ratner Screenplay: Paul Zbyszewski and Craig Rosenberg Running Time: 1:40 Rated: PG-13 (Sexual situations, profanity, violence) Theatrical Aspect Ratio: 2.35:1

After the Sunset is a mess, but it's a breezy, fun mess. No one is ever going to mistake this for great art, but it has a charismatic cast, moves with an effortless pace and, in the end, almost makes you forget that it doesn't do anything memorable. The film contains elements of a heist movie, a mismatched buddy picture, a sultry romance, and a James Bond thriller. There are all the requisite double crosses, and a twist at the end that a blind man can see coming. *After the Sunset* doesn't accomplish any of its aims exceptionally well, but it does them with just enough élan to keep the majority of the audience involved and entertained. And, if one's interest starts to wane, there's plenty to look at. Veteran cinematographer Dante Spinotti captures the natural beauty of the Caribbean with almost as much flair as he shoots Pierce Brosnan and Salma Hayek. With two such photogenic actors, no viewer need ever be bored.

After the Sunset begins with the would-be final caper in the careers of master jewel thieves Max (Brosnan) and Lola (Hayek). After relieving FBI agent Stan Lloyd (Woody Harrelson) of one of the three Napoléon diamonds, they disappear to an island paradise to enjoy their retirement. It doesn't take long before Max starts to feel like a prisoner; he's itching to try one more score, and his opportunity arrives with a cruise ship bearing another of the Napoléon diamonds. Along with the ship comes Agent Lloyd, who hooks up with a local cop, Sophie (Naomie Harris). And the island's kingpin (Don Cheadle) offers the infamous thief a lucrative partnership. The pull of committing the crime is almost too great to resist, but there is one thing holding Max back: Lola is serious about being retired. She has no intention of getting back in the business, and stealing the gem is a two-person job.

After the Sunset borders on being described as a "guilty pleasure," because, despite not being especially well written, it nevertheless offers a 100-minute, unpretentious diversion. Director Brett Ratner (*Rush Hour*) gets the tone right, and the actors play along. *After the Sunset* is a film of small moments and big laughs. If the production doesn't deliver on the level of *The Sting*, at least we don't walk out of the theater feeling stung. RECOMMENDED

Amateur [1995]

Starring: Isabelle Huppert, Martin Donovan, Elina Lowensohn
Director: Hal Hartley Screenplay: Hal Hartley Running Time: 1:45
Rated: R (Violence, profanity, sex) Theatrical Aspect Ratio: 1.85:1

As it develops, *Amateur* is a joint homage to/parody of film noir. And, as with the most reverent satires, the movie contains enough legitimate elements of the genre to be recognized as an entry. Unfortunately, this is far from a great thriller. The plot is rather stale, and, story-wise, there isn't a whole lot to hold the viewer's attention. The noir framework serves its purpose, but there's nothing great about it.

For his main character, Hartley has chosen an amnesiac. Thomas (Martin Donovan) wakes up in a cobblestoned New York City back alley with shattered glass all around him, a gash on the back of his head, and no memory of how he got in that predicament.

When he wanders into a nearby café, a woman (Isabelle Huppert) notices the blood and comes to his rescue. Isabelle is a 33-year-old ex-nun who believes herself to be a nymphomaniac even though she's still a virgin. When Thomas asks her to explain this apparent contradiction, she says she's choosey. Also folded into *Amateur* is Sofia (Elina Lowensohn), the world's hottest porn star, whose connection to Thomas is nebulous at the start. Then there are hitmen Jan (Chuck Montgomery) and Kurt (David Simonds), who have been hired by the mysterious Mr. Jacques to rub out anyone who knows too much about certain floppy disks.

Hartley's witty dialogue is a pleasure to absorb. There are times when the delivery is more important than the actual lines. The hit men discuss cellular phones like they're in the midst of a TV commercial. Stilted statements are made in the most melodramatic fashion possible, and half-baked dialogue is spoken with somber pretentiousness. To enforce the impact of this unique style, the director culls over-the-top performances from his actors, sometimes to an intentionally hilarious effect.

Amateur is a curious mixture of high art and delicious campiness, and the result is a funny, insightful, and almost-hypnotic motion picture. As the film progresses, you could care less what happens to Thomas and Isabelle, but the lure of what they'll say next draws the viewer on. Certainly, the script fails to do much with the issue of confused identities, its ostensible theme, but Hartley's style is such a pleasure to watch that it isn't a major disadvantage for the substance to be weak. RECOMMENDED

Amongst Friends [1993]

Starring: Steve Parlavecchio, Patrick McGaw, Joseph Lindsey, Mira Sorvino Director: Rob Weiss Screenplay: Rob Weiss Running Time: 1:27 Rated: R (Language, mature themes, violence) Theatrical Aspect Ratio: 1.85:1

Andy (Steve Parlavecchio), Trevor (Patrick McGaw), and Billy (Joseph Lindsey) have grown up together in the Long Island community of Five Towns. By their own admission, their friendship started almost from birth. However, relationships that were once strong begin to fracture with the onset of adulthood. A drug bust gone bad sends Trevor to prison and he emerges bitter and disillusioned. Billy becomes a big-time hood using Andy as his gopher, a role from which the somewhat-timid 23-year-old is desperate to escape.

Amongst Friends is another story about crime in

America, but instead of telling about the "have nots" of society, the film focuses on 3 boys who come from wealthy, respectable families. Bored and dissatisfied with comfortable lives where all their conventional wants are met, they crave something different and exciting. Andy's grandfather, who built his fortune as a bookie, and his gangster friends become inspirations and role models.

The 3 main characters couldn't be more different. Trevor is a dreamer and a romantic, a man to whom freedom and love mean more than all the money in the world. His feelings for Laura (Mira Sorvino) bring him back to Five Towns following a lengthy absence, and his return sets in motion the film's events. Billy is, plain and simple, a thoroughly unlikable bully. In fact, if there's an obvious flaw in any of the characters, it's that he has absolutely no redeeming characteristics. Of the 3, Andy is the most discontented. Each of his friends has something while he's still striving for that one big score to fill the gaping void. It isn't that he needs the money — he can get that from his parents any time he wants it — but the cash is a way of proving that he can hit the big time, even if it is gained through drug deals.

In the final analysis, *Amongst Friends* works not because it's an expose of upscale, suburban violence and drug use, but because it takes the time to develop its characters so that the events which swirl around them involve us. Emotional honesty is difficult for many films, but this one attains it, and when something devastating happens on screen, the reverberations shake the theater and the people sitting in it. **HIGHLY RECOMMENDED**

Amores Perros [Mexico, 2000]

Starring: Emilio Echevarría, Gael García Bernal, Goya Toledo, Álvaro Guerrero Director: Alejandro González Iñárritu Screenplay: Guillermo Arriaga Jordan Running Time: 2:31 Rated: R (Violence, profanity, sex, nudity) Theatrical Aspect Ratio: 1.85:1 In Spanish with subtitles

Amores Perros introduces us to a veritable Rogues Gallery of individuals. Of the 7 or 8 significant characters traversing Alejandro González Iñárritu's terrain, only one could be considered sympathetic. The others comprise a web of corruption and deceit. There are hit men, murderers, philanderers, thieves, betrayers, and other assorted riff-raff. Tarantino's anti-heroes are cool and suave, with always the right one-liner to offer. Iñárritu's are brutal and lacking even a modicum of charisma.

The first two we meet are Octavio (Gael García Bernal) and Susana (Vanessa Bauche). She's his sister-in-law, but that doesn't stem his ardor for her, and, because he treats her with a degree of kindness that her brutish husband, Ramiro (Marco Pérez), never shows, she can't help but be attracted to him. Octavio is determined to make enough money so that he and Susana can run away together (along with her infant son), but, in Mexico City, where poverty abounds, clean money is hard to find. Meanwhile, a couple of rungs higher on the social ladder are Daniel (Álvaro Guerrero) and Valeria (Goya Toledo). She's a world-class model who has hit the big time. Her face and body are plastered all over billboards throughout Mexico City. He's a magazine publisher who has left his wife and two children to be with her. Together, they make the perfect couple — young, good-looking, and in love — until tragedy strikes. Valeria is seriously injured in a car accident and Daniel must cope with living with a mentally and physically crippled woman whose modeling career is at an end. Finally, there's Chivo (Emilio Echevarría), a mysterious, wild-looking figure who hovers around the periphery of the other stories until his tale is finally told. Chivo is an ex-guerilla who abandoned his wife and daughter for The Cause. Now, many years later, he lives with regrets.

Amores Perros won an impressive number of awards in film festivals across the globe. Watching the film, it's not hard to understand why. Iñárritu's style contains elements of Tarantino, Peckinpah, and others, but, ultimately, the synthesis is all his own. Even though there's really no one in this film we can like, root for, or sympathize with, the intricacies of the narrative and the its themes are strong enough to ensure that we will not lose interest. *Amores Perros* is more than just a strong debut; it's good, gritty filmmaking. **RECOMMENDED**

Assassination Tango [2002]

Starring: Robert Duvall, Rubén Blades, Kathy Baker, Luciana Pedraza, Julio Oscar Mechoso, James Keane Director: Robert Duvall Screenplay: Robert Duvall Running Time: 1:54 Rated: R (Profanity, violence) Theatrical Aspect Ratio: 1.85:1

When is a hit man a terrorist? That's a question discussed in the subtext of Robert Duvall's newest movie, *Assassination Tango*, a quirky drama that I admire. For this film, Duvall wears four hats: director, writer, producer, and star, ensuring that he will bear primary responsibility for the success or failure of the project. Like 1997's *The Apostle*, this is very much Duvall's movie from top to bottom.

He plays John, a veteran hit man who is contemplating retirement so he can care for his new family: a girlfriend (Kathy Baker) and her daughter. John's latest, and perhaps last, job is to assassinate a political figure in Buenos Aires. He knows nothing about the man he is supposed to kill, nor does he care about the particulars. This is just another job for him — he wants to get in and out. Thus, there is the unspoken question: Is John acting as a terrorist? Ask his employers and they would say no; he is killing a monster. Ask the victim's backers and they would say yes. Ask John and he would shrug his shoulders. Labels don't mean much to him.

Because of a snafu in the plans, John ends up stuck in Argentina for several weeks longer than planned. While waiting for the go-ahead to kill his target, he becomes intrigued by the South American form of the tango, and convinces the dynamic Manuela (Luciana Pedraza) to teach him the steps and the philosophy. Those of us familiar with movies like this will be expecting John and Manuela to end up romantically entangled, but Duvall's writing is smarter than that. The script doesn't deny the attraction, but it deals with the situation differently from what we expect.

The film's tone is slow and deliberate. There are moments of energy, when the level of suspense is ratcheted up, but this is not primarily an action-oriented motion picture. The focus is on the "tango" portion of the title, not the "assassination." To that end, we are treated to a fair amount of dancing, and several conversations about the importance of the tango to the Argentinean culture. In large part, dialogue is *Assassination Tango*'s most obvious strength.

John isn't particularly likable, although I suppose he has a certain charm. *Assassination Tango* skims the surface of a number of genre films, but is quirky and original enough never to immerse itself fully in any of them. For those who do not demand a firm adherence to formulas and genre-driven expectations, this movie offers the chance to see something a little different. RECOMMENDED

Before the Rain [France/United Kingdom/Macedonia, 1994]
Starring: Rade Serbedzija, Katrin Cartlidge, Gregoire Colin
Director: Milcho Manchevski Screenplay: Milcho Manchevski
Running Time: 1:53 Rated: R (Violence, nudity, mature themes)
Theatrical Aspect Ratio: 2.35:1

"Time never dies. The circle is not round." As well as being a repeated line in *Before the Rain*, this statement clarifies director Milcho Manchevski's perspective. The film is an exploration of the vicious circle that is violence in the Balkans, and the way tribal and

ethnic bloodshed in that part of the world can spill over into more "civilized" countries.

Before the Rain opens and closes in Macedonia. The middle section — an interlude of sorts — takes place in England. The structure of the movie is nonchronological with the conclusion actually occurring about 40 minutes into the film. The flow of the narrative follows the "imperfect circle" pattern. Beginning and end meet and merge, but the closure is broken by one very disconcerting (and not so obvious) flashforward.

What at first appears to be several disparate stories resolves itself into a cohesive single entity, and the characters who start out as *Before the Rain*'s central figures (including a monk played by Gregoire Colin) are ultimately reduced to supporting roles. Most of the film is about — in one way or another — Pulitzer Prize-winning photographer Aleksandar (Rade Serbedzija), who became involved in the war in Bosnia by taking sides. Now, back from that war-torn place and wracked with guilt for having caused a man's death, he intends to leave England (and his English lover, played by Katrin Cartlidge) for Macedonia in hopes of making a positive difference in the violently unstable country of his birth.

The film is as rich in symbols as in narrative. Circles are everywhere, and water takes on its age-old meaning of purification. The titles of *Before the Rain*'s three chapters — "Words," "Faces," and "Pictures" — reveal aspects of the 35-odd minutes they each represent.

The visceral effectiveness of *Before the Rain* is undeniable — it brings home the global reality of violence without ever glorifying or glamorizing it. The film is loaded with chilling little touches of how this particular circle has trapped humanity. *Before the Rain* doesn't offer hope. As "Words" reminds us, communications problems are often more fundamental than language differences. In Manchevski's world, when peace exists, it's an exception, and redemption is perhaps a futile gesture. RECOMMENDED

Best Laid Plans [1999]
Starring: Alessandro Nivola, Reese Witherspoon, Josh Brolin
Director: Mike Barker Screenplay: Ted Griffin Running Time: 1:32
Rated: R (Violence, profanity, sexual situations, mature themes)
Theatrical Aspect Ratio: 1.85:1

Mike Barker's *Best Laid Plans* is a slightly overplotted, but nevertheless entertaining thriller that works primarily because it concentrates on developing characters and building relationships instead of throwing a series of improbable twists at the audience. That isn't to say there aren't a few unexpected turns in the story, but *Best Laid Plans* would still be effective without them. This is also a rare thriller that doesn't soak the screen with blood, violence, sex, and profanity. There's a little of each, but nothing compared to what we have come to expect in the post-Tarantino era.

Nick (Alessandro Nivola) and Lissa (Reese Witherspoon) are young, in love, and willing to do almost anything to get out of the dying rural town of Tropico. Nick thinks his boat has come in when his father dies, but the supposedly substantial estate evaporates when it turns out that Nick's father owed the IRS. With his finances in disarray, Nick looks for an alternative method to secure the means for his trip away from Tropico. When a co-worker at the local recycling plant offers a $10,000 opportunity for acting as a driver in a drug scam, Nick can't refuse. Unfortunately, things go bad, and Nick finds himself owing a drug dealer $15,000. His grace period to pay is a scant 5 days. With time running out, Nick and Lissa hatch a scheme to bilk Bryce (Josh Brolin), an old high school buddy of Nick's, out of the money. The plan looks foolproof — until Bryce doesn't react as expected.

Best Laid Plans is not presented linearly, but it doesn't play too many games with the chronology. The film begins in the present with a 10-minute introductory sequence designed to hook the viewer. The next hour is an extended series of flashbacks that introduce the characters and set up the situation. Finally, we're back in the present with 20 minutes to wrap things up. *Best Laid Plans* offers one surprise near the end (as seemingly all thrillers must), but it comes from an unexpected source.

These days, most thrillers are loud, brazen, and filled with MTV-style quick cuts. It's refreshing to come across a small film like *Best Laid Plans* that emphasizes story, characters, and acting over style and adrenaline (not that those qualities don't have their place). The dialogue snaps and crackles, but doesn't get carried away with its own cleverness (a flaw in too many movies like this). *Best Laid Plans* isn't the kind of motion picture that's going to linger in the mind or the memory, but, while you're in the theater watching it, the movie offers 90 minutes of solid, unpretentious entertainment. **RECOMMENDED**

Bloody Sunday [United Kingdom/Ireland, 2002]

Starring: James Nesbitt, Tim Pigott-Smith, Nicholas Farrell, Gerard McSorley Director: Paul Greengrass Screenplay: Paul Greengrass, based on the book *Eyewitness Bloody Sunday* by Don Mullan Running Time: 1:47 Rated: R (Violence, profanity) Theatrical Aspect Ratio: 1.85:1

It is said that every story has two sides, and the 1972 Bloody Sunday is no exception. The two sides — the citizens of Derry (Ireland) and the British army — have differing perspectives on what happened that afternoon. According to the latter, the military did not initiate the shooting, but returned fire after IRA members began firing at them. According to the former, the British attacked without provocation, and the resulting casualties were innocents caught in the line of fire. Official inquiries and investigations have failed to provide a clear path of culpability, and, while the evidence weighs slightly in favor of the version offered by the residents of Derry, there is no way to make a clear-cut determination of what is "the truth."

For *Bloody Sunday*, Greengrass has elected to tell the story using the citizens' version of events. Aside from this representing his personal conviction of what transpired, it is the more dramatically compelling interpretation. Greengrass' approach attempts a sort of balance — he builds to the confrontation by presenting the view from both sides. In addition to spending time with key individuals participating in the Civil Rights march, he introduces the audience to a number of British officers, including one conflicted, sympathetic man, Brigadier Maclellan (Nicholas Farrell), who tries unsuccessfully to curb the excesses of his men.

Bloody Sunday takes us through the day of January 30, 1972, beginning in the wee hours of the morning and extending until after sunset. The film's focus is on several characters. Ivan Cooper (James Nesbitt), a local Member of Parliament, is the organizer of the Civil Rights March. He believes that peaceful assembly is the route through which change can be affected. "We will march peacefully," he declares, "Until Unionist rule is put in place." Another goal is to keep the IRA out of the march, since violence begets violence. However, many of the younger marchers, such as Gerry Donaghy (Declan Duddy), are prone to rioting, needing only a spark to set them off. The British are ready for the day's activities — which are illegal under current rules that prohibit marching. Major General Ford (Tim Pigott-Smith) has decided to take a hard line, commanding Maclellan to arrest hundred of "hooligans." Troops are deployed, ready to move into position if things get out of hand. And, although the march starts out calmly enough, with between 5,000 and 20,000 citizens participating, it doesn't take long before things go badly wrong. And, in the midst of the chaos, a group of overzealous soldiers starts shooting using live ammunition, and the result is bloody carnage.

Although Greengrass brings his own perspective of the day's events to this film, he avoids the pitfalls of sermonizing, lionizing the dead, and demonizing the British. The result is a grim, startling motion picture. **RECOMMENDED**

Blow [2001]

Starring: Johnny Depp, Penélope Cruz, Franka Potente, Rachel Griffiths
Director: Ted Demme Screenplay: David McKenna and Nick Cassavetes, based on the book by Bruce Porter Running Time: 2:00
Rated: R (Pervasive drug use, profanity, violence, brief nudity)
Theatrical Aspect Ratio: 2.35:1

Blow is an effective and powerful motion picture that follows the rise and fall of drug dealer George Jung (Johnny Depp) as his story plays out against the ever-shifting tapestry of the '60s, '70s, and '80s. Based on a true story (as related in Bruce Porter's book and adapted for the screen by David McKenna and Nick Cassavetes) and employing a voiceover narrative, *Blow* shows how George's insatiable desire for material possessions leads him to betray, or be betrayed by, nearly everyone he knows or loves.

The film opens with a brief segment set in George's childhood. His hard-working father, Ray (Ray Liotta), and materialistic mother (Rachel Griffiths) are forced to declare bankruptcy when they can't make ends meet. Ray gives George some advice: "Money isn't real. It doesn't matter; it only seems like it does." That's a lesson George doesn't take to heart; by the late '60s, he's on his own and determined not to end up in the dire financial straits that paralyzed his parents. So he heads out to California with his best friend, Tuna (Ethan Suplee), to make his fortune. There, he meets the love of his life, Barbara (Franka Potente), and, with the help of Barbara's friend, Derek (Paul Reubens), gets established selling pot. Soon, "Boston George" is the King of the Beach, but he realizes that the real money is in transporting the drug to the East Coast, where college students will pay top dollar. So, using the services of Barbara, who is a stewardess (and whose bags are not checked at airports), he sets up a distribution network that nets both him and Derek $15,000 a week — until he gets caught.

While in prison, George's Colombian cellmate (Jordi Mollà) suggests that he change his product from marijuana to cocaine. After being freed from jail, George goes to Colombia, where he is introduced to the most powerful drug lord in South America, Pablo Escobar (Cliff Curtis). Escobar likes what he sees, and soon George and his new wife, Mirtha (Penelope Cruz), are supplying roughly 85% of the United States' coke. But it's a risky business, especially when the dealer is also a user.

Ultimately, the film isn't as much about drugs as it is about generational dynamics — fathers and children. The two relationships that form *Blow*'s emotional foundation are those of George and his father and George and his daughter. The tragedy of the film is that, in one way or another, George manages to betray the two people he loves the most. His failure in these relationships is the thing that haunts him and reduces him to a shadow of the man he once was. In depicting George's relationships with his father and daughter, *Blow* does an excellent job with an economy of scenes. **HIGHLY RECOMMENDED**

Boiler Room [2000]

Starring: Giovanni Ribisi, Vin Diesel, Ben Affleck, Jamie Kennedy
Director: Ben Younger Screenplay: Ben Younger Running Time: 1:57
Rated: R (Profanity) Theatrical Aspect Ratio: 1.85:1

Those who work in boiler rooms are participating in scams that routinely break SEC regulations and bilk investors out of huge amounts of money. Boiler room employees are the ultimate high-pressure salesmen. They do all their work on the phone, promising untold riches, confiding ultra-confidential "tips," and preying on the investor's greed and fear of missing out on a great opportunity. "No" is not in their vocabulary, and the only way to get rid of them is to hang up on them. Ultimately, the commodity they are offering tends to be worthless — some of the companies they sell stocks in don't exist. Boiler room brokers have two goals on any given day: make as much money as possible and avoid being arrested.

The lure of quick money is what attracts Seth Davis (Giovanni Ribisi) to the boiler room of J.T. Marlin, a "chop shop" brokerage firm located on Long Island, not on Wall Street. For all of Seth's life, he has wanted only two things: to become a millionaire and to earn his father's respect. In his quest to attain the former, however, he has endangered his chances for the latter. A 19-year-old college drop out, Seth is running a small-time illegal casino out of his apartment — a business that his dad (Ron Rifkin), a New York City judge, disapproves of. So, in an attempt to go legit, Seth joins J.T. Marlin as a trainee. But, even as he's on the fast track to wealth and success, he suspects that everything may not be on the up-and-up, and his conscience begins to prick him when he realizes he is cheating hard-working family men out of their life's savings just to earn himself a few thousand dollars in commissions.

First time writer/director Ben Younger crafted this screenplay from an insider's perspective. The attention to detail allows *Boiler Room* to achieve the same sort of insight into stock brokering that *Glengarry Glenn Ross* offered into sales. In fact, this aspect of the film is what makes *Boiler Room* a compelling movie-going experience. The characters and plot become secondary to the setting and atmosphere. There's a familiarity to the attitudes and ideas encountered here. As Seth notes, too few of us want to work hard for our money; instead, we seek the quick, easy path to excess. Also apropos, however, is an old proverb: "If it seems too good to be true, it is." And that simple adage encapsulates a philosophy that no one in this film has learned. RECOMMENDED

The Bone Collector [1999]

Starring: Denzel Washington, Angelina Jolie, Queen Latifah, Michael Rooker Director: Phillip Noyce Screenplay: Jeremy Iacone, based on the book by Jeffery Deaver Running Time: 1:57 Rated: R (Disturbing images of violence & gore, profanity) Theatrical Aspect Ratio: 2.35:1

The Bone Collector is a dark mystery/thriller that takes its characters and its audience on a twisted trek into benighted venues and disused tunnels where the sun has never shone. Director Phillip Noyce, best known for helming the two Harrison Ford/Tom Clancy films, opts to follow in David Fincher's footsteps. Those who have seen *Seven* will recognize the similarities — pervasive shadows, few daytime shots, and some interesting camera angles. The technique is used to develop a growing sense of menace, and is effective to that end.

Police detective Lincoln Rhyme (Denzel Washington) is widely considered to be a genius of forensic science. During his heyday, Rhyme was called on as an expert witness in hundreds of trials and he is said to have investigated about half the crime scenes in the city. Then 4 years ago, a tragic accident all but ended his career. In its aftermath, he is paralyzed and bedridden, able only to use one finger and everything above the shoulders. Although he is still officially a member of the force, his former colleagues have predominantly left him alone — until a new, troubling

case forces them to seek his help. This case concerns the murder of a wealthy, powerful New York City businessman, whose half-buried body was discovered near a railroad track. The patrolwoman responding to the call, Amelia Donaghy (Angelina Jolie), used a disposable camera to photograph the crime scene before an approaching rainstorm washed away the evidence. Rhyme, after looking at her handiwork, decides that she has a "natural talent for forensics," and wants her on the case.

Despite its grim and explicit nature, *The Bone Collector* contains a strong element of the old-fashioned detective mystery story. And, as is often the case in such yarns, there are some astounding leaps in logic. Throughout the picture, Rhyme lies immobile in bed, puzzling over clues and attempting to determine where the killer is going to strike next. There's more than a little Sherlock Holmes in his makeup, and his rival is the perfect Moriarty — intelligent, demented, and dangerous. Seen from this perspective, Amelia could almost be considered Rhyme's Doctor Watson. Overall, the atmosphere and suspense, coupled with strong lead performances and an interesting central relationship, allow *The Bone Collector* to work despite a storyline that no one would consider airtight. RECOMMENDED

Bound [1996]

Starring: Jennifer Tilly, Gina Gershon, Joe Pantoliano Director: The Wachowski Brothers Screenplay: The Wachowski Brothers Running Time: 1:49 Rated: R (Violence, sex, nudity, mature themes) Theatrical Aspect Ratio: 1.85:1

Bound appears to be ripe with all the elements necessary for a top-notch exploitation flick: leather, guns, gangsters, blood, and a couple of hot-to-trot lesbians. From the first scene, however, it's obvious that the writing/directing team of Andy and Larry Wachowski are aiming for something considerably higher than rudimentary titillation. And, by taking chances and twisting conventions, they have hit paydirt. *Bound* is among the best film noir entries of the decade; from beginning to end, it's solidly entertaining.

Ceasar (Joe Pantoliano) is a money launderer for the mob (sometimes in a very literal fashion — watch how he cleans up a sack of bloody bills). His live-in girlfriend, Violet (Jennifer Tilly), a closet lesbian, is itching to get free of him ("I want out! I want a new life!"). She sees her chance when an ex-con named Corky (Gina Gershon) moves in next door. Methodically, Violet seduces Corky, then, after a heated sexual encounter, the two plot how to liberate Violet along with $2 million of the mob's money that's currently in Ceasar's possession.

Saying more than that about *Bound* would be unfair, because the plot is loaded with the unexpected. For most thrillers, I'm able to predict the so-called "surprises" far in advance, but this film's well-orchestrated twists kept me off balance. Until the final scenes, it's impossible to be sure of anyone or anything. The biggest question, which is raised by the characters and stays with us, is who can be trusted? We're never sure who's on the level and who's lying. Since the Wachowskis don't feel bound by the conventions of the genre, they freely violate our expectations. Best of all, everything that transpires in *Bound* makes perfect sense — the film doesn't demand unreasonable leaps of logic to tie everything together. From the opening moments, ripe with sexual tension, to the closing shot, *Bound* offers an edge-of-the-seat experience. **HIGHLY RECOMMENDED**

The Business of Strangers [2001]

Starring: Stockard Channing, Julia Stiles, Frederick Weller
Director: Patrick Stettner Screenplay: Patrick Stettner Running
Time: 1:24 Rated: R (Profanity, sex) Theatrical Aspect Ratio: 1.85:1

Patrick Stettner's *The Business of Strangers* takes an unusual tack in addressing the issue of date rape. In the movie, Stockard Channing plays Julie, a successful business woman who is at the end of a long business trip and is looking to let off a little steam. Julia Stiles is Paula, a young woman she meets at a bar. Using alcohol as a lubricant, the two bond. Enter Nick (Frederick Weller), a head hunter whom Julie has casually known for years. Paula's reaction to Nick — one of horror and revulsion — is unexpected. She later confesses to Julie that Nick raped a friend of hers years ago at college. So, with their inhibitions loosened by too much booze, the women plot a form of revenge.

For most of its running length, *The Business of Strangers* is a sharp, compelling film that walks a tightrope between thriller and drama. The psychological interplay between Julie and Paula lies at the movie's core, and Stettner gives us about 45 minutes of it. For the most part, the movie works because the dialogue is insightful and meaningful. The conflict between the two leads is entirely verbal, but it is every bit as tense as any cinematic physical confrontation. Only at the end, when the director employs a cheat to offer one final plot twist, do things start to unravel. While the film's final turn shines a different light on

many of the events that preceded it, it also significantly reduces the complexity of Paula, transforming her into little more than a plot device.

Channing and Stiles are marvelous. Channing, a veteran performer who has had plenty of opportunities to shine, is completely at home as Julie, a woman who has become hard-as-nails to survive in a man's world. Stiles, an up-and-coming actress who is already known because of fine performances in pictures like *Save the Last Dance* and *O*, has no problem with the complexities and contradictions of Paula's character. *The Business of Strangers* is one of those films where the acting can either enhance or torpedo the storyline; Channing and Stiles ensure that the former is the case.

Disappointing though the conclusion of *The Business of Strangers* may be, it does little to blunt the film's overall impact. Stettner's screenplay still makes its point and there's plenty of material to ponder and discuss once the end credits have finished rolling. **RECOMMENDED**

Catch Me if You Can [2002]

Starring: Leonardo DeCaprio, Tom Hanks, Christopher Walken, Nathalie Baye, Amy Adams Director: Steven Spielberg Screenplay: Jeff Nathanson, based on the book by Frank Abagnale Jr. and Stan Redding Running Time: 2:20 Rated: PG-13 (Profanity, sexual situations) Theatrical Aspect Ratio: 1.85:1

Catch Me if You Can details the somewhat fictionalized tale of Frank Abagnale Jr. (Leonardo DiCaprio), who, between the ages of 16 and 21, was the world's most successful con artist. Not only did he successfully pose as an airplane pilot, a doctor, and a lawyer, but he cashed more than $2.5 million worth of fraudulent checks. Now, nearly 4 decades after being brought down, Abagnale is one of the foremost authorities on corporate security.

Soon after beginning his life of crime, Frank finds himself being pursued by FBI agent Carl Hanratty (Tom Hanks). For years, the two engage in a cat-and-mouse game, with Carl always a few steps behind Frank. But, despite his numerous failures in just missing Frank, Carl never gives up. Meanwhile, Frank frequently re-invents himself, sometimes because he needs a new cover to escape capture and sometimes out of sheer boredom. But, despite his wealth and success, he is a lonely person. His deepest connection is with his father, Frank Sr. (Christopher Walken, in a low-key and moving portrayal), whom he deeply respects. He harbors feelings of resentment towards his self-absorbed mother, Paula (Nathalie Baye), who dumped his father for a more successful man (James Brolin). His loneliness makes him vulnerable to the sweet naïveté of Brenda Strong (Amy Adams), a nurse he meets in an Atlanta hospital where he is posing as a doctor. He genuinely falls in love with her, but, when Hanratty closes in, he is forced to run . . . again.

Catch Me if You Can crosses several genres without abandoning its overall tone. There are several deeply affecting scenes, including an exchange in a bar between Frank and his father and a sequence on an airplane when Carl delivers some sad news. There are also elements of a thriller, albeit a light one, with the authorities often nearly cornering Frank, only to have him slip away. There is no question that, despite Frank's illicit behavior, he is the movie's protagonist, and we are intended to root for him. Leonardo DiCaprio's charm serves him well; Frank is charismatic and easy to like. On the other. hand, Tom Hanks does not play a bad guy. By intent, Carl is not a very interesting man, and his personal life is left largely unexplored. But he becomes a confidant for Frank, and, eventually, even though the two are on opposite sides of the law, they develop a bond.

Catch Me if You Can is not the kind of movie that was made to garner Oscar nominations. Instead, it was developed as an exercise in pure entertainment. To that end, it succeeds admirably. RECOMMENDED

The Cell [2000]

Starring: Jennifer Lopez, Vince Vaughn, Vincent D'Onofrio
Director: Tarsem Singh Screenplay: Mark Protosevich Running Time: 1:45 Rated: R (Violence, nudity, profanity, child abuse)
Theatrical Aspect Ratio: 2.35:1

Visually enticing and intellectually demanding, *The Cell* takes viewers deep into the nightmarish realm of a killer's mind, exposing audiences to a cacophony of dissonant scenes and images that are at times horrific and disturbing, but are never gratuitous. And, although the film has a clear narrative trajectory, its most compelling aspects are those that are the most disjointed.

At the heart of *The Cell* lies a new kind of technology that allows one person to enter the subconscious of another. The intent of the procedure is to facilitate the psychological analysis of deeply disturbed individuals who are unable to participate in traditional sessions due to catatonia. A team of two scientists, Miriam Kent (Marianne Jean-Baptiste) and Henry West (Dylan Baker), and one psychotherapist, Catherine Deane (Jennifer Lopez), are the only ones skilled in using the equipment — they have been experi-

menting on a young boy for the past 18 months. But, when approached by a pair of FBI agents, Peter Novak (Vince Vaughn) and Gordon Ramsey (Jake Weber), with a proposal, they find the challenge impossible to resist. Novak and Ramsey have just captured serial killer Carl Stargher (Vincent D'Onofrio), who has murdered seven times and has recently kidnapped an eighth victim. When the FBI locates Stargher, he has suffered some sort of massive psychological collapse and is in a coma. The location of his newest captive is unknown, but the FBI is aware that she has been placed in a glass tank that will automatically fill with water in 40 hours and drown her — unless Catherine can enter Stargher's mind, make contact with him, earn his trust, and learn the location of victim #8.

The Cell becomes the first serial killer feature in a long time to take the genre in a new direction. Not only does it defy formulaic expectations, but it challenges the viewer to think and consider the horrors that can turn an ordinary child into an inhuman monster. There are no easy answers, and *The Cell* doesn't pretend to offer any. Instead, director Tarsem Singh presents audiences with the opportunity to go on a harrowing journey. For those who are up to the challenge, it's worth spending time in *The Cell*.
RECOMMENDED

Cellular [2004]

Starring: Kim Basinger, Chris Evans, William H. Macy, Jason Statham, Noah Emmerich, Richard Burgi, Adam Taylor Gordon, Rick Hoffman
Director: David R. Ellis Screenplay: Chris Morgan, based on a story by Larry Cohen Running Time: 1:34 Rated: PG-13 (Profanity, violence)
Theatrical Aspect Ratio: 2.35:1

Cellular is a nearly perfectly executed "high-concept" thriller that, like *Speed* and *Phone Booth*, uses a gimmicky setup but is paced so relentlessly that you don't have time to dwell upon the obvious implausibility of the situation.

Jessica Martin (Kim Basinger) is a high school science teacher living a comfortable life in a nondescript Southern California community. One day, after sending her son, Ricky (Adam Taylor Gordon), off to school, her routine is rudely interrupted. A group of thugs, led by the implacable Greer (Jason Statham), breaks into her home, kidnaps her, and whisks her away to an unknown location. Once there, she is locked in an attic. There's a phone there, but Greer smashes it with a sledgehammer to make sure she can't use it to facilitate an escape. But the phone isn't quite dead. By touching two wires together, Jessica is able to make phone calls to random numbers. When she gets Ryan (Chris Evans) on the line, there's something in her distressed voice that keeps him from hanging up. At first, he doesn't believe her, but he nevertheless agrees to take her story to a cop named Mooney (William H. Macy), who listens patiently to the story but is then distracted. As a result, it's Ryan to the rescue when Greer's thugs head over to Ricky's school to add the boy to their hostage collection. Acting on information from Jessica about where to find her son, he ends up in a race with the bad guys to see who can find Ricky first.

Any possible cell phone cliché you can possibly imagine comes into play here: a dying battery, poor signal strength, crossed signals, ringing at inopportune moments, and dropped calls. Because it's imperative that Jessica and Ryan are not disconnected (she can't reconnect because the broken phone doesn't dial normally, and he can't call her because the criminals will answer), *Cellular* gains much of its tension by maneuvering Ryan around all sorts of obstacles to keep the call active while soliciting help from the police, looking for Jessica, and trying to prevent her son and husband from joining her. And, when Greer becomes aware of Ryan's existence, that's when things start to get ugly. *Cellular* reliably entertains for its 90-minute running time. Using the clever premise, it packs a lot of thrills into a short space while keeping the level of tension consistently high. *Cellular* is a popcorn movie, but you may end up gripping the armrest before you have emptied the bag. And don't forget to turn off your own phone — if it rings during the movie, you'll jump two feet. RECOMMENDED

Changing Lanes [2002]

Starring: Ben Affleck, Samuel L. Jackson, Toni Collette, Amanda Peet Director: Roger Michell Screenplay: Chap Taylor and Michael Tolkin Running Time: 1:40 Rated: R (Profanity) Theatrical Aspect Ratio: 2.35:1

Changing Lanes doesn't get the adrenaline pumping — but that's not a bad thing, because that isn't its goal. This is a character-centered movie — a film that makes a bold statement about societal pressures and the human condition, and how external influences can cause an otherwise decent human being to do things that are despicable. Those who go to *Changing Lanes* expecting to see a revenge thriller will probably be moderately entertained; those who look for more will find that there are greater rewards to be had.

On the one hand, we have Gavin Banek (Ben Affleck), a new partner in a high-profile Wall Street law firm that views ethics as a distraction. Unfortunately,

Gavin has a conscience of sorts, and, while he doesn't mind engaging a little lying and cheating, he feels exceedingly uncomfortable about going much further. On the other hand, we have Doyle Gipson (Samuel L. Jackson), a reformed alcoholic who is trying to put his life back together. His soon-to-be-ex-wife wants custody of their son, and intends to move to Oregon, far away from Doyle. In a last-ditch effort to prove that he can be a worthy father, Doyle is working hard to control his volcanic temper and play the part of a model citizen. Things seem to be lining up in his favor when an event brings him into contact with Gavin.

The event is a car accident which occurs when both men are in a rush to get to court — Gavin to present a judge with a Power of Appointment and Doyle to participate in a custody hearing. At the scene of the accident, Gavin doesn't want to wait around for the police — he's in too much of a hurry. So, wishing Doyle "Better luck next time," Gavin gets in his car and takes off — leaving behind Doyle and his non-functional vehicle, and (accidentally) the Power of Appointment Gavin is so eager to file. Now Doyle has something that Gavin desperately needs, and he's in no mood to return it. What follows is a cat and mouse game of one-upsmanship, as Doyle and Gavin go to increasingly unfriendly lengths to gain the upper hand. When Doyle won't give up the Power of Appointment, Gavin pays someone to hack into his financial records and bankrupt him. Doyle's response to this is potentially lethal.

The intriguing aspect of *Changing Lanes* is that both Gavin and Doyle are basically average guys caught in an extreme situation. In other circumstances, while they might not be friends, they would never be at each other's throats. Yet events drive Doyle to turn into an uncontrolled lunatic, while Gavin reflects on his misdeeds with growing disbelief: defrauding a charity, bankrupting a man, leaving the scene of an accident, forging a legal document, etc. Yet, in being brought to the edge, these men recognize things about themselves that they might otherwise not have understood. RECOMMENDED

Chopper Australia [2000]

Starring: Eric Bana, Simon Lyndon, Vince Colosimo Director: Andrew Dominik Screenplay: Andrew Dominik Running Time: 1:33 Rated: R (Violence, profanity, sexual situations) Theatrical Aspect Ratio: 1.85:1

The energetic and visceral *Chopper* is an Australian import that offers a somewhat fictionalized account of events in the life of Mark "Chopper" Read, a ruthless killer who has become a best selling author in his native country. Using the same kind of blood-and-violence-drenched mixture of comedy and suspense that enlivened well-known productions like *Pulp Fiction* and *Lock, Stock and Two Smoking Barrels*, neophyte director Andrew Dominik brings Read to life with all the fury he can muster.

In Australia, Read is a hugely controversial and immensely popular figure (his first novel sold over 250,000 copies). Dominik's intention with this movie is to present a picture of a man who is so unpredictable that no one — not the audience, not other characters in the movie, perhaps not even himself — can predict his next action. It's this kind of spontaneity that gives *Chopper* its edge. As it follows Read from a mid-'70s incarceration in a maximum security prison to another time in jail during the early '90s, *Chopper* never lets the viewer feel completely comfortable. Dominik's direction is fresh and lively, and the camerawork is exceptional.

With a movie like this, in which the main character often seems to inhabit the realm of tall tales, it's easy to question how far from the established facts *Chopper* strays. Dominik gets a preemptive strike against those who would criticize the movie on those grounds by mentioning in a pre-credits disclaimer that certain events in the film have been enhanced to generate a better narrative. It's also worth mentioning that the movie is based on a book by a man who's motto is "Never let the truth get in the way of a good story." So, although the events portrayed in *Chopper* are purportedly all true, one has to take just about everything with a grain of salt. As far as I'm concerned, it's irrelevant — the movie works, regardless of its factual accuracy or lack thereof.

The best thing about *Chopper* is the lead performance by Eric Bana, who powerfully inhabits Read's huge boots. More than anything else, he is the reason that *Chopper* is such a compelling motion picture. An hour after the end credits have rolled, he's the one — perhaps the *only* one — we remember. The film certainly isn't for everyone — those who shrink away from cinematic depictions of extreme violence will immediately be turned off — but, for those who don't mind this type of fare, *Chopper* will not be easily dismissed or forgotten. **RECOMMENDED**

City by the Sea [2002]

Starring: Robert De Niro, Frances McDormand, James Franco, Eliza Dushku Director: Michael Caton-Jones Screenplay: Ken Hixon, based on the article "Mark of a Murderer" by Michael McAlary Running Time: 1:48 Rated: R (Violence, profanity, drug use) Theatrical Aspect Ratio: 2.35:1

The City by the Sea of the title is Long Beach, New York — once a resort town like so many others, now a classic portrait of urban decay. It's a story that has been repeated in lakeside and oceanfront locales all around the country. A generation ago, certain beaches were crammed with happy families; now, many of those places have grown desolate and forgotten as vacationers have moved on to the newest trendy spot.

Homicide detective Vincent LaMarca (Robert De Niro) is a Manhattan cop investigating the death of a low-level drug dealer who went by the street name of "Picasso." Aided by his stalwart partner and friend, Reg (George Dzundza), Vincent returns to his old stomping grounds of Long Beach, from which the dead man hailed. To Vincent's shock, it appears that his son, Joey (James Franco), may be Picasso's killer. This revelation forces him to make a choice between being a cop (a job at which he has been inarguably good) and being a father (a job at which he has been inarguably bad).

Director Michael Caton-Jones employs an unhurried style atypical of cop movies. The reason for this is that the thriller/mystery elements are secondary to the film's deeper aspects — those of how fathers and sons relate to one another and how the lives of individuals can echo the life of a community. One could argue that Caton-Jones overplays the link between Vincent and Long Beach, but his depiction of the lost town is powerful and leaves a lasting impression.

If there's a weakness in *City by the Sea*, it's that the ending is too pat, the resolution too facile. But, until the closing moments, this is a motion picture of real character — a film that tells a compelling story in a way that raises issues and questions beyond what one expects from a genre picture. Those who venture into *City by the Sea* will find their 2 hours well spent.
RECOMMENDED

City of God [Brazil, 2002]

Starring: Alexandre Rodrigues, Leandro Frimino da Hora, Phellipe Haagensen, Deu Jorge, Matheus Nachtergaele, Douglas Silva Director: Fernando Meirelles Screenplay: Braulio Mantovani, based on the novel by Paulo Lins Running Time: 2:15 Rated: R (Extreme violence, sexual situations, nudity, profanity, drug content) Theatrical Aspect Ratio: 1.85:1 In Portuguese, with subtitles

The irony of calling this movie *City of God* will not be lost on the viewer, since the location in question — the slums (or *favelas*) of Rio de Janeiro — is, at the best of times, purgatory, and, at the worst of times, hell. God is nowhere to be found. Poverty is the way of life. Greed, drugs, and violence rule these streets. The latter is so pervasive that, when a gang war erupts, prepubescent children arm themselves with guns and join in the fray. The ability to use a firearm is a more important, and prevalent, trait than the ability to read and write.

The story line is not straightforward. The movie tells the tale of the rise and fall of the fearsome, sociopath gang leader Li'l Zé (Leanadro Frimino da Hora), who reigned as king of the drug lords during the 70s. The first portion of the movie illustrates some of the forces that mold Li'l Zé into the man he becomes, while the second half shows his ruthless leap to power (he kills all of his rivals), followed by the take-no-prisoners war he wages against opposing gangsters Carrot (Matheus Nachtergaele) and Knockout Ned (Deu Jorge).

The film is narrated by Rocket (Alexandre Rodrigues), a photographer who exists on the outskirts of Li'l Zé's circle. He knows the gang lord well enough to be able to relate his life's story, but is not so close to him that he has become poisoned. Rocket's telling is not linear. He generally relates the story in chronological fashion, but like many storytellers, he often stops to present tangential information about a new character or situation. Meirelles never permits these tangents to go too far astray, nor does he allow them to go on for too long.

The violence in *City of God* is extreme and shocking, even though there is virtually no blood. Death is no respecter of age in the slums of Rio de Janeiro. The immediate goal of a seven-year-old homeless boy is not finding a family or a friend, but finding a gun. When war between Li'l Zé and Knockout Ned is declared, children are quick to declare their allegiance so they can obtain a weapon and go out to kill. Despite the grim, serious nature of the subject matter, Meirelles unearths occasional moments of humor, although they are often of the gallows variety. Moments of levity are necessary to keep *City of God* from becoming unbearably bleak. If there's a message that the film espouses, it's that, in a culture where violence begets violence, only the names change. When one gang lord is deposed, another will rise in his place. And, as often as not, it's the children, more than the adults, who have to be watched. **HIGHLY RECOMMENDED**

A Civil Action [1998]

Starring: John Travolta, Robert Duvall, Tony Shalhoub, William H. Macy Director: Steven Zaillian Screenplay: Steven Zaillian based on the book by Jonathan Harr Running Time: 1:52 Rated: PG-13 (Profanity, mature themes) Theatrical Aspect Ratio: 1.85:1

A Civil Action does not enter groundbreaking territory, but it tones down the inherent melodrama of courtroom scenes to tolerable levels and does not offer any shock testimony or dramatic legal maneuvers. Indeed, the film isn't as much about a court case as it is about the legal system in general and how a sudden empathy with human suffering changes the personality of an ambulance chaser. The problem with the movie is that the transition of Jan Schlichtmann (John Travolta) from money-grubbing bottom feeder to champion of human rights happens too suddenly and without proper motivation. One moment, he's telling a group of citizens that he'll only take the case if there's a big payout; shortly thereafter, he's refusing a $25 million settlement because he wants to send a message.

Jan is the shining star at the small Boston law office comprised of him, Kevin Conway (Tony Shalhoub), and Bill Crowley (Zeljko Ivanek). They work in close concert with their accountant and financial wizard, James Gordon (William H. Macy). When Jan is offered a case in which eight children in the small town of Woburn, Massachusetts have died of leukemia, he decides to turn it down, even though he can "appreciate the theatrical value of several dead kids." The theory is that spilled chemicals from a local factory and tanning plant tainted the water and caused the cancer. Then a cursory investigation reveals that a pair of extremely wealthy corporations, W.R. Grace & Co. and Beatrice Foods, may be involved. Their deep pockets and the potential for a huge pay day cause Jan to change his mind. Soon, he is squaring off in court against William Cheeseman (Bruce Norris), the inept lawyer representing Grace, and Jerome Facher (Robert Duvall), the wily and dangerous attorney for Beatrice.

Unlike many courtroom dramas, which are grim and filled with dark tragedies and triumphant revelations, *A Civil Action* doesn't take itself too seriously, nor does it rely on the crutch of inane action sequences. There's plenty of comedy in the script. The other interesting element is that Zaillian offers some atypical insights into the workings of the legal system. *A Civil Action* does not function as an attack against lawyers, but as a hard, bitterly humorous look at the realities of the legal system. Combining a few good performances with an engaging and intelligent script, *A Civil Action* marks a rare worthwhile entry into a genre that has worn out its welcome. **RECOMMENDED**

Collateral [2004]

Starring: Tom Cruise, Jamie Foxx, Jada Pinkett Smith, Mark Ruffalo, Peter Berg, Bruce McGill, Irma P. Hall   Director: Michael Mann Screenplay: **Stuart Beattie** Running Time: **1:55** Rated: **R (Violence, profanity)** Theatrical Aspect Ratio: **2.35:1**

Collateral is a classic example of how casting against type can sometimes result in a remarkable success. Here we have Tom Cruise, who has spent the majority of his career playing the good-looking, likable, action/romantic lead, placed into the role of a grungy (graying hair and lots of stubble), soulless sociopath with penchants for existentialism and jazz. Then there's Jamie Foxx, the TV-weaned comedian of *In Living Color* and *The Jamie Foxx Show*, who plays a low-key, meek cab driver caught in a web spun by a capricious whim of fate. And, despite being so far from their respective, familiar acting backyards, both of these performers pull it off. Cruise is chillingly credible as the cold, cruel Vincent. And Foxx shows unexpected depth and humanity as Max, whose night encapsulates the cliché about being in the wrong place at the wrong time.

Although it has a unique premise, *Collateral* isn't a shockingly original motion picture. But the strength of the lead performances and the stylish direction of Michael Mann obscure the weaknesses in plotting and credibility. Although the final act of the movie feels like it was grafted on from a more traditional action picture, Mann keeps the level of tension high enough that we don't really care.

Cruise plays a contract killer who has arrived in Los Angeles to wipe out five people involved in a trial that poses problems for his employer. In order to make his way around the city, he hires Max to be his personal chauffeur for the night. Max is dubious about the prospect of having only one fare, but $600 quells his doubts. At the first stop, when a dead body falls onto the hood of his cab, he learns that Vincent isn't just in town to close a real estate deal. After·that, he quickly learns that his passenger has no intention of finding another ride, and if he wants to stay alive, his only choice is to satisfy his customer. For Max, the night spent in Vincent's company includes a number of bizarre detours, including a stop at a jazz club and a visit to the cabbie's hospitalized mother (Irma P. Hall). Plus, Vincent offers a few tips on Max's love life, opining that Max should call an earlier fare (Jada Pin-kett Smith) who left him a business card, and ask for a date. If, that is, they both survive the night.

This is not an unconventional buddy story. Max and Vincent do not bond or become close as the night wears on. Instead, this is about how extraordinary circumstances bring to the surface Max's hitherto unrecognized strengths. *Collateral* is more compelling because of the interaction between Vincent and Max than because of the gunplay, violence, and chase scenes. The screenplay seems smarter than it actually is. Acting and atmosphere define the film, but the bottom line is that there are times when style can become substance, and this is one of them. *Collateral* is a strangely involving motion picture. The performances by Cruise and Foxx are the highlights, and Mann's direction assures that boredom and disinterest will stay at bay. **RECOMMENDED**

Confidence [2003]

Starring: Edward Burns, Rachel Weisz, Andy Garcia, Dustin Hoffman, Paul Giamatti, Brian Van Holt, Franky G.   Director: James Foley Screenplay: **Doug Jung** Running Time: **1:38** Rated: **R (Violence, profanity, sexual situations)** Theatrical Aspect Ratio: **2.35:1**

The successful completion of this kind of motion picture requires nothing short of confidence on the part of the director. Confidence in the material. Confidence in the actors. And, most importantly for James Foley, confidence in himself. Done haphazardly, this could have turned into a laughably inept endeavor. But, crafted with flair and style, and without pretension, *Confidence* achieves the modest goal of being an entertaining cinematic adaptation of a B-movie script with an A-list cast.

Most of *Confidence* is told in flashbacks. This allows protagonist Jake Vig (Edward Burns) to narrate his tale. Jake's tone is self-deprecating. He knows that the con man relies upon three things: human nature, planning, and luck. Even when the first two hold true, failure of the third can ruin everything, and Murphy has stepped squarely in Jake's path. Now, he's spilling his life's story to a guy with a gun in the hope that he can keep breathing for a few more minutes.

Jake is the ringleader of a gang of four. In addition to himself, the group includes the young and brash Miles (Brian Van Holt), the pessimistic Gordo (Paul Giamatti), and the sad-sack Big Al (Louis Lombardi). Things are going fine for these guys until they pick a bad mark. Their $150,000 take turns out to belong to a shady underworld figure named King (Dustin Hoffman), and he wants restitution. After Big Al ends up slumped over his Chinese dinner with a bullet in the head, Jake decides to offer a deal: He'll pull a job for King to cover the debt. King agrees, but with two conditions: He gets to choose the mark, and one of his men, Lupus (Franky G.), goes along. To round out the group and add a little sex appeal, Jake picks up Lily (Rachel Weisz), a sultry brunette with "potential." King's chosen victim is his rival, Morgan Price (Robert Forster), and the goal is $5 million in cash. Jake meticulously plans everything, but his carefully orchestrated scheme doesn't take into account a pair of corrupt cops (Donal Logue and Luis Guzman) or the dogged Fed (Andy Garcia) who has been tracking Jake across the country.

Confidence has a high enough entertainment quotient that it's possible to overlook a great many flaws. This brash production doesn't expect a lot more from its audience than undivided attention. It plays by the genre's rules and toys with the viewer's expectations, but it never does anything truly unexpected or amazing. For those who enjoy movies about heists, cons, and double crosses, this will satisfy. Foley may be directing a script about grifters, but he isn't stealing his audience's money. RECOMMENDED

The Contender [2000]

Starring: Joan Allen, Jeff Bridges, Gary Oldman Director: Rod Lurie
Screenplay: Rod Lurie Running Time: 2:05 Rated: R (Profanity, sexual situations, nudity) Theatrical Aspect Ratio: 1.85:1

The story opens several weeks after the death of the Vice President. President Jackson Evans (Jeff Bridges) has narrowed his selection of candidates to a short list. The party favorite is up-and-coming Democratic star, Jack Hathaway (William Petersen), the popular governor of Virginia. Evans, however, is pursuing his own agenda. Midway through his second term, he is in search of a means to secure his legacy, and he believes that putting a woman in the Vice President's position is unique enough to earn him a spot in the history books. So, bucking the advice of even his key advisors, he names Ohio Senator Laine Hanson (Joan Allen) as his choice. However, his hopes for smooth sailing run afoul of Congressman Sheldon Runyon (Gary Oldman), the Republican chairman of the confirmation hearings. Runyon wants Hathaway, and will stop at nothing to derail Hanson's chances, including dredging up a 25-year-old sex scandal. Hanson finds herself embroiled in a battle where she is hampered by her own high ethical standards while her opponents have no such handicaps.

For most of its running length, *The Contender* offers a fairly straightforward account of the moves and counter-moves made by Runyon and Evans as they maneuver against one another. For either of them, a defeat means absorbing a political blow, but for Hanson, the pawn in the middle, everything is at stake — her credibility, her reputation, and her future. *The Contender* turns Hanson's confirmation process into a high-stakes game of strategy, where there are no rules. In the end, *The Contender* asks a key question: can someone with a moral code survive in the national political forum?

The Contender is not without hiccups. A subplot featuring a female FBI agent is clumsily grafted onto the main story. Although it serves a purpose — to soften the deus ex machina aspect of a key twist — Lurie never integrates it seamlessly into *The Contender*'s fabric. As a result, it remains an appendage. Additionally, the way everything is wrapped up into a nice, neat package at the end seems a little too convenient. Finally, although I'm not a big fan of using grandstanding speeches to offer a catharsis, at least in this case the speech fits the circumstances and is delivered in a suitably convincing manner. RECOMMENDED

The Cooler [2003]

Starring: William H. Macy, Alec Baldwin, Maria Bello, Shawn Hatosy, Rong Livingston, Paul Sorvino, Estella Warren, Arthur J. Nascarella
Director: Wayne Kramer Screenplay: Frank Hannah & Wayne Kramer
Running Time: 1:41 Rated: R (Sex, nudity, violence, profanity, drug use) Theatrical Aspect Ratio: 2.35:1

The Cooler, as icy a title as you're likely to find, is about the efforts of one man to find his luck (or, to be more precise, some form of luck other than that of the bad variety). Rarely has a more pathetic individual been captured and portrayed on the screen. Bernie Lootz (William H. Macy) is a loser's loser — the kind of guy who makes Wiley Coyote look fortunate. Bernie's luck is so bad that it confounds career losers. Worse, Bernie's luck is contagious. Put him next to someone who's on a roll, and he stops them cold. "People get next to me, and their luck turns," he succinctly explains. That's the reason The Shangri-La Casino in Las Vegas wants to keep Bernie in their employ. He's their "cooler." Whenever anyone starts winning, all casino mogul Shelly Kaplow (Alec Baldwin) has to do is send in Bernie.

Love comes unexpectedly into Bernie's life in the person of cocktail waitress Natalie (Maria Bello). Suddenly, after having sex with Natalie, Bernie begins to feel as if his luck is changing, and, the next day at work, his "cooling" powers fail him. This comes at a particularly inappropriate time for Shelly, whose "old school" methods of running the casino are being called into question by a mob boss (Arthur J. Nascarella) who wants to modernize the operation. And, to further complicate matters, Bernie's no-good son, Mikey (Shawn Hatosy), and his pregnant girlfriend (Estella Warren) arrive in Vegas looking to Bernie for a financial bail-out. (Really, it's just money to use for gambling and drug purchases.)

The best part of the film, unsurprisingly, is William H. Macy's low-key portrayal of Bernie, who radiates "complete loser" from frame one. The second best thing is the relationship between Bernie and Natalie, which is tender and erotic. We believe in these two characters, and we accept that they fill each other's needs. This doesn't seem like another manufactured screen romance. It feels true, and for the third act of *The Cooler* to work, that's a necessity. The other plot elements, which include Shelly playing carrot-and-stick with Bernie to get him to stick around, the mob putting pressure on Shelly, and Bernie's family problems, add texture and scope to the overall story line. And the film ends on a note of delicious irony that even the most blasé viewer will appreciate.

Director Wayne Kramer has fashioned an impressive cinematic calling card. In addition to its character, acting, and plot strengths, *The Cooler* is highly atmospheric, capturing the false glitz of Vegas with the cameras and using an evocative score. The film offers a surprisingly frank perspective of the sexual aspects of the characters' relationship, and there's a hilarious scene that might make viewers question exactly what they're hearing through paper-thin motel room walls. *The Cooler* is, without a doubt, a hot prospect.

RECOMMENDED

Copland [1997]

Starring: Sylvester Stallone, Harvey Keitel, Ray Liotta, Robert DeNiro Director: James Mangold Screenplay: James Mangold Running Time: 1:44 Rated: R (Violence, profanity, mature themes) Theatrical Aspect Ratio: 1.85:1

In *Copland,* action megastar Sylvester Stallone plays Freddy Heflin, the shy, overweight, rather dumb sheriff of the tiny town of Garrison, New Jersey. The most noticeable thing about Freddy isn't the caliber of his gun, it's the size of his paunch. And, every time Freddy confronts *Copland*'s villain, Ray Donlan (Harvey Keitel), something extraordinary happens: he meekly backs down. It's a strange thing to see Stallone playing someone whose primary characteristic is impotence.

Ultimately, *Copland* is just another story of police corruption in New York City — a Western transposed into modern times. The film takes place in Garrison, a tiny northern New Jersey town (population 1,280) that has been dubbed "Copland" because of the number of NYPD officers who live there with their families. Ray and his cronies basically own Garrison, due in large part to Freddy's passivity. He's "a wannabe who couldn't get on the force because of his bad ear," and who isn't willing to do anything to rock the boat. But Ray is a bad cop — he has his fingers in a number of illegal pies, and he has connections so high up that not even an internal affairs officer, Moe Tilden (Robert DeNiro), can touch him without concrete evidence.

In addition to the high caliber of acting, another thing that sets *Copland* apart from an average entry into the genre is Mangold's dialogue, which sparkles with intelligence. The director may not have Tarantino's gift for words, but his characters speak reasonably, not like they're reading from a sheet of paper. Even the supporting players, like Janeane Garofalo's officer Cindy Betts, say and do things in a believable manner. The overall story has problems, but Mangold is a master of the moment, and he gets us to care about the characters enough that we don't spend one-hundred minutes obsessing over flaws. As a result, *Copland* is a compelling, if imperfect, motion picture. RECOMMENDED

Copycat [1995]

Starring: Sigourney Weaver, Holly Hunter, Dermot Mulroney Director: Jon Amiel Screenplay: Ann Biderman and David Madsen Running Time: 2:03 Rated: R (Violence, post mortem photographs) Theatrical Aspect Ratio: 2.35:1

Copycat opens in a college lecture hall. Dr. Helen Hudson (Sigourney Weaver), a psychiatrist who specializes in serial killers, is giving a talk on her pet subject. Her words drive home the point: these people get turned on by what they do. They feel no remorse — only anticipation of the next kill. After finishing the seminar, Helen heads for the restrooms, where she comes face-to-face with Daryll Lee Cullem (Harry Connick Jr.), a man with murderous intentions who has been stalking her.

Thirteen months later, Helen is an agoraphobiac recovering from a nervous breakdown. She hides inside her apartment, connected to the Internet while downing pills and booze in roughly equal quantities. She's useless to herself or anyone else. Then the police, led by Mary Jane Monahan (Holly Hunter) and Reuben Goetz (Dermot Mulroney), arrive at her door. They need help tracking a serial killer who has been terrorizing young women in the San Francisco area, and who better to go to than an expert with 20 years of having "serial killers on the brain"? Although at first reluctant, Helen eventually relents and lends her experience to the investigation. Her first contribution is to identify the killer as a copycat. He is mimicking the great serial killers — the Boston Strangler, Son of Sam, the Hillside Strangler, Dahmer, and Bundy — and there's no way to tell who or how he will murder next. On top of everything, he has decided to play Internet games with Helen, the "Muse of Serial Killers."

It's a difficult task to perfect this sort of story. There are so many areas where the script can fail that it's astounding how seamlessly *Copycat* overcomes all obstacles. There are no stupid characters, contrived resolutions, or deus ex machinas. The police are smart, but so is the killer. And the movie doesn't play games with the villain's identity — we aren't left wondering whether he's one of the supposed "good guys."

The worst thing that can happen in a movie like this is for the characters to be a step behind the audience. That's not the case in *Copycat,* where the viewer is in synch with what's occurring on-screen. Tension and atmosphere are excellent, and director Jon Amiel pays careful attention to detail. Parts of this film are frightening, and will have many viewers either on the edge of their seat or hiding their eyes. And, unlike in many so-called thrillers, the ending is not a let-down. **RECOMMENDED**

Criminal [2004]

Starring: John C. Reilly, Diego Luna, Maggie Gyllenhaal, Jonathan Tucker, Peter Mullan, Zitto Kazann   Director: Gregory Jacobs Screenplay: Gregory Jacobs & Sam Lowry, based on *Nine Queens,* by Fabian Bielinsky   Running Time: 1:27   Rated: R (Profanity, violence) Theatrical Aspect Ratio: 1.85:1

Criminal is an English-language remake of the little-known *Nine Queens,* a 2000 film from Fabian Bielinsky. First-time director Gregory Jacobs and his cowriter, "Sam Lowry" (actually a pseudonym for Steven Soderbergh), have streamlined the movie for American audiences, quickening the pace and eliminating a few of the complexities. At the same time, they have left some scenes virtually unchanged.

John C. Reilly, who played Philip Baker Hall's pupil in *Hard 8,* has evolved to become the teacher here. He's Richard Giddis, a con man who has his eye on a big score. With his new, naive partner, Rodrigo (Diego Luna), in tow, he intends to bilk billionaire businessman William Hannigan (Peter Mullan at his Rupert Murdoch best) out of $750,000. In his possession is an expert forgery of a rare silver certificate, and with the help of Diego and a few hotel employees, he believes he can pull off the scam of a lifetime. Unfortunately, the hotel's concierge is Richard's sister, Valerie (Maggie Gyllenhaal), and she would like nothing better than to see her good-for-nothing brother fall on his face.

The film's strength lies in the story, and credit for that goes to Bielinsky, Jacobs, and Soderbergh. *Nine Queens* is a near-masterpiece, and the English language adaptation avoids cheapening it. Jacobs clearly appreciates the original. He's not trying to re-invent it to match his own vision. The film moves quickly and crisply, never losing the audience. Some of the twists are easily guessed, but others are not, and there are enough of them that even the most jaded viewer is guaranteed at least a surprise or two. I like well-made movies about con artists, and *Criminal,* while not at the top of the genre, ranks as a solid effort.

This is the first time Jacobs has helmed his own film, but he has been a producer and/or assistant director for Soderbergh for more than a decade. Like George Clooney, whose *Confessions of a Dangerous Mind* showed more than a hint of Soderbergh's influence, *Criminal* bears a few of the celebrated director's trademarks. Jacobs has learned his lessons well and, in putting them together on celluloid, he has created an entertaining flick that's a credit to all those involved. **RECOMMENDED**

Crimson Tide [1997]

Starring: Denzel Washington, Gene Hackman, George Dzundza, Viggo Mortensen   Director: Tony Scott   Screenplay: Michael Schiffer   Running Time: 1:55   Rated: R (Violence, post mortem photographs)   Theatrical Aspect Ratio: 2.35:1

There's a lot happening in this film. It opens with a quick synopsis of the current political situation: Russia is in the midst of a civil war and the anti-American rebels have taken control of a nuclear base. The *USS Alabama,* commanded by Captain Ramsey (Gene Hackman), is ordered off the Asian coast as the "front line and the last line of defense." Since Ramsey's usual XO has appendicitis, he must choose a new right-hand man. At the top of a short list is Ron Hunter (Denzel Washington), an officer who doesn't necessarily agree with his captain's no-thought, gut reaction method of commanding. Tension builds as orders from land make it apparent that war is imminent. A Russian sub — possibly hostile — is sighted nearby, and the crew is ready to mutiny when a fissure develops between the two men who must co-authorize a nuclear launch.

Michael Schiffer's script (as doctored by an uncredited Quentin Tarantino) works hard to incorporate elements from the likes of *The Hunt for Red October* and *Das Boot,* weaving them into his story of mutiny on a nuclear vessel. In some ways, trying to do all these things almost overburdens *Crimson Tide.* So much is going on that no single element gets the screenplay's full attention.

Denzel Washington and Gene Hackman are both in top form, and their multiple confrontations are some of *Crimson Tide*'s best moments. With these two actors going toe-to-toe, everything else fades into the background. There's little doubt that Hunter is the hero — the guy the audience is supposed to identify with — but he's shown to have a fault or two. And, while Ramsey is the obligatory human antagonist, he has his redeeming qualities, and his position on the to-launch-or-not-to-launch issue is not without merit.

Because of the contained environment, submarines make great settings for thrillers, with the throbbing of the engines sounding like a pulse. *Crimson Tide* is no exception — the atmosphere alone is sufficient to keep the audience on edge. There's not a lot that's remarkable, ground-breaking, or earth-shattering about the production, but director Tony Scott (*Top Gun, True Romance*) shows a flair for the visual. This is great, light entertainment. **RECOMMENDED**

Croupier [United Kingdom, 1998]

Starring: Clive Owen, Gina McKee, Alex Kingston Director: Mike Hodges Screenplay: Paul Mayersberg Running Time: 1:31 Rated: R (Nudity, sex, violence, profanity) Theatrical Aspect Ratio: 1.85:1

The world of the croupier (casino dealer) is seen through the eyes of Jack Manfred (Clive Owen), a writer who's looking for material to put into a new novel. By nature, Jack is an observer, not a participant. He doesn't gamble, because he knows the odds aren't good. For the most part, he likes to play by the rules. And he has a perverse addiction — he likes watching people lose. He drinks in defeat like a stimulant, and the experience of dealing often leaves him shaking afterwards. As the story unfolds, Jack begins to blur the lines between his real-life self and his fictional alter-ego, Jake. Sometimes, it's Jake, not Jack, who steps behind the tables and begins to shuffle the cards. However, while Jack is cold and detached, Jake believes in taking risks and getting involved — two things that lead to trouble.

Croupier is an unconventional thriller because it does not feature the staples of most such movies. There's some violence, but not much, and there's not a car chase to be found (in fact, for most of the film, the lead character doesn't own a car). All of the suspense is internalized — it builds slowly but consistently as we begin to understand the kinds of underhanded deeds that occur at the casino. Jack may have "the hands of a conjurer (or a cardshark)," but he'll need a peculiar kind of magic to extricate himself from a situation he agrees to be party to. His girlfriend (Gina McKee) is supportive of his writing career but despises the kind of person his casino work is turning him into. And there's a femme fatale (played by Alex Kingston), who plays on Jack's sympathies to get her way.

One of the biggest problems with modern-day thrillers is that they think a quick burst of adrenaline is a good substitute for solid plotting and intelligent dialogue. *Croupier* proves how flawed this philosophy is. The best antidote to the dumbing-down of motion pictures is to see something smart, savvy, and unpredictable — three qualities that this movie possesses in abundance. **HIGHLY RECOMMENDED**

The Crying Game [United Kingdom, 1992]

Starring: Stephen Rea, Jaye Davidson, Forest Whitaker, Miranda Richardson Director: Neil Jordan Screenplay: Neil Jordan Running Time: 1:50 Rated: R (Language, nudity, violence, mature themes) Theatrical Aspect Ratio: 2.35:1

The Crying Game, the creation of Irish director/writer Neil Jordan, loosely fits into the category of a "thriller," although to saddle it with such a label is perhaps to do it a great injustice, since this immediately causes images of the *Die Hard* series to spring to mind, and it would be hard to imagine two movies more dissimilar than *Die Hard* and *The Crying Game.*

Jordan has managed to find another dimension to the thriller, giving us not only the requisite tension and action, but a healthy — and heavy — dose of drama as well. As is typical for non-mainstream films, *The Crying Game* demands the audience's attention and moves at its own pace, never knuckling under to the pressure of its "genre." Some might complain that the first portion of the movie, where British army officer Jodi (Forest Whitaker) is held prisoner by Fergus (Stephen Rea) and his IRA cronies (including Miranda Richardson and Adrian Dunbar), is too long. If you're waiting for something explosive to happen, that may be the case, but if you're absorbing the meticulous and subtle character interaction, the pacing is perfect. There's excitement and gunplay in *The*

Crying Game, but those things are almost incidental to the themes that the movie explores. The two most basic (and potent) deal with the nature of the individual and the meaning of love.

As is often the case with European films, the acting is superlative. Stephen Rea is rock-solid throughout, giving the audience a character that we can relate to and sympathize with. Forest Whitaker, the only American in the film, is credible as Jodi, and he has surprisingly little trouble with a British accent. Miranda Richardson and Adrian Dunbar are strong in supporting roles. The real standout, however, is newcomer Jaye Davidson, whose performance is, without exaggeration, stunning.

The Crying Game is not to be missed. The script isn't especially convoluted or filled with twists and turns, but the less said the better. The film contains one surprise revelation that is central to *The Crying Game*'s resolution. Regardless of what is known — or not known — about plot details, however, the movie will still reward its viewers with a thought-provoking, superbly-rendered 110 minutes. HIGHLY RECOMMENDED

Dark Blue [2003]

Starring: Kurt Russell, Scott Speedman, Ving Rhames, Brendan Gleeson, Michael Michele, Lolita Davidovich Director: Ron Shelton Screenplay: David Ayer, based on a story by James Ellroy Running Time: 1:56 Rated: R (Violence, profanity, nudity, sexual situations) Theatrical Aspect Ratio: 2.35:1

Ron Shelton's *Dark Blue* bears more than a passing resemblance to Antoine Fuqua's *Training Day,* with perhaps a touch of *L.A. Confidential* thrown in for good measure. As with *Training Day, Dark Blue* centers on a cop who has strayed into a moral void where, in his opinion, idealism gives way to pragmatism. Unfortunately, both movies suffer third-act collapses. In neither case are the flawed endings disastrous, but for discerning viewers, the end-game melodramatics may leave a slightly bitter taste.

Sergeant Eldon Perry (Russell) is a member of the LAPD's elite Special Investigations Squad (SIS), a group of cops who aren't concerned about the means, just the ends. The hard-drinking Eldon has been given the job of breaking in a new partner, Bobby Keough (Scott Speedman, whose acting prowess is not the equal of his matinee good looks), who is the nephew of the powerful and corrupt head of the SIS, Jack Van Meter (Irish character actor Brendan Gleeson). It's an ill-kept secret that the officers in the SIS play by their own rules, but no one, not even

Internal Affairs, is willing to challenge Jack — until Deputy Chief Arthur Holland (Ving Rhames, gruff but strangely subdued) steps up and makes it known that he intends to have Eldon's badge.

The wrangling between Arthur and Eldon represents only a small fraction of *Dark Blue*'s plot, most of which deals with Eldon and Bobby's investigation into a quadruple homicide that occurs in a Korean-owned convenience store. The murders are the by-product of a robbery that was ordered by Jack. Now, eager to remain clear of any fallout, he directs Eldon to arrest two patsies and make sure they don't live long enough to tell anyone their version of things. Eldon goes along with Jack, but for the first time in recent memory, he begins to feel the stirrings of his conscience. Exacerbating things is Bobby's inability to cope with the kind of ruthlessness exhibited by both his partner and his boss.

For Ron Shelton, who is best known for his sports-themed movies (like *Bull Durham, Cobb,* and *Tin Cup,* to name a few), this represents an opportunity to break new ground. Nevertheless, the film would not have been as successful without the performance of Kurt Russell. Russell's approach to the role combines combustible rage, calculated cynicism, and a deeply buried core of humanity striving for redemption. As depicted by Russell, Eldon is never an out-and-out villain. There are nuances of warped, wounded nobility buried under the brittle exterior. He will continue to hold your attention when things around him — like the story line — lose steam and credibility. RECOMMENDED

Dead Again [1991]

Starring: Kenneth Branagh, Emma Thompson, Derek Jacobi, Andy Garcia Director: Kenneth Branagh Screenplay: Scott Frank Running Time: 1:47 Rated: R (Profanity, violence) Theatrical Aspect Ratio: 1.85:1

Over the course of 107 minutes, director Kenneth Branagh fashions a fascinating puzzle that contains its share of action, romance, dry wit, and (of course) twists & turns. And, unlike most thrillers, there's a distinct element of unpredictability to the latter. *Dead Again* contains two significant plot contortions. While it's possible, and even reasonable, for an intelligent viewer to surmise the second, the first is almost unguessable.

Dead Again is a tale of parallel stories in different time frames. The first, which transpires in post-World War II Los Angeles and is presented entirely through black-and-white flashbacks, relates the tragic romance of Roman and Margaret Strauss (Branagh and his then-wife, Emma Thompson). Roman is a world-famous composer and conductor, and Margaret is an up-and-coming musician. They meet when Roman conducts Margaret's orchestra, and it's love at first sight. They are soon married, but their fairytale existence begins to fray. Margaret is suspicious that Roman's housekeeper, Inga (Hanna Schygulla), and her son, Frankie (Gregor Hesse), may be stealing from Roman. He, in turn, is wary of her relationship with a reporter named Gray Baker (Andy Garcia), who appears to be exceeding the bounds of friendly propriety. This all leads to murder. Margaret is stabbed to death using a pair of scissors, an expensive anklet is stolen, and Roman is arrested and convicted. He goes to the electric chair claiming to be innocent.

The other part of the story occurs in 1991 Los Angeles, where a solitary private investigator, Mike Church (Branagh), has been requested by a local priest to uncover the identity of a pretty woman (Thompson) who has lost her voice and her memory. Mike's friend, newspaper man Pete (Wayne Knight), puts her photograph in the local paper, and the only respondent is a hypnotist/junk dealer named Franklyn Madison (Derek Jacobi), who believes that a trauma from the woman's past life may be causing her mute amnesia.

Although *Dead Again*'s story is complicated, Branagh presents it in a clear, straightforward manner that leaves little room for confusion. Each of the plot twists is exposed with suitable buildup, maintaining viewer interest. One of the reasons for *Dead Again*'s strong resonance and appeal is the way it toys with two issues that fascinate almost everyone: chance and fate.

Rhythm is a critical element of any psychological thriller, and *Dead Again* is no exception. However, unlike most Hitchcock wannabes, this one has it. High points and shock revelations are interspersed with exposition, and the characters are not permitted to degenerate into walking clichés. Branagh has combined all of the cinematic elements into an achievement that rivals Hitchcock's best work and stands out as one of the most intriguing and memorable thrillers of the 1990s. **MUST SEE**

Dead Presidents [1995]

Starring: Larenz Tate, Keith David, Rose Jackson, N'Bushe Wright, Chris Tucker Director: Allen & Albert Hughes Screenplay: Michael Henry Brown Running Time: 2:00 Rated: R (Violence, profanity, sex) Theatrical Aspect Ratio: 2.35:1

Although ¾ of *Dead Presidents* (the title refers to the portraits on money) takes place in the Bronx, it's the segment away from New York that drives the story. There have been any number of Vietnam tales — Oliver Stone has made a career out of that time and place — but none with quite the perspective of the Hughes Brothers'. This is the story of a black man who goes off to war as a relative innocent, and returns a decorated hero whose only scars are inside. His re-acclimatization to civilian life is difficult, but, unlike some of his friends, he never turns to drugs, and isn't averse to working hard to earn a living. Sometimes, however, good intentions and a valiant effort aren't enough. In detailing one man's actions and their consequences, *Dead Presidents* isn't just an African American tragedy — its impact is universal. People of any color can sympathize with the plight of Anthony Curtis and understand, if not agree with, the eventual choices life forces him to make.

Dead Presidents opens in 1969, as Anthony (Larenz Tate) is about to graduate from high school. Not wanting to go to college, but needing to get away from home to find himself, he enrolls in the Marine Corps, and heads off to Vietnam, leaving behind a middle-class family, a pregnant girlfriend (Rose Jackson), and a mentor/small time crook, Kirby (Keith David), who is like a second father. Joining Anthony in the military are two of his close friends, Skip (Chris Tucker) and Jose (Freddy Rodriguez). When Anthony finally comes back to the Bronx in 1973, after two tours of duty, he discovers that returning to "normal" life isn't easy or pleasant.

Even though *Dead Presidents* is more about the effects of poverty than those of racism, only the most naïve viewer could completely dissociate the two. Nevertheless, the Hughes Brothers don't overtly introduce race as an issue. Instead, this is about the failure of society, and how desperation, more than greed, can lead to radical and violent acts. The film is not perfect — certain sequences are awkward or drawn from stock, and many of the supporting characters are stereotypes — but solid storytelling and tight pacing push *Dead Presidents* through its weak spots. The result not only reaffirms the Hughes Brothers' ability as film makers, but shows they can go beyond the limits of the urban street drama they presented so forcefully in *Menace II Society*. RECOMMENDED

Deceiver [1997]

Starring: Tim Roth, Chris Penn, Michael Rooker Director: Jonas & Josh Pate Screenplay: Jonas & Josh Pate Running Time: 1:42 Rated: R (Profanity, violence) Theatrical Aspect Ratio: 2.35:1

It's Wednesday, March 27, and a murder investigation is underway in Charleston, South Carolina. The crime: a young prostitute, Elizabeth (Renee Zellweger), has been brutally slain. One half of her severed body was found in a bag at the train station. The other half was discovered in a trunk at the harbor authority, miles away. The police duo of Braxton (Chris Penn) and Kennesaw (Michael Rooker) are strapped for leads. At the moment, they have only one possible suspect: Wayland (Tim Roth), a wealthy, unemployed genius who graduated Summa Cum Laude from Princeton and appears to be the least likely character to commit such a heinous act.

That's the premise for *Deceiver,* a thriller from the Pate Brothers, Jonas and Josh. *Deceiver* plays out like a mind game between the intellectually superior Wayland and the two not-so-bright cops (captions early in the proceedings let us know that Wayland's IQ is 151; by contrast, Kennesaw's is 122 and Braxton's is 102). The setting is a police interrogation room where a lie detector test is about to be administered. Over three days, as Wayland returns to answer more questions, the drama and tension among these three characters gradually escalates until, inevitably, it boils over.

The movie, obviously fashioned in the manner of classic film noir, drips atmosphere. There are some fascinating stylistic touches; for example, although the setting is contemporary, all of the telephones are old-fashioned, rotary models. Cinematographer Bill Butler is given an opportunity to use unconventional camera work to liven up *Deceiver*'s look. Some of the things he tries (mostly those that involve the contrast between light and shadow) work exceptionally well, while others (like any of several Lazy Susan shots) seem more like unnecessary visual tricks.

One of the best things about *Deceiver* is that it never talks down to the audience. Plot points aren't hammered home, and, although the ending has its weaknesses, everything isn't spelled out in bold letters. The Pates give audience members credit for having brains, which is an increasingly rare characteristic for film makers. Occasionally gripping and never uninteresting, *Deceiver* is a fine noir effort. RECOMMENDED

The Deep End [2001]

Starring: Tilda Swinton, Goran Visnjic, Jonathan Tucker, Peter Donat Directors: Scott McGehee, David Siegel Screenplay: Scott McGehee, David Siegel, based on the novel "The Blank Wall" by Elisabeth Sanxay Holding Running Time: 1:39 Rated: R (Violence, mature themes, profanity) Theatrical Aspect Ratio: 2.35:1

The Deep End is an exceptionally involving and intelligent thriller, and, unlike many of its commercially-driven cohorts in the genre, it does not rely overmuch on narrative twists and turns. The complexity lies more in the characters than in the plot. Using one of Hitchcock's favorite devices — the "wrong man" theme — co-writers/producers/directors Scott McGehee and David Siegel have crafted a motion picture that the Master would be proud of. With each scene, McGehee and Siegel tighten the screws, heightening suspense without benefit of such cheap theatrics as gunfights or chases. The presence of so many mindless movies makes the experience of watching *The Deep End* all the more worthwhile.

Events in this film take place in and around Lake Tahoe, where Margaret Hall (Tilda Swinton) and her three children, Beau (Jonathan Tucker), Paige (Tamara Hope), and Dylan (Jordon Dorrance) live in a nice house on a wooded parcel of lakefront property. Also in residence is Margaret's father-in-law, Jack (Peter Donat). Her husband, Tom, an officer in the Navy, is away (as is often the case) at sea. Domestic problems are brewing on the homefront. Beau, a newly self-aware homosexual, is carrying on an affair with a man 12 years his senior, the rather sleazy Darby Reese (Josh Lucas). Margaret wants Darby to leave her son alone — she doesn't trust Darby and doesn't want him around. He agrees, but for a price of $5,000. When she refuses to pay, he shows up at night and encourages Beau to sneak outside so they can have sex. But Margaret has told Beau about Darby's proposal, and a fight breaks out between the two lovers. Soon, there's a dead body, a mysterious blackmailer (Goran Visnjic), and a police murder investigation. Margaret finds herself covering up for what she believes to be her son's crime, but we in the audience know a critical clue that she is unaware of.

It would be impossible to talk about why *The Deep End* succeeds without gushing rapturously about the performance of Tilda Swinton. There's Oscar buzz already for the red-haired actress, and with good reason. This is the kind of acting job that people remember all year long. Swinton's down-to-earth portrayal of Margaret is what draws us into this story and allows us to accept the coincidences and contrivances that the storyline occasionally throws in our direction. We buy into Margaret, and, through her, into everything that happens.

The Deep End is unquestionably a thriller, but, in an odd way, it's also a love story. At the film's emotional center is the question of what a mother will sacrifice for her son — what lies she will tell and what blame she will accept to keep him safe. It is said that maternal love is the fiercest kind of all, and nowhere is this more apparent than in *The Deep End*.
HIGHLY RECOMMENDED

Devil in a Blue Dress [1995]

Starring: Denzel Washington, Jennifer Beals, Tom Sizemore, Don Cheadle Director: Carl Franklin Screenplay: Carl Franklin based on the novel by Walter Mosley Running Time: 1:41 Rated: R (Violence, sex, profanity) Theatrical Aspect Ratio: 1.85:1

Beneath all the trappings — a sultry woman in blue, dead bodies, smoky back rooms, shoot-outs, and blackmail — *Devil in a Blue Dress* addresses the kind of subject matter that most crime thrillers, in their quest for pure (often prurient) entertainment, avoid. Easy Rawlins (Denzel Washington), the lead character, is black, and this is 1948 Los Angeles, where segregation and racism are the accepted way of life. As the film progresses, it becomes evident that skin color is more than a background issue — it's the first thing anyone notices, and can break careers, shatter marriages, and end lives.

Easy's not a typical private investigator — he's a bit naive and doesn't own a gun. He's not a detective by trade, but he's out of work and has a mortgage to pay (he's one of the few property-owning blacks in this time and place), so when a man of dubious connections named DeWitt Albright (Tom Sizemore) offers him $100 to locate Daphne Monet (Jennifer Beals), Easy agrees. He doesn't realize what he's gotten himself into. Daphne is the girlfriend of the richest man in L.A. (Terry Kinney), and there are a lot of people — including one talented knife-wielding gangster — looking for her. In a short time, Easy has become implicated in two murders, has been offered money by just about everyone involved, and has become a key player in a political contest where the path to victory is paved with dirty tricks and smoking guns.

If the resolution of *Devil in a Blue Dress* is a little flat, the lack of startling revelations or unexpected twists can be forgiven considering the material's depth. Capable of being viewed on more than one level, this picture has narrative texture. While *Devil in a Blue Dress* never develops the taut momentum of Franklin's previous effort, *One False Move,* it maintains audience involvement, especially after the first, somewhat slow, half-hour. And, to keep the noir elements from becoming too pervasive, the movie is sprinkled with humor.

The most interesting element of *Devil in a Blue Dress* is not the whodunit, but the "whydunit." Finding the guilty parties isn't as involving as learning their motivation, which is buried in society's perception of racial interaction. By uncovering the truth behind this mystery, Franklin illustrates that some attitudes have indeed changed for the better over the last forty years. **RECOMMENDED**

The Devil's Advocate [1997]

Starring: Al Pacino, Keanu Reeves, Charlize Theron Director: Taylor Hackford Screenplay: Jonathan Lemkin and Tony Gilroy, based on the novel by Andrew Niederman Running Time: 2:25 Rated: R (Profanity, sex, violence, nudity) Theatrical Aspect Ratio: 2.35:1

Taylor Hackford's *The Devil's Advocate* has many laudable qualities, but subtlety is not among them. The story, which postulates that the devil is walking among us today, gives Satan's human alter-ego a truly obvious name: John Milton. And, in what is arguably the most believable aspect of the movie, *The Devil's Advocate* takes lawyer-bashing to its logical extreme by making Lucifer the head of a prestigious law firm. That being said, *The Devil's Advocate* is a highly-enjoyable motion picture that's part character study, part supernatural thriller, and part morality play. Although the film isn't a landmark combination of unique elements, it has a lot of energy and the rather long 145-minute running time passes quickly.

The Devil's Advocate's protagonist is Kevin Lomax (Keanu Reeves), a Florida prosecutor-turned-defense attorney who has never lost in more than 60 cases. Kevin's approach to a trial isn't that it's a forum for justice, but a game to be won or lost — and he is willing to do anything for victory, even if he knows that his client is guilty (the official term for this kind of person is a "sleazeball"). When he successfully gains an acquittal for an accused child molester in a difficult-to-win case, he attracts the attention of a big-time New York lawyer (Ruben Santiago-Hudson), who invites Kevin and his beautiful wife, Mary Ann (Charlize Theron), to Manhattan to meet the head of his firm. Once there, Kevin finds himself being offered a very attractive job by the charismatic John

Milton (Al Pacino). But John isn't just a very powerful attorney and astute businessman — he's the devil incarnate — and he has special plans for Kevin.

Aside from Pacino's performance, the greatest strength of the film is its delicious build-up to an operatic climax. And, although huge parts of *The Devil's Advocate* are overblown and overplayed, it's never as silly as it has the potential to be — and this quality consistently keeps the picture out of the dangerous realm of self-parody. The movie's greatest weakness is its ending, which, by trying to be too clever, ends up cheating the audience of a legitimate conclusion. While there's a sense of closure, it's not an especially satisfying one. *The Devil's Advocate* certainly has problems, chief of which is the subtlety thing, but Pacino's performance is so fun to watch that it eclipses the most significant of them. RECOMMENDED

Dirty Pretty Things [UK, 2002]

Starring: Chiwetel Ejofor, Audrey Tautou, Sergi Lopez, Sophie Okonedo, Benedict Wong Director: Stephen Frears Screenplay: Steve Knight Running Time: 1:37 Rated: R (Profanity, drug use, mature themes, sexual situations) Theatrical Aspect Ratio: 1.85:1

It's impossible to deny or ignore *Dirty Pretty Things'* political perspective. Director Stephen Frears is making a statement about the inhumanity of current immigration procedures — of how people have become secondary to processes. Frears argues persuasively against nationalism — that individuals should be viewed as human beings, not as "Americans," "French," "British," "Spanish," etc. Rather than preaching, however, Frears gets his point across by using a multinational cast and peeling back the curtain that hides some of the shadier aspects of the so-called "immigrant experience." And, while the events of *Dirty Pretty Things* transpire in London, similar stories could be told in New York, Paris, or Rome.

Okwe (Chiwetel Ejofor) is a Nigerian doctor who is living illegally in London and surviving by working two jobs. By day, he is a cab driver. By night, he is behind the counter at a hotel. On those rare occasions when he finds time to sleep, he crashes at the apartment of his friend, Senay (Audrey Tautou). Senay is a Turkish immigrant who is being watched by the authorities. Under the terms of her admission to the United Kingdom, she is not allowed to rent space in her room to anyone else or to engage in paid employment for at least six months. She is doing both, and that places her in jeopardy. Meanwhile, at the hotel, Okwe discovers that the manager, Sneaky (Sergi Lopez), is running a black market organ busi-

ness. He will obtain forged passports for anyone willing to give up a kidney. He then sells that kidney to an organ "supplier" for $10,000. Okwe is shocked by this, but his friends are not, and they wonder at his naïveté. He is forced to make a moral choice when Sneaky makes him a job offer. If Okwe will put his surgical skills to use removing kidneys, Sneaky will provide forged papers for him and Senay so he can return to Nigeria and she can go to New York.

Dirty Pretty Things' depiction of life in London's immigrant culture is eye-opening — not so much in terms of what must be done by the illegal aliens to stay in England, but the matter-of-factness with which they accept their fate. Degradation is a way of life. It's easy to see how the concept of trading a kidney for a new identity would be appealing. Of course, the victims don't know that they're going to be "operated" on by someone with no surgical skills using unsterilized instruments. Infection and death are very real possibilities. The alternatives, however, which include providing sexual favors and toiling for long hours in sweat shops, aren't much more appealing.

Throughout his career, Frears has taken chances, and only on rare occasions has he missed the mark. *Dirty Pretty Things* is right on target. It's a dark and revealing movie, and while the ending may not be upbeat enough for those expecting mainstream fare, it offers a measure of hope and a catharsis. And one can disagree with the filmmaker's political position without dismissing the movie, since it deals with activities and realities that cannot be denied. HIGHLY RECOMMENDED

Disclosure [1994]

Starring: Michael Douglas, Demi Moore, Donald Sutherland Director: Barry Levinson Screenplay: Paul Attanasio based on the novel by Michael Crichton Running Time: 2:08 Rated: R (Language, sex, mature themes) Theatrical Aspect Ratio: 2.35:1

As a thriller, this movie is effective and gripping, if occasionally contrived as a result of overplotting. However, as an examination of a pervasive societal problem, *Disclosure's* success is questionable. The woman-sexually-harassing-the-man situation seems suspiciously like a male knee-jerk reaction to the issue rather than the unique "twist" it is set up to be (imagine the likely differences in a *Disclosure* penned by a female author). An incident of relatively "benign" harassment of a woman by a man is thrown in almost gratuitously.

Tom and Susan Sanders (Michael Douglas and Caroline Goodall) are a well-matched couple. Affluent and co-supportive, they have a nice house, two children, and prosperous careers. Tom is expecting a promotion when his company, Digicom, enters into a corporate merger — a merger made possible in large part because of one of Tom's projects: Arcamax, a stand-alone CD-ROM player that works twice as fast as any commercially-available product.

Tom doesn't get the raise, however. Instead, his prospective position is given to Meredith Johnson (Demi Moore), an outsider who coincidentally used to be Tom's lover. Worried that his job might be eliminated, Tom agrees to an evening meeting alone with his new boss. Once there, he discovers that she's more interested in renewing a personal relationship than discussing work. Apparently unwilling to take "no" for an answer, Meredith threatens that if Tom leaves her unsatisfied, she'll ruin him.

Disclosure is a great crowd-pleaser, scripted by men who understand exactly how a typical audience likes to be entertained. Together, Crichton, Levinson, and screenwriter Paul Attanasio create a situation, present a sympathetic protagonist and a thoroughly-dislikeable villain, bend and twist the plot, then come up with a resolution that has everyone clapping. At 128 minutes, the film is long, but its crisp pacing keeps it moving through the entire length. And the use of sexual harassment serves the dual purpose of giving Meredith her fangs and getting the audience on Tom's side. On its own terms — the fear of lost security that many thrillers prey upon — *Disclosure* works, and that's all that anyone can reasonably ask from this kind of motion picture. RECOMMENDED

Enemy of the State [1998]

Starring: Will Smith, Gene Hackman, Jon Voight Director: Tony Scott Screenplay: David Marconi Running Time: 2:08 Rated: R (Profanity, violence) Theatrical Aspect Ratio: 2.35:1

Enemy of the State is the latest entry into the suddenly-hot thriller subgenre of films that, because of convoluted plots characterized by bursts of action and unexpected twists, are fun to watch even if they defy logic. In addition to being an in-your-face experience, this kind of movie exudes self-confidence, never doubting for a moment that the viewer will buy into the premise (no matter how ludicrous it might be) and come along for the sheer exhilaration of the ride.

Robert Dean (Will Smith) is a hotshot young attorney on the fast track to prominence. There's little he won't do for a client, including tangling with known mobsters. Robert's wife, Carla (Regina King), is also a lawyer, but, unlike her husband, she's strictly by-the-

book. Her passion is the Constitution, and she doesn't like what she sees in a new piece of legislation up for a vote on Capitol Hill that will give the National Security Agency (NSA) the power to use any kind of advanced, electronic surveillance equipment without previous permission or authorization. Robert essentially ignores Carla's gripes, figuring that this kind of law will never affect him. He's wrong. The wheels are already in motion. An incriminating digital tape passed on to him without his knowledge is about to put his life and family in danger as government agents seek to clean up all evidence of a sanctioned murder.

The victim was a United States congressman. The culprit was Thomas Reynolds (Jon Voight), a high-ranking State Department official on loan to the NSA who felt that the congressman's opposition to the surveillance bill would ground it. Unfortunately for Reynolds, the killing was captured on camera by a naturalist (Jason Lee) studying geese migration. Before Reynolds' team can eliminate the witness, he slips a copy of the tape into one of Robert's shopping bags. The NSA realizes this, although Robert doesn't, and he suddenly finds himself in the crosshairs without understanding why. With his life being systematically dismantled (credit cards canceled, wife thinking he's having an affair, fired from his job), he seeks out the mysterious Brill, a shady contact who may hold the key to his situation. But who is Brill? A tough-talking stranger (Gabriel Byrne) who corners him in a lavatory? A pugnacious nerd (Gene Hackman) who threatens him with bodily harm? Or someone else?

Enemy of the State is a kinetic movie, with very few slow moments. The climax, which features an improbable standoff, is both too convenient and a little silly, but it has the virtue of wrapping everything up into a neat package. There are also more than a few gaping holes in the story's plausibility, although these generally don't become evident until long after the end credits have rolled. RECOMMENDED

Enigma [Germany/United Kingdom/United States, 2001]

Starring: Dougray Scott, Kate Winslet, Jeremy Northam, Saffron Burrows Director: Michael Apted Screenplay: Tom Stoppard, based on the novel by Robert Harris Running Time: 1:57 Rated: R (Profanity, sexual situations) Theatrical Aspect Ratio: 2.35:1

The action takes place at Bletchley Park, 60 miles north of London, where the heart of England's World War II decoding operation was located. Tom Jericho (Dougray Scott) was one of the best in the business until he suffered a nervous breakdown after being dumped by his girlfriend, Claire Romilly (Saffron

Burrows). Now, a shell of the man he once was, Jericho is back at work — the decoders need him because the Germans have altered their encryption methods, blacking out the Allies at a crucial time (a huge convoy crossing the Atlantic may be headed into a German U-boat trap). Meanwhile, Claire has vanished, and Tom, aided by her flatmate, Hester Wallace (Kate Winslet), begins to investigate her disappearance. The deeper they dig, the more their activities attract the attention of the mysterious Wigram (Jeremy Northam).

Enigma is an imperfect but entertaining thriller that probably would have been more engaging had it been allowed to expand well beyond the 2-hour running length. Parts of the film, especially during the last 45 minutes, feel rushed, as if Apted was under pressure to tell the story as quickly as possible. Economy of screen time is typically an asset in motion pictures (these days, it's also an increasingly rare commodity), but Apted cuts a few too many corners. For example, Tom Stoppard's screenplay never gives us real insight into how the codebreaking is accomplished. An attempt is made to reduce the complex procedure into layman's terms, but the analogy (which involves the name on a tombstone) is neither lucid nor effective.

Nevertheless, *Enigma* does a good job of depicting the wild energy that drives the codebreakers, as well as the strain they're under from all sides. Lives depend on their actions and the politicians and military men can't understand why the process takes so long. With its combination of intrigue, romance, and adventure set against a World War II backdrop, the movie has an undeniable appeal. Flaws aside, *Enigma* is engaging and ambitious. **RECOMMENDED**

Erin Brockovich [2000]

Starring: Julia Roberts, Albert Finney, Aaron Eckhart Director: Steven Soderbergh Screenplay: Susannah Grant Running Time: 2:10 Rated: R (Profanity) Theatrical Aspect Ratio: 1.85:1

The film opens with a car accident. The vehicle driven by Erin Brockovich (Roberts), an unemployed single mother of 3, is broadsided by a speeding car at an intersection. She takes her case to lawyer Ed Masry (Finney), who agrees to represent her on a contingency basis. However, in court, Erin's surly manner and profane vocabulary do not endear her to the jury, which finds in the defendant's favor. Both Erin and Ed go home empty-handed. Still without work and needing to pay her bills, Erin tries an unusual approach to get a job: half-bullying, half-pleading with her former attorney for a position as a file clerk. With grave reservations, Ed relents.

When a pro bono real estate case file comes across her desk, Erin becomes intrigued and begins investigating. She soon learns that the water supply of the property in question may have been contaminated with hexavalent chromium, a "highly toxic, highly carcinogenic" compound that can get into a person's DNA. Erin's efforts uncover hundreds of potential victims of Pacific Gas & Electric's illegal dumping policy, and the information she puts together is convincing enough that Ed agrees to pursue the case. But fighting a $28 billion corporation in court is a daunting and expensive prospect, and Ed isn't sure he has the resources to see it through to the end. Meanwhile, the amount of time Erin is spending working is putting a strain on her relationship with her boyfriend (Aaron Eckhart) and keeping her away from her 3 children for lengthy periods of time.

Erin Brockovich is a unique legal thriller in that, during an era when overplotted and contrived stories like those of John Grisham define the genre, this movie is not littered with throw-away plot devices designed exclusively to generate tension. With only a minor exception, Erin is not followed by shadowy figures. She does not become the target of violence and terroristic threats. *Erin Brockovich*'s suspense does not arise from the likelihood that someone will do something to harm her or her family (although the possibility certainly exists), but from the question of whether a David can succeed in today's legal world against "[Goliath's] whole family." This is the story of someone on the moral high ground fighting for what is right in a legal arena that too often favors those who have money to burn. *Erin Brockovich* is a winner — a reminder of the impact that a truly good motion picture can have. **HIGHLY RECOMMENDED**

Extreme Measures [1996]

Starring: Hugh Grant, Gene Hackman, Sarah Jessica Parker, David Morse Director: Michael Apted Screenplay: Tony Gilroy based on the novel by Michael Palmer Running Time: 1:58 Rated: R (Violence, profanity, mature themes) Theatrical Aspect Ratio: 2.35:1

Gramercy Hospital's emergency room is a picture of overcrowded chaos. Only one operating room is available, and Dr. Guy Luthan (Hugh Grant) has to make a decision: operate immediately on an injured cop whose vital signs are stable or on the drugged-out junkie who shot him, whose condition is worse. Luthan elects the former, and, while both patients survive, he's never wholly satisfied with his choice, as he later confides to Jodie (Sarah Jessica Parker), a sympathetic ER nurse.

It's moral questions like these that lift *Extreme Measures* above the level of a routine, paranoia-driven thriller. True, when you get right down to it, this movie is about a guy trying simultaneously to survive, clear his name, and bring the bad guys down, but there are more shades of gray here than in most modern-day Hitchcockian efforts. *Extreme Measures* never portrays guilt as clear-cut, and its easy to see how, by telling the same story with a script slanted towards another character's perspective, the roles of protagonist and antagonist could be reversed.

Extreme Measures is also about a doctor who crosses the line. Dr. Lawrence Myrick (Gene Hackman) is a world renowned neurosurgeon who believes he has discovered the means to heal severed spines and allow paralyzed people to walk again. Frustrated by the laws that constrain medical experimentation, he sets up an underground complex and begins to kidnap homeless people from hospital ERs to involuntarily assist him. His goal is to be known as the man who enabled the lame to walk — a very godlike ambition.

Luthan becomes involved when lab tests on one of his dead patients reveal some very strange things. Stonewalled by his bosses, who tell him to forget it or risk his promising career, he begins his own investigation. Soon, pressure is being brought to bear on him, and he discovers the price of ignoring others' warnings. Now, desperate to clear himself of a crime he didn't commit, he ends up wandering through New York City sewers and subway tunnels, dodging bullets and searching for the mysterious place where Myrick conducts his experiments.

The question that Luthan eventually has to confront is whether the ends do indeed justify the means. There's no court scene here, but, in an extended, well-played confrontation between the two leads, the morality of the entire medical profession (not to mention the validity of the Hippocratic Oath) is put on trial. The resolution is perhaps not as powerful or satisfying as we might hope, but it's not a cop-out, either. RECOMMENDED

Eyes Wide Shut [1999]

Starring: Tom Cruise, Nicole Kidman, Sydney Pollack Director: Stanley Kubrick Screenplay: Stanley Kubrick & Frederic Raphael Running Time: 2:40 Rated: R (Graphic sex, frequent nudity, profanity) Theatrical Aspect Ratio: 1.85:1

Eyes Wide Shut is Kubrick through and through, from the frequent long, unbroken takes to the camera's re-

fusal to remain static. Kubrick's style, which became increasingly personalized with every new project, is one of *Eyes Wide Shut*'s most recognizable traits. Every shot and camera angle was selected with great care. There were no happy accidents — each moment of screen time was meticulously plotted, with many scenes being re-done at a later date when the initial version did not meet with the director's approval.

The story, which deals with the various faces of sex and love, is adult in nature. The curtain rises on Dr. Bill Harford (Tom Cruise) and his wife, Alice (Nicole Kidman), as they prepare for a glamorous Christmas party given by one of Bill's friends, Victor Ziegler (Sydney Pollack). Alice isn't happy about attending, and, when her husband abandons her so he can chat with an old medical school buddy-turned-pianist (Todd Field) and flirt with a pair of models, she imbibes a few too many glasses of champagne. This makes her susceptible to the suave advances of a debonair party guest who suggests, "Don't you think that one of the charms of marriage is that it makes deception a necessity for both parties." Alice eventually fends off this seduction, but it causes her to consider fidelity in marriage — both hers and her husband's.

The next night, following a heated argument, Alice admits to Bill that she almost cheated on him once, and, had the circumstances been slightly different, she would have thrown her entire life away for one night with the man she had lusted after. This revelation shatters the stability of Bill's world; he had been confident that, no matter what, he could be sure of his wife's faithfulness. He leaves their home to visit a patient, but, instead of coming straight back, he wanders the streets of New York. A series of chance encounters leads him on an unexpected path of discovery into a sexual underworld where he finds not only perversion and pleasure, but death and danger. Soon, he is being followed and has reason to fear for his safety as well as that of his wife and his young daughter.

The key theme in *Eyes Wide Shut* is one near and dear to Kubrick's heart: the dehumanization of society. This is a concept he has returned to repeatedly during his career (most obviously in *2001*, *A Clockwork Orange*, and *Full Metal Jacket*). Here, Kubrick has something to say about the causes and effects of depersonalized sex. There is freedom in anonymity, but also isolation and a complete dearth of emotion. In terms of power and effect, *Eyes Wide Shut* approaches (but does not surpass) Kubrick's vintage work — it is thought-provoking and unsettling. Impressions and images linger long after the projector has finished weaving its peculiar magic.

HIGHLY RECOMMENDED

Fallen [1998]

Starring: Denzel Washington, John Goodman, Donald Sutherland, Embeth Davidtz Director: Gregory Hoblit Screenplay: Nicholas Kazan Running Time: 2:03 Rated: R (Violence, profanity) Theatrical Aspect Ratio: 2.35:1

A serial killer (Elias Koteas) has been on the loose in Philadephia, but Detective John Hobbes (Denzel Washington), the noblest man on the police force, has brought him to justice. Now, during his last hours on death row awaiting his inevitable date with the gas chamber, the mass murderer cryptically tells Hobbes, "What goes around really goes around." Shortly thereafter, he begins to sing "Time Is on My Side" as he's taken on his last walk. Minutes later, the State of Pennsylvania has carried out the execution and Edgar Reese is dead. But for Hobbes, the nightmare is just beginning, because Reese wasn't a normal psychopath — he was the host body for a mythical dark angel named Azazel. And, with Reese's death, Azazel is free to hop from body to body, murdering and wreaking havoc at will. Only Hobbes and a pretty, female theology teacher (Embeth Davidtz) have an inkling of what they're up against. The rest of the cops, including Hobbes' partner, Jonesy (John Goodman); Lou (James Gandolfini), a newcomer to the department; and Lieutenant Stanton (Donald Sutherland), don't have a clue, and, as a result, they are in mortal danger.

Fallen's plot is brimming with potential, not all of which is realized. Somehow, I would have expected a more frightening tale to emerge from something with this kind of premise. But the level of terror, like that of gore, is kept in check. Nevertheless, there are several creepily effective scenes as the spirit of Azazel moves from body to body when people bump against each other on crowded city sidewalks. The film also boasts a chase sequence of a kind that can best be described as unusual.

However, despite the negatives, I'm still recommending *Fallen* on the strength of its complex plot and especially its ending, which I loved. The final scenes are startling, audacious, and unexpected. It's not often that a plot development takes me by surprise the way this one did. At a time when most movies fall apart in the last 10 minutes, *Fallen* manages to buck the trend and redeem itself. **RECOMMENDED**

Fargo [1996]

Starring: William H. Macy, Steve Buscemi, Frances McDormand Director: Joel Coen Screenplay: Joel and Ethan Coen Running Time: 1:38 Rated: R (Violence, profanity) Theatrical Aspect Ratio: 1.85:1

Fargo opens, appropriately enough, in Fargo, North Dakota, with a meeting between Minnesota car salesman Jerry Lundegaard (William H. Macy) and two local thugs, Carl Showalter (Steve Buscemi) and Gaear Grimsrud (Peter Stormare). Jerry wants this pair to kidnap his wife, then ransom her for $80,000. While Jerry doesn't have that kind of money (in fact, he's strapped for cash), his father-in-law, Wade Gustafson (Harve Presnell), does. When the cash is paid out, Jerry is supposed to receive a 50% cut, as well as the safe return of his wife. That way, everyone except Wade comes out ahead. Unfortunately, with two such incompetent crooks, things are bound to go wrong, and Carl and Gaear are soon leaving a trail of dead bodies behind them. A local cop, Marge Gunderson (Frances McDormand), is given the task of investigating the murders, and it's only with an amazing assist from fate that she ends up on the right track.

A current of absurd humor runs through *Fargo*. Like David Lynch, the Coens are fascinated with what lurks behind the white picket fences of middle America. In *Fargo*, everyone falls into one of two categories — the motivated (who are greedy, duplicitous, or homicidal) or the simpleminded (everyone else).

Born and raised in Minnesota, the Coens know their home state, which accounts for their ability to reflect reality there (which is like *un*reality for most of the rest of the country). People say things like "You're darn tootin'," "aw, geez," and "what the heck." Knowing how strange the talk of Minnesotans will seem to the rest of the world, the Coens intentionally play it for deadpan comic effect.

It's easy to admire what the Coens are trying to do in *Fargo*, but more difficult to actually *like* the film. The absence of viable characters limits any dramatic impact, making this more of a laid back, lightly entertaining experience than a fully immersive one.

RECOMMENDED

Fifteen Minutes [2001]

Starring: Robert De Niro, Edward Burns, Vera Farmiga Director: John Herzfeld Screenplay: John Herzfeld Running Time: 2:00 Rated: R (Violence, profanity, nudity, sex) Theatrical Aspect Ratio: 2.35:1

Thematically, John Herzfeld's *Fifteen Minutes* has nothing new to offer. Its various elements of social commentary — about the power of the media; the country's love of violent, lurid, "real-life" TV fare; and the cult of stardom — have all been tackled before. Yet, despite its occasional lapses, the movie still works — primarily because it has the audacity to do the unexpected. Some of the concepts may be recycled, but there's something fresh and ambitious about the way they are presented. Best of all, *Fifteen Minutes* manages to develop some genuine tension, especially during the closing sequence, by which time we're convinced that *anything* can happen.

Robert De Niro plays Eddie Flemming, a New York City homicide detective (undoubtedly a big stretch for the actor). Not only is Eddie a good cop, but he's also well-liked, especially by the media. He always seems to have a statement or a scoop for the cameras, and his accessibility has made him a local celebrity. Plus, he's good friends with Robert Hawkins (Kelsey Grammer), the host of the TV tabloid show *Top Story* and is involved in a serious relationship with a newswoman (Melina Kanakaredes). Eddie's latest case brings him onto the turf of fireman Jordy Warsaw (Edward Burns), who is investigating a fire that was used to cover up a double murder. Together, Eddie and Jordy begin to piece together the puzzle, which leads them to an odd-couple of Eastern European immigrants, Oleg (Oleg Taktarov) and Emil (Karel Roden), who are killing people and making home movies of their acts. Their ultimate goal is to elminate someone famous, plead temporary insanity, then make a ton of money by selling the video tape and book rights to their story. And Eddie becomes their choice for a victim.

Fifteen Minutes takes its share of chances, not all of which work. But it doesn't feel like a cookie-cutter cop thriller, and, on top of that, it's actually about something — a trait that is becoming increasingly rare in mainstream motion pictures. *Fifteen Minutes* probably won't get you to think hard about the thin line between entertainment and exploitation, but it makes its point, and does so in a compelling way. RECOMMENDED

Fight Club [1999]

Starring: Brad Pitt, Edward Norton, Helena Bonham Carter
Director: David Fincher Screenplay: Jim Uhls, based on the novel
by Chuck Palahniuk Running Time: 2:19 Rated: R (Graphic violence,
sex, nudity, profanity) Theatrical Aspect Ratio: 2.35:1

With its kinetic style, visceral approach, compelling storyline, and powerful social message, *Fight Club* makes a commanding case to be considered the '90s version of *A Clockwork Orange*. In a time when so few motion pictures leave an impact, *Fight Club* refuses to be ignored or dismissed. The experience lingers,

demanding to be pondered and considered, and, unlike 95% of modern-day thrillers, there is a great deal here to think about and argue over. *Fight Club* presents an overload of thought-provoking material that works on so many levels as to offer grist for the mills of thousands of reviews, feature articles, and post-screening conversations.

The film begins by introducing us to our narrator, Jack, who is brilliantly portrayed by Norton. Here, the actor flows fluidly into the part of a cynical but mild-mannered employee of a major automobile manufacturer who is suffering from a bout of insomnia. When he visits his doctor for a remedy, the disinterested physician tells him to stop whining and visit a support group for testicular cancer survivors if he wants to meet people who really have problems. So Jack does exactly that — and discovers that interacting with these victims gives him an emotional release that allows him to sleep. Soon, he is addicted to attending support group meetings, and has one lined up for each night of the week. That's where he meets Marla Singer (Helena Bonham Carter), another "faker."

Then, on what can be described as the worst day of his life (an airline loses his luggage and his apartment unit explodes, destroying all of his possessions), Jack meets the flamboyant Tyler Durden (Brad Pitt), a soap salesman with an unconventional view of life. Since Jack is in need of a place to live, Tyler invites him to move in, and the two share a "dilapidated house in a toxic waste part of town." Tyler teaches Jack lessons about freedom and empowerment, and the two begin to physically fight each other as a means of release and rebirth. Soon, others find out about this unique form of therapy, and Fight Club is born — an underground organization that encourages men to beat up each other. But this is only the first step in Tyler's complex master plan.

Told in a conventional fashion, *Fight Club* would still have been engaging. However, Fincher's gritty, restless style turns it into a visual masterpiece. The overall experience is every bit as surreal as watching Kubrick's *A Clockwork Orange*. This is a tale that unfolds in an eerie alternate universe where the melodies of life have the same rhythm as in ours but are in a different key. Fincher also shows just enough restraint that his flourishes seem like important parts of the storytelling method instead of gimmicks. *Fight Club* is a memorable and superior motion picture — a rare movie that does not abandon insight in its quest to jolt the viewer. MUST SEE

Flesh and Bone [1993]

Starring: Dennis Quaid, Meg Ryan, James Caan, Gwyneth Paltrow
Director: Steve Kloves Screenplay: Steve Kloves Running Time: 2:05
Rated: R (Violence, language, sexual situations, nudity) Theatrical
Aspect Ratio: 1.85:1

One night in the early 1960s, a young boy is taken in by a West Texas family. He claims that he's lost, and, being the decent folk that they are, his benefactors decide that it's their responsibility to see that he's fed, bathed, and given a place to sleep. But this guest turns out not to be the homeless waif the family believed him to be, and, when he's discovered letting his criminal father, Roy (James Caan), into the house to rob it, a bloodbath ensues. The sole surviving member of the family is a baby girl. Father, mother, and son are all brutally gunned down — two of them in cold blood.

Thirty years later, the boy has grown into the man, Arlis Sweeny (Dennis Quaid), a vending machine stocker who roams from town-to-town following a set routine that gives him comfort and helps shield him from memories better left buried. Then, into his life comes Kay (Meg Ryan), a woman whose future is as bleak as her past, and suddenly Arlis' deeds of 30 years ago return to haunt him anew.

Flesh and Bone is film noir, complete with the characters and settings expected from the genre. It's a thriller that doesn't rely on action for its suspense. Drama — occasionally spilling over to melodrama — is the backbone. The story isn't overplotted; the only real twist is easily guessed, and, while the entire script turns on one massive coincidence, that event is so expertly buried within the context of a gripping tale that it doesn't seem so implausible when it happens. Chock it up to fate's bitterly ironic sense of humor.

Perhaps, ultimately, *Flesh and Bone* is mostly-static, and maybe its central plot element is hard to swallow. But these characters are so impressive, and their circumstances so compelling, that I didn't care about shortcomings in the story. *Flesh and Bone* is all suspenseful buildup without shoot-outs, chases, and explosions, and its conclusion doesn't demand a neatly packaged resolution. RECOMMENDED

Freeway [1996]

Starring: Reese Witherspoon, Kiefer Sutherland Director: Matthew
Bright Screenplay: Matthew Bright Running Time: 1:42 Rated: R
(Profanity, violence, sexual situations) Theatrical Aspect Ratio: 1.85:1

What happens when you cross The Brothers Grimm with David Lynch, and throw in a little Quentin Tarantino for good measure? The result, or something very much like it, can be found in Matthew Bright's brilliant, incisive satire, *Freeway*, which up-dates the children's story "Little Red Riding Hood" in new, surprising, and very adult ways. Anyone who never appreciated this fable may revise their opinion after watching *Freeway*.

The film works — and does so manifestly — because its intentions are clearly delineated. Using black humor, blood, and a pair of tremendous performances, *Freeway* hones in on its targets and calculatedly skewers them one-by-one. First up is America's welfare system. Then the judicial system. Then the penal system. And, when you put all the pieces together, you realize that *Freeway* is making a penetrating statement about the general populace's endless fascination with the lurid and violent. This movie is both grimly funny and thought-provoking.

Reese Witherspoon plays a modern-day, white trash Red Riding Hood by the name of Vanessa. She has what might be termed "domestic problems." Her mother (Amanda Plummer) is a prostitute and her stepfather (Michael T. Weiss) is a drug addict. When the cops bust both of them, Vanessa faces another round of foster care. So, instead, she runs off to find her paternal grandmother, who lives in Northern California. Her boyfriend (Bokeem Woodbine) gives her a gun as a going-away present. Shortly after she gets on I-5, her clunker of a car breaks down. A passing motorist by the name of Bob Wolverton (Kiefer Sutherland, the wolf — or Wolverton — in sheepish clothing) gives her a lift. As they drive north, she starts opening up to him, relating her sad life's story. His intentions are anything but altruistic, however, and their little trip leads to a violent off-highway confrontation. This critical event takes place well before *Freeway*'s halfway point, and opens the door for a number of surprising plot developments.

Red Riding Hood references abound, from the opening credits (which depict the Grimm story in drawings) and a TV cartoon to one of the film's last lines ("what big teeth you have"). In addition to already-noted differences between the fairy tale and *Freeway*, there's one other factor that deserves mentioning. In this "Little Red Riding Hood," the wolf makes one huge mistake — he picks a girl who certainly doesn't need a woodcutter to do her butt-kicking for her. HIGHLY RECOMMENDED

The Game [1997]

Starring: Michael Douglas, Sean Penn, Deborah Kara Unger
Director: David Fincher Screenplay: John D. Brancato, Michael Ferris,
Andrew Kevin Walker Running Time: 2:15 Rated: R (Profanity,
violence) Theatrical Aspect Ratio: 2.35:1

This is Michael Douglas' movie. Sean Penn and Deborah Kara Unger, who receive second and third billing, respectively, are supporting performers in the truest sense of the word, since neither has more than 15 to 30 minutes of screen time. Douglas, however, is omnipresent. He's in nearly every scene, and the film is told from his character's point-of-view. And Nicholas Van Orten is the kind of man that Douglas plays best — initially cool and reserved, then gradually less and less sure of himself and his circumstances. The actor's intensity in his approach to this character is palpable.

Nick is a very wealthy man. He lives in a huge mansion equipped with every creature comfort available, but, aside from his housekeeper, he is alone. His wife left him after he elevated the priority level of his work over that of his family. Now, for his 48th birthday, his brother, Conrad (Sean Penn), comes up with the perfect gift for the man who has everything: the game. Developed by a company called "Consumer Recreation Services," the game is "a profound life experience" that "provides whatever is lacking" in a person's existence. Beyond making obtuse statements like it's "an experiential book-of-the-month club," no one is willing or able to describe the game in any detail to Nick. Despite his misgivings, he agrees to participate, but events conspire to raise a vital question: is it really all a game, or is it in deadly earnest?

Figuring out all the ins and outs of *The Game* is like piecing together a jigsaw puzzle. We struggle alongside Nick to determine what's really going on, and, just when we think we have it, something happens to make us doubt our conclusion. The script has its clever moments, and it's easy to mistake this for a smart movie. However, that intelligence is only surface-deep — the seams in the plot are quite visible if you look hard enough. Nevertheless, for anyone who is willing to suspend their disbelief (which, admittedly, isn't all that hard to do), *The Game* offers the kind of taut, unpredictable ride that Hitchcock would have approved of. RECOMMENDED

Gangs of New York [2002]

Starring: Leonardo DiCaprio, Daniel Day-Lewis, Cameron Diaz, Jim Broadbent Director: Martin Scorsese Screenplay: Jay Cocks and Steven Zallian and Kenneth Lonergan Running Time: 2:44 Rated: R (Violence, profanity, sex, nudity) Theatrical Aspect Ratio: 2.35:1

Gangs of New York is a bold, epic spectacle brought to the screen using more of the old-fashioned Hollywood techniques (elaborate sets, large groups of extras) than the new ones (CGI). Visually, it is stunning, and the storyline encompasses a grand scope, using a fascinating and turbulent period of American history as the canvas upon which master cinematic painter Martin Scorsese crafts his images. Yet, despite all of this, *Gangs of New York* doesn't come close to masterpiece status. There are some great individual scenes and a tremendous performance by Daniel Day-Lewis, but the connecting material is mediocre, leading to the occasional twinge of dissatisfaction.

Following a short prologue in 1846 New York, the time line jumps ahead to the 1860s, where, set against the background of the American Civil War, the bulk of the story unspools. Amersterdam Vallon (Leonardo DiCaprio) has returned to the Five Points in lower Manhattan to settle a score. When he was a boy, he saw his father murdered in a gang war by Bill the Butcher (Daniel Day-Lewis). Bill, the head of the powerful New York "Nativists" (who are anti-black and anti-immigrant), now rules the Five Points with an iron fist, and Amsterdam has returned to extract revenge. With the help Johnny Sirocco (Henry Thomas), the only one to recognize Amsterdam as the son of the dead Priest Vallon (Liam Neeson), the young man worms his way into Bill's inner circle. But his resolve to kill Bill wavers when the flamboyant butcher takes him under his wing and treats him like a son. Meanwhile, his friendship with Johnny frays when he becomes involved with Jenny Everdeane (Cameron Diaz), an ex-flame of Bill's with whom Johnny is infatuated.

With *Gangs of New York*, Scorsese has both hit and missed. This is inarguably the most ambitious motion picture of his long career, the first time he has attempted a pure epic. There is much to appreciate about the spectacle, and about the meticulous manner in which the director has brought to life the turbulence of New York in the mid-1800s. We see here the birth pangs of the greatest American city in all of its ugliness. Yet, in presenting such a large tapestry, Scorsese occasionally seems to lose control of the flow. There are times when the movie meanders and the psychological depth of 2 of the 3 principal characters falls far below what we have come to expect from the director of the masterworks *Taxi Driver*, *Raging Bull*, and *Goodfellas*. *Gangs of New York* is an example of a production in which the whole is less than the sum of its elements. Despite some reservations, however, the movie never lost my interest, and I consider it to be worth seeing. RECOMMENDED

The General [Ireland, 1998]

Starring: Brendan Gleeson, Jon Voight, Adrian Dunbar, Maria Doyle Kennedy Director: John Boorman Screenplay: John Boorman based on the novel by Paul Williams Running Time: 2:00 Rated: R (Profanity, violence) Theatrical Aspect Ratio: 1.85:1

Gangster movies generally come in two flavors: those that portray mob personalities as vicious figures and those that dwell on the charismatic, family-oriented side of such men. *The General*, a black-and-white, cinematic biography of the recently-assassinated Irish criminal, Martin Cahill (Brendan Gleeson), falls into the latter category. Veteran director John Boorman weaves together real-life incidents and fictional anecdotes to create a fascinating portrait of a man who was both more human and more humane than the legends about him indicate.

The real Martin Cahill was at the pinnacle of Dublin's organized crime structure during the late-'80s and early '90s. Cahill was reputed to have been heavily involved in the drug trade (an assertion that Boorman's film disputes) and was known for nailing men's hands to a pool table when they wouldn't talk. By all accounts, he was also a lively, fun-loving man who could charm with a smile. Unlike American gangsters, Cahill did not leave a trail of bodies in his wake — his criminal activities were more in the line of burglary and theft than murder. Eventually, perhaps for selling rare artwork to members of the Ulster Volunteer Force, Cahill ran afoul of the IRA, and, in 1994, they assassinated him. That event bookends *The General*; the movie begins and ends with it. The film is not about Cahill's death, but about his life. 90% of *The General* focuses on Cahill as an adult, showing him plotting various crimes, carrying them out, and feuding with the local cops.

Gleeson's portrayal of Cahill is nothing short of brilliant. The actor, who is largely unknown in North America, effectively displays the numerous complex facets of his character, including the cold-hearted torturer and the loving father. Cahill is depicted as being apolitical, stealing not to fund a cause, but for his own enjoyment. And he routinely shows his contempt for all forms of "the establishment," regardless of whether they're the police, the Church, or the IRA. It's fair to say that Boorman has romanticized Cahill's life, but he and Gleeson make much more out of this character than a likable rogue. By culling a career performance from Gleeson, Boorman has crafted a memorable portrait of a man who, in his homeland, was known as both a modern-day Robin Hood and a vile gangster, and who, on screen, can be seen as either. RECOMMENDED

Get Shorty [1995]

Starring: John Travolta, Gene Hackman, Rene Russo, Danny DeVito Director: Barry Sonnenfeld Screenplay: Scott Frank based on the novel by Elmore Leonard Running Time: 1:45 Rated: R (Profanity, violence) Theatrical Aspect Ratio: 1.85:1

John Travolta is Chili Palmer, a loanshark on a mission to Los Angeles to recover $300,000 gained through an insurance fraud. Once near Hollywood, however, Chili, an avowed movie-lover (he has the lines from *Touch of Evil* memorized and can recognize *Rio Bravo* from a sound bite), becomes seduced by the thought of producing a film. So he hooks up with schlock director Harry Zimm (Gene Hackman) and scream queen Karen Flores (Rene Russo). And when Chili starts to pitch an idea, none other than big time actor Martin Weir (Danny DeVito) shows interest. Nevertheless, even as things start looking up for Chili's movie, a host of gangsters try to muscle in on his action — one way or another.

One of the great pleasures of watching *Get Shorty* is that you don't have to turn off your brain while the film is on screen. The script is smart, and makes few concessions to mentally challenged audience members. There's a lot going on beyond the obvious. Take role reversals, for example. As Chili is seduced from a criminal lifestyle by movies, his motion-picture colleagues are drawn away from film by the lure of the gangster experience. Ultimately, it turns out that the common denominator for success in either career is attitude — a quality which Chili possesses in abundance.

The ending is a little reminiscent of that of *The Player*, with a couple of big name cameos. It's a clever way to conclude a wonderfully entertaining romp. *Get Shorty* may be compared to *Pulp Fiction*, but this less profane film is likely to find wider acceptance. It's certainly more mainstream, but, at least in this case, that's not a bad thing. With *Get Shorty*, director Barry Sonnenfeld has shown that broad appeal doesn't necessarily equate with stupidity. That's a lesson Hollywood should learn. HIGHLY RECOMMENDED

The Gingerbread Man [1998]

Starring: Kenneth Branagh, Embeth Davidtz, Robert Downey Jr., Robert Duvall Director: Robert Altman Screenplay: "Al Hayes" (Robert Altman) based on an original story by John Grisham Running Time: 1:55 Rated: R (Profanity, nudity, violence) Theatrical Aspect Ratio: 1.85:1

Kenneth Branagh, stepping into a rare contemporary role, is Rick Magruder, a top-notch Savannah-based defense attorney who hasn't lost a case in 8 years. Since his successful record has resulted in part from his ability to chew cops apart on the stand, he's not one of the police department's favorite citizens. One night, following a big victory celebration, as Rick is making his way through a torrential downpour, he encounters Mallory Doss (Embeth Davidtz), a waitress whose car has just been stolen. Rick offers her a lift home and a shoulder to cry on. Soon, her whole sad story pours out: her deranged father, Dixon (Robert Duvall), has been stalking her, and she's afraid for her life. Rick, instantly sympathetic because of his infatuation, agrees to help her get an order of commitment for Dixon. But the wily old man proves to be more dangerous than the lawyer expected, and soon his 2 children are in peril. And, on top of everything else, Hurricane Geraldo is bearing down on Savannah.

The Gingerbread Man starts out strongly by defining the characters, establishing the setting, and anchoring the somewhat convoluted storyline. One of Altman's strengths is character development, so it's no surprise that we are introduced to a gallery of interesting individuals. Past the setup, as the plot gathers steam, the movie takes on the characteristics of a traditional thriller, with such familiar elements as a mysterious car that tails Nick, a drunk private investigator (Robert Downey Jr.), a damsel in distress, and children in jeopardy. Altman ratchets up the tension during this section of the film, providing a few genuine edge-of-the-seat moments.

At its best, *The Gingerbread Man* evokes memories of Alfred Hitchcock, the master of suspense who used every tool at his disposal to trick, cajole, and manipulate the audience into a state of heightened anxiety. One of the mechanisms employed here by Altman is the weather — it always seems to be raining, and the approach of the hurricane promises even more wind and water. Fortunately, the storm sequences are impressively filmed and serve to enhance the atmosphere, rather than drown it.

Although *The Gingerbread Man* has its faults, there are enough fine moments and solid performances to more than balance them out. While Altman aficionados may be disappointed by the conventional nature of the production, fans of writer John Grisham (who gets story, but not screenplay, credit) will probably feel right at home. The legal thriller has become Grisham's home field, and *The Gingerbread Man*, with an accomplished director at the helm, is as worthwhile as anything he has helped bring to the screen. The result is an entertaining and sporadically engrossing 2 hours. **RECOMMENDED**

Hard Eight [1997]

Starring: Philip Baker Hall, John C. Reilly, Gwyneth Paltrow, Samuel L. Jackson Director: Paul Thomas Anderson Screenplay: Paul Thomas Anderson Running Time: 1:41 Rated: R (Profanity, violence, sex) Theatrical Aspect Ratio: 2.35:1

Inertia. The dictionary defines it as "a property of matter by which it remains at rest or in uniform motion," and this is an apt descriptor for Paul Thomas Anderson's debut feature, *Hard Eight*. During the first half, virtually nothing happens — the characters are stuck in a stasis from which escape seems impossible. Then, during the second half, momentum carries the story to its inescapable conclusion. The dualistic nature of *Hard Eight* makes it a difficult picture to size up. At times, it's engrossing, but, on other occasions, it's a lesson in frustration.

Hard Eight opens with a fascinating, 20-minute prologue. A dapper, elderly gentleman named Sydney (Philip Baker Hall), approaches a disheveled, younger man, John (John C. Reilly), outside a roadside diner. Sydney invites John to join him for a cup of coffee and a cigarette. Inside, they talk. John's on his way back from Vegas, where he lost all his money trying to win enough to bury his mother. Sydney thinks his intentions are admirable, and offers him an opportunity: come back to Vegas and learn how to get a free room and maybe even win a little extra cash. Sydney's scam is deceptively simple and undeniably effective, and Anderson presents it with flair and an undercurrent of wry humor.

The rest of *Hard Eight* takes place 2 years later in Reno, when Sydney and John are good friends. Theirs is a father/son relationship, with John never far from Sydney's side. As John's girlfriend, waitress/prostitute Clementine (Gwyneth Paltrow), observes to the older man, "He follows you and worships you like you're a captain." Clementine's actions soon introduce new obstacles in Sydney and John's friendship, as do those of a seedy security advisor named Jimmy (Samuel L. Jackson).

Hard Eight borrows its share of conventions from noir thrillers, but this is more of a character drama than anything else. Sure, there's some violence, gunplay, and a few plot twists, but everything keeps coming back to the relationship between Sydney, an aging man with an opaque past, and John, the damaged and none-too-bright individual he takes under his wing. Clementine too is one of life's castoffs, but Sydney's interest in her is primarily as a companion for his surrogate son. As much as Sydney likes Clementine, however, that's how much he dislikes Jimmy, whose vulgar, arrogant manner marks him as trouble from the beginning. There's something almost hypnotic about the way *Hard Eight* develops — even in its slowest moments, it keeps our attention. **RECOMMENDED**

Heavenly Creatures [New Zealand, 1994]

Starring: **Melanie Lynskey, Kate Winslet** Director: **Peter Jackson** Screenplay: **Peter Jackson and Frances Walsh** Running Time: **1:38** Rated: **Not Rated** (Mature themes, sexual themes, violence) Theatrical Aspect Ratio: **2.35:1**

Heavenly Creatures is based on the true story of Pauline Rieper (Melanie Lynskey) and Juliet Hulme (Kate Winslet) set in Christchurch, New Zealand from 1952 to 1954. These two teenagers (Pauline was 15 in 1954; Juliet was 17) formed an intense and, some argued, unhealthy friendship. They were inseparable, and when a case of tuberculosis forced Juliet into quarantine, they wrote voluminous letters to each other, both as themselves and as fantasy characters they created. Eventually, their parents became concerned about the nature of this friendship, and attempted to prevent Pauline and Juliet from seeing each other. The tragic ramifications of this action, as described in the real Pauline's journal, are related in Peter Jackson's original motion picture.

This uniquely powerful film accrues much of its momentum through character interaction. Pauline and Juliet are so well-scripted and solidly portrayed that the viewer cannot help but be captivated by their relationship. While it is intentionally left ambiguous whether either of these girls is a lesbian (one sexual encounter does not define a lifestyle), no such uncertainty accompanies the exploration of how hopelessly tangled their lives and emotional well-being have become.

Fantasy plays a crucial role in *Heavenly Creatures*. It's up to the individual viewer to decide how psychotic Pauline and Juliet are (they share visions of the "4th World," a "heaven without Christians" inhabited by clay people, where the tunes of Mario Lanza perpetually fill the air). Certainly, these two are more at home living in a world apart from our own, where romance and happiness reign.

As a dysfunctional family tale, the disturbing *Heavenly Creatures* offers no facile answers as to what might have been done differently to prevent circumstances from degenerating as they did. Revealed in unforgettable fashion by a capable director, the events that unfold in this film are not easily forgotten. **HIGHLY RECOMMENDED**

Heist [2001]

Starring: **Gene Hackman, Danny DeVito, Delroy Lindo, Sam Rockwell** Director: **David Mamet** Screenplay: **David Mamet** Running Time: **1:49** Rated: **R** (Profanity, violence) Theatrical Aspect Ratio: **1.85:1**

Heist is a wonderfully written excursion into criminal activity that throws us into the deep end and asks us to sink or swim. With dizzying speed, we are shuttled through a series of double-crosses and triple-crosses, and all is not revealed until the very end. One could argue that there's one twist too many, but it works brilliantly, so who cares? *Heist* begins with a meticulously planned and flawlessly executed jewelry store robbery, proceeds to the plotting of an even bigger crime, and ends with an apparent falling out between thieves. It's fast-paced and wildly entertaining.

Dialogue has always been one of Mamet's trademarks — especially the staccato beat with which it is delivered. However, while *Heist* contains its share of brilliant one-liners (including one or two that Arnold Schwarzenegger would be proud to utter), the words are spoken in a much more "natural" manner than in any previous Mamet-directed effort. There are no strange pauses and there is no odd rhythm. Admittedly, I missed it a little, but it's the right approach for this movie.

The cast is stellar. Gene Hackman plays Joe Moore, the veteran thief who is looking for one final score to finance his exit from the business. His team is comprised of Rebecca Pidgeon, Ricky Jay, Delroy Lindo, and Sam Rockwell as the cocky newcomer. Danny DeVito shows his vicious side as Joe's fence, who suddenly wants a bigger piece of the action. Admittedly, this is not a character-driven motion picture, so none of these performers have to take their alter-egos through anything more dramatic than a perfunctory arc, but they all do solid jobs inhabiting their characters' skins.

To say anything more about the specifics of *Heist* would be to ruin the fun of discovery. It's consistently fun, occasionally funny, and will have viewers on the edges of their seats on more than one occasion. Once again, playwright-turned-filmmaker David Mamet has crafted a motion picture worth seeking out. **HIGHLY RECOMMENDED**

Identity [2003]

Starring: **John Cusack, Ray Liotta, Amanda Peet, Clea DuVall, John Hawkes, William Lee Scott, John C. McGinley, Rebecca De Mornay, Jake Busey, Alfred Molina, Pruitt Taylor Vince** Director: **James Mangold** Screenplay: **Michael Cooney** Running Time: **1:30** Rated: **R** (Violence, gore, profanity) Theatrical Aspect Ratio: **2.35:1**

An out-of-the-way motel. An introverted manager with a skeleton in the closet. Guests who lose their heads at the first signs of trouble. Sound familiar? Although the echoes of Hitchcock are certainly intentional, *Identity* is not *Psycho*, nor does it strive to be. A movie that successfully navigates the line between psychological thriller and slasher/horror movie, *Identity* ultimately metamorphoses into something unexpected and startling. What starts out as a seemingly routine excursion into genre clichés emerges into a more complex and satisfying arena than most viewers will anticipate.

Because a flood has submerged all of the "exit routes," a diverse group of strangers finds themselves stranded at an isolated motel. They include: Ed (John Cusack), a former cop who is now working as a limo driver; Caroline Suzanne (Rebecca De Mornay), the fading movie star Ed was driving; Rhodes (Ray Liotta), a corrections cop making a prisoner transfer; Maine (Jake Busey), a convicted killer in shackles; Paris (Amanda Peet), a Las Vegas hooker on her way to Florida to buy an orange grove; newlyweds Ginny (Clea DuVall) and Lou (William Lee Scott); motel manager Larry (John Hawkes); and George (John C. McGinley), an ineffectual man with a mute stepson and a seriously injured wife. As the rainy night wears on, the murders start. One by one, the motel guests are systematically picked off. Ed and Rhodes work feverishly to uncover the killer's identity before no one is left alive. The fact that he appears to have supernatural powers further complicates their investigation.

Meanwhile, elsewhere, a psychiatrist (Alfred Molina) is trying to stay the execution of his patient (Pruitt Taylor Vince), a convicted mass murderer who is due to die in less than 24 hours. While there is no doubt that the man committed the crimes for which he was sentenced, the doctor believes that the man is insane, and has devised a plan to demonstrate this to both the judge and the prosecutor.

One of the most clever aspects of *Identity* is the way in which director James Mangold and screenwriter Michael Cooney enable the two parallel stories to exist separately, then dovetail at the perfect moment. The relationship between these two plot aspects lies at the core of what *Identity* is trying to do. Early in the movie, Mangold announces that this isn't going to be a traditional horror/thriller endeavor when he uses a series of short, loosely connected flashbacks to introduce the characters and establish the action. It's an effective and economical way to get right into the action. At a short 90 minutes, the film is exactly the right length. It moves briskly, is consistently involving, and offers some very unexpected developments. For those who enjoy smart, clever films and do not demand a traditional ending that neatly wraps everything up, *Identity* is a treat. It's a popcorn movie with flair, style, and intelligence.
HIGHLY RECOMMENDED

I'm Not Scared [Italy/Spain/UK, 2003]

Starring: Aitana Sánchez-Gijón, Dino Abbrescia, Giorgio Careccia, Giuseppe Cristiano, Mattia Di Pierro, Diego Abatantuono Director: Gabriele Salvatores Screenplay: Niccolò Ammaniti and Francesca Marciano, based on the novel by Ammaniti Running Time: 1:48 Rated: R (Profanity, disturbing images) Theatrical Aspect Ratio: 2.35:1 In Italian with subtitles

I'm Not Scared, the latest movie from Italian director Gabriele Salvatores (whose *Mediterraneo* won the Best Foreign Film Oscar in 1992), tells of a crime and its impact from the point of view of a ten-year-old boy. What begins as a fairly commonplace coming-of-age story (a genre that is prevalent among imports) gradually develops into a mystery, then a thriller. By keeping our perspective in synch with that of the young protagonist, Salvatores allows the film to generate more intrigue than the plot, if presented in straightforward manner, might allow.

It's the summer of 1978, and Michele (Giuseppe Cristiano) and his family are spending the season as any rural Southern Italian family might. When he isn't required to do chores, Michele is out playing with his friends, doing dares, and riding his bicycle. One day, while searching around an abandoned building, Michele discovers a covered pit. At the bottom is a boy named Filippo (Mattia Di Pierro), who is constrained from leaving by a chain around his leg. At first, Michele is intimidated by the boy, but he eventually climbs down into the hole and makes contact. He and Filippo initiate a tentative friendship. For Michele, key questions remain. Who is Filippo? Why is he trapped in the pit? Gradually, the answers become clear, and they have disturbing implications for Michele, his mother (Aitana Sanchez-Gijon), his father (Dino Abbrescia), and a Brazilian stranger named Sergio (Diego Abatantuono), who has only recently arrived in the village.

The most impressive thing Salvatores has accomplished with *I'm Not Scared* is the successful fusion of multiple genres. The nostalgic, innocent flavor of a period-piece coming-of-age tale is very much in evidence, but it gives way to a growing sense of unease as we realize that all is not right in this seemingly idyllic village. By the final act, this has become a thriller, with the possibility of death or other dire consequences looming over the young protagonist. What makes this such an engaging experience is the screenplay's perspective. How many movies of this sort are made with the world seen through the eyes of a ten-year-old? Things that might be obvious to adults are not obvious to Michele, and Salvatores successfully keeps us in the dark with him.

RECOMMENDED

In the Company of Men [Canada, 1997]
Starring: Aaron Eckhart, Matt Malloy, Stacy Edwards Director: Neil LaBute Screenplay: Neil LaBute Running Time: 1:33 Rated: R (Mature themes, profanity) Theatrical Aspect Ratio: 1.85:1

In the Company of Men is one of those rarest of rare breeds — a movie that doesn't just ignore Hollywood conventions, but openly flouts them. The picture begins as something much different than what it concludes as, and the metamorphosis occurs so gradually that it only becomes apparent in retrospect. Shortly after *In the Company of Men* opens, the intent appears to be to center on the conflict between the sexes. Ultimately, however, this only a small piece of the much larger pie into which Neil LaBute's directorial debut slices. *In the Company of Men* widens its focus to encompass the falseness and gamesmanship that underlies many aspects of everyday human interaction. It's a cynical perspective that's all the more disturbing because it's grounded so deeply in reality. The characters here aren't cardboard cut-out stereotypes — they're the kind of people you can find anywhere inside or outside of the workplace.

Chad (Aaron Eckhart) and Howard (Matt Malloy) are two very different guys with a great deal in common. They attended the same college, work for the same corporation, and have a history of bad relationships with women. Their combined romantic record reads like a litany of injustices perpetrated on them by females. They have been duped, rejected, neglected, and intentionally misunderstood. Chad, ready to go to war against the entire gender to "restore a little dignity," has a simple, vicious suggestion for revenge. They will find a woman who has trouble getting dates, both take her out, then, after duping her into falling in love with one or both of them, they'll dump her at the same time. Howard is initially reluctant, but Chad talks him into it before locating the perfect target: an attractive-but-deaf typist

named Christine (Stacy Edwards), whose disability has caused her self-esteem to erode.

Much of LaBute's script is about manipulation and deceit, but he's smart enough to show the characters manipulating each other without turning that manipulation on the audience. Nevertheless, because we become so involved in the interaction between these people, it's impossible for us not to be enflamed by what's transpiring, or to hope that justice comes from heaven in the form of a lightning bolt.

In the Company of Men doesn't take prisoners, and "feel good" is a term *no one* will ever use to describe it. But the movie deserves high praise because what it does, it does extraordinarily well. Finally, here's a film with the guts to tell this kind of the story without turning it into a fairy tale. It's rare for any motion picture to generate such a profound sense of disquiet, but the path traversed by LaBute's characters is so bold that it's impossible not to be affected. **MUST SEE**

Insomnia [Norway, 1997]
Starring: Stellan Skarsgård, Sverre Anker Ousdal, Bjorn Floberg Director: Erik Skjoldbjærg Screenplay: Nikolaj Frobenius, Erik Skjoldbjærg Running Time: 1:37 Rated: R (Violence, profanity, nudity, sex) Theatrical Aspect Ratio: 1.85:1 In Norwegian with subtitles

Most murder mysteries take place in the dark. *Insomnia*, a compelling thriller from first-time Scandinavian director Erik Skjoldbjærg, occurs in a state of perpetual light. The setting is north of the Arctic circle in the middle of summer. At that time and place, we have entered the land of the midnight sun, a strange world where daylight holds court 24 hours a day. Yet, even in such bright circumstances, the darkest impulses of the human soul can not always be held at bay.

Jonas Engstrom (Stellan Skarsgård) and his partner, Erik Vik (Sverre Anker Ousdal), are cops from Oslo brought in to a small town to help with a murder investigation. A 17-year-old girl, Tanja (Maria Mathiesen), has been found naked and dead, and the killer has carefully removed all traces of his presence by washing her hair and scrubbing under her fingernails. Engstrom and Vik, who have a reputation as Scandinavia's most effective and tenacious investigators, are on the case immediately, and an early break allows them to set a trap for the suspect. But things go wrong, and, in the confusion of a shoot-out, Engstrom kills Vik. He is about to confess this career-damaging act to the local police chief when the man gives him an unexpected way out. From that point onward, Engstrom finds himself trapped in an increasingly-complex web of deceit as he attempts to solve the crime while covering up his own misdeed. And, as his guilty conscience and the never-ending light keep him awake at night, the lack of sleep makes him increasingly desperate and prone to error.

Although *Insomnia* is not without its share of surprises and unexpected plot twists, it does not offer the red herrings of a whodunit. Instead, it's a dissection of moral decay — of a once-decent man whose circumstances cause him to contemplate actions that place him in an increasingly indefensible situation. Along the way, he engages in the sexual molestation of a teenager and mistakes the flirtatious advances of a pretty hotel receptionist for something more serious. Engstrom is the kind of darkly complex, morally ambiguous character that American movies rarely highlight.

Insomnia works as a noir thriller of a different sort, where circumstances gradually warp a hero into a villain. Mysteries typically focus so intently on plot that there's little room for a detailed character arc, but *Insomnia* manages to balance both aspects.

HIGHLY RECOMMENDED

Insomnia [2002]
Starring: Al Pacino, Robin Williams, Hilary Swank
Director: Christopher Nolan Screenplay: Hillary Seitz, based on the
1997 screenplay by Nikolaj Frobenius and Erik Skjoldbjærg Running
Time: 1:57 Rated: R (Violence, profanity, nudity, sexual situations)
Theatrical Aspect Ratio: 2.35:1

One of the most breathtaking scenes in Christopher Nolan's *Insomnia* occurs early in the film as a small plane flies over the barren wasteland of jagged mountains and broken ice that makes up so much of the rugged terrain of America's northernmost state. For this thriller, which unites 3 Academy Award-winning actors (Al Pacino, Robin Williams, Hilary Swank) with the director of *Memento,* we're up above the Arctic Circle in the Land of the Midnight Sun. Call it *film blanche.*

For Los Angeles police detectives Will Dormer (Al Pacino) and Hap Eckhart (Martin Donovan), their latest murder investigation isn't business as usual. They have come to Alaska not only to aid the authorities of the small town of Nightmute in finding a killer, but to temporarily escape the spotlight of an Internal Affairs investigation. Will is greeted like a legend in Nightmute, especially by Officer Ellie Burr (Hilary Swank), who hero-worships him. After examining the body and getting a rundown on some basic facts about the case, Will and Hap retire to their hotel, where Hap

drops a bombshell on Will — he's going to cut a deal with I.A. Will is livid, claiming that if Hap does that, all of the criminals they put away will get out. But Hap is adamant.

The next day, Will sets a trap for the killer, an author named Walter Finch (Robin Williams), who falls into it. There's a chase along a foggy shoreline, and, when Will fires his gun at a shape in the mist, he accidentally kills his partner, whose dying words are that Will did it on purpose to stop him from testifying. Walter, concealed nearby, sees and hears everything. Later, Will decides to cover things up, pretending that their quarry shot his partner. Everyone believes Will, so it isn't difficult for him to tamper with the evidence. But Walter knows the truth, and he believes that gives him power over Will. In his mind, they're partners, and, as sleep deprivation caused by insomnia clouds Will's ability to think clearly, he is drawn into Walter's web.

For those who have not seen the earlier *Insomnia,* this motion picture delivers the goods. It's smart, well-acted, beautifully shot, and suspenseful. For those who are familiar with the source material, while there may be a sense that something is lacking, the movie still has the capacity to engage for 2 hours. *Insomnia* does not become one of those rare remakes to eclipse the original, but it doesn't disgrace it, either. Under the relentless glare of the Midnight Sun, the only darkness is in the hearts and actions of the characters. **RECOMMENDED**

The Interview [Australia, 1998]
Starring: Hugo Weaving, Tony Martin, Aaron Jeffrey Director: Craig
Monahan Screenplay: Craig Monahan, Gordon Davie Running
Time: 1:43 Rated: Not Rated (Profanity) Theatrical Aspect Ratio: 1.85:1

What starts out as a seemingly straightforward police thriller develops into something far less conventional, where even the most seasoned movie-goer will find himself or herself re-assessing the characters and the storyline that defines their interaction. *The Interview* becomes a meditation upon police procedure, justice, truth, and the (un)reliable narrator. It isn't until the final frame of the motion picture that first-time director Craig Monahan answers the question that preys upon the mind of every viewer (and, even when he does so, there's still room for interpretation).

The film opens with an unkempt man, Eddie Fleming (Hugo Weaving), being rousted out of bed when the police break down his front door. As is cursorily explained to him by Detective Sergeant John Steele (Tony Martin) and his thuggish associate,

Detective Senior Constable Wayne Prior (Aaron Jeffrey), he is wanted in association with a stolen car. After being cuffed, terrorized, and humiliated, Fleming is taken to the police station to be interviewed. That segment of the movie, which comprises most of the running length, turns into a cat-and-mouse war of wills between Fleming and Steele.

For his part, Steele believes that Fleming may be connected to a series of seemingly unrelated murders, and he uses every trick in the book to get Fleming to reveal something. Along with Prior, he plays "good cop/bad cop," all the while unaware that he is under surveillance by Internal Affairs. Meanwhile, Fleming regains the composure he lost when the police broke into his home, but is his calm demeanor merely his way of reacting to circumstances, or does he have a deeper motive? And, when he appears to let something slip by the way of a confession, is he weaving a story or recounting the facts?

In essence, Monahan is examining one of the trickiest questions of law and justice — something that applies not only in Australia, but in every society with its roots in English jurisprudence. Is it better for a guilty man to go free in order to protect against the possibility of an innocent man being sent to prison? If Fleming is blameless, then he is being horribly mistreated by the police, but if he is a serial killer, then Steele's methods seem justified — perhaps even lenient. And, because Monahan doesn't tip his hand, viewers teeter from one point-of-view to the other. **HIGHLY RECOMMENDED**

Interview with the Assassin [2002]

Starring: Raymond J. Barry, Dylan Haggerty Director: Neil Burger
Screenplay: Neil Burger Running Time: 1:34 Rated: Not Rated
(Profanity, violence) Theatrical Aspect Ratio: 1.85:1

Interview with the Assassin is a valentine to conspiracy theorists. It is also an intelligent and gripping thriller — one that uses the first-person, pseudo-documentary approach to an effective end. *Interview with the Assassin* plays with reality in such a way that it's easy to forget that what you're watching is a cleverly constructed fabrication, not a representation of something that actually happened.

There have been more conspiracy theories devised about the situations and circumstances of November 22, 1963 than about any other event in American history. According to ex-military operative Walter Ohlinger (Raymond J. Barry), Lee Harvey Oswald did not act alone. There was a second gunman on the so-

called "grassy knoll" in Dealey Plaza, and that man fired the fatal head shot. How does Walter know this? Because, he claims, he was that individual. He makes this revelation in a videotaped confession to out-of-work news cameraman Ron Kobeleski (Dylan Haggerty). Dying of cancer, Walter has decided to come clean. The two take a trip to Dallas, where Walter lays out in meticulous detail his every movement during the early afternoon of November 22, 1963. Thereafter, he and Ron embark upon a journey to find the one man who may be able to verify Walter's claim and answer Ron's paramount question: Why was President Kennedy shot?

Is Walter telling the truth or is he an insane delusional who has lost touch with reality to the point where he believes his story? Are there men following Ron and Walter, or is this paranoia? These are questions viewers will ask themselves as the film unfolds. Writer/director Neil Burger, making his feature debut, does not tip his hand early — in fact, some might argue that he doesn't tip it at all. It should be noted, however, that although the film starts out to be chillingly plausible, it grows progressively less so during the course of the proceedings. But, by the time *Interview with the Assassin* begins to strain our credulity, we're already hooked. **RECOMMENDED**

Irreversible [France, 2002]

Starring: Vincent Cassel, Albert Dupontel, Monica Bellucci, Jo Prestia
Director: Gaspar Noé Screenplay: Gaspar Noé Running Time: 1:39
Rated: Unrated (Graphic violence, graphic sexual violence, sex, nudity, profanity) Theatrical Aspect Ratio: 2.35:1 In French with subtitles

Since one of the duties of a film critic is to provide readers with enough ammunition for them to make an informed decision about whether a movie is likely to match their tastes, I must begin with a stern warning. *Irreversible* is the kind of film that will offend, outrage, and possibly even sicken about 90 percent of the mainstream viewing audience. Its brutal, unflinching depiction of violence and sexual violation is of a kind that I have never previously encountered in a movie.

Irreversible unfolds with a reverse chronology that recalls *Memento*, although, in this case, narrative places a distant second to style. There are twelve segments, all shot in single takes, that tell the story from end to beginning. The sparse story is one that Charles Bronson's *Death Wish* character would be at home in. Two men — Marcus (Vincent Cassel) and Pierre (Albert Dupontel) — are out for revenge. They are after a man called "Le Tenia" (Jo Prestia), who viciously raped and beat Marcus's girlfriend (and Pierre's ex), Alex (Monica Bellucci). When they find him, they dispose of him. Obviously, Noé's intentions here are not merely to craft a revenge flick. To begin with, most entries into that genre are exploitative. However, by making the violence as graphic and realistic as possible, the director is attempting to underline the difference between what happens in the real world and how that is often glamorized on screen. Still, one could (and many will) argue that Noé has gone too far, and that in his attempts to avoid sensationalization, he has achieved the opposite. Who but a twisted voyeur would want to sit through a nine-minute rape sequence?

Nearly everything that matters in *Irreversible* has to do with style. The reverse-time flow, the placement and movement of the handheld camera, and the choices with regard to violence are all means by which the director makes a statement. Ostensibly, the stars are real-life couple Bellucci and Vincent Cassel, but no one has a more forceful presence than the unseen (or almost unseen, since he has a cameo) Noé. There are many occasions in which the characters seem secondary to the manner in which their story is being told. Those who stay to the end will note that *Irreversible* concludes in a false paradise. Noé's approach to the closing moments is almost conventionally romantic. Unfortunately, our appreciation of this happy ending is clouded by the realization of what is to come next. We know that, within a short time, the characters' joy and zest for life will be forever, irreversibly shattered. As we are told at the outset: "Time destroys everything." This includes fairy-tale endings. Noé's backward chronology reminds us that there is no such thing as a true conclusion; there's always something yet to come.

An individual's appreciation of *Irreversible* will be based in part upon what he or she expects from movies. Those seeking light entertainment or something traditional and/or civilized probably won't make it through *Irreversible*'s 99 minutes. Those up to a challenge who attend with an open mind will find something to gnaw at the soul. Whatever else it may be, *Irreversible* is disturbingly unforgettable. It is impossible to have a blasé reaction to a film this visceral. Indifference is not an option. **HIGHLY RECOMMENDED**

The Italian Job [2003]

Starring: Mark Wahlberg, Edward Norton, Charlize Theron, Seth Green, Jason Statham, Mos Def, Donald Sutherland   Director: F. Gary Gray   Screenplay: Donna Powers & Wayne Powers, based on the 1969 screenplay by Troy Kennedy-Martin   Running Time: 1:46   Rated: PG-13 (Violence, profanity)   Theatrical Aspect Ratio: 1.85:1

The 2003 version of *The Italian Job* is less of a straightforward remake of the 1969 picture than it is a complete re-interpretation. Enough has changed that it's possible to see the two films not as the same story separated by three decades, but as distinct entities. Expectedly, there are plot similarities (the centerpiece heist contains many of the same elements, including the Minis), but the chemistry and motivations of the thieves are different, and the playful, semicomedic tone of the original has been replaced by something a little less lighthearted.

It's easy to do a heist movie wrong — the genre is littered with countless examples, some by prominent filmmakers. F. Gary Gray has discovered the right recipe: Keep things moving, develop a nice rapport between the leads, toss in the occasional surprise, and top with a sprinkling of panache. *The Italian Job* isn't a masterpiece, but it gets the job done. There are some problems (in particular, the climactic car chase — the one featuring the Minis — goes on a little too long), but for the most part, I was entertained. There's a fair amount of suspense, and I was generally impressed by the thoroughness of the caper plots.

The movie opens in Venice, where a group of six crooks are about to pull off the heist of a lifetime — $35 million in gold — and they plan to do it without holding a gun. The rogues' gallery is comprised of: Charlie (Mark Wahlberg), the young leader running his first big job; John (Donald Sutherland), the crusty veteran safecracker who is Charlie's mentor; Lyle (Seth Green), the computer whiz who was "the real inventor of Napster"; Handsome Rob (Jason Statham), who once drove across the United States just so he could set the record for the longest freeway chase; Half Ear (Mos Def), who, at age 10, put one too many M80s in a toilet bowl; and Steve (Edward Norton), who is about to betray the other five. Once they have the gold, Steve pulls a gun on John, shoots him, then leaves the others for dead. A year later, the group, now including John's daughter, Stella (Charlize Theron), a "professional vault and safe technician," tracks down Steve and plots to take away the gold he stole from them (or what's left of it).

The Italian Job has occasional busts of smart dialogue ("There are [thieves] who steal to enrich their lives, and ones who steal to define their lives."), but not enough to elevate it to the level of David Mamet's caper movie, *Heist*. And, while it boasts a less fatuous tone than the original (no Noel Coward or Benny Hill), there are times when it goes for the funny bone. *The Italian Job* delivers all that one could reasonably hope from it. RECOMMENDED

Jackie Brown [1997]

Starring: Pam Grier, Samuel L. Jackson, Robert Forster, Bridget Fonda, Robert De Niro Director: Quentin Tarantino Screenplay: Quentin Tarantino, based on the book *Rum Punch* by Elmore Leonard Running Time: 2:35 Rated: R (Profanity, violence, sex, drug use) Theatrical Aspect Ratio: 2.35:1

The story of *Jackie Brown*, which starts out slowly, develops into a twisty affair, with double-crosses and triple-crosses. And the movie is littered with occasional Tarantino trademarks: witty dialogue, unexpected gunfire, '70s pop tunes, and close-ups of womens' bare feet. Yet, for all of that, the production is something of a letdown. The sheer, in-your-face exuberance that marked *Reservoir Dogs* and especially *Pulp Fiction* is absent. The mostly-straightforward chronology of *Jackie Brown* doesn't match up favorably to the non-linear style of Tarantino's previous efforts — an approach that added tension and edginess to the narratives. And there aren't nearly as many deliciously offbeat conversations this time around. There's a Samuel L. Jackson monologue about guns, a Jackson/Chris Tucker argument regarding the merits of hiding in a car trunk, and a Jackson/Robert De Niro exchange that recalls some of the Jackson/Travolta material from *Pulp Fiction*, but that's about it.

Pam Grier is Jackie Brown, a flight attendant who gets caught transporting drugs and money into the United States. She's working for gun dealer Ordell Robbie (Samuel L. Jackson), but she keeps her mouth shut under questioning, despite pressure from Ray Nicolet (Michael Keaton), a Federal official. No longer sure whether or not he can trust Jackie, Ordell arranges for a bail bondsman, Max Cherry (Robert Forster, TV's "Banyon") to post the necessary $10,000, then plans to shoot Jackie if she proves disloyal. Jackie passes Ordell's test, however, and soon the two of them are plotting a way to smuggle $500,000 of Ordell's money into the United States without tipping off the Feds. Soon, just about everyone is after that money, including Jackie, Max, Ray, Ordell's perpetually oversexed and drugged-out girlfriend, Melanie

(Bridget Fonda), and his right-hand man, Louis (Robert De Niro).

The film, which clocks in at several minutes over the 2½ hour mark, is probably too long for the material, but the plot is convoluted enough to keep us guessing throughout (although the payoff is a letdown). Tarantino keeps things moving along nicely, with a heavier dose of humor and less violence than in *Pulp Fiction*, but, on the whole, this movie seems more like the work of one of his wannabes than something from the director himself. When it comes to recent caper films, *Jackie Brown* is a second-tier effort. It's an entertaining diversion, but not a masterpiece. RECOMMENDED

Jagged Edge [1985]

Starring: Jeff Bridges, Glenn Close, Peter Coyote, Robert Loggia Director: Richard Marquand Screenplay: Joe Eszterhas Running Time: 1:50 Rated: R (Violence, mature themes, sex, language, brief nudity) Theatrical Aspect Ratio: 1.85:1

At first glance, it might appear that *Jagged Edge* is a cleverly-scripted mystery that asks not the question "Whodunnit?" but "Did *he* do it?" However, upon closer examination, it becomes clear that the screenplay for this film is rather pedestrian: filled with clichés, formulas, and typical red herrings, and with twists that aren't as unexpected as they initially seem. Instead, what success this movie achieves is due more to solid direction and competent acting than to what spilled out of Joe Eszterhas' pen.

The chief suspect in the brutal murder of Page Forrester is her husband, Jack (Jeff Bridges), the person who stood the most to gain. Page was rich, and Jack inherits everything, making him the lone target of an investigation launched by D.A. Thomas Krasny (Peter Coyote). When a witness claims to have seen the possible murder weapon in Jack's gym locker, the widowed newspaper executive is arrested.

For his defense, Jack wants Teddy Barnes (Glenn Close), a one-time assistant under Krasny. Teddy hasn't practiced criminal law for 4 years since procedural violations allowed her to convict an innocent man. The thought of acquitting Jack — whom she believes to be innocent — seems an appropriate salve to her conscience. With the help of her investigative friend Sam Ransom (Robert Loggia), she constructs a defense, unaware that neither her client nor the DA are being straight with her.

The plot isn't all that complex, and the only reason it isn't possible to discover the truth before the climax is that the script doesn't offer enough clues. Fortunately, director Richard Marquand and his actors are up to the challenge of transforming a mediocre script into an entertaining film.

Like many entries into the genre, *Jagged Edge* works best when it's watched with a minimum of analysis. There are a fair number of gaffes, flaws, and other assorted problems, and the plot looks progressively less substantial the more closely it's examined. However, the bottom line is that the crux of the story — whether or not Jack is guilty — is engrossing, and it isn't until we know the answer that the movie really seems to let us down. **RECOMMENDED**

K-19: The Widowmaker [United States/United Kingdom, 2002]

Starring: Harrison Ford, Liam Neeson, Peter Sarsgaard
Director: Kathryn Bigelow Screenplay: Christopher Kyle Running Time: 2:15 Rated: PG-13 (Mature themes, disturbing images)
Theatrical Aspect Ratio: **2.35:1**

K-19: The Widowmaker is a war movie without a war, or at least without a hot war. The film uses the backdrop of a potential nuclear holocaust to generate a powerful sense of escalating tension. Most submarine pictures use the claustrophobic setting of the submerged vessel as an opportunity to ratchet up the suspense level during battle scenes. However, in *K-19*, there are no battles — neither of the sub-to-sub nor the sub-to-surface variety. The movie finds other ways to fray our nerves, such as setting up a situation in which there is a leak in the boat's nuclear reactor, and, if the men can't find a way to repair it or get off the ship, they will all die of radiation poisoning. And, as long as the reactor is non-functional, their engine is down and they can't move fast enough to reach a safe harbor.

Harrison Ford, whose stern demeanor is perfect for this part, is Captain Alexi Vostrikov, the man brought in to command the flagship of the Soviet submarine fleet, K-19. It's 1961, and the USSR is convinced that America is planning a first strike. By situating K-19 off the North American eastern seaboard, the Soviets believe they can nullify the United States' superior weapons advantage. Vostrikov has a difficult assignment. K-19 has been rushed into action, so all of its systems are not in perfect working order. And the crewmembers, except for one officer, Vadim Radtchenko (Peter Sarsgaard), are loyal to the former Captain, Polenin (Liam Neeson), who remains on board as the Executive Officer. When Vostrikov's

fondness for taking seemingly unnecessary chances creates unrest amongst the crew, rumbles of a mutiny begin.

K-19 contains a number of scenes that are obligatory in any submarine movie — a dive to crush depth, an uncontrolled rise to the surface, and exercises that presage real emergencies (in particular, fire fighting drills). The strained relationship between Vostrikov and Polenin is as important as any other aspect of the movie. Their interaction undergoes a number of shifts and changes, some of which seem motivated more by a necessity of the plot than by an element of one or both of their personalities. Nevertheless, they progress from wariness to open distrust to respect — a fairly common arc in movies of this nature. *K-19* will not go down in the annals of cinema as one of the great submarine stories, but it is an engaging and exciting narrative of Man confronting the Demons of his own fear and paranoia. **RECOMMENDED**

Kill Bill Volume 2 [2004]

Starring: Uma Thurman, Daryl Hannah, Michael Madsen, David Carradine, Lucy Liu, Vivica A. Fox, Gordon Liu Director: Quentin Tarantino Screenplay: Quentin Tarantino Running Time: 2:10 Rated: R (Extreme violence and gore, profanity) Theatrical Aspect Ratio: **2.35:1**

Two things are readily apparent about *Kill Bill Volume 2*. First, unlike its predecessor, this is a *complete* movie. It stands on its own. It is possible to see and enjoy *Volume 2* in a way that was not true of *Volume 1*. Viewed in retrospect, the first installment now seems like an easily discarded prologue. The real meat is in *Volume 2*. Secondly, Quentin Tarantino needs a new editor — someone who can convince him to make the really hard cuts. Sally Menke, who has held that post for all of Tarantino's movies, couldn't/wouldn't/didn't convince the egocentric filmmaker that eliminating about 30 minutes of filler from *Kill Bill Volume 2* would have made it a leaner, meaner motion picture. The running time is 130 minutes; it should have been about 90 minutes.

That's the bad news. The good news is that, despite its lugubriousness, it's still a good motion picture — a clear improvement upon volume one. There's much less action, a lot more talking, and a legitimate effort to build the characters played by Uma Thurman and David Carradine. Those in search of a kung-fu gorefest like *Volume 1* will be sorely disappointed. There are a few action sequences (about four, depending on what you count as "action"), all of which are quick and brutal. There's nothing even as sustained as the one-on-one between Thurman and Vivica A. Fox in *Volume 1*. *Volume 2* is a talky affair. Although much of the dialogue isn't vintage Tarantino (except a scene like Bill's "Superman" monologue), there's no sense that the characters are inflicted with run-on-at-the-mouth disease.

The movie picks up where *Volume 1* ended, with the Bride (Thurman) gunning for her surviving two would-be assassins and Bill (Carradine). There's not much more to the film than that. Budd (Michael Madsen) takes longer to dispatch than the Bride plans, but Elle (Daryl Hannah) goes a lot more quickly. The confrontation with Bill involves more talking than fighting, a choice that fits the circumstances. About 50 percent of the movie is used to provide backstory. We get a lengthy flashback to events leading up to the wedding chapel massacre, as well as a lengthy training sequence in which the Bride learns to become an expert assassin under the tutelage of Pai Mei (Gordon Liu). (For those unfamiliar with the Hong Kong flicks that serve as Tarantino's main inspiration for this segment of the movie, think Yoda with a bad attitude.) The background material in *Volume 2* fills out the characters nicely. The Bride even gets a name: Beatrix Kiddo. And, as hinted at during the last scene of *Volume 1*, she has a new role as well: Mommy. I enjoyed *Kill Bill Volume 2* more than *Volume 1*. The second movie is less kinetic but more satisfying. Tonally, the two films are different, which may be the result of the split. Hopefully, Tarantino's original, single-movie cut of *Kill Bill* will eventually be available on DVD. With the two parts re-knitted and much of the extraneous material removed, this could be a great motion picture, right up there with *Pulp Fiction*. As it currently stands, *Kill Bill* is a victim of its director's ego and its distributor's greed. The moments of greatness make it worth seeing, and there's certainly plenty of entertainment to be found here, but it's hard not to lament what might have been. **RECOMMENDED**

Kiss the Girls [1997]

Starring: Morgan Freeman, Ashley Judd, Cary Elwes, Tony Goldwyn
Director: Gary Fleder Screenplay: David Klass, based on the novel by James Patterson Running Time: 2:00 Rated: R (Violence, profanity, mature themes) Theatrical Aspect Ratio: 2.35:1

Kiss the Girls wouldn't be nearly as involving without the two strong performances of the leads. Morgan Freeman plays Dr. Alex Cross, a Washington, D.C. forensic pathologist who travels to Durham, N.C., when his niece, Naomi (Gina Ravera), disappears. Freeman plays Alex as an insightful, confident inves-

tigator with powerful emotions bubbling just beneath his calm, carefully-controlled exterior. Despite a less-than-enthusiastic greeting by Durham's chief of police, Alex learns that Naomi is the eighth young woman to disappear recently, all of whom fit the same description: intelligent, strong-willed, college-age, attractive, and talented. Three are already dead, but Alex suspects that the primary interest of the killer (who calls himself "Casanova") is not murder. Instead, the doctor sees him as "a collector."

Disappearance #9 is Dr. Kate McTiernan (Ashley Judd), an intern at the Carolina Regional Medical Center. As Kate, Judd adds another impressive performance to a growing resume. The actress plays her character as outwardly-tough and self-sufficient with an inner core of vulnerability. She may be a target, but she refuses to be a victim, and it's hard to miss the fire in her eyes. Nevertheless, vulnerability, whether emotional or physical, is something she has a hard time coping with. One night, Kate is abducted from her house and brought to a lightless room where she is bound and drugged. But, by taking her masked captor unawares, she escapes in what is one of *Kiss the Girls'* best filmed-sequences. Later, after surviving a fall into a river where she nearly drowns, Kate joins forces with Alex for one purpose: to bring Casanova to justice.

One thing I appreciate about *Kiss the Girls* is its willingness to spend time developing the characters before jumping into the main story. During the first 20 minutes, we gather information about both Alex and Kate. Later, the relationship between these two is developed in an intentionally ambiguous manner. There are times when it manifests itself almost as a father/daughter bond, but, on other occasions, there's a sense of latent romance. However, the film underplays this dynamic to avoid wandering off on a tangent.

The film makers, with a nod to the success of *Seven*, have apparently decided to mimic the grim atmosphere and in-your-face cinematography of that movie (light, darkness, and shadow are used to great effect here). Stylistically, *Kiss the Girls* is very similar, and the presence of Morgan Freeman only heightens the connection. Even though there are vast plot differences between the two, both are well-made and are likely to appeal to the same kind of audience. So, much like *Seven*, *Kiss the Girls* makes for a suspenseful, if somewhat bleak, 2 hours. **RECOMMENDED**

L.A. Confidential [1997]

Starring: Kevin Spacey, Russell Crowe, Guy Pearce, James Cromwell
Director: Curtis Hanson Screenplay: Curtis Hanson and Brian
Helgeland based on the novel by James Ellroy Running Time: 2:20
Rated: R (Profanity, violence, sex, nudity) Theatrical Aspect
Ratio: 2.35:1

Crooked cops. The mystery and allure of Hollywood in the '50s. Death, double-crossing, and secret alliances. Paparazzi waiting to get that one breakthrough picture. These are just some of the elements that make Curtis Hanson's *L.A. Confidential* one of the most exhilarating noir thrillers to reach the screen in recent memory. It's 1953, and the City of Angels is in the grip of an unprecedented wave of violence. Cops on the take turn their backs on crimes. The jailing of a major mob boss leaves a vacuum of power that leads to a turf war. Then comes the Night Owl Massacre, where 6 victims (including an ex-cop) are brutally gunned down at the Night Owl Café. The police begin routine investigations, but it quickly becomes apparent that this is no ordinary multiple homicide.

There are 3 cops on the job. The first, Bud White (Russell Crowe), is a "muscle" guy who believes that violence solves almost everything and is willing to bend (or even break) the rules to obtain results. The second, Jack Vincennes (Kevin Spacey), is the kind of officer who prefers the spotlight to a down-and-dirty lifestyle. He's the high-profile technical advisor to the hit TV series, *Badge of Honor,* and has a clandestine agreement with the editor (Danny DeVito) of *Hush Hush* magazine, a sleazy tabloid that publishes photos and stories showing Jack arresting celebrities in compromising positions. Finally, there's Ed Exley (Guy Pearce), a by-the-book cop who thinks he can rise through the ranks without resorting to Bud's boorish methods. Obviously, the tactics used by these 3 differ greatly, but, as they delve deeper into the murky mysteries of the L.A. police force, it becomes clear that their survival depends on working together.

The difference between *L.A. Confidential* and numerous other, more routine films of the genre begins with the script. Smart, insightful, and consistently engaging, Hanson and Brian Helgeland's faithful adaptation of James Ellroy's novel is a real treat for anyone who views film as a medium for both art and entertainment. The movie is filled with small twists and turns, but not so many that the plot becomes difficult to swallow or to follow. The subplots — and there are several — are as well-developed as the main story, and the supporting characters are presented as more than mere colorful misfits decorating the background. It takes *L.A. Confidential* nearly 2½ hours to spin its tale, but the time passes remarkably quickly. There's hardly a wasted moment in the entire movie, and director Hanson maintains tight control of every scene. **HIGHLY RECOMMENDED**

Lantana AUSTRALIAN [2001]

Starring: Anthony LaPaglia, Geoffrey Rush, Barbara Hershey, Kerry
Armstrong Director: Ray Lawrence Screenplay: Andrew Bovell, based
on his play "Speaking in Tongues" Running Time: 2:00 Rated: R
(Violence, profanity, sex) Theatrical Aspect Ratio: 2.35:1

For the briefest of moments, someone not paying attention might mistake *Lantana* for a mystery. After all, there is a body, a missing person, indications of foul play, and several police detectives. But don't be fooled — all of that is little more than a hook upon which the film's real meat can be hung. So there's a reason why *Lantana* can be considered an "unconventional murder mystery" — because it's not really a murder mystery at all. And, while the title sounds like some kind of new Latin dance, *Lantana* is actually an examination of human interaction.

Leon Zat (Anthony LaPaglia) is an Australian cop whose marriage to Sonja (Kerry Armstrong) is in the doldrums. He claims to have become emotionally numb, while she laments that she's looking for a relationship that is "passionate, challenging, [and] honest." While Leon engages in an affair with Jane O'May (Rachael Blake), Sonja emotionally unburdens herself to her psychiatrist, Valerie Somers (Barbara Hershey), stating that she believes Leon is unfaithful. She goes on to say that she doesn't mind that he's sleeping with someone else — the betrayal is that he hasn't told her. That claim will be put to the test. Meanwhile, Valerie's own marriage is on uncertain ground. Her husband, John Knox (Geoffrey Rush), has been emotionally detached from her since the death of their daughter over a year ago. Valerie's means of dealing with the death was to write a book — a project John does not agree with. Also entering the story are Jane's estranged husband, Pete (Glenn Robbins), the O'Mays' next-door neighbors, Nik and Paula Daniels (Vince Colosimo and Daniella Farinacci), and Michael (Rusell Dyskstra), a gay patient of Valerie's whom she believes may be having an affair with John. Then, one night, one of these characters vanishes, another one witnesses something, and several of the others become suspects.

Lantana argues that inertia may be the natural state of the human condition. Sometimes, only a tragedy of significant magnitude has the power to shake us out of our state of slumber, and, in some cases, even that may not be enough. Being alive and living are not the same. Through their characters, director Ray Lawrence and writer Andrew Bovell show that many humans, once happiness has evaporated, move through life in a stupor — people so easily embrace comfortable routines, giving up any hope of leading dynamic lives and instead becoming reactive. Ultimately, the achievement of sophomore director Lawrence is not what he has to add to the "whodunnit?" genre, but the observations he has to make about how people connect considering the emotional armor with which we gird ourselves. RECOMMENDED

The Last Seduction [1994]

Starring: Linda Fiorentino, Peter Berg, Bill Pullman Director: John Dahl Screenplay: Steve Barancik Running Time: 1:50 Rated: R (Sex, language, nudity, violence, mature themes) Theatrical Aspect Ratio: 1.85:1

Linda Fiorentino's Bridget Gregory does things to men that most of us wouldn't consider for what we scrape off the sidewalk. Using the word "bad" to describe her is as mammoth an understatement as calling the Sistine Chapel "nice" or the Grand Canyon "big." It has been decades since someone the likes of Bridget has graced the screen (Barbara Stanwyck in *Double Indemnity* comes to mind, although her language was never this colorful), and who knows how long it will be until our next opportunity?

Director John Dahl has fun with this material, filming the modern-day noir potboiler with such gusto that it's impossible not to fall under its spell, nor under the influence of its sultry, completely conscienceless leading lady. Dahl, the man behind the twisty Red Rock West, saturates this picture with atmosphere. Every time Bridget takes another pull on her cigarette, we're reminded of a time when 98% of new releases where in black-and-white.

Sap #1 is Bridget's husband, Clay (Bill Pullman). At her prompting, he gets involved in a drug deal that nets him $700,000. He thinks that he and his wife are going to use this to feather their nest egg, but Bridget has other plans — why split what she can have all to herself? No sooner has Bill gone into the shower than she grabs the money and runs, heading for the small upstate New York town of Beston, where people always say "hello," "please," and "thank you," and no one locks their doors at night.

Sap #2 is Mike Swale (Peter Berg), a Beston native who thinks the town is too small for him — until

Bridget arrives. To her, he's a means to an end, something to use up and throw away. To him, she's the love of his life, and he means to make her love him in return, regardless of the cost. *Big* mistake.

The Last Seduction's dialogue, scripted by Steve Barancik and spoken by the likes of Fiorentino, Pullman, Berg, and J.T. Walsh, is scintillating, often hilarious, and occasionally insightful. The best lines are about Bridget — "Anyone check you for a heartbeat lately?" and "I love you . . . I'm sure you feel the same way — I'm sure you love you, too" — or from her — "Spare me your brainless, countrified morality."

The Last Seduction is an entertaining motion picture to immerse oneself in — significant chunks of the plot fall apart on close examination, but it holds up well enough during the watching, and nothing can dispel the power of Fiorentino's performance. RECOMMENDED

The Limey [1999]

Starring: Terence Stamp, Peter Fonda, Lesley Ann Warren Director: Steven Soderbergh Screenplay: Lem Dobbs Running Time: 1:30 Rated: R (Violence, profanity) Theatrical Aspect Ratio: 1.85:1

Terence Stamp is *The Limey*, and *The Limey* is Terence Stamp. Forget about everything else in this film — the supporting cast, which features Lesley Ann Warren, Luis Guzman, and Peter Fonda, Steven Soderbergh's lively direction, and even Lem Dobbs' screenplay. Without Stamp's bravura performance, there is no movie. With it, even the thinnest premise ignites the screen with white-hot passion and energy. Stamp has done some wonderful work in a long and varied career. This is not his best film, but it may be the most forceful acting he has ever accomplished.

The movie is a visceral thriller — a stylish take on the revenge picture. Call it the art film version of *Death Wish*. There really isn't anything deeper or more meaningful going on here. However, done right, as it is here, this kind of film can be immensely entertaining and satisfying. When Stamp's Wilson finds out that his daughter, Jenny, has been killed by American drug dealers, he crosses the Atlantic and goes on a one-man killing spree, knocking off one target after another as he gets close to the bulls-eye: Jenny's lover, pop music producer Terry Valentine (Peter Fonda, playing the sleazy part with relish).

The Limey possesses several traits that allow it to work better than the average revenge thriller. The first in Stamp's performance, which blazes with intensity and energy. The actor's work here isn't just scene-stealing, it's movie-stealing. The second is Soderbergh's style, which includes flashbacks and flashforwards, with dialogue from one scene often bleeding into its successor. The third is the brilliant, snappy dialogue which often sounds scripted, but is delightful nevertheless. And the fourth is the sense of macabre, offbeat humor that suffuses the picture, reminding us not to take anything that transpires too seriously.

The film moves. It has color, energy, life, and pizzazz — all three in abundance. And, above all, it has Stamp. If *The Limey* had been a little less well-made, I'd call it a guilty pleasure. But, because it has been crafted with a great deal of attention and care, I'll drop the "guilty" and simply call it a "pleasure." **RECOMMENDED**

Lock, Stock and Two Smoking Barrels
[United Kingdom, 1998]
Starring: Jason Flemyng, Dexter Fletcher, Nick Moran, Jason Statham Director: Guy Ritchie Screenplay: Guy Ritchie Running Time: 1:43 Rated: R (Violence, profanity, drugs, brief nudity) Theatrical Aspect Ratio: 1.85:1

Surface likenesses aside, *Lock, Stock, and Two Smoking Barrels* is actually a kinder, gentler motion picture than *Pulp Fiction*. While there's as much violence, Ritchie's method is different. All of the most vicious acts occur off screen. We see the ramifications, but we miss the genuine brutality. This effectively distances the viewer from the bloodshed, allowing us to see the proceedings in an almost cartoon-like light. It's easier to laugh when the baggage of excessive, graphic violence is taken out of the equation. *Lock, Stock, and Two Smoking Barrels* contains gore, but its presentation is neither gut-wrenching nor intense.

If the criminal ranks in London are comprised of losers like this, it's a wonder that anyone gets away with anything. Eddy (Nick Moran), Tom (Jason Flemyng), Soap (Dexter Fletcher), and Bacon (Jason Statham) are a quartet of con-artists and thieves who have scraped together enough money to enter a high-stakes poker game run by the ominously-named Hatchet Harry Lonsdale (P.H. Moriarty). Eddy is an expert poker player who, because of his ability to read people's reactions, almost never loses in an honest match. But Harry doesn't believe in playing fair. With the help of his nasty assistant, Barry the Baptist (the late Lenny McLean), Harry has fixed the game. When Eddy loses a huge round, he finds himself half a million pounds in debt, with only 7 days for him and his friends to get the money. So they turn to the only possible solution: stealing from their criminal neighbors, who are led by a tough guy named Dog (Frank Harper). Dog and his crew are about to rob a group of marijuana growers who work for a local drug baron (Vas Blackwood). Also thrown into the mix are a couple of cowardly and incompetent thieves, a deadpan hitman (soccer star Vinnie Jones) and his equally deadpan son (Peter McNicholl), Eddy's irate father (Sting), a perpetually stoned girl (Suzy Ratner), and an unfortunate cop.

Ritchie's style is direct and accomplished. *Lock, Stock, and Two Smoking Barrels* keeps moving; it's kinetic, in-your-face filmmaking. This may be the first movie to capture the reckless exuberance of *Pulp Fiction* without seeming like a blatant rip-off. With memorable witticisms sprinkled throughout, the dialogue is at least as clever as the plot structure. *Lock, Stock, and Two Smoking Barrels* has plenty of laughs and a few surprises to offer to all but the most squeamish of viewers. It's a superior thriller made with the guts and gusto that too many recycled entries into the genre fail to exhibit. **HIGHLY RECOMMENDED**

The Machinist [Spain, 2004]
Starring: Christian Bale, Jennifer Jason Leigh, Aitana Sánchez-Gijón, John Sharian, Michael Ironside Director: Brad Anderson Screenplay: Scott Kosar Running Time: 1:42 Rated: R (Violence, profanity, disturbing images, sexual situations, nudity) Theatrical Aspect Ratio: 2.35:1

A noir horror movie of the most unclassic kind, Brad Anderson's *The Machinist* takes you into the unstable mind of an insomniac with a dark secret whose life has become a bleak emotional wasteland devoted only to going through the motions of working. Blessed with an extraordinary performance by Christian Bale, this movie plays out like a nightmare, and will remind some viewers of *The Fight Club, Memento,* and *Insomnia.* Although *The Machinist* may at times seem to be derivative of those films, and is inferior to them, it is nevertheless a harrowing experience for those to whom this sort of story appeals.

Bale's Trevor is, as the title implies, a machinist at an assembly-line factory. He clocks in every morning, then clocks out every afternoon, keeping basically to himself. When he returns from work, he does nothing more remarkable than frequent an airport diner where he converses with the same waitress (Aitana Sanchez-Gijon) on a daily basis, or visit his "regular" prostitute, Stevie (Jennifer Jason Leigh). But something strange is happening. A mysterious man named Ivan (John Sharian) is haunting him, and he is having strange visions. The question is whether these are figments of a deranged imagination or part of a larger external conspiracy to drive him insane. How much of what is happening is transpiring within Trevor's psyche? Who, if anyone, is real? Why has the clock stopped at 1:30? Why is the refrigerator bleeding?

Style builds suspense. The scenes around the machinery are staged in a way that radiate menace. The expectation — which is fulfilled — is that something will go horribly wrong. The camerawork and claustrophobic atmosphere are designed to externally replicate Trevor's mental state. In addition, Anderson has drastically desaturated the color, resulting in a spartan look that is only one step up from monochrome. And there's a scene with an approaching thunderstorm that is perfect in the way it is composed and presented. Even for those who are able to piece together exactly what is happening before the movie explicitly reveals everything, *The Machinist* is still capable of capturing the attention. The film is dark, but rewarding, and it never cheats the viewer. There are no sudden twists designed to blindside an audience. The reveals occur gradually, with Anderson allowing us the pleasure of putting the pieces together. *The Machinist* requires a certain kind of viewer — one who is comfortable with grimness and a certain amount of gore. Members of that group will appreciate what this picture has to offer. RECOMMENDED

Man on Fire [USA/Mexico, 2004]

Starring: Denzel Washington, Dakota Fanning, Marc Anthony, Radha Mitchell, Christopher Walken, Giancarlo Giannini, Rachel Ticotin, Jesús Ochoa, Mickey Roarke Director: Tony Scott Screenplay: Brian Helgeland, based on the novel by A. J. Quinnell Running Time: 2:12 Rated: R (Violence, profanity) Theatrical Aspect Ratio: 2.35:1

The key to *Man on Fire*'s success is unquestionable: It doesn't rush things. The slow buildup allows ample opportunity for character development and relationship building, so, when the tragedy and *Death Wish*–style retribution occur, there's a sense of urgency and meaning. Also, director Tony Scott maintains an elegiac tone. Instead of pumping up the level of testosterone, he keeps everything except his camerawork low-key, lending a mournful, not triumphant, air to the proceedings. The grim second half of *Man on Fire* is about retribution and karma, not voyeuristic satisfaction. Few will leave the theater whooping and hollering.

Denzel Washington plays Creasy, an ex–Special Forces operative who is at loose ends. Having trouble coping with his memories and oblivious to any kind of meaningful future, he drifts south of the border to Mexico, where he encounters his old pal Rayburn

(Christopher Walken), who hooks him up with a job as a bodyguard. Creasy's charge is simple: Protect Pita (Dakota Fanning), the young daughter of a Mexican businessman, Samuel (Marc Anthony), and his American wife, Lisa (Radha Mitchell). Kidnappings are frequent happenings in Mexico, and Pita is a ripe target. Initially, Creasy resists Pita's attempts to make friends, but her charm eventually wins him over, and he takes on a father-figure role. Then, one fateful day, the kidnapping attempt occurs. Creasy takes several bullets and is unable to save Pita. And, while he languishes in a hospital, the transfer of ransom money is botched. When Creasy emerges from prison, he has only one goal in mind: Kill anyone who was involved in the kidnapping.

Scott's stylistic flair may be questionable, but there's nothing wrong with his storytelling. The bond that develops between Creasy and Pita is critical to the story, and Scott never forces things. It evolves naturally as a result of their interaction. The performances, especially those of Washington and Fanning, are superlative. Washington plays an individual who runs the emotional gamut — from closed-off outsider to loving father-figure to vengeful killer. Meanwhile, Fanning avoids the obvious "too cute" trap into which many actresses of her age fall. She is sweet and likable, but never saccharine, and she shows more ability and range than in any of her previous outings. And it's nice to see Christopher Walken given an opportunity to *act* rather than *rant*.

Man on Fire is a remake of a 1987 film starring Scott Glenn. By concentrating on the emotional impact rather than the pyrotechnics, ammunition, and action/thriller elements, this new interpretation comes across as an effective piece of drama, and it doesn't cheat us with a Hollywood cop-out ending. For what *Man on Fire* delivers, it's worth enduring Scott's hyperkinetic visual techniques.

RECOMMENDED

The Man Who Wasn't There [2001]

Starring: Bob Thornton, Frances McDormand, James Gandolfini Director: Joel Coen Screenplay: Joel & Ethan Coen Running Time: 1:57 Rated: R (Violence, profanity, sexual situations) Theatrical Aspect Ratio: 1.85:1

For dour Ed Crane (Billy Bob Thornton), the life of a hair-cutter is a thankless one, probably because, in his own words, "I worked in a barber's shop, but I never considered myself a barber." It's a few years after the second World War, and Ed finds his existence to be a joyless exercise in monotonous repetition. He goes to work every day, puts in his hours, then returns home to his philandering, alcoholic wife, Doris (Frances McDormand). Ed knows that his wife is having an affair with her boss, Big Dave Brewster (James Gandolfini), but it doesn't bother him much. He just has another smoke and scowls some more. In fact, he figures out a way he can use it to his advantage. When a sleazy salesman (Jon Polito) offers Ed the opportunity to be a silent partner in a business arrangement, Ed gets the cash by anonymously blackmailing Big Dave. "Unless you pay $10,000," the note sent by Ed reads, "Everyone will know what you have been up to." Big Dave pays, but that's only the beginning of a cycle of deceit that leads to murder, cover-ups, and a singular example of judicial irony.

The thing I appreciated the most about *The Man Who Wasn't There* is the unhurried, sinuous manner in which the plot moves — it twists and turns without being obvious about its surprises, and doesn't rush to get there the way so many movies do. The pace is not so much slow as it is deliberate. The movie has a lot to offer, but only to those who are patient with it. How about, for example, oddball subplots involving an alien abduction and a *Lolita*-like attraction? The main narrative offers its share of unexpected moments, so, in true Hitchcock fashion, the viewer is never exactly sure what's going to happen next. Along the way, we are provided with a running voiceover narration by Ed that, for once, doesn't seem superfluous. Then there's the ending, which I won't talk about here except to say that it's deliciously ironic and entirely appropriate.

The Coen Brothers are known for making offbeat fare, from their brilliant debut, *Blood Simple,* to the off-the-wall comedy of *Raising Arizona,* to the snow-blinded strangeness of *Fargo*. Compared to those films, *The Man Who Wasn't There* is almost conventional. Those looking for the typical Coen outlandishness may be disappointed; on the other hand, those in search of a genuine Hitchcock homage will probably be pleased. *The Man Who Wasn't There* reminds us of how entertaining a thriller can be when it concentrates on storyline rather than the overused staples of car chases and shoot-outs. RECOMMENDED

Maria Full of Grace [USA/Columbia, 2004]

Starring: Catalina Sandino Moreno, Yenny Paola Vega, Guilied Lopez, Patricia Rae, Orlando Tobon, John Álex Toro Director: Joshua Marston Screenplay: Joshua Marston Running Time: 1:41 Rated: R (Drugs, profanity) Theatrical Aspect Ratio: 1.85:1 In Spanish with subtitles

Maria Full of Grace, the feature debut from Joshua Marston, tells the stories of three "mules" who travel from Colombia to New York with more than fifty pellets of cocaine in their bellies. It's a brilliant motion picture, not only because of the meticulous detail used in presenting the process from start to finish, but because of the clarity with which Marston develops the characters. The individuals populating *Maria Full of Grace* are three-dimensional, with understandable motives. They do not seem like constructs whose actions are determined by the needs of a screenplay. In dramatizing the situations depicted in the movie, Marston's approach is virtually flawless.

In a stunning performance, Catalina Sandino Moreno plays Maria, a 17-year-old Colombian girl who quits her grueling job as a rose de-thorner after a run-in with an unsympathetic boss. For Maria's family, this is a harsh economic blow, because everyone living in the small house — including her mother, grandmother, and unmarried sister — relies in part on Maria's wages to survive. Worse still, Maria learns that she is pregnant, but refuses to marry her baby's father. In desperate need of money, Maria investigates an "employment opportunity" that requires her to act as a mule on the Colombia-to-New York run. She is accompanied on the trip by her best friend, Blanca (Yenny Paola Vega), and Lucy (Guilied Lopez), a young woman making her third such journey.

When it comes to the nuts-and-bolts process of transporting the dope, no movie I have seen has done as thorough a job. We see how the pellets are manufactured, how the mules practice suppressing the gag reflex so they can swallow, how they are "fed" the drugs, what happens if they accidentally expel one before it is meant to be released, and the brutal consequences of a ruptured pellet.

The motivations of the three women are explored. Maria, desperately unhappy with her current lot in life, wants an opportunity for herself and her unborn child. The United States is not a wonderland, but it offers better possibilities than Colombia. Blanca agrees to become a mule because she is bored, stubborn, and seduced by the money. And Lucy, whose story is the saddest, wants to be reunited with her sister, who lives in New York. On her two previous trips she was unable to work up the courage to make contact. This may be her last opportunity.

Like many movies I have championed over the years, this one is disturbing. It is impossible to sit through *Maria Full of Grace* and not be affected by the circumstances of the characters. For that, the credit must go to Marston and his actors (especially Moreno, who, if she desires, could have an impressive career in front of the camera). The film's dramatic arc has genuine emotional impact, but there is never the slightest hint of manipulation on the part of the director. Yet, despite the dark nature of the material, *Maria Full of Grace* is not steeped in bleakness. The film ends not on a nihilistic note, but on one that could be considered hopeful. For those who appreciate serious dramas, this is one that should not be missed. **MUST SEE**

Matchstick Men [2003]

Starring: Nicolas Cage, Sam Rockwell, Alison Lohman, Bruce Altman, Bruce McGill Director: Ridley Scott Screenplay: Nicholas Griffin & Ted Griffin, based on the novel by Eric Garcia Running Time: 1:56 Rated: R (Violence, profanity, brief nudity) Theatrical Aspect Ratio: 2.35:1

Movies about confidence tricksters represent an old, although not necessarily respected, subgenre of the thriller. Many of these films are cheap and cheesy, with silly plots and "twists" that are shaky and predictable. There are a few notable exceptions, such as *The Sting* and *The Grifters*. To that elite list can be added Ridley Scott's *Matchstick Men*, which has a lot more on its agenda than the protagonists' big score — like redemption and salvation, for example.

Nicolas Cage plays Roy Waller, an obsessive/compulsive sufferer who happens to be one of the best operating grifters. Along with his partner, Frank (Sam Rockwell), there's virtually no scam he can't pull off — as long as his psychological problems remain under control. When properly medicated, Roy exhibits a few quirks — such as shutting doors three times and demanding that people take off their shoes before entering his house. But, when his pink pills run out, he becomes a mess of nervous energy, prone to facial tics and profane outbursts. Enter Dr. Klein (Bruce Altman), a psychiatrist who believes there's more to solving Roy's problems than medicating him. Soon, Dr. Klein has put Roy in touch with a 14-year-old daughter, Angela (Alison Lohman), he never knew he had. And, just as Roy is beginning to form a bond with his teenage offspring, Frank approaches Roy about pulling off a big con on an easy mark. For the first time in his life, Roy sees a possible conflict between his personal life and his professional one, and his means of bridging it is to bring Angela in on the scam. She becomes his partner, and loves every minute of it.

Matchstick Men is really two movies brilliantly spliced into one, each enriching the other. The first focuses on Cage's character — his psychological problems, his misgivings about his profession, and, most importantly, his relationship with Angela. The suddenness with which she arrives in his life opens up a world of possibilities he had never previously considered and, at the same time, makes him aware of how unprepared he is for any major life-changing decision. The second focuses on Frank and Roy's cons, which, while not monumentally unique, are interesting enough to keep us involved in the game. In addition to being moderately suspenseful (a necessity for any movie about grifters and their crimes), *Matchstick Man* also has a sly, biting sense of humor that occasionally results in laugh-aloud moments. And it's emotionally satisfying, with the association between Roy and Angela becoming central to the story line. It's fascinating to watch these two characters interact. There's a sense of discovery in this relationship, as each of these two realizes that the other fills needs they were unaware of having.

For Ridley Scott, the director of such high-intensity films as *Alien, Blade Runner, Thelma & Louise,* and *Gladiator,* this represents a departure. Scott has done character-related pieces before, but never have they been this light. For a filmmaker who has not previously ventured into comedy, Scott shows a deft hand. But, with someone of his experience, would it have been reasonable to expect anything less?

HIGHLY RECOMMENDED

Memento [2000]

Starring: Guy Pearce, Carrie-Anne Moss, Joe Pantoliano Director: Christopher Nolan Screenplay: Christopher Nolan, based on a story by Jonathan Nolan Running Time: 1:53 Rated: R (Violence, profanity, drugs) Theatrical Aspect Ratio: 2.35:1

Memento stars Australian actor Guy Pearce as Leonard Shelby, a former insurance investigator and crime victim who is trying to find the man who raped and murdered his wife (Jorja Fox). His goal is simple — he wants revenge through execution. Nothing less will satisfy him. But there's a small matter that complicates Leonard's investigation. He has no short term memory. During the attack that ended his wife's life, Leonard suffered brain damage. Now, although his long-term memory is fine, he can't remember any recent events. He can meet the same person a hundred times and won't know their name or who they are. To combat his condition, Leonard relies upon a series of annotated Polaroid snapshots — not exactly the ideal tool by which to seek out a killer who even the police can't locate. Along the way, Leonard is aided (or perhaps hindered) by the ubiquitous Teddy (Joe Pantoliano), who is always on hand to offer advice, and he becomes involved with the mysterious Natalie (Carrie-Ann Moss), whose motives may not be as straightforward as they initially appear to be.

Memento doesn't stop with a great premise. In fact, what really distinguishes this film is its brilliant, innovative structure. Nolan has elected to tell the story backwards. He starts at the end and finishes near the beginning. The main narrative is presented as a series of 3-to-8-minute segments, each of which ends where the previous one began. A second thread, which starts at an unspecified time in the past and moves forward to intersect with the main storyline, is used to buffer the "reverse" segments as well as to provide background information. (It also tells the important "Sammy Jankis" story, which becomes increasingly important the deeper we get into the film.) Although this approach might at first seem confusing, it doesn't take long to get used to it, and to understand how well it works with this material.

By presenting events in *Memento* backwards, Nolan allows us to get into the mindset of the main character. Like Leonard, we don't have a clear indication of what happened before the current segment of time. We know some things from the past, but not the recent past. Like him, we are presented with numerous cryptic clues, some of which may mean something other than what they initially appear to represent. And, although it might seem that an approach which reveals the story's conclusion in the first 5 minutes would lack tension, that's far from the case. *Memento* builds to a surprising yet completely logical finale, and there's plenty of suspense along the way to keep the viewer riveted. **MUST SEE**

The Minus Man [1999]

Starring: Owen Wilson, Brian Cox, Mercedes Ruehl, Janeane Garofalo
Director: Hampton Fancher Screenplay: Hampton Fancher, based on the novel by Lew McCreary Running Time: 1:50 Rated: R (Mature themes, drug use, profanity) Theatrical Aspect Ratio: 1.85:1

In most movies, serial killers are faceless villains or foils for the protagonist. In *The Minus Man*, Fancher (the *Bladerunner* scribe, making his directorial debut) attempts something different. His intention is not only for us to see things as Vann does, but for us to sympathize with the character. Murder is made to seem neat, painless, and almost insignificant; except

for this minor personality quirk, Vann is a nice guy. There's something twisted and broken deep within him, but he is not evil incarnate.

Vann does not see himself as a killer; he's a mailman, or the lodger in a middle-aged couple's room for rent, or the would-be boyfriend of a co-worker. Murder is something he does when the compulsion takes him, but it does not define *who* he is. He views it with a chilling matter-of-factness. "I never make a plan," he confesses, "It just happens." Owen Wilson 's portrayal is effective because it's disarming. What is it that neighbors always say about a serial killer? "He seemed like such a nice, quiet young man." That's Vann. He's hard-working, courteous, considerate, and meticulous. Yet Wilson occasionally lets us glimpse a sinister undercurrent.

The film takes place in a rural Pacific Northwest town where Vann has settled for a while. He's living in a room rented out by Doug and Jane Derwin (Brian Cox and Mercedes Ruehl). The couple's marriage is on the rocks and they're looking for someone to fill the place of their daughter, who has disappeared (we never find out exactly what happened to her). Vann fits in nicely at the Derwin household, and Doug gets him a job at the post office. There, Vann is pursued by Ferrin (Janeane Garofalo), a shy mail sorter who is attracted to him but is nervous about revealing her feelings. However, even though Vann appears to be an upstanding citizen, he hides a dark secret. A rash of mysterious deaths and disappearances starts soon after arrives.

The Minus Man is not a comfortable motion picture to sit through. The lack of overt violence and gore deepens the sense of unease. Watching Vann's tale unfold, we should be gripped by revulsion; instead, there's a strange fascination. This movie may not invite emotional participation, but it gives its audience much to ponder. **RECOMMENDED**

The Mothman Prophesies [2002]

Starring: Richard Gere, Laura Linney, Debra Messing Director: Mark Pellington Screenplay: Richard Hatem, based on the book by John A. Keel Running Time: 1:59 Rated: PG-13 (Mature themes, brief sexuality, mild profanity) Theatrical Aspect Ratio: 2.35:1

Pre-destination versus free will — it's a metaphysical debate that has obsessed religious scholars and philosophers alike through the centuries. *The Mothman Prophesies* works best if you accept the former: that the future is as immutable as the past. Admittedly, that may sound like weighty material for a movie that toes the genre line between thriller and horror movie, but director Mark Pellington is aiming for a more elevated plane.

The film opens with John and Mary Klein (Richard Gere and Debra Messing) purchasing their dream house. For John, an ace reporter at the Washington Post, happiness has finally been achieved — but it's a fleeting thing. On the way home from house-hunting, the Kleins are involved in a car accident. Mary is injured, and, at the hospital, the doctors discover that she has a rare form of brain cancer. Within weeks, she has lost her battle, but, upon her death, she leaves behind a cryptic puzzle for her husband — drawings of a strange, moth-like creature and a question: "You didn't see it, did you?"

Two years later, John has come to terms with his grief, but he is still not interested in dating. He has immersed himself in his job, which takes him away from his Georgetown home to Richmond, Virginia to interview a would-be Presidential candidate. While driving in the wee hours of the morning, he loses his way and inexplicably arrives in the small town of Point Pleasant, West Virginia, more than 400 miles distant from where he expects to be. There, from a local cop, Connie Parker (Laura Linney), he learns that a number of strange things have been happening in town — people seeing apparitions and lights in the sky, hearing strange voices, and experiencing bleeding around the eyes and ears. As John investigates, he becomes convinced that what he first believed to be hallucinations may be warnings of an impending tragedy from the same moth-like being his wife sketched — a suspicion that is re-enforced in the wake of a conversation with a reclusive author named Alexander Leek (Alan Bates).

The Mothman Prophecies is more in the nature of a supernatural thriller than a traditional horror movie. Although the film features a creature of sorts, the "Mothman" is never clearly seen, nor are its nature or intentions explained. Pellington uses a lot of clever camera trickery to give the film a stylish feel. It's an approach that not only makes *The Mothman Prophecies* look interesting, but heightens the sense of tension — all without demanding clear shots of a hideous and deranged computer fabrication. **RECOMMENDED**

Mystic River [2003]

Starring: Sean Penn, Tim Robbins, Kevin Bacon, Laurence Fishburne, Marcia Gay Harden, Laura Linney, Emmy Rossum, Tom Guiry
Director: Clint Eastwood Screenplay: Brian Helgeland, based on the novel by Dennis Lehane Running Time: 2:14 Rated: R (Violence, profanity) Theatrical Aspect Ratio: 2.35:1

With *Mystic River,* Clint Eastwood has rebounded nicely from the failure of his mediocre previous effort, *Blood Work.* This is a powerful tale of crime, guilt, and punishment — a drama that incorporates elements of whodunit mystery/thrillers and police procedurals with a richly textured three-character play.

Those three characters are Jimmy (Sean Penn), Sean (Kevin Bacon), and Dave (Tim Robbins). When we first meet them in a quiet Boston suburb, they are kids playing street hockey. A car drives up, and a gruff man gets out and identifies himself as a cop. After intimidating them, he forces Dave to get into the car, then drives off. As it turns out, the man is a pedophile, not a cop, and Dave is not seen for four days, after he escapes from his abductors.

The bulk of the story takes place some 30 years later. Over the years, Jimmy, Sean, and Dave have grown apart. Jimmy, a grocery store owner with a criminal background, is married to his second wife, Annabeth (Laura Linney), and has three daughters. The eldest of these, Katie (Emmy Rossum), is the apple of his eye. Sean, a police detective for the Massachusetts State PD, is estranged from his wife. Dave, who has never fully recovered from his abduction, has a wife, Celeste (Marcia Gay Harden), and a young son. Then, one night, events bring these three old friends back into one anothers' spheres. Katie is found murdered, and Sean and his partner, Whitey (Laurence Fishburne), are the investigating officers. One of the chief suspects turns out to be Dave, who returned home late on the night of the murder with blood on his hands and an implausible alibi. Meanwhile, as Sean begins the official investigation, Jimmy makes inquiries on his own. He is determined to find the murderer before the police do so that he can mete out his own brand of justice.

It is clear from the beginning that *Mystic River* has aspirations to be more than a conventional murder mystery. The added layer of complexity arises through the psychological depth of the characters and the importance of their past relationship. Getting the tone right for such a complex, genre-crossing story is a tricky thing, but Eastwood masters it. *Mystic River* is suffused by a slightly ominous, sad atmosphere. There are none of the cheesy shocks one often expects from murder mysteries. One could easily argue that, although plot is important, Eastwood puts a greater emphasis on character. The movie moves from one tragedy to a greater one, and we understand how every event impacts each of the protagonists.

With an intelligent, insightful screenplay and a riveting key performance, Eastwood has combined his cinematic ingredients in a mixture that cries out for Oscar consideration. *Mystic River* is haunting and melancholy, and the portraits it paints of Jimmy, Dave, and Sean will stay with you after you have left the theater. In a time when the goal of most movies is to offer instant gratification with no aftertaste, this quality should be both valued and praised.

HIGHLY RECOMMENDED

Narc [2002]

Starring: Jason Patric, Ray Liotta, Chi McBride, Alan Van Sprang, Krista Bridges Director: Joe Carnahan Screenplay: Joe Carnahan Running Time: 1:45 Rated: R (Violence, profanity, drug use) Theatrical Aspect Ratio: 1.85:1

Distilled to its base elements, *Narc* is a conventional "gritty cop" thriller of the sort that has been popularized on television by such weekly shows as *Hill Street Blues* and *NYPD Blue*. The film works less because of its relatively straightforward plot trajectory than because of its forceful lead performances and the stylistic choices made by director Joe Carnahan.

Detroit narcotics officer Nick Tellis (Jason Patric) has been off the force for 18 months following a shooting incident that left an unborn child dead and a permanent black mark on his record. Now, just as Nick is becoming restless with home life, homicide captain Cheevers (Chi McBride) offers him an opportunity at redemption and the chance to restart his career. All he has to do is solve the murder of officer Michael Calvess (Alan Van Sprang), a messy crime that has left the police without a single lead. To do this, he partners with Calvess's best friend, Henry Oak (Ray Liotta), a cop who is as known for getting results as he is for having a short trigger. The deeper Nick gets into the case, the more obsessed he becomes with determining what happened to Calvess. In the process, he loses sight of the damage the investigation is doing to his personal life. Eventually, he discovers that Henry's secrets may hold the keys to the case.

The best parts of *Narc* are those that concentrate on character development rather than police work. The investigation is a generic affair. Despite a few twists, turns, and red herrings, there's nothing remarkable about how Nick and Henry execute their jobs. But, at least during *Narc*'s first half, there's more to the film than just following clues and questioning recalcitrant suspects. We are given a window not only into Nick's home life, but into the private hell from which his loving wife, Audrey (Krista Bridges), has

rescued him. These scenes give Nick three-dimensionality, and make us care about what happens to him. If there's a disappointment to be found in *Narc*, it's that the final act becomes so focused on solving the mystery of what happened to Calvess that it forgets we care more about Nick than the corpse.

Narc is a relentless downer. The movie is about murder, abuse, and betrayal, with no distant ray of light shining like a beacon of hope. Some of Carnahan's dialogue has the rat-a-tat feel of Tarantino, but the uncompromising bluntness of the violence is pure Scorsese. This is not gratuitous bloodshed; it's the kind that makes you feel like you've been punched in the gut. *Narc*'s characters live in the shadows, and the movie works because Carnahan takes us into the darkness with them. Unfortunately, when it's all over, he leaves us there. **RECOMMENDED**

The Negotiator [1998]

Starring: Samuel L. Jackson, Kevin Spacey, John Spencer, David Morse Director: F. Gary Gray Screenplay: James DeMonaco & Kevin Fox Running Time: 2:20 Rated: R (Violence, profanity) Theatrical Aspect Ratio: 2.35:1

The Negotiator, director F. Gary Gray's entry into the summer box office sweepstakes, is what is often referred to as a "white knuckler" — a nearly-nonstop excursion into tension. Once the initial setup has been accomplished and the film kicks into high gear, it grabs the viewer's attention and holds it for the rest of the running time. *The Negotiator* deserves a place among the best action/thrillers of the year. This is a *Dog Day Afternoon* for the '90s.

The film starts by introducing us to Danny Roman (Jackson), hostage negotiator extraordinaire. Roman has a deserved reputation for being the best, although he isn't without his detractors, such as Beck (David Morse), who thinks Roman takes too many chances. Then, one day, when Roman learns a little too much about a police conspiracy to steal money from the pension fund, he is set up for the murder of his partner. Internal Affairs honcho Inspector Niebaum (the late J.T. Walsh) goes after the unjustly accused cop with a vengeance, leading Roman to believe that he will be given no chance to clear his sullied name. Desperate, he takes 4 people (2 cops and 2 civilians) hostage, including Niebaum and an old friend (Ron Rifkin), on the twentieth floor of the Chicago Administration Building. His goal: to intimidate them into telling the truth. Soon, when the police arrive to defuse the situation, Roman is in familiar territory, but on the other side of the law. This time, he's the hostage-taker and another expert negotiator, Chris Sabian (Spacey), is trying to talk him down. Both Roman and Sabian are masters of the rules of engagement, and each recognizes that, for the Chicago police force to take Roman's threats seriously, he may have to kill one of his captives.

Any resemblance to the original *Die Hard* is not coincidental. And, like in the 1988 thriller, the approach of keeping the action confined to a small area works to heighten the tension. As was the case in *Die Hard*, the main character is a cop. He has a potential ally on the outside. The Feds are an ominous, interfering presence. And the protagonist proves to be smarter and more resourceful than his better-equipped, highly-trained opponents. There are enough significant differences to keep *The Negotiator* from seeming like a *Die Hard* clone (it is, for example, much more talky), but the most important similarity — the adrenaline rush generated by a well-made thriller — is impossible to miss. RECOMMENDED

Ocean's 11 [2001]

Starring: George Clooney, Brad Pitt, Julia Roberts Director: Steven Soderbergh Screenplay: Ted Griffin, based on the 1960 screenplay by Harry Brown and Charles Lederer Running Time: 1:58 Rated: PG-13 (Profanity, violence) Theatrical Aspect Ratio: 2.35:1

The good news is that the 2001 version of *Ocean's Eleven* represents one of the rarest of Hollywood rarities: a re-make that is actually better than the original. That's not to say that this motion picture is an unqualified success — one tends to expect a little more from a director of Steven Soderbergh's caliber. However, 2001's *Ocean's Eleven* moves along at an enjoyable clip and relies on more than the notoriety of its stars. The film is an entertaining but unambitious endeavor that combines traditional caper rhythms with comic riffs.

George Clooney, he of the great smile and unforced charm, plays Danny Ocean, a con-artist and thief who is planning his next job the day he gets out of a New Jersey prison on parole. For Danny, this is the big one: a 3-casino robbery that will net more than $150 million. Even dividing the total take by 11 (the number of participants), the payout per person is enormous. Danny's crew consists of right-hand man Rusty Ryan (Brad Pitt), inside man Frank Catton (Bernie Mac), British bad guy Bashir Tarr (Don Cheadle), pick-pocket Linus Caldwell (Matt Damon), veteran con man Saul Bloom (Carl Reiner), moneybags Reuben Tishkoff (Elliot Gould), dueling brothers Turk and Virgil Malloy (Scott Caan and Casey Affleck),

electronics expert Livingston Dell (Eddie Jemison), and contortionist/gymnast Yen (Shaobo Qin). Their goal is to liberate the financial resources of the trio of Vegas casinos run by Terry Benedict (Andy Garcia) on the night of the Lennox Lewis-Wladimir Klitschko heavyweight battle. Since the money from the Bellagio, the Mirage, and the MGM Grand is all stored in the Bellagio's vault, only a single robbery is necessary. There are some obstacles — a "security system [that] rivals that of most nuclear missile silos," countless surveillance cameras, a secure elevator with multiple safeguards against unauthorized entry, armed guards, a vault door that may be impregnable, and Danny's ex-wife, Tess (Julia Roberts), who is currently Terry's girlfriend.

The movie provides an engaging 2 hours that develops in exactly the manner one would expect from this sort of production. The storyline, while certainly not a masterpiece of plotting, offers enough to keep audiences guessing and to inject a little tension into an otherwise harmless and lightweight enterprise. There are also sufficient moments of comedy to maintain an upbeat tone. The average viewer's appreciation of *Ocean's Eleven* will be influenced by expectations, and, in the case of older attendees, memories of the original. RECOMMENDED

Ocean's Twelve [2004]

Starring: George Clooney, Brad Pitt, Julia Roberts, Catherine Zeta-Jones, Casey Affleck, Scott Caan, Don Cheadle, Matt Damon, Andy Garcia, Elliott Gould, Carl Reiner, Shaobo Qin, Eddie Jemison, Bernie Mac, Vincent Cassel Director: Steven Soderbergh Screenplay: George Nolfi Running Time: 2:10 Rated: PG-13 (Profanity) Theatrical Aspect Ratio: 2.35:1

Pleasantness and affability reign supreme in Steven Soderbergh's sequel to the remake of *Ocean's Eleven*. This time around, even the bad guys don't seem so bad. Rumor has it that the atmosphere on the set of *Ocean's Twelve* was so easygoing that it was more like summer camp than a movie shoot, and much of that sense of fun comes across on-screen. Everyone who survived the first film is back for the second, including the entire complement of "Ocean's Eleven." There are two high-profile newcomers. Catherine Zeta-Jones plays Europol agent Isabel Lahiri, an ex-flame of Rusty Ryan (Brad Pitt), who is the confidante of Danny Ocean (George Clooney). The there's Vincent Cassel, who portrays "The Night Fox," a rival thief who believes that Ocean's reputation is inflated — a fact he intends to prove by challenging his rival to a thieving competition.

When the film opens, Danny is retired and living in marital bliss with his wife, Tess (Julia Roberts). It's their "second third" anniversary, and Danny's life is about to go to hell. Someone has tipped off Casino honcho Terry Benedict (Andy Garcia) about the location of Danny and his ten friends, and they all receive an ultimatum: Pay back $160 million (plus interest) in two weeks or face the consequences. So it's off to Europe for Ocean's Eleven (they're too notorious to be able to pull any heists stateside), where they have to steal enough money in 12 days to be able to fulfill their obligation to Benedict. Despite being overlong, *Ocean's Twelve* is enjoyable and will likely appeal to anyone who appreciated the 2001 film. The screenplay, by George Nolfi, starts out a little slow, but by the end of the first hour, it has hit its stride with the movie building momentum. The complicated details of the final heist are entertaining to unravel, and there's also a wonderfully wry bit of fourth wall-breaking fun that Soderbergh has at Julia Roberts's expense.

Although it functions adequately as a heist movie, *Ocean's Twelve* fairs better when seen through the lens of a comedy. The screenplay offers a lot of breezy dialogue, and while it never gets overly silly, it's clear that we're not meant to take any of the proceedings seriously. Soderbergh peppers the print with occasional directorial flourishes (freeze-frames, the use of colored filters, etc.), but for the most part, he presents the film "straight." And, on those occasions when he shows off, it's neither prolonged nor extreme enough to become distracting. One could make an argument that the filmmaker isn't so much directing his actors as he is shepherding them through the moviemaking process. There's a sense that at least some of the dialogue was improvised. The final result speaks well for the process, whatever it actually was. RECOMMENDED

One Hour Photo [2002]

Starring: Robin Williams, Connie Nielsen, Michael Vartan
Director: Mark Romanek Screenplay: Mark Romanek Running
Time: 1:35 Rated: R (Profanity, sexual situations, nudity) Theatrical
Aspect Ratio: 1.85:1

One Hour Photo is an actor's triumph — a fitting destination for Robin Williams to reach after essaying increasingly darker and more dysfunctional characters in films like *Death to Smoochy* and *Insomnia*. Any lingering doubts about Williams' ability to play a role completely straight are erased by *One Hour Photo*. The film has its share of flaws, but none of them are related to the lead actor's powerful and haunting portrayal. Williams nails it.

Sy Parrish (Williams) is the "photo guy" at the local SavMart. When he goes home, he sits alone in a spartan room and watches television. His apartment is undecorated except for one wall, which is papered with hundreds of photographs — extra copies he has made over the years of snapshots brought to him by the Yorkin family — Will (Michael Vartan), Nina (Connie Nielsen), and their son, Jakob (Dylan Smith). Sy has been living vicariously through these people for more than half a decade. His precarious mental balance begins to shift when a series of events push him past the point of instability. First, his boss (Gary Cole) shows an increasing displeasure with Sy's work. Secondly, Sy's desire to enjoy more substantive contact with the Yorkins causes him to act irrationally — buying Jakob a toy, showing up at his soccer practice, and reading the same book as Nina. Sy, whose personality is the kind for which the word "postal" was coined, decides to take matters into his own hands.

For much of its running length, *One Hour Photo* is an effective portrait of a lonely, deranged human being and the increasingly frantic rhythms of his out-of-kilter existence. As far as the audience knows, Sy has no friends, no family, no past, and no future. He crosses the line from being harmless and pathetic to being dangerous when he can no longer differentiate between fantasy and reality. There comes a time when it is no longer enough for him to watch and imagine, when the role of distant voyeur no longer satisfies him. The move from passive to active participant is not only predictable but inevitable given the psychological profile put together by filmmaker Mark Romanek. Dark and unrepentant, this excursion into the epicenter of percolating mental instability is not easily dismissed or forgotten. RECOMMENDED

Open Water [2004]

Starring: Blanchard Ryan, Daniel Travis Director: Chris Kentis
Screenplay: Chris Kentis Running Time: 1:20 Rated: R (Violence, nudity,
sexual situations) Theatrical Aspect Ratio: 1.85:1

Open Water, the second feature from director Chris Kentis, has been compared with both *Jaws* and *The Blair Witch Project.* That latter comparison is an apt one; the former is not. Aside from one coincident element — both movies feature sharks — there are few similarities between this indie horror movie and Steven Spielberg's 1975 blockbuster. On the other hand, despite the absence of a first-person approach and grainy black-and-white footage, there's more than a passing similarity to *Blair Witch.* Those who found that unexpected hit to be an instance of The Emperor's New Clothes will likely have a similar reaction to *Open Water*. But those who were creeped out by the tale of a trio of lost souls in the woods will find themselves equally terrified by what Kentis offers here.

The film starts out innocently enough, with a couple, Susan (Blanchard Ryan) and Daniel (Daniel Travis), headed to a tropical island for a vacation. Once there, they embark upon a scuba diving excursion, and that's where the problems begin. Due to an administrative snafu, they are accidentally left behind while underwater. When they surface, they find themselves all alone in the middle of the deep blue sea. Actually, they're not alone. Their company ranges from the benign (tiny fish) to the dangerous (jelly fish) to the deadly (sharks). And, as they await rescue, they must deal with a variety of problems: nausea, dehydration, hunger, hypothermia, and exhaustion.

Approximately 60 minutes of the movie's 80-minute running time is spent with Susan and Daniel floating around in the ocean. At its best, *Open Water* is suspenseful and frightening — there are several excellent "boo!" moments, and Kentis never cuts away to relieve the tension. At its worst, the film is dull. There are long stretches when little happens. The characters bicker about who's at fault and discuss the various dangers they are facing. The dialogue is neither memorable nor inspired. It's pretty pedantic, and that causes some of *Open Water*'s lulls to drag. Fortunately, even during those moments, the sense of danger lingers.

Despite its flaws, I welcome *Open Water* with great enthusiasm because it offers genuine scares and chills without the self-aware, packaged feel of many horror/thriller films. There are moments when *Open Water* literally had me on the edge of my seat (that's a real state of body, not just a cliché). There aren't many movies capable of that, especially when you consider how jaded I have become. The movie relies upon the audience's imagination for much of its horror — little blood or violence is shown on-screen. For those to whom this sounds intriguing, *Open Water* is worth a look. Just don't plan any scuba diving expeditions soon after. **RECOMMENDED**

Open Your Eyes [Spain, 1997]

Starring: Eduardo Noriega, Penelope Cruz, Chete Lera, Fele Martinez, Gerard Barray, Najwa Nimri Director: Alejandro Amenabar
Screenplay: Alejandro Amenabar, Mateo Gil Running Time: 1:57
Rated: R (Violence, sex, nudity, profanity) Theatrical Aspect
Ratio: **1.85:1** In Spanish with subtitles

Open Your Eyes touches on and passes through so many genres that it transcends categorization. At one moment, it's a melodrama. At another, it's a romance. Then film noir. Then a cautionary tale. Then a morality play. Then science fiction. Perhaps the most amazing thing is how ably and seamlessly Alejandro Amenabar blends so many diverse elements together.

Our guide through the labyrinth of *Open Your Eyes* is Cesar (Eduardo Noriega), a wealthy, self-centered, handsome dilettante who prides himself on never sleeping with the same woman twice. When his friend, Pelayo (Fele Martinez), makes the mistake of introducing Cesar to his current girlfriend, Sofia (Penelope Cruz), trouble begins brewing. Cesar, smitten by Sofia and perhaps in love for the first time in his life, sets out to lure her away from Pelayo. For her part, Sofia appears willing to succumb to Cesar's advances — until tragedy strikes. Nuria (Najwa Nimri), a woman with whom Cesar enjoyed a brief fling, becomes mad with jealousy when Cesar rejects her. While they are in a car together, Nuria accelerates to a reckless speed, then crashes the vehicle, killing herself and seriously injuring Cesar.

He lives, but at a price: his good looks are gone, marred beyond surgical repair. To avoid frightening those around him, Cesar must hide his features behind an emotionless mask. The next time he meets Sofia, she is cold and distant. However, after spending a night in a drunken stupor on the street, Cesar finds that things are looking up. Sofia, once again gentle and loving, re-enters his life. The doctors offer hope that a new technique might allow his face to be healed. But Cesar is starting to experience moments of blinding, irrational rage, and he rightly suspects that all is not as it seems.

So what's it all about? One could easily view *Open Your Eyes* as a study of dualities. Nightmares versus reality. Memories of the past versus actions in the present. Knowledge versus ignorance. Beauty versus ugliness. Madness versus sanity. All of these elements come into play as we try to piece together what's happening to Cesar. Fundamentally, *Open Your Eyes* is concerned with one issue: the vast gulf between perception and reality. When Cesar is handsome on the outside, he is rotten within. But, when the humiliation of losing his physical beauty changes him, circumstances are reversed. (Or are they?) Yet, even at that point, we have only begun to scratch the complexity of the issue, and Amenabar forces us to go much deeper. **HIGHLY RECOMMENDED**

Out of Sight [1998]

Starring: George Clooney, Jennifer Lopez, Ving Rhames, Dennis Farina
Director: Steven Soderbergh Screenplay: Scott Frank based on the
novel by Elmore Leonard Running Time: 2:03 Rated: R (Violence,
profanity, sexual themes) Theatrical Aspect Ratio: 1.85:1

Even without a solid script like the one turned in by
Scott Frank (*Dead Again*), it would almost be worth
the price of admission to see George Clooney and
Jennifer Lopez together on screen. They are two of
the most attractive and charismatic actors around,
and, in addition to having tremendous screen presence, they're good at their craft. True to form, both
are excellent in *Out of Sight,* and the constant sexual
tension between them is electric.

Clooney plays Jack Foley, one of the most successful bank robbers of our time. By applying his smile,
his charm, and his mind, he managed to make illegal
withdrawals more than 200 times (never using a gun)
before the FBI nabbed him. Now, after being broken
out of jail with the help of his best friend, Buddy
(Ving Rhames), he's on his way from Florida to Detroit for a big score — $5 million in uncut diamonds
hidden in the home of Wall Street financier Richard
Ripley (Albert Brooks), a former prison pal. But some
unfinished business is trailing Jack. During his escape, he took a female federal marshal, Karen Sisco
(Jennifer Lopez), hostage. Despite the circumstances,
the spark between them was instantaneous and undeniable, and now Jack finds himself thinking of her
constantly. For her part, even as she tracks him down,
she dreams of what it might be like to have a tryst
with him.

Everything in *Out of Sight* is smart — the dialogue,
the characters, and the storyline. The film boasts
some great scenes. In one, Jack and Karen are
crammed together in the trunk of a car. His hand
strokes her thigh as the two discuss Faye Dunaway
movies: *Bonnie and Clyde, Network,* and *Three Days
of the Condor.* In another, the two meet face-to-face
in a bar and, for the first time, openly admit the attraction that has drawn them together across the
long miles separating Florida from Michigan. The
opening bank robbery is also masterfully presented,
with Clooney oozing charisma as he asks the frightened teller, "Is this your first time being held up?"

Out of Sight contains enough to please just about
anyone who enjoys an unpredictable, character-
driven thriller. Despite a somewhat nonlinear structure that uses flashbacks to fill in story holes, the plot
is not difficult for a thinking viewer to follow. Better
still, it's compelling from start to finish. And, for the
kind of movie that this is, you couldn't ask for a more
appropriate closing scene. **HIGHLY RECOMMENDED**

Owning Mahoney [Canada/US/UK, 2003]

Starring: Philip Seymour Hoffman, Minnie Driver, Maury Chaykin,
John Hurt Director: Richard Kwietniowski Screenplay: Maurice
Chauvet, based on the book *Stung,* by Gary Stephen Ross Running
Time: 1:43 Rated: R (Profanity, brief nudity) Theatrical Aspect Ratio:
2.35:1

Owning Mahowny casts an unflinching gaze into a
window of addiction of a sort not often portrayed in
movies. Based on the true-life book *Stung,* by Gary
Stephen Ross, the film chronicles the facts of the case
of a Toronto bank vice president who stole more than
$10 million from his employer over a two-year period
in the early 1980s. All of that money funded his expanding gambling addiction, ending up in the pockets of bookies and the vaults of casinos. But *Owning
Mahowny* isn't really about how the police closed the
noose around the man's neck. Instead, it's a character
study and an examination of addiction. The two go
hand-in-hand. In order to understand Dan Mahowny
(played brilliantly by Philip Seymour Hoffman), you
have to come to grips with his addiction, and vice
versa. The two are inseparable. For Mahowny, gambling isn't a diversion, a passion, or even an obsession. It is a necessity.

Owning Mahowny is not a feel-good story about
one man's ability to overcome addiction. Instead, it illustrates a deepening spiral of compulsive behavior,
withdrawl from society, and denial. In this case, gambling is the root cause, but the same movie could be
made about a man caught in the grip of drugs, al-
chohol, sex, or anything else. For Mahowny, gambling isn't about winning or losing. Those things are
incidental, as is the money needed to play. The high
and the need are about playing the game and taking
the risk. Winnings are merely ways to prolong the experience. In the end, everything will be lost — it's just
a matter of how long it takes.

The film opens with Mahowny in debt for $10,300
to a local bookie, Frank Perlin (Maury Chaykin).
When he learns that he is being cut off until he can
pay back the money, Mahowny becomes desperate.
So he starts fudging accounts and creating fake loan
applications. Soon, he has access to a nearly endless
line of credit — enough to fund expensive binges,
trips to Atlantic City and Las Vegas, and to wager on
nearly every sporting event taking place in North
America. His gambling has driven a rift between him
and his mousy girlfriend, Belinda (Minnie Driver).

When he spends all of their "romantic" weekend in Vegas at the tables rather than with her, she realizes the seriousness of his problem. At work, no one seems to figure out what is happening. His bosses are pleased with his work ethic, and he even passes an audit.

Movies about men caught in the grip of an addiction are never pleasant to watch. But they are powerful and often instructive. *Owning Mahoney* is such a motion picture. It works for two reasons: (1) it understands the nature and patterns of addiction and doesn't try to blunt or soften them to appeal to an audience; and (2) it doesn't cop out with a happy ending. Add to that a brilliant performance by Hoffman, and you have a motion picture that never ceases to be worthwhile. **RECOMMENDED**

Panic Room [2002]

Starring: Jodie Foster, Forest Whitaker, Dwight Yoakam, Jared Leto, Kristen Stewart Director: David Fincher Screenplay: David Koepp Running Time: 1:48 Rated: R (Violence, profanity) Theatrical Aspect Ratio: 2.35:1

Critics writing reviews of *Panic Room* will likely delve into the cliché bag and pull out some of these familiar phrases: pulse-pounding, edge-of-the-seat, white-knuckler, thrill-a-minute, etc. However trite those sayings might be, they are appropriate for the latest tautly paced and slickly executed motion picture from populist auteur David Fincher. The film's gamesmanship is superior: a cat-and-mouse affair that sometimes features the skill, moves, and countermaneuvers of chess and, on other occasions, plays out like a game of chicken.

The premise is simple enough, and the kind of idea Hitchcock would have enjoyed toying with. Meg Altman (Jodie Foster) is recently divorced from her millionaire ex-husband, Stephan (Patrick Bauchau). Alone with her daughter, Sarah (Kristen Stewart), she moves into a large Brownstone in the Upper West' Side of Manhattan. It's an amazing place, with spacious rooms, and elevator, and, most interestingly, a "panic room." Designed to keep out intruders, the small chamber is protected by steel-plated walls, ceiling, and floor, and a door that is close to impervious. The panic room has its own ventilation system, a telephone line that isn't connected to the house's main one, and a bank of video cameras that show virtually every corner of the brownstone.

On the night that Meg and Sarah move in, they find themselves locked in the panic room in an attempt to escape a trio of threatening men who break into their house. Burnham (Forest Whitaker), Junior (Jared Leto), and Raoul (Dwight Yoakam) have come to steal something specific. Unfortunately, what they want is locked in the panic room with Meg and her daughter. Thus begin the games as the robbers seek to smoke out the victims. And things become further complicated when Burnham, Junior, and Raoul realize that there truly is no such thing as honor amongst thieves.

Panic Room does what all the best suspense-based thrillers accomplish: it keeps us on edge. It's not hard to become enveloped in the movie's spell. Fincher's style, which involves a restless, roaming camera, lots of shadows, and tension that builds to almost unbearable levels, pulls us in. Are there logical flaws? Undoubtedly, but they don't become apparent until long after the house lights have come back on. And the script rewards us with a rarity: protagonists and antagonists who are both smart. The resolution of *Panic Room* doesn't hinge on who makes the most stupid blunders, but on who outthinks the other. And there's a nice twist at the end. Unorthodox as it may be, it *feels* right. The suspense in *Panic Room* never ebbs, and that makes for a thoroughly entertaining — if somewhat exhausting — 108 minutes. **HIGHLY RECOMMENDED**

Payback [1999]

Starring: Mel Gibson, Maria Bello, Gregg Henry, James Coburn Director: Brian Helgeland Screenplay: Terry Hayes and Brian Helgeland based on *The Hunter* by Richard Stark Running Time: 1:42 Rated: R (Violence, torture, profanity, b&d) Theatrical Aspect Ratio: 2.35:1

Directed by Brian Helgeland in his feature debut, *Payback* is a re-make of John Boorman's 1967 edge-of-the-seat movie, *Point Blank*. Both films are based on *The Hunter*, a novel by Donald E. Westlake. Porter (Mel Gibson) is a thief and a killer, which puts him in good company with the sadistic Val Resnick (Gregg Henry). Together, the pair, along with an assist from Porter's wife (Deborah Kara Unger), pulls off a $140,000 heist. But then Resnick turns greedy, shoots Porter twice, and takes all the dough. He makes a big mistake, however: not assuring that Porter is dead. Five months later, recovered from his wounds, Porter is out for revenge. With only one ally — his girlfriend, Rosie (Maria Bello) — he decides to destroy the powerful criminal organization of which Resnick is a member.

Casting Mel Gibson as Porter is an inspired choice. *Payback*'s protagonist is an inherently dislikable fellow — a vicious killer who rips out people's nose rings, leaves behind corpses to rot, and doesn't care how many people he has to wipe out to get what he wants. However, with the appealing Gibson in this role, our natural inclination is to root for Porter, which is necessary for the film to work. If we're not on Porter's side, *Payback* becomes a litany of pointless violence. Gibson does a credible job playing a surly tough guy who's a cross between Bogart and Pacino.

Payback is surprisingly stylish for an action-oriented thriller. Its look is pure film noir, with de-saturated colors emphasizing the grayness of the city streets and gloomy interiors. The voiceover narrative (which, thankfully, isn't overused) is straight out of a potboiler, as the tough guy recounts his misfortunes with lines like "Old habits die hard — if you don't kick them, they kick you." One can almost hear Bogart uttering those words. And, while there's quite a bit more graphic bloodshed and brutality here than in any of the late screen icon's vehicles, *Payback* is a worthy '90s successor to his kind of movie. **HIGHLY RECOMMENDED**

Phone Booth [2002]
Starring: Colin Ferrell, Forest Whitaker, Katie Holmes, Radha Mitchell, Kiefer Sutherland Director: Joel Schumacher Screenplay: Larry Cohen Running Time: **1:20** Rated: **R** (Profanity, violence) Theatrical Aspect Ratio: **2.35:1**

The best way to describe *Phone Booth* is preposterous but entertaining. Due in large part to tight editing, a brisk pace, and a high level of suspense, we are able to suspend our disbelief for about 80 minutes. Afterward, even a moment's consideration will reveal an avalanche of plot holes, but it is a tribute to the filmmakers that these are not recognized until after the end credits have rolled. Hitchcock referred to this sort of film as a "refrigerator movie" (you'd think of a plausibility problem while getting a post-movie snack from the refrigerator), and he would appreciate what Schumacher has wrought here.

Stuart Shepard (Colin Farrell) is a fast-talking publicist who thinks he's on top of the world. Wearing designer suits and a fake luxury watch, he struts down the sidewalks of Manhattan with his assistant in tow, talking on a cell phone and not taking "no" for an answer. A voice-over informs us: "It used to be a mark of insanity to see people talk to themselves. Now, it's a mark of status." Then comes Stuart's daily visit to the telephone booth at 53rd and 8th, from which he calls a pretty young actress named Kelly (Katie Holmes). Stuart finds her attractive and has entertained thoughts of pursuing an affair with her. Although he hasn't done anything yet, he uses the booth so his wife (Radha Mitchell) won't see Kelly's number on his phone bill. But Stuart's daily routine has not gone un-

noticed, and as soon as he hangs up with Kelly, the booth's phone rings. A voice (that of actor Kiefer Sutherland, moonlighting from his TV series, *24*) informs Stuart that he is "guilty of inhumanity to your fellow man" and the "sin of spin — avoidance and deception." The voice states that he has a high-powered rifle trained on the phone booth from one of the many buildings with a view of the intersection, and if Stuart leaves the enclosure, he will be killed. To prove his point, the voice takes a victim. Suddenly, panic is everywhere and the police, led by a captain (Forest Whitaker), arrive and demand that Stuart hang up the phone and step out of the phone booth.

On one level, it's amazing that a movie about a man being trapped inside a phone booth could be successful, but *Phone Booth* works for many of the same reasons that *Speed* does: The script takes a seemingly dead-end premise and keeps throwing in new twists. One key to enjoying this movie is not to engage in "out of the box" thinking (or, arguably, any thinking at all) — it's better to uncover the problems and inconsistencies after the movie is over, not while it's unspooling. For those willing to accept this approach, *Phone Booth* will hold together surprisingly well while maintaining a high adrenaline level. **RECOMMENDED**

The Pledge [2001]
Starring: Jack Nicholson, Robin Wright Penn, Aaron Eckhart, Benicio Del Toro Director: Sean Penn Screenplay: Jerzy Kromolowski & Mary Olson-Kromolowski Running Time: **2:04** Rated: **R** (Violence, profanity) Theatrical Aspect Ratio: **2.35:1**

The Pledge starts out like a generic police mystery, then gradually metamorphoses into something that is part character study and part psychological thriller. Beyond the opening sequences, Sean Penn refuses to allow his movie to be pigeonholed. On the surface, it's like many things we have seen before, but the rhythm and focus are different. In the end, we come away thinking that, while *The Pledge* may not be unique, it's far from what the setup leads us to believe lies ahead. As has often been his trademark both in front of and behind the camera, Penn is not afraid to traverse the road less taken.

On the day of his retirement, Reno Detective Jerry Black (Jack Nicholson) becomes involved in a particularly sordid murder investigation. An 8-year-old girl has been sexually assaulted and brutally murdered, and, when confronting the child's mother (Patricia Clarkson) with the terrible news, Jerry vows to find the killer. Soon, the police have a man in custody, but, even after the suspect's confession and subsequent suicide, Jerry isn't convinced. He thinks there's a serial killer at work — but his colleagues, believing the case to be closed, put him out to pasture. He ends up buying a garage in an out-of-the-way Nevada town — a place where he can go fishing every day.

While there, Jerry befriends Lori (Robin Wright Penn) and her young daughter, Chrissy (Pauline Roberts). When Lori's ex-husband beats her up, Jerry opens his home as a safe haven to the pair, and they come to live with him. For a while, Jerry settles into a routine of domestic comfort — until ugly reminders of his final case begin to crop up. Soon, he is convinced that the killer is on the prowl again and that Chrissy, a dead ringer for the previous victims, is the next target. But is there really a danger, or is Jerry deluded? And, if the serial killer is real, how far will Jerry go to effect his capture? Finally, there's the question of Jerry's murky motives: is he acting to protect his "family" or because, as an ex-cop, he cannot let go of the case?

The Pledge is clever in the way that it gradually reveals things, but never gives us too much information at one time. The red herrings don't seem as cheap as they often do in murder mysteries, and Jerry is far from the infallible, all-knowing investigator. He's a flawed human being, and, only in the end do we understand the extent of that tragic character flaw. The conclusion of *The Pledge* will cause many viewers to walk out of the theaters grumbling, since there is no traditional closure. But the way in which things turn out seems right for the material and the manner in which Penn has chosen to present it. RECOMMENDED

Pulp Fiction [1994]

Starring: John Travolta, Samuel L. Jackson, Uma Thurman, Harvey Keitel Director: Quentin Tarantino Screenplay: Quentin Tarantino based on stories by Quentin Tarantino and Roger Avary Running Time: 2:29 Rated: R (Language, violence, mature themes) Theatrical Aspect Ratio: 2.35:1

This film is one wild ride. An anthology of 3 interconnected stories that take place in a modern-day Los Angeles tinted by echoes of Dashiell Hammett and Raymond Chandler, the movie impresses in every possible way. Writer/director Quentin Tarantino has merged film noir with the gangster tale and pulled them both into the '90s. *Pulp Fiction*'s 3 tales are structured to intersect and overlap at key points, even though they are not presented in chronological order. Tarantino arranges his initial scene to dovetail with his final one in a remarkable example of closure.

Those confused by the structure will see everything clearly once the final line is spoken.

"Vincent Vega and Marsellus Wallace's Wife" is the first story. It opens with Vincent (John Travolta) and Jules (Samuel L. Jackson) out on a hit for their boss, Marsellus (Ving Rhames). Along the way, Vincent confesses that he's uneasy about an upcoming job — taking out Marsellus' young wife Mia (Uma Thurman) while the main man is out of town. The source of the nervousness lies in a story circulating that Marsellus had a man thrown out a 4th story window for giving Mia a foot massage. One wrong step and Vincent could find himself in deep trouble.

"The Gold Watch" is about a boxer, Butch (Bruce Willis), who is handsomely paid by Marsellus to throw a fight. Only at the last moment does it become more profitable to renege on the deal. So, along with his French girlfriend, Fabienne (Maria de Medeiros), Butch goes on the run, hoping to live long enough to spend some of the fortune he has suddenly gained.

"The Bonnie Situation" ties together a few loose threads. It also introduces Harvey Keitel as a suave problem-solver named Wolf and Quentin Tarantino as Jim, a man worried that his wife will come home from work to find a dead body in a blood-spattered car in his garage. Sometimes, it appears, helping out Marsellus is not without its complications.

As was the case in *Reservoir Dogs*, Tarantino's crisp dialogue sparkles. The vulgarity-laced monologues and conversations ripple with humor and are ripe with points to ponder. Who else (except perhaps David Mamet) can make profanity sound so poetic? Relentless in its pace, *Pulp Fiction* is as exhausting as it is exhilarating. In between all the shootings, Mexican standoffs, and other violent confrontations exist opportunities to explore various facets of the human experience, including rebirth and redemption. With this film, every layer that you peel away leads to something deeper and richer. Tarantino makes pictures for movie-lovers, and *Pulp Fiction* is a near-masterpiece. MUST SEE

Rabbit-Proof Fence [Australia, 2002]

Starring: Everlyn Sampi, Tianna Sansbury, Laura Monaghan, David Gulpilil, Ningali Lawford, Kenneth Branagh Director: Phillip Noyce Screenplay: Christine Olsen, based on *Follow the Rabbit-Proof Fence* by Doris Pilkington Running Time: 1:34 Rated: PG (Mature themes) Theatrical Aspect Ratio: 2.35:1

In 1931 Australia, it is the official policy of the government, as determined by the Chief Protector of the Aborigine Populace, Mr. Neville (Kenneth Branagh), that all "half-caste" Aborigine children (the offspring of a white parent and an Aborigine parent) are to be taken from their families and raised in orphanages where they can be civilized with the intention of marrying them to a white person or grooming them to be a domestic servant. To Neville and those like him, this policy — separating a child from his or her family — does not seem cruel or inhuman. On the contrary, Neville states (and believes) that "in spite of himself, the native must be helped."

In the small village of Jigalong, 3 half-caste children — sisters Molly (Everlyn Sampi), who is 14 years old, and Daisy (Tianna Sansbury), who is 8, and their cousin, 10-year old Gracie (Laura Monaghan) — are taken from their mothers to live in the orphanage at Moore River, more than 1,200 miles away from their home. There, they will learn the path of "duty, service, and responsibility" that every good Christian woman should adhere to. Except that Molly, Daisy, and Gracie are not like the other girls at Moore River, and, when an opportunity presents itself, they escape. Pursued by an Aborigine tracker, Moodoo (David Gulpilil), and facing a seemingly impossible trek, they nevertheless press on, finding the rabbit-proof fence that stretches north-south across nearly all of the Australian continent and following it as a means to return to Jigalong.

Although the social injustice that led to Australia's "Stolen Generations" is very much in the forefront of *Rabbit-Proof Fence,* we are drawn into the cinematic tapestry by the real and immediate plight of the children. They are our guides through this political nightmare. *Rabbit-Proof Fence* eventually becomes a kind of road picture, with the girls making their way north and meeting all sorts of people along the way — some who help, some who hinder. There's also an element of danger, with Moodoo doggedly in pursuit and the police closing in. But Molly is smart, often outthinking or outguessing everyone, and occasionally aided by a bit of blind chance.

There is a great deal of craft evident in the way *Rabbit-Proof Fence* was put together. Under the hands of some directors, a film like this could easily turn into a travelogue; as developed by Phillip Noyce, it is an exploration of the heart and soul. And, at an economical 94 minutes, *Rabbit-Proof Fence* trims all the fat and tells its heartfelt and stirring story.

HIGHLY RECOMMENDED

The Rainmaker [1997]

Starring: **Matt Damon, Claire Danes, Danny DeVito, Jon Voight**
Director: **Francis Ford Coppola** Screenplay: **Francis Ford Coppola** based on the novel by **John Grisham** Running Time: **2:20**
Rated: **PG-13** (Mature themes, mild profanity, violence)
Theatrical Aspect Ratio: 2.35:1

In order to make an appealing movie with a lawyer as the protagonist, it's necessary to come up with a villain who can make even an attorney look good. In this case, John Grisham has found one — a big-time, sleazy insurance company. Of course, it doesn't hurt that the main character in *The Rainmaker* has his heart in the right place. Sure, Rudy Baylor (Matt Damon) may be an ambulance-chaser, but that's only an unfortunate fact of life. He's one of the few who doesn't allow the realities of practicing law to corrupt his sense of ethics.

Rudy went to law school because he believed all the myths about helping people. But, because his family had no high-placed connections, graduation found him waiting tables to pay off his student loans, rather than going to work for a prestigious firm. Eventually, Rudy hooks up with the Memphis-based ambulance-chasing outfit of Bruiser Stone (Mickey Roarke), where he's partnered with Deck Shiffler (Danny DeVito), a "para-lawyer" who knows the ropes but has failed the bar exam 6 times. Rudy is sent to the local hospital to search for new clients. What he finds instead is a young woman, Kelly Riker (Claire Danes), who has been severely beaten by her husband. The attraction between Rudy and Kelly is immediate and obvious, but she's afraid to file for divorce for fear that her husband will kill her. Pretty soon, Rudy and Deck feel the heat as a Federal probe closes in on Bruiser, so, together with only about $10,000 between them, they open up their own office.

Meanwhile, Rudy is working on his first big case: suing an insurance company for failing to make good on a claim owed to his client, a leukemia patient, Donnie Ray Black (Johnny Whitworth). When the inevitable happens and Donnie Ray dies, it becomes a wrongful death suit, with Rudy representing Donnie Ray's mother, Dot (Mary Kay Place), against a host of high-priced suits led by Leo F. Drummond (Jon Voight). But the judge, Tyrone Kipler (Danny Glover), is a fair man, and allows Rudy some latitude in presenting his case.

The Rainmaker keeps the in-trial showmanship to a minimum. While it's virtually impossible to film a courtroom drama where there aren't at least a few tricks and unexpected legal maneuvers, *The*

Rainmaker does a good job of downplaying these so that they're never too difficult to swallow. Unlike many of the other films based on a Grisham book, this one is interested in telling a story rather than ambushing the audience with cheap contrivances. **RECOMMENDED**

Ransom [1996]

Starring: Mel Gibson, Renee Russo, Gary Sinese Director: Ron Howard
Screenplay: Richard Price and Alexander Ignon Running Time: 2:01
Rated: R (Violence, profanity) Theatrical Aspect Ratio: 1.85:1

It's pretty unfair to damn *Ransom* by saying that it doesn't live up to Hitchcock's standards — how many movies do, after all? *Ransom* isn't a bad thriller, it's just not a great one. There's a little too much pointless running around, a subplot that leads nowhere, and a certain creeping predictability that argues for a shorter running length. On the other hand, strong acting, smart dialogue, and a couple of neat twists counterbalance many of *Ransom*'s weaknesses.

The script, which is based on a 1956 movie of the same name, has been re-worked by novelist Richard Price to bring it up to date. Mel Gibson is Tom Mullen, the CEO of Endeavor Airlines, the world's fourth largest carrier. He's a devoted family man, paying more than lip service to his love for his wife, Kate (Renee Russo), and son, Sean (Brawley Nolte, son of Nick). One day, at a New York City school science fair, Sean is kidnapped by a gang of 4 (Lili Taylor, Liev Schreiber, Evan Handler, and Donnie Wahlberg). Handcuffed and blindfolded, the boy is held in a small, windowless room. From this hideout, the group's ringleader, corrupt cop Jimmy Shaker (Gary Sinese), makes his $2 million ransom demand. Tom calls in the FBI. The agent in charge of the investigation, Hawkins (Delroy Lindo), advises paying the ransom. At first, Tom agrees, but, as time passes and the situation becomes more desperate, he begins to believe that Sean is already dead. Finally, no longer trusting the cops and worried that he's being played for a fool, he makes a stunning decision.

Since there's no way Sean is going to be killed (or a Disney-owned company never would have released the movie), the most compelling questions relate to how he will be recovered and whether anyone will die attempting to save him. Howard wrings a surprising amount of tension out of this cat-and-mouse material. There are times when *Ransom* is genuinely gripping, most notably during the scenes in and around Tom's fateful decision. We can also be thankful that Howard spares us a lame whodunit. We know

the kidnappers' identities from the beginning, and this eliminates the necessity of peppering the plot with distracting red herrings. The ending could have been steeped in unexpected irony, but the script opts instead for a conventional resolution. **RECOMMENDED**

Read My Lips [France, 2001]

Starring: Vincent Cassel, Emmanuelle Devos Director: Jacques
Audiard Screenplay: Jacques Audiard, Tonino Benacquista Running
Time: 1:55 Rated: Not Rated (Violence, mature themes, sexual
situations) Theatrical Aspect Ratio: 1.85:1 In French with subtitles

Read My Lips, the 4th feature from director Jacques Audiard, contains elements of a romantic thriller, but is equally powerful as a drama. The two main characters are effectively developed and fully realized. In fact, it's the protagonists — in particular, the interaction between them — that drives this motion picture forward and keeps us involved. However, unlike in many character studies, the plot is more than just a simple framework. It is complex and unpredictable, and, as a result, provides the perfect means to better get to know the characters and understand the shifting nature of their relationship.

Carla (Emmanuelle Devos) is a hearing-impaired 35-year-old woman who works as a secretary in a property development company. Her life is ruled by routine — she never goes out and is always available to babysit for her friends. She longs to move forward both in her career and in her personal life, but, encumbered by her hearing deficiency, she is unsure how to do so. One day, when her bosses decide she needs an assistant, she takes on an unskilled but charismatic 25-year-old man, Paul (Vincent Cassel). Paul is an ex-con, fresh out of jail, with no place to live. Carla is immediately attracted to Paul, and he recognizes this, and decides to manipulate the attraction for his own purposes. In return for helping her with her career goals, Paul persuades Carla to use her lip-reading abilities to aid him in casing out an apartment he intends to rob.

Audiard does a remarkable job of interweaving forceful drama with thriller elements. To bring us more into Carla's world, Audiard occasionally gives us her point-of-view, not only visually but audibly. As Carla removes her bulky hearing aid, the film's audio drops off into near-muteness, giving us a sense of what it is like to be in her position. This, like many other details employed by the director, builds strong character sympathy. **HIGHLY RECOMMENDED**

Reservoir Dogs [1992]

Starring: Harvey Keitel, Michael Madsen, Steve Buscemi, Tim Roth
Director: Quentin Tarantino Screenplay: Quentin Tarantino Running
Time: 1:36 Rated: R (Extreme violence and gore, excessive profanity)
Theatrical Aspect Ratio: 2.35:1

Reservoir Dogs grabs you by the throat and digs its claws in deep. From the moment that the unwitting viewer tumbles into the realm of Lawrence Tierney's gang of 8, they are hopelessly trapped there until the final credits roll. As the first outing for actor/director/writer Quentin Tarantino, this is a triumph, displaying all the marks of a longtime virtuoso of the genre.

A jewelry store robbery has gone wrong — badly wrong — for the thieves. One member of the gang is dead, and several are missing. The survivors, including Mr. White (Harvey Keitel), Mr. Pink (Steve Buscemi), and a critically-injured Mr. Orange (Tim Roth), are holed up in a warehouse, trying to figure out how to salvage the situation. Dissension and suspicion run high, as White and Pink discuss the possibility of a traitor in their midst, and the tension escalates when Mr. Blonde (Michael Madsen) shows up with a little surprise in the trunk of his car.

The cast is first-rate, and the parts the actors have to play are fully fleshed out. Tarantino invests each member of his group with a unique and multi-faceted personality. Not content with stereotypes, the writer/director digs deeper, bringing out the humanity in even someone as viciously sadistic and reprehensible as Mr. Blonde. To go along with the characters is a surprising plot, filled with wonderful little twists and turns, and pervaded throughout by the sense of not knowing what's around the corner. The non-chronological manner in which the story is told is confusing at first, but everything eventually sorts itself out.

Tarantino's directing influences, from John Woo to Martin Scorsese, are all in evidence, and their synthesis creates a high-voltage style that's entirely his own. The writing is crisp and clean, providing line after line of snappy dialogue designed to leave the viewer alternately pondering and laughing aloud. The gallows humor and dark comedy are among many of *Reservoir Dogs*' defining elements. This is one of those rare motion pictures that's both intelligent and visceral at the same time. **MUST SEE**

Return to Paradise [1998]

Starring: Vince Vaughn, David Conrad, Joaquin Phoenix, Anne Heche
Director: Joseph Ruben Screenplay: Wesley Strick Running Time: 1:50
Rated: R (Violence, profanity, sexual situations) Theatrical Aspect
Ratio: 2.35:1

Consider this situation: what if, by surrendering yourself to foreign authorities and agreeing to spend 3 years in a prison hellhole, you could save the life of a friend? That admittedly fascinating dilemma lies at the heart of Joseph Ruben's new morality play, *Return to Paradise*, a U.S. remake of the 1989 French feature, *Force Majeure*. And, while there are times when this movie gets bogged down in melodramatic clichés, it nevertheless represents an intriguing exploration of conscience, friendship, and sacrifice.

Return to Paradise opens during the mid-'90s in Malaysia, where 3 friends, Sheriff (Vince Vaughn), Tony (David Conrad), and Lewis (Joaquin Phoenix), are spending a 5-week vacation sampling the pleasures of "God's own bathtub": rum, drugs, and girls. At the end of their stay, Sheriff and Tony head back to New York, but Lewis, a Greenpeace activist, decides to stay behind to participate in a "Rescue the Orangutan" project. As a result, Lewis is there alone when a police raid uncovers a brick of hash that sends him to jail with a death sentence hanging over his neck.

Two years in the future, a young, persistent lawyer, Beth Eastern (Anne Heche), tracks down Sheriff and Tony to apprise them of the situation. Lewis is a week away from the hangman's noose, and the only thing that will save him is if his two accomplices agree to return with her to Malaysia, turn themselves in, and spend a term in prison. If one of them goes, it's 6 years. If both of them go, it's three apiece. If they refuse, Lewis dies. The dilemma for both men, who have established lives in New York City, is clear.

Thankfully, *Return to Paradise* does not cheat the audience when it comes to examining all of the ramifications, both pro and con, of making the crucial decision. It would have been easy for director Joseph Ruben and screenwriter Wesley Strick to simply use this conundrum as a plot device. But, while there are complications, Sheriff and Tony's decision (and the agonizing process of making it) remains at the forefront. Therein lies *Return to Paradise*'s strength, and the filmmakers recognize this. The film's ending is a little unanticipated, and, although there are a few too many surprise revelations in the last 20 minutes, they all work reasonably well to enhance, rather than diminish, the central theme. Ultimately, although *Return to Paradise* can be regarded as a suspense film (will they or won't they go back?), it is as effective when viewed as a drama. **RECOMMENDED**

Road to Perdition [2002]

Starring: Tom Hanks, Tyler Hoechlin, Paul Newman, Jude Law
Director: **Sam Mendes** Screenplay: David Self, based on the graphic
novel by Max Allan Collins and Richard Piers Rayner Running
Time: 2:00 Rated: R (Violence, profanity) Theatrical Aspect Ratio: 2.35:1

Over the course of more than 4 dozen TV shows and movies, Tom Hanks has yet to challenge himself with the most difficult role for a well-liked actor — that of a bad-to-the-bone villain. He comes close in *Road to Perdition,* but doesn't quite reach that destination. For, although Michael Sullivan is a murderer for hire, he also has a conscience and a soul, loves his family, and kills not because he likes it but because it's his job. In short, Sullivan is portrayed sympathetically. The film, director Sam Mendes' eagerly anticipated follow-up to *American Beauty,* is based on the graphic novel by Max Allan Collins and Richard Piers Rayner. As with many adaptations from this medium, *Road to Perdition* stuns with its atmosphere and visuals, but arguably underachieves in some aspects of its characterization and plotting.

The setting is 1931 in Al Capone's Chicago. (Capone doesn't appear in the final cut of *Road to Perdition,* although Anthony LaPaglia apparently plays him on the cutting room floor. Capone's right-hand man, Frank Nitti — the guy who ended up in the car in *The Untouchables* — is portrayed by Stanley Tucci.) Michael Sullivan is the number one hit man of suburban boss John Rooney (Paul Newman), who has treated Sullivan as a son since he took in the orphaned boy. In fact, Sullivan's filial relationship with Rooney is so close that the gangster's natural-born son, Connor (Daniel Craig), simmers with jealousy. One night, while Sullivan is on a job, Connor kills the other man's wife (Jennifer Jason Leigh) and youngest son. Only the older boy, Michael Jr. (Tyler Hoechlin), survives. Father and son go on the road, searching for revenge, closure, and a way to start anew. But Rooney, recognizing that Sullivan will not stop until Connor is dead, ruefully hires another hit man, Maguire (Jude Law), to eliminate Sullivan (but not "the boy").

Road to Perdition allows you to feel, smell, and breathe the air of 1930s Chicago. To some extent, cinematographer Conrad L. Hall is as big a star as any of the actors, since there are occasions when the setting overwhelms the characters. At its heart, *Road to Perdition* is a little drama about fathers, sons, and the covenants they make and break. Mendes illustrates how accomplished actors will respond to an assured director. Serious movie-goers embarking upon this journey will find that *Road to Perdition* leads to a satisfying destination. **RECOMMENDED**

Ronin [1998]

Starring: Robert De Niro, Jean Reno, Natascha McElhone, Stellan
Skarsgård Director: John Frankenheimer Screenplay: J.D. Zeik and
Richard Weisz Running Time: 2:01 Rated: R (Violence, profanity)
Theatrical Aspect Ratio: 2.35:1

Personality-wise, the mercenaries in *Ronin* fit somewhere between the Magnificent Seven and the Dirty Dozen. There are, however, only 5 of them. The most visible, and the one with the best instincts, is Sam (Robert De Niro), an ex-CIA operative who needs the money a job like this offers. Sam is joined by a Frenchman, Vincent (Jean Reno); an ex-KGB computer expert named Gregor (Stellan Skarsgård); a nervous weapons expert, Spence (Sean Bean); and an experienced driver, Larry (Skipp Sudduth). They are being paid by Deirdre (Natascha McElhone), an icy Irishwoman who is as close-mouthed about the specifics of their job as she is about Seamus (Jonathan Pryce), the man who pulls her strings. All that Sam's team knows is that they are to steal a mysterious case from its current owners before its contents are sold to a group of high-bidding Russians. However, what appears to be a straightforward ambush-and-assault operation turns ugly when betrayal and duplicity are stirred into the mix.

Despite a complex script (or perhaps because of it), there is a formula to the way *Ronin* progresses: every plot twist is accompanied by a car chase and a shoot out. So, because the storyline develops in a serpentine fashion, not only are a lot of bullets used (and, upon occasion, the artillery is a little heavier than a handgun), but there are at least 4 lengthy car chases that employ *The French Connection*'s point-of-view approach. However, while the chases are all tautly filmed, attention grabbing, and logistically complicated (especially one that features a high-speed race through a tunnel and onto an expressway *against* 4 lanes of heavy traffic), that may be one car chase too many for any movie.

Unlike many thrillers of this sort, which devolve into a series of mindless action sequences, *Ronin* manages to remain focused on the plot and the characters, even while staging increasingly complicated pyrotechnic set pieces and offering its share of white-knuckle moments. The film is consistently exciting, if a little overlong, and never fails to keep us guessing. *Ronin* also snubs a few conventions of the genre. For example, when a character departs before the mid-point, he does not suddenly re-appear later in the movie to either (a) cause trouble, (b) take revenge, or (c) save the day. That's certainly not the only reason to see this picture, but it's one of several small pleasures that, when they're all combined, make *Ronin* a significant cut above the average thriller. **HIGHLY RECOMMENDED**

Rounders [1998]

Starring: **Matt Damon, Edward Norton, Gretchen Mol, Martin Landau**
Director: **John Dahl** Screenplay: **David Levien & Brian Koppelman**
Running Time: **1:58** Rated: **R (Profanity, violence)** Theatrical Aspect Ratio: **1.85:1**

The director of *Rounders* is John Dahl, who is best known for two splendidly entertaining thrillers (*Red Rock West, The Last Seduction*) that had cable TV premieres before their theatrical runs, depriving everyone involved of a shot at Oscar consideration. Although Dahl loves twisty, intricate plots that focus as much on plot convolutions as on characters, *Rounders* is something of a departure. While there are a few surprises, the storyline is basically a straightforward sports comeback scenario, with the game in question being poker and the "athlete" being a player who suffers a debilitating loss. *Rounders* is character-centered, but it does not follow the serpentine trail used by Dahl's other films.

The story opens in New York City, where our narrator, law student and poker player Mike McDermott (Matt Damon), loses his life savings in a big game with a Russian mobster known as KGB (John Malkovich). The next time we see Mike is nine months later, and he has given up cards to appease his girlfriend (Gretchen Mol). But he still has the bug, and when an old friend of his, Worm (Edward Norton), is released from prison, he is lured into the lifestyle again. Soon, he and Worm are up to their old tricks, taking money from unsuspecting marks. But Worm owes a huge debt to KGB, and, when Mike makes the mistake of vouching for him, he finds that his life is on the line as well. Now, he has 2 days to make $15,000, or he can forget about finishing law school and living happily ever after.

Although *Rounders* offers interesting characters and a compelling plot, the most fascinating aspect of the movie is its exploration of the theory of gambling. This is one of those rare instances when the voiceover doesn't seem unnecessary or intrusive, because it's through Damon's narration that we learn the ins and outs of being successful at cards. Ultimately,

Rounders doesn't try to do anything spectacular. It's a solidly enjoyable motion picture that follows a traditional trajectory. We've seen this kind of story with boxers, baseball players, ice skaters, etc. Now it's time for the cardsharks to get their turn. However, although the storyline is predictable, the intelligent dialogue and top-drawer acting more than make up for the possible deficiency. **RECOMMENDED**

Run Lola Run [Germany, 1998]

Starring: **Franka Potente, Moritz Bleibtreu** Director: **Tom Tykwer**
Screenplay: **Tom Tykwer** Running Time: **1:21** Rated: **R (Sex, violence, profanity)** Theatrical Aspect Ratio: **1.85:1** In German with subtitles

Run Lola Run is a must-see for anyone who enjoys a fast-paced, innovative motion picture that refuses to be defined by norms of the genre. Directed by Tom Tykwer, this German import is a kinetic meditation on fate and destiny. It tells the story of Lola (Franka Potente, an actress with true screen presence), a '90s girl with Raggedy Ann hair, a large tattoo, and a voice so penetrating that when she screams, she can shatter glass. She's also athletic, because, as one might expect from the title, Lola spends most of the movie running.

Her dim-witted boyfriend, Manni (Moritz Bleibtreu), has lost 100,000 marks that he owes to the mob. Lola has 20 minutes to find that money and get it to Manni or he will be killed. So she takes to the streets, straining every resource to make the score before it's too late. Instead of just showing us one of Lola's approaches, however, Twyker gives us three to choose from, throwing us into an alley of alternate realities. You can essentially pick your own ending, each of which offers its share of irreverent surprises. Sandwiched in between the alternative storylines are soft-focus scenes of Lola and Manni reflecting on life and love. These sequences serve a dual purpose: to allow us to catch our breath and to deepen our sympathy for these two intensely likable characters.

Saturated with irony, the film moves at a blazing speed to the accompaniment of a relentless techno soundtrack; blink and you'll probably miss a thrown-in visual gag. Using an innovative mix of animation, still photography, slow motion, and normal cinematography, Twyker illustrates how the smallest change in what a person does can alter the rest of their life (not to mention the lives of others, including complete strangers they pass on the street). Critic Harlan Jacobson called this a "90-minute MTV video," but, while that statement captures the film's spirit, it greatly shortchanges *Run Lola Run*, which has as much depth as it has energy and action. **HIGHLY RECOMMENDED**

Runaway Train [1985]

Starring: Jon Voight, Eric Roberts, Rebecca De Mornay
Director: Andrei Konchalovsky   Screenplay: Djordje Milicevic, Paul Zindel and Edward Bunker, based on a screenplay by Akira Kurosawa
Running Time: 1:51   Rated: R (Profanity, violence)   Theatrical Aspect Ratio: 1.85:1

Long before Keanu Reeves was stuck on board a speeding bus, Jon Voight, Eric Roberts, and Rebecca De Mornay were trapped on a runaway train. Although *Speed* is a very good movie, *Runaway Train* is a more complete experience. The script is better-written, depending more on visceral thrills than those enhanced by special effects. The characters are better-rounded, and there is a fascinating exploration of man's primal instinct. *Runaway Train* belongs to a rare genre: the intelligent thriller. It will come as no surprise to educated movie-goers to learn that the script, credited to Djordeje Milicevic, Paul Zindel, and Edward Bunker, is based on an original screenplay devised by the Japanese master, Akira Kurosawa. One can almost imagine Kurosawa regular Toshiro Mifune in the role given to Jon Voight.

Not that Voight doesn't place his own indelible stamp on the part of Manny, a hardened criminal who is serving a life sentence in a maximum security prison in Alaska. Manny has recently spent three years locked in solitary confinement. Upon his release, he is hailed as a hero by the rest of the prison population. One of his most ardent fans is Buck (Eric Roberts), a dumb, garrulous, cocky rapist whose job pushing laundry carts becomes a critical element of Manny's escape plan. With Buck tagging along, Manny makes his way through the sewers under the prison, out into the cruel Alaskan wilderness, and to a remote train station. There, the two stowaway on a 4-engine train headed south, unaware that the engineer has died of a heart attack, and the only one else on board is Sara (Rebecca De Mornay), a female maintenance worker. The train is out of control and rushing down the tracks towards a collision with destiny.

When *Runaway Train* was produced, the action genre was undergoing a change from character-driven movies to pyrotechnics-based flicks. Of the thrillers developed after this one, only a select few — *Die Hard* and perhaps one or two others — have achieved this level of tautness without compromising

the intelligence of the plot. Best of all, in more than a decade since its release, *Runaway Train* has aged exceptionally well. It is just as compelling today as it was during the winter of 1985-86. **HIGHLY RECOMMENDED**

The Salton Sea [2002]

Starring: Val Kilmer, Vincent D'Onofrio, Adam Goldberg, Luis Guzman
Director: D.J. Caruso   Screenplay: Tony Gayton   Running Time: 1:42
Rated: R (Drug use, violence, sexual situations)   Theatrical Aspect Ratio: 1.85:1

The Salton Sea is a thriller with an edge — which is to say that it doesn't follow the stale, standard, connect-the-dots storyline which has become commonplace in movies that explore the seamy underbelly of the criminal world. Some of the elements found here are familiar — strung-out punks, dangerous drug dealers, corrupt cops, cynical FBI agents, flash-forwards, and red herrings — but screenwriter Tony Gayton and director D.J. Caruso find interesting ways to employ them.

The movie opens with a fascinating account of the history of speed (meth) since World War II, then takes us into the world of Danny Parker (Val Kilmer), who resides in the "land of the perpetual night party." At first, Danny appears to be just another user. He and his buddies, Jimmy (Peter Sarsgaard) and Kujo (Adam Goldberg) seem to have nothing better to do than hang out, absorb the punk/goth scene, and do drugs. But there's more to Danny than meets the eye — much more. In the first place, his real name is Tom Van Allen, or at least that used to be his real name. He is haunted by memories of a beautiful wife, who may or may not be real. And Danny is a police informant for a pair of crooked cops — Morgan (Doug Hutchison) and Garcetti (Anthony LaPaglia). He's also trying to make one last big score from a dealer named Pooh Bear (Vincent D'Onofrio), so he can vanish into obscurity. Or is he? The pieces don't all quite fit, and director Caruso is keeping the last one tantalizingly out of reach until he's ready to finish the puzzle.

While the strength of *The Salton Sea* is its serpentine plot, the movie also has a nice noir look. Caruso goes a little overboard in applying a distinctive visual varnish to the product by employing a variety of camera tricks (including time lapse photography, fades, etc.), but he stays clear of the ego masturbation that is common with filmmakers like Oliver Stone. For the most part, Caruso's unconventional moments work. *The Salton Sea* is dark, as befits its grim subject matter, but not unreasonably so. And it has a sense of humor, although only those with a penchant for warped jokes will absorb Caruso's stabs at comic relief. This thriller seems conventional until you start paying attention — and that's when the payoff occurs.

RECOMMENDED

Saw [2004]

Starring: Cary Elwes, Leigh Whannell, Danny Glover, Ken Leung, Dina Meyer, Michael Emerson, Monica Potter, Makenzie Vega Director: James Wan Screenplay: Leigh Whannell Running Time: 1:40 Rated: R (Violence, gore, profanity) Theatrical Aspect Ratio: 1.85:1

Saw is for hard-gore horror aficionados only. To appreciate *Saw* in its full gory, you have to have a penchant for productions that bask in the traditions of the Grand Guignol. While most of the film relies more on psychological tension and terror, there's plenty of gut-churning, visceral violence, especially during the final 15 minutes. On the strength of a grippingly original concept and 90 strong minutes of building action, *Saw* gets a recommendation — but only if you like this kind of thing.

The movie opens with Adam (Leigh Whannell) and Lawrence (Cary Elwes) chained to pipes in the bowels of a long-forgotten bathroom that hasn't been cleaned in at least 20 years and resembles a charnel house. Their shackles give them limited mobility — not enough to reach each other or the bloody corpse that lies on the floor between them. Neither has a clear memory of how they got here, and neither can answer the key question of "Why me?" Their captor has left them clues and tools: an unloaded gun, tantalizingly out of reach; a tape recorder; two saws; a cell phone; and two cigarettes. It's all part of a game, and if Adam and Lawrence don't play it right, one or both of them will end up dead. For Lawrence, the danger extends beyond his subterranean cell — his wife (Monica Potter) and daughter (Makenzie Vega) are in danger, as well.

It turns out that Adam and Lawrence are the playthings of a unique serial killer ("the Jigsaw Killer") — one who sets up his victims to bring about their own ends. And, while the perpetrator is stalking Adam and Lawrence, he in turn is being tracked by a bitter ex-cop (Danny Glover) who's looking to avenge his late partner. To say more would be criminal. *Saw* does an excellent job of building tension until the bubble bursts during the climax. There are occasional missteps that betray Wan's newness to feature directing: The pacing isn't always perfect; there are some rough edits; and he is sometimes too enamored of showy camera flourishes. Plus, Leigh Whannell's dialogue is in need of an upgrade. *Saw* is constructed like a jig-saw puzzle (mimicking the nickname of the killer), with each scene revealing a new piece. This nonlinear approach allows us to grow a realization of how deadly an antagonist Adam and Lawrence's captor is. This is an intelligent psychopath, not someone who will hold a gun on a cop while explaining his motives and waiting to be outsmarted and brought down.

The horror genre has become a minefield of clichés and recycled plots, making it difficult to generate enthusiasm about any new release. New hooks are a premium commodity, so when someone like Wan finds one, it's easy to overlook freshman mistakes. With its freshness and energy, *Saw* bucks the horror trend toward formula storytelling and proves that enough qualities in the "plus column" can overcome a weak ending. **RECOMMENDED**

The Second Time [Italy/France, 1996]

Starring: Nanni Moretti, Valeria Bruni Tedeschi, Valeria Milillo Director: Mimmo Calopresti Screenplay: Heidrun Schleef, Francesco Bruni, Mimmo Calopresti Running Time: 1:20 Rated: Not Rated (Mature themes, profanity) Theatrical Aspect Ratio: 1.85:1 In Italian with subtitles

One day, a man sees a woman. Something about her strikes him as familiar and he begins to follow her. All day, he dogs her steps — to her cafeteria at work, on the bus going home, and finally, along the street leading to the prison from which she is set free by day to participate in a work release program. The man, a university professor named Alberto Sajevo, returns home. All evening, he thinks of the woman, and the next day he sets out to meet her. Their eyes lock and they have a polite conversation, but something isn't right. Neither of them offers their real name to the other — they go by assumed identities. There's a dynamic between these two that we don't understand — perhaps they don't, either. Where are things going? Why is Alberto following her? And what are his intentions?

The Second Time is one of those stories where there's no real beginning or end. The characters' lives have been going on for a long time before we first meet them, and they'll continue after the end credits have rolled. There are no obligatory flashbacks to show us important past events and no epilogue to hint at what the future might hold. The film doesn't have much of a sense of closure, but, when it's all over, we feel that we're "up to speed" and have witnessed an important event.

Much of the credit for the film's success has to go to co-writer/director Mimmo Calopresti, who knows exactly where he wants the narrative to go, and never loses control of it. If the pacing of the second half is a little uneven, that can be attributed to the escalation in tension resulting from confrontations. The first half, however, is perfectly paced. We are brought into the situation gradually, at first mildly intrigued by the characters, then burning with curiosity. The revelation, when it occurs, is a shock, but one that makes sense when examined in retrospect. Few movies today are put together this expertly. Not only does *The Second Time* address several important issues, but it does so within a framework designed to keep viewers on the edge of their seats. **HIGHLY RECOMMENDED**

Secret Window [2004]

Starring: Johnny Depp, John Turturro, Maria Bello, Timothy Hutton, Charles S. Dutton Director: David Koepp Screenplay: David Koepp, based on "Secret Window, Secret Garden," by Stephen King Running Time: **1:42** Rated: PG-13 (Violence, gore, sexual situations, profanity) Theatrical Aspect Ratio: **2.35:1**

Secret Window introduces us to Mort Rainey (Johnny Depp), an unkempt author who is holed up in an isolated cabin somewhere in the woods, trying use writing as a form of self-therapy to forget the infidelity of his soon-to-be ex-wife, Amy (Maria Bello). Mort's life is a mess, but it's soon to become even messier. One afternoon, an ominous man calling himself John Shooter (John Turturro) arrives at Mort's door and claims that Mort plagiarized one of his stories. Mort is incredulous, and immediately dismisses the man. But Shooter will not be put off so easily, and he begins to stalk Mort, threatening dire consequences if the writer does not come to terms with him, then acting on his threats when Mort refuses to capitulate.

Secret Window offers a twist of sorts, but it's one that's consistent with the story and is only likely to surprise the inattentive viewer. Although director David Koepp doesn't telegraph things too obviously, it appears to be his intention for the viewer to be aware that there's more than one explanation for Shooter's actions. Recognizing the underlying reality of the situation does little to defuse the tension — a fair amount of suspense remains concerning what will happen to the primary characters: Mort, Shooter, Amy, Amy's lover (Timothy Hutton), and a private investigator hired by Mort (Charles S. Dutton). And Koepp thankfully doesn't wimp out and give us a "safe" ending.

The film's strength is one of perspective. It's difficult for a motion picture to effectively employ the technique of the "unreliable narrator" (this is much easier to accomplish in writing), but Koepp overcomes the obstacles with seeming ease. There's no awkwardness when the point of view shifts during the final fifteen minutes. That's also the point at which all is revealed to those who haven't figured out what's going on, and when those who have successfully "read" between the lines will be able silently exult, "I *knew* it!"

Secret Window draws inspiration equally from two of Koepp's previous projects: *The Trigger Effect* (which he wrote and directed), a talky thriller with tension percolating just under the surface, and *Panic Room* (which he wrote), about a showdown inside a New York City brownstone. The levels of violence and blood are tame enough for the MPAA to issue a PG-13 (although I dispute that because of one scene), leaving the majority of *Secret Window*'s horror in the psychological realm. It's a taut, entertaining motion picture that serves its purpose. **RECOMMENDED**

Seven [1995]

Starring: Brad Pitt, Morgan Freeman, Gwyneth Paltrow Director: David Fincher Screenplay: Andrew Kevin Walker Running Time: **2:03** Rated: R (Gory crime scenes, violence, profanity) Theatrical Aspect Ratio: **2.35:1**

Frequently, mystery/thrillers present us with a cast of about 6 or 7 characters, set up a sequence of grizzly murders, then "surprise" us by revealing which of those 6 or 7 characters is the guilty party. It's a time-honored method that's repeated in at least several movies each year. At the outset, *Seven* has all the hallmarks of this kind of motion picture. Fortunately, it turns out somewhat smarter and less predictable. Though not without flaws, *Seven* isn't transparent or moronic, and it doesn't insult the average viewer's intelligence.

The good guys are a pair of detectives at opposite ends of their careers. David Mills (Brad Pitt) is new on the job, full of energy and high ideals, and ready to "make a difference" by catching the crooks. William Somerset (Morgan Freeman) is in his last week on the job. His long years studying crime scenes and following up on clues have left him weary and jaded. To him, being a detective isn't about nabbing criminals — it's about methodically collecting and cataloguing evidence in case a prosecutor ever needs it.

The serial killer pursued by Mills and Somerset is choosing each of his victims based on which of the seven deadly sins (gluttony, greed, sloth, lust, pride, envy, wrath) they have most clearly violated. The deaths form a portion of a decidedly warped sermon.

In their quest to end this bloody, sadistic spree, the two cops appear well-paired, as together they make the perfect detective. Mills is all brawn and little brain. Somerset, on the other hand, spends long hours in the library researching Dante and Chaucer, looking for clues that will enable him to prevent the next killing.

Seven is unnecessarily gory and runs for a little too long, but neither of these elements detracts much from the film's enjoyability (unless you have a weak stomach). The same is true of several logical flaws — they're there, but not overly apparent while the film is on-screen. *Seven* may always be grim, dark, and rainy, but at least there's a little substance beneath the atmosphere. **RECOMMENDED**

Sexy Beast [United Kingdom, 2000]

Starring: **Ray Winstone, Ben Kingsley, Ian McShane** Director: **Jonathan Glazer** Screenplay: **Louis Mellis, David Scinto** Running Time: **1:28** Rated: R (Profanity, violence, sexual situations) Theatrical Aspect Ratio: **1.85:1**

The oddly-titled *Sexy Beast* (oddly titled because neither of the main characters is sexy, although both are certainly beasts) focuses on a husband's determination to honor a promise he made to his wife. The movie, the debut effort from British director Jonathan Glazer, is essentially a caper flick, although the best parts take place before the crime gets underway. The first two-thirds of this film represents a test of wills between retired criminal Gary (Ray Winstone) and gangster Don (Ben Kingsley), who wants Gary to come back to work with him on one more job. Don is abusive and unrelenting; Gary is more laid back (at times almost submissive).

Both Kingsley and Winstone give forceful performances, and their often vicious, occasionally volcanic give-and-take is a delight to behold. Winstone, whose tanned, plump body is the picture of a man who has gone soft in the lap of luxury, gives yet another in a long line of effective portrayals. As good as he is, however, he is constantly eclipsed by Kingsley, who tears into this role with a gusto we rarely see from the normally stately actor. Kingsley is so magnetic that the movie suffers noticeably when he's not on screen (unfortunately, there's a span of about 20 minutes when this is true). Satellite characters, such as Gary's wife, Deedee (Amanda Redman), and crime boss Teddy Bass (Ian McShane), enrich the plot by raising the stakes. Gary can cope with Don's threats and bullying when they are directed at him, but not when his wife is their target. The tension is effectively leavened with comedy to keep the tone from becoming too harrowing.

Although the chief pleasure of watching *Sexy Beast* lies in absorbing the performances of Winstone and (especially) Kingsley, Glazer displays a lively visual style that offers moments of surprise and gratification. *Sexy Beast* runs the gamut from relentless to playful. There's a priceless scene early in the proceedings featuring a boulder and a swimming pool that has to be seen to be believed. With a style that recalls recent films like *The Limey* and *Lock, Stock and Two Smoking Barrels*, *Sexy Beast* offers a suspenseful 90 minutes. **RECOMMENDED**

Shallow Grave [United Kingdom, 1994]

Starring: **Kerry Fox, Christopher Eccleston, Ewan McGregor** Director: **Danny Boyle** Screenplay: **John Hodge** Running Time: **1:33** Rated: R (Violence, gore, nudity, language, mature themes) Theatrical Aspect Ratio: **1.66:1**

A couple of clichés come to mind while watching Danny Boyle's deliciously diabolical feature debut, *Shallow Grave*. The first — that money is the root of all evil — is obvious. The other — that it's always the quiet ones who bear the closest watching — is only marginally more obscure.

The film starts off a little slowly with some necessary exposition to get the story jump-started. Three flatmates — Juliette (Kerry Fox), a doctor; David (Christopher Eccleston), an accountant; and Alex (Ewan McGregor), a journalist — are looking for someone to move into the vacant 4th bedroom of their suite. After interviewing an interesting range of applicants, they settle on Hugo (Keith Allen), whose outlook on life seems a good match for their own. And his willingness to pay up front with cold cash doesn't hurt.

However, Hugo's time with the trio is destined to be short. One day, he moves in; the next, he's dead, apparently of a drug overdose. Left behind in his room are his corpse, evidence of his addiction, and a suitcase full of money. This presents a dilemma for the flatmates: call the cops or dump the body and keep the cash. Because of the nature of the film, it's not hard to guess which they choose. So, while two thugs searching for Hugo begin leaving a trail of dead bodies, Juliette, David, and Alex take Hugo's remains out to the woods where they mutilate the corpse beyond recognition and bury it in a shallow grave.

There aren't any real, three-dimensional characters in *Shallow Grave,* but the stock types are played with such ability by Fox (the aloof female), Eccleston (the reclusive nerd), and McGregor (the wisecracking party boy), that it doesn't matter. Director Danny Boyle, a veteran of British TV, imbues *Shallow Grave* with a style that at times seems a little too slick.

In fact, a weakness of this film is that it occasionally tries to be too clever (bordering on smug). Several of the apparently "shocking" plot twists aren't all that surprising, but Boyle treats each new turn of John Hodge's script as if it was the most unexpected possibility. This objection is in the nature of a minor quibble, however, since it does little to detract from the viewer's overall satisfaction. Taken as a whole, *Shallow Grave* is a reasonably enjoyable (for those captivated by this sort of thing) black comedy/noir thriller. **RECOMMENDED**

The Siege [1998]

Starring: Denzel Washington, Annette Bening, Bruce Willis, Tony Shalhoub Director: Edward Zwick Screenplay: Lawrence Wright and Menno Meyjes & Edward Zwick Running Time: 1:58 Rated: R (Violence, profanity, brief nudity) Theatrical Aspect Ratio: 2.35:1

The setting is New York City, one of the most likely (and vulnerable) American targets for terrorism. When a special branch of the United States military, under the command of General William Devereaux (Bruce Willis), takes prisoner suspected terrorist mastermind Sheik Ahmed Bin Talal, Islamic fundamentalists across the world take notice. The only warning the FBI receives is a single, cryptic message: "Release him." Then all hell breaks loose in New York. A bus is destroyed, killing 25 civilians. A Broadway theater is bombed. Hostages are taken at a school. As the wave of terrorist activity crests, the President must consider if the only way to save the city and break the grip of fear is to declare martial law. Devereaux argues against that eventuality, but is nevertheless ready to lead 10,000 men into action on American soil.

Another person not in favor of martial law is Anthony Hubbard (Denzel Washington), the FBI agent in charge of investigating the terrorist activities. His staff is comprised of smart, energetic, intelligent men and women very much unlike the usual group of moronic Feds we're used to seeing in movies. Hubbard develops an uneasy alliance with CIA agent Elise Kraft (Annette Bening), whose department knows more about the situation than they're willing to reveal. Yet, as the twin threats of a catastrophic terrorist action and the implementation of martial law grow greater, Hubbard finds that time is against him.

One of the reasons that *The Siege* works so well is

that a lot is going on simultaneously, both on the surface and just beneath it. In addition to the FBI's investigation, considerable time is spent exploring the distrustful relationships that exist between various segments of the U.S. government (namely, the army, the FBI, and the CIA). This is not an attempt at a "tell all" expose of what goes into a government cover-up, but a look at the complexities inherent when so many secrets and lies are involved. *The Siege* also examines (albeit superficially) the potential for the abuse of power when the Constitution is suspended.

The Siege is many things at once: tense, exciting, disturbing, and thought provoking. In the wake of the events of September 11, 2001, one could also argue that this film is eerily prescient. **HIGHLY RECOMMENDED**

The Silence of the Lambs [1991]

Starring: Jodie Foster, Anthony Hopkins, Scott Glenn, Ted Levine Director: Jonathan Demme Screenplay: Ted Tally, based on the novel by Thomas Harris Running Time: 1:58 Rated: R (Violence, profanity, nudity) Theatrical Aspect Ratio: 1.85:1

The Silence of the Lambs opens by introducing us to FBI trainee Clarice Starling (Jodie Foster), a brilliant student who has been selected by Jack Crawford (Scott Glenn), the head of the FBI's Behavioral Science Unit, to help in the pursuit of a serial killer called Buffalo Bill, who skins his victims after murdering them. Crawford wants Clarice to approach the infamous Dr. Hannibal Lecter, or "Hannibal the Cannibal" as he has become known, and encourage Lecter to provide a profile of Buffalo Bill. Crawford claims that Lecter might be willing to open up to a woman — and he's right. The good doctor offers Clarice a quid pro quo deal. For every piece of information he shares about Buffalo Bill, Clarice must reveal one detail about her past. So, while Lecter is helping Clarice get closer to Buffalo Bill, he is also worming his way into her psyche. Perhaps surprisingly, however, she is doing the same to him.

There is little doubt that the most memorable aspect of *The Silence of the Lambs* is Anthony Hopkins' incomparable performance as Lecter. Taking over for Brian Cox, who was effective, but not especially memorable, as the good doctor in 1986's *Manhunter*, Hopkins instantly makes the role his own, capturing and conveying the charismatic essence of pure evil. To his dying day, no matter how many roles he plays in the interim, Hopkins will forever be known for this part.

Since its 1991 release, much has been written about *The Silence of the Lambs,* Hannibal Lecter, Clarice Starling, and the relationship between them.

Thomas Harris was so intrigued by the characters that he wrote the sequel, *Hannibal*, which soared into the top spot on best-seller lists countrywide as soon as it was released. *The Silence of the Lambs* may not have been the best thriller of 1991, but it was the most chilling and creepy, and there's no denying that the most celebrated aspect of the film — the Clarice/Hannibal connection — could not have been accomplished with greater skill. **HIGHLY RECOMMENDED**

A Simple Plan [1998]

Starring: Bill Paxton, Billy Bob Thornton, Bridget Fonda Director: Sam Raimi Screenplay: Scott Smith based on his novel Running Time: 2:03 Rated: R (Violence, profanity) Theatrical Aspect Ratio: 1.85:1

Beware things that are described as "simple." While this is not the central message of *A Simple Plan*, it's certainly a byproduct. From the real world, we all know that things which are supposed to be simple — a basic plumbing job, minor car repairs, etc. — frequently turn into intricate nightmares, eating up time, effort, and patience in equal quantities. In Sam Raimi's superior thriller, Hank (Bill Paxton), Jacob (Billy Bob Thorton), Lou (Brent Briscoe), and Sarah (Bridget Fonda) discover that a seemingly uncomplicated, foolproof plan to make them all rich is not without bloody ramifications.

When *A Simple Plan* begins, Hank is a happy man living out his life in a quiet, rural Midwestern town. He has everything he could possibly want: a pregnant wife he loves, a decent job, and friends and neighbors who like and respect him. Then, one winter day, something happens that is destined to change the fabric of Hank's existence. Out in the woods, he, his mentally-slow brother, Jacob, and a friend, Lou, stumble upon the snow-covered wreckage of a small plane. Inside, they find the mummified corpse of the pilot and a stash of $4.4 million in cash — "The American dream . . . in a gym bag." Hank wants to leave the money where it is and phone the authorities. Jacob and Lou, however, argue that they should claim the loot as their own, since it probably belonged to drug dealers in the first place. At first, Hank resists, but, eventually, he gives in. Soon, however, the seeds of mistrust infiltrate the small group, pitting brother against brother, and friend against friend, and, as the circle of people who know about the money expands, the threat of discovery grows, until one incident elevates the stakes to life-and-death.

Director Sam Raimi, working from a script written by Scott Smith and using groundwork laid by John Boorman (who, at one point, was set to helm this project), does a marvelous job of depicting the growing tension between the characters. While there are moments that offer shock value, Raimi's primary goal is to gradually build the suspense. He draws us into the story by making Bill Paxton's Hank a Jimmy Stewart-type of nice guy — the sort of man it's virtually impossible not to identify with — then showing his slow, gradual spiral into the abyss of greed and self-interest that captures nearly everyone who crosses *A Simple Plan*'s screen. **HIGHLY RECOMMENDED**

Snatch [United Kingdom/United States, 2000]

Starring: Benicio Del Toro, Dennis Farina, Vinnie Jones, Brad Pitt Director: Guy Ritchie Screenplay: Guy Ritchie Running Time: 1:44 Rated: R (Violence, profanity, brief nudity) Theatrical Aspect Ratio: 1.85:1

Boiled down to its essentials, *Snatch* is about a group of goons, low-level gangsters, and assorted undesirables, all of whom are after the same thing — a stolen, 84 karat diamond that's the size of a chubby baby's fist. The movie is narrated by Turkish (Jason Statham), a boxing promoter who is unwillingly pulled into the story. The diamond is initially stolen in Antwerp by Franky Four Fingers (Benicio Del Toro), who brings it to London. Once there, it is hotly pursued by the likes of an American "businessman," Cousin Avi (Dennis Farina), his blustering British cousin, Doug the Head (Mike Reid), and his hard-nosed sidekick, Bullet Tooth Tony (Vinnie Jones). Also in the hunt are ex-KGB agent Boris the Blade (Rade Serbedzija), sadistic crime boss Brick Top (Alan Ford), and a group of inept thieves with a pet dog. To further complicate matters, we are introduced to bare-knuckle boxer Mickey O'Neil (Brad Pitt), whose fortunes become integral to the convoluted narrative's eventual resolution. Part of the fun is watching how (and sometimes why) all of these characters interact, and seeing what happens when things don't go as planned.

Snatch is raucous and crude, but never boring or predictable. It is bold, brash, and cartoonish, and never takes itself seriously. In interviews, Ritchie has claimed not to have been influenced by Tarantino, but the video clerk-cum-filmmaker's trademarks are littered around *Snatch*'s colorful landscape. However, since Tarantino's style is the result of synthesizing the approaches of directors he admires, it's possible that Ritchie arrived at something similar by having the same influences. Whatever the case, most people who enjoyed *Pulp Fiction* will appreciate *Snatch*.

Like *Lock, Stock and Two Smoking Barrels*, *Snatch*

works equally well as a violent comedy or a testos-terone-fueled action film (no women have significant roles, although a few extras bare their breasts). *Snatch* finds humor in all sorts of grotesque situations — some viewers will probably be discomfited by the realization that they're laughing at such gruesome material. Some of *Snatch*'s less conventional plot elements include a dog that squeaks because it swallowed a squeeze toy, a briefcase attached to a severed arm, and a unique form of pig food. The dialogue is slick and witty, and often includes bizarre digressions (such as a lengthy discourse on a peculiar way to dispose of bodies).

For those who like this kind of movie, *Snatch* represents a diversion to be reckoned with. It's a reflection of the times, and of the kinds of films that are now considered hip and cutting edge. Ritchie came out of nowhere to make a big splash with *Lock, Stock and Two Smoking Barrels*. *Snatch* doesn't take him to the next plateau of filmmaking, but it proves that he's got some staying power. **RECOMMENDED**

The Spanish Prisoner [1997]

Starring: Campbell Scott, Rebecca Pidgeon, Steve Martin, Ben Gazzara
Director: David Mamet Screenplay: David Mamet Running Time: 1:50
Rated: PG (Violence) Theatrical Aspect Ratio: 1.85:1

Joe Ross (Campbell Scott) has just invented "The Process," a revolutionary procedure that is going to give his company control of the market (to use Hitchcock terms, this is the movie's McGuffin). But, while Joe thinks his work is worth a sizable bonus, the corporation's president, Mr. Klein (Ben Gazzara), refuses to commit to a specific figure, assuring Joe only that his effort is appreciated. While on a business trip to the Caribbean, Joe runs into Jimmy Dell (Steve Martin), a mysterious, rich stranger who offers Joe a few tips about life and business. Days later, in New York, Joe meets Jimmy again, and this begins his spiral into a strange world of deception, where nothing is what it first seems to be. Soon, like so many heroes in films like this, he finds himself in an untenable position, wrongly accused with a pile of irrefutable evidence staring him in the face. The only one he can trust is his secretary, Susan (Rebecca Pidgeon), who wants more than just a working relationship with him.

David Mamet's script supplies us with a seemingly-endless series of twists and turns, only a fraction of which are predictable. At times, the audience is a step ahead of the screenplay, but, most of the time, we're playing catch-up. Although there are plenty of holes

that Mamet has no interest is sewing up (trying to solve every riddle in *The Spanish Prisoner* is an exercise in futility), this is a smart film that develops a central character we can sympathize with — a modern version of Josef K. from Kafka's *The Trial*.

The most curious thing about *The Spanish Prisoner* is the ending. At first glance, it appears to be a common wrap-up that ties together several critical loose ends. There's a deus ex machina aspect to it which may indicate that Mamet is toying with the audience by sending up the manner in which this kind of movie must end to satisfy an audience. But are things as straightforward as they seem? Is this, in fact, the end, or is it just the latest twist in an incredibly complex con game?

Although most viewers of *The Spanish Prisoner* will be personally unfamiliar with the kind of sinister plot that Joe stumbles into, the concepts of corporate greed and backstabbing will hit closer to home. The subtext of this film is the same as the one in many other Mamet offerings — how the current business climate rewards those who act ruthlessly and punishes those who hold to a code of ethics. With a plot that would make Hitchcock proud, *The Spanish Prisoner* uses this outrageously elaborate, always-entertaining approach to illustrate these more serious concerns about what it takes to survive the '90s. **RECOMMENDED**

The Sum of All Fears [2002]

Starring: Ben Affleck, Morgan Freeman, James Cromwell Director: Phil Alden Robinson Screenplay: Paul Attanasio and Daniel Pyne, based on the novel by Tom Clancy Running Time: 2:07 Rated: PG-13 (Violence, profanity) Theatrical Aspect Ratio: 2.35:1

Any Clancy fan expecting an exact adaptation of the novel is living in a dream world. Such an endeavor would require a 5-part mini-series, not a 2-hour motion picture. About the only things that remain from the novel *The Sum of All Fears* are the plot outline and some character names. But, considering the events of 9/11/01, it's eerie to note how prescient Clancy was when he penned the book. The scenario is much like ones that we have heard discussed on TV and radio talkshows. A fringe group gets hold of a nuclear warhead and plans to detonate it at a major gathering point of American citizens — in this case, the Superbowl. The goal is not only to create mass hysteria, but to implicate the Russians, and possibly precipitate a nuclear holocaust that will wipe the world's most powerful nations off the map. The movie's logic is a little muddled here, but it's just strong enough for us not to question it while we're watching the movie. Enter Jack Ryan (Ben Affleck) and his boss, CIA director Bill Cabot (Morgan Freeman). Their job: present President Fowler (James Cromwell) with facts that others may not be aware of, and keep the lines of communication open between him and his Russian counterpart (Ciarán Hinds).

When it comes to the techno-thriller, Clancy is the king. *The Sum of All Fears* may be a stripped-down condensation of his vision, with all the delicious details removed, but the author's world-view is very much in evidence. Director Phil Alden Robinson does a competent job of escalating suspense and keeping the convoluted storyline relatively coherent — at least for viewers who pay careful attention.

Because of 9/11, *The Sum of All Fears* is more demanding than the usual escapist fare. The echoes of reality in its plot points make suspension of disbelief a facile thing, but therein lies a double-edged blade. Will viewers be able to abandon themselves to the rhythms of the story and the horrors contained therein? The movie does what all good thrillers should do — provide enough shocks and surprises to keep us guessing, and never lets up on the suspense until the end credits arrive. But now that reality and fantasy have come so close together, can audiences see one without being reminded of the other? RECOMMENDED

Swimming Pool [France/UK, 2003]

Starring: Charlotte Rampling, Ludivine Sagnier, Charles Dance, Marc Fayolle, Jean-Marie Lamour Director: François Ozon Screenplay: François Ozon, Emmanuèle Bernheim Running Time: 1:42 Rated: R (Nudity, strong sexual content) Theatrical Aspect Ratio: 1.85:1

Sarah Morton (Charlotte Rampling) is a British "crime fiction writer" who seems to have been based, at least in part, on her real-life counterparts, P. D. James and Ruth Rendell. Burned out and fed up, she pays a visit to her publisher, John Bosload (Charles Dance), in search of a little inspiration. John has just the thing for her: Spend a few weeks at his country house in France. There, she will have the peace and quiet she needs to write a new novel. She accepts his offer, and at first the secluded place, with its wooded grounds and secluded swimming pool, are perfect. Enter Julie (Ludivine Sagnier), John's rebellious, oversexed, teenage daughter, who intends to share the house with the older, more reserved woman. Sarah is not pleased, and her attempts to establish boundaries are continually flouted by Julie, who brings a new man home every night and keeps Sarah awake with the sounds of her lovemaking. Gradually, however, the relationship between the two softens, until a series of events cause a radical shift.

The tone of *Swimming Pool* is much like that of director François Ozon's *Under the Sand* (which also starred Rampling) — unhurried, deliberate, and subtly haunting. The director eschews the rat-a-tat editing techniques beloved by many of his contemporaries. Instead, he favors long, sustained shots and does not rely too much on close-ups. *Swimming Pool* is not a fast-paced motion picture, but it has a compelling quality that draws the viewer into its web and traps him or her there. Understanding, however, requires careful attention and constant vigilance. Even in retrospective, the seams between reality and fantasy are not clearly delineated, and it will probably demand a second viewing to complete *Swimming Pool*'s puzzle. A casual, inattentive audience member will either be completely confused by the ending or, even worse, might miss the twist altogether. The clues in *Swimming Pool* require thought and interpretation to decipher. Ozon does not present the answers to his audience in small, easily digestible pieces. It took me about 20 minutes of post-screening introspection before I finally "got" everything. There are plenty of hints about what's going on within the movie, but those will mostly be missed or dismissed by even alert viewers. Only at the end does Ozon provide us with a tidbit of evidence that's impossible to ignore.

Swimming Pool is not as psychologically complex as *Under the Sand* or as disturbing as the film that first brought Ozon international acclaim, *See the Sea*. But, for those willing to invest a little effort and 100 minutes of their time, the film is involving enough to make it worthwhile. There are narrative weaknesses and unmet expectations surrounding the climax that the epilogue's revelations cannot entirely dispel, but on balance, the performances and tone are more than enough to earn *Swimming Pool* a solid recommendation. Take a dip — the water's fine. RECOMMENDED

Switchback [1997]

Starring: Danny Glover, Dennis Quaid, Jared Leto, R. Lee Ermey Director: Jeb Stuart Screenplay: Jeb Stuart Running Time: 2:00 Rated: R (Violence, profanity, nude pinups) Theatrical Aspect Ratio: 2.35:1

A blizzard of exceptional proportions is bearing down on Colorado, threatening to close all routes in and out of the Rockies while burying the Centennial State beneath feet of snow. Sound familiar? Of course, it's a coincidence that *Switchback*, which uses this critical plot device, is opening in the wake of a mammoth late-October snow storm that crippled the American midwest, but it's great timing. Paramount Pictures couldn't have come up with a better release date if they'd planned it.

A baby-sitter caring for a young child is murdered, then the boy is kidnapped from his affluent parents' home. A doctor-turned-drifter wanders through Texas, trying to hitch a ride to Salt Lake City. An ex-railroad worker driving around in a cadillac (with an interior decorated by nude pin-ups) offers him a ride. A serial killer strikes in Amarillo, where the current sheriff is embroiled in a pitched battle for re-election against a powerful opponent. A mysterious FBI agent arrives claiming to be on the killer's trail while he's really pursuing his own agenda. These are the diverse strands that screenwriter Jeb Stuart weaves together into the tapestry of *Switchback*, his taut, intelligent directorial debut.

Unlike most thrillers, *Switchback* doesn't move at a breakneck pace that camouflages flaws by ceaseless action and non-stop edge-of-the-seat moments. Instead, this film progresses at a more leisurely pace, allowing us time to get to know each of the 4 main characters: Danny Glover's Bob Goodall, the cadillac driver; Jared Leto's Lane Dixon, the wandering ex-doctor; Dennis Quaid's Frank La Cross, the FBI agent; and R. Lee Ermey's Sheriff Buck Olmstead. By the time the final reel unspools, we've spent time with each of these men and have come to understand a measure of what makes them tick.

Switchback features an elaborately structured contest between the hero and the villain. As the title implies, the storyline for *Switchback* features a few unexpected curves, but it doesn't try to dazzle us with narrative contortions. In the end, the film is almost more disturbing than it is exhausting. For *Switchback*, Jeb Stuart can be credited with a job well done.

RECOMMENDED

The Tailor of Panama [2001]

Starring: Pierce Brosnan, Geoffrey Rush, Leonor Varela, Jamie Lee Curtis Director: John Boorman Screenplay: Andrew Davies & John Le Carré and John Boorman Running Time: 1:49 Rated: R (Violence, profanity, sex, nudity) Theatrical Aspect Ratio: 2.35:1

As a result of his scandalous behavior, Andy Osnard (Pierce Brosnan) is on the outs with Secret Intelligence Service MI6, and they decide to exile him to Panama, described alternatively as a "nasty web of money laundering, drug trafficking, and corruption" or as "Casablanca without heroes." Once there, Andy gets to work trying to unearth some big secret that will get London's attention. He sets his sights on uncovering the true balance of power surrounding the canal, and, as his informant, he chooses an unassuming tailor with a dark secret in his past. Harry Pendel (Geoffrey Rush) is a nice, meek man with an adoring American wife, Louisa (Jamie Lee Curtis), who minds his own business but has made an unwise investment. Now, he's $50,000 in debt and the bank is ready to call in the loan. Enter Andy, Harry's "guardian angel." If Harry will spy on his wife, who is the assistant to the Canal director, Harry will find his financial woes eliminated. Soon, Harry is spinning a fiction for Andy to keep the money flowing, and Andy is apparently eating it up, because it fuels his own agenda.

The screenplay for *The Tailor of Panama*, based on the novel by John Le Carré, is a wonderfully complex and devious affair that leaves us constantly befuddled about who's using whom and who really knows what. Some characters are a lot smarter than the initially appear to be, while others are less intelligent. And, while certain individuals aren't what they seem to be, others are. The movie sorts everything out in the end, but part of the fun is playing the game along with the characters. And, to add a sense of verisimilitude to the proceedings, much of the movie was filmed on location. (Apparently, the government deemed the consideration of having Pierce Brosnan filming in the country to be more important than the negative light in which the story portrays Panamanian politics.)

The Tailor of Panama is not an action thriller; those expecting shoot-outs and car chases will be as disappointed as those on the lookout for James Bond. Instead, this plot-centered motion picture demands that its audience thinks rather than sits passively and watches. And, although the film is primarily a serious affair, Boorman gets the opportunity to take a few shots at the American military by portraying the strategists at the Pentagon as a group of inept men who don't really know or care how accurate their information is. Over the course of a long career, Boorman has experienced his share of hits and misses. *The Tailor of Panama* belongs in the former category.

RECOMMENDED

Thirteen Days [2000]

Starring: Kevin Costner, Bruce Greenwood, Steven Culp,
Dylan Baker Director: Roger Donaldson Screenplay: David Self
Running Time: 2:24 Rated: PG-13 (Profanity) Theatrical Aspect
Ratio: 1.85:1

For 13 days in 1962, from October 16 through October 28, the world teetered on the brink of nuclear war as the United States and the Soviet Union stood toe-to-toe, neither bending, each waiting for the other to blink. *Thirteen Days* presents a dramatized (i.e., somewhat fictionalized) view from the top. The 3 main characters are JFK (Bruce Greenwood), RFK (Steven Culp), and Kenny O'Donnell (Kevin Costner). Kenny who? If you haven't heard of O'Donnell, you're not alone. O'Donnell went to Harvard with Bobby Kennedy, worked for JFK's Senate and Presidential campaigns, then became a special advisor to the President with an office next door to the Oval Office. He was definitely in Kennedy's inner circle. However, his role in the crisis appears to have been beefed up to give star Kevin Costner more screen time and greater importance. It is unlikely that some of the decisions and actions attributed to O'Donnell in this movie actually occurred in real life. Indeed, while O'Donnell's character was included to give some "balance" to the script, Costner's presence tips the scales in the wrong direction. At times, there's a sense that *Thirteen Days* should be devoting more attention to JFK and RFK and less to a lesser player like O'Donnell.

Thirteen Days includes a lot of fascinating elements, the most obvious of which is the struggle between Kennedy's advisors as the hawks and doves seek to sway the President to their point-of-view. Each side has valid objections to the other's position, and it becomes clear that both paths could lead to disaster. Some of the more zealous members of the military, disgusted by a perceived weakness in JFK's approach, seek to trap the President into a warlike position by manipulating the rules of engagement. Meanwhile, the top minds in the United States must attempt to puzzle out Moscow's seemingly contradictory responses to American actions. Are they willing to capitulate and deal beneath the table, or are they setting a trap to give them time to prepare the missiles for use? Tense moments include a confrontation between a U.S. warship and a Soviet sub, attempts by a U-2 plane to avoid missiles, and the final, frenzied negotiations as the deadline looms.

Although the movie runs a little on the long side, director Donaldson never lets the momentum flag.

The final half-hour features some weak spots, including a little too much non-historical melodrama and several over-the-top speeches. Some historians may be annoyed at the liberties taken by Self's screenplay with the established facts, but the writer claims that he spent countless hours poring over documents and listening to tapes in order to get most of the background correct. Certain aspects were dramatized to make them more accessible to viewers. This is not, after all, a documentary. For those with a thirst for a gripping political thriller with its roots in real-life events, *Thirteen Days* represents a satisfying refreshment. **RECOMMENDED**

A Time to Kill [1996]

Starring: Matthew McConaughey, Samuel L. Jackson, Sandra Bullock,
Kevin Spacey Director: Joel Schumacher Screenplay: Akiva Goldsman
based on the novel by John Grisham Running Time: 2:29 Rated: R
(Profanity, violence, mature themes) Theatrical Aspect Ratio: 2.35:1

It's possible to argue all day about how much of the race issue in *A Time to Kill* is a legitimate exploration of black/white tension, and how much is sensationalism used to spice up the story. The KKK has a prominent role, but couldn't a more moderate, less universally-despised group have filled a similar function? There are times when *A Time to Kill* preaches, but isn't Joel Schumacher aiming the sermon at the converted? The movie clearly touches on some important social issues, but it's up to the viewer to dig beneath the propaganda and unearth the messages that mean something. Then again, it's worth noting that this Hollywood production is actually saying something, rather than just churning out eye-popping special effects while relying on a regurgitated plot.

The basic setup has 10-year old Tonya Hailey, the daughter of Carl Lee Hailey (Samuel L. Jackson), being raped and beaten by two rednecks. Taking the law into his own hands, Carl Lee guns down the pair in front of dozens of witnesses in the Canton, Mississippi courthouse. In the process, he also seriously injures a local deputy (Chris Cooper). Carl Lee is arrested for the double murder, and faces trial. For his attorney, he chooses a local white lawyer, up-and-coming hotshot Jake Brigance (Matthew McConaughey). With a team that includes a sleazy divorce specialist, Harry Rex Vonner (Oliver Platt), an energetic assistant, Ellen Roarke (Sandra Bullock), and his old mentor, Lucien Wilbanks (Donald Sutherland), Jake goes up against the local D.A. (Kevin Spacey). When the KKK become involved, Jake discovers that his life, and the lives of everyone close to him, including his wife (Ashley Judd) and daughter, are in danger. And the defense of Carl Lee Hailey has just begun . . .

There's not a lot of real tension about what the verdict is going to be, although the film unsuccessfully tries to lead us astray. But there are enough interesting side-issues going on that there's no fear of a viewer losing interest. Despite certain drawbacks, *A Time to Kill* is involving, energetic, and occasionally thought-provoking. All things considered, this film will make for a worthwhile trip to the cinema for all, not just those who have time to kill. RECOMMENDED

Traffic [2000]

Starring: Michael Douglas, Catherine Zeta-Jones, Benicio Del Toro, Erika Christensen, Don Cheadle Director: Steven Soderbergh Screenplay: Stephen Gaghan, based on the min-series "Traffik" by Simon Moore Running Time: 2:25 Rated: R (Violence, drug content, profanity, sex, brief nudity) Theatrical Aspect Ratio: 1.85:1

Unlike most ensemble movies, *Traffic* does not bring all of the characters together for a dramatic finale that ties the disparate plot threads together. In fact, for the most part, the different stories do not crisscross, and, when an intersection occurs, it's an ephemeral one. The purpose of the movie is not to show how the characters interact or to illustrate some obscure point about fate and chance. Rather, it is to illuminate how far-reaching the drug trade is, and how trafficking in narcotics can impact on the lives of many different people in a variety of circumstances. *Traffic* looks at a wide sampling of aspects of the drug trade: the men who police it on both sides of the border, the government officials who carry out the so-called war, the people who get rich by distributing it, and the victims who debase themselves to get the money for their next fix. For some, drugs equate to greed, but, for others, they represent survival.

Although there are a large number of speaking parts, the action centers around four major characters. Benicio Del Toro turns in a nicely modulated performance as Javier Rodriguez, a Mexican police officer who is caught in a power struggle between two cartels. The biggest name in the cast is Michael Douglas, who plays Judge Robert Wakefield, the new U.S. Drug Czar whose personal life is thrown into turmoil when he learns that his daughter (Erika Christensen) is an addict. Finally, Catherine Zeta-Jones is Helena Ayala, the wife of a San Diego drug lord. Helena is ignorant of her husband's activities until he is arrested and she is forced to clean up the debris of his collapsing business, as well as cope with threats to her life and the life of her son.

The narrative palette of *Traffic* is rich, tightly woven, and consistently involving, with characters that are as well developed as their necessarily limited screen time allows. In many ways, *Traffic* is not meant to be a complete story, although it has a beginning and an end. Instead, it offers a glimpse into the world of drug trafficking, giving a sense of the vast scope of the battles that must be waged for any war against drugs to be winnable. Without ever preaching, *Traffic* shows the folly of believing that facile slogans like "Just say no" mean anything when faced with the kind of real-life situations underlying every drug deal. HIGHLY RECOMMENDED

Training Day [2001]

Starring: Denzel Washington, Ethan Hawke Director: Anthony Fuqua Screenplay: David Ayer Running Time: 2:00 Rated: R (Profanity, violence, drug use) Theatrical Aspect Ratio: 2.35:1

Antoine Fuqua's *Training Day* is the story of an idealistic young cop who gets a hard lesson about life in the streets from a veteran. Shining with the star power of Denzel Washington (playing the most morally ambiguous role of a fruitful career) and Ethan Hawke, *Training Day* crackles with energy. It's 2 hours long, but seems a lot shorter. However, as good as most of the movie is, it could have been better had the ending evidenced more careful scripting and less of a reliance upon contrivances.

Ethan Hawke is Jake Hoyt, an ambitious L.A. cop who wants to make detective. The fastest route to that position is to join the elite team headed by legendary undercover figure Alonzo Harris (Denzel Washington). To that end, Jake has been given one day to prove to Alonzo that he's ready for the job. At first, things don't go well — Alonzo scoffs at Jake's by-the-book attitude. "You've got to hear the street, smell it, taste it," he admonishes. Then, later, "This is street justice. It takes a wolf to catch a wolf . . . It's ugly, but it's like that." So Jake starts to learn — smoking some LSD-laced weed after Alonzo tells him, "A good narcotics officer must have narcotics in his blood." But things soon get out of hand, with Alonzo breaking the law more often than upholding it, and Jake begins to wonder what kind of hell he has lost himself in.

The movie asks hard questions and rarely gives an easy answer. It's riveting and intense, with just enough action to satisfy those who enjoy that genre and enough substance to satiate viewers who are tired of the long litany of dumb motion pictures marching through multiplexes. Unfortunately, *Training Day* doesn't deliver the complete package. The last 15 minutes are full of clichés, contrivances, and smart characters acting dumb — all in the name of providing a "pat" conclusion. The disappointing climax is not enough to take *Training Day* off the recommendation list — the rest of the film is too strong — but it diminishes its impact. **RECOMMENDED**

Trainspotting [United Kingdom, 1995]

Starring: Ewan McGregor, Ewen Bremner, Jonny Lee Miller, Kevin McKidd, Robert Carlyle Director: Danny Boyle Screenplay: John Hodge based on the novel by Irvine Welsh Running Time: **1:33** Rated: R (Profanity, drug use, sex, nudity, violence) Theatrical Aspect Ratio: **1.66:1**

"I chose not to choose life. I chose to choose something else," says the film's narrator and main character, a 20-something Edinburgh man named Mark Renton (Ewan McGregor), near the outset of *Trainspotting*. In rejecting the yuppie culture of a nuclear family, material possessions, a paying job, and dental insurance, Renton is rebelling, but this isn't just the usual disaffection of youth — it's a deeper, more pervasive dissatisfaction with a culture he views as sick and stifling.

Renton's escape is through drugs — primarily heroin, but really anything he can get his hands on. He's surrounded by his "buddies," a group of crooks, liars, and psychos who are even more twisted than he is. There's Spud (Ewan Bremner), a shy, inoffensive junkie; Sick Boy (Jonny Lee Miller), a vicious, duplicitous con artist who's obsessed with Sean Connery; Tommy (Kevin McKidd), a "virtuous" young man fighting the temptation of heroin; and Begbie (Robert Carlyle), a nutcase who gets his thrills from beating up people.

Trainspotting is careful not to present a one-sided view of drug use. After all, why would anyone use the stuff if all it leads to is misery and unhappiness? In Renton's words, to get an idea of what it's like using heroin, "Take the best orgasm you've ever had, multiply by 1,000, and you're still nowhere near it." There are no worries about the problems and concerns of everyday life, just where the next hit is going to come from. The giddiness of heroin addiction is well-illustrated during some of the film's early scenes, but it's a euphoria that gives way to tragedy.

In the end, *Trainspotting* has an anti-drug message, but it presents its case through character studies, not preaching. There are a lot of gruesome images, some of which are presented in an oddly humorous context. For example, take Renton's headfirst dive into the "worst toilet in Scotland" or Spud's reaction when he wakes up in soiled sheets. Boyle's style is distinctly his own. This is a kinetic movie, where everything, including the camera, keeps moving. This isn't an examination of the Scottish drug culture from the outside looking in, it's one from the inside looking out. **HIGHLY RECOMMENDED**

The Truth About Charlie [2002]

Starring: Thandie Newton, Mark Wahlberg, Tim Robbins Director: Jonathan Demme Screenplay: Jonathan Demme & Steve Schmidt and Peter Joshua & Jessica Bendinger Running Time: **1:44** Rated: PG-13 (Violence, sensuality, brief nudity) Theatrical Aspect Ratio: **2.35:1**

Taken on its own terms, Jonathan Demme's *The Truth About Charlie*, a '00s re-interpretation of the 1963 thriller *Charade*, is a decent — and even engaging — motion picture. It's not a great movie, or even a very good one, but, if you try not to compare it too much to the original, it works. Given the option, it's better to see *Charade*, which easily tops Demme's version for star power, if nothing else, but *The Truth About Charlie* has its own set of charms, not the least of which is Thandie Newton.

Newton is Regina Lampert, the perplexed widow of a guy named Charlie, who has about as many last names as a cat has lives. (This being a thriller, nearly every one has at least two names.) Charlie was involved in some sort of sinister plot involving betrayal, stolen diamonds, and $6 million in cash, but now he's dead and a group of nasty-looking people think Regina is hiding the money. In addition to a trio of unsavory thugs (Joong-Hoon Park, Lisa Gay Hamilton, Ted Levine) who are dogging her every move, she has to contend with a Parisian police commandant (Christine Boisson) who is unsure of her innocence and a kindly "stars-and-bars company man" named Mr. Bartholomew (Tim Robbins). Thankfully, Regina has someone to turn to in Joshua Peters (Mark Wahlberg), about whom she gushes, "You know what's wrong with you? Absolutely nothing!" That, of course, is a powerful clue that something very definitely is wrong with Joshua, and, as the body count around Regina mounts, she realizes that.

The storyline follows the typical rhythms of this sort of movie. Even if you haven't seen *Charade*, you're unlikely to be surprised by much that happens. The chief pleasure of *The Truth About Charlie* is watching Newton re-define Regina as her own. Wahlberg makes a reasonable foil for her, and there's evidence of some playful chemistry between them, but it's easy enough to determine that this is Newton's movie, and Wahlberg is along for the ride. The twisty plot is just spice added to the sauce.

From a plot standpoint, *The Truth About Charlie* doesn't venture far from the path paved by *Charade*. Militant devotees of the original will likely despise the remake, but those who view Demme's version as an affectionate homage, or those who have never seen *Charade*, will likely be entertained. I appreciate *The Truth About Charlie* in much the same way I appreciate *Charade*, proving that it is possible to like one without being disappointed by the other. **RECOMMENDED**

U-Turn [1997]

Starring: Sean Penn, Jennifer Lopez, Nick Nolte Director: Oliver Stone
Screenplay: John Ridley based on his book *Stray Dogs* Running
Time: **2:07** Rated: **R** (Violence, profanity, sexual situations) Theatrical
Aspect Ratio: **1.85:1**

U-Turn is film noir steeped in excess. Although director Oliver Stone has clearly made this motion picture with his tongue planted firmly in his cheek, he nevertheless manages to capture all of the tension and mystery necessary to hold the viewer's interest. Hence, while Stone may be poking a little good-natured fun at the genre, he has also created a highly-successful entry to it.

Film noir is always more plot-conscious than character-focused, and this is pretty much the case here. Stone and writer John Ridley have populated *U-Turn* with a variety of colorful types, only a few of whom show the beginnings of multi-dimensionality. The best-developed individual is, not surprisingly, the lead. Bobby Cooper (Sean Penn) is passing through the small town of Superior, Arizona on his way to Las Vegas to pay off a gambling debt. Bobby has already lost two fingers to the Russian mob, and he wants to avoid having to give up any more. Unfortunately, the radiator hose of his classic 1964½ Mustang chooses this moment to give out. Bobby gets the car to the only garage in the area, leaves it with the mechanic (Billy Bob Thornton) to fix, then wanders impatiently around town.

The denizens of Superior are a strange lot. There's a blind man (Jon Voight, almost unrecognizable beneath all the makeup) who doles out nuggets of wisdom, a flirtatious tease (Claire Danes) who enjoys making her boyfriend jealous, a local bully with the nickname of TNT (Joaquin Phoenix) who's spoiling for a fight, and a sheriff (Powers Boothe) who's hardly ever without a bottle in his hand. But the most bizarre citizens of the small, backwards town are Grace McKenna (Jennifer Lopez) and her grizzled husband, Jake (Nick Nolte), who lure the unsuspecting Bobby into a web of sex, vengeance, and murder.

U-Turn is definitely not for everyone — some viewers will find the juxtaposition of offbeat comedy and noir clichés too strange and others will be offended by the film's extreme violence. Nevertheless, for those who enjoy movies on the edge, *U-Turn* offers just the trajectory you might expect. **RECOMMENDED**

Unbreakable [2000]

Starring: Bruce Willis, Samuel L. Jackson, Robin Wright Penn
Director: M. Night Shyamalan Screenplay: M. Night Shyamalan
Running Time: **1:47** Rated: **PG-13** (Violence, mature themes) Theatrical
Aspect Ratio: **2.35:1**

Bruce Willis plays David Dunne, a Franklin Field security guard on his way from New York to Philadelphia by train. A horrible accident en route leaves 131 dead and only one survivor — David, who is not only alive, but doesn't have a scratch on his body. Soon thereafter, David meets Elijah Price (Samuel L. Jackson), a comic book art dealer who thinks he has an explanation for David's miraculous survival. Elijah believes that David is a real-life superhero — his body is stronger and more resilient than that of other humans and he possesses certain, as-yet untapped special abilities. Elijah makes it his purpose to convince David to accept what he is. Meanwhile, David's son (Spencer Treat Clark) is thrilled with the possibility that his dad might be like someone out of a comic book, but his wife, Audrey (Robin Wright Penn), is just interested in patching up a threadbare marriage. However, even as David begins to accept that Elijah might be correct, he discovers that, like all superheroes, he has a fatal weakness.

Looking at the screenplay, it's obvious that Shyamalan is intimately familiar with rhythms and themes of comic books. *Unbreakable* is as much an homage to the superhero books of the writer/director's youth as it is an innovative approach to the genre. Should this film be a success, it's easy to envision a number of sequels, and such a series might appeal to actor Bruce Willis because the emphasis here is on storytelling and character development rather than on action (there is only one true action sequence in the entire film). And there are additional facets of David's personality that could be explored. His half-developed, rocky relationship with his wife, for example, is tangential to the main story in *Unbreakable*, but it is instrumental in humanizing him.

Even though this film boasts more mature direction than *The Sixth Sense*, it's unlikely that it will generate the same degree of rabid repeat viewing. The earlier picture was a phenomenon; this is just a movie. As far as the superhero film is concerned, *Unbreakable* offers a fresh perspective on a genre that is typically defined by stereotypes and clichés. So, as a follow-up to *The Sixth Sense*, this may not satisfy all of Shyamalan's adherents, but, taken on its own terms, *Unbreakable* holds together. **RECOMMENDED**

Undertow [2004]

Starring: Jamie Bell, Josh Lucas, Devon Alan, Dermot Mulroney
Director: David Gordon Green Screenplay: Joe Conway, David Gordon Green Running Time: 1:47 Rated: R (Violence) Theatrical Aspect Ratio: 1.85:1

The story transpires in rural Georgia, and director David Gordon Green pulls the audience into this uninviting setting from the first frame. When it comes to establishing place and time, the director is an expert. When Green's camera takes us to a hot, dirty pig farm in the middle of nowhere, we are there. Similarly, we visit dirt roads and pathways that civilization seems to have forgotten, small towns with tiny general stores where the locals gather to gossip, and a junkyard that is a testimony to the obsolescence of man's ingenuity. Every place that appears in *Undertow* is authentic, and this is one of the movie's greatest strengths.

Green opens his film with a scene that will jar many viewers, and cause a few to glance away from the screen. Teenager Chris Munn (Jamie Bell) is seen fleeing from the gun-toting father of his would-be girlfriend. At first, it looks like a merry chase, with Chris always a few steps ahead — until he jumps off the roof of a shed and his bare foot lands on a board with a protruding nail. Chris is in constant trouble with the law, and it causes his taciturn father, John (Dermot Mulroney), to despair. John is an introverted man who moved to the middle of nowhere after the death of his wife because he couldn't stand to be around people. Chris resents the isolation, but his younger brother, 10-year-old Tim (Devon Alan), appreciates the solitude. Tim is a sickly child, whose unspecified malady prevents him from working, allowing him to fill his hours reading books. One day, the family's routines are interrupted by the arrival of Deel

(Josh Lucas), John's newly paroled brother. Deel seems to be looking to reunite with his family, but there's something in his eyes that hints at a darker motivation.

Initially, Deel fulfills the role of the "favorite uncle," allowing Chris in particular to get away with things his father would never allow. He also does his best to befriend Tim. However, it doesn't take long for his mercenary nature to be revealed, along with a nasty streak. It seems that John inherited a collection of gold coins from his and Deel's father, and now Deel wants his "fair share." One act of unpleasantness leads to another, and soon the boys are on the run, fleeing through the Georgia countryside, one step ahead of their pursuer.

Undertow will have limited appeal to mainstream audiences, who frequently do not have the patience to let a movie like this unveil its pleasures. There are allusions to everything from mythology to the Bible to the brothers Grimm. Although there is violence and danger, this is less about the chase than it is about the relationship between the siblings. Those going to *Undertow* expecting a thriller will find the proceedings slow going. However, those who are seduced by the characters and the setting will find that the 105 minutes pass quickly. **RECOMMENDED**

The Usual Suspects [1995]

Starring: Gabriel Byrne, Kevin Spacey, Stephen Baldwin, Kevin Pollak
Director: Bryan Singer Screenplay: Christopher McQuarrie Running Time: 1:46 Rated: R (Profanity, violence) Theatrical Aspect Ratio: 2.35:1

The "usual suspects" are 5 men: Dean Keaton (Gabriel Byrne), an ex-cop-turned-crook who's known for his steely demeanor and nerves of iron; Michael McManus (Stephen Baldwin), a psycho entry man; Todd Hockney (Kevin Pollak), a hardware specialist with an instinct for self-preservation; Fred Fenster (Benicio Del Toro), McManus' partner; and Verbal Klint (Kevin Spacey), a crippled con man. As the movie opens, these 5 are being bundled into a lineup. A truckload of stolen guns has been hijacked and the cops, led by U.S. Customs Special Agent Dave Kujan (Chazz Palminteri), are primed to get their man. But no one cracks, and as the criminals sit together in jail waiting to be charged or released, they hatch a plan for an elaborate emerald heist.

The story is told in 2 different time frames. In the present, looking back on events, Klint sits across a desk from Kujan, unfolding the tale as he remembers it. But the con man is an unreliable narrator, and viewers of *The Usual Suspects* are constantly kept guessing about what "truth" is. In fiction films, we're used to getting an impartial take on "reality"; this picture twists that principle. Not everything presented in *The Usual Suspects* actually happens, and some things occur differently than shown. The opening sequence, which details the climax of the gang's capers, teases the audience about what may or may not be the ultimate resolution.

As the narrative progresses, *The Usual Suspects* constantly raises the stakes. The audience is only slowly let into the story — at the beginning, everyone on-screen knows more than we do. Gradually, however, the skein of deceptions and plot devices is untangled by the switches back and forth between present and past. This film requires that a viewer pay careful attention to details. Those who get lost have only themselves to blame — *The Usual Suspects* doesn't take any prisoners. A trip to the bathroom or the snack bar will leave you floundering when you return.

Singer does an excellent job of blending humor into his noir thriller. There's enough to avoid a sense of ponderousness, but not so much that *The Usual Suspects* becomes campy. In the way it folds its various elements into a single resolution (which the astute viewer will be able to guess beforehand), Singer's film can be accused of toying with the audience. However, at times like this, when the person tugging the strings is adept at his craft, being toyed with can be a worthwhile experience. *The Usual Suspects* is an accomplished synthesis of noir elements and, as such, is an entertaining entry to the genre. **HIGHLY RECOMMENDED**

Vanilla Sky [2001]

Starring: Tom Cruise, Penelope Cruz, Kurt Russell, Cameron Diaz
Director: Cameron Crowe Screenplay: Cameron Crowe, based on *Open Your Eyes* by Alejandro Amenabar and Mateo Gil Rodríguez
Running Time: 2:10 Rated: R (Profanity, nudity, sex, violence)
Theatrical Aspect Ratio: 1.85:1

Vanilla Sky (the name refers to a painting by Monet) is the quirkily titled American remake of the 1997 Spanish language feature, *Open Your Eyes*. Like its predecessor, *Vanilla Sky* is a mind-bending excursion across genres — a warped fairy tale that dabbles in romance, mythology, horror, mystery, and science fiction. There are plenty of philosophical musings on the difference between dreams and reality, and numerous occasions in which the film dares us to tell them apart. *Vanilla Sky* gives new meaning to the familiar phrase from a children's song: "Life is but a dream."

David Aames (Tom Cruise) has the world in the palm of his hand. The majority stock owner of a big-time publishing firm, David has everything he wants — a great job with short hours, a spectacular Manhattan pad, and a gorgeous female pal named Julie (Cameron Diaz) who's willing to have sex with him whenever the urge hits (which seems to be fairly often). Then, one day, confirmed bachelor David meets Sofia (Penelope Cruz), and he suddenly discovers what love is. Unfortunately, David's blossoming relationship with Sofia fans Julie's jealousy. It seems that she doesn't share David's casual view of their sexual encounters. So, feeling hurt and betrayed, she invites David for a ride, then crashes her car, killing herself and badly injuring him. He survives, but is maimed and disfigured, and must wear a mask to hide the mass of scars and twisted flesh that comprises his once-handsome face. (With the mask on, he looks uncannily like Michael Myers, the psycho killer of the *Halloween* series.)

In many ways, the story is pure *Twilight Zone*, but Crowe's down-to-earth approach softens and grounds it, making the characters seem more genuine, even amidst the surreal setting. In addition, the screenplay closes with a less evasive explanation of what has transpired. However, the changes are minor; this is not a case in which Hollywood has butchered the end of a foreign feature in the hope of boosting ticket sales.

In the end, *Vanilla Sky* answers all the questions it poses and wraps up most (if not all) of the dangling plot threads. However, while the explanations come in the final 15 minutes, the most rewarding aspect of the film is the journey to that point — trying to outguess the script, enjoying the carefully constructed romance between David and Sofia (is anyone better than Crowe at telling a heartfelt love story?), and appreciating the details and nuances contributed by a director who knows what he's doing. The science fiction aspects of this movie may place Crowe in unfamiliar territory (he is clearly at his best when dealing with character interaction), but he rarely seems lost. **RECOMMENDED**

Veronica Guerin [US/Ireland/UK, 2003]

Starring: Cate Blanchett, Gerard McSorley, Ciaran Hinds, Brenda Fricker, Don Wycherley, Alan Devine, Gerry O'Brien Director: Joel Schumacher Screenplay: Carol Doyle and Mary Agnes Donoghue
Running Time: 1:38 Rated: R (Violence, profanity) Theatrical Aspect Ratio: 2.35:1

Veronia Guerin chronicles the last two years in the lead character's life as she movies from writing "safe" stories for her newspaper to delving into organized crime. The catalyst that transforms Guerin (Cate Blanchett) from a bystander to an activist is visiting a Dublin neighborhood and seeing children playing with used heroin needles. She begins to name names and attempt to interview some dangerous people: Martin Cahill (Gerry O'Brien), the infamous "General"; Gerry "The Monk" Hutch (Alan Devine); John Traynor (Ciaran Hinds), a.k.a. "The Coach"; and, most dangerous of all, John Gilligan (Gerard McSorley). After receiving warnings about sticking her nose where it doesn't belong, Veronica begins to receive more tangible reminders: threats to her family, a gunshot in the leg, a vicious beating, and, eventually, a hail of bullets that ends her career and life. Her June 26, 1996, death made newspapers around the world, and she became one of the most famous journalists killed in the line of duty.

With this movie, Cate Blanchett adds another fine performance to her résumé. She effortlessly brings Veronica's passion and courage to the fore, while also depicting her as loving mother, wife, and daughter, and by showing the very human side of her that fears the demons she has unleashed. As her main adversary, John Gilligan, Gerard McSorley is a frightening individual, and there's not a thing about his performance that's campy or over the top. No recent villain, real or imaginary, has unsettled me this much, and much of the credit for that must go to McSorley (who usually plays more genial parts). The film is an unusual crime story in that Veronica's lone weapon is a pen, and the only way she can fight back is by writing articles. Frankly, she doesn't do much during the course of the movie except ask questions and solicit comments. This isn't a detective story; Veronica's investigations are incomplete at the time of her murder. She doesn't match up well against the men who are after her, and it's something of a miracle that she survives for as long as she does. For the most part, this is a memorable portrayal of a woman who doggedly pursued, and died for, an ideal. And, although the final precredits sequence transforms Veronica Guerin into a martyr, the rest of the film shows her as a flawed, believable human being.

RECOMMENDED

The Village [2004]

Starring: Bryce Dallas Howard, Joaquin Phoenix, Adrien Brody, William Hurt, Sigourney Weaver, Brendan Gleeson, Judy Greer Director: M. Night Shyamalan Screenplay: M. Night Shyamalan Running Time: 1:48 Rated: PG-13 (Violence) Theatrical Aspect Ratio: 1.85:1

The Village is writer/director M. Night Shyamalan's attempt to combine the brothers Grimm with *The Twilight Zone*. Here, Little Red Riding Hood exchanges her crimson cape for a yellow one, and has to worry about the Big Bad Wolf long before she gets to Grandmother's House. Shyamalan crafts the movie to be high on tension but low on scares and action (although there are a couple of legitimate jump-in-your-seat "boo!" moments). And, for this film to really work, the viewer has to be willing to go pretty high on the suspension of disbelief curve. The film only works if Shyamalan sucks you in.

The story opens in a late-19th century American village called Covington. (We know the date because it's inscribed on a fresh tombstone: 1897.) Everyone seems to be speaking and acting as if it were at least a century earlier. Their isolation from the world at large could be part of the reason. The village is surrounded by woods, and in those woods dwell Those We Don't Speak Of, inhuman creatures who do not take kindly to intruders. As long as the villagers don't attempt to enter the woods, they are safe. Or so it is thought until Those We Don't Speak Of are glimpsed within Covington's perimeter.

At the core of *The Village* is the love story between shy, verbally challenged Lucius (Joaquin Phoenix) and blind Ivy (Bryce Dallas Howard). Theirs is a fairy-tale romance, with her knowing from the beginning that they are fated to be together, and him coming to her rescue like a knight in shining armor. Ultimately, however, their relationship becomes an exercise in sacrifice and endurance, as Ivy must risk venturing into the unknown.

The Village moves slowly, and depends more on atmosphere than on plot or action. In a way, Shyamalan seems to be relying on his reputation to pull off one of his revelations. If you're thinking that *The Village* bears a resemblance to the aliens-invade-Earth tale of *Signs,* you're right where the director wants you. *The Village* does not stand up well to over-analyzation — that's where the suspension of disbelief element comes in. This is the blockbuster equivalent of an art film, and its audience will be limited. However, for those who like the director's body of work, appreciate *The Twilight Zone,* and have a high suspension of disbelief threshold, *The Village* is likely to satisfy. **RECOMMENDED**

Where the Money Is [2000]

Starring: Paul Newman, Linda Fiorentino, Dermot Mulroney
Director: Marek Kanievska Screenplay: E. Max Frye and Topper Lilien &
Carroll Cartwright Running Time: 1:29 Rated: PG-13 (Mild profanity,
sexual situation) Theatrical Aspect Ratio: 1.85:1

The primary reason to see *Where the Money Is*, a comedy/caper from director Marek Kanievska, can be summed up in two words: star power. Star power, that is, as in Paul Newman's. At age 75, Newman still has more than his share of charm, although it's a more mature charisma than the kind he exuded in films like *Cool Hand Luke, Butch Cassidy and the Sundance Kid*, and *The Sting*.

Where the Money Is does not have a great storyline. In fact, if not for Newman, the film would likely be both forgettable and forgotten. The dialogue includes a few nice lines, but nothing special, and the story has more than a few holes that the 3 credited screenwriters (E. Max Frye, Topper Lilien, and Carroll Cartwright) don't really attempt to plug. The premise is simple: convicted bank robber Henry Manning (Newman) arrives at a nursing home after having suffered an apparent stroke. With the exception of occasional hand tremors, he never moves or speaks. But his nurse, Carol Ann McKay (Linda Fiorentino), thinks he's faking, and, with the aid of her husband, Wayne (Dermot Mulroney), she sets out to prove it. But Carol is interested in more than getting the upper hand on Harry. She wants to spice up a moribund marriage, and thinks that robbing a bank or an armored car might be the perfect antidote to boredom. And who better to be her partner than one of the most successful robbers in U.S. history?

Where the Money Is is a genial film with a fair amount of low-key humor and a caper that is characterized by its simplicity. Moments of tension and suspense are few (in fact, there are only 2 or 3). There are no big surprises or twists — the movie has the kind of direct trajectory that Hitchcock would have found disappointing. The interplay between Newman and Fiorentino is the undisputed high point. These two form a playful relationship that, while not overtly sexual, is characterized by an erotic undertone. *Where the Money Is* may not be deep, but it is fun. The objective is met. The filmmakers have given Newman a worthy vehicle in which to display his wares. He is not upstaged by the other actors or by a busy screenplay. Watching *Where the Money Is* is like spending 90 minutes in the company of an old friend. **RECOMMENDED**

With a Friend Like Harry [France, 2000]

Starring: Laurent Lucas, Sergi Lopez, Mathilde Seigner, Sophie
Guillemin Director: Dominik Moll Screenplay: Gilles Marchand,
Dominik Moll Running Time: 1:57 Rated: R (Violence, brief nudity,
profanity) Theatrical Aspect Ratio: 2.35:1 In French with subtitles

For American audiences, who have become conditioned to certain staples and formulas defining the structure of nearly every mainstream psychological thriller, *With a Friend Like Harry* may seem like a breath of fresh air. It isn't that director Dominik Moll wanders too far from familiar territory, but the manner in which he crafts the movie allows him to reject (or at least deviate from) many of the most common clichés. Consequently, *With a Friend Like Harry* is a more energetic and interesting entry than what one has come to expect from this overpopulated genre.

For Michel (Laurent Lucas) and Claire (Mathilde Seigner), the annual family summer vacation is starting off like a nightmare — the car is not air conditioned, the baby is screaming, and the kids are misbehaving. By the time they reach a rest stop, the long hours in the car have taken their toll. There, in the men's room, Michel meets Harry (Sergi Lopez), a guy he hasn't seen in 20 years. Michel doesn't remember Harry, but Harry definitely remembers Michel. In almost no time, Harry has invited himself and his girlfriend, Plum (Sophie Guillemin), for a drink at Michel and Claire's. At first, Harry is the perfect guest — offering to help out with chores and even buying Michel and Claire a new car. But there's a darker side to Harry — his interest in Michel runs deeper than is healthy, expanding into the realm of obsession. On the evidence of one juvenile poem written decades ago, Harry believes that Michel has the potential to be a great writer, and that his talent should be nurtured, regardless of the price.

Moll has fun toying with audience expectations. Several of the murders, which would be the centerpieces of similar American films, occur off-screen. On at least two occasions, there is enough ambiguity about what actually happens that it's possible to construct entirely different versions of the event. And, by constructing the ending the way he does, Moll is able to play with us while still presenting a conclusion that is satisfying and offers a sense of closure. This is the kind of motion picture that, if he was still alive, Alfred Hitchcock would almost certainly have given his approval to. **RECOMMENDED**

Young Adam [UK/France, 2003]

Starring: Ewan McGregor, Tilda Swinton, Peter Mullan, Emily Mortimer, Jack McElhone, Therese Bradley Director: David Mackenzie Screenplay: David Mackenzie, based on the novel by Alexander Trocchi Running Time: 1:33 Rated: NC-17 (Sex, nudity, violence, profanity) Theatrical Aspect Ratio: 2.35:1

Young Adam belongs to an endangered species: the compelling thriller that doesn't rely on idiotic, last-minute surprises. One of the reasons the movie works is because the question really isn't "Whodunit?" but "What Really Happened?" *Young Adam* is a little slow moving and claustrophobic (many scenes take place in the cramped belowdecks quarters on a barge), and the time line can be confusing at first. (There are no easy cues to identify flashbacks, which occur with some frequency and are not in chronological order.) The screenplay is more character-driven than plot-driven, which means that the cinemascape is not littered with contrivances. Plus, there is a lot of sex.

Joe (McGregor) is an apparently harmless young man who prefers reading a book or sitting quietly by himself to having a drink at the pub. Currently, Joe is working with the husband-and-wife team of Les (Peter Mullan) and Ella (Tilda Swinton), loading and unloading a barge that they pilot through the streams and canals of Scotland. Joe has a mysterious past that includes a relationship with a free-spirited woman named Cathie (Emily Mortimer), about whom we learn more via flashbacks as the movie progresses. When we first meet Joe, he and Les are fishing the naked dead body of a woman out of the water. Soon, Les is down at the pub boasting about the discovery (which has made the evening paper), while Joe remains behind with the objective of seducing Ella. Although the older woman resists at first, when she surrenders, she does so passionately, and soon she and Joe are involved in a sex-drenched relationship in which they can't keep their hands off each other. But, just as Ella announces her intention to divorce Les, Joe turns his attention to Ella's newly widowed sister, Gwen (Therese Bradley). Meanwhile, the investigation into the body discovered by Joe and Les takes an unsettling turn.

Young Adam, directed by David Mackenzie, uses the Scottish locales to good effect. The seemingly perpetual gray day scenes and dark night scenes (often with rain) establish an oppressive tone. This is a motion picture that relies as much upon mood as plot and characterization. In many ways, the film is a morality play, but it is equally valid as a thriller or a character study. Mackenzie's screenplay (based on the novel by Alexander Trocchi) reveals one alarming detail after another about the seemingly meek Joe until we have an entirely different picture from the one we initially envisioned. *Young Adam* has less broad-based appeal than a "traditional" thriller, but in many ways it offers a more satisfying experience. There is one scene of sexual kinkiness that may elicit some nervous chuckles, but it is important in illustrating the depths to which Joe can sink. *Young Adam* is darkly effective, and its grip lasts longer than we might be entirely comfortable with. **RECOMMENDED**

War

Black Hawk Down [2001]

Starring: **Josh Hartnett, Ewan McGregor, Tom Sizemore, Eric Bana**
Director: **Ridley Scott** Screenplay: **Ken Nolan, based on the book by Mark Bowden** Running Time: **2:23** Rated: **R (Violence, gore)** Theatrical Aspect Ratio: **2.35:1**

This is not an easy film to sit through, but it does what it sets out to do and brings the audience deep into the heart of combat. It's noisy, messy, and repetitious. There are probably more bullets and explosions than in any recent picture. Yet the illusion of "being there" is so real that, at one point, I involuntarily ducked my head to avoid being struck by something. Amazingly, director Ridley Scott manages to convey the chaos of the experience without losing the narrative.

Black Hawk Down opens with a quote by Plato: "Only the dead have seen the end of war." Then, over a color-desaturated series of images, we are presented with a brief history of why the United States was in Somalia in the early '90s. The story begins on October 2, 1993. Characters are introduced — Major General William Garrison (Sam Shepard), who is in command of the U.S. military presence in the region; Staff Sergeant Matt Eversmann (Josh Hartnett), recently promoted to commanding a team; Company Clerk John Grimes (Ewan McGregor), who is about to exchange paperwork for a gun; Lt. Colonel Danny McKnight (Tom Sizemore), in charge of a segment of the ground troops; and Master Sergeant Paul Howe (William Fichtner), who will challenge orders if he thinks they are ill-advised. Together, these men, and many others, are about to become involved in a seemingly routine mission that will go disastrously wrong.

The objective is to capture several key advisors to Mohamed Farrah Aidid, the warlord who controls Mogadishu. The United States wants Aidid out of the way, and this seems to be the best opportunity to advance that goal. But the troops, both on the ground and in the air, encounter stiffer resistance than expected, and this results in the downing of 2 black hawk helicopters. The ground troops then become divided as the raid turns into a rescue mission, and, in part because of poor planning and in part because of bad luck, the fire fight turns into a debacle.

This is a singularly effective motion picture. Sure, it could have had more character development and there are times when the gore verges on being gratuitously extreme (in particular, during the "operation" to clamp an artery), but those are minor quibbles. On the whole, *Black Hawk Down* is one hell of a ride. For better or for worse, it will leave you stunned and reeling. **HIGHLY RECOMMENDED**

Das Boot [West Germany, 1981]

Starring: **Jurgen Prochnow, Herbert Gronemeyer, Klaus Wennemann, Hubertus Bengsch** Director: **Wolfgang Petersen** Screenplay: **Wolfgang Petersen based on the novel by Lothar G. Buchheim** Running Time: **2:29** Rated: **R (Profanity, mature themes)** Theatrical Aspect Ratio: **2.35:1** In German with subtitles

During World War II in Germany, submarine duty was considered a "glamour job." It was nearly every young man's dream to be granted the privilege of serving the Fatherland aboard one of the sleek, glorious U-boats. As is often the case, the grim truth proved to be radically different from the shining fiction. Submarine service was a grueling, debilitating, dehumanizing experience, and *Das Boot* was the first motion picture to de-mythologize it completely.

The bulk of the film takes place within the boat, and follows a group of characters as they are transformed from the clean-shaven, energetic individuals who enter to the scraggly, dispirited men who eventually emerge. We see the story through the eyes of a German war correspondent (Herbert Gronemeyer) who is on board the boat for a single tour. The men are presented as he views them — a cadre of competent sailors united by bonds stronger than family or blood. The Captain (Jurgen Prochnow), an officer of great intelligence, experience, and compassion, has earned the respect of every man under his command. However, unlike in many war movies, this leader is not a tactical genius. He can, and does, make mistakes — some of which are costly. The crew is comprised of a diverse group of individuals, including a party member, a chief engineer on the verge of a breakdown, and a young man who longs for a reunion with his French fiancée.

When it comes to action, *Das Boot* is at the top of the class, and it's no wonder that, following its initial release, Wolfgang Petersen became a sought-after director. From the moment the crew first descends into the sub and we are given a tour of its innards, the sense of claustrophobia is suffocating. This feeling builds alongside the tension until the two, in concert, are almost unbearable. In later scenes, when the air supply is running out, we can feel ourselves gasping alongside the men, as if the oxygen is being siphoned out of the theater.

The battle scenes are superbly executed, not so much from a special effects perspective, but in the way that Petersen keeps us on the edge of our seats. The two standout sequences occur when the boat attacks a British caravan and when it attempts to wend its way through the treacherous straits of Gibraltar. Both are intense, nerve-wracking pieces of film making that are apt to elevate the heart rate of even the most blasé viewer. This film takes all of the drama and suspense inherent in a submarine-based story and delivers it in a near-perfect package, establishing *Das Boot* as not just a terrific adrenaline rush, but one of the best movies ever made. **MUST SEE**

Gettysburg [1993]

Starring: Martin Sheen, Tom Berenger, Jeff Daniels, Richard Jordan Director: Ronald F. Maxwell Screenplay: Ronald F. Maxwell based on the book *The Killer Angels* by Michael Shaara Running Time: 4:14 Rated: PG (Violence) Theatrical Aspect Ratio: 1.78:1

Gettysburg, Ronald F. Maxwell's re-telling of 4 hot days during the summer of 1863 (based on the Pulitzer Prize winning novel *The Killer Angels* by Michael Shaara), is a spectacle that gathers power and momentum with every scene. The film is divided into 2 parts, with an intermission in between. The first section, which begins on June 30, 1863 (the day before the start of the battle of Gettysburg) and ends during the day of July 2 with Colonel Joshua Chamberlain's legendary defense of Little Round Top, is approximately 2 hours and 20 minutes long. The second part, which takes up the remaining 1:55, concentrates primarily on July 3 and the disastrous charge of Major General George Pickett and 15,000 members of the Confederate Army against the entrenched Union position atop Cemetery Ridge.

Over 50,000 were killed or wounded during this pivotal battle of the Civil War, and *Gettysburg* takes pains to breathe life and logic into the reasons for this. Yet it does far more than that. Rather than functioning as a text book come to life, the film uses its actors to flesh out characters from history, giving not only personalities to those on both sides of the struggle, but believable causes as well. We are presented with the rare opportunity to see not only the clash of arms on the field of battle, but the clash of wills beforehand.

Historical accuracy was of great concern to the producers and director. They hired a veritable army of advisors to correct even the most minute mistakes in the script (if a general given a pale horse in the movie was known to have favored a dark horse, the mount was changed), used the actual sites in Pennsylvania as often as possible (where hiding war monuments became an art), and "recruited" more than 5,000 unpaid re-enactors to fill up the screen during the battle scenes (thus helping to keep the budget at a reasonable $20 million). The result is a movie that looks and feels real.

Epic motion pictures are a rarity these days — even more rare than films about the Civil War. *Gettysburg* should satisfy both cravings. This film is perfectly placed in the wake of Ken Burns' PBS series for any who have a re-kindled interest in this segment of American history. For those with little more than a passing interest, *Gettysburg* is still gripping enough to captivate in its own right. **MUST SEE**

Hart's War [2002]

Starring: Bruce Willis, Colin Farrell, Terrence Dashon Howard, Vicellous Reon Director: Gregory Hoblit Screenplay: Billy Ray and

Terry George Running Time: 2:05 Rated: R (Violence, profanity)
Theatrical Aspect Ratio: 2.35:1

It's December 1944 in Belgium and Lieutenant Tommy Hart (Colin Farrell), by virtue of his privileged upbringing (he's the son of a Senator), is far away from the fighting. When a routine chauffeur mission takes him into an unexpected German ambush, he ends up being tortured by the Nazis until he gives up the location of a fuel dump. After that, he is shipped to Stalag VIA, where the U.S. prisoners of war are led by Colonel William McNamara (Bruce Willis), under the watchful eye of SS Major Wilhelm Visser (Marcel Iures). McNamara is initially suspicious of Hart, rightfully assuming that he cracked under torture, and assigns him to bunk with the enlisted men rather than the officers. Hart isn't alone there for long, however — when two black officers, Lt. Lincoln Scott (Terrence Dashon Howard) and Lamar Archer (Vicellous Reon Shannon), arrive, they are also assigned to sleep with the grunts. The current of racism in the barracks is unmistakable, with one man in particular, Bedford (Cole Hauser), expressing his outrage and hatred in unmistakable terms. Shortly after setting up Archer for having a concealed weapon in his bunk, Bedford is found murdered with Scott standing over his body. McNamara requests that Visser allow the Americans to hold a court martial hearing. Visser, amused by the idea, agrees, and Hart is given the unenviable task of being Scott's lawyer, even though he has not finished law school.

The film is less of a traditional war story than it is one man's quest for redemption. After giving in to Nazi torture, Tommy Hart attempts to find the courage and opportunity to regain his honor. By defending Scott, a man he believes to be innocent, he is given this chance — even though Scott's fate seems sealed. As portrayed by Colin Farrell, Hart is a timid individual who is learning to stand up for himself.

Hart's War works uncommonly well because of the effective manner in which it blends together its various elements: the WWII prison camp setting, the courtroom aspects, and the issues of honor, racism, and redemption. This is one of those war movies that focuses on human interaction rather than battle and action sequences (there are a few of those, but not many), and it's all the stronger because of it.

RECOMMENDED

No Man's Land [France/Italy/Slovenia/United Kingdom, 2001]

Starring: **Branko Djuric, Rene Bitorajac, Simon Callow, Katrin Cartlidge**
Director: **Danis Tanovic** Screenplay: **Danis Tanovic** Running Time: 1:38

Rated: R (Violence, profanity) Theatrical Aspect Ratio: 2.35:1 In Bosnian and French with subtitles

Bosnia is the province of *No Man's Land* — a place whose horrific and catastrophic civil war few Americans understood and even fewer cared about. Part of that has to do with the fact that the conflict occurred half a world away; another part has to do with the superficial nature of the media coverage. But for Eastern Europe, the situation in the Balkans was of a more immediate concern. And, whereas Hollywood has used the Bosnian conflict to give us gung-ho, old fashioned war pictures, first-time Bosnian director Danis Tanovic has countered with the dark, sober *No Man's Land,* a movie that is by turns blackly satirical and hauntingly real.

The movie opens in the midst of a dense fog — an apt metaphor for the chaos that swirled around the former Yugoslavia — with a small group of Bosnian soldiers making their way towards the front lines. They get lost, and, when the mists clear, they are massacred by the Serbs. One survivor, Chiki (Branko Djuric), ends up in a trench in no man's land, temporarily safe from attack by the enemy, but unable to return to his side. Soon after, two Serbs stealthily make their way to the trench to search for survivors. Chiki eliminates one, but ends up in a standoff with the other, Nino (Rene Bitorajac). They endure an uneasy truce until they discover a third person, Cera (Filip Sovagovic), whose precarious situation represents a danger to all 3 survivors. And, when a United Nations force with an accompanying media caravan arrives, the situation becomes less, not more, stable.

No Man's Land is essentially comprised of two elements — the 3-character sequences in the trench, which reveal less about the individuals trapped there than about the depth of their people's blind hatred for one another. This is the Serb/Bosnian conflict in a microcosm, and is as compelling as it is difficult to watch. These characters bond, but not in the way we expect them to. The other aspect of *No Man's Land* is a broad condemnation of United Nations' "aid" — how politics and egos cause well-intentioned efforts to decay into exercises in incompetence. The media plays a prime role — the military ends up manipulating what the cameras see to serve their own ends because they are fearful of a public relations nightmare.

With the United States currently involved in attacking Afghanistan and with pro-military patriotic fervor at a post-World War II high, it is unclear how well a movie like this, with a clear anti-war message, will fare. There is no doubt, however, that, like *Platoon* and *Saving Private Ryan, No Man's Land* poses some disturbing questions about the nature of hatred and the wars it spawns. **HIGHLY RECOMMENDED**

Paradise Road [United States/United Kingdom/Australia, 1997]

Starring: Glenn Close, Cate Blanchett, Jennifer Ehle, Frances McDormand Director: Bruce Beresford Screenplay: Bruce Beresford Running Time: **1:55** Rated: R (Violence, nudity) Theatrical Aspect Ratio: **2.35:1**

The film opens in February of 1942 on a night of dining and dancing at Singapore's Raffles Hotel. It's a gala ball for soldiers stationed in the Pacific and their wives (or girlfriends). The party breaks up when it's announced that the Japanese advance has pushed the Allies back and the city is about to fall. While the men return to their units, the women evacuate, cramming aboard the *Prince Albert* for the boat trip back to Australia. They are a mixed bunch of Australians, English, and Americans, and petty quarrels break out in the close quarters. But these differences are all forgotten when Japanese planes attack and sink the ship. The waterlogged and weary survivors come ashore on the Japanese-occupied island of Sumatra, where they are rounded up and thrown into a concentration camp. There, over the course of the next 3½ years, they fight to survive and not lose hope. To this end, they form a "vocal orchestra" — a chorus that astounds audiences of fellow prisoners by performing hummed renditions of the work of Mozart, Dvorak, and Holst.

The exceptionally strong cast showcases American, British, and Australian actresses, all of whom show an astonishing willingness to appear in physically unflattering circumstances (no makeup, hair and skin caked with drying mud). The conductor of the orchestra, Adrienne Pargiter, is played with grit and zeal by Glenn Close, and represents her best screen work in years. Cate Blanchett essays Susan Macarthy, a timid nurse who finds her voice (in more ways than one) while in the camp. Jennifer Ehle, with her expressive eyes, is Rosemary Leighton-Jones, a beautiful young woman who dreams of being reunited with her true love. Frances McDormand, sporting an absurdly distracting accent, is the camp doctor.

Paradise Road is less a tearjerker than an honest examination of the bonds that are formed during extreme situations. Although there are some heart-wrenching moments, and several scenes of potentially-disturbing violence, the film never descends to the level of cheap melodrama. Instead, it opts for something deeper and more meaningful by allowing us to follow a group of well-rounded characters on a journey with a strong spiritual component. *Paradise Road* not only pays tribute to the human will to live, but it is a testament to music's lasting power to heal and uplift. **HIGHLY RECOMMENDED**

Regeneration [United Kingdom, 1997]

Starring: Jonathan Pryce, James Wilby, Jonny Lee Miller, Stuart Bunce Director: Gillies MacKinnon Screenplay: Allan Scott based on the novel by Pat Barker Running Time: **1:40** Rated: R (Violence, gore, profanity, sex, nudity) Theatrical Aspect Ratio: **1.85:1**

Regeneration is Gillies MacKinnon's look at the horrors of war (specifically, World War I) and the effects they have on the men who must endure them. *Regeneration* does not argue that war is wrong, but it asks us to question, without looking through a haze of patriotic pride, when a nation's political, economic, or moral position is in enough jeopardy to warrant the horrifying debt of blood that will inevitably be incurred.

The majority of *Regeneration*, which is adapted from a novel by Pat Barker, takes place within the walls of Craiglockart, a Scottish hospital for those whose war wounds are to the mind and spirit, not the body. The story centers around 4 men: established poet and war hero Siegfried Sassoon (James Wilby), neophyte writer Wilfred Owen (Stuart Bunce), shell-shocked officer Billy Prior (Jonny Lee Miller), and the doctor who treats them all, William Rivers (Jonathan Pryce). Sassoon has been sent to Craiglockart to discredit him, because his current philosophy, that the war has become one of "aggression and conquest" is a source of embarrassment to his senior officers. While there, he strikes up a friendship with Owen, and the two spend many hours talking about writing. Meanwhile, Prior, who is fighting to break through a memory blockage, is romancing a local munitions plant worker (Tanya Allen). And Rivers, who is gradually taking on the burdens of all his patients, is on the way to a breakdown. His character arc — from a strong, self-assured psychiatrist to a stammering, conscience-stricken man — is the film's most dramatic.

Rivers is the individual who provides the film with its glue, and actor Jonathan Pryce breathes life into him. Rivers represents one of the actor's finest portrayals, a once-confident doctor who slowly crumbles under the onslaught of pain he absorbs from the men under his care. There is no melodrama here, just good acting and solid writing. Rivers is allowed to retain his dignity. The other primary performances, especially that of Jonny Lee Miller, are solid.

Although *Regeneration* is not as devastating a motion picture experience as *Saving Private Ryan,* it touches upon many of the same subjects. This movie is more cerebral and reserved, but it makes at least one telling point about the dehumanizing experience of war — often, the deepest wounds endured in battle are not those done to the body, but those suffered by the mind. Doctors may be able to regenerate flesh, but mending a broken spirit requires considerably more time, energy, and skill. RECOMMENDED

Ride with the Devil [1999]

Starring: Tobey Maguire, Skeet Ulrich, Jewel, Jeffrey Wright
Director: Ang Lee Screenplay: James Schamus, based on *Woe To Live On* by Daniel Woodrell Running Time: 2:15 Rated: R (Violence, occasional profanity, brief nudity) Theatrical Aspect Ratio: 2.35:1

The 4 main characters — Jake Roedel (Tobey Maguire), Jack Bull Chiles (Skeet Ulrich), George Clyde (Simon Baker-Denny), and Daniel Holt (Jeffrey Wright) — are members of the "Missouri Irregulars," a poorly organized, rag-tag group that wages guerrilla warfare against Union loyalists. Like their jayhawker enemies, these bushwhackers often attack without warning or mercy, killing men and burning whole villages with seeming impunity. Roedel and Chiles fight out of loyalty to the Confederacy and because they hate the Yankees (both have lost loved ones to Federalists). Clyde, the prototypical Southern gentleman, is at war to preserve his way of life. And, Holt, the most interesting man in the group, is an ex-slave who fights for the South out of a sense of allegiance to Clyde, who purchased then freed him. Holt does not believe in Clyde's cause, but he will fight alongside his friend for as long as they both continue to breathe.

The story develops over the course of a winter, while the four men hide out in a crudely built shelter on the property of a pro-Confederacy family, the Evanses. A young widow in the household, Sue Lee Shelly (Jewel), becomes involved with Chiles, and Clyde spends much of his time visiting a local lady friend. This gives Roedel and Holt an opportunity to get to know one another, and sets up the inevitable tragedy when combat occurs and not all of the participants escape with their lives. After the Irregulars stage a bloody raid on Lawrence, Kansas (a Union stronghold), they are hunted down by Northern troops and cut to pieces. Injured survivors seek shelter with friendly families and are forced to re-evaluate their participation in the war.

As the film progresses, Ang Lee increasingly stresses the pointlessness of the Irregulars' struggle.

The only thing they are accomplishing is killing people. Nothing they do has any impact on the war. This truth occurs to everyone, beginning with Sue Lee and ending with Roedel, as disillusionment convinces each of them of the folly of continuing the fight. *Ride with the Devil* also illustrates the horrible excesses that some men go to in the name of a cause.

Ride with the Devil is a different sort of Civil War story. It takes us away from the big battles of the East and to a place where things are less cleanly defined. Although Missouri was not a battleground where the Union and Confederate armies repeatedly clashed, it was nevertheless rent by strife. As was true almost everywhere else, ideological gulfs often divided families. This is the terrain into which Lee has ventured, and the resulting motion picture offers yet another effective and affecting portrait of the United States' most important and difficult conflict. RECOMMENDED

Saving Private Ryan [1998]

Starring: Tom Hanks, Tom Sizemore, Matt Damon, Edward Burns
Director: Steven Spielberg Screenplay: Robert Rodat Running Time: 2:50 Rated: R (Extreme and graphic gore & violence, profanity) Theatrical Aspect Ratio: 1.85:1

Saving Private Ryan opens with a 30-minute cinematic tour de force that is without a doubt one of the finest half-hours ever committed to film. This sequence, a soldier's-eye view of the D-Day invasion of Normandy, is brilliant not only in terms of technique but in the depth of viewer reaction it generates. It is certainly the most violent, gory, visceral depiction of war that I have ever witnessed on screen. Steven Spielberg spares the viewer nothing of the horrors of battle, using every tactic at his disposal to convey the chaos and senseless waste that lies at the core of any engagement. We are presented with unforgettable, bloody images of bodies being cut to pieces by bullets, limbs blown off, entrails spilling out, and a variety of other assorted examples of carnage.

The D-Day invasion at "Bloody Omaha" Beach forms a prologue to the main story. Following the opening half-hour sequence, we learn that 2 of the 4 Ryan brothers died in this action, while a third perished elsewhere. The mother receives all 3 telegrams on the same day. The U.S. army chief of staff, General George C. Marshall (Harve Presnell), is stirred by the grief-stricken woman's plight, and decides to send a group of men into the French countryside to find and rescue the fourth son, paratrooper Private James Ryan (Matt Damon).

Captain John Miller (Tom Hanks), a hero and survivor of the Omaha Beach battle, is chosen to lead the team of 8 men whose goal is, in Miller's words, like finding "a needle in a stack of needles." His hand-picked team includes 6 men who have served with him throughout the war and one newcomer: Upham (Jeremy Davies), a French/German/English transla-tor who has never seen active combat. Together, they strike out across the French countryside, heading in the general direction of Cherbourg. Along the way, they learn that skirmishes in small towns can be as deadly as the attack on the beach.

In *Saving Private Ryan,* there are no human vil-lains, and the enemy isn't so much the Germans as it is the implacable, destructive specter of war. The film's central question (When is one life more impor-tant than another?) is never really answered. For those who are willing to brave the movie's shocking and unforgettable images, *Saving Private Ryan* offers a singular motion picture experience. **MUST SEE**

The Thin Red Line [1998]

Starring: **Sean Penn, James Caviezel, Ben Chaplin, Elias Koteas, Nick Nolte** Director: **Terrence Malick** Screenplay: **Terrence Malick based on the novel by James Jones** Running Time: **2:50** Rated: **R** (Violence, profanity) Theatrical Aspect Ratio: **2.35:1**

The Thin Red Line is the story of the Guadalcanal conflict as seen from the American side of the front line. There are 5 main characters and a host of sec-ondary ones. The commanding officer is Lt. Colonel Gordon Tall (Nick Nolte), who's involved in this battle for all the glory he can commandeer. To that end, he has no problem ordering scores of men to throw away their lives by attacking a seemingly-impreg-nable position. Captain James Staros (Elias Koteas), the commander of "C" Company who is known for his kindness to his men, refuses a direct order from Tall when he believes it's a suicide mission. Sgt. Ed-ward Welsh (Sean Penn) has a reputation for being cold and hard, but, on the battlefield, he displays his humanity by risking his own life to get pain killers to a mortally wounded soldier. Private Witt (James Caviezel), despite nearly being courtmartialed for go-ing AWOL, distinguishes himself in combat. And Pri-vate Bell (Ben Chaplin) performs acts of astounding bravery as his memories of his perfect marriage to a beautiful woman (Miranda Otto) fuel his desire to re-turn home alive.

One of the things that *The Thin Red Line* does well is to illustrate the terror and chaos of war. The char-acters here aren't macho guys marching into a hail of bullets for the glory of the moment. They're scared

men staring death in the face — a death that waits concealed in the beauty of a grassy hill. You can see the panic in their eyes when violence shatters the serenity of the countryside. There is valor in *The Thin Red Line,* but that's not the point of the film, and the characters who perform the great deeds don't feel like heroes.

After the battle for the hill is over, Malick doesn't seem to know where to go with the movie. The final hour is a fragmentary narrative about random events that occur afterwards. It isn't compelling and there are times when it borders on being incoherent. A battle occurs towards the end of the film, but most of it apparently happens off screen. One moment, a massive force of Japanese troops is advancing; the next, it's all over and a commanding officer is ad-dressing the survivors.

Although *The Thin Red Line* will not go down as the kind of war movie classic that *Saving Private Ryan* will, there are still many reasons to see this motion picture, especially for those who appreciate epic battle stories. See it for Malick's unparalleled visual style, for the primary character portrayals, and for the effectively chaotic, in-your-face combat sequences. The movie has the capacity to engage on both an in-tellectual and a visceral level. **RECOMMENDED**

Three Kings [1999]

Starring: **George Clooney, Mark Wahlberg, Ice Cube, Spike Jonze** Director: **David O. Russell** Screenplay: **David O. Russell based on a story by John Ridley** Running Time: **1:54** Rated: **R** (Profanity, violence, gore) Theatrical Aspect Ratio: **2.35:1**

Just as the Gulf War wasn't a traditional conflict, so *Three Kings* is not a traditional war picture — there are no big battles and only a few small-scale skirmishes. Instead, this is more of an action/adventure film, and a fairly good one at that. The characters are well devel-oped, the situations are effectively realized, and, most importantly, there's some thought-provoking content just beneath the surface. Until the ending, *Three Kings* is a surprisingly solid effort.

Three Kings should probably be called *Four Kings,* since there are 4 main characters (although it would wreck the Biblical allusion). Archie Gates (George Clooney), Troy Barlow (Mark Wahlberg), Chief Elgin (Ice Cube), and Vig (Spike Jonze) are soldiers stuck in Iraq during March 1991, just after the ceasefire decla-ration. Early in the film, after Troy shoots a gun-toting Iraqi soldier, Vig sums up their experience by saying, "I didn't think I'd get to see anyone get shot in this war. Take a picture." Meanwhile, Archie, who is only weeks away from retirement, isn't being cooperative with the reporter (Nora Dunn) he has been asked to escort. He is told curtly by a superior, "This is a media war. You'd better get on board." The boredom lifts for all 4 men when they come into possession of a map that shows the possible location of a secret bunker where Saddam Hussein may have hidden millions of dollars in gold bullion stolen from Kuwait. With mercenary intentions, Archie, Troy, Vig, and the Chief set out one morning with the intention of striking it rich. Reality deals them a harsh blow, however. Once away from the army camp, they come across Saddam's troops brutally massacring those Iraqi citizens who have followed George Bush's exhortation to throw off their leader's yoke. Expecting American aid, they rebelled against Saddam, only to discover that no foreign help would be forthcoming.

As action/adventure movies go, *Three Kings* is reasonably effective. It's about mercenaries who start out with hardened, cynical hearts but who grow to feel deeply for the plight of the people around them. The action sequences are expertly directed, and David O. Russell develops tension because we're never sure who's going to survive or what's going to happen next. There are also several scenes of graphic brutality that underscore the basic inhumanity of any armed conflict. *Three Kings* is solidly structured until the end, which has a tacked-on feel. The conclusion and epilogue both seem like they were added to please Hollywood executives who might not otherwise have greenlighted the project. Overall, however, *Three Kings* makes for an interesting and occasionally exhilarating examination of modern war and human brutality. RECOMMENDED

A Very Long Engagement [France, 2004]

Starring: Audrey Tautou, Gaspard Ulliel, Dominique Pinon, Clovis Cornillac, Jérôme Kircher, Albert Dupontel, Chantal Neuwirth, Denis Lavant, Dominique Bettenfeld, Jean-Pierre Darroussin, Marion Cotillard Director: Jean-Pierre Jeunet Screenplay: Jean-Pierre Jeunet, Guillaume Laurant, based on the novel by Sébastien Japrisot Running Time: 2:13 Rated: R (Violence, sexual situations, brief nudity) Theatrical Aspect Ratio: 2.35:1 In French with subtitles

A Very Long Engagement is Jean-Pierre Jeunet's follow-up to his international success, *Amélie*. However, despite the return of elfin star Audrey Tautou, this is nothing like a sequel. Based on the novel by Sébastien Japrisot, *A Very Long Engagement* tells a darker tale. Whereas *Amélie* was optimistic and life-affirming, this movie spends much of its time in the bloody, muddy trenches of World War I, where death is a more likely companion than life, and optimism is only for the unrealistic.

The year is 1920. The war has ended. The trenches have been filled in and are overgrown by weeds and farmers' crops. For Mathilde (Tautou), however, there is no closure. Her fiancé, Manech (Gaspard Ulliel), has been missing for more than three years. She has been told that he died in early 1917, but her intuition tells her that he may still be alive. So she begins an investigation of her own, tracking down official government documents, putting ads in newspapers to attract the attention of survivors who may have known Manech, and hiring a private investigator. The hunt is slow, but a picture gradually begins to emerge.

Manech was court-martialed for "self-mutilation," and sentenced to death. Along with four others facing the same punishment, he was sent to the oddly named trench of Bingo Crepuscule. The five men, after being served a last meal, were expelled from the trench into the no-man's land between the French and the Germans. According to eyewitness accounts, none survived. But no one actually *saw* Manech die, and this fuels Mathilde's unrealistic belief that her lover somehow escaped. Meanwhile, as she continues her investigation, it appears that someone else is attempting something similar. Except, in this case, the witnesses aren't talking, they're dying.

A Very Long Engagement starts slowly, but builds to a satisfying conclusion. It's grittier than fans of *Amélie* might appreciate, but they should recognize that before that romantic fable, Jeunet was known for black comedies. This film finds a middle ground. Despite the war scenes, it is not unremittingly bleak, and there are times when it is darkly funny. *A Very Long Engagement* makes points about the absurdity of war, but balances those out by adopting the phrase "love conquers all." And, although one could argue that the movie doesn't demand its full 2¼-hour running length to tell its story, and that some extraneous material could have been trimmed, the only thing "very long" about this film is in the title. RECOMMENDED

We Were Soldiers [2002]

Starring: Mel Gibson, Madeleine Stowe, Sam Elliott, Greg Kinnear Director: Randall Wallace Screenplay: Randall Wallace, based on *We Were Soldiers Once, and Young* by Hal Moore and Joe Galloway Running Time: 2:18 Rated: R (War violence, profanity) Theatrical Aspect Ratio: 2.35:1

We Were Soldiers is the latest in the new breed of war movies — films that throw the viewer into the midst of the chaos and brutality of the fray, giving audiences a taste of the violent, visceral nature of an armed conflict, while still allowing moments of honor and heroism to stand out. The film tells of the November 1965 battle in the Ia Drang Valley (aka "The Valley of Death"), which was the first major engagement between American and North Vietnamese troops. Before taking the story to Vietnam, however, director Randall Wallace allows us to spend some time with the American soldiers at home. This becomes crucial to the movie's later success, as it humanizes the men, presenting them as more than faceless fodder for enemy bullets. If only briefly, we see their wives and children. Then they ship off, and, in seemingly no time, are trapped and outnumbered, fighting for their lives.

The commanding officer is Lt. Colonel Hal Moore (Mel Gibson), the leader of the 1st Battalion of the 7th Cavalry. He is a student of history and a master of tactics, and his motto is to leave no man behind. Before departing for Vietnam, he has spent sleepless nights poring over books detailing previous military engagements there, and he is determined not to repeat the mistakes of those who preceded him. In the midst of battle, Moore is at his best, inspiring confidence in his men by never expecting more of them than he is willing and able to give. He seems to be everywhere, bolstering spirits and improvising defenses for each new attack by the enemy. The men under his command include daredevil helicopter pilot Snakeshit Crandall (Greg Kinnear); the gentle and well-liked Lieutenant Jack Geoghegan (Chris Klein), whose wife has just given birth; and the crusty Sergeant Major Basil Plumley (Sam Elliott in the R. Lee Ermey role), Moore's right-hand man. Another key participant is photojournalist Joe Galloway (Barry Pepper), who is temporarily forced to exchange his camera for a gun.

Once, war movies were very much arm's length affairs, but, in an era when so many lines have been crossed and so many barriers broken, such an approach no longer works. As a result, the in-your-face style of *We Were Soldiers* results in a suspenseful, intense, and exhausting cinematic experience. There are times when the film is grueling and times when it is exhilarating. The movie has the ability to keep viewers on the edges of their seats and to wring tears from their eyes. It's an amazing experience, and a second success from the team that previously cooperated to give us an Oscar-winning motion picture (*Braveheart*). Their subject, both then and now, is about the courageous of spirit and brave of heart.

HIGHLY RECOMMENDED

Western

The Ballad of Little Jo [1993]

Starring: Suzy Amis, Bo Hopkins, Ian McKellen Director: Maggie Greenwald Screenplay: Maggie Greenwald Running Time: 2:00 Rated: R (Nudity, mature themes, violence) Theatrical Aspect Ratio: 1.85:1

Once Josephine Monaghan (Suzy Amis) lost her virginity and gave birth to a bastard, her future was ruined. With her past sins hanging over her like a hangman's noose, she has no choice but to flee the constrained, pampered socialite's world she knew in the East, and head West. There she discovers that the best life she can lead as a woman is that of a prostitute, so she makes the bold decision to grab at freedom and independence by masquerading as a man. Whiskers and muscles aren't necessary. The mere appearance of a female as a male in a time when it's "illegal to dress improper to your sex" is enough to convince just about everyone.

Loosely based on the true-life story of a woman about whom little is known, the story of *Little Jo* is a masterpiece of detail and intelligence. Maggie Greenwald has done her homework, piecing together an engrossing tale that movies quickly enough to keep the easily-distracted involved, but not so rapidly that it misses the nuances of the situation. Touches of humor are mixed nicely with drama as of *Little Jo* explores the entire spectrum of human emotions. And just because Jo has chosen to live life as a man doesn't mean that she can't yearn for her lost femininity.

The focal point of this film is Jo. As played by Suzy Amis, the character is not perfectly developed, but the actress gets better as the movie unfolds. I was particularly unimpressed with her early scenes (when she's openly female), but after the "transformation," she settled into the role. Amis is not an especially emotive actress, and her Jo is reserved — perhaps occasionally too much so. The most effective scenes are those of quiet emotion, such as when Jo sheds a tear.

If you like films about the "new Old West," *The Ballad of Little Jo* is a worthwhile choice. Even for those who aren't particularly fond of Westerns, this movie still has a lot to offer. Keeping the conventions of the genre to a minimum, it strikes out in bolder directions, reflecting personalities and lifestyles through the eyes of a woman whom everyone accepts as a man. *The Ballad of Little Jo* loses its focus on a number of occasions, but never for very long, and never in a manner that jeopardizes the viewer's overall enjoyment of Maggie Greenwald's film. **RECOMMENDED**

Dances with Wolves [1990]

Starring: Kevin Costner, Mary McDonnell, Graham Greene, Rodney A. Grant Director: Kevin Costner Screenplay: Michael Blake, based on his novel Running Time: 3:03 Rated: PG-13 (Violence, animal deaths, discreet sex & nudity) Theatrical Aspect Ratio: 2.35:1

Dances with Wolves has been called a "revisionist western" — a movie that reversed the traditional roles of Cowboys and Indians. In fact, it's nothing of the sort. While it is true that the Sioux tribe is portrayed with the kind of balance and sensitivity rarely accorded to Native Americans in any movie, the Pawnee do not fare as well (as Sioux enemies, they are presented in much the same fashion that Indians were back in the '50s and '60s). And the American soldiers are depicted as genuine, imperfect human beings, not as thoughtless, vicious brutes. *Dances with Wolves* did not subvert the entire genre; it just twisted a few of the conventions.

Dances with Wolves opens with a brief Civil War prologue in which the protagonist, Lt. John Dunbar (Costner), establishes himself as a hero by providing a diversion so that a group of Union soldiers can overcome an entrenched Rebel position. Because of his bravery, he is offered a station anywhere he wants. He chooses the frontier, so he can see it before it is gone. For over a month, Dunbar is alone at Fort Sedgewick. His only companions are a friendly wolf that he names Two Socks and his faithful mount, Cisco.

The story moves into high gear with the arrival of the Sioux, led by the thoughtful Kicking Bird (Graham Greene) and the tempestuous Wind in His Hair (Rodney A. Grant). At first, there is mutual distrust, but, as Dunbar and the Sioux interact and begin to communicate (each learning a few words of the other's language), they form a truce, then a bond. His interaction with them becomes even easier when Stands With A Fist (Mary McDonnell), a white woman who has lived with the Sioux since childhood, is able to act as an interpreter. Eventually, Dunbar leaves Fort Sedgewick and moves into the Sioux camp. He falls in love with Stands With A Fist, becomes a respected member of the tribe with his own Sioux name ("Dances With Wolves"), and is able to forget the life he left behind — until the day when Fort Sedgewick is garrisoned and the soldiers find him: an out-of-uniform officer "gone Injun."

Dances with Wolves works on many levels. It's a rousing adventure, a touching romance, and a stirring drama. Although *Dances with Wolves* contains several well-executed battle scenes, there's little doubt that the most breathtaking sequence is the buffalo hunt, where the Sioux riders race alongside thousands of rampaging buffalo and bring several of them down. It's a high adrenaline sequence that marks the moment when Dunbar finally rejects his old culture to embrace his new one. Not just during that sequence, but for three hours, *Dances with Wolves* transports us to another world, and that's the mark of a great motion picture. **MUST SEE**

The Hi-Lo Country [1998]

Starring: Woody Harrelson, Billy Crudup, Patricia Arquette, Cole Hauser Director: Stephen Frears Screenplay: Walon Green based on the book by Max Evans Running Time: 1:54 Rated: R (Violence, profanity, sexual situations) Theatrical Aspect Ratio: 2.35:1

The Hi-Lo Country is a curious marriage of genres. This movie illustrates the result of grafting film noir onto a western. It's what happens when a femme fatale hops into the saddle and the sack with a cowboy. Unusual as the mix may be, it is ultimately successful. While the setting and scenery are exactly what one might expect from a western, the fast-paced action has been replaced by a slowly-escalating tension and the unshakable sensation of impending doom. And the voiceover narrative, with its promise of violence, would be at home in a crime thriller.

The Hi-Lo Country takes place in New Mexico shortly after the curtain has dropped on World War II. The two main characters, Big Boy Matson (Woody Harrelson) and Pete Calder (Billy Crudup), are old school cowboys. In spite of, or perhaps because of, their vast personality difference, they're the best of friends. Together, they share dreams and a workload, and ultimately fall for the same woman: Mona Birk (Patricia Arquette), the raven-haired siren whose smell and looks mesmerize Big Boy and Pete.

Although Mona flirts with Pete, she's in love with Big Boy. Pete realizes that this makes her untouchable, but even a relationship with a pretty Mexican-American girl, Josepha (Penélope Cruz), can't banish her from his thoughts. But the complications don't stop there. Mona is married to Les Birk (John Diehl), an older man who works for the biggest landowner in the district, Jim Ed Love (Sam Elliot). Big Boy resents Love's business ways, and takes out his anger on anyone who is employed by the man, including his own brother, Little Boy (Cole Hauser). As a mark of his contempt for Les, Big Boy gradually becomes unconcerned about concealing his relationship with Mona, guaranteeing that the cuckolded husband will learn of his wife's unfaithfulness and be forced to take steps to defend his own honor.

Admittedly, *The Hi-Lo Country* is encumbered by a somewhat uneven narrative. There are long stretches when things move forward forcefully, but, in between, there are transitional sequences when the proceedings grind to a halt. Flow-related hiccups aside, Frears' picture offers numerous small pleasures. In particular, it's fascinating to observe how Frears brings together two seemingly-unrelated genres in a film that, for the most part, succeeds in paying homage to both. **RECOMMENDED**

High Noon [1952]

Starring: Gary Cooper, Thomas Mitchell, Lloyd Bridges, Katy Jurado, Grace Kelly Director: Fred Zinnemann Screenplay: Carl Foreman Running Time: 1:25 Rated: Not Rated (Violence) Theatrical Aspect Ratio: 1.33:1

High Noon contains many of the elements of the traditional Western: the gun-toting bad guys, the moral lawman, the pretty girl, and the climactic gunfight. But it's in the way these elements are blended together, with the slight spin put on them by Zinnemann and screenwriter Carl Foreman, that makes *High Noon* unlike any other Western.

Cooper plays Marshal Will Kane, and, when *High Noon* opens, it's a little after 10 o'clock in the morning, and he is being married to Amy Fowler (Grace Kelly), a woman less than half his age. At the same time, trouble has arrived in Kane's sleepy Western town. Three outlaws, the henchmen of convicted murderer Frank Miller (Ian MacDonald), are waiting at the railroad station, where Miller, recently freed from prison, is expected on the noon train. He has one goal: revenge, and the target of his hatred is Kane, the man who brought him down. Kane's friends, including the town's mayor (Thomas Mitchell), the local judge (Otto Kruger), and the former Marshal, Martin Howe (Lon Chaney), urge him to flee, but he can't. Against the wishes of his Quaker wife and with no one in the town willing to stand beside him, Kane prepares to face Miller and his gang alone.

High Noon is about loyalty and betrayal. Loyalty on Kane's part — even when everyone deserts him, he stands his ground, though it seems inevitable that the action will cost him his life. And betrayal on the town's part. Many of the locals are agreed that they owe their prosperity to Kane, but they will not help him or defend him, because they believe his cause to be hopeless. There are even those who welcome Miller's return. In the end, Kane is forced into the showdown on his own, until, at a crucial moment, Amy proves herself to be a worthy wife.

The movie transpires virtually in real time, with a minute on screen equaling one in the theater. In one of many departures from the traditional Western, there is little action until the final 10 minutes, when Kane shoots it out with Miller's gang. *High Noon*'s tension comes through Kane's desperation, aided in no small part by Elmo Williams' brilliant editing as the clock ticks down to 12. For a motion picture with so little action, the suspense builds to almost unbearable levels.

As is true of nearly every great film, all of the elements mix together in *High Noon*. The Western may be one of the few truly American art forms, and *High Noon* shows exactly how much potential it can embrace. **MUST SEE**

The Missing [2003]

Starring: Tommy Lee Jones, Cate Blanchett, Evan Rachel Wood, Jenna Boyd, Aaron Eckhart, Val Kilmer, Eric Schweig, Jay Tavare Director: Ron Howard Screenplay: Ken Kaufman, based on the novel *The Last Ride,* by Thomas Eidson Running Time: 2:18 Rated: R (Violence) Theatrical Aspect Ratio: 2.35:1

The Missing takes place in 1885 New Mexico, as the Old West is gradually becoming civilized. For someone like Maggie Gilkeson (Cate Blanchett), who lives with her lover, Brake Baldwin (Aaron Eckhart), and two daughters, Lily (*Thirteen*'s Evan Rachel Wood) and Dot (Jenna Boyd), the loneliness of the frontier can be dangerous if marauders come calling. After Brake is killed and Lily is kidnapped by a group of army deserters led by an Aztec mystic named Chidin (Eric Schweig), Maggie is forced to put aside her enmity for her estranged father, Samuel Jones (Tommy Lee Jones), so he can lead her to her daughter. As a young man, Samuel abandoned Maggie and his wife so he could "go native" and live with a tribe of Aztecs. Now, with the end looming just beyond the horizon, he is seeking to make amends. So, accompanied by Dot, who will not be left behind, the two of them journey southward, hoping to head off the raiders before they cross the border into Mexico.

Much of the movie is devoted to Samuel and Maggie's pursuit of Chidin, and what happens after they track him down. Along the way, father and daughter gradually reconnect, with Samuel's willingness to sacrifice acting as a tonic to Maggie's pride and long-nursed anger. In some ways, the film's broad story line recalls John Ford's classic Western *The Searchers*. There must be something about the idea of a long pursuit through the unspoiled lands of the Old West that appeals to filmmakers, since it recurs frequently throughout the genre.

For the most part, *The Missing* is a compelling, involving story. It contains a few nicely unexpected moments, and the characters and their relationships are effectively realized. The movie also does not fall into the trap of overexplaining things. Good acting is another of the film's strengths — especially that of Cate Blanchett as the fiercely independent Maggie, Tommy Lee Jones as the aging warrior Samuel, and Evan Rachel Wood as the mistreated Lily, who discovers a hitherto unexpected inner strength. *The Missing* is not without its share of problems. In the first place, the supernatural elements of the movie are poorly integrated. At times, they seem more than a little hokey, especially during a scene in which Samuel must help Maggie fight off a curse. Another flaw in the film is the number of brief subplots that seemingly go nowhere. Although Westerns will almost never be as popular as they were during their heyday, they (like musicals) seem to be undergoing something of a minor revival. The perspectives are much different — it's no longer sufficient to have a simple story of cowboys against Indians — but the time period and wildness of the frontier still make for an impressive backdrop. *The Missing* is a worthy effort and makes for an enjoyable (if slightly overlong) two-plus hours. RECOMMENDED

The Newton Boys [1998]

Starring: Matthew McConaughey, Ethan Hawke, Vincent D'Onofrio, Skeet Ulrich Director: Richard Linklater Screenplay: Claude Stanush, Clark McBay, Richard Linklater Running Time: 2:02 Rated: PG-13 (Violence, profanity) Theatrical Aspect Ratio: 2.35:1

The Newton Boys illustrates that it's possible to make a film about gangsters and gunplay without an abundance of bloodshed, violence, and death. In fact, for this account, which depicts "the true story of the most successful bank robbers in the history of the United States," director Richard Linklater has consciously kept the tone playful. That's not to say that *The Newton Boys* doesn't have its grim moments, but Linklater limits the shadows. The result is a fast-paced, entertaining motion picture that replaces gritty tension with a lightly dramatic character interaction that occasionally borders on straight comedy.

The real Newton Boys started their crime spree in 1919, and finished it 5 years later, in 1924. During that time, the 4 brothers — Joe (Skeet Ulrich), Jesse (Ethan Hawke), Willis (Matthew McConaughey), and Dock (Vincent D'Onofrio) — and explosives expert Glasscock (Dwight Yoakam) broke into more than 80 banks and committed the largest train robbery in U.S. history — the famous June 12, 1924 Rondout Robbery. Their illegal activities took them from their native Texas, through dozens of small towns and major cities all across the country, and into Canada. Linklater's film recounts the Newton gang's exploits with all of the fondness of a grandfather relating a favorite story to a child.

One thing that differentiates the Newton Boys from America's numerous, other well-known bandits is that they never killed anyone. They used guns, but rarely fired them, and almost never at a living target. All they wanted was the money, and they were often kind to the men they held at gunpoint. Moreover, they viewed themselves as champions of the under-trodden — little thieves stealing from big thieves (the companies insuring the banks). Linklater presents all

four brothers as happy, good-natured fellows — the kind of guys no one would mind hanging out with. RECOMMENDED

Open Range [2003]

Starring: Robert Duvall, Kevin Costner, Annette Bening, Michael Gambon, Michael Jeter, Diego Luna, James Russo, Abraham Benrubi, Dean McDermott Director: Kevin Costner Screenplay: Craig Storper, based on *The Open Range Men,* by Lauran Paine Running Time: 2:20 Rated: PG-13 (Violence) Theatrical Aspect Ratio: 2.35:1

Like most recent Westerns (not that there are an abundance to choose from), *Open Range* belongs to the "revisionist" category, which is to say that it turns some of the Western conventions upside down. In this film it's pretty clear who the protagonists are, but they're not morally upright gunslingers wearing white hats. They have pasts that haunt them, and they aren't beyond killing for a less-than-pure motive like revenge. Also, the centerpiece gunfight is as chaotic, unpleasant, and gritty as anything ever committed to film. This isn't two people facing each other on a deserted street with tumbleweeds blowing around. It's quick, brutal, and bloody.

The year is 1882, and the Old West is gradually being modernized. The frontier, like so many other things, is becoming a relic of the past. The post–Civil War race westward is wiping away the Indians and populating the land with towns where the rule of the gun is more important than the law. Free grazing, in which roaming cattle are allowed to feed wherever they roam, is still legal, but it is increasingly looked down upon by property owners who don't want their prime acres stripped clean. The conflict between a group of free-grazing cattlemen and a wealthy, unscrupulous rancher lies at the center of *Open Range*.

Boss Spearman (Robert Duvall) has ridden with Charley Waite (Kevin Costner) for a decade. Recently, they have taken on two apprentices: the gentle giant Mose (Abraham Benrubi), and the orphan Button (Diego Luna). All is going well until they reach a town "owned" by Denton Baxter (Michael Gambon), who doesn't like free grazers and wants Boss's herd. So, with the help of the corrupt local marshal, Poole (James Russo), he contrives to have Boss and his fellows murdered. Things don't go exactly as planned. Mose is killed and Button is badly injured, but Boss and Charley escape unscathed and with an appetite for vengeance. They take Button to the local doctor's house, where Sue Barlow (Annette Bening), the sister of Doc Barlow (Dean McDermott), cares for him. Then, with the connivance of a local named Percy (the late Michael Jeter), they plot their first move against Baxter and Poole.

With its emphasis on realism over legend, the film's texture is just about perfect. Fans of classic Westerns will find much here that's comfortable and familiar, while those who are less than enthused by the "sameness" of the genre will discover that Costner has uncovered a new way to look at an old story. The tone is melancholy, but, unlike in pictures like *Unforgiven* and *High Noon,* there is room for hope and redemption. The movie's major action sequence owes a nod to Kurosawa and is not infected with the rapid-fire editing style that too many filmmakers have become enamored with. There's something a little old-fashioned about *Open Range,* despite its modern approach to Western motifs, and that's a welcome quality. RECOMMENDED

The Wild Bunch [1969]

Starring: William Holden, Ernest Borgnine, Robert Ryan, Edmond O'Brien Director: Sam Peckinpah Screenplay: Sam Peckinpah and Walon Green based on a story by Walon Green and Roy N. Sickner Running Time: 2:25 Rated: R (Violence, language, mature themes, brief nudity) Theatrical Aspect Ratio: 2.35:1

The movie opens during 1913 in the small south Texas town of San Rafael. The Wild Bunch — a gang of 6 — has moved in to pull off a robbery. What they don't know is that it's a setup — the sacks of money are filled with washers and there are dozens of gun-toting bounty hunters hidden in ambush. Things turn bloody and numerous innocent citizens are caught in the crossfire. The gang escapes with the bounty hunters hot on their trail.

Leading the Wild Bunch is Pike (William Holden), an aging outlaw who enjoys planning his capers as much as carrying them out. He's beginning to feel his age, however — an old wound makes it nearly impossible for him to mount his horse and he wonders how many more jobs he'll be good for. Pike's right-hand man is Dutch (Ernest Borgnine), another grizzled veteran of the robbery circuit. The gang is rounded out by Sykes (Edmond O'Brien), Angel (Jaime Sanchez), and the Gorch Brothers (Warren Oates and Ben Johnson). One member of the Bunch is missing, however. Thornton (Robert Ryan), once Pike's closest friend, was arrested as a result of a past screw-up, and now commands the mercenaries hunting his old buddies.

It's possible to view *The Wild Bunch* as a straight action picture, albeit a highly stylized one — Peckinpah's use of multiple angles and quick cuts is amazing. All the traditional elements of the genre are present: shoot-outs, male bonding, and a high body count. The director's methods of orchestrating tension are such that the movie has its fair share of edge-of-the-seat moments. But there's a lot more here. *The Wild Bunch* has level upon level of complexity even beyond the obvious metaphor of Vietnam, and has been structured to satisfy the more discriminating movie-goer.

Not only does *The Wild Bunch* illustrate Peckinpah's mastery of his medium, but it presents a story that is effective on nearly every level: the emotional, the visual, and the visceral. There aren't many epic motion pictures of this scope these days, so it's a rare treat to look back more than 2 decades and see something that is as potent and relevant today as when it was first released. MUST SEE

Appendix:
Easter Eggs, Extended Editions and Director's Cuts

EASTER EGGS

In DVD terminology, an "Easter egg" is a hidden special feature that cannot be accessed via a conventional on-screen menu. Many Easter eggs can be opened by finding and clicking on a secret icon, and the means by which that icon is found can vary from simple to complex. Most Easter eggs are inconsequential — gag reels, bloopers, and short interviews being popular. But there are times, such as the *Memento* reverse-chronology egg, where they are worth the effort to seek out. The majority of DVDs do not contain Easter eggs. Hidden features are typically the province of big-budget movies aimed at children and teenagers. It's rare, although not unheard of, for a foreign, independent, or adult-oriented movie to contain eggs. This list represents a "cheat sheet" leading to 77 Easter eggs on 37 movies (all of which are reviewed in other sections of this book). If you happen to be renting one of these titles, you may want to take a few minutes to see what hidden features can be found. I have placed ** next to those I believe to be especially fun to watch.

Almost Famous — Bootleg Cut
- Outtakes: On disc 2, go to "Special Features," then "Cast," then "Fairuza Balk." When her bio is displayed, hit the UP arrow. One of her photos will turn red. Hit ENTER/SELECT.

Army of Darkness, Director's Cut
- Storyboards: Go to "Commentary" and turn it ON, then go to "Subtitles" and turn them ON.

Storyboards will be displayed at the bottom of each scene. Note: In the two-disc set, this is a menu option, not an Easter egg.

Blue Velvet
- Musical montage: On the "Main Menu" screen, highlight "Play Movie," then hit the LEFT arrow. A new menu item, "Strange World," will be highlighted. Hit ENTER/SELECT.

Cast Away
- Joke comment: On disc 2, go to "Stills and Galleries," then highlight "Raft Escape." Hit the LEFT arrow. A depiction of the "Angel Wings" FedEx slogan will be displayed. Hit ENTER/SELECT.

Charlie's Angels
- Gag reel: On the third "Special Features" page, highlight the "<" and then hit the RIGHT arrow. Sam Rockwell's eyes will be highlighted. Hit ENTER/SELECT.

Citizen Kane
- Interview with Ruth Warrick: On disc 1, go to "Special Features," highlight "Post Production," then hit the RIGHT arrow to highlight the sled. Hit ENTER/SELECT.

Die Another Day
- Various angles of Halle Berry dripping wet: On disc 2, go to "Image database," then "Sets &

locations." Hit the RIGHT arrow until there is a photo of Halle Berry rising out of the water. Then hit the UP arrow.

Dinosaur

- **Multiple features: All on disc 2. For "Development," "Creating the Characters," "Production Process," and "Publicity"— all have "Dino Fossil" icons. Use arrow keys to highlight this icon on each of the menus, then hit ENTER/SELECT.

Fast Times at Ridgemont High

- Spicoli quotes: Go to "Bonus Materials," hit the UP arrow to highlight the footprints, then hit ENTER/SELECT.

Fight Club

- Fake *Fight Club* Merchandise Catalog: On disc 2, go to "Advertising," then "Promotional Gallery." Hit the DOWN arrow, and a happy face will appear. Hit ENTER/SELECT.
- **Fake warning: On disc 1, as the disc starts up, there are the usual "FBI Warning" and "Attention" pages. There is then another "Warning" page that is clearly made up. There is no way to pause the page, so it may be necessary to restart the movie multiple times to read all the way through it.

Finding Nemo

- Short video: On disc 2, go to "Special Features," then go to "Behind the Scenes." Highlight "Studio Tours" and hit the UP arrow. Hit ENTER/SELECT.
- Short video: On disc 1, go to "Bonus Features," highlight the arrow at bottom of the screen, then hit the DOWN arrow. Hit ENTER/SELECT.
- Short video: On disc 1, go to "Bonus Features," then "Visual Comentary." While on the fish that looks like it's in a TV, hit the UP arrow, then hit ENTER/SELECT.
- **Fake commercial: On disc 2, go to "Bonus Features" and navigate to the curved arrow at the bottom. Hit the DOWN arrow, then hit ENTER/SELECT.
- Short video: On disc 2, go to "Bonus Features," then "Mr. Ray's Encyclopedia." Navigate to the curved arrow at the bottom, then hit the DOWN arrow. Hit ENTER/SELECT.

- Bruce's oath: On disc 1, go to "Bonus Features," then highlight the fish in the TV on the lower left. Hit the LEFT arrow, then hit ENTER/SELECT.
- Bruce's comment: On disc 1, go to the "Set Up" menu, then highlight "Subtitles." Hit the LEFT arrow, then hit ENTER/SELECT.
- Bruce's speech: On disc 1, go to "Bonus Features," then go to "Virtual Commentary Includes Deleted Scenes," followed by "Virtual Commentary Index." Highlight "Play All," then hit the LEFT arrow. Hit ENTER/SELECT.

A Fish Called Wanda

- Press UP at "Languages." The treasure chest should be highlighted. Select it by pressing ENTER. You will view a looping aquarium segment.

The Girl Next Door

- **On side B, go to the "Special Features" section of the DVD. When you get there, go to the gag reel and push right and you should see three blue Xs. Then, when you select them, you should see the old Sex-ed movie.

Gladiator

- Chicken Run mock *Gladiator* trailer: On disc 2, go to "Trailers and TV Spots." Hit the LEFT arrow, then hit ENTER/SELECT.
- CGI Rhino — abandoned concept: On disc 2, go to the second menu screen. Enter "Original Storyboards." Once there, press "More." On the next screen, enter the deleted sequence storyboard called "Rhino Fight." You will see the first page of the storyboard. Hit the UP arrow. Hit ENTER/SELECT.

Glengarry Glen Ross, Collector's Edition

- Auditions: On disc 2, go to "Special Features," then scroll down to highlight "Main Menu." Hit the LEFT arrow, then hit ENTER/SELECT.

Godfather DVD Collection

- Foreign language audio clips: On the bonus disc (disc 5), go to "Set Up." Once there, hit the RIGHT arrow when highlighting any of the options. Hit ENTER/SELECT.
- **Sopranos* clip of characters watching *Godfather* bootleg: On disc 5, go to "Galleries," then go to "DVD Credits." The cursor will be on "Next."

Hit ENTER/SELECT three times. The cursor will have moved to the "Previous" option. Move it to "Next" and hit ENTER/SELECT.

- **Caan does Brando: On disc 5, go to the "Family Tree" and select Santino's branch. Hit through to Sonny's picture, then hit ENTER/SELECT. At the biography of James Caan, highlight the picture and hit ENTER/SELECT.
- Puzo and $$: On disc 5, go to "Film Makers," then go to "Mario Puzo." Hit the LEFT arrow several times until a large green "$" sign appears. Hit ENTER/SELECT.

Insomnia (U.S. Version)

- **Avalanche video: Choose "Special Features," then "Production Diaries." Highlight "Features" at the bottom of the screen, then hit the LEFT arrow followed by ENTER/SELECT.

The Lord of the Rings: The Fellowship of the Ring: Extended Edition

- **MTV Awards parody: On disc 1 of the four-disc Special Extended Edition (not the two-disc set), go to "Select a Scene," then highlight scene #27. Hit the DOWN arrow, then ENTER/SELECT.
- Two Towers Preview: On disc 2 of the four-disc set, go to "Select a Scene," then go to scene #48. A screen will appear with "Fan Club Credits" in the center. Go to the list of chapters to the right and highlight #48. Hit the DOWN arrow, then ENTER/SELECT.

The Lord of the Rings: The Two Towers: Extended Edition

- **Gollum's MTV Award speech: On disc 1 of the 4-disc set, go to "Select a Scene," then highlight scene #30. Hit the DOWN arrow then ENTER/SELECT.

The Lord of the Rings: The Return of the King: Extended Editon

- **Elijah Wood *Punk'd* interview: On disc 1 of the four-disc set, go to "Select a Scene," then highlight scene #36. Hit the DOWN arrow, then ENTER/SELECT.
- **Siller & Vaughn pitch a sequel: On disc 2 of the four-disc set, go to "Select a Scene," then go to scene #78. A screen will appear with "Fan Club Credits" in the center. Go to the list of chapters to the right and highlight #78. Hit the DOWN arrow, then ENTER/SELECT.

Magnolia

- Bloopers: On disc 1, go to "Set Up," then go to "Color Bars." After 20 seconds of color bars, the Easter egg will begin.

Memento, Limited Edition

- **Movie in chronological order: Complicated! On disc 2 of the Limited Edition set (only), hit random answers in the psychology quiz until a page of objects is displayed. Select the clock, then hit ENTER/SELECT. Choose the answer "c" five times (regardless of what you think the "real" answer should be). When you reach the question where you are asked to put the pictures in order of a woman fixing a flat tire, place them in reverse order (3, 4, 1, 2). The movie will start playing in chronological order, staring from reverse credits. Note: During this option it is not possible to fast-forward or rewind.

A Mighty Wind

- Hidden Features Menu: Go to "Special Features," then highlight "Continue" and hit the UP arrow until the guitar string is highlighted. Hit ENTER/SELECT.

Monsters, Inc.

- Gag reel: On disc 2, go through the door marked "Monsters Only." On the next screen, highlight an arrow pointing to the right, then hit the RIGHT arrow, then hit ENTER/SELECT.
- Atrium features: On disc 2, go through the the door marked "Humans Only," then go to "Production Tour." Jump to chapter 7 (hit the "next chapter" button six times). Seven mystery doors will appear.
- Paper airplane contest: On disc 2, go through the door marked "Humans Only," then go to "Pixar." Next, highlight "Pixar Fun Factory Tour" and hit the DOWN arrow to highlight the "M" logo. Next, hit the LEFT arrow, then ENTER/SELECT.

Moulin Rouge (All on disc 2)

- Zidler's can-can: Go to the second menu and highlight "Back." Hit the RIGHT arrow, then ENTER/SELECT.

- The Hammer: Go to "The Story is about," then go to "Old Story Lines and Script Comparisons." Highlight "Return" and hit the RIGHT arrow, followed by ENTER/SELECT.
- Surprise from Baz: Go to "The Stars." Once the video introduction has ended, type 9 and then 17 (on some controls, "17" may be "10+" followed by "7"). You should not need to hit ENTER/SELECT at any time, including between the numbers.
- Leguizamo short clip: Go to "The Stars," then hit "More." Highlight "John Leguizamo as Toulouse Lautrec," the hit the UP arrow, followed by ENTER/SELECT.
- The magic of ADR: Go to "The Design" on the second menu, then go to "Set Design." Go to "Spectacular Spectacular." Hit the RIGHT arrow two times, then hit the UP arrow. Finally, hit SELECT/ENTER.
- Kidman rehearses: Go to "The Design" on the second menu, then go to "Set Design." Go to "The Gothic Tower." Hit the RIGHT arrow five times, then hit the UP arrow. Finally, hit SELECT/ENTER.
- Ewan loses the mic: Go to "The Design" on the second menu, then go to "Costume Design." Go to "A Courtesan's Wardrobe." Hit the RIGHT arrow four times, then hit the UP arrow. Finally, hit SELECT/ENTER.
- More can-can: Go to "The Design" on the second menu, then go to "Costume Design." Go to "The Bohemians." Hit the RIGHT arrow five times, then hit the UP arrow. Finally, hit SELECT/ENTER
- Throwing in the hats: Go to "The Design" on the second menu, then go to "Smoke and Mirrors." Next, type 5 and then 18 (on some controls, "18" may be "10+" followed by "8").
- Nipple powdering (PG version): Go to "The Design" on the second menu. Next, type 18, then 99 (on some controls, "18" may be "10+" followed by "8"; "99" may be achieved by hitting "10+" nine times followed by "9").
- The tango: Go to "Dance" on the second menu, then go to "The Dance" again. Highlight "A Word From Baz" and hit the RIGHT arrow, followed by ENTER/SELECT.
- Baz dances to "Like a Virgin": Go to "Dance" on the second menu, then go to "Choreography." Highlight "Main Menu" and hit the RIGHT arrow, followed by ENTER/SELECT.

- Weather report: Go to "The Music," then go to "The Lady Marmalade Phenomenon." Highlight "Main Menu" and hit the RIGHT arrow followed by ENTER/SELECT.
- Mom's house: Go to "Marketing" on the second menu, then go to "Photo Gallery." Highlight "Mary Ellen Mark." Hit the RIGHT arrow, followed by ENTER/SELECT.
- **"Your Song" a.k.a. "Can't Stop the Giggles." Go to "The Cutting Room" and highlight "Main Menu." Hit the LEFT arrow, followed by ENTER/SELECT.

Nurse Betty

- **Final soap opera episode: Go to "Special Features," then go to "Reason to Love." Highlight the first episode, then hit the UP arrow, followed by ENTER/SELECT.

Pirates of the Caribbean:
The Curse of the Black Pearl

- Time-lapse video of cave construction: On disc 2, go to "Fly on the Set." Highlight "Play All" and hit the RIGHT arrow, followed by ENTER/SELECT.
- Foreign movie trailer: On disc 2, go to "Below Deck," then go to "Scene Index." On the second page of "Scene Index," highlight "Pirate Ships." Hit the LEFT arrow, followed by ENTER/SELECT.
- **Keith Richards interview: On disc 2, go to "Moonlight Serenade Scene Progression." Highlight "Main Menu," then hit the DOWN arrow, followed by ENTER/SELECT.
- CGI chase sequence: On disc 2, to to "Below Deck." Highlight "Set Sail" and hit the LEFT arrow twice, followed by ENTER/SELECT.

The Princess Bride: Special Edition

- Quick quotes: On the main menu, there are four jewels in the four corners of the screen. Navigate using your arrow buttons until the upper-left jewel is highlighted. Hit ENTER/SELECT.

Requiem for a Dream

- **Tappy's life story: On the main menu, hit the DOWN arrow to highlight "Hear Tappy's Amazing Life Story." Hit ENTER/SELECT.
- **Tappy's secret #3: Go to "Chapter Selection,"

then go to the video cassette spine for Chapters 21–24. Hit the UP arrow twice, then hit ENTER/SELECT. (I had to try this a few times before getting it right, but it's worth the effort.)

Reservoir Dogs

- Reservoir dolls: On disc 2, go to "Special Features," then go to "K BILLY." Highlight the rightmost button and hit ENTER/SELECT.

Spider-Man

- Interview with the Romitas: On disc 2, go to "Web of Spider-Man," then go to "The Evolution Of Spiderman." Highlight "Artists Gallery," then hit the RIGHT arrow, followed by ENTER/SELECT.
- CGI bloopers: On disc 1, go to "Commentaries." Use the LEFT arrow to highlight the picture of Harry Osborn, then hit ENTER/SELECT.
- Comic book character Bio: On disc 1, go to "Special Features," then go to "Character Files." Choose any actor except Cliff Robertson. Hit the RIGHT arrow to access the second filmography page, then hit the UP arrow. Hit SELECT/ENTER.
- Interview about the Web Effects: On disc 2, go to "Web of Spider-Man," then go to "DVD-ROM." Hit the UP arrow, followed by ENTER/SELECT.

Star Wars Episode 1: The Phantom Menace

- **Bloopers: On disc 1, go to "Options." Enter "11," then "3," then "8." (On some remotes, it may be necessary to enter "10+" and then "1" to get "11.") At no time should it be necessary to hit ENTER/SELECT.
- Pre-Pod race documentary: On disc 2, go to "Deleted Scenes and Documentaries," then go to "Deleted Scenes Only." Next, go to "Complete Podrace Grid Sequence" and highlight "Documentary." Hit the RIGHT arrow, followed by ENTER/SELECT.
- Pod race lap 2 documentary: On disc 2, go to "Deleted Scenes and Documentaries," then go to "Deleted Scenes Only." Next, go to "Extended Podrace Lap 2" and highlight "Documentary." Hit the RIGHT arrow, followed by ENTER/SELECT.

Star Wars Episode II: Attack of the Clones

- **Bloopers: On disc 1, go to "Options." Enter "11," then "3," then "8." (On some remotes, it may be necessary to enter "10+" and then "1" to get "11.") At no time should it be necessary to hit ENTER/SELECT.

Star Wars Trilogy

- Bloopers: On the bonus disc (disc 4), go to "Video Games and Still Galleries." Enter "11," then "3," then "8." (On some remotes, it may be necessary to enter "10+" and then "1" to get "11.") At no time should it be necessary to hit ENTER/SELECT.

Thirteen

- Deleted scene: On the "Full Screen" side of the DVD, to to "Special Features." Highlight "Making Of," then hit the RIGHT arrow, followed by ENTER/SELECT.

Vanilla Sky

- Bloopers: Go to "Special Features," then go to "Photo Galleries." Highlight "Audio Introduction by Photographer Neal Preston," then hit the UP arrow. "Special Features" will be highlighted. Hit the RIGHT arrow, followed by ENTER/SELECT.

X-Men

- **Special guest star in an outtake: Go to "Special Features," then go to "Theatrical Trailers & TV Spots." Hit the LEFT arrow, followed by ENTER/SELECT.
- Concept drawings of unused characters: Go to "Special Features," then go to "Art Gallery." Highlight "Main Menu," then hit the UP arrow, followed by ENTER/SELECT.

EXTENDED EDITIONS AND DIRECTOR'S CUTS

The Abyss [1989, Director's Cut]

Starring: Ed Harris, Mary Elizabeth Mastrantonio, Michael Biehn
Director: **James Cameron** Screenplay: **James Cameron** Running Time: 2:26 (Theatrical); 2:51 (Director's) Rated: PG-13 (Violence, brief nudity, profanity) Theatrical Aspect Ratio: 2.35:1

James Cameron's *The Abyss* may be the most extreme example of an available movie that demonstrates how the vision of a director, once fully realized on-screen, can transform a good motion picture into a great one. When *The Abyss* was first released in 1989, it was rushed into theaters in a version that was truncated and incomplete. The ending eliminated a key thematic element (that of humankind's ability to save itself from its own folly), and left plot holes unplugged. Cameron, aware that the theatrical version was deeply flawed, went to work on a director's cut. This rendering, which lasts about 25 minutes longer than the one that played in theaters, provides the missing components of the climax and adds additional character definition. In addition to incorporating deleted scenes, Cameron spent money on new special effects (something that is now regularly done, but was unique at the time), so that his preferred cut would have the desired impact.

The Abyss is the story of underwater extraterrestrials and those who make first contact with them. The lead characters, a husband-and-wife team played by Ed Harris and Mary Elizabeth Mastrantonio, work on an underwater search mission trying to locate a missing U.S. nuclear submarine. A hurricane, accidents, and the appearance of a UFO (Underwater Flying Object) combine to create a dangerous work environment. To further complicate matters, the head Navy SEAL (Michael Biehn) on the operation is showing signs of mental instability caused by pressure sickness. Meanwhile, above the waves, World War III looms.

Cameron blends these elements into a taut tale that, while not matching the likes of *Das Boot* for underwater tension, is nevertheless riveting. For two hours the theatrical version of the film matches its director's cut counterpart. Then the deviations begin. The shorter version of the film rushes the encounter with the aliens. The deteriorating political situation has been nixed, keeping themes one-dimensional. The director's cut takes its time during this part of the movie, giving us a greater understanding of the aliens' goals and showing a lot more of what is happening on the surface. Cameron's message, lost in the theatrical version, comes across clearly.

Fortunately for those who are interested in *The Abyss*, the director's cut is as widely available as the theatrical version. (The Special Edition DVD contains both.) When the longer *Abyss* was released on home video, it was successful, and led to Cameron providing the same treatment to his earlier, more successful movie, *Aliens*. To date, *The Abyss* remains a template to which directors, when unsatisfied with the theatrical cut of their movie, look for inspiration.

Theatrical Version: RECOMMENDED
Director's Cut: HIGHLY RECOMMENDED

Alien [1979, Director's Cut]

Starring: Tom Skerritt, Sigourney Weaver, Veronica Cartwright, Harry Dean Stanton, John Hurt, Ian Holm, Yaphet Kotto Director: **Ridley Scott** Screenplay: **Dan O'Bannon** Running Time: 1:57 (Theatrical); 1:56 (Director's) Rated: R (Violence, gore, profanity) Theatrical Aspect Ratio: 2.35:1

Alien is the original "haunted house in space" movie, and is just as creepy today as it was when it was first released. For the film's 25th anniversary, director Ridley Scott agreed to take a second look at the film and develop a director's cut. Although pleased with the theatrical edition that arrived in cinemas in 1979, Scott decided there were places where changes were warranted, and the result offers an alternative view of this influential motion picture.

The story is unchanged: Upon receiving a distress signal, the crew of a deep space commercial towing ship elects to investigate. A mishap on the planet's surface leads to a life-and-death struggle for one of the crew members. When, in critical condition, he is brought back aboard the ship without going through proper quarantine procedures, he unwittingly becomes the conduit by which a lethal alien finds its way into this small population of humans. One-by-one, as it grows, it picks them off.

Instead of taking the usual route of adding back deleted scenes, Scott elected to re-edit all of *Alien*. Some of his original trims are returned to the screen (including a key sequence with the ship's captain, Dallas, begging for a mercy killing), but Scott eliminates more material than he incorporates. As a result, the director's cut is a minute shorter than the theatrical version. The new, tighter rendition enhances the tension, but not by a substantial amount.

It's hard to say which is the definitive version of the

film. *Alien* fans will treasure both, but the casual viewer will notice few, if any, changes. Some director's cuts represent grand reshaping of films. That's not the case with *Alien*, where Scott went to work with a scalpel, not a chisel. Consequently, the restructuring is subtle. It works, but so does the original cut. The reasons to seek out the new version are prosaic: The print has been cleaned up, and the sound has been remastered. In terms of content, there's no overriding reason to prefer one to the other. Both offer plenty of tension and scares, which is all one hopes for when viewing this movie.

Theatrical Version: HIGHLY RECOMMENDED
Director's Cut: HIGHLY RECOMMENDED

Apocalypse Now [1979, Director's Cut]

Starring: Martin Sheen, Marlon Brando, Robert Duvall, Frederic Forrest, Sam Bottoms, Albert Hall, Laurence Fishburne Director: Francis Ford Coppola Screenplay: John Milius and Francis Ford Coppola, based on Joseph Conrad's *Heart of Darkness* Running Time: 2:33 (Theatrical); 3:21 (Director's) Rated: R (Violence, profanity, drugs, nudity, sexual situations) Theatrical Aspect Ratio: 2.35:1

In its initial 1979 form, Francis Ford Coppola's anti-war *Apocalypse Now* is flawed, but undeniably powerful. The primary problem with the film is the ending, where the climactic confrontation between Captain Benjamin Willard (Martin Sheen) and Colonel Kurtz (Marlon Brando) lacks focus. However, considering the onset and postproduction turmoil surrounding this movie, it's amazing that the result works as well as it does. As a meditation on the insanity of war, it's tough to find a better example than the first three-quarters of *Apocalypse Now*. Until the arrival of *Platoon*, it was rightfully used as the standard against which all Vietnam war movies were measured.

Apocalypse Now transpires during the Vietnam War and chronicles the journey by Willard up the fictional Nung River into Cambodia. His mission: to locate the renegade Kurtz, who has set himself up as a god to the natives, and terminate him with "extreme prejudice." The farther he gets from civilization, the more bizarre and extreme the circumstances become.

In retrospect, Coppola should have left the film untouched. By revisiting the movie some 20 years after its release, he has done the production a disservice. For the "Redux" version of *Apocalypse Now*, Coppola has spliced in nearly 50 minutes of previously unused footage, and for the most part, it's easy to see why that material wasn't included in the first place. The two biggest add-ins — a hallucinogenic romp with naked Playmates during a hurricane, and a visit to a French plantation — are shockingly bad. The acting is awful, the pacing is poor, and these scenes do little more than kill the momentum of the upriver journey. Why Coppola, looking back at *Apocalypse Now* through the lens of two decades, thought these sequences would improve his movie is a mystery.

One or two of the re-introduced scenes are effective. In particular, those near the end featuring Brando beef up Kurtz's characterization and help to clarify his motivations. They part some of the fog surrounding the murky climax. Ultimately, however, more damage is done by including so much pointless material than can be counterbalanced by the few moments that enhance the proceedings. Filmmakers, of course, have every right to revisit movies made earlier in their careers. But by choosing to tinker with *Apocalypse Now*, it appears that Coppola failed to understand that "more" doesn't always mean "better."

The director's cut of *Apocalypse Now* retains some of the original's power, but its overall effectiveness is undercut by its length and turgid, erratic pacing. It is unwieldy and difficult to watch in one sitting. Take away the naked Playmates and the interminable philosophizing with French aristocrats and you're left with a solid motion picture — which also happens to be close to the 1979 cut. Unless you're obsessed with completeness, the theatrical version is the way to go.

Theatrical Version: RECOMMENDED
Director's Cut: RECOMMENDED WITH RESERVATIONS

Army of Darkness [1993, Director's Cut]

Starring: Bruce Campbell, Embeth Davidz, Marcus Gilbert Director: Sam Raimi Screenplay: Sam and Ivan Raimi Running Time: 1:21 (Theatrical); 1:36 (Director's) Rated: R (Violence, gore, profanity) Theatrical Aspect Ratio: 1.85:1

Army of Darkness is the third installment of Sam Raimi's *Evil Dead* trilogy, and the most openly jokey of the series. Raimi's stalwart hero, Ash (Bruce Campbell), finds himself in medieval times, battling the forces of evil while attempting to find a way back home. His foes include a girlfriend who has been turned into a harpy and an army of skeletons who act suspiciously like members of the Three Stooges. *Army of Darkness* is properly identified as a "horror comedy," but the accent is more on the second element than the first. Scares are infrequent in this film; laughter is not.

For the director's cut, Raimi was given the opportunity to rectify some of the changes imposed upon him as a result of studio interference. Many of the changes are small, but there are two significant alterations. The first occurs during the final battle between the humans and the "deadites." In the theatrical version, this was a relatively quick affair. For the director's cut, Raimi re-introduces about ten minutes of additional footage, reshaping the scope of the struggle, making it more "epic" in nature. And there's a different, darker ending. Instead of seeing Ash return to his department store job to duel a she-demon in the aisles, he ends up somewhere completely different.

Although I enjoyed the theatrical cut of *Army of Darkness,* the director's cut is the better edition. The rushed feeling associated with the studio-approved version (which had a running length of about 80 minutes) is not evident in Raimi's interpretation. And, although the theatrical ending is the happier one, the apocalyptic conclusion of the director's cut fits better with Raimi's overall vision of the *Evil Dead* trilogy. Ash is a hero, but he's the kind of hero who is always getting beaten down.

Fans of the *Evil Dead* movies likely already own copies of both versions of *Army of Darkness*, but first-time viewers are advised to pass up the shorter version and experience what Raimi intended from the beginning. Since *Army of Darkness* first came out, Raimi's Hollywood stock has risen dramatically (he directed the first two *Spider-Man* movies), giving him complete creative control over future projects. The availability of the *Army of Darkness* director's cut restores the film to what Raimi intended it to be.

Theatrical Version: RECOMMENDED

Director's Cut: RECOMMENDED

The Butterfly Effect [2004, Director's Cut]

Starring: Ashton Kutcher, Amy Smart, William Lee Scott, Elden Henson, John Patrick Amedori, Eric Stoltz, Logan Lerman   Directors: Eric Bress, J. Mackye Gruber   Screenplay: J. Mackye Gruber & Eric Bress   Running Time: 1:53 (Theatrical); 2:00 (Director's)   Rated: R (Violence, profanity, sexual situations, nudity)   Theatrical Aspect Ratio: 1.85:1

The Butterfly Effect is a science fiction tale from Eric Bress and J. Mackye Gruber that is sure to entice anyone who enjoys stories about alternate universes and time-travel paradoxes. As flawed as the movie is — and it could have used a little more polishing on the word processor before going in front of the cameras — *The Butterfly Effect* is compelling because of the chances it takes. Following one character through a series of alternate realities, the film adopts the tenet of chaos theory: that even the smallest action of one person can have a dramatic ripple effect. So, by doing

something seemingly minor, Ashton Kutcher's character impacts not only his own future, but those of many of his friends.

At the time the movie was initially released, I gave it a favorable review, but remarked that a weakness was the ending, which seemed too pat. For a movie as dark as *The Butterfly Effect* often is, the manner in which the directors conclude it is out of character with the bulk of the production. The director's cut DVD rectifies this.

Test screenings conducted by New Line Cinema revealed that potential viewers hated the downbeat way in which Bress and Guber concluded the story, even though this *Twilight Zone*–inspired denouement is perfect for the tale that precedes it. For the DVD, the original, bleak ending has been restored, and it smoothes over one of *The Butterfly Effect*'s noticeable imperfections. (Nothing, however, can be done about the variability of Ashton Kutcher's performance.) Other inserts are mostly minor and relate, in one way or another, to the ending.

The overall flow and direction of the film have not changed, but the director's cut is less optimistic than the theatrical version (which is gloomy enough in its own right). *The Butterfly Effect* is not for everyone, but for those who enjoy this kind of speculative science fiction fare, skip the theatrical edition and go straight for the director's cut. It satisfies in a way that only a movie that has not been compromised to meet least common denominator standards can.

Theatrical Version: RECOMMENDED

Director's Cut: RECOMMENDED

Dances with Wolves [1990, Director's Cut]

Starring: Kevin Costner, Mary McDonnell, Graham Greene, Rodney A. Grant   Director: Kevin Costner   Screenplay: Michael Blake, based on his novel   Running Time: 3:03 (Theatrical); 3:56 (Director's)   Rated: PG-13 (Violence, brief nudity, discreet sex)   Theatrical Aspect Ratio: 2.35:1   In English and Lakota, with subtitles

When it was released in 1990, *Dances with Wolves* was referred to as "Costner's Folly." For his directorial debut, not only did the actor venture into a genre (the Western) that had been considered dead for some time, but he did so with a cut that was three hours long. A quick box office death was predicted, but Costner had the last laugh. *Dances with Wolves* went on to break the $100 million mark in gross receipts and, in early 1991, it won the Best Picture Oscar (the first of two Westerns to be granted that citation during a three-year period).

What viewers didn't know at the time was that

Costner's preferred version was actually four hours long. This was the cut that he released to theaters overseas. However, it was only after the DVD had become an accepted format that the longer *Dances with Wolves* was made available in the American home video market.

Nothing in Costner's director's cut is mandatory viewing, but there's no denying that the added scenes (which are sprinkled liberally throughout the production) add depth to the characters and breadth to the scenes. As is often the case with epic movies that are broadened by the introduction of large amounts of new material, this one has a tendency to become ponderous at times. Overall, however, there isn't an extreme impact to the movie's pace. Many pictures, upon gaining about 50 minutes of unused footage, become erratic or unwieldy.

So which is the better version of *Dances with Wolves*? It probably depends upon your taste. If you have patience, the director's cut offers the greater feel for the world Costner is re-creating. But there are strong arguments in favor of the theatrical edition, the chief of which is its relative brevity. One could argue that three hours is the right length for this movie, and that the additional 50 minutes represents fat that was rightfully excised in the editing room. The shorter film moves more briskly but loses some of the story's nuances in the process. So, if you have the time, I would recommend the director's cut. Otherwise, the theatrical version will still catapult you to all the right places.

Theatrical Version: MUST SEE
Director's Cut: MUST SEE

Das Boot [Germany, 1981, Director's Cut]
Starring: Jurgen Prochnow, Herbert Gronemeyer, Klaus Wennemann, Hubertus Bengsch, Martin Semmelrogge, Bernd Tauber, Erwin Leder, Martin May   Director: Wolfgang Petersen   Screenplay: Wolfgang Petersen, based on the novel by Lothar-G. Buchheim   Running Time: 2:29 (Theatrical); 3:30 (Director's); 4:53 (Uncut)   Rated: R (Profanity, mature themes)   Theatrical Aspect Ratio: 2.35:1 In German with subtitles

The international success of Wolfgang Petersen's 1981 thriller, *Das Boot*, about life aboard a German U-boat during World War II, led the director to a successful Hollywood career. The film was praised around the world, earning six Oscar nominations — an unusually large total for a foreign language motion picture. What much of the world did not know at the time, however, was that the 2½ hour version of *Das Boot* released in movie theaters represents only a fraction of the whole story. In fact, the full version of *Das Boot*, which was shown on German TV as a miniseries, is five hours long.

To date, three versions of *Das Boot* have been released on DVD. The theatrical version still packs a visceral punch, but considering all that has been eliminated (roughly 50 percent), it seems bare-bones, especially to someone who has watched either of the longer cuts. The shortest edition of *Das Boot* is heavily focused on plot and tension, with minimal room for character development. The 1997 director's cut, which was put together by Petersen after he had gained the clout to oversee the project, restores one hour of material, almost all of it character-based. This version of *Das Boot* is the superior one. It has all of the suspense of the original, but in a richer package. We get to know the men on the submarine; they are no longer interchangeable faces. Finally, there's the five-hour miniseries, which has a tendency to drag. This one adds in a lot more backstory, and is for completists only. If you have seen and loved the theatrical version and director's cut, this is worth a look to see what's missing.

In any of its incarnations, *Das Boot* is an incredible motion picture experience. Petersen took authenticity to an extreme, re-creating the inside of a German U-boat in its exact dimensions, without concern for how difficult it would be to move and position the cameras. The result captures the inherent claustrophobia of the situation, and this adds to the tension when the U-boat comes under attack. *Das Boot* is a true white-knuckle experience, especially when seen in circumstances where the sound system allows the popping of bolts to sound like gunshots. With the life of every character onboard, from the captain down to the lowliest crewman, in danger, it's easy to understand why the 3½-hour version is the superior one. Stronger character development almost always enhances thrillers.

Theatrical Version: HIGHLY RECOMMENDED
Director's Cut: MUST SEE
Uncut Miniseries: HIGHLY RECOMMENDED

The Lord of the Rings: The Fellowship of the Ring
[New Zealand/U.S., 2001, Extended Cut]
Starring: Elijah Wood, Ian McKellen, Viggo Mortensen, Sean Astin   Director: Peter Jackson   Screenplay: Fran Walsh & Philippa Boyens & Peter Jackson, based on the novel by J.R.R. Tolkien   Running Time: 2:58 (Theatrical); 3:28 (Extended)   Rated: PG-13 (Violence, mature themes)   Theatrical Aspect Ratio: 2.35:1

The extended version of *The Lord of the Rings: The Fellowship of the Ring* incorporates 30 minutes of previously deleted scenes into the text of Peter Jackson's adaptation of the first book in J.R.R. Tolkien's seminal fantasy trilogy. The results are astounding. Although the theatrical edition of the film was, at the time, without peer in its genre, the larger canvas allows the story to breathe. The film's quiet moments, which are crucial to character development, expand and bring greater depth to each of the fellowship's participants. Relationships are strengthened and motives are made clearer.

Although there are numerous small adds and edits throughout the film, there are three major areas that Jackson has expanded. The first is the beginning. The sequences surrounding Bilbo's birthday party are lengthened, and a voice-over by Bilbo is introduced. By using this approach, Jackson provides a fuller sense of the land from which the hobbits hail. Later, during the Rivendell segments, we are given a better sense of the politics involved in the fellowship, and are led to understand something of the weight on Aragorn's shoulders. Finally, the visit to Lothlorien has been revised and extended to more closely follow Tolkien's written version.

One could make an argument that the 30 minutes were excised from the theatrical version to quicken the pace. This is indeed the case, but the trade-off of having so many important additional scenes seems worth the sacrifice of an additional half hour. There is no fat in the extended edition of *The Fellowship of the Ring*. In fact, for home video viewing, this is the preferred rendering. The aids to character development and understanding of Middle Earth's crisis pay dividends not only in gaining a greater appreciation of this film, but of the trilogy as a whole.

Peter Jackson has said that the director's cut of *The Fellowship of the Ring* is the one that was shown in theaters; he made the extended edition as a gift to the fans. Yet in almost every way, the longer version is superior. Given a choice, I would invest the additional 30 minutes and see the more complete cinematic re-creation of the introductory chapter of *The Lord of the Rings*.

Theatrical Version: MUST SEE
Extended Version: MUST SEE

The Lord of the Rings: The Two Towers

[New Zealand/U.S., 2002, Extended Cut]
Starring: Elijah Wood, Ian McKellen, Viggo Mortensen, Sean Astin, Bernard Hill Director: Peter Jackson Screenplay: Fran Walsh & Philippa Boyens & Peter Jackson, based on the novel by J.R.R. Tolkien

Running Time: 2:59 (Theatrical); 3:43 (Extended) Rated: PG-13 (Violence, mature themes) Theatrical Aspect Ratio: 2.35:1

By adding 30 minutes of additional footage to *The Fellowship of the Ring*, director Peter Jackson crafted a home video version of his epic that surpassed the theatrical one. Using the same template, Jackson returned to the editing room for the middle chapter of *The Lord of the Rings*, but this time he incorporated nearly 45 minutes of expunged scenes. And it proves to be too much. Although the extended version of *The Two Towers* is still a great cinematic experience, and I would not wish to be accused of steering potential viewers away, it is not the equal of the theatrical cut. It is perhaps a must-see only for die-hard fans who are more concerned about completeness than pacing or momentum.

Having said that, there are some valuable additions to *The Two Towers*. It's just that there's also a lot of extraneous material that bogs down the narrative. By its nature, *The Fellowship of the Ring* is a more reflective movie. The action is just getting started. By the time *The Two Towers* has arrived, we're in the middle of things and the viewer is likely to have less tolerance for lengthy static periods or talky exposition scenes. *The Two Towers* contains both, and there are times when one might be tempted, however reluctantly, to murmur, "Get on with it!"

The two biggest additions to *The Two Towers* are the least successful. In the first, much of the dialogue between Merry, Pippin, and Treebeard that was cut from the theatrical version has been restored. Although this brings the screenplay closer to the book, it has the side effect of causing the movie to grind to a halt every time these characters are on-screen. Treebeard isn't an energetic creature, and a lot of his scenes share that characteristic. While the additional Faramir scenes are more defensible, since they flesh out the character of Denethor's younger son (and even include a glimpse of the Steward of Gondor in a flashback), they still slow things down. Their placement, rather than their content, is the problem.

Both versions of *The Two Towers* represent superior cinema, and there is every reason for a viewer who craves more of Jackson's filmed version to seek out the longer cut. But for the casual viewer who wants to experience the best rendering of this chapter of the story, the theatrical telling is the better choice.

Theatrical Version: MUST SEE
Extended Version: HIGHLY RECOMMENDED

The Lord of the Rings: The Return of the King

[New Zealand/U.S., 2003, Extended Cut]
Starring: Elijah Wood, Ian McKellen, Viggo Mortensen, Sean Astin, Bernard Hill   Director: Peter Jackson   Screenplay: Fran Walsh & Philippa Boyens & Peter Jackson, based on the novel by J.R.R. Tolkien   Running Time: 3:21 (Theatrical); 4:11 (Extended)   Rated: PG-13 (Violence, mature themes)   Theatrical Aspect Ratio: 2.35:1

For the special DVD edition of *The Return of the King*, Peter Jackson has pulled out all of the stops, re-introducing 50 minutes of deleted footage into the narrative: 20 minutes more than in *The Fellowship of the Ring*, and five minutes more than in *The Two Towers*. The result transforms the viewing experience. Watching a movie that clocks in at 4 hours, 11 minutes is a lot different from watching one that's 3 hours, 21 minutes. The impact of the additional footage is a mixed bag. Some of what Jackson has added is valuable, and makes *The Return of the King* a better motion picture experience. Some, however, does little more than protract an already long movie. As a fan, I treasure the special edition of *The Return of the King* because it gives me more time to spend with characters I have grown to love. But I sense that some casual viewers may grow impatient. The theatrical cut is leaner and meaner, but there are some scenes in the extended version that are too worthwhile to miss.

First, the good stuff. The most invaluable sequence in the extended edition occurs near the beginning, and reveals the fate of Saruman. While I understand Peter Jackson's reasoning for eliminating this from the theatrical version, it plugs a gaping hole. For two films, Saruman is the trilogy's most visible villain. Then, suddenly, he simply vanishes (with only a line from Treebeard to explain his absence). The long edition corrects this oversight. Other highlights include Gandalf's battle with the Witch-King and some nice "courtship" scenes between Eowyn and Faramir (which explain their hand-holding at the coronation).

On the other hand, there are sequences that would have been better left on the cutting room floor. Chief among these are the scenes with Frodo and Sam in the orc army. These are poorly executed, which is a rarity for anything found in this three-movie set. The acting is mediocre, and they play like bad comedy. Also of limited value is the confrontation between Aragorn and the Mouth of Sauron. And one could argue that Aragorn's seizing of the corsair ships hurts the film dramatically. Although it fills in what could be considered to be a narrative hole, it diminishes the impact of the ships' arrival at Minas Tirith.

It's hard to fault Jackson for packing so much new material into *The Return of the King*. This is, after all, his farewell to Middle Earth (unless legal issues are resolved and he is able to make *The Hobbit*). It's a wonderful way to say good-bye. Both versions of the film have different strengths and, with productions this fabulous, making note of weaknesses is nit-picking. Whichever you choose, you can't go wrong.

Theatrical Version: MUST SEE
Extended Version: MUST 150

Index of Titles

Index of Directors

Index of Foreign Films

VIETNAM

WEST GERMANY